MW01698456

About Pearson

Pearson is the world's learning company, with presence across 70 countries worldwide. Our unique insights and world-class expertise comes from a long history of working closely with renowned teachers, authors and thought leaders, as a result of which, we have emerged as the preferred choice for millions of teachers and learners across the world.

We believe learning opens up opportunities, creates fulfilling careers and hence better lives. We hence collaborate with the best of minds to deliver you class-leading products, spread across the Higher Education and K12 spectrum.

Superior learning experience and improved outcomes are at the heart of everything we do. This product is the result of one such effort.

Your feedback plays a critical role in the evolution of our products and you can contact us at reachus@pearson.com. *We look forward to it.*

ORGANIZATIONAL BEHAVIOR

UPDATED 18TH EDITION

Stephen P. Robbins
—San Diego State University

Timothy A. Judge
—The Ohio State University

Neharika Vohra
—Indian Institute of Management Ahmedabad

Pearson

Microsoft and/or its respective suppliers make no representations about the suitability of the information contained in the documents and related graphics published as part of the services for any purpose. All such documents and related graphics are provided "as is" without warranty of any kind. Microsoft and/or its respective suppliers hereby disclaim all warranties and conditions with regard to this information, including all warranties and conditions of merchantability, whether express, implied or statutory, fitness for a particular purpose, title and non-infringement. In no event shall Microsoft and/or its respective suppliers be liable for any special, indirect or consequential damages or any damages whatsoever resulting from loss of use, data or profits, whether in an action of contract, negligence or other tortious action, arising out of or in connection with the use or performance of information available from the services.

The documents and related graphics contained herein could include technical inaccuracies or typographical errors. Changes are periodically added to the information herein. Microsoft and/or its respective suppliers may make improvements and/or changes in the product(s) and/or the program(s) described herein at any time. Partial screen shots may be viewed in full within the software version specified.

Microsoft® and Windows® are registered trademarks of the Microsoft Corporation in the U.S.A. and other countries. This book is not sponsored or endorsed by or affiliated with the Microsoft Corporation.

The rights of Stephen P. Robbins and Timothy A. Judge to be identified as the authors of this work have been asserted by them in accordance with the Copyright, Designs and Patents Act 1988.

Acknowledgments of third-party content appear on the appropriate page within the text, which constitutes an extension of this copyright page.

PEARSON and ALWAYS LEARNING are exclusive trademarks owned by Pearson Education, Inc. or its affiliates in the U.S. and/or other countries.

Authorized adaptation from the United States edition, entitled *Organizational Behavior,* Global Edition, Updated 18th Edition, ISBN 978-1-292-40306-9 by Stephen P. Robbins; Timothy A. Judge, published by Pearson Education, Ltd., Copyright © 2022.

Indian Subcontinent Adaptation

Copyright © 2022 Pearson India Education Services Pvt. Ltd

This book is sold subject to the condition that it shall not, by way of trade or otherwise, be lent, resold, hired out, or otherwise circulated without the publisher's prior written consent in any form of binding or cover other than that in which it is published and without a similar condition including this condition being imposed on the subsequent purchaser and without limiting the rights under copyright reserved above, no part of this publication may be reproduced, stored in or introduced into a retrieval system, or transmitted in any form or by any means (electronic, mechanical, photocopying, recording or otherwise), without the prior written permission of both the copyright owner and the publisher of this book.

ISBN 978-93-560-6427-0

First Impression, 2022
Eight Impression,2025
Nineth Impression

This edition is manufactured in India and is authorized for sale only in India, Bangladesh, Bhutan, Pakistan, Nepal, Sri Lanka and the Maldives. Circulation of this edition outside of these territories is UNAUTHORIZED.

Published by Pearson India Education Services Pvt. Ltd, CIN: U72200TN2005PTC057128.

Head Office: 1st Floor, Berger Tower, Plot No. C-001A/2, Sector 16B, Noida - 201 301, Uttar Pradesh, India.

Registered Office: Featherlite, 'The Address' 5th Floor, Survey No 203/10B, 200 Ft MMRD Road, Zamin Pallavaram, Chennai – 600044, Phone: 044-66540100
Website: in.pearson.com, Email: companysecretary.india@pearson.com

Printed in India at: Rahul Print O Pack

Brief Contents

Contents

4 *Personality and Values* 146

3 The Group

9 *Foundations of Group Behavior* 356

10 *Understanding Work Teams* 396

11 *Power and Politics* 432

12 *Communication* 470

13 *Leadership* 512

14 *Foundations of Organization Structure* 558

4 The Organization System

15 *Organizational Culture* 596

16 *Organizational Change and Stress Management* 638

About the Authors

Stephen P. Robbins

Ph.D. University of Arizona

Stephen P. Robbins is Professor Emeritus of Management at San Diego State University and the world's best-selling textbook author in the areas of both management and organizational behavior. His books are used at more than a thousand U.S. colleges and universities; have been translated into 19 languages; and have adapted editions for Canada, Australia, South Africa, and India. Dr. Robbins is also the author of the best-selling books *The Truth about Managing People*, 2nd ed. (Financial Times/Prentice Hall, 2008) and *Decide & Conquer* (Financial Times/Prentice Hall, 2004).

In his "other life," Dr. Robbins actively participates in masters' track competitions. Since turning 50 in 1993, he's won 18 national championships and 12 world titles, and set numerous U.S. and world age-group records at 60, 100, 200, and 400 meters. In 2005, Dr. Robbins was elected into the USA Masters' Track & Field Hall of Fame.

Timothy A. Judge

Ph.D. University of Illinois at Urbana-Champaign

Timothy A. Judge is currently the Joseph A. Alutto Chair in Leadership Effectiveness at the Department of Management and Human Resources, Fisher College of Business, The Ohio State University. He has held academic positions at the University of Notre Dame, University of Florida, University of Iowa, Cornell University, Charles University in the Czech Republic, Comenius University in Slovakia, and University of Illinois at Urbana-Champaign. Dr. Judge's primary research interests are in (1) personality, moods, and emotions; (2) job attitudes; (3) leadership and influence behaviors; and (4) careers (person–organization fit, career success). Dr. Judge has published more than 154 articles in these and other major topics in journals such as the *Academy of Management Journal* and the *Journal of Applied Psychology*. He is a fellow of several organizations, including the American Psychological Association and the Academy of Management. Among the many professional acknowledgments of his work, most recently Dr. Judge was awarded the Academy of Management Human Resources Division's Scholarly Achievement Award for 2014. Dr. Judge is a co-author of *Essentials of Organizational Behavior*, 14th ed., with Stephen P. Robbins, and *Staffing Organizations*, 8th ed., with Herbert G. Heneman III. He is married and has three children—a daughter who is a health care social worker, a daughter who is studying for a master's degree, and a son in middle school.

Neharika Vohra

Ph.D. University of Manitoba

Neharika Vohra is Professor at the Indian Institute of Management Ahmedabad. Dr. Vohra's research interests have focused on leadership, diversity and inclusion, corporate social responsibility, innovation, small and medium business growth and sustainability, and employee attitudes. Dr. Vohra has been involved in leadership development at the middle-and-senior management level of large national and multinational organizations. She has been involved in the training of more than 15,000 managers over the last 15 years. Dr. Vohra is currently on the board of three companies, two consulting organizations, and three top-ranked academic institutions in India.

Dr. Vohra has worked on the Indian adaptation of with *Stephen P. Robbins and Mary Coulter: Management, 11e* (Prentice Hall, 2012) and *Stephen P. Robbins and Timothy Judge: Organizational Behavior* (15th edition onwards). Dr. Vohra has published more than 40 papers in international and national journals such as *Science, Journal of Personality and Social Psychology,* and *American Psychologist.* She has served as the editor of *Vikalpa: Journal for Decision Makers* for four years and Associate Editor of the *Indian Journal of Abstracts and Reviews.* Dr. Vohra is also on the editorial board of several international journals. Other than being involved in academic duties, Dr. Vohra enjoys reading, traveling, and gardening. She is also passionate about self-work and curriculum innovations.

Preface

The World's Most Successful Organizational Behavior Text Is Better Than Ever

This matrix identifies which features and end-of-chapter material will help you develop specific skills employers are looking for in job candidates.

Employability Skills Matrix (ESM)

	Myth or Science?	Career OBjectives	An Ethical Choice	Point/ Counterpoint	Experiential Exercise	Ethical Dilemma	Case Incident 1	Case Incident 2
Critical Thinking		✓	✓	✓	✓	✓	✓	✓
Communication	✓	✓			✓		✓	
Collaboration					✓		✓	
Knowledge Application and Analysis			✓	✓	✓	✓	✓	✓
Social Responsibility		✓	✓	✓	✓	✓	✓	✓

(*Employability Skills Matrix* for Chapter 2)

Employability

A new **Employability Skills Matrix** at the beginning of each chapter provides students with a visual guide to features that support the development of skills employers are looking for in today's business graduates, helping students to see from the start of class the relevance of the course to their career goals.

Additional Application Practice in End-of-Chapter

Experiential Activities, **Ethical Dilemmas**, and **two Cases** are included at the end of each chapter. Also, **five Comprehensive Cases** at the end of the textbook provide more practice than any other text available.

ETHICAL DILEMMA BYOD

"What's your cell phone number? Good, I'll call you about the meeting." If you're like many people in the world who have used a smartphone for years, or one of the 1.3 billion people who bought one recently, chances are you've used it for work. In fact, your employer may have even invited—or asked—you to use your smartphone, tablet, or laptop in your job. Such is the bring-your-own-device (BYOD) trend, which started out of friendly convenience but now carries major ethical issues. For instance:

(Page 495)

EXPERIENTIAL EXERCISE Choosing the Right Modes of Communication

Pair up with someone you never worked with before. In this exercise, you will pretend to be Gerard, the head of the accounting department in the company. During an intense week, you receive the following email from the human resources director.

Subject: A difficult situation with an employee

We believe that your department would environment for this employee to feel mo on the job. Two colleagues from HR will ass the employee in the transition process, whic to begin next month. All the people involved demonstrated great collaboration with us, sure you will do the same. Sorry for the short we are facing strict deadlines this month.

(Page 494)

CASE INCIDENT 1 Warning: Collaboration Overload

"Regardless of what you're giving us, we're dying by e-mail," an executive told Jamie McLellan, a CTO at an advertising agency. McLellan invested in many different collaboration tools with the goal of helping the employees work more efficiently. Many organizations have taken this same approach through open-plan offices, such as those in many knowledge-intensive companies like Facebook, which has a notorious 430,000-square-foot open office space. Among these tools, employees can use them to create internal team websites, chat, and share documents. However, almost

spent collaborating with one's work) translates to c

Collaboration overloa decision making within c number of collaboratio ing communication com involved in decision m requiring more meetings Although there is much need to tone down the ri

(Page 219)

Relevant Examples

Every chapter is filled with examples to make OB more meaningful and help students recognize course concepts in action. **Profiles of real company leaders** throughout illustrate how course concepts have helped their success.

The **OB Poll** in each chapter highlights statistics that challenge common assumptions.

OB POLL

Percentage of Men and Women Working

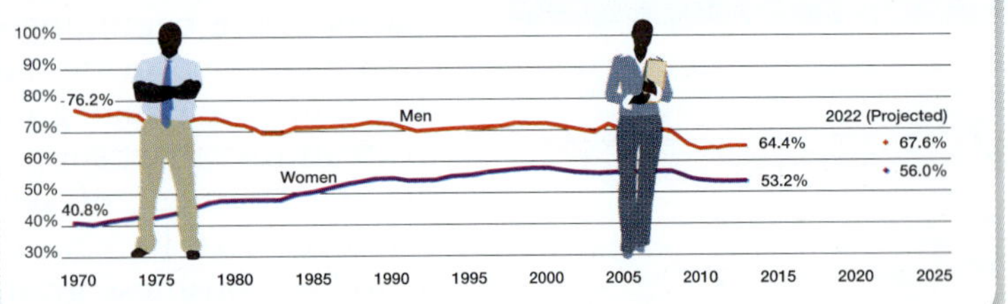

Sources: Based on U.S. Bureau of Labor Statistics, "Women in the Labor Force: A Datebook," 2014, www.bls.gov/opub/reports/cps/women-in-the-labor-force-a-databook-2014.pdf; and U.S. Bureau of Labor Statistics, "Economic News Release," 2013, http://www.bls.gov/news.release/ecopro.t02.htm.

(Page 58

The **Point/Counterpoint** feature presents opposing positions on hot topics in Organizational Behavior to help students learn to think critically.

(Page 708)

Nonunion Positions and the Gig Economy Are Bad for Workers

POINT

What do Uber, Etsy, and Amazon Turk all have in common? All of these platforms are fuel for short-term freelance work, and a reflection of what economists have dubbed the gig economy. Fifty years ago, employers expected workers to stay with a company for 30 years. In exchange for their loyalty, employees were given more opportunities and a pension. Unlike the labor market of today, companies promoted from within. As this practice fell by the wayside, employers hired employees for shorter and shorter periods. Now, many new jobs are not long-term or even short-term positions: They're gigs. Employees work as independent contractors, using third-party platforms to connect to clients. Because these employees do not have a traditional employment contract, they have complete flexibility: They can work as much or

COUNTERPOINT

While the gig economy has its drawbacks, these platforms exist for a reason. Employers and employees alike are fed up with traditional employment. Yes, some people who work through freelance apps use it as a primary source of income. But there are just as many, if not more, who just want a flexible second job to get a little extra cash. If these positions were like the services they are replacing (e.g., cab companies), then gig employees would have to agree to specific policies regarding sick days and work a set schedule.

I'm also skeptical of this idea that freelancers are replacing traditional employment. Yes, some city-level data shows that gig-based jobs increased while payroll jobs decreased. But there are also more data from 2010 to 2014 that suggest that contractor and payroll jobs have increased in most sectors that support freelance platforms. For

Career OBjectives

Is it wrong that I'd rather have guys on my team?

Please don't call me sexist; women are great colleagues and equally effective managers, but I'd rather have men on my team. It's more relaxing for me, and for the other guys I think, because we naturally understand each other and can talk freely. The teams with all men that I've been in have all been very productive.

—Jiten

Dear Jiten,

With all the talk currently focused on gender diversity in organizations, your of team diversity's potential for higher morale, trust, and satisfaction. Notice that these are *values* as opposed to the reported *reality* from the paragraph above. Ellison concluded that there is a "mismatch between the kind of workplace people think they would like and the actual workplace that would make them happier."

Don't think this is your ticket to male-only teams, though. Happiness aside, this study found that diverse teams realized significantly greater rev-

You would be better off putting your efforts into creating an egalitarian atmosphere and choosing your teammates based on what they can contribute to your team.

Sources: Based on C. Diaz-Garcia, A. Gonzalez-Moreno, and F. Jose Saez-Martinez, "Gender Diversity within R&D Teams: Its Impact on Radicalness of Innovation," *Innovation-Management Policy & Practice* 15, no. 2 (2013): 149–60; S. Hoogedoorn, H. Oosterbeek, and M. van Praag, "The Impact of Gender Diversity on the Performance of Business Teams: Evidence from a Field Experiment," *Manage-*

The recently added **Career OBjectives** provide advice, in question-and-answer format, to help students think through how OB concepts can help them address issues they may face in today's workforce.

(Page 403)

Key Changes to the Eighteenth Edition

- *NEW* Employability matrix at the beginning of every chapter provides students with a visual guide to features that support the development of skills employers are looking for in today's business graduates, helping students to see from the start of class the relevance of the course to their career goals.
- *NEW* Application and Employability section in every chapter summarizes the relevance of each chapter for students' employability, the skills learned from chapter features, and the skills to be learned in the end-of-chapter material.
- *NEW AND UPDATED Opening Vignettes* in every chapter bring current business trends and events to the forefront.
- *NEW AND UPDATED* content in every chapter reflects the most current developments in OB research. This new content includes the following topics:
  - Expatriate Readjustment
  - Deviance and Counterproductive Work Behaviors
  - Customer Satisfaction
  - Emotional Labor
  - Mindfulness
  - Unemployment/Job Search
  - Behavioral Ethics
  - Deonance Theory
  - Third-Party Observations of Injustice
  - Job Enrichment
  - Voice
  - Abusive Supervision
  - Executive Board Composition
  - Espoused and Enacted Climates
  - High-Performance Work Systems
  - Human Capital Resources
  - Sleep Deprivation
  - Recovery Experiences
  - Job Demands
- *NEW* photos and captions in over 75 percent of chapters link the chapter content to contemporary, real-life worldwide situations to enhance students' understanding of hands-on application of concepts.
- *NEW* Point/Counterpoint features reflect ongoing tensions between perspectives in OB, focusing students' attention on new topics in 5 of 18 chapters.
- The following end-of-chapter material is either completely new or substantially revised and updated for each chapter (along with assisted-graded writing questions), bringing the most contemporary thinking to the attention of students:
  - *Experiential Exercise* (9 of 18 total)
  - *Ethical Dilemma* (9 of 18 total)
  - *Case Incidents* (25 of 36 total)
- Updated References throughout every chapter.

Chapter-by-Chapter Changes

Chapter 1: What Is Organizational Behavior?

- Revised *Learning Objectives*
- New *Opening Vignette* (Road Warriors)
- New research in The Importance of Interpersonal Skills and Big Data
- New major section: Employability Skills
- New *Case Incident 1* (L'Oréal around the Globe)
- New *Case Incident 2* (So, How Engaged Are Employees? The Data Says It All)

Chapter 2: Diversity in Organizations

- New *Opening Vignette* (A Lack of Diversity in the Tech Industry)
- New section on Expatriate Adjustment
- Revised/updated sections: Demographic Characteristics, Tenure, Sexual Orientation and Gender Identity, and Ability
- New research in Stereotype Threat; Discrimination in the Workplace; Age, Sex, Race, and Ethnicity; Hidden Disabilities; Religion; Sexual Orientation and Gender Identity; and Intellectual Abilities
- Updated *OB Poll* (Gender Pay Gap: Narrowing but Still There)
- Revised *Implications for Managers*
- Updated *An Ethical Choice* (Global Diversity: Affirmative Action)
- New *Ethical Dilemma* (Voiding the "License to Discriminate")
- New *Case Incident 1* (Encouraging Female Engineers)

Chapter 3: Attitudes and Job Satisfaction

- New *Opening Vignette* (In the Legoland Wonderland)
- Revised/updated sections: Attitudes, Organizational Commitment, Perceived Organizational Support, Employee Engagement, and Organizational Citizenship Behavior (OCB)
- New research in Job Satisfaction and Involvement, Employee Engagement, Personality, Customer Satisfaction, and Counterproductive Work Behavior (CWB)
- New international research in Attitudes, Job Conditions, and Corporate Social Responsibility (CSR)
- Updated *Exhibit 3-2* (Worst Jobs of 2016 for Job Satisfaction)
- New *Experiential Exercise* (Job Attitudes Situational Interview)
- New *Case Incident 1* (Jobs, Money, and Satisfaction)

Chapter 4: Personality and Values

- Revised *Learning Objectives*
- New *Opening Vignette* (Leading the "Quiet Revolution")
- New major section on Personality, Job Search, and Unemployment
- Revised/updated section: The Big Five Personality Model
- New research in Conscientiousness at Work, Emotional Stability at Work, Extraversion at Work, Openness at Work, Agreeableness at Work, and Proactive Personality
- Updated *Myth or Science?* (We Can Accurately Judge Individuals' Personalities a Few Seconds after Meeting Them)
- New *Exhibit 4-6* (Comparison of Hofstede's Framework and the GLOBE Framework)
- Revised *Implications for Managers*
- Revised *Summary*
- Revised *Questions for Review*
- New *Case Incident 2* (Personality Matters!)

Chapter 5: Perception, Learning and Individual Decision Making

- New *Opening Vignette* (Individual Intuition Igniting Innovation)
- Revised section on Halo and Horns Effects

- Revised/updated sections: Context, Attribution Theory, Selective Perception, Confirmation Bias, and Three Ethical Decision Criteria
- New research in Context, Bounded Rationality, Intuition, Escalation of Commitment, Risk Aversion, Personality, Gender, and Three Ethical Decision Criteria
- New international research in Contrast Effects
- New section on Decision Making in Times of Crisis
- New *Point/Counterpoint* (Implicit Assessment)
- New *Experiential Exercise* (Fake News?)
- New *Case Incident 1* (Warning: Collaboration Overload)
- New *Case Incident 2* (How Do Employees Justify Cyberloafing?)

Chapter 6: Emotions and Moods

- New *Opening Vignette* (Objections Sustained)
- Revised/updated sections: What Are Emotions and Moods?, The Basic Emotions, Moral Emotions, Do Emotions Make Us Ethical?, and Emotion Regulation Techniques
- New research in The Function of Emotions, Do Emotions Make Us Ethical?, Stress, Age, Sex, Emotional Labor, Affective Events Theory, Emotional Intelligence, and Emotion Regulation Techniques
- New international research in The Basic Emotions, Experiencing Moods and Emotions, Emotional Labor, Emotional Intelligence, and Emotion Regulation Techniques
- Updated *OB Poll* (Emotional States)
- Updated *Experiential Exercise* (Mindfulness at Work)
- New *Case Incident 1* (Hiring an Emotionally Intelligent Employee)
- New *Case Incident 2* (Anger: A Dangerous Emotion at Work)

Chapter 7: Motivation Concepts

- Revised *Learning Objectives*
- New *Opening Vignette* (When Goals Go out of Control)
- New sections on Equity Theory/Organizational Justice and Others' Reactions to Injustice
- Revised/updated sections: Hierarchy of Needs Theory, Two-Factor Theory, McClelland's Theory of Needs, Other Contemporary Theories of Motivation, and Expectancy Theory
- New research in McClelland's Theory of Needs, Self-Determination Theory, Goal-Setting Theory, Goal Commitment, Task Characteristics, Implementing Goal Setting, Equity Theory/Organizational Justice, and Job Engagement
- New international research in McClelland's Theory of Needs, Self-Determination Theory, and Equity Theory/Organizational Justice
- Revised *Summary*
- Revised *Implications for Managers*
- Revised *Questions for Review*
- New *Ethical Dilemma* (Follies of Reward)
- New *Case Incident 1* ("Human and Authentic": Motivation at Schoenen Torfs)
- New *Case Incident 2* (Laziness Is Contagious)

Chapter 8: Motivation: From Concepts to Applications

- New *Opening Vignette* (Employees Trading Places)
- New section on Job Enrichment
- Revised/updated sections: Relational Job Design, Flextime, Job Sharing, Telecommuting, and How to Pay: Rewarding Individual Employees through Variable-Pay Programs
- New research in The Job Characteristics Model, Flextime, Telecommuting, Participative Management, Using Rewards to Motivate Employees, How to Pay: Rewarding Individual Employees through Variable-Pay Programs, Bonus, and Employee Stock Ownership Plan
- New international research in The Job Characteristics Model, Flextime, How to Pay: Rewarding Individual Employees through Variable-Pay Programs, and Flexible Benefits: Developing a Benefits Package
- New *Point/Counterpoint* (Gainsharing: Fair Shares?)
- Updated *OB Poll* (Who Works from Home?)
- Updated *An Ethical Choice* (Workers' Cooperatives)
- New *Experiential Exercise* (Developing a Motivation Plan for Your Museum Security Guards)
- New *Ethical Dilemma* (You Want Me to Do *What*?)
- New *Case Incident 1* (We Talk, But They Don't Listen)
- New *Case Incident 2* (Will More Money Fill the Gap?)

Chapter 9: Foundations of Group Behavior

- New *Opening Vignette* (The Rolling Stones: A Supergroup)
- New research in Social Identity, Group Development, Role Expectations, Negative Norms and Group Outcomes, Status and Stigmatization, and Group Property 6: Diversity
- New international research in Group Property 4: Size and Dynamics and Group Property 6: Diversity
- New *Point/Counterpoint* (Diverse Work Groups Are Smarter and More Innovative)
- New *Ethical Dilemma* (It's Obvious, They're Chinese)
- New *Case Incident 1* (The Dangers of Groupthink)

Chapter 10: Understanding Work Teams

- New *Opening Vignette* (A Solution to Growing Pains)
- Revised/updated section: Diversity of Members
- New research in Multiteam Systems, Adequate Resources, Leadership and Structure, Team Composition, Common Plan and Purpose, Team Identity, Team Cohesion, Conflict Levels, and Training: Creating Team Players
- New international research in Conflict Levels
- New section on Crises and Extreme Contexts
- New section on Team Trust
- New *Experiential Exercise* (How to Resolve Social Loafing in Your Team?)
- New *Ethical Dilemma* (When Your Cycling Skills Matter!)
- New *Case Incident 1* (Trusting Someone You Can't See)

Chapter 11: Power and Politics

- New *Opening Vignette* (A Tale of Presidential Corruption)
- New research in Coercive Power, Social Network Analysis: A Tool for Assessing Resources, Applying Power Tactics, and Interviews and IM
- New international research in Performance Evaluations and IM
- New *Ethical Dilemma* (Sexual Harassment and Office Romances)
- New *Case Incident 1* (Power and Gender Diversity)
- New *Case Incident 2* (Where Flattery Will Get You)

Chapter 12: Communication

- New *Opening Vignette* (Workplace Communication: Too Much of a Good Thing?)
- Revised/updated section: Social Media Websites
- New research in Upward Communication, The Grapevine, Meetings, E-Mail, Information Overload, Language, and Silence
- New international research in Cultural Barriers
- New section on Communicating in Times of Crisis
- New *Experiential Exercise* (Choosing the Right Modes of Communication)
- New *Case Incident 1* (Do Men and Women Speak the Same Language?)
- New *Case Incident 2* (Shoulders Back, It's Interview Time)

Chapter 13: Leadership

- New *Opening Vignette* (From Wacky Vision to Total Hotel Industry Disruption)
- New section on Abusive Supervision
- Revised/updated sections: Trait Theories, Behavioral Theories, Leader–Member Exchange (LMX) Theory, How Charismatic Leaders Influence Followers, How Transformational Leadership Works, Evaluation of Transformational Leadership, Responsible Leadership, Authentic Leadership, and Ethical Leadership
- New research in Trait Theories, Leader–Member Exchange (LMX) Theory, What Is Charismatic Leadership?, Are Charismatic Leaders Born or Made?, How Charismatic Leaders Influence Followers, Does Effective Charismatic Leadership Depend on the Situation?, Transactional and Transformational Leadership, How Transformational Leadership Works, Evaluation of Transformational Leadership, Transformational versus Transactional Leadership, Authentic Leadership, Ethical Leadership, Servant Leadership, The Role of Time, and Training Leaders
- New international research in Leader–Member Exchange (LMX) Theory, Are Charismatic Leaders Born or Made?, How Transformational Leadership Works, Evaluation of Transformational Leadership, Authentic Leadership, Ethical Leadership, and Servant Leadership
- New section on Leading in Times of Crisis
- Revised *Implications for Managers*
- New *Experiential Exercise* (What's in a Leader?)
- New *Ethical Dilemma* (Innocent, but What about Trust?)
- New *Case Incident 1* (Sharing Is Performing)
- New *Case Incident 2* (Andrea Illy: Leading a Family Company Responsibly)

Chapter 14: Foundations of Organization Structure

- Revised *Learning Objectives*
- New *Opening Vignette* (Samsung: Transforming a Hierarchy)
- Revised/updated sections: Departmentalization, The Simple Structure, The Virtual Structure, and The Leaner Organization: Downsizing
- New research in Work Specialization, Centralization, Boundary Spanning, The Bureaucracy, The Divisional Structure, The Virtual Structure, The Leaner Organization: Downsizing, Technology, and Organizational Designs and Employee Behavior
- New international research in Boundary Spanning
- New *Point/Counterpoint* (Open-Air Offices Inspire Creativity and Enhance Productivity)
- Revised *Questions for Review*
- New *Case Incident 2* (Turbulence on United Airlines)

Chapter 15: Organizational Culture

- New *Opening Vignette* ("Uniform" Culture)
- Updated/revised sections: A Definition of Organizational Culture, Culture Creates Climate, Barriers to Acquisitions and Mergers, and Top Management
- New *Exhibit 15-2* (The Effect of Culture on Organizational Outcomes)
- New research in A Definition of Organizational Culture, Do Organizations Have Uniform Cultures?, Strong versus Weak Cultures, The Functions of Culture, Culture Creates Climate, The Ethical Dimension of Culture, Culture as an Asset, Barriers to Diversity, Toxicity and Dysfunctions, Symbols, and Developing an Ethical Culture
- New international research in Culture Creates Climate, Culture and Innovation, and Barriers to Acquisitions and Mergers
- Updated *Myth or Science?* (An Organization's Culture Is Forever)
- Updated *An Ethical Choice* (A Culture of Compassion)
- Revised *Implications for Managers*
- New *Point/Counterpoint* (Organizational Culture Can Be "Measured")
- New *Experiential Exercise* (Creating a Green Culture)
- Updated *Case Incident 1* (Culture of Fear)

Chapter 16: Human Resources Policies and Practices

- New *Opening Vignette* (An Unusual Perk)
- Updated/revised sections: Types of Training, Improving Performance Evaluations, and The Leadership Role of HR
- New research in Recruitment Practices, Selection Practices, Application Forms, Background Checks, Assessment Centers, Interviews, Interpersonal Skills, Evaluating Effectiveness, and The Leadership Role of HR
- New international research in Who Should Do the Evaluating?
- Updated *An Ethical Choice* (HIV/AIDS and the Multinational Organization)
- New *Experiential Exercise* (Responding to Employees' Requests of Flexibility)
- New *Ethical Dilemma* (Should I Pay the Staff More and Reduce Company's Profit?)

Chapter 17: Organizational Change and Stress Management

- New *Opening Vignette* (Stress and Well-Being)
- Revised/updated sections: Change, Forces for Change, Process Consultation, Stimulating Innovation, Stressors, and Physiological Symptoms
- Updated *Exhibit 17-7* (Work Is One of the Top Sources of Stress)
- New research in Implementing Changes Fairly; Selecting People Who Accept Change; Sources of Innovation; Context and Innovation; Stressors; Personal Factors; Perception; Physiological Symptoms; Managing Stress; Individual Approaches; Selection and Placement, and Training; Goal Setting; Redesigning Jobs; Employee Sabbaticals; and Wellness Programs
- New international research in Implementing Changes Fairly, Demands and Resources, Cultural Differences, Physiological Symptoms, and Psychological Symptoms
- New *Experiential Exercise* (Making Employees Less Resistant to Change)
- New *Ethical Dilemma* (The Fear of Redundancy and Ceasing Operations)
- New *Case Incident 2* (Sweat the Stress)

Chapter 18: Conflict and Negotiation

- New *Opening Vignette* (Bargaining Chips)
- Revised/updated sections: Stage III: Intentions, Stage V: Outcomes, and Managing Functional Conflict
- New research in Types of Conflict, Stage IV: Behavior, Integrative Bargaining, Personality Traits in Negotiations, Moods and Emotions in Negotiations, and Gender Differences in Negotiations
- New international research in Loci of Conflict and Culture in Negotiations
- New *Exhibit 18-7* (Integration of Two Bargaining Strategies within One Negotiation Episode)
- New *Point/Counterpoint* (Nonunion Positions and the Gig Economy Are Bad for Workers)
- New *Ethical Dilemma* (The Case of the Overly Assertive Employee)
- New *Case Incident 2* (Start-up Stress)

Instructor Resource Center

At www.pearsoned.co.in/stephenprobbins instructors can easily register to gain access to a variety of instructor resources available with this text in downloadable format. If assistance is needed, our dedicated technical support team is ready to help with the media supplements that accompany this text.

The following supplements are available with this text:

- Instructor's Resource Manual
- Test Bank
- PowerPoint Presentation

This title is available as an eBook and can be purchased.

Acknowledgments

Getting this book into your hands was a team effort. It took faculty reviewers and a talented group of designers and production specialists, editorial personnel, and marketing and sales staff.

The eighteenth edition was peer reviewed by many experts in the field. Their comments, compliments, and suggestions have significantly improved the final product. The authors would also like to extend their sincerest thanks to these instructors.

The authors wish to thank David Richard Glerum and Bridget Christine McHugh of the Ohio State University for help with several key aspects of this revision.

We owe a debt of gratitude to all those at Pearson who have supported this text over the past 30 years and who have worked so hard on the development of this latest edition. We want to thank Kris Ellis-Levy, Senior Portfolio Manager; Claudia Fernandes, Senior Content Producer; and Andrea Archer and Angela Urquhart, Project Managers, Thistle Hill Publishing Services. We would also like to thank Becky Brown, Senior Product Marketer; Nicole Price, Field Marketing Manager; and their sales staff, who have been selling this text over its many editions. Thank you for the attention you've given to this text.

Global Edition Acknowledgments

Pearson would like to thank the following people for their work on the Global Edition:

Contributors

Iva Bimpli, University of Leeds
Timothy Campbell, Stafford Global
Hussein Ismail, Lebanese American University
Michele Kehoe, National College of Ireland
John Opute, London South Bank University
Stephanie Pougnet, Ecole hôtelière de Lausanne, University of Applied Sciences Western Switzerland (HES-SO)
Andrew Richardson, University of Leeds
Jon and Diane Sutherland
Randall Zindler, Lancaster University Management School

Reviewers

Maria Adamson, Queen Mary University of London
Charbel N. Aoun, Lebanese American University
Nishat Babu, Aston University
Pawan Budhwar, Aston University
Robin Cheng, Taylor's University
Roberta Fida, University of East Anglia
Renate Grau, University of Applied Sciences and Arts, Northwestern Switzerland
Elham Hasham, Notre Dame University–Louaize
Stephanie K. Jones, Maastricht School of Management
Michele Kehoe, National College of Ireland
Yong Wooi Keong, Sunway University
Wen-Dong Li, The Chinese University of Hong Kong
Neelofer Mashood, Middlesex University Dubai
Catherine Ng, Hong Kong Baptist University
John Opute, London South Bank University
Riani Rachmawati, University of Indonesia
Sununta Siengthai, Asian Institute of Technology

Enterprises like writing a book simply cannot be undertaken without the undying support and encouragement from family. I would like to acknowledge the support I have received from my family members, those who live with me and those who live far away. Working on this book required a lot of time spent away from them and a lot of time ruminating over what to write, what to include, and thus, being silent and lost in thought. I express my heartfelt gratitude towards Kishor Dattani for being the support and Sugatha Nair for helping me keep all the files in place. This work would never have been completed without the patient and solid support of Anindita Malhotra of Pearson. Several friends in various companies have shared their experiences and I thank them all. I also want to acknowledge the appreciation that I have received from various readers and users of the previous editions of Organization Behavior. The appreciation and feedback kept me motivated to work further on this book.

—Neharika Vohra

1 What Is Organizational Behavior?

Source: T. Schneider.shutterstock.com

LEARNING OBJECTIVES

After studying this chapter, you should be able to:

1-1 Demonstrate the importance of interpersonal skills in the workplace.

1-2 Define *organizational behavior* (*OB*).

1-3 Show the value of OB to systematic study.

1-4 Identify the major behavioral science disciplines that contribute to OB.

1-5 Demonstrate why few absolutes apply to OB.

1-6 Identify managers' challenges and opportunities in applying OB concepts.

1-7 Compare the three levels of analysis in this text's OB model.

1-8 Describe the key employability skills gained from studying OB that are applicable to other majors or future careers.

MANAGING A 100-YEAR-OLD COMPANY: ITC LTD.

Popular Indian brands like Ashirvaad, Savlon, Sunbean, Wills and many more are owned by the conglomerate ITC which a vast portfolio in multiple business segments like fast moving consumer goods (FMCG), hotels, paperboards and packaging, agri business, and information technology. The company pioneered the concept of e-Choupal—an initiative that leverages the power of internet to empower farmers by improving farm productivity, replenishing natural resources and providing efficient market access—impacting 4 million farmers and helping them with real time information and getting better prices for their produce. ITC is a professionally managed company that is not owned by a family. Its values include trusteeship and nation orientation.

Often ranked among the best companies to work for, ITC has been nominated as India's most admired company. As of 2021, the gross sales value of ITC has been ₹74,979 crores, and its 36,500 workforce are spread across over 70 locations in India. Over the 100 years of its existence, ITC reinvented itself from being a tobacco company to its present avatar as one of India's foremost private sector companies. In 2012, it was reported for not having had even one senior manager leaving the organization over the past 15 years. Analysis of reviews of ITC employees on various employee review portals mostly reveals employee satisfaction. Employees particularly are happy with the training they receive as skill and knowledge enhancement, both on the job and in the classroom. Managers are expected to work in and lead more than one business so that by the time the senior management retires, internal resources are well-groomed and properly trained talent to be promoted to the next level. As a result, the senior management at ITC is largely comprised of its loyal employees who have moved up the ladder within the organization rather than those hired laterally. A fine example of this is Mr. Sanjiv Puri the current chairman of the ITC who has been with company since 1986. Although ITC is not known to be a high paymaster compared to its competitors. However, most employees state that they continue working for ITC because of the professional work culture and the associated perks like professional growth. While employees are not so satisfied with the work-life balance at the company, they still prefer to stay because of the opportunities they get to explore within the company.

Albeit the challenges of managing a diversified conglomerate are many. Not always and not all not always of ITC employees are satisfied. For example, those working in the infotech business of ITC, find that the culture sometimes laid back and a few of their senior managers do not understand the nuances of running IT-based businesses. From running agri-based businesses to luxury hotels and IT businesses, the needs of employees are varied because of the trends of respective industries they serve and the nature of employment in each business. One disgruntled ITC infotech employee has stated in the online Q&A platform, Quora.com, that "the senior management runs it like a grocery shop". Another employee of the same division finds "not enough challenge at work and terms his manager as lazy and slow-moving". But again, there is another employee from ITC Hotels who describes being a part of ITC as receiving the best-in-class training and exposure. On a brighter note, the Chairman and MD of ITC hotels was chosen to be the Impact Person for 2020 for transforming the company from a slow-moving tobacco company to a fast-moving conglomerate. Over the two years of the COVID-19 pandemic, ITC launched 120 new products in the market—many of them in the hygiene and health segment.

Sources: Based on Gavagai (January 15, 2020), "We analyzed 834 employee reviews about ITC", retrieved on March 25, 2022 from https://www.gavagai.io; Basu, A. (2017), "People First: ITC keeps its staff motivated with employee-centric policies", ©*Business Today.in (March 12, 2017)*, retrieved on March 23, 2022 from https://www.businesstoday.in; Mukherjee, W. (2012), "ITC: Zero attrition at senior management since 15 years; remuneration & reward strategy cited as main reasons", ©*ET Bureau (January 18, 2012)* retrieved on March 25, 2022 from https://economictimes.indiatimes.com; "About ITC", retrieved on March 25, 2022 from https://www.itcportal.com; Quora.com (2017), "I have offers from ITC Infotech and Robert Bosch (RBEI), which would I have to choose?" retrieved on March 25, from https://www.quora.com.

A glimpse of a large and established business, such as ITC Ltd., reflects the complexity of running organizations. It highlights several issues of interest to those of us seeking to understand organizational behaviour including motivation, ethics, turnover, justice, emotions, culture. Throughout this text, you'll learn how organizational challenges often cut across areas like these, which is exactly why the systematic approach pursued in this text and in your course is important.

The Importance of Interpersonal Skills

1-1 Demonstrate the importance of interpersonal skills in the workplace.

Until the late 1980s, business school curricula emphasized the technical aspects of management, focusing on economics, accounting, finance, and quantitative techniques. Coursework in human behavior and people skills received relatively less attention. Since then, however, business schools have realized the significant role that interpersonal skills play in determining a manager's effectiveness. In fact, a survey of over 2,100 CFOs across 20 industries indicated that a lack of interpersonal skills is the top reason why some employees fail to advance.[1]

Incorporating OB principles into the workplace can yield many important organizational outcomes. For one, companies known as good places to work—such as Lupin, Tata Motors, Infosys, Mindtree, Google, Facebook, LinkedIn, and TCS[2]—have been found to generate superior financial performance.[3] Second, developing managers' interpersonal skills helps organizations attract and keep high-performing employees, which is important because outstanding employees are always in short supply and costly to replace. Third, strong associations exist between the quality of workplace relationships and employee job satisfaction, stress, and turnover. One very large study of hundreds of workplaces and more than 200,000 respondents showed that social relationships among coworkers and supervisors were strongly related to overall job satisfaction. Positive social relationships were also associated with lower stress at work and lower intentions to quit.[4] Additional research suggests that positive work relationships help employees to flourish, leading to improvements in job and life satisfaction, positive emotions at work, and perceptions that one's work has meaning.[5] Fourth, increasing the OB element in organizations can foster social responsibility awareness. Accordingly, universities have begun to incorporate social entrepreneurship education into their curriculum in order to train future leaders in addressing social issues within their organizations.[6] This is especially important because there is a growing need for understanding the means and outcomes of corporate social responsibility (CSR).[7]

We understand that in today's competitive and demanding workplace, managers can't succeed on their technical skills alone. They also have to exhibit good people skills. This text has been written to help both managers and potential managers develop people skills and to acquire the knowledge that understanding human behavior provides.

IBM Chief Executive Virginia Rometty has the interpersonal skills required to succeed in management. Communication and leadership skills distinguish managers such as Rometty, who is shown here at a panel discussion in Washington, D.C. Rometty is an innovative leader capable of driving IBM's entrepreneurial culture, and her skills have helped her rise to the top of her profession.

Source: Jonathan Ernst/Reuters/Alamy Stock Photo

Management and *Organizational Behavior*

1-2 Define *organizational behavior (OB)*.

manager An individual who achieves goals through other people.

organization A consciously coordinated social unit, composed of two or more people, that functions on a relatively continuous basis to achieve a common goal or set of goals.

Let's begin by briefly defining the terms *manager* and *organization*. First, the most notable characteristic of **managers** is that they get things done through other people. They make decisions, allocate resources, and direct the activities of others to attain goals. Managers are sometimes called *administrators*, especially in nonprofit organizations. They do their work in an **organization**, which is a consciously coordinated social unit composed of two or more people, that functions on a relatively continuous basis to achieve a common goal or set of goals. By this definition, manufacturing and service firms are organizations, and so are schools; hospitals; churches; military units; nonprofits; police departments; and local, state, and federal government agencies.

More than ever, new hires and other employees are placed into management positions without sufficient management training or informed experience. According to a large-scale survey, more than 58 percent of managers reported that they had not received any training, and 25 percent admitted that they were not ready to lead others when they were given the role.[8] Added to that challenge, the demands of the job have increased: The average manager has seven direct reports (five was once the norm), and less time than before to spend directly supervising them.[9] Considering that a Gallup poll found organizations chose the wrong candidate for management positions 82 percent of the time,[10] we conclude that the more you can learn about people and how to manage them, the better prepared you will be to be the right management candidate. OB will help you get there. Let's start by identifying a manager's primary activities.

planning A process that includes defining goals, establishing strategy, and developing plans to coordinate activities.

organizing Determining what tasks are to be done, who is to do them, how the tasks are to be grouped, who reports to whom, and where decisions are to be made.

leading A function that includes motivating employees, directing others, selecting the most effective communication channels, and resolving conflicts.

controlling Monitoring activities to ensure that they are being accomplished as planned and correcting any significant deviations.

The work of managers can be categorized into four different activities: **planning**, **organizing**, **leading**, and **controlling**. The *planning* function encompasses defining an organization's goals, establishing an overall strategy for achieving those goals, and developing a comprehensive set of plans to integrate and coordinate activities. Evidence indicates the need for planning increases the most as managers move from lower-level to midlevel management.[11]

When managers engage in designing their work unit's structure, they are *organizing*. The organizing function includes determining what tasks are to be done, who is to do them, how the tasks are to be grouped, who reports to whom, and where decisions are to be made.

Every organization contains people, and it is management's job to direct and coordinate those people, which is the *leading* function. When managers motivate employees, direct their activities, select the most effective communication channels, or resolve conflicts, they're engaging in leading.

To ensure that the activities are going as they should, management must monitor the organization's performance and compare it with previously set goals. If there are any significant deviations, it is management's job to get the organization back on track. This monitoring, comparing, and potential correcting is the *controlling* function.

Management Roles

Henry Mintzberg, now a prominent management scholar, undertook a careful study of executives early in his career to determine what they did on their jobs. On the basis of his observations, Mintzberg concluded that managers perform

Exhibit 1-1 Minztberg's Managerial Roles

Role	Description
Interpersonal	
Figurehead	Symbolic head; required to perform a number of routine duties of a legal or social nature
Leader	Responsible for the motivation and direction of employees
Liaison	Maintains a network of outside contacts who provide favors and information
Informational	
Monitor	Receives a wide variety of information; serves as nerve center of internal and external information of the organization
Disseminator	Transmits information received from outsiders or from other employees to members of the organization
Spokesperson	Transmits information to outsiders on organization's plans, policies, actions, and results; serves as expert on organization's industry
Decisional	
Entrepreneur	Searches organization and its environment for opportunities and initiates projects to bring about change
Disturbance handler	Responsible for corrective action when organization faces important, unexpected disturbances
Resource allocator	Makes or approves significant organizational decisions
Negotiator	Responsible for representing the organization at major negotiations

Source: H. Mintzberg, *The Nature of Managerial Work*, 1st ed., © 1973, pp. 92–93. Reprinted and electronically reproduced by permission of Pearson Education, Inc., New York, NY.

10 different, highly interrelated roles or sets of behaviors, thus serving a critical function in organizations.[12] As shown in Exhibit 1-1, these 10 roles are primarily (1) interpersonal, (2) informational, or (3) decisional. Although much has changed in the world of work since Mintzberg developed this model, research indicates the roles have changed very little.[13]

Interpersonal Roles All managers are required to perform duties that are ceremonial and symbolic in nature. For instance, when the president of a college hands out diplomas at commencement or a factory supervisor gives a group of high school students a tour of the plant, they are acting in a *figurehead* role. Another key interpersonal role all managers have is a *leadership* role. This role includes hiring, training, motivating, and disciplining employees. The third role within the interpersonal grouping is the *liaison* role, or contacting and fostering relationships with others who provide valuable information. The sales manager who obtains information from the quality-control manager in his own company has an internal liaison relationship. When that sales manager has contact with other sales executives through a marketing trade association, he has external liaison relationships.

Informational Roles To some degree, all managers collect information from outside organizations and institutions, typically by scanning the news media and talking with other people to learn of changes in the public's tastes and what competitors may be planning. Mintzberg called this the *monitor* role. Managers also act as a conduit to transmit information to organizational members. This is the *disseminator* role. In addition, managers perform a *spokesperson* role when they represent the organization to outsiders.

Decisional Roles Mintzberg identified four roles that require making choices. In the *entrepreneur* role, managers initiate and oversee new projects that will improve their organization's performance. As *disturbance handlers*, managers take corrective action in response to unforeseen problems. As *resource allocators*, managers are responsible for allocating human, physical, and monetary resources. Finally, managers perform a *negotiator* role, in which they discuss issues and bargain with other units (internal or external) to gain advantages for their own unit.

Management Skills

Another way to consider what managers do is to look at the skills or competencies they need to achieve their goals. Researchers have identified a number of skills that differentiate effective from ineffective managers.[14] Each of these skills is important, and all are needed to become a well-rounded and effective manager.

technical skills The ability to apply specialized knowledge or expertise.

Technical Skills **Technical skills** encompass the ability to apply specialized knowledge or expertise. When you think of the skills of professionals such as civil engineers or oral surgeons, you typically focus on the technical skills they have learned through extensive formal education. Of course, professionals don't have a monopoly on technical skills, and not all technical skills have to be learned in schools or other formal training programs. All jobs require some specialized expertise, and many people develop their technical skills on the job.

human skills The ability to work with, understand, and motivate other people, both individually and in groups.

Human Skills The ability to understand, communicate with, motivate, and support other people, both individually and in groups, defines **human skills**. Many people may be technically proficient but poor listeners, unable to understand the needs of others, or weak at managing conflicts. Managers must have good human skills because they need to get things done through other people.

conceptual skills The mental ability to analyze and diagnose complex situations.

Conceptual Skills Managers must have the mental ability to analyze and diagnose complex situations. These tasks require **conceptual skills**. Decision making, for instance, requires managers to identify problems, develop alternative solutions to correct those problems, evaluate those alternative solutions, and select the best one. After they have selected a course of action, managers must be able to organize a plan of action and then execute it. The abilities to integrate new ideas with existing processes and to innovate on the job are also crucial conceptual skills for today's managers.

Effective versus Successful Managerial Activities

Fred Luthans and his associates looked at what managers do from a somewhat different perspective.[15] They asked, "Do managers who move up most quickly in an organization do the same activities and with the same emphasis as managers who do the best job?" You might think the answer is yes, but that's not always the case.

Luthans and his associates studied more than 450 managers, all engaged in four managerial activities:

1. **Traditional management.** Decision making, planning, and controlling.
2. **Communication.** Exchanging routine information and processing paperwork.
3. **Human resources management.** Motivating, disciplining, managing conflict, staffing, and training.
4. **Networking.** Socializing, politicking, and interacting with outsiders.

When you see this icon, Global OB issues and research are being discussed in the paragraph.

The "average" manager spent 32 percent of his or her time in traditional management activities, 29 percent communicating, 20 percent in human resources management activities, and 19 percent networking. However, the time and effort that different *individual* managers spent on those activities varied a great deal. As shown in Exhibit 1-2, among managers who were *successful* (defined in terms of speed of promotion within their organization), networking made the largest relative contribution to success, and human resources management activities made the least relative contribution. Among *effective* managers (defined in terms of quantity and quality of their performance and the satisfaction and commitment of employees), communication made the largest relative contribution and networking the least. Other studies in Australia, Israel, Italy, Japan, and the United States confirm the link between networking, social relationships, and success within an organization.[16] The connection between communication and effective managers is also clear. Managers who explain their decisions and seek information from colleagues and employees—even if the information turns out to be negative—are the most effective.[17]

This research offers important insights. *Successful* (in terms of promotion) managers give almost the opposite emphases to traditional management, communication, human resources management, and networking as do *effective* managers. This finding challenges the historical assumption that promotions are based on performance, and it illustrates the importance of networking and political skills in getting ahead in organizations.

Exhibit 1-2 Allocation of Activities by Time

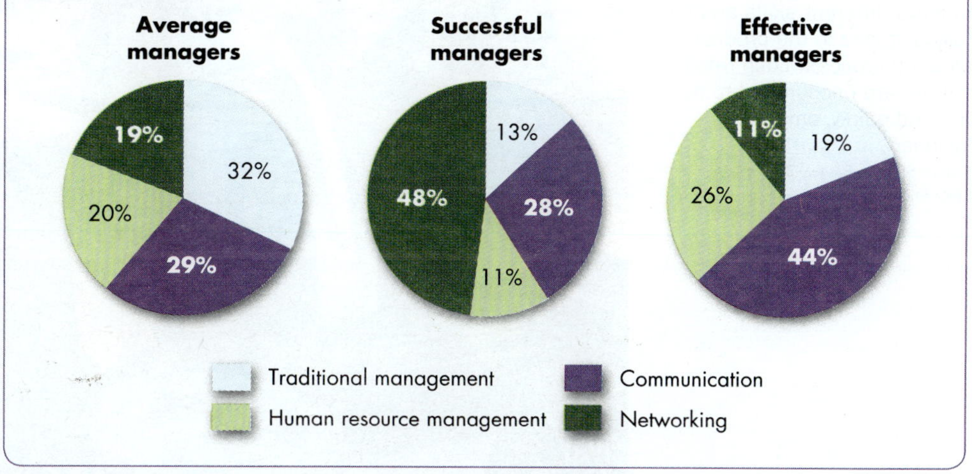

Source: Based on F. Luthans, R. M. Hodgetts, and S. A. Rosenkrantz, *Real Managers* (Cambridge, MA: Ballinger, 1988).

organizational behavior (OB) A field of study that investigates the impact that individuals, groups, and structure have on behavior within organizations for the purpose of applying such knowledge toward improving an organization's effectiveness.

Now that we've established what managers do, we need to study how best to do these things. **Organizational behavior (OB)** is a field of study that investigates the impact that individuals, groups, and structure have on behavior within organizations for the purpose of applying such knowledge toward improving an organization's effectiveness. That's a mouthful, so let's break it down.

OB is a field of study, meaning that it is a distinct area of expertise with a common body of knowledge. It focuses on three determinants of behavior in organizations: individuals, groups, and structure. In addition, OB applies the knowledge gained about individuals, groups, and the effect of structure on behavior in order to make organizations work more effectively.

To sum up our definition, OB is the study of what people do in an organization and the way their behavior affects the organization's performance. Because OB is concerned specifically with employment-related situations, it examines behavior in the context of job satisfaction, absenteeism, employment turnover, productivity, human performance, and management. Although debate exists about the relative importance of each, OB includes these core topics:

- Motivation
- Leader behavior and power
- Interpersonal communication
- Group structure and processes
- Attitude development and perception
- Change processes
- Conflict and negotiation
- Work design[18]

Manufacturer and retailer Lush Cosmetics incorporates standard benefits, training, and a good working environment with the chance to learn different skills and be fully engaged in the product creation process. Lush retail outlets are encouraged to be fun and quirky, employees included.

Source: Stephen Barnes/Business/Alamy Stock Photo

Complementing Intuition with Systematic Study

1-3 Show the value of OB to systematic study.

Whether you've explicitly thought about it before or not, you've been "reading" people almost all your life by watching their actions and interpreting what you see, or by trying to predict what people might do under different conditions. This casual approach to reading others can often lead to erroneous predictions, but using a systematic approach can improve your accuracy.

Underlying the systematic approach in this text is the belief that behavior is not random. Rather, we can identify fundamental consistencies underlying the behavior of all individuals and modify them to reflect individual differences.

These fundamental consistencies are very important. Why? Because they allow predictability. Behavior is generally predictable, and the *systematic study* of behavior is a way to make reasonably accurate predictions. When we use the term **systematic study**, we mean looking at relationships, attempting to attribute causes and effects, and basing our conclusions on scientific evidence—that is, on data gathered under controlled conditions and measured and interpreted in a rigorous manner.

systematic study Looking at relationships, attempting to attribute causes and effects, and drawing conclusions based on scientific evidence.

Evidence-based management (EBM) complements systematic study by basing managerial decisions on the best available scientific evidence. For example, we want doctors to make decisions about patient care based on the latest available evidence, and EBM argues that managers should do the same, thinking more scientifically about management problems. A manager might pose a question, search for the best available evidence, and apply the relevant information to the question or case at hand. You might wonder what manager would not base decisions on evidence, but the vast majority of management decisions are still made "on the fly," with little to no systematic study of available evidence.[19]

evidence-based management (EBM) Basing managerial decisions on the best available scientific evidence.

Systematic study and EBM add to **intuition**, or those "gut feelings" about what makes others (and ourselves) "tick." Of course, the things you have come to believe in an unsystematic way are not necessarily incorrect. Jack Welch (former CEO of General Electric) noted, "The trick, of course, is to know when to go with your gut." But if we make *all* decisions with intuition or gut instinct, we're likely working with incomplete information—like making an investment decision with only half the data about the potential for risk and reward.

intuition An instinctive feeling not necessarily supported by research.

Relying on intuition is made worse because we tend to overestimate the accuracy of what we think we know. Surveys of human resources managers have also shown that many managers hold so-called commonsense opinions regarding effective management that have been flatly refuted by empirical evidence.

We find a similar problem in chasing the business and popular media for management wisdom. The business press tends to be dominated by fads. As a writer for *The New Yorker* put it, "Every few years, new companies succeed, and they are scrutinized for the underlying truths they might reveal. But often there is no underlying truth; the companies just happened to be in the right place at the right time."[20] Although we try to avoid it, we might also fall into this trap. It's not that the business press stories are all wrong; it's that without a systematic approach, it's hard to separate the wheat from the chaff.

Myth or Science?

Management by Walking around Is the Most Effective Management

This is mostly a myth, but with a caveat. Management by walking around (MBWA) is an organizational principle made famous with the 1982 publication of *In Search of Excellence* and based on a 1970s initiative by Hewlett-Packard—in other words, it's a dinosaur. Years of research indicate that effective management practices are not built around MBWA. But the idea of requiring managers at all levels of the organization to wander around their departments to observe, converse, and hear from employees continues as a common business practice.

Many companies expecting managers and executives to do regular "floor time" have claimed benefits from increased employee engagement to deeper management understanding of company issues. A recent three-year study also suggested that a modified form of MBWA may significantly improve safety in organizations because employees become more mindful of following regulatory procedures when supervisors observe and monitor them frequently.

While MBWA sounds helpful, its limitations suggest that modern practices focused on building trust and relationships are more effective for management. Limitations include available hours, focus, and application.

1. **Available hours.** Managers are charged with planning, organizing, coordinating, and controlling; yet even CEOs—the managers who should be the most in control of their time—report spending 53 percent of their average 55-hour workweek in time-wasting meetings.
2. **Focus.** MBWA turns management's focus toward the concerns of employees. This is good, but only to a degree. As noted by Jeff Weiner, CEO of LinkedIn, "Part of the key to time management is carving out time to think, as opposed to constantly reacting. And during that thinking time, you're not only thinking strategically, thinking proactively, thinking longer-term, but you're literally thinking about what is urgent versus important." Weiner and other CEOs argue that meetings distract them from their purpose.
3. **Application.** The principle behind MBWA is that the more managers know their employees, the more effective those managers will be. This is not always (or even often) true. As we'll learn in Chapter 5, knowing something (or thinking we know it) should not always lead us to act on *only* that information because our internal decision making is subjective. We need objective data to make the most effective management decisions.

Based on the need for managers to dedicate their efforts to administering and growing businesses, and given the proven effectiveness of objective performance measures, it seems the time for MBWA is gone. Yet there is that one caveat: Managers should know their employees well. As Rick Russell, CEO of Greer Laboratories, says, "Fostering close ties with your lieutenants is the stuff that gets results. You have to rally the troops. You can't do it from a memo." Management should therefore not substitute walking around for true management.

Sources: Based on G. Luria and I. Morag, "Safety Management by Walking Around (SMBWA): A Safety Intervention Program Based on Both Peer and Manager Participation," *Accident Analysis and Prevention* (March 2012): 248–57; J. S. Lublin, "Managers Need to Make Time for Face Time," *The Wall Street Journal*, March 17, 2015, http://www.wsj.com/articles/managers-need-to-make-time-for-face-time-1426624214; and R. E. Silverman, "Where's the Boss? Trapped in a Meeting," *The Wall Street Journal*, February 14, 2012, B1, B9.

Big Data

Data has been used to evaluate behavior since at least 1749, when the word *statistic* was coined to mean a "description of the state."[21] Statistics back then were used for purposes of governance, but since the data collection methods were clumsy and simplistic, so were the conclusions. Big data—the extensive use of statistical compilation and analysis—didn't become possible until computers were sophisticated enough to store and manipulate large amounts of information. Let's look at the roots of the application of big data for business, which originated in the marketing department of online retailers.

Background It's difficult to believe now, but not long ago companies treated online shopping as a virtual point-of-sale experience: Shoppers browsed websites anonymously, and sellers tracked sales data only on what customers bought. Gradually, though, online retailers began to track and act on information about customer preferences that was uniquely available through the Internet shopping experience, information that was far superior to data gathered in simple store transactions. This enabled them to create more targeted marketing strategies than ever before. The bookselling industry is a case in point: Before online selling, brick-and-mortar bookstores could collect data about book sales only to create projections about consumer interests and trends. With the advent of Amazon, suddenly a vast array of information about consumer preferences—what customers bought, what they looked at, how they navigated the site, and what they were influenced by (such as promotions, reviews, and page presentation)—became available for tracking. The challenge for Amazon then was to identify which statistics were *persistent,* giving relatively constant outcomes over time, and which were *predictive,* showing steady causality between certain inputs and outcomes. The company used these statistics to develop algorithms to forecast which books customers would like to read next. Amazon could then base its wholesale purchase decisions on the feedback customers provided, both through these passive collection methods and through solicited recommendations for upcoming titles.

Current Usage No matter how many terabytes of data firms can collect or from how many sources, the reasons for data analytics include *predicting* any event, from a book purchase to a spacesuit malfunction; detecting how much *risk* is incurred at any time, from the risk of a fire to that of a loan default; and *preventing* catastrophes large and small, from a plane crash to an overstock of product.[22] With big data HDFC bank for bill payments, tax collection, and fraud management[23] and also hand out loans in less than 30 seconds. The smart city initiative of Central Government of India relies on the use of big data to provide services to the residents.[24] Reliance Jio uses big data analytics to carve out its future strategy.[25]

Naturally, big data has been used by technology companies like Google and Facebook, who rely on advertising dollars for revenue and thus need to predict user behavior. Companies like Netflix and Uber similarly use big data to predict where and when customers may want to use their services, although their revenue comes from subscribers to their services. Insurance firms predict behavior to assess risks, such as the chance of traffic accidents, in order to set customer premiums. Oyo, a hotel room aggregator uses analytics to drive engagement and strategy for enhancing customer experience, engagement with room and hotel owners etc.[26] Rivigo, a company that has solved for logistics and supply chain uses big data capabilities to analyse the movement of its 2500 trucks and location of drivers to cut down on transition time.[27] Another interesting use of big data is in the field of higher education. While no university in India has still used big data, the Ashford School in the U.K. has implemented big data tools, such as Socrative, Nearpod and Classroom Monitor for observing the performance and behaviour of its students.[28]

Online retailers like eBay and Amazon that market tangible products through online platforms also rely on big data to predict what will sell. For organizations like Nielson Holdings, which tracks television and radio watching, the results of data analyses *are* the product they sell. Still other organizations collect big data but do not use it directly. These are often organizations whose primary business is not online. Kroger, a U.S. grocery store chain, collects electronic information from 55 million customers who have loyalty cards and sells the data to vendors who stock Kroger's shelves.[29] Sometimes technology companies simply sell their data; Twitter sells 500 million tweets a day to four data assimilation companies.[30]

New Trends While accessibility to data increases organizations' ability to predict human behavioral trends, the use of big data for understanding, helping, and managing people is relatively new but holds promise. In fact, research on 10,000 workers in China, Germany, India, the United Kingdom, and the United States indicated that employees expect the next transformation in the way people work will rely more on technological advancements than on any other factor, such as demographic changes.[31] Organizations are also beginning to focus more on fast data, emphasizing a consistent influx of actionable data that can be used to guide business decisions in real time.[32]

It is good news for the future of business that researchers, the media, and company leaders have identified the potential of data-driven management and decision making. A manager who uses data to define objectives, develop theories of causality, and test those theories can determine which employee activities are relevant to the objectives.[33] Big data has implications for correcting management assumptions and increasing positive performance outcomes. It is applied increasingly toward making effective decisions (Chapter 5) and managing human resources (HR; Chapter 16). It is quite possible that the best use of big data in managing people will come from organizational behavior and psychology research, where it might even help employees with mental illnesses monitor and change their behavior.[34]

Limitations As technological capabilities for handling big data have increased, so have issues of privacy. This is particularly true when data collection includes surveillance instruments. For instance, an experiment in Brooklyn, New York, has been designed to improve the quality of life for residents, but the researchers will collect intensive data from infrared cameras, sensors, and smartphone Wi-Fi signals.[35] Through similar methods of surveillance monitoring, a bank call center and a pharmaceutical company found that employees were more productive with more social interaction, so they changed their break-time policies so more people took breaks together. They then saw sales increase and turnover decrease. Bread Winners Café in Dallas, Texas, constantly monitors all employees in the restaurant through surveillance and uses the data to promote or discipline its servers.[36]

These big data tactics and others might yield results—and research indicates that, in fact, electronic performance monitoring does increase task performance and citizenship behavior (helping behaviors toward others), at least in the short term.[37] But critics point out that after Frederick Taylor introduced surveillance analytics in 1911 to increase productivity through monitoring and feedback controls, his management control techniques were surpassed by Alfred Sloan's greater success with management outcomes, achieved by providing meaningful work to employees.[38] This brings up a larger concern: What do people think about big data when *they* are the source of the data? Organizations using big data run the risk of offending the very people they are trying to influence: employees and customers. The use of Arogya Setu app as a must for building residents and all those entering the building during the pandemic was both be seen as a means to ensure safety to all it was also seen as a means of surveillance[39] and could have the potential for misuse and curtailing of individual liberties.

We must keep in mind that big data will always be limited in predicting behavior, curtailing risk, and preventing catastrophes. In contrast to the replicable results we can obtain in the sciences through big data analytics, human behavior is often capricious and predicated on innumerable variables. Otherwise, our decision making would have been taken over by artificial intelligence by now! But that will never be a worthy goal.[40] Management is more than the sum of data.

Therefore, we are not advising you to throw intuition out the window. In dealing with people, leaders often rely on hunches, and sometimes the outcomes are excellent. At other times, human tendencies get in the way. Alex Pentland, a celebrated MIT data scientist, proposes a new science termed *social physics*, which is based on improving the way ideas and behaviors travel. Studies on social physics would lead to subtler forms of data collection and analysis than some of the more intrusive surveillance methods mentioned previously, while still informing managers on how to help employees focus their energies.[41] The prudent use of big data, along with an understanding of human behavioral tendencies, can contribute to sound decision making and ease natural biases. What we are advising is to use evidence as much as possible to inform your intuition and experience. That is the promise of OB.

Disciplines That Contribute to OB

1-4 Identify the major behavioral science disciplines that contribute to OB.

OB is an applied behavioral science built on contributions from a number of behavioral disciplines, mainly psychology and social psychology, sociology, and anthropology. Psychology's contributions have been principally at the individual or micro level of analysis, while the other disciplines have contributed to our understanding of macro concepts such as group processes and organization. Exhibit 1-3 is an overview of the major contributions to the study of organizational behavior.

Psychology

psychology The science that seeks to measure, explain, and sometimes change the behavior of humans and other animals.

Psychology seeks to measure, explain, and sometimes change the behavior of humans and other animals. Contributors to the knowledge of OB are learning theorists; personality theorists; counseling psychologists; and, most important, industrial and organizational psychologists.

Early industrial/organizational psychologists studied the problems of fatigue, boredom, and other working conditions that could impede efficient work performance. More recently, their contributions have expanded to include learning, perception, personality, emotions, training, leadership effectiveness, needs and motivational forces, job satisfaction, decision-making processes, performance appraisal, attitude measurement, employee-selection techniques, work design, and job stress.

Social Psychology

social psychology An area of psychology that blends concepts from psychology and sociology to focus on the influence of people on one another.

Social psychology, generally considered a branch of psychology, blends concepts from both psychology and sociology to focus on people's influence on one another. One major study area is *change*—how to implement it and how to reduce barriers to its acceptance. Social psychologists also contribute to measuring, understanding, and changing attitudes; identifying communication patterns; and building trust. They have made important contributions to our study of group behavior, power, and conflict.

Exhibit 1-3 Toward an OB Discipline

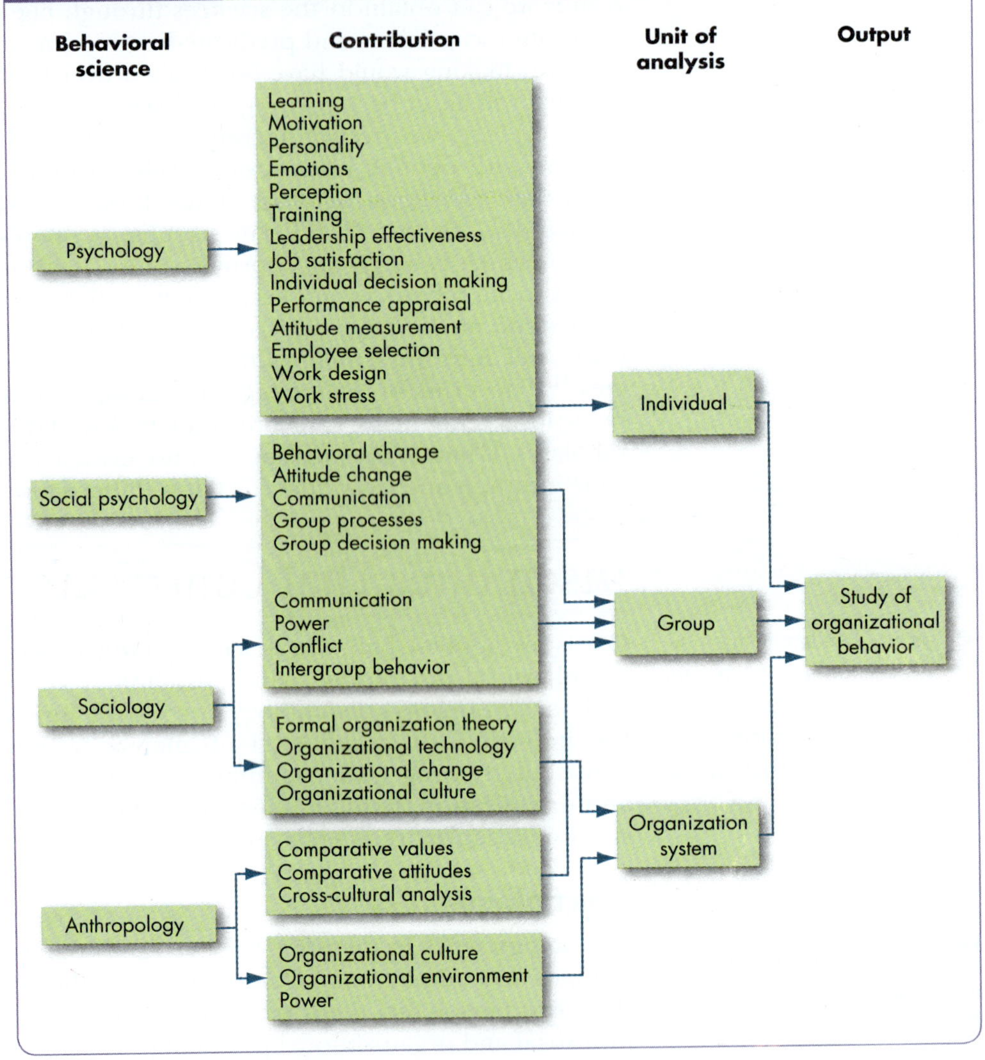

Sociology

sociology The study of people in relation to their social environment or culture.

While psychology focuses on the individual, **sociology** studies people in relation to their social environment or culture. Sociologists have contributed to OB through their study of group behaviors in organizations, particularly formal and complex organizations. Perhaps most important, sociologists have studied organizational culture, formal organization theory and structure, organizational technology, communications, power, and conflict.

Anthropology

anthropology The study of societies to learn about human beings and their activities.

Anthropology is the study of societies to learn about human beings and their activities. Anthropologists' work on cultures and environments has helped us understand differences in fundamental values, attitudes, and behavior among people in different countries and within different organizations. Much of our current understanding of organizational culture, organizational climate, and differences among national cultures is a result of the work of anthropologists or those using their methods.

There Are Few Absolutes in OB

1-5 Demonstrate why few absolutes apply to OB.

Laws in the physical sciences—chemistry, astronomy, physics—are consistent and apply in a wide range of situations. They allow scientists to generalize about the pull of gravity or to be confident about sending astronauts into space to repair satellites. Human beings are complex, and few, if any, simple and universal principles explain organizational behavior. Because we are not alike, our ability to make simple, accurate, and sweeping generalizations about ourselves is limited. Two people often act very differently in the same situation, and the same person's behavior changes in different situations. For example, not everyone is motivated by money, and people may behave differently at a religious service than they do at a party.

contingency variables Situational factors or variables that moderate the relationship between two or more variables.

That doesn't mean, of course, that we can't offer reasonably accurate explanations of human behavior or make valid predictions. It does mean that OB concepts must reflect situational, or contingency, conditions. We can say x leads to y, but only under conditions specified in z—the **contingency variables**. The science of OB was developed by applying general concepts to a particular situation, person, or group. For example, OB scholars would avoid stating that everyone likes complex and challenging work (a general concept). Why? Because not everyone wants a challenging job. Some people prefer routine over varied work or simple over complex tasks. A job attractive to one person may not be to another; its appeal is contingent on the person who holds it. Often, we'll find both general effects (money does have some ability to motivate most of us) and contingencies (some of us are more motivated by money than others, and some situations are more about money than others). We'll best understand OB when we realize how both (general effects, and the contingencies that affect them) often guide behavior.

Challenges and Opportunities

1-6 Identify managers' challenges and opportunities in applying OB concepts.

Understanding organizational behavior has never been more important for managers. Take a quick look at the dramatic changes in organizations. The typical employee is getting older, the workforce is becoming increasingly diverse, and global competition requires employees to become more flexible and cope with rapid change.

As a result of these changes and others, employment options have adapted to include new opportunities for workers. Exhibit 1-4 details some of the types of options individuals may find offered to them by organizations or for which they would like to negotiate. Under each heading in the exhibit, you will find a grouping of options from which to choose—or combine. For instance, at one point in your career, you may find yourself employed full-time in an office in a localized, nonunion setting with a salary and bonus compensation package, while at another point you may wish to negotiate for a flextime, virtual position and choose to work from overseas for a combination of salary and extra paid time off.

In short, today's challenges bring opportunities for managers to use OB concepts. In this section, we review some of the most critical issues confronting

Exhibit 1-4 Employment Options

Categories of Employment	Types of Employment	Places of Employment	Conditions of Employment	Compensation for Employment
Employed	Full-time	Anchored (office/cubicle)	Local	Salary
Underemployed/underutilized	Part-time	Floating (shared space)	Expatriate	Hourly
Re-employed	Flextime	Virtual	Short-term assignee	Overtime
Unemployed/jobless	Job share	Flexible	Flexpatriate	Bonus
Entrepreneur	Contingent	Work from home	International business traveler	Contract
Retired	Independent contractor		Visa employee	Time off
Job seeking	Temporary		Union/nonunion employee	Benefits
Furloughed	Reduced hours			
Laid off	Intern			

Sources: Based on J. R. Anderson, E. Binney, N. M. Davis, G. Kraft, S. Miller, T. Minton-Eversole, . . . and A. Wright, "Action Items: 42 Trends Affecting Benefits, Compensation, Training, Staffing and Technology," *HR Magazine* (January 2013): 33; M. Dewhurst, B. Hancock, and D. Ellsworth, "Redesigning Knowledge Work," *Harvard Business Review* (January–February 2013): 58–64; E. Frauenheim, "Creating a New Contingent Culture," *Workforce Management* (August 2012): 34–39; N. Koeppen, "State Job Aid Takes Pressure off Germany," *The Wall Street Journal*, February 1, 2013, A8; and M. A. Shaffer, M. L. Kraimer, Y.-P. Chen, and M. C. Bolino, "Choices, Challenges, and Career Consequences of Global Work Experiences: A Review and Future Agenda," *Journal of Management* (July 2012): 1282–1327.

managers for which OB offers solutions—or at least meaningful insights toward solutions.

Economic Pressures

When the U.S. economy plunged into a deep and prolonged recession in 2008, virtually all other large economies around the world followed suit. Layoffs and job losses were widespread, and those who survived the ax were often asked to accept pay cuts. When times are bad, as they were during the recession, managers are on the frontlines with employees who are asked to make do with less, who worry about their futures, and who sometimes must be fired. The difference between good and bad management can be the difference between profit and loss or ultimately between business survival and failure.

Managing employees well when times are tough is just as hard as when times are good, if not harder. In good times, understanding how to reward, satisfy, and retain employees is at a premium. In bad times, issues like stress, decision making, and coping come to the forefront.

Continuing Globalization

Organizations are no longer constrained by national borders. Samsung, the largest South Korean business conglomerate, sells most of its products to organizations in other countries, Burger King is owned by a Brazilian firm, and

McDonald's sells hamburgers in more than 118 countries on six continents. Even what is arguably the U.S. company with the strongest U.S. identity—Apple—employs twice as many workers outside the United States as it does inside the country. And all major automobile makers now manufacture cars outside their borders; Honda builds cars in Ohio, Ford in Brazil, Volkswagen in Mexico, and both Mercedes and BMW in the United States and South Africa.

The world has become a global village. In the process, the manager's job has changed. Effective managers anticipate and adapt their approaches to the global issues we discuss next.

Increased Foreign Assignments You are increasingly likely to find yourself in a foreign assignment—transferred to your employer's operating division or subsidiary in another country. Once there, you'll have to manage a workforce with very different needs, aspirations, and attitudes than those you are used to back home. To be effective, you will need to understand everything you can about your new location's culture and workforce—and demonstrate your cultural sensitivity—before introducing alternate practices.

Working with People from Different Cultures Even in your own country, you'll find yourself working with bosses, peers, and other employees born and raised in different cultures. What motivates you may not motivate them. Or your communication style may be straightforward and open, which others may find uncomfortable and threatening. To work effectively with people from different cultures, you need to understand how their culture and background have shaped them and how to adapt your management style to fit any differences.

Overseeing Movement of Jobs to Countries with Low-Cost Labor It is increasingly difficult for managers in advanced nations, where the minimum wage can be as high as $16.88 an hour, to compete against firms that rely on workers from

Guy Woolaert, senior vice president and chief technical and innovation officer of The Coca-Cola Company, has worked effectively with people from many cultures. He learned from his 20 years of assignments abroad in Europe, the Pacific, and other geographic regions how to adapt his management style to reflect the values of different countries.

Source: Robin Nelson/ZUMA Press, Inc./Alamy Stock Photo

developing nations where labor is available for as little as $0.03 an hour.[42] In a global economy, jobs tend to be created where lower costs give businesses a comparative advantage, although labor groups, politicians, and local community leaders see the exporting of jobs as undermining the job market at home. Managers face the difficult task of balancing the interests of their organizations with their responsibilities to the communities in which they operate.

Adapting to Differing Cultural and Regulatory Norms To be effective, managers need to know the cultural norms of the workforce in each country where they do business. For instance, a large percentage of the workforce enjoys long holidays in some countries. There will be country and local regulations to consider, too. Managers of subsidiaries abroad need to be aware of the unique financial and legal regulations applying to guest companies or else risk violating them. Violations can have implications for operations in that country and also for political relations between countries. Managers also need to be cognizant of differences in regulations for competitors in that country; understanding the laws can often lead to success rather than failure. For example, knowing local banking laws allowed one multinational firm—the Bank of China—to seize control of a storied (and very valuable) London building, Grosvenor House, from under the nose of the owner, the Indian hotel group Sahara. Management at Sahara contends that the loan default that led to the seizure was a misunderstanding regarding one of their other properties in New York.[43] Globalization can get complicated.

Workforce Demographics

The workforce has always adapted to variations in economies, longevity and birth rates, socioeconomic conditions, and other changes that have widespread impact. People adapt to survive, and OB studies the way those adaptations affect individuals' behavior. For instance, even though the 2008 global recession ended years ago, some trends from those years are continuing: Some people who had long been unemployed left the workforce altogether,[44] while others have cobbled together several part-time jobs[45] or settled for on-demand work.[46] Additional options that have been particularly popular for younger

OB POLL

Percentage of Men and Women Working

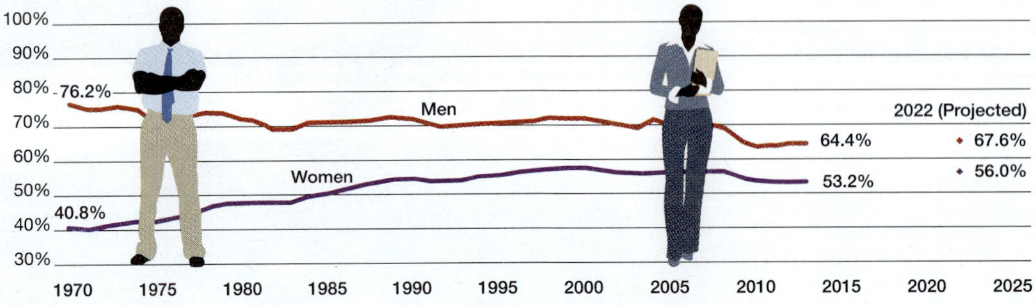

Sources: Based on U.S. Bureau of Labor Statistics, "Women in the Labor Force: A Datebook," 2014, www.bls.gov/opub/reports/cps/women-in-the-labor-force-a-databook-2014.pdf; and U.S. Bureau of Labor Statistics, "Economic News Release," 2013, http://www.bls.gov/news.release/ecopro.t02.htm.

educated workers have included obtaining specialized industry training after college,[47] accepting full-time jobs that are lower-level,[48] and starting their own companies.[49] As students of OB, we can investigate what factors lead employees to make various choices and how their experiences affect their perceptions of their workplaces. This understanding can help us predict organizational outcomes.

Longevity and birth rates have also changed the dynamics in organizations. Global longevity rates have increased six years in a very short time (since 1990),[50] while birth rates are decreasing for many developed countries, trends that together indicate a lasting shift toward an older workforce. OB research can help explain what this means for attitudes, organizational culture, leadership, structure, and communication. Socioeconomic shifts have a profound effect on workforce demographics. Equal access to work and education, regardless of gender identity or sexual orientation, has been deemed a human rights issue by the United Nations.[51] OB researchers study how people from diverse backgrounds fare in the workplace, the unique challenges and benefits they experience, as well as how their conditions can be improved. This is just one illustration of how cultural and socioeconomic changes affect the workplace, and it is one of many. We will discuss how OB can provide understanding and insight on workforce issues throughout this text.

Workforce Diversity

workforce diversity The concept that organizations are becoming more heterogeneous in terms of gender, age, race, ethnicity, sexual orientation, and other characteristics.

One of the most important challenges for organizations is **workforce diversity**, a trend by which organizations are becoming more heterogeneous in terms of employees' gender, age, race, ethnicity, sexual orientation, and other characteristics. Managing this diversity is a global concern. Though we have more to say about diversity in Chapter 2, we start here by saying that diversity presents great opportunities and poses challenging questions for managers and employees. How can we leverage differences within groups for competitive

Global food and drinks giant Danone has focused on customer-led corporate culture and behavior. It maintains a high visibility through sponsorship, advertising, and other promotional activities. Its customer-responsive culture aims to appeal to all age groups, and it includes participants and audiences for their annual Danone Nations Cup, won in 2016 by Germany.
Source: CrowdSpark/Alamy Stock Photo

advantage? Should we treat all employees alike? Should we recognize individual and cultural differences? What are the legal requirements in each country? Does increasing diversity even matter?

Customer Service

Service employees include technical support representatives, fast-food workers, salesclerks, nurses, automobile repair technicians, consultants, financial planners, and flight attendants. The shared characteristic of their jobs is substantial interaction with an organization's customers. OB can help managers increase the success of these customer interactions by showing how employee attitudes and behavior influence customer satisfaction.

Many organizations have failed because their employees failed to please customers. Management needs to create a customer-responsive culture. OB can provide considerable guidance in helping managers create such cultures—in which employees establish rapport with customers, put customers at ease, show genuine interest, and are sensitive to a customer's individual situation.[52]

People Skills

As you proceed through the chapters of this text, we'll present relevant concepts and theories that can help you explain and predict the behavior of people at work. You'll also gain insights into specific people skills you can use on the job. For instance, you'll learn ways to design motivating jobs, techniques for improving your management skills, and how to create more effective teams.

Networked Organizations

Networked organizations allow people to communicate and work together even though they may be thousands of miles apart. Independent contractors can telecommute via computer and change employers as the demand for their services changes. Software programmers, graphic designers, systems analysts, technical writers, photo researchers, book and media editors, and medical transcribers are just a few examples of people who can work from home or other nonoffice locations.

The manager's job is different in a networked organization. Motivating and leading people and making collaborative decisions online require different techniques than when individuals are physically present in a single location. As more employees do their jobs by linking to others through networks, managers must develop new skills. OB can provide valuable insights to help hone those skills.

Social Media

As we will discuss in Chapter 12, social media in the business world is here to stay. Despite its pervasiveness, many organizations continue to struggle with employees' use of social media in the workplace. In February 2015, a Texas pizzeria fired an employee before she showed up for her first day of work after she tweeted unflattering comments about her future job. In December 2014, Nordstrom fired an Oregon employee who had posted a personal Facebook comment seeming to advocate violence against white police officers.[53] These examples show that social media is a difficult issue for today's managers, presenting both a challenge and an opportunity for OB.

For instance, how much should HR look into a candidate's social media presence? Should a hiring manager read the candidate's Twitter feeds or do a quick perusal of her Facebook profile? We will discuss this issue later in the text.

Once employees are on the job, many organizations have policies about accessing social media at work—when, where, and for what purposes. But what about the impact of social media on employee well-being? One recent study found that subjects who woke up in a positive mood and then accessed Facebook frequently found their mood decreased during the day. Subjects who checked Facebook frequently over a two-week period reported a decreased level of satisfaction with their lives.[54] Managers—and the field of OB—are trying to increase employee satisfaction and therefore improve and enhance positive organizational outcomes. We will discuss these issues further in Chapters 3 and 4.

Employee Well-Being at Work

The typical employee in the 1960s and 1970s showed up at a specified workplace Monday through Friday and worked for clearly defined 8- or 9-hour chunks of time. That's no longer true for a large segment of today's workforce because the definition of the workplace has expanded to include anywhere a laptop or smartphone can go. Even if employees work flexible hours at home or from half a continent away, managers still need to consider their well-being at work.

One of the biggest challenges to maintaining employee well-being is the new reality that many workers never get away from the virtual workplace. While communication technology allows many technical and professional employees to do their work at home or on the beach in Tahiti, it also means that many feel like they're not part of a team. "The sense of belonging is very challenging for virtual workers, who seem to be all alone out in cyberland," said Ellen Raineri of Kaplan University.[55] Another challenge is that organizations are asking employees to put in longer hours. According to one study, one in four employees shows signs of burnout, and two in three report high stress levels and fatigue.[56] This may actually be an underestimate because workers report maintaining "always on" access for their managers through e-mail and texting. Employee well-being is challenged by heavy outside commitments. Millions of single-parent employees and employees with dependent parents face significant challenges in balancing work and family responsibilities, for instance.

As a result of their increased responsibilities in and out of the workplace, employees want jobs that give them flexibility in their work schedules so they can better manage work–life conflicts.[57] In fact, 56 percent of men and women in a recent study reported that work–life balance, more than money, recognition, and autonomy, was their definition of career success.[58] Most college and university students say attaining balance between personal life and work is a primary career goal; they want a life as well as a job. Organizations that don't help their employees achieve work–life balance will find it increasingly difficult to attract and retain the most capable and motivated individuals.

As you'll see in later chapters, the field of OB offers a number of suggestions to guide managers in designing workplaces and jobs that can help employees deal with work–life conflicts.

Twitter employees rave about their company's culture, which creates a positive work environment where smart and friendly colleagues learn; share values, ideas, and information; and work together to help the company grow and succeed. At Twitter's San Francisco headquarters, employees like Jenna Sampson, community relations manager, enjoy free meals, yoga classes, and a rooftop garden.
Source: Noah Berger/Reuters

Positive Work Environment

positive organizational scholarship An area of OB research that studies how organizations develop human strengths, foster vitality and resilience, and unlock potential.

A real growth area in OB research is **positive organizational scholarship** (also called positive organizational behavior), which studies how organizations develop human strengths, foster vitality and resilience, and unlock potential. Researchers in this area say too much of OB research and management practice has been targeted toward identifying what's wrong with organizations and their employees. In response, they try to study what's *good* about them.[59] Some key topics in positive OB research are engagement, hope, optimism, and resilience in the face of strain. Researchers hope to help practitioners create positive work environments for employees.

Positive organizational scholars have studied a concept called reflected best-self by asking employees to think about when they were at their personal best in order to understand how to exploit their strengths. The idea is that we all have things at which we are unusually good, yet we focus too often on addressing our limitations and rarely think about how to exploit our strengths.[60]

Although positive organizational scholarship does not deny the value of the negative (such as critical feedback), it does challenge researchers to look at OB through a new lens and pushes organizations to exploit employees' strengths rather than dwell on their limitations. One aspect of a positive work environment is the organization's culture, the topic of Chapter 15. Organizational culture influences employee behavior so strongly that organizations have begun to employ a culture officer to shape and preserve the company's personality.[61]

Ethical Behavior

ethical dilemmas and ethical choices Situations in which individuals are required to define right and wrong conduct.

In an organizational world characterized by cutbacks, expectations of increasing productivity, and tough competition, it's not surprising many employees feel pressured to cut corners, break rules, and engage in other questionable practices. They increasingly face **ethical dilemmas and ethical choices**, in which they are required to identify right and wrong conduct. Should they blow the whistle if they uncover illegal activities in their company? Do they follow orders with which they don't personally agree? Do they play politics to advance their careers?

What constitutes good ethical behavior has never been clearly defined and, in recent years, the line differentiating right from wrong has blurred. We see people all around us engaging in unethical practices: Elected officials pad expense accounts or take bribes; corporate executives inflate profits to cash in lucrative stock options; and university administrators look the other way when winning coaches encourage scholarship athletes to take easy courses or even, in the case of the University of North Carolina–Chapel Hill, sham courses with fake grades.[62] When caught, people give excuses such as "everyone does it" or "you have to seize every advantage."

Determining the ethically correct way to behave is especially difficult for both managers and employees in a global economy because different cultures have different perspectives on certain ethical issues.[63] The definition of fair treatment of employees in an economic downturn varies considerably across cultures, for instance. As we'll see in Chapter 2, perceptions of religious, ethnic, and gender diversity also differ across countries.

Today's manager must create an ethically healthy climate for employees in which they can do their work productively with minimal ambiguity about right and wrong behaviors. Companies that promote a strong ethical mission, encourage employees to behave with integrity, and provide strong leadership can influence employees to behave ethically.[64] Classroom training sessions in ethics have also proven helpful in maintaining a higher level of awareness of the implications of employee choices as long as the training sessions are given on an ongoing basis.[65] In upcoming chapters, we'll discuss the actions managers can take to create an ethically healthy climate and help employees sort through ambiguous situations.

Coming Attractions: Developing an OB Model

1-7 Compare the three levels of analysis in this text's OB model.

We conclude this chapter by presenting a general model that defines the field of OB and stakes out its parameters, concepts, and relationships. By studying the model, you will have a good picture of how the topics in this text can inform your approach to management issues and opportunities.

An Overview

model An abstraction of reality, a simplified representation of some real-world phenomenon.

A **model** is an abstraction of reality, a simplified representation of some real-world phenomenon. Exhibit 1-5 presents the skeleton of our OB model. It proposes three types of variables (inputs, processes, and outcomes) at three levels of analysis (individual, group, and organizational). In the chapters to follow, we will proceed from the individual level (Chapters 2 through 8), to group behavior (Chapters 9 through 14), to the organizational system (Chapters 15 through 18). The model illustrates that inputs lead to processes, which lead to outcomes; we will discuss these interrelationships at each level of analysis. Notice that the model also shows that outcomes can influence inputs in the future, which highlights the broad-reaching effect that OB initiatives can have on an organization's future.

An Ethical Choice

Vacation: All I Ever Wanted

Do you work to live, or live to work? Those of us who think it's a choice might be wrong. Almost one-third of 1,000 respondents in a study by Kelton Research cited workload as a reason for not using allotted vacation days. Consider Ken Waltz, a director for Alexian Brothers Health System. He has 500 hours (approximately 3 months) in banked time off and no plans to spend it. "You're on call 24/7 and these days, you'd better step up or step out," he says, referring to today's leaner workforce. "It's not just me—it's upper management.... It's everybody."

Many people feel pressure, spoken or unspoken, to work through their vacation days. Employers expect workers to do more with less, putting pressure on workers to use all available resources—chiefly their time—to meet manager expectations. In today's economy, there is always a ready line of replacement workers, and many employees will do everything possible to stay in their manager's good graces.

The issue of vacation time is an ethical choice for the employer *and* for the employee. Many organizations have "use it or lose it" policies whereby employees forfeit the paid time off they have accrued for the year if they haven't used it. When employees forfeit vacation, the risk of burnout increases. Skipping vacation time can wear you down emotionally, leading to exhaustion, negative feelings about your work, and a reduced feeling of accomplishment. You may find you are absent more often, contemplate leaving your job, and grow less likely to want to help anyone (including your managers). Even though these are negative consequences for your employer as well as for you personally, the employee must often take charge of the situation. Here are some ways you can maintain your well-being and productivity:

1. **Recognize your feelings.** We solve few problems without first recognizing them. According to a recent study by ComPsych involving 2,000 employees, two in three identified high levels of stress, out-of-control feelings, and extreme fatigue.
2. **Identify your tendency for burnout.** Research on 2,089 employees found that burnout is especially acute for newcomers and job changers. Burnout symptoms should level off after 2 years, but each individual experiences stress differently.
3. **Talk about your stressors.** Thomas Donohoe, a researcher on work–life balance, recommends talking with trusted friends or family. On the job, discussing your stress factors in an appropriate manner can help you reduce job overload.
4. **Build in high physical activity.** Research found an increase in job burnout (and depression) was highest for employees who did not engage in regular physical activity, while it was almost negligible for employees who did engage in regular physical activity.
5. **Take brief breaks throughout your day.** For office employees, the current suggestion from experts is to spend at least 1 to 2 minutes of every hour standing up to combat the effects of all-day sitting. Donohoe also suggests snack breaks, walks, or short naps to recharge.
6. **Take your vacation!** Studies suggest that recovery from stress can happen only if employees are (1) physically away from work and (2) not occupied by work-related duties. That means telling your manager that you will log off your e-mail accounts and shut off your phone for the duration of the vacation.

It is not always easy to look beyond the next deadline. But to maximize your long-term productivity and avoid stress, burnout, and illness—all of which are ultimately harmful to employer aims and employee careers alike—you should not succumb to vacation deficit disorder. Educate your managers. Your employer should thank you for it.

Sources: Based on B. B. Dunford, A. J. Shipp, R. W. Boss, I. Angermeier, and A. D. Boss, "Is Burnout Static or Dynamic? A Career Transition Perspective of Employee Burnout Trajectories," *Journal of Applied Psychology* 97, no. 3 (2012): 637–50; E. J. Hirst, "Burnout on the Rise," *Chicago Tribune*, October 29, 2012, 3-1, 3-4; B. M. Rubin, "Rough Economy Means No Vacation," *Chicago Tribune*, September 3, 2012, 4; and S. Toker and M. Biron, "Job Burnout and Depression: Unraveling Their Temporal Relationship and Considering the Role of Physical Activity," *Journal of Applied Psychology* 97, no. 3 (2012): 699–710.

Exhibit 1-5 **A Basic OB Model**

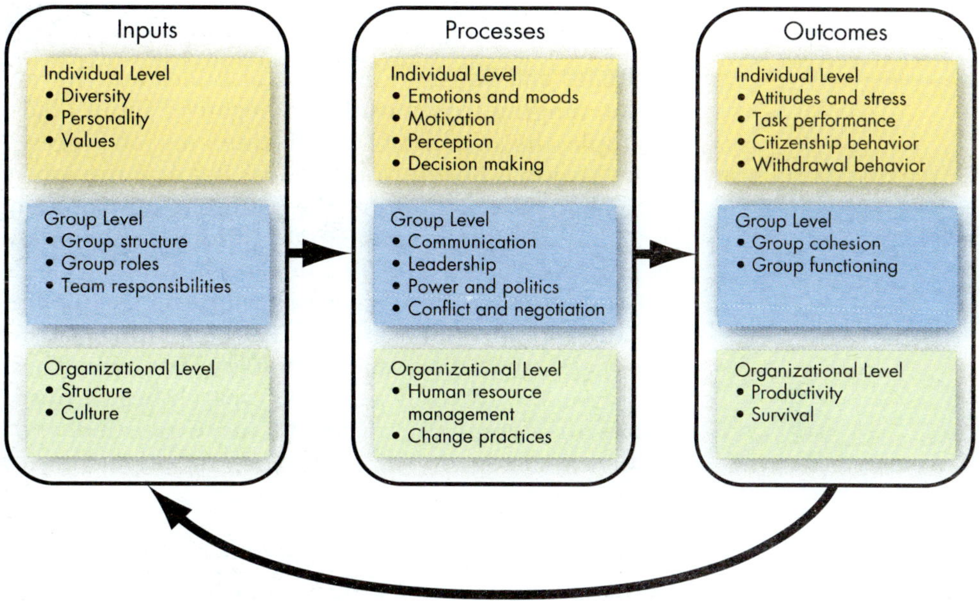

Inputs

inputs Variables that lead to processes.

Inputs are variables like personality, group structure, and organizational culture that lead to processes. These variables set the stage for what will occur in an organization later. Many are determined in advance of the employment relationship. For example, individual diversity characteristics, personality, and values are shaped by a combination of an individual's genetic inheritance and childhood environment. Group structure, roles, and team responsibilities are typically assigned immediately before or after a group is formed. Organizational structure and culture are usually the result of years of development and change as the organization adapts to its environment and builds up customs and norms.

Processes

processes Actions that individuals, groups, and organizations engage in as a result of inputs and that lead to certain outcomes.

If inputs are like the nouns in OB, processes are like the verbs. **Processes** are actions that individuals, groups, and organizations engage in as a result of inputs and that lead to certain outcomes. At the individual level, processes include emotions and moods, motivation, perception, and decision making. At the group level, they include communication, leadership, power and politics, and conflict and negotiation. At the organizational level, processes include human resources management and change practices.

Outcomes

outcomes Key factors that are affected by other variables.

Outcomes are the key variables that you want to explain or predict and that are affected by other variables. What are the primary outcomes in OB? Scholars have emphasized individual-level outcomes, such as attitudes and stress, task performance, citizenship behavior, and withdrawal behavior. At the group level, cohesion and functioning are the dependent variables. At the organizational level, we look at overall productivity and survival. Because these outcomes will be covered in all the chapters, we'll briefly discuss each here so you can understand the goal of OB.

Attitudes and Stress Employee attitudes are the evaluations that employees make, ranging from positive to negative, about objects, people, or events. For example, the statement "I really think my job is great" is a positive job attitude, and "My job is boring and tedious" is a negative job attitude. **Stress** is a psychological process that occurs in response to environmental pressures.

stress A psychological process that occurs in response to environmental pressures.

Some people might think influencing employee attitudes and stress is purely soft stuff and not the business of serious managers, but as we will show, attitudes often have behavioral consequences that relate directly to organizational effectiveness. The belief that satisfied employees are more productive than dissatisfied employees has been a basic tenet among managers for years, though only now has research begun to support it. Ample evidence shows that employees who are more satisfied and treated fairly are more willing to engage in the above-and-beyond citizenship behavior so vital in the contemporary business environment.

Task Performance The combination of effectiveness and efficiency at doing your core job tasks is a reflection of your level of **task performance**. If we think about the job of a factory worker, task performance could be measured by the number and quality of products produced in an hour. The task performance of a teacher would be the level of education that students obtain. The task performance of consultants might be the timeliness and quality of the presentations they offer to the client. All these types of performance relate to the core duties and responsibilities of a job and are often directly related to the functions listed on a formal job description.

task performance The combination of effectiveness and efficiency at doing core job tasks.

Obviously task performance is the most important human output contributing to organizational effectiveness, so in every chapter we devote considerable time to detailing how task performance is affected by the topic in question.

Organizational Citizenship Behavior (OCB) The discretionary behavior that is not part of an employee's formal job requirements, and that contributes to the psychological and social environment of the workplace, is called **organizational citizenship behavior (OCB)**, or simply citizenship behavior. Successful organizations have employees who do more than their usual job duties—who provide performance *beyond* expectations. In today's dynamic workplace, where tasks are increasingly performed by teams and where flexibility is critical, employees who engage in good citizenship behaviors help others on their team, volunteer for extra work, avoid unnecessary conflicts, respect the spirit as well as the letter of rules and regulations, and gracefully tolerate occasional work-related impositions and nuisances.

organizational citizenship behavior (OCB) Discretionary behavior that contributes to the psychological and social environment of the workplace.

Organizations want and need employees who will do things that aren't in any job description. Evidence indicates organizations that have such employees outperform those that don't. Absence in India has been reported to increase stress, disrupt work of others, and reduce quality of output.[66]

Withdrawal Behavior We've already mentioned behavior that goes above and beyond task requirements, but what about behavior that in some way is below task requirements? **Withdrawal behavior** is the set of actions that employees

withdrawal behavior The set of actions employees take to separate themselves from the organization.

take to separate themselves from the organization. There are many forms of withdrawal, ranging from showing up late or failing to attend meetings to absenteeism and turnover.

Employee withdrawal can have a very negative effect on an organization. The cost of employee turnover alone has been estimated to run into the thousands of dollars, even for entry-level positions. Absenteeism also costs organizations significant amounts of money and time every year. For instance, a recent survey found the average direct cost to U.S. employers of unscheduled absences is 8.7 percent of payroll.[67] And in Sweden, an average of 10 percent of the country's workforce is on sick leave at any given time.[68]

It's obviously difficult for an organization to operate smoothly and attain its objectives if employees fail to report to their jobs. The workflow is disrupted, and important decisions may be delayed. In organizations that rely heavily on assembly-line production, absenteeism can be considerably more than a disruption; it can drastically reduce the quality of output or even shut down the facility. Levels of absenteeism beyond the normal range have a direct impact on any organization's effectiveness and efficiency. A high rate of turnover can also disrupt the efficient running of an organization when knowledgeable and experienced personnel leave and replacements must be found to assume positions of responsibility. Research indicates that, in general, turnover is significantly harmful for organizational performance.[69]

All organizations have some turnover, of course. Turnover rates vary greatly by country and in part reflect the economy of that country. The U.S. national turnover rate in 2014 averaged about 40 percent; often the average is around 3 percent per month.[70] Is this good or bad? To answer that question, we need to know why there is turnover. Turnover includes voluntary terminations by the employee (quitting); involuntary terminations by the employer without cause (layoffs and discharges); and other separations, including involuntary terminations with cause (firing). The yearly average for quitting in 2014 was about 20 percent, layoffs and discharges averaged about 14 percent, and other separations averaged about 4 percent for the year. Therefore, about half the turnover was due to employees quitting their jobs; about 35 percent was due to layoffs and discharges; and the remainder was for other reasons, including firings.

While high turnover often impairs an organization's ability to achieve its goals, quitting is not all bad. In fact, U.S. Federal Reserve Chairwoman Janet Yellen has discussed the positive aspect of turnover for the economy: People quit because they are optimistic about their outside prospects.[71] If the "right" people are leaving—the poorer performers—quits can actually be positive for an organization. They can create opportunities to replace underperforming individuals with others who have higher skills or motivation, open up increased opportunities for promotions, and bring new and fresh ideas to the organization. In today's changing world of work, reasonable levels of employee-initiated turnover improve organizational flexibility and employee independence, and they can lessen the need for management-initiated layoffs. While it is reasonable to conclude that high turnover often indicates high employee withdrawal (and thus has a negative effect on organizational performance), zero turnover is not necessarily the goal. It's also important for organizations to assess which employees are leaving, and why.

So why do employees withdraw from work through counterproductive behaviors or quitting? As we will show later in the text, reasons include negative job attitudes, emotions, moods, and negative interactions with coworkers and supervisors.

Career OBjectives

What do I say about my termination?

I got fired! When prospective employers find out, they'll never hire me. Is there anything I can say to turn this around?

— Manish

Dear Manish:

Under this dark cloud, there are some silver linings: (1) Firing, or involuntary termination, happens to just about everyone at least once in a career, and (2) there is a worldwide job shortage of skilled workers. You might be amazed to know that, historically, individuals from age 18 to 44 have changed jobs an average of 11 times over their early careers. In fact, you can probably expect to stay in a job for less than three years, which means you'll have a lot of jobs in your lifetime.

Therefore, you shouldn't feel hopeless; you are likely to find your next job soon. ManpowerGroup's recent survey of over 37,000 employers in 42 countries found that 36 percent of organizations have talent shortages, the highest percentage in 7 years.

Still, we know you are worried about how to present the facts of your involuntary termination to prospective employers. If you give a truthful, brief account of the reason for your termination, you can position yourself well. Here are some additional suggestions:

- *Remember your soft skills count; in fact, they top the lists of employer requirements for all industries.* According to Chuck Knebl, a communications manager for the job placement company WorkOne, use your résumé and cover letter, interviews, and thank-you notes to showcase your communication skills. Employers report they are also looking for a teamwork attitude, positivity, personal responsibility, and punctuality, so use every opportunity to demonstrate these traits.
- *Although your soft skills count, don't forget your technical skills; employers agree they are equally important.* Knebl advises you to use your résumé to list your technical abilities and be prepared to elaborate upon request. Need some more skills? Job training has been shown to be helpful and can sometimes be free through colleges and unemployment offices.
- *Emphasize your ongoing training and education, especially as they relate to new technology; top performers are known to be continuous learners.* Also, if you've kept up with recent trends in social media, show it, but don't go on about your friend's tweet to Rihanna.

Best wishes for your success!

Sources: Based on Bureau of Labor Statistics, United States Department of Labor, Employment Projections, http://www.bls.gov/emp/ep_chart_001.htm; G. Jones, "How the Best Get Better and Better," *Harvard Business Review* (June 2008): 123–27; ManpowerGroup, "The Talent Shortage Continues/2014," http://www.manpowergroup.com/wps/wcm/connect/0b882c15-38bf-41f3-8882-44c33d 0e2952/2014_Talent_Shortage_WP_US2.pdf?MOD=AJPERES; J. Meister, "Job Hopping Is the 'New Normal' for Millennials: Three Ways to Prevent a Human Resource Nightmare," *Forbes* (August 14, 2012), http://www.forbes.com/sites/jeannemeister/2012/08/14/job-hopping-is-the-new-normal-for-millennials-three-ways-to-prevent-a-human-resource-nightmare/; and N. Schulz, "Hard Unemployment Truths about 'Soft' Skills," *The Wall Street Journal*, September 19, 2012, A15.

The opinions provided here are of the managers and authors only and do not necessarily reflect those of their organizations. The authors or managers are not responsible for any errors or omissions, or for the results obtained from the use of this information. In no event will the authors or managers, or their related partnerships or corporations thereof, be liable to you or anyone else for any decision made or action taken in reliance on the opinions provided here.

group cohesion The extent to which members of a group support and validate one another while at work.

Group Cohesion Although many outcomes in our model can be conceptualized as individual-level phenomena, some relate to the way groups operate. **Group cohesion** is the extent to which members of a group support and validate one another at work. In other words, a cohesive group is one that sticks together. When employees trust one another, seek common goals, and work together to achieve these common ends, the group is cohesive; when employees are divided among themselves in terms of what they want to achieve and have little loyalty to one another, the group is not cohesive.

There is ample evidence showing that cohesive groups are more effective.[72] These results are found both for groups studied in highly controlled laboratory settings and for work teams observed in field settings. This fits with our intuitive sense that people tend to work harder in groups that have a common purpose. Companies attempt to increase cohesion in a variety of ways, ranging from brief icebreaker sessions to social events like picnics, parties, and outdoor adventure-team retreats. Throughout the text, we assess whether these specific efforts are likely to result in increases in group cohesiveness. We'll also consider ways that picking the right people to be on the team in the first place might be an effective way to enhance cohesion.

group functioning The quantity and quality of a group's work output.

Group Functioning In the same way that positive job attitudes can be associated with higher levels of task performance, group cohesion should lead to positive group functioning. **Group functioning** refers to the quantity and quality of a group's work output. Similar to how the performance of a sports team is more than the sum of individual players' performance, group functioning in work organizations is more than the sum of individual task performances.

What does it mean to say that a group is functioning effectively? In some organizations, an effective group is one that stays focused on a core task and achieves its ends as specified. Other organizations look for teams that are able to work together collaboratively to provide excellent customer service. Still others put more of a premium on group creativity and the flexibility to adapt to changing situations. In each case, different types of activities will be required to get the most from the team.

productivity The combination of the effectiveness and efficiency of an organization.

effectiveness The degree to which an organization meets the needs of its clientele or customers.

efficiency The degree to which an organization can achieve its ends at a low cost.

Productivity The highest level of analysis in OB is the organization as a whole. An organization is productive if it achieves its goals by transforming inputs into outputs at the lowest cost. Thus, **productivity** requires both **effectiveness** and **efficiency**.

A hospital is *effective* when it meets the needs of its clientele successfully. It is *efficient* when it can do so at a low cost. If a hospital manages to achieve higher output from its present staff by reducing the average number of days a patient is confined to a bed or increasing the number of staff–patient contacts per day, we say the hospital has gained productive efficiency. A business firm is effective when it attains its sales or market share goals, but its productivity also depends on achieving those goals efficiently. Popular measures of organizational efficiency include return on investment, profit per dollar of sales, and output per hour of labor.

Service organizations must include customer needs and requirements in assessing their effectiveness. Why? Because a clear chain of cause and effect runs from employee attitudes and behavior to customer attitudes and profitability. For example, a recent study of six hotels in China indicated that negative employee attitudes decreased customer satisfaction and ultimately harmed the organization's profitability.[73]

organizational survival The degree to which an organization is able to exist and grow over the long term.

Survival The final outcome we will consider is **organizational survival**, which is simply evidence that the organization is able to exist and grow over the long term. The survival of an organization depends not just on how productive the organization is but also on how well it fits with its environment. A company that is very productive in making goods and services of little value to the market is unlikely to survive for long, so survival also relies on perceiving the market successfully, making good decisions about how and when to pursue opportunities, and successfully managing change to adapt to new business conditions.

Having reviewed the input, process, and outcome model, we're going to change the figure up a little bit by grouping topics together based on whether

Exhibit 1-6 The Plan of the Text

	The Individual	The Group	The Organization
Inputs	• Diversity in organizations (Ch. 2) • Personality and values (Ch. 5)	• Group structure (Ch. 9 & 10) • Group roles (Ch. 9 & 10) • Team responsibilities (Ch. 9 & 10)	• Structure (Ch. 15) • Culture (Ch. 16)
Processes	• Emotions and moods (Ch. 4) • Motivation (Ch. 7 and 8) • Perception and decision making (Ch. 6)	• Communication (Ch. 11) • Leadership (Ch. 12) • Power and politics (Ch. 13) • Conflict and negotiation (Ch. 14)	• Human resource management (Ch. 17) • Change practices (Ch. 18)
Outcomes	• Attitudes (Ch. 3) and stress (Ch. 18) • Task performance (all) • Citizenship behavior (all) • Withdrawal behavior (all)	• Group cohesion (Ch. 9 & 10) • Group functioning (Ch. 9 & 10)	• Productivity (all) • Survival (all)

we study them at the individual, group, or organizational level. As you can see in Exhibit 1-6, we deal with inputs, processes, and outcomes at all three levels of analysis, but we group the chapters as shown here to correspond with the typical ways research has been done in these areas. For example, it is easier to understand one unified presentation about how personality leads to motivation, which leads to performance, than to jump around levels of analysis. Each level builds on the one that precedes it, so after going through them in sequence, you will have a good idea of how the human side of organizations functions.

Employability Skills

1-8 Describe the key employability skills gained from studying OB that are applicable to other majors or future careers.

Challenges relevant to OB can be found in just about every function of business, from finance and accounting to management and marketing. Without a doubt, at some point in your career, you will come across an issue that hinges to a large degree on the behavior of people in organizations. A review of the great challenges that most businesses face reveals that OB is an essential piece of the puzzle in solving many problems that involve managing integrity/social responsibility, resource management, competition among businesses, bolstering customer and employee loyalty, reducing uncertainty, complying with government regulation, managing risks, and finding the right staff—all while growing revenue and increasing profit.[74]

But OB is not relevant to business majors only; it is important for all students, no matter what their majors are. At first glance, for example, it might not seem as if a university student with a microbiology degree would have any need to take an OB class. But what happens after that student graduates? Wouldn't knowledge of OB principles and concepts help him or her apply to and be successful at a job as a biology technician with Battelle? What about a graduate with a nursing degree working at the Mayo Clinic? A computer science graduate who is about to begin work with Cisco? OB principles matter for students of all majors and can help increase employability as well as interpersonal skills in the workplace. These skills can even help you to become successful in your classes as you interact with other students and your professors! Clearly, the knowledge of OB concepts such as stress management, change, attitudes, emotions, and motivation, among others, can help you navigate your interactions with your classmates as you continue to learn.

People, along with their behaviors, differences, attitudes, emotions, moods, personalities, values, intentions, thoughts, and motivations, are inextricably linked to life in the workplace. As Benjamin Schneider notes, "The people make the place."[75] These employees interact and communicate with one another within and across work groups, departments, teams, and organizations to help accomplish the organization's goals. Leaders within these organizations (along with the employees themselves) seek to effect change, establish an organizational culture, and set policies and procedures: processes that inevitably involve leadership, politicking, conflict, and negotiation. Given the pervasiveness of OB in organizational life, entry-level employees and working professionals would therefore benefit from having solid foundational skills in OB, such as communication, collaboration, critical thinking, problem solving, social responsibility, and knowledge application and analysis.

In this section, we explore the career employability skills that a course in OB can help expand for those who select *any* major—from English, to engineering, to political science.

Employability Skills That Apply across Majors

Throughout this text, you'll learn and practice many skills that hiring managers identify as important to success in a variety of business settings, including small and large firms, nonprofit organizations, and public service. These skills will also be useful if you plan to start your own business, for example:

- *Critical thinking* involves purposeful and goal-directed thinking used to define and solve problems and to make decisions or form judgments related to a particular situation or set of circumstances. It involves cognitive, metacognitive, and dispositional components that may be applied differently in specific contexts.
- *Communication* is defined as effective use of oral, written, and nonverbal communication skills for multiple purposes (e.g., to inform, instruct, motivate, persuade, and share ideas); effective listening; using technology to communicate; and being able to evaluate the effectiveness of communication efforts—all within diverse contexts.
- *Collaboration* is a skill in which individuals can actively work together on a task, constructing meaning and knowledge as a group through dialogue and negotiation that results in a final product reflective of their joint, interdependent actions.
- *Knowledge application and analysis* is defined as the ability to learn a concept and then apply that knowledge appropriately in another setting to achieve a higher level of understanding.
- *Social responsibility* includes skills related to both business ethics and corporate social responsibility. Business ethics includes sets of guiding principles that influence the way individuals and organizations behave within the society that they operate. Corporate social responsibility is a form of ethical behavior that requires that organizations understand, identify, and eliminate unethical economic, environmental, and social behaviors.

Each of the chapters in the text start with what we refer to as the employability skills matrix (ESM). As you can see on the next page, this matrix links the five employability skills that were just defined with special features in each chapter, including Myth or Science?, Career Objectives, An Ethical Choice, Point/Counterpoint, Experiential Exercise, Ethical Dilemma, and Case Incident. Within these sections, you will be primed to think critically and apply your knowledge to consider special cases and concepts. You will also learn how to improve your collaboration and communication skills by learning what you might do or say in these given situations to navigate the work world positively and effectively. You will be confronted with ethical dilemmas in which you will consider the ethics of particular behaviors in the workplace. We recommend that you review and consider the ESM in advance of reading the chapter so that you have a better idea of the skills you will be developing from each section. All five of these skills are critical to success in careers that are relevant to OB and other majors alike. In the chapters to come, you will engage in a variety of activities and become exposed to several cases in which you will be developing these skills.

Employability Skills Matrix (ESM)

	Myth or Science?	Career OBjectives	An Ethical Choice	Point/ Counterpoint	Experiential Exercise	Ethical Dilemma	Case Incident 1	Case Incident 2
Critical Thinking				✓	✓	✓	✓	✓
Communication	✓	✓	✓		✓		✓	✓
Collaboration	✓	✓			✓	✓		✓
Knowledge Application and Analysis		✓		✓	✓	✓	✓	✓
Social Responsibility			✓		✓	✓	✓	

Summary

Managers need to develop their interpersonal, or people, skills to be effective in their jobs. Organizational behavior (OB) investigates the impact that individuals, groups, and structure have on behavior within an organization, and it applies that knowledge to make organizations work more effectively.

Implications for Managers

- Resist the inclination to rely on generalizations; some provide valid insights into human behavior, but many are erroneous. Get to know the person, and understand the context.
- Use metrics rather than hunches to explain cause-and-effect relationships.
- Work on your interpersonal skills to increase your leadership potential.
- Improve your technical skills and conceptual skills through training and staying current with OB trends like big data and fast data.
- OB can improve your employees' work quality and productivity by showing you how to empower your employees, design and implement change programs, improve customer service, and help your employees balance work–life conflicts.

The Battle of the Texts

POINT

Walk into your nearest major bookstore and you'll see shelves of management books whose titles tell us the topics we apparently need to know about:

- *The Secret* (Blanchard & Miller, 2014)
- *Turn the Ship Around!* (Marquet, 2013)
- *The Way You Do Anything Is the Way You Do Everything* (Evans, 2014)
- *Leadership Safari* (Iannucci, 2014)
- *Business Is a Baby* (Noh, 2014)
- *Think Like a Freak* (Dubner & Levitt, 2014)
- *Spiraling Upward* (Wallbridge, 2015)
- *Refire! Don't Retire* (Blanchard & Shaevitz, 2015)
- *Top Dog* (Bronson & Merryman, 2015)

Popular books on organizational behavior often have cute titles and are fun to read, but they make the job of managing people seem like it's just a matter of having a good slogan and five easy steps. If you dig into the texts, you'll find that most are based on the author's opinions rather than substantive research. Most become popular in part because people largely agree with the opinions they are reading and enjoy the author's writing style. Often, the writers are presentation speakers or consultants whose real business is in delivering ideas to you. When the author is a veteran from the business world, it is doubtful that one person's experience translates into an effective management practice for everyone. Even when the authors are numbers-oriented, as are the *Think Like a Freak* authors Steven Levitt and Stephen Dubner, their conclusions for management are not management research based. So why do we base our own management philosophies on these books when, with a little effort, we can access knowledge produced by thousands of scientific studies on human behavior in organizations?

Organizational behavior is a complex subject. Few if any simple statements about human behavior are generalizable to all people in all situations. Would you try to apply leadership insights you got from a book about *Star Wars* or *Breaking Bad* to managing software engineers in the twenty-first century? Surely not. Neither should we try to apply leadership insights that aren't based on research about the type of workplaces in which we function.

COUNTERPOINT

People want to know about management—the good, the bad, and the ugly. People who have experience or high interest write about the topics that interest readers, and publishers put out the best of these texts. When books become popular, we know people are learning from them and finding good results by applying the author's management ideas. Texts like these can provide people with the secrets to management that others have worked out through experience. Isn't it better to learn about management from people in the trenches instead of the latest obscure references from academia? Many of the most important insights we gain in life aren't necessarily the product of careful empirical research studies.

Unhelpful management guides sometimes do get published, and once in a while they become popular. But do they outnumber the esoteric research studies published in scholarly journal articles every year? Far from it; sometimes it seems that for every popular business text, there are thousands of scholarly journal articles. Many of these articles can hardly be read by individuals in the workplace—they are buried in academic libraries, riddled with strange acronyms and insider terms, and light on practical application. Often they apply to specific management scenarios, so they are even less generalizable. For example, a few recent management and OB studies were published in 2015 with the following titles:

- "Transferring Management Practices to China: A Bourdieusian Critique of Ethnocentricity" (Siebers, Kamoche, & Li, 2015)
- "Cross-Cultural Perceptions of Clan Control in Korean Multinational Companies: A Conceptual Investigation of Employees' Fairness Monitoring Based on Cultural Values" (Yang, 2015)
- "The Resistible Rise of Bayesian Thinking in Management: Historical Lessons from Decision Analysis" (Cabantous & Gond, 2015)
- "A Model of Rhetorical Legitimation: The Structure of Communication and Cognition Underlying Institutional Maintenance and Change" (Harmon, Green, & Goodnight, 2016)

We don't mean to poke fun at these studies, but our point is that all ways of creating knowledge can be criticized. If business books are sometimes light reading, academic articles can be esoteric and even less relevant. Popular books can add to our understanding of how people work and how to manage them best. We shouldn't assume they are not of value. And while there is no one right way to learn the science and art of managing people in organizations, the most enlightened managers gather insights from multiple sources: their own experience; research findings; observations of others; and, yes, the popular business press. Authors and academics have an important role to play, and it isn't fair to condemn business books with catchy titles.

CHAPTER REVIEW

QUESTIONS FOR REVIEW

1-1 What is the importance of interpersonal skills in the workplace?

1-2 What is the definition of organizational behavior (OB)?

1-3 How does systematic study contribute to our understanding of OB?

1-4 What are the major behavioral science disciplines that contribute to OB?

1-5 Why are there so few absolutes in OB?

1-6 What are the challenges and opportunities for managers in using OB concepts?

1-7 What are the three levels of analysis in our OB model?

EXPERIENTIAL EXERCISE I'm a Team Leader; I Don't Need Any Help.

Students will create teams of approximately four or five members and consider the following scenario. One of the team members is the CEO of a startup that creates robots for technology-assisted surgery, and the others are members of the board of directors. One of your teams, headed by Mark, a team leader with a PhD in robotics from a prestigious university, is experiencing problems in the development of a new robot prototype for heart surgery. The board decided to participate in some of their meetings to understand more.

Here the notes that you wrote down in one of their meetings:

- *The meeting starts with Mark communicating general information about the company's current projects. He then reviews the team's progress and members start to discuss a major problem they are facing that is preventing the robot from working as required.*
- *Shubhra and Ramesh say that they have reviewed all the steps of robot development to understand where the problem was but were not able to discover anything unusual.*
- *Geeta and Manish describe the different attempts they have been making in the previous weeks, which resulted in no significant improvements in the robot functioning.*
- *All of them propose to Mark that he consult with technical specialists outside the team and ask for help. Mark disagrees; he has some notion of how to fix the problem.*
- *The team members say that an external eye on the project would still be helpful. Mark seems to not hear their requests and quickly terminates the meeting, promising to have a solution in ten days on his own.*

Your team should discuss what recommendations you can offer Mark based on your notes. The following questions can serve as the basis for class discussion.

Questions

1-8. What do you think explains Mark's attitude and why he is reluctant to ask for external help?

1-9. Should the board intervene in managing this situation? What help can be given to Mark to improve his work attitude?

1-10. Let us suppose that the board decides to introduce to the team headed by Mark another team member who has experienced similar problems in the past. How do you think the rest of the team and Mark will react to this change? What can be done to favor a smooth integration of this new component of the team?

ETHICAL DILEMMA There's a Drone in Your Soup

It is 2020, and drones are everywhere. Alibaba quadcopters have been delivering special ginger tea to customers in Beijing, Shanghai, and Guangzhou for years; Amazon's octocopters finally deliver packages in most major cities within 30 minutes without knocking down pedestrians; and college students everywhere welcome late-night nachos from Taco Bell Tacocopters. Indoor drones are still in the pioneering phase—backyard enthusiasts are building tiny versions, but no large-scale commercial efforts have been made to address indoor utility drones. That's all about to change.

You work for a multinational technology corporation on a sprawling, 25-acre headquarters campus, with offices in 2 million square feet of interior space in one large building and four additional smaller (but still large) buildings. The official Head of Interior Spaces is your boss; you're the leader of the Consideration of New Things team. In a meeting with your team, your boss says, "I've just heard from my friend at Right To Drones Too (R2D2) that his group has perfected their inside drone. It's small and light but can carry up to 10 pounds. It includes a camera, a speaker, and a recorder."

Your team expresses surprise; no one even knew an inside utility drone was under development, and governments worldwide are still haggling over regulations for drones. Your boss goes on enthusiastically, "I've seen the little drones, and I think you'll be impressed—not only can they scoot across the quad, but they can fetch things off tables, grab me a latté, attend meetings for me, check over your shoulders to see what you're working on … anything! They're really accurate, agile, and super quiet, so you'll barely even know they're around. My friend wants us to have the first 100 drones here for free, and he's willing to send them over tomorrow. I figure we can hand them out randomly, although of course we'll each have one."

Your boss sits back, smiling and expecting applause. You glance at your team members and are relieved to see doubt and hesitation on their faces.

"Sounds, uh, great," you reply. "But how about the team takes the afternoon to set the ground rules?"

Questions

1-11. How might the R2D2 drones influence employee behavior? Do you think they will cause people to act more or less ethically? Why?

1-12. Who should get the drones initially? How can you justify your decision ethically? What restrictions for use should these people be given, and how do you think employees, both those who get drones and those who don't, will react to this change?

1-13. How will your organization deal with sabotage or misuse of the drones? The value of an R2D2 drone is $2,500.

1-14. Many organizations already use electronic monitoring of employees, including sifting through website visits and e-mail correspondence, often without the employees' direct knowledge. In what ways might drone monitoring be better or worse for employees than covert electronic monitoring of Web or e-mail activity?

CASE INCIDENT 1 L'Oréal around the Globe

With more than 88,000 employees and a massive presence spread across 150 countries on five continents of the globe, L'Oréal is the world's largest beauty company. The company has had a successful global expansion strategy since its inception, growing from a local producer of a hair dye for French hairdressers in 1909 to a global giant today. Around the globe, the company has a mix of different operations, ranging from corporate offices, to manufacturing sites, to distribution centers, to retail stores. In line with its expansion strategy, the company has acquired numerous popular beauty companies and brands over the years, including European, American, and Asian brands. According to L'Oréal, this aspect of its expansion strategy is especially important for bolstering its brand portfolio and ensuring future organic growth.

However, global expansion has its own challenges, among which is successfully managing employees across cultures and regions, all separated by different norms, languages, and traditions. There are many examples of companies that have failed in foreign markets due to their inability to manage the cultural differences among their global units and establish effective communication between its international subsidiaries. According to Geert Hofstede, a Dutch social psychologist known for his pioneering research on cross-cultural groups (see Chapter 4), there are cultural differences between different countries and regions, especially between Western and Eastern cultures. Similarly, Jeanne M. Brett, a professor at the Kellogg School of Management, notes that communication styles vary from one culture to another, which can increase the possibilities of conflict and misunderstanding between employees from different cultures. In fact, a recent study by L'Oréal in the United Kingdom found that cultural differences across international markets are the biggest reason why employers are unable to provide ample foreign assignments to their employees.

Global companies need to create effective strategies that can increase harmony and unity among their workers across the globe. They can build cultural sensitivity—being aware and sensitive to the cultural differences between different groups of people—by ensuring that employees learn about each other's norms and cultures. L'Oréal has invested heavily in workforce initiatives that aim to build stronger connections between its people around the globe. L'Oréal tries to base itself on "global careers" by promoting and encouraging its staff to rotate among the company's locations around the world. The result is stronger collaboration and partnerships between different international workgroups that contributes to organizational effectiveness in global settings. At its foundation is a strong dedication to employee diversity, underpinned by L'Oréal's long history of building diverse, multicultural teams, raising cultural awareness, and improving unity between its people, something that its competitors have found much more challenging.

Questions

1-15. What are the challenges for L'Oréal as it expands to international locations? Name some challenges not listed in the case.

1-16. What do you think of the L'Oréal' study mentioned in the case? What did you find most interesting in the study? Should L'Oréal continue to conduct such studies?

1-17. What is your opinion on using international careers to overcome cultural challenges. What alternative means can you think of?

Sources: Hofstede Insights, "Country Comparison," www.hofstede-insights.com/country-comparison/, accessed June 2, 2020; H. Hae-Jung and Y. Doz, "L'Oréal Masters Multiculturalism," *Harvard Business Review*, 91 (June 2013): 114–19; R. Knight, "How to Run a Meeting of People from Different Cultures," *Harvard Business Review Digital Articles* (2015): 2–7; L'Oréal Group, "Promoting Diversity & Inclusion," www.loreal.com/group/diversity-and-inclusion, accessed April 8, 2020; L'Oréal UK and Ireland, "Freedom to Go Beyond, That's the Beauty of L'Oréal," www.loreal.co.uk/sites/default/files/cms/loreal_uk_global_careers_report.pdf, accessed April 8, 2020.

CASE INCIDENT 2 So, How Engaged Are Employees? The Data Says It All

Given the prime role it plays in organizational success, employee engagement has of late been the focus of many research studies and reports. An engaged worker is one who feels passionate and enthusiastic about their job and their workplace. Studies show that engagement can have a significant impact on organizational outcomes. For example, research conducted across the retail giant Marks & Spencer over a four-year period showed that an improved employee engagement led to an increase of £62 million in sales every year compared to stores with low employee engagement. A similar study at Sainsbury's, one of the biggest grocery stores in the United Kingdom, demonstrated that employee engagement led to a 15 percent increase in a store's year-on-year growth.

However, despite its obvious importance, employee engagement is still a challenge in many companies around the world. A global study by Qualtrics in 2020 showed that employee engagement scores are below the employee engagement average of 53 percent in many countries. For example, the United Kingdom, Singapore, Germany, South Korea, and Japan scored 50 percent, 47 percent, 41 percent, 40 percent, and 35 percent respectively on employee engagement.

Low levels of engagement at work could spell trouble in the long run; employees who are disengaged at work are often demotivated and less productive, all of which can slow down business performance and reduce a company's competitiveness in the market. Many experts say that businesses should consider employee engagement as a top priority and develop strategies to foster it in the workplace. However, this outcome is heavily dependent on understanding and measuring the drivers of employee engagement at work, which leads us to a vital issue—data collection. To this end, businesses need to employ the right data measurement tools for assessing and managing employee engagement levels at work.

Employee and engagement surveys are a prime example of data measurement tools. Focusing on the assessment of employee attitudes about various aspects of the business environment, these surveys can take the form of advanced online surveys, which are administered frequently to employees and promise to offer frequent, real-time data, or they can be the more traditional yearly surveys, which run the risk of slowing down the management's response time in improving engagement at work. A recent article by Eric O'Rourke, Scott Judd, and Adam Grant in the *Harvard Business Review* lists a number of benefits of employee surveys, foremost among them being that they are excellent predictors of employee behavior with a high degree of accuracy. Based on what surveys say about how their employees may act in the future, companies can use this information to make better decisions at work.

Despite the strategic importance of data collection, studies show that many companies have yet to leverage the power of data in decision making across companies. Employers often fail to act on the data filled by employees in the surveys, and in many cases employees may not be surveyed at all. It has been argued that improving employee engagement requires a fundamental change to a corporate culture that recognizes the value of generating data for making better-informed decisions. It follows that generating data about employee engagement represents one of the best practices for improved performance, and companies who discover the power of employee data too late may find themselves at a disadvantage in the marketplace.

Questions

1-18. In your opinion, how does measuring employee engagement through a survey provide managers with insights in improving staff performance? What other types of tools can you use to gather data on employee engagement?

1-19. In which instances would collecting data about employees lead to infringement of employee privacy?

1-20. The case mentions that many companies do not do any type of assessment of their employees' attitudes at work. What are the dangers of failing to gather such feedback?

Sources: Richard Barrett, *The Values-Driven Organization: Cultural Health and Employee Well-Being as a Pathway to Sustainable Performance* (UK: Routledge, 2017); T. Davenport and N. Mittal, "How CEOs Can Lead a Data-Driven Culture," *Harvard Business Review* (March 23, 2020), hbr.org/2020/03/how-ceos-can-lead-a-data-driven-culture, accessed April 10, 2020; Scott Judd, Eric O'Rourke, and Adam Grant, "Employee Surveys Are Still One of the Best Ways to Measure Engagement," *Harvard Business Review* (March 14, 2018), hbr.org/2018/03/employee-surveys-are-still-one-of-the-best-ways-to-measure-engagement, accessed April 10, 2020; H. Ismail, A. Iqbal, and L. Nasr, "Employee Engagement and Job Performance in Lebanon: The Mediating Role of Creativity," *International Journal of Productivity and Performance Management* 68(3) (2019): 506–23; Qualtrics, "2020 Employee Experience Trends," Singapore, www.qualtrics.com/m/assets/au/wp-content/uploads/2020/01/FINAL_SG_EX_Trends_Report_Ebook.pdf, accessed October 7, 2020.

ENDNOTES

[1] "Survey: Few CFOs Plan to Invest in Interpersonal Skills Development for Their Teams," Accountemps press release, June 19, 2013, http://accountemps.rhi.mediaroom.com/2013-06-19-Survey-Few-CFOs-Plan-to-Invest-in-Interpersonal-Skills-Development-for-Their-Teams.

[2] J. Kauflin, "The Best Places to Work in 2017," *Forbes*, December 7, 2016, http://www.forbes.com/sites/jeffkauflin/2016/12/07/the-best-places-to-work-in-2017/#4a3abb3673e3.

[3] I. S. Fulmer, B. Gerhart, and K. S. Scott, "Are the 100 Best Better? An Empirical Investigation of the Relationship between Being a 'Great Place to Work' and Firm Performance," *Personnel Psychology* 56, no. 4 (2003): 965–93.

[4] S. E. Humphrey, J. D. Nahrgang, and F. P. Morgeson, "Integrating Motivational, Social, and Contextual Work Design Features: A Meta-Analytic Summary and Theoretical Extension of the Work Design Literature," *Journal of Applied Psychology* 92, no. 5 (2007): 1332–56.

[5] A. E. Colbert, J. E. Bono, and R. K. Purvanova, "Flourishing via Workplace Relationships: Moving beyond Instrumental Support," *Academy of Management Journal* 59, no. 4 (2016): 1199–223.

[6] T. L. Miller, C. L. Wesley II, and D. E. Williams, "Educating the Minds of Caring Hearts: Comparing the Views of Practitioners and Educators on the Importance of Social Entrepreneurship Competencies," *Academy of Management Learning & Education* 2, no. 3 (2012): 349–70.
[7] H. Aguinis and A. Glavas, "What We Don't Know about Corporate Social Responsibility: A Review and Research Agenda," *Journal of Management* 38, no. 4 (2012): 932–68.
[8] D. Meinert, "Background on Bosses," *HR Magazine*, August 2014, 29.
[9] Ibid.
[10] Ibid.
[11] A. I. Kraut, P. R. Pedigo, D. D. McKenna, and M. D. Dunnette, "The Role of the Manager: What's Really Important in Different Management Jobs," *Academy of Management Executive* 19, no. 4 (2005): 122–29.
[12] C. Matheson, "Understanding the Policy Process: The Work of Henry Mintzberg," *Public Administration Review* 69, no. 6 (2009): 1148–61; S. Segal, "A Heideggerian Perspective on the Relationship between Mintzberg's Distinction between Engaged and Disconnected Management: The Role of Uncertainty in Management," *Journal of Business Ethics* 103, no. 3 (2011): 469–83; H. Mintzberg, "Productivity Is Killing American Enterprise," *Harvard Business Review* (July–August 2007): 25; and H. Mintzberg, "Rebuilding Companies as Communities," *Harvard Business Review* (July–August 2009): 140–43.
[13] Ibid.
[14] D. Bartram, "The Great Eight Competencies: A Criterion-Centric Approach to Validation," *Journal of Applied Psychology* 90, no. 6 (2005): 1185–203; and S. E. Scullen, M. K. Mount, and T. A. Judge, "Evidence of the Construct Validity of Developmental Ratings of Managerial Performance," *Journal of Applied Psychology* 88, no. 1 (2003): 50–66.
[15] For the original study, see F. Luthans, "Successful vs. Effective Real Managers," *Academy of Management Executive* 2, no. 2 (1988): 127–32. A great deal of research by Fred Luthans and others has used this study as a basis. See, for example, F. Shipper and J. Davy, "A Model and Investigation of Managerial Skills, Employees' Attitudes, and Managerial Performance," *Leadership Quarterly* 13, no. 2 (2002): 95–120.
[16] P. Wu, M. Foo, and D. B. Turban, "The Role of Personality in Relationship Closeness, Developer Assistance, and Career Success," *Journal of Vocational Behavior* 73, no. 3 (2008): 440–48; and A. M. Konrad, R. Kashlak, I. Yoshioka, R. Waryszak, and N. Toren, "What Do Managers Like to Do? A Five-Country Study," *Group & Organization Management* 26, no. 4 (2001): 401–33.
[17] L. Dragoni, H. Park, J. Soltis, and S. Forte-Trammell, "Show and Tell: How Supervisors Facilitate Leader Development among Transitioning Leaders," *Journal of Applied Psychology* 99, no. 1 (2014): 66–86.
[18] For a review of what one researcher believes *should* be included in organizational behavior based on survey data, see J. B. Miner, "The Rated Importance, Scientific Validity, and Practical Usefulness of Organizational Behavior Theories: A Quantitative Review," *Academy of Management Learning & Education* 2, no. 3 (2003): 250–68.
[19] D. M. Rousseau, *The Oxford Handbook of Evidence-Based Management* (New York: Oxford University Press, 2014).
[20] J. Surowiecki, "The Fatal-Flaw Myth," *The New Yorker*, July 31, 2006, 25.
[21] Z. Karabell, "Everyone Has a Data Point," *The Wall Street Journal*, February 19, 2014, A11.
[22] E. Morozov, "Every Little Byte Counts," *The New York Times Book Review*, May 18, 2014, 23.
[23] Chawla, V. (2020), "HDFC Bank Uses Advanced Analytics For 10 Second Loan Approvals: Smita Bhagat, Country Head", *Analytics India Magazine (February 26, 2020)*, retrieved on March 22, 2022 from https://analyticsindiamag.com.
[24] Centre for Internet and Society, "*Big Data and Governance in India*", retrieved on March 12, 2022 from https://cis-india.org.
[25] Bhatia, R. (2017), "Is Big Data turning the wheels at Reliance Jio—inside the youngest mobile operator's big data strategy", *Analytics India Magazine (August 7, 2017)*, retrieved on March 22, 2022 from https://analyticsindiamag.com.
[26] Kumar, A. (2018), "How OYO Rooms is using analytics and data science to enhance customer experience", *Express Computer (July 25, 2018)*, retrieved on March 13, 2022, from https://www.expresscomputer.in.
[27] Tandon, S. (2018), "How two Indian startups are using big data to get ahead—and stay there", *Quartz India (May 7, 2018)*, retrieved on March 25, 2022, from https://qz.com.
[28] Sharma, R (2021), "Top 5 Interesting Big Data Applications in Education [2022]", *Upgrad (January 6, 2021)*, retrieved on March 25, 2022 from https://www.upgrad.com.
[29] V. Monga, "What Is All That Data Worth?" *The Wall Street Journal*, October 13, 2014, B3, B6.
[30] E. Dwoskin and Y. Koh, "Twitter Pushes Deeper into Data," *The Wall Street Journal*, April 16, 2014, B2.
[31] "What Will Transform the Way People Work?" *HR Magazine* (December 2014): 16.
[32] J. Hugg, "Fast Data: The Next Step after Big Data," *InfoWorld*, June 11, 2014, http://www.infoworld.com/article/2608040/big-data/fast-data–the-next-step-after-big-data.html; A. Lorentz, "Big Data, Fast Data, Smart Data," *Wired*, April 17, 2013, https://www.wired.com/insights/2013/04/big-data-fast-data-smart-data/; and J. Spencer, "Which Do We Need More: Big Data or Fast Data?," *Entrepreneur*, March 12, 2015, https://www.entrepreneur.com/article/243123.
[33] N. Bloom, R. Sadun, and J. Van Reenan, "Does Management Really Work? How Three Essential Practices Can Address Even the Most Complex Global Practices," *Harvard Business Review* (November 2012): 77–82.
[34] C. Cole, "Changing Neurobiology with Behavior," *Association for Psychological Science: Observer* 27, no. 6 (2014): 29–32.
[35] E. Dwoskin, "Big Data Knows When You Turn off the Lights," *The Wall Street Journal*, October 21, 2014, B1–B2.
[36] S. Lohr, "Unblinking Eyes Track Employees," *The New York Times*, June 22, 2014, 1, 15.
[37] D. B. Bhave, "The Invisible Eye? Electronic Performance Monitoring and Employee Job Performance," *Personnel Psychology* 67, no. 3 (2003): 605–35.
[38] R. Karlgaard, "Danger Lurking: Taylor's Ghost," *Forbes*, May 26, 2014, 34.
[39] German Institute for Global and Area Studies (2021), "*Digital Surveillance and the Threat to Civil Liberties in India*", retrieved

on March 24, 2022, from https://www.giga-hamburg.de.
[40] W. Isaacson, "Of Man and Machine," *The Wall Street Journal*, September 27–28, 2015, C1–C2.
[41] Morozov, "Every Little Byte Counts."
[42] M. Boesler, "Here's How America's Minimum Wage Stacks up Against Countries Like India, Russia, Greece, and France," *Business Insider*, August 19, 2013, http://www.businessinsider.com/a-look-at-minimum-wages-around-the-world-2013-8, accessed May 15, 2017.
[43] C. Karmin and S. Chaturvedi, "Grosvenor House Is Seized," *The Wall Street Journal*, March 4, 2015, C8.
[44] V. McGrane, "The Downside of Lower Unemployment," *The Wall Street Journal*, February 3, 2014, A2.
[45] A. Lowrey, "Long Out of Work, and Running Out of Options," *The New York Times*, April 4, 2014, B1, B4.
[46] L. Weber and R. E. Silverman, "On-Demand Workers: 'We Are Not Robots,'" *The Wall Street Journal*, January 28, 2015, B1, B7.
[47] C. Porter and M. Korn, "Can This Online Course Get Me a Job?," *The Wall Street Journal*, March 4, 2014, B7.
[48] D. Belkin and M. Peters, "For New Grads, Path to a Career Is Bumpy," *The Wall Street Journal*, May 24–25, 2014, A5.
[49] N. Kitsantonis, "A Hands-On Approach to the Greek Economy," *The New York Times*, March 25, 2014, B3.
[50] G. Naik, "Global Life Expectancy Rises by Six Years," *The Wall Street Journal*, December 18, 2014, A10.
[51] United Nations, *Gender Equality*, https://www.un.org/en/sections/issues-depth/gender-equality/index.html, accessed April 16, 2020.
[52] I. O. Karpen, "Service-Dominant Orientation: Measurement and Impact on Performance Outcomes," *Journal of Retailing* 91, no. 1 (2015): 89–108.
[53] J. Greenwald, "Tips for Dealing with Employees Whose Social Media Posts Reflect Badly on Your Company," *Forbes*, March 6, 2015, www.forbes.com/sites/entrepreneursorganization/2015/03/06/tips-for-dealing-with-employees-whose-social-media-posts-reflect-badly-on-your-company/.
[54] E. Jaffe, "Using Technology to Scale the Scientific Mountain," *Association for Psychological Science: Observer* 27, no. 6 (2014): 17–19.
[55] N. Fallon, "No Face Time? No Problem: How to Keep Virtual Workers Engaged," *Business News Daily*, October 2, 2014, http://www.businessnewsdaily.com/7228-engaging-remote-employees.html.
[56] E. J. Hirst, "Burnout on the Rise," *Chicago Tribune*, October 19, 2012, http://articles.chicagotribune.com/2012-10-29/business/ct-biz-1029-employee-burnout-20121029_1_employee-burnout-herbert-freudenberger-employee-stress.
[57] S. Shellenbarger, "Single and off the Fast Track," *The Wall Street Journal*, May 23, 2012, D1, D3.
[58] M. Mithel, "What Women Want," *Business Today*, March 8, 2013, http://businesstoday.intoday.in/story/careers-work-life-balance-women/1/193135.html.
[59] F. Luthans and C. M. Youssef, "Emerging Positive Organizational Behavior," *Journal of Management* 33, no. 3 (2007): 321–49; C. M. Youssef and F. Luthans, "Positive Organizational Behavior in the Workplace: The Impact of Hope, Optimism, and Resilience," *Journal of Management* 33, no. 5 (2007): 774–800; and J. E. Dutton and S. Sonenshein, "Positive Organizational Scholarship," in C. Cooper and J. Barling (eds.), *Encyclopedia of Positive Psychology* (Thousand Oaks, CA: Sage, 2007).
[60] L. M. Roberts, G. Spreitzer, J. Dutton, R. Quinn, E. Heaphy, and B. Barker, "How to Play to Your Strengths," *Harvard Business Review* (January 2005): 1–6; and L. M. Roberts, J. E. Dutton, G. M. Spreitzer, E. D. Heaphy, and R. E. Quinn, "Composing the Reflected Best Self-Portrait: Becoming Extraordinary in Work Organizations," *Academy of Management Review* 30, no. 4 (2005): 712–36.
[61] "Five Jobs That Won't Exist in 10 Years . . . and One New Title You'll Start to See," *HR Magazine*, February 2014, 16.
[62] Editorial Board, "NCAA Should Punish the University of North Carolina for Cheating Scandal," *Chicago Tribune*, November 7, 2014, http://www.chicagotribune.com/news/opinion/editorials/ct-north-carolina-sports-scandal-edit-1108-20141107-story.html, accessed March 11, 2015.
[63] W. Bailey and A. Spicer, "When Does National Identity Matter? Convergence and Divergence in International Business Ethics," *Academy of Management Journal* 50, no. 6 (2007): 1462–80; and A. B. Oumlil and J. L. Balloun, "Ethical Decision-Making Differences between American and Moroccan Managers," *Journal of Business Ethics* 84, no. 4 (2009): 457–78.
[64] D. M. Mayer, M. Kuenzi, R. Greenbaum, M. Bardes, and R. Salvador, "How Low Does Ethical Leadership Flow? Test of a Trickle-Down Model," *Organizational Behavior and Human Decision Processes* 108, no. 1 (2009): 1–13; and A. Ardichvili, J. A. Mitchell, and D. Jondle, "Characteristics of Ethical Business Cultures," *Journal of Business Ethics* 85, no. 4 (2009): 445–51.
[65] D. Meinert, "Managers' Influence," *HR Magazine*, April 2014, 25.
[66] Society for Human Resource Management. "Total Financial Impact of Employee Absences Across the United States, China, Australia, Europe, India and Mexico", retrieved on March 25, 2022 from https://www.shrm.org.
[67] "Unplanned Absence Costs Organizations 8.7 Percent of Payroll, Mercer/Kronos Study," June 28, 2010, www.mercer.com/press-releases/1383785.
[68] W. Hoge, "Sweden's Cradle-to-Grave Welfare Starts to Get Ill," *International Herald Tribune*, September 25, 2002, 8.
[69] T.-Y. Park and J. D. Shaw, "Turnover Rates and Organizational Performance: A Meta-Analysis," *Journal of Applied Psychology* 98, no. 2 (2013): 268–309.
[70] "Job Openings and Labor Turnover Survey/2014 Revised," http://www.bls.gov/jlt/revisiontables.htm, accessed March 13, 2015.
[71] N. Shah, "Good Sign for Jobs: Less Caution, More Quitting," *The Wall Street Journal*, February 10, 2014, A2.
[72] M. Casey-Campbell and M. L. Martens, "Sticking It All Together: A Critical Assessment of the Group Cohesion-Performance Literature," *International Journal of Management Reviews* 11, no. 2 (2009): 223–46.
[73] X. Zhao and A. S. Mattila, "Examining the Spillover Effect of Frontline Employees' Work-Family Conflict on Their Affective Work Attitudes and Customer Satisfaction," *International Journal of Hospitality Management* 33 (2013): 310–15.
[74] W. F. Cascio and H. Aguinis, "Research in Industrial and Organizational

Psychology from 1963 to 2007: Changes, Choices, and Trends," *Journal of Applied Psychology* 93, no. 5 (2008): 1062–81; G. George, J. Howard-Grenville, A. Joshi, and L. Tihanyi, "Understanding and Tackling Societal Grand Challenges through Management Research," *Academy of Management Journal* 59, no. 6 (2016): 1880–95; and L. W. Porter and B. Schneider, "What Was, What Is, and What May Be in OP/OB," *Annual Review of Organizational Psychology and Organizational Behavior* 1, no. 1 (2014): 1–21.

[75] B. Schneider, "The People Make the Place," *Personnel Psychology* 40 (1987): 437–53; and B. Schneider, H. W. Goldstein, and D. B. Smith, "The ASA Framework: An Update," *Personnel Psychology* 48 (1995): 747–73.

2 Diversity in Organizations

Source: StockImageFactory.com.shutterstock.com

LEARNING OBJECTIVES

After studying this chapter, you should be able to:

2-1 Describe the two major forms of workplace diversity.

2-2 Demonstrate how workplace discrimination undermines organizational effectiveness.

2-3 Describe how the key biographical characteristics are relevant to Organizational Behavior (OB).

2-4 Explain how other differentiating characteristics factor into OB.

2-5 Demonstrate the relevance of intellectual and physical abilities to OB.

2-6 Describe how organizations manage diversity effectively.

This matrix identifies which features and end-of-chapter material will help you develop specific skills employers are looking for in job candidates.

Employability Skills Matrix (ESM)

	Myth or Science?	Career OBjectives	An Ethical Choice	Point/ Counterpoint	Experiential Exercise	Ethical Dilemma	Case Incident 1	Case Incident 2
Critical Thinking		✓	✓	✓	✓	✓	✓	✓
Communication	✓	✓			✓		✓	
Collaboration					✓		✓	
Knowledge Application and Analysis			✓	✓	✓	✓	✓	✓
Social Responsibility		✓	✓	✓	✓	✓	✓	✓

A LACK OF DIVERSITY IN THE TECH INDUSTRY

The tech industry has been notorious for failing on the diversity and inclusion front. Apple, Facebook, Google, and Microsoft may be the biggest technology companies across the world, yet the diversity reports they have posted for the past five years consistently present the same picture, an industry dominated by white and Asian men.

There has been some progress since 2014. Facebook, for instance, says the percentage of its female employees globally has increased from 15 to 23 percent. However, ethnic diversity remains low. Over the same time period, the proportion of U.S. technical employees at Google and Microsoft who are African American or Latinx (of Latin American descent) rose by only about 1 percent. The share of African American technical workers at Apple is 6 percent, less than half the 13 percent proportion of African Americans in the U.S. population. Ageism also continues to be a challenge; when tech workers hit 45, their job offers drop and salaries start to fall.

Global research and advisory firm, 451 Research, reports that India leads all other countries with 34 percent of the IT workforce comprising of women under the age of 30. Even more promising is the pipeline of graduates in the STEM domain at almost 50:50 for male to female ratio. However, the number is not as encouraging at the middle and senior management levels.[1] Women in AI-related jobs occupy 27.8 percent of the

AI/Analytics workforce in India.[2] In a recent study conducted in the top 20 IT companies, reveals that at the senior level the women workforce strength is around 30 percent, and most of these companies have set the goal to be at 45 to 50 percent in the next 24 months.[3]

In the United Kingdom too, data on diversity in the tech industry is disappointing, lagging far behind the Financial Times Stock Exchange 100 Index (FTSE 100). About 8.5 percent of senior executives in technology are from a minority background, while women make up just 12.6 percent of board members in the sector, compared with the 30 percent female representation achieved by FTSE 100 businesses. The picture is similar across Europe. According to the 2019 State of European Tech Report, there was a record investment of about €30 billion in the industry across the continent, yet 92 percent of the investment went to all-male founding teams, and funding to all-female teams actually dropped. Of the hundreds of founders that responded to the survey, 84 percent self-identify as white, and just 0.9 percent are of African descent. And 82 percent of founders are university educated, as compared to the 35 percent of people across Europe.

The status quo is particularly troubling because of how technology now affects every sector, from transport, to finance, to government, to healthcare. If only today's tech-literate workers can access these growing employment opportunities, swaths of the general population will be left behind. The products and services they make will be skewed too. The lack of inclusion affects the design of the goods and services that the industry creates. For instance, voice recognition initially did not respond to women because the designers who tested the products were male. Facial recognition is notoriously poor at recognizing darker and female faces, again partly because of biased training data. A more diverse workforce will lead to better products that can address a wider range of customers, who may include people from different ethnic and socio economic backgrounds as well as the elderly and the disabled.

Sources: M. Murgia, "How to Increase Diversity in the Tech Sector," *Financial Times*, November 13, 2019; and C. Warner, "Why Is European Tech Still Failing on Diversity and Inclusion," *Forbes*, November 25, 2019, www.forbes.com/sites/checkwarner/2019/11/25/why-is-european-tech-still-failing-on-diversity-and-inclusion/?sh=681dac4c17cb.

The barriers and hardships facing women such as those in the tech industry are substantial, and they are examples of why diversity is so important for organizations. In this chapter, we look at how organizations should work to maximize the potential contributions of a diverse workforce. Because each of us is different from others in myriad ways, we consider diversity in many different forms. We also show how individual differences in abilities affect employee behavior and effectiveness in organizations.

World over, despite a predominantly male working population, there has been a rise in a more diverse workforce. For example, the U.S. during 1950s showed only 26.9 percent women occupied paid work positions, but over the 7 decades the number has increased to 45.8 percent.[4] Puzzlingly though, India has seen a decrease in the percentage of women participating in the workforce from 34.1 percent in 1999–2000 to 27.2 percent in 2011–12 to 23.5 percent in 2019.[5,6,7]

Not surprisingly, a 2019 salary index report in India shows that women in India earn less than 20 percent as compared to men.[8] The complexities of the gender pay gap in India can be linked to the prevalent socioeconomic structures that define gender roles. The gap in payments to women is distributed across several industries such as IT, finance and manufacturing. The story is no different in the unorganized sectors like agricultural and construction where the pay gap is a significantly high for the wages offered to men versus women.[9]

Further, the gender pay gap can also be analyzed by looking at the frequency of supervisory positions held by males compared to females. The salary index report also revealed major differences between wages received by supervisors and non-supervisors employed in the financial sector, leading to believe that more experienced women often face higher inequality in pay.

A recent study shows that during the pandemic women faced a further blow and only 65 percent of women received a pay rise or bonus for taking on extra responsibilities or a new role compared to 70 per cent of men.[10]

Diversity

2-1 Describe the two major forms of workplace diversity.

We are, each of us, unique. This is obvious enough, but managers sometimes forget they need to recognize the individual differences in their employees in order to capitalize on their unique strengths. In this chapter, we'll learn how individual characteristics like age, gender, race, ethnicity, and abilities can influence employee performance. We'll also see how managers can develop awareness about these characteristics and manage their diverse workforces effectively. But first, let's consider an overview of the changing workforce.

Demographic Characteristics

The predominantly white, male managerial workforce of the past has given way to a gender-balanced, multiethnic workforce. For instance, in 1950, only 29.6 percent of the U.S. workforce was female,[11] but by 2016, women comprised 46.8 percent.[12] Both in the United States and internationally, women today are much more likely than before to be employed full time, have an advanced education, and earn wages comparable to those of men (see the OB Poll).[13] The pay gap between women and men could be because of lower female representation at senior levels and the types of jobs that have traditionally been dominated by either gender. It is also argued that a gender pay gap is not the same as an equal pay gap. Different pay for people performing the same job

OB POLL

Gender Pay Gap: Narrowing but Still There

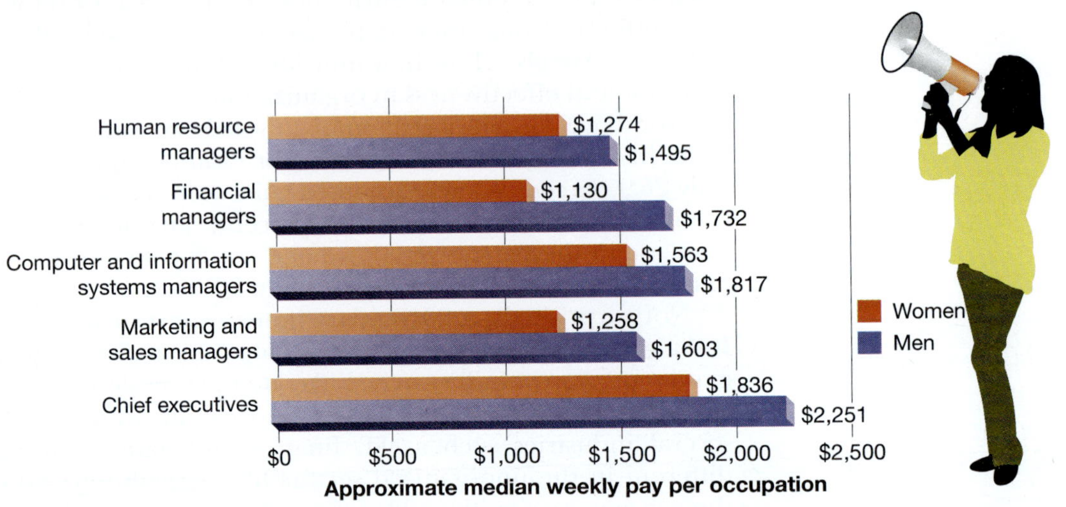

Source: US Bureau of Labor Statistics, *Highlights of Women's Earnings in 2015* (Report No. 1604, November 2016): https://www.bls.gov/opub/reports/womens-earnings/2015/pdf/home.pdf.

has been illegal in the United Kingdom since 1970. It appears that the gender pay difference demonstrates a demographic pay gap, and the solutions to the two issues seem to be rather different.[14]

Levels of Diversity

surface-level diversity Differences in easily perceived characteristics, such as gender, race, ethnicity, age, or disability, that do not necessarily reflect the ways people think or feel but that may activate certain stereotypes.

deep-level diversity Differences in values, personality, and work preferences that become progressively more important for determining similarity as people get to know one another better.

Although much has been said about diversity in age, race, gender, ethnicity, religion, and disability status, experts now recognize that these demographic characteristics are just the tip of the iceberg.[15] These characteristics mostly reflect **surface-level diversity**, not thoughts and feelings, and can lead employees to make stereotypes and assumptions about others from certain demographic backgrounds. However, evidence has shown that people are less concerned about demographic differences if they see themselves as sharing more important characteristics, such as personality and values, that represent **deep-level diversity**.[16]

Managing diversity involves everyone and benefits everyone. Consider the following example. Philip and Sharon are managers who do not seem to have much in common. Philip is a recently hired young man with a marketing degree from an Eastern European–dominant neighborhood in London. Sharon is an older woman from rural Manchester who started as a secretary after college and worked her way up the hierarchy. At first, these coworkers may notice their surface-level differences in education, ethnicity, regional background, and gender. However, as they get to understand one another, they may find they are both deeply committed to their families, share a common way of thinking about work problems, like to work collaboratively, and are interested in international assignments. These deep-level similarities can overshadow the more superficial differences between them, and research suggests they will work together. Additionally, increasing support for equal opportunities and diversity should be viewed as mutually supportive and the combination as important. Diversification with culturally related countries might lead to greater homogeneity of perception, particularly if it concentrates on individuals rather than groups and includes improvement of opportunities for all individuals. In effect, managing diversity involves everyone and benefits everyone as separate groups are not singled out.

Throughout this text, we will encounter differences between deep- and surface-level diversity in various contexts. Diversity is an important concept in OB because individual differences shape preferences for rewards, communication styles, reactions to leaders, negotiation styles, and many other aspects of behavior in organizations. Unfortunately, increased diversity may also mean increases in discriminatory practices, which we will discuss next.

An Ethical Choice

Global Diversity: Affirmative Action

Across the globe, support for affirmative action is aimed at bridging inequalities in several facets of life, including bridging inequalities in employment pay, promoting diversity, favoring members of a disadvantaged group who suffer or have suffered from discrimination within a culture—it varies from region to region. In a historic move in the United States, While the public sector has had quotas and affirmative action towards people from the less disadvantaged sections of the society in India, the private sector has started paying attention to it only recently. Notably, 62 out of the BSE 100 companies in India mention or take into consideration caste in their recruitment as compared to less than even ten years ago when companies were caste blind[17]. Industry associations such as ASSOCHAM, CII and FICCI have provided scholarships, free education and vocational training to 1.73 lakh, 1.36 lakh and 6.5 lakh SC/ST students, respectively. However only 1.27 lakh ST/SC students gained employment.[18] Sometimes, affirmative action is required to give an unfairly disadvantaged workforce segment an opportunity to succeed, whether it is achieved through percentages or by hiring prospective employees from the desired group.

In the United Kingdom, the Equality Act 2010 promotes positive action with respect to employment. As an example, Section 158 of the Equality Act 2010 builds on existing legislation or positive action and extends it to include other protected statuses, such as age and disability. In Australia, the Affirmative Action (Equal Employment Opportunity for Women) Act 1986 requires all private sector employers in Australia with more than 100 employees to report annually on programs they have developed to improve women's employment opportunities. In South Africa, the Employment Equity Act seeks to eliminate unfair discrimination in employment and thereby achieve a diverse workforce where no one feels disadvantaged. Also in place is the broad-based Black Economic Empowerment, a legislative framework to help reverse the legacy of apartheid.

Ordinarily, affirmative action is needed to give an unfairly disadvantaged workforce segment or group an opportunity to succeed, but success will depend on the sincerity and consistency of purpose of governments and business organizations as well as the attitude of the individual or group concerned. However, it is evident that resources are scarce and will continue to be so—there are only so many jobs to go around. CEOs and HR managers must balance the ethics of affirmative action against the need to strengthen their workforce for the good of their organization and society at large.

Sources: Based on "100,000 Jobs Mission Hires over 200,000 Veterans," *Veteran Jobs Mission* press release (February 9, 2015), https://www.veteranjobsmission.com/press-releases/750; D. C. Baldridge and M. L. Swift, "Withholding Requests for Disability Accommodation: The Role of Individual Differences and Disability Attributes," *Journal of Management* (March 2013): 743–62; "Walmart Celebrates More Than 40,000 Hires in First Year of Veterans Commitment," Walmart Foundation press release (May 21, 2014), http://news.walmart.com/news-archive/2014/05/21/walmart-celebrates-more-than-40-000-hires-in-first-year-of-veterans-commitment; B. Yerbak and C. V. Jackson, "Battling to Get More Vets in the Work Force," *Chicago Tribune* (October 28, 2012), http://articles.chicagotribune.com/2012-10-28/business/ct-biz-1028-vets-20121028_1_train-veterans-unemployment-rate-war-zone; "Veterans Unemployment Drops but Remains High," *HR Magazine*, February 2013, 16; J. Sheridan Alison "Affirmative Action in Australia—Employment Statistics Can't Tell the Whole Story," *Women in Management Review* 10, no. 2 (1995): 26–34; T. Jarrett, The Equality Act 2010 and Positive Action, *Library House of Commons, Business and Transport Section*, last updated, 24 October 2013.

Discrimination

2-2 Demonstrate how workplace discrimination undermines organizational effectiveness.

discrimination Noting of a difference between things; often we refer to unfair discrimination, which means making judgments about individuals based on stereotypes regarding their demographic group.

stereotyping Judging someone on the basis of our perception of the group to which that person belongs.

Although diversity presents many opportunities for organizations, diversity management includes working to eliminate unfair **discrimination.** To discriminate is to note a difference between things, which in itself isn't necessarily bad. Noticing one employee is more qualified is necessary for making hiring decisions; noticing another is taking on leadership responsibilities exceptionally well is necessary for making promotion decisions. Usually when we talk about discrimination, though, we mean allowing our behavior to be influenced by stereotypes about *groups* of people. **Stereotyping** is judging someone on the basis of our perception of the group to which that person belongs. To use a machine metaphor, you might think of stereotypes as the fuel that powers the discrimination engine. Stereotypes can be insidious not only because they may affect the perpetrators of discrimination but also because they can affect how potential targets of discrimination see themselves.

Stereotype Threat

Let's say that you are sitting in a restaurant, waiting for the blind date your coworker arranged to find you in the crowded room. How do you think your coworker described you to this person? Now consider how you would describe yourself to this new person if you'd talked on the phone before the date. What identifiable groups would you mention as a shorthand way for your date to know a bit about you so he or she could recognize you in the restaurant?

Chances are good that you'd mention your race, something about how you express your gender (such as the way you dress), how old you are, and maybe what you do for a living. You might also mention how tall you are if you are remarkably tall or short, and—if you're candid—you might mention something about your build (heavyset, petite, in between). Overall, you'd give cues to your blind date about characteristics that are *distinctive*, or that stand out, about you. What you tell someone about yourself says a lot about what you think about yourself. Just as we stereotype others, we also stereotype ourselves.

stereotype threat The degree to which we are concerned with being judged by or treated negatively based on a certain stereotype.

Stereotype threat describes the degree to which we agree internally with the generally negative stereotyped perceptions of our groups. Along with that comes a fear of being judged when we are identified with the negative connotations of that group. This can happen when we are a minority in a situation. For instance, an older worker applying for a job in a predominately millennial-age workforce may assume the interviewer thinks he is out of touch with current trends. What creates a stereotype threat is not whether the worker is or is not up to date with trends, but whether he agrees internally that older workers (the group he identifies with) are out of date (the stereotype). The negative stereotypes about the older worker, extending to such beliefs among outgroups that they have lower dexterity and physical ability, may increase their apprehension and thus lead older employees to take on more demanding jobs. In essence, they put in extra effort and time that would otherwise have been superfluous just to avoid a stereotype threat.

People become their own worst enemies when they feel stereotype threat. Ironically, they may unconsciously exaggerate the stereotype, like an older job applicant who talks about aging, rambles during the conversation, and discloses too much.[19] Second, employees may engage in self-handicapping, in which they avoid effort so that they can attribute their potential failure to other sources, such as stress or "having a bad day."[20] Third, people may overcompensate for the stereotype threat they feel or work to avoid confirming the stereotype. A Bengali worker who keeps his opinions to himself and does not participate in any informal office discussions around upcoming elections maybe attempting to overcome the stereotype threat of Bengalis being argumentative and opinionated. This may happen even if the workplace has many ethnic minority employees because minorities perceive stereotypes about each other.[21] Stereotype threat can serve as a "brain drain" for employees, causing them to deplete their working memories so that they do not perform as well on employment tests or training.[22]

Stereotype threat has serious implications for the workplace. Stereotype threat can occur during preemployment tests and assessments, performance evaluations, and everyday workplace exchanges. It can lead to underperformance on tests, performance evaluations, training exercises, negotiations, and everyday interactions with others as well as to disengagement, poor job attitudes, a reluctance to seek feedback, and poor performance in the employees experiencing the threat.[23] Although the occurrence of stereotype threat is not inevitable and occurs infrequently in testing environments, we should still put in efforts to combat it in the workplace by treating employees as individuals and not highlighting group differences. The following organizational changes can be successful in reducing stereotype threat: increasing awareness of how stereotypes may be perpetuated (especially when developing policies and practices), reducing differential and preferential treatment through objective assessments, confronting microaggressions against minority groups, and adopting transparent practices that signal the value of all employees.[24]

Discrimination in the Workplace

To review, unfair discrimination assumes that everyone in a group is the same rather than looking at the characteristics of individuals within the group. This discrimination is often very harmful for employees, as we've just discussed, as well as for organizations.

Exhibit 2-1 provides definitions and examples of some forms of discrimination in organizations. Although many are prohibited by law and therefore are not part of organizations' official policies, the practices persist. Tens of thousands of cases of employment discrimination are documented every year, and many more go unreported. Because discrimination has increasingly come under both legal scrutiny and social disapproval, most overt forms have faded, which may have resulted in an increase in more covert forms like incivility or exclusion, especially when leaders look the other way.[25]

As you can see, discrimination can occur in many ways, and its effects can vary depending on organizational context and the personal biases of employees. Some forms of discrimination, exclusion and incivility, for example, are especially hard to root out because they may occur simply because the actor isn't aware of the effects of his or her actions. Like stereotype threat, actual discrimination can lead to increased negative consequences for employers, including reduced productivity and organizational citizenship behavior (OCB), more conflict, increased turnover, and even increased risk-taking behavior.[26] Unfair discrimination also leaves qualified job candidates out of initial hiring and promotions. Thus, even if an employment discrimination lawsuit is never

Exhibit 2-1 Forms of Discrimination

Type of Discrimination	Definition	Examples from Organizations
Discriminatory policies or practices	Actions taken by representatives of the organization that deny equal opportunity to perform or unequal rewards for performance.	Older workers may be targeted for layoffs because they are highly paid and have lucrative benefits.
Sexual harassment	Unwanted sexual advances and other verbal or physical conduct of a sexual nature that create a hostile or offensive work environment.	Salespeople at one company went on company-paid visits to strip clubs, brought strippers into the office to celebrate promotions, and fostered pervasive sexual rumors.
Intimidation	Overt threats or bullying directed at members of specific groups of employees.	African-American employees at some companies have found nooses hanging over their work stations.
Mockery and insults	Jokes or negative stereotypes; sometimes the result of jokes taken too far.	Arab-Americans have been asked at work whether they were carrying bombs or were members of terrorist organizations.
Exclusion	Exclusion of certain people from job opportunities, social events, discussions, or informal mentoring; can occur unintentionally.	Many women in finance claim they are assigned to marginal job roles or are given light workloads that don't lead to promotion.
Incivility	Disrespectful treatment, including behaving in an aggressive manner, interrupting the person, or ignoring his or her opinions.	Female lawyers note that male attorneys frequently cut them off or do not adequately address their comments.

Sources: Based on J. Levitz and P. Shishkin, "More Workers Cite Age Bias after Layoffs," *The Wall Street Journal,* March 11, 2009, D1–D2; W. M. Bulkeley, "A Data-Storage Titan Confronts Bias Claims," *The Wall Street Journal,* September 12, 2007, A1, A16; D. Walker, "Incident with Noose Stirs Old Memories," *McClatchy-Tribune Business News,* June 29, 2008; D. Solis, "Racial Horror Stories Keep EEOC Busy," *Knight-Ridder Tribune Business News,* July 30, 2005, 1; H. Ibish and A. Stewart, *Report on Hate Crimes and Discrimination against Arab Americans: The Post-September 11 Backlash, September 11, 2001–October 11, 2001* (Washington, DC: American-Arab Anti-Discrimination Committee, 2003); A. Raghavan, "Wall Street's Disappearing Women," *Forbes,* March 16, 2009, 72–78; and L. M. Cortina, "Unseen Injustice: Incivility as Modern Discrimination in Organizations," *Academy of Management Review* 33, no. 1 (2008): 55–75.

filed, a strong business case can be made for aggressively working to eliminate unfair discrimination.

Whether it is overt or covert, intentional or unintentional, discrimination is one of the primary factors that prevent diversity. On the other hand, recognizing diversity opportunities can lead to an effective diversity management program and ultimately to a better organization. *Diversity* is a broad term, and the phrase *workplace diversity* can refer to any characteristic that makes people different from one another. The following section covers some important surface-level characteristics that differentiate members of the workforce.

2-3 Describe how the key biographical characteristics are relevant to Organizational Behavior (OB).

Biographical Characteristics

biographical characteristics Personal characteristics—such as age, gender, race, and length of tenure—that are objective and easily obtained from personnel records. These characteristics are representative of surface-level diversity.

Biographical characteristics such as age, gender, race, and disability are some of the most obvious ways employees differ. Let's begin by looking at factors that are easily definable and readily available—data that can be obtained, for the most part, from an employee's human resources (HR) file. Variations in surface-level characteristics may be the basis for discrimination against classes of employees, so it is worth knowing how related they actually are to work outcomes. As a general rule, many biographical differences are not important to actual work outcomes, and far more variation occurs *within* groups sharing biographical characteristics than between them.

Age

Age in the workforce is likely to be an issue of increasing importance during the next decade for many reasons. For one, the workforce is aging worldwide in most developed countries;[27] by 2014–2024 projections, the average annual growth rate of workers over age 54 in the labor force is expected to be 1.8 percent, which is over three times greater than that of the overall labor force.[28] In the United States, the proportion of the workforce age 55 and older is 22 percent and increasing,[29] and legislation has, for all intents and purposes, outlawed mandatory retirement. The United States and Australia, among other countries, have laws directed against age discrimination.[30] Most workers today no longer have to retire at age 70, and 62 percent of workers age 45 to 60 plan to delay retirement.[31]

The stereotypes of older workers as being behind the times, grumpy, and inflexible are changing. In India more than 65 percent below the age of 35 of which 50 percent is below the age of 25. In 2020, the average age of an Indian is 28.4 years, compared to 37 for China and 48 for Japan; and, by 2030.[32] Managers often see a number of positive qualities that older workers

Myth or Science?

Bald Is Better

Surprisingly, it appears true that bald is better for men in the workplace. A recent study showed that observers believe a male's shaved head indicates greater masculinity, dominance, and leadership potential than longer or thinning hair. Thinning hair was perceived as the least powerful look, and other studies have agreed that male-pattern baldness (when some hair remains) is not considered advantageous. Why is this?

In some respects, the reported youthful advantage of a shaved head is counterintuitive. Because we have more hair when we are young, and contemporary culture considers youthfulness a desirable characteristic in the workplace (if you doubt this, see the discussions on aging in this chapter), it would make more sense for a hairless head to be a distinct disadvantage. Yet the media is loaded with images of powerful men with shaved heads—military heroes, winning athletes, and action heroes. No wonder study participants declared that the men with shaved heads were an inch taller and 13 percent stronger than the same men with hair.

A bald head has become the hallmark of some important business leaders, notably Jeff Bezos of Amazon, Lloyd Blankfein of Goldman Sachs, Marc Andreessen of Netscape, and "Shark Tank" investor Daymond John. Men who shave their heads report it can give them a business advantage, whether or not it makes them look younger (which is debatable). According to psychologist Caroline Keating, just as older silverback gorillas are "typically the powerful actors in their social groups," so it is in the office, where baldness may "signal who is in charge and potentially dangerous." Research professor Michael Cunningham agrees, adding that baldness "is nature's way of telling the rest of the world you are a survivor." Men with shaved heads convey aggressiveness, competitiveness, and independence, he adds. Will you join the 13 percent of men who shave their heads? Though we don't wish to advocate head shaving for this reason, it does demonstrate how biased we continue to be in judging people by superficial characteristics. Time will tell if this situation ever improves.

Sources: Based on D. Baer, "People Are Psychologically Biased to See Bald Men as Dominant Leaders," *Business Insider* (February 13, 2015), http://www.businessinsider.com/bald-men-signals-dominance-2015-2; J. Misener, "Men with Shaved Heads Appear More Dominant, Study Finds," *The Huffington Post* (October 1, 2012), www.huffingtonpost.com/2012/10/01/bald-men-dominant-shaved-heads-study_n_1930489.html; A. E. Mannes, "Shorn Scalps and Perceptions of Male Dominance," *Social Psychological and Personality Science*, (2012), doi: 10.1177/1948550612449490; and R. E. Silverman, "Bald Is Powerful," *The Wall Street Journal* (October 3, 2012), B1, B6.

bring to their jobs, such as experience, judgment, a strong work ethic, and commitment to quality. The Public Utilities Board, the water agency of Singapore, reports that 27 percent of its workforce is over age 55 because older workers bring workforce stability.[33] And industries like health care, education, government, and nonprofits often welcome older workers.[34] But older workers are still perceived as less adaptable and less motivated to learn new technology.[35] When organizations seek individuals who are open to change and training, the perceived negatives associated with age clearly hinder the initial hiring of older workers and increase the likelihood they will be let go during cutbacks.

Now let's look at the evidence. What effect does age actually have on turnover, absenteeism, productivity, and satisfaction? Regarding turnover, the older you are, the less likely you are to quit your job.[36] As workers get older, they have fewer alternate job opportunities because their skills have become more specialized. Within organizations, older workers' longer tenure tends to provide them with higher wages, longer paid vacations, and benefits that may bind them to their employers.

It may seem likely that age is positively correlated to absenteeism, but this isn't true. Most studies show that older employees have lower rates of avoidable absence versus younger employees.[37] Furthermore, older workers do not have more psychological problems or day-to-day physical health problems than younger workers.[38]

The majority of studies have shown "virtually no relationship between age and job performance," according to Director Harvey Sterns of the Institute for Life-Span Development and Gerontology.[39] Indeed, some studies indicate that older adults perform better. In Munich, a 4-year study of 3,800 Mercedes-Benz workers found that "the older workers seemed to know better how to avoid severe errors," said Matthias Weiss, the academic coordinator of the study.[40] Related to performance, there is a conception that creativity lessens as people age. Researcher David Galenson, who studied the ages of peak creativity, found that people who create through experimentation do "their greatest work in their 40s, 50s, and 60s. These artists rely on wisdom, which increases with age." There is evidence that age-diverse teams and organizations perform better than those with similar ages, primarily because both older and younger workers bring a complementary, diverse set of knowledge, skills, and abilities to their teams.[41]

What about age and satisfaction? Regarding life satisfaction, which we will discuss further in later chapters, there is a cultural assumption that older people are more prone to depression and loneliness. Actually, a study of adults ages 18 to 94 found that positive moods increased with age. "Contrary to the popular view that youth is the best time of life, the peak of emotional life may not occur until well into the seventh decade," researcher Laura Carstensen said.[42]

Regarding job satisfaction, an important topic in Chapter 3, a review of more than 800 studies found that older workers tend to be more satisfied with their work, report better relationships with coworkers, and are more committed to their organizations.[43] Other studies, however, have found that job satisfaction increases up to middle age, at which point it begins to drop off. When we separate the results by job type, though, we find that satisfaction tends to increase continually among professionals as they age, whereas among nonprofessionals, it falls during middle age and then rises again in the later years.

In sum, we can see that the surface-level characteristic of an employee's age is an unfounded basis for discrimination and that an age-diverse workforce is a benefit to an organization.

Sex

Few issues initiate more debates, misconceptions, and unsupported opinions than whether women perform as well on jobs as men.

The best place to begin to consider this topic is with the recognition that few, if any, differences between men and women affect job performance.[44] Though men may have slightly higher math ability and women slightly higher verbal ability, the differences are fairly small, and there are no consistent male–female differences in problem-solving ability, analytical skills, or learning ability.[45] One meta-analysis of job performance studies found that women scored slightly higher than men on performance measures.[46] A separate meta-analysis of 95 leadership studies indicated that women and men are rated equally effective as leaders.[47]

Yet biases and stereotypes persist. In the hiring realm, managers are influenced by gender bias when selecting candidates for certain positions.[48] For instance, men are preferred in hiring decisions for male-dominated occupations, particularly when men are doing the hiring.[49] Once on the job, men and women may be offered a similar number of developmental experiences, but females are less likely to be assigned challenging positions by men, assignments that could help them achieve higher organizational positions.[50] Men are more likely to be chosen for leadership roles even though men and women are equally effective leaders, a phenomenon which has been referred to as the "glass ceiling" (and applies to any underrepresented group that faces obstacles to advancement).[51] In fact, as of April 2020, women hold only 6 percent of CEO positions in S&P 500 companies.[52] Furthermore, a study of 20 organizations in Spain, for example, suggested that women are generally selected for leadership roles that require handling organizational crises, positions in which they are usually set up to fail, a phenomenon commonly referred to as the glass cliff.[53] According to Naomi Sutherland, senior partner in diversity at recruiter Korn Ferry, "Consciously or subconsciously, companies are still hesitant to take the risk on someone who looks different from their standard leadership profile."[54]

These stereotypes counter the evidence which suggests that females are effective leaders in organizations: not only does research from hundreds of studies suggest that women are rated as effective leaders in organizations, but that women's representation in leadership positions is actually predictive of financial performance in hundreds of thousands of organizations.[55] Sex discrimination has a pervasive negative impact. Notably, women still earn less money than men for the same positions,[56] even in traditionally female roles.[57] Furthermore, the sex differences in promotions, bonuses, and salaries (across 97 different studies and nearly 400,000 people) are 14 times larger than their differences on performance evaluations.[58] Working mothers also face "maternal wall bias," meaning they are often not considered for new positions after they have children, and both men and women experience discrimination for their family caregiving roles.[59] Women who receive fewer challenging assignments and development opportunities from biased managers tend to curtail their management aspirations.[60] Women who are assertive in the workplace tend to be liked less and perceived as less hirable.[61]

We've seen that there are many misconceptions and contradictions about male and female workers. Thankfully, many countries, including Australia, the United Kingdom, and the United States, have laws against sex discrimination.

Other countries, such as Belgium, France, Norway, and Spain, are seeking gender diversity through laws to increase the percentage of women on boards of directors.[62] Gender biases and gender discrimination are still serious issues, but there are indications that the situation is improving.

Race and Ethnicity

Race is a controversial issue in society and in organizations. We define *race* as the heritage people use to identify themselves; *ethnicity* is the additional set of cultural characteristics that often overlaps with race. Typically, we associate race with biology, and ethnicity with culture, but there is a history of self-identifying for both classifications. Laws against race and ethnic discrimination are in effect in many countries, including Australia, the United Kingdom, and the United States.[63]

Race and ethnicity have been studied as they relate to employment outcomes such as hiring decisions, performance evaluations, pay, and workplace discrimination. Individuals may slightly favor colleagues of their own race in performance evaluations, promotion decisions, and pay raises, although such differences are not found consistently, especially when highly structured methods of decision making are employed.[64] Also, some industries have remained less racially diverse than others. For instance, U.S. advertising and media organizations suffer from a lack of racial diversity in their management ranks even though their client base is increasingly ethnically diverse.[65] In the United Kingdom, there have been demands that the Government stop auditing and start acting against racial discrimination. Research suggests that many BAME (Black, Asian, and Minority Ethnic) professionals in UK organizations, including universities, are among the most qualified and experienced in their teams and functions, but they struggle to achieve the career progression they are qualified for. In the education sector, where the numbers of ethnic minority students are rising, figures published by the Higher Education Statistics Agency in 2017 showed there were no Black academics in the manager, director, and senior official categories in 2015–16.[66]

Members of racial and ethnic minorities report higher levels of discrimination in the workplace.[67] Black people generally fare worse than white people in employment decisions (a finding that may not apply outside the United States). They receive lower ratings in employment interviews, lower job performance ratings, less pay, and fewer promotions.[68] While this does not necessarily prove overt racial discrimination, black people are often discriminated against even in controlled experiments. For example, one study of low-wage jobs found that black applicants with no criminal history received fewer job offers than did white applicants with criminal records.[69] Even applicants with black-sounding names were 50 percent less likely than those with white-sounding names to receive interview callbacks in one large randomized experiment.[70]

positive diversity climate In an organization, an environment of inclusiveness and an acceptance of diversity.

As we discussed before, discrimination—for any reason—leads to increased turnover, which is detrimental to organizational performance. While better representation of all racial groups in organizations remains a goal, an individual of minority status is much less likely to leave the organization if there is a feeling of inclusiveness, known as a **positive diversity climate**.[71] A positive climate for diversity can also lead to increased sales, commitment, and retention, suggesting there are organizational performance gains associated with reducing racial and ethnic discrimination.[72]

How do we move beyond the destructiveness of discrimination? The answer is in understanding one another's viewpoint. Evidence suggests that some people find interacting with other racial groups uncomfortable unless there are clear behavioral scripts to guide their behavior,[73] so creating diverse work groups focused on mutual goals could be helpful, along with developing a positive diversity climate.

Disabilities

Workplace policies, both official and circumstantial, regarding individuals with physical or mental disabilities vary from country to country. Countries such as Australia, the United States, the United Kingdom, and Japan have specific laws to protect individuals with disabilities.[74] These laws have resulted in greater acceptance and accommodation of people with physical or mental impairments. In the United States, for instance, the representation of individuals with disabilities in the workforce rapidly increased with the passage of the Americans with Disabilities Act (ADA, 1990).[75] According to the ADA, employers are required to make reasonable accommodations so their workplaces will be accessible to individuals with physical or mental disabilities.

The U.S. Equal Employment Opportunity Commission (EEOC), the federal agency responsible for enforcing employment discrimination laws, classifies a person as *disabled* who has any physical or mental impairment that substantially limits one or more major life activities. One of the most controversial aspects of the ADA is the provision that requires employers to make reasonable accommodations (e.g., comfort and assistance animals) for people with psychiatric disabilities.[76] Examples of recognized disabilities include missing limbs, seizure disorder, Down syndrome, deafness, schizophrenia, alcoholism, diabetes, depression, and chronic back pain. These conditions share almost no common features, so there's no specific definition about how each condition is related to employment.

Since it was first introduced in the United Kingdom some 20 years ago, discrimination law has defined disability using the following formulation: "A disabled person is someone who suffers from a physical or mental impairment which has a substantial and long-term adverse effect on his ability to carry our normal day to day activities."

The final clause ("normal day-to-day activities") has always been the subject of controversy, and the courts have always interpreted it as referring to ordinary, everyday tasks that the average man or woman in the street performs. An individual is not disabled for the purposes of the Equity Act (formerly the Disability Discrimination Act) because you cannot play football or because you cannot climb a mountain. The impairment must stop you from basic, common daily activities like getting dressed, making breakfast, and getting to work.

The controversy arises because this often means that someone is not classified as disabled and hence has no case in law when their impairment prevents them from carrying out an aspect of their work that does not fall under the definition of normal day-to-day activities. In the United Kingdom, a number of cases involve dismissal because of an inability to lift heavy weights, which is not a "normal day-to-day activity" and hence is not the basis for successful disability discrimination claims. It is interesting to see how the case law further develops in this area from the perspective of the United States and the United Kingdom.

The impact of disabilities on employment outcomes has been explored from a variety of perspectives. On one hand, when disability status is randomly manipulated among hypothetical candidates, disabled individuals are rated as having superior personal qualities like dependability.[77] Another review suggested that workers with disabilities receive higher performance evaluations. However, individuals with disabilities tend to encounter lower performance expectations and are less likely to be hired.[78] Mental disabilities may impair performance more than physical disabilities: Individuals with common mental health issues such as depression and anxiety are significantly more likely to be absent from work.[79]

The elimination of discrimination against the disabled workforce has long been problematic. In Europe, for instance, policies to motivate employers have failed to boost the workforce participation rate for workers with disabilities, and outright quota systems in Germany, France, and Poland have backfired.[80] However, the recognition of the talents and abilities of individuals with disabilities has made a positive impact. In addition, technology and workplace advancements have greatly increased the scope of available jobs for those with all types of disabilities. Managers need to be attuned to the true requirements of each job and match the skills of the individual to them, providing accommodations when needed. But what happens when employees do not disclose their disabilities? Let's discuss this next.

Hidden Disabilities

As we mentioned earlier, disabilities include observable characteristics like missing limbs, illnesses that require a person to use a wheelchair, and blindness. Other disabilities may not be obvious, at least at first. Unless an individual decides to disclose a disability that isn't easily observable, it can remain hidden at the discretion of the employee. These are called *hidden disabilities* (or invisible disabilities). Hidden, or invisible, disabilities generally fall under the categories of sensory disabilities (for example, impaired hearing), autoimmune disorders (like rheumatoid arthritis), chronic illness or pain (like carpal tunnel syndrome), cognitive or learning impairments (like attention deficit hyperactivity disorder [ADHD]), sleep disorders (like insomnia), and psychological challenges (like PTSD).[81]

As a result of recent changes to the Americans with Disabilities Act Amendments Act (ADAAA) of 2008, U.S. organizations must accommodate employees with a very broad range of impairments. However, employees must disclose their conditions to their employers in order to be eligible for workplace accommodations and employment protection. Many employees do not want to disclose their invisible disabilities, so they are prevented from getting the workplace accommodations they need in order to thrive in their jobs. Research indicates that individuals with hidden disabilities are afraid of being stigmatized or ostracized if they disclose their disabilities to others in the workplace, and they believe that their managers will think they are less capable of strong job performance.[82] Add this to the challenge of receiving a diagnosis for a condition that one did not previously have and these fears are compounded even more so than if the diagnosis was made for employees when they were younger.[83]

In some ways, a hidden disability is not truly invisible. For example, a person with undisclosed autism will still exhibit the behaviors characteristic of the condition, such as difficulty with verbal communication and lack of adaptability.[84] You may observe behaviors that lead you to suspect an individual has a hidden disability. Unfortunately, you may attribute the behavior to other causes—for instance, you may incorrectly ascribe the slow, slurred speech of a coworker to an alcohol problem rather than to the long-term effects of a stroke.

As for the employee, research suggests that disclosure helps all—the individual, others, and organizations. Disclosure may increase the job satisfaction and well-being of the individual, help others understand and assist the individual to succeed in the workplace, and allow the organization to accommodate the situation so that the employee and the organization achieve top performance.[82]

Other Differentiating Characteristics

2-4 Explain how other differentiating characteristics factor into OB.

The last set of characteristics we'll look at includes tenure, religion, sexual orientation and gender identity, and cultural identity. These characteristics illustrate deep-level differences that provide opportunities for workplace diversity as long as discrimination can be overcome.

Tenure

Except for gender and racial differences, few issues are more subject to misconceptions and speculations than the impact of seniority and *tenure*, meaning time spent in a job, organization, or field.

Extensive reviews have been conducted of the seniority–productivity relationship.[86] The evidence demonstrates a positive relationship between organizational tenure (i.e., how long an employee has been in his or her organization) and job performance. As such, organizational tenure appears to be a good predictor of employee performance, although there is some evidence that the relationship is not linear: Differences in organizational tenure are more important to job performance for relatively new or inexperienced employees than among those who have been on the job longer. To use a National Football League (NFL) analogy, a second-year quarterback has more of an edge over a rookie than a tenth-year quarterback has over one in his ninth year. Job tenure, on the other hand (i.e., how long an employee has been in his or her job), demonstrates a weak, inconsistent effect on employee outcomes, indicating that employees may lose desire for further career advancement.

Religion

Religious and nonreligious people question each other's belief systems, and people of different religious faiths often conflict. There are few—if any—countries in which religion is a nonissue in the workplace. For this reason, employers are prohibited by law from discriminating against employees based on religion in many countries, including Australia, the United Kingdom, and the United States.[87]

Islam is one of the most popular religions in the world, and it is the majority religion in many countries. However, in the India, Muslims are a minority group that is growing. In India, all religious groups grew between 1951 and 2011. For example, Hindus increased from 304 million (30.4 crore) to 966 million (96.6 crore), Muslims grew from 35 million (3.5 crore) to 172 million (17.2 crore), and Christians rose from 8 million (0.8 crore) to 28 million (2.8 crore). Sikhs, India's fourth-largest religious group, have increased from 7 million (70 lakh) to nearly 21 million (2.1 crore). As per projection, as of 2020 about 15 percent of Indians are Muslim (vs. 14.2 percent in the 2011 census), 79 percent are Hindu (vs. 79.8 percent in 2011), and 2 percent are Christian and Sikhs (in line with 2011.[88] One's own religious commitment predicts whether or not an employee will intervene when observing religious discrimination.[89]

Faith can be an employment issue wherever religious beliefs prohibit or encourage certain behaviors. The behavioral expectations can be informal, such as employees leaving work early on the evening of Dhanteras or the day before Diwali. Or they maybe systemic such as in UAE where the workweek is from Sunday to Thursday so that Friday maybe spent to mark the sacred day of worship.

Religious discrimination has been a growing source of discrimination claims across the world. The Hijab controversy in Karnataka in India, the head scarf ban in France, Samantha Elauf being denied a job in USA because she wore a head scarf and other countries where Hijab has either been banned or been a source of discrimination in job offers has brought to light the complexity of the situation. Even courts across the world are not always sure how to guide public action in such cases.[90,91,92]

Sexual Orientation and Gender Identity

While much has changed, the full acceptance and accommodation of lesbian, gay, bisexual, transgender, and questioning (LGBTQ) employees remains a work in progress. In the United States, a Harvard University study sent fictitious but realistic résumés to 1,700 actual entry-level job openings. The applications were identical with one exception: Half mentioned involvement in gay organizations during college, and the other half did not. The applications without the mention received 60 percent more callbacks than the ones with it.[93] Another study suggests that the hirability perceptions of lesbian and gay candidates made by women are actually higher than those for heterosexuals, suggesting that the bias is complicated and nuanced.[94]

Perhaps as a result of perceived discrimination, many LGBTQ employees do not disclose their status. For example, John Browne, former CEO of British Petroleum (BP), hid his sexual orientation until he was 59, when the press threatened to disclose that he was gay. Fearing the story would result in turmoil for the company, he resigned. Browne wrote recently, "Since my outing in 2007, many societies around the world have done more to embrace people who are lesbian, gay, bisexual, or transgender. But the business world has a long way to go."[95]

U.S. federal law does not prohibit discrimination against employees based on sexual orientation, although 29 states and more than 160 municipalities do. For states and municipalities that protect against discrimination based on sexual orientation, roughly as many claims are filed for sexual orientation discrimination as for sex and race discrimination.[96] Some other countries are more progressive: For instance, Australia has laws against discriminating on the basis of sexual preference, and the United Kingdom has similar laws regarding sexual orientation.[97] However, the distinctions in these laws may not be broad enough—researchers have acknowledged a new acronym, QUILTBAG, to describe individuals who are queer/questioning, undecided, intersex, lesbian, transgender, bisexual, asexual, or gay.[98]

The rights and freedoms of LGBT citizens are significantly influenced by the prevailing cultural traditions and religions of people living in some regions of the world, such as the Middle East and some Asian countries. Several Middle Eastern countries have received strong international criticism for discriminating against this group. The Human Rights Watch believes the main argument can be made by framing the situation of people in terms of their rights violation and protection. Southern and East Africa, the Middle East, and South Asia remain very conservative in this regard while Western Europe tends to be permissive and has prohibited discrimination at the workplace based on

Career OBjectives

Should I come out at work?

I'm gay, but no one at my workplace knows it. How much should I be willing to tell? I want to be sure to have a shot at the big positions in the firm.

— Ryan

Dear Ryan:

Unfortunately, you are right to be concerned. Here are some suggestions:

- *Look for an inclusive company culture*. Apple CEO Tim Cook said, "I've had the good fortune to work at a company that loves creativity and innovation and knows it can only flourish when you embrace people's differences. Not everyone is so lucky." Recent research has focused on discovering new methods to counteract a discrimination culture in the United States, the United Kingdom, and Australia.
- *Choose your moral ground*. Do you feel you have a responsibility to "come out" to help effect social change? Do you have a right to keep your private life private? The balance is a private decision. A recent study by the U.S. Human Rights Campaign indicated that only half of LGBT employees nationwide disclose their status.
- *Consider your future in top management*. Corporate-level leaders are urged to be open with peers and employees. As Ernst & Young global vice chairperson Beth Brooke said about her decades of staying closeted, the pressure to be "authentic" adds stress if you are keeping your gay status a secret.
- *Weigh your options*. The word from people at the top who are gay (some who have come out and others who have not) is mixed. Brooke said, "Life really did get better" after she announced her status in a company-sponsored video. Mark Stephanz, a vice chairman at Bank of America Merrill Lynch, agreed, remarking that "most people still deal with you the same way they always do." Yet Deena Fidas, deputy director for the largest LGBT civil rights group in the United States, reported that being gay in the workplace is still "far from being a 'nonissue.'"
- *Be aware of international and national laws*. Sadly, some nations and states are intolerant. You will need to study the laws to be sure you will be safe from repercussions when you reveal your status.

So think about your decision from both an ethical and a self-interested point of view. Your timing depends not only on what you think are your ethical responsibilities but also on your context—where you work, the culture of your organization, and the support of the people within it. Thankfully, globalization is ensuring that the world becomes increasingly accepting and fair.

Good luck in your career!

Sources: Based on M. D. Birtel, "'Treating' Prejudice: An Exposure-Therapy Approach to Reducing Negative Reactions Toward Stigmatized Groups," *Psychological Science* (November 2012): 1379–86; L. Cooper and J. Raspanti, "The Cost of the Closet and the Rewards of Inclusion," Human Rights Campaign report (May 2014), http://hrc-assets.s3-website-us-east-1.amazonaws.com//files/assets/resources/Cost_of_the_Closet_May2014.pdf; N. Rumens and J. Broomfield, "Gay Men in the Police: Identity Disclosure and Management Issues," *Human Resource Management Journal* (July 2012): 283–98; and A. M. Ryan and J. L. Wessel, "Sexual Orientation Harassment in the Workplace: When Do Observers Intervene?" *Journal of Organizational Behavior* (May 2012): 488–509.

The opinions provided here are of the managers and authors only and do not necessarily reflect those of their organizations. The authors or managers are not responsible for any errors or omissions, or for the results obtained from the use of this information. In no event will the authors or managers, or their related partnerships or corporations thereof, be liable to you or anyone else for any decision made or action taken in reliance on the opinions provided here.

sexual orientation.[99] As a first step in the United States, the federal government has prohibited discrimination against *government* employees based on sexual orientation. The EEOC recently held that sex-stereotyping against lesbian, gay, and bisexual individuals represents gender discrimination enforceable under the Civil Rights Act of 1964.[100] Even in the absence of federal legislation, many organizations have implemented policies and procedures that cover sexual orientation. IBM, once famous for requiring all employees to wear white shirts and ties, has changed its ultraconservative environment. Former vice president Ted Childs said, "IBM ensures that people who are gay, lesbian, bisexual or transgender feel safe, welcomed and valued within the global walls of our business.... The contributions that are made by [gay and transgender] IBMers accrue directly to our bottom line and ensure the success of our business."[101]

IBM is not alone. Surveys indicate that more than 90 percent of Fortune 500 companies have policies that cover sexual orientation. As for gender identity, companies are increasingly adopting policies to govern the way their organizations treat transgender employees. In 2001, only eight companies in the Fortune 500 had policies on gender identity. That number is now more than 250.

Among the Fortune 1000, however, some noteworthy companies do not currently have domestic-partner benefits or nondiscrimination clauses for LGBT employees, including Berkshire Hathaway, currently number 4 in the *Fortune* rankings of the largest U.S. companies.[102] Some companies claim that they do not need to provide LGBT benefits for religious reasons. Recently, the U.S. Supreme Court allowed that Hobby Lobby, a retail arts and crafts chain, does not need to provide contraception insurance coverage due to the religious objections of its founding family, and many fear that this ruling will pave the way for overt LGBT discrimination by organizations.[103] Some organizations that claim to be inclusive don't live up to the claim. For example, a recent study of five social cooperatives in Italy indicated that these so-called inclusive organizations actually expect individuals to remain quiet about their status.[104]

Thus, while times have certainly changed, sexual orientation and gender identity remain individual differences that organizations must address in eliminating discrimination and promoting diversity.

Cultural Identity

We have seen that people sometimes define themselves in terms of race and ethnicity. Many people carry a strong *cultural identity* as well, a link with the culture of family ancestry or youth that lasts a lifetime, no matter where the individual may live in the world. People choose their cultural identity, and they also choose how closely they observe the norms of that culture. Cultural norms influence the workplace, sometimes resulting in clashes. Organizations must adapt.

Workplace practices that coincided with the norms of a person's cultural identity were commonplace years ago, when societies were less mobile. People looked for work near familial homes and organizations established holidays, observances, practices, and customs that suited the majority. Organizations were generally not expected to accommodate each individual's preferences.

In India's as a result of a Supreme Court ruling in 2018 consensual homosexual acts does not constitute a crime. The ruling of the Supreme Court reversed Section 377 of the Indian Penal Code.[105] For foreign managers interacting with subordinate employees in the United Arab Emirates, avoiding conflict and confrontation is paramount. Managers rarely disappoint their subordinates with a simple "no," believing that blunt truth sometimes destroys harmony. While Italian and French managers may be familiar with such indirectness, Americans and Australians may come across as brutally candid.[106]

An organization seeking to be sensitive to the cultural identities of its employees should look beyond accommodating its majority groups and instead create as much of an individualized approach to practices and norms as possible. Often, managers can provide the bridge of workplace flexibility to meet both organizational goals and individual needs.

Ability

2-5 Demonstrate the relevance of intellectual and physical abilities to OB.

Contrary to what we were taught in grade school, we weren't all created equal in our abilities. For example, regardless of how motivated you are, you may not be able to act as well as Ranbeer Kapoor, play ciricket as well as Virat Kohli, or write as well as Aravind Adiga, J. K. Rowling. Of course, all of us have strengths and weaknesses that make us relatively superior or inferior to others in performing certain tasks or activities. From management's standpoint, the challenge is to understand the differences and thus increase the likelihood that a given employee will perform the job well.

ability An individual's capacity to perform the various tasks in a job.

What does *ability* mean? As we use the term, **ability** is an individual's current capacity to perform the various tasks in a job. Overall abilities are essentially made up of two sets of factors: intellectual and physical.

Intellectual Abilities

intellectual abilities The capacity to do mental activities—thinking, reasoning, and problem solving.

Intellectual abilities are abilities needed to perform mental activities—thinking, reasoning, and problem solving. Most societies place a high value on intelligence, and for good reason. Smart people generally earn more money and attain higher levels of education. They are also more likely to emerge as leaders of groups. However, assessing and measuring intellectual ability are not always simple. IQ tests are designed to ascertain a person's general intellectual abilities, but the origins, influence factors, and testing of intelligence quotient (IQ) are controversial.[107] So, too, are popular college admission tests, such as the SAT and ACT, and graduate admission tests in business (GMAT), law (LSAT), and medicine (MCAT). The firms that produce these tests do not claim that they assess intelligence, but experts confirm that they do.[108]

The seven most frequently cited dimensions making up intellectual abilities are number aptitude, verbal comprehension, perceptual speed, inductive reasoning, deductive reasoning, spatial visualization, and memory.[109] Exhibit 2-2 describes these dimensions.

Exhibit 2-2 Dimensions of Intellectual Ability

Dimension	Description	Job Example
Number aptitude	Ability to do speedy and accurate arithmetic	Accountant: Computing the sales tax on a set of items
Verbal comprehension	Ability to understand what is read or heard and the relationship of words to each other	Plant manager: Following corporate policies on hiring
Perceptual speed	Ability to identify visual similarities and differences quickly and accurately	Fire investigator: Identifying clues to support a charge of arson
Inductive reasoning	Ability to identify a logical sequence in a problem and then solve the problem	Market researcher: Forecasting demand for a product in the next time period
Deductive reasoning	Ability to use logic and assess the implications of an argument	Supervisor: Choosing between two different suggestions offered by employees
Spatial visualization	Ability to imagine how an object would look if its position in space were changed	Interior decorator: Redecorating an office
Memory	Ability to retain and recall past experiences	Salesperson: Remembering the names of customers

Intelligence dimensions are positively correlated, so if you score high on verbal comprehension, for example, you are also more likely to score high on spatial visualization. The correlations aren't perfect, meaning people do have specific abilities that predict important work-related outcomes when considered individually. However, they are high enough that researchers also recognize a general factor of intelligence, **general mental ability (GMA)**.[110] Evidence supports the idea that the structures and measures of intellectual abilities generalize across cultures. Someone in Venezuela or Sudan, for instance, does not have a different set of mental abilities than a U.S. or Czech individual. There is some evidence that IQ scores vary to some degree across cultures, but those differences become much smaller when we take into account educational and economic differences.[111]

general mental ability (GMA) An overall factor of intelligence, as suggested by the positive correlations among specific intellectual ability dimensions.

Jobs differ in the demands they place on intellectual abilities. Research consistently indicates a correspondence between cognitive ability and task performance. Where employee tasks are highly routine and there are few or no opportunities to exercise discretion, a high IQ is not as important to performing well. However, that does not mean people with high IQs cannot have an impact on traditionally less complex jobs.[112]

It might surprise you that the intelligence test most widely used in hiring decisions takes only 12 minutes to complete. It's the Wonderlic Cognitive Ability Test. There are different forms of the test, but each has 50 questions and the same general construct. Here are two questions to try:

- When rope is selling at \$0.10 a foot, how many feet can you buy for \$0.60?
- Assume the first two statements below are true. Is the final one true, false, or not certain?

  a. The boy plays baseball.
  b. All baseball players wear hats.
  c. The boy wears a hat.

The Wonderlic measures both speed (almost nobody has time to answer every question) and power (the questions get harder as you go along), so the average score is quite low—about 21 of 50. Because the Wonderlic is able to provide valid information cheaply (for \$5 to \$10 per applicant), many organizations use it in hiring decisions, including Publix supermarkets, Manpower staffing systems, BP, and Dish satellite systems.[113] Most of these companies don't give up other hiring tools, such as application forms or interviews. Rather, they add the Wonderlic for its ability to provide valid data on applicants' intelligence levels.

While intelligence is a big help in performing a job well, it doesn't make people happier or more satisfied with their jobs.[114] In fact, research suggests that those with higher cognitive ability and who are high performers in the workplace might be victimized, bullied, and mistreated by their peers due to envy and social comparison.[115]

Physical Abilities

Although the changing nature of work suggests intellectual abilities are increasingly important for many jobs, **physical abilities** have been and will remain valuable. Research on hundreds of jobs has identified nine basic abilities needed in the performance of physical tasks.[116] These are described in Exhibit 2-3. High employee performance is likely to be achieved when the extent to which a job requires each of the nine abilities matches the abilities of employees in that job.

physical abilities The capacity to do tasks that demand stamina, dexterity, strength, and similar characteristics.

Exhibit 2-3 Nine Basic Physical Abilities

Strength Factors	
1. Dynamic strength	Ability to exert muscular force repeatedly or continuously over time
2. Trunk strength	Ability to exert muscular strength using the trunk (particularly abdominal) muscles
3. Static strength	Ability to exert force against external objects
4. Explosive strength	Ability to expend a maximum of energy in one or a series of explosive acts
Flexibility Factors	
5. Extent flexibility	Ability to move the trunk and back muscles as far as possible
6. Dynamic flexibility	Ability to make rapid, repeated flexing movements
Other Factors	
7. Body coordination	Ability to coordinate the simultaneous actions of different parts of the body
8. Balance	Ability to maintain equilibrium despite forces pulling off balance
9. Stamina	Ability to continue maximum effort requiring prolonged effort over time

In sum, organizations are increasingly aware that an optimally productive workforce includes all types of people and does not automatically exclude anyone on the basis of personal characteristics. The potential benefits of diversity are enormous for forward-thinking managers. For example, a pilot program of software company SAP in Germany, India, and Ireland has found that employees with autism achieve excellent performance in precision-oriented tasks like debugging software.[117] Of course, integrating diverse people into an optimally productive workforce takes skill. We will discuss how to bring the talents of a diverse workforce together in the next section.

Implementing Diversity Management Strategies

2-6 Describe how organizations manage diversity effectively.

diversity management The process and programs by which managers make everyone more aware of and sensitive to the needs and differences of others.

Having discussed a variety of ways in which people differ, we now look at how a manager can and should manage these differences. **Diversity management** makes everyone more aware of and sensitive to the needs and differences of others.[118] This definition highlights the fact that diversity programs include and are meant for everyone. Diversity is much more likely to be successful when we see it as everyone's business than when we believe it helps only certain groups of employees.

Attracting, Selecting, Developing, and Retaining Diverse Employees

One method of enhancing workforce diversity is to target recruitment messages to specific demographic groups that are underrepresented in the workforce. This means placing advertisements in publications geared toward those groups; pairing with colleges, universities, and other institutions with significant numbers of underrepresented minorities, as Microsoft is doing to encourage women to undertake technology studies;[119] and forming partnerships with associations like the Society of Women Engineers or the National Minority Supplier Development Council.

Research has shown that women and minorities have greater interest in employers that make special efforts to highlight a commitment to diversity in their recruiting materials. Diversity advertisements that fail to show women and minorities in positions of organizational leadership send a negative message about the diversity climate at an organization.[120] Of course, to show the pictures, organizations must actually have diversity in their management ranks.

Some companies have been actively working toward recruiting less-represented groups. Etsy, an online retailer, hosts engineering classes and provides grants for aspiring women coders and then hires the best.[121] McKinsey & Co., Bain & Co., Boston Consulting Group, and Goldman Sachs have also actively recruited women who left the workforce to start families by offering phase-in programs and other benefits.[122]

Diversity in Groups

Most contemporary workplaces require extensive work in group settings. When people work in groups, they need to establish a common way of looking at and accomplishing the major tasks, and they need to communicate with one another often. If they feel little sense of membership and cohesion in their groups, all group attributes are likely to suffer.

In some cases, diversity in traits can hurt team performance, whereas in others it can facilitate performance.[123] Whether diverse or homogeneous teams are more effective depends on the characteristic of interest. Demographic diversity (in gender, race, and ethnicity) does not appear to either help or hurt team performance in general, although racial diversity in management groups may increase organizational performance in the right conditions.[124]

Teams of individuals who are highly intelligent, conscientious, and interested in working in team settings are more effective. Thus, diversity on these variables is likely to be a bad thing—it makes little sense to try to form teams that mix in members who are lower in intelligence or conscientiousness, and who are uninterested in teamwork. In other cases, diversity can be a strength. Groups of individuals with different types of expertise and education are more effective than homogeneous groups. Similarly, a group made entirely of assertive people who want to be in charge or a group whose members all prefer to follow the lead of others will be less effective than a group that mixes leaders and followers.

Regardless of the composition of the group, differences can be leveraged to achieve superior performance. The most important factor is to emphasize the similarities among members.[125]

Expatriate Adjustment

According to a 2013 survey by Mercer, a global consulting firm, 70 percent of multinational organizations were expecting to increase short-term international assignments and 55 percent were looking to increase their long-term assignments. These organizations note that they do so in order to provide technical and managerial skills not available locally, provide career and leadership development opportunities, ensure knowledge transfer, and fulfill specific project needs.[126]

The experience of moving to a different country and adjusting to its new cultural, interactive, and work-related norms is a major undertaking for both the expatriate (i.e., the employee on international assignment) and the host country nationals. If it is not handled properly, poor adjustment can result in employee dissatisfaction, poor performance, prejudice, and misunderstanding.[127]

Several factors can be targeted to ensure that the adjustment process goes smoothly. For one, feelings of empowerment along with the motivation to interact with those of other cultures were found in one study to be related to ease of adjustment, increased satisfaction, and reduced intentions to leave prematurely.[128] Although adjustment tends to increase over time in a curvilinear fashion for all expatriates, those with previous culture-specific work experience as well as higher self-esteem and self-efficacy tend to adjust and be promoted more quickly.[129] A review of 66 studies on nearly 9,000 expatriates suggests that several other factors work in concert to affect different forms of adjustment, including language ability, relational skills, role clarity and autonomy, organizational support, and familial support.[130] These studies suggest that organizations should select employees for international assignments who are capable of adjusting quickly and then ensure they have the support they need for their assignment.

Effective Diversity Programs

Organizations use a variety of diversity programs in recruiting and selection policies, as well as training and development practices. Effective, comprehensive workforce programs encouraging diversity have three distinct components. First, they teach managers about the legal framework for equal employment opportunity and encourage fair treatment of all people regardless of their demographic characteristics. Second, they teach managers how a diverse workforce is better able to serve a diverse market of customers and clients. Third, they foster personal development practices that bring out the skills and abilities of all workers, acknowledging how differences in perspective can be a valuable way to improve performance for everyone.[131]

EasyJet has a hugely diverse workforce and employs people from 50 different nationalities. These employees give valuable insights into the different markets and destinations in which the airline operates.
Alex Segre/Alamy Stock Photo

Most negative reactions to employment discrimination are based on the idea that discriminatory treatment is unfair. Regardless of race or gender, people are generally in favor of diversity-oriented programs, including affirmative action programs (AAPs), to increase the representation of minority groups and to ensure that everyone has a fair opportunity to show their skills and abilities.

Organizational leaders should examine their workforce to determine whether target groups have been underutilized. If groups of employees are not proportionally represented in top management, managers should look for any hidden barriers to advancement. Managers can often improve recruiting practices, make selection systems more transparent, and provide training for those employees who have not had adequate exposure to diversity material in the past. The organization should also clearly communicate its policies to employees so they can understand how and why certain practices are followed. Communications should focus as much as possible on qualifications and job performance; emphasizing certain groups as needing more assistance could backfire.

Research also indicates that a tailored approach will be needed for international organizations. For instance, a case study of the multinational Finnish company TRANSCO found it was possible to develop a consistent global philosophy for diversity management. However, differences in legal and cultural factors across nations forced the company to develop unique policies to match the cultural and legal frameworks of each country in which it operated.[132]

Summary

This chapter looked at diversity from many perspectives. We paid particular attention to three variables—biographical characteristics, abilities, and diversity programs. Diversity management must be an ongoing commitment that crosses all levels of the organization. Policies to improve the climate for diversity can be effective, and diversity management can be learned.

Implications for Managers

- Increase awareness of stereotypes, how they are perpetuated, and how covert discrimination can manifest in organizations.
- Understand your organization's antidiscrimination policies thoroughly and share them with all employees.
- Assess and challenge your own stereotype beliefs to increase your objectivity.
- Fully evaluate what accommodations a person with disabilities will need and then fine-tune a job to that person's abilities.
- Seek to understand and respect the unique biographical characteristics of each individual; a fair but individualistic approach yields the best performance.
- Look beyond readily observable biographical characteristics and consider the individual's capabilities before making management decisions; remain open and encouraging for individuals to disclose any hidden disabilities.
- Strive to promote diversity in recruitment and selection practices.
- Develop a comprehensive diversity management program that weaves diversity considerations into the organization's operations.

Affirmative Action Programs Have Outlived Their Usefulness

POINT

U.S. Supreme Court Justice Sonia Sotomayor is arguably the Court's strongest supporter of affirmative action—in theory. In a recent case upholding the Michigan ban on affirmative action for underrepresented races in state university admission practices, Justice Sotomayor refused to use the term. "Affirmative action," she said, has the connotation of "intentional preferential treatment based on race alone." Yes, it does. Isn't that the point?

Affirmative action programs (AAPs) were needed to get the process of workplace diversity started, but that was all a long time ago. The practice, now outlawed in Arizona, California, Florida, Michigan, Nebraska, New Hampshire, Oklahoma, and Washington, raises the percentage of minority individuals but does not create a positive diversity climate. Here's why:

- *Affirmative action lowers the standards for everyone by shifting the criteria for hiring from experience, education, and abilities to quotas based on race or other nonperformance attributes.* Performance standards for the organization are then effectively lowered. Groups not helped by the initiative will be resentful, which can lead to workplace discrimination. Individuals "helped" into the organization also suffer from perceptions of low self-competence ("I don't know if I would have made it here if not for AAP") and stereotype threat ("I'm afraid others can't see me as competent because I was let in by the AAP").
- *Research indicates that minorities are not helped by AAP in pursuing higher education.* In fact, a large-scale study showed that minority law students who attended schools best matched to their LSAT scores performed better than those who went to higher-ranked schools than their scores would warrant without affirmative action.
- *Some of the world's AAPs have resulted in strife.* For example, Sri Lanka has suffered from civil wars partially caused by affirmative action that further polarized the Tamils and Shinalese. In Africa, the quota system to help blacks created a climate of race entitlement and marginalization of Indians. In fact, most countries have struggled with issues arising from affirmative action policies.

Affirmative action has outlived its usefulness in creating diversity, and it is time to create true equality by focusing on merit-based achievements.

COUNTERPOINT

Affirmative action was enacted to ensure equality, and it's still needed today. When the United States was considering the issue for black minorities back in 1965, President Lyndon B. Johnson said, "You do not take a person who, for years, has been hobbled by chains and liberate him, bring him up to the starting line of a race and then say, 'You are free to compete with all the others,' and still justly believe that you have been completely fair." Dr. Martin Luther King Jr. agreed that, in order to create equal opportunity, proactive measures are needed as long as some people remain at a disadvantage. Therefore, what we should be asking is: Are minority groups faring as well as majority groups in the United States? No, they are not—not by any indicator.

South Africa has affirmative action for blacks through the Equal Employment Act; China has "preferential policies" that require that ethnic minorities and women be appointed to top government positions; Israel has a class-based affirmative action policy to promote women, Arabs, blacks, and people with disabilities; India has a policy of reservation, a form of affirmative action, for underrepresented castes; Sri Lanka has the "standardization" affirmative action policy to help those in areas with lower rates of education; Malaysia's New Economic Policy (NEP) provides advantage for the majority group, the Malays, who have lower income; Brazil, Finland, France, New Zealand, and Romania have education AAPs; Germany's Basic Law has AAPs for women and those with handicaps; Russia has quotas for women and ethnic minorities; and Canada's Employment Equity Act provides affirmative action to women, the disabled, aboriginal people, and visible minorities.

To be certain, fairness is in the eye of the beholder. Affirmative action provides opportunity, but then it is up to the individual to meet the expectations of schools or employers. As blogger Berneta Haynes wrote, "I'm not ashamed to admit that without affirmative action, I'm not certain I would be on the precipice of the law career that I'm at right now. As an African-American woman from a poor family, I have little doubt that affirmative action helped me get into college, earn a degree, and enroll in law school."

If we change anything about affirmative action, we should expand the program until the achievements of underserved groups fully match those of long-overprivileged groups.

Sources: Based on D. Desilver, "Supreme Court Says States Can Ban Affirmative Action: 8 Already Have," Pew Research Center *Thinktank* (April 22, 2014), http://www.pewresearch.org/fact-tank/2014/04/22/supreme-court-says-states-can-ban-affirmative-action-8-already-have/; B. Haynes, "Affirmative Action Helped Me," *Inside Higher Ed* (March 12, 2013), www.insidehighered.com/views/2013/03/12/affirmative-action-helped-me-and-benefits-society-essay; D. Leonhardt, "Rethinking Affirmative Action," *The New York Times* (October 13, 2012), www.nytimes.com/2012/10/14/sunday-review/rethinking-affirmative-action.html?pagewanted=all; L. M. Leslie, D. M. Mayer, and D. A. Kravitz, "The Stigma of Affirmative Action: A Stereotyping-Based Theory and Meta-Analytic Test of the Consequences for Performance," *Academy of Management Journal* 57, no. 4 (2014): 964-89; and B. Zimmer, "Affirmative Action's Hazy Definitions," *The Wall Street Journal* (April 26-27, 2014), C4.

CHAPTER REVIEW

QUESTIONS FOR REVIEW

2-1 What are the two major forms of workplace diversity?

2-2 How does workplace discrimination undermine organizational effectiveness?

2-3 How are the key biographical characteristics relevant to OB?

2-4 How do other differentiating characteristics factor into OB?

2-5 What are the relevant points of intellectual and physical abilities to organizational behavior?

2-6 How can organizations manage diversity effectively?

APPLICATION AND EMPLOYABILITY

Diversity, in a variety of forms, is important to the application of OB in the workplace. First, workplace discrimination can undermine the effectiveness of an organization and can lead to many poor outcomes. Beyond biographical characteristics, other factors such as intellectual and physical abilities are important to OB. Knowledge of diversity in OB can help you and your organization manage diversity effectively and can help you work effectively with coworkers who may be different than you in a variety of ways. In this chapter, you improved your critical thinking skills and learned various ways to approach issues of social responsibility through encountering how even minor elements of one's appearance (e.g., baldness) can affect perceptions in the workplace, the considerations to make when deciding whether one should come out at work, and the usefulness and ethics surrounding affirmative action programs. In the following section, you will have more opportunities to develop these skills by recognizing the differences and similarities between you and your classmates, considering how moral licensing and tokenism operate in organizations, determining whether diversity training is effective, and examining the so-called encore career.

EXPERIENTIAL EXERCISE Helping Each Other and Finding Out We Aren't That Different

Break into teams of four or five while trying to maximize internal diversity. Student take turns sharing with the others a problem that they are currently facing in their lives. Any problem can be presented; the only requirement is that the problem should be meaningful and important for the presenter. It can be a problem that students are facing at school, at work, in their sports or leisure activities, or in their personal life. Sample problems are: How can I find an internship? How can I improve my language abilities? Where could I travel for the weekend? And so forth. After each request is shared, all the other team members are asked to use their intellect, experience, network, or skills to figure out if they can help resolve the problem. Each problem must be discussed for a maximum of 7 minutes, and the presenter is invited to write down the advice received. After all the students' problems are discussed, team members are invited to discuss if and to what extent they are facing, or have faced in the past, problems similar to those of their classmates, regardless of their country of origin or educational background. The following questions can help in the team discussion (remind them that all information discussed will remain in the room):

2-7. Do you think that sharing personal problems and helping one another can create a positive climate that favors inclusion and appreciation of each other? What does this exercise teach you about how to manage diversity at work?

2-8. How could this experience be replicated in the workplace for discussing organization-related problems faced by people from different departments? Would you consider establishing a weekly meeting based on this exercise? Discuss the reasons for and reasons against establishing such a ritual.

Source: Inspired by the reciprocity ring exercise described in A. Grant, *Give and Take: Why Helping Others Drives Our Success* (Orion Publishing Co., 2013).

ETHICAL DILEMMA Voiding the "License to Discriminate"

In the recently completed Olympics the Indian women's hockey team displayed great talent and missed the bronze medal in the final competition. Despite the loss the PM congratulated the team and motivated them to do better next time. He made a special mention of the leader Vandana Katariya. However, the entire sporting community remained silent on the attacks that were made on her house in Haridwar and on the social media because of her caste. While there were members of the public who did support Vandana and spoke against the caste-based attacks there was no stand taken by the officials.[133]

In the workplace, tokenism refers to minority members being hired into a position because they are different from other members and sometimes to serve as proof that the organization or group is nondiscriminatory. Once in their positions, tokens are given work that would be stereotypically suitable for their demographic. For example, women may be given stereotypically female tasks instead of other tasks that they would be perfectly capable of performing. By engaging in tokenism, organizations may fall prey to a moral licensing effect, where employers are more likely to engage in prejudicial or unethical behavior when they have initially behaved in a morally acceptable way (such as in believing that selecting or including one minority member is "proof" that the group is nondiscriminatory).

Questions

2-9. Can you think of other examples in which tokenism might emerge in the workplace? What are they?

2-10. Organizations use a variety of diversity management strategies to make employees more aware of and sensitive to the needs of others. Do you think that these same practices may inadvertently (or intentionally) lead to tokenism or moral licensing? Why or why not?

2-11. What do you think can be done to limit tokenism in workgroups and organizations?

Sources: Based on I. Blanken, N. van de Ven, and M. Zeelenberg, "A Meta-Analytic Review of Moral Licensing," *Personality and Social Psychology Bulletin* 41, no. 4 (2015): 540–558; Z. Clay, "Tokenism and Black America," *Clutch: News & Opinion*, April 2013, https://www.clutchmagonline.com/2013/04/dealing-with-tokenism-in-black-america/; R. Kanter, *Men and Women of the Corporation* (New York: Basic Books, 1977); and L. Zimmer, "Tokenism and Women in the Workplace: The Limits of Gender-Neutral Theory," *Social Problems* 35, no. 1 (1988): 64–77.

CASE INCIDENT 1 Encouraging Female Engineers

When Jess Stone tells people she is training to become an engineer, they often remark that she does not look like the kind of person who would "fix a boiler." According to the 23-year-old, who works for aerospace company Airbus, there's "a bit of a misunderstanding around the term engineer. Oily overalls? These ideas are so outdated."

While 47 percent of the UK workforce is female, the figure for those working in core engineering occupations is just 12 percent. In engineering businesses, it is only 9 percent, according to EngineeringUK. "Times have changed. There has been progress but it's still a male bastion," says Margaret Craddock, who has spent 33 years in the sector. She recalls one eager salesman visiting her site office 30 years ago and asking her, when she was the co-owner of a machinery business, "Is there anybody important here?" More recently, she has also heard men ask women in the sector, "Are you a real engineer?"

In her current role as BatchLine Division lead with Dyer Engineering, a fabrication and machining business in County Durham, Craddock does come across women, but mostly in engineering purchasing departments. "But when you get to welding and machining, it's a harsh environment. It's noisy, it's dangerous," she says.

With a retiring workforce and technology creating new opportunities, engineering in Britain is suffering from severe skills shortages, and new blood is urgently needed. According to EngineeringUK's 2018 report, the sector has an annual demand for 124,000 engineers and technicians with core engineering skills but faces a shortfall of up to 59,000 every year.

Engineering offers exciting prospects and fascinating work. "I really enjoy the technical challenges," says Emilie Weaving, a mechanical development engineer working for construction equipment manufacturer JCB. Salaries are also good. According to EngineeringUK, graduates with an engineering and technology degree had an average starting salary of around €30,000, above the all-subject average of €24,500. Despite eager recruits like Ms. Weaving and Ms. Stone, the lack of diversity in UK engineering, which is also reflected in the low intake of people from black, Asian, and minority ethnic backgrounds, is a concern for the sector.

When it comes to international comparisons, the United Kingdom scores poorly. According to Hayaatun Sillem, Chief Executive of the Royal Academy of Engineering, it "has the lowest proportion of female professional engineers of any European country." But that is not to say that this is only a British issue; proportions are low across the continent.

Recruitment isn't the only issue; there's also a retention problem. A 2017 report from the Institution of Mechanical Engineers said that within a few years of gaining an engineering degree, just under half of the United Kingdom's female engineering graduates were leaving the profession, while two-thirds of male engineers remained. Clearly, this is a huge waste of women's potential.

Questions

2-12. What factors may have caused the low participation rate of females in engineering?

2-13. What could be done to attract more women and other groups that are underrepresented in the profession?

2-14. Retention of women engineers is also an issue. How could this be improved?

Sources: Adapted from C. Tighe, "Female Engineers Flourish but Numbers Stay Stubbornly Low," *Financial Times*, October 4, 2019; and J. Miller, "Diverse Recruitment Bottleneck Hinders German Engineering," *Financial Times*, November 20, 2019.

CASE INCIDENT 2 The Encore Career

In India, retired bureaucrats, scientists, and professors are highly valued in high value projects and R&D. The same in true in other rapidly developing economies like Cambodia, Vietnam and Myanmar where, senior-level managers who have the expertise and experience to support and accelerate business growth in sectors like manufacturing, information technology, energy and construction are sought after.[134]

Unfortunately, older workers face a variety of discriminatory attitudes in the workplace. Researchers scanned more than 100 publications on age discrimination to determine what types of age stereotypes were most prevalent across studies. They found that stereotypes inferred that older workers are lower performers. Research indicates that they are not, however, and organizations are realizing the benefits of this needed employee group.

Dale Sweere, HR director for engineering firm Stanley Consultants, is one of the growing number of management professionals actively recruiting older workers. Sweere says older workers "typically hit the ground running much quicker and they fit into the organization well." They bring to the job a higher skill level earned through years of experience, remember an industry's history, and know the aging customer base.

Tell that to the older worker who is unemployed. Older workers have long been sought by government contractors, financial firms, and consultants, according to Cornelia Gamlem, president of consulting firm GEMS Group Ltd., and she actively recruits them. However, the U.S. Bureau of Labor Statistics reports that the average job search for an unemployed worker over age 55 is 56 weeks, versus 38 weeks for the rest of the unemployed population.

Enter the encore career, also known as unretirement. Increasingly, older workers who aren't finding fulfilling positions are seeking to opt out of traditional roles. After long careers in the workforce, an increasing number are embracing flexible, work-from-home options such as customer service positions. For instance, Olga Howard, 71, signed on as an independent contractor for 25–30 hours per week with Arise Virtual Solutions, handling questions for a financial software company after her long-term career ended. Others are starting up new businesses. Chris Farrell, author of *Unretirement*, said, "Older people are starting businesses more than any other age group." Others funnel into nonprofit organizations, where the pay may not equal the individual's previous earning power, but the mission is strong. "They need the money and the meaning," said Encore.org CEO Marc Freedman. Still others are gaining additional education, such as Japan's "silver entrepreneurs," who have benefited from the country's tax credits for training older workers.

Individuals who embark on a second-act career often report they are very fulfilled. However, the loss of workers from their long-standing careers may be undesirable. "In this knowledge economy, the retention of older workers gives employers a competitive edge by allowing them to continue to tap a generation of knowledge and skill," said Mark Schmit, executive director of the Society for Human Resource Management (SHRM) Foundation.

Questions

2-15. What changes in employment relationships are likely to occur as the population ages?

2-16. Do you think increasing age diversity will create new challenges for managers? What types of challenges do you expect will be most profound?

2-17. How can organizations cope with differences related to age discrimination in the workplace? How can older employees help?

Sources: Based on N. Eberstadt and M. W. Hodin, "America Needs to Rethink 'Retirement'," *The Wall Street Journal,* March 11, 2014, A15; S. Giegerich, "Older Job-Seekers Must Take Charge, Adapt," *Chicago Tribune,* September 10, 2012, 2–3; R. J. Grossman, "Encore!" *HR Magazine,* July 2014, 27–31; T. Lytle, "Benefits for Older Workers," *HR Magazine,* March 2012, 53–58; G. Norman, "Second Acts after 65," *The Wall Street Journal,* September 24, 2014, A13; D. Stipp, "The Anti-Aging Revolution," *Fortune,* June 14, 2010, 124–30; R. A. Posthuma and M. A. Campion, "Age Stereotypes in the Workplace: Common Stereotypes, Moderators, and Future Research Directions," *Journal of Management* 35 (2009): 158–88; and P. Sullivan, "Older, They Turn a Phone into a Job," *The New York Times,* March 25, 2014, F3.

ENDNOTES

[1] 451 Research. "Women in Tech: India Leads the Way". *Retrieved from https:// go.451research.com* (Accessed on April 13, 2022).

[2] Gupta, B. (2020). "Study: Gender Diversity In Analytics—2020". *Analytics India Magazine (March 2, 2020).* Retrieved from https://analyticsindiamag.com https://go.451research.com (Accessed on April 11, 2022).

[3] Verma, P. (2022). "Gender gap is closing fast across India's top IT companies". *The Economic Times (February 12, 2022).* Retrieved from https://economictimes.indiatimes.com (Accessed on April 11, 2022).

[4] U.S. Census Bureau, DataFerrett, Current Population Survey, December 2016; S. Ricker, "The Changing Face of U.S. Jobs," *Career-Builder, March 26, 2015,* www.thehiringsite.careerbuilder.com/2015/03/26/9-findingsdiversity-americas-workforce.

[5] Mehrotra, S. & Sinha, S. (2019). "Towards higher female work participation in India: what can be done?" *CSE Working Paper 2019-02 ©Azim Premji University (January 2019).* Retrieved from https://cse.azimpremjiuniversity.edu.in (Accessed on April 11, 2022).

[6] Verick, S. "Women's labour force participation in India: Why is it so low?" *Intenational Labour Organization.* Retrieved from https://www.ilo.org (Accessed on April 11, 2022).

[7] Kathuria, S. (2021). "Enhancing women's employment is key to economic recovery". *©Hindustan Times (January 19, 2021).* Retrieved from https://www.hindustantimes.com (Accessed on April 11, 2022).

[8] Monsterindia.com. "Monster Salary Index". Retrieved from https://media.monsterindia.com (Accessed pn April 22, 2022).

[9] Chakraborty, N. (2019). "What is gender pay gap and why it is so wide in India?" *Livemint©The Mint (December 3, 2019).* Retrieved from https://www.livemint.com (Accessed on April 11, 2022).

[10] Panache. "Pandemic hurt gender pay-gap in India further; more women failed to get deserving pay hikes, bonuses." *©The Economic Times (December 9, 2021).* Retrieved from https://economictimes.indiatimes.com (Accessed on April 11, 2022).

[11] M. Toossi, "A Century of Change: The U.S. Labor Force, 1950–2050," *Bureau of Labor Statistics,* May 2002, www.bls.gov/opub/2002/05/art2full.pdf.

[12] U.S. Census Bureau, DataFerrett, *Current Population Survey,* December 2016; S. Ricker, "The Changing Face of U.S. Jobs," *CareerBuilder,* March 26, 2015, www.thehiringsite.careerbuilder.com/2015/03/26/9-findings-diversity-americas-workforce.

[13] L. Colley, "Not Codgers in Cardigans! Female Workforce Participation and Aging Public Services," *Gender Work and Organization* 20, no. 3 (2013): 327–48; and M. DiNatale and S. Boraas, "The Labor Force Experience of Women from Generation X," *Monthly Labor Review,* March 2002, 1–15.

[14] J. Faragher, "Reporting Requirements Will Take Gender Pay Rows from the Red Carpet to the UK Shop Floor," *People Management,* February 2017: 27–30.

[15] A. H. Eagly and J. L. Chin, "Are Memberships in Race, Ethnicity, and Gender Categories Merely Surface Characteristics?" *American Psychologist* 65, no. 9 (2010): 934–35.

[16] W. J. Casper, J. H. Wayne, and J. G. Manegold, "Who Will We Recruit? Targeting Deep- and Surface-Level Diversity with Human Resource Policy Advertising," *Human Resource Management* 52, no. 3 (2013): 311–32; S. L. Gaertner and J. F. Dovidio, *Reducing Intergroup Bias: The Common Ingroup Identity Model* (Philadelphia: Psychology Press, 2000).

[17] Business Line (2017). "Corporates have stepped up affirmative action practices, but more can be done". *©The Hindu (February 20, 2017).* Retrieved from https://www.thehindubusinessline.com (Accessed on April 11, 2022).

[18] Ketan, A. (2021). "A distant dream". *©The Telegraph Online.* Retrieved from https://www.telegraphindia.com (Accessed on April 11, 2022).

[19] C. T. Kulik, "Spotlight on the Context: How a Stereotype Threat Framework Might Help Organizations to Attract and Retain Older Workers," *Industrial and Organizational Psychology* 7, no. 3 (2014): 456–61.
[20] S. J. Spencer, C. Logel, and P. G. Davies, "Stereotype Threat," *Annual Review of Psychology* 67 (2016): 415–37.
[21] E. J. Kenny and R. B. Briner, "Stereotype Threat and Minority Ethnic Employees: What Should Our Research Priorities Be?" *Industrial and Organizational Psychology* 7, no. 3 (2014): 425–29; and Spencer, Logel, and Davies, "Stereotype Threat."
[22] J. A. Grand, "Brain Drain? An Examination of Stereotype Threat Effects during Training on Knowledge Acquisition and Organizational Effectiveness," *Journal of Applied Psychology*, 102, no. 2 (2017): 115–50; and Spencer, Logel, and Davies, "Stereotype Threat."
[23] G. M. Walton, M. C. Murphy, and A. M. Ryan, "Stereotype Threat in Organizations: Implications for Equity and Performance," *Annual Review of Organizational Psychology and Organizational Behavior* 2 (2015): 523–50.
[24] G. Czukor and M. Bayazit, "Casting a Wide Net? Performance Deficit, Priming, and Subjective Performance Evaluation in Organizational Stereotype Threat Research," *Industrial and Organizational Psychology* 7, no. 3 (2014): 409–12; K. S. Jones and N. C. Carpenter, "Toward a Sociocultural Psychological Approach to Examining Stereotype Threat in the Workplace," *Industrial and Organizational Psychology* 7, no. 3 (2014): 429–32; Kulik, "Spotlight on the Context"; C. T. Kulik, S. Perera, and C. Cregan, "Engage Me: The Mature-Age Worker and Stereotype Threat," *Academy of Management Journal* 59, no. 6 (2016): 2132–56 ; and O. R. Shewach, P. R. Sackett, and S. Quint, "Stereotype Threat Effects in Settings with Features Likely versus Unlikely in Operational Test Settings: A Meta-analysis," *Journal of Applied Psychology* (in press).
[25] L. M. Cortina, "Unseen Injustice: Incivility as Modern Discrimination in Organizations," *Academy of Management Review* 33, no. 1 (2008): 55–75; and C. M. Harold and B. C. Holtz, "The Effects of Passive Leadership on Workplace Incivility," *Journal of Organizational Behavior* 36, no. 1 (2015): 16–38.
[26] N. A. Bowling and T. A. Beehr, "Workplace Harassment from the Victim's Perspective: A Theoretical Model and Meta-Analysis," *Journal of Applied Psychology* 91, no. 5 (2006): 998–1012; and J. P. Jamieson, K. Koslov, M. K. Nock, and W. B. Mendes, "Experiencing Discrimination Increases Risk Taking," *Psychological Science* 24, no. 2 (2012): 131–39.
[27] C. T. Kulik, S. Ryan, S. Harper, and G. George, "Aging Populations and Management," *Academy of Management Journal* 57, no. 4 (2014): 929–35.
[28] M. Toossi, "Labor Force Projections to 2024: The Labor Force Is Growing, but Slowly," *Monthly Labor Review*, December 2015, https://www.bls.gov/opub/mlr/2015/article/labor-force-projections-to-2024.htm.
[29] A. Tergesen, "Why Everything You Know about Aging Is Probably Wrong," *The Wall Street Journal*, December 1, 2014, B1–B2.
[30] L. Turner and A. Suflas, "Global Diversity—One Program Won't Fit All," *HR Magazine,* May 2014, 59–61.
[31] L. Weber, "Americans Rip Up Retirement Plans," *The Wall Street Journal*, January 31, 2013, http://online.wsj.com/article/SB10001424127887323926104578276241741448064.html.
[32] Wikipedia. "Demographics of India". Retrieved from https://en.wikipedia.org (Accessed on April 11, 2022).
[33] M. Chand and R. L. Tung, "The Aging of the World's Population and Its Effects on Global Business," *Academy of Management Perspectives* 28, no. 4 (2014): 409–29.
[34] S. Shellenbarger, "Work & Family Mailbox," *The Wall Street Journal*, January 29, 2014, D2.
[35] N. E. Wolfson, T. M. Cavanaugh, and K. Kraiger, "Older Adults and Technology-Based Instruction: Optimizing Learning Outcomes and Transfer," *Academy of Management Learning & Education* 13, no. 1 (2014): 26–44.
[36] T. W. H. Ng and D. C. Feldman, "Re-examining the Relationship between Age and Voluntary Turnover," *Journal of Vocational Behavior* 74, no. 3 (2009): 283–94.
[37] T. W. H. Ng and D. C. Feldman, "The Relationship of Age to Ten Dimensions of Job Performance," *Journal of Applied Psychology* 93, no. 2 (2008): 392–423.
[38] T. W. H. Ng and D. C. Feldman, "Evaluating Six Common Stereotypes about Older Workers with Meta-Analytical Data," *Personnel Psychology* 65, no. 4 (2012): 821–58.
[39] A. Tergesen, "Why Everything You Know about Aging Is Probably Wrong," *The Wall Street Journal*, December 1, 2014, B1–B2.
[40] Ibid.
[41] Ibid.; A. Burmeister, M. Wang, and A. Hirschi, "Understanding the Motivational Benefits of Knowledge Transfer for Older and Younger Workers in Age-Diverse Coworker Dyads: An Actor-Partner Interdependence Model," *Journal of Applied Psychology* (in press); Y. Li, Y. Gong, A. Burmeister, M. Wang, V. Alterman, A. Alonso, and S. Robinson, "Leveraging Age Diversity for Organizational Performance: An Intellectual Capital Perspective," *Journal of Applied Psychology* (in press).
[42] A. Tergesen, "Why Everything You Know about Aging Is Probably Wrong."
[43] T. W. H. Ng and D. C. Feldman, "The Relationship of Age with Job Attitudes: A Meta-Analysis," *Personnel Psychology* 63, no. 3 (2010): 677–718.
[44] E. Zell, Z. Krizan, and S. R. Teeter, "Evaluating Gender Similarities and Differences Using Metasynthesis," *American Psychologist* 70, no. 1 (2015): 10–20.
[45] J. B. Allendorfer, C. J. Lindsell, M. Siegel, C. L. Banks, J. Vannest, S. K. Holland, and J. P. Szaflarski, "Females and Males Are Highly Similar in Language Performance and Cortical Activation Patterns during Verb Generation," *Cortex* 48, no. 9 (2012): 1218–33; and A. Ardila, M. Rosselli, E. Matute, and O. Inozemtseva, "Gender Differences in Cognitive Development," *Developmental Psychology* 47, no. 4 (2011): 984–90.
[46] P. L. Roth, K. L. Purvis, and P. Bobko, "A Meta-Analysis of Gender Group Differences for Measures of Job Performance in Field Studies," *Journal of Management* 38, no. 2 (2012): 719–39.
[47] S. C. Paustian-Underdahl, L. S. Walker, and D. J. Woehr, "Gender and Perceptions of Leadership Effectiveness: A Meta-Analysis of Contextual Moderators," *Journal of Applied Psychology* 99, no. 6 (2014): 1129–45.
[48] R. E. Silverman, "Study Suggests Fix for Gender Bias on the Job," *The Wall Street Journal*, January 9, 2013, D4.
[49] A. J. Koch, S. D. D'Mello, and P. R. Sackett, "A Meta-Analysis of Gender Stereotypes and Bias in Experimental Simulations of Employment Decision Making," *Journal of Applied Psychology* 100, no. 1 (2015): 128–61.
[50] E. B. King, W. Botsford, M. R. Hebl, S. Kazama, J. F. Dawson, and A. Perkins, "Benevolent Sexism at Work: Gender Differences in the Distribution of Challenging Developmental Experiences," *Journal of Management* 38, no. 6 (2012): 1835–66.
[51] K. S. Lyness and D. E. Thompson, "Above the Glass Ceiling? A Comparison of Matched Samples of Female and Male Executives," *Journal of Applied Psychology* 82 (1997): 359–75; C. Hymowitz and T. D. Schellhardt, "The Glass Ceiling," *The Wall*

Street Journal (March 24, 1986): D1, 4–5; B. Zimmer, "The Phrase 'Glass Ceiling' Stretches Back Decades," *The Wall Street Journal* (April 3, 2015), https://www.wsj.com/articles/the-phrase-glass-ceiling-stretches-back-decades-1428089010.
[52]Catalyst, *List: Women CEOs of the S&P 500*, accessed April 16, 2020, https://www.catalyst.org/research/women-ceos-of-the-sp-500/.
[53] L. Gartzia, M. K. Ryan, N. Balluerka, and A. Aritzeta, "Think Crisis—Think Female: Further Evidence," *European Journal of Work and Organizational Psychology* 21, no. 4 (2014): 603–28; M. K. Ryan and S. A. Haslam, "The Glass Cliff: Evidence That Women Are Over-represented in Precarious Leadership Positions," *British Journal of Management* 16, no. 2 (2005): 81–90; M. K. Ryan and S. A. Haslam, "The Glass Cliff: Exploring the Dynamics Surrounding the Appointment of Women to Precarious Leadership Positions," *Academy of Management Review* 32, no. 2 (2007): 549–72.
[54] P. Wechsler, "58 women CFOs in the Fortune 500: Is This progress?" *Fortune*, February 24, 2015, http://fortune.com/2015/02/24/58-women-cfos-in-the-fortune-500-is-this-progress/.
[55]J. M. Hoobler, C. R. Masterson, S. M. Nkomo, and E. J. Michel, "The Business Case for Women Leaders: Meta-analysis, Research Critique, and Path Forward," *Journal of Management* 44, no. 6 (2018): 2473–99; S. C. Paustian-Underdahl, L. Slattery Walker, and D. J. Woehr, "Gender and Perceptions of Leadership Effectiveness: A Meta-analysis of Contextual Moderators," *Journal of Applied Psychology* 99, no. 6 (2014): 1129–45.
[56] A. Damast, "She Works Hard for Less Money," *Bloomberg Businessweek*, December 24, 2012–January 6, 2013, 31–32.
[57] B. Casselman, "Male Nurses Earn More," *The Wall Street Journal*, February 26, 2013, A2.
[58]A. Joshi, J. Son, and H. Roh, "When Can Women Close the Gap? A Meta-Analytic Test of Sex Differences in Performance and Rewards," *Academy of Management Journal* 58, no. 5 (2015): 1516–45.
[59] A. J. C. Cuddy, "Increasingly, Juries Are Taking the Side of Women Who Face Workplace Discrimination," *Harvard Business Review*, September 2012, 95–100.
[60] J. M. Hoobler, G. Lemmon, and S. J. Wayne, "Women's Managerial Aspirations: An Organizational Development Perspective," *Journal of Management* 40, no. 3 (2014): 703–30.
[61]M. J. Williams and L. Z. Tiedens, "The Subtle Suspension of Backlash: A Meta-Analysis of Penalties for Women's Implicit and Explicit Dominance Behavior," *Psychological Bulletin*, 142, no. 2 (2016): 165–97.
[62] Turner and Suflas, "Global Diversity—One Program Won't Fit All."
[63] Ibid.
[64] G. N. Powell and D. A. Butterfield, "Exploring the Influence of Decision Makers' Race and Gender on Actual Promotions to Top Management," *Personnel Psychology* 55, no. 2 (2002): 397–428.
[65] T. Vega, "With Diversity Still Lacking, Industry Focuses on Retention," *The New York Times*, September 4, 2012, B3.
[66]D. Hack-Polay, "It's Time to Stop Auditing and Start Acting on Racial Discrimination," *People Management*, December 2017/January 2018: 20.
[67]D. R. Avery, P. F. McKay, and D. C. Wilson, "What Are the Odds? How Demographic Similarity Affects the Prevalence of Perceived Employment Discrimination," *Journal of Applied Psychology* 93, no. 2 (2008): 235–49.
[68]P. Bobko and P. L. Roth, "Reviewing, Categorizing, and Analyzing the Literature on Black-White Mean Differences for Predictors of Job Performance: Verifying Some Perceptions and Updating/Correcting Others," *Personnel Psychology* 66, no. 1 (2013): 91–126; and P. F. McKay and M. A. McDaniel, "A Reexamination of Black-White Mean Differences in Work Performance: More Data, More Moderators," *Journal of Applied Psychology* 91, no. 3 (2006): 538–54.
[69]S. Mullainathan, "The Measuring Sticks of Racial Bias," *The New York Times*, January 4, 2015, 6.
[70]M. Bertrand and S. Mullainathan, "Are Emily and Brendan More Employable Than Latoya and Tyrone? Evidence on Racial Discrimination in the Labor Market from a Large Randomized Experiment," *American Economic Review*, 94 (2004): 991–1013.
[71]B. R. Ragins, J. A. Gonzalez, K. Ehrhardt, and R. Singh, "Crossing the Threshold: The Spillover of Community Racial Diversity and Diversity Climate to the Workplace," *Personnel Psychology* 65, no. 4 (2012): 755–87.
[72]P. F. McKay, D. R. Avery, and M. A. Morris, "Mean Racial-Ethnic Differences in Employee Sales Performance: The Moderating Role of Diversity Climate," *Personnel Psychology* 61, no. 2 (2008): 349–74; and P. F. McKay, D. R. Avery, S. Tonidandel, M. A. Morris, M. Hernanez, and M. R. Hebl, "Racial Differences in Employee Retention: Are Diversity Climate Perceptions the Key?" *Personnel Psychology* 60, no. 1 (2007): 35–62.
[73]D. R. Avery, J. A. Richeson, M R. Hebl, and N. Ambady, "It Does Not Have to Be Uncomfortable: The Role of Behavioral Scripts in Black-White Interracial Interactions," *Journal of Applied Psychology* 94, no. 6 (2009): 1382–93.
[74]Turner and Suflas, "Global Diversity—One Program Won't Fit All."
[75]Information on the Americans with Disabilities Act can be found on their website at www.ada.gov, accessed July 28, 2015.
[76]S. G. Goldberg, M. B. Killeen, and B. O'Day, "The Disclosure Conundrum: How People with Psychiatric Disabilities Navigate Employment," *Psychology, Public Policy, and Law* 11, no. 3 (2005): 463–500; M. L. Ellison, Z. Russinova, K. L. MacDonald-Wilson, and A. Lyass, "Patterns and Correlates of Workplace Disclosure among Professionals and Managers with Psychiatric Conditions," *Journal of Vocational Rehabilitation* 18, no. 1 (2003): 3–13; and C. Hunter, M.-L. Verreynne, N. Pachana, and P. Harpur, "The Impact of Disability-Assistance Animals on the Psychological Health of Workplaces: A Systematic Review," *Human Resource Management Review* 29 (2019): 400–17.
[77]B. S. Bell and K. J. Klein, "Effect of Disability, Gender, and Job Level on Ratings of Job Applicants," *Rehabilitation Psychology* 46, no. 3 (2001): 229–46; and E. Louvet, "Social Judgment toward Job Applicants with Disabilities: Perception of Personal Qualities and Competences," *Rehabilitation Psychology* 52, no. 3 (2007): 297–303.
[78]J. E. Beatty, D. C. Baldridge, S. A. Boehm, M. Kukarni, and A. J. Colella, "On the Treatment of Persons with Disabilities in Organizations: A Review and Research Agenda," *Human Resource Management* 58 (2019): 119–37; S. Bonaccio, C. E. Connelly, I. R. Gellatly, A. Jetha, and K. A. Martin Ginis, "The Participation of People with Disabilities in the Workplace across the Employment Cycle: Employer Concerns and Research Evidence," *Journal of Business and Psychology* 35 (2020): 135–58; and L. R. Ren, R. L. Paetzold, and A. Colella, "A Meta-Analysis of Experimental Studies on the Effects of Disability on Human Resource Judgments," *Human Resource Management Review* 18, no. 3 (2008): 191–203.
[79]S. Almond and A. Healey, "Mental Health and Absence from Work: New Evidence from the UK Quarterly Labour

Force Survey," *Work, Employment, and Society* 17, no. 4 (2003): 731–42.
[80]P. T. J. H. Nelissen, K. Vornholt, G. M. C. Van Ruitenbeek, U. R. Hulsheger, and S. Uitdewilligen, "Disclosure or Nondisclosure—Is This the Question?" *Industrial and Organizational Psychology* 7, no. 2 (2014): 231–35.
[81]M. Santuzzi, P. R. Waltz, and L. M. Finkelstein, "Invisible Disabilities: Unique Challenges for Employees and Organizations," *Industrial and Organizational Psychology* 7, no. 2 (2014): 204–19.
[82]Ibid.
[83]T. D. Johnson and A. Joshi, "Dark Clouds or Silver Linings? A Stigma Threat Perspective on the Implications of an Autism Diagnosis for Workplace Well-Being," *Journal of Applied Psychology* 101, no. 3 (2015): 430–49.
[84]R. A. Schriber, R. W. Robins, and M. Solomon, "Personality and Self-Insight in Individuals with Autism Spectrum Disorder," *Journal of Personality and Social Psychology* 106, no. 1 (2014): 112–30.
[85]C. L. Nittrouer, R. C. E. Trump, K. R. O'Brien, and M. Hebl, "Stand Up and Be Counted: In the Long Run, Disclosing Helps All," *Industrial and Organizational Psychology* 7, no. 2 (2014): 235–41.
[86]T. W. H. Ng and D. C. Feldman, "Organizational Tenure and Job Performance," *Journal of Management* 36, no. 5 (2010): 1220–50; T. W. H. Ng and D. C. Feldman, "Does Longer Job Tenure Help or Hinder Job Performance?" *Journal of Vocational Behavior* 83, no. 3 (2013): 305–14.
[87]Turner and Suflas, "Global Diversity—One Program Won't Fit All."
[88] Kramer, S. (2021). "Population growth and religious composition". *©Pew Research Center (September 21, 2021).* Retrieved from https://www.pewforum.org (Accessed on April 15, 2022).
[89]S. Ghumman, A. M. Ryan, and J. S. Park, "Religious Harassment in the Workplace: An Examination of Observer Intervention," *Journal of Organizational Behavior* 37, no. 2 (2016): 279–306.
[90] The Hindu (February 9, 2022). "Watch | Karnataka's hijab controversy explained". *Retrieved from https://www.thehindu.com* (Accessed on April 12, 2022).
[91] Lang, C. (2021). "Who Gets to Wear a Headscarf? The Complicated History Behind France's Latest Hijab Controversy". *©Time (May 19, 2021).* Retrieved from https://time.com (Accessed on April 13, 2022).
[92] A. Liptak, "In a Case of Religious Dress,Justices Explore the Obligations of Employers," from *The New York Times (February 25, 2015)*, http://www.nytimes.com.
[93]A. Tilcsik, "Pride and Prejudice: Employment Discrimination against Openly Gay Men in the United States," *American Journal of Sociology* 117, no. 2 (2011): 586–626.
[94] B. A. Everly, M. M. Unzueta, and M. J. Shih, "Can Being Gay Provide a Boost in the Hiring Process? Maybe if the Boss Is Female," *Journal of Business Psychology* 31, no. 2 (2016): 293–306.
[95]J. Browne, "What One CEO Learned by Being Outed," *The Wall Street Journal*, June 7–8, 2014, C3.
[96] U.S. Equal Employment Opportunity Commission, "Facts about Discrimination in Federal Government Employment Based on Marital Status, Political Affiliation, Status as a Parent, Sexual Orientation, or Transgender (Gender Identity) Status," (Washington, DC: Author, 2013), www.eeoc.gov/federal/otherprotections.cfm.
[97] Turner and Suflas, "Global Diversity—One Program Won't Fit All."
[98] V. Priola, D. Lasio, S. De Simone, and F. Serri, "The Sound of Silence: Lesbian, Gay, Bisexual, and Transgender Discrimination in 'Inclusive Organizations,'" *British Journal of Management* 25, no. 3 (2012): 488–502.
[99] P. Gerber and J. Gory, "The UB Human Rights Committee and LGBT Rights: What Is It Doing? What Could It Be Doing?", *Human Rights Law Review* 14, no. 3 (2014): 403–39.
[100] U.S. Equal Employment Opportunity Commission, "Sex-Based Discrimination," (Washington, DC: Author, 2013), www.eeoc.gov/laws/types/sex.cfm.
[101] C. Burns, "The Costly Business of Discrimination," *Center for American Progress*, March 2012, www.scribd.com/doc/81214767/The-Costly-Business-of-Discrimination.
[102] Human Rights Campaign Foundation, *HRC Corporate Equality Index 2017: Rating Workplaces on Lesbian, Gay, Bisexual and Transgender Equality* (Washington, DC: Author, 2017), http://assets.hrc.org//files/assets/resources/CEI-2017-FinalReport.pdf.
[103] P. Levy, "Does the Hobby Lobby Decision Threaten Gay Rights?" *Newsweek*, July 9, 2014, http://www.newsweek.com/does-hobby-lobby-decision-threaten-gay-rights-258098.
[104] Priola, Lasio, De Simone, and Serri, "The Sound of Silence."
[105] Rautray, S. (2018). "Section 377: Supreme Court rewrites history, homosexuality no longer a crime". *©The Economic Times (September 6, 2018).* Retrieved from https://economictimes.indiatimes.com (Accessed on April 13, 2022).
[106] H. Deresky, *International Management: Managing across Borders and Cultures* (Harlow: Pearson Education Limited, 2014); Latham & Watkins LLP, *Doing Business in the United Arab Emirates* (Qatar: LW.com, 2014).
[107] R. E. Nisbett, J. Aronson, C. Blair, W. Dickens, J. Flynn, D. F. Halpern, and E. Turkheimer, "Intelligence: New Findings and Theoretical Developments," *American Psychologist* 67, no. 2 (2012): 130–59.
[108] L. S. Gottfredson, "The Challenge and Promise of Cognitive Career Assessment," *Journal of Career Assessment* 11, no. 2 (2003): 115–35.
[109] M. D. Dunnette and E. A. Fleishman (eds.), *Human Performance and Productivity: Human Capability Assessment* (New York and London: Psychology Press/Taylor & Francis Group, 2014).
[110] M. J. Ree and T. R. Carretta, "g2K," *Human Performance* 15, nos. 1–2 (2002): 3–23; and W. J. Schneider and D. A. Newman, "Intelligence Is Multidimensional: Theoretical Review and Implications of Specific Cognitive Abilities," *Human Resource Management Review* 25, no. 1 (2015): 12–27.
[111] N. Barber, "Educational and Ecological Correlates of IQ: A Cross-National Investigation," *Intelligence* 33, no. 3 (2005): 273–84.
[112] N. Schmitt, "Personality and Cognitive Ability as Predictors of Effective Performance at Work," *Annual Review of Organizational Psychology and Organizational Behavior* 1 (2014): 45–65.
[113] A. Hollis, "What Companies Will Make You Take a Wonderlic Test?" *Beat the Wonderlic Blog*, August 2, 2016, https://beatthewonderlic.com/blogs/news/what-companies-will-make-you-take-a-wonderlic-test.
[114]Y. Ganzach, "Intelligence and Job Satisfaction," *Academy of Management Journal* 41, no. 5 (1998): 526–39; and Y. Ganzach, "Intelligence, Education, and Facets of Job Satisfaction," *Work and Occupations* 30, no. 1 (2003): 97–122.
[115]J. M. Jensen, P. C. Patel, and J. L. Raver, "Is it Better to Be Average? High and Low Performance as Predictors of

Employee Victimization," *Journal of Applied Psychology*, 99, no. 2 (2014): 296–309; E. Kim and T. M. Glomb, "Get Smarty Pants: Cognitive Ability, Personality, and Victimization," *Journal of Applied Psychology* 95, no. 5 (2010): 889–901; and E. Kim and T. M. Glomb, "Victimization of High Performers: The Roles of Envy and Work Group Identification," *Journal of Applied Psychology* 99, no. 4 (2014): 619–34.

[116] J. J. Caughron, M. D. Mumford, and E. A. Fleishman, "The Fleishman Job Analysis Survey: Development, Validation, and Applications," in M. A. Wilson, W. Bennett Jr., S. G. Gibson, and G. M. Alliger (eds.), *The Handbook of Work Analysis: Methods, Systems, Applications and Science of Work Measurement in Organizations* (New York: Routledge/ Taylor & Francis Group, 2012); and P. D. Converse, F. L. Oswald, M. A. Gillespie, K. A. Field, and E. B. Bizot, "Matching Individuals to Occupations Using Abilities and the O*Net: Issues and an Application in Career Guidance," *Personnel Psychology* 57, no. 2 (2004): 451–87.

[117] S. S. Wang, "Companies Find Autism Can Be a Job Skill," *The Wall Street Journal*, March 28, 2014, B1–B2.

[118] Q. M. Roberson, "Diversity in the Workplace: A Review, Synthesis, and Future Research Agenda," *Annual Review of Organizational Psychology and Organizational Behavior* 6 (2019): 69–88.

[119] N. Wingfield, "Microsoft Chief Backpedals on Women's Pay," *The Wall Street Journal*, October 10, 2014, B1, B7.

[120] D. R. Avery, "Reactions to Diversity in Recruitment Advertising: Are the Differences Black and White?" *Journal of Applied Psychology* 88, no. 4 (2003): 672–79; P. F. McKay and D. R. Avery, "What Has Race Got to Do with It? Unraveling the Role of Racioethnicity in Job Seekers' Reactions to Site Visits," *Personnel Psychology* 59, no. 2 (2006): 395–429; and D. R. Avery and P. F. McKay, "Target Practice: An Organizational Impression Management Approach to Attracting Minority and Female Job Applicants," *Personnel Psychology* 59, no. 1 (2006): 157–87.

[121] A. Overholt, "More Women Coders," *Fortune*, February 25, 2013, 14.

[122] L. Kwoh, "McKinsey Tries to Recruit Mothers Who Left the Fold," *The Wall Street Journal*, February 20, 2013, B1, B7.

[123] S. T. Bell, "Deep-Level Composition Variables as Predictors of Team Performance: A Meta–Analysis," *Journal of Applied Psychology* 92, no. 3 (2007): 595–615; S. K. Horwitz and I. B. Horwitz, "The Effects of Team Diversity on Team Outcomes: A Meta-Analytic Review of Team Demography," *Journal of Management* 33, no. 6 (2007): 987–1015; G. L. Stewart, "A Meta-Analytic Review of Relationships between Team Design Features and Team Performance," *Journal of Management* 32, no. 1 (2006): 29–54; and A. Joshi and H. Roh, "The Role of Context in Work Team Diversity Research: A Meta-Analytic Review," *Academy of Management Journal* 52, no. 3 (2009): 599–627.

[124] G. Andrevski, O. C. Richard, J. D. Shaw, and W. J. Ferrier, "Racial Diversity and Firm Performance: The Mediating Role of Competitive Intensity," *Journal of Management* 40, no. 3 (2014): 820–44.

[125] A. C. Homan, J. R. Hollenbeck, S. E. Humphrey, D. Van Knippenberg, D. R. Ilgen, and G. A. Van Kleef, "Facing Differences with an Open Mind: Openness to Experience, Salience of Intragroup Differences, and Performance of Diverse Work Groups," *Academy of Management Journal* 51, no. 6 (2008): 1204–22.

[126] R. Maurer, "International Assignments Expected to Increase in 2013," *Society for Human Resource Management: Global HR*, May 14, 2013, https://www.shrm.org/ResourcesAndTools/hr-topics/global-hr/Pages/International-Assignments-Increase-2013.aspx.

[127] P. Bhaskar-Shrinivas, D. A. Harrison, M. A. Shaffer, and D. M. Luk, "Input-Based and Time-Based Models of International Adjustment: Meta-Analytic Evidence and Theoretical Extensions," *Academy of Management Journal* 48, no. 2 (2005): 257–81; and J. Bonache, H. Langinier, and C. Zárraga-Oberty, "Antecedents and Effects of Host Country Nationals Negative Stereotyping of Corporate Expatriates: A Social Identity Analysis," *Human Resource Management Review* 26, no. 1 (2016): 59–68.

[128] B. M. Firth, G. Chen, B. L. Kirkman, and K. Kim, "Newcomers Abroad: Expatriate Adaptation during Early Phases of International Assignments," *Academy of Management Journal* 57, no. 1 (2014): 280–300.

[129] J. Zhu, C. R. Wanberg, D. A. Harrison, and E. W. Diehn, "Ups and Downs of the Expatriate Experience? Understanding Work Adjustment Trajectories and Career Outcomes," *Journal of Applied Psychology* 101, no. 4 (2016): 549–68.

[130] Bhaskar-Shrinivas, Harrison, Shaffer, and Luk, "Input-Based and Time-Based Models of International Adjustment."

[131] C. L. Holladay and M. A. Quiñones, "The Influence of Training Focus and Trainer Characteristics on Diversity Training Effectiveness," *Academy of Management Learning and Education* 7, no. 3 (2008): 343–54; and R. Anand and M. Winters, "A Retrospective View of Corporate Diversity Training from 1964 to the Present," *Academy of Management Learning and Education* 7, no. 3 (2008): 356–72.

[132] A. Sippola and A. Smale, "The Global Integration of Diversity Management: A Longitudinal Case Study," *International Journal of Human Resource Management* 18, no. 11 (2007): 1895–1916.

[133] Taneja, N. (2021). "Ministers to Hockey India, all are quiet on casteist attack on Dalit player Vandana Katariya". ©*The Print (August 8, 2021)*. Retrieved from https://theprint.in (Accessed on April 13, 2022).

[134] Michael Page (Blog). "Job hunting over 50 in India: it isn't over yet". Retrieved from https://www.michaelpage.co.in (Accessed on April 12, 2022).

3 Attitudes and Job Satisfaction

Source: Richard McDowell/Alamy Stock Photo

LEARNING OBJECTIVES

After studying this chapter, you should be able to:

3-1 Contrast the three components of an attitude.

3-2 Summarize the relationship between attitudes and behavior.

3-3 Compare the major job attitudes.

3-4 Define *job satisfaction*.

3-5 Summarize the main causes of job satisfaction.

3-6 Identify three outcomes of job satisfaction.

3-7 Identify four employee responses to job dissatisfaction.

This matrix identifies which features and end-of-chapter material will help you develop specific skills employers are looking for in job candidates.

Employability Skills Matrix (ESM)

	Myth or Science?	Career OBjectives	An Ethical Choice	Point/ Counterpoint	Experiential Exercise	Ethical Dilemma	Case Incident 1	Case Incident 2
Critical Thinking		✓	✓	✓	✓	✓	✓	✓
Communication	✓	✓	✓		✓	✓		
Collaboration			✓	✓				
Knowledge Application and Analysis	✓	✓			✓		✓	✓
Social Responsibility	✓		✓	✓		✓	✓	✓

IN THE LEGOLAND WONDERLAND

Imagine working in a workplace divided into flexible work zones with no specific seating arrangements and no offices for managers, where you can choose to work in different settings that can support the activities or tasks you are performing, within an environment that can provide the ambience that helps you perform at your best. Imagine a workplace that has a variety of spaces that support different types of individual work as well as teamwork, a workplace that includes a library, quiet-zone booths (which are do-not-disturb places), areas that are equipped with high partitions for "head down" work, as well as small, closed rooms for complete privacy and circular "study caves" carved out of a wall for individual contemplation or rest. A workplace where technology enhances job satisfaction and innovation plays a key role, and where creativity is constantly stimulated in various ways. A workplace that, apart from the workspace, includes a wellness center (containing gyms, massage rooms, a swimming pool, a multi-use indoor sports pitch, and more), a rooftop garden split over multiple floors, and cafes where you can grab healthy and reenergizing food and beverages. This has been the vision, and ultimately the reality, for Lego's work environment set-up.

Some will wonder, why go to such lengths to create such an office environment? Lego shares a philosophy with Google, Microsoft, and Facebook that their staff must be encouraged to be creative and to *become*, and they seek to achieve this by providing exemplary working environments. They have embedded in their organizational culture the belief that employees' momentum and wellbeing is key to improving job satisfaction. Sophie Patrikios, Senior Director of Consumer Services at Lego, has stated that the leadership at Lego is always supportive and driven by a clear vision; it is not fixated on numbers but on the core values of the company deriving from its vision. Conversely, behaviors that are not in line with the values and the vision of the company have no place in it. The company seeks to instill its values and vision by encouraging management to allow space for creativity and initiative.

Many at Lego will aver that thinking and behaving like this is in the company's DNA, linked to their famous bricks, an outlet for creativity of many a child (and adult). Others would add that this company has an authentic reverence for its employees, seeking not just to appeal to their minds in motivating performance but also to their hearts. More prosaically, others will see this as a way to re-engineer traditional HR to ensure a happy workforce for an ultimately profitable workplace. But if all these play an important role in employees' overall job satisfaction—and of course they do—how do these elements actually affect the way they formulate their attitudes about the company's human resource management philosophy and approach?

Sources: "Best Places to Work 2020," Glassdoor, https://www.glassdoor.com/Award/Best-Places-to-Work-LST_KQ0,19.htm; Alex Hern, *The Guardian*, "Google Submits Plans for 'Landscraper' London Headquarters," June 1, 2017, https://www.theguardian.com/technology/2017/jun/01/google-submits-plans-million-sq-ft-london-hq-construction-kings-cross; The Long + Short, "Hot Desks: Inside LEGO's Imaginative London Office," July 11, 2016, https://thelongandshort.org/spaces/lego-creative-london-hq; Indeed, "Lego Group Company Reviews by Employees, https://www.indeed.co.uk/cmp/The-Lego-Group/reviews; *Financial Times*, "Happy Workplaces Help Companies Perform Better," December 20, 2017, https://www.ft.com/content/6081b1fc-d0b2-11e5-92a1-c5e23ef99c77; Inside, "A Great Company Culture Example: LEGO," December 20, 2017, https://inside.6q.io/company-culture-example-lego/.

It's a truism to say that a happy worker is a productive worker. As the chapter-opening vignette shows, however, what contributes to the development of job attitudes varies and may change over time. What factors besides organizational culture, leadership, and infrastructure affect job attitudes?[1] Does having a satisfying job really matter? Before we tackle these important questions, it's important to define what we mean by attitudes generally and by job attitudes in particular.

Attitudes

3-1 Contrast the three components of an attitude.

attitudes Evaluative statements or judgments concerning objects, people, or events.

cognitive component The opinion or belief segment of an attitude.

affective component The emotional or feeling segment of an attitude.

behavioral component An intention to behave in a certain way toward someone or something.

Attitudes are evaluative statements—either favorable or unfavorable—about objects, people, or events. They reflect how we feel about something. When you say, "I like my job," you are expressing your attitude about your work.

Attitudes are complex. If you ask people about their attitude toward religion, Lady Gaga, or an organization, you may get a simple response, but the underlying reasons are probably complicated. To fully understand attitudes, we must consider their fundamental properties or components.

Typically, researchers assume that attitudes have three components: cognition, affect, and behavior.[2] The statement "My pay is low" is a **cognitive component** of an attitude—a description of or belief in the way things are. It sets the stage for the more critical part of an attitude—its **affective component**. Affect is the emotional or feeling segment of an attitude reflected in the statement, "I am angry over how little I'm paid." Affect can lead to behavioral outcomes. The **behavioral component** of an attitude describes an intention to behave a certain way toward someone or something—as in, "I'm going to look for another job that pays better."

Viewing attitudes as having three components—affect, behavior, and cognition (e.g., the ABCs of attitudes)—helps understand their complexity and the potential relationship between attitudes and behavior. For example, imagine you (just now) realized that someone treated you unfairly. Aren't you likely to have almost instantaneous feelings occurring along with this realization? Thus, cognition and affect are intertwined.

Exhibit 3-1 illustrates how the three components of an attitude are related. In this example, an employee didn't get a promotion he thought he deserved. His attitude toward his supervisor is illustrated as follows: The employee thought he deserved the promotion (cognition), he strongly dislikes his supervisor (affect), and he has complained and taken action (behavior).

In organizations, attitudes are important for their behavioral component. For example, if workers vary in how committed they are to their organizations and this commitment can lead to whether or not they stay or leave their jobs, we should try to understand how this commitment is formed and how it might be changed. Some research from the Netherlands suggests that, with organizational commitment, prior cognition and behavior both cause affect, although these components are often difficult to separate.[3]

Attitudes and Behavior

3-2 Summarize the relationship between attitudes and behavior.

Early research on attitudes assumed that they were causally related to behavior—that is, the attitudes people hold determine what they do. However, one researcher—Leon Festinger—argued that attitudes *follow* behavior. Other researchers have agreed that attitudes predict future behavior.[4]

Exhibit 3-1 The Components of an Attitude

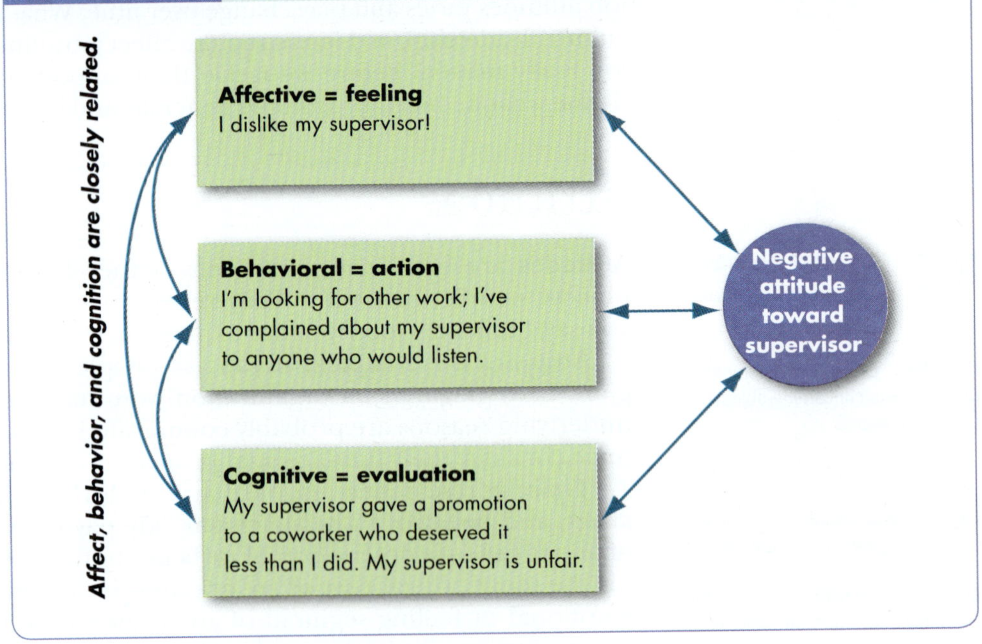

cognitive dissonance Any incompatibility between two or more attitudes or between behavior and attitudes.

Did you ever notice how people change what they say so it doesn't contradict what they do? Perhaps a friend of yours consistently argued that her apartment complex was better than yours until another friend in your complex asked her to move in with him; once she moved to your complex, you noticed her attitude toward her former apartment became more critical. Cases of attitude following behavior illustrate the effects of **cognitive dissonance**,[5] contradictions individuals might perceive between their attitudes and their behavior.

People seek a stable consistency among their attitudes and between their attitudes and their behavior.[6] Any form of inconsistency is uncomfortable, and individuals therefore attempt to reduce or minimize it. When there is dissonance, people alter either their attitudes or behavior to minimize the dissonance, or they develop a rationalization for the discrepancy. Recent research found, for instance, that the attitudes of employees who had emotionally challenging work events improved after they talked about their experiences with coworkers. Social sharing helped these workers adjust their attitudes to behavioral expectations.[7]

No individual can avoid dissonance. You know texting while walking is unsafe, but you do it anyway and convince yourself that nothing bad will happen. Or you give someone advice you have trouble following yourself. The desire to reduce dissonance depends on three factors, including the *importance* of the elements creating dissonance and the degree of *influence* we believe we have over the elements. The third factor is the *rewards* of dissonance; high rewards accompanying high dissonance tend to reduce tension inherent in the dissonance (dissonance is less distressing if accompanied by something good, such as a higher pay raise than expected). Individuals are more motivated to reduce dissonance when the attitudes are important or when they believe the dissonance is due to something they can control.

The most powerful moderators of the attitude–behavior relationship are the *importance* of the attitude, its *correspondence to behavior,* its *accessibility*, the

Westin Hotels strives for consistency between employee attitudes and behavior through a global wellness program to help employees improve their health. Shown here is Westin's executive chef, Frank Tujague, whose cooking demonstrations give employees direct experience with healthy ingredients and cooking techniques.
Source: Diane Bondareff/AP Images

presence of *social pressures*, and whether a person has *direct experience* with the attitude.[8] Important attitudes reflect our fundamental values, self-interest, or identification with individuals or groups we value. These attitudes tend to show a strong relationship to our behavior. However, discrepancies between attitudes and behaviors tend to occur when social pressures to behave in certain ways hold exceptional power, as in most organizations. You're more likely to remember attitudes you frequently express, and attitudes that our memories can easily access are more likely to predict our behavior. The attitude–behavior relationship is also likely to be much stronger if an attitude refers to something with which we have direct personal experience.

Job Attitudes

3-3 Compare the major job attitudes.

We have thousands of attitudes, but Organizational Behavior (OB) focuses on a very limited number that form positive or negative evaluations that employees hold about their work environments. Much of the research has looked at three attitudes: job satisfaction, job involvement, and organizational commitment.[9] Other important attitudes include perceived organizational support and employee engagement.

Job Satisfaction and Job Involvement

job satisfaction A positive feeling about one's job resulting from an evaluation of its characteristics.

When people speak of employee attitudes, they usually mean **job satisfaction**, a positive feeling about a job resulting from an evaluation of its characteristics. A person with high job satisfaction holds positive feelings about the work, while a person with low satisfaction holds negative feelings. Because OB researchers give job satisfaction high importance, we'll review this attitude in detail later.

An Ethical Choice

Office Talk

You are working peacefully in your cubicle when your coworker invades your space, sitting on your desk and nearly overturning your coffee. As she talks about the morning meeting, do you: (a) stop what you're doing and listen, or (b) explain that you're in the middle of a project and ask to talk some other time?

Your answer may reflect your attitude toward office talk, but it should be guided by whether your participation is ethical. Sometimes, office conversations can help employees to process information and find solutions to problems. Other times, office talk can be damaging to everyone. Consider the scenario from two perspectives: oversharing and venting.

More than 60 percent of 514 professional employees recently surveyed indicated they encounter individuals who frequently share too much about themselves. Some are self-centered, narcissistic, and "think you want to know all the details of their lives," according to psychologist Alan Hilfer.

Despite the drawbacks, oversharers can be strong contributors. Billy Bauer, director of marketing for manufacturer Royce Leather, is an oversharer who boasts about his latest sales—which may push other employees to work harder. Employees can also contribute to teamwork when they share personal stories related to organizational goals.

Now let's look at this the other way. According to Yale Professor Amy Wrzesniewski, when it comes to office talk, some people are often "the first people to become offended" when they think the organization is making wrong decisions. They can become emotional, challenging, and outspoken about their views. If they are not heard, they can increase their venting or withdraw.

Yet these people can be top-performing employees: They are often highly engaged, inspiring, and strong team players who are more likely to work harder than others. Venting their frustrations helps restore a positive attitude to keep them high performing. Research indicates that venting to coworkers can also build camaraderie.

Guidelines for acceptable office conversation are almost nonexistent in the contemporary age of openness, personalization, and transparency, so you must decide what kinds of office talk are ethical and productive. Knowing who is approaching you for conversation, why they are approaching you, what they may talk about, and how you may keep the discussion productive and ethical can help you choose whether to engage or excuse yourself.

Sources: Based on S. Shellenbarger, "Office Oversharers: Don't Tell Us about Last Night," *The Wall Street Journal,* June 25, 2014, D2; A. S. McCance, C. D. Nye, L. Wang, K. S. Jones, and C. Chiu, "Alleviating the Burden of Emotional Labor: The Role of Social Sharing," *Journal of Management* (February 2013): 392–415; S. Shellenbarger, "When It Comes to Work, Can You Care Too Much?" *The Wall Street Journal,* April 30, 2014, D3; and F. Gino, "Teams Who Share Personal Stories are More Effective," *Harvard Business Review*, April 25, 2016, https://hbr.org/2016/04/teams-who-share-personal-stories-are-more-effective.

job involvement The degree to which a person identifies with a job, actively participates in it, and considers performance important to self-worth.

psychological empowerment Employees' belief in the degree to which they affect their work environment, their competence, the meaningfulness of their job, and their autonomy in their work.

Related to job satisfaction is **job involvement**, the degree to which people identify psychologically with their jobs and consider their perceived performance levels important to their self-worth.[10] Employees with high job involvement strongly identify with and care about the kind of work they do. Another closely related concept is **psychological empowerment**, or employees' beliefs in the degree to which they influence their work environment, their competencies, the meaningfulness of their job, and their autonomy.[11]

Research suggests that psychological empowerment strongly predicts job attitudes and strain, while it moderately predicts performance behaviors. A meta-analysis spanning 43 studies and over 15,000 employees found that empowerment tended to be more predictive of these outcomes when considering all four beliefs (i.e., impact, competence, meaningfulness, and self-determination) together instead of each one separately, although some evidence suggests meaningfulness empowerment beliefs have a strong effect on attitudes and strain, even after taking the other factors into account.[12]

Organizational Commitment

organizational commitment The degree to which an employee identifies with a particular organization and its goals and wishes to maintain membership in the organization.

An employee with strong **organizational commitment** identifies with his or her organization and its goals and wishes to remain a member. Emotional attachment to an organization and belief in its values is the gold standard for employee commitment.[13]

Employees who are committed will be less likely to engage in work withdrawal even if they are dissatisfied because they feel that they should work hard out of a sense of loyalty or attachment. They do not have other options, or it would be difficult to leave.[14] Even if employees are not currently happy with their work, they may decide to continue with the organization if they are committed enough.

Perceived Organizational Support

perceived organizational support (POS) The degree to which employees believe an organization values their contribution and cares about their well-being.

Perceived organizational support (POS) is the degree to which employees believe that the organization values their contributions and cares about their well-being. An excellent example is R&D engineer John Greene, whose POS is sky-high because CEO Marc Benioff and 350 fellow Salesforce.com employees covered all his medical expenses and stayed in touch with him throughout his recovery after he was diagnosed with leukemia. No doubt stories like this are part of the reason Salesforce.com was in the top 25 of *Fortune*'s 100 Best Companies to Work For in 2017.[15]

power distance The degree to which people in a country accept that power in institutions and organizations is distributed unequally.

People perceive their organizations as supportive when rewards are deemed fair, employees have a voice in decisions, and they see their supervisors as supportive.[16] POS is a predictor, but there are some cultural influences. POS is important in countries where the **power distance**, the degree to which people in a country accept that power in institutions and organizations is distributed unequally, is lower. In low power-distance countries like the United States, people are more likely to view work as an exchange than as a moral obligation, so employees look for reasons to feel supported by their organizations. In high power-distance countries like China, employee POS perceptions are not as deeply based on demonstrations of fairness, support, and encouragement.[17]

Employee Engagement

employee engagement The degree of enthusiasm an employee feels for the job.

Employee engagement is an employee's involvement with, satisfaction with, and enthusiasm for the work he or she does. To evaluate engagement, we might ask employees whether they have access to resources and opportunities to learn new skills, whether they feel their work is important and meaningful, and whether interactions with coworkers and supervisors are rewarding.[18] Highly engaged employees have a passion for their work and feel a deep connection to their companies; disengaged employees have essentially checked out, putting time but not energy or attention into their work. Engagement becomes a real concern for most organizations because surveys indicate that few employees—between 17 percent and 29 percent—are highly engaged by their work.

Engagement levels determine many measurable outcomes. Reviews of the research on employee engagement suggest that employee engagement is moderately related to employee and organizational performance. A study of nearly 8,000 business units in 36 companies found that units whose employees reported high-average levels of engagement achieved higher levels of customer satisfaction, were more productive, brought in higher profits, and experienced lower levels of turnover and accidents than at other business units.[19] Molson Coors, for example, found engaged employees were five times less likely to have safety incidents, and

Performers smiling at guests at Main Street U.S.A. in Disney's Magic Kingdom are committed to the company and its goal of giving visitors a magical and memorable experience. Through careful hiring and extensive training, Disney ensures that employees identify with its priority of pleasing customers by creating an unforgettable experience for them.

Source: Blaine Harrington/Age Fotostock/Alamy Stock Photo

when an accident did occur, it was much less serious and less costly for an engaged employee than for a disengaged one ($63 per incident versus $392). Caterpillar set out to increase employee engagement and recorded a resulting 80 percent drop in grievances and a 34 percent increase in highly satisfied customers.[20]

Such promising findings have earned employee engagement a following in many business organizations and management consulting firms. However, the concept generates active debate about its usefulness, partly because of the difficulty of separating it from related constructs. For example, some note that employee engagement has been used to refer at different times to a variety of different organizational phenomena, including psychological states, personality traits, and behaviors. They suggest, "The meaning of employee engagement is ambiguous among both academic researchers and among practitioners who use it in conversations with clients." Another reviewer called engagement "an umbrella term for whatever one wants it to be."[21] Another study found that many of the survey questions used to measure employee engagement are similar to those found in satisfaction, commitment, and involvement measures.[22] Other meta-analytic research suggests that the relationship between employee engagement and job attitudes is extremely strong, leading one to question whether or not they are measuring distinct concepts.[23] For the most part, research suggests that employee engagement predicts important outcomes. For the most part, however, the amassed work to date calls into question how distinct it is from other job attitudes. Thus, there is still work to be done.

Are These Job Attitudes All That Distinct?

You might wonder whether job attitudes are, in fact, distinct. If people feel like their work is central to their being (high job involvement), isn't it probable that they like it, too (high job satisfaction)? Won't people who think their organization is supportive (high perceived organizational support) also feel committed to it (strong organizational commitment)? Evidence suggests these attitudes *are* highly related, perhaps to a confusing degree as mentioned in the prior section.

There is some distinctiveness among attitudes, but they overlap greatly for various reasons, including the employee's personality. Generally, if you know someone's level of job satisfaction, you know most of what you need to know about how that person sees the organization. Next, we will consider the implications of job satisfaction and then job dissatisfaction.

Job Satisfaction

3-4 Define *job satisfaction.*

We have already discussed job satisfaction briefly. Now let's dissect the concept more carefully. How do we measure job satisfaction? What causes an employee to have a high level of job satisfaction? How do satisfied employees affect an organization? Before you answer these questions, a look at the list of worst jobs for job satisfaction (Exhibit 3-2) may give you some indications. You may be surprised that they are not all low-paying jobs.

Measuring Job Satisfaction

Our definition of job satisfaction—a positive feeling about a job resulting from an evaluation of its characteristics—is broad. Yet that breadth is appropriate. A job is more than just shuffling papers, writing programming code, waiting on customers, or driving a truck. Jobs require interacting with coworkers and bosses, following organizational rules and policies, determining the power structure, meeting performance standards, living with less-than-ideal working conditions, adapting to new technology, and so forth. An employee's assessment of satisfaction with the job is thus a complex summation of many discrete elements. How, then, do we measure it?

Two approaches are popular. The single global rating is a response to one question, such as "All things considered, how satisfied are you with your job?"

Exhibit 3-2 **Worst Jobs of 2016 for Job Satisfaction***

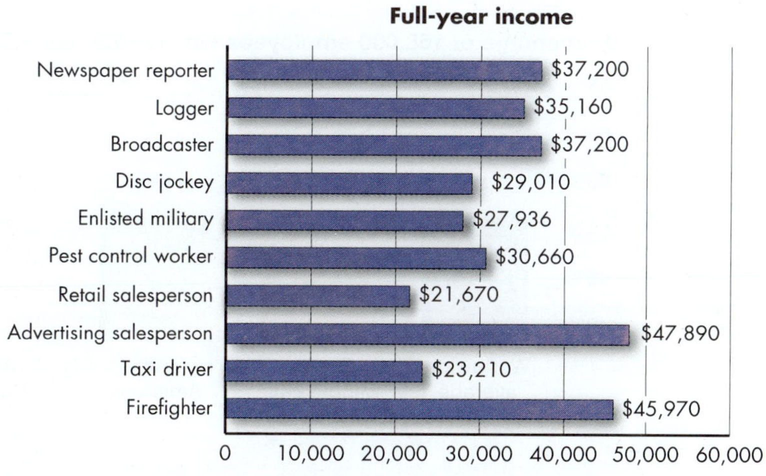

*Based on physical demands, work environment, income, stress, and hiring outlook.

Source: Based on CareerCast.com (2016), http://www.careercast.com/jobs-rated/worst-jobs-2016.

Respondents circle a number between 1 and 5 on a scale from "highly satisfied" to "highly dissatisfied." The second method, the summation of job facets, is more sophisticated. It identifies key elements in a job such as the type of work, skills needed, supervision, present pay, promotion opportunities, culture, and relationships with coworkers. Respondents rate these on a standardized scale, and researchers add the ratings to create an overall job satisfaction score.

Is one of these approaches superior? Summing up responses to a number of job factors seems, based on one's intuition, likely to achieve a more accurate evaluation of job satisfaction. Research doesn't entirely support this approach, however.[24] This is one of those rare instances in which simplicity seems to work as well as complexity, making one method essentially as valid as the other. Both methods can be helpful. The single global rating method isn't very time consuming, while the summation of job facets helps managers zero in on problems and deal with them faster and more accurately.

How Satisfied Are People in Their Jobs?

Are most people satisfied with their jobs? You may want to consider the OB Poll before you answer. Job satisfaction levels can remain quite consistent over time. India has consistently been shown to be among the highest on job satisfaction across various surveys. While these surveys reveal that a large number is seemingly dissatisfied with their salary, reports suggest that there is an overall satisfaction with jobs. In a study that compared satisfaction over three years 2011–2013, it was found that the level of satisfaction remained consistent over the years.[25] Even during the pandemic with uncertainty lurking around life and health, Indian employees continued to show high level of satisfaction with their work.[26] Job satisfaction rates tend to vary in different cultures worldwide, and, of course, there are always competing measurements that offer alternative viewpoints.

The facets of job satisfaction levels can vary widely. As shown in Exhibit 3-3, people have typically been more satisfied with their jobs overall, the work itself,

OB POLL

Happy Places

Percentage of 168,000 employees who responded YES to "Are you happy in your job?"

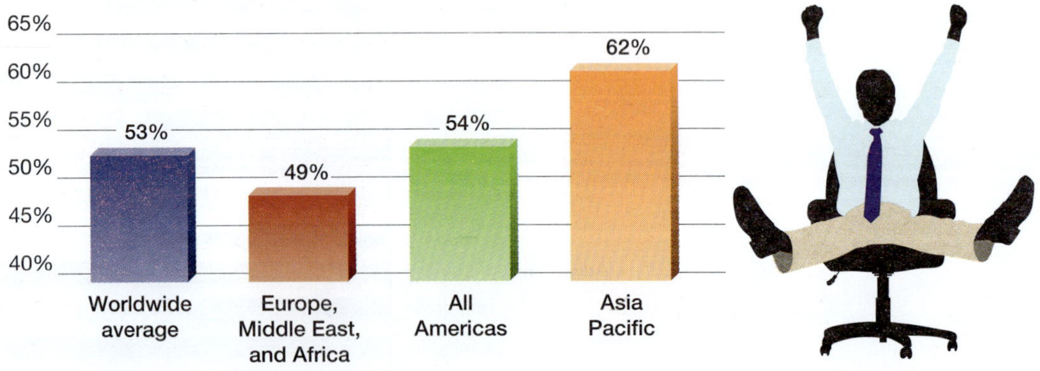

Sources: Based on Statista (2013), http://www.statista.com/statistics/224508/employee-job-satisfaction-worldwide/; Kelly Services Group (2012), http://www.kellyocg.com/uploadedFiles/Content/Knowledge/Kelly_Global_Workforce_Index_Content/Acquisition%20and%20Retention%20in%20the%20War%20for%20Talent%20Report.pdf.

Exhibit 3-3 Average Job Satisfaction Levels by Facet

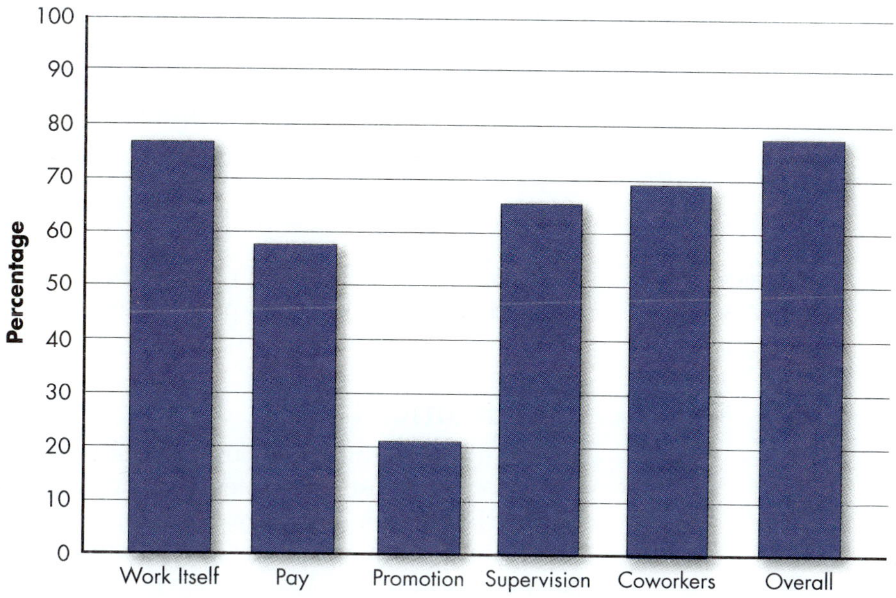

and their supervisors and coworkers than they have been with their pay and promotion opportunities.

There are some cultural differences in job satisfaction. Exhibit 3-4 provides the results of a global study of job satisfaction levels of workers in 15 countries,

Exhibit 3-4 Average Levels of Employee Job Satisfaction by Country

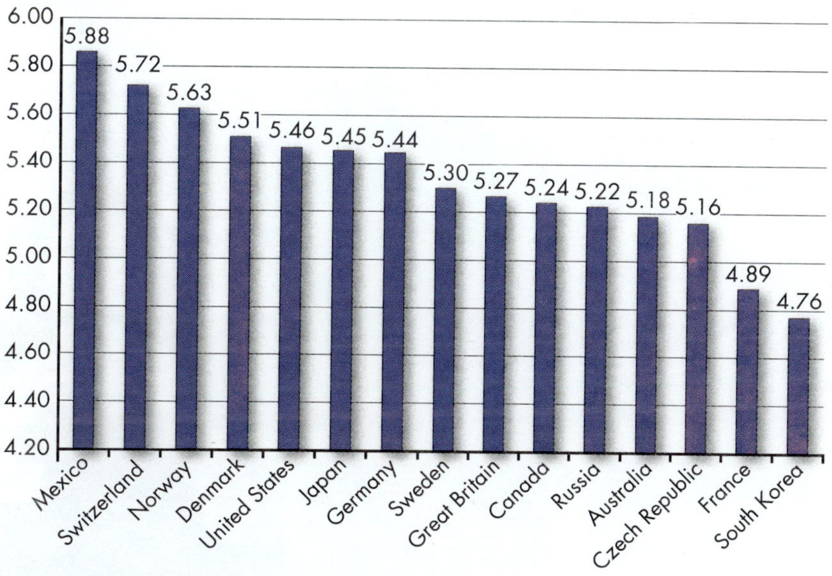

Source: Based on J. H. Westover, "The Impact of Comparative State-Directed Development on Working Conditions and Employee Satisfaction," *Journal of Management & Organization* 19, no. 4 (2013): 537–54.

with the highest levels in Mexico and Switzerland. Do employees in these cultures have better jobs? Or are they simply more positive (and less self-critical)? Conversely, the lowest score in the study was for South Korea. Autonomy is low in South Korean culture, and businesses tend to be rigidly hierarchical in structure. Does this make for low job satisfaction?[27] It is difficult to discern all the factors influencing the scores, but considering how businesses are responding to changes brought on by globalization may give us clues.

What Causes Job Satisfaction?

3-5 Summarize the main causes of job satisfaction.

Think about the best job you've ever had. What made it great? The reasons can differ greatly. Let's discuss some characteristics that likely influence job satisfaction, starting with job conditions.

Job Conditions

Generally, interesting jobs that provide training, variety, independence, and control satisfy most employees. Interdependence, feedback, social support, and positive interactions with coworkers and even customers are also strongly related to job satisfaction, even after accounting for characteristics of the work itself.[28] As you may have guessed, managers also play a big role in employees' job satisfaction. One review of nearly 70,000 employees from 23 countries found that the quality of exchange between the leaders and their employees is more strongly related to job satisfaction in more individualistic (e.g., Western) cultures than it is in more collectivistic (e.g., Asian) cultures.[29] However, another meta-analysis demonstrated that leader emotional intelligence (see Chapter 6) is more strongly related to job satisfaction in more collectivistic cultures.[30]

Thus, job conditions—especially the intrinsic nature of the work itself, social interactions, and supervision—are important predictors of satisfaction and

Employees at Google enjoy the 20 percent time they can devote to creative work. They say that it allows them to try new things and motivates them to giving their best for the rest of the 80 percent of the time.
Source: Google innovation Lab. PA Images/ Alamy Stock Photo

employee well-being.[31] Although each is important, and although their relative value varies across employees, the intrinsic nature of the work is most important.[32]

Personality

core self-evaluation (CSE) Believing in one's inner worth and basic competence.

As important as job conditions are to job satisfaction, personality also plays an important role.[33] People who have a positive **core self-evaluation (CSE)**—who believe in their inner worth and basic competence—are more satisfied with their jobs than people with negative CSEs. For those in collectivist cultures, those with high CSEs may realize particularly high job satisfaction.[34]

In a study conducted in 2019, for 34 countries having the highest and the lowest job satisfaction across the globe, India recorded the highest with 89 percent job satisfaction, Mexico followed with 85 percent, followed by the U.S.A at 78 percent. China and the U.K. showed a job satisfaction level of 74 percent, while France and Germany recorded 68 percent and 71 percent, respectively. Japan showed the lowest with 42 percent. What is interesting is that of the many reasons for dissatisfaction at work, a bad work culture and cutthroat competition contributed to the Japanese employees' poor job satisfaction level.[35]

Pay

You've probably noticed that pay comes up often when people discuss job satisfaction. Pay does correlate with job satisfaction and overall happiness for many people, but the effect can be smaller once an individual reaches a standard level of comfortable living. Look at Exhibit 3-5. It shows the relationship between the average pay for a job and the average level of job satisfaction. Money does motivate people, as we will discover in Chapter 5. But what motivates us is not necessarily the same as what makes us happy.

Exhibit 3-5 **Relationship between Average Pay in Job and Job Satisfaction of Employees in That Job**

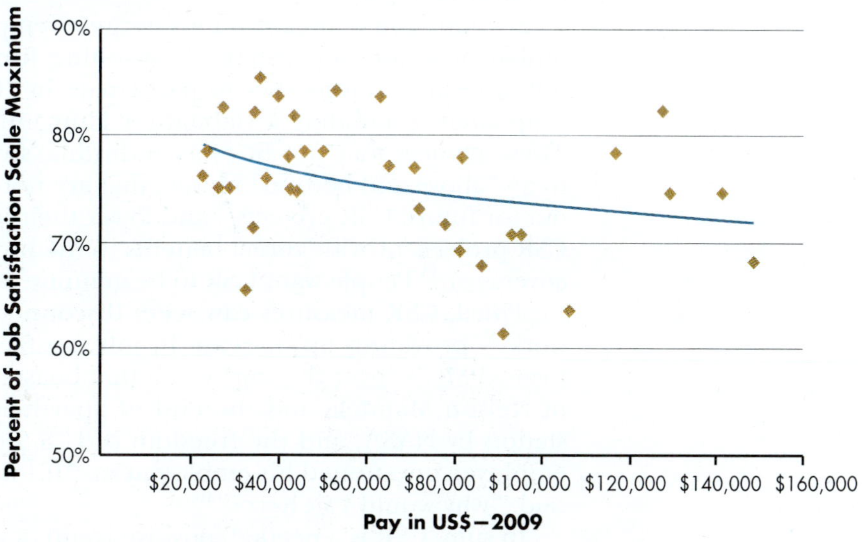

Source: Based on T. A. Judge, R. F. Piccolo, N. P. Podsakoff, J. C. Shaw, and B. L. Rich, "The Relationship between Pay and Job Satisfaction: A Meta-Analysis of the Literature," *Journal of Vocational Behavior* 77, no. 2 (2010): 157–67.

Corporate Social Responsibility (CSR)

corporate social responsibility (CSR) An organization's self-regulated actions to benefit society or the environment beyond what is required by law.

Would you be as happy to work for an organization with a stated social welfare mission as one without? An organization's commitment to **corporate social responsibility (CSR)**, or its self-regulated actions to benefit society or the environment beyond what is required by law, increasingly affects employee job satisfaction. Organizations practice CSR in several ways, including environmental sustainability initiatives, nonprofit work, and charitable giving.

CSR is good for the planet and good for people. Research suggests that American and Australian employees whose personal values fit with their organization's CSR mission are often more satisfied.[36] In fact, of 59 large and small organizations surveyed, 86 percent reported they have happier employees because of their CSR programs.[37]

The relationship between CSR and job satisfaction is particularly strong for millennials. "The next generation of employees is seeking out employers that are focused on the triple bottom line: people, planet, and revenue," said Susan Cooney, founder of philanthropy firm Givelocity.[38] CSR allows workers to serve a higher purpose or contribute to a mission. According to researcher Amy Wrzesniewski, people who view their work as part of a higher purpose often realize higher job satisfaction.[39] However, an organization's CSR efforts must be well governed and its initiatives must be sustainable for long-term job satisfaction benefits.[40]

Although the link between CSR and job satisfaction is strengthening, not all employees find value in CSR.[41] Therefore, organizations need to address a few issues to be most effective. First, not all projects are equally meaningful for every person's job satisfaction, yet participation for all employees is sometimes expected. For instance, as per a report of Latham and Watkins on pro bono opportunities in India while there is no pro bono work required of lawyers in India there are some law firms who allow their lawyers to bill some of their pro bono work."[42] Requiring these activities may decrease overall job satisfaction for those who do not wish to volunteer their time but are required to do so.

Second, some organizations require employees to contribute in a prescribed manner. For instance, consulting firm entreQuest's CEO, Joe Mechlinksi, requires employees to participate in "Give Back Days" by serving in a soup kitchen, building a Habitat for Humanity house, or mentoring children. These choices may not fit every individual's vision of CSR. Pressuring people to go "above and beyond" in ways that are not natural for them can burn them out for future CSR projects[43] and lower their job satisfaction, particularly when CSR projects provide direct benefits to the organization (such as positive press coverage).[44] People want CSR to be genuine and authentic.

Third, CSR measures can seem disconnected from the employee's actual work,[45] providing no increase in job satisfaction. After watching consulting firm KPMG's "over the top" video that boasted of involvement in the election of Nelson Mandela and the end of apartheid, the launch of the first space station by NASA, and the freedom of U.S. hostages in Iran, one anonymous employee questioned his employment. "If I want to really make a change," he said, "why would I sit here?"[46]

In sum, CSR is a needed, positive trend of accountability and serving. It can also contribute significantly to increased employee job satisfaction when managed well.

Outcomes of Job Satisfaction

3-6 Identify three outcomes of job satisfaction.

Having discussed some of the causes of job satisfaction, we now turn to some specific outcomes.

Job Performance

As several studies have concluded, happy workers are more likely to be productive workers. Some researchers used to believe the relationship between job satisfaction and job performance was a myth, but a review of 300 studies suggested the correlation is quite robust.[47] Individuals with higher job satisfaction perform better, and organizations with more satisfied employees tend to be more effective than those with fewer.

Organizational Citizenship Behavior (OCB)

It seems logical that job satisfaction should be a major determinant of an employee's organizational citizenship behavior (known as OCB or as citizenship behavior; see Chapter 1).[48] OCBs include people talking positively about their organizations, helping others, and going beyond the normal expectations of their jobs. Evidence suggests job satisfaction *is* moderately correlated with OCB; people who are more satisfied with their jobs are more likely to engage in citizenship behavior.[49]

Why does job satisfaction lead to OCB? One reason is trust. Research in 18 countries suggests that managers reciprocate employees' OCB with trusting behaviors of their own.[50] Individuals who feel that their coworkers support them are also more likely to engage in helpful behaviors than those who have antagonistic coworker relationships.[51] Personality matters, too. Individuals with certain personality traits (extraversion and conscientiousness; see Chapter 5) are more satisfied with their work, which in turn leads them to engage in more

Luxury automotive companies like Lamborghini understand that giving customers the ability to customize the car is key to gaining their satisfaction and loyalty. The company thus launched the "Lamborghini Ad Personam" program with a dedicated staff in charge of meeting any customer's wish with a range of combinations from colors to materials to make each car unique.
Source: dpa picture alliance/Alamy Stock Photo

OCB.[52] Individuals who receive positive feedback on their OCB from their peers are more likely to continue their citizenship activities.[53]

Customer Satisfaction

Because customer satisfaction is a key outcome in the service industry, it's reasonable to ask whether employee satisfaction is related to positive customer outcomes. For employees with regular customer contact, the answer appears to be yes. Satisfied employees and managers appear to increase customer satisfaction and loyalty.[54] Recent research suggests that employee and customer satisfaction are reciprocally related and that the inward effect of customer satisfaction on employee satisfaction might be *stronger* than the employee–customer relationship.[55]

A number of companies are acting on this evidence. Online shoe retailer Zappos is so committed to finding customer service employees who are satisfied

Career OBjectives

How can I make my job better?

Honestly, I hate my job. But there are reasons I should stay: This is my first job out of college, it pays pretty well, and it will establish my career. Is there any hope, or am I doomed until I quit?

— Manish

Dear Manish:

You're not doomed! You can work on your attitude to either improve your experience or find a positive perspective. In other words, if you can turn "I hate my job" into "this is what I'm doing to make my situation better," your job satisfaction is likely to improve. Try this:

- *Write down everything you hate about your job, but wait until you have a few days off so you can get a more objective viewpoint.* Be specific. Keep asking yourself why, as in, "Why do I dislike my office mate?" Also, consider your history: Was the job always a problem? Or perhaps circumstances have changed?
- *Now write down everything you like about the job.* Again, be specific. Think about the environment, the people, and the work separately. Find something positive, even if it's just the coffee in the break room.
- *Compare your lists for clues about your attitude and job satisfaction.* Look for mentions of the work or the people. Job satisfaction is generally more strongly related to how interesting your work is than it is to other factors. People, especially your supervisor, are important to your attitude toward work as well.
- *Read your lists aloud to a few trusted friends (you don't want to rant about your boss with your coworkers).* Ask them to help process your grievances. Are there deal breakers like harassment?
- *Decide whether you can talk with your manager about this.* According to Roy L. Cohen, author of *The Wall Street Professional's Survival Guide*, "consider whether how you're being treated is unique to you or shared by your colleagues." If everyone has the same problem, especially if the problem is the boss, you probably shouldn't approach your manager. But changes can be made in most situations.

Based on the sources of your grievances and your ability to make changes in the workplace, you may choose to address the issues, or develop skills for your next job. Meanwhile, don't sabotage yourself with sloppy performance and complaints. Instead, look for positive reinforcement, join a professional organization, or volunteer. Happy employees are healthier. You deserve to be one of them.

Sources: Based on "Employee Engagement," *Workforce Management* (February 2013): 19; A. Hurst, "Being 'Good' Isn't the Only Way to Go," *The New York Times*, April 20, 2014, 4; R. E. Silverman, "Work as Labor or Love?" *The Wall Street Journal*, October 18, 2012, D3; H. J. Smith, T. F. Pettigrew, G. M. Pippin, and S. Bialosiewicz, "Relative Deprivation: A Theoretical and Meta-Analytic Review," *Personality and Social Psychology Review* 16 (2012): 203–32; and A. Tugend, "Survival Skills for a Job You Detest," *The Wall Street Journal*, April 7, 2012, B5.

The opinions provided here are of the managers and authors only and do not necessarily reflect those of their organizations. The authors or managers are not responsible for any errors or omissions, or for the results obtained from the use of this information. In no event will the authors or managers, or their related partnerships or corporations thereof, be liable to you or anyone else for any decision made or action taken in reliance on the opinions provided here.

with the job that it offers a $2,000 bribe to quit the company after training, figuring the least satisfied will take the cash and go.[56] Zappos employees are empowered to "create fun and a little weirdness" to ensure that customers are satisfied, and it works: Of the company's more than 24 million customers, 75 percent are repeat buyers. For Zappos, employee satisfaction has a direct effect on customer satisfaction.

Life Satisfaction

Until now, we've treated job satisfaction as if it were separate from life satisfaction, but they may be more related than you think, with evidence suggesting that they mutually influence one another.[57] Research in Europe indicated that job satisfaction is positively correlated with life satisfaction, and your attitudes and experiences in life spill over into your job approaches and experiences.[58] Life satisfaction decreases when people become unemployed, according to research in Germany, and not just because of the loss of income.[59] For most individuals, work is an important part of life, and therefore it makes sense that our overall happiness depends in no small part on our happiness in our work (our job satisfaction).

The Impact of Job Dissatisfaction

3-7 Identify four employee responses to job dissatisfaction.

What happens when employees dislike their jobs? One theoretical model—the exit–voice–loyalty–neglect framework—is helpful for understanding the consequences of dissatisfaction. Exhibit 3-6 illustrates employees' four responses to job dissatisfaction, which differ along two dimensions: constructive/destructive and active/passive. The responses are as follows:[60]

exit Dissatisfaction expressed through behavior directed toward leaving the organization.

- **Exit.** *The exit response* directs behavior toward leaving the organization, including looking for a new position or resigning. To measure the effects

Exhibit 3-6 **Responses to Dissatisfaction**

	Constructive	Destructive
Active	VOICE	EXIT
Passive	LOYALTY	NEGLECT

of this response to dissatisfaction, researchers study individual terminations and *collective turnover*, the total loss to the organization of employee knowledge, skills, abilities, and other characteristics.[61]

voice Dissatisfaction expressed through active and constructive attempts to improve conditions.

loyalty Dissatisfaction expressed by passively waiting for conditions to improve.

neglect Dissatisfaction expressed through allowing conditions to worsen.

- **Voice.** *The voice response* includes actively and constructively attempting to improve conditions, including suggesting improvements, discussing problems with superiors, and undertaking union activity.
- **Loyalty.** *The loyalty response* means passively but optimistically waiting for conditions to improve, including speaking up for the organization in the face of external criticism and trusting the organization and its management to "do the right thing."
- **Neglect.** *The neglect response* passively allows conditions to worsen and includes chronic absenteeism or lateness, reduced effort, and an increased error rate.

Exit and neglect behaviors are linked to performance variables such as productivity, absenteeism, and turnover. But this model expands employee responses to include voice and loyalty—constructive behaviors that allow individuals to tolerate unpleasant situations or improve working conditions. The model helps us understand various situations. For instance, union members often express dissatisfaction through the grievance procedure or formal contract negotiations. These voice mechanisms allow them to continue in their jobs while acting to improve the situation.

As helpful as this framework is, it is quite general. We will next address counterproductive work behavior, a behavioral response to job dissatisfaction.

Counterproductive Work Behavior (CWB)

counterproductive work behavior (CWB) Actions that actively damage the organization, including stealing, behaving aggressively toward coworkers, or being late or absent.

Substance abuse, stealing at work, undue socializing, gossiping, absenteeism, and tardiness are examples of behaviors that are destructive to organizations. They are indicators of a broader syndrome called **counterproductive work behavior (CWB)**, also termed deviant behavior in the workplace, or simply employee withdrawal (see Chapter 1).[62] Like other behaviors we have discussed, CWB doesn't just happen—the behaviors often follow negative and sometimes long-standing attitudes. Therefore, if we can identify the predictors of CWB, we may lessen the probability of its effects.

Generally, job dissatisfaction predicts CWB. People who are not satisfied with their work become frustrated, which lowers their performance[63] and makes them more prone to CWB.[64] However, some research also suggests that this relationship might be stronger for men than for women, given that men tend to exhibit more aggressiveness and less impulse control.[65] Individual personality traits also matter. A study of Chinese knowledge workers revealed that CWB was prevalent and that personality variables, including agreeableness, neuroticism, conscientiousness, and locus of control, were a more important predictor than demographic and job characteristics.[66] CWB can be a response to abusive supervision from managers, which then increases the abuse, thus starting a vicious cycle.[67]

One important point about CWB is that dissatisfied employees often choose one or more of these specific behaviors due to idiosyncratic factors. One worker might quit. Another might use work time to surf the Internet or take work supplies home for personal use. In short, workers who don't like their jobs "get even" in various ways. Because those ways can be quite creative, controlling only one behavior with policies and punishments leaves the root cause untouched. Employers should seek to correct the source of the problem—the dissatisfaction—rather than try to control the different responses.

According to some research, sometimes CWB is an emotional reaction to perceived unfairness, a way to try to restore an employee's sense of equity exchange.[68] Therefore, CWB has complex ethical implications. For example, is someone who takes a box of markers home from the office for his children acting ethically? Some people consider this stealing. Others may want to look at moderating factors such as the employee's contribution to the organization before they decide. Does the person generously give extra time and effort to the organization, with little thanks or compensation? If so, they might see CWB as part of an attempt to "even the score."

As a manager, you can take steps to mitigate CWB. You can poll employee attitudes, for instance, identify areas for workplace improvement, and attempt to measure CWB. Several reviews suggest that self-reports of CWB can be just as effective as reports from coworkers or supervisors, partly because of differences in observability of CWB.[69] Creating strong teams, integrating supervisors within them, providing formalized team policies, and introducing team-based incentives may help lower the CWB "contagion" that lowers the standards of the group.[70]

Absenteeism We find a consistent negative relationship between satisfaction and absenteeism, but the relationship is moderate to weak.[71] Generally, when numerous alternative jobs are available, dissatisfied employees have high absence rates, but when there are few alternatives, dissatisfied employees have the same (low) rate of absence as satisfied employees.[72] Organizations that provide liberal sick leave benefits are encouraging all their employees—including those who are highly satisfied—to take days off. You can find work satisfying yet still want to enjoy a three-day weekend if those days come free with no penalties.

Turnover The relationship between job satisfaction and turnover is stronger than between satisfaction and absenteeism.[73] Overall, a pattern of lowered job satisfaction is the best predictor of intent to leave. Turnover also has a workplace environment connection. If the climate within an employee's immediate workplace is one of low job satisfaction leading to turnover, there will be a contagion effect. This suggests that managers consider the job satisfaction (and turnover) patterns of coworkers when assigning workers to a new area.[74]

The satisfaction–turnover relationship is affected by alternative job prospects. If an employee accepts an unsolicited job offer, job dissatisfaction was less predictive of turnover because the employee more likely left in response to "pull" (the lure of the other job) than "push" (the unattractiveness of the current job). Similarly, job dissatisfaction is more likely to translate into turnover when other employment opportunities are plentiful. When employees have high "human capital" (high education, high ability), job dissatisfaction is more likely to translate into turnover because they have, or perceive, many available alternatives.[75]

Some factors help break the dissatisfaction–turnover relationship. Employees' embeddedness—connections to the people or groups they are involved with at work—can help lower the probability of turnover, particularly in

Myth or Science?

Happy Workers Means Happy Profits

There are exceptions, of course, but this statement is basically true. A glance at *Fortune*'s Best Companies to Work For list, where companies are chosen by the happiness inducements they provide, reveals recognizable profit leaders: Google, SAS, Edward Jones, and REI, to name a few. However, all happiness is not created equal.

An employee who is happy because her coworker did most of the work on her team's project isn't necessarily going to work harder, for instance. Some happiness-inducers also seem unrelated to profit increases, such as Google's bowling alley and Irish pub, Facebook's free chocolate lunches, and Salesforce.com's off-the-charts parties. Traditional benefits programs also don't necessarily yield higher job satisfaction, productivity, and profits. Research indicates employees highly value paid time off, a retirement plan such as a 401(k), and lower health premiums. But many companies offer these benefits and are nowhere near the Fortune 500 organizations in profits.

It turns out that the value of keeping happiness in the profit equation may be felt in the level of employee engagement. As Julie Gebauer, a managing director for consulting firm Towers Watson, said, "It's not just about making them happy—that's not a business issue. Engagement is." Job engagement "represents employees' commitment ... and the level of discretionary effort they are willing to put forth at work," wrote Jack in the Box's Executive VP Mark Blankenship. Happy employees with higher job engagement are willing to work hard, make customers happy, and stay with the company—three factors that affect the bottom line in a big way. Conversely, a review of 300 studies revealed that turnover rates resulting from poor attitudes or low engagement led to poorer organizational performance.

So the moral of the story seems to be this: Treat others as we want to be treated in the workplace. It's just good business.

Sources: Based on M. H. Blankenship, "Happier Employees + Happier Customers = More Profit," *HR Magazine,* July 2012, 36–38; A. Edmans, "The Link between Job Satisfaction and Firm Value, with Implications for Corporate Social Responsibility," *Academy of Management Perspectives* (November 2012): 1–19; "Getting Them to Stay," *Workforce Management* (February 2013): 19; J. K. Harter et al., "Causal Impact of Employee Work Perceptions on the Bottom Line of Organizations," *Perspectives on Psychological Science* (July 2010): 378–89; T.-Y. Park and J. D. Shaw, "Turnover Rates and Organizational Performance: A Meta-Analysis," *Journal of Applied Psychology* (March 2013): 268–309; and J. Waggoner, "Do Happy Workers Mean Higher Profit?" *USA Today,* February 20, 2013, B1–B2.

collectivist (group-oriented) cultures.[76] Embedded employees seem less likely to want to consider alternative job prospects.

Managers Often "Don't Get It"

Given the evidence we've just reviewed, it should come as no surprise that job satisfaction can affect the bottom line. One study by a management consulting firm separated large organizations into those with high morale (more than 70 percent of employees expressed overall job satisfaction) and medium or low morale (fewer than 70 percent). The stock prices of companies in the high-morale group grew 19.4 percent compared with 10 percent for the medium- or low-morale group. Despite these results, many managers are unconcerned about employee job satisfaction. Others overestimate how satisfied employees are, so they don't think there's a problem when there is. In one study of 262 large employers, 86 percent of senior managers believed their organizations treated employees well, but only 55 percent of employees agreed. Another study found 55 percent of managers thought morale was good in their organization compared to only 38 percent of employees.[77]

Regular surveys can reduce gaps between what managers *think* employees feel and what they *really* feel. A gap in understanding can affect the bottom line in small franchise sites as well as in large companies. As manager of a KFC restaurant in Houston, Jonathan McDaniel surveyed his employees every three months. Some results led him to make changes, such as giving employees greater say about which workdays they had off. However, McDaniel believed the process itself was valuable. "They really love giving their opinions," he said. "That's the most important part of it—that they have a voice and that they're heard." Surveys are no panacea, but if job attitudes are as important as we believe, organizations need to use every reasonable method to find out how job attitudes can be improved.[78]

Summary

Managers should be interested in their employees' attitudes because attitudes influence behavior and indicate potential problems. Creating a satisfied workforce is hardly a guarantee of successful organizational performance, but evidence strongly suggests that managers' efforts to improve employee attitudes will likely result in positive outcomes, including greater organizational effectiveness, higher customer satisfaction, and increased profits.

Implications for Managers

- Of the major job attitudes—job satisfaction, job involvement, organizational commitment, perceived organizational support (POS), and employee engagement—remember that an employee's job satisfaction level is the best single predictor of behavior.
- Pay attention to your employees' job satisfaction levels as determinants of their performance, turnover, absenteeism, and withdrawal behaviors.
- Measure employee job attitudes at regular intervals to determine how employees are reacting to their work.
- To raise employee satisfaction, evaluate the fit between each employee's work interests and the intrinsic parts of the job; then create work that is challenging and interesting to the individual.
- Consider the fact that high pay alone is unlikely to create a satisfying work environment.

Employer–Employee Loyalty Is an Outdated Concept

POINT

The word *loyalty* is horribly outdated. Long gone are the days when an employer would keep an employee for life, as are the days when an employee would want to work for a single company for an entire career.

Professor Linda Gratton says, "Loyalty is dead—killed off through shortening contracts, outsourcing, automation, and multiple careers. Faced with what could be 50 years of work, who honestly wants to spend that much time with one company? Serial monogamy is the order of the day." Many employers agree; only 59 percent of employers report feeling loyal to their employees, while a mere 32 percent believe their employees are loyal to them.

The loyalty on each side of the equation is weak. For the most part, this is warranted—why retain employees who are subpar performers? It's only a matter of the employer handling the loyalty of employees with respect. Admittedly, some breaches happen. For example, Renault ended the 31-year career of employee Michel Balthazard (and two others) on false charges of espionage. When the wrongness of the charges became public, Renault halfheartedly offered the employees their jobs back and a lame apology: "Renault thanks them for the quality of their work at the group and wishes them every success in the future."

As for employees' loyalty to their employers, that is worth little nowadays. One manager with Deloitte says the current employee attitude is, "I'm leaving, I had a great experience, and I'm taking that with me." There just isn't an expectation of loyalty. In fact, only 9 percent of recent college graduates would stay with an employer for more than a year if they didn't like the job, research indicated. But there is nothing wrong with this. A "loyal" employee who stays with the organization but isn't satisfied with the job can do a lot of damage. At best, this person will be less productive. At worst, he or she can engage in years' worth of damaging CWB. For the worker, staying with an organization forever—no matter what—can limit career and income prospects.

The sooner we see the employment experience for what it is (mostly transactional, mostly short term to medium term), the better off we'll be. The workplace is no place for fantasies of loyalty.

COUNTERPOINT

Agreed: The word *loyalty* is outdated when it refers to employers and employees. But the basic concept is valid in the workplace. We now just measure loyalty with finer measurements such as *organizational trust* and *organizational commitment*. There certainly are employers and employees who show little loyalty to each other, but that isn't the norm.

Says management guru Tom Peters, "Bottom line: loyalty matters. A lot. Yesterday. Today. Tomorrow." University of Michigan's Dave Ulrich says, "Leaders who encourage loyalty want employees who are not only committed to and engaged in their work but who also find meaning from it." Commitment. Engagement. Trust. These are some of the building blocks of loyalty.

It is true that the employer-employee relationship has changed. For example, (largely) gone are the days when employers provided guaranteed payout pensions to which employees contributed nothing. But is that such a bad thing? Many employers have helped employees take charge of their own retirement plans.

It's not that loyalty is dead but rather that employers are loyal to a different kind of employee. True, employers no longer refuse to fire a long-tenured but incompetent employee, which is a good thing. These employees can bring down everyone's productivity and morale. In a globalized world where customer options are plentiful, organizations with "deadwood"—people who don't contribute—will not be competitive enough to survive. Companies are instead loyal to employees who do their jobs well, and that is as it should be.

In short, employees become loyal—trusting, engaged, and committed—when organizations and their people act decently. Employers with superior managers who empower their employees obtain high levels of this kind of loyalty. A true reciprocal relationship is a stronger business model than employees staying with an organization for years in exchange for an organization's caretaking. Bonds of trust and loyalty rest on the relationships of individuals. Workplace psychologist Binna Kandola observes, "Workplaces may have changed but loyalty is not dead—the bonds between people are too strong."

Sources: Based on "If You Started a Job and You Didn't Like It, How Long Would You Stay?" *USA Today,* June 11, 2012, 1B; O. Gough and S. Arkani, "The Impact of the Shifting Pensions Landscape on the Psychological Contract," *Personnel Review* 40, no. 2 (2011): 173–84; "Loyalty Gap Widens," *USA Today,* May 16, 2012, 1B; P. Korkki, "The Shifting Definition of Worker Loyalty," *The New York Times,* April 24, 2011, BU8; I. Macsinga, C. Sulea, P. Sarbescu, and C. Dumitru, "Engaged, Committed and Helpful Employees: The Role of Psychological Empowerment," *Journal of Psychology* 149, no. 3 (2015): 263–76; M. Top, M. Akdere, and M. Tarcan, "Examining Transformational Leadership, Job Satisfaction, Organizational Commitment and Organizational Trust in Turkish Hospitals: Public Servants versus Private Sector Employees," *International Journal of Human Resource Management* 26, no. 9 (2015): 1259–82; and "Is Workplace Loyalty an Outmoded Concept?" *Financial Times,* March 8, 2011, www.ft.com/, accessed July 29, 2015.

CHAPTER REVIEW

QUESTIONS FOR REVIEW

3-1 What are the three components of attitudes?

3-2 Does behavior always follow from attitudes?

3-3 What are the major job attitudes?

3-4 How do we measure job satisfaction?

3-5 What causes job satisfaction?

3-6 What are three outcomes of job satisfaction?

3-7 How do employees respond to job satisfaction?

APPLICATION AND EMPLOYABILITY

As we saw in the chapter-opening discussion of baristas, your knowledge, skills, and abilities determine how well you do in the workplace—and your job attitudes matter, too. Job satisfaction, job involvement, employee engagement, organizational commitment, and perceived organizational support all affect how you, your coworkers, and your boss behave and perform in the workplace. First, the job attitudes of your work unit also affect the bottom line—attitudes affect customer service and sales performance. Second, job attitudes and satisfaction can be assessed in a variety of ways to keep a "pulse" on the workforce of your organization. Third, knowledge of what causes job attitudes and the consequences/outcomes of job attitudes can help you set policies, practices, and procedures (when you are in a supervisory position) or engage in behaviors (if you are an employee) that will help you improve attitudes in your workplace. In this chapter, you improved your critical thinking skills and considered various situations relevant to social responsibility in the workplace, including whether happy workers lead to improved profit margins, how you can move forward if you hate your job, the pitfalls and benefits of office gossip and venting, and whether employee loyalty is a relic of the past. In the following section, you will continue to improve your critical thinking skills and apply your knowledge about job attitudes to reexamine attitudes you've held in a current or previous job, examine the ethics of employee tell-all websites, and evaluate carefully the impact of self-service kiosks and job crafting on job attitudes.

EXPERIENTIAL EXERCISE Job Attitudes Situational Interview

Each class member is to think about an event in which she or he felt satisfied or dissatisfied (or committed or not committed) in the workplace (students can imagine one even if they have never been employed). Each student writes this experience down in as much detail as possible on a small piece of paper. When finished, each student exchanges her or his paper with another student. These students take turns asking and recording the answers to the following questions (asking follow-up questions as needed):

1. What sorts of feelings were you experiencing at the time? What were you thinking when this was going on? Did you think about doing anything in that moment?
2. What targets were your feelings or thoughts directed toward? For example, were they directed toward your organization? Toward the job? Coworkers? Pay and benefits?
3. What led you to your feelings of satisfaction and commitment in that moment?
4. What did you (actually) do in response to your experience? What was the outcome?

The students can then reassemble as a class to share their findings and discuss the following questions.

Questions

3-8. Do you think it is possible for the affective, cognitive, or behavioral components of job attitudes to conflict with one another? Why or why not?

3-9. Can job attitudes be directed toward different targets? Why or why not? What implications does this have for the behavioral outcomes of satisfaction and commitment?

3-10. Do you believe that job attitudes can change over time? Or does each person have a typical level of job attitudes that she or he exhibits from one job to the next?

ETHICAL DILEMMA Tell-All Websites

"Arrogant, condescending, mean-spirited, hateful ... and those traits describe the nicest people at Netflix," writes one anonymous employee. "Management is awful ... good old boys club," writes a Coca-Cola market development manager. And the reviews keep rolling in; Coca-Cola has 1,600 employee reviews, and some companies, like Google, have double that number on Glassdoor, one of the Internet sites that allows anyone to rate their employers.

Websites like Glassdoor are thriving; employees increasingly join the forums and seem to relish the chance to speak freely. The app Memo, which claimed 10,000 new members in about 3 months, allows users to post, comment, and share links. They will soon be able to upload photographs and documents, which will raise new security concerns for organizations.

Ryan Janssen, CEO of Memo's parent company, Collectively, says apps like Memo, Yik Yak, and Whisper allow bosses access to candid feedback they cannot otherwise get. Janssen said, "The employee's natural reaction [when managers ask for feedback directly] is to tell you what you want to hear." There is certainly truth to this—studies indicate that employees "put on a happy face" for their bosses. When people know their posts aren't anonymous, "People put on this weird, fake professional face," he said.

Organizations are aware that people watch what they say when they can be identified, and many have used anonymous job attitude surveys for this reason. Still, evaluations from these surveys are often more glowing, and less detailed, than anonymous website feedback. Some organizations have therefore altered the frequency and scope of surveys to obtain more depth. Others have their own intranet platforms to solicit concerns and complaints.

Beyond the personally unethical aspect of posting scathing denouncements about people or organizations online—sharing details with the world that you would not share in person—issues of organizational ethics come into play. While companies like Visa, Boeing, and Hewlett-Packard have tried to discourage employees from anonymously venting on websites and apps, such mandates may violate the employees' right of free speech. And how anonymous are anonymous posts? Posts on Glassdoor and other forums eliminate a person's name, but can't bosses sometimes determine which subordinate posted the comments? Managers everywhere need to decide how much management sleuthing is ethical and what consequences, if any, can be forced on subordinates for anonymous posts.

Grant Vodori, cofounder of a digital marketing agency in Chicago, has been successful in obtaining candid answers from his employees through polls taken several times each week. "It's sometimes a little bit scary," he said, asking himself, "Do I really want to know the answer to this?"

Questions

3-11. Do you think employees have a right to say what they want to about their organizations online as opposed to in private?

3-12. How would you react if you learned one of your employees posted unflattering comments about you as a manager? Would your reaction be any different if the employee posted unflattering comments about you as a person?

3-13. Do you feel it is acceptable to post comments anonymously, or do you think people should include their names? Why or why not?

Sources: Based on L. Gilman, "Memo App Lets Workers Vent Anonymously about the Boss," *The Wall Street Journal,* January 21, 2015, B7; Glassdoor.com; A. S. McCance, C. D. Nye, L. Wang, K. S. Jones, and C. Chiu, "Alleviating the Burden of Emotional Labor: The Role of Social Sharing," *Journal of Management* (February 2013): 392–415; R. E. Silverman, "Are You Happy in Your Job? Bosses Push Weekly Surveys," *The Wall Street Journal,* December 3, 2014, B1, B4; and R. E. Silverman, "Workers Really Do Put on a Happy Face for the Boss," *The Wall Street Journal,* January 29, 2015, D4.

CASE INCIDENT 1 Jobs, Money, and Satisfaction

When two caretaker jobs were advertised on the tiny island of Great Blasket, Ireland's most westerly point, there was no shortage of interest; it drew responses from Alaska to South Africa. But this was no high-paying job on a luxury resort island. The position was described as intense and tough, with no electricity, Wi-Fi, or hot showers, and life was described as "back to basics," involving candles, stoves, wildlife, and nature. The posts included free accommodation and food, but it is unlikely the applicants were particularly interested in the pay or benefits. The previous post holders had left jobs in Dublin and a demanding work commute for what they considered their dream job. No doubt many of the applicants also saw it as a once-in-a-lifetime opportunity.

Of a like mind as those applicants for the caretaker jobs, Meenakshi was a high-flying executive who discovered that she had more important priorities in life than money. Having endured yet another late and stressful night working as an investment banker, she finally decided there was more to life. Meenakshi quit her job of 20 years, and six months later she was teaching in a primary school. "I feel refreshed," she said. "I love teaching, genuinely enjoy my work, and have had more holidays in the last year than I managed in the previous ten." As for money, Meenakshi earns less than one quarter of what she used to as an investment banker.

It's not just in the pursuit of dream jobs where people are willing to forgo money. One study reported that 49 percent of the 2,000 employees it surveyed were prepared to take a reasonable pay cut for a more flexible work schedule. Fifty-six percent said they would take a pay cut for better health benefits. Another report collected data from German, French, UK, and U.S. employees and found that those who were happy with their jobs cited meaningful work—not compensation—as the most important factor. It seems millennials may even sacrifice money simply to get a better job title. The CEO of an employment agency claimed she had seen millennial candidates forgo nearly €10,000 in salary for what they consider a more valuable title.

But Peter Weber, an industrial designer, makes an interesting point: "There is no way I could consider taking a pay cut. I have a family to take care of and bills to pay. It's only a choice for people who already have enough money." Money may not be everything in life, but it *is* something.

Questions

3-14. If you could choose between a highly paid job that you didn't like or your dream job that paid comparatively little, which would you choose, and why?

3-15. What other factors are important to you besides compensation?

3-16. Explore the possible causes of Meenakshi's job dissatisfaction as an investment banker, why she is more satisfied as a teacher, and the likely outcomes of her newly found job satisfaction.

Sources: R. Carroll, "Dream Job? Hundreds Apply to Work on Remote Irish Island," *The Guardian*, January 14, 2020; A. Mahdawi, "Would You Take a Pay Cut to Get a Better Job Title? It's Not as Stupid as It Sounds," *The Guardian*, March 1, 2019; Wrike, "Wrike Happiness Index, Compensation" cdn.wrike.com/ebook/2019_US_Happiness_Index_Compensation.pdf; and WorldatWork, "Survey Finds Half of Workers Would Take Pay Cut for More Flexible Schedule," May 29, 2019, www.worldatwork.org/workspan/articles/survey-finds-half-of-workers-would-take-pay-cut-for-more-flexible-schedule, accessed January 28, 2020.

CASE INCIDENT 2 Job Crafting

Consider for a moment a midlevel manager, Fatima, who seems to be doing well. She's consistently making her required benchmarks and goals, she has built successful relationships with colleagues, and senior management has identified her as having "high potential." But she isn't satisfied in her job. She'd be interested in understanding how her organization can use social media in marketing efforts at all levels of the organization, for example, but her job doesn't allow her to work on this idea. She wants to quit and find something that better suits her passions, but in her economic situation this may not be an option. So she has decided to proactively reconfigure her current job.

Fatima is part of a movement toward job crafting, which is the process of deliberately reorganizing your job so that it better fits your motives, strengths, and passions. So how did Fatima craft her job? She first noticed that she was spending too much of her time monitoring her team's performance and answering questions, and not enough time working on the creative projects that inspire her. She then considered how to modify her relationship with the team so that her activities incorporated her passion for social media strategies with the team's activities more centered on developing new marketing. She also identified members of her team who might be able to help her implement her new strategies and directed her interactions with these individuals toward her new goals. As a result, her engagement in her work increased, and she developed new ideas that were recognized and advanced within the organization. In sum, she found that by actively and creatively examining her work, she was able to shape her job into one that is truly satisfying.

As you may have noted, Fatima exhibited a proactive personality—she was eager to develop her own options and find her own resources. Proactive individuals are often self-empowered and are therefore more likely to seek workable solutions when they are not satisfied. Research leads us to believe that Fatima will be successful in her customized job and that she will experience increased well-being. To the extent possible, all employees should feel encouraged to be proactive in creating their best work situations.

Questions

3-17. Should organizations work to create jobs that are satisfying to individual employees?

3-18. Are the principles of job crafting described here relevant to your job or studies? Why or why not?

3-19. Are there any potential drawbacks to the job-crafting approach? If so, how can they be minimized?

Sources: Based on A. B. Bakker, M. Tims, and D. Derks, "Proactive Personality and Job Performance: The Role of Job Crafting and Work Engagement," *Human Relations* (October 2012): 1359–78; A. Wrzesniewski, J. M. Berg, and J. E. Dutton, "Turn the Job You Have into the Job You Want," *Harvard Business Review* (June 2010): 114–17; A. Wrzesniewski and J. E. Dutton, "Crafting a Job: Revisioning Employees as Active Crafters of Their Work," *Academy of Management Review* 26 (2010): 179–201; and G. R. Slemp and D. A. Vella-Brodrick, "Optimising Employee Mental Health: The Relationship between Intrinsic Need Satisfaction, Job Crafting, and Employee Well-Being," *Journal of Happiness Studies* 15, no. 4 (2014): 957–77.

ENDNOTES

[1] A. Gengler, "Chained to Your Desk No More," *CNNMoney*, April 2014, 53.

[2] S. J. Breckler, "Empirical Validation of Affect, Behavior, and Cognition as Distinct Components of Attitude," *Journal of Personality and Social Psychology* 47 (1984): 1191–205; M. J. Rosenberg and C. I. Hovland, "Cognitive, Affective and Behavioral Components of Attitude," in M. J. Rosenberg, C. I. Hovland, W. J. McGuire, R. Abelson, and J. Brehm (eds.), *Attitude Organization and Change* (New Haven, CT: Yale University Press, 1960).

[3] O. N. Solinger, J. Hofmans, and W. van Olffen, "The Dynamic Microstructure of Organizational Commitment," *Journal of Occupational and Organizational Psychology* 88 (2015): 773–96.

[4] See L. S. Glasman and D. Ablarracín, "Forming Attitudes That Predict Future Behavior: A Meta-Analysis of the Attitude-Behavior Relation," *Psychological Bulletin* 132, no. 5 (2006): 778–822.

[5] L. Festinger and J. M. Carlsmith, "Cognitive Consequences of Forced Compliance," *Journal of Abnormal and Social Psychology* 58 (1959): 203–10.

[6] See, for instance, L. R. Fabrigar, R. E. Petty, S. M. Smith, and S. L. Crites, "Understanding Knowledge Effects on Attitude-Behavior Consistency: The Role of Relevance, Complexity, and Amount of Knowledge," *Journal of Personality and Social Psychology* 90, no. 4 (2006): 556–77; and D. J. Schleicher, J. D. Watt, and G. J. Greguras, "Reexamining the Job Satisfaction–Performance Relationship: The Complexity of Attitudes," *Journal of Applied Psychology* 89, no. 1 (2004): 165–77.

[7] A. S. McCance, C. D. Nye, L. Wang, K. S. Jones, and C. Chiu, "Alleviating the Burden of Emotional Labor: The Role of Social Sharing," *Journal of Management*, February 2013, 392–415.

[8] Glasman and Albarracín, "Forming Attitudes That Predict Future Behavior"; K. B. Starzyk, L. R. Fabrigar, A. S. Soryal, and J. J. Fanning, "A Painful Reminder: The Role of Level and Salience of Attitude Importance in Cognitive Dissonance," *Personality and Social Psychology Bulletin* 35, no. 1 (2009): 126–37.

[9] D. A. Harrison, D. A. Newman, and P. L. Roth, "How Important Are Job Attitudes? Meta-analytic Comparisons of Integrative Behavioral Outcomes and Time Sequences," *Academy of Management Journal* 49 (2006): 305–25; D. A. Newman, D. L. Joseph, and C. L. Hulin, "Job Attitudes and Employee Engagement: Considering the Attitude 'A-Factor,'" in S. L. Albrecht (ed.), *Handbook of Employee Engagement: Perspectives, Issues, Research and Practice* (Northampton, MA: Edward Elgar, 2010): 43–61.

[10] S. P. Brown, "A Meta-Analysis and Review of Organizational Research on Job Involvement," *Psychological Bulletin* 120, no. 2 (1996): 235–55; T. M. Lodahl and M. Kejner, "The Definition and Measurement of Job Involvement," *Journal of Applied Psychology* 49, no. 1 (1965): 24–33.

[11] G. M. Spreitzer, "Psychological Empowerment in the Workplace: Construct Definition, Measurement, and Validation," *Academy of Management Journal* 38 (1995): 1442–65; G. M. Spreitzer, "Taking Stock: A Review of More Than Twenty Years of Research on Empowerment at Work," in J. Barling and C. L. Cooper (eds.), *Handbook of Organizational Behavior* (Thousand Oaks, CA: Sage, 2008): 54–72.

[12] S. E. Seibert, G. Wang, and S. H. Courtright, "Antecedents and Consequences of Psychological and Team Empowerment in Organizations: A Meta-Analytic Review," *Journal of Applied Psychology* 96, no. 5 (2011): 981–1003.

[13] Z. A. Mercurio, "Affective Commitment as a Core Essence of Organizational Commitment: An Integrative Literature Review," *Human Resource Development Review* 14, no. 4 (2015): 389-414; O. N. Solinger, W. van Olffen, and R. A. Roe, "Beyond the Three-Component Model of Organizational Commitment," *Journal of Applied Psychology* 93 (2008): 70–83.

[14] A. Cooper-Hakim and C. Viswesvaran, "The Construct of Work Commitment: Testing an Integrative Framework," *Psychological Bulletin* 131, no. 2 (2005): 241–59; Solinger, van Olffen, and Roe, "Beyond the Three-Component Model of Organizational Commitment."

[15] "100 Best Companies to Work For," *Fortune*, February 2017, www.fortune.com/best-companies/, accessed March 8, 2017.

[16] L. Rhoades, R. Eisenberger, and S. Armeli, "Affective Commitment to the Organization: The Contribution of Perceived Organizational Support," *Journal of Applied Psychology* 86, no. 5 (2001): 825–36.

[17] J.-L. Farh, R. D. Hackett, and J. Liang, "Individual-Level Cultural Values as Moderators of Perceived Organizational Support–Employee Outcome Relationships in China: Comparing the Effects of Power Distance and Traditionality," *Academy of Management Journal* 50, no. 3 (2007): 715–29; L. Zhong, S. J. Wayne, and R. C. Liden, "Job Engagement, Perceived Organizational Support, High-Performance Human Resource Practices, and Cultural Value Orientations: A Cross-Level Investigation," *Journal of Organizational Behavior* 37, no. 6 (2016): 823–44.

[18] B. L. Rich, J. A. Lepine, and E. R. Crawford, "Job Engagement: Antecedents and Effects on Job Performance," *Academy of Management Journal* 53 (2010): 617–35.

[19] M. S. Christian, A. S. Garza, and J. E. Slaughter, "Work Engagement: A Quantitative Review and Test of Its Relations with Task and Contextual Performance," *Personnel Psychology* 64 (2011): 89–136; J. K. Harter, F. L. Schmidt, and T. L. Hayes, "Business-Unit-Level Relationship between Employee Satisfaction, Employee Engagement, and Business Outcomes: A Meta-Analysis," *Journal of Applied Psychology* 87, no. 2 (2002): 268–79.

[20] N. R. Lockwood, *Leveraging Employee Engagement for Competitive Advantage* (Alexandria, VA: Society for Human Resource Management, 2007); and R. J. Vance, *Employee Engagement and Commitment* (Alexandria, VA: Society for Human Resource Management, 2006).

[21] W. H. Macey and B. Schneider, "The Meaning of Employee Engagement," *Industrial and Organizational Psychology* 1 (2008): 3–30; A. Saks, "The Meaning and Bleeding of Employee Engagement: How Muddy Is the Water?" *Industrial and Organizational Psychology* 1 (2008): 40–43.

[22] D. A. Newman and D. A. Harrison, "Been There, Bottled That: Are State and Behavioral Work Engagement New and Useful Construct 'Wines'?" *Industrial and Organizational Psychology* 1 (2008): 31–35.

[23] Newman, Joseph, and Hulin, "Job Attitudes and Employee Engagement."

[24] S. Highhouse and A. S. Becker, "Facet Measures and Global Job Satisfaction," *Journal of Business and Psychology* 8, no. 1 (1993): 117–27; M. S. Nagy, "Using a Single-Item Approach to Measure Facet Job Satisfaction," *Journal of Occupational and Organizational Psychology* 75 (2002): 77–86; M. Roznowski, "Examination of the Measurement Properties of the Job Descriptive Index with Experimental Items," *Journal of Applied Psychology* 74 (1989): 805–14; J. P. Wanous and M. J. Hudy, "Single-Item Reliability: A Replication and Extension," *Organizational Research Methods* 4, no. 4 (2001): 361–75; J. P. Wanous, A. E. Reichers, and M. J. Hudy, "Overall Job Satisfaction: How Good Are Single-Item Measures?" *Journal of Applied Psychology* 82, no. 2 (1997): 247–52.

[25] Paycheck.in. "Job Satisfaction in India". Retrieved from https://paycheck.in (Accessed on April 20, 2022).
[26] Levanon, G. (2021). "Job Satisfaction Stays High Despite Pandemic, Economic Crisis". Retrieved from https://www.forbes.com (Accessed on April 19, 2022).
[27] World Business Culture, "Doing Business in South Korea," www.worldbusinessculture.com/Business-in-South-Korea.html, accessed July 29, 2015.
[28] S. E. Humphrey, J. D. Nahrgang, and F. P. Morgeson, "Integrating Motivational, Social, and Contextual Work Design Features: A Meta-Analytic Summary and Theoretical Extension of the Work Design Literature," *Journal of Applied Psychology* 92, no. 5 (2007): 1332–56; D. S. Chiaburu and D. A. Harrison, "Do Peers Make the Place? Conceptual Synthesis and Meta-Analysis of Coworker Effect on Perceptions, Attitudes, OCBs, and Performance," *Journal of Applied Psychology* 93, no. 5 (2008): 1082–103; and W. J. Shepherd, R. E. Ployhart, and J. Kautz, "The Neglected Role of Collective Customer Perceptions in Shaping Collective Employee Satisfaction, Service Climate, Voluntary Turnover, and Involuntary Turnover: A Cautionary Note," *Journal of Applied Psychology* (in press).
[29] T. Rockstuhl, J. H. Dulebohn, S. Ang, and L. M. Shore, "Leader-Member Exchange (LMX) and Culture: A Meta-Analysis of Correlates of LMX across 23 Countries," *Journal of Applied Psychology* 97, no. 6 (2012): 1097–130.
[30] C. Miao, R. H. Humphrey, and S. Qian, "Leader Emotional Intelligence and Subordinate Job Satisfaction: A Meta-Analysis of Main, Mediator, and Moderator Effects," *Personality and Individual Differences* 102 (2016): 13–24.
[31] A. L. Rubenstein, Y. Zhang, K. Ma, H. M. Morrison, and D. F. Jorgensen, "Trait Expression through Perceived Job Characteristics: A Meta-analytic Path Model Linking Personality and Job Attitudes," *Journal of Vocational Behavior* 112 (2019): 141–57.
[32] K. M. Dawson, K. E. O'Brien, and T. A. Beehr, "The Role of Hindrance Stressors in the Job Demand-Control-Support Model of Occupational Stress: A Proposed Theory Revision," *Journal of Organizational Behavior* 37, no. 3 (2016): 397–415.
[33] P. Steel, J. Schmidt, F. Bosco, and K. Uggerslev, "The Effects of Personality on Job Satisfaction and Life Satisfaction: A Meta-analytic Investigation Accounting for Bandwidth-Fidelity and Commensurability," *Human Relations* 72, no. 2 (2019): 217–47.
[34] C.-H. Chang, D. L. Ferris, R. E. Johnson, C. C. Rosen, and J. A. Tan, "Core Self-Evaluations: A Review and Evaluation of the Literature," *Journal of Management* 38, no. 1 (2012): 81–128; T. A. Judge and J. E. Bono, "Relationship of Core Self-Evaluations Traits—Self-Esteem, Generalized Self-Efficacy, Locus of Control, and Emotional Stability—with Job Satisfaction and Job Performance: A Meta-Analysis," *Journal of Applied Psychology* 86, no. 1 (2001): 80–92.
[35] Buchholz, K. (2020). "This chart shows which countries have the highest and lowest job satisfaction". *©World Economic Forum in collaboration with Statista (June 10, 2020).* Retrieved from https://www.weforum.org (Accessed on April 20, 2022).
[36] S. Du, C. B. Bhattacharya, and S. Sen, "Corporate Social Responsibility, Multi-Faceted Job-Products, and Employee Outcomes," *Journal of Business Ethics* 131 (2015): 319–35; J. Spanjol, L. Tam, and V. Tam, "Employer-Employee Congruence in Environmental Values: An Exploration of Effects on Job Satisfaction and Creativity," *Journal of Business Ethics* 130 (2015): 117–30.
[37] D. Thorpe, "Why CSR? The Benefits of Corporate Social Responsibility Will Move You to Act," *Forbes* (May 18, 2013), http://www.forbes.com/sites/devinthorpe/2013/05/18/why-csr-the-benefits-of-corporate-social-responsibility-will-move-you-to-act/.
[38] N. Fallon, "What Is Corporate Responsibility?" *Business News Daily* (December 22, 2014), http://www.businessnewsdaily.com/4679-corporate-social-responsibility.html.
[39] R. Feintzeig, "I Don't Have a Job. I Have a Higher Calling," *The Wall Street Journal,* February 25, 2015, B1, B4.
[40] See I. Filatotchev and C. Nakajima, "Corporate Governance, Responsible Managerial Behavior, and Corporate Social Responsibility: Organizational Efficiency versus Organizational Legitimacy?" *The Academy of Management Perspectives* 28, no. 3 (2014): 289–306.
[41] A. Hurst, "Being 'Good' Isn't the Only Way to Go," *The New York Times,* April 20, 2014, 4.
[42] Latham & Watkins LLP. "Pro Bono Practices and Opportunities in India". Retrieved from https://www.lw.com (Accessed on April 26, 2022).
[43] M. C. Bolino, H.-H. Hsiung, J. Harvey, and J. A. LePine, "'Well, I'm Tired of Tryin'! Organizational Citizenship Behavior and Citizenship Fatigue," *Journal of Applied Psychology* 100, no. 1 (2015): 56–74.
[44] G. E. Newman and D. M. Cain, "Tainted Altruism: When Doing Some Good Is Evaluated as Doing Worse Than Doing No Good at All," *Psychological Science* 25, no. 3 (2014): 648–55.
[45] Ibid.
[46] Ibid.
[47] T. A. Judge, C. J. Thoresen, J. E. Bono, and G. K. Patton, "The Job Satisfaction–Job Performance Relationship: A Qualitative and Quantitative Review," *Psychological Bulletin* 127, no. 3 (2001): 376–407.
[48] See P. M. Podsakoff, S. B. MacKenzie, J. B. Paine, and D. G. Bachrach, "Organizational Citizenship Behaviors: A Critical Review of the Theoretical and Empirical Literature and Suggestions for Future Research," *Journal of Management* 26, no. 3 (2000): 513–63.
[49] B. J. Hoffman, C. A. Blair, J. P. Maeriac, and D. J. Woehr, "Expanding the Criterion Domain? A Quantitative Review of the OCB Literature," *Journal of Applied Psychology* 92, no. 2 (2007): 555–66.
[50] B. S. Reiche, P. Cardona, Y.-T. Lee, M. A. Canela, E. Akinnukawe, J. P. Briscoe, … and H. Wilkinson, "Why Do Managers Engage in Trustworthy Behavior? A Multilevel Cross-Cultural Study in 18 Countries," *Personnel Psychology* 67, no. 1 (2014): 61–98.
[51] D. S. Chiaburu and D. A. Harrison, "Do Peers Make the Place? Conceptual Synthesis and Meta-Analysis of Coworker Effect on Perceptions, Attitudes, OCBs, and Performance," *Journal of Applied Psychology* 93, no. 5 (2008): 1082–103.
[52] R. Ilies, I. S. Fulmer, M. Spitzmuller, and M. D. Johnson, "Personality and Citizenship Behavior: The Mediating Role of Job Satisfaction," *Journal of Applied Psychology* 94 (2009): 945–59; T. A. Judge, D. Heller, and M. K. Mount, "Five-Factor Model of Personality and Job Satisfaction: A Meta-Analysis," *Journal of Applied Psychology* 87, no. 3 (2002): 530–41.
[53] G. L. Lemoine, C. K. Parsons, and S. Kansara, "Above and Beyond, Again and Again: Self-Regulation in the Aftermath of Organizational Citizenship Behaviors," *Journal of Applied Psychology* 100, no. 1 (2015): 40–55.
[54] R. G. Netemeyer, J. G. Maxham III, and D. R. Lichtenstein, "Store Manager Performance and Satisfaction: Effects on Store Employee Performance and Satisfaction, Store Customer Satisfaction, and Store Customer Spending Growth," *Journal of Applied Psychology* 95, no. 3 (2010): 530–45; E. P. Piening, A. M. Baluch, and T. O. Salge, "The Relationship between Employees' Perceptions of Human Resource Systems and Organizational Performance: Examining Mediating Mechanisms and Temporal Dynamics," *Journal of Applied Psychology* 98, no. 6 (2013): 926–47; M. Schulte, C. Ostroff, S. Shmulyian, and A. Kinicki, "Organizational Climate Configurations: Relationships to Collective Attitudes, Customer Satisfaction, and Financial

Performance," *Journal of Applied Psychology* 94 (2009): 618–34.

[55] A. R. Zablah, B. D. Carlson, D. T. Donavan, J. G. Maxham, and T. J. Brown, "A Cross-Lagged Test of the Association between Customer Satisfaction and Employee Job Satisfaction in a Relational Context," *Journal of Applied Psychology* 101, no. 5 (2016): 743–55.

[56] B. Taylor, "Why Amazon Is Copying Zappos and Paying Employees to Quit," *Harvard Business Review*, April 14, 2014, https://hbr.org/2014/04/why-amazon-is-copying-zappos-and-paying-employees-to-quit/.

[57] N. A. Bowling, K. J. Eschleman, and Q. Wang, "A Meta-Analytic Examination of the Relationship between Job Satisfaction and Subjective Well-Being," *Journal of Occupational and Organizational Psychology* 83, no. 4 (2010): 915–34; B. Erdogan, T. N. Bauer, D. M. Truxillo, and L. R. Mansfield, "Whistle While You Work: A Review of the Life Satisfaction Literature," *Journal of Management* 38, no. 4 (2012): 1038–83; Steel et al., "The Effects of Personality on Job Satisfaction and Life Satisfaction."

[58] Y. Georgellis and T. Lange, "Traditional versus Secular Values and the Job-Life Satisfaction Relationship across Europe," *British Journal of Management* 23 (2012): 437–54.

[59] O. Stavrova, T. Schlosser, and A. Baumert, "Life Satisfaction and Job-Seeking Behavior of the Unemployed: The Effect of Individual Differences in Justice Sensitivity," *Applied Psychology: An International Review* 64, no. 4 (2014): 643–70.

[60] A. Davis-Blake, J. P. Broschak, and E. George, "Happy Together? How Using Nonstandard Workers Affects Exit, Voice, and Loyalty among Standard Employees," *Academy of Management Journal* 46, no. 4 (2003): 475–85; A. O. Hirschman, *Exit, Voice, and Loyalty: Responses to Decline in Firms, Organizations, and States* (Cambridge, MA: Harvard University Press, 1970); J. B. Olson-Buchanan and W. R. Boswell, "The Role of Employee Loyalty and Formality in Voicing Discontent," *Journal of Applied Psychology* (December 2002): 1167–74; and J. Zhou and J. M. George, "When Job Dissatisfaction Leads to Creativity: Encouraging the Expression of Voice," *Academy of Management Journal* (August 2001): 682–96.

[61] A. J. Nyberg and R. E. Ployhart, "Context-Emergent Turnover (CET) Theory: A Theory of Collective Turnover," *Academy of Management Review* 38 (2013): 109–31.

[62] L. K. Treviño, N. A. den Nieuwenboer, and J. J. Kish-Gephart, "(Un)Ethical Behavior in Organizations," *Annual Review of Psychology* 65 (2014): 635–60; and P. E. Spector, S. Fox, L. M. Penney, K. Bruursema, A. Goh, and S. Kessler, "The Dimensionality of Counterproductivity: Are All Counterproductive Behaviors Created Equal?" *Journal of Vocational Behavior* 68, no. 3 (2006): 446–60.

[63] P. A. O'Keefe, "Liking Work Really Does Matter," *The New York Times*, September 7, 2014, 12.

[64] T. A. Judge, B. A. Scott, and R. Ilies, "Hostility, Job Attitudes, and Workplace Deviance: Test of a Multilevel Model," *Journal of Applied Psychology* 91, no. 1 (2006): 126–38.

[65] N. A. Bowling and G. N. Burns, "Sex as a Moderator of the Relationships between Predictor Variables and Counterproductive Work Behavior," *Journal of Business Psychology* 30 (2015): 193–205.

[66] H. Peng, "Counterproductive Work Behavior among Chinese Knowledge Workers," *International Journal of Selection and Assessment* 20, no. 2 (2012): 119–38.

[67] H. Lian, D. L. Ferris, R. Morrison, and D. J. Brown, "Blame It on the Supervisor or the Subordinate? Reciprocal Relations between Abusive Supervision and Organizational Deviance," *Journal of Applied Psychology* 99, no. 4 (2014): 651–64.

[68] R. Folger and D. P. Skarlicki, "Beyond Counterproductive Work Behavior: Moral Emotions and Deontic Retaliation versus Reconciliation," in S. Fox and P. E. Spector (eds.), *Counterproductive Work Behavior: Investigations of Actors and Targets* (Washington, DC: American Psychological Association, 2005): 83–105.

[69] C. M. Berry, N. C. Carpenter, and C. L. Barratt, "Do Other-Reports of Counterproductive Work Behavior Provide an Incremental Contribution over Self-Reports? A Meta-Analytic Comparison," *Journal of Applied Psychology* 97, no. 3 (2012): 613–36; and N. C. Carpenter, B. Rangel, G. Jeon, and J. Cottrell, "Are Supervisors and Coworkers Likely to Witness Employee Counterproductive Work Behavior? An Investigation of Observability and Self-Observer Convergence," *Personnel Psychology* (in press).

[70] Diestel, Wegge, and Schmidt, "The Impact of Social Context on the Relationship between Individual Job Satisfaction and Absenteeism."

[71] R. D. Hackett, "Work Attitudes and Employee Absenteeism: A Synthesis of the Literature," *Journal of Occupational Psychology* 62 (1989): 235–48; and J. F. Ybema, P. G. W. Smulders, and P. M. Bongers, "Antecedents and Consequences of Employee Absenteeism: A Longitudinal Perspective on the Role of Job Satisfaction and Burnout," *European Journal of Work and Organizational Psychology* 19 (2010): 102–24.

[72] J. P. Hausknecht, N. J. Hiller, and R. J. Vance, "Work-Unit Absenteeism: Effects of Satisfaction, Commitment, Labor Market Conditions, and Time," *Academy of Management Journal* 51, no. 6 (2008): 1123–245.

[73] G. Chen, R. E. Ployhart, H. C. Thomas, N. Anderson, and P. D. Bliese, "The Power of Momentum: A New Model of Dynamic Relationships between Job Satisfaction Change and Turnover Intentions," *Academy of Management Journal*, February 2011, 159–81; and R. W. Griffeth, P. W. Hom, and S. Gaertner, "A Meta-Analysis of Antecedents and Correlates of Employee Turnover: Update, Moderator Tests, and Research Implications for the Next Millennium," *Journal of Management* 26, no. 3 (2000): 479.

[74] W. Felps, T. R. Mitchell, D. R. Hekman, T. W. Lee, B. C. Holtom, and W. S. Harman, "Turnover Contagion: How Coworkers' Job Embeddedness and Job Search Behaviors Influence Quitting," *Academy of Management Journal* 52, no. 3 (2009): 545–61; and D. Liu, T. R. Mitchell, T. W. Lee, B. C. Holtom, and T. R. Hinkin, "When Employees Are Out of Step with Coworkers: How Job Satisfaction Trajectory and Dispersion Influence Individual- and Unit-Level Voluntary Turnover," *Academy of Management Journal* 55, no. 6 (2012): 1360–80.

[75] T. H. Lee, B. Gerhart, I. Weller, and C. O. Trevor, "Understanding Voluntary Turnover: Path-Specific Job Satisfaction Effects and the Importance of Unsolicited Job Offers," *Academy of Management Journal* 51, no. 4 (2008): 651–71.

[76] K. Jiang, D. Liu, P. F. McKay, T. W. Lee, and T. R. Mitchell, "When and How Is Job Embeddedness Predictive of Turnover? A Meta-Analytic Investigation," *Journal of Applied Psychology* 97 (2012): 1077–96; and C. M. Porter, R. A. Posthuma, C. P. Maertz Jr., J. R. W. Joplin, J. Rigby, M. Gordon, and K. Graves, "On-the-job and Off-the-job Embeddedness Differentially Influence Relationships between Informal Job Search and Turnover," *Journal of Applied Psychology* 104, no. 5 (2019): 678–89.

[77] K. Holland, "Inside the Minds of Your Employees," *The New York Times*, January 28, 2007, B1; "Study Sees Link between Morale and Stock Price," *Workforce Management*, February 27, 2006, 15; and "The Workplace as a Solar System," *The New York Times*, October 28, 2006, B5.

[78] E. White, "How Surveying Workers Can Pay Off," *The Wall Street Journal*, June 18, 2007, B3.

4 Personality and Values

Source: Rick Kern/Stringer/Getty Images

LEARNING OBJECTIVES

After studying this chapter, you should be able to:

4-1 Describe the differences between person–job fit and person–organization fit.

4-2 Describe personality, the way it is measured, and the factors that shape it.

4-3 Describe the strengths and weaknesses of the Myers-Briggs Type Indicator (MBTI) personality framework and the Big Five model.

4-4 Discuss how the concepts of core self-evaluation (CSE), self-monitoring, and proactive personality contribute to the understanding of personality.

4-5 Describe how personality affects job search and unemployment.

4-6 Describe how the situation affects whether personality predicts behavior.

4-7 Contrast terminal and instrumental values.

4-8 Compare Hofstede's five value dimensions and the GLOBE framework.

Employability Skills Matrix (ESM)

	Myth or Science?	Career OBjectives	An Ethical Choice	Point/ Counterpoint	Experiential Exercise	Ethical Dilemma	Case Incident 1	Case Incident 2
Critical Thinking	✓	✓	✓	✓	✓	✓	✓	✓
Communication	✓				✓			✓
Collaboration					✓		✓	✓
Knowledge Application and Analysis	✓	✓	✓	✓	✓	✓	✓	✓
Social Responsibility		✓	✓	✓		✓		✓

LEADING THE "QUIET REVOLUTION"

As vice chair (business innovations), Beth Comstock (shown here), has been "lighting up GE." She has been rated in 2016 as the forty-eighth most powerful woman in business and has held executive positions at NBCUniversal as well as GE throughout her decades-spanning career. Today, her position requires that she forecast future opportunities for GE and gather the right teams to foster new business models. Not only is she in charge of business model innovation, but she also oversees many aspects of GE's sales, marketing, and communication functions.

To many, someone this successful *must* appear to need an extroverted personality or be sociable, gregarious, and assertive. However, you may be surprised to hear that Beth considers herself to be an introvert: "I'm definitely a more introverted leader, but I've worked hard during my career to make sure I put myself out there because I [understand] that business is an extroverted activity." Comstock illustrates how even though traits such as extroversion can greatly help an individual succeed in the business world, adapting to the situation goes a long way. Furthermore, introversion itself has some unique benefits, Beth notes, "There are also a lot of great things about being more introverted—you observe things more, you aren't always the first to speak. I've come to learn that leadership is about understanding things are never perfectly balanced and how to best use that tension moving forward."

Beth's insights into leadership are quite telling and may be extended beyond the study of leadership and personality. Life isn't as perfectly balanced or black and white as it may seem. Certain personality traits may be useful in some contexts and useless in others. There has been a renewed focus on the power of introversion in a world that idolizes extroversion. In her 2012 book, *Quiet: The Power of Introverts in a World That Can't Stop Talking*, Susan Cain delves into these ideas and has since sold 2 million copies worldwide. In 2015, she met with 50 GE executives for a fireside discussion of her book. Responding to a question an executive asked about any advice that could be given to his introverted daughter who was en route to college, Cain says "Take time to find your tribe ... It's a difficult world when the social currency is how gregarious you are." As an introvert, getting out there and finding a group you can belong to is so important, as the world seems to value extraversion.

Cain's work has sparked a renewed interest in what it means to be introverted or extroverted, navigating a world that on the whole values extraverted behavior, and whether introverts make effective leaders. Although extraverted traits can be helpful in some situations, the advice for introverts to "be more extroverted" has perhaps been misguided. Psychologists and Organizational Behavior (OB) experts alike are beginning to realize that there are valuable skills unique to both introversion and extraversion.

Beyond our personalities, which describe our behavioral tendencies, our values and belief systems also matter in relation to what we do and how we do it in the workplace. For example, Beth has a track record of investing in women-led start-ups because she is a big believer in supporting female entrepreneurs and founders. By investing in these organizations, she is acting in support of her values. In fact, all her investments to date have been in women-led companies.

Sources: Based on G. Colvin, "How Beth Comstock Is Lighting up GE," *Fortune*, September 14, 2016, http://fortune.com/beth-comstock-general-electric-most-powerful-women/; L. M. Holson, "Instigating a 'Quiet Revolution' of Introverts," *The New York Times*, July 26, 2015, Section ST, p. 10; D. Schawbel, "Beth Comstock: Being an Introverted Leader in an Extroverted Business World," *Forbes*, October 20, 2016, https://www.forbes.com/sites/danschawbel/2016/10/20/beth-comstock-being-an-introverted-leader-in-an-extroverted-business-world/2/#3a47817a1c6f; and V. Zarya, "Why GE Vice Chair Beth Comstock Is Investing in These Women-Led Startups," *Fortune*, May 18, 2016, http://fortune.com/2016/05/18/beth-comstock-women-led-startups/.

Personality is indeed a strong factor for many life and work outcomes. Personality plays a major role in success in the workplace, although the effects are not always direct; sometimes they are nuanced. We will explain extraversion, conscientiousness, openness, agreeableness, and neuroticism: the traits which comprise the Big Five, the most well-defined and supported personality framework to-date. We'll also review frameworks that describe an individual's personality and tendencies.

Linking an Individual's Personality and Values to the Workplace

4-1 Describe the differences between person-job fit and person-organization fit.

Thirty years ago, organizations were concerned with personality, in part because they used it to match individuals to specific jobs. That concern has expanded to include how well the individual's personality *and* values match the organization. Why? Because managers today are less interested in an applicant's ability to perform a *specific* job than with his or her *flexibility* to meet changing situations and maintain commitment to the organization. Still, one of the first types of fit managers look for is person–job fit.

Person–Job Fit

personality-job fit theory A theory that identifies six personality types and proposes that the fit between personality type and occupational environment determines satisfaction and turnover.

The effort to match job requirements with personality characteristics is described by John Holland's **personality–job fit theory**, one of the more proven theories in use internationally.[1] The Vocational Preference Inventory questionnaire contains 160 occupational titles. Respondents indicate which they like or dislike, and their answers form personality profiles. Holland presented six personality types and proposed that satisfaction and the propensity to leave a position depend on how well individuals match their personalities to a job. Exhibit 4-1 describes the six types, their personality characteristics, and examples of the congruent occupations for each.

There are cultural implications for person–job fit that speak to workers' expectations that jobs will be tailored. In individualistic countries where workers expect to be heard and respected by management, increasing person–job fit by tailoring the job to the person increases the individual's job satisfaction. However, in collectivistic countries, person–job fit is a weaker predictor of job satisfaction because people do not expect to have a job tailored to them, so they value person–job fit efforts less. Therefore, managers in collectivistic cultures should not violate cultural norms by designing jobs for individuals; rather, they should seek people who will likely thrive in jobs that have already been structured.[2]

Person–Organization Fit

We've noted that researchers have looked at matching people to organizations and jobs. If an organization has a dynamic and changing environment and needs employees able to change tasks readily and move easily between teams, it's more important that employees' personalities fit with the overall organization's culture than with the characteristics of any specific job.

person-organization fit A theory that people are attracted to and selected by organizations that match their values, and leave when there is no compatibility.

Person–organization fit essentially means people are attracted to and are selected by organizations that match their values, and they leave organizations that are not compatible with their personalities.[3] Using the Big Five terminology, for instance, we could expect that extraverts fit well with aggressive and team-oriented

Exhibit 4-1 Holland's Typology of Personality and Congruent Occupations

Type	Personality Characteristics	Congruent Occupations
Realistic: Prefers physical activities that require skill, strength, and coordination	Shy, genuine, persistent, stable, conforming, practical	Mechanic, drill press operator, assembly-line worker, farmer
Investigative: Prefers activities that involve thinking, organizing, and understanding	Analytical, original, curious, independent	Biologist, economist, mathematician, news reporter
Social: Prefers activities that involve helping and developing others	Sociable, friendly, cooperative, understanding	Social worker, teacher, counselor, clinical psychologist
Conventional: Prefers rule-regulated, orderly, and unambiguous activities	Conforming, efficient, practical, unimaginative, inflexible	Accountant, corporate manager, bank teller, file clerk
Enterprising: Prefers verbal activities in which there are opportunities to influence others and attain power	Self-confident, ambitious, energetic, domineering	Lawyer, real estate agent, public relations specialist, small business manager
Artistic: Prefers ambiguous and unsystematic activities that allow creative expression	Imaginative, disorderly, idealistic, emotional, impractical	Painter, musician, writer, interior decorator

cultures, people high on agreeableness match better with a supportive organizational climate, and highly open people fit better in organizations that emphasize innovation rather than standardization.[4] Following these guidelines when hiring should yield employees who fit better with the organization's culture, which should, in turn, result in higher employee satisfaction and reduced turnover. Research on person–organization fit also looked at whether people's values match the organization's culture. A match predicts high job satisfaction, commitment to the organization, and task performance, as well as low turnover.[5]

It is more important than ever for organizations to manage their image online because job seekers view company websites as part of their pre-application process. Applicants want to see a user-friendly website that provides information about company philosophies and policies. For example, millennials in particular may react positively when they perceive that an organization is committed to work-life balance. The website is so important to the development of perceived person–organization fit that improvements to its style (usability) and substance (policies) can lead to more applicants.[6]

Other Dimensions of Fit

Although person–job fit and person–organization fit are considered the most salient dimensions for workplace outcomes, other avenues of fit are worth examining. These include *person–group fit* and *person–supervisor fit*.[7] Person–group fit is important in team settings, where the dynamics of team interactions significantly affect work outcomes. Person–supervisor fit has become an important area of research because poor fit in this dimension can lead to lower job satisfaction and reduced performance.

All dimensions of fit are sometimes broadly referred to as person–environment fit. Each dimension can predict work attitudes, which are partially based on culture. A recent meta-analysis of person–environment fit in East Asia, Europe, and North America suggested the dimensions of person–organization and person–job fit are the strongest predictors of positive work attitudes and performance in North America. These dimensions are important to a lesser degree in Europe, and they are the least important in East Asia.[8]

Decathlon India—a large format store that sells fitness equipment, goods and accessories for more than 70 sports—believes in person-job fit. Thus, while hiring, the passion of the person to play sports is seen as an essential qualification. The selection of all possible candidates begins with playing a team sport.
Source: Harry Wedzinga.shutterstock.com

Personality

4-2 Describe personality, the way it is measured, and the factors that shape it.

Why are some people quiet and passive, while others are loud and aggressive? Are certain personality types better adapted than others for certain jobs? Before we can answer these questions, we need to address a more basic one: What is personality?

What Is Personality?

When we speak of someone's personality, we use many adjectives to describe how they act and seem to think; in fact, participants in a recent study used 624 distinct adjectives to describe people they knew.[9] As organizational behaviorists, however, we organize personality characteristics by overall traits, describing the growth and development of a person's personality.

personality The sum of ways in which an individual reacts to and interacts with others.

Defining Personality For our purposes, think of **personality** as the sum of ways in which an individual reacts to and interacts with others. We most often describe personality in terms of the measurable traits a person exhibits.

Measuring Personality Personality assessments have been increasingly used in diverse organizational settings. In India, psychometric assessments are used for recruitment and competency mapping by several companies including Cognizant, Ford Motors, Tata Motors, TVS Sundaram, Deloitte, etc. In a historic move, the Central Board of Secondary Education (CBSE) mandated that in all its 19,500 affiliated schools, the teaching and non-teaching staff should undergo a psychometric evaluation which tests among other things the personality measures.[10] Personality tests are useful in hiring decisions and help managers forecast who is best for a job.[11]

The most common means of measuring personality is through self-report surveys in which individuals evaluate themselves on a series of factors, such as "I worry a lot about the future." In general, when people know their personality scores are going to be used for hiring decisions, they rate themselves as about half a standard deviation more conscientious and emotionally stable than if they are taking the test to learn more about themselves.[12] Another problem is accuracy; a candidate who is in a bad mood when taking the survey may have inaccurate scores.[13]

Research indicates that culture influences the way we rate ourselves. People in individualistic countries trend toward self-enhancement, while people in collectivist countries like India, Taiwan, China, and South Korea trend toward self-diminishment. Self-enhancement does not appear to harm a person's career in individualistic countries, but it does in collectivist countries, where humility is valued. Underrating (self-diminishment) may harm a person's career in both collectivistic and individualistic communities.[14]

Observer-ratings surveys provide an independent assessment of personality. Here, a coworker or another observer does the rating. Though the results of self-reports and observer-ratings surveys are strongly correlated, research suggests that observer-ratings surveys predict job success more than self-ratings alone.[15] However, each can tell us something unique about an individual's

Career OBjectives

How do I ace the personality test?

I just landed a second-round interview with a great company, and I'm super excited. And super nervous because I've read a few articles about how more and more companies are using personality testing. Do you have tips for how I can put my best foot forward?

— ***Lavisha***

Dear Lavisha:

Congratulations! It's natural for you to want to understand the tests your prospective employer uses. You've probably deduced that it's possible to respond in a favorable manner. For example, if a statement says, "I am always prepared," you know that employers are looking for an applicant who agrees with this statement. You might think responding in the most favorable way possible increases your chances of getting hired, and you might be right.

There are a few caveats, however. First, some companies build in "lie scales" that flag individuals who respond to statements in an extremely favorable manner. It's not always easy to detect them, but clues usually appear across several items. If you respond in the most favorable way to a long list of items, then you might pop up on the lie scale.

Second, high scores on every trait are not desirable for every kind of job. Some employers might be more interested in low scores on a particular trait or pay more attention to a total profile that would be hard to "game." For example, agreeableness is not a good predictor of job performance for jobs that are competitive in nature (sales, coach, trader).

Third, there is an ethical perspective you should consider. How are you going to feel once you are in the organization if you have not represented yourself correctly in the hiring process? What is your general attitude toward lying? How are you going to make sure your behavior fits the traits you tried to portray?

Finally, perhaps you should look at the assessment differently. The organization—and you—should be looking for a good match. If you are not a good match and are hired, you are likely to be unsuccessful, and miserable in the process. However, if you have a good, honest match, you can arrive for your first day confident and ready for success.

In the end, you might increase your chances of getting hired by responding to a personality test in a favorable manner. However, we still think honesty is the best policy—for you and for your future employer!

Sources: Based on M. N. Bing, H. K. Davison, and J. Smothers, "Item-Level Frame-of-Reference Effects in Personality Testing: An Investigation of Incremental Validity in an Organizational Setting," *International Journal of Selection and Assessment* 22, no. 2 (2014): 165–78; P. R. Sackett and P. T. Walmsley, "Which Personality Attributes Are Most Important in the Workplace?" *Perspectives on Psychological Science* 9, no. 5 (2014): 538–51; and L. Weber, "To Get a Job, New Hires Are Put to the Test," *The Wall Street Journal*, April 15, 2015, A1, A10.

The opinions provided here are of the authors only. The authors are not responsible for any errors or omissions, or for the results obtained from the use of this information. In no event will the authors or their related partnerships or corporations thereof be liable to you or anyone else for any decision made or action taken in reliance on the opinions provided here.

behavior, so a combination of self-reports and observer reports predicts performance better than any one type of information. The implication is clear: Use both observer ratings and self-report ratings of personality when making important employment decisions.

Personality Determinants An early debate centered on whether an individual's personality is the result of heredity or environment. Personality appears to be a result of both; however, research tends to support the importance of heredity over environment.

heredity Factors determined at conception; one's biological, physiological, and inherent psychological makeup.

Heredity refers to factors determined at conception. Physical stature, facial features, gender, temperament, muscle composition and reflexes, energy level, and biological rhythms are either completely or substantially influenced by parentage—by your biological parents' biological, physiological, and inherent psychological makeup. The heredity approach argues that the ultimate explanation of an individual's personality is the molecular structure of the genes, which are located on the chromosomes. A review of 134 studies found that there is some truth to this approach, with about 40 percent of personality being attributable to heredity and the other 60 percent attributable to the environment.[16]

This is not to suggest that personality never changes. People's scores on dependability tend to increase over time, as when young adults start families and establish careers. However, strong individual differences in dependability remain; everyone tends to change by about the same amount, so their rank order stays roughly the same.[17] Furthermore, personality is more changeable in adolescence and more stable among adults.[18]

Early work on personality tried to identify and label enduring characteristics that describe an individual's behavior, including shy, aggressive, submissive, lazy, ambitious, loyal, and timid. When someone frequently exhibits these characteristics and they are relatively enduring over time and across

Energetic, charismatic, decisive, ambitious, adaptable, courageous, and industrious are personality traits used to describe Richard Branson, founder of Virgin Group. These traits helped Branson, shown here promoting Virgin Trains, build one of the most recognized and respected global brands in travel, entertainment, and lifestyle.

Source: Joe Pepler/REX/AP Images

personality traits Enduring characteristics that describe an individual's behavior.

situations, we call them **personality traits.**[19] The more consistent the characteristic over time and the more frequently it occurs in diverse situations, the more important the trait is in describing the individual.

Personality Frameworks

4-3 Describe the strengths and weaknesses of the Myers-Briggs Type Indicator (MBTI) personality framework and the Big Five model.

Throughout history, people have sought to understand what makes individuals behave in different ways. Many of our behaviors stem from our personalities, so understanding the components of personality helps us predict behavior. Important theoretical frameworks and assessment tools help us categorize and study the dimensions of personality.

The most widely used and best known personality frameworks are the Myers-Briggs Type Indicator (MBTI) and the Big Five Personality Model. Both describe a person's total personality through exploration of the facets of personality. Other frameworks, such as the Dark Triad, explain certain aspects, but not the total, of an individual's personality. We discuss each below, but let's begin with the dominant frameworks.

The Myers-Briggs Type Indicator

Myers-Briggs Type Indicator (MBTI) A personality test that taps four characteristics and classifies people into one of sixteen personality types.

The **Myers-Briggs Type Indicator (MBTI)** is one of the most widely used personality assessment instruments in the world.[20] It is a 100-question personality test that asks people how they usually feel or act in situations. Respondents are classified as extraverted or introverted (E or I), sensing or intuitive (S or N), thinking or feeling (T or F), and judging or perceiving (J or P):

- *Extraverted (E) versus Introverted (I).* Extraverted individuals are outgoing, sociable, and assertive. Introverts are quiet and shy.
- *Sensing (S) versus Intuitive (N).* Sensing types are practical and prefer routine and order, and they focus on details. Intuitives rely on unconscious processes and look at the big picture.
- *Thinking (T) versus Feeling (F).* Thinking types use reason and logic to handle problems. Feeling types rely on their personal values and emotions.
- *Judging (J) versus Perceiving (P).* Judging types want control and prefer order and structure. Perceiving types are flexible and spontaneous.

The MBTI describes personality types by identifying one trait from each of the four pairs. For example, Introverted/Intuitive/Thinking/Judging people (INTJs) are visionaries with original minds and great drive. They are skeptical, critical, independent, determined, and often stubborn. ENFJs are natural teachers and leaders. They are relational, motivational, intuitive, idealistic, ethical, and kind. ESTJs are organizers. They are realistic, logical, analytical, and decisive, perfect for business or mechanics. The ENTP type is innovative, individualistic, versatile, and attracted to entrepreneurial ideas. This person tends to be resourceful in solving challenging problems but may neglect routine assignments.

According to the Myers & Briggs Foundation, introverts account for over 50 percent of the E/I responses in the U.S. population. Indeed, two of the three most common MBTI types are introverts: ISFJ and ISTJ. ISFJs are nurturing and responsible, and ISTJs are dutiful and logical. The least common types are INFJ (insightful and protective) and ENTJ (focused and decisive).[21]

The MBTI is used in a variety of organizational settings. It is taken by over 2.5 million people each year, and 89 of the Fortune 100 companies use it.[22]

Evidence is mixed about its validity as a measure of personality; however, most of the evidence is against it.[23] As Professor Dan Ariely noted about MBTI results, "Next time, just look at the horoscope. It is just as valid and takes less time."[24]

One problem with the MBTI is that the model forces a person into one type or another; that is, you're either introverted or extraverted. There is no in-between. Another problem is with the reliability of the measure: When people retake the assessment, they often receive different results. An additional problem is in the difficulty of interpretation. There are levels of importance for each of the MBTI facets, and there are separate meanings for certain combinations of facets, all of which require trained interpretation that can leave room for error. Finally, results from the MBTI tend to be unrelated to job performance. The MBTI can thus be a valuable tool for increasing self-awareness and providing career guidance, but because results tend to be unrelated to job performance, managers should consider using the Big Five Personality Model, discussed next, as the personality selection test for job candidates instead.

The Big Five Personality Model

The MBTI may lack strong supporting evidence, but an impressive body of research supports the **Big Five Model**, which proposes that five basic dimensions underlie all others and encompass most of the significant variation in human personality.[25] Test scores of these traits do a very good job of predicting how people behave in a variety of real-life situations[26] and remain relatively stable for an individual over time, with some daily variations.[27] These are the Big Five factors:

Big Five Model A personality model that proposes five basic dimensions encompass most of the differences in human personality.

- *Conscientiousness.* The **conscientiousness** dimension is a measure of personal consistency and reliability. A highly conscientious person is responsible, organized, dependable, and persistent. Those who score low on this dimension are easily distracted, disorganized, and unreliable.
- *Emotional stability.* The **emotional stability** dimension taps a person's ability to withstand stress. People with emotional stability tend to be calm, self-confident, and secure. High scorers are more likely to be positive and optimistic and to experience fewer negative emotions; they are generally happier than low scorers. Emotional stability is sometimes discussed as its converse, neuroticism. Low scorers (those with high neuroticism) are hypervigilant and vulnerable to the physical and psychological effects of stress. Those with high neuroticism tend to be nervous, anxious, depressed, and insecure.
- *Extraversion.* The **extraversion** dimension captures our relational approach toward the social world. Extraverts tend to be gregarious, assertive, and sociable. They experience more positive emotions than do introverts, and they more freely express these feelings. On the other hand, introverts (low extraversion) tend to be more thoughtful, reserved, timid, and quiet.
- *Openness to experience.* The **openness to experience** dimension addresses the range of interests and fascination with novelty. Open people are creative, curious, and artistically sensitive. Those at the low end of the category are conventional and find comfort in the familiar.
- *Agreeableness.* The **agreeableness** dimension refers to an individual's propensity to defer to others. Agreeable people are cooperative, warm, and trusting. You might expect agreeable people to be happier than disagreeable people. They are, but only slightly. When people choose organizational team members, agreeable individuals are usually their first choice. In contrast, people who score low on agreeableness are cold and antagonistic.

conscientiousness A personality dimension that describes someone who is responsible, dependable, persistent, and organized.

emotional stability A personality dimension that characterizes someone as calm, self-confident, and secure (positive) versus nervous, depressed, and insecure (negative).

extraversion A personality dimension describing someone who is sociable, gregarious, and assertive.

openness to experience A personality dimension that characterizes someone in terms of imagination, sensitivity, and curiosity.

agreeableness A personality dimension that describes someone who is good natured, cooperative, and trusting.

General Motors CEO Mary Barra is unusual in that she appears to score high on all the Big Five personality dimensions. Her unique combination of traits has helped her become the first female CEO of a major global automaker.

Source: Michael Buholzer/Photoshot/Newscom

How Do the Big Five Traits Predict Behavior at Work? There are many relationships between the Big Five personality dimensions and job performance,[28] and we are learning more about them every day. Let's explore one trait at a time, beginning with the strongest predictor of job performance—conscientiousness.

Conscientiousness at Work As researchers have stated, "Personal attributes related to conscientiousness ... are important for success across many jobs, spanning across low to high levels of job complexity, training, and experience."[29] Employees who score higher in conscientiousness develop higher levels of job knowledge, probably because highly conscientious people learn more (conscientiousness may be related to grade point average [GPA]),[30] and these levels correspond with higher levels of job performance.[31] Conscientious people are also more able to maintain their job performance even when faced with abusive supervision, according to a recent study in India.[32] Prior reviews also suggest that conscientious people tend to be more likely to engage in more organizational citizenship behaviors (OCBs), less likely to engage in counterproductive work behaviors (CWBs) or think about leaving the organization, and can adapt to changing task demands and situations.[33] Conscientious people also engage in less unsafe behavior and tend to have fewer accidents than those who are less conscientious.[34]

Conscientiousness is important to overall organizational success. As Exhibit 4-2 shows, a study of the personality scores of 313 Chief Executive Officer (CEO) candidates in private equity companies (of whom 225 were hired) found conscientiousness—in the form of persistence, attention to detail, and setting high standards—was more important to success than other traits.[35]

Like any trait, conscientiousness has pitfalls. Extremely conscientious individuals can be too deliberate and perfectionistic, resulting in diminished happiness and performance, which includes task performance, safety performance, and OCB.[36] They may also become too focused on their own work to help others in the organization.[37] Finally, they are often less creative, especially artistically.[38]

Exhibit 4-2 Traits That Matter Most to Business Success at Buyout Companies

Most Important	Less Important
Persistence	Strong oral communication
Attention to detail	Teamwork
Efficiency	Flexibility/adaptability
Analytical skills	Enthusiasm
Setting high standards	Listening skills

Source: Based on S. N. Kaplan, M. M. Klebanov, and M. Sorensen, "Which CEO Characteristics and Abilities Matter?" *The Journal of Finance* 67, no. 3 (2012): 973–1007.

Conscientiousness is the best predictor of job performance. However, the other Big Five traits are also related to aspects of performance and have other implications for work and for life, as Exhibit 4-3 summarizes.

Emotional Stability at Work Of the Big Five traits, emotional stability is most strongly related to life satisfaction, job satisfaction, and reduced burnout and intentions to quit.[39] People with high emotional stability can adapt to unexpected or changing demands in the workplace.[40] At the other end of the spectrum, neurotic individuals, who may be unable to cope with these

Exhibit 4-3 Model of How Big Five Traits Influence OB Criteria

BIG FIVE TRAITS	WHY IS IT RELEVANT?	WHAT DOES IT AFFECT?
Emotional stability →	• Less negative thinking and fewer negative emotions • Less hypervigilant →	• Higher job and life satisfaction • Lower stress levels • More adaptable to change
Extraversion →	• Better interpersonal skills • Greater social dominance • More emotionally expressive →	• Higher performance • Enhanced leadership • Higher job and life satisfaction
Openness →	• Increased learning • More creative • More flexible and autonomous →	• Enhanced Training Performance • Enhanced leadership
Agreeableness →	• Better liked • More compliant and conforming →	• Higher performance • Lower levels of deviant behavior
Conscientiousness →	• Greater effort and persistence • More drive and discipline • Better organized and planning →	• Higher performance • Enhanced leadership • Greater longevity

demands, may experience burnout.[41] These people also tend to experience work–family conflict, which can affect work outcomes.[42] Given these negative, straining effects, neurotic employees are more likely to engage in CWBs, less likely to engage in OCBs, and less likely to be motivated at work.[43]

Extraversion at Work People with extraverted personality traits tend to perform well in jobs that require interpersonal interaction. They are socially dominant, "take charge" people who are usually more assertive than introverts.[44] Extraversion is a relatively strong predictor of leadership emergence and behaviors in groups.[45] Extraverts also tend to have generally high job satisfaction and reduced burnout.[46] Some negatives are that extraverts can appear to be self-aggrandizing, egoistic, or too dominating and that their social behavior can be disadvantageous for jobs that do not require frequent social interaction.[47]

Openness at Work Open people tend to be the most creative and innovative compared with the other traits.[48] Open people are more likely to be effective leaders and more comfortable with ambiguity—they cope better with organizational change and are more adaptable.[49] While openness isn't related to initial performance on a job, individuals higher in openness are less susceptible to a decline in performance over a longer time period.[50] Open people also experience less work–family conflict.[51]

Agreeableness at Work Agreeable individuals are better liked than disagreeable people; they should perform well in interpersonally oriented jobs such as customer service. They experience less work–family conflict and are less susceptible to turnover.[52] They also contribute to organizational performance by engaging in OCB.[53] Disagreeable people, on the other hand, are more likely to engage in CWBs, as are people low in conscientiousness.[54] Agreeableness is associated with lower levels of career success, perhaps because highly agreeable people consider themselves less marketable and are less willing to assert themselves.[55]

In general, the Big Five personality factors appear in almost all cross-cultural studies,[56] including studies in China, India, Israel, Germany, Japan, Spain, Nigeria, Norway, Pakistan, and the United States. However, a study of illiterate indigenous people in Bolivia suggested that the Big Five framework may be less applicable when studying the personalities of small, remote groups.[57]

Research indicates that the Big Five traits have the most verifiable links to important organizational outcomes, but they are not the only traits a person exhibits, nor are they the only ones with OB implications. Let's discuss some other traits, known collectively as the Dark Triad.

The Dark Triad

Outside the Big Five framework, researchers have identified three other socially *undesirable* traits, which we all have in varying degrees, are also relevant to organizational behavior: Machiavellianism, narcissism, and psychopathy. Because of their negative nature, researchers have labeled these the **Dark Triad**—though they do not always occur together.[58]

Dark Triad A constellation of negative personality traits consisting of Machiavellianism, narcissism, and psychopathy.

The Dark Triad may sound sinister, but these traits are not clinical pathologies hindering everyday functioning. They might be expressed particularly strongly when an individual is under stress and unable to moderate any inappropriate responses. Sustained high levels of dark personality traits can cause individuals to derail their careers and personal lives.[59]

Machiavellianism The degree to which an individual is pragmatic, maintains emotional distance, and believes that ends can justify means.

Machiavellianism Dinesh is a young bank manager in Delhi. He's received three promotions in the past 4 years and makes no apologies for the aggressive tactics he's used. "This is who I am, this is what I do. I do whatever to get ahead. I am clever and smart," he says. Dinesh would be termed Machiavellian.

The personality characteristic of **Machiavellianism** (often abbreviated *Mach*) is named after Niccolo Machiavelli, who wrote in the sixteenth century about how to gain and use power. An individual high in Machiavellianism is pragmatic, maintains emotional distance, and believes ends can justify means. "If it works, use it" is consistent with a high-Mach perspective. High Machs manipulate more, win more, and are persuaded less by others but persuade others more than do low Machs.[60] They are more likely to act aggressively and engage in CWBs as well. Surprisingly, Machiavellianism does not positively predict overall job performance.[61] High-Mach employees, by manipulating others to their advantage, win in the short term at a job, but they lose those gains in the long term because they are not well liked.

Machiavellian tendencies may have ethical implications. One study showed that high-Mach job seekers were less positively affected by the knowledge that an organization engaged in a high level of corporate social responsibility (CSR),[62] suggesting that high-Mach people may care less about sustainability issues. Another study found that Machs' ethical leadership behaviors were less likely to translate into followers' work engagement because followers see through these behaviors and realize it is a case of surface acting.[63]

Narcissism Sabrina likes to be the center of attention. She often looks at herself in the mirror, has extravagant dreams about her future, and considers herself a person of many talents. Sabrina is a narcissist. The trait is named for the Greek myth about Narcissus, a youth so vain and proud he fell in love with his own image. In psychology, **narcissism** describes a person who has a grandiose sense of self-importance, requires excessive admiration, and is arrogant. Narcissists often have fantasies of grand success, a tendency to exploit situations and people, a sense of entitlement, and a lack of empathy.[64] However, narcissists can be hypersensitive and fragile people.[65] They may also experience more anger.[66]

OB POLL

Does Business School Make You Narcissistic?

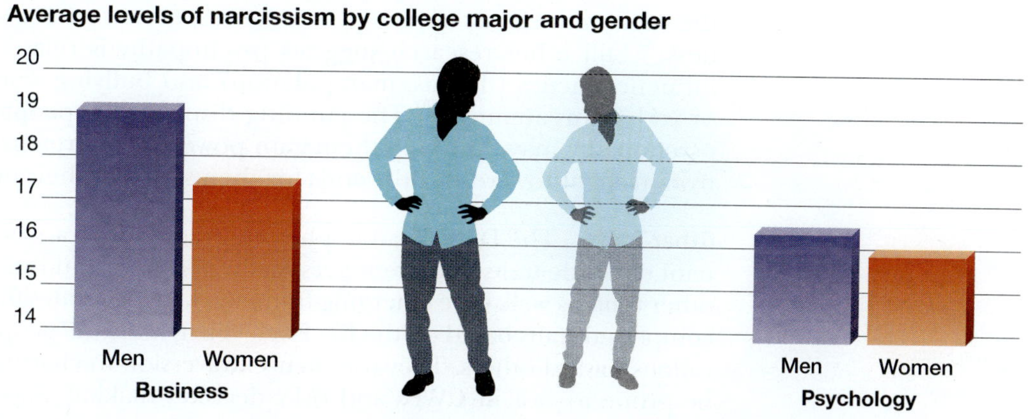

Source: Based on J. W. Westerman, J. Z. Bergman, S. M. Bergman, and J. P. Daly, "Are Universities Creating Millennial Narcissistic Employees? An Empirical Examination of Narcissism in Business Students and Its Implications," *Journal of Management Education* 36 (2012), 5–32.

While narcissism seems to be relatively unrelated to job effectiveness or OCB,[67] it is one of the largest predictors of increased CWB in individualistic cultures—but not in collectivist cultures that discourage self-promotion.[68] Narcissists commonly think they are overqualified for their positions.[69] When they receive feedback about their performance, they often tune out information that conflicts with their positive self-perception, but they will work harder if rewards are offered.[70]

On the bright side, narcissists may be more charismatic than others.[71] They also might be found in business more often than in other fields (see OB Poll). They are more likely to be chosen for leadership positions, and medium ratings of narcissism (neither extremely high nor extremely low) are positively correlated with leadership effectiveness.[72] Some evidence suggests that narcissists are more adaptable and make better business decisions than others when the issue is complex.[73] A study of Norwegian bank employees found those scoring high on narcissism enjoyed their work more.[74]

Special attention has been paid to narcissistic CEOs who make more acquisitions, pay higher premiums for those acquisitions, respond less clearly to objective measures of performance, and respond to media praise by making even more acquisitions.[75] Research using data compiled over 100 years has shown that narcissistic CEOs of baseball organizations generate higher levels of manager turnover, although members of external organizations see them as more influential.[76]

Narcissism and its effects are not confined to CEOs or celebrities. Like the effects of Machiavellianism, those of narcissism vary by context, but are evident in all areas of life.

psychopathy The tendency for a lack of concern for others and a lack of guilt or remorse when actions cause harm.

Psychopathy Psychopathy is part of the Dark Triad, but in organizational behavior, it does not connote clinical mental illness. In the OB context, **psychopathy** is defined as a lack of concern for others and a lack of guilt or remorse when actions cause harm.[77] Measures of psychopathy attempt to assess the motivation to comply with social norms; impulsivity; willingness to use deceit to obtain desired ends; and disregard, that is, lack of empathic concern for others.

The literature is not consistent about whether psychopathy is important to work behavior. One review found little correlation between measures of psychopathy and job performance or CWBs.[78] Another found that antisocial personality, which is closely related to psychopathy, was positively related to advancement in the organization but unrelated to other aspects of career success and effectiveness.[79] Still other research suggests psychopathy is related to the use of hard influence tactics (threats, manipulation) and bullying work behavior (physical or verbal threatening).[80] The cunning displayed by people who score high on psychopathy may thus help them gain power in an organization but keep them from using it toward healthy ends for themselves or their organizations.

Other Traits The Dark Triad is a helpful framework for studying the three dominant dark-side traits in current personality research, and researchers are exploring other traits as well. One emerging framework incorporates five additional aberrant compound traits based on the Big Five.[81] First, *antisocial* people are indifferent and callous toward others. They use their extraversion to charm people, but they may be prone to violent CWBs and risky decision making. Second, *borderline* people have low self-esteem and high uncertainty. They are unpredictable in their interactions at work, are inefficient, and may have low job satisfaction. Their low self-esteem can lead to clinical depression.[82] Third, *schizotypal* individuals are eccentric and disorganized. In the workplace, they can be highly creative, although they are susceptible to work stress. Fourth, *obsessive-compulsive* people are perfectionists and can be stubborn, yet they attend to details, carry a strong work ethic, and may be motivated by achievement. Fifth, *avoidant* individuals feel inadequate and hate criticism. They can function only in environments requiring little interaction.

Personality traits have both positive and negative aspects. The degree of each trait—those in the Big Five, the Dark Triad, and others—in a person, and the combination of traits, matter a great deal to organizational outcomes. It would be easy to make quick management decisions based on our observations, but it is important to keep discussions on personality in perspective and to consider other theories.

Other Personality Attributes Relevant to OB

4-4 Discuss how the concepts of core self-evaluation (CSE), self-monitoring, and proactive personality contribute to the understanding of personality.

As we've discussed, studies of traits have much to offer to the field of OB. Now we'll look at other attributes that are powerful predictors of behavior in organizations: core self-evaluations, self-monitoring, and proactive personality.

Core Self-Evaluations (CSEs)

core self-evaluation (CSE) Bottom-line conclusions individuals have about their capabilities, competence, and worth as a person.

Core self-evaluations (CSEs) are bottom-line conclusions individuals have about their capabilities, competence, and worth as a person. People who have positive CSEs like themselves and see themselves as effective and in control of their environment. Those with negative CSEs tend to dislike themselves, question their capabilities, and view themselves as powerless over their environment.[83] As we discussed in Chapter 3, CSEs relate to job satisfaction because people who are positive on this trait see more challenge in their jobs and attain more complex jobs.

People with positive CSEs perform better than others because they set more ambitious goals, are more committed to their goals, and persist longer in attempting to reach them.[84] People who have high CSEs provide better customer service, are more popular coworkers, and may have careers that begin on a better footing and ascend more rapidly over time.[85] They perform especially well if they feel their work provides meaning and is helpful to others.[86] Therefore, people with high CSEs may thrive in organizations with high corporate social responsibility (CSR). However, it is possible for one's CSE to be too high—research suggests when it is, one may begin to become less popular with coworkers.[87]

Self-Monitoring

Sarah is always in trouble at work. Although she's competent, hardworking, and productive, she receives average ratings in performance reviews and seems to have made a career out of irritating her bosses. Sarah's problem is that she's politically inept and unable to adjust her behavior to fit changing situations. As she said, "I'm true to myself. I don't remake myself to please others." Sarah is a low self-monitor.

self-monitoring A personality trait that measures an individual's ability to adjust their behavior to external, situational factors.

Self-monitoring describes an individual's ability to adjust behavior to external, situational factors.[88] High self-monitors show considerable adaptability in adjusting their behavior to external situational factors. They are highly sensitive to external cues and can behave differently in varying situations, sometimes presenting striking contradictions between their public personae and their private selves. Low self-monitors like Sarah can't disguise themselves in that way. They tend to display their true dispositions and attitudes in every situation; hence, there is high behavioral consistency between who they are and what they do.

Richa Kar, founder of Zivame, is confident, capable, and effective. Her high core self-evaluations enabled her to use her education and past experience, to starting an online lingerie business in her early 30s putting her own and family's money into the business. Zivame continues to grow each day in its service to women and is backed by 11 investors.[89,90]
Source: sdx15.shutterstock.com

Evidence indicates that high self-monitors pay closer attention to the behavior of others and are more capable of conforming than are low self-monitors.[91] High self-monitor employees show less commitment to their organizations but receive better performance ratings and are more likely to emerge as leaders.[92] High self-monitor managers tend to be more mobile in their careers, receive more promotions (both internal and cross-organizational), and are more likely to occupy central positions in organizations.[93] However, self-monitoring can be considered a mixed blessing: despite the aforementioned positive benefits, self-monitors may be seen as inauthentic, self-serving, or unprincipled.[94]

Proactive Personality

proactive personality People who identify opportunities, show initiative, take action, and persevere until meaningful change occurs.

Did you ever notice that some people take the initiative to improve their current circumstances or create new ones? These are proactive personalities.[95] Those with a **proactive personality** identify opportunities, show initiative, take action, and persevere until meaningful change occurs, unlike those who generally react to situations. Proactive individuals have many desirable behaviors that organizations covet. They have higher levels of job performance[96] and creativity,[97] do not need much oversight, and are given more autonomy as a result.[98] They tend to be satisfied with their jobs, committed to their organizations, and tend to engage in more networking behaviors.[99] Proactive individuals often achieve career success, although they are also more likely to be envied by their coworkers (and prone to social undermining or the withholding of help from coworkers).[100]

A proactive personality may be important for work teams. One study of 95 Research and Development (R&D) teams in 33 Chinese companies revealed that teams with high-average levels of proactive personality were more innovative.[101] Proactive individuals are also more likely to exchange information with others in a team, which builds trust relationships.[102] Like other traits,

Myth or Science?

We Can Accurately Judge Individuals' Personalities a Few Seconds after Meeting Them

Surprisingly, this statement appears to be true.

Research indicates that individuals can accurately appraise others' personalities only a few seconds after first meeting them, or sometimes even from a photo. This "zero acquaintance" approach shows that, regardless of the way in which people first meet someone, whether in person or online, their first judgments about the other's personality have some validity. In one study, for example, individuals were asked to introduce themselves in, on average, 7.4 seconds. Observers' ratings of those individuals' extraversion were significantly correlated with the individuals' self-reported extraversion. Other research suggests personalities can be surmised from online profiles at zero acquaintance as well. One study even found that participants could determine the personality traits of individuals at the ends of the trait spectrum from viewing only photos.

Some traits, such as extraversion, are easier to perceive than others upon initial acquaintance, but less obvious traits like self-esteem are also often judged accurately by others. Even being forced to make intuitive, quick judgments rather than deliberate evaluations does not seem to undermine the accuracy of the appraisals.

Situations make a difference in the accuracy of the judgments for some personality traits. For example, although neuroticism is perhaps the most difficult trait to detect accurately, a recent study found neuroticism could be judged much more accurately when the situation made the individual react nervously. This makes sense when you consider that some situations activate or draw out a trait much more readily than others. Almost everybody looks calm when they're about to fall asleep!

The moderate accuracy of these "thin slices" (quick inferences from short experiences) helps to explain the moderate validity of employment interviews, which we discuss in Chapter 16. Specifically, research shows that interviewers make up their minds about candidates within 2 minutes of first meeting them. While this is hardly an ideal way to make important employment decisions, the research on personality shows these judgments do have some level of validity. It is important to keep in mind, however, that though we can ascertain people's personalities quickly, we should keep an open mind and suspend judgment. There is always more to people than first meets the eye.

Sources: Based on A. Beer, "Comparative Personality Judgments: Replication and Extension of Robust Findings in Personality Perception Using an Alternative Method," *Journal of Personality Assessment* 96, no. 6 (2014): 610–18; M. Gladwell, *Blink: The Power of Thinking Without Thinking* (Boston, MA: Back Bay Books, 2007); S. Hirschmüller, B. Egloff, S. C. Schmukle, S. Nestler, and M. D. Back, "Accurate Judgments of Neuroticism at Zero Acquaintance: A Question of Relevance," *Journal of Personality* 83, no. 2 (2015): 221–28; S. Hirschmüller, B. Egloff, S. Nestler, and D. Mitja, "The Dual Lens Model: A Comprehensive Framework for Understanding Self–Other Agreement of Personality Judgments at Zero Acquaintance," *Journal of Personality and Social Psychology* 104 (2013): 335–53; and J. M. Stopfer, B. Egloff, S. Nestler, and M. D. Back, "Personality Expression and Impression Formation in Online Social Networks: An Integrative Approach to Understanding the Processes of Accuracy, Impression Management, and Meta-Accuracy," *European Journal of Personality* 28 (2014): 73–94.

proactive personality is affected by the context. One study of bank branch teams in China found that if a team's leader was not proactive, the benefits of the team's proactivity became dormant or, worse, was suppressed by the leader.[103] In terms of pitfalls, one study of 231 Flemish unemployed individuals found that proactive individuals abandoned their job searches sooner. It may be that proactivity includes stepping back in the face of failure.[104]

In short, these personality traits predict many important organizational outcomes. However, there has been a renewed interest in how personality is related to employability, job search, and unemployment. The next section is an integrative example that will demonstrate recent research on the relationship between personality, job search, and unemployment.

Personality, Job Search, and Unemployment

4-5 Describe how personality affects job search and unemployment.

As we have discussed, there are many ways in which various personality traits (from several different frameworks) affect on-the-job outcomes. But how does personality affect our behaviors when we are not working? How does personality influence our job search outcomes and operate during our periods of unemployment? You can imagine that these periods may be more exciting for those who have a proactive personality, as introduced in the prior section.[105] But the influence of personality is more nuanced than that.

A relevant question involves the behaviors of those who are unemployed and looking for a job: What personality characteristics predict job search behaviors (e.g., networking intensity) among the unemployed? Many studies of unemployed job seekers have found that conscientiousness and extraversion were predictive of networking intensity, general job search intensity, interview callbacks, and job offers, even after controlling for demographic characteristics and the time spent unemployed.[106] Conscientiousness is such a powerful predictor that in one study of 4,000 British adolescents, the less conscientious of them were twice as likely to be unemployed than those with higher conscientiousness levels.[107] Research in Finland suggests that time structure (i.e., ensuring that your time is structured and purposefully used) is also important for enabling the unemployed to cope effectively with unemployment, with conscientiousness strongly predicting the creation of time structure even above and beyond contextual factors that might impede time structure (e.g., household demands, having children).[108] Overall, one review suggests that conscientiousness and extraversion are the two strongest predictors of job search behavior, although self-esteem and self-efficacy (parts of CSE) are also important.[109]

Additional work on unemployed university students suggests that positive affectivity is also important in getting interviews, job offers, and becoming employed—primarily because the positive affect enables the students to have a clearer and more open perspective toward the job search process, engage in more self-monitoring of their motivation, and reduce procrastination.[110] Negative affectivity and hostility can have the reverse effect—in one sample of Finnish employees tracked over 15 years, unemployed individuals became more hostile and remained unemployed longer as a result of being hostile.[111]

It appears that extraversion, conscientiousness, and positive affectivity tend to have a substantial effect on becoming employed and coping with unemployment (with negative affectivity and hostility having equivalent negative effects). If you find yourself in a situation where you are unemployed, can you expect your personality to change? Or can you change your behavior to act in a way that goes against your traits? First, it appears as if "approach" and "avoidance" traits (e.g., traits that lead to approaching challenges head-on or avoiding them) have an effect on job search—for example, extraversion, conscientiousness, proactive personality, and positive affect have a positive effect, whereas negative affect, hostility, and low self-esteem and self-efficacy have a negative effect.[112] As such, it might be worthwhile to try to adopt an "approach" orientation—take the challenge head on, try to stay positive and organized, and build your network! Second, some research in Germany suggests that your personality *can* change after unemployment—in a sample of nearly 7,000 unemployed adults who were tracked over 4 years, significant patterns of change in agreeableness, conscientiousness, and openness were uncovered.[113] As we will discuss further in the next section, the situation and context matters as well. The experience of unemployment is not the same for everyone across the board—it can be different for new entrants to the labor market (college graduates), those who have just lost their jobs, and those who are employed and seeking jobs.[114] Can we expect the effect of personality to differ in each of these contexts?

Personality and Situations

4-6 Describe how the situation affects whether personality predicts behavior.

Earlier we discussed how research shows that heredity is more important than the environment in developing our personalities. The environment is not irrelevant, though. Some personality traits, such as the Big Five, can be effective in many environments or situations. For example, research indicates conscientiousness is helpful to the performance of most jobs, and extraversion is related to emergence as a leader in most situations. However, we are learning that the effect of particular traits on organizational behavior may depend on the situation. Two theoretical frameworks, situation strength and trait activation, help explain how this works.

Situation Strength Theory

Imagine you are in a meeting with your department. How likely are you to walk out, shout at someone, or turn your back on everyone? Probably highly unlikely. Now imagine working from home. You might work in your pajamas, listen to loud music, or take a catnap. From these examples, you can see that many situations vary in their "strength."

situation strength theory A theory indicating that the way personality translates into behavior depends on the strength of the situation.

Situation strength theory proposes that the way personality translates into behavior depends on the strength of the situation. By *situation strength,* we mean the degree to which norms, cues, or standards dictate appropriate behavior.[115] Strong situations show us what the right behavior is, pressure us to exhibit it, and discourage the wrong behavior. In weak situations, conversely, "anything goes," and thus we are freer to express our personality in behavior. Thus, personality traits better predict behavior in weak situations than in strong ones.

Researchers have analyzed situation strength in organizations in terms of four elements:[116]

1. **Clarity,** or the degree to which cues about work duties and responsibilities are available and clear. Jobs high in clarity produce strong situations because individuals can readily determine what to do. For example, the job of janitor probably provides higher clarity about each task than the job of nanny.
2. **Consistency,** or the extent to which cues regarding work duties and responsibilities are compatible with one another. Jobs with high consistency represent strong situations because all the cues point toward the same desired behavior. The job of acute care nurse, for example, probably has higher consistency than the job of manager.
3. **Constraints,** or the extent to which individuals' freedom to decide or act is limited by forces outside their control. Jobs with many constraints represent strong situations because an individual has limited individual discretion. Bank examiner, for example, is probably a job with stronger constraints than forest ranger.
4. **Consequences,** or the degree to which decisions or actions have important implications for the organization or its members, clients, suppliers, and so on. Jobs with important consequences represent strong situations because the environment is probably heavily structured to guard against mistakes. A surgeon's job, for example, has higher consequences than a foreign-language teacher's.

Some researchers have speculated that organizations are strong situations because they impose rules, norms, and standards that govern behavior. These constraints are usually appropriate. For example, we would not want an employee to feel free to engage in sexual harassment, follow questionable accounting procedures, or come to work only when the mood strikes.

Beyond the basics, though, it is not always desirable for organizations to create strong situations for their employees for several reasons. First, the elements of situation strength are often determined by organization rules and guidelines, which adds some objectivity to them. However, the perception of these rules influences how the person will respond to the situation's strength. For instance, a person who is usually self-directed may view step-by-step instructions (high clarity) for a simple task as a lack of faith in his ability. Another person who is a rule-follower might appreciate the detailed instructions. Their responses (and work attitudes) will reflect their perception of and reaction to the situation.[117]

Second, jobs with myriad rules and tightly controlled processes can be dull or demotivating. Imagine that all work was executed with an assembly-line approach. Some people may prefer the routine, but many prefer having some variety and freedom. Third, strong situations might suppress the creativity, initiative, and discretion prized by some organizational cultures. One study, for example, found that in weak organizational situations, employees were more likely to behave proactively in accordance with their values.[118] Work is increasingly complex and interrelated globally. Creating strong rules to govern diverse systems might be not only difficult but also unwise. Fourth, situational strength is not an all-or-nothing characteristic—organizations can be strong in some areas and weak in others. For example, a workplace can have weak norms for how work should be done (low strength), but very strong norms against CWB (high strength).[119] In sum, managers need to recognize the role of situation strength in the workplace and find the appropriate balance.

Trait Activation Theory

trait activation theory (TAT) A theory that predicts that some situations, events, or interventions "activate" a trait more than others.

Another important theoretical framework toward understanding personality and situations is **trait activation theory (TAT)**. TAT predicts that some situations, events, or interventions "activate" a trait more than others. Using TAT, we can foresee which jobs suit certain personalities. For example, a commission-based compensation plan would likely activate individual differences because extraverts are more reward-sensitive, than, say, open people. Conversely, in jobs that encourage creativity, differences in openness may better predict desired behavior than differences in extraversion. See Exhibit 4-4 for specific examples.

TAT also applies to personality tendencies. For example, a recent study found that people learning online responded differently when their behavior was being electronically monitored. Those who had a high fear of failure had higher apprehension from the monitoring than others and learned significantly less. In this case, a feature of the environment (electronic monitoring) activated a trait (fear of failing), and the combination of the two meant lowered job performance.[120] TAT can also work in a positive way. One study found that, in a supportive environment, everyone behaved prosocially, but in a harsh environment, only people with prosocial tendencies exhibited them.[121]

Exhibit 4-4 Trait Activation Theory: Jobs in Which Certain Big Five Traits Are More Relevant

Detail Orientation Required	Social Skills Required	Competitive Work	Innovation Required	Dealing with Angry People	Time Pressure (Deadlines)
Jobs scoring high (the traits listed here should predict behavior in these jobs)					
Air traffic controller	Clergy	Coach/scout	Actor	Correctional officer	Broadcast news analyst
Accountant	Therapist	Financial manager	Systems analyst	Telemarketer	Editor
Legal secretary	Concierge	Sales representative	Advertising writer	Flight attendant	Airline pilot
Jobs scoring low (the traits listed here should not predict behavior in these jobs)					
Forester	Software engineer	Postal clerk	Court reporter	Composer	Skincare specialist
Masseuse	Pump operator	Historian	Archivist	Biologist	Mathematician
Model	Broadcast technician	Nuclear reactor operator	Medical technician	Statistician	Fitness trainer
Jobs that score high activate these traits (make them more relevant to predicting behavior)					
Conscientiousness (+)	Extraversion (+) Agreeableness (+)	Extraversion (+) Agreeableness (–)	Openness (+)	Extraversion (+) Agreeableness (+) Neuroticism (–)	Conscientiousness (+) Neuroticism (–)

Note: A plus (+) sign means that individuals who score high on this trait should do better in this job. A minus (–) sign means that individuals who score low on this trait should do better in this job.

Together, situation strength and trait activation theories show that the debate over nature versus nurture might best be framed as nature *and* nurture. Not only does each affect behavior, but they interact with one another. Put another way, personality and the situation both affect work behavior, but when the situation is right, the power of personality to predict behavior is even higher.[122]

Having discussed personality traits, we now turn to values. Values are often very specific and describe belief systems rather than behavioral tendencies. Some beliefs or values reflect a person's personality, but we don't always act consistently with our values.

Values

4-7 Contrast terminal and instrumental values.

values Basic convictions that a specific mode of conduct or end-state of existence is personally or socially preferable to an opposite or converse mode of conduct or end-state of existence.

value system A hierarchy based on a ranking of an individual's values in terms of their intensity.

Is capital punishment right or wrong? Is a desire for power good or bad? The answers to these questions are value-laden.

Values represent basic convictions that "a specific mode of conduct or end-state of existence is personally or socially preferable to an opposite or converse mode of conduct or end-state of existence."[123] Values contain a judgmental element because they carry an individual's ideas about what is right, good, or desirable. They have both content and intensity attributes. The content attribute says a mode of conduct or end-state of existence is *important*. The intensity attribute specifies *how important* it is. When we rank values in terms of intensity, we obtain that person's **value system**. We all have a hierarchy of values according to the relative importance we assign to values such as freedom, pleasure, self-respect, honesty, obedience, and equality.

Values tend to be relatively stable and enduring.[124] Many of the values we hold are established in our early years—by parents, teachers, friends, and others. If we question our values, they may change, but more often they are reinforced. There is also evidence linking personality to values, implying our values may be partly determined by genetically transmitted traits.[125] Open people, for example, may be more politically liberal, whereas conscientious people may place a greater value on safe and ethical conduct. To explore the topic further, we will discuss the importance and organization of values first.

The Importance and Organization of Values

Values lay the foundation for understanding attitudes and motivation, and they influence our perceptions. We enter an organization with preconceived notions of what "ought" and "ought not" to be. These notions contain our interpretations of right and wrong and our preferences for certain behaviors or outcomes. Regardless of whether they clarify or bias our judgment, our values influence our attitudes and behaviors at work.

While values can sometimes augment decision making, at times they can cloud objectivity and rationality.[126] Suppose you enter an organization with the view that allocating pay based on performance is right, while allocating pay based on seniority is wrong. How will you react if you find the organization you've just joined rewards seniority and not performance? You're likely to be disappointed—this can lead to job dissatisfaction and a decision not to exert a high level of effort because "It's probably not going to lead to more money anyway." Would your attitudes and behavior be different if your values aligned with the organization's pay policies? Most likely.

Terminal versus Instrumental Values

terminal values Desirable end-states of existence; the goals a person would like to achieve during their lifetime.

instrumental values Preferable modes of behavior or means of achieving one's terminal values.

How can we organize values? One researcher—Milton Rokeach—argued that we can separate them into two categories.[127] One set, called **terminal values**, refers to desirable end-states. These are the goals a person would like to achieve during a lifetime. The other set, called **instrumental values**, refers to preferable modes of behavior, or means of achieving the terminal values. Some examples of terminal values are prosperity and economic success, freedom, health and well-being, world peace, and meaning in life. Examples of instrumental values are autonomy and self-reliance, personal discipline, kindness, and goal-orientation. Each of us places value on both the ends (terminal values) and the means (instrumental values). A balance between the two is important, as is an understanding of how to strike this balance.

Generational Values

Researchers have integrated several analyses of work values into groups that attempt to capture the shared views of different cohorts or generations in the U.S. workforce.[128] You will surely be familiar with the labels, some of which are used internationally. It is important to remember that, while categories are helpful, they represent trends, not the beliefs of individuals.

Exhibit 4-5 segments employees by the era during which they entered the workforce. Because most people start work between the ages of 18 and 23, the eras also correlate closely with employee age.

Though it is fascinating to think about generational values, remember these classifications lack solid research support. Early research was plagued by methodological problems that made it difficult to assess whether differences actually exist. Reviews suggest many of the generalizations are either overblown or incorrect.[129] Differences across generations often do not support popular conceptions of how generations differ. For example, the value placed on leisure

Exhibit 4-5 Dominant Work Values in Today's Workforce

Cohort	Entered the Workforce	Approximate Current Age	Dominant Work Values
Boomers	1965–1985	50s to 70s	Success, achievement, ambition, dislike of authority; loyalty to career
Xers	1985–2000	Mid-30s to 50s	Work-life balance, team-oriented, dislike of rules; loyalty to relationships
Millennials	2000 to present	To mid-30s	Confident, financial success, self-reliant but team-oriented; loyalty to both self and relationships

has increased over generations from the baby boomers to the millennials and work centrality has declined, but research did not find that millennials had more altruistic work values.[130] Generational classifications may help us understand our own and other generations better, but we must also appreciate their limits.

An Ethical Choice

Do You Have a Cheating Personality?

Stories of widespread cheating have been on the rise, leading many experts to conclude that the incidence of cheating is increasing. In 2012, a major cheating scandal was uncovered at Harvard University, where more than 125 students were found to be involved in an organized cheating scheme.

Like most complex behaviors, cheating in school, at work, and in life is a product of the person and the situation. As for the person, research reveals certain traits are related to the tendency to cheat, including high levels of narcissism, low levels of conscientiousness and agreeableness, and high levels of competitiveness.

As for the situation, cheating increases when it is easier to cheat (such as on take-home exams), when there is greater pressure to cheat, and when clear standards are lacking or are not reinforced (such as when an organization's sexual harassment policy is not communicated to employees).

How can this research help inform you as a student and employee?

1. **Recognize situations that are more likely to provoke pressures to cheat.** Being explicit and open with yourself about your response to pressure should keep you from succumbing to a moral blind spot, in which you engage in behavior without considering its ethical undertones. Remember that technological advancements in the detection of cheating increase the probability of getting caught.
2. **If you score high on certain traits that predispose you to cheat, this does not mean you are destined to cheat.** However, you should realize that you may be more susceptible and therefore need to avoid certain environments, especially unethical ones.

Sources: Based on M. J. Cooper and C. Pullig, "I'm Number One! Does Narcissism Impair Ethical Judgment Even for the Highly Religious?" *Journal of Business Ethics* 112 (2013): 167–76; H. E. Hershfield, T. R. Cohen, and L. Thompson, "Short Horizons and Tempting Situations: Lack of Continuity to Our Future Selves Leads to Unethical Decision Making and Behavior," *Organizational Behavior and Human Decision Processes* 117 (2012): 298–310; C. H. Hsiao, "Impact of Ethical and Affective Variables on Cheating: Comparison of Undergraduate Students with and without Jobs," *Higher Education* 69, no. 1 (2015): 55–77; M. Carmichael, "Secret E-mail Searches on Harvard Cheating Scandal Broader Than Initially Described," *Boston Globe* (April 2, 2013), www.boston.com/metrodesk/2013/04/02/secret-mail-searches-harvard-cheating-scandal-broader-than-initially-described/Mgz0mc8hSk3lgW GjxLwsJP/story.html; P. E. Mudrack, J. M. Bloodgood, and W. H. Turnley, "Some Ethical Implications of Individual Competitiveness," *Journal of Business Ethics* 108 (2012): 347–59; and R. Pérez-Peña, "Studies Find More Students Cheating, with High Achievers No Exception," *The New York Times*, September 8, 2012, A13.

Cultural Values

4-8 Compare Hofstede's five value dimensions and the GLOBE framework.

Unlike personality, which is largely genetically determined, values are learned. They are passed down through generations and vary by cultures. As researchers have sought to understand cultural value differences, two important frameworks that have emerged are from Geert Hofstede and the GLOBE studies.

Hofstede's Framework

One of the most widely referenced approaches for analyzing variations among cultures was done in the late 1970s by Geert Hofstede.[131] Hofstede surveyed more than 116,000 IBM employees in 40 countries about their work-related values and found that managers and employees varied on five value dimensions of national culture:

power distance A national culture attribute that describes the extent to which a society accepts that power in institutions and organizations is distributed unequally.

individualism A national culture attribute that describes the degree to which people prefer to act as individuals rather than as members of groups.

collectivism A national culture attribute that describes a tight social framework in which people expect others in groups of which they are a part to look after them and protect them.

masculinity A national culture attribute that describes the extent to which the culture favors traditional masculine work roles of achievement, power, and control. Societal values are characterized by assertiveness and materialism.

femininity A national culture attribute that indicates little differentiation between male and female roles; a high rating indicates that women are treated as the equals of men in all aspects of the society.

uncertainty avoidance A national culture attribute that describes the extent to which a society feels threatened by uncertain and ambiguous situations and tries to avoid them.

- *Power distance.* **Power distance** describes the degree to which people in a country accept that power in institutions and organizations is distributed unequally. A high rating on power distance means large inequalities of power and wealth exist and are tolerated in the culture, as in a class or caste system that discourages upward mobility. A low power distance rating characterizes societies that stress equality and opportunity.
- *Individualism versus collectivism.* **Individualism** is the degree to which people prefer to act as individuals rather than as members of groups and believe in an individual's rights above all else. **Collectivism** emphasizes a tight social framework in which people expect others in groups of which they are a part to look after them and protect them.
- *Masculinity versus femininity.* Hofstede's construct of **masculinity** is the degree to which the culture favors traditional masculine roles such as achievement, power, and control, as opposed to viewing men and women as equals. A high masculinity rating indicates the culture has separate roles for men and women, with men dominating the society. A high **femininity** rating means the culture sees little differentiation between male and female roles and treats women as the equals of men in all respects.
- *Uncertainty avoidance.* The degree to which people in a country prefer structured over unstructured situations defines their **uncertainty avoidance**. In cultures scoring high on uncertainty avoidance, people have increased anxiety about uncertainty and ambiguity and use laws and controls to reduce uncertainty. People in cultures low on uncertainty avoidance are more accepting of ambiguity, are less rule oriented, take more risks, and accept change more readily.
- *Long-term versus short-term orientation.* This typology measures a society's devotion to traditional values. People in a culture with **long-term orientation** look to the future and value thrift, persistence, and tradition. In a **short-term orientation**, people value the here and now; they also accept change more readily and don't see commitments as impediments to change.

long-term orientation A national culture attribute that emphasizes the future, thrift, and persistence.

short-term orientation A national culture attribute that emphasizes the present and accepts change.

In recent years, Hofstede has proposed an additional dimension, *indulgence versus restraint*, which refers to a national culture attribute that emphasizes enjoying life and having fun vs. regulating conduct through strict social norms.[132] Although fairly new as a dimension, some research supports its distinction from other values and shows that it is correlated with a society's level of prosociality (behavior showing the intent to benefit others or society in general).[133]

How do different countries score on Hofstede's dimensions? Power distance is higher in Malaysia than in any other country. The United States is very individualistic; in fact, it's the most individualistic nation of all (closely followed by Australia and Great Britain). Guatemala is the most collectivistic nation. The country with the highest masculinity rank by far is Japan, and the country with the highest femininity rank is Sweden. Greece scores the highest in uncertainty avoidance, while Singapore scores the lowest. Hong Kong has one of the longest-term orientations; Pakistan has the shortest-term orientation.

Research across 598 studies with more than 200,000 respondents has investigated the relationship of Hofstede's cultural values and a variety of organizational criteria at both the individual and national level of analysis.[134] Overall, the five original culture dimensions were found to be equally strong predictors of relevant outcomes. The researchers also found measuring individual scores resulted in much better predictions of most outcomes than assigning all people in a country the same cultural values. In sum, this research suggests Hofstede's framework may be a valuable way of thinking about differences among people, but we should be cautious about assuming all people from a country have the same values.

The GLOBE Framework

Begun in 1993, the Global Leadership and Organizational Behavior Effectiveness (GLOBE) research program is an ongoing cross-cultural investigation of leadership and national culture. Using data from 825 organizations in 62 countries, the GLOBE team identified nine dimensions on which national cultures differ.[135] Some dimensions—such as power distance, individualism/collectivism, uncertainty avoidance, gender

According to Hofstede's framework, many Asian countries have a strong collectivist culture that fosters a team-based approach to work. These employees in a department store outlet in Busan, South Korea, are likely to consider the success of their team as more important than personal success on the job.
Source: Yonhap News/YNA/Newscom

differentiation (like masculinity versus femininity), and future orientation (like long-term versus short-term orientation)—resemble the Hofstede dimensions. The main difference is that the GLOBE framework added dimensions, such as humane orientation (the degree to which a society rewards individuals for being altruistic, generous, and kind to others) and performance orientation (the degree to which a society encourages and rewards group members for performance improvement and excellence). In Exhibit 4-6, the linkages between dimensions from the GLOBE framework and Hofstede's dimensions are outlined. As can be seen in the exhibit, the GLOBE framework also differentiated between these dimensions as they relate to practices (what is currently done) and values (what the society idealizes and aspires toward).

Comparison of Hofstede's Framework and the GLOBE Framework

Both frameworks have a great deal in common and often lead to similar conclusions. For example, a review of the organizational commitment literature shows both the Hofstede and GLOBE individualism/collectivism dimensions operated similarly. Specifically, both frameworks showed organizational commitment tends to be lower in individualistic countries.[136] However, the GLOBE study (or framework) expands upon the Hofstede framework in a number of ways, methodologically and theoretically. For example, as can be seen in Exhibit 4-6, various aspects of the values are disentangled into narrower dimensions.

Exhibit 4-6 Comparison of Hofstede's Dimensions and the GLOBE Framework

Hofstede's Dimensions	GLOBE
Power Distance: Extent to which a society accepts an unequal distribution of power.	**Power Distance:** Extent to which a society accepts an unequal distribution of power.
Uncertainty Avoidance: Extent to which a society feels threatened by and avoids ambiguity.	**Uncertainty Avoidance:** Extent to which a society seeks orderliness, structure, and laws to avoid ambiguity.
Long-Term Orientation: Extent to which a society emphasizes the future and persistence (vs. the present and change).	**Future Orientation:** Extent to which a society believes their actions can influence the future.
Collectivism: Extent to which a society emphasizes acting as a tight-knit collective (vs. as independent individuals).	**Institutional Collectivism:** Extent to which a society supports collective action and resource distribution. **In-Group Collectivism:** Extent to which a society values loyalty, pride, patriotism, and cohesion.
Masculinity: Extent to which a society favors traditional, masculine roles such as power and control (vs. little differentiation of gender roles).	**Gender Egalitarianism:** Extent to which a society de-emphasizes traditional gender roles. **Assertiveness:** Extent to which a society emphasizes confidence and advocating for what one wants.
	Humane Orientation: Extent to which a society values caring, friendliness, altruism, fairness, kindness, and generosity.
	Performance Orientation: Extent to which a society values producing results, excellence, and productivity.

Adapted from R. Hadwick, "Should I Use GLOBE or Hofstede? Some Insights That Can Assist Cross-Cultural Scholars, and Others, Choose the Right Study to Support Their Work," paper presented at *Australian & New Zealand Academy of Management*, Wellington, NZ (December 2011); R. J. House, P. J. Hanges, M. Javidan, P. W. Dorfman, and V. Gupta, *Culture, Leadership, and Organizations: The GLOBE Study of 62 Societies* (Thousand Oaks, CA, 2004); X. Shi and J. Wang, "Interpreting Hofstede Model and GLOBE Model: Which Way to Go for Cross-Cultural Research?" *International Journal of Business and Management* 6, no. 5 (2011): 93–99.

Summary

Personality matters to organizational behavior. It does not explain all behavior, but it sets the stage. Emerging theory and research reveal how personality matters more in some situations than others. The Big Five has been a particularly important advancement, though the Dark Triad and other traits matter as well. Every trait has advantages and disadvantages for work behavior, and there is no perfect constellation of traits that is ideal in every situation. Personality can help you to understand why people (including yourself!) act, think, and feel the way we do, and the astute manager can put that understanding to use by taking care to place employees in situations that best fit their personalities. An understanding of personality can also help you understand what strengths you may have (and should strive for) when searching for a job.

Values often underlie and explain attitudes, behaviors, and perceptions. Values tend to vary internationally along dimensions that can predict organizational outcomes; however, an individual may or may not hold values that are consistent with the values of the national culture.

Implications for Managers

- Consider applicants' and employees' fit to the job and organization in employment decisions. Their personalities, values, and other characteristics may be useful to understanding whether they will flourish in particular assignments, jobs, teams, or organizations.
- Consider screening job candidates for conscientiousness—and the other Big Five traits—depending on the criteria your organization finds most important. Other aspects, such as core self-evaluation or narcissism, may be relevant in certain situations.
- Although the MBTI has faults, you can use it in training and development to help employees better understand each other, open communication in work groups, and possibly reduce conflicts.
- Emphasize the ideal personality and values of your organization in your recruitment materials and practices. This may help attract people whose values and personality types match your organization/or job vacancies.
- Understand that situation strength and the context (e.g., trait activating features) can affect behavior. Take stock of the environmental features in your organization that may influence the behavior of applicants, customers, employees, and even leaders.
- An understanding of differences in cultural values can equip you to interact with others from cultures that are different from your own.

Millennials Are More Narcissistic Than Their Parents

POINT

Millennials have some great virtues: As a group, they are technologically savvy, socially tolerant, and engaged. They value their quality of life as equal to their career, seeking a balance between home and work. In these ways, millennials surpass their baby boomer parents, who are less technologically adept, less tolerant, and more localized, and who have a history of striving to get ahead at all costs. However, millennials have a big Achilles' heel—they are more narcissistic.

Several large-scale, longitudinal studies found that millennials are more likely than baby boomers to have seemingly inflated views of themselves, and psychologists have found narcissism has been growing since the early 1980s. More millennials rate themselves as above average on attributes such as academic ability, leadership, public speaking ability, and writing ability. Millennials are also more likely to agree they would be "very good" spouses (56 percent, compared to 37 percent among 1980 graduates), parents (54 percent; 36 percent for 1980 graduates), and workers (65 percent; 49 percent for 1980 graduates).

Cliff Zukin, a senior faculty fellow at Rutgers University, believes the reason is in the childhood upbringing of millennials. "This is the most affirmed generation in history," he said. "They were raised believing they could do anything they wanted to, and that they have skills and talents to bring to a job setting." Jean M. Twenge, author of *Generation Me*, agrees. "People were not saying, 'Believe in yourself' and 'You are special' in the '60s."

Narcissism is bad for society, and particularly bad for the workplace. "[Narcissists] tend to be very self-absorbed; they value fun in their personal and their work life," one administrator said. "I can't expect them to work on one project for any amount of time without getting bored."

COUNTERPOINT

Wasn't "The Me Generation" generations ago? Honestly, every generation thinks they are better than the ones that come after! "You can find complaints [about the younger generation] in Greek literature, in the Bible," Professor Cappelli of the Wharton School observed. "There's no evidence Millennials are different. They're just younger." While millennials are the twenty-somethings of today, what *is* universally true is that young people share certain characteristics ... *because* they are young.

A recent study shows the similarity between how millennials and baby boomers thought about themselves at the same stage of life. As college freshmen, 71 percent of millennials thought they were above average academically, and 63 percent of baby boomers thought the same thing when they were college freshmen. Similarly, 77 percent of millennials believed they were above average in the drive to achieve, versus 68 percent for baby boomers. In other words, "Every generation is Generation Me."

In some ways, millennials may be less narcissistic than baby boomers today. As one manager observed, "[Millennials] don't have that line between work and home that used to exist, so they're doing Facebook for the company at night, on Saturday or Sunday. We get incredible productivity out of them." Millennials also may be more altruistic. For example, 29 percent of millennials believe individuals have a responsibility to remain involved in issues and causes for the good of all, while only 24 percent of baby boomers feel the same level of responsibility.

Rather than comparing different generations, it is more accurate to compare people at one life stage with others at the same life stage. Research supports that people in their twenties tend to be more narcissistic than people in their fifties. Millennials are in their twenties, and many of their parents are in their fifties, and millennials are no more narcissistic than baby boomers were in their youth.

Sources: Based on J. M. Twenge, W. K. Campbell, and E. C. Freeman, "Generational Differences in Young Adults' Life Goals, Concern for Others, and Civic Orientation, 1966–2009," *Journal of Personality and Social Psychology* 102 (2012): 1045–62; M. Hartman, "Millennials at Work: Young and Callow, Like Their Parents," *The New York Times*, March 25, 2014, F4; J. Jin and J. Rounds, "Stability and Change in Work Values: A Meta-Analysis of Longitudinal Studies," *Journal of Vocational Behavior* 80 (2012): 326–39; C. Lourosa-Ricardo, "How America Gives," *The Wall Street Journal,* December 15, 2014, R3; "Millennials Rule," *The New York Times Education Life,* April 12, 2015, 4; G. Ruffenach, "A Generational Gap: Giving to Charity," *The Wall Street Journal,* January 20, 2015, R4; and S. W. Lester, R. L. Standifer, N. J. Schultz, and J. M. Windsor, "Actual versus Perceived Generational Differences at Work: An Empirical Examination," *Journal of Leadership & Organizational Studies* 19 (2012): 341–54.

CHAPTER REVIEW

QUESTIONS FOR REVIEW

4-1 What is personality? How do we typically measure it? What factors determine personality?

4-2 What are the strengths and weaknesses of the Myers-Briggs Type Indicator (MBTI) and the Big Five personality model?

4-3 How do the concepts of core self-evaluation (CSE), self-monitoring, and proactive personality help us to understand personality?

4-4 What are the strongest predictors of job search behavior?

4-5 How does the situation or environment affect the degree to which personality predicts behavior?

4-6 What is the difference between terminal and instrumental values?

4-7 What are the differences between person–job fit and person–organization fit?

4-8 How do Hofstede's five value dimensions and the GLOBE framework differ?

APPLICATION AND EMPLOYABILITY

An insight into your personality and values, along with how these are important in the workplace, can help you improve your employability skills. First, the workplace is a complex system filled with many interacting people. By understanding how these people have different values and behavioral tendencies, you will be better able to anticipate conflict and how to work among people with different personalities. Understanding that many organizations measure and assess personality is critical to knowing which elements of your personality to focus on developing to become more employable, depending on the position or work that you are interested in. Conversely, understanding how the situation either constrains or activates the expression of these behavioral traits or tendencies is also important for becoming more adaptable in the workplace. Understanding how people have values that vary in terms of their importance to organizations can help you make better decisions in deciding which companies you would like to work for and understanding how you fit with the culture in an organization you would like to work for. Cultures around the globe vary on the values that are important to them. Being aware of these different cultural values and spending time abroad can help you improve your cultural intelligence and interact more effectively with those of different cultural backgrounds.

In this chapter, you developed your critical thinking and knowledge application and analysis skills by finding out how to do well on personality tests, finding out how personalities can be accurately judged within seconds after meeting someone, gaining insight into whether you have a cheating personality (and what you can do about it), and debating whether millennials are more narcissistic as a generation. In the next section, you will develop these skills by exploring what values are most important to you and your classmates, questioning whether political ideology should be used in hiring, examining the pitfalls of being nice, and determining how to adapt to personality clashes at work.

EXPERIENTIAL EXERCISE Your Best Self

The object of this game is to end up with the labels that best represent each person's values. The following rows represent 11 rounds of play. Break the class into groups of four students (if the number of students is not divisible by four, then we suggest three). Play begins with the person in the group whose name comes first in alphabetical order. That student picks one of the values in round one that represents him- or herself, crosses it off this list, and writes it down on a piece of paper. Values can be used by only one person at a time. Moving clockwise, the next person does the same, and so forth, for round one until all the values have been taken.

For round two, the first player can either add a second value from the round two row, or take a value from one of the other players by adding it to his or her list while the other player crosses off the value. The player whose value has been taken selects two new values from the one and two rows. Play proceeds clockwise.

The rest of the rounds continue the same way, with a new row available for each round. At the end of the rounds, students rank the importance of the values they have accumulated to themselves.

1.	Freedom	Integrity	Spirituality	Respect
2.	Loyalty	Achievement	Fidelity	Exploration
3.	Affection	Challenge	Serenity	Justice
4.	Charity	Discipline	Security	Mastery
5.	Prudence	Diversity	Kindness	Duty
6.	Wisdom	Inspiration	Harmony	Joy
7.	Depth	Compassion	Excellence	Tolerance
8.	Honesty	Success	Growth	Modesty
9.	Courage	Dedication	Empathy	Openness
10.	Faith	Service	Playfulness	Learning
11.	Discovery	Independence	Humor	Understanding

Questions

4-9. What are your top three values? How well do they represent you? Did you feel pressure to choose values that might seem most socially acceptable?

4-10. Is there a value you would claim for yourself that is not on the list?

4-11. It is often argued that values are meaningful only when they conflict and we must choose between them. Do you think that was one of the objectives of this game? Do you agree with the premise of this argument for the game?

ETHICAL DILEMMA Personal Values and Ethics in the Workplace

Satish Jha was born in a small rural village in Bihar. He spent his childhood years working on his family's farm. He belonged community that highly regarded values such as honesty and respect, but the people of the community were desperately poor. Eventually, Satish had moved to Patna to find a job.

As a young man, Satish left his village and took on the challenging task of finding a job for himself in a the city. He took the help of a distant relative who worked at Patna Railway Station, and was able get the job of a helper at the railway canteen. Satish worked dedicatedly and showed a flair for cooking. Gradually, he rose to the level of assistant cook in the canteen.

One day a customer asked Satish if he would like to take the job of a cook and move to Dubai. As the customer assured him that he was friends with the senior cook at the canteen and was also in terms with Satish's distant relative. Satish confirmed the association with both and was showed interest in availing himself of the opportunity. A few days later, the customer returned with a bunch of papers and informed Satish that the latter had been offered the job of a cook in a restaurant in Dubai with a salary of ₹50,000 per month, and in this connection, Satish needed to sign the papers to apply for his passport and file the visa application too.

But the customer also mentioned Satish needed to pay the a charge of ₹20,000 for the efforts put in processing Satish's papers. Satish felt unsure and uncomfortable about the amount that was being charged. He told the customer that he would think about it. But the customer persuaded him to take a quick decision because opportunities as such do not wait. The customer also said that money was the charge for the combined efforts of his, the senior cook's and the distant relative put together. Confusion and despair made Satish take a loan to pay the money.

Later in the month, one evening as Satish was preparing to leave the canteen, he noticed the owner of the canteen being questioned by the police. After some time, the police arrested both the senior cook in the canteen and Satish's distant relative. Utterly disheartened and financially broke, Satish still furnished the bail for both of them who once vouched their association with the customer who cheated Satish. Both of the senior cook and the distant relative were sorry that they could not return the money to Satish because the customer had disappeared with the money.

Questions

4-12. What could Satish have done differently?

4-13. Could the canteen owner do something differently to curtail such behaviour in the future?

4-14. How would you have acted if you had been in a similar situation?

CASE INCIDENT 1 On the Costs of Being Nice

Agreeable people tend to be kinder and more accommodating in social situations, which you might think could add to their success in life. However, one downside of agreeableness is potentially lower earnings. Research has shown the answer to this and other puzzles; some of them may surprise you.

First, and perhaps most obvious, agreeable individuals are less adept at a type of negotiation called distributive bargaining. As we discuss in Chapter 18, distributive bargaining is less about creating win–win solutions and more about claiming as large a share of the pie as possible. Because salary negotiations are generally distributive, agreeable individuals often negotiate lower salaries for themselves than they might otherwise get.

Second, agreeable individuals may choose to work in industries or occupations that earn lower salaries, such as the "caring" industries of education and health care. Agreeable individuals are also attracted to jobs both in the public sector and in nonprofit organizations. Third, the earnings of agreeable individuals also may be reduced by their lower drive to emerge as leaders and by their tendency to engage in lower degrees of proactive task behaviors, such as thinking of ways to increase organizational effectiveness.

While being agreeable certainly doesn't appear to help your paycheck, it does provide other benefits. Agreeable individuals are better liked at work, more likely to help others at work, and generally happier at work and in life.

Nice guys and gals may finish last in terms of earnings, but wages do not define a happy life and, on that front, agreeable individuals have the advantage.

Questions

4-15. Do you think employers must choose between agreeable employees and top performers? Why or why not?

4-16. The effects of personality often depend on the situation. Can you think of some job situations in which agreeableness is an important virtue and some in which it is harmful to job performance?

4-17. In some research we've conducted, the negative effect of agreeableness on earnings has been stronger for men than for women (that is, being agreeable hurt men's earnings more than women's). Why do you think this might be the case?

Sources: Based on T. A. Judge, B. A. Livingston, and C. Hurst, "Do Nice Guys—and Gals—Really Finish Last? The Joint Effects of Sex and Agreeableness on Income," *Journal of Personality and Social Psychology* 102 (2012): 390–407; J. B. Bernerth, S. G. Taylor, H. J. Walker, and D. S. Whitman, "An Empirical Investigation of Dispositional Antecedents and Performance-Related Outcomes of Credit Scores," *Journal of Applied Psychology* 97 (2012): 469–78; J. Carpenter, D. Doverspike, and R. F. Miguel, "Public Service Motivation as a Predictor of Attraction to the Public Sector," *Journal of Vocational Behavior* 80 (2012): 509–23; and A. Neal, G. Yeo, A. Koy, and T. Xiao, "Predicting the Form and Direction of Work Role Performance from the Big 5 Model of Personality Traits," *Journal of Organizational Behavior* 33 (2012): 175–92.

CASE INCIDENT 2 Personality Matters!

Most employers rely heavily on screening resumes when shortlisting candidates for interviews. Employers look especially for a job fit based on the extent to which the experience, skills, and education featured in a resume match the requirements of an advertised job vacancy. A strong match greatly increases the chances that the candidate in question will be called for a job interview. However, for most top employers, technical skills are only one part of the hiring process; today, many companies want to ensure that the candidate hired for the job not only matches the skills and education required but also possesses the suitable personality for the job.

In an article titled "Hire for Attitude, Train for Skill," professional speaker and university lecturer Jackie Freiberg says that highly successful companies are those that primarily focus on finding employees with the right personality. Such companies have realized that skills can be trained and upgraded, but the personality of an employee is much more difficult to change; hence, top employers need to be sure that they have found the candidate with the right personal characteristics before they make the decision to hire. There are a number of methods that recruiters can use to assess employees' personality, from the more traditional one-on-one interview to more advanced methods such as personality tests. In one-on-one interviews, recruiters may ask questions about a candidate's previous job to develop an understanding of the job applicant's character in relation to their confidence, optimism, independence, honesty, etc. In a behavioral interview, the interviewer asks employees about how they had acted or behaved in a specific job situation in a past job, such as the way they handled an angry customer. The answers may unintentionally reveal information about their attitudes and personality; anger, arrogance, and negligence may all be put on display by the candidates in the course of their narratives.

Recognizing that interviews alone may not be enough to assess personality, many companies have been using formal personality tests in combination with interviews to improve their hiring decisions. In a global study involving 1,406 HR professionals from companies around the world, 62 percent of respondents confirmed the use of personality assessments in hiring candidates. And there are numerous personality tests that recruiters can choose and buy off the market, such as the popular Caliper Profile test, used by the thousands of companies around the world.

Despite the popularity of personality tests in recruitment, experts say that they are not without problems. According to research by Frank L. Schmidt, a management and organizations professor emeritus at the University of Iowa, personality tests are actually poor at predicting job performance. His own findings have demonstrated that personality tests work best when combined with other types of selection tests, such as cognitive ability or integrity tests, which have better predictive validity. The main reason that the results of personality tests should be taken with a grain of salt is the simple fact that candidates can lie and fake their answers. Personality tests can also fail because the design of some of the tests may be too crude and simplistic to measure employees' personality or may not have been even intended to be used in hiring to begin with. Experts therefore recommend that personality tests be used not to make a decision but only to inform decision-making.

Questions

4-18. Think of the last person that you closely worked with, either at work or on a personal project. Would you describe that person as someone who typically displays extroverted or introverted behavior? What kind of jobs do you think fits them best, and why?

4-19. Based on what you have read in the chapter about the Myers and Briggs Indicator test, do you believe that companies should rely on it to hire employees?

4-20. Do you think that the personality of a job seeker affects job search outcomes? How so?

Sources: J. Freiberg, "Hire for Attitude, Train for Skill," *Executive Excellence,* 15, no. 6 (1998): 7; Katie Jacobs, "Is Psychometric Testing Still Fit for Purpose?", *People Management,* February 22, 2018, www.peoplemanagement.co.uk/long-reads/articles/psychometric-testing-fit-purpose, accessed June 1, 2020; W. Martin, "The Problem with Using Personality Tests for Hiring," *Harvard Business Review Digital Articles* (August 27, 2014): 2–5, hbr.org/2014/08/the-problem-with-using-personality-tests-for-hiring, accessed June 1, 2020; Dori Meinert, "What Do Personality Tests Really Reveal?," *SHRM,* June 1, 2015, www.shrm.org/hr-today/news/hr-magazine/pages/0615-personality-tests.aspx, accessed June 1, 2020; W. Mondy, *Human Resource Management,* 11th edition (Boston: Pearson, 2010); Tracy M. Kantrowitz, PhD, "Global Assessment Trends 2014," www.cebglobal.com/content/dam/cebglobal/us/EN/regions/uk/tm/pdfs/Report/gatr-2014.pdf, accessed May 29, 2020.

ENDNOTES

[1]J. L. Holland, *Making Vocational Choices: A Theory of Careers*, 2nd ed. (Englewood Cliffs, NJ: Prentice-Hall, 1985); A. L. Kristof-Brown, R. D. Zimmerman, and E. C. Johnson, "Consequences of Individuals' Fit at Work: A Meta-Analysis of Person-Job, Person-Organization, Person-Group, and Person-Supervisor Fit," *Personnel Psychology* 58 (2005): 281–342; and C. Ostroff, "Person-Environment Fit in Organizational Settings," in S. W. J. Kozlowski (ed.), *The Oxford Handbook of Organizational Psychology*, Vol. 1 (Oxford, UK: Oxford University Press, 2012): 373–408.

[2]M. Rokeach, *The Nature of Human Values* (New York: The Free Press, 1973).

[3]See, for example, N. R. Lockwood, F. R. Cepero, and S. Williams, *The Multigenerational Workforce* (Alexandria, VA: Society for Human Resource Management, 2009).

[4]E. Parry and P. Urwin, "Generational Differences in Work Values: A Review of Theory and Evidence," *International Journal of Management Reviews* 13, no. 1 (2011): 79–96.

[5]J. M. Twenge, S. M. Campbell, B. J. Hoffman, and C. E. Lance, "Generational Differences in Work Values: Leisure and Extrinsic Values Increasing, Social and Intrinsic Values Decreasing," *Journal of Management* 36, no. 5 (2010): 1117–42.

[6]Y. Lee and J. Antonakis, "When Preference Is Not Satisfied but the Individual Is: How Power Distance Moderates Person-Job Fit," *Journal of Management* 40, no. 3 (2014): 641–57.

[7]See W. Arthur Jr., S. T. Bell, A. J. Villado, and D. Doverspike, "The Use of Person-Organization Fit in Employment Decision-Making: An Assessment of Its Criterion-Related Validity," *Journal of Applied Psychology* 91, no. 4 (2006): 786–801; and J. R. Edwards, D. M. Cable, I. O. Williamson, L. S. Lambert, and A. J. Shipp, "The Phenomenology of Fit: Linking the Person and Environment to the Subjective Experience of Person–Environment Fit," *Journal of Applied Psychology* 91, no. 4 (2006): 802–27.

[8]A. Leung and S. Chaturvedi, "Linking the Fits, Fitting the Links: Connecting Different Types of PO Fit to Attitudinal Outcomes," *Journal of Vocational Behavior*, October 2011, 391–402.

[9]D. Leising, J. Scharloth, O. Lohse, and D. Wood, "What Types of Terms Do People Use When Describing an Individual's Personality?" *Psychological Science* 25, no. 9 (2014): 1787–94.

[10]Central Tests (May 29, 2019). "Demystifying the use of psychometric assessments for school staff in India". Retrieved from https://www.centraltest.com (Accessed on April 15, 2022).

[11]M. R. Barrick, M. K. Mount, and T. A. Judge, "Personality and Performance at the Beginning of the New Millennium: What Do We Know and Where Do We Go Next?" *International Journal of Selection and Assessment* 9, nos. 1–2 (2001): 9–30; and P. R. Sackett and P. T. Walmsley, "Which Personality Attributes Are Most Important in the Workplace?" *Perspectives on Psychological Science* 9, no. 5 (2014): 538–51.

[12]S. A. Birkeland, T. M. Manson, J. L. Kisamore, M. T. Brannick, and M. A. Smith, "A Meta-Analytic Investigation of Job Applicant Faking on Personality Measures," *International Journal of Selection and Assessment* 14, no. 14 (2006): 317–35.

[13]S. A. Golder and M. W. Macy, "Diurnal and Seasonal Mood Vary with Work, Sleep, and Day Length across Diverse Cultures," *Science* 333 (2011): 1878–81; and R. E. Wilson, R. J. Thompson, and S. Vazire, "Are Fluctuations in Personality States More Than Fluctuations in Affect?" *Journal of Research in Personality* (in press), http://dx.doi.org/10.1016/j.jrp.2016.06.006.

[14]K. L. Cullen, W. A. Gentry, and F. J. Yammamarino, "Biased Self-Perception Tendencies: Self-Enhancement/Self-Diminishment and Leader Derailment in Individualistic and Collectivistic Cultures," *Applied Psychology: An International Review* 64, no. 1 (2015): 161–207.

[15]D. H. Kluemper, B. D. McLarty, and M. N. Bing, "Acquaintance Ratings of the Big Five Personality Traits: Incremental Validity beyond and Interactive Effects with Self-Reports in the Prediction of Workplace Deviance," *Journal of Applied Psychology* 100, no. 1 (2015): 237–48; and I. Oh, G. Wang, and M. K. Mount, "Validity of Observer Ratings of the Five-Factor Model of Personality Traits: A Meta-Analysis," *Journal of Applied Psychology* 96, no. 4 (2011): 762–73.

[16]T. Vukasović and D. Bratko, "Heritability of Personality: A Meta-Analysis of Behavior Genetic Studies," *Psychological Bulletin* 141, no. 4 (2015): 769–85.

[17]S. Srivastava, O. P. John, and S. D. Gosling, "Development of Personality in Early and Middle Adulthood: Set Like Plaster or Persistent Change?" *Journal of Personality and Social Psychology* 84, no. 5 (2003): 1041–53; and B. W. Roberts, K. E. Walton, and W. Viechtbauer, "Patterns of Mean-Level Change in Personality Traits across the Life Course: A Meta-Analysis of Longitudinal Studies," *Psychological Bulletin* 132, no. 1 (2006): 1–25.

[18]S. E. Hampson and L. R. Goldberg, "A First Large Cohort Study of Personality Trait Stability over the 40 Years between Elementary School and Midlife," *Journal of Personality and Social Psychology* 91, no. 4 (2006): 763–79.

[19]L. R. James and M. D. Mazerolle, *Personality in Work Organizations* (Thousand Oaks, CA: Sage, 2002); and D. P. McAdams and B. D. Olson, "Personality Development: Continuity and Change Over the Life Course," *Annual Review of Psychology* 61 (2010): 517–42.

[20]CPP, "Myers-Briggs Type Indicator (MBTI)," https://www.cpp.com/products/mbti/index .aspx, accessed March 22, 2017.

[21]The Myers & Briggs Foundation, "How Frequent Is My Type?," http://www.myersbriggs.org/my-mbti-personality-type/my-mbti-results /how-frequent-is-my-type.asp, accessed April 24, 2015.

[22]A. Grant, "Goodbye to MBTI, the Fad That Won't Die," *Huffington Post*, (September 17, 2013), http://www.huffingtonpost.com/adam-grant/goodbye-to-mbti-the-fad-t_b_3947014.html.

[23]See, for instance, D. J. Pittenger, "Cautionary Comments Regarding the Myers-Briggs Type Indicator," *Consulting Psychology Journal: Practice and Research* 57, no. 3 (2005): 10–221; L. Bess and R. J. Harvey, "Bimodal Score Distributions and the Myers-Briggs Type Indicator: Fact or Artifact?" *Journal of Personality Assessment* 78, no. 1 (2002): 176–86; R. M. Capraro and M. M. Capraro, "Myers-Briggs Type Indicator Score Reliability across Studies: A Meta-Analytic Reliability Generalization Study," *Educational & Psychological Measurement* 62, no. 4 (2002): 590–602;

and R. C. Arnau, B. A. Green, D. H. Rosen, D. H. Gleaves, and J. G. Melancon, "Are Jungian Preferences Really Categorical? An Empirical Investigation Using Taxometric Analysis," *Personality & Individual Differences* 34, no. 2 (2003): 233–51.

[24]D. Ariely, "When Lame Pick-Up Lines Actually Work," *The Wall Street Journal*, July 19–20, 2014, C12.

[25]See, for example, O. P. John, L. P. Naumann, and C. J. Soto, "Paradigm Shift to the Integrative Big Five Trait Taxonomy: History, Measurement, and Conceptual Issues," in O. P. John, R. W. Robins, and L. A. Pervin (eds.), *Handbook of Personality: Theory and Research*, 3rd ed. (New York, NY: Guilford, 2008): 114–58; and M. R. Barrick and M. K. Mount, "Yes, Personality Matters: Moving On to More Important Matters," *Human Performance* 18, no. 4 (2005): 359–72.

[26]W. Fleeson and P. Gallagher, "The Implications of Big Five Standing for the Distribution of Trait Manifestation in Behavior: Fifteen Experience-Sampling Studies and a Meta-Analysis," *Journal of Personality and Social Psychology* 97, no. 6 (2009): 1097–114.

[27]T. A. Judge, L. S. Simon, C. Hurst, and K. Kelley, "What I Experienced Yesterday Is Who I Am Today: Relationship of Work Motivations and Behaviors to Within-Individual Variation in the Five-Factor Model of Personality," *Journal of Applied Psychology* 99, no. 2 (2014): 199–221; Roberts, Walton, and Viechtbauer, "Patterns of Mean-Level Change in Personality Traits across the Life Course."

[28]See, for instance, Barrick, Mount, and Judge, "Personality and Performance at the Beginning of the new Millennium."

[29]P. R. Sackett and P. T. Walmsley, "Which Personality Attributes Are Most Important in the Workplace?," *Perspectives on Psychological Science* 9, no. 5 (2014): 538–51.

[30]A. E. Poropat, "A Meta-Analysis of the Five-Factor Model of Personality and Academic Performance," *Psychological Bulletin* 135, no. 2 (2009): 322–38.

[31]M. R. Barrick and M. K. Mount, "The Big Five Personality Dimensions and job Performance: A Meta-Analysis," *Personnel Psychology* 44 (1991): 1–26.

[32]A. K. Nandkeolyar, J. A. Shaffer, A. Li, S. Ekkirala, and J. Bagger, "Surviving an Abusive Supervisor: The Joint Roles of Conscientiousness and Coping Strategies," *Journal of Applied Psychology* 99, no. 1 (2014): 138–50.

[33]D. S. Chiaburu, I.-S. Oh, C. M. Berry, N. Li, and R. G. Gardner, "The Five-Factor Model of Personality Traits and Organizational Citizenship Behaviors: A Meta-Analysis," *Journal of Applied Psychology* 96, no. 6 (2011): 1140–66; J. L. Huang, K. L. Zabel, A. M. Ryan, and A. Palmer, "Personality and Adaptive Performance at Work: A Meta-Analytic Investigation," *Journal of Applied Psychology* 99, no. 1 (2014): 162–79; Kluemper, McLarty, and Bing, "Acquaintance Ratings of the Big Five Personality Traits"; and R. D. Zimmerman, "Understanding the Impact of Personality Traits on Individuals' Turnover Intentions: A Meta-Analytic Path Model," *Personnel Psychology* 61 (2008): 309–48.

[34]J. M. Beus, L. Y. Dhanani, and M. A. McCord, "A Meta-Analysis of Personality and Workplace Safety: Addressing Unanswered Questions," *Journal of Applied Psychology* 100, no. 2 (2015): 481–98.

[35]S. N. Kaplan, M. M. Klebanov, and M. Sorensen, "Which CEO Characteristics and Abilities Matter?" *The Journal of Finance* 67, no. 3 (2012): 973–1007.

[36]N. T. Carter, D. K. Dalal, A. S. Boyce, M. S. O'Connell, M.-C. Kung, and K. Delgado, "Uncovering Curvilinear Relationships between Conscientiousness and Job Performance: How Theoretically Appropriate Measurement Makes and Empirical Difference," *Journal of Applied Psychology* 99, no. 4 (2014): 564–86; and N. T. Carter, L. Guan, J. L. Maples, R. L. Williamson, and J. D. Miller, "The Downsides of Extreme Conscientiousness for Psychological Well-Being: The Role of Obsessive Compulsive Tendencies," *Journal of Personality* 84, no. 4 (2016): 510–22.

[37]M. K. Shoss, K. Callison, and L. A. Witt, "The Effects of Other-Oriented Perfectionism and Conscientiousness on Helping at Work," *Applied Psychology: An International Review* 64, no. 1 (2015): 233–51.

[38]C. Robert and Y. H. Cheung, "An Examination of the Relationship between Conscientiousness and Group Performance on a Creative Task," *Journal of Research in Personality* 44, no. 2 (2010): 222–31; and M. Batey, T. Chamorro-Premuzic, and A. Furnham, "Individual Differences in Ideational Behavior: Can the Big Five and Psychometric Intelligence Predict Creativity Scores?" *Creativity Research Journal* 22, no. 1 (2010): 90–97.

[39]K. M. DeNeve and H. Cooper, "The Happy Personality: A Meta-Analysis of 137 Personality Traits and Subjective Well-Being," *Psychological Bulletin* 124, no. 2 (1998): 197–229; T. A. Judge, D. Heller, and M. K. Mount, "Five-Factor Model of Personality and Job Satisfaction: A Meta-Analysis," *Journal of Applied Psychology* 87, no. 3 (2002): 530–41; B. W. Swider and R. D. Zimmerman, "Born to Burnout: A Meta-Analytic Path Model of Personality, Job Burnout, and Work Outcomes," *Journal of Vocational Behavior* 76 (2010): 487–506; and Zimmerman, "Understanding the Impact of Personality Traits on Individuals' Turnover Intentions."

[40]Huang, Ryan, Zabel, and Palmer, "Personality and Adaptive Performance at Work."

[41]Swider and Zimmerman, "Born to Burnout."

[42]T. D. Allen, R. C. Johnson, K. N. Saboe, E. Cho, S. Dumani, and S. Evans, "Dispositional Variables and Work-Family Conflict: A Meta-Analysis," *Journal of Vocational Behavior* 80 (2012): 17–26.

[43]Chiaburu, Oh, Berry, Li, and Gardner, "The Five-Factor Model of Personality Traits and Organizational Citizenship Behaviors"; T. A. Judge and R. Ilies, "Relationship of Personality to Performance Motivation: A Meta-Analytic Review," *Journal of Applied Psychology* 87, no. 4 (2002): 797–807; and Kluemper, McLarty, and Bing, "Acquaintance Ratings of the Big Five Personality Traits."

[44]R. J. Foti and M. A. Hauenstein, "Pattern and Variable Approaches in Leadership Emergence and Effectiveness," *Journal of Applied Psychology* 92, no. 2 (2007): 347–55.

[45]D. S. DeRue, J. D. Nahrgang, N. Wellman, and S. E. Humphrey, "Trait and Behavioral Theories of Leadership: An Integration and Meta-Analytic Test of Their Relative Validity," *Personnel Psychology* 64 (2011): 7–52; and T. A. Judge, J. E. Bono, R. Ilies, and M. W. Gerhardt, "Personality and Leadership: A Qualitative and Quantitative Review," *Journal of Applied Psychology* 87, no. 4 (2002): 765–80.

[46]Judge, Heller, and Mount, "Five-Factor Model of Personality and Job Satisfaction"; and Swider and R. Zimmerman, "Born to Burnout."

[47]M. A. McCord, D. L. Joseph, and E. Grijalva, "Blinded by the Light: The Dark Side of Traditionally Desirable Personality Traits," *Industrial and Organizational Psychology: Perspectives on Science and Practice* 7, no. 1 (2014): 130–7.

[48]M. M. Hammond, N. L. Neff, J. L. Farr, A. R. Schwall, and X. Zhao, "Predictors of Individual-Level Innovation at Work: A Meta-Analysis," *Psychology of Aesthetics, Creativity, and the Arts* 5, no. 1 (2011): 90–105.

[49]Huang, Ryan, Zabel, and Palmer, "Personality and Adaptive Performance at Work"; and Judge, Bono, Ilies, and Gerhardt, "Personality and Leadership."

[50]Barrick and Mount, "The Big Five Personality Dimensions and Job Performance"; and A. Minbashian, J. Earl, and J. E. H. Bright, "Openness to Experience as a Predictor of Job Performance Trajectories," *Applied Psychology: An International Review* 62, no. 1 (2013): 1–12.

[51]Allen, Johnson, Saboe, Cho, Dumani, and Evans, "Dispositional Variables and Work-Family Conflict."

[52]Allen, Johnson, Saboe, Cho, Dumani, and Evans, "Dispositional Variables and Work-Family Conflict"; and Zimmerman, "Understanding the Impact of Personality Traits on Individuals' Turnover Intentions."

[53]Chiaburu, Oh, Berry, Li, and Gardner, "The Five-Factor Model of Personality Traits and Organizational Citizenship Behaviors"; and R. Ilies, I. S. Fulmer, M. Spitzmuller, and M. D. Johnson, "Personality and Citizenship Behavior: The Mediating Role of Job Satisfaction," *Journal of Applied Psychology* 94, no. 4 (2009): 945–59.

[54]Kluemper, McLarty, and Bing, "Acquaintance Ratings of the Big Five Personality Traits."

[55]R. Fang, B. Landis, Z. Zhang, M. H. Anderson, J. D. Shaw, and M. Kilduff, "Integrating Personality and Social Networks: A Meta-Analysis of Personality, Network Position, and Work Outcomes in Organizations," *Organization Science* 26, no. 4 (2015): 1243–60.

[56]See, for instance, S. Yamagata, A. Suzuki, J. Ando, Y. Ono, K. Yutaka, N. Kijima, et al., "Is the Genetic Structure of Human Personality Universal? A Cross-Cultural Twin Study from North America, Europe, and Asia," *Journal of Personality and Social Psychology* 90, no. 6 (2006): 987–98; and R. R. McCrae, P. T. Costa Jr., T. A. Martin, V. E. Oryol, A. A. Rukavishnikov, I. G. Senin, et al., "Consensual Validation of Personality Traits across Cultures," *Journal of Research in Personality* 38, no. 2 (2004): 179–201.

[57]M. Gurven, C. von Ruden, M. Massenkoff, H. Kaplan, and M. L. Vie, "How Universal Is the Big Five? Testing the Five-Factor Model of Personality Variation among Forager-Farmers in the Bolivian Amazon," *Journal of Personality and Social Psychology* 104, no. 2 (2013): 354–70.

[58]J. F. Rauthmann, "The Dark Triad and Interpersonal Perception: Similarities and Differences in the Social Consequences of Narcissism, Machiavellianism, and Psychopathy," *Social Psychological and Personality Science* 3 (2012): 487–96.

[59]P. D. Harms and S. M. Spain, "Beyond the Bright Side: Dark Personality at Work," *Applied Psychology: An International Review* 64, no. 1 (2015): 15–24.

[60]P. K. Jonason, S. Slomski, and J. Partyka, "The Dark Triad at Work: How Toxic Employees Get Their Way," *Personality and Individual Differences* 52 (2012): 449–53.

[61]E. H. O'Boyle, D. R. Forsyth, G. C. Banks, and M. A. McDaniel, "A Meta-Analysis of the Dark Triad and Work Behavior: A Social Exchange Perspective," *Journal of Applied Psychology* 97 (2012): 557–79.

[62]L. Zhang and M. A. Gowan, "Corporate Social Responsibility, Applicants' Individual Traits, and Organizational Attraction: A Person–Organization Fit Perspective," *Journal of Business and Psychology* 27 (2012): 345–62.

[63]D. N. Hartog and F. D. Belschak, "Work Engagement and Machiavellianism in the Ethical Leadership Process," *Journal of Business Ethics* 107 (2012): 35–47.

[64]E. Grijalva and P. D. Harms, "Narcissism: An Integrative Synthesis and Dominance Complementarity Model," *The Academy of Management Perspectives* 28, no. 2 (2014): 108–27.

[65]D. C. Maynard, E. M. Brondolo, C. E. Connelly, and C. E. Sauer, "I'm Too Good for This Job: Narcissism's Role in the Experience of Overqualification," *Applied Psychology: An International Review* 64, no. 1 (2015): 208–32.

[66]Grijalva and Harms, "Narcissism: An Integrative Synthesis and Dominance Complementarity Model."

[67]B. J. Brummel and K. N. Parker, "Obligation and Entitlement in Society and the Workplace," *Applied Psychology: An International Review* 64, no. 1 (2015): 127–60.

[68]E. Grijalva and D. A. Newman, "Narcissism and Counterproductive Work Behavior (CWB): Meta-Analysis and Consideration of Collectivist Culture, Big Five Personality, and Narcissism's Facet Structure," *Applied Psychology: An International Review* (2015): 93–126.

[69]Maynard, Brondolo, Connelly, and Sauer, "I'm Too Good for This Job."

[70]Grijalva and Harms, "Narcissism: An Integrative Synthesis and Dominance Complementarity Model."

[71]J. J. Sosik, J. U. Chun, and W. Zhu, "Hang on to Your Ego: The Moderating Role of Leader Narcissism on Relationships between Leader Charisma and Follower Psychological Empowerment and Moral Identity," *Journal of Business Ethics*, February 12, 2013; and B. M. Galvin, D. A. Waldman, and P. Balthazard, "Visionary Communication Qualities as Mediators of the Relationship between Narcissism and Attributions of Leader Charisma," *Personnel Psychology* 63, no. 3 (2010): 509–37.

[72]D. Meinert, "Narcissistic Bosses Aren't All Bad, Study Finds," *HR Magazine*, March 2014, 18.

[73]K. A. Byrne and D. A. Worthy, "Do Narcissists Make Better Decisions? An Investigation of Narcissism and Dynamic Decision-Making Performance," *Personality and Individual Differences*, July 2013, 112–17.

[74]C. Andreassen, H. Ursin, H. Eriksen, and S. Pallesen, "The Relationship of Narcissism with Workaholism, Work Engagement, and Professional Position," *Social Behavior and Personality* 40, no. 6 (2012): 881–90.

[75]A. Chatterjee and D. C. Hambrick, "Executive Personality, Capability Cues, and Risk Taking: How Narcissistic CEOs React to Their Successes and Stumbles," *Administrative Science Quarterly* 56 (2011): 202–37.

[76]C. J. Resick, D. S. Whitman, S. M. Weingarden, and N. J. Hiller, "The Bright-Side and Dark-Side of CEO Personality: Examining Core Self-Evaluations, Narcissism, Transformational Leadership, and Strategic Influence," *Journal of Applied Psychology* 94, no. 6 (2009): 1365–81.

[77]O'Boyle, Forsyth, Banks, and McDaniel, "A Meta-Analysis of the Dark Triad and Work Behavior," 558.

[78]Ibid.

[79]B. Wille, F. De Fruyt, and B. De Clercq, "Expanding and Reconceptualizing Aberrant Personality at Work: Validity of Five-Factor Model Aberrant Personality Tendencies to Predict Career Outcomes," *Personnel Psychology* 66 (2013): 173–223.

[80]Jonason, Slomski, and Partyka, "The Dark Triad at Work," 449–53; and H. M. Baughman, S. Dearing, E. Giammarco, and P. A. Vernon, "Relationships between Bullying Behaviours and the Dark Triad: A Study with Adults," *Personality and Individual Differences* 52 (2012): 571–75.

[81]B. Wille, F. De Fruyt, and B. De Clercq, "Expanding and Reconceptualizing Aberrant Personality at Work: Validity of Five-Factor Model Aberrant Personality Tendencies to Predict Career Outcomes," *Personnel Psychology* 66 (2013): 173–223.

[82]U. Orth and R. W. Robins, "Understanding the Link between Low Self-Esteem and Depression," *Current Directions in Psychological Science* 22, no. 6 (2013): 455–60.

[83]T. A. Judge and J. E. Bono, "A Rose by Any Other Name . . . Are Self-Esteem, Generalized Self-Efficacy, Neuroticism, and Locus of Control Indicators of a Common Construct?," in B. W. Roberts and R. Hogan (eds.), *Personality Psychology in the Workplace* (Washington, DC: American Psychological Association, 2001), 93–118.

[84]T. A. Judge, J. E. Bono, A. Erez, and E. A. Locke, "Core Self-Evaluations and Job and Life Satisfaction: The Role of Self-Concordance and Goal Attainment," *Journal of Applied Psychology* 90, no. 2 (2005): 257–68.

[85]A. N. Salvaggio, B. Schneider, L. H. Nishi, D. M. Mayer, A. Ramesh, and J. S. Lyon, "Manager Personality, Manager Service Quality Orientation, and Service Climate: Test of a Model," *Journal of Applied Psychology* 92, no. 6 (2007): 1741–50; B. A. Scott and T. A. Judge, "The Popularity Contest at Work: Who Wins, Why, and What Do They Receive?" *Journal of Applied Psychology* 94, no. 1 (2009): 20–33; and T. A. Judge and C. Hurst, "How the Rich (and Happy) Get Richer (and Happier): Relationship of Core Self-Evaluations to Trajectories in Attaining Work Success," *Journal of Applied Psychology* 93, no. 4 (2008): 849–63.

[86]A. M. Grant and A. Wrzesniewksi, "I Won't Let You Down . . . or Will I? Core Self-Evaluations, Other-Orientation, Anticipated Guilt and Gratitude, and Job Performance," *Journal of Applied Psychology* 95, no. 1 (2010): 108–21.

[87]X. Zheng, B. Wu, C. S. Li, P. Zhang, and N. Tang, "Reversing the Pollyanna Effect: The Curvilinear Relationship between Core Self-Evaluation and Perceived Social Acceptance," *Journal of Business and Psychology* (in press).

[88]D. V. Day and D. J. Schleicher, "Self-Monitoring at Work: A Motive-Based Perspective," *Journal of Personality* 74, no. 3 (2006): 685–714; S. Kudret, B. Erdogan, and T. N. Bauer, "Self-monitoring Personality Trait at Work: An Integrative Narrative Review and Future Directions," *Journal of Organizational Behavior* 40 (2019): 193–208.

[89]Wings (2021). "Richa Kar: The Woman Behind The Success of Zivame!" *Team leverage Edu (March 3, 2021).* Retrieved from https://leverageedu.com (Accessed on April 15, 2022).

[90]Cruchbase. "Zivame.com". Retrieved from https://www.crunchbase.com (Accessed on April 15, 2022).

[91]F. J. Flynn and D. R. Ames, "What's Good for the Goose May Not Be as Good for the Gander: The Benefits of Self-Monitoring for Men and Women in Task Groups and Dyadic Conflicts," *Journal of Applied Psychology* 91, no. 2 (2006): 272–81; and M. Snyder, *Public Appearances, Private Realities: The Psychology of Self-Monitoring* (New York, NY: W. H. Freeman, 1987).

[92]D. V. Day, D. J. Shleicher, A. L. Unckless, and N. J. Hiller, "Self-Monitoring Personality at Work: A Meta-Analytic Investigation of Construct Validity," *Journal of Applied Psychology* 87, no. 2 (2002): 390–401.

[93]H. Oh and M. Kilduff, "The Ripple Effect of Personality on Social Structure: Self-Monitoring Origins of Network Brokerage," *Journal of Applied Psychology* 93, no. 5 (2008): 1155–64; and A. Mehra, M. Kilduff, and D. J. Brass, "The Social Networks of High and Low Self-Monitors: Implications for Workplace Performance," *Administrative Science Quarterly* 46, no. 1 (2001): 121–46.

[94]Kudret et al., "Self-monitoring Personality Trait at Work"; and A. M. Kleinbaum, A. H. Jordan, and P. G. Audia, "An Altercentric Perspective on the Origins of Brokerage in Social Networks: How Perceived Empathy Moderates the Self-Monitoring Effect," *Organization Science*, 26 (2015): 1–17.

[95]T. S. Bateman and J. M. Crant, "The Proactive Component of Organizational Behavior: A Measure and Correlates," *Journal of Organizational Behavior* 14 (1993): 103–18.

[96]K. Tornau and M. Frese, "Construct Clean-up in Proactivity Research: A Meta-Analysis on the Nomological Net of Work-Related Proactivity Concepts and Their Incremental Values," *Applied Psychology: An International Review* 62, no. 1 (2013): 44–96.

[97]F. Li, T. Chen, N. Y-F. Chen, Y. Bai, and J. M. Crant, "Proactive yet Reflective? Materializing Proactive Personality into Creativity through Job Reflective Learning and Activated Positive Affective States," *Personnel Psychology* (in press); N. Rodrigues and T. Rebelo, "Predicting innovative performance through proactive personality: Examining its criterion validity and incremental validity over the five-factor model," *International Journal of Selection and Assessment* 27 (2019): 1–8.

[98]S. Han, C. M. Harold, and M. Cheong, "Examining Why Employee Proactive Personality Influences Empowering Leadership: The Roles of Cognition- and Affect-Based Trust," *Journal of Occupational and Organizational Psychology* 92 (2019): 352–83; W.-D. Li, D. Fay, M. Frese, P. D. Harms, and X. Y. Gao, "Reciprocal Relationship between Proactive Personality and Work Characteristics: A Latent Change Score Approach," *Journal of Applied Psychology* 99, no. 5 (2014): 948–65.

[99]J. P. Thomas, D. S. Whitman, and C. Viswesvaran, "Employee Proactivity in Organizations: A Comparative Meta-Analysis of Emergent Proactive Constructs," *Journal of Occupational and Organizational Psychology* 83 (2010): 275–300.

[100]P. D. Converse, P. J. Pathak, A. M. DePaul-Haddock, T. Gotlib, and M. Merbedone, "Controlling Your Environment and Yourself: Implications for Career Success," *Journal of Vocational Behavior* 80 (2012): 148–59; J. Sun, W.-D. Li, Y. Li, R. C. Liden, S. Li, and X. Zhang, "Unintended Consequences of Being Proactive? Linking Proactive Personality to Coworker Envy, Helping, and Undermining, and the Moderating Role of Prosocial Motivation," *Journal of Applied Psychology* (in press).

[101]G. Chen, J. Farh, E. M. Campbell-Bush, Z. Wu, and X. Wu, "Teams as Innovative Systems: Multilevel Motivational

Antecedents of Innovation in R&D Teams," *Journal of Applied Psychology* 98 (2013): 1018–27.
[102]Y. Gong, S.-Y. Cheung, M. Wang, and J.-C. Huang, "Unfolding the Proactive Process for Creativity: Integration of the Employee Proactivity, Information Exchange, and Psychological Safety Perspectives," *Journal of Management* 38, no. 5 (2012): 1611–33.
[103]Z. Zhang, M. Wang, and S. Junqi, "Leader-Follower Congruence in Proactive Personality and Work Outcomes: The Mediating Role of Leader-Member Exchange," *Academy of Management Journal* 55 (2012): 111–30.
[104]G. Van Hoye and H. Lootens, "Coping with Unemployment: Personality, Role Demands, and Time Structure," *Journal of Vocational Behavior* 82 (2013): 85–95.
[105]D. J. Brown, R. T. Cober, K. Kane, P. E. Levy, and J. Shalhoop, "Proactive Personality and the Successful Job Search: A Field Investigation with College Graduates," *Journal of Applied Psychology* 91, no. 3 (2006): 717–26.
[106]D. B. Turban, C. K. Stevens, and F. K. Lee, "Effects of Conscientiousness and Extraversion on New Labor Market Entrants' Job Search: The Mediating Role of Metacognitive Activities and Positive Emotions," *Personnel Psychology* 62 (2009): 553–73; and C. R. Wanberg, R. Kanfer, and J. T. Banas, "Predictors and Outcomes of Networking Intensity Among Unemployed Job Seekers," *Journal of Applied Psychology* 85, no. 4 (2000): 491–503.
[107]M. Egan, M. Daly, L. Delaney, C. J. Boyce, and A. M. Wood, "Adolescent Conscientiousness Predicts Lower Lifetime Unemployment," *Journal of Applied Psychology* 102, no. 4 (2017): 700–9.
[108]G. Van Hoye and H. Lootens, "Coping with Unemployment: Personality, Role Demands, and Time Structure," *Journal of Vocational Behavior* 82, no. 2 (2013): 85–95.
[109]R. Kanfer, C. R. Wanberg, and T. M. Kantrowitz, "Job Search and Employment: A Personality-Motivational Analysis and Meta-Analytic Review," *Journal of Applied Psychology* 86, no. 5 (2001): 837–55.
[110]S. Côté, A. M. Saks, and J. Zikic, "Trait Affect and Job Search Outcomes," *Journal of Vocational Behavior* 68, no. 2 (2006): 233–52; and D. B. Turban, F. K. Lee, S. P. Da Motta Veiga, D. L. Haggard, and S. Y. Wu, "Be Happy, Don't Wait: The Role of Trait Affect in Job Search," *Personnel Psychology* 66 (2013): 483–514.
[111]C. D. Crossley and J. M. Stanton, "Negative Affect and Job Search: Further Examination of the Reverse Causation Hypothesis," *Journal of Vocational Behavior* 66, no. 3 (2005): 549–60; and C. Hakulinen, M. Jokela, M. Hintsanen, L. Pulkki-Råback, M. Elovainio, T. Hintsa, . . . and L. Keltikangas-Järvinen, "Hostility and Unemployment: A Two-Way Relationship?," *Journal of Vocational Behavior* 83, no. 2 (2013): 153–60.
[112]R. D. Zimmerman, W. R. Boswell, A. J. Shipp, B. B. Dunford, and J. W. Boudreau, "Explaining the Pathways between Approach-Avoidance Personality Traits and Employees' Job Search Behavior," *Journal of Management* 38, no. 5 (2012): 1450–75.
[113]C. J. Boyce, A. M. Wood, M. Daly, and C. Sedikides, "Personality Change Following Unemployment," *Journal of Applied Psychology* 100, no. 4 (2015): 991–1011.
[114]W. R. Boswell, R. D. Zimmerman, and B. W. Swider, "Employee Job Search: Toward an Understanding of Search Context and Search Objectives, *Journal of Management* 38, no. 1 (2012): 129–63.
[115]R. D. Meyer, R. S. Dalal, and R. Hermida, "A Review and Synthesis of Situational Strength in the Organizational Sciences," *Journal of Management* 36 (2010): 121–40.
[116]Ibid.
[117]K. R. Keeler, W. Kong, R. S. Dalal, and J. M. Cortina, "Situational Strength Interactions: Are Variance Patterns Consistent with Theory?" *Journal of Applied Psychology* (in press); R. D. Meyer, R. S. Dalal, I. J. Jose, R. Hermida, T. R. Chen, R. P. Vega, . . . and V. P. Khare, "Measuring Job-Related Situational Strength and Assessing Its Interactive Effects with Personality on Voluntary Work Behavior," *Journal of Management* 40, no. 4 (2014): 1010–41.
[118]A. M. Grant and N. P. Rothbard, "When in Doubt, Seize the Day? Security Values, Prosocial Values, and Proactivity under Ambiguity," *Journal of Applied Psychology* 98, no. 5 (2013): 810–9.
[119]R. S. Dalal et al., "Extending Situational Strength Theory to Account for Situation-Outcome Mismatch," *Journal of Business and Psychology* 35 (2020): 273–96.
[120]A. M. Watson, T. F. Thompson, J. V. Rudolph, T. J. Whelan, T. S. Behrend, et al., "When Big Brother Is Watching: Goal Orientation Shapes Reactions to Electronic Monitoring During Online Training," *Journal of Applied Psychology* 98 (2013): 642–57.
[121]Y. Kim, L. Van Dyne, D. Kamdar, and R. E. Johnson, "Why and When Do Motives Matter? An Integrative Model of Motives, Role Cognitions, and Social Support as Predictors of OCB," *Organizational Behavior and Human Decision Processes* 121 (2013): 231–45.
[122]T. A. Judge and C. P. Zapata, "The Person-Situation Debate Revisited: Effect of Situation Strength and Trait Activation on the Validity of the Big Five Personality Traits in Predicting Job Performance," *Academy of Management Journal* 58, no. 4 (2015): 1149–79.
[123]G. R. Maio, J. M. Olson, M. M. Bernard, and M. A. Luke, "Ideologies, Values, Attitudes, and Behavior," in J. Delamater (ed.), *Handbook of Social Psychology* (New York: Springer, 2003), 283–308.
[124]See, for instance, A. Bardi, J. A. Lee, N. Hofmann-Towfigh, and G. Soutar, "The Structure of Intraindividual Value Change," *Journal of Personality and Social Psychology* 97, no. 5 (2009): 913–29.
[125]S. Roccas, L. Sagiv, S. H. Schwartz, and A. Knafo, "The Big Five Personality Factors and Personal Values," *Personality and Social Psychology Bulletin* 28, no. 6 (2002): 789–801.
[126]B. C. Holtz and C. M. Harold, "Interpersonal Justice and Deviance: The Moderating Effects of Interpersonal Justice Values and Justice Orientation," *Journal of Management*, February 2013, 339–65.
[127]J. C. Carr, A. W. Pearson, M. J. Vest, and S. L. Boyar, "Prior Occupational Experience, Anticipatory Socialization, and Employee Retention, *Journal of Management* 32, no. 32 (2006): 343–59; B. J. Hoffman and D. J. Woehr, "A Quantitative Review of the Relationship between Person-Organization fit and Behavioral Outcomes," *Journal of Vocational Behavior* 68 (2006): 389–99; and M. L. Verquer, T. A. Beehr, and S. E. Wagner, "A Meta-Analysis of Relations between Person–Organization Fit and Work Attitudes," *Journal of Vocational Behavior* 63, no. 3 (2003): 473–89
[128]K. H. Ehrhart, D. M. Mayer, and J. C. Ziegert, "Web-Based Recruitment in the Millennial Generation: Work-Life Balance, Website Usability, and Organizational Attraction," *European Journal of Work and Organizational Psychology* 21, no. 6 (2012): 850–74.
[129]Kristof-Brown, Zimmerman, and Johnson, "Consequences of Individuals' Fit at Work"; and Ostroff, "Person-Environment Fit in Organizational Settings."
[130]I.-S. Oh, R. P. Guay, K. Kim, C. M. Harold, J. H. Lee, C.-G. Heo, and K.-H.

Shin, "Fit Happens Globally: A Meta-Analytic Comparison of the Relationships of Person-Environment Fit Dimensions with Work Attitudes and Performance across East Asia, Europe, and North America," *Personnel Psychology* 67 (2014): 99–152.

[131]See The Hofstede Centre, www.geert-hofstede.com.

[132]G. Hofstede, G. J. Hofstede, and M. Minkov, *Cultures and Organizations: Software of the Mind*, 3rd edition (New York: McGraw-Hill, 2010); Hofstede Insights, *National Culture*, https://hi.hofstede-insights.com/national-culture, accessed April 23, 2020.

[133]Q. Guo, Z. Liu, X. Li, and X. Qiao, "Indulgence and Long Term Orientation Influence Prosocial Behavior at National Level," *Frontiers in Psychology* 9, no. 1798 (2018): 1–10; A. Maleki and M. de Jong, "A Proposal for Clustering the Dimensions of Culture," *Cross-Cultural Research* 48, no. 2 (2014): 107–43.

[134]V. Taras, B. L. Kirkman, and P. Steel, "Examining the Impact of Culture's Consequences: A Three-Decade, Multilevel, Meta-Analytic Review of Hofstede's Cultural Value Dimensions," *Journal of Applied Psychology* 95, no. 5 (2010): 405–39.

[135]M. Javidan and R. J. House, "Cultural Acumen for the Global Manager: Lessons from Project GLOBE," *Organizational Dynamics* 29, no. 4 (2001): 289–305; and R. J. House, P. J. Hanges, M. Javidan, and P. W. Dorfman (eds.), *Leadership, Culture, and Organizations: The GLOBE Study of 62 Societies* (Thousand Oaks, CA: Sage, 2004).

[136]J. P. Meyer, D. J. Stanley, T. A. Jackson, K. J. McInnis, E. R. Maltin, et al., "Affective, Normative, and Continuance Commitment Levels across Cultures: A Meta-Analysis," *Journal of Vocational Behavior* 80 (2012): 225–45.

5 Perception, Learning and Individual Decision Making

Source: David Lyon/Alamy Stock Photo

LEARNING OBJECTIVES

After studying this chapter, you should be able to:

5-1 Explain the factors that influence perception.

5-2 Describe attribution theory.

5-3 Explain the link between perception and decision making.

5-4 Contrast the rational model of decision making with bounded rationality and intuition.

5-5 Explain how individual differences and organizational constraints affect decision making.

5-6 Contrast the three ethical decision criteria.

5-7 Describe the three-stage model of creativity.

Employability Skills Matrix (ESM)

	Myth or Science?	Career OBjectives	An Ethical Choice	Point/ Counterpoint	Experiential Exercise	Ethical Dilemma	Case Incident 1	Case Incident 2
Critical Thinking	✓	✓		✓	✓	✓	✓	✓
Communication			✓		✓	✓	✓	
Collaboration		✓			✓		✓	
Knowledge Application and Analysis	✓	✓	✓	✓	✓	✓	✓	✓
Social Responsibility	✓	✓	✓	✓	✓	✓	✓	✓

INDIVIDUAL INTUITION IGNITING INNOVATION

Richard Branson, Sir James Dyson, and Ella Woodward are three entrepreneurs and very successful business owners operating in completely different industries, but they have one thing in common—a strong, innovative, entrepreneurial intuition. Richard Branson, the English business tycoon, investor, and philanthropist; Sir James Dyson, the British inventor, industrial designer, and founder of the Dual Cyclone bagless vacuum cleaner; and Ella Woodward, the English food writer and founder of the brand Deliciously Ella, have all made key business decisions based on their intuition and "gut feeling," leading to innovative, creative market offerings that ultimately resulted in successful business ventures and strong brand names within the United Kingdom as well as the global marketplace. Richard Branson has admitted to making decisions based on creative instinct, James Dyson has confessed to trusting intuition based on market research, and Ella Woodward has drawn on her emotions and drive in response to a diagnosis of postural tachycardia syndrome to make decisions.

Of course, their business ventures' successes have not been the outcome solely of the entrepreneurs' intuitive decision-making; sound analytical skills and well-informed judgment have played a major role as well. Dyson's decision-making has been based on the knowledge of and expertise in technology, Branson's is based on his knowledge of the market, and Woodward's is based on her knowledge of the targeted consumer.

Intuition has often been on their side, but not always. Consider, for example, the case of Virgin Cola. In 1994, Virgin Group founder Richard Branson was looking to broaden Virgin's offerings and to bring a rival to Coca-Cola and Pepsi brands. After numerous ups and (mainly) downs, Virgin Drinks U.S.A., the company dealing with Virgin Cola's U.S. market, closed in April 2001, having managed to establish a measly 0.5 percent share of the market by volume. In 2012, the production of Virgin Cola was ceased entirely, and no company acquired the UK Virgin Cola licence in its place.

The hope was to take over Coca-Cola and Pepsi's market shares and even dominate the soft drinks market, but the actual facts revealed a failure in the product, which some attribute to a lack of market research and market knowledge and even misinterpretation of consumer behavior. Others argue that this is a case of what is known as bounded rationality, which involves oversimplifying a decision that was complex at that time. Still others state that it was simply a case of bad judgment in the first place. Wherever the truth lies, Branson does not fear taking risks or the unknown; he continues to be intrigued and inspirited by them. And these traits have made him the business magnate that he is.

Decision making is a complex task and process, particularly in a corporate environment, as it requires and engages both intuition (and therefore affective reasoning) as well as rationalized judgments. The two aspects work in a symbiotic manner, but differently from one individual to another. These individual differences are linked to personality differences, the risk perceptions of the individuals, and the way they approach and understand creativity and innovation. Richard Branson, Sir James Dyson, and Ella Woodward have all displayed excellent intuition in their enterprising activities, but they all have great experience and knowledge of the way an idea can be transformed into a business venture.

Sources: Management Today, "Relying on Intuition—Should You Always Trust Your Gut Feelings?", October 1, 2013, https://www.managementtoday.co.uk/relying-intuition-always-trust-gut-feelings/article/1155928; BBC, "Trusting Your Gut: Smart Management or a Fool's Errand?", September 20, 2013, http://www.bbc.com/capital/story/20130923-should-you-trust-your-gut; *Business Insider*, "Richard Branson Leadership Rules for Being a Great Leader," October 19, 2015, http://uk.businessinsider.com/richard-branson-leadership-rules-2015-10?r=US&IR=T; CNBC, "Richard Branson: Great Entrepreneurs Share 5 Skills, January 31, 2017, https://www.cnbc.com/2017/01/31/richard-branson-successful-entrepreneurs-share-these-5-skills.html; Entrepreneur, Rod Kurtz, "Richard Branson on Being Richard Branson," December 17, 2012, https://www.entrepreneur.com/article/225295; Elizabeth Grice, "Deliciously Ella: 'There's a pressure to be sparkly and shiny all the time,'" *The Telegraph*, January 23, 2016, http://www.telegraph.co.uk/food-and-drink/features/deliciously-ella-interview-new-book-Deliciously-Ella-Every-Day/; Carole Cadwalladr, "James Dyson Interview: Vacuums Are Already Smarter Than People," *The Guardian*, May 9, 2014, https://www.theguardian.com/technology/2014/may/09/james-dyson-interview-engineering-education.

Virgin Cola illustrates how pervasive and tricky intuitive decision making is within organizations. As we will see later in the chapter, decision making hinges on several criteria and can be fostered through many means. To better understand what influences us and our organizations, we start at the roots of our thought processes: our perceptions and the way they affect our decision making.

What Is Perception?

5-1 Explain the factors that influence perception.

perception A process by which individuals organize and interpret their sensory impressions to give meaning to their environment.

Perception is a process by which we organize and interpret sensory impressions to give meaning to our environment. What we perceive can be substantially different from objective reality. For example, all employees in a firm may view it as a great place to work—favorable working conditions, interesting job assignments, good pay, excellent benefits, understanding and responsible management—but, as most of us know, it's very unusual to find universal agreement across people.

Why is perception important in the study of Organizational Behavior (OB)? It is important because people's behavior is based on their perception of what reality is, not on reality itself. *The world as it is perceived is the world that is behaviorally important.* In other words, our perception becomes the reality from which we act. To understand what all of us have in common in our interpretations of reality, we need to begin with the factors that influence our perceptions.

Factors That Influence Perception

Many factors shape and sometimes distort perception. These factors can reside in the *perceiver*, the object or *target* being perceived, or the *situation* in which the perception is made (see Exhibit 5-1).

Perceiver When you look at a target, your interpretation of what you see is influenced by your personal characteristics—attitudes, personality, motives, interests, past experiences, and expectations.[1] In some ways, we hear what we want to hear[2] and we see what we want to see—not because it's the truth, but because it conforms to our thinking. For instance, research indicates that supervisors perceived employees who started work earlier in the day as more conscientious and therefore as higher performers; however, supervisors who were night owls *themselves* were less likely to make that erroneous assumption.[3] Some perceptions created by attitudes like these can be counteracted by objective evaluations, but others can be more insidious. Consider, for instance, observer perceptions of a recent shooting in New York. There were two eyewitnesses—one said a police officer chased and shot a fleeing man; the other said a handcuffed man lying on the ground was shot. Neither perceived the situation correctly: The man was attempting to attack a police officer with a hammer when he was shot by another officer.[4]

Exhibit 5-1 **Factors That Influence Perception**

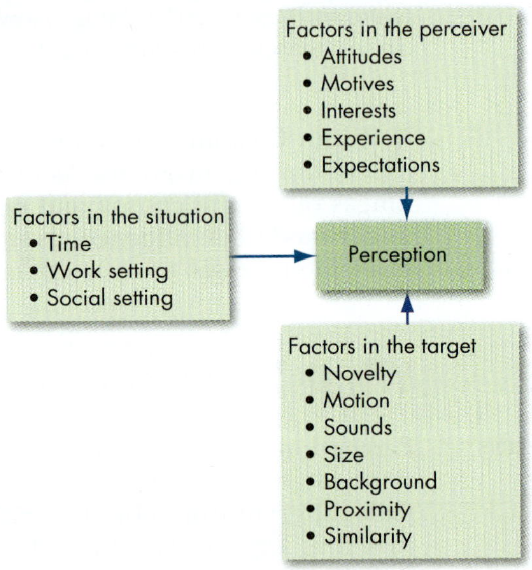

Target The characteristics of the target also affect what we perceive. Because we don't look at targets in isolation, the relationship of a target to its background influences perception, as does our tendency to group close things and similar things together.[5] We can perceive members of any group that has clearly distinguishable characteristics as alike in other, often unrelated ways. These assumptions can be harmful, as when people who have criminal records are prejudged in the workplace even when it is known they were wrongly arrested.[6] Sometimes differences can work in our favor, though, such as when we are drawn to targets that are different from what we expect. For instance, participants in a recent study respected a professor wearing a T-shirt and sneakers in the classroom more than the same professor dressed traditionally. The professor stood out from the norm for the classroom setting and was therefore perceived as an individualist.[7]

Context Context matters too. The time at which we see an object or event can influence our attention, as can location, light, heat, or situational factors. For instance, you may not notice someone dressed up for a formal event that you attended on a Saturday night. Yet if you were to notice that person dressed the same way for your Monday morning management class, he or she would likely catch your attention, if the students do not normally wear formal attire to class. Neither the perceiver nor the target has changed between Saturday night and Monday morning, but the situation is different.

People are usually not aware of the factors that influence their view of reality. In fact, people are not even that perceptive about their *own* abilities.[8] Thankfully, awareness and objective measures can reduce our perception distortions. For instance, when people are more aware of their own racial biases, they are more motivated to control their own prejudice and more attuned to perceiving their own biases.[9] Let's next consider *how* we make perceptions of others.

Person Perception: Making Judgments about Others

5-2 Describe attribution theory.

The perception concepts most relevant to OB include *person perceptions*, or the perceptions people form about each other. Many of our perceptions of others are formed by first impressions and small cues that have little supporting evidence. This is particularly troublesome—but common—when we infer another person's morality. Research indicates we form our strongest impressions based on what we perceive about another's moral character, but our initial information about this can be sketchy and unfounded.[10] Let's unravel some of our other human tendencies that interfere with correct person perception, beginning with the evidence behind attribution theory.

Attribution Theory

Nonliving objects such as desks, machines, and buildings are subject to the laws of nature, but they have no beliefs, motives, or intentions. People do. When we observe people, we attempt to explain their behavior. Our perception and judgment of a person's actions are influenced by the assumptions we make about that person's state of mind.

attribution theory An attempt to explain the ways we judge people differently, depending on the meaning we attribute to a behavior, such as determining whether an individual's behavior is internally or externally caused.

Attribution theory tries to explain the ways we judge people differently depending on the meaning we attribute to a behavior.[11] For instance, consider what you think when people smile at you. Do you think they are cooperative, exploitative, or competitive? We assign meaning to smiles and other expressions in many ways.[12] Attribution theory also tries to explain what we do as a result of our attributions. For example, recent research suggests that supervisors are more likely to exploit or treat subordinates poorly (e.g., making them work extra hours, giving them tedious tasks) if they judge them as being "passionate" about their work.[13] In other words, they think it is okay if they make them work harder if they see them as passionate.

Attribution theory suggests that when we observe an individual's behavior, we attempt to determine whether it was internally or externally caused. That determination depends largely on three factors: (1) distinctiveness, (2) consensus, and (3) consistency.[14] Let's clarify the differences between internal and external causation, and then we'll discuss the determining factors.

Internally caused behaviors are those an observer believes to be under the personal behavioral control of another individual. *Externally* caused behavior is what we imagine the situation forced the individual to do. If an employee is late for work, you might attribute that to his overnight partying and subsequent oversleeping. This is an internal attribution. But if you attribute his lateness to a traffic snarl, you are making an external attribution.

Now let's discuss the three determining factors. *Distinctiveness* refers to whether an individual displays different behaviors in different situations. Is the employee who arrives late today also one who regularly "blows off" other kinds of commitments? What we want to know is whether this behavior is unusual. If it is, we are likely to give it an external attribution. If it is not, we will probably judge the behavior to be internal.

If everyone who faces a similar situation responds in the same way, we can say the behavior shows *consensus*. The behavior of our tardy employee meets this criterion if all employees who took the same route were also late. From an attribution perspective, if consensus is high, you would probably give an external attribution to the employee's tardiness, whereas if other employees who took the same route made it to work on time, you would attribute his lateness to an internal cause.

An observer looks for *consistency* in a person's actions. Does the person respond the same way over time? Coming in 10 minutes late for work is not perceived the same for an employee who hasn't been late for several months as for an employee who is late three times a week. The more consistent the behavior, the more we are inclined to attribute it to internal causes.

Exhibit 5-2 summarizes the key elements in attribution theory. It tells us, for instance, that if an employee, Katelyn, generally performs at about the same level on related tasks as she does on her current task (low distinctiveness), other employees frequently perform differently—better or worse—than Katelyn on that task (low consensus), and Katelyn's performance on this current task is consistent over time (high consistency), anyone judging Katelyn's work will likely hold her primarily responsible for her task performance (internal attribution).

fundamental attribution error The tendency to underestimate the influence of external factors and overestimate the influence of internal factors when making judgments about the behavior of others.

self-serving bias The tendency for individuals to attribute their own successes to internal factors and put the blame for failures on external factors.

Errors or biases distort attributions. When we make judgments about the behavior of other people, we tend to underestimate the influence of external factors and overestimate the influence of internal or personal factors.[15] This **fundamental attribution error** can explain why a sales manager attributes the poor performance of her sales agents to laziness rather than to a competitor's innovative product line. Individuals and organizations tend to attribute their own successes to internal factors such as ability or effort while blaming failure on external factors such as bad luck or difficult coworkers. People tend to attribute ambiguous information as relatively flattering, accept positive feedback, and reject negative feedback. This is called **self-serving bias.**[16]

The evidence on cultural differences in perception is mixed, but most suggests there are differences across cultures in the attributions people make, with collectivist cultures making external attributions more frequently than internal attributions.[17] A study of customer service employees from the same hotel chain in China and Canada examined the different reactions to mistreatment by customers based on cultural values. Analysis revealed that individualism and collectivism accounted for the reactions. North American employees responded with direct, active, and target-specific reactions such as acts of sabotage toward

Exhibit 5-2 Attribution Theory

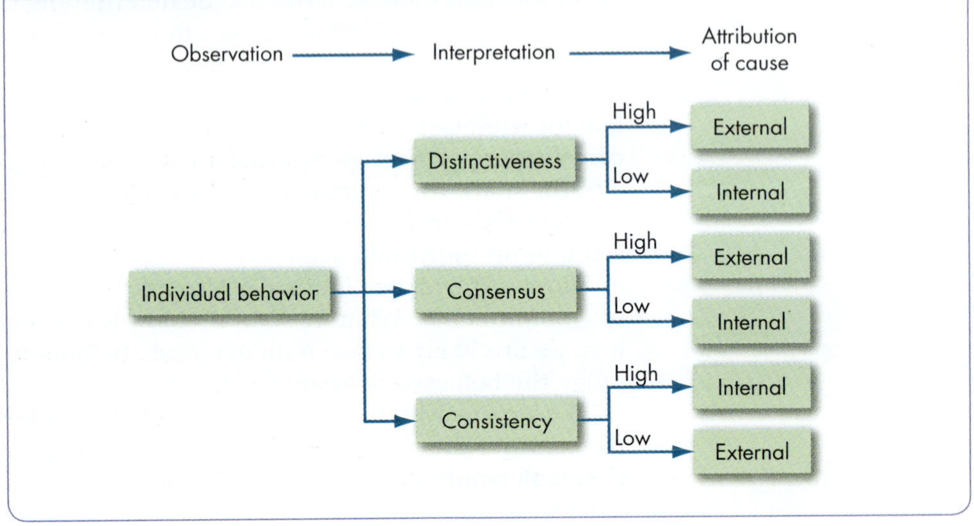

the source of the mistreatment. However, East Asian employees were more indirect, passive, and target-general in their response, including the withdrawal of organizational citizenship behavior from customers as whole.[18]

Self-serving biases may be less common in East Asian cultures, but evidence suggests they still operate there.[19] Studies indicate Chinese managers assess blame for mistakes using the same distinctiveness, consensus, and consistency cues Western managers use.[20] They also become angry and punish those deemed responsible for failure, a reaction shown in many studies of Western managers. It may just take more evidence for Asian managers to conclude someone else should be blamed.

The concept of attribution theory significantly advances our understanding of person perception by helping us identify why we draw certain conclusions

Career OBjectives

So what if I'm a few minutes late to work?

I'm often late to work; something always comes up at the last minute. But my boss is such a jerk about it! He's threatening to install a time clock. This is so insulting—I'm in management, I'm a professional, I'm on salary, and I do the work! Please tell me how to talk some sense into him.

—Ankita

Dear Ankita,

This issue seems to be very frustrating to you, and we'd like to help you eliminate that dissatisfaction. Let's start by analyzing why you and your boss think differently on the issue. You and he certainly perceive the situation differently—he sees your lateness as a violation, and you see it as a natural occurrence. In many other jobs, precise timing may not be expected, valued, or needed. Perhaps your boss is trying to highlight the value he places on punctuality. Or maybe he sees your lateness as unethical behavior that cheats your organization of your valuable work time.

According to Ann Tenbrunsel, director of the Institute for Ethical Business Worldwide, the way we look at our decisions changes our perception of our behaviors. You view your tardiness as something that just happens, not part of a decision process. What if you looked at your tardiness as a daily ethical decision? Your organization has a start time to which you agreed as a condition of your employment, so coming in late is a deviation from the standard. There *are* actions you can take throughout your early morning that control your arrival time. So, by this model, your behavior is unethical.

Your situation is not uncommon; we all have moral blind spots, or situations with ethical ramifications we don't see. Also, as we said earlier, other organizations may not care about your arrival time, so it's not always an ethical situation. But for situations where ethics are in play, research indicates punishment doesn't work. Reframing the decisions so we see the ethical implications does work. Try these steps to gain insight:

- *Look at the motives for your decisions during your morning routine.* Can you see where you make choices?
- *Consider your past actions.* When you think back about your early morning decisions, do you find yourself justifying your delays? Justification signals that our decisions might be suspect.
- *Look at the facts.* How do the reasons for your past delays reflect attitudes you have unconsciously acted on?

If you can see the ethical aspect of your daily lateness, you can work to meet the expectation. Think briefly about the ethics of your morning choices when you first wake up, and you'll be much more likely to be on time.

Sources: Based on C. Moore and A. E. Tenbrunsel, "'Just Think about It'? Cognitive Complexity and Moral Choice," *Organizational Behavior and Human Decision Processes* 123, no. 2 (2014): 138–49; A. Tenbrunsel, Ethical Systems, *www.ethicalsystems.org/content/ann-tenbrunsel*, accessed May 7, 2015; review and podcast of *Blind Spots: Why We Fail to Do What's Right and What to Do about It*, May 4, 2015, *http://press.princeton.edu/titles/9390.html*, accessed May 7, 2015.

The opinions provided here are of the authors only. The authors are not responsible for any errors or omissions, or for the results obtained from the use of this information. In no event will the authors or their related partnerships or corporations thereof be liable to you or anyone else for any decision made or action taken in reliance on the opinions provided here.

from people's behavior. Having introduced person perception, let's consider the common shortcuts we use to simplify our processing of others' behavior.

Common Shortcuts in Judging Others

Shortcuts for judging others often allow us to make accurate perceptions rapidly and provide valid data for making predictions. However, they can and do sometimes result in significant distortions.

Selective Perception Any characteristic that makes a person, an object, or an event stand out will increase the probability we will perceive it. Why? Because it is impossible for us to assimilate everything we see; we can take in only certain stimuli. Thus, you are more likely to notice cars like your own, and your boss may reprimand some people and not others doing the same thing. Because we can't observe everything going on around us, we use **selective perception**. But we don't choose randomly: We make selections based on our interests, background, experience, and attitudes. Seeing what we want to see, we sometimes draw unwarranted conclusions from an ambiguous situation.

selective perception The tendency to choose to interpret what one sees based on one's interests, background, experience, and attitudes.

Halo and Horns Effects When we draw a positive impression about an individual based on a single characteristic, such as intelligence, sociability, or appearance, a **halo effect** is operating.[21] The **horns effect**, on the other hand, is when we draw a *negative* impression from a single characteristic. These effects are easy to demonstrate. If you think someone was, say, sociable, what else would you infer? You probably wouldn't say the person was introverted, right? You might assume the person was loud, happy, or quick-witted when in fact the word *sociable* does not include those other positive attributes. Managers need to be careful not to draw inferences from small clues.

halo effect The tendency to draw a positive general impression about an individual based on a single characteristic.

horns effect The tendency to draw a negative general impression about an individual based on a single characteristic.

Contrast Effects An adage among entertainers is "Never follow an act that has kids or animals in it." Why? Audiences love children and animals so much that you'll look bad in comparison. This example demonstrates how the **contrast effect** can distort perceptions. We don't evaluate a person in isolation. Our reaction is influenced by other people we have recently encountered.

contrast effect Evaluation of a person's characteristics that is affected by comparisons with other people recently encountered who rank higher or lower on the same characteristics.

For example, research on 22 teams in a Chinese hospitality organization that was undergoing radical organizational change and new leader appointments suggests that transformational leadership (see Chapter 13) is more effective in improving support for the changes among followers when the former leader was *not* transformational—when the former leader *was* transformational, the new leader behaviors were not as effective.[22]

Stereotyping When we judge someone based on our perception of the group to which he or she belongs, we are **stereotyping**.[23]

stereotyping Judging someone based on one's perception of the group to which that person belongs.

We deal with our complex world's unmanageable number of stimuli by using stereotypes or shortcuts called *heuristics* to make decisions quickly. For example, it does make sense to assume that Allison from finance will be able to help you figure out a forecasting problem. The challenge occurs when we generalize inaccurately or too much. Stereotypes can be deeply ingrained and powerful enough to influence life-and-death decisions. One study that controlled for a wide array of factors (such as aggravating or mitigating circumstances) showed that the degree to which black defendants in murder trials looked "stereotypically black" essentially doubled their odds of receiving

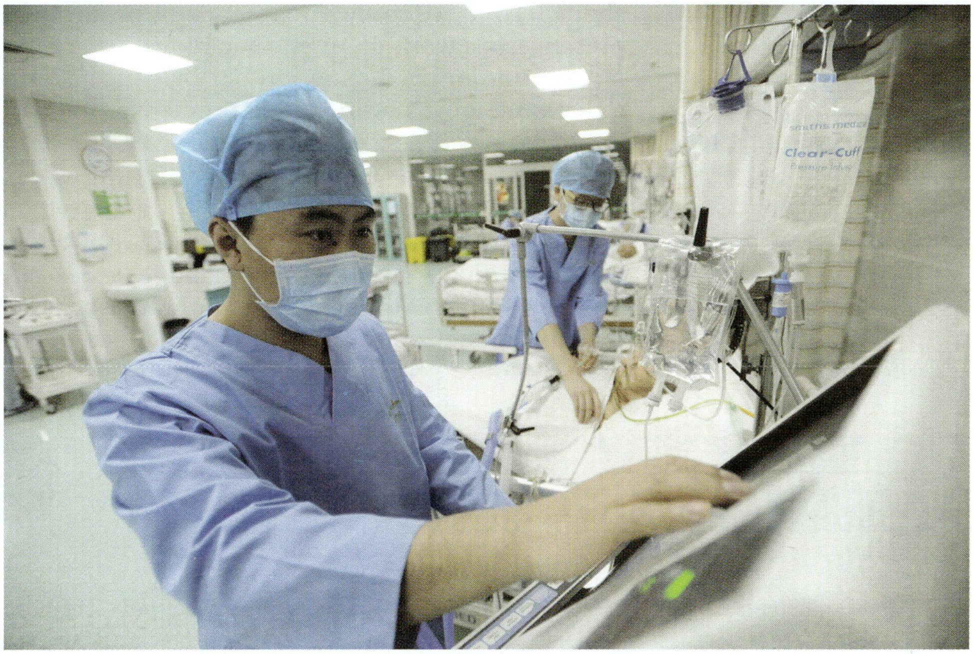

Male nurses face experience negative stereotypes based on their gender. Male nurses in many countries report that gender stereotyping generalizes inaccurately that nursing is a profession for women only because men lack the patience, empathy, and compassion required to succeed as a nurse.
Source: Zhang Wenkui Xinhua News Agency/ Newscom

a death sentence if convicted.[24] Another study found that students tended to assign higher scores for leadership potential and effective leadership to whites than to minorities, supporting the stereotype of whites as better leaders.[25]

One problem with stereotypes is that they *are* widespread generalizations, although they may not contain a shred of truth when applied to a particular person or situation. We must monitor ourselves to make sure we're not unfairly applying a stereotype in our evaluations and decisions. Stereotypes are an example of the warning, "The more useful, the more danger from misuse."

It should be obvious by now that our perceptions, many of which are near-instantaneous and without conscious deliberation, color our outlook. Sometimes they have little impact on anyone, but more often our perceptions greatly influence our decisions. The first step toward increasing the effectiveness of organizational decision making is to understand the perception process on an individualized level, a topic we discuss next.

Specific Applications of Shortcuts in Organizations

People in organizations are always judging each other. Managers must appraise their employees' performances. We evaluate how much effort our coworkers are putting into their jobs. Team members immediately "size up" a new person. In many cases, our judgments have important consequences for the organization. Let's look at the most obvious applications.

Employment Interview Few people are hired without an interview. But interviewers make perceptual judgments that are often inaccurate and draw early impressions that quickly become entrenched.[26] Research shows that we form impressions of others within a tenth of a second, based on our first glance.[27] Most interviewers' decisions change very little after the first 4 or 5 minutes of an interview. Thus, information elicited early in the interview carries greater weight than does information elicited later, and a "good applicant" is probably characterized more by the absence of unfavorable characteristics than by the presence of favorable ones. Our individual intuition about a job candidate is not reliable in predicting job performance, so collecting input from multiple independent evaluators can be predictive.[28]

self-fulfilling prophecy A situation in which a person inaccurately perceives a second person and the resulting expectations cause the second person to behave in ways consistent with the original perception.

Performance Expectations People attempt to validate their perceptions of reality even when these perceptions are faulty. The terms **self-fulfilling prophecy** and *Pygmalion effect* describe how an individual's behavior is determined by others' expectations.[29] If a manager expects big things from her people, they're not likely to let her down. Similarly, if she expects only minimal performance, the employees will likely meet those low expectations. Expectations become reality. The self-fulfilling prophecy has been found to affect

Myth or Science?

All Stereotypes Are Negative

This statement is false. Positive stereotypes exist as much as negative ones.

A study of Princeton University students shows, for example, that even today we believe Germans are better workers, Italians and African Americans are more loyal, Jews and Chinese are more intelligent, and Japanese and English are more courteous. What is surprising is that positive stereotypes are not always positive.

We may be more likely to "choke" (fail to perform) when we identify with positive stereotypes because they induce pressure to perform at the stereotypical level. For example, men are commonly believed to have higher math ability than women. A study showed that when this stereotype is activated before men take a math test, their performance on the test decreases. The belief that white men are better at science and math than women or minorities caused white men in another study to leave science, technology, engineering, and math majors. One study used basketball to illustrate the complexity of stereotypes. Researchers provided evidence to one group of undergraduates that whites were better free throw shooters than blacks. Another group was provided evidence that blacks were better free throw shooters than whites. A third group was given no stereotypic information. The undergraduates in all three groups then shot free throws while observers watched. The people who performed the worst were those in the negative stereotype condition (black undergraduates who were told whites were better and white undergraduates who were told blacks were better). However, the positive stereotype group (black undergraduates who were told blacks were better and white undergraduates who were told whites were better) also did not perform well. The best performance was turned in by those in the group without stereotypic information.

"Choking" is not the only negative thing about positive stereotypes. Research revealed that when women or Asian Americans heard positive stereotypes about themselves ("women are nurturing"; "Asians are good at math"), they felt depersonalized and reacted negatively to the individual expressing the positive stereotype. Another study showed that positive stereotypes about African Americans solidified negative stereotypes because any stereotype tends to reinforce group-based differences, whether positive or negative.

Stereotypes are understandable. To function, we need shortcuts; however, shortcuts run both ways. Because stereotypes are socially learned, we need to be vigilant about not accepting or propagating them among our coworkers and peers.

Sources: Based on A. C. Kay, M. V. Day, M. P. Zanna, and A. D. Nussbaum, "The Insidious (and Ironic) Effects of Positive Stereotypes," *Journal of Experimental Social Psychology* 49 (2013): 287–91; J. O. Sly and S. Cheryan, "When Compliments Fail to Flatter: American Individualism and Responses to Positive Stereotypes," *Journal of Personality and Social Psychology* 104 (2013): 87–102; M. J. Tagler, "Choking under the Pressure of a Positive Stereotype: Gender Identification and Self-Consciousness Moderate Men's Math Test Performance," *Journal of Social Psychology* 152 (2012): 401–16; M. A. Beasley and M. J. Fischer, "Why They Leave: The Impact of Stereotype Threat on the Attrition of Women and Minorities from Science, Math and Engineering Majors," *Social Psychology of Education* 15 (2012): 427–48; and A. Krendl, I. Gainsburg, and N. Ambady, "The Effects of Stereotypes and Observer Pressure on Athletic Performance," *Journal of Sport & Exercise Psychology* 34 (2012): 3–15.

the performance of students, soldiers, accountants, and a number of other occupations.[30]

Performance Evaluations We'll discuss performance evaluations in Chapter 16, but note that they very much depend on the perceptual process.[31] An employee's future is closely tied to his or her appraisal—promotion, pay raises, and continuation of employment are among the outcomes. Although the appraisal can be objective (for example, a salesperson is appraised on how many dollars of sales he generates in his territory), many jobs are evaluated subjectively. Subjective evaluations, though often necessary, are problematic because of the errors we've discussed—selective perception, contrast effects, halo effects, and so on. Sometimes performance ratings say as much about the evaluator as they do about the employee!

Learning

5-3 Define learning and outline the principles of the three major theories of learning.

All complex behavior is learned. If we want to explain and predict behavior, we need to understand how people learn. In this section, we define *learning*, present three popular learning theories, and describe how managers can facilitate employee learning.

A Definition of Learning

learning A relatively permanent change in behavior that occurs as a result of experience.

What is **learning**? A psychologist's definition is considerably broader than the layperson's view that "it's what we did when we went to school." In actuality, each of us is continuously "going to school." Learning occurs all the time. Therefore, a generally accepted definition of *learning* is "any relatively permanent change in behavior that occurs as a result of experience."[32] Ironically, we can say that changes in behavior indicate that learning has taken place and that learning is a change in behavior.

The previous definition suggests that we can see changes taking place, but we can't see the learning itself. The concept is theoretical and, hence, not directly observable:

> You have seen people in the process of learning, you have seen people who behave in a particular way as a result of learning and some of you (in fact, I guess the majority of you) have "learned" at some time in your life. In other words, we infer that learning has taken place if an individual behaves, reacts, responds as a result of experience in a manner different from the way he formerly behaved.[33]

Our definition has several components that deserve clarification. First, learning involves change. Change may be good or bad from an organizational point of view. People can learn unfavorable behaviors—to hold prejudices or to shirk their responsibilities, for example—as well as favorable behaviors. Second, the change must become ingrained. Immediate changes may be only reflexive or a result of fatigue (or a sudden burst of energy) and thus may not represent learning. Third, some form of experience is necessary for learning. Experience may be acquired directly through observation or practice, or it may be acquired indirectly, as through reading. The crucial test still remains: Does this experience result in a relatively permanent change in behavior? If the answer is "yes," we can say that learning has taken place.

Theories of Learning

How do we learn? Three theories have been offered to explain the process by which we acquire patterns of behavior. These are classical conditioning, operant conditioning, and social learning.

classical conditioning A type of conditioning in which an individual responds to some stimulus that would not ordinarily produce such a response.

Classical Conditioning **Classical conditioning** Grew out of experiments to teach dogs to salivate in response to the ringing of a bell, conducted in the early 1900s by Russian physiologist Ivan Pavlov.[34] A simple surgical procedure allowed Pavlov to measure accurately the amount of saliva secreted by a dog. When Pavlov presented the dog with a piece of meat, the dog exhibited a noticeable increase in salivation. When Pavlov withheld the presentation of meat and merely rang a bell, the dog did not salivate. Then Pavlov proceeded to link the meat and the ringing of the bell. After repeatedly hearing the bell before getting the food, the dog began to salivate as soon as the bell rang. After a while, the dog would salivate merely at the sound of the bell, even if no food was offered. In effect, the dog had learned to respond—that is, to salivate—to the bell. Let's review this experiment to introduce the key concepts in classical conditioning.

In Pavlov's experiment, the meat was an *unconditioned stimulus*; it invariably caused the dog to react in a specific way. The reaction that took place whenever the unconditioned stimulus occurred was called the *unconditioned response* (or the noticeable increase in salivation, in this case). The bell was an artificial stimulus, or what we call the *conditioned stimulus*. Although it was originally neutral, after the bell was paired with the meat (an unconditioned stimulus), it eventually produced a response when presented alone. The last key concept is the *conditioned response*. This describes the behavior of the dog; it salivated in reaction to the bell alone.

Using these concepts, we can summarize classical conditioning. Essentially, learning a conditioned response involves building up an association between a conditioned stimulus and an unconditioned stimulus. When the stimuli, one compelling and the other one neutral, are paired, the neutral one becomes a conditioned stimulus and, hence, takes on the properties of the unconditioned stimulus.

Classical conditioning can be used to explain why nursery rhymes often bring back pleasant memories of childhood and feelings of euphoria. In an organizational setting, we can also see classical conditioning operating. For example, at one manufacturing plant, every time the top executives from the head office were scheduled to make a visit, the plant management would clean up the administrative offices and wash the windows. This went on for years. Eventually, employees would turn on their best behavior and look prim and proper whenever the windows were cleaned—even in those occasional instances when the cleaning was not paired with a visit from the top brass. People had learned to associate the cleaning of the windows with a visit from the head office.

Classical conditioning is passive. Something happens, and we react in a specific way. It is elicited in response to a specific, identifiable event. As such, it can explain simple reflexive behaviors. But most behavior—particularly the complex behavior of individuals in organizations—is emitted rather than elicited. That is, it's voluntary rather than reflexive. For example, employees *choose* to arrive at work on time, ask their boss for help with problems, or "goof off" when no one is watching. The learning of those behaviors is better understood by looking at operant conditioning.

operant conditioning A type of conditioning in which desired voluntary behavior leads to a reward or prevents a punishment.

Operant Conditioning **Operant conditioning** argues that behavior is a function of its consequences. People learn to behave to get something they want or to avoid something they don't want. Operant behavior means voluntary or learned behavior in contrast to reflexive or unlearned behavior. The tendency to repeat such behavior is influenced by the reinforcement or lack of reinforcement brought about by the consequences of the behavior. Therefore, reinforcement strengthens a behavior and increases the likelihood that it will be repeated.

What Pavlov did for classical conditioning, the Harvard psychologist B. F. Skinner did for operant conditioning.[35] Skinner argued that creating pleasing consequences to follow specific forms of behavior would increase the frequency of that behavior. He demonstrated that people will most likely engage in desired behaviors if they are positively reinforced for doing so; that rewards are most effective if they immediately follow the desired response; and that behavior that is not rewarded, or is punished, is less likely to be repeated. For example, we know a professor who places a mark by a student's name each time the student makes a contribution to class discussions. Operant conditioning would argue that this practice is motivating because it conditions a student to expect a reward (earning class credit) each time she demonstrates a specific behavior (speaking up in class). The concept of operant conditioning was part of Skinner's broader concept of **behaviorism**, which argues that behavior follows stimuli in a relatively unthinking manner. In Skinner's form of radical behaviorism, concepts such as feelings, thoughts, and other states of mind are rejected as causes of behavior. In short, people learn to associate stimulus and response, but their conscious awareness of this association is irrelevant.[36]

behaviorism A theory that argues that behavior follows stimuli in a relatively unthinking manner.

You see apparent illustrations of operant conditioning everywhere. For example, any situation in which it is either explicitly stated or implicitly suggested that reinforcements are contingent on some action on your part involves the use of operant learning. Your instructor says that if you want a high grade in the course, you must supply correct answers on the test. A commissioned salesperson wanting to earn a sizable income finds that doing so is contingent on generating high sales in her territory. Of course, the linkage can also work to teach the individual to engage in behaviors that work against the best interests of the organization. Assume that your boss tells you that if you will work overtime during the next 3-week busy season you'll be compensated for it at your next performance appraisal. However, when performance-appraisal time comes, you find that you are given no positive reinforcement for your overtime work. The next time your boss asks you to work overtime, what will you do? You'll probably decline! Your behavior can be explained by operant conditioning: If a behavior fails to be positively reinforced, the probability that the behavior will be repeated declines.

Social Learning Individuals can learn by observing what happens to other people and just by being told about something as well as through direct experiences. For example, much of what we have learned comes from watching models—parents, teachers, peers, motion picture and television performers, bosses, and so forth. This view that we can learn through both observation and direct experience is called **social-learning theory**.[37]

social-learning theory The view that people can learn through observation and direct experience.

Although social-learning theory is an extension of operant conditioning—that is, it assumes that behavior is a function of consequences—it also acknowledges the existence of observational learning and the importance of perception in learning. People respond to how they perceive and define consequences, not to the objective consequences themselves.

The influence of models is central to the social-learning viewpoint. Four processes have been found to determine the influence that a model will have on an individual:

1. **Attentional processes.** People learn from a model only when they recognize and pay attention to its critical features. We tend to be most influenced by models that are attractive, repeatedly available, important to us, or similar to us in our estimation.
2. **Retention processes.** A model's influence depends on how well the individual remembers the model's action after the model is no longer readily available.
3. **Motor reproduction processes.** After a person has seen a new behavior by observing the model, the watching must be converted to doing. This process then demonstrates that the individual can perform the modeled activities.
4. **Reinforcement processes.** Individuals are motivated to exhibit the modeled behavior if positive incentives or rewards are provided. Behaviors that are positively reinforced are given more attention, learned better, and performed more often.

Shaping: A Managerial Tool

5-4 Define shaping and show how it can be used in OB.

shaping behavior Systematically reinforcing each successive step that moves an individual closer to the desired response.

Because learning takes place on the job as well as prior to it, managers are concerned with how they can teach employees to behave in ways that most benefit the organization. When we attempt to mold individuals by guiding their learning in graduated steps, we are **shaping behavior**. Consider a situation in which an employee's behavior is significantly different from that sought by management. If management rewarded the individual only when he showed desirable responses, there might be very little reinforcement taking place. In such a case, shaping offers a logical approach toward achieving the desired behavior.

We *shape* behavior by systematically reinforcing each successive step that moves the individual closer to the desired response. If an employee who has chronically been a half-hour late for work comes in only 20 minutes late, we can reinforce that improvement. Reinforcement would increase as responses more closely approximated the desired behavior.

Methods of Shaping Behavior There are four ways to shape behavior: through positive reinforcement, negative reinforcement, punishment, and extinction.

Following a response with something pleasant is called *positive reinforcement*. This would describe, for instance, a boss who praises an employee for a job well done. Following a response by the termination or withdrawal of something unpleasant is called *negative reinforcement*. If your college instructor asks a question and you don't know the answer, looking through your lecture notes is likely to preclude your being called on. This is a negative reinforcement because you have learned that looking busily through your notes prevents the instructor from calling on you. *Punishment* is causing an unpleasant condition in an attempt to eliminate an undesirable behavior. Giving an employee a 2-day suspension from work without pay for showing up drunk is an example of punishment. Eliminating any reinforcement that is maintaining a behavior is called *extinction*. When the behavior is not reinforced, it tends to be

An Ethical Choice

"You Can't Teach an Old Dog New Tricks!"

This statement is false. It reflects the widely held stereotype that older workers have difficulty adapting to new methods and techniques. Studies consistently demonstrate that older employees are perceived as being relatively inflexible, resistant to change, and less willing and able to be trained than their younger counterparts.[38] But these perceptions are mostly wrong.

Evidence does indicate that older workers (typically defined as people aged 50 and over) are less confident of their learning abilities (perhaps due to acceptance of societal stereotypes). Moreover, older workers do seem to be somewhat less efficient in acquiring complex or demanding skills, and, on average, they are not as fast in terms of reaction time or in solving problems. That is, they may take longer to train. However, once trained, research indicates that older workers actually learn more than their younger counterparts, and they are better at transferring what they have learned to the job.[39] And age actually improves some intellectual abilities, such as verbal ability, and older brains are packed with more so-called expert knowledge—meaning they tend to have better outlines for how to solve problems.[40]

The ability to acquire the skills, knowledge, or behavior necessary to perform a job at a given level—that is, trainability—has been the subject of much research. And the evidence indicates that there are differences between people in their trainability. A number of individual-difference factors (such as low ability and reduced motivation) have been found to impede learning and training outcomes. However, age has not been found to influence these outcomes. In fact, older employees actually benefit more from training. Still, the stereotypes persist.[41]

gradually extinguished. College instructors who wish to discourage students from asking questions in class can eliminate this behavior in their students by ignoring those who raise their hands to ask questions. Hand raising will become extinct when it is invariably met with an absence of reinforcement.

Both positive and negative reinforcement result in learning. They strengthen a response and increase the probability of repetition. In the preceding illustrations, praise strengthens and increases the behavior of doing a good job because praise is desired. The behavior of "looking busy" is similarly strengthened and increased by its terminating the undesirable consequence of being called on by the teacher. However, both punishment and extinction weaken behavior and tend to decrease its subsequent frequency. In shaping behavior, a critical issue is the timing of reinforcements. This is an issue we'll consider now.

continuous reinforcement
Reinforcing a desired behavior each time it is demonstrated.

intermittent reinforcement
Reinforcing a desired behavior often enough to make the behavior worth repeating but not every time it is demonstrated.

Schedules of Reinforcement The two major types of reinforcement schedules are *continuous* and *intermittent*. A **continuous reinforcement** schedule reinforces the desired behavior each and every time it is demonstrated. Take, for example, the case of someone who historically has had trouble arriving at work on time. Every time he is not tardy, his manager might compliment him on his desirable behavior. With **intermittent reinforcement**, on the other hand, not every instance of the desirable behavior is reinforced, but reinforcement is given often enough to make the behavior worth repeating. This latter schedule can be compared to the workings of a slot machine, which people will continue to play even when they know it is adjusted to give a considerable return to the casino. The intermittent payoffs occur just often enough to reinforce the behavior of slipping in coins and pulling the handle. Evidence indicates that the intermittent, or varied, form of reinforcement tends to promote more resistance to extinction than does the continuous form.[42]

An intermittent reinforcement can be of a ratio or interval type. *Ratio schedules* depend on how many responses the subject makes. The individual is reinforced after giving a certain number of specific types of behavior. *Interval schedules* depend on how much time has passed since the previous reinforcement. With interval schedules, the individual is reinforced on the first appropriate behavior after a particular time has elapsed. A reinforcement can also be classified as fixed or variable.

fixed-interval schedule Spacing rewards at uniform time intervals.

When rewards are spaced at uniform time intervals, the reinforcement schedule is a **fixed-interval schedule**. The critical variable is time, which is held constant. This is the predominant schedule for most salaried workers. When you get your paycheck on a monthly or other predetermined time basis, you're rewarded on a fixed-interval reinforcement schedule.

variable-interval schedule Distributing rewards in time so that reinforcements are unpredictable.

If rewards are distributed in time so that reinforcements are unpredictable, the schedule is a **variable-interval schedule**. When an instructor advises her class that pop quizzes will be given during the term (the exact number of which is unknown to the students) and the quizzes will account for 20 percent of the term grade, she is using a variable-interval schedule. Similarly, a series of randomly timed unannounced visits to a company office by the corporate audit staff is an example of a variable-interval schedule.

fixed-ratio schedule Initiating rewards after a fixed or constant number of responses.

In a **fixed-ratio schedule**, after a fixed or constant number of responses are given, a reward is initiated. For example, a piece-rate incentive plan is a fixedratio schedule; the employee receives a reward based on the number of work pieces generated. If the piece rate for a zipper installer in a dressmaking factory is INR 120 per dozen, the reinforcement (money in this case) is fixed to the number of zippers sewn into garments. After every dozen is sewn in, the installer has earned another INR 120.

variable-ratio schedule Varying the reward relative to the behavior of the individual.

When the reward varies relative to the behavior of the individual, he or she is said to be reinforced on a **variable-ratio schedule**. Salespeople on commission are examples of individuals on such a reinforcement schedule. On some occasions, they may make a sale after only 2 calls on a potential customer. On other occasions, they might need to make 20 or more calls to secure a sale. The reward, then, is variable in relation to the number of successful calls the salesperson makes. Exhibit 5-3 summarizes the schedules of reinforcement.

Reinforcement Schedules and Behavior Continuous reinforcement schedules can lead to early satiation, and under this schedule, behavior tends to weaken rapidly when reinforcers are withheld. However, continuous reinforcers are appropriate for newly emitted, unstable, or low-frequency responses. In contrast, intermittent reinforcers preclude early satiation because they don't follow every response. They are appropriate for stable or high-frequency responses.

In general, variable schedules tend to lead to higher performance than fixed schedules (see Exhibit 5-4). For example, as noted previously, most employees in organizations are paid on fixed-interval schedules. But such a schedule does not clearly link performance and rewards. The reward is given for time spent on the job rather than for a specific response (performance). In contrast, variable-interval schedules generate high rates of response and more stable and

Exhibit 5-3 Schedules of Reinforcement

Reinforcement Schedule	Nature of Reinforcement	Effect on Behavior	Example
Continuous	Reward given after each desired behavior	Fast learning of new behavior but rapid extinction	Compliments
Fixed-interval	Reward given at fixed time intervals	Average and irregular performance with rapid extinction	Weekly paychecks
Variable-interval	Reward given at variable time intervals	Moderately high and stable performance with slow extinction	Pop quizzes
Fixed ratio	Reward given at fixed amounts of output	High and stable performance attained quickly but also with rapid extinction	Piece-rate pay
Variable-ratio	Reward given at variable amounts of output	Very high performance with slow extinction	Commissioned sales

consistent behavior because of the high correlation between performance and reward and because of the uncertainty involved—the employee tends to be more alert because there is a surprise factor.

Behavior Modification A now-classic study took place a number of years ago with freight packers at Emery Air Freight (now part of FedEx).[43] Emery's management wanted packers to use freight containers for shipments whenever possible because of specific economic savings. When packers were asked about the percentage of shipments contained, the standard reply was 90 percent. An analysis by Emery found, however, that the actual container utilization rate was only 45 percent. In order to encourage employees to use containers, management established a program of feedback and positive reinforcements. Each packer was instructed to keep a checklist of daily packings, both containerized and noncontainerized. At the end of each day, the packer computed the container utilization rate. Almost unbelievably, container utilization jumped to more than 90 percent on the first day of the program and held at that level. Emery reported that this simple program of feedback and positive reinforcements saved the company $2 million over a 3-year period.

OB Mod The application of reinforcement concepts to individuals in the work setting.

This program at Emery Air Freight illustrates the use of behavior modification, or what has become more popularly called **OB Mod.**[44] It represents the application of reinforcement concepts to individuals in the work setting. The typical OB Mod program follows a five-step problem-solving model: (1) identify critical behaviors; (2) develop baseline data; (3) identify behavioral consequences; (4) develop and implement an intervention strategy; and (5) evaluate performance improvement.[45]

Everything an employee does on the job is not equally important in terms of performance outcomes. The first step in OB Mod, therefore, is to identify the critical behaviors that make a significant impact on the employee's job performance. These are those 5 to 10 percent of behaviors that may account for up to 70 or 80 percent of each employee's performance. Freight packers using containers whenever possible at Emery Air Freight is an example of a critical behavior.

The second step requires the manager to develop some baseline performance data. This is obtained by determining the number of times the identified behavior

Exhibit 5-4 Intermittent Schedules of Reinforcement

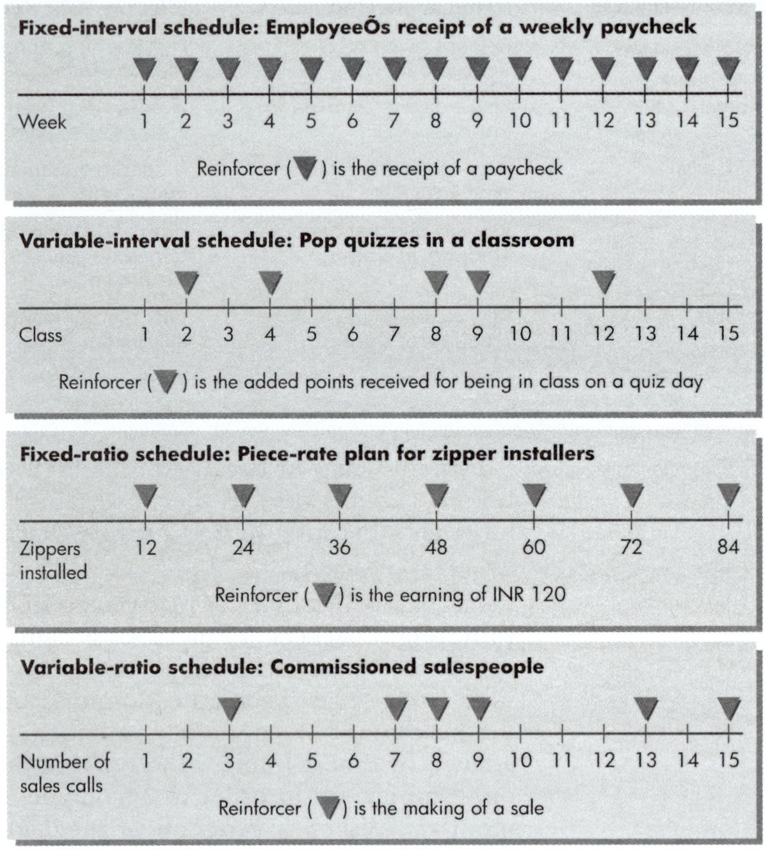

is occurring under present conditions. In the Emery freightpacking example, this was the revelation that 45 percent of all shipments were containerized.

The third step is to perform a functional analysis to identify the behavioral contingencies or consequences of performance. This tells the manager the antecedent cues that emit the behavior and the consequences that are currently maintaining it. At Emery Air Freight, social norms and the greater difficulty in packing containers were the antecedent cues. This encouraged the practice of packing items separately. Moreover, the consequences for continuing the behavior, prior to the OB Mod intervention, were social acceptance and escaping more demanding work.

Once the functional analysis is complete, the manager is ready to develop and implement an intervention strategy to strengthen desirable performance behaviors and weaken undesirable behaviors. The appropriate strategy will entail changing some elements of the performance–reward linkage—structure, processes, technology, groups, or the task—with the goal of making high-level performance more rewarding. In the Emery example, the work technology was altered to require the keeping of a checklist. The checklist plus the computation, at the end of the day, of a container-utilization rate acted to reinforce the desirable behavior of using containers.

The final step in OB Mod is to evaluate performance improvement. In the Emery intervention, the immediate improvement in the container-utilization rate demonstrated that behavioral change took place. That it rose to 90 percent and held at that level further indicates that learning took place. That is, the employees underwent a relatively permanent change in behavior.

A number of organizations have used OB Mod to improve employee productivity; to reduce errors, absenteeism, tardiness, and accident rates; and to improve friendliness toward customers.[46] For instance, a clothing manufacturer saved $60,000 in 1 year due to fewer absences. A packing firm improved productivity 16 percent, cut errors by 40 percent, and reduced accidents by more than 43 percent—resulting in savings of over $1 million. A bank successfully used OB Mod to increase the friendliness of its tellers, which led to a demonstrable improvement in customer satisfaction.

Problems with OB Mod and Reinforcement Theory Although the effectiveness of reinforcements in the form of rewards and punishments has a lot of support in the literature, that doesn't necessarily mean that Skinner was right or that OB Mod is the best way to reward people. What if the power of reinforcements isn't due to operant conditioning or behaviorism? One problem with behaviorism is, as research shows, that thoughts and feelings immediately follow environmental stimuli, even those explicitly meant to shape behavior. This is contrary to the assumptions of behaviorism and OB Mod, which assume that people's innermost thoughts and feelings in response to the environment are irrelevant.

Think about praise from a supervisor. For example, assume your course instructor compliments you for asking a good question. A behaviorist would argue that this shapes your behavior because you find the stimulus (the compliment) pleasant and therefore respond by attempting to ask other questions that will generate the same reward. However, imagine, for example, that you had to weigh the pleasant feelings produced by your professor's praise against the snickers of jealous classmates who whispered "brown noser." Your choice of what to do would likely be dictated by weighing the value of these stimuli, which may be a rather complex mental process involving thinking and feeling.

Also, is it really shaping if the compliment was given without an intention of molding behavior? Isn't it perhaps overly restrictive to view all stimuli as motivated to obtain a particular response? Is the only reason we tell someone we love them because we wish to obtain a reward or to mold their behavior?

Because of these problems, among others, operant conditioning and behaviorism have been superseded by other approaches that emphasize cognitive processes.[47] There is no denying, though, the contribution of these theories to our understanding of human behavior.

The Link between Perception, Learning and Individual Decision Making

5-5 Explain the link between perception and decision making.

decisions Choices made from among two or more alternatives.

Individuals make **decisions**, choices from among two or more alternatives. Ideally, decision making would be an objective process, but the way individuals make decisions and the quality of their choices are largely influenced by their perceptions. Individual decision making is an important factor of behavior at all levels of an organization.

problem A discrepancy between the current state of affairs and some desired state.

Decision making occurs as a reaction to a **problem**. That is, a discrepancy exists between the current state of affairs and some desired state, requiring us to consider alternative courses of action. If your car breaks down and you rely on it to get to work, you have a problem that requires a decision on your part. Unfortunately, most problems don't come neatly labeled. One person's *problem* is another person's *satisfactory state of affairs.* One manager may view her division's 2 percent decline in quarterly sales to be a serious problem requiring immediate action on her part. Her counterpart in another division, who also had a 2 percent sales decrease, might consider it quite acceptable. So awareness that a problem exists and that a decision might or might not be needed is a perceptual issue.

Every decision requires us to interpret and evaluate information. We typically receive data from multiple sources that we need to screen, process, and interpret. Which data are relevant to the decision, and which are not? Our perceptions will answer that question. We also need to develop alternatives and evaluate their strengths and weaknesses. Again, our perceptual process will affect the outcome. Finally, we should consider how our perceptions of the situation influence our decisions. For instance, how good are you at saying no? Research indicates that we perceive that saying no is uncomfortable, and often after saying no we will feel obligated to say yes to subsequent requests. In fact, people are so uncomfortable saying no that they may agree to unethical acts. When student participants in a study asked 108 strangers to write the word *pickle* in library books, half of them did it![48]

Decision Making in Organizations

5-6 Contrast the rational model of decision making with bounded rationality and intuition.

Business schools train students to follow rational decision-making models. While such rationalistic models have merit, they don't always describe how people make decisions. OB improves the way we make decisions in organizations by addressing the decision-making errors people commit in addition to the perception errors we've discussed. First, we describe some decision-making constructs and then outline a few of the most common errors.

The Rational Model, Bounded Rationality, and Intuition

In OB, generally accepted constructs of decision making are employed by each of us to make determinations. These constructs are rational decision making, bounded rationality, and intuition. Though their processes make sense, they may not lead to the most accurate (or best) decisions. More important, sometimes one strategy may lead to a better outcome than another in a given situation.

rational A style of decision making characterized by making consistent, value-maximizing choices within specified constraints.

rational decision-making model A decision-making model that describes how individuals should behave to maximize some outcome.

Rational Decision Making We often think the best decision maker is **rational** and makes consistent, value-maximizing choices within specified constraints.[49] Rational decisions follow a six-step **rational decision-making model**[50] (see Exhibit 5-5).

Exhibit 5-5 **Steps in the Rational Decision-Making Model**

1. Define the problem.
2. Identify the decision criteria.
3. Allocate weights to the criteria.
4. Develop the alternatives.
5. Evaluate the alternatives.
6. Select the best alternative.

The rational decision-making model assumes the decision maker has complete information, can identify all relevant options in an unbiased manner, and chooses the option with the highest utility.[51] However, most decisions don't follow the rational model; people are usually content to find an acceptable or reasonable solution to a problem rather than an optimal one. We tend to limit our choices to the neighborhood of the problem's symptom and the current alternative at hand. As one expert in decision making put it, "Most significant decisions are made by judgment, rather than by a defined prescriptive model."[52] People are remarkably unaware of making suboptimal decisions.[53]

Bounded Rationality Often, we don't follow the rational decision-making model for a reason: Our limited information-processing capability makes it impossible to assimilate all the information necessary to optimize, even if the information is readily obtainable.[54] Many problems don't have an optimal solution because they are too complicated to fit the rational decision-making model, so people *satisfice:* They seek solutions that are satisfactory and sufficient. We tend to reduce complex problems to a level we can readily understand.

bounded rationality A simplified process of making decisions by perceiving and interpreting the essential features of problems without capturing their complexity.

Because the human mind cannot formulate and solve complex problems with full rationality, we operate within the confines of **bounded rationality**. We construct simplified models that extract the essential features from problems without capturing all their complexity. We can then behave rationally within the limits of the simple model.

How does bounded rationality work for the typical individual? Once we've identified a problem, we begin to search for criteria and alternatives. The criteria are unlikely to be exhaustive. We identify alternatives that are highly visible and that usually represent familiar criteria and tried-and-true solutions. Next, we begin reviewing the alternatives, focusing on choices that differ little from the current

Nintendo president Satoru Iwata (right) and DeNA president Isao Moriyasu operated within the confines of bounded rationality in deciding to form an alliance to develop and operate new game applications for mobile devices. The alliance brings Nintendo's games and characters to the mobile user market and strengthens DeNA's mobile gaming business.
Source: Akio Kon/Bloomberg/Getty Images

state until we identify one that is "good enough"—that meets an acceptable level of performance. Thus ends our search. Therefore, the solution represents a satisficing choice—the first *acceptable* one we encounter—rather than an optimal one.

Satisficing is not always bad—a simple process may frequently be more sensible than the traditional rational decision-making model.[55] To use the rational model, you need to gather a great deal of information about all the options, compute applicable weights, and then calculate values across a huge number of criteria. All these processes can cost time, energy, and money. Sometimes a fast-and-frugal process of solving problems might be your best option.

Bounded rationality can also be of concern in ethical decision making (as discussed later in this chapter). Not only are we prone to make systematic and predictable errors in ethical decisions,[56] but our perceptions of whether we have the freedom or *right* to behave in a particular way are bounded by our *duties* toward the people our actions affect.[57] For example, you *want* to take the last doughnut in the break room but you know that you *shouldn't* in case someone has not had one yet. Researchers have identified many ways in which the automatic effects of our bounded rationality can be circumvented in an ethical context: Be sure to triangulate on the focal issue by asking multiple questions, drawing on multiple sources, considering the sources from which you derive information, and leaving more time to decide.[58]

intuitive decision making An unconscious process created out of distilled experience.

Intuition Perhaps the least rational way of making decisions is **intuitive decision making**, an unconscious process created from distilled experience.[59] Intuitive decision making occurs outside conscious thought; relies on holistic associations, or links between disparate pieces of information; is fast; and is *affectively charged*, meaning it engages the emotions.[60] While intuition isn't rational, it isn't necessarily wrong, nor does it always contradict rational analysis; the two can complement each other.

Does intuition help effective decision making? Researchers are divided, but most experts are skeptical, in part because intuition is hard to measure and

Intuition plays an important role in the investment buying decisions of Warren Buffett, chair and CEO of Berkshire Hathaway. Buffett begins exploring investment alternatives by using his intuition as a guide in selecting a firm he understands and finds interesting before he starts analyzing the firm, its industry, and its valuation.
Source: Huang Jihui/Xinhua/Alamy Stock Photo

analyze (although expertise-based intuitive decisions tend to be more effective and accurate).[61] Probably the best advice from one expert is: "Intuition can be very useful as a way of setting up a hypothesis but is unacceptable as 'proof.'" Use hunches derived from your experience to speculate, yes, but always make sure to test those hunches with objective data and rational, dispassionate analysis.[62]

As you can see, the more we use objective processes for decision making, the more likely we are to correct some of the problems with our perceptual process. Just as there are biases and errors in the perception process, it stands to reason there are identifiable biases and errors in our decision making, which we will outline next.

Common Biases and Errors in Decision Making

Decision makers engage in bounded rationality, but they also allow systematic biases and errors to creep into their judgments.[63] To minimize effort and avoid trade-offs, people tend to rely too heavily on experience, impulses, gut feelings, and convenient rules of thumb. Shortcuts can distort rationality. The following are the most common biases in decision making. Exhibit 5-6 provides some suggestions for avoiding these biases and errors.

Overconfidence Bias We tend to be overconfident about our abilities and the abilities of others; also, we are usually not aware of this bias.[64] For example, when people say they're 90 percent confident about the range a certain number might take, their estimated ranges contain the correct answer only about 50 percent of the time—and experts are no more accurate in setting up confidence intervals than are novices.[65]

Exhibit 5-6 Reducing Biases and Errors

Focus on Goals. Without goals, you can't be rational, you don't know what information you need, you don't know which information is relevant and which is irrelevant, you'll find it difficult to choose between alternatives, and you're far more likely to experience regret over the choices you make. Clear goals make decision making easier and help you eliminate options that are inconsistent with your interests.

Look for Information That Disconfirms Your Beliefs. One of the most effective means for counteracting overconfidence and the confirmation and hindsight biases is to actively look for information that contradicts your beliefs and assumptions. When we overtly consider various ways we could be wrong, we challenge our tendencies to think we're smarter than we actually are.

Don't Try to Create Meaning out of Random Events. The educated mind has been trained to look for cause-and-effect relationships. When something happens, we ask why. And when we can't find reasons, we often invent them. You have to accept that there are events in life that are outside your control. Ask yourself if patterns can be meaningfully explained or whether they are merely coincidence. Don't attempt to create meaning out of coincidence.

Increase Your Options. No matter how many options you've identified, your final choice can be no better than the best of the option set you've selected. This argues for increasing your decision alternatives and for using creativity in developing a wide range of diverse choices. The more alternatives you can generate, and the more diverse those alternatives, the greater your chance of finding an outstanding one.

Source: Based on S. P. Robbins, *Decide & Conquer: Making Winning Decisions and Taking Control of Your Life* (Upper Saddle River, NJ: Financial Times/Prentice Hall, 2004), 164–68.

Individuals whose intellectual and interpersonal abilities are *weakest* are most likely to overestimate their performance and ability.[66] There's also a negative relationship between entrepreneurs' optimism and performance of their new ventures: the more optimistic, the less successful.[67] The tendency to be too confident about their ideas might keep some from planning how to avoid problems that arise.

Investor overconfidence operates in a variety of ways.[68] Finance professor Terrance Odean says, "People think they know more than they do, and it costs them." Investors, especially novices, overestimate not just their skill in processing information but also the quality of the information. Most investors will do only as well as or just slightly better than the market.

Overconfidence has a relationship with leadership emergence (which we discuss in the chapter on leadership). People are more likely to select the overconfident as leaders as they tend to ease their sense of ambiguity, and overconfidence fits the perceiver's understanding of what it means to be a leader.[69] Furthermore, overconfidence bias is more likely to emerge in leaders who are powerful, ambitious, and of a higher social class and, in some cases, lead to higher firm performance.[70] However, despite initial benefits, overconfidence may eventually backfire: as overconfidence is revealed (the person's behaviors are not as good as they say they are or their claims are falsifiable), people begin to perceive the overconfident person negatively, which damages their reputation.[71]

anchoring bias A tendency to fixate on initial information, from which one then fails to adjust adequately for subsequent information.

Anchoring Bias **Anchoring bias** is a tendency to fixate on initial information and fail to adequately adjust for subsequent information.[72] As we discussed earlier in the chapter, the mind appears to give a disproportionate amount of emphasis to the first information it receives in employment interviews. Anchors are widely used by people in professions in which persuasion skills are important—advertising, management, politics, real estate, and law.

Any time a negotiation takes place, so does anchoring. When a prospective employer asks how much you made in your prior job, your answer typically anchors the employer's offer. (Remember this when you negotiate your salary, but set the anchor only as high as you truthfully can.) The more precise your anchor, the smaller the adjustment. Some research suggests people think of making an adjustment after an anchor is set as rounding off a number: If you suggest a salary of ₹5,50,000, your boss will consider ₹5,00,000 to ₹6,00,000 a reasonable range for negotiation, but if you mention ₹5,56,500, your boss is more likely to consider ₹5,55,000 to ₹5,60,000 the range of likely values.[73]

confirmation bias The tendency to seek out information that reaffirms past choices and to discount information that contradicts past judgments.

Confirmation Bias The rational decision-making process assumes we objectively gather information. But we don't. We *selectively* gather it. **Confirmation bias** represents a case of selective perception: We seek out (and accept) information that reaffirms our past choices and current views, and we discount (or are skeptical of) information that contradicts or challenges them.[74] We even tend to seek sources most likely to tell us what we want to hear, and we give too much weight to supporting information and too little to contradictory. Those who feel a strong need to be accurate in deciding are less prone to confirmation bias. Confirmation bias applies to person perception (discussed earlier in this chapter): once we settle on a trait attribution, we seek out and accept information that reaffirms this perception.[75] For example, if your supervisor sees you as unreliable, they are more likely to notice when you are unreliable than when you are reliable.

Availability Bias More people are afraid of flying than they are of driving in a car. But if flying on a commercial airline were as dangerous as driving, the equivalent of two 747s filled to capacity would crash every week, killing all aboard. Because the media give more attention to air accidents, we tend to overstate the risk of flying and understate the risk of driving.

availability bias The tendency for people to base their judgments on information that is readily available to them.

Availability bias is our tendency to base judgments on readily available information. A combination of readily available information and our previous direct experience with similar information has a particularly strong impact on our decision making. Also, events that evoke emotions, are particularly vivid, or are more recent tend to be more available in our memory. This can lead us to overestimate the chances of unlikely events, such as being in an airplane crash, suffering complications from medical treatment, or getting fired.[76] Availability bias can also explain why managers give more weight in performance appraisals to recent employee behaviors than to behaviors of 6 or 9 months earlier.[77]

Escalation of Commitment Another distortion that creeps into decisions is a tendency to escalate commitment, often for increasingly nonrational reasons.[78] **Escalation of commitment** refers to our staying with a decision even if there is clear evidence that it is wrong. Consider a friend who has been dating someone for several years. Although he admits things aren't going too well, he says he is still going to marry her. His justification: "I have a lot invested in the relationship!"

escalation of commitment An increased commitment to a previous decision despite negative information.

When is escalation most likely to occur? Evidence indicates that it occurs when individuals view themselves as responsible for the outcome or when they feel like they will eventually succeed.[79] The fear of personal failure even biases the way we search for and evaluate information so that we choose only information that supports our dedication.[80] It doesn't appear to matter whether we chose the failing course of action or it was assigned to us—we feel responsible and escalate in either case. Also, the sharing of decision authority—such as when others review the choice we made—can lead to higher escalation.[81]

We usually think of escalation of commitment as ungrounded. However, persistence in the face of failure is responsible for many of history's greatest feats: the building of the Pyramids, the Great Wall of China, the Panama Canal, and the Empire State Building among them. On a smaller scale, the desire to consider yourself a "good person" can lead you to experience escalation toward a prosocial goal.[82] Researchers suggest that a balanced approach includes frequent evaluation of the spent costs and whether the next step is worth the anticipated costs.[83] What we want to combat is thus the tendency to escalate commitment *automatically*.

Randomness Error Most of us like to think we have some control over our world. Our tendency to believe we can predict the outcome of random events is the **randomness error**.

randomness error The tendency of individuals to believe that they can predict the outcome of random events.

Decision making suffers when we try to create meaning in random events, particularly when we turn imaginary patterns into superstitions.[84] These can be completely contrived ("I never make important decisions on Friday the 13th") or they can evolve from a reinforced past pattern of behavior (Tiger Woods often wears a red shirt during a golf tournament's final round because he won many junior tournaments wearing red shirts). Decisions based on random occurrences can handicap us when they affect our judgment or bias our major decisions.

risk aversion The tendency to prefer a sure gain of a moderate amount over a riskier outcome, even if the riskier outcome might have a higher expected payoff.

Risk Aversion Mathematically speaking, we should find a 50–50 flip of the coin for ₹100 to be worth as much as a sure promise of ₹50. After all, the expected value of the gamble over many trials is ₹50. However, nearly everyone but committed gamblers would rather have the sure thing than a risky prospect.[85] For many people, a 50–50 flip of a coin even for ₹200 might not be worth as much as a sure promise of ₹50, even though the gamble is mathematically worth twice as much! This tendency to prefer a sure thing over a risky outcome is **risk aversion**.

Overall, the framing of a decision has an effect on whether or not people will engage in risk-averse behavior—when decisions are framed positively, such as a potential gain of ₹50, people will be more risk averse (conversely, when the decision is framed in a negative manner, such as a loss of ₹50, people will engage in riskier behaviors).[86] CEOs at risk of termination are exceptionally risk averse, even when a riskier investment strategy is in their firms' best interests.[87] Organizations have a stronger hold on employees who are more risk averse because these employees tend to perceive that they have more to lose and are less likely to leave the organization.[88]

Risk preference is sometimes reversed: People take chances when trying to prevent a negative outcome.[89] They may thus risk losing a lot of money at trial rather than settle for less out of court. Stressful situations can make risk preferences stronger. People under stress are more likely to engage in risk-seeking behavior to avoid negative outcomes and in risk-averse behavior when seeking positive outcomes.[90]

hindsight bias The tendency to believe falsely, after an outcome of an event is actually known, that one would have accurately predicted that outcome.

Hindsight Bias **Hindsight bias** is the tendency to believe falsely, after the outcome is known, that we would have accurately predicted it.[91] When we have feedback on the outcome, we seem good at concluding it was obvious.

For instance, the original home video rental industry, renting movies at brick-and-mortar stores, collapsed as online distribution outlets ate away at the market.[92] Some have suggested that if rental companies like Blockbuster had leveraged their brand to offer online streaming and kiosks, they could have avoided failure. While that seems obvious now in hindsight, tempting us to think we would have predicted it, many experts failed to predict industry trends in advance. Though criticisms of decision makers may have merit, as Malcolm Gladwell, author of *Blink* and *The Tipping Point*, writes, "What is clear in hindsight is rarely clear before the fact."[93]

We are all susceptible to biases like hindsight bias, but are we all susceptible to the same degree? It is not likely. Our individual differences play a significant role in our decision-making processes, while our organizations constrain the range of our available decision choices.

Influences on Decision Making: Individual Differences and Organizational Constraints

5-7 Explain how individual differences and organizational constraints affect decision making.

We turn here to factors that influence the way people make decisions and the degree to which they are susceptible to errors and biases. We discuss individual differences and then organizational constraints.

Individual Differences

As we discussed, decision making in practice is characterized by bounded rationality, common biases and errors, and the use of intuition. Individual differences such as personality also create deviations from the rational model.

Personality Research suggests that personality influences our decisions. Let's look at conscientiousness and self-esteem.

Specific facets of conscientiousness—particularly achievement-striving and dutifulness—may affect escalation of commitment.[94] First, achievement-oriented people hate to fail, so they escalate their commitment, hoping to forestall failure. Dutiful people, however, are more inclined to do what they see as best for the organization, so they are less likely to escalate their commitment. Second, achievement-striving individuals appear more susceptible to hindsight bias, perhaps because they have a need to justify their actions.[95] We don't have evidence yet on whether dutiful people are immune to this bias.

People with high self-esteem (a general perception of being good enough) are strongly motivated to maintain it, so they use the self-serving bias to preserve it. They blame others for their failures while taking credit for successes.[96] In a more extreme case, those with the personality trait of grandiosity, a facet of narcissism (see Chapter 4), tend to engage in the self-serving bias.[97]

Gender Who makes better decisions, men or women? It depends on the situation. When the situation isn't stressful, decision making by men and women is about equal in quality. In stressful situations, it appears that men become more egocentric and make more risky decisions, while women become more empathetic and their decision making improves.[98] Research on rumination, or reflecting at length, offers further insights into gender differences in decision making.[99] Women spend more time than men analyzing the past, present, and future. They're more likely to overanalyze problems before deciding and to rehash a decision once made. This can make problems harder to solve, increase regret over past decisions, and increase depression. Women are nearly twice as likely as men to develop depression,[100] but why women ruminate more than men is not clear; some research points to differences in the hypothalamus, pituitary, and adrenal gland responses.[101] However, the gender difference seems to lessen with age. Differences are largest during young adulthood and smallest after age 65, when both men and women ruminate the least.[102]

Mental Ability We know people with higher levels of mental ability can process information more quickly, solve problems more accurately, and learn faster, so you might expect them to be less susceptible to common decision errors. However, mental ability appears to help people avoid only some of them.[103] Smart people are just as likely to fall prey to anchoring, overconfidence, and escalation of commitment, probably because being smart doesn't alert you to the possibility that you're too confident or emotionally defensive. It's not that intelligence never matters. Once warned about decision-making errors, more intelligent people learn to avoid them more quickly.

Cultural Differences The rational model makes no acknowledgment of cultural differences, nor does the bulk of OB research literature on decision making. But Indonesians, for instance, don't necessarily make decisions the same way Australians do. Therefore, we need to recognize that the cultural background of a decision maker can significantly influence the selection of problems, the depth of analysis, the importance placed on logic and rationality, and whether organizational decisions should be made autocratically by an individual manager or collectively in groups.[104]

Cultures differ in time orientation, the value they place on rationality, their belief in the ability of people to solve problems, and their preference for collective decision making. First, differences in time orientation help us understand, for instance, why managers in Egypt make decisions at a much slower and more deliberate pace than their U.S. counterparts. Second, the value to appear rational is much more in North America as compared to collective cultures as in India and Iran. A North American manager might decide intuitively but know it's important to appear to proceed in a rational fashion because rationality is highly valued in the West. In countries such as Iran, where rationality is not paramount over other factors, it is not necessary for efforts to appear rational.

Third, some cultures emphasize solving problems, while others focus on accepting situations as they are. The United States falls in the first category; Thailand and Indonesia are examples of the second. Because problem-solving managers believe they can and should change situations to their benefit, U.S. managers might identify a problem long before their Thai or Indonesian counterparts would choose to recognize it as such.

Fourth, decision making in Japan is much more group-oriented than in the United States. The Japanese value conformity and cooperation, so before Japanese CEOs make an important decision, they collect a large amount of information to use in consensus-forming group decisions.

Organizational Constraints

Organizations can constrain decision makers, creating deviations from the rational model. For instance, managers shape decisions to reflect the organization's performance evaluation and reward systems, to comply with formal regulations, and to meet organizationally imposed time constraints. Precedents can also limit decisions.

Performance Evaluation Systems Managers are influenced by the criteria on which they are evaluated. If a division manager believes the manufacturing plants under his responsibility are operating best when he hears nothing negative, the plant managers will spend a good part of their time ensuring that negative information doesn't reach him.

Reward Systems The organization's reward systems influence decision makers by suggesting which choices have better personal payoffs. If the organization rewards risk aversion, managers are more likely to make conservative decisions. For instance, for over half a century (the 1930s through the mid-1980s), General Motors consistently gave promotions and bonuses to managers who kept a low profile and avoided controversy. These executives became adept at dodging tough issues and passing controversial decisions on to committees, which harmed the organization over time.

Formal Regulations David, a shift manager at a Taco Bell restaurant in San Antonio, Texas, describes constraints he faces on his job: "I've got rules and regulations covering almost every decision I make—from how to make a burrito to how often I need to clean the restrooms. My job doesn't come with much freedom of choice." David's situation is not unique. All but the smallest organizations create rules and policies to program decisions and get individuals to act in the intended manner. In doing so, they limit decision choices.

System-Imposed Time Constraints Almost all important decisions come with explicit deadlines. For example, a report on new-product development may have to be ready for executive committee review by the first of the month. Such conditions often make it difficult, if not impossible, for managers to gather all information before making a final choice.

Historical Precedents Decisions aren't made in a vacuum; they have context. Individual decisions are points in a stream of choices; those made in the past are like ghosts that haunt and constrain current choices. It's common knowledge that the largest determinant of the size of any given year's budget is last year's budget. Choices made today are largely a result of choices made over the years.

Decision Making in Times of Crisis

During the COVID-19 pandemic of 2020, employees and leaders of businesses alike were forced to make extremely difficult decisions amidst chaos, confusion, and uncertainty.[105] As Anjali Lai, a senior analyst at Forrester eloquently described, "unprecedented levels of uncertainty paired with a rapid flow of new information means [people forged] ahead with neither a template to follow, nor the luxury of pondering every decision."[106] Decision makers are particularly susceptible to biases and distortion during times of crisis. For example, expert credit-rating agencies are more likely to provide negative or pessimistic ratings of creditworthiness during times of crisis, even when the creditworthiness of these target people or organizations would not be affected by the crisis.[107] Furthermore, decisions made during times of crisis are more likely to be emotionally charged and intuitive.[108] Not only does the strain of the crisis add an additional layer of anxiety and negative emotions to typical decisions, but the decisions in and of themselves may become highly charged, such as how doctors and nurses had to make extremely tough decisions as to who would receive treatment during the COVID-19 pandemic.[109] Relatedly, justice and ethics in decision making (see the following section for more discussion) play a huge role in times of crisis. Indeed, perceptions of justice are incredibly important during times of crisis, influencing employee attitudes and customer reactions alike.[110] As Lai noted, "choices and actions expose the company's priorities and values to ever-watchful consumers. To the business leaders navigating these decisions, our guidance is clear: treat your employees and customers as your North Star."[111]

What about Ethics in Decision Making?

5-8 Contrast the three ethical decision criteria.

As discussed in the prior section, ethical considerations should be important to organizational decision making, but not just during times of crisis. In this section, we present three ways to frame decisions ethically and then address the important issue of the effect of lying on decision making.

Three Ethical Decision Criteria

utilitarianism An ethical perspective in which decisions are made to provide the greatest good for all.

The first ethical yardstick is **utilitarianism**, which proposes making decisions solely based on their *outcomes*, ideally to provide the greatest good for all.[112] This view dominates business decision making and is consistent with goals such as rationality, efficiency, productivity, and high profits.[113] Keep in mind that utilitarianism is not always as objective as it sounds. A recent study indicated that the ethicality of utilitarianism is influenced in ways we don't realize. Participants were given a moral dilemma: The weight of five people bends a footbridge so it is low to some train tracks. A train is about to hit the bridge. The choice is to let all five people perish, or push the one heavy man off the bridge to save four people. In the United States, South Korea, France, and Israel, 20 percent of respondents chose to push the man off the bridge; in Spain, 18 percent chose to do so; and in Korea, none did. These might speak to cultural utilitarian values, but a minor change, asking people to answer in a non-native language they knew, caused more participants to push the man overboard: In one group, 33 percent pushed the man, and in another group 44 percent did.[114] The emotional distance of answering in a non-native language thus seemed to foster a utilitarian viewpoint. It appears that even our view of what we consider pragmatic is changeable.

Another ethical criterion is to make decisions consistent with fundamental liberties and privileges, as set forth in documents such as the Constitution of India. An emphasis on *rights* in decision making means respecting and protecting the basic rights of individuals, such as the right to privacy, free speech, and due process. This criterion protects **whistle-blowers**[115] when they reveal an organization's unethical practices to the press or government agencies, using their right to free speech.

whistle-blowers Individuals who report unethical practices by their employer to outsiders.

A third criterion is to impose and enforce rules fairly and impartially to ensure *justice* or an equitable distribution of benefits and costs.[116] This criterion is often approached from a **deonance** standpoint (employees feel as if they *ought* to behave in a certain way, as laid out in rules, laws, norms, or moral principles).[117] For example, some employees might feel as if they *should not* steal from their workplace because it is ethically "wrong" by moral norms, principles, or standards or it is forbidden by rules or laws. Notably, this "ought force" is present regardless of whether organizational rules exist; often, a decision is regarded as unfair or unjust because it violates a moral norm or principle.

deonance A perspective in which ethical decisions are made because you "ought to" in order to be consistent with moral norms, principles, standards, rules, or laws.

Decision makers, particularly in for-profit organizations, feel comfortable with utilitarianism. The "best interests" of the organization and its stockholders can justify a lot of questionable actions, such as large layoffs. However, while raising prices, selling products with questionable effects on consumer health, closing inefficient plants, laying off large numbers of employees, and moving production overseas to cut costs can be justified in utilitarian terms, there may no longer be a single measure by which good decisions are judged. This presents a challenge because satisfying individual rights and social justice creates far more ambiguities than clear-cut utilitarian effects on efficiency and profits. Indeed, the ethical-decision making process itself is complex and the traditional perspective of viewing these criteria as completely separate is giving way to one that views them as interrelated and contingent upon whether decisions are made about the self or judging others' behavior.[118]

This is where corporate social responsibility (CSR) comes in to effect a positive change. As we can see by looking at utilitarian ideals, organizations may approach decisions in a certain way when they are looking only at a balance sheet. However, public pressure on organizations to behave responsibly has meant sustainability issues now affect the bottom line: Consumers increasingly choose to purchase goods and services from organizations with effective CSR initiatives, high performers are attracted to work at CSR organizations, governments offer incentives to organizations for sustainability efforts, and so forth. CSR is now beginning to make good business sense, folding ethics into utilitarian computations.

behavioral ethics Analyzing how people behave when confronted with ethical dilemmas.

Researchers are turning increasingly to **behavioral ethics**—an area of study that analyzes how people behave when confronted with ethical dilemmas. Their research tells us that, while ethical standards exist collectively in societies and organizations, and individually in the form of personal ethics, we do not always follow ethical standards promoted by our organizations, and we sometimes violate our own standards. Our ethical behavior varies widely from one situation to the next.

How might we increase ethical decision making in organizations? First, seemingly superficial aspects of the environment—such as lighting, outward displays of wealth and status, and cleanliness—can affect ethical behavior in organizations.[119] Managers must first realize that ethical behavior can be affected by these signals; for example, if signs of status and money are everywhere, an employee may perceive those, rather than ethical standards, to be of the highest importance. Second, managers should encourage conversations about moral issues; they may serve as a reminder and increase ethical decision making. One study found that simply asking business school students to think of an ethical situation had powerful effects when they were making ethical choices later.[120] We should be aware of our own moral "blind spots"—the tendency to see ourselves as more moral than we are and others as less moral than they are. An environment that encourages open discussions and does not penalize people for coming forward is key to overcoming blind spots and increasing the ethicality of decision making.[121]

Behavioral ethics research stresses the importance of culture to ethical decision making. There are few global standards for ethical decision making,[122] as contrasts between Asia and the West illustrate. What is ethical in one culture may be unethical in another. For example, because bribery is more common in countries such as India, a Canadian working in India might face a dilemma: Should I pay a bribe to secure business if it is an accepted part of that country's culture? Although some companies, such as IBM, explicitly address this issue, many do not. Without sensitivity to cultural differences as part of the definition of ethical conduct, organizations may encourage unethical conduct without even knowing it.

Lying

Are you a liar? Many of us would not like to be labeled as a liar. But if a liar is merely someone who lies, we are all liars. We lie to ourselves, and we lie to others. We lie consciously and unconsciously. We tell big lies and create small deceptions. Lying is one of the top unethical activities we may indulge in daily, and it undermines all efforts toward sound decision making.

Although lying might depend on both situational characteristics and individual differences, a large volume of research suggests that lying and dishonest behavior are very common.[123] Perhaps one of the reasons we lie is because lying is difficult for others to detect. In more than 200 studies, individuals correctly identified people who were lying only 47 percent of the time, which is less than random picking.[124] This seems to be true no matter what lie-detection technique is employed. For example, one technique used by police officers is based on the theory that people look up and to the right when they lie. Unfortunately, researchers who tested the technique could not substantiate the underlying theory.[125]

Another technique is to study a person's body language, but researchers found that the probability of detecting lying based solely on body language was less than a random guess. Psychologist Maria Hartwig observed, "The common-sense notion that liars betray themselves through body language appears to be little more than a cultural fiction."[126] Still another technique is to study facial expressions. Here again, many researchers could not support the technique with evidence. Research professor Nicholas Epley concluded, "Reading people's expressions can give you a little information, but you can get so much more just by talking to them."[127]

What about our words? Liars may indeed give verbal cues, but which cues apply to which people is a matter of debate. Whether liars tell better stories, or conversely give fewer details, is not certain. Law enforcers analyze an individual's words, looking for emphatic or repeated phrases to indicate lying. Detecting lies from our written words is even trickier because there are fewer cues. However, that doesn't stop lie-detection speculation for written

An Ethical Choice

Choosing to Lie

Mark Twain wrote, "The wise thing is for us diligently to train ourselves to lie thoughtfully." Not everyone agrees that lying is wrong. But we probably agree that people do lie, including each of us, to varying degrees. And most of us probably agree that if we lied less, organizations and society would be better off. So how can we get ourselves to lie less often? Research conducted by behavioral scientists suggests some steps to recovery.

1. **Stop lying to ourselves.** We lie to ourselves about how much we lie. Specifically, many studies reveal that we deem ourselves much less likely to lie than we judge others to be. At a collective level, this is impossible—everyone can't be below average in their propensity to lie. So step 1 is to admit the truth: We underestimate the degree to which we lie, we overestimate our morality compared to that of others, and we tend to engage in "moral hypocrisy"—we think we're more moral than we are.
2. **Trust, but verify.** Lying is learned at a very young age. When a toy was placed out of view, an experimenter told young children not to look at the toy and went out of sight. More than 80 percent of the children looked at the toy. When asked whether they had looked, 25 percent of 2½-year-olds lied compared to 90 percent of 4-year-olds. Why do we learn to lie? Because we often get away with it. Negotiation research shows that we are more likely to lie in the future when our lies have succeeded or gone undetected in the past. Managers need to eliminate situations in which lying is available to employees.
3. **Reward honesty.** "The most difficult thing is to recognize that sometimes we too are blinded by our own incentives," writes author Dan Ariely, "because we don't see how our conflicts of interest work on us." So if we want more honesty, we have to provide greater incentives for the truth and more disincentives for lying and cheating.

Sources: Based on D. Ariely, *The Honest Truth about Dishonesty: How We Lie to Everyone—and Especially Ourselves* (New York: Harper, 2012); K. Canavan, "Even Nice People Cheat Sometimes," *The Wall Street Journal,* August 8, 2012, 4B; M. H. Bazerman and Ann E. Tenbrunsel, *Blind Spots: Why We Fail to Do What's Right and What to Do about It* (Princeton, NJ: Princeton University Press, 2012); A. D. Evans and K. Lee, "Emergence of Lying in Very Young Children," *Developmental Psychology* (2013); and L. Zhou, Y. Sung, and D. Zhang, "Deception Performance in Online Group Negotiation and Decision Making: The Effects of Deception Experience and Deception Skill," *Group Decision and Negotiation* 22 (2013): 153–72.

communications. Some say that in e-mail messages, liars omit personal pronouns, use noncommittal expressions, change tenses, skip topics, provide too much detail, or add qualifying statements.[128] Yet a person who regularly does those things when writing may not be lying.

The best hope for lie detection is to read a combination of cues unique to the person. Perhaps it is true that a mother can sometimes tell when her child is lying, for instance, because the mother knows how the child changes his behavior when he's stressed. Although we may feel that our lying is "written all over our face," as Epley says, "[t]he mind comes through the mouth."[129] Lie detection is also easier if the person is a bad liar without a lot of experience. According to Tyler Cohen Wood of the Defense Intelligence Agency's Science and Technology Directorate, "The majority of people prefer to tell the truth. That's why when they are lying, the truth is going to leak out."[130] Research indicates that, while we do not consciously discern lying in others, we are able to sense on some level when lying is happening.[131]

Although people often try to justify lying as necessary in certain situations (e.g., sales) or because honesty can be difficult,[132] lying is deadly to decision making, whether we sense the lies or not. Managers and employees simply cannot make good decisions when facts are misrepresented and people give false motives for their behaviors. Lying is a big ethical problem as well. From an organizational perspective, using fancy lie-detection techniques and entrapping liars when possible yield unreliable results.[133] The most lasting solution comes from organizational behavior, which studies ways to prevent lying by working with our natural propensities to create environments not conducive to lying.

Creativity, Creative Decision Making, and Innovation in Organizations

5-9 Describe the three-stage model of creativity.

creativity The ability to produce novel and useful ideas.

Although alternatives to solving problems may often be clear or readily available, sometimes a decision maker also needs **creativity**, the ability to produce novel and useful ideas. Novel ideas are different from what's been done before but are appropriate for the problem.

Creativity allows the decision maker to appraise and understand problems fully, including seeing problems others can't see. Although all aspects of organizational behavior are complex, that is especially true for creativity. To simplify, Exhibit 5-7 provides a three-stage model of creativity in organizations. The core of the model is *creative behavior*, which has both *causes* (predictors of creative behavior) and *effects* (outcomes of creative behavior). In this section, we discuss the three stages of creativity, starting with the center, creative behavior.

Creative Behavior

Creative behavior occurs in four steps, each of which leads to the next:[134]

problem formulation The stage of creative behavior that involves identifying a problem or opportunity requiring a solution that is yet unknown.

1. **Problem formulation.** Any act of creativity begins with a problem that the behavior is designed to solve. Thus, **problem formulation** is the stage of creative behavior in which we identify a problem or opportunity that requires a solution that is yet unknown. For example, Marshall Carbee and John Bennett founded Eco Safety Products after discovering that even

Exhibit 5-7 Three-Stage Model of Creativity in Organizations

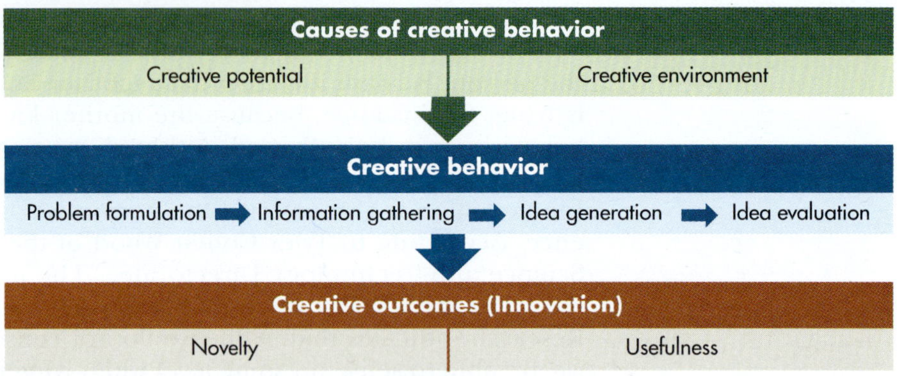

paints declared safe by the Environmental Protection Agency (EPA) emitted hazardous chemical compounds. Thus, Eco's development of artist-safe soy-based paint began with identifying a safety problem with paints currently on the market.[135]

2. **Information gathering.** Given a problem, the solution is rarely directly at hand. We need time to learn more and to process that learning. Thus, **information gathering** is the stage of creative behavior when knowledge is sought and possible solutions to a problem incubate in an individual's mind. Information gathering leads us to identifying innovation opportunities.[136] Niklas Laninge of Hoa's Tool Shop, a Stockholm-based company that helps organizations become more innovative, argues that creative information gathering means thinking beyond usual routines and comfort zones. For example, have lunch with someone outside your field to discuss the problem. "It's so easy, and you're forced to speak about your business and the things that you want to accomplish in new terms. You can't use buzzwords because people don't know what you mean," Laninge says.[137]

information gathering The stage of creative behavior when possible solutions to a problem incubate in an individual's mind.

3. **Idea generation. Idea generation** is the process in which we develop possible solutions to a problem from relevant information and knowledge. Curiosity has been found to be a driver of idea generation: when you are curious about something, you are more likely to link earlier ideas or earlier solutions to help solve the current problem.[138]

idea generation The process of creative behavior that involves developing possible solutions to a problem from relevant information and knowledge.

4. **Idea evaluation.** Finally, it's time to choose from the ideas we have generated. Thus, **idea evaluation** is the process of creative behavior in which we evaluate potential solutions to identify the best one. Sometimes the method of choosing can be innovative. When Dallas Mavericks owner Mark Cuban was unhappy with the team's uniforms, he asked fans to help design and choose the best uniform. Cuban said, "What's the best way to come up with creative ideas? You ask for them. So we are going to crowd source the design and colors of our uniforms."[139] Generally, you want those who evaluate ideas to be different from those who generate them, to eliminate the obvious biases.

idea evaluation The process of creative behavior involving the evaluation of potential solutions to problems to identify the best one.

Causes of Creative Behavior

Having defined creative behavior, the main stage in the three-stage model, we now look back to the causes of creativity: creative potential and creative environment.

Creative Potential Is there such a thing as a creative personality? Indeed. While creative genius is rare—whether in science (Stephen Hawking), performing arts (Martha Graham), or business (Steve Jobs)—most people have some of the characteristics shared by exceptionally creative people. The more of these characteristics we have, the higher our creative potential. Innovation is one of the top organizational goals for leaders (see OB Poll). Consider these facets of potential:

1. **Intelligence and Creativity** Intelligence is related to creativity.[140] Smart people are more creative because they are better at solving complex problems. However, intelligent individuals may also be more creative because they have greater "working memory"; that is, they can recall more information related to the task at hand.[141] Along the same lines, research in the Netherlands indicates that an individual's high need for cognition (desire to learn) is correlated with greater creativity.[142]
2. **Personality and Creativity** The Big Five personality trait of openness to experience (see Chapter 4) correlates with creativity, probably because open individuals are less conformist in action and more divergent in thinking.[143] Other traits of creative people include proactive personality, self-confidence, risk taking, tolerance for ambiguity, and perseverance.[144] Hope, self-efficacy (belief in your capabilities), and positive affect also predict an individual's creativity.[145] Research in China suggests that people with high core self-evaluations are better able than others to maintain creativity in negative situations.[146] Perhaps counterintuitively, some research supports the "mad genius" theory that some people with mental illness are wildly creative partially due to their psychopathology; history certainly provides examples, such as Vincent Van Gogh, John Forbes Nash, and others. However, the converse isn't true—people who are creative may have less psychopathology as a group than the general population.[147]

OB POLL

Is Innovation More Talk than Show?

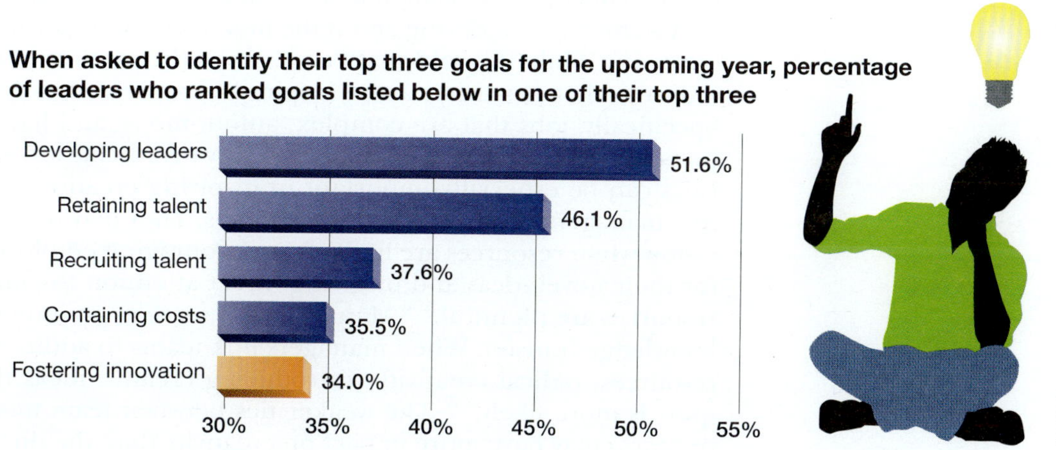

Source: Based on T. Henneman, "Bright Ideas," *Workforce Management* (January 2013), 18–25.

3. **Expertise and Creativity** *Expertise* is the foundation for all creative work and thus is the single most important predictor of creative potential. Film writer, producer, and director Quentin Tarantino spent his youth working in a video rental store, where he built up an encyclopedic knowledge of movies. The potential for creativity is enhanced when individuals have abilities, knowledge, proficiencies, and similar expertise to their field of endeavor. For instance, you wouldn't expect someone with minimal knowledge of programming to be very creative as a software engineer. The expertise of others is important, too. People with larger social networks have greater exposure to diverse ideas and informal access to the expertise and resources of others.[148]
4. **Ethics and Creativity** Although creativity is linked to many desirable individual characteristics, it is not correlated with ethicality. People who cheat may be more creative than those who behave ethically, according to recent research. It may be that dishonesty and creativity can both stem from a rule-breaking desire.[149]

Creative Environment Most of us have creative potential we can learn to apply, but as important as creative potential is, by itself it is not enough. We need to be in an environment where creative potential can be realized.[150] What environmental factors affect whether creative potential translates into creative behaviors?

First, and perhaps most important, is *motivation.* If you aren't motivated to be creative, it is unlikely you will be. Intrinsic motivation, or the desire to work on something because it's interesting, exciting, satisfying, and challenging (discussed in more detail in the next chapter), correlates moderately with creative outcomes.[151]

It is also valuable to work in an environment that rewards and recognizes creative work. A study of health care teams found that team creativity translated into innovation only when the climate actively supported innovation.[152] The organization should foster the free flow of ideas, including providing fair and constructive judgment. Freedom from excessive rules encourages creativity; employees should have the freedom to decide what work is to be done and how to do it. One study in China revealed that both structural empowerment (in which the structure of the work unit allows sufficient employee freedom) and psychological empowerment (which lets the individual feel personally enabled to decide) were related to employee creativity.[153] However, research in Slovenia found that creating a competitive climate where achievement is valued at any cost stymies creativity.[154]

You may be wondering about the link between organizational resources and creativity. While it is said that "necessity is the mother of invention," research indicates that creativity can be inspired by an abundance of resources as well. Specifically, jobs that are complex, autonomous, and have clear role expectations for innovation are related to innovative behavior—these job characteristics can be especially important in inspiring creative behavior.[155] It appears that managers greatly affect the outcomes. They may be able to heighten innovation when resources are limited by encouraging employees to find resources for their novel ideas and by giving direct attention to appropriate tools when resources are plentiful.[156] Managers also serve as an important bridge role for knowledge transfer. When managers link teams to additional information and resources, radical creativity (introducing creative ideas that break the status quo) is more likely.[157] The weaker ties between team members and manager networks may have more impact on creativity than the direct, stronger ties that team members have with their own networks because the weaker sources provide more divergent thinking.[158]

What is the role of culture? A recent nation-level study suggests that countries scoring high on Hofstede's culture dimension of individuality (see Chapter 4) are more creative.[159] Western countries like the United States, Italy, and Belgium score high on individuality, and South American and eastern countries like China, Colombia, and Pakistan score low. Does this mean Western cultures are more creative? Some evidence suggests this is true. One study compared the creative projects of German and Chinese college students, some of whom were studying in their homeland and some of whom were studying abroad. An independent panel of Chinese and German judges determined that the German students were most creative and that Asian German students were more creative than domestic Chinese students. This suggested that the German culture was more creative.[160] However, even if some cultures are more creative on average, there is always strong variation within cultures. Put another way, there are millions of Chinese more creative than their U.S. counterparts.

Good leadership matters to creativity, too.[161] One study of more than 100 teams working in a large bank revealed that when the leader behaved in a punitive, unsupportive manner, the teams were less creative.[162] On the other hand, when leaders are encouraging in tone, run their units in a transparent fashion, and encourage the development of their employees, the individuals they supervise are more creative.[163]

As we will learn in Chapter 10, more work today is being done in teams, and many people believe diversity will increase team creativity. Past research has suggested that diverse teams are not more creative. More recently, however, one study of Dutch teams revealed that when team members were explicitly asked to understand and consider the point of view of the other team members (an exercise called perspective taking), diverse teams *were* more creative than those with less diversity.[164] Leadership might make the difference. One study of 68 Chinese teams reported that diversity was positively related to team creativity only when the team's leader was inspirational and instilled members with confidence.[165]

There are other worthwhile findings regarding creativity. One study in a multinational drug company found that teams from diverse business functions were more creative when they shared knowledge of each other's areas of expertise.[166] However, if team members have a similar background, creativity may be heightened only when the members are sharing specific, detailed information,[167] because general information may be dismissed by members with the same expertise. As you might expect, newcomers to a team can be a rich source of creative ideas, although unfortunately they are often expected to contribute less early on.[168] Putting individuals who are resistant to change into teams that are supportive of change can increase total creativity,[169] perhaps because of the group's positive influence. Collectively, these studies show that diverse teams *can* be more creative, especially if they are intentionally led.

Creative Outcomes (Innovation)

The final stage in our model of creativity is the outcome. Creative behavior does not always produce an innovative outcome. An employee might generate a creative idea and never share it. Management might reject a creative solution. Teams might squelch creative behaviors by isolating those who propose different ideas. One study showed that most people have a bias against accepting creative ideas because ideas create uncertainty. When people feel uncertain, their ability to see any idea as creative is blocked.[170]

We can define *creative outcomes* as ideas or solutions judged to be novel and useful by relevant stakeholders. Novelty itself does not generate a creative outcome if it isn't useful. Thus, "off-the-wall" solutions are creative only if they help solve the problem. The usefulness of the solution might be self-evident (the iPad), or it might be considered successful only by the stakeholders initially.[171]

An organization may harvest many creative ideas from its employees and call itself innovative. However, as one expert stated, "Ideas are useless unless used." Soft skills help translate ideas into results. One researcher found that, in a large agribusiness company, creative ideas were most likely to be implemented when an individual was motivated to translate the idea into practice—and had strong networking ability.[172] These studies highlight an important fact: Creative ideas do not implement themselves; translating them into creative outcomes is a social process that requires utilizing other concepts addressed in this text, including power and politics, leadership, and motivation.

Summary

Individuals base their behavior not on the way their external environment actually is but rather on the way they see it or believe it to be. An understanding of the way people make decisions can help us explain and predict behavior, but few important decisions are simple or unambiguous enough for the rational model's assumptions to apply. We find individuals looking for solutions that satisfice rather than optimize, injecting biases and prejudices into the decision process and relying on intuition. Managers should encourage creativity in employees and teams to create a route to innovative decision making.

Implications for Managers

- Behavior follows perception, so to influence behavior at work, assess how people perceive their work. Often behaviors we find puzzling can be explained by understanding the initiating perceptions.
- Make better decisions by recognizing perceptual biases and decision-making errors we tend to commit. Learning about these problems doesn't always prevent us from making mistakes, but it does help.
- Adjust your decision-making approach to the national culture you're operating in and to the criteria your organization values. If you're in a country that doesn't value rationality, don't feel compelled to follow the decision-making model or to try to make your decisions appear rational. Adjust your decision approach to ensure compatibility with the organizational culture.
- Combine rational analysis with intuition. These are not conflicting approaches to decision making. By using both, you can improve your decision-making effectiveness.
- Try to enhance your creativity. Actively look for novel solutions to problems, attempt to see problems in new ways, use analogies, and hire creative talent. Try to remove work and organizational barriers that might impede creativity.

Implicit Assessment

POINT

As mentioned earlier in this chapter, some decisions are made intuitively–they are made nonconsciously, quickly, and emotionally in the moment. So isn't it likely that we may be acting prejudicially toward others without even realizing it?

Project Implicit, an initiative at Harvard started by Tony Greenwald, Mahzarin Banaji, and Brian Nosek, sought to uncover hidden biases that are outside our conscious awareness. Much of this research has used the Implicit Association Test (IAT), which successfully enabled researchers to examine how quickly people make prejudicial associations (e.g., black and negative, or white and positive) versus nonprejudicial associations (e.g., black and positive, or white and negative). The differences between decision speeds (in milliseconds) for these two associations provides an estimate of one's prejudice or bias.

The IAT has been very helpful in furthering research on nonconscious decision making and prejudice, suggesting that "milliseconds matter" in understanding nonconscious, intuitive behavior. On average, a database of 1.5 million participants in the Project Implicit website research has revealed that white people in the southeastern United States tend to be the most prejudiced and that, overall, white people on average score somewhere between a slight and moderate preference for whites over those of other racial makeups.

The IAT has helped us understand that people prefer women over men and mothers over fathers implicitly, but as soon as women are judged within a "male" domain, the preferences shift: We tend to prefer male authority figures and leaders over female ones. A 2009 meta-analysis of nearly 15,000 people found that the IAT was moderately related to predicting future prejudiced judgments, behaviors, and physiological indices.

COUNTERPOINT

Although intuition certainly plays a role in decision making, can a test actually tell us whether we are prejudiced? Is the number of milliseconds it takes to select an association between two concepts enough to tell someone that he or she is biased? This link between the IAT and biased behavior has long been questioned by scholars, notably Hart Blanton.

Beyond the ethical implications of using a test to label someone as prejudiced or biased, which Emily Bazelon of *The New York Times* has likened to taking our societal discussions of bias and changing them "from a psychological observation to a political accusation," Blanton notes that there are many issues with the measure itself: "The IAT isn't even predicting the IAT two weeks later ... how can a test predict behavior if it can't even predict itself?" One study has also determined that it is impossible to separate true variability in the IAT versus variability due to faking (when people are instructed to fake the IAT).

In an updated meta-analysis published in 2015, Blanton and colleagues found that the IAT does very little to predict behavior, perceptions, policy preferences, nonverbal behaviors, and response times (although sometimes small effects can have societally large effects); the only element that the IAT seemed to predict moderately well was brain activity of some kind. Blanton has also sparked debate by reanalyzing data from influential IAT tests from the earlier 2000s and found that some of the findings were smaller than anticipated and have changed substantially because of outliers and other factors (although this was debated by the original authors).

Sources: Based on T. Bartlett, "Can We Really Measure Implicit Bias? Maybe Not," *The Chronicle of Higher Education,* January 5, 2017, http://www.chronicle.com/article/Can-We-Really-Measure-Implicit/238807; E. Bazelon, "How 'Bias' Went from a Psychological Observation to a Political Accusation," *The New York Times,* October 18, 2016, https://nyti.ms/2jDe6WL; H. Blanton, J. Jaccard, J. Klick, B. Mellers, G. Mitchell, and P. E. Tetlock, "Strong Claims and Weak Evidence: Reassessing the Predictive Validity of the IAT," *Journal of Applied Psychology* 94, no. 3 (2009): 567–82; D. Chugh, "Societal and Managerial Implications of Implicit Social Cognition: Why Milliseconds Matter," *Social Justice Research* 17, no. 2 (2004): 203–22; A. G. Greenwald, T. A. Poehlman, E. L. Uhlmann, and M. R. Banaji, "Understanding and Using the Implicit Association Test: III. Meta-Analysis of Predictive Validity," *Journal of Personality and Social Psychology* 97, no. 1 (2009): 17–41; J. Kluger, "There's a Test That May Reveal Racial Bias in Police–and in All of Us," *Time,* July 8, 2016, http://time.com/4398505/implicit-association-racism-test/; C. Mooney, "Across America, Whites Are Biased and They Don't Even Know It," *The Washington Post,* December 8, 2014, https://www.washingtonpost.com/news/wonk/wp/2014/12/08/across-america-whites-are-biased-and-they-dont-even-know-it/?utm_term=.ef02a0e7ce3b; F. L. Oswald, G. Mitchell, H. Blanton, J. Jaccard, and P. E. Tetlock, "Predicting Ethnic and Racial Discrimination: A Meta-Analysis of IAT Criterion Studies," *Journal of Personality and Social Psychology* 105, no. 2 (2013): 171–93; Project Implicit website, 2011, accessed March 29, 2017, https://implicit.harvard.edu/implicit/; J. Röhner and T. Ewers, "Trying to Separate the Wheat from the Chaff: Construct- and Faking-Related Variance on the Implicit Association Test (IAT)," *Behavioral Research* 48 (2016): 243–58; and T. Shatseva, "Don't Think You're Sexist? Sorry, We All Are," *Popular Science*, December 2, 2016, http://www.popsci.com/dont-think-youre-sexist-sorry-we-all-are.

CHAPTER REVIEW

QUESTIONS FOR REVIEW

5-1 What are the factors that influence our perception?

5-2 What is attribution theory?

5-3 What is the link between perception and decision making?

5-4 How is the rational model of decision making different from bounded rationality and intuition?

5-5 How do individual differences and organizational constraints influence decision making?

5-6 What are the three ethical decision criteria, and how do they differ?

5-7 What are the parts of the three-stage model of creativity?

APPLICATION AND EMPLOYABILITY

Our perception is our first window into the world—it gives us a sense of the world around us, who we are interacting with, where we are, and what we should or should not be doing. These perceptions are instrumental in guiding our decision making. In the world of business, the prevailing assumption is that, when we make business decisions, we do so rationally. However, additional research counters this assumption because many people are limited by their own perception and biases in the workplace. Following this line of thought, becoming aware of your own biases and limitations to your decision making can help you make better, more informed decisions and, in turn, make you more employable. This understanding can help you improve not only your ethical decision making but also your creative performance. In this chapter, you developed your social responsibility as well as your knowledge application and analysis skills by challenging the assumption that all stereotypes are negative, pondering the ethicality of workplace tardiness, learning how to confront situations in which we might be more prone to lying, and examining the feasibility of measuring prejudicial intuitions. In the section that follows, you will continue to develop these skills, along with your communication and critical thinking skills, by gaining insight into your own perception and decision making through playing the Mafia game, confronting cheating as a decision, examining the perils of collaboration overload, and examining how boredom and repetitive tasks can lead to unethical decisions.

EXPERIENTIAL EXERCISE Fake News?

In 2019, the United Kingdom held a general election. In its aftermath, there were calls for politicians to be more truthful and transparent when electioneering. The pro-democracy pressure group Compassion in Politics even went as far as suggesting that a law should be created that would see politicians jailed if they lied to the public during elections or when in office. They felt that current laws have not kept up with changes in politics and particularly the growth of online campaigning.

Social media has been accused of spreading false information, misquotes, distortions of the truth, and outright lies during numerous elections and political debates across the world. The tone of many of the social media messages has been at odds with politicians' outward appearance of being caring, compassionate, and respectful.

But just how do misleading claims affect our perceptions of politicians or leaders? Do they ultimately have any impact on our decision making when we vote, support, or endorse them? Singapore invoked its Protection from Online Falsehoods and Manipulation Act (POFMA) for the first time in November 2019 to counter false and misleading information on Facebook. The problem is that, despite legal action and retraction, the damage to perception has been done and decisions have already been influenced.

The class should be split into groups of four or five. Each group should try to identify an example of when they had their perceptions changed and their decisions subsequently altered by something that turned out to be untrue. This can either be something said or done, social media messages, fake news, or rumors that were deliberately spread to influence and change opinion.

The case that a group chooses does not have to be based in their own country, and they can focus on broadcast, print, or online media sources. The groups should consider

1. the importance of the misleading statement and how it affected decision making.
2. how the misleading statement was revealed to be untrue. (What were the motives of the disclosing individuals or organization?)
3. whether the long-term impact of the incident was significant.
4. whether the incident has made it more or less likely that the group will be suspicious of statements in the future.

Once the group has finished their discussion, they can answer the following questions:

Questions

5-8. Was it easy to tell when the person making the misleading statement was not being truthful? Why or why not? How could you tell?

5-9. To what extent was the misleading statement believed and what were the long-term consequences?

5-10. What led you to perceive this statement as the truth?

Source: Compassion in Politics website, https://www.compassioninpolitics.com/; Faye Brown, "MPs Could Be Jailed for Lying to the Public under New Law," *Metro,* December 11, 2019, https://metro.co.uk/2019/12/11/mps-jailed-lying-public-new-law-11751567/?ito=cbshare?ito=cbshare.

ETHICAL DILEMMA Max's Burgers: The Dollar Value of Ethics

In July 2011, Nassar Group, a well-diversified conglomerate operating in Dubai, bought the rights to manage Max's Burgers' network of franchised outlets in Dubai. Max's Burgers is an emerging American fast-food chain with franchised outlets across the globe. The move was a personal project of Houssam Nassar, the Group's managing director and a businessman with an excellent reputation.

Dubai's fast-food market is overwhelmed with franchised restaurants. Meat quality at Max's Burgers, however, was lower than the standards set by franchisors. This was all about to change, because Nassar did not intend to jeopardize his reputation and image. Accordingly, as the new operator of Max's Burgers outlets, he issued a directive instructing the warehouse manager to decline any frozen meat shipment that did not comply with the franchisor's set standards.

A few weeks after Nassar Group took over the management of Max's Burgers, a frozen meat shipment was delivered to the Max's Burgers main warehouse. Upon measuring the temperature of the meat, the warehouse manager found that it was a few degrees outside acceptable limits. In terms of governmental regulations, a couple of degrees' difference in temperature would present no risk to customers' health; however, such a difference could have a minimal effect on the taste and texture of the meat.

Prior to the change of management, and for many years before, the warehouse manager had had no second thoughts about accepting such a shipment: no food poisoning claim was ever filed against Max's Burgers, and taste inconsistencies never bothered anyone enough to complain. Further, the company supplying the meat to Max's Burgers was owned by a relative of the warehouse manager.

With the new directive in place, however, the warehouse manager was unsure about his decision. Even though he knew that Nassar would have no way of finding out that the received meat was noncompliant, he wasn't sure about his decision this time around.

Questions

5-11. Does the decision to accept or refuse the frozen meat shipment call for ethical or legal considerations? Why?

5-12. Identify the stakeholders who will be influenced by the decision to accept or refuse the frozen meat shipment.

5-13. What type of decision-making framework would you advise the warehouse manager to adopt in order to help him reach an optimal decision? How will your suggestion help?

Sources: "The Dollar Value of Ethics!", Charbel Aoun, Instructor and AVP for Human Resources, Lebanese American University, Beirut, Lebanon. The case was adapted to provide materials for class discussions. The author does not intend to illustrate either effective or ineffective handling of a situation. To protect confidentiality, the author may have disguised certain names and other identifying information without jeopardizing the fundamentals of the case.

CASE INCIDENT 1 Warning: Collaboration Overload

"Regardless of what you're giving us, we're dying by e-mail," an executive told Jamie McLellan, a CTO at an advertising agency. McLellan invested in many different collaboration tools with the goal of helping the employees work more efficiently. Many organizations have taken this same approach through open-plan offices, such as those in many knowledge-intensive companies like Facebook, which has a notorious 430,000-square-foot open office space. Among these tools, employees can use them to create internal team websites, chat, and share documents. However, almost everyone tended to stick to what they knew and were used to using: e-mail, with the employees sending and receiving between 3,000 to 5,000 e-mails *per month.*

This influx of various collaboration mechanisms has led to a real problem for organizations: collaboration overload. According to data spanning two decades, employees spend about 50 percent or more of their time collaborating with others. Although this may seem beneficial on the surface, this pattern has many drawbacks that aren't readily apparent. For one, nearly 20 to 35 percent of collaborations that actually add value come from only 3 to 5 percent of employees. Unfortunately, people become known for their capabilities and willingness to help, and thus the scope of their positions increases in a phenomenon known as escalating citizenship. Another major problem with collaboration overload is that time and energy spent collaborating with others (rather than working on one's work) translates to depleted personal resources.

Collaboration overload can have drastic effects on decision making within organizations. By increasing the number of collaboration tools and therefore increasing communication complexity, the number of people involved in decision making increases exponentially, requiring more meetings, e-mails, and instant messages. Although there is much evidence that suggests we may need to tone down the richness, variety, and depth of our communication due to how little "deep" work can get done, there seems to be an escalation of commitment to the cult of collaboration, with not many offices agreeing to become at least partially unplugged.

Questions

5-14. In what ways do you think collaboration overload can have an impact on decision making?

5-15. What biases do you think play into managers continued use of collaboration tools and modes?

5-16. How does collaboration overload (e.g., requiring employees to use multiple collaboration mechanisms or become employed in open-office environments) compare to the three ethical decision criteria (i.e., utilitarianism, liberties/rights, and deonance) discussed in this chapter?

Sources: Based on "The Collaboration Curse," *The Economist* (Schumpeter Blog), January 23, 2016, http://www.economist.com/news/business/21688872-fashion-making-employees-collaborate-has-gone-too-far-collaboration-curse; R. Cross, R. Rebele, and A. Grant, "Collaborative Overload," *Harvard Business Review,* January–February, 2016, https://hbr.org/2016/01/collaborative-overload; J. Greene, "Beware Collaboration-Tool Overload," March 12, 2017, https://www.wsj.com/articles/beware-collaboration-tool-overload-1489370400; and M. Mankins, "Collaboration Overload Is a Symptom of a Deeper Organizational Problem," *Harvard Business Review,* March 27, 2017, https://hbr.org/2017/03/collaboration-overload-is-a-symptom-of-a-deeper-organizational-problem.

CASE INCIDENT 2 How Do Employees Justify Cyberloafing?

It is a quiet, normal day in the office, your manager is off site, and you have just finished all duties for the day—but there are 3 hours left before you go home for the day. You decide to browse for some holiday packages that you have been looking for. You have just engaged in the act of cyberloafing.

Cyberloafing is the usage of the Internet and social network platforms while at work, thus engaging in non-work online activities while on the clock. But are you really stealing company time? Many companies consider cyberloafing to be unethical and even illegal. They say that the consequences of cyberloafing can range from brief employee distraction (leading to inefficiency) to a more serious drain on company resources (for example, decreased profits) and even compromised security (due to, for example, slower network performance or computer viruses). On the other hand, some research suggests that cyberloafing is an opportunity to be more productive as it results in employees feeling less bored and mentally exhausted, being more engaged, and even allowing a measure of stress release while at work.

From the employees' end, the act of cyberloafing might be rationalized as personal time earned on the basis of having accrued sufficient credits previously through the effort and time they put into completing their task, or it may result in feelings of guilt. In organizational contexts that contractually restrict, filter (for example, WebTitan or firewall settings), or prohibit the use of the Internet while "on the clock," feelings of guilt are intensified. Research conducted by Vivien Lim on 188 adults with access to the Internet at the workplace found that employees "neutralize" their subsequent engagement in the act of cyberloafing when they perceive that the organization in which they work is somehow unjust. Neutralization is the idea that individuals are entitled to deviant behavior—including cyberloafing—if they have accrued good credits in the past that can be "cashed in" later to excuse that behavior.

Organizational and managerial research suggest that treating employees fairly and reciprocating employees' investment of time and effort while ensuring a productive workplace can make it difficult for employees to legitimize inappropriate behavior such as cyberloafing. In addition, some studies suggest that the terminology should evolve, as employees now seek "work–life flexibility," where an employee controls the amount of time they dedicate to work and life, integrating the two as necessary.

Questions

5-17. How do you think the act of cyberloafing can affect your individual performance in the workplace?

5-18. Do you think Internet browsing at the workplace is an acceptable behavior? Why, or why not?

5-19. How do you think innovation and creativity can assist companies with cyberloafing?

Sources: Vivien Lim, "The Moderating Effect of Neutralization Technique on Organizational Justice and Cyberloafing" (2005), PACIS 2005 Proceedings, http://aisel.aisnet.org/pacis2005/18; WebTitan, "New Study Confirms the High Cost of Cyberloafing," August 31, 2017, https://www.webtitan.com/blog/new-study-confirms-high-cost-cyberloafing/; M. Anandarajan, T. S. H. Teo, and C. A. Simmers, "The Internet and the Workplace Transformation," *Advances in Management Information Systems*, Vol. 7 (2015); Emily Lowe-Calverley and Rachel Grieve, "How Can Bosses Put a Stop to Workers Idly Browsing Online?" BBC, August 20, 2017, http://www.bbc.com/capital/story/20170818-how-can-bosses-put-a-stop-to-workers-idly-browsing-online; Emily Lowe-Calverley and Rachel Grieve, "Some Workers 'Cyberloaf' if They Think They Can Get Away with It, so Employers Need to Get Creative," Phys.org, August 9, 2017, https://phys.org/news/2017-08-workers-cyberloaf-employers-creative.html; *Harvard Business Review*, "There's No Shame in Cyberloafing," December 2011, https://hbr.org/2011/12/theres-no-shame-in-cyberloafing.

ENDNOTES

[1] R. Rau, E. N. Carlson, M. D. Back, M. Barranti, J. E. Gebauer, L. J. Human, D. Leising, and S. Nestler, "What Is the Structure of Perceiver Effects? On the Importance of Global Positivity and Trait-Specificity across Personality Domains and Judgment Contexts," *Journal of Personality and Social Psychology* (in press); D. Wood, P. Harms, and S. Vazire, "Perceiver Effects as Projective Tests: What Your Perceptions of Others Say about You," *Journal of Personality and Social Psychology* 99 (2010): 174–90.

[2] E. Bernstein, "Honey, You Never Said ...," *The Wall Street Journal*, March 24, 2015, D1, D4.

[3] K. C. Yam, R. Fehr, and C. M. Barnes, "Morning Employees Are Perceived as Better Employees: Employees' Start Times Influence Supervisor Performance Ratings," *Journal of Applied Psychology* 99, no. 6 (2014): 1288–99.

[4] J. Dwyer, "Witness Accounts in Midtown Hammer Attack Show the Power of False Memory," *The New York Times*, May 14, 2015, http://www.nytimes.com/2015/05/15/nyregion/witness-accounts-in-midtown-hammer-attack-show-the-power-of-false-memory.html?_r=1.

[5] See, for instance, T. Masuda, P. C. Ellsworth, B. Mesquita, J. Leu, S. Tanida, and E. Van de Veerdonk, "Placing the Face in Context: Cultural Differences in the Perception of Facial Emotion," *Journal of Personality and Social Psychology* 94, no. 3 (2008): 365–81.

[6] G. Fields and J. R. Emshwiller, "Long after Arrests, Records Live On," *The Wall Street Journal*, December 26, 2014, A1, A10.

[7] S. S. Wang, "The Science of Standing Out," *The Wall Street Journal*, March 18, 2014, D1, D4.

[8] E. Zell and Z. Krizan, "Do People Have Insight into Their Abilities? A Metasynthesis," *Perspectives on Psychological Science* 9, no. 2 (2014): 111–25.

[9] S. P. Perry, M. C. Murphy, and J. F. Dovidio, "Modern Prejudice: Subtle, but Unconscious? The Role of Bias Awareness in Whites' Perceptions of Personal and Others' Biases," *Journal of Experimental Social Psychology* 61 (2015): 64–78.

[10] G. P. Goodwin, J. Piazza, and P. Rozin, "Moral Character Predominates in Person Perception and Evaluation," *Journal of Personality and Social Psychology* 106, no. 1 (2014): 148–68.

[11] P. Harvey, K. Madison, M. Martinko, T. R. Crook, and T. A. Crook, "Attribution

Theory in the Organizational Sciences: The Road Traveled and the Path Ahead," *The Academy of Management Perspectives* 28, no. 2 (2014): 128–46; and M. J. Martinko, P. Harvey, and M. T. Dasborough, "Attribution Theory in the Organizational Sciences: A Case of Unrealized Potential," *Journal of Organizational Behavior* 32, no. 1 (2011): 144–49.

[12]C. M. de Melo, P. J. Carnevale, S. J. Read, and J. Gratch, "Reading People's Minds from Emotion Expressions in Interdependent Decision Making," *Journal of Personality and Social Psychology* 106, no. 1 (2014): 73–88; and P. Meindl, K. M. Johnson, and J. Graham, "The Immoral Assumption Effect: Moralization Drives Negative Trait Attributions," *Personality and Social Psychology Bulletin* 42, no. 4 (2016): 540–53.

[13]J. Y. Kim, T. H. Campbell, S. Shepherd, and A. C. Kay, "Understanding Contemporary Forms of Exploitation: Attributions of Passion Serve to Legitimize the Poor Treatment of Workers," *Journal of Personality and Social Psychology* 118, no. 1 (2020): 121–48.

[14]H. H. Kelley, "Attribution Theory in Social Psychology," in D. Levine (ed.), *Nebraska Symposium on Motivation*, Vol. 15 (Lincoln: University of Nebraska, 1967): 129–238; and K. Sanders and H. Yang, "The HRM Process Approach: The Influence of Employees' Attribution to Explain the HRM-Performance Relationship," *Human Resource Management* 55, no. 2 (2016): 201–17.

[15]Kelley, "Attribution Theory in Social Psychology"; and J. M. Moran, E. Jolly, and J. P. Mitchell, "Spontaneous Mentalizing Predicts the Fundamental Attribution Error," *Journal of Cognitive Neuroscience* 26, no. 3 (2014): 569–76.

[16]See, for instance, N. Epley and D. Dunning, "Feeling 'Holier Than Thou': Are Self-Serving Assessments Produced by Errors in Self or Social Prediction?," *Journal of Personality and Social Psychology* 76, no. 6 (2000): 861–75; E. G. Hepper, R. H. Gramzow, and C. Sedikides, "Individual Differences in Self-Enhancement and Self-Protection Strategies: An Integrative Analysis," *Journal of Personality* 78, no. 2 (2010): 781–814; and J. Shepperd, W. Malone, and K. Sweeny, "Exploring Causes of the Self-Serving Bias," *Social and Personality Psychology Compass* 2, no. 2 (2008): 895–908.

[17]See, for instance, A. H. Mezulis, L. Y. Abramson, J. S. Hyde, and B. L. Hankin, "Is There a Universal Positivity Bias in Attributions? A Meta-Analytic Review of Individual, Developmental, and Cultural Differences in the Self-Serving Attributional Bias," *Psychological Bulletin* 130, no. 5 (2004): 711–47; C. F. Falk, S. J. Heine, M. Yuki, and K. Takemura, "Why Do Westerners Self-Enhance More Than East Asians?," *European Journal of Personality* 23, no. 3 (2009): 183–203; and F. F. T. Chiang and T. A. Birtch, "Examining the Perceived Causes of Successful Employee Performance: An East–West Comparison," *International Journal of Human Resource Management* 18, no. 2 (2007): 232–48; M. Feinberg, R. Fang, S. Liu, and K. Peng, "A World of Blame to Go Around: Cross-cultural Determinants of Responsibility and Punishment Judgments," *Personality and Social Psychology Bulletin* 45, no. 4 (2019): 634–51.

[18]R. Shao and D.P. Skarlicki, "Service Employees' Reactions to Mistreatment by Customers: A Comparison between North America and East Asia," *Personnel Psychology* 67, no. 1 (2014): 23–59.

[19]J. D. Brown, "Across the (Not So) Great Divide: Cultural Similarities in Self-Evaluative Processes," *Social and Personality Psychology Compass* 4, no. 5 (2010): 318–30.

[20]A. Zhang, C. Reyna, Z. Qian, and G. Yu, "Interpersonal Attributions of Responsibility in the Chinese Workplace: A Test of Western Models in a Collectivistic Context," *Journal of Applied Social Psychology* 38, no. 9 (2008): 2361–77; and A. Zhang, F. Xia, and C. Li, "The Antecedents of Help Giving in Chinese Culture: Attribution, Judgment of Responsibility, Expectation Change and the Reaction of Affect," *Social Behavior and Personality* 35, no. 1 (2007): 135–42.

[21]J. P. Forgas and S. M. Laham, "Halo Effects," in R. F. Pohl (ed.), *Cognitive Illusions: Intriguing Phenomena in Thinking, Judgment and Memory*, 2nd ed. (New York: Routledge, 2017): 276–90; P. Rosenzweig, *The Halo Effect* (New York: The Free Press, 2007); and I. Dennis, "Halo Effects in Grading Student Projects," *Journal of Applied Psychology* 92, no. 4 (2007): 1169–76.

[22]H. H. Zhao, S. E. Seibert, M. S. Taylor, C. Lee, and W. Lam, "Not Even the Past: The Joint Influence of Former Leader and New Leader during Leader Succession in the Midst of Organizational Change," *Journal of Applied Psychology* 101, no. 12 (2016): 1730–8.

[23]A.-S. Chaxel, "How Do Stereotypes Influence Choice?," *Psychological Science* 26, no. 5 (2015): 641–5; and S. Kanahara, "A Review of the Definitions of Stereotype and a Proposal for a Progressional Model," *Individual Differences Research* 4, no. 5 (2006): 306–21.

[24]J. L. Eberhardt, P. G. Davies, V. J. Purdic-Vaughns, and S. L. Johnson, "Looking Deathworthy: Perceived Stereotypicality of Black Defendants Predicts Capital-Sentencing Outcomes," *Psychological Science* 17, no. 5 (2006): 383–86.

[25]A. S. Rosette, G. J. Leonardelli, and K. W. Phillips, "The White Standard: Racial Bias in Leader Categorization," *Journal of Applied Psychology* 93, no. 4 (2008): 758–77.

[26]R. E. Frieder, C. H. Van Iddekinge, and P. H. Raymark, "How Quickly Do Interviewers Reach Decisions? An Examination of Interviewers' Decision-making Time across Applicants," *Journal of Occupational and Organizational Psychology* 89 (2016): 223–48; H. M. Gray, "To What Extent, and under What Conditions, Are First Impressions Valid," in N. Ambady & J. J. Skowronski (eds.), *First Impressions* (New York: Guilford, 2008): 106–28; and B. W. Swider, M. R. Barrick, and T. B. Harris, "Initial Impressions: What They Are, What They Are Not, and How They Influence Structured Interview Outcomes," *Journal of Applied Psychology* 101, no. 5 (2016): 625–38.

[27]J. Willis and A. Todorov, "First Impressions: Making Up Your Mind after a 100ms Exposure to a Face," *Psychological Science* 17, no. 7 (2006): 592–98.

[28]N. Eisenkraft, "Accurate by Way of Aggregation: Should You Trust Your Intuition-Based First Impressions?" *Journal of Experimental Social Psychology* 49, no. 2 (2013): 277–79.

[29]N. M. Kierein and M. A. Gold, "Pygmalion in Work Organizations: A Meta-Analysis," *Journal of Organizational Behavior* 21, no. 8 (2000): 913–28; and J. S. Livingston, "Pygmalion in Management," *Harvard Business Review* 81 (2003): 97–106.

[30]Kierein and Gold, "Pygmalion in Work Organizations"; D. B. McNatt and T. A. Judge, "Boundary Conditions of the Galatea Effect: A Field Experiment and Constructive Replication," *Academy of Management Journal* 47, no. 4 (2004): 550–65; and X. M. Bezuijen, P. T. van den Berg, K. van Dam, and H. Thierry, "Pygmalion and Employee Learning: The Role of Leader Behaviors," *Journal of Management* 35 (2009): 1248–67.

[31]H. J. Bernardin, S. Thomason, M. R. Buckley, and J. S. Kane, "Rater Rating-Level Bias and Accuracy in Performance Appraisals: The Impact of Rater

Personality, Performance Management Competence, and Rater Accountability," *Human Resource Management* 55, no. 2 (2016): 321–40; and J. R. Spence and L. Keeping, "Conscious Rating Distortion in Performance Appraisal: A Review, Commentary, and Proposed Framework for Research," *Human Resource Management Review* 21 (2011): 85–95.

[32] See H. M. Weiss, "Learning Theory and Industrial and Organizational Psychology," in M. D. Dunnette and L. M. Hough (eds.), *Handbook of Industrial & Organizational Psychology*, 2nd ed., vol. 1 (Palo Alto, CA: Consulting Psychologists Press, 1990), pp. 172–173.

[33] W. McGehee, "Are We Using What We Know About Training? Learning Theory and Training," *Personnel Psychology*, Spring 1958, p. 2.

[34] I. P. Pavlov, *The Work of the Digestive Glands*, trans. W. H. Thompson (London: Charles Griffin, 1902). See also the special issue of *American Psychologist*, September 1997, pp. 933–972, commemorating Pavlov's work.

[35] B. F. Skinner, *Contingencies of Reinforcement* (East Norwalk, CT: Appleton-Century-Crofts, 1971).

[36] J. A. Mills, *Control: A History of Behavioral Psychology* (New York: New York University Press, 2000).

[37] A. Bandura, *Social Learning Theory* (Upper Saddle River, NJ: Prentice Hall, 1977).

[38] T. Maurer, K. Wrenn, and E. Weiss, "Toward Understanding and Managing Stereotypical Beliefs About Older Workers' Ability and Desire for Learning and Development," *Research in Personnel and Human Resources Management* 22 (2003), pp. 253–285.

[39] J. A. Colquitt, J. A. LePine, and R. A. Noe, "Toward an Integrative Theory of Training Motivation: A Meta-Analytic Path Analysis of 20 Years of Research," *Journal of Applied Psychology* 85, no. 5 (2000), pp. 678–707.

[40] S. Begley, "The Upside of Aging," *New York Times*, February 16, 2007, pp. W1, W4.

[41] Wrenn and Maurer, "Beliefs About Older Workers' Learning and Development Behavior," pp. 223–242.

[42] A. D. Stajkovic and F. Luthans, "A Meta-analysis of the Effects of Organizational Behavior Modification on Task Performance, 1975–95," *Academy of Management Journal*, October 1997, pp. 1122–1149.

[43] "At Emery Air Freight: Positive Reinforcement Boosts Performance," *Organizational Dynamics*, Winter 1973, pp. 41–50.

[44] F. Luthans and R. Kreitner, *Organizational Behavior Modification and Beyond: An Operant and Social Learning Approach* (Glenview, IL: Scott, Foresman, 1985); Stajkovic and Luthans, "A Meta- Analysis of the Effects of Organizational Behavior Modification on Task Performance, 1975–95," pp. 1122–1149; and A. D. Stajkovic and F. Luthans, "Behavioral Management and Task Performance in Organizations: Conceptual Background, Meta-Analysis, and Test of Alternative Models," *Personnel Psychology*, Spring 2003, pp. 155–192.

[45] A. D. Stajkovic and F. Luthans, "A Meta-analysis of the Effects of Organizational Behavior Modification on Task Performance, 1975–95," *Academy of Management Journal*, October 1997, p. 1123.

[46] See F. Luthans and A. D. Stajkovic, "Reinforce for Performance: The Need to Go Beyond Pay and Even Rewards," *Academy of Management Executive*, May 1999, pp. 49–57; and A. D. Stajkovic and F. Luthans, "Differential Effects of Incentive Motivators on Work Performance," *Academy of Management Journal* 44, no. 3 (2001), pp. 580–590.

[47] E. A. Locke, "Beyond Determinism and Materialism, or Isn't It Time We Took Consciousness Seriously?" *Journal of Behavior Therapy & Experimental Psychiatry* 26, no. 3 (1995), pp. 265–273.

[48] E. Bernstein, "The Right Answer Is 'No,'" *The Wall Street Journal*, March 11, 2014, D1–D2.

[49] E. Shafir and R. A. LeBoeuf, "Rationality," *Annual Review of Psychology* 53 (2002): 491–517.

[50] For a review of the rational decision-making model, see M. H. Bazerman and D. A. Moore, *Judgment in Managerial Decision Making*, 7th ed. (Hoboken, New Jersey: Wiley, 2008).

[51] J. G. March, *A Primer on Decision Making* (New York: The Free Press, 2009); and D. Hardman and C. Harries, "How Rational Are We?" *Psychologist* (February 2002): 76–79.

[52] M. H. Bazerman and D. A. Moore, *Judgment in Managerial Decision Making*, 7th ed. (Hoboken, New Jersey: Wiley, 2008).

[53] J. E. Russo, K. A. Carlson, and M. G. Meloy, "Choosing an Inferior Alternative," *Psychological Science* 17, no. 10 (2006): 899–904.

[54] D. Chugh and M. H. Bazerman; "Bounded Awareness: What You Fail to See Can Hurt You," *Mind & Society* 6 (2007): 1–18; N. Halevy and E. Y. Chou, "How Decisions Happen: Focal Points and Blind Spots in Interdependent Decision Making," *Journal of Personality and Social Psychology* 106, no. 3 (2014): 398–417; and D. Kahneman, "Maps of Bounded Rationality: Psychology for Behavioral Economics," *The American Economic Review* 93, no. 5 (2003): 1449–75.

[55] G. Gigerenzer, "Why Heuristics Work," *Perspectives on Psychological Science* 3, no. 1 (2008): 20–29; and A. K. Shah and D. M. Oppenheimer, "Heuristics Made Easy: An Effort-Reduction Framework," *Psychological Bulletin* 134, no. 2 (2008): 207–22.

[56] M. C. Kern and D. Chugh, "Bounded Ethicality: The Perils of Loss Framing," *Psychological Science* 20, no. 3 (2009): 378–84.

[57] R. Folger, D. B. Ganegoda, D. B. Rice, R. Taylor, and D. X. H. Wo, "Bounded Autonomy and Behavioral Ethics: Deonance and Reactance as Competing Motives," *Human Relations* 66, no. 7 (2013): 905–24; and R. Folger and D. R. Glerum, "Justice and Deonance: 'You Ought to be Fair,'" in M. Ambrose and R. Cropanzano (eds.), *The Oxford Handbook of Justice in the Workplace* (New York: Oxford, 2015): 331–50.

[58] T. Zhang, P. O. Fletcher, F. Gino, and M. H. Bazerman, "Reducing Bounded Ethicality: How to Help Individuals Notice and Avoid Unethical Behavior," *Organizational Dynamics* 44 (2015): 310–7.

[59] See A. W. Kruglanski and G. Gigerenzer, "Intuitive and Deliberate Judgments Are Based on Common Principles," *Psychological Review* 118 (2011): 97–109.

[60] E. Dane and M. G. Pratt, "Exploring Intuition and Its Role in Managerial Decision Making," *Academy of Management Review* 32, no. 1 (2007): 33–54; and J. A. Hicks, D. C. Cicero, J. Trent, C. M. Burton, and L. A. King, "Positive Affect, Intuition, and Feelings of Meaning," *Journal of Personality and Social Psychology* 98 (2010): 967–79.

[61] E. Salas, M. A. Rosen, and D. DiazGranados, "Expertise-Based Intuition and Decision Making in Organizations," *Journal of Management* 36, no. 4 (2010): 941–73.

[62] C. Akinci and E. Sadler-Smith, "Intuition in Management Research: A Historical Review," *International Journal of Management Reviews* 14 (2012): 104–22.

[63] S. P. Robbins, *Decide & Conquer: Making Winning Decisions and Taking Control of Your Life* (Upper Saddle River, NJ: Financial Times/Prentice Hall, 2004), 13.

[64] S. Ludwig and J. Nafziger, "Beliefs about Overconfidence," *Theory and Decision* 70, no. 4 (2011): 475–500.

[65]C. R. M. McKenzie, M. J. Liersch, and I. Yaniv, "Overconfidence in Interval Estimates: What Does Expertise Buy You," *Organizational Behavior and Human Decision Processes* 107 (2008): 179–91.

[66]R. P. Larrick, K. A. Burson, and J. B. Soll, "Social Comparison and Confidence: When Thinking You're Better Than Average Predicts Overconfidence (and When It Does Not)," *Organizational Behavior and Human Decision Processes* 102 (2007): 76–94.

[67]K. M. Hmieleski and R. A. Baron, "Entrepreneurs' Optimism and New Venture Performance: A Social Cognitive Perspective," *Academy of Management Journal* 52, no. 3 (2009): 473–88.

[68]R. Frick and A. K. Smith, "Overconfidence Game," *Kiplinger's Personal Finance* 64, no. 3 (2010): 23.

[69]R. Ronay, J. K. Oostrom, N. Lehmann-Willenbrock, S. Mayoral, and H. Rusch, "Playing the Trump Card: Why We Select Overconfident Leaders and Why It Matters," *The Leadership Quarterly* (in press).

[70]P. Belmi, M. A. Neale, D. Reiff, and R. Ulfe, "The Social Advantage of Miscalibrated Individuals: The Relationship between Social Class and Overconfidence and Its Implications for Class-based Inequality," *Journal of Personality and Social Psychology* 118, no. 2 (2020): 254–82; I. Vitanova, "Nurturing Overconfidence: The Relationship between Leader Power, Overconfidence, and Firm Performance," *The Leadership Quarterly* (in press).

[71]E. R. Tenney, N. L. Meikle, D. Hunsaker, D. A. Moore, and C. Anderson, "Is Overconfidence a Social Liability? The Effect of Verbal versus Nonverbal Expressions of Confidence," *Journal of Personality and Social Psychology* 116, no. 3 (2019): 396–415.

[72]See, for instance, J. P. Simmons, R. A. LeBoeuf, and L. D. Nelson, "The Effect of Accuracy Motivation on Anchoring and Adjustment: Do People Adjust from Their Provided Anchors?" *Journal of Personality and Social Psychology* 99 (2010): 917–32.

[73]C. Janiszewski and D. Uy, "Precision of the Anchor Influences the Amount of Adjustment," *Psychological Science* 19, no. 2 (2008): 121–27.

[74]See E. Jonas, S. Schultz-Hardt, D. Frey, and N. Thelen, "Confirmation Bias in Sequential Information Search after Preliminary Decisions," *Journal of Personality and Social Psychology* 80, no. 4 (2001): 557–71; and W. Hart, D. Albarracín, A. H. Eagly, I. Brechan, M. Lindberg, and L. Merrill, "Feeling Validated versus Being Correct: A Meta-Analysis of Selective Exposure to Information," *Psychological Bulletin* 135 (2009): 555–88.

[75]K. A. Costabile and S. Madon, "Downstream Effects of Dispositional Influences on Confirmation Biases," *Personality and Social Psychology Bulletin* 45, no. 4 (2019): 557–70.

[76]T. Pachur, R. Hertwig, and F. Steinmann, "How Do People Judge Risks: Availability Heuristic, Affect Heuristic, or Both?," *Journal of Experimental Psychology: Applied* 18 (2012): 314–30.

[77]G. Morgenson, "Debt Watchdogs: Tamed or Caught Napping?" *The New York Times*, December 7, 2009, 1, 32.

[78]B. M. Staw, "The Escalation of Commitment to a Course of Action," *Academy of Management Review* (October 1981): 577–87.

[79]D. J. Sleesman, "Pushing through the Tension While Stuck in the Mud: Paradox Mindset and Escalation of Commitment," *Organizational Behavior and Human Decision Processes* 155 (2019): 83–96.

[80]K. F. E. Wong and J. Y. Y. Kwong, "The Role of Anticipated Regret in Escalation of Commitment," *Journal of Applied Psychology* 92, no. 2 (2007): 545–54.

[81]D. J. Sleesman, D. E. Conlon, G. McNamara, and J. E. Miles, "Cleaning Up the Big Muddy: A Meta-Analytic Review of the Determinants of Escalation of Commitment," *Academy of Management Journal* 55 (2012): 541–62.

[82]R. L. Schaumberg and S. S. Wiltermuth, "Desire for a Positive Moral Self-Regard Exacerbates Escalation of Commitment to Initiatives with Prosocial Aims," *Organizational Behavior and Human Decision Processes* 123, no. 2 (2014): 110–23.

[83]H. Drummond, "Escalation of Commitment: When to Stay the Course?," *The Academy of Management Perspectives* 28, no. 4 (2014): 430–46.

[84]See, for instance, A. James and A. Wells, "Death Beliefs, Superstitious Beliefs and Health Anxiety," *British Journal of Clinical Psychology* (March 2002): 43–53; and U. Hahn and P. A. Warren, "Perceptions of Randomness: Why Three Heads Are Better Than One," *Psychological Review* 116 (2009): 454–61.

[85]See, for example, D. J. Keys and B. Schwartz, "Leaky Rationality: How Research on Behavioral Decision Making Challenges Normative Standards of Rationality," *Psychological Science* 2, no. 2 (2007): 162–80; and U. Simonsohn, "Direct Risk Aversion: Evidence from Risky Prospects Valued below Their Worst Outcome," *Psychological Science* 20, no. 6 (2009): 686–92.

[86]A. Kühberger, "The Influence of Framing on Risky Decisions: A Meta-Analysis," *Organizational Behavior and Human Decision Processes* 75, no. 1 (1998): 23–55; and A. Kühberger, M. Schulte-Mecklenbeck, and J. Perner, "The Effects of Framing, Reflection, Probability, and Payoff on Risk Preference in Choice Tasks," *Organizational Behavior and Human Decision Processes* 78, no. 3 (1999): 204–31.

[87]A. Chakraborty, S. Sheikh, and N. Subramanian, "Termination Risk and Managerial Risk Taking," *Journal of Corporate Finance* 13 (2007): 170–88.

[88]D. G. Allen, K. P. Weeks, and K. R. Moffitt, "Turnover Intentions and Voluntary Turnover: The Moderating Roles of Self-Monitoring, Locus of Control, Proactive Personality, and Risk Aversion," *Journal of Applied Psychology* 90, no. 5 (2005): 980–90; and C. Vandenberghe, A. Panaccio, and A. K. B. Ayed, "Continuance Commitment and Turnover: Examining the Moderating Role of Negative Affectivity and Risk Aversion," *Journal of Occupational and Organizational Psychology* 84 (2011): 403–24.

[89]P. Bryant and R. Dunford, "The Influence of Regulatory Focus on Risky Decision-Making," *Applied Psychology: An International Review* 57, no. 2 (2008): 335–59.

[90]A. J. Porcelli and M. R. Delgado, "Acute Stress Modulates Risk Taking in Financial Decision Making," *Psychological Science* 20, no. 3 (2009): 278–83.

[91]R. L. Guilbault, F. B. Bryant, J. H. Brockway, and E. J. Posavac, "A Meta-Analysis of Research on Hindsight Bias," *Basic and Applied Social Psychology* 26, nos. 2–3 (2004): 103–17; and L. Werth, F. Strack, and J. Foerster, "Certainty and Uncertainty: The Two Faces of the Hindsight Bias," *Organizational Behavior and Human Decision Processes* 87, no. 2 (2002): 323–41.

[92]J. Bell, "The Final Cut?" *Oregon Business* 33, no. 5 (2010): 27.

[93]E. Dash and J. Creswell, "Citigroup Pays for a Rush to Risk," *The New York Times*, November 20, 2008, 1, 28; S. Pulliam, S. Ng, and R. Smith, "Merrill Upped Ante as Boom in Mortgage Bonds Fizzled," *The Wall Street Journal*, April 16, 2008, A1, A14; and M. Gladwell, "Connecting the Dots," *The New Yorker*, March 10, 2003.

[94]H. Moon, J. R. Hollenbeck, S. E. Humphrey, and B. Maue, "The Tripartite Model of Neuroticism and the Suppression of Depression and Anxiety within an

Escalation of Commitment Dilemma," *Journal of Personality* 71 (2003): 347–68; and H. Moon, "The Two Faces of Conscientiousness: Duty and Achievement Striving in Escalation of Commitment Dilemmas," *Journal of Applied Psychology* 86 (2001): 535–40.

[95]J. Musch, "Personality Differences in Hindsight Bias," *Memory* 11 (2003): 473–89.

[96]M. D. Coleman, "Emotion and the Self-Serving Bias," *Current Psychology* (December 2011): 345–54.

[97]M. Tamborski, R. P. Brown, and K. Chowning, "Self-Serving Bias or Simply Serving the Self? Evidence for a Dimensional Approach to Narcissism," *Personality and Individual Differences* 52, no. 8 (2012): 942–6.

[98]T. Huston, "Are Women Better Decision Makers?" *The New York Times*, October 19, 2014, 9.

[99]A. Borders and K. A. Hennebry, "Angry Rumination Moderates the Association between Perceived Ethnic Discrimination and Risky Behaviors," *Personality and Individual Differences* 79 (2015): 81–86; and J. S. Hyde, A. H. Mezulis, and L. Y. Abramson, "The ABCs of Depression: Integrating Affective, Biological, and Cognitive Models to Explain the Emergence of the Gender Difference in Depression," *Psychological Review* 115, no. 2 (2008): 291–313.

[100]H. Connery and K. M. Davidson, "A Survey of Attitudes to Depression in the General Public: A Comparison of Age and Gender Differences," *Journal of Mental Health* 15, no. 2 (April 2006): 179–89.

[101]A. Shull, S. E. Mayer, E. McGinnis, E. Geiss, I. Vargas, and N. L. Lopez-Duran, "Trait and State Rumination Interact to Prolong Cortisol Activation to Psychosocial Stress in Females," *Psychoneuroendocrinology* 74 (2016): 324–32.

[102]M. Elias, "Thinking It Over, and Over, and Over," *USA Today*, February 6, 2003, 10D.

[103]K. E. Stanovich and R. F. West, "On the Relative Independence of Thinking Biases and Cognitive Ability," *Journal of Personality and Social Psychology* 94, no. 4 (2008): 672–95.

[104]N. J. Adler, *International Dimensions of Organizational Behavior*, 4th ed. (Cincinnati, OH: South-Western Publishing, 2002), 182–89; and J. F. Yates and S. de Oliveira, "Culture and Decision Making," *Organizational Behavior and Human Decision Processes* 136 (2016): 106–18.

[105]A. Lai, "For Businesses, Decision-Making during the COVID-19 Crisis Requires a Bias toward People, Not Profit," *Forbes* (March 19, 2020), https://www.forbes.com/sites/forrester/2020/03/19/decision-making-during-the-covid-19-crisis-requires-a-bias-toward-people-not-profit/#3b3d5e454ddc; B. Lincoln and R. Santorum, "Doctors, Nurses Must Make Hard Decisions in Pandemic. Let's Protect Them from Lawsuits," *USA Today* (April 22, 2020), https://www.usatoday.com/story/opinion/2020/04/22/pandemic-congress-should-protect-doctors-others-lawsuits-column/2995082001/.

[106]Lai, "For Businesses, Decision-Making during the COVID-19 Crisis Requires a Bias toward People, Not Profit."

[107]P. M. Vaaler and G. McNamara, "Crisis and Competition in Expert Organizational Decision Making: Credit-Rating Agencies and Their Response to Turbulence in Emerging Economies," *Organization Science* 15, no. 6 (2004): 687–703.

[108]L. Sayegh, W. P. Anthony, and P. L. Perrewé, "Managerial Decision-Making under Crisis: The Role of Emotion in an Intuitive Decision Process," *Human Resource Management Review* 14 (2004): 179–99.

[109]Santorum, "Doctors, Nurses Must Make Hard Decisions in Pandemic."

[110]S. Harvey and V. Y. Haines III, "Employer Treatment of Employees during a Community Crisis: The Role of Procedural and Distributive Justice," *Journal of Business and Psychology* 20, no. 1 (2005): 53–68.

[111]Lai, "For Businesses, Decision-Making during the COVID-19 Crisis Requires a Bias toward People, Not Profit."

[112]R. Audi, "Can Utilitarianism Be Distributive? Maximization and Distribution as Criteria in Managerial Decisions," *Business Ethics Quarterly* 17, no. 4 (2007): 593–611; and K. V. Kortenkamp and C. F. Moore, "Ethics under Uncertainty: The Morality and Appropriateness of Utilitarianism When Outcomes Are Uncertain," *American Journal of Psychology* 127, no. 3 (2014): 367–82.

[113]See, for example, I. Patil, M. M. Zucchelli, W. Kool, S. Campbell, F. Fornasier, M. Calò, G. Silani, M. Cikara, and F. Cushman, "Reasoning Supports Utilitarian Resolutions to Moral Dilemmas across Diverse Measures," *Journal of Personality and Social Psychology* (in press).

[114]A. Lukits, "Hello and Bonjour to Moral Dilemmas," *The Wall Street Journal*, May 13, 2014, D4.

[115]J. Hollings, "Let the Story Go: The Role of Emotion in the Decision-Making Process of the Reluctant, Vulnerable Witness or Whistle-Blower," *Journal of Business Ethics* 114, no. 3 (2013): 501–12.

[116]D. E. Rupp, P. M. Wright, S. Aryee, and Y. Luo, "Organizational Justice, Behavioral Ethics, and Corporate Social Responsibility: Finally the Three Shall Merge," *Management and Organization Review* 11 (2015): 15–24.

[117]R. Folger, "Fairness as Deonance," in S. W. Gilliland, D. D. Steiner, and D. P. Skarlicki (eds.), *Research in Social Issues in Management: Theoretical and Cultural Perspectives on Organizational Justice*, Vol. 1 (Charlotte, NC: Information Age, 2001): 3–31; R. Folger, "Deonanace: Behavioral Ethics and Moral Obligation," in D. DeCremer and A. E. Tenbrunsel (eds.), *Series in Organization and Management: Behavioral Business Ethics; Shaping an Emerging Field* (New York: Routledge, 2011): 123–42; and Folger and Glerum, "Justice and Deonance."

[118]M. Hennig and M. Hütter, "Revisiting the Divide between Deontology and Utilitarianism in Moral Dilemma Judgment: A Multinomial Modeling Approach," *Journal of Personality and Social Psychology* 118, no. 1 (2020): 22–56; M.-H. Li and L.-L. Rao, "Do People Believe That They Are More Deontological Than Others?" *Personality and Social Psychology Bulletin* 45, no. 8 (2019): 1308–20; A. Mata, "Social Metacognition in Moral Judgment: Decisional Conflict Promotes Perspective Taking," *Journal of Personality and Social Psychology* (in press).

[119]L. L. Shu and F. Gino, "Sweeping Dishonesty under the Rug: How Unethical Actions Lead to Forgetting of Moral Rules," *Journal of Personality and Social Psychology* 102 (2012): 1164–77.

[120]B. C. Gunia, L. Wang, L. Huang, J. Wang, and J. K. Murnighan, "Contemplation and Conversation: Subtle Influences on Moral Decision Making," *Academy of Management Journal* 55 (2012): 13–33.

[121]R. F. West, R. J. Meserve, and K. E. Stanovich, "Cognitive Sophistication Does Not Attenuate the Bias Blind Spot," *Journal of Personality and Social Psychology* 103 (2012): 506–19.

[122]J. B. Cullen, K. P. Parboteeah, and M. Hoegl, "Cross-National Differences in Managers' Willingness to Justify Ethically Suspect Behaviors: A Test of Institutional Anomie Theory," *Academy of Management Journal* 47, no. 3 (2004): 411–21.

[123]A. Vrij, M. Hartwig, and P. A. Granhag, "Reading Lies: Nonverbal Communication and Deception," *Annual Review of Psychology* 70 (2019): 295–317.

[124]N. Klein and H. Zhou, "Their Pants Aren't on Fire," *The New York Times,* March 25, 2014, D3.
[125]Ibid.
[126]Ibid.
[127]Ibid.
[128]E. Bernstein, "Lie Detection for Your Email," *The Wall Street Journal,* May 20, 2014, D1.
[129]Klein and Zhou, "Their Pants Aren't on Fire."
[130]E. Bernstein, "Lie Detection for Your Email," *The Wall Street Journal,* May 20, 2014, D1.
[131]L. ten Brinke, D. Simson, and D. R. Carney, "Some Evidence for Unconscious Lie Detection," *Psychological Science* 25, no. 5 (2014): 1098–105.
[132]B.C. Gunia and E. E. Levine, "Deception as Competence: The Effect of Occupational Stereotypes on the Perception and Proliferation of Deception," *Organizational and Human Decision Processes* 152 (2019): 122–37; J. J. Lee, N. Llewellyn, and A. Whittle, "Lies, Defeasibility and Morality-in-Action: The Interactional Architecture of False Claims in Sales, Telemarketing and Debt Collection Work," *Human Relations* 72, no. 4 (2019): 834–58; M. Ong, B. Parmar, and E. Amit, "Lay Theories of Effortful Honesty: Does the Honesty–Effort Association Justify Making a Dishonest Decision?" *Journal of Applied Psychology* 104, no. 5 (2019): 659–77.
[133]S. D. Levitt and S. J. Dubner, "Traponomics," *The Wall Street Journal,* May 10–11, 2014, C1, C2.
[134]N. Anderson, K. Potocnik, and J. Zhou, "Innovation and Creativity in Organizations: A State-of-the-Science Review, Prospective Commentary, and Guiding Framework," *Journal of Management* 40, no. 5 (2014): 1297–333.
[135]"Is Your Art Killing You?," Investorideas.com, May 13, 2013, www.investorideas.com/news/2013/renewable-energy/05134.asp.
[136]M. M. Gielnik, A.-C. Kramer, B. Kappel, and M. Frese, "Antecedents of Business Opportunity Identification and Innovation: Investigating the Interplay of Information Processing and Information Acquisition," *Applied Psychology: An International Review* 63, no. 2 (2014): 344–81.
[137]G. Anderson, "Three Tips to Foster Creativity at Your Startup," *ArcticStartup,* May 8, 2013, downloaded May 14, 2013, from http://www.arcticstartup.com/.
[138]L. Paine Hagtvedt, K. Dossinger, S. H. Harrison, and L. Huang, "Curiosity Made the Cat More Creative: Specific Curiosity as a Driver of Creativity," *Organizational Behavior and Human Decision Processes* 150 (2019): 1–13.
[139]Z. Harper, "Mark Cuban Wants You to Design the New Dallas Mavericks Uniforms," CBSSports.com, May 13, 2013, http://sports.yahoo.com/blogs/nba-ball-dont-lie/mark-cuban-wants-designs-dallas-mavericks-uniforms-214849952.html.
[140]K. H. Kim, "Meta-Analyses of the Relationship of Creative Achievement to Both IQ and Divergent Thinking Test Scores," *The Journal of Creative Behavior* 42, no. 2 (2008): 106–30.
[141]C. K. W. De Dreu, B. A. Nijstad, M. Baas, I. Wolsink, and M. Roskes, "Working Memory Benefits Creative Insight, Musical Improvisation, and Original Ideation through Maintained Task-Focused Attention," *Personality and Social Psychology Bulletin* 38 (2012): 656–69.
[142]C.-H. Wu, S. K. Parker, and J. P. J. de Jong, "Need for Cognition as an Antecedent of Individual Innovation Behavior," *Journal of Management* 40, no. 6 (2014): 1511–34.
[143]M. M. Hammond, N. L. Neff, J. L. Farr, A. R. Schwall, and X. Zhao, "Predictors of Individual-Level Innovation at Work: A Meta-analysis," *Psychology of Aesthetics, Creativity, and the Arts* 5, no. 1 (2011): 90–105; and S. M. Wechsler, C. Vendramini, and T. Oakland, "Thinking and Creative Styles: A Validity Study," *Creativity Research Journal* 24 (April 2012): 235–42.
[144]Y. Gong, S. Cheung, M. Wang, and J. Huang, "Unfolding the Proactive Processes for Creativity: Integration of the Employee Proactivity, Information Exchange, and Psychological Safety Perspectives," *Journal of Management* 38 (2012): 1611–33; and Hammond, Neff, Farr, Schwall, and Zhao, "Predictors of Individual-Level Innovation at Work."
[145]A. Rego, F. Sousa, C. Marques, and M. P. E. Cunha, "Retail Employees' Self-Efficacy and Hope Predicting Their Positive Affect and Creativity," *European Journal of Work and Organizational Psychology* 21, no. 6 (2012): 923–45.
[146]H. Zhang, H. K. Kwan, X. Zhang, and L.-Z. Wu, "High Core Self-Evaluators Maintain Creativity: A Motivational Model of Abusive Supervision," *Journal of Management* 40, no. 4 (2012): 1151–74.
[147]D. K. Simonton, "The Mad-Genius Paradox: Can Creative People Be More Mentally Healthy but Highly Creative People More Mentally Ill?," *Perspectives on Psychological Science* 9, no. 5 (2014): 470–80.
[148]C. Wang, S. Rodan, M. Fruin, and X. Xu, "Knowledge Networks, Collaboration Networks, and Exploratory Innovation," *Academy of Management Journal* 57, no. 2 (2014): 484–514.
[149]F. Gino and S. S. Wiltermuth, "Evil Genius? Dishonesty Can Lead to Greater Creativity," *Psychological Science* 25, no. 4 (2014): 973–81.
[150]D. van Knippenberg and G. Hirst, "A Motivational Lens Model of Person x Situation Interactions in Employee Creativity," *Journal of Applied Psychology* (in press).
[151]S. N. de Jesus, C. L. Rus, W. Lens, and S. Imaginário, "Intrinsic Motivation and Creativity Related to Product: A Meta-Analysis of the Studies Published between 1990–2010," *Creativity Research Journal* 25 (2013): 80–84; and Hammond, Neff, Farr, Schwall, and Zhao, "Predictors of Individual-Level Innovation at Work."
[152]A. Somech and A. Drach-Zahavy, "Translating Team Creativity to Innovation Implementation: The Role of Team Composition and Climate for Innovation," *Journal of Management* 39 (2013): 684–708.
[153]L. Sun, Z. Zhang, J. Qi, and Z. X. Chen, "Empowerment and Creativity: A Cross-Level Investigation," *Leadership Quarterly* 23 (2012): 55–65.
[154]M. Cerne, C. G. L. Nerstad, A. Dysvik, and M. Skerlavaj, "What Goes Around Comes Around: Knowledge Hiding, Perceived Motivational Climate, and Creativity," *Academy of Management Journal* 57, no. 1 (2014): 172–92.
[155]Hammond, Neff, Farr, Schwall, and Zhao, "Predictors of Individual-level Innovation at Work."
[156]S. Sonnenshein, "How Organizations Foster the Creative Use of Resources," *Academy of Management Journal* 57, no. 3 (2014): 814–48.
[157]V. Venkataramani, A. W. Richter, and R. Clarke, "Creative Benefits from Well-Connected Leaders: Leader Social Network Ties as Facilitators of Employee Radical Creativity," *Journal of Applied Psychology* 99, no. 5 (2014): 966–75.
[158]J. E. Perry-Smith, "Social Network Ties beyond Nonredundancy: An Experimental Investigation of the Effect of Knowledge Content and Tie Strength on Creativity," *Journal of Applied Psychology* 99, no. 5 (2014): 831–46.
[159]T. Rinne, D. G. Steel, and J. Fairweather, "The Role of Hofstede's Individualism in National-Level Creativity," *Creativity Research Journal* 25 (2013): 129–36.
[160]X. Yi, W. Hu, H. Scheithauer, and W. Niu, "Cultural and Bilingual Influences

on Artistic Creativity Performances: Comparison of German and Chinese Students," *Creativity Research Journal* 25 (2013): 97–108.

[161]Hammond, Neff, Farr, Schwall, and Zhao, "Predictors of Individual-Level Innovation at Work."

[162]D. Liu, H. Liao, and R. Loi, "The Dark Side of Leadership: A Three-Level Investigation of the Cascading Effect of Abusive Supervision on Employee Creativity," *Academy of Management Journal* 55 (2012): 1187–212.

[163]J. B. Avey, F. L. Richmond, and D. R. Nixon, "Leader Positivity and Follower Creativity: An Experimental Analysis," *Journal of Creative Behavior* 46 (2012): 99–118; and A. Rego, F. Sousa, C. Marques, and M. E. Cunha, "Authentic Leadership Promoting Employees' Psychological Capital and Creativity," *Journal of Business Research* 65 (2012): 429–37.

[164]I. J. Hoever, D. van Knippenberg, W. P. van Ginkel, and H. G. Barkema, "Fostering Team Creativity: Perspective Taking as Key to Unlocking Diversity's Potential," *Journal of Applied Psychology* 97 (2012): 982–96.

[165]S. J. Shin, T. Kim, J. Lee, and L. Bian, "Cognitive Team Diversity and Individual Team Member Creativity: A Cross-Level Interaction," *Academy of Management Journal* 55 (2012): 197–212.

[166]A. W. Richter, G. Hirst, D. van Knippenberg, and M. Baer, "Creative Self-Efficacy and Individual Creativity in Team Contexts: Cross-Level Interactions with Team Informational Resources," *Journal of Applied Psychology* 97 (2012): 1282–90.

[167]X. Huang, J. J. P.-A. Hsieh, and W. He, "Expertise Dissimilarity and Creativity: The Contingent Roles of Tacit and Explicit Knowledge Sharing," *Journal of Applied Psychology* 99, no. 5 (2014): 816–30.

[168]T. B. Harris, N. Li, W. R. Boswell, X.-A. Zhang, and Z. Xie, "Getting What's New from Newcomers: Empowering Leadership, Creativity, and Adjustment in the Socialization Context," *Personnel Psychology* 67 (2014): 567–604.

[169]A. H. Y. Hon, M. Bloom, and J. M. Crant, "Overcoming Resistance to Change and Enhancing Creative Performance," *Journal of Management* 40, no. 3 (2014): 919–41.

[170]J. S. Mueller, S. Melwani, and J. A. Goncalo, "The Bias against Creativity: Why People Desire but Reject Creative Ideas," *Psychological Science* 23 (2012): 13–17.

[171]T. Montag, C. P. Maertz, and M. Baer, "A Critical Analysis of the Workplace Creativity Criterion Space," *Journal of Management* 38 (2012): 1362–86.

[172]M. Baer, "Putting Creativity to Work: The Implementation of Creative Ideas in Organizations," *Academy of Management Journal* 55 (2012): 1102–19.

6 Emotions and Moods

Source: Victor J. Blue/Bloomberg/Getty Images

LEARNING OBJECTIVES

After studying this chapter, you should be able to:

6-1 Differentiate between emotions and moods.

6-2 Identify the sources of emotions and moods.

6-3 Show the impact that emotional labor has on employees.

6-4 Describe affective events theory.

6-5 Describe emotional intelligence.

6-6 Identify strategies for emotion regulation.

6-7 Apply concepts about emotions and moods to specific OB issues.

Employability Skills Matrix (ESM)

	Myth or Science?	Career OBjectives	An Ethical Choice	Point/ Counterpoint	Experiential Exercise	Ethical Dilemma	Case Incident 1	Case Incident 2
Critical Thinking			✓	✓	✓	✓	✓	✓
Communication	✓	✓		✓			✓	
Collaboration	✓	✓		✓			✓	
Knowledge Application and Analysis			✓	✓	✓	✓	✓	✓
Social Responsibility		✓	✓	✓		✓		

OBJECTIONS SUSTAINED

Daraprim is a drug that is used to treat toxoplasmosis, a lethal condition that is caused by a parasitic infection. In September 2015, the drug was selling for $13.50 a pill by an organization that held the production and distribution rights. No one could have guessed that the price of the drug would be raised more than 5,000 percent overnight to $750 a pill (hundreds of thousands of dollars annually, in patient costs). The CEO of Turing Pharmaceuticals, Martin Shkreli, after acquiring the original rights-holding company, agreed to the price hike because the prior pill was no longer profitable at $13.50 per pill.

This change in price resulted in immediate, unrelenting outrage from the public, earning him unflattering titles such as "the most hated man in America," "everything that is wrong with capitalism," and "pharma-bro." Not only was the act of raising the Daraprim prices offensive to many, but the tenacity and brazenness with which he defended the price hike were especially provocative. Shkreli tweeted at members of Congress after being called to testify at a hearing focused on high drug prices, held by the House Committee on Oversight and Government Reform. He noted sarcastically that they were "busy whining to healthcare reporters" about the hearing.

Shkreli was not the only one to engage in price hikes of this sort—notably, Mylan's CEO Heather Bresch raised the prices of EpiPens (devices used to treat anaphylaxis, a life-threatening allergic reaction that at least one in 50 Americans experiences at some point in their life) more than 1,000 percent in a 7-year period. Demonstrators, such as the ones shown in the accompanying photograph protesting Paulson & Co.'s investment in Mylan, have come out in full force across all walks of life in recent years to protest these decisions. Politicians, such as Senator Richard Blumenthal of Connecticut, are also expressing their distaste at such drug profiteering: "Sadly, this case is just the latest in a greedy trend of skyrocketing prescription drug prices that are hurting consumers, limiting health options, and strangling our economy."

These cases of drug profiteering highlight an uneasy tension between what is moral and what is legal: Although setting drug prices in this fashion is legal, it was considered by many to be immoral given the potential for increasing the suffering of many who may not have access to the drug. However, Shkreli defended his actions, noting that he could "see how it looks greedy" but he thinks "there's a lot of altruistic properties" to his company's tactics, namely, that it was "dramatically increasing the access to Daraprim, [and] lowering co-pays." This line of reasoning was rejected, however, by The Pharmaceutical Research and Manufacturers of America (PhRMA) on Twitter. As Katie Thomas, columnist from the *New York Times* notes, "almost no one actually pays those prices. Insurers and pharmacy-benefit managers, who manage drug plans for insurers, negotiate discounts and rebates, which lowers the effective cost of a drug," thus painting a more complicated picture of drug pricing than what appears on the surface.

Regardless, public outrage will continue as long as there are perceptions of unfairness, harm, and deception. Even with PhRMA beginning a new advertising campaign that focuses on pharmaceutical innovation and the excitement surrounding new forms of treatment, Jeremy Greene, historian of medicine at Johns Hopkins University, notes, "What does it matter to the average American that there are new and exciting treatments for cancer if there's no confidence they'll be able to afford them or [have] access [to] them?"

Sources: Based on A. E. Cha, "CEO Martin Shkreli: 4,000 Percent Drug Price Hike Is 'Altruistic,' Not Greedy," *The Washington Post*, September 22, 2015, https://www.washingtonpost.com/news/to-your-health/wp/2015/09/22/turing-ceo-martin-shkreli-explains-that-4000-percent-drug-price-hike-is-altruistic-not-greedy/; U. W. Chohan, "Martin Shkreli and the Outrage of Inequality," *The Conversation,* January 7, 2016, http://theconversation.com/martin-shkreli-and-the-outrage-of-inequality-52812; C. Y. Johnson, "'Pharma Bro' Martin Shkreli Responds to a Subpoena with Sarcastic Tweets," *The Washington Post,* January 21, 2016, https://www.washingtonpost.com/news/wonk/wp/2016/01/21/pharma-bro-martin-shkreli-is-responding-to-a-subpoena-with-sarcastic-tweets/; B. Popken, "Martin Shkreli Weighs In on EpiPen Scandal, Calls Drug Makers 'Vultures,'" *NBC News*, August 19, 2016, http://www.nbcnews.com/business/consumer/martin-shkreli-weighs-epipen-scandal-calls-drug-makers-vultures-n634451; K. Thomas, "The Complex Math Behind Spiraling Prescription Drug Prices," *The New York Times,* August 24, 2016, https://www.nytimes.com/2016/08/25/business/high-drug-prices-explained-epipen-heart-medications.html?_r=0; and Z. Thomas and T. Swift, "Who Is Martin Shkreli—'the Most Hated Man in America'?" *BBC News*, September 23, 2015, http://www.bbc.com/news/world-us-canada-34331761.

Similar cases in India spurred up during April 2021, in the midst of the deadly second wave of COVID-19 virus, drug companies and scams around drugs abounded. Hapless relatives of COVID patients ran from door to door trying to get Remdesivir, considered a key life-saving drug. While the efficacy of Remdesivir was still not established, drug companies, scammers took advantage of the desperation of people to jack up the prices of the drug.[1] The public outpour on the unabated operating of black economy had people up in arms on the social media and outside the hospitals. Seeing the number of people suffering, the mood of the nurses in a large COVID hospital was sombre. While they battled the effects of the coronavirus in their nursing homes, they expressed helplessness that they could not provide the required medicines because of shortages. The anger of the relatives also affected the emotional well-being of the staff at the hospitals. A doctor in the same hospital shared, "I feel very sad that because of the profiteering motive of some elements of the society and system, we are unable to provide treatment to them despite the best of our intentions and obviously the patients do not trust us."[2] The doctors and nurses shared that angry relatives are not even able to discriminate that they drug scammers and the staff at the hospital were not the same party.

As the outrage over profiteering during crisis illustrates, emotions can greatly influence our attitudes toward others, our decision making, and our behaviors. It can even spark conflict with potentially disastrous consequences. In truth, we cannot set aside our emotions, but we can acknowledge and work with them. And not all emotions have negative influences on us.

Given the obvious role emotions play in our lives, it might surprise you that, until recently, the field of Organizational Behavior (OB) has not given the topic of emotions much attention. Why? Generally because emotions in the workplace were historically thought to be detrimental to performance. Although managers knew emotions were an inseparable part of everyday life, they tried to create organizations that were emotion-free. Researchers tended to focus on strong negative emotions—especially anger—that interfered with an employee's ability to work effectively.

Thankfully, this type of thinking is changing. Certainly, some emotions can hinder performance, particularly those exhibited at the wrong time. Other emotions are neutral, and some are constructive. Employees bring their emotions to work every day, so no study of OB would be comprehensive without considering the role of emotions in workplace behavior.

What Are Emotions and Moods?

6-1 Differentiate between emotions and moods.

affect A term used to describe a broad range of feelings that people experience.

emotions Intense, discrete, and short-lived feeling experiences that are often caused by a specific event.

moods Feelings that tend to be longer-lived and less intense than emotions and that lack a contextual stimulus.

First, we need to discuss three terms that are closely intertwined: *affect, emotions,* and *moods.* **Affect** is a generic term that covers a broad range of feelings, including both emotions and moods.[3] **Emotions** are intense, discrete, and short-lived feeling experiences that are often caused by a specific event.[4] **Moods** are longer-lived and less intense feelings than emotions and often arise without a specific event acting as a stimulus.[5] Exhibit 6-1 shows the relationships among affect, emotions, and moods.

Affect, emotions, and moods are separable in theory; in practice the distinction isn't always defined. When we review the OB topics on emotions and moods, you may see more information about emotions in one area and moods in another. This is simply the state of the research. Let's start with a review of the basic emotions.

Exhibit 6-1 Affect, Emotions, and Moods

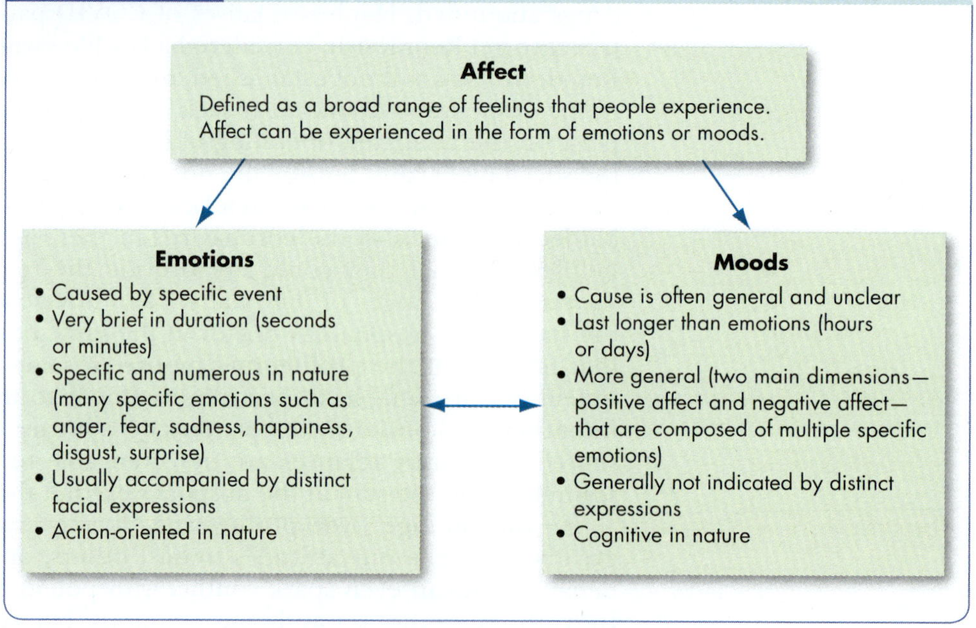

The Basic Emotions

How many emotions are there? There are dozens, including anger, contempt, enthusiasm, envy, fear, frustration, disappointment, embarrassment, disgust, happiness, hate, hope, jealousy, joy, love, pride, surprise, and sadness. Numerous researchers have tried to limit them to a fundamental set.[6] Other scholars argue that by thinking in terms of "basic" emotions, we lose sight of the bigger picture because emotions can mean different things in different contexts and may vary across cultures.[7]

Psychologists have tried to identify basic emotions by studying how we express them. Facial expressions have proved difficult to interpret.[8] One problem is that some emotions are too complex to be easily represented on our faces. Second, although people can, for the most part, recognize emotions across cultures at better-than-chance levels, this accuracy is worse for cultural groups with less exposure to one another.[9] Cultures also have norms that govern emotional expression, so the way we *recognize* an emotion isn't always the same as the way we *show* it. For example, in collectivist countries, where emotional restraint is the norm, people focus more strongly on the eyes, whereas in individualistic countries, where emotional expression is the norm, people focus more strongly on the position of the mouth.[10]

It's unlikely psychologists or philosophers will ever completely agree on a set of basic emotions or even on whether there is such a thing. Still, many researchers agree on six universal emotions—anger, fear, sadness, happiness, disgust, and surprise.[11] We sometimes mistake happiness for surprise, but rarely do we confuse happiness and disgust.

Moral Emotions

We may tend to think our internal emotions are innate. For instance, if someone jumped out at you from behind a door, wouldn't you feel surprised? Maybe you would, but you may also feel any of the other five universal emotions—anger,

Myth or Science?

Smile, and the Work World Smiles with You

It is true that a smile is not always an emotional expression. Smiles are used as social currency in most organizations to create a positive atmosphere, and a smile usually evokes an unconscious reflexive return smile. However, anyone who has ever smiled at an angry manager knows this doesn't always work. In truth, the giving and withholding of smiles is often an unconscious power play of office politics.

Research on the "boss effect" suggests that the amount of power and status a person feels over another person dictates who will smile. Subordinates generally smile more often than their bosses smile back at them. This may happen in part because workers are increasingly expected to show expressions of happiness with their jobs. However, the relationship is complex and varies by national culture: In one study, Chinese workers reflexively smiled only at bosses who had the power to give them negative job evaluations, while U.S. participants smiled most at managers perceived to have higher social power. Other researchers found that when individuals felt powerful, they usually didn't return even a high-ranking individual's smile. Conversely, when people felt powerless, they returned everyone's smiles. "Your feelings about power and status seem to dictate how much you are willing to return a smile to another person," cognitive neuroscientist Evan Carr affirmed.

The science of smiling transcends the expression of emotion. While an angry manager may not smile back, a happy manager might not either, according to "boss effect" research. "The relationship of what we show on our face and how we feel is a very loose one," said Arvid Kappas, a professor of emotion research at Jacobs University Bremen in Germany. This suggests that, when we want to display positive emotions to others, we should do more than smile, as service representatives do when they try to create happy moods in their customers with excited voice pitch, encouraging gestures, and energetic body movement.

The science of smiling is an area of current research, but it is clear already that knowing about the "boss effect" suggests many practical applications. For one, managers and employees can be made more aware of ingrained tendencies toward others and, through careful self-observation, change their habits. Comprehensive displays of positive emotion using voice inflection, gestures, and word choice may also be more helpful in building good business relationships than the simple smile.

Sources: Based on R. L. Hotz, "Too Important to Smile Back: The 'Boss Effect,'" *The Wall Street Journal,* October 16, 2012, D2; P. Jaskunas, "The Tyranny of the Forced Smile," *The New York Times,* February 15, 2015, 14; and E. Kim and D. J. Yoon, "Why Does Service with a Smile Make Employees Happy? A Social Interaction Model," *Journal of Applied Psychology* 97 (2012): 1059–67.

moral emotions Emotions that have moral implications.

fear, sadness, happiness, or disgust—depending on the circumstance. Our experiences of emotions are closely tied to our interpretations of events. One area in which researchers have been furthering this idea is through the study of **moral emotions**, that is, emotions that have moral implications because of our instant judgment of the situation that evokes them.[12] Examples of moral emotions include sympathy for the suffering of others, guilt about our own immoral behavior, anger about injustice done to others, and contempt for those who behave unethically.

Another example is the disdain we feel about violations of moral norms, called *moral disgust.* Moral disgust is unique from other forms of disgust. Say you stepped in cow dung by mistake—you might feel disgusted by it, but you wouldn't feel moral disgust—you probably wouldn't make a moral judgment. In contrast, say that you watched a video of a police officer making a sexist or racist slur. You might feel disgusted in a different way because it offends your sense of right and wrong. In fact, you might feel a variety of emotions based on your moral judgment of the situation.[13]

Research indicates that our responses to moral emotions differ from our responses to other emotions.[14] When we feel moral anger, for instance, we may be more likely to confront the situation that causes it than when we just feel angry. However, we cannot assume our emotional reactions to events on a moral level will be the same as someone else's. Moral emotions are developed during childhood as children learn moral norms and standards, so moral emotions depend on the situation and normative context more so than other emotions. Because morality is a construct that differs from one culture to the next, so do moral emotions. Therefore, we need to be aware of the moral aspects of situations that trigger our emotions and make certain we understand the context before we act, especially in the workplace.[15]

You can think about this research in your own life to see how moral emotions operate. Consider a time when you have done something that hurt someone else. Did you feel angry or upset with yourself? Or think about a time when you have seen someone else treated unfairly. Did you feel contempt for the person acting unfairly, or did you engage in a cool, rational calculation of the justice of the situation? Most people who think about these situations have some sense of an emotional stirring that might prompt them to engage in ethical actions like donating money to help others, apologizing and attempting to make amends, or intervening on behalf of those who have been mistreated. In sum, we can conclude that people who are behaving ethically are at least partially making decisions based on their emotions and feelings.

Emotions can be fleeting, but moods can endure, and for quite a while. To understand the impact of emotions and moods in organizations, we next classify the many distinct emotions into broader mood categories.

The Basic Moods: Positive and Negative Affect

As a first step toward studying the effect of moods and emotions in the workplace, we will classify emotions into two categories: positive and negative. Positive emotions—such as joy and gratitude—express a favorable evaluation or feeling. Negative emotions—such as anger and guilt—express the opposite. Keep in mind that emotions can't be neutral. Being neutral is being nonemotional.[16]

When we group emotions into positive and negative categories, they become *mood states* because we are now looking at them more generally instead of isolating one particular emotion. In Exhibit 6-2, excited is a pure marker of high positive affect, while boredom is a pure marker of low positive affect. Nervous is a pure marker of high negative affect; relaxed is a pure marker of low negative affect. Finally, some emotions—such as contentment and sadness—are in between. You'll notice this model does not include all emotions. Some, such as surprise, don't fit well because they're not as clearly positive or negative.

positive affect A mood dimension that consists of specific positive emotions such as excitement, enthusiasm, and elation at the high end and boredom, sluggishness, and tiredness at the low end.

negative affect A mood dimension that consists of emotions such as nervousness, stress, and anxiety at the high end.

So we can think of **positive affect** as a mood dimension consisting of positive emotions such as excitement, enthusiasm, and elation at the high end (high positive affect). **Negative affect** is a mood dimension consisting of nervousness, stress, and anxiety at the high end (high negative affect).[17] While we rarely experience both positive and negative affect at the same time, over time people do differ in how much they experience each. Some people (we might call them emotional or intense) may experience quite a bit of high positive and high negative affect over, say, a week's time. Others (we might call them unemotional or phlegmatic) experience little of either. And still others may experience one much more predominately than the other.

Exhibit 6-2 The Structure of Mood

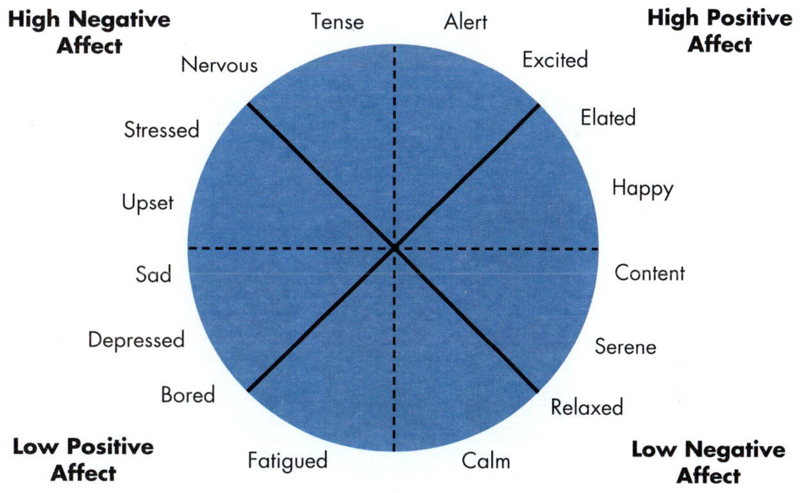

Experiencing Moods and Emotions

positivity offset The tendency of most individuals to experience a mildly positive mood at zero input (when nothing in particular is going on).

As if it weren't complex enough to consider the many distinct emotions and moods that a person might identify, the reality is that we all experience moods and emotions differently. For most people, positive moods are somewhat more common than negative moods. Indeed, research finds a **positivity offset**, meaning that at zero input (when nothing in particular is going on), most individuals experience a mildly positive mood.[18] This appears to be true for employees in a wide range of job settings. For example, one study of customer service representatives in a British call center revealed that people reported experiencing positive moods 58 percent of the time despite the stressful environment.[19] Another research finding is that negative emotions lead to negative moods. Perhaps this happens because people think about events that created strong negative emotions five times as long as events that created strong positive ones.[20]

Does the degree to which people experience positive and negative emotions vary across cultures? Yes (see the OB Poll). The reason is not that people of various cultures are inherently different: People in most cultures appear to experience certain positive and negative emotions, and people interpret them in much the same way worldwide. We all view negative emotions such as hate, terror, and rage as dangerous and destructive, and we desire positive emotions such as joy, love, and happiness. However, an individual's experience of emotions appears to be culturally shaped. Some cultures value certain emotions more than others, which leads individuals to change their perspective on experiencing these emotions.

There is much to be learned in exploring the value differences. Some cultures embrace negative emotions, such as Japan and Russia, while others emphasize positive emotions and expressions, such as Mexico and Brazil.[21] There may also be a difference in the value of negative emotions between collectivist and individualist countries. The difference may be the reason negative emotions are less detrimental to the health of those of Eastern, as opposed to

OB POLL

Emotional States

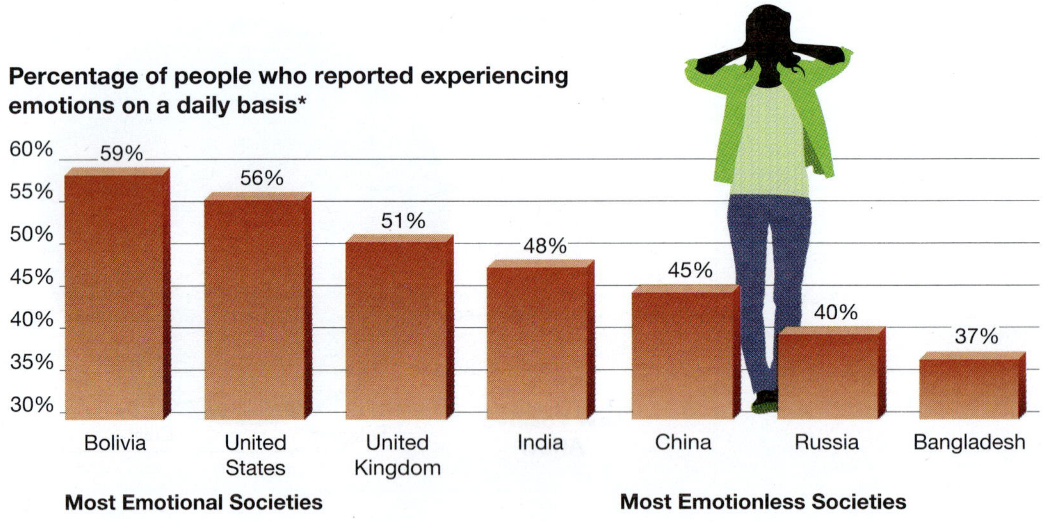

*Respondents in 148 countries worldwide during 2014 were asked whether they experienced five positive (well-rested, treated with respect, enjoyment, smiling and laughing, learning or doing something interesting) and five negative emotions (anger, stress, sadness, physical pain, worry) daily.

Source: Based on J. Clifton, "Latin Americans Lead World in Emotions," Gallup (August 27, 2015), http://www.gallup.com/poll/184631/latin-americans-lead-world-emotions.aspx.

Western, cultures.[22] For example, the Chinese consider negative emotions—while not always pleasant—as potentially more useful and constructive than do people in the United States.

There may be merit to the Eastern perspective: Research has suggested that negative affect can have benefits. For example, research in Germany suggests that valuing negative affect often allows people to accept present circumstances and cope, reducing the negative effects on physical and psychological health and decision making.[23] Negative affect may also allow managers to think more critically and fairly.[24]

Now that we've identified the basic emotions, the basic moods, and our experience of them, let's explore the function of emotions and moods, particularly in the workplace.

The Function of Emotions

In some ways, emotions are a mystery. What function do they serve? As we discussed, OB researchers have been finding that emotions can be critical to an effectively functioning workplace. For example, a large number of reviews suggest that happy employees tend to have positive job attitudes, to engage in less withdrawal and counterproductive work behaviors, to engage in more task and citizenship performance, and even to be more successful than their unhappy counterparts.[25] Individuals who tend to experience positive affect consistently as part of their personalities (see Chapter 4) tend to have positive job attitudes, experience good social integration with their supervisor and coworkers, experience good treatment from their organizations, and engage in more task and citizenship performance.[26] Let's discuss two critical areas—rationality and ethicality—in which emotions can enhance performance.

Do Emotions Make Us Irrational? How often have you heard someone say, "Oh, you're just being emotional"? You might have been offended. Observations like this suggest that rationality and emotion are in conflict and that by exhibiting emotion you are acting irrationally. The perceived association between the two is so strong that some researchers argue that displaying emotions such as sadness to the point of crying is so toxic to a career that we should leave the room rather than allow others to witness it.[27] This perspective suggests that the demonstration or even experience of emotions can make us seem weak, brittle, or irrational. However, this is wrong. Our emotions actually make our thinking more rational. Why? Because our emotions provide important information about how we understand the world around us and they help guide our behaviors. For instance, individuals in a negative mood may be better able to discern truthful from inaccurate information than are people in a happy mood.[28]

Consider Phineas Gage, a railroad worker in Vermont. One September day in 1848, a 3-foot, 7-inch iron bar propelled by an explosive charge flew into his lower-left jaw and out through the top of his skull. Remarkably, Gage survived his injury, was able to read and speak, and performed well above average on cognitive ability tests. However, he completely lost his ability to experience emotion, which eventually took away his ability to reason. After the accident, he often behaved erratically and against his self-interests. He drifted from job to job, eventually joining a circus. In commenting on Gage's condition, one expert noted, "Reason may not be as pure as most of us think it is or wish it were ... emotions and feelings may not be intruders in the bastion of reason at all: They may be enmeshed in its networks, for worse *and* for better."[29]

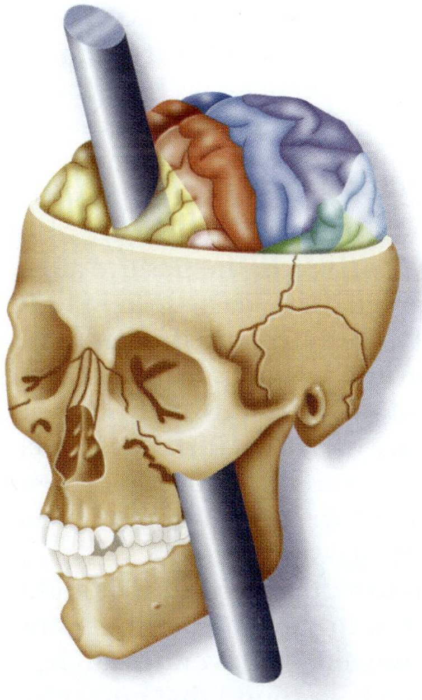

By studying brain injuries, such as the injury experienced by Phineas Gage, whose skull is illustrated here, researchers discovered an important link between emotions and rational thinking. They learned that our emotions provide us with valuable information that helps our thinking process.

Source: BSIP/Science Source

Do Emotions Make Us Ethical? A growing body of research has begun to examine moral emotions and moral attitudes.[30] It was previously believed that, like decision making in general, most ethical decision making was based on higher-order cognitive processes, but the research on moral emotions increasingly questions this perspective. Numerous studies suggest that moral judgments are largely based on feelings rather than on cognition, even though we tend to see our moral boundaries as logical and reasonable, not as emotional.

To some degree, our beliefs are shaped by the groups we belong to, which influence our perceptions of the ethicality of certain situations, resulting in unconscious responses and shared moral emotions. Unfortunately, these shared emotions may allow us to justify purely emotional reactions as rationally "ethical" just because we share them with others.[31] We also tend to judge (and punish) outgroup members (anyone who is not in our group) more harshly for moral transgressions than ingroup members, even when we are trying to be objective.[32] In addition, we tend to glorify ingroup members (anyone who is part of our group) and are more lenient when judging their misdeeds, often leading to a double-standard in ethicality.[33]

When we can identify the sources of emotions and moods, we are better able to predict behavior and manage people well. Let's explore that topic next.

Sources of Emotions and Moods

6-2 Identify the sources of emotions and moods.

Have you ever said, "I got up on the wrong side of the bed today"? Have you ever snapped at a coworker or family member for no reason? If you have, you probably wonder where those emotions and moods originated. Here we discuss some of the primary influences.

Personality

Moods and emotions have a personality trait component, meaning that some people have built-in tendencies to experience certain moods and emotions more frequently than others do. People also experience the same emotions with different intensities; the degree to which they experience them is called their **affect intensity**.[34] Affectively intense people experience both positive and negative emotions more deeply: When they're sad, they're really sad, and when they're happy, they're really happy.

affect intensity Individual differences in the strength with which individuals experience their emotions.

Time of Day

Moods vary by the time of day. However, research suggests most of us follow the same pattern. Levels of positive affect tend to peak in the late morning (10 A.M. to noon) and then remain at that level until early evening (around 7 P.M.). Starting about 12 hours after waking, positive affect begins to drop until midnight, and then, for those who remain awake, the drop accelerates until positive mood picks up again after sunrise.[35]As for negative affect, most research suggests it fluctuates less than positive affect,[36] but the general trend is for it to increase over the course of a day, so that it is lowest early in the morning and highest late in the evening.[37]

A fascinating study assessed moods by analyzing millions of tweets (i.e., Twitter messages) from around the globe.[38] The researchers noted the presence of words connoting positive affect (happy, enthused, excited) and negative (sad, angry, anxious) affect. You can see the trends they observed in the positive affect part of Exhibit 6-3. Daily fluctuations in mood followed a similar pattern in most countries. These results are comparable to what has been reported in previous research. A major difference, though, happens in the evening. Whereas most research suggests that positive affect tends to drop after 7 P.M., this study suggests that it *increases* before the midnight decline. We'll have to wait for further research to see which description is accurate. The negative affect trends in this study were more consistent with past research, showing that negative affect is lowest in the morning and tends to increase over the course of the day and evening.

You may wonder what happens for people who work the third shift at night. When our internal circadian process is out of line with our waking hours, our moods and well-being are likely to be negatively affected. However, researchers studying how the body's inner clock can be adjusted have found that governing our exposure to light may allow us to shift our circadian rhythms.[39] Thus, by manipulating light and darkness, someone who is awake at night might have a similar mood cycle to someone who sleeps at night.

Day of the Week

Are people in their best moods on the weekends? In most cultures, they are—for example, U.S. adults tend to experience their highest positive affect on Friday, Saturday, and Sunday, and their lowest on Monday.[40] As shown in Exhibit 6-4,

Exhibit 6-3 **Time of Day Effects on Mood of U.S. Adults as Rated from Tweets**

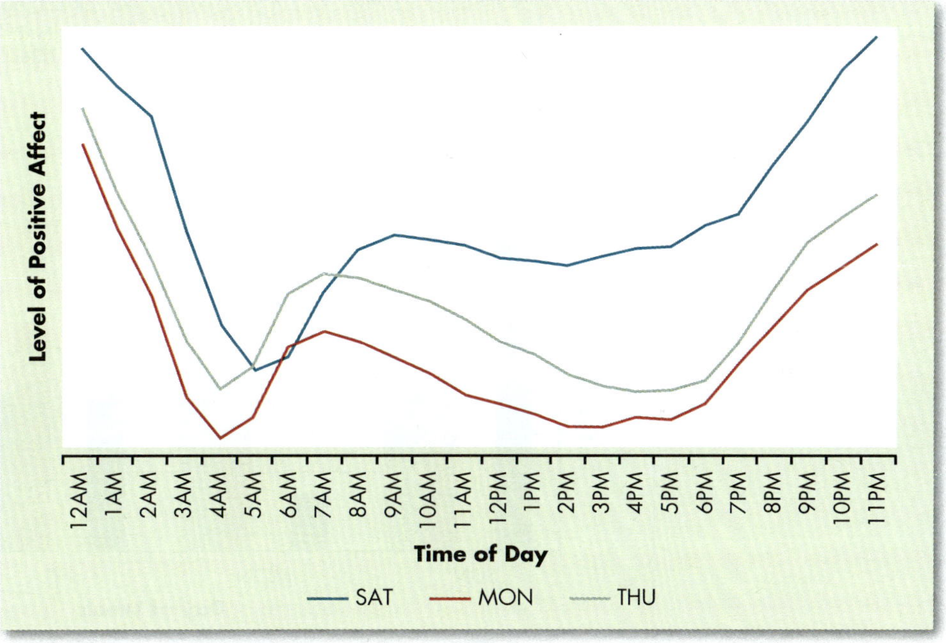

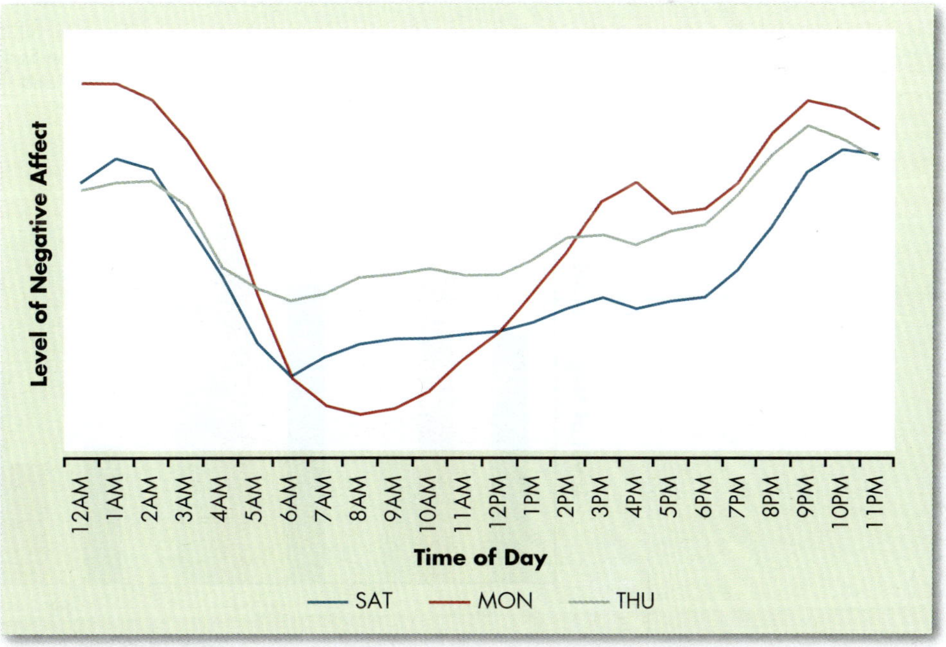

Note: Based on analysis of U.S. tweets (i.e., Twitter postings) and coding of words that represent positive feelings (delight, enthusiasm) and negative feelings (fear, guilt). Lines represent percentage of total words in tweets that convey these moods.

Sources: Based on S. A. Golder and M. W. Macy, "Diurnal and Seasonal Mood Vary with Work, Sleep, and Daylength across Diverse Cultures," *Science* 333 (2011): 1878–81; A. Elejalde-Ruiz, "Seize the Day," *Chicago Tribune,* September 5, 2012, downloaded June 20, 2013 from http://articles.chicagotribune.com/.

Exhibit 6-4 Day-of-Week Mood Effects across Four Cultures

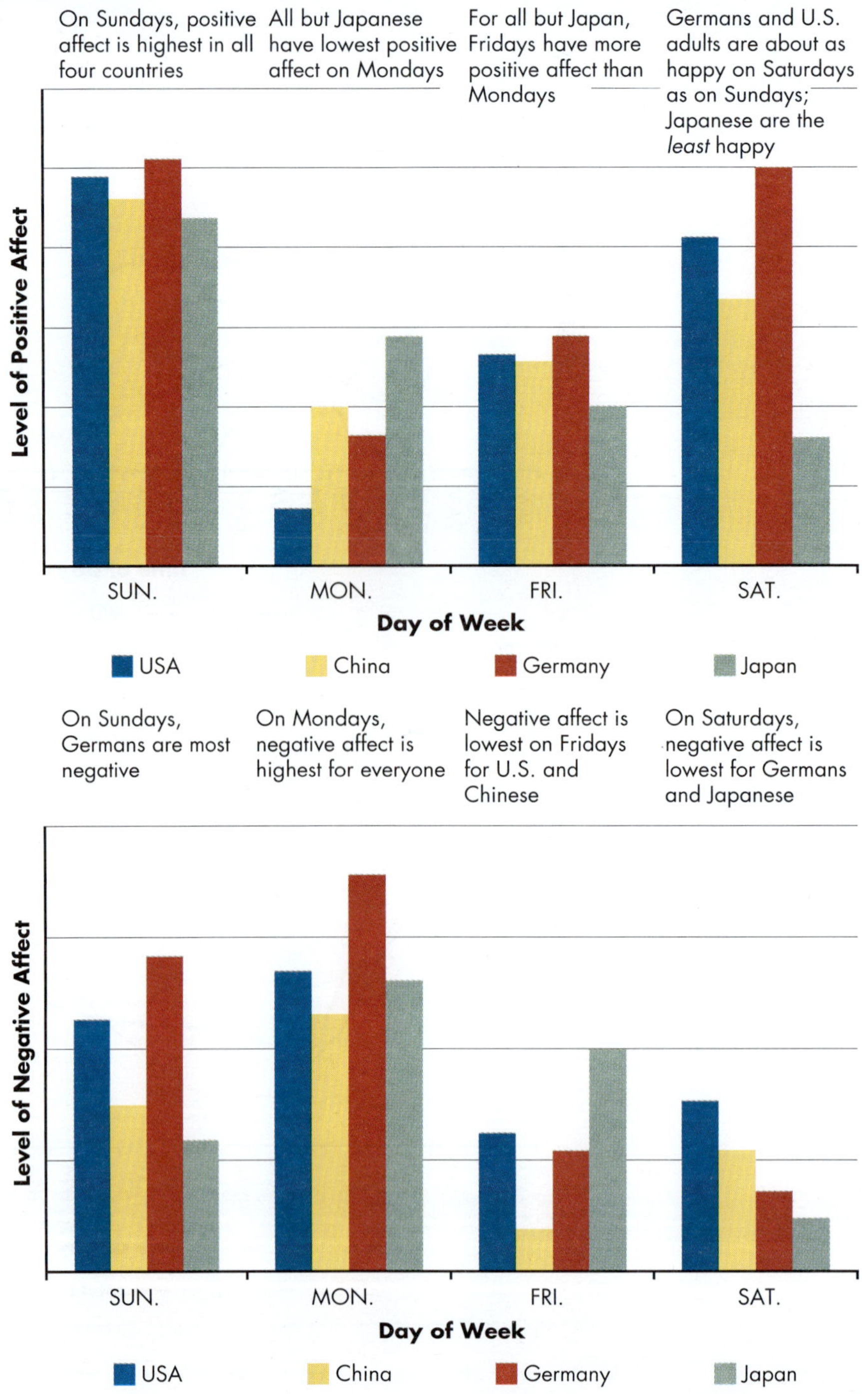

Source: Based on S. A. Golder and M. W. Macy, "Diurnal and Seasonal Mood Vary with Work, Sleep, and Daylength across Diverse Cultures," *Science* 333 (2011): 1878–81; A. Elejalde-Ruiz, "Seize the Day," *Chicago Tribune*, September 5, 2012, downloaded June 20, 2013 from http://articles.chicagotribune.com/.

again based on the study of tweets, that tends to be true in several other cultures as well. For Germans and the Chinese, positive affect is highest from Friday to Sunday and lowest on Monday. This isn't the case in all cultures, however. As the exhibit shows, in Japan, positive affect is higher on Monday than on either Friday or Saturday.

As for negative affect, Monday is the highest negative-affect day across most cultures. In some countries, however, negative affect is lower on Friday and Saturday than on Sunday. It may be that, while Sunday is enjoyable as a day off (and thus we have higher positive affect), we also get a bit stressed about the week ahead (which is why negative affect is higher).

Weather

When do you think you would be in a better mood—when it's 70 degrees and sunny, or on a gloomy, cold, rainy day? Many people believe that their mood is tied to the weather. However, a large and detailed body of evidence suggests weather has little effect on mood, at least for most people.[41] One expert concluded, "Contrary to the prevailing cultural view, these data indicate that people do not report a better mood on bright and sunny days (or, conversely, a worse mood on dark and rainy days)."[42]

illusory correlation The tendency of people to associate two events when in reality there is no connection.

Illusory correlation, which occurs when we associate two events that, in reality, have no connection, explains why people tend to *think* weather influences them. For example, employees may be more productive on bad weather days, a study in Japan and the United States recently indicated, but not because of mood—instead, the worse weather removed some work distractions.[42]

Stress

As you might imagine, stressful events at work (a nasty e-mail, impending deadline, loss of a big sale, reprimand from the boss, etc.) negatively affect moods. A review of nearly 100 studies on 25,000 employees suggests that the effects of chronic stress also build over time. As the authors of one such study note, "A constant diet of even low-level stressful events has the potential to cause workers to experience gradually increasing levels of strain over time."[44] Mounting levels of stress can worsen our moods as we experience more negative emotions. Although sometimes we thrive on it, most of us find stress usually takes a toll on our mood. In fact, when situations are overly emotionally charged and stressful, we have a natural response to disengage, to literally look away.[45]

Social Activities

Do you tend to be happiest when out with friends? For most people, social activities increase a positive mood and have little effect on a negative mood. But do people in positive moods seek out social interactions, or do social interactions cause people to be in good moods? It seems both are true,[46] although the *type* of social activity does matter. Activities that are physical (skiing or hiking with friends), informal (going to a party), or epicurean (eating with others) are more strongly associated with increases in positive mood than events that are formal (attending a meeting) or sedentary (watching TV with friends).[47]

Sleep

U.S. adults report sleeping less than adults did a generation ago.[48] According to researchers and public health specialists, a large portion of the U.S. workforce suffers from sleep deprivation: 41 million workers sleep less than 6 hours per night. Sleep quality affects moods and decision making, and increased fatigue puts workers at risk of disease, injury, and depression.[49] Poor or reduced sleep also makes it difficult to control emotions. Even one bad night's sleep makes us angrier and risk-prone,[50] possibly because poor sleep impairs job satisfaction[51] and makes us less able to make ethical judgments.[52]

On the positive side, increased regular sleep enhances creativity, performance, and career success. University of California–San Diego researchers calculated that, for employees who do not sleep enough, "a one-hour increase in long-run average sleep increases wages by 16 percent, equivalent to more than a year of schooling."[53] Other researchers are trying to reduce how much sleep is needed for high functioning through drug therapy, hoping to find "something better than caffeine," said Ying-Hui Fu of the University of California–San Francisco.[54]

Exercise

You often hear that people should exercise to improve their mood. Does "sweat therapy" really work? It appears so. Research consistently shows that exercise enhances peoples' positive moods.[55] Exercise can also help protect against persistent negative moods and improve the ability to recover from negative experiences.[56]

Age

Do young people experience more extreme positive emotions (so-called youthful exuberance) than older people? Surprisingly, no. Older adults tend to focus on more positive stimuli (and on less negative stimuli) than younger adults, a finding confirmed across nearly 100 studies. These older adults tend to self-regulate by actively trying to increase the positivity (and decrease the negativity) in their attention and memory.[57]

Gender

Many believe women are more emotional than men. Is there any truth to this? Evidence does confirm women experience emotions more intensely, tend to "hold on to" emotions longer than men, and display more frequent expressions of both positive and negative emotions, except anger.[58] Evidence from a study of participants from 37 different countries found that men consistently reported higher levels of powerful emotions like anger, whereas women reported more powerless emotions like sadness and fear.[59] As one review notes, however, some of these findings (such as that women tend to experience more shame and guilt than men) may be due to how emotions are measured and contextualized, and what the emotions are targeted for.[60] Thus, there are some apparent gender differences in the experience and expression of emotions, but these may be obscured by how emotions are measured.

People also tend to attribute men's and women's emotions in ways that might be based on stereotypes of typical emotional reactions. One study showed that when viewing pictures of faces, participants interpreted the women's emotional

Yoga is known to increase positive moods and results in happier, healthier, and more productive employees. Many companies encourage yoga and meditation at workplace can help reduce stress, improve efficiency and create a more positive environment in the office.
Source: yurakrasil.shutterstock.com

expressions as being dispositional (related to personality), whereas the men's expressions were interpreted as situational.[61] For example, a picture of a sad woman led observers to believe she had an emotional personality, whereas a picture of sadness in a man was more likely to be attributed to having a bad day. Another study showed that participants were quicker to detect angry expressions on male faces and happy expressions on female faces; neutral faces in men were attributed as being more angry and neutral faces in women were interpreted as being happy.[62]

It might seem by now that we all—leaders, managers, and employees alike—operate as unwitting slaves to our emotions and moods. On an internal experiential level, this may be true. Yet we know from our workplace experiences that people aren't expressing every brief emotion that flits through their consciousness. Let's put together what we've learned about emotions and moods with workplace coping strategies, beginning with emotional labor.

Emotional Labor

6-3 Show the impact that emotional labor has on employees.

If you've ever had a job in retail or in sales, or waited on tables in a restaurant, you know the importance of projecting a friendly demeanor and smiling. Even though there were days when you didn't feel cheerful, you knew management expected you to be upbeat when dealing with customers, so you faked it.

emotional labor An employee's organizationally desired emotions during interpersonal transactions at work.

Every employee expends physical and mental labor by putting body and mind, respectively, into the job. But jobs also require **emotional labor**, an employee's expression of organizationally desired emotions during interpersonal transactions at work. Emotional labor is a key component of effective job performance. We expect flight attendants to be cheerful, funeral directors to be sad, and doctors to be emotionally neutral. At the least, your managers expect you to be courteous, not hostile, in your interactions with coworkers.

One of Apple's "geniuses," the title given to Apple store employees, meets with customers. Employees' smiles when meeting with customers are expressions of emotional labor that Apple requires and considers appropriate for their jobs.
Source: Melanie Stetson Freeman/The Christian Science Monitor/Getty Images

felt emotions An individual's actual emotions.

displayed emotions Emotions that are organizationally required and considered appropriate in a given job.

The way we experience an emotion is obviously not always the same as the way we show it. To analyze emotional labor, we divide emotions into *felt* or *displayed emotions.*[63] **Felt emotions** are our actual emotions. In contrast, **displayed emotions** are those the organization requires workers to show and considers appropriate in a given job. They're not innate; they're learned, and they may or may not coincide with felt emotions. For instance, research suggests that in U.S. workplaces, it is expected that employees should typically display positive emotions like happiness and excitement and suppress negative emotions like fear, anger, disgust, and contempt.[64]

Effective managers have learned to look serious when they give an employee a negative performance evaluation, and to look calm when they are berated by their bosses, because the organization expects these displays. Of course, there are no display rules for many workplace situations. Does your employer dictate what emotions you display when you are, say, heading out for lunch? Probably not. Many workplaces have explicit display rules, but usually only for interactions that matter, particularly between employees and customers. Regarding employee and customer interactions, you might expect that the more an employer dictates salespeople's emotional displays, the higher the sales. Employees under very high or very low display rules do not perform as well in sales situations as employees who have moderate display rules and a high degree of discretion in their roles.[65]Displaying fake emotions requires us to suppress real ones. **Surface acting** is hiding feelings and emotional expressions in response to display rules. A worker who smiles at a customer even when he doesn't feel like it is surface acting. **Deep acting** is trying to modify our true feelings based on display rules. Surface acting deals with *displayed* emotions, and deep acting deals with *felt* emotions. One study of employees in both the United States and Singapore examined the types of employees who engage in different levels of surface and deep acting: the surface actors, deep actors, non-actors (who rarely engage in either type of acting), low-actors (who infrequently engage in either type of acting), and regulators (who frequently engage in both types of acting).[66]

surface acting Hiding one's feelings and forgoing emotional expressions in response to display rules.

deep acting Trying to modify one's true feelings based on display rules.

New employees of the ward office in the city of Daejeon, South Korea, practice smiling during their training on how to be kind public employees. The strategy of surface acting, or "putting on a face," is an appropriate technique that the employees learn for modifying their emotions and helping them create positive interactions with customers.
Source: Yonhap News/YNA/Newscom

Displaying emotions we don't really feel can be exhausting. Surface acting is associated with increased stress and decreased job satisfaction.[67] Daily surface acting can also lead to emotional exhaustion at home, work–family conflict, absenteeism, and insomnia.[68] On the other hand, deep acting has a positive relationship with job satisfaction (especially when the work is challenging), job performance, and even better customer treatment and tips.[69]

emotional dissonance Inconsistencies between the emotions people feel and the emotions they project.

The disparity between employees having to project one emotion *while feeling another* is called **emotional dissonance**. Bottled-up feelings of frustration, anger, and resentment can lead to emotional exhaustion. Long-term emotional dissonance is a predictor for job burnout, declines in job performance, and lower job satisfaction.[70] However, research from Germany and Australia suggests that employees who have a high capacity for self-control, who get a good night's sleep every day, and who have strong relationships with their customers or clients tend to be buffered to some degree from the negative side effects of emotional dissonance.[71]

Affective events theory, discussed in the next section, fits a job's emotional labor requirements into a construct with implications for work events, emotional reactions, job satisfaction, and job performance.

6-4 Describe affective events theory.

Affective Events Theory

affective events theory (AET) A model suggesting that workplace events cause emotional reactions on the part of employees, which then influence workplace attitudes and behaviors.

We've seen that emotions and moods are an important part of our personal and work lives. But how do they influence our job performance and satisfaction? **Affective events theory (AET)** proposes that employees react emotionally to things that happen to them at work, and these reactions influence their job performance and satisfaction.[72] Say that you just found out your company is downsizing. You might experience a variety of negative emotions, causing you to worry that you'll lose your job. Because it is out of your hands, you may feel insecure and fearful, and spend much of your time worrying rather than working. Needless to say, your job satisfaction will also be down.

Prior research supports the notion that the extent to which one's personality is negative or positive is related to emotional reactions when experiencing workplace events and that these are related to workplace attitudes and behaviors.[73] However, we experience some events more often than others, so does this have an effect on the types of affective reactions, attitudes, and behaviors at work? Some research supports the idea that it does, given that interpersonal mistreatment by customers of part-time workers accounted for nearly 50 percent of negative affective work events.[74]

In sum, AET offers two important messages.[75] First, emotions provide valuable insights into how workplace events influence employee performance and satisfaction. Second, employees and managers shouldn't ignore emotions or the events that cause them, even when they appear minor, because they accumulate. Emotional intelligence is another framework that helps us understand the impact of emotions on job performance, so we will look at that topic next.

Emotional Intelligence

6-5 Describe emotional intelligence.

As the CEO of an international talent company, Terrie Upshur-Lupberger was at a career pinnacle. So why was she resentful and unhappy? A close friend observed, "Terrie, you were out on the skinny branch—you know, the one that breaks easily in a strong wind. You were so busy and overwhelmed and out of touch with your own values, cares, and guiding beliefs that you failed to pay attention to the branch that was about to break."[76] According to Upshur-Lupberger, she had failed to notice that her moods constantly swung toward frustration and exhaustion. Her job satisfaction, productivity, and relationships suffered. Worse, she was too busy to realize the deficiencies until she was completely depleted. She said, "I learned that, as a leader, you either pay attention to and manage the moods (including your own) in the organization, or . . . you ignore them and pay the price." Upshur-Lupberger learned the value of emotional intelligence.

emotional intelligence (EI) The ability to detect and to manage emotional cues and information.

Emotional intelligence (EI) is a person's ability to (1) perceive emotions in the self and others, (2) understand the meaning of these emotions, and (3) regulate his or her own emotions accordingly,[77] as shown in Exhibit 6-5. People who know their own emotions and are good at reading emotional cues—for instance, knowing why they're angry and how to express themselves without violating norms—are most likely to be effective.[78]

Several studies suggest that EI plays an important role in job performance, although the survey items are often strikingly similar to other items from personality, intelligence, and self-perception tests.[79] Other reviews suggest that EI is related to teamwork effectiveness as well as deviant and citizenship behavior.[80] South Korean managers with high EI tend to have better sales figures than those with low EI because they were able to create more cohesive stores and improved sales-directed behavior.[81] A study undertaken on project managers in the Australian defense industry examined the contribution of EI to project success. The results indicated that EI has a positive impact on project success and that important mediating factors are satisfaction and trust. Senior managers can use this information about work attitudes to enhance performance in complex project situations.[82]

Exhibit 6-5 **A Cascading Model of Emotional Intelligence**

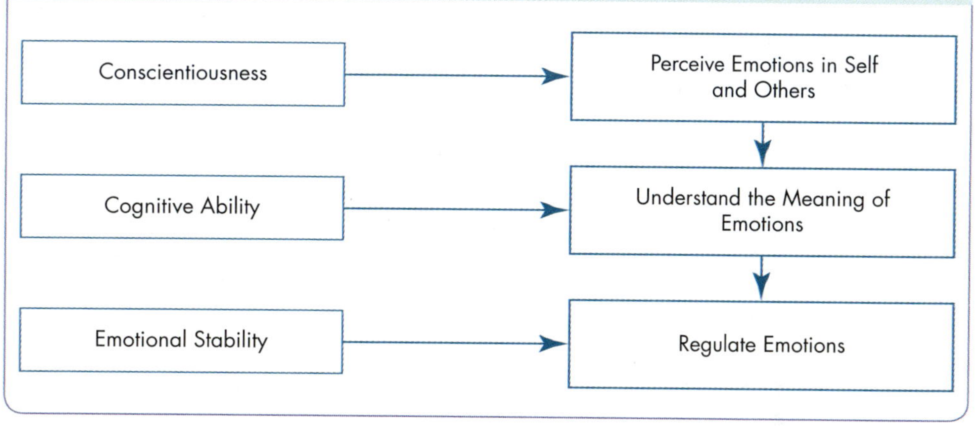

Source: Based on D. L. Joseph and D. A. Newman, "Emotional Intelligence: An Integrative Meta-Analysis and Cascading Model," *Journal of Applied Psychology* 95, no. 1 (2010): 54–78.

Although the field is progressing in its understanding of EI, many questions have not been answered.[83] One relates to a better understanding of EI. For example, we need to be precise when we talk about EI—are we referring to EI in general? Or to regulating emotions, understanding emotions, or perceiving emotions specifically? A second question is about the reliability of EI testing. For example, part of the reason EI has only a modest correlation with job effectiveness is that it is hard to measure—mostly it is measured with self-report inventories, which, of course, are often far from objective! A third question is one of the most important for managers in organizations: can EI be learned? Several reviews of dozens of studies suggest that EI can be trained and developed as a skill—although paradoxically, the people who need it the most are the ones least likely to actually seek it out![84]

All questions aside, EI is wildly popular among consulting firms and in the popular press, and it has accumulated some support in the research literature. Love it or hate it, one thing is for sure—EI is here to stay. So might be our next topic, emotion regulation, which is increasingly studied as an independent concept.[85]

Emotion Regulation

6-6 Identify strategies for emotion regulation.

Have you ever tried to cheer yourself up when you're feeling down, or calm yourself when you're feeling angry? If so, you have engaged in *emotion regulation.* The central idea behind emotion regulation is to identify and modify the emotions you feel. Recent research suggests that emotion management ability is a strong predictor of task performance for some jobs and for organizational citizenship behavior (OCB).[86] Therefore, in our study of OB, we are interested in *whether* and *how* emotion regulation should be used in the workplace. We begin by identifying which individuals might naturally employ it.

Emotion Regulation Influences and Outcomes

As you might suspect, not everyone is equally good at regulating emotions.[87] Individuals who are higher in the personality trait of neuroticism have more trouble doing so and often find their moods are beyond their ability to control.

An Ethical Choice

Should Managers Use Emotional Intelligence (EI) Tests?

As we discussed in this chapter, the concept of emotional intelligence has raised some debate. One of the decisions for managers is whether to use EI tests in the selection process. Here are some ethical considerations:

- *There is no commonly accepted test.* For instance, researchers have recently used the Mayer–Salovey–Caruso Emotional Intelligence Test (MSCEIT), the Trait Emotional Intelligence Questionnaire, and the Situational Judgment Test of Emotional Intelligence (SJT of EI) in studies. Researchers feel EI tests may need to be culturally specific because emotional displays vary by culture; thus, the interpretation of emotional cues differs. For example, a recent study comparing the emotional intelligence scores for Indian and North American executives using the Emotional Competence Inventory (ECI-2) test found the results similar but not the same, suggesting the need for modification.
- *Applicants may react negatively to taking an EI test in general or to parts of it.* The face recognition test, for example, may seem culturally biased to some if the subject photos are not diverse. Also, participants who score high on EI tests tend to consider them fair; applicants who score lower may not perceive the tests to be fair and can thus view the hiring organizations unfavorably—even if they score well on other assessments.
- *EI tests may not be predictive of performance for all types of jobs.* In a study of 600 Romanian participants, results indicated that EI was valid for salespeople, public servants, and CEOs of public hospitals, but these were all roles requiring significant social interaction. EI tests may need to be tailored for each position category or not be used when the position description does not warrant such tests.
- *It remains somewhat unclear what EI tests are actually measuring.* They may reflect personality or intelligence, in which case other measures might be better. Also, some EI tests may predict job performance, but many of these tests include personality constructs and measures of general mental ability.
- *There is not enough research on how emotional intelligence affects, for instance, counterproductive work behavior (CWB).* It may not be prudent to test and select applicants who are rated high on EI when we aren't yet certain that everything about EI leads to desired workplace outcomes.

These concerns suggest that EI tests should be avoided in hiring decisions. However, because research has indicated that emotional intelligence does predict job performance to some degree, managers should not be too hasty to dismiss them altogether. Rather, those wishing to use EI in hiring decisions should be aware of these issues to make informed and ethical decisions about not only whom to hire but how.

Sources: Based on D. Iliescu, A. Ilie, D. Ispas, and A. Ion, "Emotional Intelligence in Personnel Selection: Applicant Reactions, Criterion, and Incremental Validity," *International Journal of Selection and Assessment* (September 2012): 347–58; D. L. Joseph, J. Jin, D. A. Newman, and E. H. O'Boyle, "Why Does Self-Reported Emotional Intelligence Predict Job Performance? A Meta-Analytic Investigation of Mixed EI," *Journal of Applied Psychology* 100, no. 2 (2015): 298–342; R. Sharma, "Measuring Social and Emotional Intelligence Competencies in the Indian Context," *Cross Cultural Management* 19 (2012): 30–47; and S. Sharma, M. Gangopadhyay, E. Austin, and M. K. Mandal, "Development and Validation of a Situational Judgment Test of Emotional Intelligence," *International Journal of Selection and Assessment* (March 2013): 57–73.

Individuals who have lower levels of self-esteem are also less likely to try to improve their sad moods, perhaps because they are less likely than others to feel they deserve to be in a good mood.[88]

The workplace environment influences an individual's tendency to employ emotion regulation. In general, diversity in work groups increases the likelihood that you will regulate your emotions. For example, younger employees are likely to regulate their emotions when their work groups include older members.[89] Racial diversity also has an effect: If diversity is low, the minority employee will engage in emotion regulation, perhaps to "fit in" with the majority employees as much as possible; if diversity is high and many different races are represented, the majority employee will employ emotion regulation, perhaps to integrate him- or herself with the whole group.[90] These findings suggest a beneficial outcome of diversity—it may cause us to regulate our emotions more consciously and effectively.

While regulating your emotions might seem beneficial, research suggests there is a downside to trying to change the way you feel. Changing your emotions takes effort and, as we noted when discussing emotional labor, this effort can be exhausting. Sometimes attempts to change an emotion actually make the emotion stronger; for example, trying to talk yourself out of being afraid can make you focus more on what scares you, which makes you more afraid.[91] From another perspective, research suggests that avoiding negative emotional experiences is less likely to lead to positive moods than does seeking out positive emotional experiences.[92] For example, you're more likely to experience a positive mood if you have a pleasant conversation with a friend than if you avoid an unpleasant conversation with a hostile coworker.

Emotion Regulation Techniques

Researchers of emotion regulation often study the strategies people employ to change their emotions (for example, as we discussed earlier in the chapter, *deep acting* and *surface acting* are emotion regulation techniques). One technique of emotion regulation is *emotional suppression*, or suppressing initial emotional responses to situations. This response seems to facilitate practical thinking in the short term. However, it appears to be helpful only when a strongly negative event would illicit a distressed emotional reaction during a crisis.[93] For example, a soldier in battle may suppress initial emotional distress after a shooting and thus be able to make clearer decisions about how to proceed. A portfolio manager might suppress an emotional reaction to a sudden drop in the value of a stock and can therefore clearly decide how to plan. Suppression used in crisis situations appears to help an individual recover from the event emotionally, while suppression used as an everyday emotion regulation technique can take a toll on mental ability, emotional ability, health, and relationships.[94] Thus, unless we're truly in a crisis, acknowledging rather than suppressing our emotional responses to situations and reevaluating events after they occur yield the best outcomes.[95]

Cognitive reappraisal, or reframing our outlook on an emotional situation, is one way to regulate emotions effectively.[96] Cognitive reappraisal ability seems to be the most helpful to individuals in situations where they cannot control the sources of stress.[97] A recent study illustrates the potentially powerful effect of this technique. Israeli participants who were shown anger-inducing information about the Israeli-Palestinian conflict after they were primed to reappraise the situation showed more inclination toward conciliation and less inclination toward aggressive tactics against Palestinians than the control group, not only immediately after the study but up to 5 months later. This result suggests that cognitive reappraisal may allow people to change their emotional responses, even when the subject matter is as highly emotionally charged as the Israeli-Palestinian conflict.[98]

Another technique with potential for emotion regulation is *social sharing*, or venting. Research shows that the open expression of emotions can help individuals to regulate their emotions as opposed to keeping emotions "bottled up." Social sharing can reduce anger reactions when people can talk about the facts of a bad situation, their feelings about the situation, or any positive aspects of the situation.[99] Caution must be exercised, though, because expressing your frustration affects other people. In fact, whether venting emotions helps the "venter" feel better depends very much upon the listener's response. If the listener doesn't respond (many refuse to respond to venting), the venter feels worse. If the listener responds with expressions of support or validation, the venter feels better. Therefore, if we are going to vent to a coworker, we need to choose someone who will respond sympathetically. Venting to the perceived offender rarely improves things and can result in heightening the negative emotions.[100]

mindfulness Reception, attention, and awareness of the present moment, events, and experiences.

A final emotion regulation technique, **mindfulness**—receptively paying attention to and being aware of the present moment, events, and experiences—has started to become popular in organizations.[101] Mindfulness has roots in traditional Buddhist meditative techniques—in fact, it is the literal translation of the Vedic word *sati*, or "intentness of mind."[102] Claims of the impact of mindfulness have been quite head-turning. For example, past research suggests that mindfulness can slow aging, bolster test performance, and aid in facilitating neuroplasticity (i.e., producing actual changes in the brain).[103] The key mechanisms responsible for its effectiveness can be found in being able to separate oneself from the moment, decrease the use of automatic thoughts, and increase awareness of one's own body.[104] Initial research on mindfulness in Germany and the Netherlands suggests that it reduces emotional exhaustion in the workplace and improves job satisfaction by causing employees to engage in *surface acting*.[105] Other preliminary studies suggest that mindfulness can lead to improved job performance, work-life balance, and sleep quality (which leads one to be refreshed after work) as well as reduced turnover intentions, retaliatory behaviors (after experiencing injustice), and counterproductive work behaviors.[106] However, studies on employee mindfulness are new and we have yet to realize fully its causes and outcomes, along with the most effective methods for achieving and sustaining mindful states. Many mindfulness studies do not agree about how they conceptualize mindfulness and do not use the best methodological practices and measures.[107]

While emotion regulation techniques can help us cope with difficult workplace situations, research indicates that the effect varies. For example, a recent study in Taiwan found that all participants who worked for abusive supervisors reported emotional exhaustion and work-withdrawal tendencies but to different degrees based on the emotion regulation strategies they employed. Employees who used suppression techniques suffered greater emotional exhaustion and work withdrawal than employees who used cognitive reappraisal. This suggests that more research on the application of techniques needs to be done to help employees increase their coping skills.[108]

Thus, while there is much promise in emotion regulation techniques, the best route to a positive workplace is to recruit positive-minded individuals and train leaders to manage their moods, job attitudes, and performance.[109] The best leaders manage emotions as much as they do tasks and activities. The best employees can use their knowledge of emotion regulation to decide when to speak up and how to express themselves effectively.[110] The key is to be adaptive: try to be aware of your emotions and use the regulation techniques best suited for the situation.[111]

Ethics of Emotion Regulation

Emotion regulation has important ethical implications. On one end of the continuum, some people might argue that controlling your emotions is unethical because it requires a degree of acting. On the other end, people might argue that all emotions should be controlled so you can take a dispassionate perspective. Both arguments—and all arguments in between—have ethical pros and cons that you will have to decide for yourself. Consider the reasons for emotion regulation and the outcomes. Are you regulating your emotions so you don't react inappropriately, or are you regulating your emotions so no one knows what you are thinking? Consider this: You may be able to "fake it 'til you make it." Recent research has found that acting like you are in a good mood might *put* you in a good mood. In one study, a group of participants was asked to hold only an efficient conversation with a barista serving them at Starbucks, while another group was asked to act happy. The happy actors reported later that they were in much better moods.[112]

Now that we have studied the role of emotions and moods in organizational behavior, let's consider the opportunities for more specific applications that our understanding provides.

OB Applications of Emotions and Moods

6-7 Apply concepts about emotions and moods to specific OB issues.

Our understanding of emotions and moods can affect many aspects of organizational behavior, including the selection process, decision making, creativity, motivation, leadership, negotiation, customer service, job attitudes, deviant workplace behavior, and safety. Let's think through each of these.

The Selection Process

One implication from the evidence on EI is that employers should consider it a factor in hiring employees, especially for jobs that demand a high degree of social interaction. In fact, more employers *are* starting to use EI measures to hire people. For example, a study of U.S. Air Force recruiters showed that top-performing recruiters exhibited high levels of EI. Using these findings, the Air Force revamped its selection criteria. A follow-up investigation found hires who had high EI scores were 2.6 times more successful than those who didn't.[113] In a study of IT professionals in India it was found that there was a positive relationship between emotional intelligence and job performance. Emotional intelligence explained 31.9 percent difference in the performance of male IT professionals and 26.7% among female IT professionals.[114] A second implication is that applicant emotions are sometimes, knowingly or not, used in selection decisions. As an example, Hong Kong Chinese applicants are more likely to try to appear calm, rather than excited, during the selection process and Hong Kong Chinese employers are more likely to hire calm applicants.[115]

Decision Making

Moods and emotions have effects on decision making that managers should understand. Positive emotions and moods seem to help people make sound decisions. Positive emotions also enhance problem-solving skills, so positive people find better solutions.[116]

OB researchers continue to debate the role of negative emotions and moods in decision making. One recent study suggested that people who are saddened by events may make the same decisions as before, while people

A leader of high emotional intelligence, Starbucks CEO Howard Schultz bounds on stage before addressing 10,000 Starbucks managers at the firm's Global Leadership Conference. Schultz's optimism, excitement, and enthusiasm energize employees and motivate them to accept his vision of the company's future.
Source: F. Carter Smith/Bloomberg/Getty Images

who are angered by events might make stronger (though not necessarily better) choices than before.[117] Another study found that participants made choices reflecting more originality in a negative mood.[118] Still other research indicated that individuals in a negative mood may take higher risks than they do when in a positive mood.[119] Taken together, these and other studies suggest negative (and positive) emotions affect decision making but that there are other variables that require further research.[120]

Creativity

As we see throughout this text, one goal of leadership is to maximize employee productivity through creativity. Creativity is influenced by emotions and moods, but there are two schools of thought on the relationship. Much research suggests that people in good moods tend to be more creative than people in bad moods.[121] People in good moods produce more ideas and more options, and others think their ideas are original.[122] It seems that people experiencing positive moods or emotions are more flexible and open in their thinking, which may explain why they are more creative.[123] Supervisors should actively try to keep employees happy because doing so creates more good moods (employees like their leaders to encourage them and provide positive feedback on a job well done), which in turn leads people to be more creative.[124]

Some researchers, however, do not believe a positive mood makes people more creative. They argue that, when people are in positive moods, they may relax ("If I'm in a good mood, things must be going okay, and I don't need to think of new ideas") and not engage in the critical thinking necessary for some forms of creativity.[125] Individuals who worry more may perform better on creative tasks than those who worry less.

Determining which perspective is correct may lie in thinking of moods somewhat differently. Rather than looking at positive or negative affect, it's possible to conceptualize moods as active feelings like anger, fear, or elation and contrast these with deactivating moods like sorrow, depression, or serenity. All the activating moods, whether positive *or* negative, seem to lead to more creativity, whereas deactivating moods lead to less.[126] We discussed earlier that other factors such as fatigue may boost creativity. A study of 428 students found they performed best on a creative problem-solving task when they were fatigued, suggesting that tiredness may free the mind to consider novel solutions.[127]

Motivation

Several studies have highlighted the importance of moods and emotions on motivation. One study asked two groups of people to solve word puzzles. The first group saw a funny video clip intended to put them in a good mood first. The other group was not shown the clip and started working on the puzzles right away. The positive-mood group reported higher expectations of being able to solve the puzzles, worked harder at them, and did solve more as a result.[128] Another study looked at the moods of insurance sales agents in Taiwan.[129] Agents in a good mood were found to be more helpful toward their coworkers and felt better about themselves. These factors in turn led to superior performance in the form of higher sales and better supervisor reports of performance.

Giving people performance feedback—whether real or fake—influences their mood, which then influences their motivation.[130] A cycle can be created in which positive moods cause people to be more creative, leading to positive feedback from those observing their work. The feedback further reinforces the positive mood, which makes people perform even better, and so on. Overall, the findings suggest a manager may enhance employee motivation—and performance—by encouraging good moods.

Leadership

Research indicates that putting people in a good mood makes good sense. Leaders who focus on inspirational goals generate greater optimism, cooperation, and enthusiasm in employees, leading to more positive social interactions with coworkers and customers.[131] A study with Taiwanese military participants indicates that, by sharing emotions, transformational leaders inspire positive emotions in their followers that in turn lead to higher task performance.[132]

Leaders are perceived as more effective when they share positive emotions, and followers are more creative in a positive emotional environment. What about when leaders are sad? Research found that leader displays of sadness increased the analytic performance of followers, perhaps because followers attended more closely to tasks to help the leaders.[133] Another interesting study examined over 300 halftime locker room speeches from high school and college basketball teams, finding that leader's sharing of negative emotions (e.g., anger) can help *improve* team performance. However, these emotions had to be at the right level of intensity—too negative and intense, and the display would backfire.[134]

Corporate executives know emotional content is critical for employees to buy into their vision of the company's future and accept change. When higher-ups offer new visions, especially with vague or distant goals, it is often difficult for employees to accept the changes they will bring. By arousing emotions and linking them to an appealing vision, leaders may help managers and employees alike to accept change and feel connected to the new plan.

Negotiation

Have you considered the potential of using emotions and moods to enhance your negotiation skills? Several studies suggest that a negotiator who feigns anger has an advantage over an opponent. Why? Because when a negotiator shows anger, the opponent concludes that the negotiator has conceded all he or she can and so gives in.[135] However, anger should be used selectively in negotiation: Angry negotiators who have less information or less power than their opponents have significantly worse outcomes.[136]

As in the use of any emotion, context matters. Displaying a negative emotion (such as anger) can be effective, but feeling bad about your performance appears to impair future negotiations. Individuals who do poorly in negotiation experience negative emotions, develop negative perceptions of their counterparts, and are less willing to share information or be cooperative in future negotiations.[137]

Altogether, the best negotiators are probably those who remain emotionally detached. One study of people who suffered damage to the emotional centers of their brains suggested that unemotional people may be the best negotiators because they're not likely to overcorrect when faced with negative outcomes.[138]

Customer Service

emotional contagion The process by which peoples' emotions are caused by the emotions of others.

Workers' emotional states influence the level of customer service they give, which in turn influences levels of repeat business and customer satisfaction.[139] This result is primarily due to **emotional contagion**—the "catching" of emotions from others.[140] When someone experiences positive emotions and laughs and smiles at you, you tend to respond positively. Of course, the opposite is true as well.

Studies indicate a matching effect between employee and customer emotions. In the employee-to-customer direction, research finds that customers who catch the positive moods or emotions of employees shop longer. In the other direction, when an employee feels unfairly treated by a customer, it's harder for him to display the positive emotions his organization expects.[141] High-quality customer service makes demands on employees because it often puts them in a state of emotional dissonance, which can be damaging to the employee and the organization. Managers can interrupt negative contagion by fostering positive moods.

Work-Life Satisfaction

There is good news and bad news about the relationship between moods and work-life satisfaction: Both are affected by work and home events. Ever hear the advice, "Never take your work home with you," meaning you should forget about work once you go home? That's easier said than done. The good news is that a positive mood at work can apparently spill over to your off-work hours, and a negative mood at work can be restored to a positive mood after a break. Several studies have shown that people who had a good day at work tend to be in a better mood at home that evening, and vice versa.[142] Other research has found that, although people do emotionally take their work home with them, by the next day the effect is usually gone.[143] The bad news is that the moods of your household may interfere with yours. As you might expect, one study found that if one member of a couple was in a negative mood during the workday, the negative mood spilled over to the spouse at night.[144]

Career OBjectives

How do I turn down the volume on my screaming boss?

My boss is a yeller. One time, he kicked my chair and yelled for me to get out of the office just because I'd forgotten to tell him that lunch had been delivered. His rage makes me so mad I want to yell back, but I don't because it isn't professional. Is there a way to get him to think before he fumes?

— ***Lata***

Dear Lata:

We feel for you! Actually, your internal anger response is perfectly normal. Almost everyone has an emotional reaction to screaming and other situations of workplace incivility like swearing and rude behavior, and a majority of employees react somehow. For example, 66 percent of participants in a recent study reported that their performance declined when they were the recipients of incivility, and 25 percent admitted they took their frustration out on customers. Another study found that verbal aggression reduces victims' working memory, making even simple instructions difficult to follow. So you're right to want to strategize how to calm the situation since it hurts you, your coworkers, and the company.

The good news is that you can work on your reactions to deescalate an episode. Experts suggest empathizing with your boss (often we find if we try to understand where someone is coming from, it helps us deal with the emotions more effectively), apologizing if you've done something wrong, and not talking back (incivility is never cured by payment in kind). Find situations where you can laugh over mutual frustrations and don't take his outbursts personally.

The bad news is that you probably can't change his emotional response to incidents, but you may be able to help him see the error of his ways by modeling better behavior. Of course, there are situations in which you cannot and should not tolerate uncivil behavior (such as when you are being threatened or when the behavior becomes truly abusive). In those cases, you may need to deal with the situation more directly by first calmly confronting your boss or, if that fails, seeing someone in human resources. But short of that breaking point, our experience and the research suggest that your best response is not to respond outwardly but rather to rethink the way you are responding inwardly.

As the British poster says, "Keep calm and carry on!"

Sources: Based on C. Porath and C. Pearson, "The Price of Incivility," *Harvard Business Review* (January–February 2013): 114–21; A. Rafaeli et al., "When Customers Exhibit Verbal Aggression, Employees Pay Cognitive Costs," *Journal of Applied Psychology* (September 2012): 931–50; S. Shellenbarger, "'It's Not My Fault!' A Better Response to Criticism at Work," *The Wall Street Journal*, June 18, 2014, D1, D4; and S. Shellenbarger, "When the Boss Is a Screamer," *The Wall Street Journal*, August 15, 2012, D1, D2.

The opinions provided here are of the authors only. The authors are not responsible for any errors or omissions or for the results obtained from the use of this information. In no event will the authors, or their related partnerships or corporations thereof, be liable to you or anyone else for any decision made or action taken in reliance on the opinions provided here.

Deviant Workplace Behaviors

Anyone who has spent much time in an organization realizes people can behave in ways that violate established norms and threaten the organization, its members, or both. As we saw in Chapter 1, these actions are called counterproductive work behaviors (CWBs).[145] They can be traced to negative emotions and can take many forms. People who feel negative emotions are more likely than others to engage in short-term deviant behavior at work, such as gossiping or excessively surfing the Internet instead of working,[146] although negative emotions can also lead to more serious forms of CWB.

For instance, envy is an emotion that occurs when you resent someone for having something you don't have but strongly desire—such as a better work assignment, larger office, or higher salary. It can lead to malicious deviant behaviors. An envious employee could undermine other employees and take all the credit for things others accomplished. Angry people look for other people to blame for their bad mood, interpret other people's behavior as hostile, and have trouble considering others' points of view.[147] It's also not hard to see how these thought processes can lead directly to verbal or physical aggression.

A recent study in Pakistan found that anger correlated with more aggressive CWBs such as abuse against others and production deviance, while sadness did not. Neither anger nor sadness predicted workplace withdrawal, which suggests that managers need to take employee expressions of anger seriously; employees may stay with an organization and continue to act aggressively toward others.[148] Once aggression starts, it's likely that other people will become angry and aggressive, so the stage is set for a serious escalation of negative behavior. Therefore, managers need to stay connected with their employees to gauge emotions and emotional intensity levels.

Safety and Injury at Work

Research relating negative affectivity to increased injuries at work suggests employers might improve health and safety (and reduce costs) by ensuring that workers aren't engaged in potentially dangerous activities when they're in a bad mood. Bad moods can contribute to injury at work in several ways.[149] Individuals in negative moods tend to be more anxious, which can make them less able to cope effectively with hazards. A person who is always fearful will be more pessimistic about the effectiveness of safety precautions because she feels she'll just get hurt anyway, or she might panic or freeze up when confronted with a threatening situation. Negative moods also make people more distractible, and distractions can obviously lead to careless behaviors.

Selecting positive team members can contribute toward a positive work environment because positive moods transmit from team member to team member. One study of 130 leaders and their followers found that leaders who are charismatic transfer their positive emotions to their followers through a contagion effect.[150] It makes sense, then, to choose team members predisposed to positive moods.

Summary

Emotions and moods are similar because both are affective in nature. But they're also different—moods are more general and less contextual than emotions. The time of day, stressful events, and sleep patterns are some of the factors that influence emotions and moods. OB research on emotional labor, affective events theory, emotional intelligence, and emotion regulation helps us understand how people deal with emotions. Emotions and moods have proven relevant for virtually every OB topic we study, with implications for managerial practices.

Implications for Managers

- Recognize that emotions are a natural part of the workplace, and good management does not mean creating an emotion-free environment.
- To foster effective decision making, creativity, and motivation in employees, model positive emotions and moods as much as is authentically possible.
- Provide positive feedback to increase the positivity of employees. Of course, it also helps to hire people who are predisposed to positive moods.
- In the service sector, encourage positive displays of emotion, which make customers feel more positive and thus improve customer service interactions and negotiations.
- Understand the role of emotions and moods to significantly improve your ability to explain and predict your coworkers' and others' behavior.

Sometimes Yelling Is for Everyone's Good

POINT

Anger is discussed throughout this chapter for a reason: It's an important emotion. There are benefits to expressing anger. For one, research indicates that only employees who are committed to their organizations tend to express their anger, and generally only to leaders who created the situation. This type of expression of anger could lead to positive organizational change. Second, suppressed anger can lower job satisfaction and lead to a feeling of hopelessness about things improving.

Even with these findings, we hear a lot about not responding emotionally to work challenges. Work cultures teach us to avoid showing any anger at all lest we be seen as poor workers or, worse, unprofessional or even deviant or violent. While, of course, there *are* times when the expression of anger is harmful or unprofessional, we've taken this view so far that we now teach people to suppress perfectly normal emotions and to ignore the effectiveness of some emotional expression.

Emerging research shows that suppressing anger takes a terrible internal toll on individuals. One Stanford University study found, for example, that when individuals were asked to wear a poker face during the showing of a movie clip depicting the atomic bombings of Japan during World War II, they were much more stressed in conversations after the video. Other research shows that college students who suppress emotions like anger have more trouble making friends and are more likely to be depressed, and that employees who suppress anger feel more stressed by work.

For the good of organizations and their employees, we should encourage people not to hold back their emotions but to share them constructively.

COUNTERPOINT

Yes, anger is a common emotion. But it's also a toxic one for the giver and the receiver. Angry outbursts can compromise the heart and contribute to diabetes, among other ill effects. The experience of another's anger and its close correlate, hostility, is also linked to many counterproductive behaviors in organizations. The Bureau of Labor Statistics estimates that 16 percent of fatal workplace injuries result from workplace violence. That is why many organizations have developed counteractive techniques—to blunt the harmful effects of anger in the workplace.

To reduce outcomes, many companies develop policies that govern conduct such as yelling, shouting profanities, and making hostile gestures. Others institute anger management programs. For example, one organization conducted mandatory in-house workshops that showed individuals how to deal with conflicts in the workplace before they boil over. The director who instituted the training said that it "gave people specific tools for opening a dialogue to work things out." MTS Systems, a Minnesota engineering firm, engages an outside consulting company to conduct anger management programs for its organization. Typically, MTS consultants hold an 8-hour seminar that discusses sources of anger, conflict resolution techniques, and organizational policies. This is followed by one-on-one sessions with individual employees that focus on cognitive behavioral techniques to manage their anger. The outside trainer charges around $10,000 for the seminar and one-on-one sessions. The financial cost, though, is worth it for the emotional benefits the participants receive. "You want people to get better at communicating with each other," says MTS manager Karen Borre.

In the end, everyone wins when organizations seek to diminish both the experience and the expression of anger at work. The work environment becomes less threatening and stressful to employees and customers. Employees are likely to feel safer, and the angry employee is often helped as well.

Sources: Based on B. Carey, "The Benefits of Blowing Your Top," *The New York Times,* July 6, 2010, D1; R. Y. Cheung and I. J. Park, "Anger Suppression, Interdependent Self-Construal, and Depression among Asian American and European American College Students," *Cultural Diversity and Ethnic Minority Psychology* 16, no. 4 (2010): 517–25; D. Geddes and L. T. Stickney, "The Trouble with Sanctions: Organizational Responses to Deviant Anger Displays at Work," *Human Relations* 64, no. 2 (2011): 201–30; J. Fairley, "Taking Control of Anger Management," *Workforce Management* (October 2010): 10; L. T. Stickney and D. Geddes, "Positive, Proactive, and Committed: The Surprising Connection between Good Citizens and Expressed (vs. Suppressed) Anger at Work," *Negotiation and Conflict Management Research* 7, no. 4 (November 2014): 243–64; and J. Whalen, "Angry Outbursts Really Do Hurt Your Health, Doctors Find," *The Wall Street Journal,* March 24, 2015, D1, D4.

CHAPTER REVIEW

QUESTIONS FOR REVIEW

6-1 How are emotions different from moods?

6-2 What are the sources of emotions and moods?

6-3 What impact does emotional labor have on employees?

6-4 What is affective events theory?

6-5 What is emotional intelligence?

6-6 What are some strategies for emotion regulation?

6-7 How do you apply concepts about emotions and moods to specific OB issues?

APPLICATION AND EMPLOYABILITY

An understanding, or even awareness of, others' emotions and moods can help improve your effectiveness in the workplace. As we have seen, employees react to events as they happen in the workplace, and these affective reactions can have a large impact on outcomes that are important to organizations. Employees may need to regulate their emotions (especially in positions that require interacting with clients), and this regulation may have an impact on employee performance and well-being. Employees may vary on emotional intelligence, a skill, ability, or set of competencies that is related to many outcomes in the workplace. In this chapter, you have improved many skills, including your communication and collaboration skills, by discovering the impact of a smile (and the air of office politics surrounding it), learning how to deal with an angry boss, deciding whether to use an EI test to assess applicants before hiring, and discussing the benefits and pitfalls of yelling in the workplace. In the following section, you will have more opportunities to develop your critical thinking and knowledge application skills by learning mindfulness techniques for emotion regulation and stress reduction, considering the ethics of data mining microexpressions of emotion, learning to consider and adapt to management emotions, and becoming aware of the insidious effects of boredom and the remedies to being bored.

EXPERIENTIAL EXERCISE Mindfulness at Work

The concept of mindfulness emphasizes trying to focus your mind in the present moment, immersing yourself in what's going on around you. Core principles include suspending immediate judgment of the environment and your own thoughts, and keeping yourself open to what is around you. The benefits of mindfulness can reach beyond reducing stress to include increased creativity, longer spans of attention, reductions in procrastination, and improved performance.

The Procedure

Start this exercise individually and then come together into groups of three or four individuals to discuss what you have found. Although full workplace mindfulness interventions can take several weeks, some basic starting exercises can be done in a relatively short period and give you a feeling for what a full course of mindfulness would be like. Here are three simple exercises to try. For all these, everyone needs to put everything away (especially phones, tablets, and computers!) and focus on what is going on in the immediate environment.

- *Mindful breathing:* Clear your head of everything except thoughts of your own breaths. Concentrate on how you are inhaling and exhaling. It is sometimes helpful to count how long each breath takes. Try to maintain this mindful breathing for 3 minutes. The group will then take 3 minutes to discuss how this made them feel.

- *Mindful listening:* Now clear your head of everything except what is going on in the immediate environment. Try to hear as many sounds around you as you can, without judging or evaluating them. Try to maintain this mindful listening for 3 minutes. The group will then take 3 minutes to discuss some of the details they noticed.
- *Mindful thinking:* As with listening, clear your head of everything, but now focus just on your ideas about mindfulness and stress. Do not talk about or write down what you're thinking (yet); just focus your whole quiet attention on this exercise and what it means. Try to maintain this mindful thinking for 3 minutes. The group will then take 3 minutes to talk about what this experience was like.

As noted earlier, these are just brief examples of what mindfulness exercises are like. In a full mindfulness program, you would go through several sessions of up to an hour each. Now that you have an idea of what it feels like to do mindfulness work, consider the following questions in your groups:

6-8. Were there any aspects of the mindfulness practice sessions that you found especially pleasant or useful? Were there any aspects of the sessions that you found unpleasant or uncomfortable?

6-9. What concerns might you have about implementing a mindfulness intervention in the workplace? What are some of the obstacles you might face in trying to have employees engage in a mindfulness stress reduction program?

6-10. Bring the class together and discuss your responses.

Sources: Based on E. Langer, "Mindfulness in the Age of Complexity," *Harvard Business Review*, March 2014, 68–73; H. J. E. M. Alberts and U. R. Hülsheger, "Applying Mindfulness in the Context of Work: Mindfulness-Based Interventions," in J. Reb and P. W. B. Atkins, *Mindfulness in Organizations* (Cambridge, UK: Cambridge University Press, 2015), 17–41; K. A. Aikens, J. Astin, K. R. Pelletier, K. Levanovich, C. M. Baase, Y. Y. Park, and C. M. Bodnar, "Mindfulness Goes to Work: Impact of an Online Workplace Intervention," *Journal of Occupational and Environmental Medicine 56* (2014): 721–31.

ETHICAL DILEMMA Data Mining Emotions

Did anyone ever tell you that you wear your heart on your sleeve? It's a popular expression, but obviously no one is looking at your sleeve to read your emotions. Instead, we tend to study a person's facial expressions to "read" their emotions. Most of us think we're rather good at reading faces, but we couldn't say exactly how we make our interpretations, and we don't know whether they are accurate. But what if we could use technology to know how another person is feeling? Would it be ethical to do so in the workplace and then act on our findings?

Technology is not quite ready to do this. Face reading is a complex science. Paul Ekman, a noted psychologist, may be the best human face reader in the world. He has been studying the interpretation of emotions for over 40 years and developed a catalog of over 5,000 muscle movements and their emotional content. His work even spawned a television series called *Lie to Me,* in which the main characters analyzed microexpressions—expressions that occur in a fraction of a second—to assist in corporate and governmental investigations. Using Ekman's Facial Coding System, technology firms like Emotient Inc. have been developing algorithms to match microexpressions to emotions. These organizations are currently looking for patterns of microexpressions that might predict behavior.

Honda, Procter & Gamble (P&G), Coca-Cola, and Unilever have tried the technology to identify the reactions to new products, with mixed results. For one thing, expressions can change instantly, so it is challenging to discern which emotions prevail. A person watching a commercial, for instance, may smile, furrow his brow, and raise his eyebrows all in the space of 30 seconds, indicating expressiveness, confusion, and surprise in turn. Second, it is difficult to know whether a person will act on these fleeting emotions. Third, the technology might misinterpret the underlying emotions or their causes.

The potential applications of this technology to the workplace include surveillance, gauging reactions to organization announcements, and lie detection. Cameras could be in every meeting room, hallway, and even on employees' computer screens. Emotion monitoring could be an announced event—say, every Monday from 8 to 9 A.M.—or random. Monitoring could be conducted with or without the knowledge of employees; for instance, data on the emotional reactions of every employee in an organizational announcement meeting could be read and interpreted through a camera on the wall.

So far, the most reliable workplace application seems to be using the technology to capture inconsistencies (lying). Even the pioneer of facial emotion recognition, Ekman, said, "I can't control usage [of his technology]. I can only be certain that what I'm providing is at least an accurate depiction of when someone is concealing emotion."

For each usage, there is an ethical consideration and a responsibility, particularly if a manager is going to act on the findings or infer the employee's future behavior. The fact that the technology has not yet fully evolved for workplace application allows time for ethical guidelines to be developed. Foremost among the ethical concerns is privacy. "I can see few things more invasive than trying to record someone's emotions in a database," said privacy advocate Ginger McCall. Concerns about ethical usage are also highly important if managers use the technology to make decisions about employees. For example, what if a manager learns from the software that an employee is unhappy and thus decides to look for a work reassignment for the employee, when actually the employee is unhappy about his spouse? Former U.S. counterterrorism detective Charles Lieberman advises, "Recognize [the technology's] limitations—it can lead you in the right direction but is not definitive."

Questions

6-11. What do you think are the best workplace applications for emotion reading technology?

6-12. What are the ethical implications of reading faces for emotional content in the workplace?

6-13. Assuming you could become better at detecting the real emotions of others from facial expressions, do you think it would help your career? Why or why not?

Sources: Based on Paul Ekman profile, Being Human, http://www.beinghuman.org/mind/paul-ekman, accessed April 17, 2015; E. Dwoskin and E. M. Rusli, "The Technology That Unmasks Your Hidden Emotions," *The Wall Street Journal,* January 29, 2015, B1, B8; and D. Matsumoto and H. S. Hwang, "Reading Facial Expressions of Emotion," Psychological Science Agenda, May 2011, http://www.apa.org/science/about/psa/2011/05/facial-expressions.aspx.

CASE INCIDENT 1 Hiring an Emotionally Intelligent Employee

Emotional intelligence is our ability to identify and manage our own emotions and to understand and influence other people's emotions. These qualities provide us with the ability to build better relationships, manage difficult emotions, increase creativity and innovation, and lead others effectively.

People are hired by organizations because of where they went to college, the test scores and grades achieved, their technical skills and certifications, not because they are effective team players or can get along with others. Being smart is not just all about intellect, and companies are increasing interested in job applicants who display emotional intelligence (EI). The challenge facing organizations is how to hire emotionally intelligent employees. Guidance has been provided by McKee on undertaking this process.

Don't:

- **Use personality tests as a means of testing for EI:** These tests are designed to test personality traits and types. These tests are not effective as they do not measure abilities such as self-awareness, achievement orientation, empathy, or inspirational leadership, which are at the core of emotional intelligence.
- **Use a self-report test.** These types of tests are problematic as a candidate may have a low level of self-awareness and he or she will more than likely record what they believe the organization would like to hear.
- **Use a 360-degree feedback instrument,** even if it is valid and even if it measures EI competencies. The 360-degree feedback method involves a process where employees receive feedback from those who work with them, including their manager, team members, peers, and support staff. It is important to the process that this information is both anonymous and confidential. This system provides an opportunity for professional development by identifying strengths and weaknesses but not evaluation. When these instruments are used as a method of evaluation, people may carefully select the respondents and even prepare them on how to score.

Do:

- **Get references and talk to referees.** Letters of reference do not give enough insight into a person's EI. It is important to actually talk to the referee and to ask specific questions about particular EI competencies. You should encourage the referee to give you lots of examples about how the candidate treats other people. When you actually talk to a referee, you can ask specific and pointed questions about how the candidate demonstrated various EI competencies. Ask for lots of examples especially about how the candidate treats other people.
- **Interview for emotional intelligence.** Many interviewers think they are already doing this and that it is easy. Interviewers should not allow candidates to be vague in their responses and need to ask good follow-up questions. It should be kept in mind that people often talk about what they ideally would do and what they would like to be and have a low level of self-awareness.

To overcome the some of the challenges of learning about a candidate's competencies a *behavioural event interview* should be conducted. Firstly, the candidate should be put at ease and asked a few general questions. Then they should be asked about a challenging situation that they mastered successfully. The candidate should be informed to tell the story briefly and then at greater length be questioned about what they thought, felt, and did throughout. This process should be repeated as the candidate is asked to recount an unsuccessful situation that created a learning experience. This may be followed by another successful story as the interview closes. As the stories are told the interviewer will gain an insight into the candidate's self-awareness, self-regulation, capacity for empathy, and overall level of EI. This helps one to "see" the candidates' EI through the lens of real experiences.

These strategies are subjective by nature but will help in selecting more emotionally intelligent candidates for your business who will be better at managing emotions, be more productive, have a greater self-awareness, have better quality relationships, and be more effective communicators.

Questions

6-14. What is emotional intelligence? What benefits are identified in the case of hiring an emotionally intelligent employee?

6-15. Comment on McKee's recommendations on what not to do when using EI as means of employee selection.

6-16. Identify a time that you successfully completed a task and record what you thought, how you felt and what you did at this time. Then do the same for a task that you were not successful at completing. What insight into your EI did these experiences provide you with?

Sources: A. McKee, "How to Hire for Emotional Intelligence," *Harvard Business Review*, February 5, 2016; Linda Le Phan, "Emotional Intelligence: 5 Reasons Companies Are Starting to Care More," Kununu, June 19, 2017, https://transparency.kununu.com/emotional-intelligence-5-reasons-compnaies-care-about-it; Jayson DeMers, "5 Reasons You Need Emotionally Intelligent Employees (and How to Find Them)," Entrepreneur, https://www.entrepreneur.com/article/292094.

CASE INCIDENT 2 Anger: A Dangerous Emotion at Work

Work-related anger emotions are a serious problem for many companies. Anger at work may lead to a number of detrimental organizational outcomes: job demotivation, job dissatisfaction, unhealthy employee relations, decreased productivity, and higher rates of absences and employee turnover. It usually arises as a hostile response or reaction to a stressful issue or event beyond an employee's ability to cope. This may include anything from the background noise of a phone ringing in the office to larger work-related matters such as excessive workload, but all of them can lead to work-related stress and cause an employee to lose their temper.

Anger is believed to be one of the most commonly experienced emotions at work around the globe. According to surveys in the United Kingdom, 45 percent of all staff lose their temper at work. Anger reactions may take several forms, ranging from a simple "argh!" gesture in response to a challenging task in the workplace to more severe extreme anger reactions, or so-called "office rage"—extreme, visible anger demonstrated by an employee at work. The latter is becoming a growing problem in many firms today. One research study conducted by Canon Europe found that, on average, as many as 83 percent of European workers have witnessed one of their colleagues visibly lose their temper in the workplace. Italy leads among the countries surveyed—as much as 94 percent of Italian workers have seen a colleague lose their temper at work.

Lucy Beresford, a psychotherapist and occupational stress expert who was part of the Canon Europe study, has noted that office rage is becoming a major and a growing concern in many parts of Europe and advises companies to be proactive about resolving such problems. According to the study, the biggest cause for anger at work was "pointless meetings," which was followed by other major triggers—ill-mannered colleagues, unsupportive bosses and colleagues, office politics, unpleasant office temperature, and faulty printers and computers. Each of those reasons has many implications about what employers can do to reduce and tackle office rage and anger at work.

Finally, anger can have a bad impact on employees' personal health; there have even been studies suggesting a correlation between excessive anger at the workplace and lung problems. It is important to note that not all employees experience the same level or intensity of anger; it can differ due to a multitude of factors including genes, personality, and a person's values. Regardless, experts agree that anger at work is best avoided; in most cases, anger will not help in resolving an issue and may even worsen the problem.

Many companies have been actively implementing anger management programs at the workplace in an effort to reduce and manage workplace anger. Companies have begun to offer employee assistance program services in the form of counseling sessions to help employees control and manage feelings of anger. According to the Society for Human Resource Management, most of these anger management sessions are designed to help angry employees develop skills related to stress reduction, communication, conflict resolution, and problem-solving. Many companies take a reactive approach—they await for an incident to happen and then offer a fix—but experts advise that companies be on the lookout for warning signs and offer assistance before negative incidents actually take place. For example, an employee who has been increasingly argumentative is a warning signal that employers must act by referring that employee to an anger management session. Increased complaints at work is another warning signal, indicating that employee relations may be deteriorating at the workplace. Companies that intercede proactively by dealing with anger problems from the onset, well before the situation progresses to more severe consequences, will be more capable of maintaining their organizational effectiveness.

Questions

6-17. Do you think that personal differences in terms of gender and personality play a role in the expression of emotions such as anger? Why or why not?

6-18. Based on the figures and statistics that you read in the case, do you think that companies are doing enough to reduce anger at work? Why should managers be concerned about managing anger at work? What approaches or techniques can you think of to reduce anger at work?

6-19. Reflecting on what you have read in the chapter, suggest ways that employees can use emotional regulation to decrease anger at work.

Sources: Linda Wasmer Andrews, "When It's Time for Anger Management," SHRM website, June 1, 2005, www.shrm.org/hr-today/news/hr-magazine/pages/0605andrews.aspx, accessed June 5, 2020; Alison Birrane, "Need to Smash a Printer with a Baseball Bat? Now You Can," BBC Worklife, September 14, 2016, www.bbc.com/worklife/article/20160913-need-to-smash-a-printer-with-a-baseball-bat-now-you-can, accessed May 12, 2020; J. Booth, J. L. Ireland, S. Mann, M. Eslea, and L. Holyoak, "Anger Expression and Suppression at Work: Causes, Characteristics and Predictors," *International Journal of Conflict Management* 28, no. 3 (2017): 368–82, doi:http://dx.doi.org.ezproxy.lau.edu.lb:2048/10.1108/IJCMA-06-2016-0044; British Association of Anger Management, "Anger Statistics," www.angermanage.co.uk/anger-statistics/, accessed May 12, 2020; R. Geffner, M. Braverman, J. Galasso, and J. Marsh (eds.), *Aggression in Organizations: Violence, Abuse, and Harassment at Work and in Schools* (New York: Routledge, 2005); P. Lehrer, "Anger, Stress, Dysregulation Produces Wear and Tear on the Lung," *Thorax* 61, no. 10 (2006): 833–34, doi.org/10.1136/thx.2006.057182; G. McMahon, "Anger at Work," *Training Journal* (2008): 61–65; Celia Richardson and Ed Halliwell, *Boiling Point: Problem Anger and What We Can Do about It,* Mental Health Foundation, www.mentalhealth.org.uk/sites/default/files/boilingpoint.pdf, accessed October 7, 2020; E. Stuart and C. Hancock, *Issues in Healthcare Risk Management* (Oxford, UK: Healthcare Governance Ltd., 2008).

ENDNOTES

[1] Hizbullah, M., Sharma, M. and Singh, D. (2020). "Caught profiteering off Covid lifesaving drugs". ©*India Today (July 16, 2020).* Retrieved from https://www.indiatoday.in (Accessed on April 21, 2022).

[2] Constructed based on authors conversations with several stakeholders of a hospital in May 2021.

[3] S. G. Barsade and D. E. Gibson, "Why Does Affect Matter in Organizations?" *Academy of Management Perspectives* 21, no. 1 (2007): 36–59; and H. A. Elfenbein, "Emotion in Organizations," *The Academy of Management Annals* 1, no. 1 (2007): 315–86.

[4] Ibid.

[5] Ibid.

[6] See, for example, G. J. Boyle, E. Helmes, G. Matthews, and C. E. Izard, "Multidimensional Measures of Affects: Emotions and Mood States," in G. J. Boyle, D. H. Saklofske, and G. Matthews (eds.), *Measures of Personality and Social Psychological Constructs* (New York, NY: Elsevier, 2015): 3–15; and M. T. Jarymowicz and K. K. Imbir, "Toward a Human Emotions Taxonomy (Based on Their Automatic vs. Reflective Origin)," *Emotion Review* 7, no. 2 (2015): 183–8.

[7] R. C. Solomon, "Back to Basics: On the Very Idea of 'Basic Emotions,'" *Journal for the Theory of Social Behaviour* 32, no. 2 (2002): 115–44.

[8] P. Ekman, *Emotions Revealed: Recognizing Faces and Feelings to Improve Communication and Emotional Life* (New York: Times Books/Henry Holt and Co., 2003).

[9] H. A. Elfenbein and N. Ambady, "On the Universality and Cultural Specificity of Emotion Recognition: A Meta-Analysis," *Psychological Bulletin* 128, no. 2 (2002): 203–35.

[10] M. Yuki, W. W. Maddux, and T. Masuda, "Are the Windows to the Soul the Same in the East and West? Cultural Differences in Using the Eyes and Mouth as Cues to Recognize Emotions in Japan and the United States," *Journal of Experimental Social Psychology* 43, no. 2 (2007): 303–11.

[11] Ekman, *Emotions Revealed: Recognizing Faces and Feelings to Improve Communication and Emotional Life*; and J. L. Tracy and D. Randles, "Four Models of Basic Emotions: A Review of Ekman and Cordaro, Izard, Levenson, and Panksepp and Watt," *Emotion Review* 3, no. 4 (2011): 397–405.

[12] R. Greenbaum, J. Bonner, T. Gray, and M. Mawritz, "Moral Emotions: A Review and Research Agenda for Management Scholarship," *Journal of Organizational Behavior* 41 (2020): 95–114.

[13] P. S. Russell and R. Giner-Sorolla, "Bodily Moral Disgust: What It Is, How It Is Different from Anger, and Why It Is an Unreasoned Emotion," *Psychological Bulletin* 139, no. 2 (2013): 328–51.

[14] H. A. Chapman and A. K. Anderson, "Things Rank and Gross in Nature: A Review and Synthesis of Moral Disgust," *Psychological Bulletin* 139, no. 2 (2013): 300–27.

[15] T. Krettenauer, J. B. Asendorpf, and G. Nunner-Winkler, "Moral Emotion Attributions and Personality Traits as Long-Term Predictors of Antisocial Conduct in Early Adulthood: Findings from a 20-Year Longitudinal Study," *International Journal of Behavioral Development* 27 (2013): 192–201; T. Krettenauer, T. Colasante, M. Buchmann, and T. Malti, "The Development of Moral Emotions and Decision-Making from Adolescence to Early Adulthood: A 6-Year Longitudinal Study," *Journal of Youth & Adolescence* 43 (2014): 583–96; and J. P. Tangney, J. Stuewig, and D. J. Mashek, "Moral Emotions and Moral Behavior," *Annual Review of Psychology* 58 (2007): 345–72.

[16] A. Ben-Ze'ev, *The Subtlety of Emotions* (Cambridge, MA: MIT Press, 2000), 94.

[17] R. Cropanzano, H. M. Weiss, J. M. S. Hale, and J. Reb, "The Structure of Affect: Reconsidering the Relationship between Negative and Positive Affectivity," *Journal of Management* 29, no. 6 (2003): 831–57.

[18] T. A. Ito and J. T. Cacioppo, "Variations on a Human Universal: Individual Differences in Positivity Offset and Negativity Bias," *Cognition and Emotion* 19, no. 1 (2005): 1–26.

[19] D. Holman, "Call Centres," in D. Holman, T. D. Wall, C. Clegg, P. Sparrow, and A. Howard (eds.), *The Essentials of the New Work Place: A Guide to the Human Impact of Modern Working Practices* (Chichester, UK: Wiley, 2005), 111–32.

[20] Ben-Ze'ev, *The Subtlety of Emotions.*

[21] S. D. Pressman, M. W. Gallagher, S. J. Lopez, and B. Campos, "Incorporating Culture into the Study of Affect and Health," *Psychological Science* 25, no. 12 (2014): 2281–83.

[22] K. B. Curhan, T. Simms, H. R. Markus, S. Kitayama, M. Karasawa, N. Kawakami, ... and C. D. Ryff, "Just How Bad Negative Affect Is for Your Health Depends on Culture," *Psychological Science* 25, no. 12 (2014): 2277–80.

[23] O. Burkeman, "The Power of Negative Thinking," *The New York Times,* August 5, 2012, 9; G. Luong, C. Wrzus, G. G. Wagner, and M. Riediger, "When Bad Moods May Not Be So Bad: Valuing Negative Affect Is Associated with Weakened Affect-Health Links," *Emotion* 16, no. 3 (2016): 38–401.

[24] E. Jaffe, "Positively Negative," *Association for Psychological Science Observer,* November 2012, 13–17.

[25] S. Lyubomirsky, L. King, and E. Diener, "The Benefits of Frequent Positive Affect: Does Happiness Lead to Success?" *Psychological Bulletin* 131, no. 6 (2005): 803–55; K. M. Shockley, D. Ispas, M. E. Rossi, and E. L. Levine, "A Meta-Analytic Investigation of the Relationship between State Affect, Discrete Emotions, and Job Performance," *Human Performance* 25 (2012): 377–411; and C. J. Thoresen, S. A. Kaplan, A. P. Barsky, C. R. Warren, and K. de Chermont, "The Affective Underpinnings of Job Perceptions and Attitudes: A Meta-Analytic Review and Integration," *Psychological Bulletin* 129, no. 6 (2003): 914–45.

[26] T. W. H. Ng and K. L. Sorensen, "Dispositional Affectivity and Work-Related Outcomes: A Meta-Analysis," *Journal of Applied Social Psychology* 39, no. 6 (2009): 1255–87.

[27] L. M. Poverny and S. Picascia, "There Is No Crying in Business," *Womensmedia.com,* October 20, 2009, retrieved from http://www.susanpicascia.com/noCrying.html.

[28] M.-A. Reinhard and N. Schwartz, "The Influence of Affective States on the Process of Lie Detection," *Journal of Experimental Psychology* 18 (2012): 377–89.

[29] K. D. McCaul and A. B. Mullens, "Affect, Thought and Self-Protective Health Behavior: The Case of Worry and Cancer Screening," in J. Suls and K. A. Wallston (eds.), *Social Psychological Foundations of Health and Illness* (Malden, MA: Blackwell, 2003): 161.

[30] J. Haidt, "The New Synthesis in Moral Psychology," *Science* 316 (May 18, 2007): 998, 1002; I. E. de Hooge, R. M. A. Nelissen, S. M. Breugelmans, and M. Zeelenberg, "What Is Moral about Guilt?

Acting 'Prosocially' at the Disadvantage of Others," *Journal of Personality and Social Psychology* 100 (2011): 462–73; and C. A. Hutcherson and J. J. Gross, "The Moral Emotions: A Social-Functionalist Account of Anger, Disgust, and Contempt," *Journal of Personality and Social Psychology* 100 (2011): 719–37.
[31]A. Arnaud and M. Schminke, "The Ethical Climate and Context of Organizations: A Comprehensive Model," *Organization Science* 23, no. 6 (2012): 1767–80; and P. C. Kelley and D. R. Elm, "The Effect of Context on Moral Intensity of Ethical Issues: Revising Jones's Issue-Contingent Model," *Journal of Business Ethics* 48, no. 2 (2003): 139–54.
[32]N. Angier, "Spite Is Good. Spite Works," *The Wall Street Journal,* April 1, 2014, D1, D3; A. Gopnik, "Even Children Get More Outraged at 'Them' Than at 'Us'," *The Wall Street Journal,* August 30–31, 2014, C2; J. I. Krueger and T. E. DiDonato, "Social Categorization and the Perception of Groups and Group Differences," *Social and Personality Psychology Compass* 2, no. 2 (2008): 733–50; and D. A. Yudkin, T. Rothmund, M. Twardawski, N. Thalla, and J. J. Van Bavel, "Reflexive Intergroup Bias in Third-Party Punishment," *Journal of Experimental Psychology: General* 145, no. 11 (2016): 1448–59.
[33]E. Castano, "On the Perils of Glorifying the In-group: Intergroup Violence, In-group Glorification, and Moral Disengagement," *Social and Personality Psychology Compass* 2, no. 1 (2008): 154–70.
[34]E. Diener, R. J. Larsen, S. Levine, and R. A. Emmons, "Intensity and Frequency: Dimensions Underlying Positive and Negative Affect," *Journal of Personality and Social Psychology* 48 (1985): 1253–65; and D. C. Rubin, R. M. Hoyle, and M. R. Leary, "Differential Predictability of Four Dimensions of Affect Intensity," *Cognition and Emotion* 26 (2012): 25–41.
[35]B. P. Hasler, M. S. Mehl, R. R. Bootzin, and S. Vazire, "Preliminary Evidence of Diurnal Rhythms in Everyday Behaviors Associated with Positive Affect," *Journal of Research in Personality* 42 (2008): 1537–46; and D. Watson, *Mood and Temperament* (New York: Guilford Press, 2000).
[36]Watson, *Mood and Temperament.*
[37]A. A. Stone, J. E. Schwartz, D. Schkade, N. Schwarz, A. Krueger, and D. Kahneman, "A Population Approach to the Study of Emotion: Diurnal Rhythms of a Working Day Examined with the Day Reconstruction Method," *Emotion* 6 (2006): 139–49.
[38]S. A. Golder and M. W. Macy, "Diurnal and Seasonal Mood Vary with Work, Sleep, and Daylength across Diverse Cultures," *Science* 333 (2011): 1878–81.
[39]G. D. Block, "Fixes for Our Out-of Sync Body Clocks," *The Wall Street Journal,* August 16–17, 2014, C3; A.-M. Chang, N. Santhi, M. St. Hilaire, C. Gronfier, D. S. Bradstreet, J. F. Duffy, ... and C. A. Czeisler, "Human Responses to Bright Light of Different Durations," *The Journal of Physiology* 590, no. 13 (2012): 3103–12; and T. L. Shanahan, J. M. Zeitzer, and C. A. Czeisler, "Resetting the Melatonin Rhythm with Light in Humans," *Journal of Biological Rhythms* 12, no. 6 (1997): 556–67.
[40]Golder and Macy, "Diurnal and Seasonal Mood Vary with Work, Sleep, and Daylength across Diverse Cultures."
[41]J. J. A. Denissen, L. Butalid, L. Penke, and M. A. G. van Aken, "The Effects of Weather on Daily Mood: A Multilevel Approach," *Emotion* 8, no. 5 (2008): 662–67; M. C. Keller, B. L. Fredrickson, O. Ybarra, S. Côté, K. Johnson, J. Mikels, A. Conway, and T. Wagner, "A Warm Heart and a Clear Head: The Contingent Effects of Weather on Mood and Cognition," *Psychological Science* 16 (2005): 724–31; and Watson, *Mood and Temperament.*
[42]D. Watson, *Mood and Temperament* (New York: Guilford Press, 2000).
[43]J. J. Lee, F. Gino, and B. R. Staats, "Rainmakers: Why Bad Weather Means Good Productivity," *Journal of Applied Psychology* 99, no. 3 (2014): 504–13.
[44]M. T. Ford, R. A. Matthews, J. D. Wooldridge, V. Mishra, U. M. Kakar, and S. R. Strahan, "How Do Occupational Stressor-Strain Effects Vary with Time? A Review and Meta-Analysis of the Relevance of Time Lags in Longitudinal Studies," *Work & Stress* 28, no. 1 (2014): 9–30; and J. A. Fuller, J. M. Stanton, G. G. Fisher, C. Spitzmüller, S. S. Russell, and P. C. Smith, "A Lengthy Look at the Daily Grind: Time Series Analysis of Events, Mood, Stress, and Satisfaction," *Journal of Applied Psychology* 88, no. 6 (December 2003): 1019–33.
[45]G. Schaffer, "What's Good, When, and Why?" *Association for Psychological Science Observer,* November 2012, 27–29; see also J. D. Nahrgang, F. P. Morgeson, and D. A. Hofmann, "Safety at Work: A Meta-Analytic Investigation of the Link Between Job Demands, Job Resources, Burnout, Engagement, and Safety Outcomes," *Journal of Applied Psychology* 96, no. 1 (2011): 71–94.
[46]A. M. Isen, "Positive Affect as a Source of Human Strength," in L. G. Aspinwall and U. Staudinger (eds.), *The Psychology of Human Strengths* (Washington, DC: American Psychological Association, 2003), 179–95.
[47]Watson, *Mood and Temperament.*
[48]*Sleep in America Poll* (Washington, DC: National Sleep Foundation, 2005), www.kintera.org/atf/cf/%7Bf6bf2668-a1b4-4fe8-8d1a-a5d39340d9cb%7D/2005_summary_of_findings.pdf.
[49]D. Meinert, "Sleepless in Seattle ... and Cincinnati and Syracuse," *HR Magazine,* October 2012, 55–57.
[50]E. Bernstein, "Changing the Clocks Wasn't Good for Your Relationships," *The Wall Street Journal,* March 10, 2015, D1, D2.
[51]B. A. Scott and T. A. Judge, "Insomnia, Emotions, and Job Satisfaction: A Multilevel Study," *Journal of Management* 32, no. 5 (2006): 622–45.
[52]Bernstein, "Changing the Clocks Wasn't Good for Your Relationships."
[53]B. Arends, "To Sleep, Perchance to Earn," *The Wall Street Journal,* September 20–21, 2014, B8.
[54]S. Reddy, "Husband and Wife Scientists Troll Genetics for Clues to Restful Shut Eye for All," *The Wall Street Journal,* June 10, 2014, D1, D2.
[55]A. L. Rebar, R. Stanton, D. Geard, C. Short, M. J. Duncan, and C. Vandelanotte, "A Meta-Meta-Analysis of the Effect of Physical Activity on Depression and Anxiety in Non-Clinical Adult Populations," *Health Psychology Review* 9, no. 3 (2015): 366–78.
[56]E. E. Bernstein, J. E. Curtiss, G. W. Y. Wu, P. J. Barreira, and R. J. McNally, "Exercise and Emotion Dynamics: An Experience Sampling Study," *Emotion* 19, no. 4 (2019): 637–44.
[57]M. Mather, "The Affective Neuroscience of Aging," *Annual Review of Psychology* 67 (2016): 213–38.
[58]M. G. Gard and A. M. Kring, "Sex Differences in the Time Course of Emotion," *Emotion* 7, no. 2 (2007): 429–37;

M. Jakupcak, K. Salters, K. L. Gratz, and L. Roemer, "Masculinity and Emotionality: An Investigation of Men's Primary and Secondary Emotional Responding," *Sex Roles* 49 (2003): 111–20; and D. P. Johnson and M. A. Whisman, "Gender Differences in Rumination: A Meta-Analysis," *Personality and Individual Differences* 55, no. 4 (2013): 367–74.

[59]A. H. Fischer, P. M. Rodriguez Mosquera, A. E. M. van Vianen, and A. S. R. Manstead, "Gender and Culture Differences in Emotion," *Emotion* 4 (2004): 84–87.

[60]N. M. Else-Quest, A. Higgins, C. Allison, and L. C. Morton, "Gender Differences in Self-Conscious Emotional Experience: A Meta-Analysis," *Psychological Bulletin* 138, no. 5 (2012): 947–81.

[61]L. F. Barrett and E. Bliss-Moreau, "She's Emotional. He's Having a Bad Day: Attributional Explanations for Emotion Stereotypes," *Emotion* 9 (2009): 649–58.

[62]D. V. Becker, D. T. Kenrick, S. L. Neuberg, K. C. Blackwell, and D. M. Smith, "The Confounded Nature of Angry Men and Happy Women," *Journal of Personality and Social Psychology* 92 (2007): 179–90.

[63]A. A. Grandey, "Emotion Regulation in the Workplace: A New Way to Conceptualize Emotional Labor," *Journal of Occupational Health Psychology* 5, no. 1 (2000): 95–110; and A. R. Hochschild, *The Managed Heart: Commercialization of Human Feeling* (Berkeley: University of California Press, 1983); M. W. Kramer and J. A. Hess, "Communication Rules for the Display of Emotions in Organizational Settings," *Management Communication Quarterly*, August 2002, 66–80; and J. M. Diefendorff and E. M. Richard, "Antecedents and Consequences of Emotional Display Rule Perceptions," *Journal of Applied Psychology* April 2003, 284–94.

[64]J. M. Diefendorff and G. J. Greguras, "Contextualizing Emotional Display Rules: Examining the Roles of Targets and Discrete Emotions in Shaping Display Rule Perceptions," *Journal of Management* 35 (2009): 880–98.

[65]P. S. Christoforou and B. E. Ashforth, "Revisiting the Debate on the Relationships between Display Rules and Performance: Considering the Explicitness of Display Rules," *Journal of Applied Psychology* 100, no. 1 (2015): 249–61.

[66]A. S. Gabriel, M. A. Daniels, J. M. Diefendorff, and G. J. Greguras, "Emotional Labor Actors: A Latent Profile Analysis of Emotional Labor Strategies," *Journal of Applied Psychology* 100, no. 3 (2015): 863–79.

[67]J. D. Kammeyer-Mueller, A. L. Rubenstein, D. M. Long, M. A. Odio, B. R. Buckman, Y. Zhang, and M. D. K. Halvorsen-Ganepola, "A Meta-Analytic Structural Model of Dispositional Affectivity and Emotional Labor," *Personnel Psychology* 66 (2013): 47–90.

[68]H. Nguyen, M. Groth, and A. Johnson, "When the Going Gets Tough, the Tough Keep Working: Impact of Emotional Labor on Absenteeism," *Journal of Management* 42, no. 3 (2016): 615–43; and D. T. Wagner, C. M. Barnes, and B. A. Scott, "Driving It Home: How Workplace Emotional Labor Harms Employee Home Life," *Personnel Psychology* 67 (2014): 487–516.

[69]U. R. Hülsheger, J. W. B. Lang, A. F. Schewe, and F. R. H. Zijlstra, "When Regulating Emotions at Work Pays Off: A Diary and an Intervention Study on Emotion Regulation and Customer Tips in Service Jobs," *Journal of Applied Psychology* 100, no. 2 (2015): 263–77; J. L. Huang, D. S. Chiaburu, X., Li, N., and Grandey, A. A., "Rising to the Challenge: Deep Acting Is More Beneficial When Tasks Are Appraised as Challenging," *Journal of Applied Psychology* 100, no. 5 (2015): 1398–1408; J. D. Kammeyer-Mueller et al., "A Meta-Analytic Structural Model of Dispositional Affectivity and Emotional Labor"; and Y. Zhan, M. Wang, and J. Shi, "Interpersonal Process of Emotional Labor: The Role of Negative and Positive Customer Treatment," *Personnel Psychology* 69, no. 3 (2016): 525–57.

[70]A. A. Grandey, "When 'The Show Must Go On,'" *Academy of Management Journal* 46 (2003): 86–96.

[71]S. Diestel, W. Rivkin, and K.-H. Schmidt, "Sleep Quality and Self-Control Capacity as Protective Resources in the Daily Emotional Labor Process: Results from Two Diary Studies," *Journal of Applied Psychology* 100, no. 3 (2015): 809–27; and K. L. Wang and M. Groth, "Buffering the Negative Effects of Employee Surface Acting: The Moderating Role of Employee-Customer Relationship Strength and Personalized Services," *Journal of Applied Psychology* 99, no. 2 (2014): 341–50.

[72]S. Ohly and A. Schmitt, "What Makes Us Enthusiastic, Angry, Feeling at Rest or Worried? Development and Validation of an Affective Work Events Taxonomy Using Concept Mapping Methodology," *Journal of Business Psychology* 30 (2015): 15–35; and H. M. Weiss and R. Cropanzano, "Affective Events Theory: A Theoretical Discussion of the Structure, Causes and Consequences of Affective Experiences at Work," *Research in Organizational Behavior* 18 (1996): 1–74.

[73]C. D. Fisher, "Antecedents and Consequences of Real-Time Affective Reactions at Work," *Motivation and Emotion* 26, no. 1 (2002): 3–30; A. A. Grandey, A. P. Tam, and A. L. Brauburger, "Affective States and Traits in the Workplace: Diary and Survey Data from Young Workers," *Motivation and Emotion* 26, no. 1 (2002): 31–55.

[74]Grandey, Tam, and Brauburger, "Affective States and Traits in the Workplace."

[75]N. M. Ashkanasy, C. E. J. Hartel, and C. S. Daus, "Diversity and Emotion: The New Frontiers in Organizational Behavior Research," *Journal of Management* 28, no. 3 (2002): 324.

[76]T. Upshur-Lupberger, "Watch Your Mood: A Leadership Lesson," *The Huffington Post*, April 22, 2015, http://www.huffingtonpost.com/terrie-upshurlupberger/watch-your-mood-a-leaders_b_7108648.html.

[77]D. L. Joseph and D. A. Newman, "Emotional Intelligence: An Integrative Meta-Analysis and Cascading Model," *Journal of Applied Psychology* 95, no. 1 (2010): 54–78; and P. Salovey and D. Grewal, "The Science of Emotional Intelligence," *Current Directions in Psychological Science* 14, no. 6 (2005): 281–5.

[78]D. Geddes and R. R. Callister, "Crossing the Line(s): A Dual Threshold Model of Anger in Organizations," *Academy of Management Review* 32, no. 3 (2007): 721–46.

[79]D. L. Joseph, J. Jin, D. A. Newman, and E. H. O'Boyle, "Why Does Self-Reported Emotional Intelligence Predict Job Performance? A Meta-Analytic Investigation of Mixed EI," *Journal of Applied Psychology* 100, no. 2 (2015): 298–342; and Joseph and Newman, "Emotional Intelligence."

[80]C. I. C. Chien Farh, M.-G. Seo, and P. E. Tesluk, "Emotional Intelligence,

Teamwork Effectiveness, and Job Performance: The Moderating Role of Job Context," *Journal of Applied Psychology* 97, no. 4 (2012): 890–900; and D. Greenidge, D. Devonish, and P. Alleyne, "The Relationship between Ability-Based Emotional Intelligence and Contextual Performance and Counterproductive Work Behaviors: A Test of the Mediating Effects of Job Satisfaction," *Human Performance* 27 (2014): 225–42.

[81]C. P. M. Wilderom, Y. Hur, U. J. Wiersma, P. T. Van Den Berg, and J. Lee, "From Manager's Emotional Intelligence to Objective Store Performance: Through Store Cohesiveness and Sales-Directed Employee Behavior," *Journal of Organizational Behavior* 36 (2015): 825–44.

[82]A. Rezvani, A. Chang, A. Wiewiora, N. M. Askanasy, P. J. Jordan, and R. Zolin, "Manager Emotional Intelligence and Project Success: The Mediating Role of Job Satisfaction and Trust," *International Journal of project Management* 34, no. 7 (2016): 1112–22.

[83]S. Côté, "Emotional Intelligence in Organizations," *Annual Review of Organizational Psychology and Organizational Behavior* 1 (2014): 59–88.

[84]S. Hodzic, J. Scharfen, P. Ripoll, H. Holling, and F. Zenasni, "How Efficient Are Emotional Intelligence Trainings: A Meta-analysis," *Emotion Review* 10, no. 2 (2018): 138–48; I. Kotsou, D. Nelis, J. Grégoire, and M. Mikolajczak, "Emotional Plasticity: Conditions and Effects of Improving Emotional Competence in Adulthood," *Journal of Applied Psychology* 96, no. 4 (2011): 827–39; V. Mattingly and K. Kraiger, "Can Emotional Intelligence Be Trained? A Meta-analytical Investigation," *Human Resource Management Review* 29 (2019): 140–55; O. J. Sheldon, D. Dunning, and D. R. Ames, "Emotionally Unskilled, Unaware, and Uninterested in Learning More: Reactions to Feedback about Deficits in Emotional Intelligence," *Journal of Applied Psychology* 99, no. 1 (2014): 125–37.

[85]S. L. Koole, "The Psychology of Emotion Regulation: An Integrative Review," *Cognition and Emotion* 23 (2009): 4–41; H. A. Wadlinger and D. M. Isaacowitz, "Fixing Our Focus: Training Attention to Regulate Emotion," *Personality and Social Psychology Review* 15 (2011): 75–102.

[86]D. H. Kluemper, T. DeGroot, and S. Choi, "Emotion Management Ability: Predicting Task Performance, Citizenship, and Deviance," *Journal of Management* (2013): 878–905.

[87]D. J. Hughes, I. K. Kratsiotis, K. Niven, and D. Holman, "Personality Traits and Emotion Regulation: A Targeted Review and Recommendations," *Emotion* 20, no. 1 (2020): 63–67.

[88]J. V. Wood, S. A. Heimpel, L. A. Manwell, and E. J. Whittington, "This Mood Is Familiar and I Don't Deserve to Feel Better Anyway: Mechanisms Underlying Self-Esteem Differences in Motivation to Repair Sad Moods," *Journal of Personality and Social Psychology* 96 (2009): 363–80.

[89]E. Kim, D. P. Bhave, and T. M. Glomb, "Emotion Regulation in Workgroups: The Roles of Demographic Diversity and Relational Work Context," *Personnel Psychology* (2013): 613–44.

[90]Ibid.

[91]S. L. Koole, "The Psychology of Emotion Regulation: An Integrative Review," *Cognition and Emotion* 23 (2009): 4–41.

[92]L. K. Barber, P. G. Bagsby, and D. C. Munz, "Affect Regulation Strategies for Promoting (or Preventing) Flourishing Emotional Health," *Personality and Individual Differences* 49 (2010): 663–66.

[93]J. L. Jooa and G. Francesca, "Poker-Faced Morality: Concealing Emotions Leads to Utilitarian Decision Making," *Organizational Behavior and Human Decision Processes* 126 (2015): 49–64.

[94]Ibid.

[95]T. L. Webb, E. Miles, and P. Sheeran, "Dealing with Feeling: A Meta-Analysis of the Effectiveness of Strategies Derived from the Process Model of Emotion Regulation," *Psychological Bulletin* 138, no. 4 (2012): 775–808; S. Srivastava, M. Tamir, K. M. McGonigal, O. P. John, and J. J. Gross, "The Social Costs of Emotional Suppression: A Prospective Study of the Transition to College," *Journal of Personality and Social Psychology* 96 (2009): 883–97; Y. Liu, L. M. Prati, P. L. Perrewé, and R. A. Brymer, "Individual Differences in Emotion Regulation, Emotional Experiences at Work, and Work-Related Outcomes: A Two-Study Investigation," *Journal of Applied Social Psychology* 40 (2010): 1515–38; and H. A. Wadlinger and D. M. Isaacowitz, "Fixing Our Focus: Training Attention to Regulate Emotion," *Personality and Social Psychology Review* 15 (2011): 75–102.

[96]J. J. Gross, E. Halperin, and R. Porat, "Emotion Regulation in Intractable Conflicts," *Current Directions in Psychological Science* 22, no. 6 (2013): 423–29.

[97]A. S. Troy, A. J. Shallcross, and I. B. Mauss, "A Person-by-Person Situation Approach to Emotion Regulation: Cognitive Reappraisal Can Either Help or Hurt, Depending on the Context," *Psychological Science* 24, no. 12 (2013): 2505–14.

[98]E. Halperin, R. Porat, M. Tamir, and J. J. Gross, "Can Emotion Regulation Change Political Attitudes in Intractable Conflicts? From the Laboratory to the Field," *Psychological Science*, January 2013, 106–11.

[99]A. S. McCance, C. D. Nye, L. Wang, K. S. Jones, and C. Chiu, "Alleviating the Burden of Emotional Labor: The Role of Social Sharing," *Journal of Management* 39, no. 2 (2013): 392–415.

[100]F. Nils and B. Rimé, "Beyond the Myth of Venting: Social Sharing Modes Determine the Benefits of Emotional Disclosure," *European Journal of Social Psychology* 42 (2012): 672–81; and J. D. Parlamis, "Venting as Emotion Regulation: The Influence of Venting Responses and Respondent Identity on Anger and Emotional Tone," *International Journal of Conflict Management* 23 (2012): 77–96.

[101]T. M. Glomb, M. K. Duffy, J. E. Bono, and T. Yang, "Mindfulness at Work," *Research in Personnel and Human Resources Management* 30 (2011): 115–57; P. Hyland, R. A. Lee, and M. Mills, "Mindfulness at Work: A New Approach to Improving Individual and Organizational Performance," *Industrial and Organizational Psychology* 8, no. 4 (2015): 576–602; and K. M. Sutcliffe, T. J. Vogus, and E. Dane, "Mindfulness in Organizations: A Cross-Level Review," *Annual Review of Organizational Psychology and Organizational Behavior* 3 (2016): 55–81.

[102]Glomb, Duffy, Bono, and Yang, "Mindfulness at Work."

[103]E. Epel, J. Daubenmier, J. T. Moskowitz, S. Folkman, and E. Blackburn, "Can Meditation Slow Rate of Cellular Aging? Cognitive Stress, Mindfulness, and Telomeres," *Annals of the New York Academy of Sciences* 1172 (2009): 34–53; B. K. Hölzel, J. Carmody, M. Vangel, C. Congleton, S. M. Yerramsetti, T. Gard, and S. W. Lazar,

"Mindfulness Practice Leads to Increases in Regional Brain Gray Matter Density," *Psychiatry Research: Neuroimaging* 191, no. 1 (2011): 36–43; and M. D. Mrazek, M. S. Franklin, D. T. Phillips, B. Baird, and J. W. Schooler, "Mindfulness Training Improves Working Memory Capacity and GRE Performance While Reducing Mind Wandering," *Psychological Science* 24 (2013): 776–81.

[104]Glomb, Duffy, Bono, and Yang, "Mindfulness at Work."

[105]U. R. Hülsheger, H. J. E. M. Alberts, A. Feinholdt, and J. W. B. Lang, "Benefits of Mindfulness at Work: The Role of Mindfulness in Emotion Regulation, Emotional Exhaustion, and Job Satisfaction," *Journal of Applied Psychology* 98, no. 2 (2013): 310–25.

[106]E. Dane and B. J. Brummel, "Examining Workplace Mindfulness and its Relations to Job Performance and Turnover Intention," *Human Relations* 67, no. 1 (2013): 105–28; U. R. Hülsheger, A. Feinholdt, and A. Nübold, "A Low-Dose Mindfulness Intervention and Recovery from Work: Effects of Psychological Detachment, Sleep Quality, and Sleep Duration," *Journal of Occupational and Organizational Psychology* 88 (2015): 464–89; S. Krishnakumar and M. D. Robinson, "Maintaining an Even Keel: An Affect-Mediated Model of Mindfulness and Hostile Work Behavior," *Emotion* 15, no. 5 (2015): 579–89; E. C. Long and M. S. Christian, "Mindfulness Buffers Retaliatory Responses to Injustice: A Regulatory Approach," *Journal of Applied Psychology* 100, no. 5 (2015): 1409–22; and A. Michel, C. Bosch, and M. Rexroth, "Mindfulness as a Cognitive-Emotional Segmentation Strategy: An Intervention Promoting Work-Life Balance," *Journal of Occupational and Organizational Psychology* 87 (2014): 733–54.

[107]S. D. Jamieson and M. R. Tuckey, "Mindfulness Interventions in the Workplace: A Critique of the Current State of the Literature," *Journal of Occupational Health Psychology* 22, no. 2 (2017): 180–93.

[108]S.-C. S. Chi and S.-G. Liang, "When Do Subordinates' Emotion-Regulation Strategies Matter? Abusive Supervision, Subordinates' Emotional Exhaustion, and Work Withdrawal," *Leadership Quarterly*, February 2013, 125–37.

[109]R. H. Humphrey, "How Do Leaders Use Emotional Labor?" *Journal of Organizational Behavior*, July 2012, 740–44.

[110]A. M. Grant, "Rocking the Boat but Keeping It Steady: The Role of Emotion Regulation in Employee Voice," *Academy of Management Journal* 56, no. 6 (2013): 1703–23.

[111]E. S. Blanke, A. Brose, E. K. Kalokerinos, Y. Erbas, M. Riediger, and P. Kuppens, "Mix It to Fix It: Emotion Regulation Variability in Daily Life," *Emotion* 20, no. 3 (2020): 473–85; L. Pruessner, S. Barnow, D. V. Holt, J. Joormann, and K. Schulze, "A Cognitive Control Framework for Understanding Emotion Regulation Flexibility," *Emotion* 20, no. 1 (2020): 21–29.

[112]S. Reddy, "Walk This Way: Acting Happy Can Make It So," *The Wall Street Journal*, November 18, 2014, D3.

[113]C. Cherniss, "The Business Case for Emotional Intelligence," *Consortium for Research on Emotional Intelligence in Organizations* (1999), http://www.eiconsortium.org/pdf/business_case_for_ei.pdf.

[114]Priyam Dhani, Tanu Sharma, Effect of Emotional Intelligence on Job Performance of IT employees: *A gender study, Procedia Computer Science, Volume 122, 2017, Pages 180–185, ISSN 1877–0509,* https://doi.org/10.1016/j.procs.2017.11.358. (Accessed on April 25, 2022).

[115]L. Z. Bencharit, Y. Wan Ho, H. H. Fung, D. Y. Yeung, N. M. Stephens, R. Romero-Canyas, and J. L. Tsai, "Should Job Applicants Be Excited or Calm? The Role of Culture and Ideal Affect in Employment Settings," *Emotion* 19, no. 3 (2019): 377–401.

[116]See A. M. Isen, "Positive Affect and Decision Making," in M. Lewis and J. M. Haviland-Jones (eds.), *Handbook of Emotions*, 2nd ed. (New York: Guilford, 2000), 261–77.

[117]N. Nunez, K. Schweitzer, C. A. Chai, and B. Myers, "Negative Emotions Felt during Trial: The Effect of Fear, Anger, and Sadness on Juror Decision Making," *Applied Cognitive Psychology* 29, no. 2 (2015): 200–9.

[118]S. N. Mohanty and D. Suar, "Decision Making under Uncertainty and Information Processing in Positive and Negative Mood States," *Psychological Reports* 115, no. 1 (2014): 91–105.

[119]S.-C. Chuang and H.-M. Lin, "The Effect of Induced Positive and Negative Emotion and Openness-to-Feeling in Student's Consumer Decision Making," *Journal of Business and Psychology* 22, no. 1 (2007): 65–78.

[120]D. van Knippenberg, H. J. M. Kooij-de Bode, and W. P. van Ginkel, "The Interactive Effects of Mood and Trait Negative Affect in Group Decision Making," *Organization Science* 21, no. 3 (2010): 731–44.

[121], King, and Diener, "The Benefits of Frequent Positive Affect"; and M. Baas, C. K. W. De Dreu, and B. A. Nijstad, "A Meta-Analysis of 25 Years of Mood-Creativity Research: Hedonic Tone, Activation, or Regulatory Focus," *Psychological Bulletin* 134 (2008): 779–806.

[122]. J. Grawitch, D. C. Munz, and E. K. Elliott, "Promoting Creativity in Temporary Problem-Solving Groups: The Effects of Positive Mood and Autonomy in Problem Definition on Idea-Generating Performance," *Group Dynamics* 7, no. 3 (September 2003): 200–13.

[123]Lyubomirsky, King, and Diener, "The Benefits of Frequent Positive Affect."

[124]N. Madjar, G. R. Oldham, and M. G. Pratt, "There's No Place Like Home? The Contributions of Work and Nonwork Creativity Support to Employees' Creative Performance," *Academy of Management Journal* 45, no. 4 (2002): 757–67.

[125]J. M. George and J. Zhou, "Understanding When Bad Moods Foster Creativity and Good Ones Don't: The Role of Context and Clarity of Feelings," *Journal of Applied Psychology* 87, no. 4 (August 2002): 687–97; and J. P. Forgas and J. M. George, "Affective Influences on Judgments and Behavior in Organizations: An Information Processing Perspective," *Organizational Behavior and Human Decision Processes* 86, no. 1 (2001): 3–34.

[126]C. K. W. De Dreu, M. Baas, and B. A. Nijstad, "Hedonic Tone and Activation Level in the Mood-Creativity Link: Toward a Dual Pathway to Creativity Model," *Journal of Personality and Social Psychology* 94, no. 5 (2008): 739–56; J. M. George and J. Zhou, "Dual Tuning in a Supportive Context: Joint Contributions of Positive Mood, Negative Mood, and Supervisory Behaviors to Employee Creativity," *Academy of Management Journal* 50, no. 3 (2007): 605–22.

[127]M. B. Wieth and R. T. Zacks, "Time of Day Effects on Problem Solving: When the Non-Optimal Is Optimal," *Thinking & Reasoning* 17 (2011): 387–401.
[128]A. Erez and A. M. Isen, "The Influence of Positive Affect on the Components of Expectancy Motivation," *Journal of Applied Psychology* 87, no. 6 (2002): 1055–67.
[129]W. Tsai, C.-C. Chen, and H. Liu, "Test of a Model Linking Employee Positive Moods and Task Performance," *Journal of Applied Psychology* 92, no. 6 (2007): 1570–83.
[130]R. Ilies and T. A. Judge, "Goal Regulation across Time: The Effect of Feedback and Affect," *Journal of Applied Psychology* 90, no. 3 (May 2005): 453–67.
[131]J. E. Bono, H. J. Foldes, G. Vinson, and J. P. Muros, "Workplace Emotions: The Role of Supervision and Leadership," *Journal of Applied Psychology* 92, no. 5 (2007): 1357–67.
[132]S. G. Liang and S.-C. S. Chi, "Transformational Leadership and Follower Task Performance: The Role of Susceptibility to Positive Emotions and Follower Positive Emotions," *Journal of Business and Psychology* (2013): 17–29.
[133]V. A. Visser, D. van Knippenberg, G. van Kleef, and B. Wisse, "How Leader Displays of Happiness and Sadness Influence Follower Performance: Emotional Contagion and Creative versus Analytical Performance," *Leadership Quarterly*, (2013): 172–88.
[134]B. M. Staw, K. A. DeCelles, and P. de Goey, "Leadership in the Locker Room: How the Intensity of Leaders' Unpleasant Affective Displays Shapes Team Performance," *Journal of Applied Psychology* (in press).
[135]G. A. Van Kleef, C. K. W. De Dreu, and A. S. R. Manstead, "The Interpersonal Effects of Emotions in Negotiations: A Motivated Information Processing Approach," *Journal of Personality and Social Psychology* 87, no. 4 (2004): 510–28; and G. A. Van Kleef, C. K. W. De Dreu, and A. S. R. Manstead, "The Interpersonal Effects of Anger and Happiness in Negotiations," *Journal of Personality and Social Psychology* 86, no. 1 (2004): 57–76.
[136]E. van Dijk, G. A. Van Kleef, W. Steinel, and I. van Beest, "A Social Functional Approach to Emotions in Bargaining: When Communicating Anger Pays and When It Backfires," *Journal of Personality and Social Psychology* 94, no. 4 (2008): 600–14.
[137]K. M. O'Connor and J. A. Arnold, "Distributive Spirals: Negotiation Impasses and the Moderating Role of Disputant Self-Efficacy," *Organizational Behavior and Human Decision Processes* 84, no. 1 (2001): 148–76.
[138]B. Shiv, G. Loewenstein, A. Bechara, H. Damasio, and A. R. Damasio, "Investment Behavior and the Negative Side of Emotion," *Psychological Science* 16, no. 6 (2005): 435–39.
[139]W.-C. Tsai and Y.-M. Huang, "Mechanisms Linking Employee Affective Delivery and Customer Behavioral Intentions," *Journal of Applied Psychology* (2002): 1001–08.
[140]See P. B. Barker and A. A. Grandey, "Service with a Smile and Encounter Satisfaction: Emotional Contagion and Appraisal Mechanisms," *Academy of Management Journal* 49, no. 6 (2006): 1229–38; and S. D. Pugh, "Service with a Smile: Emotional Contagion in the Service Encounter," *Academy of Management Journal* (2001): 1018–27.
[141]D. E. Rupp and S. Spencer, "When Customers Lash Out: The Effects of Customer Interactional Injustice on Emotional Labor and the Mediating Role of Emotions, *Journal of Applied Psychology* 91, no. 4 (2006): 971–78; and Tsai and Huang, "Mechanisms Linking Employee Affective Delivery and Customer Behavioral Intentions."
[142]R. Ilies and T. A. Judge, "Understanding the Dynamic Relationships among Personality, Mood, and Job Satisfaction: A Field Experience Sampling Study," *Organizational Behavior and Human Decision Processes* 89 (2002): 1119–39.
[143]T. A. Judge and R. Ilies, "Affect and Job Satisfaction: A Study of Their Relationship at Work and at Home," *Journal of Applied Psychology* 89 (2004): 661–73.
[144]Z. Song, M. Foo, and M. A. Uy, "Mood Spillover and Crossover among Dual-Earner Couples: A Cell Phone Event Sampling Study," *Journal of Applied Psychology* 93, no. 2 (2008): 443–52.
[145]See R. J. Bennett and S. L. Robinson, "Development of a Measure of Workplace Deviance," *Journal of Applied Psychology* June 2000, 349–60; see also P. R. Sackett and C. J. DeVore, "Counterproductive Behaviors at Work," in N. Anderson, D. S. Ones, H. K. Sinangil, and C. Viswesvaran (eds.), *Handbook of Industrial, Work & Organizational Psychology*, vol. 1 (Thousand Oaks, CA: Sage, 2001), 145–64.
[146]K. Lee and N. J. Allen, "Organizational Citizenship Behavior and Workplace Deviance: The Role of Affect and Cognition," *Journal of Applied Psychology* 87, no 1 (2002): 131–42; T. A. Judge, B. A. Scott, and R. Ilies, "Hostility, Job Attitudes, and Workplace Deviance: Test of a Multilevel Mode," *Journal of Applied Psychology* 91, no. 1 (2006): 126–38; and S. Kaplan, J. C. Bradley, J. N. Luchman, and D. Haynes, "On the Role of Positive and Negative Affectivity in Job Performance: A Meta-Analytic Investigation," *Journal of Applied Psychology* 94, no. 1 (2009): 152–76.
[147]S. C. Douglas, C. Kiewitz, M. Martinko, P. Harvey, Y. Kim, and J. U. Chun, "Cognitions, Emotions, and Evaluations: An Elaboration Likelihood Model for Workplace Aggression," *Academy of Management Review* 33, no. 2 (2008): 425–51.
[148]A. K Khan, S. Ouratulain, and J. R. Crawshaw, "The Mediating Role of Discrete Emotions in the Relationship between Injustice and Counterproductive Work Behaviors: A Study in Pakistan," *Journal of Business and Psychology* (2013): 49–61.
[149]Kaplan, Bradley, Luchman, and Haynes, "On the Role of Positive and Negative Affectivity in Job Performance"; and J. Maiti, "Design for Worksystem Safety Using Employees' Perception about Safety," *Work—A Journal of Prevention Assessment & Rehabilitation* 41 (2012): 3117–22.
[150]J. E. Bono and R. Ilies, "Charisma, Positive Emotions and Mood Contagion," *The Leadership Quarterly* 17, no. 4 (2006): 317–34.

7 Motivation Concepts

Source: Rick Wilking/Reuters/Alamy Stock Photo

LEARNING OBJECTIVES

After studying this chapter, you should be able to:

7-1 Describe the three key elements of motivation.

7-2 Compare the early theories of motivation.

7-3 Contrast the elements of self-determination theory and goal-setting theory.

7-4 Understand the differences among self-efficacy theory, reinforcement theory, and expectancy theory.

7-5 Describe the forms of organizational justice, including distributive justice, procedural justice, informational justice, and interactional justice.

7-6 Identify the implications of employee job engagement for managers.

7-7 Describe how the contemporary theories of motivation complement one another.

Employability Skills Matrix (ESM)

	Myth or Science?	Career OBjectives	An Ethical Choice	Point/ Counterpoint	Experiential Exercise	Ethical Dilemma	Case Incident 1	Case Incident 2
Critical Thinking				✓	✓	✓	✓	✓
Communication		✓			✓			✓
Collaboration	✓	✓			✓			
Knowledge Application and Analysis	✓	✓	✓	✓	✓	✓	✓	✓
Social Responsibility	✓	✓	✓		✓	✓	✓	

WHEN GOALS GO OUT OF CONTROL

In 2018, Tata Starbucks announced that they would achieve 40 percent gender diversity at all levels in all their stores by 2022. In 2019, they ensured hundred percent gender parity for all employees, which essentially means that all employees are paid the same amount of money for the same kind of work. In 2020, an increase in female workforce from 16 percent to 34 percent was observed. The steep rise was achieved by instituting a number of changes which included flexible working hours for young mothers, structured career paths for part-timers.[1] Two of the key developments were setting up of lactation rooms for nursing women and safe travel arrangements for women.[2] In addition, all women-managed stores were opened as a means to challenge the mindset that women are not capable of managing on their own.[3] Starbucks' actions and results attests to the power of setting specific, challenging goals.

Goal-setting theory has had an undeniable impact on the study of motivation in organizational behavior. A voluminous literature suggests that goal setting can help improve motivation and performance in employees, and many organizations recognize this and try to harness their power. But sometimes goal setting may not be used in the "right" way and can lead to perceptions of unfairness or injustice from employees, who may even engage in counterproductive work behaviors (like cheating) to accomplish the goal.

For example, in September 2016, it was revealed that over 5,000 employees of the Wells Fargo bank "cheated the system" by opening more than 2 million unauthorized customer accounts using personally identifiable information to meet "indiscriminate" sales goals. Essentially, an employee would move funds from cardholders' accounts into new accounts to meet their sales goals. To make matters worse, nearly 15,000 customers were charged interest, overdraft, and annual fees for accounts they never authorized to be opened.

Although likely satirical or exaggerated, early cartoon YouTube videos using the site xtranormal.com perhaps tapped into employees' underlying perceptions of injustice. For example, one 2011 depiction of a conversation between a banking manager and supervisor provides insight into these unrealistic goals: "Please share with me how you plan to hit 400 checking accounts and 2,000 solutions this month," asks the supervisor. The manager answers, "Well, I plan to work 90 hours a week for the next four weeks." "That's not good enough," responds the supervisor. Susan Fischer, one bank manager from Phoenix, recalled, "[T]he challenges that I faced were the astronomical goals that were set... it was the pressure of having to hold the team accountable to very unrealistic standards." Not only have these events upset customers, clients, and employees alike, but shareholders were irate as well: Prior to an annual shareholders meeting, the Sisters of St. Francis of Philadelphia, an order of nuns who were also shareholders in Wells Fargo, wanted to see "real, systematic change in culture, ethics, values and financial sustainability," further characterizing the perceptions of injustice.

Despite these challenges, Wells Fargo tried to repair their relationships with their customers, employees, and all involved. It appears as if the current goal system is on its way out, and the organization has already engaged in remedial action. Wells Fargo has since fired most of the employees who participated in the practices and will also be paying millions in fines and refunds to the customers affected. Paradoxically, some research suggests that, when organizations go above and beyond to repair damaged relationships after ethical transgressions or injustices, sometimes employees and customers can become *more* satisfied than if the transgressions never occurred at all.

Sources: Based on M. Egan, "5,300 Wells Fargo Employees Fired over 2 Million Phony Accounts," *CNN Money*, September 9, 2016, http://money.cnn.com/2016/09/08/investing/wells-fargo-created-phony-accounts-bank-fees/?iid=EL; M. Egan, "Wells Fargo Still Faces over a Dozen Probes Tied to Fake Account Scandal," *CNN Money*, March 31, 2017, http://money.cnn.com/2017/03/31/investing/wells-fargo-investigations-fake-account-scandal/; E. A. Locke and G. P. Latham, "Building a Practically Useful Theory of Goal Setting and Task Motivation," *American Psychologist* 57, no. 9 (2002): 705–17; L. D. Ordóñez, M. E. Schweitzer, A. D. Galinsky, and M. H. Bazerman, "Goals Gone Wild: The Systematic Side Effects of Over-Prescribing Goal Setting," *Academy of Management Perspectives* 31, no. 1 (2017): 6–16; M. P. Regan, "Wells Fargo Scandal Gets Cartoonish," *Bloomberg: Gadfly,* October 21, 2016, https://www.bloomberg.com/gadfly/articles/2016-10-21/psst-regulators-watch-videos-for-bank-scandal-after-wells-fargo; M. Schminke, J. Caldwell, M. L. Ambrose, and S. R. McMahon, "Better Than Ever? Employee Reactions to Ethical Failures in Organizations, and the Ethical Recovery Paradox," *Organizational Behavior and Human Decision Processes* 123 (2014): 206–19; B. Scudamore, "Why I'm Spending My Spring Break with 500 of My Closest Co-Workers," *Inc.*, March 14, 2017, http://www.inc.com/brian-scudamore/we-put-500-employees-on-a-plane-to-hawaii-for-1-very-good-reason.html; S. Woolley, "Next Time Your Boss Sets a Crazy Sales Goal, Show Him This," *Bloomberg,* September 14, 2016, https://www.bloomberg.com/news/articles/2016-09-14/how-sales-targets-encourage-wrongdoing-inside-america-s-companies.

As we read in the chapter-opening vignette, motivation is a powerful force: It can drive employees through encouragement and reward to accomplish challenging goals. It can also drive employees to cheat when they experience injustice or are threatened by unattainable goals. As a manager, navigating and attempting to predict these forces becomes a challenge, but knowing more about different theories of motivation can help increase an understanding of how motivation may operate and how employees become motivated.

Motivation is one of the most frequently researched topics in organizational behavior (OB).[4] In one survey, 69 percent of workers reported wasting time at work every day, and nearly a quarter said they waste between 30 and 60 minutes each day. How? Usually by surfing the Internet (checking the news and visiting social network sites) and chatting with coworkers.[5] Although times change, the problem of motivating a workforce stays the same.

In this chapter, we'll review the basics of motivation, assess motivation theories, and provide an integrative model that fits these theories together. But first, look at the potential that a little motivation to ask for a raise can yield, shown in the OB Poll.

OB POLL

Asking for a Raise: Business Executives

Note: Survey of 3,900 executives from 31 countries.

Source: Based on Accenture, "The Path Forward" (2012), http://www.accenture.com/SiteCollectionDocuments/PDF/Accenture-IWD-Research-Deck-2012-FINAL.pdf#zoom=50, 36.

Motivation Defined

7-1 Describe the three key elements of motivation.

The same young student who struggles to read a textbook for more than 20 minutes may devour a Harry Potter book in a day. The difference is the situation. As we analyze the concept of motivation, keep in mind that the level of motivation varies both between individuals and within individuals at different times.

motivation The processes that account for an individual's intensity, direction, and persistence of effort toward attaining a goal.

We define **motivation** as the processes that account for an individual's *intensity, direction*, and *persistence* of effort toward attaining a goal.[6] While general motivation is concerned with effort toward *any* goal, we'll narrow the focus to *organizational* goals.

Intensity describes how hard a person tries. This is the element most of us focus on when we talk about motivation. However, high intensity is unlikely to lead to favorable job performance outcomes unless the effort is channeled in a *direction* that benefits the organization. Therefore, we consider the quality of effort as well as its intensity. Effort directed toward, and consistent with, the organization's goals is the kind of effort we should be seeking. Finally, motivation has a *persistence* dimension. This measures how long a person can maintain effort. Motivated individuals stay with a task long enough to achieve their goals.

Early Theories of Motivation

7-2 Compare the early theories of motivation.

Three theories of employee motivation formulated during the 1950s are probably the best known. Although they are now of questionable validity (as we'll discuss), they represent a foundation of motivation theory, and many practicing managers still use their terminology.

Hierarchy of Needs Theory

hierarchy of needs Abraham Maslow's hierarchy of five needs—physiological, safety, social, esteem, and self-actualization—in which, as each need is substantially satisfied, the next need becomes dominant.

The best-known theory of motivation is Abraham Maslow's **hierarchy of needs**,[7] which hypothesizes that within every human being there is a hierarchy of five needs. Recently, a sixth need has been proposed for a highest level—intrinsic values—which is said to have originated from Maslow, but it has yet to gain widespread acceptance.[8] The original five needs are:

1. **Physiological.** Includes hunger, thirst, shelter, sex, and other bodily needs.
2. **Safety-security.** Security and protection from physical and emotional harm.
3. **Social-belongingness.** Affection, belongingness, acceptance, and friendship.
4. **Esteem.** Internal factors such as self-respect, autonomy, and achievement, and external factors such as status, recognition, and attention.
5. **Self-actualization.** Drive to become what we are capable of becoming; includes growth, achieving our potential, and self-fulfillment.

According to Maslow, as each need becomes substantially satisfied, the next one becomes dominant. So if you want to motivate someone, you need to understand what level of the hierarchy that person is currently on and focus on satisfying needs at or above that level. We depict the hierarchy as a pyramid in Exhibit 7-1 because this is its best-known presentation, but Maslow referred to the needs only in terms of levels.

Exhibit 7-1 Maslow's Hierarchy of Needs

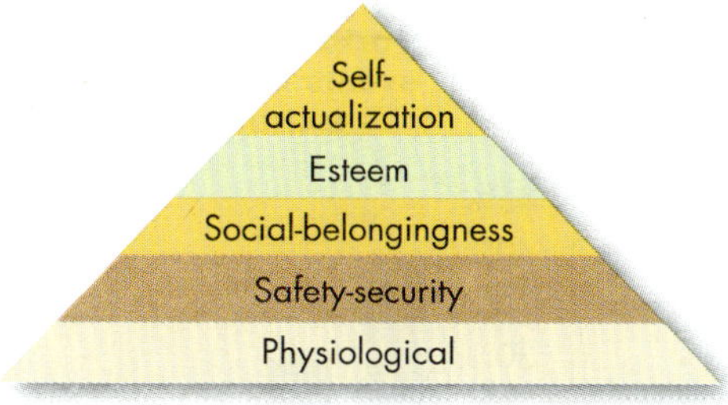

Source: Based on H. Skelsey, "Maslow's Hierarchy of Needs—the Sixth Level," *Psychologist* (2014): 982–83.

Maslow's theory has received long-standing wide recognition, particularly among practicing managers. It is intuitively logical and easy to understand, and some research has validated it.[9] Unfortunately, however, most research does not, and it hasn't been frequently researched since the 1960s.[10] But old theories, especially intuitively logical ones, die hard. It is thus important to be aware of the prevailing public acceptance of the hierarchy when discussing motivation.

Two-Factor Theory

Believing an individual's relationship to work is basic, and that the attitude toward work can determine success or failure, psychologist Frederick Herzberg wondered, "What do people want from their jobs?" He asked people to describe, in detail, situations in which they felt exceptionally *good* or *bad* about their jobs. The responses differed significantly and led Hertzberg to his **two-factor theory** (also called *motivation-hygiene theory*, but this term is not used much today).[11]

two-factor theory A theory that relates intrinsic factors to job satisfaction and associates extrinsic factors with dissatisfaction. Also called motivation-hygiene theory.

As shown in Exhibit 7-2, intrinsic factors such as advancement, recognition, responsibility, and achievement seem related to job satisfaction. Respondents who felt good about their work tended to attribute these factors to their situations, while dissatisfied respondents tended to cite extrinsic factors, such as supervision, pay, company policies, and work conditions.

To Herzberg, the data suggest that the opposite of satisfaction is not dissatisfaction, as was traditionally believed. Removing dissatisfying characteristics from a job does not necessarily make the job satisfying. Herzberg proposed a dual continuum: The opposite of "satisfaction" is "no satisfaction," and the opposite of "dissatisfaction" is "no dissatisfaction" (see Exhibit 7-3).

Under two-factor theory, the factors that lead to job satisfaction are separate and distinct from those that lead to job dissatisfaction. Therefore, managers who seek to eliminate factors that can create job dissatisfaction may bring about peace but not necessarily motivation. They will be placating rather than motivating their workers. Conditions such as quality of supervision, pay, company policies, physical work conditions, relationships with others, and job security are **hygiene factors**. When they're adequate, people will not be dissatisfied; neither will they be satisfied. If we want to *motivate* people on their jobs, we should emphasize factors associated with the work itself or with outcomes directly derived from it, such as promotional opportunities, personal growth opportunities, recognition, responsibility, and achievement. These are the characteristics people find intrinsically rewarding.

hygiene factors Factors—such as company policy and administration, supervision, and salary—that, when adequate in a job, placate workers. When these factors are adequate, people will not be dissatisfied.

Exhibit 7-2 Comparison of Satisfiers and Dissatisfiers

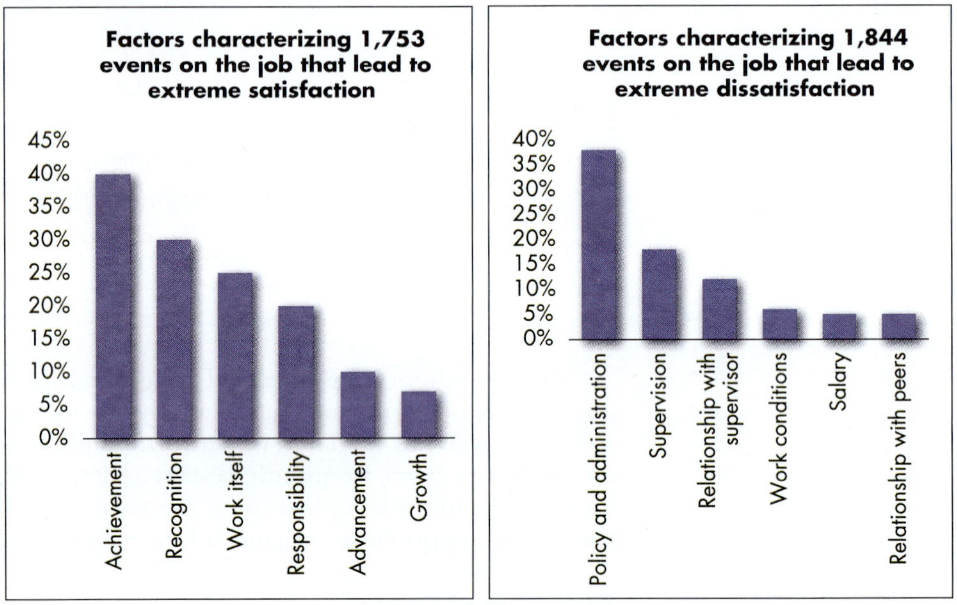

Source: Based on Harvard Business Review, "Comparison of Satisfiers and Dissatisfiers," An exhibit from One More Time: How Do You Motivate Employees? by Frederick Herzberg, January 2003. Copyright © 2003 by the Harvard Business School Publishing Corporation. All rights reserved.

The two-factor theory has not been well supported in research. Criticisms center on Herzberg's original methodology and his assumptions, such as how the participants may be biased in thinking back to times when they felt good or bad about their jobs.[12] Furthermore, if hygiene and motivational factors are equally important to a person, both should be capable of motivating.

Regardless of the criticisms, Herzberg's theory has been quite influential and has been used in many studies in Asian countries, such as Japan and India.[13] Few managers worldwide are unfamiliar with its recommendations.

Exhibit 7-3 Contrasting View of Satisfaction and Dissatisfaction

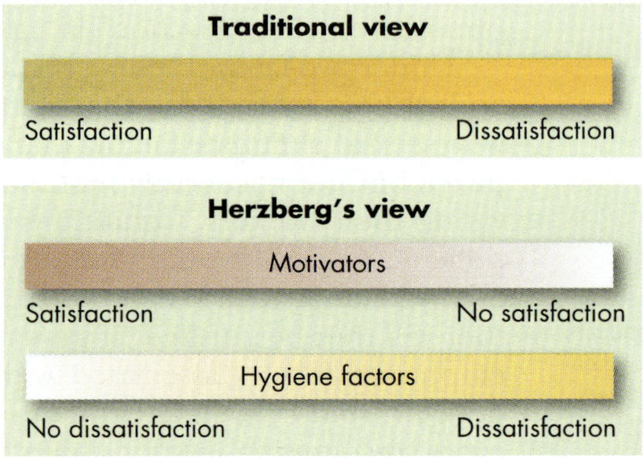

McClelland's Theory of Needs

You have one beanbag and five targets set up in front of you, each farther away than the last. Target A sits almost within arm's reach. If you hit it, you get ₹20. Target B is a bit farther out and pays ₹40, but only about 80 percent of the people who try can hit it. Target C pays ₹80, and about half the people who try can hit it. Very few people can hit Target D, but the payoff is ₹160 for those who do. Finally, Target E pays ₹320, but it's almost impossible to achieve. Which would you try for? If you selected C, you're likely to be a high achiever. Why? Read on.

McClelland's theory of needs A theory that states achievement, power, and affiliation are three important needs that help explain motivation.

need for achievement (nAch) The need to excel or achieve to a set of standards.

need for power (nPow) The need to make others behave in a way in which they would not have behaved otherwise.

need for affiliation (nAff) The desire for friendly and close interpersonal relationships.

McClelland's theory of needs was developed by David McClelland and his associates.[14] Compared to Maslow's hierarchy, these needs are more akin to motivating factors than strict needs for survival. There are three:

- **Need for achievement (nAch)** is the drive to excel, to achieve in relationship to a set of standards.
- **Need for power (nPow)** is the need to make others behave in a way they would not have otherwise.
- **Need for affiliation (nAff)** is the desire for friendly and close interpersonal relationships.

McClelland and subsequent researchers focused most of their attention on nAch. In general, high achievers perform best when they perceive their probability of success as 0.5—that is, a 50–50 chance. They dislike gambling with high odds because they get no achievement satisfaction from success that comes by pure chance. Similarly, they dislike low odds (high probability of success) because then there is no challenge to their skills. They like to set goals that require stretching themselves a little.

McClelland's theory has research support across cultures, particularly (when cultural dimensions including power distance are considered).[15] Based on prior nAch research, we can predict some relationships between nAch and

Entrepreneur Fred DeLuca is a high achiever motivated by work that demands a high degree of personal responsibility. He cofounded a Subway sandwich shop in 1965 at the age of 17 to help finance his college education and grew the company into the world's largest fast-food franchise, with almost 44,000 shops in more than 100 countries.

Source: Geoff Caddick/EMPPL PA Wire/AP Images

job performance. First, when employees have a high level of nAch, they tend to exhibit more positive moods and be more interested in the task at hand.[16] Second, employees high on nAch tend to perform very well in high-stakes conditions on the job, like work walkthroughs or sales encounters.[17]

The need for achievement has received a great deal of research attention and acceptance in a wide array of fields, including organizational behavior, psychology, and general business.[18] The nPow also has research support, but it may be more familiar to people in broad terms (e.g., a need to obtain power) than in relation to the original definition (e.g., a need to make others behave in a way that you want them to).[19] We will discuss power much more in Chapter 11. The nAff is also well established and accepted in research—for example, one recent study of 145 teams from Korean organizations suggests that, out

Career OBjectives

Why won't he take my advice?

The new guy in the office is nice enough, but he's straight out of college, and I have 20 years of experience in the field. I'd like to help him out, but he won't take it no matter how I approach him. Is there anything I can do to motivate him to accept my advice? He badly needs a few pointers.

— James

Dear James:

It's great that you want to help, and surely you have wisdom to offer. But let's start with this: When is the last time you took someone else's advice? Chances are it's easier for you to remember the last time you *didn't* take someone's advice than when you did. That's because we want success on our own terms, and we don't like the idea that a ready answer was out there all along (and we missed it). "When somebody says, 'You should do something,' the subtext is: 'You're an idiot for not already doing it,'" said psychologist Alan Goldberg. "Nobody takes advice under those conditions." So under what conditions *do* people take advice?

There are two parts to the motivation equation for advice: what your coworker wants to hear, and how you can approach him. For the first part, keep this rule in mind: He wants to hear that whatever decisions he's made are brilliant. If he hears anything different from that, he's likely to tune you out or keep talking until you come over to his side.

For the second part, your coworker's motivation to accept and, more important, act on advice has a lot to do with how you approach him. Are you likely to "impart your wisdom to the younger generation"? Anything like "I wish I had known this when I was just starting out like you" advice will likely have him thinking you (and your advice) are out of date. Are you going to give "if I were you, I would do this" advice? He may resent your intrusion. According to research, what is most likely to work is a gentle suggestion, phrased as a request. Ravi Dhar, a director at Yale, said, "Interrogatives have less reactance and may be more effective." You might say, for instance, "Would you consider trying out this idea?"

Take heart. The problem isn't that we don't like advice—we do, as long as we seek it. According to research, we are more motivated toward advice when we are facing important decisions, so good timing may work in your favor. When he does ask, you may suggest that he writes down the parameters of his choices and his interpretations of the ethics of each decision. Researcher Dan Ariely has found that we are much more motivated to make morally right decisions when we've considered the moral implications in a forthright manner. In this way, your coworker may motivate himself to make the right decisions.

Keep trying!

Sources: Based on D. Ariely, "What Price for the Soul of a Stranger?" *The Wall Street Journal*, May 10–11, 2014, C12; J. Queenan, "A Word to the Wise," *The Wall Street Journal*, February 8–9, 2014, C1–C2; and S. Reddy, "The Trick to Getting People to Take the Stairs? Just Ask," *The Wall Street Journal*, February 17, 2015, R4.

The opinions provided here are of the managers and authors only and do not necessarily reflect those of their organizations. The authors or managers are not responsible for any errors or omissions, or for the results obtained from the use of this information. In no event will the authors or managers, or their related partnerships or corporations thereof, be liable to you or anyone else for any decision made or action taken in reliance on the opinions provided here.

of all the needs, groups composed of employees with a high nAff tend to perform the best, exhibit the most open communication, and experience the least amount of conflict.[20] Both nAff and nPow tend to be closely related to managerial success. The best managers may be high in their need for power and low in their need for affiliation.[21]

Additional research on Cameroonian and German adults suggests that our personalities may affect whether we can satisfy these needs. For example, a high degree of neuroticism can prevent one from fulfilling the nAff, whereas agreeableness supports fulfillment of this need; interestingly, extraversion had no significant effect.[22]

The degree to which we have each of the three needs is difficult to measure, and therefore the theory is difficult to put into practice. A behavior may be directed at satisfying many different needs, and many different behaviors may be directed at satisfying one given need, making needs difficult to isolate and examine.[23] It is more common to find situations in which managers aware of these motivational drivers label employees based on observations made over time. Therefore, the concepts are helpful, but they are not often used objectively.

Contemporary Theories of Motivation

7-3 Contrast the elements of self-determination theory and goal-setting theory.

Contemporary theories of motivation have one thing in common: Each has a reasonable degree of valid supporting documentation. We call them "contemporary theories" because they represent the latest thinking in explaining employee motivation. This doesn't mean they are unquestionably right, however.

Self-Determination Theory

"It's strange," said Marcia. "I started work at the Humane Society as a volunteer. I put in 15 hours a week helping people adopt pets. I loved coming to work; but then, 3 months ago, they hired me full-time at $11 an hour. I'm doing the same work I did before. But I'm not finding it as much fun."

self-determination theory A meta-theory of motivation at work that is concerned with autonomy, intrinsic motivation, extrinsic motivation, and the satisfaction of psychological work needs.

cognitive evaluation theory A sub-theory of self-determination theory in which extrinsic rewards for behavior tend to decrease the overall level of motivation, if the rewards are seen as controlling or reduce their sense of competence.

Does Marcia's reaction seem counterintuitive? There's an explanation for it. It can be found in **self-determination theory**, which proposes (in part) that people prefer to feel they have control over their actions, and anything that makes a previously enjoyed task feel more like an obligation than a freely chosen activity undermines motivation.[24] The theory is widely used in psychology, management, education, and medical research.

Much research on self-determination theory in OB has focused on **cognitive evaluation theory**, a complementary theory hypothesizing that extrinsic rewards reduce intrinsic interest in a task. When people are paid for work, it feels less like something they *want* to do and more like something they *have* to do. Self-determination theory proposes that, in addition to being driven by a need for autonomy, people seek ways to achieve competence and make positive connections with others. Of all the three needs, however, the autonomy need is the most important for attitudinal and affective outcomes, whereas the competence need appears to be most important for predicting performance.[25]

What does self-determination theory suggest about providing rewards? It suggests that some caution in the use of extrinsic rewards to motivate is wise and that pursuing goals from intrinsic motives (such as a strong interest in the work itself) is more sustaining to human motivation than are extrinsic rewards. Similarly, cognitive evaluation theory suggests that providing extrinsic incentives may, in many cases, undermine intrinsic motivation. For example, if a computer programmer values writing code because she likes to solve problems, a bonus for writing a certain number of lines of code every day could feel coercive, and her intrinsic motivation would suffer. She may or may not increase her number of lines of code per day in response to the extrinsic motivator. In support, a recent meta-analysis confirms that intrinsic motivation contributes to the quality of work, while incentives contribute to the quantity of work. Although intrinsic motivation predicts performance regardless of incentives, it may be less of a predictor when incentives are tied to performance directly (such as with monetary bonuses) rather than indirectly.[26]

self-concordance The degree to which people's reasons for pursuing goals are consistent with their interests and core values.

A more recent outgrowth of self-determination theory is **self-concordance**, which considers how strongly people's reasons for pursuing goals are consistent with their interests and core values. OB research suggests that people who pursue work goals for intrinsic reasons are more satisfied with their jobs, feel they fit into their organizations better, and may perform better.[27] Across cultures, if individuals pursue goals because of intrinsic interest, they are more likely to attain goals, are happier when they do so, and are happy even when they are unable to attain them.[28] Why? Because the process of striving toward goals is fun regardless of whether the goal is achieved. Recent research reveals that when people do not enjoy their work for intrinsic reasons, those who work because they feel obligated to do so can still perform acceptably, though

Myth or Science?

Helping Others and Being a Good Citizen Is Good for Your Career

We might think we should motivate employees to display organizational citizenship behavior (OCB), and that helping others would benefit their careers. We would probably also believe our own OCB will yield us career benefits. Surprisingly, there is some evidence that these assumptions are false, at least in certain organizations. Why?

In some organizations, employees are evaluated more on *how* their work gets done than on how much they do. If they possess the requisite knowledge and skills, or if they demonstrate the right behaviors on the job (for example, always greeting customers with a smile), they are determined by management to be motivated, "good" performers. In these situations, OCBs are considered as the next higher level of good employee behavior. Employees' careers thus benefit because of their helpfulness toward coworkers.

In other organizations, however, employees are evaluated more on *what* gets done. Here, employees are determined to be "good" performers if they meet objective goals such as billing clients a certain number of hours or reaching a certain sales volume. When managers overlook employee OCB, frown on helpful behaviors, or create an overly competitive organizational culture, employees become unmotivated to continue their helpful actions. Those who still engage in OCB can find their career progress is slowed when they take time away from core tasks to be helpful.

The upshot? There may be a tradeoff between being a good performer and being a good citizen. In organizations that focus more on behaviors, following your motivation to be a good citizen can help to accomplish your career goals. However, in organizations that focus more on objective outcomes, you may need to consider the cost of your good deeds.

Sources: Based on D. M. Bergeron, "The Potential Paradox of Organizational Citizenship Behavior: Good Citizens at What Cost?" *Academy of Management Review* 32, no. 4 (2007); and D. M. Bergeron, A. J. Shipp, B. Rosen, and S. A. Furst, "Organizational Citizenship Behavior and Career Outcomes: The Cost of Being a Good Citizen," *Journal of Management* 39, no. 4 (2013): 958–84.

they experience higher levels of strain.[29] Research on Australian, British, and American employees suggests that organizations can increase certain behaviors of interest from their employees, such as environmentally sustainable behaviors (e.g., conserving energy and commuting), by connecting them with goals that are important to them.[30]

What does all this mean? For individuals, it means you should choose your job for reasons other than extrinsic rewards. For organizations, it means managers should provide intrinsic as well as extrinsic incentives. Managers need to make the work interesting, provide recognition, link organizational and employee goals, and support employee growth and development. Employees who feel that what they do is within their control and a result of free choice are likely to be more motivated by their work and committed to their employers.[31] Furthermore, employees can satisfy many of these needs through helping others.[32]

Goal-Setting Theory

goal-setting theory A theory stating that specific and difficult goals, with feedback, lead to higher performance.

You've likely heard this sentiment several times: "Just do your best. That's all anyone can ask." But what does "do your best" mean? Do we ever know whether we've achieved that vague goal? Research on **goal-setting theory**, proposed by Edwin Locke, reveals the impressive effects of goal specificity, challenge, and feedback on performance. Under the theory, intentions to work toward a goal are considered a major source of work motivation.[33]

Goal-setting theory is well supported. Evidence strongly suggests that *specific* goals increase performance; that *difficult* goals, when accepted, result in higher performance than do easy goals; and that *feedback* leads to higher performance than does nonfeedback.[34] Why? First, specificity itself seems to act as an internal stimulus. When a trucker commits to making 12 round-trip hauls between Toronto and New York each week, this intention gives him a specific objective to attain. All things being equal, he will outperform a counterpart with no goals or the generalized goal "do your best."

Second, if factors such as acceptance of goals are held constant, the more difficult the goal, the higher the level of performance. Of course, it's logical to assume easier goals are more likely to be accepted. But once a hard task has been accepted, we can expect the employee to exert a high level of effort to try to achieve it.

In six years since its inception, Mukesh Bansal and Ankit Nagori have grown cult.fit, a health and fitness platform to provide a mix of online and offline services, in 200+ centres in more than 20 cities across India.[35] The challenging goal of "making health easy" for all Indians motivates employees to exert a high level of effort in giving customers challenging, caring, and meaningful advice and service.[36]

Source: Shashank.Agarwal.shutterstock.com

Third, people do better when they get feedback on how well they are progressing toward their goals because it helps identify discrepancies between what they have done and what they want to do next—that is, feedback guides behavior. For example, managers who coach their sales employees can directly facilitate sales goal attainment if the managers are good at coaching.[37] But all feedback is not equally potent. Self-generated feedback—with which employees can monitor their own progress or receive feedback from the task process itself—is more powerful than externally generated feedback.[38]

If employees can participate in the setting of their own goals, will they try harder? The evidence is mixed, although across studies it appears that they will not perform any better.[39] In some studies, participatively set goals yielded superior performance; in others, individuals performed best when assigned goals by their boss. One study in China found, for instance, that participative team goal setting improved team outcomes.[40] Another study found that participation results in more achievable goals for individuals.[41] Without participation, the individual pursuing the goal needs to clearly understand the goal's purpose and importance.[42]

Three personal factors influence the goals–performance relationship: *goal commitment, task characteristics,* and *national culture.*

Goal Commitment Goal-setting theory assumes an individual is committed to the goal and determined not to lower or abandon it. The individual (1) believes he or she can achieve the goal and (2) wants to achieve it.[43] Goal commitment is most likely to occur when employees expect that their efforts will pay off in goal attainment, when people of higher status are watching and aware of the goal, when accomplishing the goal is attractive to them, and when they actively participate in goal setting.[44]

Task Characteristics Goals themselves seem to affect performance more strongly when tasks are simple rather than complex, and when the tasks are independent rather than interdependent.[45] On interdependent tasks, group goals along with delegation of tasks are preferable. Paradoxically, goal abandonment following an initial failure is more likely for individuals who self-affirm their core values, possibly because they internalize the implications of failure more strongly than others do.[46]

National Culture Setting specific, difficult, individual goals may have different effects in different cultures. In collectivistic and high power-distance cultures, achievable moderate goals can be more motivating than difficult ones.[47] Assigned goals appear to generate greater goal commitment in high than in low power-distance cultures.[48] However, research has not shown that group-based goals are more effective in collectivist than in individualist cultures. More research is needed to assess how goal constructs might differ across cultures.

Although goal setting has positive outcomes, it's not unequivocally beneficial. For example, some goals may be *too* effective.[49] When learning something is important, goals related to performance undermine adaptation and creativity because people become too focused on outcomes and ignore the learning process. Nor are all goals equally effective. For rote tasks with quantifiable standards of productivity, goals that reward quantity can be highly motivating. For other jobs that require complex thinking and personal investment, goals and rewards for quantity may not be effective.[50] And individuals may fail to give up on an unattainable goal even when it might be beneficial to do so.

promotion focus A self-regulation strategy that involves striving for goals through advancement and accomplishment.

prevention focus A self-regulation strategy that involves striving for goals by fulfilling duties and obligations.

Research has found that people differ in the way they regulate their thoughts and behaviors during goal pursuit.[51] Generally, people fall into one of two categories, though they could belong to both. Those with a **promotion focus** strive for advancement and accomplishment, and approach conditions that move them closer toward desired goals. This concept is similar to the approach side of the approach-avoidance framework discussed in Chapter 4. Those with a **prevention focus** strive to fulfill duties and obligations and avoid conditions that pull them away from desired goals. Aspects of this concept are similar to the avoidance side of the approach-avoidance framework. Although you would be right in noting that both strategies are in the service of goal accomplishment, the way they get there is quite different. As an example, consider studying for an exam. You could engage in promotion-focused activities such as reading class materials, or you could engage in prevention-focused activities such as refraining from doing things that would get in the way of studying, such as playing video games.

You may ask, "Which is the better strategy?" Well, the answer depends on the outcome you are striving for. A promotion (but not a prevention) focus is related to higher levels of task performance, citizenship behavior, and innovation; a prevention (but not a promotion) focus is related to safety performance. Ideally, it's probably best to be both promotion- *and* prevention-oriented.[52] Keep in mind that a person's job satisfaction is more heavily affected by low success when that person has an avoidance (prevention) outlook,[53] so set achievable goals, remove distractions, and provide structure for these individuals.[54]

Implementing Goal Setting How do managers make goal-setting theory operational? That's often left up to the individual. Some managers set aggressive performance targets—what General Electric called "stretch goals." Some leaders, Baba Kalyani of Bharat Forge and Mukesh Ambani of Reliance Industries, are known for their demanding performance goals. But many managers don't set goals. When asked whether their jobs had clearly defined goals, a minority of survey respondents said yes.[55]

management by objectives (MBO) A program that encompasses specific goals, participatively set, for an explicit time period, with feedback on goal progress.

A more systematic way to utilize goal setting is with **management by objectives (MBO)**, an initiative most popular in the 1970s but still used today.[56] MBO emphasizes participatively set goals that are tangible, verifiable, and measurable. As Exhibit 7-4 shows, the organization's overall objectives are translated into specific cascading objectives for each level (divisional, departmental, individual). But because lower-unit managers jointly participate in setting their own goals, MBO works from the bottom up as well as from the top down. The result is a hierarchy that links objectives at one level to those at the next. For the individual employee, MBO provides specific personal performance objectives.

Four ingredients are common to MBO programs: goal specificity, participation in decision making (including the setting of goals or objectives), an explicit time period, and performance feedback.[57] Many elements in MBO programs match the propositions of goal-setting theory.

You'll find MBO programs in many business, health care, educational, government, and nonprofit organizations, and many of these programs have led to a performance gain.[58] A version of MBO, called management by objectives and results (MBOR), has been used for 30 years in the governments of Denmark, Norway, and Sweden.[59] However, the popularity of these programs does not mean they always work.[60] When MBO fails, the culprits tend to be unrealistic expectations, lack of commitment by top management, and inability or unwillingness to allocate rewards based on goal accomplishment.

Exhibit 7-4 Cascading of Objectives

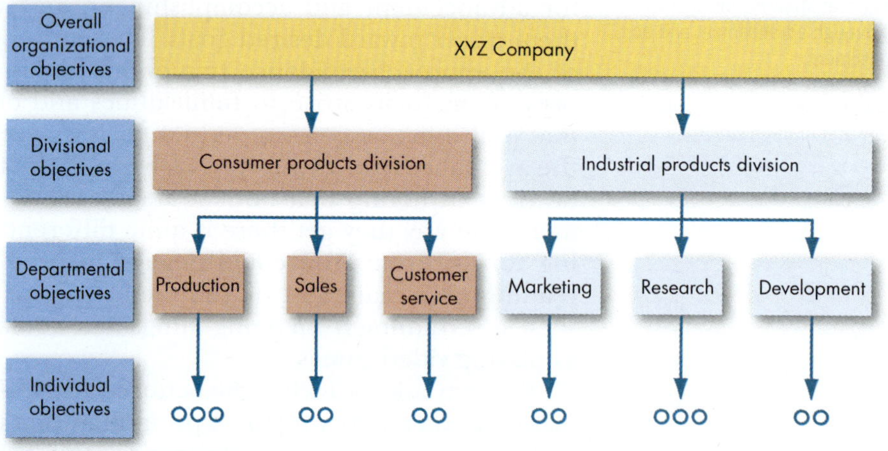

Goal Setting and Ethics The relationship between goal setting and ethics is quite complex: If we emphasize the attainment of goals, what is the cost? The answer is probably found in the standards we set for goal achievement. For example, when money is tied to goal attainment, we may focus on getting the money and become willing to compromise ourselves ethically. If we are instead primed with thoughts about how we are spending our time when we are pursuing the goal, we are more likely to act more ethically.[61] However, this result is limited to thoughts about how we are spending our time. If we are put under time pressure and worry as a result, thoughts about time turn against us. Time pressure often increases as we are nearing a goal, which can tempt us to act unethically to achieve it.[62] Specifically, we may forego mastering tasks and adopt avoidance techniques so we don't look bad,[63] both of which can incline us toward unethical choices.

Other Contemporary Theories of Motivation

7-4 Understand the differences among self-efficacy theory, reinforcement theory, and expectancy theory.

Self-determination theory and goal-setting theory are well supported contemporary theories of motivation. But they are far from the only noteworthy OB theories on the subject. Self-efficacy, reinforcement, and expectancy theories reveal different aspects of our motivational processes and tendencies. We begin with the concept of self-efficacy.

Self-Efficacy Theory

self-efficacy theory An individual's belief that they are capable of performing a task.

Self-efficacy theory, a component of *social cognitive theory* or *social-learning theory,* refers to an individual's belief that he or she is capable of performing a task.[64] The higher your self-efficacy, the more confidence you have in your ability to succeed. So, in difficult situations, people with low self-efficacy are more likely to lessen their effort or give up altogether, while those with high self-efficacy will try harder to master the challenge.[65] Self-efficacy can (but not always) create a positive spiral in which those with high efficacy become more engaged in their tasks and then in turn increase performance, which increases efficacy further.[66] One study introduced a further explanation: Self-efficacy was associated with a higher level of focused attention, which led to increased task performance.[67]

Feedback influences self-efficacy; individuals high in self-efficacy seem to respond to negative feedback with increased effort and motivation, while those low in self-efficacy are likely to lessen their effort after negative feedback.[68] Changes in self-efficacy over time are related to changes in creative performance as well.[69] How can managers help their employees achieve high levels of self-efficacy? By bringing goal-setting theory and self-efficacy theory together.

Goal-setting theory and self-efficacy theory don't compete with each other; they complement each other. As Exhibit 7-5 shows, employees whose managers set difficult goals for them have a higher level of self-efficacy and set higher goals for their own performance. Why? Setting difficult goals for people communicates your confidence in them.

Increasing Self-Efficacy in Yourself The researcher who developed self-efficacy theory, Albert Bandura, proposes four ways that self-efficacy can be increased:[70]

1. Enactive mastery.
2. Vicarious modeling.
3. Verbal persuasion.
4. Arousal.

The most important source of increasing self-efficacy is *enactive mastery*—that is, gaining relevant experience with the task or job. If you've been able to do the job successfully in the past, you're more confident that you can do it in the future.

Exhibit 7-5 **Joint Effects of Goals and Self-Efficacy on Performance**

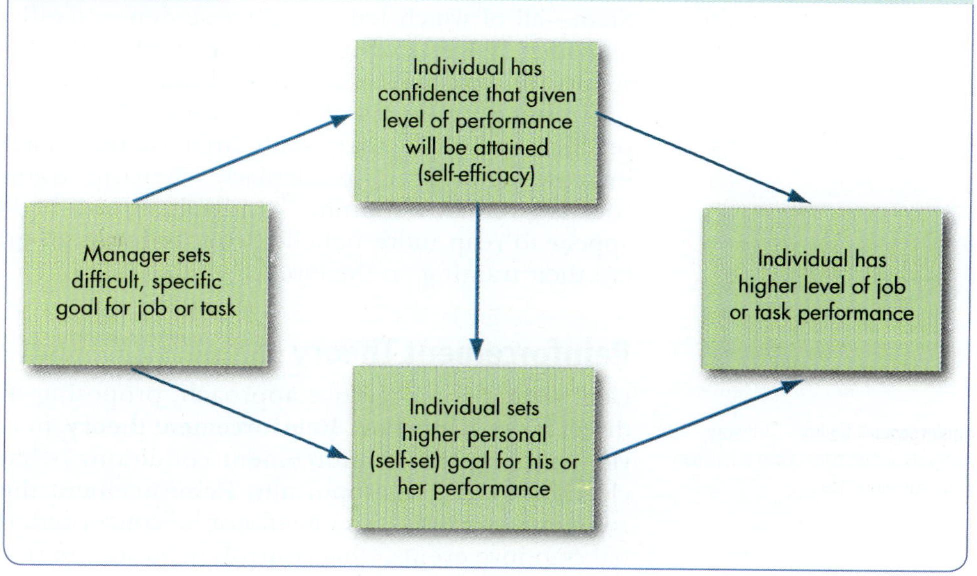

Source: Based on E. A. Locke and G. P. Latham, "Building a Practically Useful Theory of Goal Setting and Task Motivation: A 35-Year Odyssey," *American Psychologist* (September 2002): 705–17.

The second source is *vicarious modeling*—becoming more confident because you see someone else doing the task. If your friend quits smoking, it increases your confidence that you can quit, too. Vicarious modeling is most effective when you see yourself as similar to the person you are observing. Watching Tiger Woods play a difficult golf shot might not increase your confidence in being able to play the shot yourself, but watching a golfer with a handicap similar to yours is persuasive.

The third source is *verbal persuasion*: We become more confident when someone convinces us we have the skills necessary to be successful. Motivational speakers use this tactic.

Fourth, *arousal* increases self-efficacy. Arousal leads to an energized state, so we get "psyched up," feel up to the task, and perform better. But if the task requires a steady, lower-key perspective (say, carefully editing a manuscript), arousal may in fact hurt performance even as it increases self-efficacy because we might hurry through the task.

Intelligence and personality are absent from Bandura's list, but they too can increase self-efficacy.[71] People who are intelligent, conscientious, and emotionally stable are so much more likely to have high self-efficacy that some researchers argue that self-efficacy is less important than prior research would suggest.[72] They believe it is partially a by-product in a smart person with a confident personality.

Influencing Self-Efficacy in Others The best way for a manager to use verbal persuasion is through the *Pygmalion effect,* a term based on a Greek myth about a sculptor (Pygmalion) who fell in love with a statue he carved. The Pygmalion effect is a form of *self-fulfilling prophecy* in which believing something can make it true. Here, it is often used to describe "that what one person expects of another can come to serve a self-fulfilling prophecy."[73] An example should make this clear. In some studies, teachers were told their students had very high IQ scores when, in fact, they spanned a range from high to low. Consistent with the Pygmalion effect, the teachers spent more time with the students they *thought* were smart, gave them more challenging assignments, and expected more of them—all of which led to higher student self-efficacy and better achievement outcomes.[74] This strategy has been used in the workplace too, with replicable results and enhanced effects when leader–subordinate relationships are strong.[75]

Training programs often make use of enactive mastery by having people practice and build their skills. In fact, one reason training works is that it increases self-efficacy, particularly when the training is interactive and feedback is given after training.[76] Individuals with higher levels of self-efficacy also appear to reap more benefits from training programs and are more likely to use their training on the job.[77]

Reinforcement Theory

reinforcement theory A theory suggesting that behavior is a function of its consequences.

Goal setting is a cognitive approach, proposing that an individual's purposes direct his or her action. **Reinforcement theory**, in contrast, takes a behavioristic view, arguing that reinforcement conditions behavior.[78] The two theories are clearly at odds philosophically. Reinforcement theorists see behavior as environmentally caused. You need not be concerned, they would argue, with internal cognitive events; what controls behavior are reinforcers—any consequences that, when they immediately follow responses, increase the probability that the behavior will be repeated.

Reinforcement theory ignores the inner state of the individual and concentrates solely on what happens when he or she takes some action. Because it does not concern itself with what initiates behavior, it is not, strictly speaking, a theory of motivation. But it does provide a powerful means of analyzing what controls behavior, and therefore we typically consider it in discussions of motivation.

Operant Conditioning/Behaviorism and Reinforcement *Operant conditioning theory*, probably the most relevant component of reinforcement theory for management, argues that people learn to behave to get something they want or to avoid something they don't want. Unlike reflexive or unlearned behavior, operant behavior is influenced by the reinforcement or lack of reinforcement brought about by consequences. Reinforcement strengthens a behavior and increases the likelihood it will be repeated.

B. F. Skinner, one of the most prominent advocates of operant conditioning, demonstrated that people will most likely engage in desired behaviors if they are positively reinforced for doing so; rewards are most effective if they immediately follow the desired response; and behavior that is not rewarded, or is punished, is less likely to be repeated. The concept of operant conditioning was part of Skinner's broader concept of **behaviorism**, which argues that behavior follows stimuli in a relatively unthinking manner. Skinner's form of radical behaviorism rejects feelings, thoughts, and other states of mind as causes of behavior. In short, people learn to associate stimulus and response, but their conscious awareness of this association is irrelevant.[79]

behaviorism A theory stating that behavior follows stimuli in a relatively unthinking manner.

You can see illustrations of operant conditioning everywhere. For instance, a commissioned salesperson wanting to earn a sizable income finds doing so is contingent on generating high sales in his territory, so he sells as much as possible. Of course, the linkage can also teach individuals to engage in behaviors that work against the best interests of the organization. Assume your boss says that if you work overtime during the next three-week busy season, you'll be compensated for it at your next performance appraisal. However, when performance appraisal time comes, you are given no positive reinforcement for your overtime work. The next time your boss asks you to work overtime, what will you do? You'll probably decline!

Social-Learning Theory and Reinforcement Individuals can learn by being told or by observing what happens to other people, as well as through direct experience. Much of what we have learned comes from watching models—parents, teachers, peers, film and television performers, bosses, and so forth.[80] The view that we can learn through both observation and direct experience is called **social-learning theory**.[81]

social-learning theory The view that we can learn through both observation and direct experience.

Although social-learning theory is an extension of operant conditioning—that is, it assumes behavior is a function of consequences—it also acknowledges the effects of observational learning and perception. People respond to the way they perceive and define consequences, not to the objective consequences themselves.

Tech Mahindra, in 2018, rolled out facial recognition technology that recorded the attendance of their employees and the "mood of the workforce".[82] Bangalore-based EmpMonitor takes screenshots of the laptop of the employee laptop and collects the browsing history and the apps used by the employee during work hours.

An Ethical Choice

Motivated by Big Brother

Technology is a great thing. The Internet provides us with instant access to an abundance of information, and smartphones allow us to stay connected with others through e-mail, texting, and tweeting. Yet that ease of connectivity has also given employees the sinking feeling they are being watched—and they are right. But is tracking employees ethical?

Some companies are using technology to track their employees' activities, and some of this tracking is done in the name of science. For example, Bank of America Corp. wanted to learn whether face-to-face interaction made a difference to the productivity of its call center teams, so it asked around 100 workers to wear badges for a few weeks that tracked their whereabouts. Discovering that the most productive workers interacted most frequently with others, the company scheduled work breaks for groups rather than individually. This is a nice outcome, but how did the monitoring affect the behavior and motivation of the workers?

Other companies track employees to ensure that they are hard at work, which risks completely demotivating some. Accurate Biometrics, for example, uses computer monitoring to oversee its telecommuters. Says Timothy Daniels, VP of operations, looking at websites his employees have visited "enables us to keep a watchful eye without being overinvasive." Currently, around 70 percent of organizations monitor their employees.

Practically speaking, managers may not want to adopt technologies that demotivate their employees through micromanagement. Perhaps more important, though, how can they use monitoring technology ethically in workplace applications? First and foremost, employees should be informed that their activities will be tracked. Second, the purpose of tracking should be made clear to employees. Are workers being monitored to learn something that might help them and the organization as a whole? Or are they being monitored to ensure that they never slack off? Finally, it should be made clear which behaviors are inappropriate. Taking a legitimate work break is different from spending hours on a social networking site. These guidelines should increase the likelihood that monitoring programs are accepted and perceived to be fair.

Sources: Based on S. Shellenbarger, "Working from Home without Slacking Off," *The Wall Street Journal,* July 13–15, 2012, 29; R. Richmond, "3 Tips for Legally and Ethically Monitoring Employees Online," *Entrepreneur,* May 31, 2012, http://www.entrepreneur.com/article/223686; and R. E. Silverman, "Tracking Sensors Invade the Workplace," *The Wall Street Journal,* March 7, 2003, www.wsj.com.

Models are central to the social-learning viewpoint. Four processes determine their influence on an individual:

1. **Attentional processes.** People learn from a model only when they recognize and pay attention to its critical features. We tend to be most influenced by models that are attractive, repeatedly available, important to us, or similar to us (in our estimation).
2. **Retention processes.** A model's influence depends on how well the individual remembers the model's action after the model is no longer readily available.
3. **Motor reproduction processes.** After a person has seen a new behavior by observing the model, watching must be converted to doing. This process demonstrates that the individual can perform the modeled activities.
4. **Reinforcement processes.** Individuals are motivated to exhibit the modeled behavior if positive incentives or rewards are provided. Positively reinforced behaviors are given more attention, learned better, and performed more often.

At Thai Takenaka, a leading construction firm in Thailand, experienced employees teach younger workers construction management skills, building techniques, and the basics of craftsmanship through training by "looking, touching, and realization." This social-learning view helps employees succeed in meeting the firm's high standards of quality and efficiency.
Source: */Kyodo/Newscom

Expectancy Theory

expectancy theory A theory stating that the strength of a tendency to act in a certain way depends on the strength of an expectation that the act will be followed by a given outcome and on the attractiveness of that outcome to the individual.

One of the most widely accepted explanations of motivation is Victor Vroom's **expectancy theory**.[83] Although it has critics, most evidence supports the theory.[84]

Expectancy theory argues that the strength of our tendency to act a certain way depends on the strength of our expectation of a given outcome and its attractiveness. In practical terms, employees will be motivated to exert a high level of effort when they believe that it will lead to a good performance appraisal, that a good appraisal will lead to organizational rewards such as salary increases and/or intrinsic rewards, and that the rewards will satisfy their personal goals. The theory therefore focuses on three relationships (see Exhibit 7-6):

1. **Expectancy: the effort–performance relationship.** The probability perceived by the individual that exerting a given amount of effort will lead to performance.
2. **Instrumentality: the performance–reward relationship.** The degree to which the individual believes performing at a particular level will lead to the attainment of a desired outcome.

Exhibit 7-6 Expectancy Theory

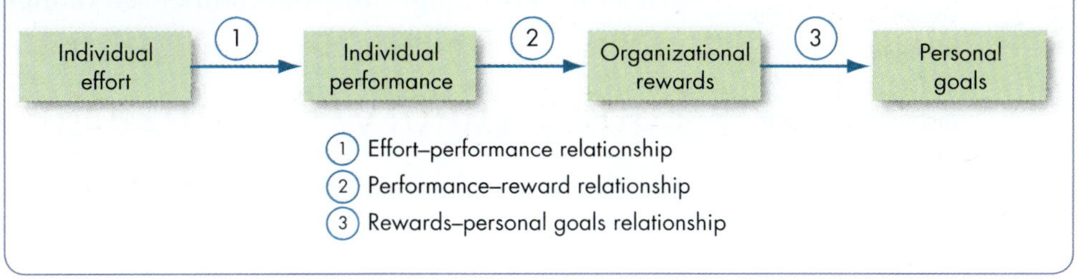

3. **Valence: the rewards–personal goals relationship.** The degree to which organizational rewards satisfy an individual's personal goals or needs and the attractiveness of those potential rewards for the individual.

Expectancy theory helps explain why a lot of workers aren't motivated on their jobs and do only the minimum necessary to get by. Let's frame the theory's three relationships as questions that employees need to answer in the affirmative if their motivation is to be maximized.

First, *if I give maximum effort, will it be recognized in my performance appraisal?* For many employees, the answer is no. Why? Their skill level may be deficient, which means no matter how hard they try, they're not likely to be high performers. Or the organization's performance appraisal system may be designed to assess nonperformance factors such as loyalty, initiative, or courage, which means more effort won't necessarily result in a higher evaluation. Another possibility is that employees, rightly or wrongly, perceive the boss doesn't like them. Thus, they expect a poor appraisal, regardless of effort. These examples suggest that people will be motivated only if they perceive a link between their effort and their performance.

Second, *if I get a good performance appraisal, will it lead to organizational rewards?* Many organizations reward things besides performance. When pay is based on factors such as having seniority, being cooperative, or "kissing up" to the boss, employees are likely to see the performance–reward relationship as weak and demotivating.

Finally, *if I'm rewarded, are the rewards attractive to me?* The employee works hard in the hope of getting a promotion but gets a pay raise instead. Or the employee wants a more interesting and challenging job but receives only a few words of praise. Unfortunately, many managers are limited in the rewards they can distribute, which makes it difficult to tailor rewards to individual employee needs. Some managers incorrectly assume all employees want the same thing, thus overlooking the motivational effects of differentiating rewards. In these cases, employee motivation is not maximized.

As a vivid example of how expectancy theory can work, consider stock analysts. They make their living trying to forecast a stock's future price; the accuracy of their buy, sell, or hold recommendations is what keeps them employed. But the dynamics are not so simple. Analysts place few sell ratings on stocks, although many stocks are both falling and rising in a steady market. Expectancy theory provides an explanation: Analysts who place a sell rating on a company's stock should balance the benefits they receive by being accurate against the risks they run by drawing that company's ire. What are these risks? They include public rebuke, professional blackballing, and exclusion from information. When analysts place a buy rating on a stock, they face no such trade-off because, obviously, companies love it when analysts recommend that investors buy their stock. So the incentive structure suggests the expected outcome of buy ratings is higher than the expected outcome of sell ratings, and that's why buy ratings vastly outnumber sell ratings.[85]

7-5 Describe the forms of organizational justice, including distributive justice, procedural justice, informational justice, and interactional justice.

Equity Theory/Organizational Justice

Aneesha is a student working toward a bachelor's degree in finance. To gain some work experience and increase her marketability, she accepted a summer internship in the finance department at a pharmaceutical company. She is

Exhibit 7-7 Equity Theory

Ratio Comparisons*	Perception
$\frac{O}{I_A} < \frac{O}{I_B}$	Inequity due to being underrewarded
$\frac{O}{I_A} = \frac{O}{I_B}$	Equity
$\frac{O}{I_A} > \frac{O}{I_B}$	Inequity due to being overrewarded

*Where $\frac{O}{I_A}$ represents the employee and $\frac{O}{I_B}$ represents relevant others

quite pleased at the pay: ₹20,000 a month is more than other students in her cohort receive for their summer internships. At work she meets Biprajeet, a recent graduate working as a middle manager in the same finance department. Biprajeet makes ₹40,000 a month.

On the job, Aneesha is a go-getter. She's engaged, satisfied, and always seems willing to help others. Biprajeet is the opposite. He often seems disinterested in his job and entertains thoughts about quitting. When pressed one day about why he is unhappy, Biprajeet cites his pay as the main reason. Specifically, he tells Aneesha that, compared to managers at other pharmaceutical companies, he makes much less. "It isn't fair," he complains. "I work just as hard as they do, yet I don't make as much. Maybe I should go work for the competition."

How could someone making ₹40,000 a month be less satisfied with his or her pay than someone making ₹20,000 a month and be less motivated as a result? The answer lies in **equity theory** and, more broadly, in principles of organizational justice.[86] According to equity theory, employees compare what they get from their job (their "outcomes," such as pay, promotions, recognition, or a bigger office) to what they put into it (their "inputs," such as effort, experience, and education). They take the ratio of their outcomes to their inputs and compare it to the ratio of others, usually someone similar like a coworker or someone doing the same job. This is shown in Exhibit 7-7. If we believe our ratio is equal to those with whom we compare ourselves, a state of equity exists and we perceive our situation as fair, although some research suggests that inputs and outputs matter as a function of age: the older you become, the more you value task contributions (inputs) than what you get from them (outputs).[87]

equity theory A theory stating that individuals compare their job inputs and outcomes with those of others and then respond to eliminate any inequities.

Based on equity theory, employees who perceive inequity will make one of six choices:[88]

1. **Change inputs** (exert less effort if underpaid or more if overpaid).
2. **Change outcomes** (individuals paid on a piece-rate basis can increase their pay by producing a higher quantity of units of lower quality).
3. **Distort perceptions of self** ("I used to think I worked at a moderate pace, but now I realize I work a lot harder than everyone else").
4. **Distort perceptions of others** ("Mike's job isn't as desirable as I thought").
5. **Choose a different referent** ("I may not make as much as my brother-in-law, but I'm doing a lot better than my Dad did when he was my age").
6. **Leave the field** (quit the job).

Equity theory has support from some researchers but not from all.[89] There are some concerns with the propositions. First, inequities created by overpayment do not seem to significantly affect behavior in most work situations. So don't expect an employee who feels overpaid to give back part of his salary or put in more hours to make up for the inequity. Although individuals may sometimes perceive that they are overrewarded, they restore equity by rationalizing their situation ("I'm worth it because I work harder than everyone else"). Second, not everyone is equally equity-sensitive, for various reasons, including feelings of entitlement.[90] Others prefer the outcome–input ratios to be lower than the referent comparisons. Predictions from equity theory are not likely to be very accurate about these "benevolent types."[91]

organizational justice An overall perception of what is fair in the workplace, composed of distributive, procedural, informational, and interpersonal justice.

Although equity theory's propositions have not all held up, the hypothesis serves as an important precursor to the study of **organizational justice** or, more simply, fairness in the workplace.[92] Organizational justice is concerned more broadly with how employees feel authorities and decision makers at work treat them. For example, Westside stores provide great customer service. Its secret! Empowering employees to make decisions that directly affect how they work as well as including them in the decision-making process, giving them a sense of motivation through procedural justice. Employees are empowered to provide excellent customer service. When a distraught customer arrived at how the color had bled for a dress, she had bought 6 months after she bought the dress the customer service just took back the dress and asked if she would like the money back or want a store credit. For the most part, employees evaluate how fairly they are treated, as shown in Exhibit 7-8.

Exhibit 7-8 **Model of Organizational Justice**

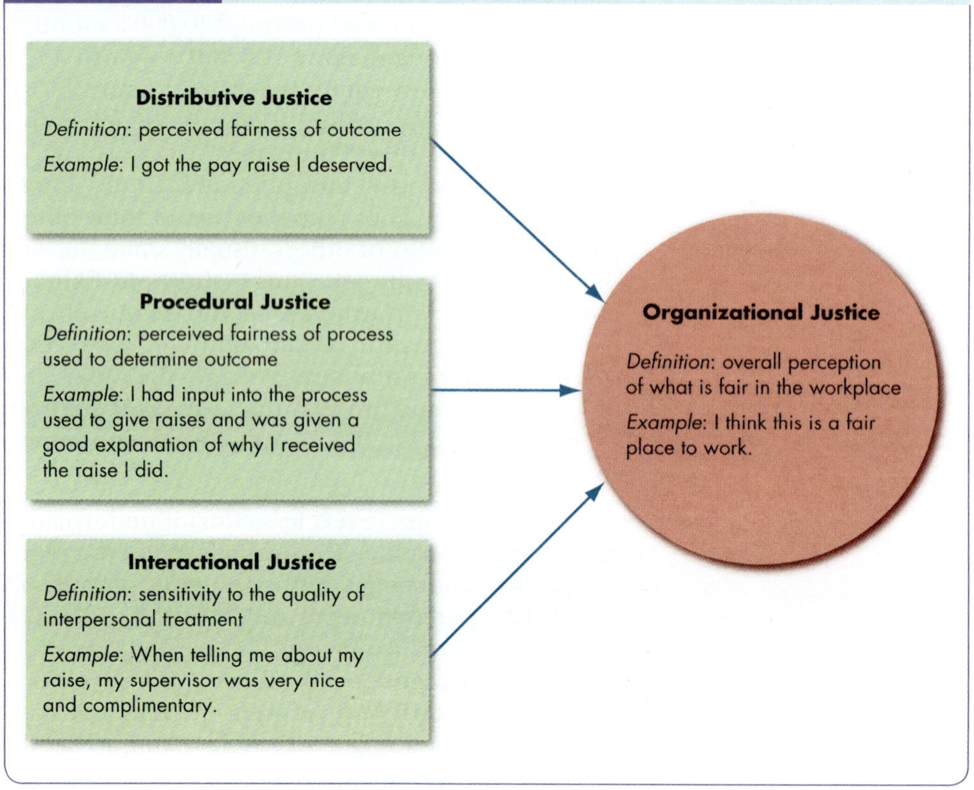

Distributive Justice

distributive justice Perceived fairness of the amount and allocation of rewards among individuals.

Distributive justice is concerned with the fairness of the outcomes, such as pay and recognition, that employees receive.[93] Outcomes can be allocated in many ways. For example, we could distribute raises equally among employees, or we could base raises on which employees need money the most. As we said in our discussion about equity theory, however, employees tend to perceive their outcomes are fairest when they are distributed equitably.

Does the same logic apply to teams? At first glance, distributing rewards equally among team members would seem to be best for boosting morale and teamwork—that way, no one is favored more than another. A study of U.S. National Hockey League teams suggests otherwise. Differentiating the pay of team members based on their inputs (how well they performed in games) attracted better players to the team, made it more likely that they would stay, and increased team performance.[94]

The way we have described things so far, it would seem that individuals gauge distributive justice and equity in a rational, calculative way as they compare their outcome–input ratios to those of others. But the experience of justice, and especially of injustice, is often not so cold and calculated. Instead, people base distributive judgments on a feeling or an emotional reaction to the way they think they are being treated relative to others, and their reactions are often "hot" and emotional rather than cool and rational.[95]

Consider the case of the two sports coaches who reportedly assaulted five trainees at the National Sports Academy in Bijapur District of Chhattisgarh. The reason of assault being the trainees' complaint that they were discriminated and not being given enough attention to. The matter has been reported to the police.[96]

Procedural Justice

procedural justice The perceived fairness of the process used to determine the distribution of rewards.

Although employees care a lot about *what* outcomes are distributed (distributive justice), they also care about *how* they are distributed. While distributive justice looks at *what* outcomes are allocated, **procedural justice** examines *how*.[97] For one, employees perceive that procedures are fairer when they are given a say in the decision-making process. Having direct influence over how decisions are made, or at the very least being able to present our opinion to decision makers, creates a sense of control and makes us feel empowered (we discuss empowerment more in the next chapter). Employees also perceive that procedures are fairer when decision makers follow several rules, including making decisions in a consistent manner (across people and over time), avoiding bias (not favoring one group or person over another), using accurate information, considering the groups or people that their decisions affect, acting ethically, and remaining open to appeals or correction.

If outcomes are favorable and individuals get what they want, they care less about the process, so procedural justice doesn't matter as much when distributions are perceived to be fair. It's when outcomes are unfavorable that people pay close attention to the process. If the process is judged to be fair, then employees are more accepting of unfavorable outcomes.[98] If employees are given a voice when experiencing unfavorable outcomes, an element of fair process, they will feel better about the situation, even when the outcomes continue to be poor.[99]

Think about it. If you are hoping for a raise and your manager informs you that you did not receive one, you'll probably want to know how raises were

Nordstrom is legendary for its customer service. Its secret? Empowering employees to make decisions that directly affect how they work as well as including them in the decision-making process, giving them a sense of motivation through procedural justice. Employees such as this cosmetician at a Nordstrom in Seattle, Washington, are empowered to provide excellent customer service. Legend has it that one Nordstrom representative drove all the way to an airport to bring a customer the bags she left at the store!
Source: B. O'Kane/Alamy Stock Photo

determined. If it turns out your manager allocated raises based on merit and you were simply outperformed by a coworker, then you're more likely to accept your manager's decision than if raises were based on favoritism. Of course, if you get the raise in the first place, then you'll be less concerned with how the decision was made.

Interactional Justice

Beyond outcomes and procedures, research has shown that employees care about two other types of fairness that have to do with the way they are treated during interactions with others. Both of these fall within the category of *interactional justice* (see Exhibit 7-8).[100]

informational justice The degree to which employees are provided truthful explanations for decisions.

Informational Justice The first type is **informational justice**, which reflects whether managers provide employees with explanations for key decisions and keep them informed of important organizational matters. The more detailed and candid managers are with employees, the more fairly treated those employees feel.

It may seem obvious that managers should be honest with their employees and not keep them in the dark about organizational matters; however, many managers are hesitant to share information. This is especially the case with bad news, which is uncomfortable for both the manager delivering it and the employee receiving it. Explanations for bad news are beneficial when they take the form of excuses after the fact ("I know this is bad, and I wanted to give you the office, but it wasn't my decision") rather than justifications ("I decided to give the office to Sam, but having it isn't a big deal").[101]

Interpersonal Justice The second type of justice relevant to interactions between managers and employees is **interpersonal justice**, which reflects whether employees are treated with dignity and respect. Compared to the other forms of justice we've discussed, interpersonal justice is unique because it can occur in everyday interactions between managers and employees.[102] This quality allows managers to take advantage of (or miss out on) opportunities to make their employees feel fairly treated. Many managers may view treating employees politely and respectfully as too soft, and instead choose more aggressive tactics out of a belief that doing so will be more motivating. Although displays of negative emotions such as anger may be motivating in some cases,[103] managers sometimes take this too far. Consider former Rutgers University men's basketball coach Mike Rice, who was caught on video verbally and even physically abusing players and was subsequently fired.[104]

Justice Outcomes

After all this talk about types of justice, how much does justice really matter to employees? A great deal, as it turns out. When employees feel fairly treated, they respond in many positive ways. All the types of justice discussed in this section have been linked to higher levels of task performance and citizenship behaviors such as helping coworkers, as well as lower levels of counterproductive behaviors such as shirking job duties.[105] Distributive and procedural justice are more strongly associated with task performance, while informational and interpersonal justice are more strongly associated with citizenship behavior. Even more physiological outcomes, such as how well employees sleep and the state of their health, have been linked to fair treatment.[106]

Why does justice have these positive effects? Fair treatment enhances commitment to the organization and makes employees feel that the organization cares about their well-being. In addition, employees who feel fairly treated trust their supervisors more, which reduces uncertainty and fear of being exploited by the organization. Fair treatment elicits positive emotions, which in turn prompts behaviors like citizenship.[107]

Despite all attempts to enhance fairness, perceived injustices are still likely to occur. Fairness is often subjective; what one person sees as unfair, another may see as perfectly appropriate. In general, people see allocations or procedures favoring themselves as fair.[108] However, if an organization is not consistent in how justly it treats its employees, and employees feel like they are on a rollercoaster of abuse and fair treatment, then they are more likely to become detached, cooperate less, and have lower job attitudes.[109]

Others' Reactions to Injustice Your coworker' reactions to injustice can be just as important as your own. Research is beginning to suggest that *third-party*, or observer, reactions to injustice can have a substantial effect. Let's say that you read about massive, unannounced layoffs at a restaurant chain you frequent. You find out that employees were let go without any warning and were not given any assistance in finding alternative arrangements. Would you continue to go to this restaurant? Research suggests that you may not.[110] People also make attributions when judging justice rule violations. Research suggests that violation of justice norms is gendered: Women are judged more harshly when they violate interactional norms than when they violate procedural norms.[111]

Why and how do we make judgments like this? One such model of third-party injustice suggests that several factors play into how we react: (1) our own traits and characteristics, (2) the transgressor's and victim's traits and characteristics (including an attribution of blame), and (3) the specifics of the justice event or situation.[112] In turn, those who observed mistreatment perceive unfairness and react accordingly. For example, a coworker watches your supervisor berate you: If you deserved it, the coworker would probably be content; if you didn't, the coworker would probably be angry with your supervisor.[113] Research also suggests that how your coworkers and supervisors treat *customers* also affects your justice perceptions. Two studies in health care organizations found that patient mistreatment by one's supervisor led to employee distrust and less cooperative behavior.[114]

Promoting Justice

How can an organization affect the justice perceptions and rule adherence of its managers? This depends on the motivation of each manager. Some managers are likely to calculate justice by their degree of adherence to the justice rules of the organization. These managers will try to gain greater subordinate compliance with behavioral expectations, create an identity of being fair to their employees, or establish norms of fairness. Other managers may be motivated in justice decisions by their emotions. When they have a high positive affect and/or a low negative affect, these managers are most likely to act fairly.

It might be tempting for organizations to adopt strong justice guidelines in attempts to mandate managerial behavior, but this isn't likely to be universally effective. In cases where managers have more rules and less discretion, those who calculate justice are more likely to act fairly, but managers whose justice behavior follows from their affect may act more fairly when they have greater discretion.[115]

Culture and Justice

Across nations, the same basic principles of procedural justice are respected: Workers around the world prefer rewards based on performance and skills over rewards based on seniority.[116] However, inputs and outcomes are valued differently in various cultures.[117]

We may think of justice differences in terms of Hofstede's cultural dimensions (see Chapter 4). One large-scale study of over 190,000 employees in 32 countries and regions suggested that justice perceptions are most important to people in countries with individualistic, feminine, uncertainty avoidance, and low power-distance values.[118] Organizations can tailor programs to meet these justice expectations. For example, in countries that are highest in individualism, such as Australia and the United States, competitive pay plans and rewards for superior individual performance enhance feelings of justice. In countries dominated by uncertainty avoidance, such as France, fixed pay compensation and employee participation may help employees feel more secure. The dominant dimension in Sweden is femininity, so relational concerns are considered important. Swedish organizations may therefore want to provide work-life balance initiatives and social recognition. Austria, in contrast, has a strong low power-distance value. Ethical concerns may be foremost to individuals in perceiving justice in Austrian organizations, so it will be important for organizations to justify inequality between leaders and workers and to provide symbols of ethical leadership.

We can also look at other cultural factors. Some cultures emphasize status over individual achievement as a basis for allocating resources. Materialistic cultures are more likely to see cash compensation and rewards as the most relevant outcomes of work, whereas relational cultures will see social rewards and status as important outcomes. International managers must consider the cultural preferences of each group of employees when determining what is fair in different contexts.

Job Engagement

7-6 Identify the implications of employee job engagement for managers.

job engagement The investment of an employee's physical, cognitive, and emotional energies into job performance.

When Joseph reports to his job as a hospital nurse, it seems that everything else in his life goes away, and he becomes completely absorbed in what he is doing. His emotions, thoughts, and behavior are all directed toward patient care. In fact, he can get so caught up in his work that he isn't even aware of how long he's been there. Because of this total commitment, he is more effective in providing patient care and feels uplifted by his time at work.

Joseph has a high level of **job engagement**, the investment of an employee's physical, cognitive, and emotional energies into job performance.[119] Practicing managers and scholars have become interested in facilitating job engagement, believing factors deeper than liking a job or finding it interesting drives performance. Studies attempt to measure this deeper level of commitment. For example, one review found higher levels of engagement were associated with task performance and citizenship behavior.[120]

What makes people more likely to be engaged in their jobs? One key is the degree to which an employee believes it is meaningful to engage in work. This is partially determined by job characteristics and access to sufficient resources to work effectively.[121] Another factor is a match between the individual's values and those of the organization.[122] Leadership behaviors that inspire workers to a greater sense of mission also increase employee engagement.[123]

One of the critiques of the concept of engagement is that the construct is partially redundant with job attitudes like satisfaction or stress.[124] Other critics note there may be a dark side to engagement, as evidenced by positive relationships between engagement and work–family conflict.[125] It is possible individuals might grow so engaged in their work roles that family responsibilities become an unwelcome intrusion. Also, an overly high level of engagement can lead to a loss of perspective and ultimately burnout. Additional research exploring how engagement relates to these negative outcomes may help clarify whether some highly engaged employees might be getting "too much of a good thing."

Integrating Contemporary Theories of Motivation

7-7 Describe how the contemporary theories of motivation complement one another.

Our job might be simpler if, after presenting a half dozen theories, we could say only one was found valid. But many of the theories in this chapter are complementary. We now tie them together to help you understand their interrelationships.

Exhibit 7-9 integrates much of what we know about motivation. Its foundation is the expectancy model that was shown in Exhibit 7-8. Let's walk through Exhibit 7-9. (We will look at job design more closely in Chapter 8.)

We begin by explicitly recognizing that opportunities can either aid or hinder individual effort. The individual effort box on the left also has another arrow leading into it, from the person's goals. Consistent with goal-setting theory, the goals–effort loop is meant to remind us that goals direct behavior.

Exhibit 7-9 **Integrating Contemporary Theories of Motivation**

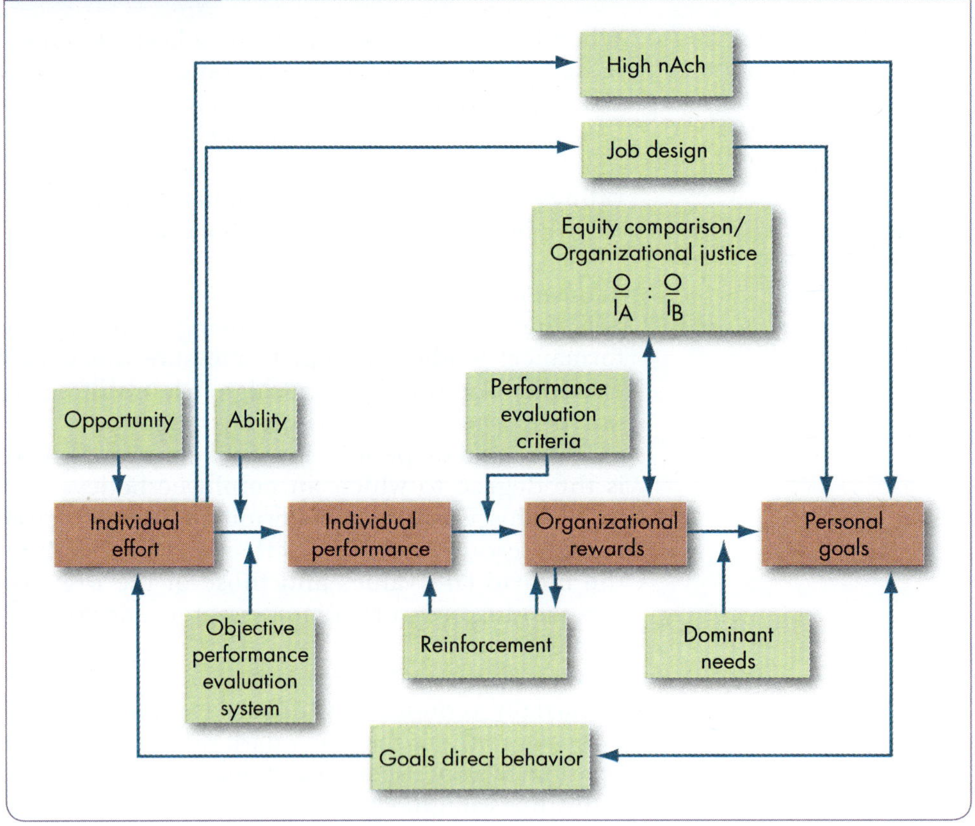

Expectancy theory predicts employees will exert a high level of effort if they perceive a strong relationship between effort and performance, performance and reward, and rewards and satisfaction of personal goals. Each of these relationships is, in turn, influenced by other factors. For effort to lead to good performance, the individual must have the ability to perform and perceive the performance appraisal system as fair and objective. The performance–reward relationship will be strong if the individual perceives that performance (rather than seniority, personal favorites, or other criteria) is rewarded. If cognitive evaluation theory were fully valid in the actual workplace, we would predict that basing rewards on performance should decrease the individual's intrinsic motivation. The final link in expectancy theory is the rewards–goals relationship. Motivation is high if the rewards for high performance satisfy the dominant needs consistent with individual goals.

A closer look at Exhibit 7-9 also reveals that the model considers achievement motivation, job design, reinforcement, and equity theories/organizational justice. A high achiever is not motivated by an organization's assessment of performance or organizational rewards, hence the jump from effort to personal goals for those with a high nAch. Remember, high achievers are internally driven as long as their jobs provide them with personal responsibility, feedback, and moderate risks. They are not concerned with the effort–performance, performance–reward, or rewards–goal linkages.

Reinforcement theory enters the model by recognizing that the organization's rewards reinforce the individual's performance. If employees see a reward system as "paying off" for good performance, the rewards will reinforce and encourage good performance. Rewards also play a key part in organizational justice research. Individuals judge the favorability of their outcomes (for example, their pay) relative to what others receive but also with respect to how they are treated: When people are disappointed in their rewards, they are likely to be sensitive to the perceived fairness of the procedures used and the consideration given to them by their supervisors.

Summary

Motivation describes the processes (e.g., intensity, direction, and persistence) underlying how employees and other individuals in the workplace direct their efforts toward a goal. Although not well supported, many early foundational theories of motivation focused on the needs that employees have along with the consequences of need satisfaction. More contemporary theories focus on topics such as intrinsic and extrinsic motivation; setting goals in organizations; self-efficacy; reinforcement; and our expectations regarding effort, performance, reward, and outcome relationships. Beyond these theories, various forms of organizational justice (e.g., distributive, procedural, and interactional), all deriving from equity theory, are important in motivating employees. Motivation is key to understanding employees' contributions to their work, including their job engagement. Overall, motivation underlies how and why employees exert effort to engage in performance activities, which in turn meet personal or organizational goals.

Implications for Managers

- Make sure extrinsic rewards for employees are not viewed as coercive but instead provide information about competence and relatedness.
- Either set or inspire your employees to set specific, difficult goals and provide quality, developmental feedback on their progress toward those goals.
- Try to align or tie employee goals to the goals of your organization.
- Model the types of behaviors you would like to see performed by your employees.
- Expectancy theory offers a powerful explanation of performance variables such as employee productivity, absenteeism, and turnover.
- When making decisions regarding resources in your organization, make sure to consider how the resources are being distributed (and who is affected), the fairness of the decision, and whether your actions demonstrate that you respect those involved.

Goals Get You to Where You Want to Be

POINT

Of course this is a true statement. Goal-setting theory is one of the best-supported theories in the motivation literature. Study after study has consistently shown the benefits of goals. Want to excel on a test, lose a certain amount of weight, secure a job with a particular income level, or improve your golf game? If you want to be a high performer, merely set a specific, difficult goal and let nature take its course. That goal will dominate your attention, cause you to focus, and make you try harder.

All too often, people are told by others to simply "do their best." Could anything be more vague? What does "do your best" actually mean? Maybe you feel that your "best" on one day is to muster a grade of 50 percent on an exam, while your "best" on another day is 80 percent. But if you were given a more difficult goal—say, to score a 95 on the exam—and you were committed to that goal, you would ultimately perform better.

Edwin Locke and Gary Latham, the researchers best known for goal-setting theory, put it best when they said: "The effects of goal setting are very reliable." In short, goal-setting theory is among the most valid and practical theories of motivation in organizational psychology.

COUNTERPOINT

Sure, a lot of research has shown the benefits of goal setting, but those studies ignore the harm that's often done. For one, how often have you set a "stretch" goal, only to see yourself later fail? Goals create anxiety and worry about reaching them, and they often create unrealistic expectations as well. Imagine those who set a goal to earn a promotion in a certain period of time (a specific, difficult goal), only to find themselves laid off once a recession hit. Or how about those who envision a retirement of leisure yet are forced to take on a part-time job or delay retirement altogether to continue making ends meet. When too many influential factors are out of our control, our difficult goals become impossible.

Or consider this: Goals can lead to unethical behavior and poorer performance. How many reports have you heard over the years about teachers who "fudged" students' test scores to achieve educational standards? When Ken O'Brian, a professional quarterback for the New York Jets, was penalized for every interception he threw, he achieved his goal of fewer interceptions quite easily—by refusing to throw the ball even when he should have.

In addition to this anecdotal evidence, research has directly linked goal setting to cheating. We should heed the warning of Professor Maurice E. Schweitzer—"Goal-setting is like a powerful medication"—before blindly accepting that specific, difficult goal.

Sources: Based on E. A. Locke and G. P. Latham, "Building a Practically Useful Theory of Goal Setting and Task Motivation," *American Psychologist* 57 (2002): 705–71; A. Tugend, "Expert's Advice to the Goal-Oriented: Don't Overdo It," *The New York Times*, October 6, 2012, B5; and C. Richards, "Letting Go of Long-Term Goals," *The New York Times*, August 4, 2012, B4.

CHAPTER REVIEW

QUESTIONS FOR REVIEW

7-1 What are the three key elements of motivation?

7-2 What are some early theories of motivation? How applicable are they today?

7-3 What are the similarities and differences between self-determination theory and goal-setting theory?

7-4 What are the key principles of self-efficacy theory, reinforcement theory, and expectancy theory?

7-5 What are some of the different types of organizational justice and what are their outcomes?

7-6 Why is employee job engagement important to managers?

7-7 How do the contemporary theories of motivation compare to one another?

APPLICATION AND EMPLOYABILITY

Motivation is a fundamental aspect of organizational behavior. It drives effortful work processes toward the accomplishment of work tasks and the realization of work goals. Therefore, by gaining an understanding of the traditional and contemporary theories of motivation and how workplace decisions affect motivation, you can develop your management skills and become more employable. An understanding of equity theory and organizational justice can help you understand just how much of an impact fairness has in the workplace as well as help you consider others' fairness perspectives when making organizational decisions. In this chapter, you developed your knowledge application and analysis skills; gained an understanding of social responsibility issues by learning how helping others is good (and bad) for your career, how to interact with others who won't take your advice, and how electronic monitoring is used in the workplace; and debated whether goal setting works. In the following section, you will continue to develop these skills as well as your critical thinking by considering unjust situations in the workplace and developing recommendations for handling unfairness; learning to recognize the "folly of rewarding A, while hoping for B"; discussing how CEO pay can be demotivating and unfair to employees; and considering laziness in the workplace, especially how it can escalate and spread to others.

EXPERIENTIAL EXERCISE Organizational Justice Task

Break the class into groups of three or four.

Questions

7-8. Each person should recall an instance in which he or she was (a) treated especially fairly and (b) treated especially unfairly. Work-related instances are preferable, but nonwork examples are fine too. What do the stories have in common?

7-9. Spend several minutes discussing whether the instance was more distributive, procedural, informational, or interpersonal in nature. What was the source of the fair/unfair treatment? How did each student feel, and how did he or she respond?

7-10. Each group should develop a set of recommendations for handling the unfair situations in a positive manner, and select a leader group who will briefly summarize the unfair instances, along with the group's recommendations for handling them better. The discussion should reflect the four types of justice discussed in this chapter (distributive, procedural, informational, and interpersonal).

ETHICAL DILEMMA Follies of Reward

Most of the time, we have good intentions when we try to reward others. We might give a bonus to an employee who has done an exceptionally good job all year. Or our reward systems might be a little more institutionalized. For example, a movie theater might reward an employee for eliciting charity donations from moviegoers, or a realtor might receive a commission for each house she sells.

Sometimes, however, even with good intentions, we may be rewarding the wrong thing. In a classic article of the same title, Steven Kerr outlines this "Folly of Rewarding A, While Hoping for B." For example, if you go to the doctor's office, the doctor can make two types of errors: (1) pronouncing you well when you are actually sick and (2) pronouncing you sick when you are actually well. If the doctor commits the first error, the consequences are grave—there could be a threat of a lawsuit, malpractice, or negligence. If the doctor commits the second error, the consequences have much less of an impact—the doctor generates more income, establishes a more regular customer base, and is rewarded by society for taking a "conservative" approach to diagnosis. These reward and punishment differences persist, even when there is the chance that treatment without due cause can cause more harm than good. However, shouldn't society seek to minimize both types of errors and instead seek medical diagnostic accuracy as a goal?

In a more recent example, one study found that a monthly perfect attendance award program across five industrial laundry plants did not work the way it was intended to: When participants became ineligible for the award, they showed up less frequently. The employees became so focused on attendance that their efficiency decreased by 8 percent because many of them would become ineligible for the reward after coming in late or missing a day during the month period. The plant was rewarding attendance and hoping for good performance.

Questions

7-11. How do you think we might be able to recognize when we are rewarding the wrong thing? What steps can organizations take to recognize these instances?

7-12. Is rewarding the unintended behavior or outcome always unethical? Why or why not?

7-13. Do you think it is possible for a reward program to start out rewarding the appropriate behavior at its inception but then begin to reward the wrong thing over time? Why or why not?

Sources: Based on T. Gubler, I. Larkin, and L. Pierce, "Motivational Spillovers from Awards: Crowding Out in a Multitasking Environment," *Organization Science* 27, no. 2 (2016): 286–303; and S. Kerr, "On the Folly of Rewarding A, While Hoping for B," *Academy of Management Journal* 18, no. 4 (1975): 769–83.

CASE INCIDENT 1 "Human and Authentic": Motivation at Schoenen Torfs

For several decades, Belgian shoe retailer Torfs was a decent place to work. The family-owned chain of stores was fair and caring to employees. But it was a traditional "top-down" company. "It was more, 'The company says how it has to be, and the coworkers just execute'," recalls Els Van Keymeulen, HR Manager at Torfs. "They have to follow."

Things began to change in the mid-1990s under Wouter Torfs, the third-generation leader of Torfs. As part of a broad plan for the shoe company to take larger strides in the market, Wouter Torfs started empowering his employees. He began to bring all employees together twice a year to share information about the company's direction. And gradually, these meetings became more interactive and engaging. In 2009, for example, Torfs employees were asked to help come up with the company's values. They defined the values as a family feel, a focus on results, and "*goesting*," a Flemish word that roughly translates to "enthusiasm."

The company's *goesting* was in full force when store employees were asked to get into small groups and design a sneaker. "Things got crazy," Van Keymeulen says of the activity. "The energy that generated was amazing." The winning designs were put into production and sold in all the stores—the first time Torfs sold its own shoe.

The company also involves itself with philanthropic efforts such as helping to build an orphanage in South Africa, providing aid to schoolchildren in Nepal, and organizing a fundraising campaign at its stores after Nepal was struck by an earthquake.

CEO Wouter Torfs says, "We are very proactive when it comes to the happiness of our employees, because happy employees result in happy customers. It is not easy to find and retain the right people in retail, but with our reputation for looking after the wellbeing of our teams, we attract them. It's also rare for people to leave our company."

In June 2019, the level of employee involvement, excitement, and social purpose earned Torfs the "Best Employer in Europe" award from Great Place to Work. The GPTW company overview commented, "Torfs is a place where you come to work with a smile, where you have fun with your colleagues, where you can be proud of the fruits of your efforts and where you get the confidence and room for self-development".

Since taking the helm nearly 30 years ago, Wouter Torfs has tripled the number of stores to 75, relocating dozens from city centers to the outskirts; doubled staff numbers; and increased turnover from €9 million to €146 million. But it has not all been plain sailing; the costs associated with the firm's online business has decimated profits recently. Yet this is unlikely to put a dent in the company's commitment to service and to its employees' happiness and loyalty.

Questions

7-14. List the different methods Torfs is using to motivate its employees.

7-15. Which motivation theories described in this chapter support the use of these methods?

7-16. Do you think the motivation techniques used at this chain of shoe stores would also be useful, for example, at an advertising agency? A pharmaceutical company? A fast-food restaurant?

Sources: Great Place to Work, "Torfs: Company Overview," www.greatplacetowork.be/en/certified-companies/torfs, accessed February 5, 2020; W. Kay, "Generations Filling Shoes: Wouter Torfs," *CEO Magazine*, May 30, 2019; Retail Detail, "Increasing Online Costs Decimate Torfs Profit," August 2, 2019, www.retaildetail.eu/en/news/fashion/increasing-online-costs-decimate-torfs-profit; E. Frauenheim, "The Basics and Beyond in Europe," *Great Place to Work*, June 3, 2015, http://www.greatplacetowork.net/publications-and-events/blogs-and-news/2046-the-basics-and-beyond-in-europe.

CASE INCIDENT 2 Laziness Is Contagious

Being lazy is often a quality that is shunned or looked down on in the workplace. When someone is unwilling to put energy into their work, they are, essentially, not engaged with their job. It is still unclear whether someone can have a "lazy" personality, but we can all most likely recall times when we did not want to or commit to putting forth the energy needed to do our work. In many cases, this leads to procrastination or excessive delegation, resulting in a failure to meet tight deadlines. One laziness behavior includes fleeing the scene when one does not want to work; another one is playing the victim and making excuses to make up for a lack of effort.

Although there has not been much research on laziness (perhaps anyone who has attempted to has not been able to muster the effort!), the research that does exist suggests that trait attributions of laziness are complex. For example, people tend to acknowledge that they have more personality traits than others (e.g., "I am a very complex, multifaceted person"). Although someone would not hesitate to say that they are "very energetic," people tend to qualify laziness with "diminutive" words (e.g., "I am a little bit lazy"). Similar peculiar effects emerge when considering others' attributions as well. Even though halo biases (see Chapter 5) can emerge for positive attributions of others (e.g., "She could have easily lied to me about accidentally giving an extra twenty dollars in change back to the customer when she first started working here. She is a fantastic, industrious, and honest person!"), horns biases do not occur as broadly as these positive traits when considering laziness (e.g., a supervisor witnessing an employee lying when she first started working there may think that she will lie in many circumstances but will not see this person as lazy).

Even more worrisome, laziness can subtly escalate or catch on with others. For instance, one lazy behavior can lead to another, and sunk costs can add up to the point where you reason you will simply start over tomorrow. Recent research suggests that laziness can be contagious—participants, unaware of their shifts toward laziness, start to endorse the same lazy behaviors and decisions that fictional, computer-generated participants made. The implications here are very intriguing: "[F]or example, if your lazy boss rewards you for having invested more effort in your work, will you become more or less lazy?"

Regardless of the negative air surrounding laziness, some have found merit in its practice. For example, Michael Lewis, author of *Moneyball*, asserts that laziness is not necessarily a bad thing and has even helped him succeed: "My laziness serves as a filter.... Something has to be really good before I'll decide to work on it."

Questions

7-17. Do you consider laziness to be more of a personality trait or more of a motivational state that we experience from time to time? Why? Is there a potential that it could be a little bit of both?

7-18. Do you agree or disagree with Michael Lewis that there is an upside to laziness? Why or why not?

7-19. How do you think managers and organizations can "manage laziness" so that the negative effects are minimized and the positive effects maximized? What sorts of programs and initiatives could an organization implement to achieve these goals?

Sources: Based on J. Boitnott, "5 Kinds of Lazy Employees and How to Handle Them," *Entrepreneur*, May 17, 2016, https://www.entrepreneur.com/article/275845; W.-Y. Cheung, T. Wildschut, C. Sedikides, and B. Pinter, "Uncovering the Multifaceted Self in the Domain of Negative Traits: On the Muted Expression of Negative Self-Knowledge," *Personality and Social Psychology Bulletin* 40, no. 4 (2014), 513-25; M. Gräf and C. Unkelbach, "Halo Effects in Trait Assessment Depend on Information Valence: Why Being Honest Makes You Industrious, but Lying Does Not Make You Lazy," *Personality and Social Psychology Bulletin* 42, no. 3 (2016): 290–310; A. MacMillan, "Why Laziness May Be Contagious," *Time*, March 30, 2017, http://time.com/4718737/laziness-impatience-contagious-personality/; J. Selk, "Laziness Isn't a Personality Flaw—It's Just a Habit," *Forbes*, July 10, 2014, https://www.forbes.com/sites/jasonselk/2014/07/10/laziness-isnt-a-personality-flaw-its-just-a-habit/#810a5c301627; and M. Zetlin, "Being Lazy Is the key to Success, According to the Best-Selling Author of 'Moneyball,'" *Inc.*, March 20, 2017, http://www.inc.com/minda-zetlin/why-being-lazy-makes-you-successful-according-to-the-bestselling-author-of-money.html.

ENDNOTES

[1] Kumar, A. (2018). "Women in workforce: What it would take to achieve gender parity in India". *Your Story Journal (October 9, 2018).* Retrieved from https://yourstory.com (Accessed on April 14, 2022).

[2] Bahl, S. (2021). "How Is Starbucks Availing Equal Representation To All Women". *Business World, BW People.in (December 8, 2021).* Retrieved from http://bwpeople.businessworld.in (Accessed on April 14, 2022).

[3] Starbucks Stories & News (2020). "Starbucks opens two all-female stores in India". *Starbucks (August 21, 2020).* Retrieved from https://stories.starbucks.com (Accessed on April 15, 2022).

[4] See, for example, W. F. Cascio and H. Aguinis, "Research in Industrial and Organizational Psychology from 1963 to 2007: Changes, Choices, and Trends," *Journal of Applied Psychology* 93, no. 5 (2008): 1062–81; and C. C. Pinder, *Work Motivation in Organizational Behavior*, 2nd ed. (London, UK: Psychology Press, 2008).

[5] A. Gouveia, "The 2013 Wasting Time at Work Survey: Everything You've Always Wanted to Know about Wasting Time in the Office," Salary.com, 2013, http://www.salary.com/2013-wasting-time-at-work-survey/.

[6] See, for instance, Pinder, *Work Motivation in Organizational Behavior*.

[7] A. H. Maslow, "A Theory of Human Motivation," *Psychological Review* 50 (1943), 370–96; and R. J. Taormina and J. H. Gao, "Maslow and the Motivation Hierarchy: Measuring Satisfaction of the Needs," *American Journal of Psychology* 126, no. 2 (2013): 155–57.

[8] H. S. Guest, "Maslow's Hierarchy of Needs—The Sixth Level," *The Psychologist* 27, no. 12 (2014): 982–83.

[9] Ibid.

[10] T. R. Mitchell and D. Daniels, "Motivation," in W. Borman, D. Ilgen, and R. Klimoski (eds.), *Handbook of Psychology: Industrial/Organizational Psychology*, Vol. 12 (New York: Wiley, 2002): 225–54.

[11] V. M. Bockman, "The Herzberg Controversy," *Personnel Psychology* 24, no. 2 (1971): 155–89; and F. Herzberg, "The Motivation-Hygiene Concept and Problems of Manpower," *Personnel Administrator* 27 (1964): 3–7.

[12] N. Bassett-Jones and G. C. Lloyd, "Does Herzberg's Motivation Theory Have Staying Power?," *Journal of Management Development* 24, no. 10 (2005): 929–43.

[13] See, for instance, V. S. R. Vijayakumar and U. Saxena, "Herzberg Revisited: Dimensionality and Structural Invariance of Herzberg's Two Factor Model," *Journal of the Indian Academy of Applied Psychology* 41, no. 2 (2015): 291–98; and R. Worthley, B. MacNab, R. Brislin, K. Ito, and E. L. Rose, "Workforce Motivation in Japan: An Examination of Gender Differences and Management Perceptions," *The International Journal of Human Resource Management* 20, no. 7 (2009): 1503–20.

[14] D. C. McClelland, *Human Motivation* (Cambridge, UK: Cambridge University Press, 1987); and D. C. McClelland, J. W. Atkinson, R. A. Clark, and E. L. Lowell, *The Achievement Motive* (New York: Appleton-Century-Crofts, 1953).

[15] H. van Emmerick, W. L. Gardner, H. Wendt, et al., "Associations of Culture and Personality with McClelland's Motives: A Cross-Cultural Study of Managers in 24 Countries," *Group and Organization Management* 35, no. 3 (2010): 329–67.

[16] R. Eisenberger, J. R. Jones, F. Stinglhamber, L. Shanock, and A. T. Randall, "Flow Experiences at Work: For High Need Achievers Alone?" *Journal of Organizational Behavior* 26, no. 7 (2005): 755–75.

[17] A. K. Kirk and D. F. Brown, "Latent Constructs of Proximal and Distal

Motivation Predicting Performance under Maximum Test Conditions," *Journal of Applied Psychology* 88, no. 1 (2003): 40–49; and R. B. Soyer, J. L. Rovenpor, and R. E. Kopelman, "Narcissism and Achievement Motivation As Related to Three Facets of the Sales Role: Attraction, Satisfaction, and Performance," *Journal of Business and Psychology* 14, no. 2 (1999): 285–304.
[18] See, for instance, F. Yang, J. E. Ramsay, O. C. Schultheiss, and J. S. Pang, "Need for Achievement Moderates the Effect of Motive-Relevant Challenge on Salivary Cortisol Changes," *Motivation and Emotion* (2015): 321–34; M. S. Khan, R. J. Breitnecker, and E. J. Schwarz, "Adding Fuel to the Fire: Need for Achievement Diversity and Relationship Conflict in Entrepreneurial Teams," *Management Decision* 53, no. 1 (2015): 75–79; M. G. Koellner and O. C. Schultheiss, "Meta-Analytic Evidence of Low Convergence between Implicit and Explicit Measures of the Needs for Achievement, Affiliation, and Power," *Frontiers in Psychology* 5, no. 826 (2014): 1-20; and T. Bipp and K. van Dam, "Extending Hierarchical Achievement Motivation Models: The Role of Motivational Needs for Achievement Goals and Academic Performance," *Personality and Individual Differences* 64 (2014): 157–62.
[19] Koellner and Schultheiss, "Meta-Analytic Evidence of Low Convergence between Implicit and Explicit Measures of the Needs for Achievement, Affiliation, and Power."
[20] J. S. Chun and J. N. Choi, "Members' Needs, Intragroup Conflict, and Group Performance," *Journal of Applied Psychology* 99, no. 3 (2014): 437–50.
[21] D. G. Winter, "The Motivational Dimensions of Leadership: Power, Achievement, and Affiliation," in R. E. Riggio, S. E. Murphy, and F. J. Pirozzolo (eds.), *Multiple Intelligences and Leadership* (Mahwah, NJ: Lawrence Erlbaum, 2002): 119–38.
[22] J. Hofer, H. Busch, and C. Schneider, "The Effect of Motive-Trait Interaction on Satisfaction of the Implicit Need for Affiliation among German and Cameroonian Adults," *Journal of Personality* 83, no. 2 (2015): 167–78.
[23] J. T. Austin and J. B. Vancouver, "Goal Constructs in Psychology: Structure, Process, and Content," *Psychological Bulletin* 120 (1996): 338–75.
[24] E. Deci and R. Ryan (eds.), *Handbook of Self-Determination Research* (Rochester, NY: University of Rochester Press, 2002); R. Ryan and E. Deci, "Self-Determination Theory and the Facilitation of Intrinsic Motivation, Social Development, and Well-Being," *American Psychologist* 55, no. 1 (2000): 68–78; and M. Gagné and E. L. Deci, "Self-Determination Theory and Work Motivation," *Journal of Organizational Behavior* 26, no. 4 (2005): 331–62.
[25] A. Van den Broeck, D. L. Ferris, C.-H. Chang, and C. C. Rosen, "A Review of Self-Determination Theory's Basic Psychological Needs at Work," *Journal of Management* 42, no. 5 (2016): 1195–229.
[26] C. P. Cerasoli, J. M. Nicklin, and M. T. Ford, "Intrinsic Motivation and Extrinsic Incentives Jointly Predict Performance: A 40-Year Meta-Analysis," *Psychological Bulletin* 140, no. 4 (2014): 980–1008.
[27] J. E. Bono and T. A. Judge, "Self-Concordance at Work: Toward Understanding the Motivational Effects of Transformational Leaders," *Academy of Management Journal* 46, no. 5 (2003): 554–71.
[28] K. M. Sheldon, A. J. Elliot, and R. M. Ryan, "Self-Concordance and Subjective Well-being in Four Cultures," *Journal of Cross-Cultural Psychology* 35, no. 2 (2004): 209–23.
[29] L. M. Graves, M. N. Ruderman, P. J. Ohlott, and Todd J. Webber, "Driven to Work and Enjoyment of Work: Effects on Managers' Outcomes," *Journal of Management* 38, no. 5 (2012): 1655–80.
[30] K. L. Unsworth and I. M. McNeill, "Increasing Pro-Environmental Behaviors by Increasing Self-Concordance: Testing an Intervention," *Journal of Applied Psychology* 102, no. 1 (2017): 88–103.
[31] Van den Broeck, Ferris, Chang, and Rosen, "A Review of Self-Determination Theory's Basic Psychological Needs at Work."
[32] M. E. L. Zeijen, P. Petrou, A. B. Bakker, and B. R. van Gelderen, "Dyadic Support Exchange and Work Engagement: An Episodic Test and Expansion of Self-Determination Theory," *Journal of Occupational and Organizational Psychology* (in press).
[33] E. A. Locke and G. P. Latham, "Building a Practically Useful Theory of Goal Setting and Task Motivation," *American Psychologist* 57, no. 9 (2002): 705–17; and E. A. Locke and G. P. Latham, "New Directions in Goal-Setting Theory," *Current Directions in Psychological Science* 15, no. 5 (2006): 265–68; B. M. Wilkowski, A. Fetterman, S. Lappi, L. Z. Williamson, E. F. Leki, E. Rivera, and B. P. Meier, "Lexical Derivation of the PINT Taxonomy of Goals: Prominence, Inclusiveness, Negativity Prevention, and Tradition," *Journal of Personality and Social Psychology* (in press).
[34] Ibid.
[35] Vashney, R. (2021). "[The Turning Point] Why Mukesh Bansal, Ankit Nagori chose to focus on health with Cult.fit". *YourStory (June 12, 2021).* Retrieved from https://yourstory.com (Accessed on April 12, 2022).
[36] cult.fit. "Careers". Retrieved from https://www.cult.fit (Accessed on April 12, 2022).
[37] J. J. Dahling, S. R. Taylor, S. L. Chau, and S. A. Dwight, "Does Coaching Matter? A Multilevel Model Linking Managerial Coaching Skill and Frequency to Sales Goal Attainment," *Personnel Psychology* 69, no. 4 (2016): 863–94.
[38] C. Gabelica, P. Van den Bossche, M. Segers, and W. Gijselaersa, "Feedback, a Powerful Lever in Teams: A Review," *Educational Research Review* 7, no. 2 (2012): 123–44.
[39] A. Kleingeld, H. van Mierlo, and L. Arends, "The Effect of Goal Setting on Group Performance: A Meta-Analysis," *Journal of Applied Psychology* 96, no. 6 (2011): 1289–304.
[40] J. Lee and F. Wei, "The Mediating Effect of Psychological Empowerment on the Relationship between Participative Goal Setting and Team Outcomes—A Study in China," *International Journal of Human Resource Management* 22, no. 2 (2011): 279–95.
[41] S. W. Anderson, H. C. Dekker, and K. L. Sedatole, "An Empirical Examination of Goals and Performance-to-Goal Following the Introduction of an Incentive Bonus Plan with Participative Goal Setting," *Management Science* 56, no. 1 (2010): 90–109.
[42] T. S. Bateman and B. Bruce, "Masters of the Long Haul: Pursuing Long-Term Work Goals," *Journal of Organizational Behavior* 33, no. 7 (2012): 984–1006.
[43] Ibid.
[44] H. J. Klein, M. J. Wesson, J. R. Hollenbeck, and B. J. Alge, "Goal Commitment and the Goal-Setting Process: Conceptual Clarification and Empirical Synthesis," *Journal of Applied Psychology* 84, no. 6 (1999): 885–96; H. J. Klein, R. B. Lount, H. M. Park, and B. J. Linford, "When Goals Are Known: The Effects of Audience Relative Status on Goal Commitment and Performance," *Journal of Applied Psychology* 105, no. 4 (2020): 372–89.
[45] Kleingeld, van Mierlo, and Arends, "The Effect of Goal Setting on Group Performance"; and Locke and Latham, "Building a Practically Useful Theory of Goal Setting and Task Motivation."
[46] K. D. Vohs, J. K. Park, and B. J. Schmeichel, "Self-Affirmation Can Enable Goal

Disengagement," *Journal of Personality and Social Psychology* 104, no. 1 (2013): 14–27.
[47]D. F. Crown, "The Use of Group and Groupcentric Individual Goals for Culturally Heterogeneous and Homogeneous Task Groups: An Assessment of European Work Teams," *Small Group Research* 38, no. 4 (2007): 489–508; and J. Kurman, "Self-Regulation Strategies in Achievement Settings: Culture and Gender Differences," *Journal of Cross-Cultural Psychology* 32, no. 4 (2001): 491–503.
[48]C. Sue-Chan and M. Ong, "Goal Assignment and Performance: Assessing the Mediating Roles of Goal Commitment and Self-Efficacy and the Moderating Role of Power Distance," *Organizational Behavior and Human Decision Processes* 89, no. 2 (2002): 1140–61.
[49]L. D. Ordóñez, M. E. Schweitzer, A. D. Galinsky, and M. H. Bazerman, "Goals Gone Wild: The Systematic Side Effects of Overprescribing Goal Setting," *Academy of Management Perspectives* 23, no. 1 (2009): 6–16; and E. A. Locke and G. P. Latham, "Has Goal Setting Gone Wild, or Have Its Attackers Abandoned Good Scholarship?" *Academy of Management Perspectives* 23, no. 1 (2009): 17–23.
[50]Cerasoli, Nicklin, and Ford, "Intrinsic Motivation and Extrinsic Incentives Jointly Predict Performance."
[51]E. T. Higgins, "Promotion and Prevention: Regulatory Focus as a Motivational Principle," *Advances in Experimental Social Psychology* 30 (1998): 1–46; and E. T. Higgins and J. F. M. Cornwell, "Securing Foundations and Advancing Frontiers: Prevention and Promotion Effects on Judgment & Decision Making," *Organizational Behavior and Human Decision Processes* 136 (2016): 56–67.
[52]K. Lanaj, C. D. Chang, and R. E. Johnson, "Regulatory Focus and Work-Related Outcomes: A Review and Meta-Analysis," *Psychological Bulletin* 138, no. 5 (2012): 998–1034.
[53]D. L. Ferris, R. E. Johnson, C. C. Rosen, E. Djurdjevic, C.-H. Chang, and J. A. Tan, "When Is Success Not Satisfying? Integrating Regulatory Focus and Approach/Avoidance Motivation Theories to Explain the Relation between Core Self-Evaluation and Job Satisfaction," *Journal of Applied Psychology* 98, no. 2 (2013): 342–53.
[54]M. Roskes, A. J. Elliot, and C. K. W. De Dreu, "Why Is Avoidance Motivation Problematic, and What Can Be Done about It?" *Current Directions in Psychological Science* 23, no. 2 (2014): 133–38.
[55]"KEYGroup Survey Finds Nearly Half of All Employees Have No Set Performance Goals," *IPMA-HR Bulletin* (March 10, 2006): 1; S. Hamm, "SAP Dangles a Big, Fat Carrot," *BusinessWeek* (May 22, 2006): 67–68; and "P&G CEO Wields High Expectations but No Whip," *USA Today*, February 19, 2007, 3B.
[56]P. Drucker, *The Practice of Management* (New York: Harper, 1954).
[57]See, for instance, H. Levinson, "Management by Whose Objectives?," *Harvard Business Review* 81, no. 1 (2003): 107–16.
[58]See, for example, E. Lindberg and T. L. Wilson, "Management by Objectives: The Swedish Experience in Upper Secondary Schools," *Journal of Educational Administration* 49, no. 1 (2011): 62–75; R. Rodgers and J. E. Hunter, "Impact of Management by Objectives on Organizational Productivity," *Journal of Applied Psychology* 76, no. 2 (1991): 322–36; and A. C. Spaulding, L. D. Gamm, and J. M. Griffith, "Studer Unplugged: Identifying Underlying Managerial Concepts," *Hospital Topics* 88, no. 1 (2010): 1–9.
[59]M. B. Kristiansen, "Management by Objectives and Results in the Nordic Countries: Continuity and Change, Differences and Similarities," *Public Performance and Management Review* 38, no. 3 (2015): 542–69.
[60]See, for instance, M. Tanikawa, "Fujitsu Decides to Backtrack on Performance-Based Pay," *New York Times*, March 22, 2001, W1; and W. F. Roth, "Is Management by Objectives Obsolete?" *Global Business and Organizational Excellence* 28 (May/June 2009): 36–43.
[61]F. Gino and C. Mogilner, "Time, Money, and Morality," *Psychological Science* 25, no. 2 (2014): 414–21.
[62]V. Lopez-Kidwell, T. J. Grosser, B. R. Dineen, and S. P. Borgatti, "What Matters When: A Multistage Model and Empirical Examination of Job Search Effort," *Academy of Management Journal* 56, no. 6 (2012): 1655–78.
[63]J. W. Beck and A. M. Schmidt, "State-Level Goal Orientations as Mediators of the Relationship between Time Pressure and Performance: A Longitudinal Study," *Journal of Applied Psychology* 98, no. 2 (2013): 354–63.
[64]A. Bandura, *Social Foundations of Thought and Action: A Social Cognitive Theory* (Englewood Cliffs, NJ: Prentice Hall, 1986); A. Bandura, *Self-Efficacy: The Exercise of Control* (New York: W. H. Freeman, 1997); and A. Bandura, "Social Cognitive Theory: An Agentic Perspective," *Annual Review of Psychology* 52 (2001): 1–26.
[65]A. Bandura, "Cultivate Self-Efficacy for Personal and Organizational Effectiveness," in E. Locke (ed.), *Handbook of Principles of Organizational Behavior* (Malden, MA: Blackwell, 2004): 120–36; S. D. Brown, R. W. Lent, K. Telander, and S. Tramayne, "Social Cognitive Career Theory, Conscientiousness, and Work Performance: A Meta-Analytic Path Analysis," *Journal of Vocational Behavior* 79, no. 1 (2011): 81–90.
[66]M. Salanova, S. Llorens, and W. B. Schaufeli, "Yes I Can, I Feel Good, and I Just Do It! On Gain Cycles and Spirals of Efficacy Beliefs, Affect, and Engagement," *Applied Psychology* 60, no. 2 (2011): 255–85. Compare with J. B. Vancouver, C. M. Thompson, and A. A. Williams, "The Changing Signs in the Relationships Among Self-Efficacy, Personal Goals, and Performance," *Journal of Applied Psychology* 86, no. 4 (2001): 605–20; and J. B. Vancouver and J. D. Purl, "A Computational Model of Self-Efficacy's Various Effects on Performance: Moving the Debate Forward," *Journal of Applied Psychology* 102, no. 4 (2017): 599–616.
[67]J. R. Themanson and P. J. Rosen, "Examining the Relationships between Self-Efficacy, Task-Relevant Attentional Control, and Task Performance: Evidence from Event-Related Brain Potentials," *British Journal of Psychology* 106, no. 2 (2015): 253–71.
[68]A. P. Tolli and A. M. Schmidt, "The Role of Feedback, Causal Attributions, and Self-Efficacy in Goal Revision," *Journal of Applied Psychology* 93, no. 3 (2008): 692–701.
[69]P. Tierney and S. M. Farmer, "Creative Self-Efficacy Development and Creative Performance over Time," *Journal of Applied Psychology* 96, no. 2 (2011): 277–93.
[70]S. L. Anderson and N. E. Betz, "Sources of Social Self-Efficacy Expectations: Their Measurement and Relation to Career Development," *Journal of Vocational Behavior* 58, no. 1 (2001): 98–117; M. Ben-Ami, J. Hornik, D. Eden, et al., "Boosting Consumers' Self-Efficacy by Repositioning the Self," *European Journal of Marketing* 48 (2014): 1914–38; L. De Grez and D. Van Lindt, "Students' Gains in Entrepreneurial Self-Efficacy: A Comparison of 'Learning-by-Doing' versus Lecture-Based Courses," *Proceedings of the 8th European Conference on Innovation and Entrepreneurship* (2013): 198–203; and K. S. Hendricks, "Changes in Self-Efficacy Beliefs over Time: Contextual Influences of Gender, Rank-Based Placement, and Social Support in a Competitive Orchestra Environment,"

Psychology of Music 42, no. 3 (2014): 347–65.

[71] T. A. Judge, C. L. Jackson, J. C. Shaw, B. Scott, and B. L. Rich, "Self-Efficacy and Work-Related Performance: The Integral Role of Individual Differences," *Journal of Applied Psychology* 92, no. 1 (2007): 107–27.

[72] Ibid.

[73] A. M. Paul, "How to Use the 'Pygmalion' Effect," *Time,* April 1, 2013, http://ideas.time.com/2013/04/01/how-to-use-the-pygmalion-effect/.

[74] A. Friedrich, B. Flunger, B. Nagengast, K. Jonkmann, and U. Trautwein, "Pygmalion Effects in the Classroom: Teacher Expectancy Effects on Students' Math Achievement," *Contemporary Educational Psychology* 41 (2015): 1–12.

[75] L. Karakowsky, N. DeGama, and K. McBey, "Facilitating the Pygmalion Effect: The Overlooked Role of Subordinate Perceptions of the Leader," *Journal of Occupational and Organizational Psychology* 85, no. 4 (2012): 579–99; and P. Whiteley, T. Sy, and S. K. Johnson, "Leaders' Conceptions of Followers: Implications for Naturally Occurring Pygmalion Effects," *Leadership Quarterly* 23, no. 5 (2012): 822–34.

[76] G. Chen, B. Thomas, and J. C. Wallace, "A Multilevel Examination of the Relationships among Training Outcomes, Mediating Regulatory Processes, and Adaptive Performance," *Journal of Applied Psychology* 90, no. 5 (2005): 827–41; A. Gegenfurtner, C. Quesada-Pallares, and M. Knogler, "Digital Simulation-Based Training: A Meta-Analysis," *British Journal of Educational Technology* 45, no. 6 (2014): 1097–114; and C. L. Holladay and M. A. Quiñones, "Practice Variability and Transfer of Training: The Role of Self-Efficacy Generality," *Journal of Applied Psychology* 88, no. 6 (2003): 1094–103.

[77] E. C. Dierdorff, E. A. Surface, and K. G. Brown, "Frame-of-Reference Training Effectiveness: Effects of Goal Orientation and Self-Efficacy on Affective, Cognitive, Skill-Based, and Transfer Outcomes," *Journal of Applied Psychology* 95, no. 6 (2010): 1181–91; R. Grossman and E. Salas, "The Transfer of Training: What Really Matters," *International Journal of Training and Development* 15, no. 2 (2011): 103–20; and D. S. Stanhope, S. B. Pond III, and E. A. Surface, "Core Self-Evaluations and Training Effectiveness: Prediction through Motivational Intervening Mechanisms," *Journal of Applied Psychology* 98, no. 5 (2013): 820–31.

[78] M. L. Ambrose and C. T. Kulik, "Old Friends, New Faces: Motivation Research in the 1990s," *Journal of Management* 25, no. 3 (1999): 231–92; and B. F. Skinner, *Contingencies of Reinforcement* (New York: Appleton-Century-Crofts, 1969).

[79] M. J. Goddard, "Critical Psychiatry, Critical Psychology, and the Behaviorism of B. F. Skinner," *Review of General Psychology* 18, no. 3 (2014): 208–15.

[80] Y. Rofcanin, M. Las Heras, M. J. Bosch, G. Wood, and F. Mughal, "A Closer Look at the Positive Crossover between Supervisors and Subordinates: The Role of Home and Work Engagement," *Human Relations* 72, no. 11 (2019): 1776–804; J. Wu, R. C. Liden, C. Liao, and S. J. Wayne, "Does Manager Servant Leadership Lead to Follower Serving Behaviors? It Depends on Follower Self-Interest," *Journal of Applied Psychology* (in press).

[81] A. Bandura, *Social Learning Theory* (New York: General Learning, 1971); and J. R. Brauer and C. R. Tittle, "Social Learning Theory and Human Reinforcement," *Sociological Spectrum* 32, no. 2 (2012): 157–77.

[82] Mohandas, S. & Srinivasa, D.N. (2020). "The Boss Will See You Now - The Growth of Workplace Surveillance in India, is Data Protection Legislation the Answer?" *The Centre For Internet & Society (December 31, 2020).* Retrieved from https://cis-india.org (Accessed on April 15, 2022).

[83] W. Van Eerde and H. Thierry, "Vroom's Expectancy Models and Work-Related Criteria," *Journal of Applied Psychology* 81, no. 5 (1996): 575–86; and V. H. Vroom, *Work and Motivation* (New York: Wiley, 1964).

[84] R. Kanfer, M. Frese, and R. E. Johnson, "Motivation Related to Work: A Century of Progress," *Journal of Applied Psychology* 102, no. 3 (2017): 338–55; J. C. Naylor, R. D. Pritchard, and D. R. Ilgen, *A Theory of Behavior in Organizations* (New York: Academic, 1980); and Van Eerde and Thierry, "Vroom's Expectancy Models and Work-Related Criteria."

[85] J. Nocera, "The Anguish of Being an Analyst," *The New York Times,* March 4, 2006, B1, B12.

[86] J. S. Adams, "Inequity in Social Exchange," in L. Berkowitz (ed.), *Advances in Experimental Social Psychology,* Vol. 2 (New York: Academic, 1965), 267–99.

[87] T. Kollmann, C. Stockmann, J. M. Kensbock, and A. Peschl, "What Satisfies Younger Versus Older Employees, and Why? An Aging Perspective on Equity Theory to Explain Interactive Effects of Employee Age, Monetary Rewards, and Task Contributions on Job Satisfaction," *Human Resource Management* 59 (2020): 101–15.

[88] Ibid.

[89] M. C. Bolino and W. H. Turnley, "Old Faces, New Places: Equity Theory in Cross-Cultural Contexts," *Journal of Organizational Behavior* 29, no. 1 (2008): 29–50; and R. T. Mowday and K. A. Colwell, "Employee Reactions to Unfair Outcomes in the Workplace: The Contributions of Equity Theory to Understanding Work Motivation," in L. W. Porter, G. A. Bigley, and R. M. Steers (eds.), *Motivation and Work Behavior* (Burr Ridge, IL: McGraw-Hill, 2003), 65–113.

[90] B. K. Miller, "Entitlement and Conscientiousness in the Prediction of Organizational Deviance," *Personality and Individual Differences* 82 (2015): 114–19; and H. J. R. Woodley and N. J. Allen, "The Dark Side of Equity Sensitivity," *Personality and Individual Differences* 67 (2014): 103–08.

[91] J. M. Jensen, P. C. Patel, and J. L. Raver, "Is It Better to Be Average? High and Low Performance as Predictors of Employee Victimization," *Journal of Applied Psychology* 99, no. 2 (2014): 296–309.

[92] J. A. Colquitt, J. Greenberg, and C. P. Zepata-Phelan, "What Is Organizational Justice? A Historical Overview," in J. Greenberg and J. A. Colquitt (eds.), *Handbook of Organizational Justice* (Mahwah, NJ: Lawrence Erlbaum, 2005): 3–56; and J. Greenberg, "Organizational Justice: The Dynamics of Fairness in the Workplace," in S. Zedeck (ed.), *APA Handbook of Industrial and Organizational Psychology: Maintaining, Expanding, and Contracting the Organization,* Vol. 3 (Washington, D.C.: APA, 2011): 271–327.

[93] Ibid.

[94] C. O. Trevor, G. Reilly, and B. Gerhart, "Reconsidering Pay Dispersion's Effect on the Performance of Interdependent Work: Reconciling Sorting and Pay Inequality," *Academy of Management Journal* 55, no. 3 (2012): 585–610.

[95] See, for example, R. Cropanzano, J. H. Stein, and T. Nadisic, *Social Justice and the Experience of Emotion* (New York: Routledge/Taylor and Francis Group, 2011); I. SimanTov-Nachlieli and P. Bamberger, "Pay Communication, Justice, and Affect: The Asymmetric Effects of Process and Outcome Pay Transparency on Counterproductive Work Behavior," *Journal of Applied Psychology* (in press).

[96] Tigga, S. (2022). "No Action So Far Against 'Casteist' Coaches Who Assaulted Athletes at Bastar National Sports Academy". *The Wire (February 24,*

2022). Retrieved from https://thewire.in (Accessed on April 15, 2022).

[97] G. S. Leventhal, "What Should Be Done with Equity Theory? New Approaches to the Study of Fairness in Social Relationships," in K. Gergen, M. Greenberg, and R. Willis (eds.), *Social Exchange: Advances in Theory and Research* (New York: Plenum, 1980): 27–55; E. A. Lind and T. R. Tyler, *The Social Psychology of Procedural Justice* (New York: Plenum, 1988); and J. Thibaut and L. Walker, *Procedural Justice: A Psychological Analysis* (Hillsdale, NJ: Erlbaum, 1975); R. Outlaw, J. A. Colquitt, M. D. Baer, and H. Sessions, "How Fair versus How Long: An Integrative Theory-based Examination of Procedural Justice and Procedural Timeliness," *Personnel Psychology* 72 (2019): 361–91.

[98] J. Brockner, B. M. Wiesenfeld, and K. A. Diekmann, "Towards a 'Fairer' Conception of Process Fairness: Why, When, and How May Not Always Be Better Than Less," *Academy of Management Annals* 3 (2009): 183–216.

[99] R. Folger, "Distributive and Procedural Justice: Combined Impact of 'Voice' and Improvement on Experienced Inequity," *Journal of Personality and Social Psychology* 35 (1977): 108–19; and R. Folger, D. Rosenfield, J. Grove, and L. Corkran, "Effects of 'Voice' and Peer Opinions on Responses to Inequity," *Journal of Personality and Social Psychology* 37 (1979): 2253–71.

[100] R. J. Bies and J. F. Moag, "Interactional Justice: Communication Criteria on Fairness," in R. J. Lewicki, B. H. Sheppard, and M. H. Bazerman (eds.), *Research on Negotiations in Organizations*, Vol. 1, (Greenwich, CT: JAI, 1986): 43–55.

[101] J. C. Shaw, E. Wild, and J. A. Colquitt, "To Justify or Excuse? A Meta-Analytic Review of the Effects of Explanations," *Journal of Applied Psychology* 88, no. 3 (2003): 444–58.

[102] R. J. Bies, "Are Procedural and Interactional Justice Conceptually Distinct?," in J. Greenberg and J. A. Colquitt (eds.), *Handbook of Organizational Justice* (Mahwah, NJ: Erlbaum, 2005): 85–112; and B. A. Scott, J. A. Colquitt, and E. L. Paddock, "An Actor-Focused Model of Justice Rule Adherence and Violation: The Role of Managerial Motives and Discretion," *Journal of Applied Psychology* 94, no. 3 (2009): 756–69.

[103] G. A. Van Kleef, A. C. Homan, B. Beersma, D. V. Knippenberg, B. V. Knippenberg, and F. Damen, "Searing Sentiment or Cold Calculation? The Effects of Leader Emotional Displays on Team Performance Depend on Follower Epistemic Motivation," *Academy of Management Journal* 52, no. 3 (2009): 562–80.

[104] "Rutgers Fires Mike Rice," ESPN, 2013, http://espn.go.com/sportsnation/post/_/id/9129245/rutgers-fires-mike-rice.

[105] J. A. Colquitt, D. E. Conlon, M. J. Wesson, C. O. L. H. Porter, and K. Y. Ng, "Justice at the Millenium: A Meta-Analytic Review of 25 Years of Organizational Justice Research," *Journal of Applied Psychology* 86, no. 3 (2001): 425–45; J. A. Colquitt, B. A. Scott, J. B. Rodell, D. M. Long, C. P. Zapata, D. E. Conlon, and M. J. Wesson, "Justice at the Millennium, A Decade Later: A Meta-Analytic Test of Social Exchange and Affect-Based Perspectives," *Journal of Applied Psychology* 98, no. 2 (2013): 199–236; and N. E. Fassina, D. A. Jones, and K. L. Uggerslev, "Meta-Analytic Tests of Relationships between Organizational Justice and Citizenship Behavior: Testing Agent-System and Shared-Variance Models," *Journal of Organizational Behavior* 29 (2008): 805–28.

[106] J. M. Robbins, M. T. Ford, and L. E. Tetrick, "Perceived Unfairness and Employee Health: A Meta-Analytic Integration," *Journal of Applied Psychology* 97, no. 2 (2012): 235–72.

[107] J. A. Colquitt, J. A. LePine, R. F. Piccolo, C. P. Zapata, and B. L. Rich, "Explaining the Justice-Performance Relationship: Trust as Exchange Deepener or Trust as Uncertainty Reducer?," *Journal of Applied Psychology* 97, no. 1 (2012): 1–15.

[108] K. Leung, K. Tong, and S. S. Ho, "Effects of Interactional Justice on Egocentric Bias in Resource Allocation Decisions," *Journal of Applied Psychology* 89, no. 3 (2004): 405–15; and L. Francis-Gladney, N. R. Manger, and R. B. Welker, "Does Outcome Favorability Affect Procedural Fairness as a Result of Self-Serving Attributions," *Journal of Applied Social Psychology* 40, no. 1 (2010): 182–94.

[109] F. K. Matta, B. A. Scott, Z. A. Guo, and J. G. Matusik, "Exchanging One Uncertainty for Another: Justice Variability Negates the Benefits of Justice," *Journal of Applied Psychology* 105, no. 1 (2020): 97–110; Y.-R. Wang, M. T. Ford, Y. Wang, and J. Jin, "Shifts and Variability in Daily Interpersonal Justice Are Associated with Psychological Detachment and Affect at Home," *Journal of Vocational Behavior* (in press).

[110] D. P. Skarlicki, J. H. Ellard, and B. R. C. Kelln, "Third-Party Perceptions of a Layoff: Procedural, Derogation, and Retributive Aspects of Justice," *Journal of Applied Psychology* 83, no. 1 (1998): 119–27.

[111] S. Caleo, "Are Organizational Justice Rules Gendered? Reactions to Men's and Women's Justice Violations," *Journal of Applied Psychology* 101, no. 10 (2016): 1422–35.

[112] D. P. Skarlicki and C. T. Kulik, "Third-Party Reactions to Employee (Mis) treatment: A Justice Perspective," *Research in Organizational Behavior* 26 (2005): 183–229; and E. E. Umphress, A. L. Simmons, R. Folger, R. Ren, and R. Bobocel, "Observer Reactions to Interpersonal Injustice: The Roles of Perpetrator Intent and Victim Perception," *Journal of Organizational Behavior* 34 (2013): 327–49.

[113] M. S. Mitchell, R. M. Vogel, and R. Folger, "Third Parties' Reactions to the Abusive Supervision of Coworkers," *Journal of Applied Psychology* 100, no. 4 (2015): 1040–55; and J. O'Reilly, K. Aquino, and D. Skarlicki, "The Lives of Others: Third Parties' Responses to Others' Injustice," *Journal of Applied Psychology* 101, no. 2 (2016): 171–89.

[114] B. B. Dunford, C. L. Jackson, A. D. Boss, L. Tay, and R. W. Boss, "Be Fair, Your Employees Are Watching: A Relational Response Model of External Third-Party Justice," *Personnel Psychology* 68 (2015): 319–52.

[115] This section is based on B. A. Scott, A. S. Garza, D. E. Conlon, and Y. J. Kim, "Why Do Managers Act Fairly in the First Place? A Daily Investigation of 'Hot' and 'Cold' Motives and Discretion," *Academy of Management Journal* 57, no. 6 (2014): 1571–91.

[116] F. F. T. Chiang and T. Birtch, "The Transferability of Management Practices: Examining Cross-National Differences in Reward Preferences," *Human Relations* 60, no. 9 (2007): 1293–330; and M. J. Gelfand, M. Erez, and Z. Aycan, "Cross-Cultural Organizational Behavior," *Annual Review of Psychology* 58 (2007): 479–514.

[117] M. C. Bolino and W. H. Turnley, "Old Faces, New Places: Equity Theory in Cross-Cultural Contexts," *Journal of Organizational Behavior* 29, no. 1 (2008): 29–50.

[118] R. Shao, D. E. Rupp, D. P. Skarlicki, and K. S. Jones, "Employee Justice across Cultures: A Meta-Analytic Review," *Journal of Management* 39, no. 1 (2013): 263–301.

[119] B. L. Rich, J. A. LePine, and E. R. Crawford, "Job Engagement: Antecedents and Effects on Job Performance," *Academy of Management Journal* 53, no. 3 (2010): 617–35.

[120] M. S. Christian, A. S. Garza, and J. E. Slaughter, "Work Engagement: A Quantitative Review and Test of Its Relations with Task and Contextual Performance," *Personnel Psychology* 64, no. 1 (2011): 89–136.
[121] E. R. Crawford, J. A. LePine, and B. L. Rich, "Linking Job Demands and Resources to Employee Engagement and Burnout: A Theoretical Extension and Meta-Analytic Test," *Journal of Applied Psychology* 95, no. 5 (2010): 834–48.
[122] Rich, LePine, and Crawford, "Job Engagement."
[123] F. O. Walumbwa, P. Wang, H. Wang, J. Schaubroeck, and B. J. Avolio, "Psychological Processes Linking Authentic Leadership to Follower Behaviors," *Leadership Quarterly* 21, no. 5 (2010): 901–14.
[124] D. A. Newman and D. A. Harrison, "Been There, Bottled That: Are State and Behavioral Work Engagement New and Useful Construct "Wines'?," *Industrial and Organizational Psychology* 1, no. 1 (2008): 31–35; and A. J. Wefald and R. G. Downey, "Job Engagement in Organizations: Fad, Fashion, or Folderol," *Journal of Organizational Behavior* 30, no. 1 (2009): 141–45.
[125] J. M. George, "The Wider Context, Costs, and Benefits of Work Engagement," *European Journal of Work and Organizational Psychology* 20, no. 1 (2011): 53–59; and J. R. B. Halbesleben, J. Harvey, and M. C. Bolino, "Too Engaged? A Conservation of Resources View of the Relationship between Work Engagement and Work Interference with Family," *Journal of Applied Psychology* 94, no. 6 (2009): 1452–65.

8 Motivation: From Concepts to Applications

Source: Angelika Warmuth/dpa picture alliance archive/Alamy Stock Photo

LEARNING OBJECTIVES

After studying this chapter, you should be able to:

8-1 Describe how the job characteristics model motivates by changing the work environment.

8-2 Compare the main ways jobs can be redesigned.

8-3 Explain how specific alternative work arrangements can motivate employees.

8-4 Describe how employee involvement measures can motivate employees.

8-5 Demonstrate how the different types of variable-pay programs can increase employee motivation.

8-6 Show how flexible benefits turn benefits into motivators.

8-7 Identify the motivational benefits of intrinsic rewards.

Employability Skills Matrix (ESM)

	Myth or Science?	Career OBjectives	An Ethical Choice	Point/ Counterpoint	Experiential Exercise	Ethical Dilemma	Case Incident 1	Case Incident 2
Critical Thinking	✓		✓	✓	✓	✓	✓	✓
Communication		✓		✓	✓	✓	✓	
Collaboration		✓		✓	✓		✓	
Knowledge Application and Analysis	✓	✓	✓	✓	✓	✓	✓	✓
Social Responsibility			✓			✓	✓	

EMPLOYEES TRADING PLACES

If you were given the chance to try something new, something other than the job in the career path you've selected, would you take it? What if you were *encouraged* to do so? This is exactly what some organizations are implementing through their job rotation programs, which enable employees to shift periodically from one task or job to another. The idea is that such assignments have myriad benefits, such as helping employees learn new skills (and gain deeper insight into those they already have), maintaining employee motivation, countering career stagnation, building a flexible and cross-trained workforce, fostering healthy competition, recognizing hidden talents, and sparking employees' curiosity or interest for new roles they may be good at but might not have considered possible.

Intel Corporation lets their employees (such as the one shown) take on temporary assignments to get a better feel and sense of the "hardware" that contributes to Intel's work infrastructure. What's even more interesting is that Intel has developed an internal database (Intel's Developmental Opportunity Tool [DOT]) with which employees can search for hundreds of temporary assignment listings that they can take on. The program's overseer, Amreen Madhani, notes that DOT allows employees to "test-drive a job or make connections in different departments." The success of DOT has led to thousands of successful temporary placements. Before DOT, Madhani asserts, Intel was "so siloed. Everyone had their own tools, but there was limited visibility to employees across the organization. We wanted an enterprise-wide solution."

Taking on job rotation assignments, however, is not always smooth or easy. For example, Elizabeth Wright Korytkowski, a benefits specialist with Intel, took on a four-month, software services group position. She "felt like a deer in the headlights" given the shock, change, and difficulty of taking on such an assignment. Since then, however, she has gained familiarity with software and tools she wouldn't have otherwise been exposed to and has since been promoted.

The advent of job rotation approaches is a welcome trend for both employers and employees—in fact, *employer* and *employee* may be antiquated words decades from now. Randstad's Workplace 2025 survey asked employers and employees to choose a new word that they thought better represented *employees* and that they would like to see used by the year 2025. 47 percent of employers and 57 percent of employees felt that the term *contributor* was the most appropriate word. The survey results are striking regarding perceptions of the role of the "contributor" in the next decade: 76 percent of workers say that they're just as committed when they are working on different types of tasks or functions; 85 percent agree that what matters is providing skills and results, not the role assigned; only 5 percent believe that job experience or seniority is critical; and over 70 percent of millennials and Generation Z employees agree that periodically changing career paths increases their potential.

Job rotation programs appear to provide a great benefit to organizations and *contributors* alike. As Terri Lodwick, president of Executive Women International (EWI) notes, job rotation allows employees to "get to see how they fit into the entire organization, not just their little cubicle."

Sources: Based on D. Coker, "How Job Rotation Is Beneficial for the Organization," *The HR Digest*, October 31, 2016, https://www.thehrdigest.com/job-rotation-beneficial-organization/; B. Fetherstonhaugh, "Developing a Strategy for a Life of Meaningful Labor," *Harvard Business Review*, September 5, 2016, https://hbr.org/2016/09/developing-a-strategy-for-a-life-of-meaningful-labor; F. Gino, "Let Your Workers Rebel," *Harvard Business Review*, October 24, 2016, https://hbr.org/cover-story/2016/10/let-your-workers-rebel; D. Parrey, "How to Create High-Profile Opportunities for High-Potential Employees," *Institute for Corporate Productivity: The Productivity Blog*, May 14, 2013, https://www.i4cp.com/productivity-blog/2013/05/14/how-to-create-high-profile-opportunities-for-high-potential-employees; Randstad, *Workplace 2025: From Employee to Contributor: The Worker of the Future*, October 2016, https://www.randstadusa.com/workforce360/workplace-2025/infographic/?utm_source=pr&utm_medium=pr&utm_term=client&utm_content=rusa&utm_campaign=wp2025+infographic; and L. Weber and L. Kwoh, "Managing & Careers: Co-Workers Change Places," *The Wall Street Journal*, February 21, 2012, B8.

As a result of this switch, it is clear that a number of firms are switching to job rotation methods; task characteristics, job design elements, work arrangements, and a sense of agency are all powerful motivators within the realm of work. These elements can be altered or changed perhaps just by letting workers try something new. However, the process of motivating is more complex than it may seem on the surface and requires an understanding of many job design and redesign elements, along with a consideration of the motivation concepts described in the previous chapter.

In Chapter 7, we focused on motivation theories. While it's important to understand these underlying concepts, it's also important to see how you can use them as a manager. In this chapter, we apply motivation concepts to practices, beginning with job design.

Motivating by Job Design: The Job Characteristics Model

8-1 Describe how the job characteristics model motivates by changing the work environment.

The way work is structured has a bigger impact on an individual's motivation than might first appear. **Job design** suggests that the way elements in a job are organized can influence employee effort,[1] and the job characteristics model, discussed next, can serve as a framework to identify opportunities for changes to those elements.

job design The way the elements in a job are organized.

job characteristics model (JCM) A model proposing that any job can be described in terms of five core job dimensions: skill variety, task identity, task significance, autonomy, and feedback.

skill variety The degree to which a job requires a variety of different activities.

task identity The degree to which a job requires completion of a whole and identifiable piece of work.

task significance The degree to which a job has a substantial impact on the lives or work of other people.

autonomy The degree to which a job provides substantial freedom and discretion to the individual in scheduling the work and in determining the procedures to be used in carrying it out.

feedback The degree to which carrying out the work activities required by a job results in the individual obtaining direct and clear information about the effectiveness of their performance.

The Job Characteristics Model

The **job characteristics model (JCM)** describes jobs in terms of five core job dimensions:[2]

1. **Skill variety** is the degree to which a job requires different activities using specialized skills and talents. The work of a garage owner-operator who does electrical repairs, rebuilds engines, does bodywork, and interacts with customers scores high on skill variety. The job of a body shop worker who sprays paint 8 hours a day scores low on this dimension.
2. **Task identity** is the degree to which a job requires completion of a whole and identifiable piece of work. A cabinetmaker who designs furniture, selects the wood, builds the furniture, and finishes the pieces has a job that scores high on task identity. A job scoring low on this dimension is operating a lathe solely to make table legs.
3. **Task significance** is the degree to which a job affects the lives or work of other people. The job of a nurse helping patients in a hospital intensive care unit scores high on task significance; sweeping floors in a hospital scores low.
4. **Autonomy** is the degree to which a job provides the worker freedom, independence, and discretion in scheduling work and determining the procedures for carrying it out. A sales manager who schedules his own work and tailors his sales approach for each customer without supervision has a highly autonomous job. An account representative who is required to follow a standardized sales script with potential customers has a job low on autonomy.
5. **Feedback** is the degree to which carrying out work activities generates direct and clear information about your own performance. A job with high feedback is testing and inspecting iPads. Installing components of iPads as they move down an assembly line provides low feedback.

Exhibit 8-1 The Job Characteristics Model

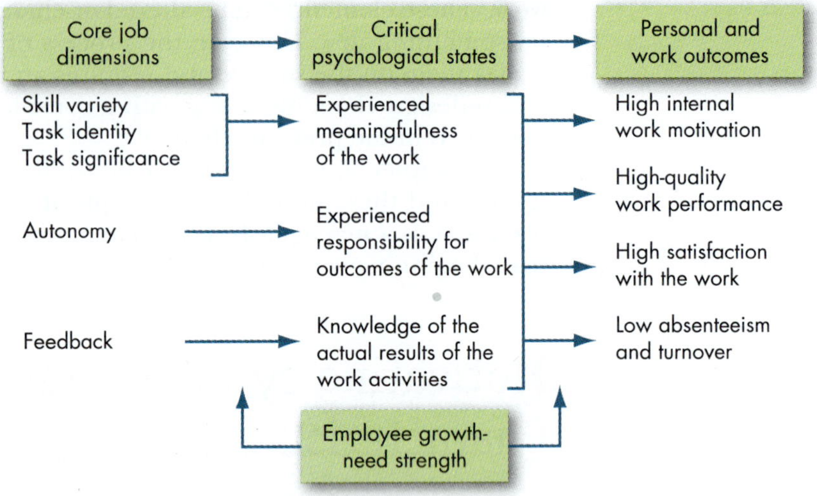

Source: Based on J. L. Pierce, I. Jussila, and A. Cummings, "Psychological Ownership within the Job Design Context: Revision of the Job Characteristics Model," *Journal of Organizational Behavior* 30, no. 4 (2009): 477–96.

Exhibit 8-1 presents the JCM. Note how the first three dimensions—skill variety, task identity, and task significance—combine to create meaningful work the employee will view as important, valuable, and worthwhile. Jobs with high autonomy give employees a feeling of personal responsibility for results; feedback shows them how effectively they are performing. The JCM proposes that individuals obtain internal rewards when they learn (knowledge of results in the model) that they personally have performed well (experienced responsibility) on a task they care about (experienced meaningfulness). The more these three psychological states are present, the greater will be employees' motivation, performance, and satisfaction, and the lower their absenteeism and likelihood of leaving. As Exhibit 8-1 indicates, individuals with a high growth need are more likely to experience the critical psychological states when their jobs are enriched—and are more likely to respond to them more positively.

Much evidence supports the relationship between the presence of these job characteristics and higher job satisfaction and organizational commitment through increased motivation.[3] In general, research concurs with the theory behind the JCM, although studies have introduced potential modifiers. One study suggested that when employees were other-oriented (concerned with the welfare of others at work), the relationship between intrinsic job characteristics and job satisfaction was weaker,[4] meaning that our job satisfaction comes less from these characteristics when we care about others. Another study proposed that the degree of psychological ownership we feel toward our work enhances our motivation, particularly if the feelings of ownership are shared among a work group.[5] Other research has explored the JCM in unique settings such as in virtual work situations, finding that if individuals work together online but not in person, their experience of meaningfulness, responsibility, and knowledge of results can suffer. Thankfully, managers can mitigate these negative effects for employees by consciously developing personal relationships with them and increasing their sense of task significance, autonomy, and feedback.[6]

motivating potential score (MPS) A predictive index that suggests the motivating potential in a job.

We can combine the core dimensions of the JCM into a single predictive index, called the **motivating potential score (MPS)** and calculated as follows:

$$\text{MPS} = \frac{\text{skill variety} + \text{task identity} + \text{task significance}}{3} \times \text{autonomy} \times \text{feedback}$$

To be high on motivating potential, jobs must be high on at least one of the three factors that lead to experienced meaningfulness and high on both autonomy and feedback. If jobs score high on motivating potential, the model predicts that motivation, performance, and satisfaction will improve and that absence and turnover will be reduced. Think about your job. Do you have the opportunity to work on different tasks, or is your day routine? Are you able to work independently, or do you have a supervisor or coworker looking over your shoulder constantly? Your answers indicate your job's motivating potential.

Research has also examined the role that leadership (to be discussed further in Chapter 12) affects employee perceptions of job characteristics. For instance, one study found that ethical leaders improve employees' effort and job performance because they bolster the task significance of their employees.[7] Research in government, private, and military research and development (R&D) organizations in Taiwan reached a similar conclusion—that supportive leadership behaviors improved the job characteristics of R&D professionals.[8]

Job Redesign

8-2 Compare the main ways jobs can be redesigned.

"Every day was the same thing," Frank said. "Stand on that assembly line. Wait for an instrument panel to be moved into place. Unlock the mechanism and drop the panel into the Jeep ... as it moved by on the line. Then I plugged in the harnessing wires. I repeated that for eight hours a day. I don't care that they were paying me 24 dollars an hour. I was going crazy. Finally, I just said this isn't going to be the way I'm going to spend the rest of my life. My brain was turning to JELL-O. So I quit. Now I work in a print shop and I make less than 15 dollars an hour. But let me tell you, the work I do is really interesting. The job changes all the time, I'm continually learning new things, and the work really challenges me! I look forward every morning to going to work again."

The repetitive tasks in Frank's job at the Jeep plant provided little variety, autonomy, or motivation. In contrast, his job in the print shop is challenging and stimulating. From an organizational perspective, the failure of Frank's first employer to redesign his job into a more satisfying one led to increased turnover. Redesigning jobs therefore has important practical implications—reduced turnover and increased job satisfaction among them. Let's look at some ways to put the JCM into practice to make jobs more motivating.

Job Rotation and Job Enrichment

job rotation The periodic shifting of an employee from one task to another.

Job Rotation If employees suffer from over-routinization of their work, one alternative is **job rotation**, or the periodic shifting of an employee from one task to another with similar skill requirements at the same organizational level (also called cross-training).[9] Manufacturers also use job rotation as needed to respond more flexibly to the volume of incoming orders. New managers are sometimes rotated through jobs, too, to help them get a picture of a whole organization.[10] For these reasons, job rotation can be applied in any setting where cross-training is feasible, from manufacturing floors to hospital wards. At Singapore Airlines, for instance, a ticket agent may temporarily take on the duties of a baggage handler, both to be cross-trained and to get exposure to different aspects of the organization. Extensive job rotation is among the reasons that Singapore Airlines is rated one of the best airlines in the world.[11]

The use of job rotation has been shown to increase job satisfaction and organizational commitment.[12] Evidence from Italy, Britain, and Turkey shows that job rotation is associated with higher levels of organizational performance in manufacturing settings.[13] It reduces boredom, increases motivation, and helps employees understand how their work contributes to the organization. It may also increase safety and reduce repetitive-based work injuries, but this is currently a topic of much study and debate, with mixed findings.[14]

Myth or Science?

Money Can't Buy Happiness

Or maybe you've probably heard that money *does* buy happiness. Both may be true. Economist Richard Easterlin argued that once basic financial needs have been met, more money doesn't really do much to make a person happy. Researchers set the limit at around $75,000, recently prompting one CEO to give away all his earnings above that amount to his employees!

This is by no means the last word, nor is it a directive to be unhappy until you make $75,000 and no happier afterward. More recent research worldwide indicates the exact opposite: The more money, the better. The authors said, "If there is a satiation point, we are yet to reach it."

Given these mixed findings, the relationship between happiness and income is probably not direct. In fact, other research suggests your *level* of income is less important than *how* you spend it. Think about why you may be motivated by money. Do you envision the number of zeroes in your bank account increasing? Probably not. You're probably more motivated by what you can buy with the money than by the money itself. From research, we know:

- *Giving money away makes people happier than spending it on themselves.* In one study, students were given money and told to either give it away or spend it on themselves. Then the study asked people to give away their own money. Either way, people were happier giving away the money, even if the givers were relatively poor. What seems to matter is not the amount but how much impact you think your donation will have on others.
- *People are happier when they spend money on experiences rather than products.* Research professor Thomas Gilovich says that we think to ourselves, "I have a limited amount of money, and I can either go there, or I can have this. If I go there, it'll be great, but it'll be over in no time. If I buy this thing, at least I'll always have it. That is factually true, but not psychologically true. We adapt to our material goods."
- *People are happier when they buy time, but only if they use it well.* Outsource tasks when you can, for instance, and "think of it as 'windfall time' and use it to do something good," says researcher Elizabeth Dunn.

Saying that money brings more happiness when spent on our experiences (and the time to do them) may seem counterintuitive until we think about it closely. What did you think of your cell phone when you bought it compared to what you think of it now? Chances are you were interested and engaged when you bought it, but now it is an everyday object. For experiences, what did you think of your greatest vacation when you were on it, and what do you think of it now? Both the experience at the time and the recollection now may bring a smile to your face.

Sources: Based on A. Blackman, "Can Money Buy Happiness?" *The Wall Street Journal,* November 10, 2014, R1, R2; D. Kurtzleben, "Finally: Proof That Money Buys Happiness (Sort Of)," *USNews.com,* April 29, 2013; and A. Novotney, "Money Can't Buy Happiness," *Monitor on Psychology* (July/August 2012): 24–26.

Job rotation does have drawbacks. Training costs increase when each rotation necessitates a round of training. Second, moving a worker into a new position reduces overall productivity for that role. Third, job rotation creates disruptions when members of the work group must adjust to new employees. Fourth, supervisors may have to spend more time answering questions and monitoring the work of recently rotated employees.

Job Enrichment Think back to some of the motivation concepts from Chapter 7, including developing and nurturing intrinsic motivation. This major focus of self-determination theory can be put into action through the process of job enrichment. In **job enrichment**, high-level responsibilities are added to the job to increase a sense of purpose, direction, meaning, and intrinsic motivation.[15]

job enrichment Adding high-level responsibilities to a job to increase intrinsic motivation.

Enriching a job in this way is different from enlarging it, or adding more tasks and requirements. It involves adding another layer of responsibility and meaning. Job enrichment has its roots in Herzberg's theories of providing hygiene, or motivating factors, to the job to increase motivation. Sometimes, enrichment is not rigidly controlled by management; employees, especially those in occupations experiencing high industry growth, have been known to enrich their own jobs (and become satisfied as a result).[16]

Early reviews suggest that job enrichment can be effective at reducing turnover, almost twice as effective as giving employees a "realistic preview" of the work before they join the organization.[17] In a survey of over 20,000 British employees, job enrichment practices were related to organizations' financial performance, labor productivity, absenteeism, and output quality through improvements in job satisfaction.[18]

Relational Job Design

While redesigning jobs on the basis of job characteristics theory is likely to make work more intrinsically motivating, research is focusing on how to make jobs more prosocially motivating to people. In other words, how can managers design work so employees are motivated to promote the well-being of the organization's beneficiaries (customers, clients, patients, and employees)? This view, **relational job design**, shifts the spotlight from the employee to those whose lives are affected by the job that employee performs.[19] It also motivates individuals toward increased job performance and job satisfaction, especially when coupled with autonomy.[20]

relational job design Constructing jobs so employees see the positive difference they can make in the lives of others directly through their work.

One way to make jobs more prosocially motivating is to connect employees more closely with the beneficiaries of their work by relating stories from customers who have found the company's products or services to be helpful. For example, the medical device manufacturer Medtronic invites people to describe how its products have improved, or even saved, their lives and shares these stories with employees during annual meetings, which provides the employees a powerful reminder of the impact of their work. For another example, researchers found that when university fundraisers briefly interacted with the undergraduates who would receive the scholarship money they raised, they persisted 42 percent longer and raised nearly twice as much money as those who didn't interact with potential recipients.[21] The positive impact was apparent even when fundraisers met with just a single scholarship recipient.

Personal contact with beneficiaries may not always be necessary. Once a child's chemotherapy comes to an end at one of the many cancer centers

A woman's collective at an hill station in India, put the name of the knitter or painter on all the craft products they sold. The customers value the fact that they can relate to the woman who knitted their cap or painted their *diya*.
Source: clicksabhi.shutterstock.com

across the United States and he or she has successfully defeated cancer, it has become tradition for the child to ring a bell, the sound of which is often broadcast throughout many areas of the hospital. The mere act of hearing this bell is inspiring to the staff. Dr. ZoAnn Dryer of the Texas Children's Cancer Center notes, "Every time that bell rings, it's like you know what, somebody else has done it. That's what this is all about."[22]

Why do these connections have such positive consequences? Meeting beneficiaries firsthand—or even just seeing pictures of them—allows employees to see that their actions affect a real person and have tangible consequences. It makes customers or clients more memorable and emotionally vivid, which leads employees to consider the effects of their work actions more. Connections allow employees to take the perspective of beneficiaries, which fosters higher levels of commitment.

You might be wondering whether connecting employees with the beneficiaries of their work is already covered by the idea of task significance in job characteristics theory. However, some differences make beneficiary contact unique. For one, many jobs might be perceived as being high in significance, yet employees in those jobs never meet the individuals affected by their work. Second, beneficiary contact seems to have a distinct relationship with prosocial behaviors such as helping others. For example, one study found that lifeguards who read stories about how their actions benefited swimmers were rated as more helpful by their bosses; this was not the case for lifeguards who read stories about the personal benefits of their work for themselves.[23] The upshot? There are many ways you can design jobs to be more motivating, and your choice should depend on the outcomes you'd like to achieve.

Relational job design, with its focus on prosocial motivation, is an especially salient topic for organizations with corporate social responsibility (CSR) initiatives. As we discussed in earlier chapters, CSR efforts often include invitations for employees to volunteer their time and effort, sometimes using the skills they gained on the job (like Home Depot employees when they help rebuild homes) but often not (such as when bank employees help rebuild homes with groups like Habitat for Humanity). In both cases, the employees may be able to interact with the beneficiaries of their efforts, and research indicates that corporate-sponsored volunteer programs enhanced the JCM dimensions of meaningfulness and task significance and motivated employees to volunteer.[24] While this motivation for prosocial behavior is noteworthy, however, it is not the same as relational job design: For one, the CSR efforts occur through volunteering (not on the job). Also, the work employees are providing is not usually the same work they do at their jobs (Home Depot workers do not build homes on the job). However, relational job design holds intriguing possibilities for CSR initiatives.

Alternative Work Arrangements

8-3 Explain how specific alternative work arrangements can motivate employees.

As you are probably aware, there are many approaches to motivating people, and we've discussed some of them. Another approach to motivation is to consider alternative work arrangements such as flextime, job sharing, and telecommuting.[25] These are likely to be especially important for a diverse workforce of dual-earner couples, single parents, and employees caring for a sick or aging relative.

Flextime

Susan is the classic "morning person." Every day she rises at 5:00 A.M. sharp, full of energy. However, as she puts it, "I'm usually ready for bed right after the 7:00 P.M. news."

Susan's work schedule as a claims processor at The Hartford Financial Services Group is flexible. Her office opens at 6:00 A.M. and closes at 7:00 P.M., and she schedules her 8-hour day within this 13-hour period. Because she is a morning person whose 7-year-old son gets out of school at 3:00 P.M. every day, Susan opts to work from 6:00 A.M. to 3:00 P.M. "My work hours are perfect. I'm at the job when I'm mentally most alert, and I can be home to take care of my son after he gets out of school."

flextime Flexible work hours.

Susan's schedule is an example of **flextime**, short for flexible work time or flexible work arrangements.[26] Flextime employees must work a specific number of hours per week but may vary their hours of work, within limits. As Exhibit 8-2 shows, each day consists of a common core, usually 6 hours, with a flexibility band surrounding it. The core may be 9:00 A.M. to 3:00 P.M., and the office opens at 6:00 A.M. and closes at 6:00 P.M. Employees must be at their jobs during the common core period, but they may accumulate their other 2 hours around that. Some flextime programs allow employees to accumulate extra hours and turn them into days off.

Flextime has become extremely popular. According to recent surveys, a majority (54 to 56 percent) of U.S. organizations offer some form of flextime—and reap benefits from it as well. Thirty-three percent of organizations report an increase in participation and 23 percent indicate an increase in productivity (conversely, 5 percent or less indicated a decrease in participation and productivity).[27] It appears as if flextime has become an important job design element for many employees—53 percent of employees cite flexible arrangements as a very important aspect of their job satisfaction, 55 percent of employees were unlikely to seek job opportunities elsewhere within the year, and 34 percent stated that they would remain with their current employer because of flexible arrangements.[28] In countries such as Germany, Belgium, the

Exhibit 8-2 Possible Flextime Staff Schedules

Schedule 1

Percent Time:	100% = 40 hours per week
Core Hours:	9:00 A.M.–5:00 P.M., Monday through Friday (1 hour lunch)
Work Start Time:	Between 8:00 A.M. and 9:00 A.M.
Work End Time:	Between 5:00 P.M. and 6:00 P.M.

Schedule 2

Percent Time:	100% = 40 hours per week
Work Hours:	8:00 A.M.–6:30 P.M., Monday through Thursday (1/2 hour lunch)
	Friday off
Work Start Time:	8:00 A.M.
Work End Time:	6:30 P.M.

Schedule 3

Percent Time:	90% = 36 hours per week
Work Hours:	8:30 A.M.–5:00 P.M., Monday through Thursday (1/2 hour lunch)
	8:00 A.M.–Noon Friday (no lunch)
Work Start Time:	8:30 A.M. (Monday–Thursday); 8:00 A.M. (Friday)
Work End Time:	5:00 P.M. (Monday–Thursday); Noon (Friday)

Schedule 4

Percent Time:	80% = 32 hours per week
Work Hours:	8:00 A.M.–6:00 P.M., Monday through Wednesday (1/2 hour lunch)
	8:00 A.M.–11:30 A.M. Thursday (no lunch)
	Friday off
Work Start Time:	Between 8:00 A.M. and 9:00 A.M.
Work End Time:	Between 5:00 P.M. and 6:00 P.M.

Netherlands, and France, employers are not allowed to refuse an employee's request for either a part-time or a flexible work schedule by law as long as the request is reasonable, such as to care for an infant child.[29]

Most of the evidence for flextime stacks up favorably. One review of over 40 studies suggests that flextime is related to positive work outcomes in general, but only weakly—the effects are much stronger when considering reductions in absenteeism and, to a lesser degree, improvements in productivity and schedule satisfaction.[30] Flextime tends to reduce absenteeism because employees can schedule their work hours to align with personal demands, reducing tardiness and absences, and they can work when they are most productive. Flextime can also help employees balance work and family lives; it is a popular criterion for judging how family friendly a workplace is. Much less promising, the empirical evidence from over 100,000 employees suggests that, although flextime is weakly effective at reducing the extent to which work interferes with family, it does not affect situations in which family interferes with work.[31] However, flextime's effects on work-life balance are more nuanced than they might appear. A British survey showed that men use flexitime to increase flexibility and control over work while maintaining earning capacity. However, the practical limitations of using flexitime may create difficulties for women due to the constraints of their greater household contribution.[32] These studies suggest that if flextime is used too much, it can undermine goal accomplishment.

Flextime's major drawback is that it's not applicable to every job or every worker. Managers and supervisors already have a high degree of autonomy in their jobs, so it is not as effective for them as it is for general employees.[33] It also appears that people who have a strong desire to separate their work and family lives are less apt to use flextime.[34] Those who ask for it are often stigmatized, which may be avoided if the majority of the organization's leaders adopt flexible hours to signal that flextime is acceptable.[35] Flextime is intuitively a worthwhile business practice, so these findings suggest additional research is needed to determine individual differences in the use of various aspects of flextime.

Job Sharing

job sharing An arrangement that allows two or more individuals to split a traditional 40-hour-a-week job.

Job sharing allows two or more individuals to split a traditional full-time job.[36] One employee might perform the job from 8:00 A.M. to noon and the other from 1:00 P.M. to 5:00 P.M., or the two could work full but alternate days. For example, top Ford engineers Julie Levine and Julie Rocco engaged in a job-sharing program that allowed both to spend time with their families while redesigning the Explorer crossover. Typically, one of them would work late afternoons and evenings while the other worked mornings. They both agreed that the program worked well, although making it feasible required a great deal of time and preparation.[37]

Only 18 percent of U.S. organizations offered job sharing in 2014, a 29 percent decrease since 2008.[38] Reasons it is not more widely adopted include the difficulty of finding compatible partners to job-share and the historically negative perceptions of individuals not completely committed to their jobs and employers. However, eliminating job sharing for these reasons might be shortsighted. Job sharing allows an organization to draw on the talents of more than one individual for a given job. It opens the opportunity to acquire skilled workers—for instance, retirees and parents with young children—who might not be available on a full-time basis. From employees' perspectives, job sharing can increase motivation and satisfaction if they can work when they wouldn't normally be able to do so. An employer's decision to use job sharing is often based on policy and financial reasons. Two part-time employees sharing a job can be less expensive in terms of salary and benefits than one full-timer, but this may not be the case because training, coordination, and administrative costs can be high. Ideally, employers should consider each employee and job separately, seeking to match the skills, personality, and needs of the employee with the tasks required for the job and taking into account that individual's motivating factors.

Telecommuting

Since the COVID-19 pandemic of 2020, working from home might be the "new normal."[39] During this time, a large portion of the nearly 9,000 employees from a Gallup panel indicated that they were working from home during the pandemic, especially those of middle- to upper-class backgrounds.[40] Furthermore, a Gartner survey found that 74 percent of the executives surveyed would keep at least a portion of their work force remote after the pandemic.[41]

Although people rarely had a choice in the matter during the COVID-19 pandemic, is working from home effective? Do employees like working from home? For some, it might be close to the ideal job: no rush hour traffic, flexible hours, freedom to dress as you please, and few interruptions. **Telecommuting** refers to working at home—or anywhere else the employee chooses that is outside the workplace—at least 2 days a week through virtual devices linked to the employer's office.[42] A sales manager working from home is telecommuting, but a sales manager working from her car on a business trip is not.

telecommuting Working from home at least 2 days a week through virtual devices that are linked to the employer's office.

Telecommuting seems to mesh with the cultural transition to knowledge work (which often can be performed anywhere) and, as the OB Poll indicates, people with more education are more apt to work from home. However, telecommuting has been a popular topic lately not for its potential but for its organizational acceptance, or lack thereof. Despite the benefits of telecommuting, large organizations such as Yahoo! and Best Buy have eliminated it.[43] Yahoo! CEO Marissa Mayer discussed how telecommuting may undermine corporate culture, noting, "People are more productive when they're alone, but they're more collaborative and innovative when they're together."[44]

What kinds of jobs lend themselves to telecommuting? Writers, attorneys, analysts, and employees who spend most their time on computers or the telephone—including telemarketers, customer service representatives, reservation agents, and product support specialists—are candidates. As telecommuters, they can access information on their computers at home as easily as in the company's office.

Telecommuting has several benefits. It is positively related to objective and supervisor rated performance and job satisfaction; to a lesser degree, it reduces role stress and turnover intentions.[45] Employees who work virtually more than 2.5 days a week tend to experience the benefits of reductions in work-family conflict more intensely than those who are in the office the majority of their workweek.[46] Beyond the benefits to organizations and their employees, telecommuting has potential benefits to society. One study estimated that if people in the United States telecommuted half the time, carbon emissions would be reduced by approximately 51 metric tons per year. Environmental savings could come from lower office energy consumption, fewer traffic jams that emit greenhouse gases, and a reduced need for road repairs.[47]

Telecommuting has several downsides too. In today's team-focused workplace, telecommuting may lead to social loafing (i.e., employees shirking responsibility in a team setting), especially when the employees have many family responsibilities but their teammates do not.[48] Your manager working remotely can affect your performance negatively.[49] Managers are also challenged to handle the demotivation of office workers who feel they are unfairly denied the freedom of telecommuters.[50] Contrary to Mayer's conclusions for Yahoo!, research indicates that more creative tasks may actually be best suited for telecommuting, whereas dull repetitive tasks like data entry decrease motivation and thus performance for remote workers.[51]

From the employee's standpoint, telecommuting can increase feelings of isolation as well as reduce job satisfaction and coworker relationship quality.[52] Research indicates that if you are forced to work from home, although you may experience less work–family conflict in general, you might still experience it if you work hours beyond the contracted workweek and are constantly "on call."[53] Telecommuters are also vulnerable to the "out of sight, out of

Career OBjectives

How can I get flextime?

My job is great, but I can't understand why management won't allow flextime. After all, I often work on a laptop in the office! I could just as easily be working on the same laptop at home without interruptions from my colleagues. I know I'd be more productive. How can I convince them to let me?

—Sophia

Dear Sophia:

We can't help but wonder two things: (1) Is the ban on working from home a company policy or your manager's policy, and (2) do you want flextime or telecommuting? If you work for Yahoo!, for instance, you may not be able to convince anyone to let you work from home after CEO Marissa Mayer's very public decree against the policy. If the ban is your manager's policy—or even your division's policy—in an organization open to alternative work arrangements, you just may be able to get your way.

That leads us to the second question, about flextime versus telecommuting. If you want flextime as you stated and just want to work from home during some noncore hours (say, work in the office for 6 hours a day and work another 2 hours a day from home), your employer may be more likely to grant your wish than if you want to telecommute completely (work all your hours from home).

Research indicates that employees are most likely to be granted work-from-home privileges because of a direct sympathetic relationship with their managers (not because of a company policy). Employees are also more likely to gain acceptance for partial than for full telecommuting (either flextime or by alternating days). It helps if you have a legitimate need to be home and if you do knowledge-based work. Jared Dalton, for instance, telecommutes 2 days a week as a manager for accounting firm Ernst & Young, and his wife Christina telecommutes on 2 different days so they can oversee the care of their infant.

If it sounds like flextime depends on favoritism, you might be right. It's also a reflection, however, of the state of telecommuting: Only 38 percent of U.S. organizations permit *some* of their employees to work from home regularly. To be one of the lucky few:

- *Check your organization's flexible options policies.*
- *Develop a plan for working from home to show your manager.* Include how many hours per week, which days of the week, and where you will work, and explain how your manager can retain oversight of you.
- *Assemble evidence on your productivity.* Have you worked from home before? If so, show how much you achieved. You stated you would be more productive at home: How much more?
- *Outline your reasons for working from home.* Do you need to help care for an aging relative, for instance? Would working from home save you commuting time you could use for work?
- *Address management's concerns.* Research indicates the biggest ones are the possibility of abuse of the system and issues of fairness.
- *Consider your relationship with your manager.* Has he or she been supportive of you in the past? Is your manager approachable?

When you're ready, discuss your request with your manager. Remember, pitching the idea of telecommuting is the same as pitching any idea—you've got to think about what's in it for your employer, not for yourself.

Sources: Based on "The 2015 Workplace Flexibility Study," *WorkplaceTrends.com*, February 3, 2015, https://workplacetrends.com/the-2015-workplace-flexibility-study/; T. S. Bernard, "For Workers, Less Flexible Companies," *The New York Times*, May 20, 2014, B1, B7; and C. C. Miller and L. Alderman, "The Flexibility Gap," *The New York Times*, December 14, 2014, 1, 5.

The opinions provided here are of the managers and authors only and do not necessarily reflect those of their organizations. The authors or managers are not responsible for any errors or omissions, or for the results obtained from the use of this information. In no event will the authors or managers, or their related partnerships or corporations thereof, be liable to you or anyone else for any decision made or action taken in reliance on the opinions provided here.

mind" effect: Employees who aren't at their desks miss meetings and don't share in day-to-day informal workplace interactions, which may put them at a disadvantage when it comes to raises and promotions because they're perceived as not putting in the requisite face time, unless telework is the norm in

OB POLL

Who Works from Home?

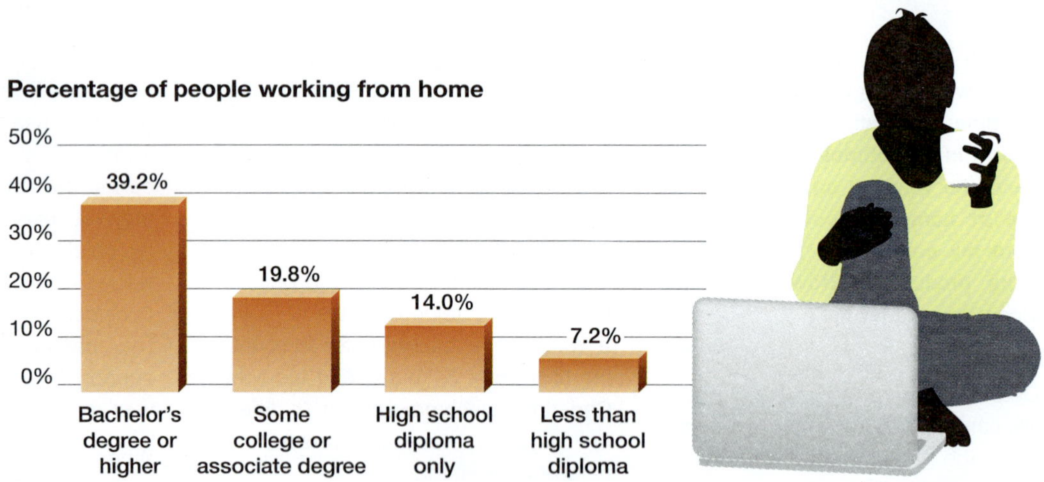

Source: Bureau of Labor Statistics, Table 6, from Economic News Release, "American Time Use Survey Summary," June 24, 2016, https://www.bls.gov/news.release/atus.t06.htm.

the organization, there is still common contact with the supervisor, and it is clear that the employee is working (e.g., they have a heavy workload and are productive).[54]

If telecommuting is here to stay, what can employees and employers do to ensure the arrangements are effective? Apart from ensuring the arrangement is right for the position (as described above),[55] self-leadership, including proactive, goal-setting, and personal performance management are related to success in telework.[56] Further, using smart collaboration tools, communicating frequently, having clear and transparent policies, and building trust among virtual team members can help improve the effectiveness of telework for the whole team.[57]

Employee Involvement

8-4 Describe how employee involvement measures can motivate employees.

employee involvement and participation (EIP) A participative process that uses the input of employees to increase employee commitment to organizational success.

Employee involvement and participation (EIP)[58] is a process that uses employees' input to increase their commitment to organizational success. If workers are engaged in decisions that increase their autonomy and control over their work lives, they will become more motivated, more committed to the organization, more productive, and more satisfied with their jobs (and less likely to leave their jobs).[59] These benefits don't stop with individuals—when teams are given more control over their work, morale and performance increase as well.[60]

To be successful, EIP programs should be tailored to local and national norms.[61] A study of four countries, including India and the United States, confirmed the importance of modifying practices to reflect national culture.[62] While U.S. employees readily accepted EIP programs, managers in

India who tried to empower their employees were rated low by those employees. These reactions are consistent with India's high power-distance culture, which accepts and expects differences in authority. The work culture in India may not be in as much transition as it is in China, in which some employees are becoming less high power-distance oriented. Chinese workers who were very accepting of traditional Chinese cultural values showed few benefits from participative decision making. However, Chinese workers who were less traditional were more satisfied and had higher performance ratings under participative management.[63] Another study conducted in China showed that involvement increased employees' thoughts and feelings of job security, which enhanced their well-being.[64] These differences within China may well reflect the current transitional nature of Chinese culture. For example, research in urban China indicated that some aspects of EIP programs, namely, those that favor consultation and expression but not participation in decision making, yield higher job satisfaction.[65]

Examples of Employee Involvement Programs

Let's look at two major forms of employee involvement—participative management and representative participation—in more detail.

participative management A process in which subordinates share a significant degree of decision-making power with their immediate superiors.

Participative Management Common to all **participative management** programs is joint decision making, in which subordinates share a significant degree of decision-making power with their immediate superiors.[66] This sharing can occur either formally through, say, briefings or surveys, or informally through daily consultations as a way to enhance motivation through trust and commitment.[67] Participative management has, at times, been considered a panacea or cure-all for poor morale and low productivity—indeed, evidence suggests that participative management reduces the negative effects of job insecurity on satisfaction and turnover intentions.[68] Participative management techniques such as quality circles have been found in one review to have a moderate effect on job performance.[69] For participative management to be effective, however, followers must have trust and confidence in their leaders and be prepared for the change in management style, whereas leaders should avoid coercive techniques, stress the organizational consequences of decision making to their followers, and review progress periodically.[70]

Studies of the participation–organizational performance relationship have yielded more mixed findings.[71] Organizations that institute participative management may realize higher stock returns, lower turnover rates, and higher labor productivity, although these effects are typically not large.[72]

representative participation A system in which workers participate in organizational decision making through a small group of representative employees.

Representative Participation Most countries in western Europe require companies to practice **representative participation.**[73] Representative participation redistributes power within an organization, putting labor's interests on a more equal footing with the interests of management and stockholders by including a small group of employees as participants in decision making. In the United Kingdom, Ireland, Australia, and New Zealand, representative participation was originally the only EIP program, formed to allow employee representatives to discuss issues outside union agreements, and the representatives were all from the union. However, representative groups are now increasingly a mix of union and nonunion, separate from the union arrangement.[74]

Bernd Osterloh, chair of Volkswagen's works councils, speaks to production line workers at company headquarters in Wolfsburg, Germany. Volkswagen (VW) includes employees in decision making by allowing them to participate in discussions about work rules, the company's finances and business plans, and workplace productivity and safety.
Source: Fabian Bimmer/Reuters

The two most common forms of representation are works councils and board representatives. Works councils are groups of nominated or elected employees who must be consulted when management makes decisions about employees. Board representatives are employees who sit on a company's board of directors and represent employees' interests.

The influence of representative participation on working employees seems to be mixed, but generally an employee would need to feel his or her interests are well represented and make a difference to the organization for motivation to increase. Thus, representative participation as a motivational tool is surpassed by more direct participation methods.

In sum, EIP programs clearly have the potential to increase employees' intrinsic motivation. The opportunity to make and implement decisions—and then see them work out—can contribute to all desirable organizational outcomes. Giving employees control over key decisions, along with ensuring that their interests are represented, can enhance feelings of procedural justice. But like any other initiatives, EIP programs must be designed carefully.

Using Rewards to Motivate Employees

8-5 Demonstrate how the different types of variable-pay programs can increase employee motivation.

As we saw in Chapter 3, pay is not the only factor driving job satisfaction. However, it does motivate people, and companies often underestimate its importance. Although not as important as enjoyment of one's work and the job fitting well with other areas of an employee's life, approximately 60 percent of respondents to an American Psychological Association survey indicated that they were staying with their current employer because of the pay and benefits.[75]

Given that pay is so important, will the organization lead, match, or lag the market in pay? How will individual contributions be recognized? In this section, we consider (1) what to pay employees (decided by establishing a pay structure), and (2) how to pay individual employees (decided through variable-pay plans).

What to Pay: Establishing a Pay Structure

There are many ways to pay employees. The process of initially setting pay levels entails balancing *internal equity*—the worth of the job to the organization (usually established through a technical process called job evaluation), and *external equity*—the competitiveness of an organization's pay relative to pay in its industry (usually established through pay surveys). Obviously, the best pay system reflects what the job is worth and also stays competitive relative to the labor market.

Some organizations prefer to pay above the market, while some may lag the market because they can't afford to pay market rates or they are willing to bear the costs of paying below market (namely, higher turnover because people are lured to better-paying jobs). Some companies that have realized impressive gains in income and profit margins have done so in part by holding down employee wages.[76]

Pay more, and you may get better-qualified, more highly motivated employees who will stay with the organization longer. A study covering 126 large organizations found employees who believed they were receiving a competitive pay level experienced higher morale and were more productive, and customers were more satisfied as well.[77] Trident a traditional manufacturing company in early 2021 adopted objectives and key results', as the method to align and engage employees with the goals they set and achieve. Employees receive variable pay linked to their achievement of goals.[78] But pay is often the highest single operating cost for an organization, which means paying too much can make the organization's products or services too expensive. It's a strategic decision an organization must make, with clear trade-offs.

Cary Chin works at the front desk for Gravity Payments, a credit card processing firm in Seattle, where the cost of living is extremely high. Gravity's CEO Dan Price established a new pay structure for all employees of a $70,000 base salary to improve their quality of life and motivate them to work harder on achieving high customer satisfaction.

Source: Ted S. Warren/AP Images

In the case of Walmart, it appears that its strategic decision on pay did not work. While annual growth in U.S. stores slowed to around 1 percent in 2011, one of Walmart's larger competitors, Costco, grew around 8 percent. The average worker at Costco made approximately $45,000 compared to approximately $17,500 for the average worker at Walmart-owned Sam's Club. Costco's strategy was that it will get more if it pays more—and higher wages resulted in increased employee productivity and reduced turnover. Given the recent Walmart decision to increase worker wages throughout the organization, perhaps its executives agree.[79]

However, companies often face challenge with multiple age-groups working in the system, it is difficult to decide which is a better motivator-high pay or added benefits. Recognizing this challenge, Diageo has devised multiple strategies for its employees. The rewards are a mix of "creating a culture of purpose, needs agile and flexible compensation and benefit plans, and learning opportunities" says Aziz, the CHRO of Diageo.[80]

How to Pay: Rewarding Individual Employees through Variable-Pay Programs

"Why should I put any extra effort into this job?," asked Anne, a fourth-grade elementary schoolteacher in Denver, Colorado. "I can excel or I can do the bare minimum. It makes no difference. I get paid the same. Why do anything above the minimum to get by?" Comments like Anne's have been voiced by schoolteachers for decades because pay increases were tied to seniority. Recently, however, many states have altered their compensation systems to motivate teachers by linking pay to results in the classroom, and other states are considering such programs.[81] Many organizations, public and private, are moving away from pay based on seniority or credentials.

variable-pay program A pay plan that bases a portion or all of an employee's pay on some individual and/or organizational measure of performance.

Piece-rate, merit-based, bonus, profit-sharing, and employee stock ownership plans are all forms of a **variable-pay program** (also known as pay for performance), which bases a portion of an employee's pay on some individual and/or organizational measure of performance.[82] The variable portion may be all or part of the paycheck, and it may be paid annually or upon attainment of benchmarks. It can also be either optional for the employee or an accepted condition of employment.[83] Variable-pay plans have long been used to compensate salespeople and executives, but the scope of variable-pay jobs has broadened. Some universities in India increased the per article published rate for faculty and have realized high gains in research productivity.

Around the world, about 84 percent of companies offer some form of variable-pay plan.[84] Most organizations (70 percent) use a combination of organization-, department-, team-, and individual-level awards, whereas less than a third use only organization-wide or department-, team-, or individual-level awards exclusively.[85] For 2017 exempt workers (e.g., salaried workers who are not covered under the Fair Labor Standards Act [FLSA]), organizations are projecting to reward employees 11.6 percent of their salaries, on average, with a variable-pay method.[86]

Unfortunately, not all employees see a strong connection between pay and performance. although it seems that the type of plan matters. As we stated, teacher pay-for-performance plans are starting to be used more frequently, particularly those that are based on student test scores; recent research on thousands of teachers in the United States has shown that these programs (1) are not having a positive impact on teacher motivation or teaching practices and

(2) have actually led to higher levels of stress, along with counterproductive work behaviors, such as cheating and even bullying of students to perform better on tests.[87]

Empirically, the results of pay-for-performance plans are mixed; the context and receptivity of the individual to the plan plays a large role. For instance, one study of 438 Chinese and Taiwanese supervisor–subordinate dyads found that employee creativity and intrinsic motivation was bolstered by pay-for-performance plans, but only when employees trusted management and when *guanxi* (specific, personal connections between subordinates, supervisors, and coworkers) played less of a role in human resources (HR) practices.[88] Leadership (see Chapter 12) also plays a role, with pay-for-performance plans leading to performance more clearly when contingent reward leadership and other positive leadership behaviors are used.[89] Extraverted and emotionally stable individuals tend to be more receptive to and perform better under pay for performance, whereas conscientious employees were not as receptive.[90]

Secrecy plays a role in the motivational success of variable-pay plans. In some government and nonprofit agencies, pay amounts are either specifically or generally made public, but most U.S. organizations encourage or require pay secrecy.[91] Is this good or bad? Unfortunately, it's bad: Pay secrecy has a detrimental effect on job performance. Even worse, it adversely affects high performers more than other employees. It very likely increases employees' perception that pay is subjective, which can be demotivating. Individual pay amounts may not need to be broadcast to restore the balance, but if general pay categories are made public and employees feel variable pay is linked objectively to their performance, the motivational effects of variable pay can be retained.[92]

The fluctuation in variable pay is what makes these programs attractive to management. It turns part of an organization's fixed labor costs into a variable cost, thus reducing expenses when performance declines. For example, when the U.S. economy encountered a recession in 2001 and again in 2008, companies with variable pay could reduce their labor costs much faster than others could.[93] Over time, low performers' pay stagnates, while high performers enjoy pay increases commensurate with their contributions. However, it appears that the organization's return on pay for performance varies over time as well. One study of shareholder returns of the U.S. S&P's 500 firms between 1998 and 2005 suggests that, although pay-for-performance plans (including stock options and bonuses) are most effective for CEOs when they start out, their relationship with shareholder returns slowly decreases over time; the relationship between traditional plans and shareholder returns increases over time.[94]

Let's examine the different types of variable-pay programs in more detail.

piece-rate pay plan A pay plan in which workers are paid a fixed sum for each unit of production completed.

Piece-Rate Pay The **piece-rate pay plan** has long been popular as a means of compensating production workers with a fixed sum for each unit of production completed, but it can be used in any organizational setting where the outputs are similar enough to be evaluated by quantity.[95] A pure piece-rate plan provides no base salary and pays the employee only for what he or she produces. Ballpark workers selling peanuts and soda are frequently paid piece-rate. If they sell 40 bags of peanuts at ₹10 each for their earnings, their take is ₹400. The more peanuts they sell, the more they earn. Alternatively, piece-rate plans are sometimes distributed to sales teams, so a ballpark worker makes money on a portion of the total number of bags of peanuts sold by the group during a game.

Piece-rate plans are known to produce higher productivity and wages, so they can be attractive to organizations and motivating for workers.[96] In fact, one major Chinese university increased its piece-rate pay for articles by professors and realized an increase of 50 percent in research productivity.[97] In the workplace, employees most likely to be motivated by piece-rate plans are managers and more tenured workers. Low-performing workers are generally not interested in piece-rate pay, for obvious reasons—they won't get paid much!

The chief concern of both individual and team piece-rate workers is financial risk. A recent experiment in Germany found that 68 percent of risk-averse individuals prefer an individual piece-rate system, and that lower performers prefer team piece-rate pay. Why? The authors suggested risk-averse and high-performing individuals would rather take their chances on pay based on what they can control (their own work) because they are concerned others will slack off in a team setting.[98] What about using both? Recent work suggests that doing so might address the limitations of using either in isolation: across more than 22,000 European establishments, using both plans (combined with an EIP approach, as described earlier) led to substantial increases in employee innovation.[99] This is a valid concern, as we will discuss in the next chapter. Organizations, on the other hand, should verify that their piece-rate plans are indeed motivating to individuals. European research has suggested that when the pace of work is determined by uncontrollable outside factors such as customer requests rather than internal factors such as coworkers, targets, and machines, a piece rate plan is not motivating.[100] Either way, managers must be mindful of the motivation for workers to decrease quality and thus increase their speed of output.

Thus, while piece-rate plans can be a powerful motivator in many organizational settings, an obvious limitation is that they're not feasible for many jobs. An emergency room (ER) doctor and nurse can earn significant salaries regardless of the number of patients they see or their patients' outcomes. Would it be better to pay them only if their patients fully recover? It seems unlikely that most would accept such a deal, and it might cause unanticipated consequences as well (such as ERs turning away patients with terminal diseases or life-threatening injuries). Although incentives are motivating and relevant for some jobs, it is unrealistic to think they work universally.

merit-based pay plan A pay plan based on performance appraisal ratings.

Merit-Based Pay A **merit-based pay plan** pays for individual performance based on performance appraisal ratings.[101] A main advantage is that high performers can get bigger raises. If designed correctly, merit-based plans let individuals perceive a strong relationship between their performance and their rewards.[102]

Most large organizations have merit pay plans, especially for salaried employees. Merit pay is slowly taking hold in the public sector. For example, most U.S. government employees are unionized, and the unions that represent them have usually demanded that pay raises be based solely on seniority. Claiming a new era of accountability, however, New Jersey governor Chris Christie implemented merit pay for teachers. The Newark teacher's union approved the plan, which included funding from Facebook CEO Mark Zuckerberg.[103] In another unusual move, New York City's public hospital system pays doctors based on how well they reduce costs, increase patient satisfaction, and improve the quality of care.[104]

Such merit and performance-based pay does not exist even in the public sector in India. However, in a first ever move the Maharashtra government has announced in January 2018 that it will rank and grade all its 7.5 lakh state employees on the basis of their performance and has formulated a new 100-point performance marking system for the purpose.[105]

A move away from merit pay, on the other hand, is coming from some organizations that don't feel it separates high and low performers enough. "There's a very strong belief and there's evidence and academic research that shows that variable pay does create focus among employees," said Ken Abosch, a compensation manager at human resources consulting firm Aon Hewitt. But when the annual review and raise are months away, the motivation of this reward for high performers diminishes. Even companies that have retained merit pay are rethinking the allocation.[106]

Although you might think a person's average level of performance is the key factor in merit pay decisions, the projected level of future performance also plays a role. One study found that National Basketball Association (NBA) players whose performance was on an upward trend were paid more than their average performance would have predicted. Managers of all organizations may unknowingly be basing merit pay decisions on how they *think* employees will perform, which may result in overly optimistic (or pessimistic) pay decisions.[107]

Despite their intuitive appeal, merit pay plans have several limitations. One is that they are typically based on an annual performance appraisal and thus are only as valid as the performance ratings, which are often subjective. This brings up issues of discrimination, as we discussed in Chapter 2. Research indicates that black employees receive lower performance ratings than white employees, women's ratings are higher than men's, and there are demographic differences in the distribution of salary increases, even with all other factors equal.[108] Another limitation is that the pay-raise pool of available funds fluctuates on economic or other conditions that have little to do with individual performance. For instance, a high performing sales executive at a manufacturing organization in Pune was given a pay raise only of ₹1500. Why? Because the pay-raise pool was very small. Yet that amount is more of a cost-of-living increase than a pay-for-performance one. Unions typically resist merit pay plans. Relatively few teachers are covered by merit pay for this reason. Instead, seniority-based pay, which gives all employees the same raises, predominates.

The concept and intention of merit pay—that employees are paid for performance—is sound. For employee motivation purposes, however, merit pay should be only one part of a performance recognition program.

bonus A pay plan that rewards employees for recent performance rather than historical performance.

Bonus An annual **bonus** is a significant component of total compensation for many jobs.[109] Once reserved for upper management, bonus plans are now routinely offered to employees in all levels of the organization. The incentive effects should be higher than those of merit pay because, rather than paying for previous performance now rolled into base pay, bonuses reward recent performance (merit pay is cumulative, but the increases are generally much smaller than bonus amounts). When times are bad, firms can cut bonuses to reduce compensation costs. Workers on Wall Street, for example, saw their average bonus drop by more than a third as their firms faced greater scrutiny.[110]

Bonus plans have a clear upside: They are motivating for workers. As an example, a recent study in India found that when a higher percentage of overall pay was reserved for the potential bonuses of managers and employees, productivity increased.[111] This example also highlights the downside of bonuses: They leave employees' pay more vulnerable to cuts. This is problematic especially when employees depend on bonuses or take them for granted. "People have begun to live as if bonuses were not bonuses at all but part of their expected annual income," said Jay Lorsch, a Harvard Business School professor. KeySpan Corp., a 9,700-employee utility company in New York, combined yearly bonuses with a smaller merit-pay raise. Elaine Weinstein, KeySpan's senior vice president of human resources, credits the plan with changing the culture from "entitlement to meritocracy."[112]

The way bonuses and rewards are categorized also affects peoples' motivation. In 2021, PWC gave two-week salary to all its 15,000 employees working in India as a bonus for being resilient during COVID-19 waves.[113] Although it is a bit manipulative, splitting rewards and bonuses into categories—even if the categories are meaningless—may increase motivation.[114] Why? Because people are more likely to feel they missed out on a reward if they don't receive one from each category, and then work harder to earn rewards from more categories. Short-term bonuses can also have an effect: In a high-tech manufacturing factory, cash, family meal vouchers, and employee recognition (see later in this chapter) all increased performance by 5 percent, and *nonmoney*-based bonuses were actually more effective at improving performance.[115]

profit-sharing plan An organization-wide program that distributes compensation based on some established formula designed around a company's profitability.

Profit-Sharing Plan A **profit-sharing plan** distributes compensation based on some established formula designed around a company's profitability.[116] Compensation can be direct cash outlays or, particularly for top managers, allocations of stock options. When you read about executives like Mark Zuckerberg, who accepts a modest $1 salary, remember that many executives are granted generous stock options. In fact, Zuckerberg has made as much as $2.3 billion after cashing out some of his stock options.[117] Of course, the clear majority of profit-sharing plans are not so grand in scale. For example, Jacob Luke started his own lawn-mowing business at age 13. He employed his brother Isaiah and friend Marcel and paid them each 25 percent of the profits he made on each yard.

Chinese Internet firm Tencent Holdings rewards employees with attractive incentives that include cash bonuses for lower-ranking employees. The young men shown here were among 5,000 employees who received a special bonus tucked in red envelopes and personally handed out by Tencent's CEO and cofounder Pony Ma.

Source: Keita Wen sz/ICHPL Imaginechina/AP Images

Studies generally support the idea that organizations with profit-sharing plans have higher levels of profitability than those without them.[118] These plans have also been linked to higher levels of employee commitment, especially in small organizations.[119] Profit sharing at the organizational level appears to have positive impacts on employee attitudes; employees report a greater feeling of psychological ownership.[120] Recent research in Canada indicates that profit-sharing plans motivate individuals to higher job performance when they are used in combination with other pay-for-performance plans.[121] Obviously, profit sharing does not work when there is no reported profit per se, such as in

An Ethical Choice

Workers' Cooperatives

Workers' cooperatives are aimed at creating sustainable jobs for their owners/workers/members in order to generate wealth for their local community. Therefore, they differ from other enterprises in that their owners/workers/members seek to enhance their capacity to produce and serve their needs first, before pursuing profit maximization. Democratically, each worker owns one share, and all shares are owned by the workers. Workers' cooperatives are well established in most countries in Europe but can also be found in countries like Australia, New Zealand, Israel, and India.

The basis for the institutionalization of the modern cooperative movement was established in 1844 on the core principle of "one member, one vote," when a group of weavers founded their food cooperative, the Rochdale Society of Equitable Pioneers, which diversified rapidly by opening its own mills and a solidary savings fund. Promoting similar values of benevolent assistance, Friedrich Wilhelm Raiffeisen, a pioneer of the cooperative movement, founded a German association for self-procurement of food during the starvation winter of 1846–47 and created the first cooperative lending bank in 1864. Today, Raiffeisenbanken and the International Raiffeisen Union (IRU) are powerful cooperative networks in Europe.

Employees who can decide how to allocate their own resources best, with their own considerations of work–family balance, are more committed to their jobs. As cooperative workers can make such decisions, they commit to their work, making their cooperatives successful. Additionally, cooperatives allow individual members to benefit from a pool of collective resources, allowing them to better market their products and negotiate prices. Cooperatives help enterprises' creation, development, and sustainability. Striking the balance between individual autonomy and common responsibility, between capitalism and socialism, the cooperative model is also sometimes viewed as immune to global economic crises.

One for all, all for one? Mondragón, which employs 80,000 people in 27 countries, was founded in Spain with the ideals of worker participation, solidarity, and equality; however, as it grew bigger, decision-making became more centralized, salary differentials increased, and job satisfaction dropped below that of employees of similarly sized private-owned companies—for example, a senior manager at Mondragón earns eight times the lowest-paid worker in the cooperative. In 2013, when Fagor, one of its constituents, had to declare bankruptcy after having run up debts of over €850m ($1.2 billion), Mondragón decided not to lend Fagor any more money. Almost 5,500 workers lost their jobs in Spain, France, China, Poland, and Morocco. Such issues raise key questions: What are the limits of cooperative ideals? Is the cooperative model just some ethical window-dressing for ruthless businesses to hide behind?

Sources: G. Cheney, I. Santa Cruz, A.-M. Peredo, and E. Nazaredo, "Worker Cooperatives as an Organizational Alternative: Challenges, Achievements and Promise in Business Governance and Ownership," *Organization* 21, no. 5 (2014): 591–603; The International Co-operative Alliance, https://ica.coop/en/international-co-operative-alliance; "Trouble in Workers' Paradise," *The Economist*, November 9, 2013, https://www.economist.com/news/business/21589469-collapse-spains-fagor-tests-worlds-largest-group-co-operatives-trouble-workers; International Labour Organization, Statistics on Cooperatives (2013); J. Schaffer, "Historical Dictionary of the Cooperative Movement" (Scarecrow Press, 1999); S. Kim, M. Las Heras, and M.-J. Bosch, "A Matter of Love: Exploring What Enables Work-Family Enrichment," *International Business Research* 9, no. 8 (2016): 24–36.

nonprofit organizations, or often in the public sector. However, profit sharing may make sense for many organizations, large or small.

employee stock ownership plan (ESOP) A company-established benefits plan in which employees acquire stock, often at below-market prices, as part of their benefits.

Employee Stock Ownership Plan An **employee stock ownership plan (ESOP)** is a company-established benefit plan in which employees acquire stock, often at below-market prices, as part of their benefits.[122] Research on ESOPs indicates they increase firm performance as well as employee innovation and organizational identification.[123] ESOPs have the potential to increase job satisfaction only when employees psychologically experience ownership.[124] Even so, ESOPs may not inspire lower absenteeism or greater motivation,[125] perhaps because the employee's actual monetary benefit comes with cashing in the stock at a later date. Relatedly, in a study of nearly three thousand Chinese firms, ESOPs were not as strongly related with firm performance when combined with executive stock ownership plans and when employees had no control rights (e.g., no "say" in the management of the business).[126] Furthermore, a study of nearly two thousand European firms suggests that stock ownership predicts return-on-investment only when the employees trust the managers and are culturally low on uncertainty avoidance (see Chapter 4).[127] Thus, employees need to be kept regularly informed of the status of the business and have the opportunity to influence it positively to feel motivated toward higher personal performance.[128]

ESOPs for top management can reduce unethical behavior. For instance, CEOs are less likely to manipulate firm earnings reports to make themselves look good in the short run when they have an ownership share.[129] ESOPs are also tools that can be used for community wealth building, such as the Cleveland model of networked worker cooperatives in Ohio.[130] Of course, not all companies want ESOPs, and they won't work in all situations, but they can be an important part of an organization's motivational strategy.

Evaluation of Variable Pay Do variable-pay programs increase motivation and productivity? Generally, yes, but that doesn't mean everyone is equally motivated by them.[131] Many organizations have more than one variable-pay element in operation, such as an ESOP and bonuses, so managers should evaluate the effectiveness of the plan in terms of the employee motivation gained from each element separately and from all elements together. Managers should monitor their employees' performance-reward expectancy because a combination of elements that makes employees feel that their greater performance will yield them greater rewards will be the most motivating.[132]

Using Benefits to Motivate Employees

8-6 Show how flexible benefits turn benefits into motivators.

Now that we have discussed what and how to pay employees, let's discuss two other motivating factors organizations must decide: (1) what benefits and choices to offer (such as flexible benefits), and (2) how to construct employee recognition programs. Like pay, benefits are both a provision and a motivator. Whereas organizations of yesteryear issued a standard package to every employee, contemporary leaders understand that each employee values benefits differently. A flexible program turns the benefits package into a motivational tool.

Flexible Benefits: Developing a Benefits Package

Akhtar is married and has three young children; his wife is at home full-time. His Citigroup colleague Valley is married too, but her husband has a high-paying job with the federal government, and they have no children. Akhtar is concerned about having a good medical plan and enough life insurance to support his family in case it's needed. In contrast, Valley's husband already has her medical needs covered on his plan, and life insurance is a low priority. Valley is more interested in extra vacation time and long-term financial benefits such as a tax-deferred savings plan.

A standardized benefits package is unlikely to meet the needs of Akhtar and Valley well. Citigroup can cover both sets of needs, however, with flexible benefits.

flexible benefits A benefits plan that allows each employee to put together a benefits package individually tailored to their own needs and situation.

Consistent with expectancy theory's thesis that organizational rewards should be linked to each employee's goals, **flexible benefits** individualize rewards by allowing each employee to choose the compensation package that best satisfies his or her current needs and situation. Flexible benefits can accommodate differences in employee needs based on age, marital status, partner's benefits status, and number and age of dependents.

Benefits in general can be a motivator for a person to go to work and for a person to choose one organization over another. But are flexible benefits more motivating than traditional plans? It's difficult to tell. Some organizations that have moved to flexible plans report increased employee retention, job satisfaction, and productivity. However, flexible benefits may not substitute for higher salaries when it comes to motivation, as research in China suggests.[133] As more organizations worldwide adopt flexible benefits, the individual motivation they produce will likely decrease (the plans will be seen as a standard work provision). The downsides of flexible benefit plans may be obvious: They may be costlier to administrate, and identifying the motivational impact of different provisions is challenging.

Given the intuitive motivational appeal of flexible benefits, it may be surprising that their use is not yet global. In China, only a limited percentage of companies offer flexible plans,[134] as in other Asian countries.[135] Almost all major corporations in the United States offer them, and a recent survey of 211 Canadian organizations found that 60 percent offer flexible benefits, up from 41 percent in 2005.[136] A similar survey of firms in the United Kingdom found that nearly all major organizations offer flexible benefits programs, with options ranging from supplemental medical insurance to holiday trading (with coworkers), discounted bus travel, and child care assistance.[137]

Using Intrinsic Rewards to Motivate Employees

8-7 Identify the motivational benefits of intrinsic rewards.

We have discussed motivating employees through job design and by the extrinsic rewards of pay and benefits. On an organizational level, are those the only ways to motivate employees? Not at all! We would be remiss if we overlooked the intrinsic rewards that organizations can provide, such as employee recognition programs, discussed next.

Employee Recognition Programs

Laura makes $8.50 per hour working at her fast-food job in Pensacola, Florida, and the job isn't very challenging or interesting. Yet Laura talks enthusiastically about the job, her boss, and the company that employs her. "What I like is the fact that Guy [her supervisor] appreciates the effort I make. He compliments me regularly in front of the other people on my shift, and I've been chosen Employee of the Month twice in the past six months. Did you see my picture on that plaque on the wall?"

employee recognition program A plan to encourage specific employee behaviors by formally appreciating specific employee contributions.

Organizations are increasingly realizing what Laura knows: Recognition programs and other ways of increasing an employee's intrinsic motivation work. An **employee recognition program** is a plan to encourage specific behaviors by formally appreciating specific employee contributions.[138] Employee recognition programs range from a spontaneous and private thank-you to widely publicized formal programs in which the procedures for attaining recognition are clearly identified.

As companies and government organizations face tighter budgets, nonfinancial incentives become more attractive. Everett Clinic in Washington State uses a combination of local and centralized initiatives to encourage managers to recognize employees.[139] Employees and managers give "Hero Grams" and "Caught in the Act" cards to colleagues for exceptional accomplishments at work. Part of the incentive is simply to receive recognition, but there are also drawings for prizes based on the number of cards a person receives. Multinational corporations like Symantec Corporation, Intuit, and Panduit have also increased their use of recognition programs. Symantec claims it increased engagement 14 percent in less than a year due to the Applause recognition program administered by Globoforce, a corporation that implements employee recognition programs.[140] Centralized programs across multiple offices in different countries can help ensure that all employees, regardless of where they work, can be recognized for their contribution to the work environment.[141] Recognition programs are common in Canadian and Australian firms as well.[142]

Research suggests that financial incentives may be more motivating in the short term, but in the long run nonfinancial incentives work best.[143] Surprisingly, there is not a lot of research on the motivational outcomes or global use of employee recognition programs. However, recent studies indicate that employee recognition programs are associated with self-esteem, self-efficacy, and job satisfaction,[144] and the broader outcomes from intrinsic motivation are well documented.

An obvious advantage of recognition programs is that they are inexpensive: Praise is free![145] With or without financial rewards, they can be highly motivating to employees. Despite the increased popularity of such programs, though, critics argue they are highly susceptible to political manipulation by management. When applied to jobs for which performance factors are relatively objective, such as sales, recognition programs are likely to be perceived by employees as fair. In most jobs, however, performance criteria aren't self-evident, which allows managers to manipulate the system and recognize their favorites. Abuse can undermine the value of recognition programs and demoralize employees, and even cause the person recognized to be ostracized. As one study in a northern Chinese manufacturing company showed, once a top performer is recognized, other members of the team whose contributions are not recognized may begin to distance themselves from that member.[146] These members may have unfair procedural justice perceptions (see Chapter 7) and begin to ostracize that employee as a result. Therefore, where formal recognition programs are used, care must be taken to ensure fairness. Where they are not, it is important to motivate employees by consistently recognizing their performance efforts.

Summary

As we've seen in this chapter, understanding what motivates individuals is ultimately key to organizational performance. Employees whose differences are recognized, who feel valued, and who can work in jobs tailored to their strengths and interests will be motivated to perform at the highest levels. Employee participation can also increase employee productivity, commitment to work goals, motivation, and job satisfaction. However, we cannot overlook the powerful role of organizational rewards in influencing motivation. Pay, benefits, and intrinsic rewards must be designed carefully and thoughtfully to enhance employee motivation toward positive organizational outcomes.

Implications for Managers

- Recognize individual differences. Spend the time necessary to understand what's important to each employee. Design jobs to align with individual needs and maximize their motivation potential.
- Use goals and feedback. You should give employees firm, specific goals, and they should get feedback on how well they are faring in pursuit of those goals.
- Allow employees to participate in decisions that affect them. Employees can contribute to setting work goals, choosing their own benefits packages, and solving productivity and quality problems.
- Link rewards to performance. Rewards should be contingent on performance, and employees must perceive the link between the two.
- Check the system for equity. Employees should perceive that individual effort and outcomes explain differences in pay and other rewards.

Gainsharing: Fair Shares?

POINT

Gainsharing is an employment benefit whereby a company's profits are shared with employees based upon their contribution to the gains that are achieved. Therefore, it is considered an incentive to make employees perform their best at work.

Employees who know that they will receive financial rewards if the company does well have a vested interest in their company's success. Gainsharing reinforces the employees' feelings of being recognized by their employer as responsible for their company's profitability. It gives employees a sense of ownership and accountability. Therefore, it empowers employees as they become business partners and feel more attached to their employer and adhere better to the company's objectives.

As gainsharing is a variable incentive, it seems only fair that the better you work, the better you are rewarded. It is also a self-funded system based on savings generated by improved performance. Provided that each individual's job performance is sufficiently tracked and recorded, you can tie individuals' performance to the company's bottom line. It thus fosters a culture of continuous improvement and helps promote positive change.

One other positive impact of gainsharing is that it sends the message that all of the employees contribute to the company's success and are working together on the same cooperative team toward this end. Gainsharing can therefore reinforce group cohesion and a collaborative work culture within a company—provided all employees are rewarded equivalently.

COUNTERPOINT

Usually, gainsharing plans result in stocks, bonds, or straight cash being distributed as a percentage of annual pay; for example, 1–2 percent for basic employees and up to 40 percent for senior executives. Thus, what if a top executive makes a critical decision that will increase the company's profit within a year, and by extension their related annual bonus, but with an outcome that might be detrimental in the long run? In addition, less money is shared with employees in lower-paying jobs, and higher amounts in bonuses are shared with highly compensated employees. Is this fair?

The distribution formula behind any gainsharing system is key. Each employee needs to identify the extent to which their contribution really makes an impact, and more particularly, which part of the work that they delivered counts the most. Consider when happy, loyal patrons leave tips in a restaurant—should waiters share these tips with kitchen co-workers, seasonal and extra service staff, and the restaurant managers? In what proportion? Ultimately, it is the waiter who personalized the service, smiled at the guests, reformulated the order, and made upselling suggestions—all ways by which the waiter has performed better. Thus, gainsharing requires employees' participation and employers' transparency regarding performance measures and the distribution formula.

Finally, because it results in all employees getting involved, gainsharing may increase the level of organizational stress, as everyone has more of a financial stake in the company's success.

Sources: R. J. Bullock and E. E. Lawler, "Gainsharing: A Few Questions, and Fewer Answers," *Human Resource Management* 23, no. 1 (1984): 23–40; J. Cloutier, D. Morin, and S. Reynaud, "Les Régimes de Rémunération Variable: Comment les Choisir et les Gérer?", *Gestion* 35, no. 1 (2010): 31–44; D. De Cremer and T. Tao, "Huawei: A Case Study of When Profit Sharing Works," *Harvard Business Review*, September 24, 2013, https://hbr.org/2015/09/huawei-a-case-study-of-when-profit-sharing-works; S. Fernandez, "Applying the Principles of Psychology in the Restaurant and Hotel Industry," ehotelier.com, April 13, 2017, https://ehotelier.com/insights/2017/04/13/applying-principles-psychology/.

CHAPTER REVIEW

QUESTIONS FOR REVIEW

8-1 How does the job charactieristics model motivate individuals?

8-2 What are the major ways that jobs can be redesigned?

8-3 What are the motivational benefits of the specific alternative work arrangements?

8-4 How can employee involvement measures motivate employees?

8-5 How can the different types of variable-pay programs increase employee motivation?

8-6 How can flexible benefits motivate employees?

8-7 What are the motivational benefits of intrinsic rewards?

APPLICATION AND EMPLOYABILITY

Organizations and human resource departments can alter or supplement tasks, duties, and responsibilities in many ways to make them more motivating to employees. This chapter on job design and redesign, alternative work arrangements, employee involvement and participation, and rewards and benefits is directly applicable to how OB can make you more employable. Future OB and HR professionals can use this toolkit in their future work assignments to reduce turnover, improve employee satisfaction and retention, and reduce conflict in the workplace. In this chapter so far, you have developed your critical thinking and knowledge and application skills by pondering whether money can "buy" happiness, considered whether flextime would be viable for your work situation, examined ethical issues underlying sweatshops and worker safety, and debated whether face time matters when considering telecommuting. In this section, you will continue to develop these skills, along with your communication skills, by working with a group to design an organizational development and compensation plan for automotive sales consultants; considering the effects of illegitimate tasks; forging an action plan for when employees provide feedback but their supervisors do not listen; and considering the value of small, frequent pay raises.

EXPERIENTIAL EXERCISE Developing a Motivation Plan for Your Museum Security Guards

Break the class into groups of three to five.

You are part of a team of human resource professionals working for an important museum of contemporary arts. You have been asked to develop a motivation plan for the museum security guards. Security guards are essential for the operations of the museum as they prevent works of art from being damaged by curious visitors and also carry out basic operations of the museum, like opening and closing the sites. However, the curator of the museum has noticed that some of security guards lack motivation, with negative repercussions on the visitors' museum experience. Last week, for example, the curator was told that one of the guards was looking at his smartphone and did not notice a visitor almost touching an important masterpiece. Luckily, the imprudent visitor was stopped by other people. You are worried that the repetitive and sometimes uninteresting duties of security guards are diminishing their motivation and attention on the job.

Using what you have read in this chapter, answer the following questions as a group.

Questions

8-8. Reflect on the characteristics of the security guard role according to the job characteristic model (i.e., skill variety, task identity, task significance, autonomy, and feedback). Then, write down three to five recommendations, addressing each of the five characteristics, that the curator of the museum can follow in order to enhance the motivation of security guards.

8-9. Job crafting is a recent approach in job design. It involves giving employees greater discretion over several components of their job to let them change the way they do their work and make it more meaningful, interesting, and satisfying. Would you consider such an approach for enhancing the motivation of security guards? What changes could security guards make to their profession to make it more interesting?

8-10. Smartphones are a useful tool for enhancing employees' productivity and responsiveness to work-related messages but, as shown in this example, they are also a potential distraction that can cause errors and inappropriate organizational behavior. As a team, think about a possible corporate digital philosophy aimed at regulating the use of smartphones during working hours and establishing when smartphone use is allowed and forbidden.

ETHICAL DILEMMA You Want Me to Do *What*?

You're a bright, female investment analyst about to give a major presentation to a group of bankers supporting a corporate acquisition. After walking in and meeting the bankers before you give the presentation, you're asked by your boss to "be a dear and serve them coffee." Imagine the insult and awkwardness of such a situation—what do you do? Do you carry through with the task, sacrificing your dignity or doing something wrong because you can't afford to lose the job? Or do you speak up?

A group of Swiss occupational health researchers have recently started a program of research on *illegitimate tasks*, or tasks that violate "norms about what can reasonably be expected from a given person" in a job. Therefore, illegitimate tasks are unethical and violate or offend one's professional and task identity. What might cause supervisors and managers within organizations to allocate these kinds of tasks? One study points to a variety of organizational characteristics, including competition for resources among departments or units, unfair resource allocation procedures, and an unclear decisional structure.

Researchers have found that these sorts of tasks can have some nasty outcomes. For one, illegitimate tasks lead to increased stress and CWB, even after controlling for the effort-reward imbalance, organizational justice, and personality traits. Illegitimate tasks can literally keep you up at night: One study found that, on days in which these tasks were performed, the employees took longer to fall asleep and woke up more often in the middle of the night. Another study found that these tasks lead to high negative affect and psychological detachment at the end of the workday. Other studies found that illegitimate tasks lead to lowered self-esteem and job satisfaction from day to day, along with increases in anger and depression. Illegitimate tasks can also cause people to want to leave their jobs, although if their leader was appreciative of them, they were less likely to want to leave.

Questions

8-11. How do you think employees should respond when given illegitimate tasks? How can an organization monitor the tasks it assigns to employees and ensure that the tasks are legitimate? Explain your answer.

8-12. Is there ever a case in which illegitimate tasks should be tolerated or "rightfully" given? Explain your answer.

8-13. How should the criterion of "legitimacy" be determined? Explain.

Sources: Based on E. Apostel, C. J. Syrek, and C. H. Antoni, "Turnover Intention as a Response to Illegitimate Tasks: The Moderating Role of Appreciative Leadership," *International Journal of Stress Management* (in press); L. Björk, E. Bejerot, N. Jacobshagen, and A. Härenstam, "I Shouldn't Have to Do This: Illegitimate Tasks as a Stressor in Relation to Organizational Control and Resource Deficits," *Work & Stress* 27, no. 3 (2013): 262–77; E. M. Eatough, L. L. Meier, I. Igic, A. Elfering, P. E. Spector, and N. K. Semmer, "You Want Me to Do What? Two Daily Diary Studies of Illegitimate Tasks and Employee Well-Being," *Journal of Organizational Behavior* 37 (2016): 108–27; D. Pereira, N. K. Semmer, and A. Elfering, "Illegitimate Tasks and Sleep Quality: An Ambulatory Study," *Stress and Health* 30 (2014): 209–21; N. K. Semmer, F. Tschan, L. L. Meier, S. Facchin, and N. Jacobshagen, "Illegitimate Tasks and Counterproductive Work Behavior," *Applied Psychology: An International Review* 59, no. 1 (2010): 70–96; S. Sonnentag and T. Lischetzke, "Illegitimate Tasks Reach into Afterwork Hours: A Multilevel Study," *Journal of Occupational Health Psychology* (in press); and M. Valcour, "How to Know Whether You're Giving Your Team Needless Work," *Harvard Business Review*, August 26, 2016, https://hbr.org/2016/08/how-to-know-whether-youre-giving-your-team-needless-work.

CASE INCIDENT 1 We Talk, But They Don't Listen

It's a great feeling to be sought for your opinion and participation when your organization needs to make an important decision. But what happens when the organization's managers don't listen? Management consultant Liz Ryan perhaps put it best: "When you work for a company that is not interested in your opinion, you can tell. They make it obvious. Once you know in your gut that your boss is not interested in your opinion, what other choice do you have than to find another job?"

Some suggest that these bosses perhaps should be let go. Given that bad members can lower employee satisfaction and engagement, supervisors who exercise this form of control often emphasize politics over productivity and abuse their power, while employees complain because of the lack of support they are getting. They are "thrown under the bus" and forced out of the loop, and communication is all one way.

Giving employees a chance to voice their opinions as part of the process leads to improved justice perceptions and satisfaction, and thus regularly not listening to feedback can be an issue. For example, one study found that both employees *and* managers recognize that paying lip service to employees and soliciting their suggestions without taking their advice occurs. Employees who became aware of this feigned interest were more reluctant to offer input later, experienced more conflicts with colleagues, bullied others, and refused to participate in meetings. Conversely, employees who had their ideas implemented spoke up more often and had better interpersonal relationships with their coworkers.

Questions

8-14. Do you think sometimes managers are justified in not taking their employee's advice? Why or why not?

8-15. How should managers handle their employees' dissatisfaction with not having their advice put into practice?

8-16. Which do you think is the most effective form of employee involvement and participation (EIP) program, participative management or representative management? Is it possible to implement elements of both? Why or why not?

Sources: Based on G. de Vries, K. A. Jehn, and B. W. Terwel, "When Employees Stop Talking and Start Fighting: The Detrimental Effects of Pseudo Voice in Organizations," *Journal of Business Ethics* 105, no. 2 (2012): 221–30; H. R. Huhman, "5 Signs It's Time to Fire a Company Manager," *Entrepreneur*, May 28, 2014, https://www.entrepreneur.com/article/234184; and L. Ryan, "The Real Reason Good Employees Quit," *Forbes*, March 31, 2017, https://www.forbes.com/sites/lizryan/2017/03/31/the-real-reason-good-employees-quit/#1fe3cfa34b4e.

CASE INCIDENT 2 Will More Money Fill the Gap?

In a referendum on June 23, 2016, a majority of UK voters decided that they wanted to leave the European Union. While negotiations will be lengthy and complex, it is anticipated that the United Kingdom will leave by March 2019. Being a member of the European Union meant that people from other EU nations were free to move to the United Kingdom for work. This was seen as a positive for the pro-Brexit campaign, with supporters stressing the benefits of controlling the movement of labor. But the question now is, will UK businesses find local workers to fill these soon-to-be vacant jobs?

According to the Office of National Statistics, in 2016, 7 percent—2.2 million—of the UK labor market were EU nationals. While these workers were employed across all sectors, the majority are employed in the lower-skilled jobs, such as cleaning, farming, hospitality, and food retail. If these workers are unable to work in the United Kingdom, organizations need to think about how they can encourage UK workers to take their place. Food retailer and restaurant chain Pret a Manger claims that only 1 in 50 applicants for their vacant jobs is British, so this is going to be a real challenge for them. This is supported by the UK Government, which believes that it will be years before British workers will be ready to fill these low-skilled jobs.

Pay could well be part of the solution; workers in these roles typically only receive minimum wage. It is anticipated that the UK hospitality pay bill will increase by £1.4 billion in the first year after Brexit as UK workers begin to fill the vacant roles. There will undoubtedly be a great deal of pressure to establish a new pay structure for the increasing numbers of UK workers. Some organizations may be happier to do this, believing that higher wages will lead to higher productivity through increased commitment and higher retention rates. However, considering the pressure to remain competitive, there may be more cost-effective ways to increase recruitment and motivate and retain workers.

Employers will need to improve the extrinsic rewards, which may motivate in the short term, while also increasing the intrinsic ones, which may provide better long-term results. Some organizations in the food retail industry are more effective than others at accomplishing this. In 2015, McDonalds UK came last in an employee fast-food poll, with some complaining about the lack of job rotation. In the same poll, one Pret a Manger employee complained about the inequity of the pay scheme, as pay is partly based on a mystery shopper evaluation that could be ruined by the poor performance of a colleague. Greggs, the sandwich and fast-food chain, came top in the poll, with praise for their higher-than-average pay, social activities, and profit-share scheme.

The results from the survey above would suggest a number of possible improvements. A merit-based pay system would ensure that those employees putting in the extra effort would be individually rewarded. The praise the employee receives and the additional money would satisfy both extrinsic and intrinsic motivation. Job rotation would require employees to undertake additional training, which many would see as an intrinsic reward, while giving the organization greater flexibility within the workforce. As demonstrated by Greggs, these changes may need to go hand in hand with a review of pay and other employee benefits if the organizations hope to recruit (and retain) sufficient new UK workers.

Questions

8-17. Can relational job design be factored into the roles carried out by the workers in food retail?

8-18. What are some of the potential issues faced by a business looking to implement job rotation?

8-19. Using the Job Characteristics model as a framework may identify changes that need to be made which will make the jobs in hospitality and food retail more attractive. How might this be problematic for jobs in these industries?

Sources: Zoe Catchpole, "Brexit Secretary: It Will Take Years for Brits to Fill Low-skilled EU Migrant Jobs," SkyNews, http://news.sky.com/story/it-will-take-years-for-brits-to-fill-low-skilled-eu-migrant-jobs-says-brexit-secretary-10777345; Julia Kollewe, "The British Jobs Brexit Makes Hard to Fill," *The Guardian*, March 25, 2017, https://www.theguardian.com/business/2017/mar/25/brexit-eu-nationals-exodus-jobs-recruitment; International immigration and the labour market, UK: 2016, Office for National Statistics, https://www.ons.gov.uk/peoplepopulationandcommunity/populationandmigration/internationalmigration/articles/migrationandthelabourmarketuk/2016; Rebecca Burn-Callander, "Employees Send McDonald's to Bottom of Top 10 Ranking of Fast Food Chains," *The Telegraph*, http://www.telegraph.co.uk/finance/jobs/11786866/Its-official-Flipping-burgers-at-McDonalds-is-the-worst-fast-food-job-in-the-UK.html.

ENDNOTES

[1] A. M. Grant, Y. Fried, and T. Juillerat, "Work Matters: Job Design in Classic and Contemporary Perspectives," in S. Zedeck (ed.), *APA Handbook of Industrial and Organizational Psychology: Building and Developing the Organization*, Vol. 1 (Washington DC: APA, 2011): 417–53; and S. K. Parker, F. P. Morgeson, and G. Johns, "One Hundred Years of Work Design Research: Looking Back and Looking Forward," *Journal of Applied Psychology* 102, no. 3 (2017): 403–20.

[2] J. R. Hackman and G. R. Oldham, "Motivation through the Design of Work: Test of a Theory," *Organizational Behavior and Human Performance* 16 (1976): 250–79.

[3] S. E. Humphrey, J. D. Nahrgang, and F. P. Morgeson, "Integrating Motivational, Social, and Contextual Work Design Features: A Meta-Analytic Summary and Theoretical Extension of the Work Design Literature," *Journal of Applied Psychology* 92, no. 5 (2007): 1332–56.

[4] B. M. Meglino and A. M. Korsgaard, "The Role of Other Orientation in Reactions to Job Characteristics," *Journal of Management* 33, no. 1 (2007): 57–83.

[5] J. L. Pierce, I. Jussila, and A. Cummings, "Psychological Ownership within the Job Design Context: Revision of the Job Characteristics Model," *Journal of Organizational Behavior* 30, no. 4 (2009): 477–96.

[6] C. B. Gibson, J. L. Gibbs, T. L. Stanko, P. Tesluk, and S. G. Cohen, "Including the 'I' in Virtuality and Modern Job Design: Extending the Job Characteristics Model to Include the Moderating Effect of Individual Experiences of Electronic Dependence and Copresence," *Organization Science* 22, no. 6 (2011): 1481–99.

[7] R. F. Piccolo, R. Greenbaum, D. N. Den Hartog, and R. Folger, "The Relationship between Ethical Leadership and Core Job Characteristics," *Journal of Organizational Behavior* 31 (2010): 259–78.

[8] Q.-J. Yeh, "Leadership, Personal Traits and Job Characteristics in R&D Organizations: A Taiwanese Case,"

Leadership & Organization Development Journal 16, no. 6 (1995): 16–26.
[9] M. A. Campion, L. Cheraskin, and M. J. Stevens, "Career-Related Antecedents and Outcomes of Job Rotation," *Academy of Management Journal* 37, no. 6 (1994): 1518–42.
[10] T. Silver, "Rotate Your Way to Higher Value," *Baseline* (March/April 2010): 12; and J. J. Salopek, "Coca-Cola Division Refreshes Its Talent with Diversity Push on Campus," *Workforce Management Online,* March 2011, www.workforce.com.
[11] Skytrax website review of Singapore Airlines, http://www.airlinequality.com/ratings/singapore-airlines-star-rating/, accessed April 3, 2017.
[12] Campion, Cheraskin, and Stevens, "Career-Related Antecedents and Outcomes of Job Rotation"; and S.-Y. Chen, W.-C. Wu, C.-S. Chang, and C.-T. Lin, "Job Rotation and Internal Marketing for Increased Job Satisfaction and Organisational Commitment in Hospital Nursing Staff," *Journal of Nursing Management* 23, no. 3 (2015): 297–306.
[13] A. Christini and D. Pozzoli, "Workplace Practices and Firm Performance in Manufacturing: A Comparative Study of Italy and Britain," *International Journal of Manpower* 31, no. 7 (2010): 818–42; and K. Kaymaz, "The Effects of Job Rotation Practices on Motivation: A Research on Managers in the Automotive Organizations," *Business and Economics Research Journal* 1, no. 3 (2010): 69–86.
[14] S.-H. Huang and Y.-C. Pan, "Ergonomic Job Rotation Strategy Based on an Automated RGB-D Anthropometric Measuring System," *Journal of Manufacturing Systems* 33, no. 4 (2014): 699–710; and P. C. Leider, J. S. Boschman, M. H. W. Frings-Dresen, et al., "Effects of Job Rotation on Musculoskeletal Complaints and Related Work Exposures: A Systematic Literature Review," *Ergonomics* 58, no. 1 (2015): 18–32.
[15] Grant, Fried, and Juillerat, "Work Matters."
[16] M. T. Ford and J. D. Wooldridge, "Industry Growth, Work Role Characteristics, and Job Satisfaction: A Cross-Level Mediation Model," *Journal of Occupational Health Psychology* 17, no. 4 (2012): 493–504.
[17] G. M. McEvoy and W. F. Cascio, "Strategies for Reducing Employee Turnover: A Meta-Analysis," *Journal of Applied Psychology* 70, no. 2 (1985): 342–53.
[18] S. Wood, M. Van Veldhoven, M. Croon, and L. M. de Menezes, "Enriched Job Design, High Involvement Management and Organizational Performance: The Mediating Roles of Job Satisfaction and Well-Being," *Human Relations* 65, no. 4 (2012): 419–46.
[19] A. M. Grant, "Leading with Meaning: Beneficiary Contact, Prosocial Impact, and the Performance Effects of Transformational Leadership," *Academy of Management Journal* 55 (2012): 458–76; and A. M. Grant and S. K. Parker, "Redesigning Work Design Theories: The Rise of Relational and Proactive Perspectives," *Annals of the Academy of Management* 3, no. 1 (2009): 317–75.
[20] J. Devaro, "A Theoretical Analysis of Relational Job Design and Compensation," *Journal of Organizational Behavior* 31 (2010): 279–301; D. P. Bhave, F. Halldórsson, E. Kim, and A. M. Lefter, "The Differential Impact of Interactions outside the Organization on Employee Well-being," *Journal of Occupational and Organizational Psychology* 92 (2019): 1–29.
[21] A. M. Grant, E. M. Campbell, G. Chen, K. Cottone, D. Lapedis, and K. Lee, "Impact and the Art of Motivation Maintenance: The Effects of Contact with Beneficiaries on Persistence Behavior," *Organizational Behavior and Human Decision Processes* 103, no. 1 (2007): 53–67.
[22] E. Francis and S. Schwartz, "The Sound of 'Success': Young Patients Ring Bell to Mark End of Cancer Treatment," *ABC News,* November 18, 2016, http://abcnews.go.com/Health/sound-success-young-patients-ring-bell-mark-end/story?id=43645402.
[23] A. M. Grant, "The Significance of Task Significance: Job Performance Effects, Relational Mechanisms, and Boundary Conditions," *Journal of Applied Psychology* 93, no. 1 (2008): 108–24.
[24] K. Pajo and L. Lee, "Corporate-Sponsored Volunteering: A Work Design Perspective," *Journal of Business Ethics* 99, no. 3 (2011): 467–82.
[25] M. C. Bolino, T. K. Kelemen, and S. H. Matthews, "Working 9-to-5? A Review of Research on Nonstandard Work Schedules," *Journal of Organizational Behavior* (in press).
[26] See, for instance, T. D. Allen, R. C. Johnson, K. M. Kiburz, and K. M. Shockley, "Work-Family Conflict and Flexible Work Arrangements: Deconstructing Flexibility," *Personnel Psychology* 66 (2013): 345–76; and B. B. Baltes, T. E. Briggs, J. W. Huff, J. A. Wright, and G. A. Neuman, "Flexible and Compressed Workweek Schedules: A Meta-Analysis of Their Effects on Work-Related Criteria," *Journal of Applied Psychology* 84, no. 4 (1999): 496–513.
[27] Society for Human Resource Management (SHRM), *2016 Employee Benefits: Looking Back at 20 Years of Employee Benefits Offerings in the U.S.* (Alexandria, VA: SHRM, 2016); and Society for Human Resource Management (SHRM), *2016 Strategic Benefits—Flexible Work Arrangements* (Alexandria, VA: SHRM, 2016).
[28] Society for Human Resource Management (SHRM), *Employee Job Satisfaction and Engagement: Revitalizing a Changing Workforce* (Alexandria, VA: SHRM, 2016).
[29] R. Waring, "Sunday Dialogue: Flexible Work Hours," *The New York Times,* January 19, 2013, www.nytimes.com.
[30] Baltes, Briggs, Huff, Wright, and Neuman, "Flexible and Compressed Workweek Schedules."
[31] Allen, Johnson, Kiburz, and Shockley, "Work-Family Conflict and Flexible Work Arrangements."
[32] D. Wheatley, "Employee Satisfaction and Use of Flexible Working Arrangements," *Work, Employment and Society* 31, no. 4 (2017): 567–85.
[33] Baltes, Briggs, Huff, Wright, and Neuman, "Flexible and Compressed Workweek Schedules."
[34] K. M. Shockley and T. D. Allen, "Investigating the Missing Link in Flexible Work Arrangement Utilization: An Individual Difference Perspective," *Journal of Vocational Behavior* 76, no. 1 (2010): 131–42.
[35] C. L. Munsch, C. L. Ridgeway, and J. C. Williams, "Pluralistic Ignorance and the Flexibility Bias: Understanding and Mitigating Flextime and Flexplace Bias at Work," *Work and Occupations* 41, no. 1 (2014): 40–62.
[36] See, for instance, B. J. Freeman and K. M. Coll, "Solutions to Faculty Work Overload: A Study of Job Sharing," *The Career Development Quarterly* 58 (2009): 65–70.
[37] J. LaReau, "Ford's 2 Julies Share Devotion—and Job," *Automotive News* (October 25, 2010): 4.
[38] S. Adams, "Workers Have More Flextime, Less Real Flexibility, Study Shows," *Forbes,* May 2, 2014, http://www.forbes.com/sites/susanadams/2014/05/02/workers-have-more-flextime-less-real-flexibility-study-shows/.
[39] K. Guyot and I. V. Sawhill, "Telecommuting Will Likely Continue Long after the Pandemic," *Brookings: Up Front* [blog post], April 6, 2020, https://www.brookings.edu/blog/up-front/2020/04/06/telecommuting-will-likely-continue-long-after-the-pandemic/;

T. Knutson, "Telecommuting Surge Likely to Last Past COVID-19 Crisis, Predicts Brookings Report," *Forbes*, April 8, 2020, https://www.forbes.com/sites/tedknutson/2020/04/08/telecommuting-surge-likely-to-last-past-covid-19-crisis-says-brookings-report/#44861f7f74ca.

[40] R. V. Reeves and J. Rothwell, "Class and COVID: How the Less Affluent Face Double Risks," *Brookings: Up Front* [blog post], March 27, 2020, https://www.brookings.edu/blog/up-front/2020/03/27/class-and-covid-how-the-less-affluent-face-double-risks/.

[41] Gartner, *Gartner CFO Survey Reveals 74% Intend to Shift Some Employees to Remote Work Permanently*, press release (Arlington, VA: April 3, 2020).

[42] F. Bélanger and R. W. Collins, "Distributed Work Arrangements: A Research Framework," *Information Society* 14 (1998): 137–52; R. S. Gajendran and D. A. Harrison, "The Good, the Bad, and the Unknown about Telecommuting: Meta-Analysis of Psychological Mediators and Individual Consequences," *Journal of Applied Psychology* 92, no. 6 (2007): 1524–41; and B. A. Lautsch and E. E. Kossek, "Managing a Blended Workforce: Telecommuters and Non-Telecommuters," *Organizational Dynamics* 40, no. 1 (2010): 10–17; T. D. Golden and R. S. Gajendran, "Unpacking the Role of a Telecommuter's Job in Their Performance: Examining Job Complexity, Problem Solving, Interdependence, and Social Support," *Journal of Business and Psychology* 34 (2019): 55–69.

[43] B. Belton, "Best Buy Copies Yahoo, Reins in Telecommuting." *USA Today*, March 6, 2013, www.usatoday.com.

[44] C. Tkaczyk, "Marissa Mayer Breaks Her Silence on Yahoo's Telecommuting Policy," *Fortune*, April 13, 2013, http://fortune.com/2013/04/19/marissa-mayer-breaks-her-silence-on-yahoos-telecommuting-policy/.

[45] Gajendran and Harrison, "The Good, the Bad, and the Unknown about Telecommuting."

[46] Ibid.

[47] J. Kotkin, "Marissa Mayer's Misstep and the Unstoppable Rise of Telecommuting," *Forbes*, March 26, 2013.

[48] S. J. Perry, N. M. Lorinkova, E. M. Hunter, A. Hubbard, and J. T. McMahon, "When Does Virtuality Really 'Work'? Examining the Role of Work-Family and Virtuality in Social Loafing," *Journal of Management* 42, no. 2 (2016): 449–79.

[49] T. D. Golden and A. Fromen, "Does It Matter Where Your Manager Works? Comparing Managerial Work Mode (Traditional, Telework, Virtual) across Subordinate Work Experiences and Outcomes," *Human Relations* 64, no. 11 (2011): 1451–75.

[50] C. A. Bartel, A. Wrzesniewski, and B. M. Wiesenfeld, "Knowing Where You Stand: Physical Isolation, Perceived Respect, and Organizational Identification among Virtual Employees," *Organization Science* 23, no. 3 (2011): 743–57; and S. M. B. Thatcher and J. Bagger, "Working in Pajamas: Telecommuting, Unfairness Sources, and Unfairness Perceptions," *Negotiation and Conflict Management Research* 4, no. 3 (2011): 248–76.

[51] E. G. Dutcher, "The Effects of Telecommuting on Productivity: An Experimental Examination; the Role of Dull and Creative Tasks," *Journal of Economic Behavior & Organization* 84, no. 1 (2014): 355–63.

[52] See, for example, Bartel, Wrzesniewski, and Wiesenfeld, "Knowing Where You Stand"; Gajendran and Harrison, "The Good, the Bad, and the Unknown about Telecommuting"; and M. Virick, N. DaSilva, and K. Arrington, "Moderators of the Curvilinear Relation between Extent of Telecommuting and Job and Life Satisfaction: The Role of Performance Outcome Orientation and Worker Type," *Human Relations* 63, no. 1 (2010): 137–54.

[53] J. Delanoeije, M. Verbruggen, and L. Germeys, "Boundary Role Transitions: A Day-to-Day Approach to Explain the Effects of Home-Based Telework on Work-to-Home Conflict and Home-to-Work Conflict," *Human Relations* 72, no. 12 (2019): 1843–68; L. M. Lapierre, E. F. Van Steenbergen, M. C. W. Peeters, and E. S. Kluwer, "Juggling Work and Family Responsibilities When Involuntarily Working More from Home: A Multiwave Study of Financial Sales Professionals," *Journal of Organizational Behavior* 37, no. 6 (2016): 804–22; and M. C. Noonan and J. L. Glass, "The Hard Truth about Telecommuting," *Monthly Labor Review* (2012): 1459–78.

[54] T. D. Golden and K. A. Eddleston, "Is There a Price Telecommuters Pay? Examining the Relationship between Telecommuting and Objective Career Success," *Journal of Vocational Behavior* (in press); J. Welch and S. Welch, "The Importance of Being There," *BusinessWeek*, April 16, 2007, 92; Z. I. Barsness, K. A. Diekmann, and M. L. Seidel, "Motivation and Opportunity: The Role of Remote Work, Demographic Dissimilarity, and Social Network Centrality in Impression Management," *Academy of Management Journal* 48, no. 3 (2005): 401–19.

[55] Bolino et al., "Working 9-to-5?"

[56] T. Müller and C. Niessen, "Self-Leadership in the Context of Part-Time Teleworking," *Journal of Organizational Behavior* 40 (2019): 883–98.

[57] E. Frauenheim, "COVID-19: Learning to Love Telecommuting," *Great Place to Work* [blog], March 17, 2020, https://www.greatplacetowork.com/resources/blog/covid-19-silver-lining-learning-to-love-telecommuting; M. Tarallo, "How to Create an Effective Teleworking Program," *Society for Human Resource Management* [blog], April 19, 2018, https://www.shrm.org/resourcesandtools/hr-topics/employee-relations/pages/how-to-create-an-effective-teleworking-program.aspx.

[58] J. Cotton, *Employee Involvement: Methods for Improving Performance and Work Attitudes* (Newbury Park, CA: Sage, 1993); and A. Cox, S. Zagelmeyer, and M. Marchington, "Embedding Employee Involvement and Participation at Work," *Human Resource Management Journal* 16, no. 3 (2006): 250–67.

[59] See, for example, A. Kim and K. Han, "All for One and One for All: A Mechanism through Which Broad-Based Employee Stock Ownership and Employee-Perceived Involvement Practice Create a Productive Workforce," *Human Resource Management* 58 (2019): 571–84.

[60] See, for example, the literature on empowerment, such as S. E. Seibert, S. R. Silver, and W. A. Randolph, "Taking Empowerment to the Next Level: A Multiple-Level Model of Empowerment, Performance, and Satisfaction," *Academy of Management Journal* 47, no. 3 (2004): 332–49; M. M. Butts, R. J. Vandenberg, D. M. DeJoy, B. S. Schaffer, and M. G. Wilson, "Individual Reactions to High Involvement Work Processes: Investigating the Role of Empowerment and Perceived Organizational Support," *Journal of Occupational Health Psychology* 14, no. 2 (2009): 122–36; and M. T. Maynard, L. L. Gilson, and J. E. Mathieu, "Empowerment—Fad or Fab? A Multilevel Review of the Past Two Decades of Research," *Journal of Management* 38, no. 4 (2012): 1231–81.

[61] See, for instance, A. Sagie and Z. Aycan, "A Cross-Cultural Analysis of Participative Decision-Making in Organizations," *Human Relations* 56, no. 4 (2003): 453–73; and J. Brockner, "Unpacking Country Effects: On the Need to Operationalize the Psychological Determinants of Cross-National Differences," in R. M. Kramer and

B. M. Staw (eds.), *Research in Organizational Behavior* 25 (Oxford, UK: Elsevier, 2003), 336–40.
[62] C. Robert, T. M. Probst, J. J. Martocchio, R. Drasgow, and J. J. Lawler, "Empowerment and Continuous Improvement in the United States, Mexico, Poland, and India: Predicting Fit on the Basis of the Dimensions of Power Distance and Individualism," *Journal of Applied Psychology* 85, no. 5 (2000): 643–58.
[63] Z. X. Chen and S. Aryee, "Delegation and Employee Work Outcomes: An Examination of the Cultural Context of Mediating Processes in China," *Academy of Management Journal* 50, no. 1 (2007): 226–38.
[64] G. Huang, X. Niu, C. Lee, and S. J. Ashford, "Differentiating Cognitive and Affective Job Insecurity: Antecedents and Outcomes," *Journal of Organizational Behavior* 33, no. 6 (2012): 752–69.
[65] Z. Cheng, "The Effects of Employee Involvement and Participation on Subjective Wellbeing: Evidence from Urban China," *Social Indicators Research* 118, no. 2 (2014): 457–83.
[66] A. Bar-Haim, *Participation Programs in Work Organizations: Past, Present, and Scenarios for the Future* (Westport, CT: Quorum, 2002); and J. S. Black and H. B. Gregersen, "Participative Decision-Making: An Integration of Multiple Dimensions," *Human Relations* 50, no. 7 (1997): 859–78.
[67] Black and Gregersen, "Participative Decision-Making."
[68] D. Collins, "The Ethical Superiority and Inevitability of Participatory Management as an Organizational System," *Organization Science* 8, no. 5 (1997): 489–507; and T. M. Probst, "Countering the Negative Effects of Job Insecurity through Participative Decision Making: Lessons from the Demand-Control Model," *Journal of Occupational Health Psychology* 10, no. 4 (2005): 320–9.
[69] G. M. Pereira and H. G. Osburn, "Effects of Participation in Decision Making on Performance and Employee Attitudes: A Quality Circle Meta-Analysis," *Journal of Business and Psychology* 22 (2007): 145–53.
[70] C. M. Linski, "Transitioning to Participative Management," *Organization Development Journal* 32, no. 3 (2014): 17–26.
[71] See, for instance, A. Pendleton and A. Robinson, "Employee Stock Ownership, Involvement, and Productivity: An Interaction-Based Approach," *Industrial and Labor Relations Review* 64, no. 1 (2010): 3–29.
[72] D. K. Datta, J. P. Guthrie, and P. M. Wright, "Human Resource Management and Labor Productivity: Does Industry Matter?," *Academy of Management Journal* 48, no. 1 (2005): 135–45; C. M. Riordan, R. J. Vandenberg, and H. A. Richardson, "Employee Involvement Climate and Organizational Effectiveness," *Human Resource Management* 44, no. 4 (2005): 471–88; and J. Kim, J. P. MacDuffie, and F. K. Pil, "Employee Voice and Organizational Performance: Team versus Representative Influence," *Human Relations* 63, no. 3 (2010): 371–94.
[73] C. J. Travers, *Managing the Team: A Guide to Successful Employee Involvement* (Oxford, UK: Wiley-Blackwell, 1994).
[74] Office of the Secretary, United States Department of Labor, "Inspecting Nonunion Models for Employee Voice," *Futurework: Trends and Challenges for Work in the 21st Century*, accessed April 4, 2017, https://www.dol.gov/oasam/programs/history/herman/reports/futurework/conference/relations/nonunion.htm.
[75] American Psychological Association and Harris Interactive, *Workforce Retention Survey*, August 2012, http://www.apaexcellence.org/assets/general/2012-retention-survey-final.pdf.
[76] D. A. McIntyre and S. Weigley, "8 Companies That Most Owe Workers a Raise," *USA Today*, May 13, 2013, www.usatoday.com/story/money/business/2013/05/12/8-companies-that-most-owe-workers-a-raise/2144013/.
[77] M. Sabramony, N. Krause, J. Norton, and G. N. Burns, "The Relationship between Human Resource Investments and Organizational Performance: A Firm-Level Examination of Equilibrium Theory," *Journal of Applied Psychology* 93, no. 4 (2008): 778–88.
[78] HR Katha (2021). "How Trident Group adopted OKR-based pay for 14,000 employees". *HRK News (January 15, 2021).* Retrieved from https://www.hrkatha.com (Accessed on April 20, 2022).
[79] C. Isidore, "Walmart Ups Pay Well above Minimum Wage," *CNN Money*, February 19, 2015, http://money.cnn.com/2015/02/19/news/companies/walmart-wages/.
[80] HR Katha. "Employee Experience Strategy for a Multilingual Workforce". *HRK WhitePapers.* Retrieved from https://www.hrkatha.com (Accessed on April 20, 2022).
[81] See, for example, B. Martinez, "Teacher Bonuses Emerge in Newark," *The Wall Street Journal*, April 21, 2011, A15; K. Taylor, "Differing Results When Teacher Evaluations Are Tied to Test Scores," *The New York Times*, March 23, 2015, A16; and D. Weber, "Seminole Teachers to Get Bonuses Instead of Raises," *Orlando Sentinel*, January 19, 2011, www.orlandosentinel.com.
[82] G. T. Milkovich, J. M. Newman, and B. Gerhart, *Compensation* (11th ed., New York: McGraw-Hill, 2013).
[83] See, for example, M. Damiani and A. Ricci, "Managers' Education and the Choice of Different Variable Pay Schemes: Evidence from Italian Firms," *European Management Journal* 32, no. 6 (2014): 891–902.
[84] S. Miller, "Bonus Binge: Variable Pay Outpaces Salary," *Society for Human Resource Management*, August 11, 2016, https://www.shrm.org/resourcesandtools/hr-topics/compensation/pages/variable-pay-outpaces-raises.aspx.
[85] Ibid.
[86] *U.S. Companies Holding the Line on Pay Raises for 2017, Willis Towers Watson Survey Finds*, Willis Towers Watson Press Release, August 24, 2016, http://www.globenewswire.com/news-release/2016/08/24/866587/0/en/U-S-companies-holding-the-line-on-pay-raises-for-2017-Willis-Towers-Watson-survey-finds.html.
[87] A. M. Paul, "Atlanta Teachers Were Offered Bonuses for High Test Scores. Of Course They Cheated," *The Washington Post*, April 16, 2015, https://www.washingtonpost.com/posteverything/wp/2015/04/16/atlanta-teachers-were-offered-bonuses-for-high-test-scores-of-course-they-cheated/?utm_term=.e4df48aeb80b; N P. von der Embse, A. M. Schoemann, S. P. Kilgus, M. Wicoff, and M. Bowler, "The Influence of Test-Based Accountability Policies on Teacher Stress and Instructional Practices: A Moderated Mediation Model," *Educational Psychology* 37, no. 3 (2017): 312–31; and K. Yuan, V.-N. Le, D. F. McCaffrey, J. A. Marsh, L. S. Hamilton, B. M. Stecher, and M. G. Springer, "Incentive Pay Programs Do Not Affect Teacher Motivation or Reported Practices: Results from Three Randomized Studies," *Educational Evaluation and Policy Analysis* 35, no. 1 (2013): 3–22.
[88] Y. Zhang, L. Long, T.-Y. Wu, and X. Huang, "When Is Pay for Performance Related to Employee Creativity in the Chinese Context? The Role of Guanxi HRM Practice, Trust in Management, and Intrinsic Motivation," *Journal of Organizational Behavior* 36, no. 5 (2015): 698–719.
[89] J. H. Han, K. M. Bartol, and S. Kim, "Tightening Up the Performance-Pay Linkage: Roles of Contingent Reward

Leadership and Profit-Sharing in the Cross-Level Influence of Individual Pay-for-Performance," *Journal of Applied Psychology* 100, no. 2 (2015): 417–430; and D. Pohler and J. A. Schmidt, "Does Pay-for-Performance Strain the Employment Relationship? The Effect of Manager Bonus Eligibility on Nonmanagement Employee Turnover," *Personnel Psychology* 69, no. 2 (2016): 395–429.

[90] I. S. Fulmer and W. J. Walker, "More Bang for the Buck? Personality Traits As Moderators of Responsiveness to Pay-for-Performance," *Human Performance* 28 (2015): 40–65.

[91] E. Belogolovsky and P. A. Bamberger, "Signaling in Secret: Pay for Performance and the Incentive and Sorting Effects of Pay Secrecy," *Academy of Management Journal* 57, no. 6 (2014): 1706–33.

[92] Ibid.

[93] B. Wysocki Jr., "Chilling Reality Awaits Even the Employed," *The Wall Street Journal,* November 5, 2001, A1; and J. C. Kovac, "Sour Economy Presents Compensation Challenges," *Employee Benefit News,* July 1, 2008, 18.

[94] W. Hou, R. L. Priem, and M. Goranova, "Does One Size Fit All? Investigating Pay–Future Performance Relationships over the 'Seasons' of CEO Tenure," *Journal of Management* 43, no. 3 (2017): 864–91.

[95] See, for instance, M. K. Judiesch and F. L. Schmidt, "Between-Worker Variability in Output under Piece-Rate versus Hourly Pay Systems," *Journal of Business and Psychology* 14, no. 4 (2000): 529–52.

[96] P. M. Wright, "An Examination of the Relationships among Monetary Incentives, Goal Level, Goal Commitment, and Performance," *Journal of Management* 18, no. 4 (1992): 677–93.

[97] J. S. Heywood, X. Wei, and G. Ye, "Piece Rates for Professors," *Economics Letters* 113, no. 3 (2011): 285–87.

[98] A. Baker and V. Mertins, "Risk-Sorting and Preference for Team Piece Rates," *Journal of Economic Psychology* 34 (2013): 285–300.

[99] E. Della Torre, M. Salimi, and A. Giangreco, "Crowding-out or Crowding-in? Direct Voice, Performance-Related Pay, and Organizational Innovation in European Firms," *Human Resource Management* 59 (2020): 185–99.

[100] A. Clemens, "Pace of Work and Piece Rates," *Economics Letters* 115, no. 3 (2012): 477–79.

[101] S. L. Rynes, B. Gerhart, and L. Parks, "Personnel Psychology: Performance Evaluation and Pay for Performance," *Annual Review of Psychology* 56, no. 1 (2005): 571–600.

[102] Ibid.

[103] K. Zernike, "Newark Teachers Approve a Contract with Merit Pay," *The New York Times,* November 14, 2012, www.nytimes.com/.

[104] "Paying Doctors for Performance," *The New York Times,* January 27, 2013, A16.

[105] Raja, V. (2018). "In a First, Maharashtra Will Rank 7.5 Lakh Govt. Employees on Performance!" *The Better India (January 29, 2018).* Retrieved from https://www.thebetterindia.com (Accessed on April 20, 2022).

[106] S. Halzack, "Companies Look to Bonuses Instead of Salary Increases in an Uncertain Economy," *Washington Post,* November 6, 2012, http://articles.washingtonpost.com/.

[107] C. M. Barnes, J. Reb, and D. Ang, "More Than Just the Mean: Moving to a Dynamic View of Performance-Based Compensation," *Journal of Applied Psychology* 97, no. 3 (2012): 711–18.

[108] E. J. Castillo, "Gender, Race, and the New (Merit-Based) Employment Relationship," *Industrial Relations* 51, no. S1 (2012): 528–62.

[109] Rynes, Gerhart, and Parks, "Personnel Psychology."

[110] P. Furman, "Ouch! Top Honchos on Wall Street See Biggest Cuts to Bonuses," *New York Daily News,* February 18, 2013, www.nydailynews.com.

[111] N. Chun and S. Lee, "Bonus Compensation and Productivity: Evidence from Indian Manufacturing Plant-Level Data," *Journal of Productivity Analysis* 43, no. 1 (2015): 47–58.

[112] E. White, "Employers Increasingly Favor Bonuses to Raises," *The Wall Street Journal,* August 28, 2006, B3; and J. S. Lublin, "Boards Tie CEO Pay More Tightly to Performance," *The Wall Street Journal,* February 21, 2006, A1, A14.

[113] Comsultancy.in (March 25, 2021). "PwC India gives entire staff bonus for pandemic resilience". Retrieved from https://www.consultancy.in (Accessed on April 20, 2022).

[114] S. S. Wiltermuth and F. Gino, "'I'll Have One of Each': How Separating Rewards into (Meaningless) Categories Increases Motivation," *Journal of Personality and Social Psychology* (January 2013): 1–13.

[115] L. Bareket-Bojmel, G. Hochman, and D. Ariely, "It's (Not) All about the Jacksons: Testing Different Types of Short-Term Bonuses in the Field," *Journal of Management* 43, no. 2 (2017): 534–54.

[116] M. J. Roomkin, *Profit Sharing and Gain Sharing* (Metuchen, NJ: Rutgers University Press, 1990).

[117] "Mark Zuckerberg Reaped $2.3 Billion on Facebook Stock Options," *Huffington Post,* April 26, 2013, www.huffingtonpost.com.

[118] D. D'Art and T. Turner, "Profit Sharing, Firm Performance, and Union Influence in Selected European Countries," *Personnel Review* 33, no. 3 (2004): 335–50; and D. Kruse, R. Freeman, and J. Blasi, *Shared Capitalism at Work: Employee Ownership, Profit and Gain Sharing, and Broad-Based Stock Options* (Chicago: University of Chicago Press, 2010).

[119] A. Bayo-Moriones and M. Larraza-Kintana, "Profit-Sharing Plans and Affective Commitment: Does the Context Matter?" *Human Resource Management* 48, no. 2 (2009): 207–26; and G. W. Florkowski and M. H. Schuster, "Support for Profit Sharing and Organizational Commitment," *Human Relations* 45, no. 5 (1992): 507–23.

[120] N. Chi and T. Han, "Exploring the Linkages between Formal Ownership and Psychological Ownership for the Organization: The Mediating Role of Organizational Justice," *Journal of Occupational and Organizational Psychology* 81, no. 4 (2008): 691–711.

[121] Han, Bartol, and Kim, "Tightening Up the Performance-Pay Linkage."

[122] ESOP Association, *ESOP Association's Position on President's Panel on Federal Tax Reform Recommendation on Retirement Savings.* Washington, DC: Author.

[123] R. P. Garrett, "Does Employee Ownership Increase Innovation?," *New England Journal of Entrepreneurship* 13, no. 2, (2010): 37–46; Mullins et al., "Broad-Based Employee Stock Ownership"; E. H. O'Boyle, P. C. Patel, and E. Gonzalez-Mulé, "Employee Ownership and Firm Performance: A Meta-Analysis," *Human Resource Management Journal* 26, no. 4 (2016): 425–48; T. A. Paterson and T. W. Welbourne, "I Am Therefore I Own: Implications of Organization-Based Identity for Employee Stock Ownership," *Human Resource Management* 59 (2020): 175–83.

[124] D. McCarthy, E. Reeves, and T. Turner, "Can Employee Share-Ownership Improve Employee Attitudes and Behaviour?," *Employee Relations* 32, no. 4 (2010): 382–95.

[125] A. Pendleton, "Shared Capitalism at Work: Employee Ownership, Profit and Gain Sharing, and Broad-Based Stock Options," *Industrial & Labor Relations Review* 64, no. 3 (2011): 621–22.

[126] T. Ren, Y. Xiao, H. Yang, and S. Liiu, "Employee Ownership Heterogeneity and Firm Performance in China," *Human Resource Management* 58 (2019): 621–39.
[127] S. Kang and A. Kim, "Employee Stock Ownership and Financial Performance in European Countries: The Moderating Effects of Uncertainty Avoidance and Social Trust," *Human Resource Management* 58 (2019): 641–55.
[128] A. Pendleton and A. Robinson, "Employee Stock Ownership, Involvement, and Productivity: An Interaction-Based Approach," *Industrial and Labor Relations Review* 64, no. 1 (2010): 3–29.
[129] X. Zhang, K. M. Bartol, K. G. Smith, M. D. Pfarrer, and D. M. Khanin, "CEOs on the Edge: Earnings Manipulation and Stock-Based Incentive Misalignment," *Academy of Management Journal* 51, no. 2 (2008): 241–58.
[130] S. Dubb, "Community Wealth Building Forms: What They Are and How to Use Them at the Local Level," *Academy of Management Perspectives* 30, no. 2 (2016): 141–52.
[131] C. B. Cadsby, F. Song, and F. Tapon, "Sorting and Incentive Effects of Pay for Performance: An Experimental Investigation," *Academy of Management Journal* 50, no. 2 (2007): 387–405.
[132] Han, Bartol, and Kim, "Tightening Up the Performance-Pay Linkage."
[133] Z. Lin, J. Kelly, and L. Trenberth, "Antecedents and Consequences of the Introduction of Flexible Benefit Plans in China," *The International Journal of Human Resource Management*, 22, no. 5 (2011): 1128–45.
[134] Ibid.
[135] R. C. Koo, "Global Added Value of Flexible Benefits," *Benefits Quarterly* 27, no. 4 (2011): 17–20.
[136] P. Stephens, "Flex Plans Gain in Popularity," *CA Magazine*, January/February 2010, 10.
[137] D. Lovewell, "Flexible Benefits: Benefits on Offer," *Employee Benefits*, March 2010, S15.
[138] L. E. Tetrick and C. R. Haimann, "Employee Recognition," in A. Day, E. K. Kelloway, and J. J. Hurrell Jr. (eds.), *Workplace Well-Being: How to Build Psychologically Healthy Workplaces* (Hoboken, NJ: Wiley, 2014), 161–74.
[139] L. Shepherd, "Special Report on Rewards and Recognition: Getting Personal," *Workforce Management*, September 2010: 24–29.
[140] www.globoforce.come/our-clients, accessed June 4, 2015.
[141] L. Shepherd, "On Recognition, Multinationals Think Globally," *Workforce Management*, September 2010, 26.
[142] R. J. Long and J. L. Shields, "From Pay to Praise? Non-Case Employee Recognition in Canadian and Australian Firms," *International Journal of Human Resource Management* 21, no. 8 (2010): 1145–72.
[143] S. E. Markham, K. D. Scott, and G. H. McKee, "Recognizing Good Attendance: A Longitudinal, Quasi-Experimental Field Study," *Personnel Psychology* 55, no. 3 (2002): 641; and S. J. Peterson and F. Luthans, "The Impact of Financial and Nonfinancial Incentives on Business Unit Outcomes over Time," *Journal of Applied Psychology* 91, no. 1 (2006): 156–65.
[144] C. Xu and C. Liang, "The Mechanisms Underlying an Employee Recognition Program," in L. Hale and J. Zhang (eds.), *Proceedings of the International Conference on Public Human Resource Management and Innovation* (2013): 28–35.
[145] A. D. Stajkovic and F. Luthans, "Differential Effects of Incentive Motivators on Work Performance," *Academy of Management Journal* 4, no. 3 (2001): 587. See also F. Luthans and A. D. Stajkovic, "Provide Recognition for Performance Improvement," in E. A. Locke (ed.), *Handbook of Principles of Organizational Behavior* (Malden, MA: Blackwell, 2004): 166–80.
[146] X. Zheng, H. H. Zhao, X. Liu, and N. Li, "Network Reconfiguration: The Implications of Recognizing Top Performers in Teams," *Journal of Occupational and Organizational Psychology* 92 (2019): 825–47.

9 Foundations of Group Behavior

Source: ZUMA Press Inc/Alamy Stock Photo

LEARNING OBJECTIVES

After studying this chapter, you should be able to:

9-1 Distinguish between the different types of groups.

9-2 Describe the punctuated-equilibrium model of group development.

9-3 Show how role requirements change in different situations.

9-4 Demonstrate how norms exert influence on an individual's behavior.

9-5 Show how status and size differences affect group performance.

9-6 Describe how issues of cohesiveness and diversity can be integrated for group effectiveness.

9-7 Contrast the strengths and weaknesses of group decision making.

Employability Skills Matrix (ESM)

	Myth or Science?	Career OBjectives	An Ethical Choice	Point/ Counterpoint	Experiential Exercise	Ethical Dilemma	Case Incident 1	Case Incident 2
Critical Thinking	✓	✓		✓	✓	✓	✓	✓
Communication	✓	✓	✓		✓	✓	✓	✓
Collaboration	✓	✓	✓	✓	✓	✓	✓	✓
Knowledge Application and Analysis		✓		✓	✓	✓	✓	✓
Social Responsibility	✓	✓	✓			✓	✓	✓

THE ROLLING STONES: A SUPERGROUP

The Rolling Stones are one of the world's most successful rock bands. Formed in London in 1962, the group has sold more than 240 million albums worldwide and is reportedly worth around €850 million. Many would think that after so long, having achieved so much, and suffering from various health issues, it would be time to retire. Not the Stones. In February 2020, 15 additional dates for their "No Filter Tour" were announced.

So what has made the group so extraordinary and kept them together for close to 60 years despite their many public feuds? Their story provides key lessons for working in groups.

Cohesion is the invisible force that keeps a group together and is a basis for high performance as a unit. And nowhere is cohesion better demonstrated than by the career of the Rolling Stones. In the beginning, it was music—a shared passion for American R&B—that brought them together. The album *Best of Muddy Waters* provided the initial spark when Keith Richards and Mick Jagger met at a railway station in their hometown of Dartford, Kent, in 1960. One of the tracks on it—"Rollin' Stone"—gave the group their name.

Early cohesion came from the group spending a lot of time together. The band lived, played, and went everywhere together, piled in the back of a van along with their kit. Shared experiences and especially early success helped reinforce the team's match for each other. Cohesion grew as the team recognized that each member of the band was a master of his own instrument or voice.

The Stones also represented a fusion of different personalities. On stage, Jagger is a natural showman. He also takes the lead as the driving force in the Stones' organization and their highly lucrative business empire. In contrast with Jagger's vision and need for a clear plan, Richards claims his only ambition has been to be in the Rolling Stones and to make records. Taking things day by day, "happy to just wake up," he writes music and lives much more loosely. If Jagger is the band's CEO, Richards is its musical spirit. In his words, "Mick's Rock, I'm Roll."

These differences between Jagger and Richards are kept in balance by the solid, straightforward nature of drummer Charlie Watts and the diplomatic approach of guitarist Ronnie Wood. With his infectious enthusiasm, coupled with the instinct of a seasoned peace negotiator, Wood has acted as middleman between Jagger and Richards more than once.

The Stones have developed a set of practices and rules to help them keep performing at the highest level. For example, they have evolved and adopted a method of decision making that works for them. In many instances, Jagger can take the lead, taking input from the others but with Richards effectively having veto rights.

The Rolling Stones keep going together because they can and because they still want to. As long as the fans want to see them perform, the Stones will play. The buzz of performance is the ultimate—and only—satisfaction. On stage they are free to share what Richards calls the real release: "Once we're up there doing it, it's sheer fun and joy."

Sources: Adapted from *Superteams*, Penguin Portfolio (Tu, K. 2012) Copyright © Khoi Tu, 2012, Reproduced by permission of Penguin Books Ltd; and J. Lawrence, "With Touring Still A Focal Point, The Rolling Stones, AC/DC And U2 Fight For Top Honors In Rock And Roll History," www.forbes.com, December 30, 2014; www.rollingstones.com accessed February 20, 2020; S. Andrew, "The Rolling Stones Are Headed Back on Tour." CNN International, February 6, 2020; www.therichest.com, "The Rolling Stones Net Worth," accessed February 20, 2020.

As individuals, we all belong to groups based on our occupations, race, gender, and many other categories. Being part of a group can greatly influence how people behave, and the impact could be positive or negative—or both. In the chapter-opening vignette above, the Rolling Stones offer an exceptional example of group cohesiveness. Spending a lot of time in each other's company and being in constant interaction can bring members of a group closer together. If members of a group display different viewpoints (and the Rolling Stones have certainly had their share of public disagreements), this may lead to more group conflict, but acknowledgment of and respect for the role each individual plays within the group goes a long way toward building and maintaining group cohesion. In addition, individuals who emerge as group leaders can encourage the rest of the group to focus on common goals, especially when they show that they value the input of all members.

Yet tensions among members of a group may not be overcome by group cohesiveness or lack of role conflict, as many other bands have demonstrated. Some groups can exert a powerful positive influence, and others can create bias. The objectives of this chapter and Chapter 10 are to familiarize you with group and team concepts, provide you with a foundation for understanding how groups and teams work, and show you how to create effective working units. Let's begin by defining a group.

Defining and Classifying Groups

9-1 Distinguish between the different types of groups.

group Two or more individuals, interacting and interdependent, who have come together to achieve particular objectives.

informal group A group that is not defined by an organization's structure; such a group appears in response to other needs, such as social clubs or interest groups.

formal group A designated work group defined by an organization's structure.

In organizational behavior, a **group** is two or more individuals, interacting and interdependent, who have come together to achieve particular objectives. Groups can be either formal or informal. A **formal group** is defined by the organization's structure, with designated work assignments and established tasks. In formal groups, the behaviors that team members should engage in are stipulated by and directed toward organizational goals. The six members of an airline flight crew are a formal group, for example. In contrast, an **informal group** is neither formally structured nor organizationally determined. Informal groups in the work environment meet the need for social contact. Three employees from different departments who regularly have lunch or coffee together are an informal group. These types of interactions among individuals, though informal, deeply affect their behavior and performance.

Social Identity

People often feel strongly about their groups, partly because, as research indicates, shared experiences amplify our perception of events.[1] Also, according to research in Australia, sharing painful experiences, in particular, increases our felt bond and trust with others.[2] Why do people form groups, and why do they feel so strongly about them? Consider the celebrations that follow when a sports team wins a national championship. The winner's supporters are elated, and sales of team-related shirts, jackets, and hats skyrocket. Fans of the losing team feel dejected, even embarrassed. Why? Even though fans have little to do with the actual performance of the sports team, their self-image can be wrapped up in their identification with the group. Our tendency to personally invest in the accomplishments of a group is the territory of **social identity theory**.

social identity theory Perspective that considers when and why individuals consider themselves members of groups.

Social identity theory proposes that people have emotional reactions to the failure or success of their group because their self-esteem gets tied to whatever happens to the group.[3] When your group does well, you bask in reflected glory, and your own self-esteem rises. When your group does poorly, you might feel bad about yourself, or you might reject that part of your identity, similar to fair-weather fans. If your group is devalued and disrespected, your social identity might feel threatened, and you might endorse deviant behaviors to restore your group's standing.[4] Social identities can even lead people to experience pleasure as a result of seeing another group suffer. We often see these feelings of *schadenfreude* in the joy fans experience when a hated team loses.[5]

OB POLL

Most People Report Drinking with Coworkers Is Acceptable

Note: Society for Human Resources Management (SHRM) survey of 501 individuals and how drinking is viewed in their organization at a range of work-related activities.

Source: Based on S. M. Heathfield, "To Drink or Not to Drink: Does Alcohol Drinking Mix Safely with Work Events?," *About.com Guide,* 2013, http://humanresources.about.com/od/networking/qt/drink_i3.htm.

People develop many identities through the course of their lives. You might define yourself in terms of the organization you work for, the city you live in, your profession, your religious background, your ethnicity, and/or your gender. Since 2011, over 100,00 nationals have become Irish citizens. The top 10 nationalities are Polish, Indian, Nigerian, Romanian, Filipino, Pakistani, Chinese, Ukrainian, South African, and Bangladeshi. At a recent ceremony, the new Irish citizens were advised to "not forget your own country, your own people, your own traditions."[6] We may thus pick and choose which of our social identities are salient to the situation, or we may find that our social identities are in conflict, such as the identities of business leader and parent.[7]

Our social identities help us understand who we are and where we fit in with other people, and research indicates they bring us better health and lower levels of depression because we become less likely to attribute negative situations to internal or insurmountable reasons.[8] To experience these good outcomes, however, we need to feel that our social identities are positive.[9]

Until now, we've discussed social identities primarily in a cultural context. However, the identity we may feel with respect to our organization is only one aspect of our work-related identities (see OB Poll). Within our organizations and work groups, we can develop many identities through (1) *relational* identification, when we connect with others because of our roles, and (2) *collective* identification, when we connect with the aggregate characteristics of our groups. We can identify with groups within our team, our work group, and our organizations. Often, our identification with our work groups is stronger than with our organizations, but both are important to positive outcomes in attitudes and behaviors. The strength of our identification may vary, depending on how unique a group is within an organization.[10] Low identification to the group may lead to problems. If we have low identification with our organizations, we may experience decreased satisfaction and engage in fewer organizational citizenship behaviors (OCBs).[11] Similarly, we are less likely to apply to organizations that do not correspond to our collective identities.[12] Immigrant workers, for example, often experience strained and threatened identities when they do not have inclusive, supportive supervisors or when they do not feel like they are a part of the local community. This often leads to high turnover rates for immigrants and migrants.[13] Even the words that leaders use matter; when CEOs use "we" or "us" language (instead of "I" language), this signals to employees and stakeholders alike that they are a part of a group. One study of German organizations spanning 16 years found that use of collective language was correlated with increased sales and return-on-investment.[14]

In a study conducted in India, it has been observed that the prevalence of caste-based discrimination and gender inequality has affected the social identity of doctors. The study reveals gender- and caste-based discrimination is worse among doctors belonging to lower caste compared to doctors from upper castes due to a lower rate of return to experience, between genders, for lower caste doctors. However, policy implications and caste-based reservation to remove caste-based discrimination, has improved the share of low-caste aspirants in the healthcare profession has risen from about 12 percent in 1999 to above 50 percent in 2009.[15]

Ingroups and Outgroups

ingroup favoritism Perspective in which we see members of our ingroup as better than other people, and people not in our group as all the same.

outgroup The inverse of an ingroup, which can mean everyone outside the group but is more usually an identified other group.

Ingroup favoritism occurs when we see members of our group as better than other people, and people not in our group as all the same. Recent research suggests that people with low openness and/or low agreeableness are more susceptible to ingroup favoritism.[16]

Whenever there is an ingroup, there is by necessity an **outgroup**, which is sometimes everyone else but is usually an identified group known by the ingroup's members. For example, if my ingroup is the Republican Party in U.S. politics, my outgroup might be anyone in the world who is not a Republican, but it's more likely to be the other U.S. political parties, or perhaps just Democrats.

When there are ingroups and outgroups, there is often animosity between them. One of the most powerful sources of ingroup–outgroup feelings is the practice of religion, even in the workplace. A study in Kenya examined the effects of interfaith dialog in the workplace in the achievement of organizational goals. Employees of different faiths have the potential to clash when they come into contact. Diverse faiths may enhance or jeopardize organizational cohesiveness and goal achievement. In the Diamond Trust Bank and Cooperative Bank of Kenya, the workforce, which consists of Christians, Muslims, and Hindus, meets once a week to pray. Faith may, in some environments, provide a framework for intercultural communication.[17]

On a final note, you may remember discussing *the threat of technological unemployment* in the chapter on perception and individual decision making. Despite fear of job loss to automation, recent research suggests that the rise of automation and a robot workforce may lead to a *less prejudiced workforce*. By classifying employees into human and non-human, a new *panhumanist social identity* (i.e., seeing humanity as a common social identity, where humans are a part of the ingroup) may emerge that can reduce human-to-human prejudice, discrimination, and inequality.[18]

Social Identity Threat

Ingroups and outgroups pave the way for *social identity threat*, which is akin to stereotype threat (see Chapter 5). With social identity threat, individuals believe they will be personally negatively evaluated due to their association with a devalued group, and they may lose confidence and performance effectiveness. One study found, for example, that when subjects from high and low socioeconomic backgrounds took a high-pressure math test, the low-status subjects who felt social identity threat could be as confident as the high-status subjects only when they were first deliberately encouraged about their abilities.[19]

Stages of Group Development

9-2 Describe the punctuated-equilibrium model of group development.

punctuated-equilibrium model A set of phases that temporary groups go through that involves transitions between inertia and activity.

Temporary groups with finite deadlines pass through a unique sequencing of actions (or inaction) called the **punctuated-equilibrium model**, shown in Exhibit 9-1. The stages in this model include the following: (1) The first meeting sets the group's direction, (2) the first phase of group activity is one of inertia and thus slower progress, (3) a transition takes place exactly when the group has used up half its allotted time, (4) this transition initiates major changes, (5) a second phase of inertia follows the transition, and (6) the group's last meeting is characterized by markedly accelerated activity.[20] Alternative models suggest that teams progress through a formation stage, a conflict resolution or "storming" stage, a "norming" stage where members agree on roles and make decisions, and a "performing" stage where members begin to work collaboratively. The forming, storming, norming, and performing stages may occur at phase one of the punctuated equilibrium model, while a second performing and conforming stage may occur in the second phase, following a short period of reforming group norms and expectations.[21]

Let's discuss each stage of the punctuated-equilibrium model. At the first meeting, the group's general purpose and direction is established and then a framework of behavioral patterns and assumptions through which the group will approach its project emerges, sometimes in the first few seconds of the group's existence. Once set, the group's direction is solidified and is unlikely to be reexamined throughout the first half of its life. This is a period of inertia—the

Exhibit 9-1 The Punctuated-Equilibrium Model

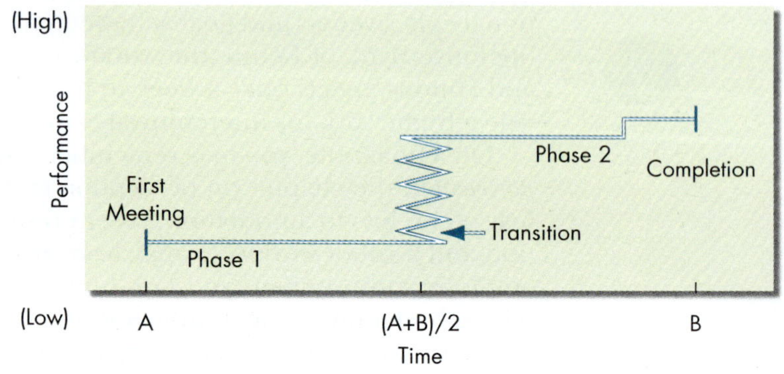

group tends to stand still or become locked into a fixed course of action, even if it gains new insights that challenge initial patterns and assumptions.

One of the most interesting discoveries in studies was that groups experienced a transition precisely halfway between the first meeting and the official deadline—whether members spent an hour on their project or 6 months. The midpoint appears to work like an alarm clock, heightening members' awareness that their time is limited and they need to get moving. This transition ends phase 1 and is characterized by a concentrated burst of changes, dropping of old patterns, and adoption of new perspectives. The transition sets a revised direction for phase 2, a new equilibrium or period of inertia in which the group executes plans created during the transition period.

The group's last meeting is characterized by a final burst of activity to finish its work. In summary, the punctuated-equilibrium model characterizes groups as exhibiting long periods of inertia interspersed with brief revolutionary changes triggered primarily by members' awareness of time and deadlines. This is not the only model of group stages by far, but it is a dominant theory with strong support. Keep in mind, however, that this model doesn't apply to all groups but is suited to the finite quality of temporary task groups working under a time deadline.[22]

Group Property 1: Roles

9-3 Show how role requirements change in different situations.

role A function assumed by someone occupying a given position in a group.

Work groups shape members' behavior, and they also help explain individual behavior as well as the performance of the group itself. Some defining group properties are *roles, norms, status, size, cohesiveness, and diversity*. We'll discuss each in the sections that follow. Let's begin with the first group property, roles.

Shakespeare said, "All the world's a stage, and all the men and women merely players."* Using the same metaphor, all group members are actors, each playing a **role**, a set of expected behavior patterns attributed to someone occupying a given position in a social unit. We are required to play a number of diverse roles, both on and off our jobs. As we'll see, one of the tasks in understanding behavior is grasping the role a person is currently playing.

Mahesh is a plant manager with Mahindra Automobiles, a large car manufacturer in Pune. He fulfills a number of roles—employee, member of middle management, and electrical engineer. Off the job, Mahesh holds more roles: husband, father, Hindu, cricket player, member of the Gymkhana, and treasurer of his homeowners' association. Many of these roles are compatible; some create conflicts. How does Mahesh's commitment to the organization clash with the time required by his residential society in resolving some conflicts? There are also times when members of the residential society pressure him to get sponsorships for their society functions from his company? A recent offer of promotion requires Mahesh to relocate, yet his family wants to stay in Pune. Can the role demands of his job be reconciled with the demands of his husband and father roles?

Different groups impose different role requirements on individuals. Like Bill, we all play a number of roles, and our behavior varies with each. But how do we know each role's requirements? We draw on our role perceptions to frame our ideas of appropriate behaviors and to learn the expectations of our groups.

*William Shakespeare, *As You Like It*, D. C. Heath & Company, 1904.

Role Perception

role perception An individual's view of how they are supposed to act in a given situation.

Our view of how we're supposed to act in a given situation is a **role perception**. We get role perceptions from stimuli all around us—for example, friends, books, films, and television, as when we form an impression of politicians from *House of Cards*. Apprenticeship programs allow beginners to watch an expert so they can learn to act as they should.

Role Expectations

role expectations How others believe a person should act in a given situation.

Role expectations are the way others believe you should act in a given context. A Supreme Court judge is viewed as having propriety and dignity, while a football coach may be seen as aggressive, dynamic, and inspiring to the players. Role expectations can influence the way people perform their work. For example, creative role expectations can lead people to be more creative in their work.[23]

psychological contract An unwritten agreement that sets out what a manager expects from an employee, and vice versa.

In the workplace, we look at role expectations through the perspective of the **psychological contract**: an unwritten agreement that exists between employees and employers. This agreement sets out mutual expectations.[24] Management is expected to treat employees justly, provide acceptable working conditions, clearly communicate what is a fair day's work, and give feedback on how well employees are doing. Employees are expected to demonstrate a good attitude, follow directions, and show loyalty to the organization. When a psychological contract also focuses on relationships between employers (or supervisors) and employees, employees may also be more likely to engage in organizational citizenship behaviors (OCBs).[25]

What happens if management is derelict in its part of the bargain? We can expect negative effects on employee performance and satisfaction. One study among restaurant managers found that violations of the psychological contract were related to greater intentions to quit, while another study of a variety of different industries found psychological contracts were associated with lower levels of productivity, higher levels of theft, and greater work withdrawal.[26]

In a specialized store for women sarees, Nalli, the salespersons are friendly, knowledgeable about each saree in the store, and display patience while the customer chooses from among various options. The sales representatives are expected to individually attend to each customer to make them feel special.[27]

Source: mrinalpal.shutterstock.com

There is evidence that perceptions of psychological contracts vary across cultures. In France, where people are individualistic and power is more asymmetric, contracts are perceived as self-interested yet favoring the more powerful party. In Canada, where people are individualistic but power is more symmetric, contracts are perceived as self-interested yet focused on balanced reciprocity. In China, where people are collectivistic and power is more asymmetric, contracts are perceived as going beyond the work context into employees' lives. And in Norway, where people are collectivistic but power is more symmetric, contracts are perceived as more relational and based on trust.[28]

Role Conflict

role conflict A situation in which an individual is confronted by divergent role expectations.

interrole conflict A situation in which the expectations of an individual's different, separate groups are in opposition.

When compliance with one role requirement may make it difficult to comply with another, the result is **role conflict.**[29] At the extreme, two or more role expectations may be contradictory. For example, if you, as a manager, were to provide a performance evaluation of a person you mentored, your roles as evaluator and mentor may conflict. Similarly, we can experience **interrole conflict**[30] when the expectations of our different, separate groups are in opposition. An example can be found in work–family conflict, which Bill experiences when expectations placed on him as a husband and father differ from those placed on him as an executive with EMM Industries. Bill's wife and children want to remain in Phoenix, while EMM expects its employees to be responsive to the company's needs and requirements. Although it might be in Bill's financial and career interests to accept a relocation, the conflict centers on choosing between family and work role expectations. Indeed, a great deal of research demonstrates that work–family conflict is one of the most significant sources of stress for most employees.[31]

Within organizations, most employees are simultaneously in occupations, work groups, divisions, and demographic groups, and these identities can conflict when the expectations of one clash with the expectations of another.[32] During mergers and acquisitions, employees can be torn between their identities as members of their original organization and of the new parent company.[33] Multinational organizations have also been shown to lead to dual identification—with the local division and with the international organization.[34]

Role Play and Assimilation

The degree to which we comply with our role perceptions and expectations—even when we don't agree with them initially—can be surprising. One of the most illuminating role and identity experiments was done a number of years ago by psychologist Philip Zimbardo and his associates.[35] They created a "prison" in the basement of the Stanford psychology building; hired emotionally stable, physically healthy, law-abiding students who scored "normal average" on personality tests; randomly assigned them the role of either "guard" or "prisoner"; and established some basic rules.

It took little time for the prisoners to accept the authority positions of the guards and for the mock guards to adjust to their new authority roles. Consistent with social identity theory, the guards came to see the prisoners as a negative outgroup, and they developed stereotypes about the "typical" prisoner personality type. After the guards crushed a rebellion attempt on the second day, the prisoners became increasingly passive. Whatever the guards dished out, the prisoners took. The prisoners actually began to believe and act like

Myth or Science?

Gossip and Exclusion Are Toxic for Groups

The statement above is not necessarily true, but it is counterintuitive. Let's explore the conditions.

What is gossip? Most of us might say gossip is talking about others, sharing rumors, and speculating about others' behaviors; gossip affects a person's reputation. We might also say gossip is malicious, but according to researchers, it can serve positive social functions, too. Prosocial gossip can expose behavior that exploits other people, which can lead to positive changes. For example, if Julie tells Chris that Alex is bullying Summer, then Chris has learned about Alex's poor behavior through gossiping. Chris might refuse to partner with Alex on a work project, which might limit Alex's opportunities with the organization, preventing him from bullying more people. Alternatively, as the gossip spreads, Alex might feel exposed for his behavior and conform to group expectations against bullying behavior. In fact, according to research, Alex is likely to cooperate with the group in response to the gossip, and others hearing and spreading the gossip are likely also to cooperate by not acting on their impulses toward bad behavior.

What about excluding Alex? There are two types of exclusion in the workplace: leaving someone out of a group and ostracizing an individual. Both lead to the same end—the person isn't part of the group. While simply leaving someone out of a group might not send a message of exclusion, ostracism certainly does. Ostracism is more of a felt punishment than gossip because it is more direct. Research indicates that ostracized individuals cooperate to a greater degree when they are around the group to show a willingness to conform, hoping to be invited back into the group.

Can gossip and ostracism work together? Yes, according to a recent study. When subjects were given an opportunity to gossip about the work of another subject, that subject cooperated more than before; when the opportunity to gossip was paired with the ability to ostracize, that subject cooperated to a much greater degree.

Thus, gossip and exclusion may provide groups with benefits, at least when the gossip is confined to truthful work-related discussion, when the opportunity still exists to rejoin the group with full standing, and when the group norms are positive.

Sources: Based on M. Cikara and J. J. Van Bavel, "The Neuroscience of Intergroup Relations: An Integrative Review," *Perspectives on Psychological Science* 9, no. 3 (2014): 245–74; M. Feinberg, R. Willer, and M. Schultz, "Gossip and Ostracism Promote Cooperation in Groups," *Psychological Science* 25, no. 3 (2014): 656–64; and I. H. Smith, K. Aquino, S. Koleva, and J. Graham, "The Moral Ties That Bind...Even to Out-Groups: The Interactive Effect of Moral Identity and the Binding Moral Foundations," *Psychological Science* (2014): 1554–62.

they were inferior and powerless. Every guard, at some time during the simulation, engaged in abusive, authoritative behavior. One said, "I was surprised at myself.... I made them call each other names and clean the toilets out with their bare hands. I practically considered the prisoners cattle, and I kept thinking: 'I have to watch out for them in case they try something.'" Surprisingly, during the entire experiment—even after days of abuse—not one prisoner said, "Stop this. I'm a student like you. This is just an experiment!" The researchers had to end the study after only 6 days because of the participants' pathological reactions.

What can we conclude from this study? Like the rest of us, the participants had learned stereotyped conceptions of guard and prisoner roles from the mass media and their own personal experiences in power and powerless relationships gained at home (parent–child), in school (teacher–student), and in other situations. This background allowed them to assume roles easily and rapidly and, with a vague notion of the social identity of their roles and no prior personality pathology or training for the parts they were playing, to execute extreme forms of behavior consistent with those roles.

A reality television show that was a follow-up to the Stanford experiment was conducted by the BBC.[36] The BBC results were dramatically different from those of the Stanford experiment, partially because the show used a less intense simulated prison setting. The "guards" were far more careful in their behavior, limiting their aggressive treatment of "prisoners" and expressing concerns about how their actions might be perceived. In short, they did not fully take on their authority roles, possibly because they knew their behavior was being observed by millions of viewers. These results suggest that less intense situations evoke less extreme behavior, and abuse of roles can be limited when people are made conscious of their behavior.

Group Property 2: Norms

9-4 Demonstrate how norms exert influence on an individual's behavior.

norms Acceptable standards of behavior within a group that are shared by the group's members.

Did you ever notice that golfers don't speak while their partners are putting? Why not? The answer is norms.

All groups have established **norms**—acceptable standards of behavior shared by members that express what they ought to do and ought not to do under certain circumstances. It's not enough for group leaders to share their opinions—even if members adopt the leaders' views, the effect may last only 3 days![37] When agreed to by the group, norms influence behavior with a minimum of external controls. Different groups, communities, and societies have different norms, but they all have them.[38] Norms are established through the social perception of group members—such as when a group leader says "this is what we should do" and rewards that action when it does happen, and the rest of the group unanimously puts the suggestion into practice.[39] Let's discuss the levels of influence that norms can exert over us, starting with our emotions.

Norms and Emotions

Have you ever noticed how the emotions of one member of your family, especially strong emotions, can influence the emotions of the other members? A family can be a highly normative group. So can a task group whose members work together on a daily basis, because frequent communication can increase the power of norms. A recent study found that, in a task group, individuals' emotions influenced the group's emotions, and vice versa. This may not be surprising, but researchers also found that norms dictated the *experience* of emotions for the individuals and for the groups—in other words, people grew to interpret their shared emotions in the same way.[40] As we discovered in Chapters 4 and 5, our emotions and moods can shape our perspective, so the normative effect of groups can have a powerful influence on group attitudes and outcomes.

Norms and Conformity

conformity The adjustment of one's behavior to align with the norms of the group.

As a member of a group, you desire acceptance and stability. Thus, you may conform to group norms when you perceive that others are doing so or if you experience conflict or frustration.[41] Considerable evidence suggests that groups can place strong pressures on individual members to change their attitudes and behaviors to match the group's standard.[42] The impact that group pressures for **conformity** can have on an individual member's judgment was demonstrated in studies by Solomon Asch and others.[43] Asch made up groups of seven or eight people who were asked to compare two cards. One card had one line, and the

Exhibit 9-2 Examples of Cards Used in Asch's Study

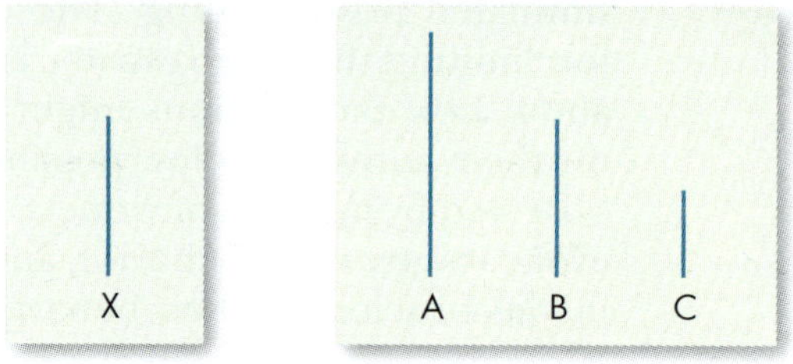

other had three lines of varying length, one of which was identical to the line on the one-line card, as Exhibit 9-2 shows. The difference in line length was obvious; in fact, under ordinary conditions, subjects were incorrect less than 1 percent of the time in announcing which of the three lines matched the single line.

The experiment began with sets of matching exercises. Everyone gave the right answers. On the third set, however, the first subject, who was part of the research team, gave an obviously wrong answer—for example, saying "C" in Exhibit 9-2 was the same as "X." The next subject, also on the research team, gave the same wrong answer, and so forth. Now the dilemma confronting the subject, who didn't know any of the subjects were on the research team, was this: Should he or she publicly state a perception that differed from the announced position of the others or give an incorrect answer that agreed with the others?

The results over many experiments showed 75 percent of subjects gave at least one answer that conformed—that they knew was wrong but was consistent with the replies of other group members—and the average conformer gave wrong answers 37 percent of the time. This suggests that we feel the pressure toward conformity with group norms. Other recent research with moral decision making indicated an even stronger effect of conformity when subjects found the nonconforming ideas not just incorrect but objectionable.[44] Does that mean we are mere robots? Certainly not. The flip side of the 37 percent of conforming responses is the 63 percent of independent responses, and 95 percent gave the correct (nonconforming) response at least once. Therefore, we feel the pressure to conform, but it is not a perfect predictor of what we will do. Furthermore, we don't tend to like the pressure we feel to conform. Asch wrote, "Those who participated in this challenging experiment agreed nearly without exception that independence was preferable to conformity."[45]

Do individuals conform to the pressures of all groups to which they belong? Obviously not, because people belong to many groups whose norms vary and sometimes are contradictory. People conform to their **reference groups**, in which a person is aware of other members, defines him- or herself as a member or would like to be a member, and feels group members are significant to him or her. The implication, then, is that all groups do not impose equal conformity pressures on their members.

reference groups Important groups to which individuals belong or hope to belong and with whose norms individuals are likely to conform.

Norms and Behavior

Norms can cover any aspect of group behavior.[46] As we've mentioned, norms in the workplace significantly influence employee behavior. This may seem intuitive, but full appreciation of the influence of norms on worker behavior did not

An Ethical Choice

Using Peer Pressure as an Influence Tactic

We've all experienced peer pressure, and it can be hard to behave differently from your friends and coworkers. As more work in organizations is performed in groups and teams, the possibilities and pitfalls of such pressure have become an increasingly important ethical issue for managers.

Peer pressure can be a positive force in some ways. In groups where high effort and performance are the norms, peer pressure from coworkers, whether direct or indirect, can encourage high performance from those not meeting expectations. A group with a norm toward behaving ethically could also use peer pressure to minimize negative behavior. Thus, peer pressure can promote all sorts of good behaviors, from donating to charity to volunteering at the local soup kitchen.

However, peer pressure can also be destructive. It can create a feeling of exclusion in those who do not go along with group norms and can be very stressful and hurtful for those who don't see eye-to-eye with the rest of the group. Peer pressure itself can be an unethical practice that unduly influences workers' behavior and thoughts. And while groups might pressure others into good behavior, they can just as easily sway them to bad behavior.

Should you use group peer pressure? As a leader, you may need to. One survey found that only 6 percent of leaders reported being able to successfully influence their employees on their own. Peer pressure hastens a group toward consensus, and levels of peer pressure predict how much the leader can control the group. If you use peer pressure to encourage individuals to work toward team goals and behave consistently with organizational values, it can enhance ethical performance. But your behavior should emphasize acceptance and rewarding of positive behavior, rather than rejection and exclusion, as a means of getting everyone to behave consistently in the group.

Sources: Based on E. Estrada and E. Vargas-Estrada, "How Peer Pressure Shapes Consensus, Leadership, and Innovations in Social Groups," *Scientific Reports* 3 (2013), article number 2905; A. Verghese, "The Healing Power of Peer Pressure," *Newsweek,* March 14, 2011, www.newsweek.com; J. Meer, "Brother, Can You Spare a Dime? Peer Pressure in Charitable Solicitation," *Journal of Public Economics* 95, no. 7–8 (2011): 926–41; and L. Potter, "Lack Influence at Work? Why Most Leaders Struggle to Lead Positive Change," *Yahoo,* May 14, 2013, http://finance.yahoo.com/news/lack-influence-why-most-leaders-121500672.html.

occur until the Hawthorne Studies conducted between 1924 and 1932 at the Western Electric Company's Hawthorne Works in Chicago.[47]

In the studies, the researchers first examined the relationship between the physical environment and productivity. As they increased the light level for the experimental group of workers, output rose for that unit and the control group. But as they dropped the light level, productivity continued to increase. In fact, productivity in the experimental group decreased only when the light intensity had been reduced to that of moonlight, leading researchers to believe that group dynamics, rather than the environment, influenced behavior.

The researchers next isolated a small group of women assembling telephones so their behavior could be observed more carefully. Over the next several years, this small group's output increased steadily, and the number of personal and sick absences was approximately one-third of that in the regular production department. It became evident that this group's performance was significantly influenced by its "special" status. The members thought they were in an elite group, and that management showed concern about their interests by engaging in experimentation. In essence, workers in both the illumination and assembly experiments were really reacting to the increased attention they received.

A wage incentive plan was then introduced in the bank wiring observation room. The most important finding was that employees did not individually maximize their output. Rather, their role performance became controlled by

Research suggests that social networking site Facebook may be detrimental to the psychosocial well-being of its younger users. A study on Italian adolescents that aimed to determine how personality traits and social influence processes relate to the use of Facebook—which involved a total of 968 participants—found that emotional stability, extraversion, conscientiousness, and norms directly predicted problematic Facebook use.
Source: pixinoo/Shutterstock

a group norm. Members were afraid that if they significantly increased their output, the unit incentive rate might be cut, the expected daily output might be increased, layoffs might occur, or slower workers might be reprimanded. So the group established its idea of a fair output—neither too much nor too little. Members helped each other ensure their reports were nearly level, and the norms that the group established included a number of behavioral "don'ts." *Don't* be a rate-buster, turning out too much work. *Don't* be a chiseler, turning out too little work. *Don't* squeal on any of your peers. The group enforced its norms with name calling, ridicule, and even punches to the upper arms of violators. It thus operated well below its capability, using norms that were tightly established and strongly enforced.

Positive Norms and Group Outcomes

One goal of every organization with corporate social responsibility (CSR) initiatives is for the organization's values (or the values of the CEO and executives) to hold normative sway over employees.[48] After all, if employees aligned their thinking with the organization's positive norms, these norms would become stronger and the probability of positive impact would grow exponentially. We might expect the same outcomes from political correctness (PC) norms. But what *is* the effect of strong positive norms on group outcomes? The popular thinking is that, to increase creativity in groups, for instance, norms should be loosened. However, research on gender-diverse groups indicates that strong PC norms increase group creativity. Why? Clear expectations about male-female interactions reduce uncertainty about group expectations,[49] which allows the members to express their creative ideas more easily, without combating stereotype norms.

Positive group norms may well beget positive outcomes, but only if other factors are present, too. For instance, in a recent study a high level of group extraversion predicted helping behaviors more strongly when there were positive cooperation norms.[50] As powerful as norms can be, though, not everyone is equally susceptible to positive group norms. In a study of Italian adolescents, gender, group norms, and social identity predicted perceived frequency of the use of the social networking site Facebook. In addition, the personality traits of emotional stability, extraversion, conscientiousness, and norms directly predicted problematic Facebook use.[51]

Negative Norms and Group Outcomes

Lalit is frustrated by a coworker who constantly spreads malicious and unsubstantiated rumors about him. Rashmi is tired of a member of her work group who, when confronted with a problem, takes out his frustration by yelling and screaming at her and other members. And Komal recently quit her job as a dental hygienist after being sexually harassed by her employer.

What do these illustrations have in common? They represent employees exposed to acts of deviant workplace behavior.[52] As we discussed in Chapter 3, counterproductive work behavior (CWB) or **deviant workplace behavior** (also called *antisocial behavior* or *workplace incivility*) is voluntary behavior that violates significant organizational norms and, in so doing, threatens the well-being of the organization or its members. Exhibit 9-3 provides a typology of deviant workplace behaviors, with examples of each.

deviant workplace behavior Voluntary behavior that violates significant organizational norms and, in so doing, threatens the well-being of the organization or its members. Also called antisocial behavior or workplace incivility.

Few organizations will admit to creating or condoning conditions that encourage and maintain deviant behaviors. Yet they exist. As we discussed before, a work group can become characterized by positive or negative attributes. When those attributes are negative, such as when a work group is high in psychopathy and aggression, the characteristics of deceit, amorality, and intent to harm others are pronounced.[53] Second, employees have been reporting an increase in rudeness and disregard toward others by bosses and coworkers in recent years. Workplace incivility, like many other deviant behaviors, has many negative outcomes for the victims.[54] Nearly half of employees who have

Exhibit 9-3 **Typology of Deviant Workplace Behavior**

Category	Examples
Production	Leaving early Intentionally working slowly Wasting resources
Property	Sabotage Lying about hours worked Stealing from the organization
Political	Showing favoritism Gossiping and spreading rumors Blaming coworkers
Personal aggression	Sexual harassment Verbal abuse Stealing from coworkers

Sources: Based on S. H. Appelbaum, G. D. Iaconi, and A. Matousek, "Positive and Negative Deviant Workplace Behaviors: Causes, Impacts, and Solutions," *Corporate Governance* 7, no. 5 (2007): 586–98; and R. W. Griffin and A. O'Leary-Kelly, *The Dark Side of Organizational Behavior* (New York: Wiley, 2004).

suffered this incivility say that it has led them to think about changing jobs; 12 percent actually quit because of it.[55] Also, a study of nearly 1,500 respondents found that, in addition to increasing turnover intentions, incivility at work increased reports of psychological stress and physical illness.[56] Employees that are repeatedly subjected to incivility feel a sense of injustice and may lash out at the organization by engaging in deviant behaviors.[57] Research suggests that a lack of sleep, which is often caused by heightened work demands and which hinders a person's ability to regulate emotions and behaviors, can also lead to deviant behavior. As organizations have tried to do more with less, pushing their employees to work extra hours, they may be indirectly facilitating deviant behavior.[58]

Like norms in general, employees' antisocial actions are shaped by the group context within which they work. Evidence demonstrates deviant workplace behavior is likely to flourish where it's supported by group norms.[59] For example, workers who socialize either at or outside work with people who are frequently absent from work are more likely to be absent themselves.[60] Thus when deviant workplace norms surface, employee cooperation, commitment, and motivation are likely to suffer.

What are the consequences of workplace deviance for groups? Some research suggests a chain reaction occurs in groups with high levels of dysfunctional behavior.[61] The process begins with negative behaviors like shirking, undermining coworkers, or being generally uncooperative. As a result of these behaviors, the group collectively starts to have negative moods. These negative moods then result in poor coordination of effort and lower levels of group performance.

Norms and Culture

Do people in collectivist cultures have different norms than people in individualist cultures? Of course they do[62]—even to the extent that some norms are undetectable or not understood by outgroup members.[63] But did you know that our orientation may be changed, even after years of living in one society? In a recent experiment, an organizational role-playing exercise was given to a neutral group of subjects; the exercise stressed either collectivist or individualist norms. Subjects were then given a task of their personal choice or were assigned one by an ingroup or outgroup person. When the individualist-primed subjects were allowed personal choice of the task, or the collectivist-primed subjects were assigned the task by an ingroup person, they became more highly motivated.[64]

Group Property 3: Status, and Group Property 4: Size and Dynamics

9-5 Show how status and size differences affect group performance.

We've discussed how the roles we play and the norms we internalize tend to dictate our behavior in groups. However, those are not the only two factors that influence who we are in a group and how the group functions. Have you ever noticed how groups tend to stratify into higher- and lower-status members? Sometimes the status of members reflects their status outside the group setting, but not always. Also, status often varies between groups of different sizes. Let's examine how these factors affect a work group's efficacy.

Group Property 3: Status

status A socially defined position or rank given to groups or group members by others.

Status—a socially defined position or rank given to groups or group members by others—permeates every society. Even the smallest group shows differences in member status over time. Status is a significant motivator and has major behavioral consequences when individuals perceive a disparity between what they believe their status is and what others perceive it to be.

status characteristics theory A theory stating that differences in status characteristics create status hierarchies within groups.

What Determines Status? According to **status characteristics theory**, status tends to derive from one of three sources:[65]

1. **The power a person wields over others.** Because they likely control the group's resources, people who control group outcomes tend to be perceived as high status.
2. **A person's ability to contribute to a group's goals.** People whose contributions are critical to the group's success tend to have high status.
3. **An individual's personal characteristics.** Someone whose personal characteristics are positively valued by the group (good looks, intelligence, money, or a friendly personality) typically has higher status than someone with fewer valued attributes.

Status and Norms Status has some interesting effects on the power of norms and pressures to conform. High-status individuals may be more likely to deviate from norms when they have low identification (social identity) with the group.[66] They also eschew pressure from lower-ranking members of other groups. For instance, physicians actively resist administrative decisions made by lower-ranking medical insurance company employees.[67] High-status people are also better able to resist conformity pressures than their lower-status peers. An

Sourav Ganguly, presently the President of Board of Cricket Council in India (BCCI), welcomed his ex-Team India colleague, Rahul Dravid, as the Head Coach for the cricket team in 2022. In praise of Rahul Dravid, Ganguly said, "The BCCI welcomes Rahul Dravid as the Head Coach of India's senior men's team. Rahul has had an illustrious playing career and is one of the greats of the game. He has also served Indian cricket as Head of National Cricket Academy (NCA) with distinction. Rahul's effort at the NCA has nurtured several young cricketing talents who have gone on to represent the country at the international stage."[68] Ganguly's words reflects the high equitable status displayed by him.
Source: Saikat Paul.shutterstock.com

individual who is highly valued by a group but doesn't need or care about the group's social rewards is particularly able to disregard conformity norms.[69] In general, bringing high-status members into a group may improve performance, but only up to a point, perhaps because these members may introduce counterproductive norms.[70]

Status and Group Interaction People tend to become more assertive when they seek to attain higher status in a group.[71] They speak out more often, criticize more, state more commands, and interrupt others more often. Lower-status members tend to participate less actively in group discussions; when they possess expertise and insights that could aid the group, failure to fully utilize these members reduces the group's overall performance. But that doesn't mean a group of only high-status individuals would be preferable. Adding *some* high-status individuals to a group of mid-status individuals may be advantageous because group performance suffers when too many high-status people are in the mix.[72] Regardless of one's status, however, accurate knowledge of the status hierarchy (i.e., "who is who in my group") leads to better performance and results in effective within-group networking.[73]

Status Inequity It is important for group members to believe the status hierarchy is equitable. Perceived inequity creates disequilibrium, which inspires various types of corrective behaviors. Hierarchical groups can lead to resentment among those at the lower end of the status continuum. Large differences in status within groups are also associated with poorer individual performance, lower health, and more pronounced intentions for the lower-status members to leave the group.[74]

Groups generally agree within themselves on status criteria; hence, there is usually high concurrence on group rankings of individuals. Business executives may use personal income or the growth rate of their companies as determinants of status. Government bureaucrats may use the size of their budgets, and blue-collar workers may use their years of seniority. Managers who occupy central positions in their social networks are typically seen as higher in status by their subordinates, and this position actually translates into greater influence over the group's functioning.[75]

Groups generally form an informal status order based on ranking and command of needed resources.[76] Individuals can find themselves in conflicts when they move between groups whose status criteria are different, or when they join groups whose members have heterogeneous backgrounds. Cultures also differ in their criteria for conferring status upon individuals. When groups are heterogeneous, status differences may initiate conflict as the group attempts to reconcile the separate hierarchies. As we'll see in Chapter 10, this can be a problem when management creates teams of employees from varied functions.

Status and Stigmatization Although it's clear that your own status affects the way people perceive you, the status of people with whom you are affiliated can also affect others' views of you. Studies have shown that people who are stigmatized can "infect" others with their stigma. This "stigma by association" effect can result in negative opinions and evaluations of the person affiliated with the stigmatized individual, even if the association is brief and purely coincidental. Even if the person who is stigmatized calls the group members out for this, other low status members will still tend to legitimize their beliefs and continue to withhold support to the stigmatized.[77] Of course, many of the foundations of cultural status differences have no merit in the first place. For example, men interviewing for a job were viewed as less qualified when they were sitting next to an obese woman in a waiting room. Another study looking at the effects of being associated with an overweight person found that even when onlookers were told the target person and the overweight person were unrelated, the target person was still devalued. Similarly, leaders of predominantly African American work groups also suffer from stigma by association, resulting in lower performance appraisals by their peers.[78]

Group Status Early in life, we acquire an "us and them" mentality.[79] You may have correctly surmised that if you are in an outgroup, your group is of lower status in the eyes of the associated ingroup's members. Culturally, sometimes ingroups represent the dominant forces in a society and are given high status, which can create discrimination against their outgroups. Low-status groups, perhaps in response to this discrimination, are likely to leverage ingroup favoritism to compete for higher status.[80] When high-status groups then feel the discrimination from low-status groups, they may increase their bias against the outgroups.[81] With each cycle, the groups become more polarized.

Group Property 4: Size and Dynamics

Does the size of a group affect the group's overall behavior? Yes, but the effect depends on what dependent variables we examine.[82] Groups with a dozen or more members are good for gaining diverse input.[83] If the goal is fact-finding or idea-generating, then larger groups should be more effective.[84] Smaller groups of about seven members are better at doing something productive.[85]

social loafing The tendency for individuals to expend less effort when working collectively than when working individually.

Group dynamics are also important for characterizing groups. One of the most important findings concerning group dynamics involves **social loafing**, the tendency for individuals to expend less effort when working collectively than when alone.[86] Social loafing directly challenges the assumption that the productivity of the group as a whole should at least equal the sum of the productivity of the individuals in it, no matter what the group size.

What causes social loafing? It may be a belief that others in the group are not carrying their fair share. If you see others as lazy or inept, you can reestablish equity by reducing your effort. But simply failing to contribute may not be enough for someone to be labeled a free rider. Instead, the group must believe the social loafer is acting in an exploitive manner (benefitting at the expense of other team members).[87] Another explanation for social loafing is the diffusion of responsibility. Because group results cannot be attributed to any single person, the relationship between an individual's input and the group's output is clouded. Individuals may then be tempted to become free riders and coast on the group's efforts.[88]

The implications for Organizational Behavior (OB) are significant. When managers use collective work situations, they must also be able to identify individual efforts. Greater performance diversity creates greater social loafing the longer a group is together, which decreases satisfaction and performance.[89]

Social loafing appears to have a Western bias.[90] It's consistent with individualist cultures, such as the United States and Canada, that are dominated by self-interest. It is *not* consistent with collectivist societies, in which individuals are motivated by group goals. When research is compared across cultures, groups from Eastern cultures had significantly lower rates of social loafing.

Young employees of Alibaba's Tmall online shopping site celebrate their group's achievement of increasing the volume of sales orders during China's "Singles Day" shopping event. Although social loafing is consistent with individualistic cultures, in collectivist societies such as China, employees are motivated by group goals and perform better in groups than they do when they are working individually.
Source: Han Chuanhao Xinhua News Agency/Newscom

Research indicates that the stronger an individual's work ethic is, the less likely that person is to engage in social loafing.[91] Also, the greater the level of conscientiousness and agreeableness in a group, the more likely that performance will remain high whether there is social loafing or not.[92] There are ways to prevent social loafing: (1) set group goals, so the group has a common purpose to strive toward; (2) increase intergroup competition, which focuses on the shared group outcome; (3) engage in peer evaluations; (4) select members who have high motivation and prefer to work in groups; and (5) base group rewards in part on each member's unique contributions.[93] Recent research indicates that social loafing can be counteracted by publicly posting individual performance ratings for group members, too.[94] Although no magic bullet will prevent social loafing, these steps should help minimize its effect.

Group Property 5: Cohesiveness, and Group Property 6: Diversity

9-6 Describe how issues of cohesiveness and diversity can be integrated for group effectiveness.

For a group to be highly functioning, it must act cohesively as a unit, but not because all the group members think and act alike. In some ways, the properties of cohesiveness and diversity need to be valued way back at the tacit establishment of roles and norms—will the group be inclusive of all its members, regardless of differences in backgrounds? Let's discuss the importance of group cohesiveness first.

Group Property 5: Cohesiveness

cohesiveness The shared bond driving group members to work together and to stay in the group.

Groups differ in their **cohesiveness**—the shared bond driving group members to work together and to stay in the group.[95] Some work groups are cohesive because the members have spent a great deal of time together, the group's small size or purpose facilitates high interaction, or external threats have brought members close together.

Exhibit 9-4 **Relationship among Group Cohesiveness, Performance Norms, and Productivity**

Performance Norms	Cohesiveness: High	Cohesiveness: Low
High	High productivity	Moderate productivity
Low	Low productivity	Moderate to low productivity

Cohesiveness affects group productivity. Studies consistently show that the relationship between cohesiveness and productivity depends on the group's performance-related norms.[96] If norms for quality, output, and cooperation with outsiders are high, a cohesive group will be more productive than a less cohesive group. But if cohesiveness is high and performance norms are low, productivity will be low. If cohesiveness is low and performance norms are high, productivity increases, but less than in the high-cohesiveness/high-norms situation. When cohesiveness and performance-related norms are both low, productivity tends to fall into the low-to-moderate range. These conclusions are summarized in Exhibit 9-4.

What can you do to encourage group cohesiveness? Here are some ideas: (1) Make the group smaller, (2) encourage agreement with group goals, (3) increase the time members spend together, (4) increase the group's status and the perceived difficulty of attaining membership, (5) stimulate competition with other groups, (6) give rewards to the group rather than to individual members, and (7) physically isolate the group.[97]

Group Property 6: Diversity

diversity The extent to which members of a group are similar to, or different from, one another.

The final property of groups that we consider is **diversity** in the group's membership, or the degree to which members of the group are similar to, or different from, one another. Overall, studies identify both costs and benefits from group diversity.

Diversity appears to increase group conflict, especially in the early stages of a group's tenure; this often lowers group morale and raises dropout rates. One study compared groups that were culturally diverse and homogeneous (composed of people from the same country). On a wilderness survival test, the groups performed equally well, but the members from the diverse groups were less satisfied with their groups, were less cohesive, and had more conflict.[98] Another study examined the effect of differences in tenure on the performance of 67 engineering research and development groups.[99] When most people had roughly the same level of tenure, performance was high, but as tenure diversity increased, performance dropped off. There was an important qualifier: Higher levels of tenure diversity were not related to lower performance for groups when there were effective team-oriented human resources (HR) practices. More specifically, groups in which members' values or opinions differ tend to experience more conflict, but leaders who can get the group to focus on the task at hand and encourage group learning are able to reduce these conflicts and enhance discussion of group issues.[100] Gender diversity can also be a challenge to a group, but if inclusiveness is stressed, group conflict and dissatisfaction are lowered.[101]

You may have correctly surmised that the type of group diversity matters. Surface-level diversity—in observable characteristics such as national origin, race, and gender—alerts people to possible deep-level diversity—in underlying attitudes, values, and opinions. One researcher argues, "The mere presence of diversity you can see, such as a person's race or gender, actually cues a team that there's likely to be differences of opinion."[102] Surface-level diversity may subconsciously cue team members to be more open-minded in their views.[103] For example, two studies of MBA student groups found surface-level diversity led to greater openness. The effects of deep-level diversity are less understood. Research in Korea indicates that putting people with a high need for *power* with those with a low need for power can reduce unproductive group competition, whereas putting individuals with a similar need for *achievement* may increase task performance.[104]

Although differences can lead to conflict, they also provide an opportunity to solve problems in unique ways. One study of jury behavior found diverse juries were more likely to deliberate longer, share more information, and make fewer factual errors when discussing evidence. Altogether, the impact of diversity on groups is mixed. It is difficult to be in a diverse group in the short term. However, if members can weather their differences, over time diversity may help them be more open-minded and creative and to perform better. For example, gender diversity has been found to improve group performance in Chinese work groups.[105] On the other hand, even positive effects are unlikely to be especially strong. As one review stated, "The business case (in terms of demonstrable financial results) for diversity remains hard to support based on the extant research."[106] Yet other researchers argue that we shouldn't overlook the effects of homogeneity, many of which can be detrimental.[107]

faultlines The perceived divisions that split groups into two or more subgroups based on individual differences such as sex, race, age, work experience, and education.

One possible side effect in diverse teams—especially those that are diverse in terms of surface-level characteristics—is **faultlines**, or perceived divisions that split groups into two or more subgroups based on individual differences such as sex, race, age, work experience, and education.

For example, let's say that group A is composed of three men and three women. The three men have approximately the same amount of work experience and background in marketing. The three women have about the same amount of work experience and background in finance. Group B has three men and three women, but they all differ in terms of their experience and backgrounds. Two of the men are experienced, while the other is new. One of the women has worked at the company for several years, while the other two are new. In addition, two of the men and one woman in group B have backgrounds in marketing, while the other man and the remaining two women have backgrounds in finance. It is thus likely that a faultline will result in subgroups of males and females in group A but not in group B, based on the differentiating characteristics.

Research on faultlines has shown that splits are generally detrimental to group functioning and performance. Subgroups may compete with each other, which takes time away from core tasks and harms group performance. Groups that have subgroups learn more slowly, make more risky decisions, are less creative, and experience higher levels of conflict. Subgroups may not trust each other. Satisfaction with subgroups is generally high, but the overall group's satisfaction is lower when faultlines are present.[108]

Are faultlines ever a good thing? One study suggested that faultlines based on differences in skill, knowledge, and expertise could be beneficial when the groups were in organizational cultures that strongly emphasized results. Why? A results-driven culture focuses people's attention on what's important to the company rather than on problems arising from subgroups.[109] Another study showed that problems stemming from strong faultlines based on gender and educational major were counteracted when their roles were crosscut and the group as a whole was given a common goal to strive for. Together, these strategies force collaboration between members of subgroups and focus their efforts on accomplishing a goal that transcends the boundary imposed by the faultline.[110] Faultlines that are split along task-relevant characteristics may boost performance in certain organizations by promoting division of labor.[111]

Overall, although research on faultlines suggests that diversity in groups is potentially a double-edged sword, recent work indicates they can be strategically employed to improve performance.

Group Decision Making

9-7 Contrast the strengths and weaknesses of group decision making.

The belief—characterized by juries—that two heads are better than one has long been accepted as a basic component of the U.S. legal system and those of many other countries. Many decisions in organizations are made by groups, teams, or committees. We'll discuss the advantages of group decision making, along with the unique challenges that group dynamics bring to the decision-making process. Finally, we'll offer some techniques for maximizing the group decision-making opportunity.

Groups versus the Individual

Decision-making groups may be widely used in organizations, but are group decisions preferable to those made by an individual alone? The answer depends on a number of factors. Let's begin by looking at the strengths and weaknesses of group decision making.

Strengths of Group Decision Making Groups generate *more complete information and knowledge.* By aggregating the resources of several individuals, groups bring more input as well as heterogeneity into the decision process. They offer *increased diversity of views.* This opens up the opportunity to consider more approaches and alternatives. Finally, groups lead to increased *acceptance of a solution.* Group members who participate in making a decision are more likely to support it enthusiastically and to encourage others to accept it later.

Weaknesses of Group Decision Making Group decisions are time-consuming because groups typically take more time to reach a solution. There are *conformity pressures.* The desire by group members to be accepted and considered an asset to the group can squash any overt disagreement. Group discussion can be *dominated by one or a few members.* If they're low- and medium-ability members, the group's overall effectiveness will suffer. Also, setting a norm that allows "lone dissenters," or group members who have divergent opinions, can reduce conformity and the influence of dominating members.[112] Finally, group decisions suffer from *ambiguous responsibility.* In an individual decision, it's clear who is accountable for the final outcome. In a group decision, the responsibility of any single member is diluted.

Effectiveness and Efficiency Whether groups are more effective than individuals depends on how you define effectiveness and who is making the evaluation. As discussed in the chapter on perception and individual decision making, the accuracy of evaluators can be affected by general perceptions of group cohesion and trust.[113] Group decisions are generally more *accurate* than the decisions of the average individual in a group, but they are less accurate than the judgments of the most accurate person.[114] In terms of *speed*, individuals are superior. If *creativity* is important, groups tend to be more effective. And if effectiveness means the degree of *acceptance* of achievable solutions, the nod again goes to the group.[115]

But we cannot consider effectiveness without also assessing efficiency. With few exceptions, group decision making consumes more work hours than having an individual tackle the same problem. The exceptions tend to be instances in which, to achieve comparable quantities of diverse input, the single decision maker must spend a great deal of time reviewing files and talking to other people who have unique information that could lead to a better solution.[116] Research suggests that groups may be inefficient in decision making if information is heavily dispersed among group members and effectively "hidden." It is very difficult to compile this information to make the best decision, and groups in these situations are encouraged to openly and collaboratively share information to solve the problem.[117] In deciding whether to use groups, then, managers must assess whether increases in effectiveness are more than enough to offset the reductions in efficiency.

In summary, groups are an excellent vehicle for performing many steps in the decision-making process and offer both breadth and depth of input for information gathering. If group members have diverse backgrounds, the alternatives generated should be more extensive and the analysis more critical. When the final solution is agreed on, there are more people in a group decision to support and implement it. These pluses, however, may be more than offset by the time consumed by group decisions, the internal conflicts they create, and the pressures they generate toward conformity. We must be careful to define the types of conflicts, however. Research in Korea indicates that group conflicts about tasks may increase group performance, while conflicts in relationships may decrease performance.[118] In some cases, therefore, we can expect individuals to make better decisions than groups.

Groupthink and Groupshift

Two by-products of group decision making, groupthink and groupshift, can affect a group's ability to appraise alternatives objectively and achieve high-quality solutions.

groupthink A phenomenon in which the norm for consensus overrides the realistic appraisal of alternative courses of action.

groupshift A change between a group's decision and an individual decision that a member within the group would make; the shift can be toward either conservatism or greater risk but it generally is toward a more extreme version of the group's original position.

Groupthink relates to norms and describes situations in which group pressures for conformity deter the group from critically appraising unusual, minority, or unpopular views. Groupthink attacks many groups and can dramatically hinder their performance.[119] **Groupshift** describes the way group members tend to exaggerate their initial positions when discussing a given set of alternatives to arrive at a solution. In some situations, caution dominates and there is a conservative shift, while in other situations groups tend toward a risky shift.[120] Let's look at each phenomenon in detail.

Groupthink Groupthink appears closely aligned with the conclusions Solomon Asch drew in his experiments with a lone dissenter. Individuals who hold

Career OBjectives

Can I fudge the numbers and not take the blame?

I've got a great work group, except for one thing: The others make me omit negative information about our group's success that I'm in charge of as the treasurer. They gang up on me, insult me, and threaten me, so in the end I report what they want. They say omitting the negative information is not really wrong, and it doesn't violate our organization's rules, but on my own I would report everything. I need to stay in the group or I'll lose my job. If we are called out on the numbers, can I just put the blame on the whole group?

— Jayant

Dear Jayant:

The short answer is that, because you are in a leadership role in the group, you may not have the option of blaming the others. Further, you may be held individually accountable as a leader for the outcomes of this situation.

Your dilemma is not unusual. Once we think of ourselves as part of a collective, we want to stay in the group and can become vulnerable to pressures to conform. The pressure you're getting from multiple members can make you aware that you're in the minority in the group, and taunting can make you feel like an outsider or lesser member; therefore threats to harm your group standing may feel powerful.

So you have a choice: Submit to the pressure and continue misrepresenting your group's success, or adhere to the responsibility you have as the treasurer and come clean. From an ethical standpoint, we hope you don't consider the first option an acceptable choice. To make a change, you may be able to use social identification to your advantage. Rather than challenging the group as a whole, try meeting with individual group members to build trust, talking to each as fellow members of a worthy group that can succeed without any ethical quandaries. Don't try to build a coalition; instead, build trust with individuals and change the climate of the group to value ethical behavior. Then the next time you need to report the numbers, you can call upon the group's increased ethical awareness to gain support for your leadership decisions.

Sources: Based on M. Cikara and J. J. Van Bavel, "The Neuroscience of Intergroup Relations: An Integrative Review," *Perspectives on Psychological Science* 9, no. 3 (2014): 245–74; M. A. Korsgaard, H. H. Brower, and S. W. Lester, "It Isn't Always Mutual: A Critical Review of Dyadic Trust," *Journal of Management* 41, no. 1 (2015): 47–70; and R. L. Priem and P. C. Nystrom, "Exploring the Dynamics of Workgroup Fracture: Common Ground, Trust-with-Trepidation, and Warranted Distrust," *Journal of Management* 40, no. 3 (2014): 674–795.

The opinions provided here are of the managers and authors only and do not necessarily reflect those of their organizations. The authors or managers are not responsible for any errors or omissions, or for the results obtained from the use of this information. In no event will the authors or managers, or their related partnerships or corporations thereof, be liable to you or anyone else for any decision made or action taken in reliance on the opinions provided here.

a position different from that of the dominant majority are under pressure to suppress, withhold, or modify their true feelings and beliefs. As members of a group, we find it more pleasant to be in agreement—to be a positive part of the group—than to be a disruptive force, even if disruption would improve effectiveness. Groups that are more focused on performance than learning are especially likely to fall victim to groupthink and to suppress the opinions of those who do not agree with the majority.[121]

Does groupthink attack all groups? No. It seems to occur most often when there is a clear group identity, when members hold a positive image of their group that they want to protect, and when the group perceives a collective threat to its positive image.[122] One study showed that those influenced by groupthink were more confident about their course of action early on;[123] however, groups that believe too strongly in the correctness of their course of action are more likely to suppress dissent and encourage conformity than groups that are more skeptical about their course of action.

What can managers do to minimize groupthink?[124] First, they can monitor group size. People grow more intimidated and hesitant as group size increases, and although there is no magic number that will eliminate groupthink, individuals are likely to feel less personal responsibility when groups are larger than about 10 members. Managers should also encourage group leaders to play an impartial role. Leaders should actively seek input from all members and avoid expressing their own opinions, especially in the early stages of deliberation. In addition, managers should appoint one group member to play the role of devil's advocate, overtly challenging the majority position and offering divergent perspectives. Yet another suggestion is to use exercises that stimulate active discussion of diverse alternatives without threatening the group or intensifying identity protection. Have group members delay discussion of possible gains so they can first talk about the dangers or risks inherent in a decision. Requiring members to focus initially on the negatives of an alternative makes the group less likely to stifle dissenting views and more likely to gain an objective evaluation.

Groupshift or Group Polarization There are differences between group decisions and the individual decisions of group members.[125] In groups, discussion leads members toward a more extreme view of the position they already held. Conservatives become more cautious, and more aggressive types take on more risk. We can view this group polarization as a special case of groupthink. The group's decision reflects the dominant decision-making norm—toward greater caution or more risk—that develops during discussion.

The shift toward polarization has several explanations.[126] It's been argued, for instance, that discussion makes the members more comfortable with each other and thus more willing to express extreme versions of their original positions. Another argument is that the group diffuses responsibility. Group decisions free any single member from accountability for the group's final choice, so a more extreme position can be taken. It's also likely that people take extreme positions because they want to demonstrate how different they are from the outgroup.[127] People on the fringes of political or social movements take on ever-more-extreme positions just to prove they are really committed to the cause, whereas those who are more cautious tend to take moderate positions to demonstrate how reasonable they are.

So how should you use the findings on groupshift? Recognize that group decisions exaggerate the initial position of individual members, the shift has been shown more often to be toward greater risk, and which way a group will shift is a function of the members' prediscussion inclinations.

We now turn to the techniques by which groups make decisions. These reduce some of the dysfunctional aspects of group decision making.

Group Decision-Making Techniques

interacting groups Typical groups in which members interact with each other face-to-face.

The most common form of group decision making takes place in **interacting groups**.[128] Members meet face-to-face and rely on both verbal and nonverbal interaction to communicate. But as our discussion of groupthink demonstrated, interacting groups often censor themselves and pressure individual members toward conformity of opinion. Brainstorming and the nominal group technique can reduce problems inherent in the traditional interacting group.

brainstorming An idea-generation process that specifically encourages any and all alternatives while withholding any criticism of those alternatives.

Brainstorming **Brainstorming** can overcome the pressures for conformity that dampen creativity[129] by encouraging any and all alternatives while withholding criticism. In a typical brainstorming session, a half-dozen to a dozen people sit around a table. The group leader states the problem in a clear manner so all participants understand. Members then freewheel as many alternatives as they can in a given length of time. To encourage members to "think the unusual," no criticism is allowed, even of the most bizarre suggestions, and all ideas are recorded for later discussion and analysis.

Brainstorming may indeed generate ideas—but not very efficiently. Research consistently shows individuals working alone generate more ideas than a group in a brainstorming session. One reason for this is "production blocking." When people are generating ideas in a group, many are talking at once, which blocks individuals' thought process and eventually impedes the sharing of ideas.[130]

nominal group technique A group decision-making method in which individual members meet face-to-face to pool their judgments in a systematic but independent fashion.

Nominal Group Technique The **nominal group technique** may be more effective. This technique restricts discussion and interpersonal communication during the decision-making process. Group members are all physically present, as in a traditional meeting, but they operate independently. Specifically, a problem is presented and then the group takes the following steps:

1. **Before any discussion takes place,** each member independently writes down ideas about the problem.
2. **After this silent period,** each member presents one idea to the group. No discussion takes place until all ideas have been presented and recorded.
3. **The group discusses the ideas** for clarity and evaluates them.
4. **Each group member silently and independently rank-orders** the ideas. The idea with the highest aggregate ranking determines the final decision.

The chief advantage of the nominal group technique is that it permits a group to meet formally but does not restrict independent thinking. Research generally shows nominal groups outperform brainstorming groups.[131]

Each of the group decision techniques has its own set of strengths and weaknesses. The choice depends on the criteria you want to emphasize and the cost–benefit trade-off. As Exhibit 9-5 indicates, an interacting group is good for achieving commitment to a solution, brainstorming develops group cohesiveness, and the nominal group technique is an efficient means for generating a large number of ideas.

Exhibit 9-5 Evaluating Group Effectiveness

	Type of Group		
Effectiveness Criteria	**Interacting**	**Brainstorming**	**Nominal**
Number and quality of ideas	Low	Moderate	High
Social pressure	High	Low	Moderate
Money costs	Low	Low	Low
Speed	Moderate	Moderate	Moderate
Task orientation	Low	High	High
Potential for interpersonal conflict	High	Low	Moderate
Commitment to solution	High	Not applicable	Moderate
Development of group cohesiveness	High	High	Moderate

Summary

We can draw several implications from our discussion of groups. First, norms control behavior by establishing standards of right and wrong. Second, status inequities create frustration and can adversely influence productivity and willingness to remain with an organization. Third, the impact of size on a group's performance depends on the type of task. Fourth, cohesiveness may influence a group's level of productivity, depending on the group's performance-related norms. Fifth, diversity appears to have a mixed impact on group performance, with some studies suggesting that diversity can help performance and others suggesting the opposite. Sixth, role conflict is associated with job-induced tension and job dissatisfaction.[132] Groups can be carefully managed toward positive organizational outcomes and optimal decision making. The next chapter will explore several of these conclusions in greater depth.

Implications for Managers

- Recognize that groups can have a dramatic impact on individual behavior in organizations, to either positive or negative effect. Therefore, pay special attention to roles, norms, and cohesion—to understand how these are operating within a group is to understand how the group is likely to behave.
- To decrease the possibility of deviant workplace activities, ensure that group norms do not support antisocial behavior.
- Pay attention to the status aspect of groups. Because lower-status people tend to participate less in group discussions, groups with high status differences are likely to inhibit input from lower-status members and reduce their potential.
- Use larger groups for fact-finding activities and smaller groups for action-taking tasks. With larger groups, provide measures of individual performance.
- To increase employee satisfaction, make certain people perceive their job roles accurately.

Diverse Work Groups Are Smarter and More Innovative

POINT

Birds of a feather flock together, but when it comes to business, it may be better for pigeons to flock with crows. Employees may feel more comfortable working with people who are similar to them, but this comfort may come at the cost of success.

Time after time, research demonstrates that more diverse companies have the most success. A global analysis of 2,400 companies demonstrated that the presence of at least one female employee on an executive board leads to higher net income growth and return on equity. Diversity at lower levels of the organization may also be helpful: Companies with more diverse work groups have higher financial returns than companies with fewer minority or female employees.

Diverse groups think smarter. When people are asked to work with people who are different from them, they are forced out of their comfort zone, leading to more critical thinking and innovation. In mock juries, for example, more ethnically heterogenous juries made more accurate decisions and supported their decisions with more facts from the case. Teams of heterogenous financial professionals also performed better on tasks where they were asked to price stocks in a stock market simulation. In addition, a recent analysis of research and design teams in Spain found that teams with greater gender diversity created more innovative products. Other types of diversity may also be beneficial. In a murder mystery task, groups with a mix of organizational tenure were more likely to guess the correct suspect. When cultural diversity of businesses in the United Kingdom were analyzed, more culturally diverse leadership teams created more new products.

So the next time you're worried about working with someone you don't have a lot in common with, remember the words of Maya Angelou: "In diversity there is beauty and there is strength."

COUNTERPOINT

There is some evidence that having diverse leadership may benefit companies. What about the research showing that diversity is linked to lower employee morale and well-being, slower decision making, and increased conflict? Organizations with more diverse work groups are also more likely to be sued for discrimination.

Sometimes more diverse tasks can boost innovation and critical thinking skills, but those advantages may not be worth forcing employees to work with people they feel uncomfortable with. When employees are forced to participate in diversity initiatives, it can lead to more stress. Over half feel that they have to modify their behavior significantly to feel like they fit in. If employees try to act like their peers rather than acknowledging their differences, it doesn't just lead to stress. Research has shown that any advantages on task creativity disappear when team members don't openly discuss and acknowledge their differing backgrounds.

Even if employees feel comfortable enough to express themselves, that's no guarantee that they will actually get along. Group members with diverse racial, gender, and educational backgrounds might have a slight advantage over homogenous groups in some tasks. Yet they can be less effective when group members have different values. When group members have different values because, for example, they have different cultural backgrounds, it may be difficult for the group to overcome these differences.

It may be tempting to think that a diverse team is better, but remember, there's a reason like attracts like.

Sources: Based on S. Bailey, "Why Diversity Is Bad for Business (and Inclusion Is the Answer)," *Forbes*, May 20, 2014, https://www.forbes.com/sites/sebastianbailey/2014/05/20/why-we-should-prioritize-the-i-in-d-and-i/#2c6b0e54600d; D. Rock, H. Grant, and J. Grey, "Diverse Teams Feel Less Comfortable—and That's Why They Perform Better," *Harvard Business Review*, September 22, 2016, https://hbr.org/2016/09/diverse-teams-feel-less-comfortable-and-thats-why-they-perform-better; and D. Rock and H. Grant, "Why Diverse Teams Are Smarter," *Harvard Business Review*, November 4, 2016, https://hbr.org/2016/11/why-diverse-teams-are-smarter.

CHAPTER REVIEW

QUESTIONS FOR REVIEW

9-1 What are the different types of groups?

9-2 What are the key components of the punctuated-equilibrium model?

9-3 How do role requirements change in different situations?

9-4 How do group norms influence an individual's behavior?

9-5 How do status and size differences affect group performance?

9-6 How can cohesiveness and diversity support group effectiveness?

9-7 What are the strengths and weaknesses of group (versus individual) decision making?

APPLICATION AND EMPLOYABILITY

Groups have a powerful influence on individuals, leading to both positive and negative consequences. Peer pressure and norms may be beneficial when they help individuals perform better and engage in prosocial behaviors. Yet groups may also exert influences that harm other groups, encourage conformity, and lead to poor decision making. By gaining an understanding of group behaviors, you can better understand how to encourage positive outcomes and avoid negative outcomes in the workplace among your coworkers, supervisors, and subordinates. In this chapter, you learned valuable lessons about communication, collaboration, and social responsibility when facing peer pressure from coworkers, listening to gossip about a peer, and deciding whether peer pressure is an ethically sound strategy for motivating employees. You also utilized your critical thinking skills while exploring the advantages and pitfalls of diverse work groups. In the next section, you will continue to develop these skills, as well as apply your knowledge and analytical skills to surviving the wild alone and in a group, assess whether to violate a psychological contract, explore the downfalls of hoping for a consensus in American politics, and explore how a group divided affected a military campaign.

EXPERIENTIAL EXERCISE Surviving the Wild: Join a Group or Go It Alone?

You are a member of a hiking party. After reaching base camp on the first day, you decide to take a quick sunset hike by yourself. After a few exhilarating miles, you turn around for the return to camp. On your way back, you realize you are lost. You shout for help, to no avail. It is now dark—and getting cold.

Your Task

Without communicating with anyone else in your group, read the following scenarios and choose the best answer. Keep track of your answers on a sheet of paper. You have 10 minutes to answer the 10 questions.

Questions

9-8. The first thing you decide to do is to build a fire. However, you have no matches, so you use the bow-and-drill method. What is the bow-and-drill method?

a. A dry, soft stick is rubbed between the hands against a board of supple green wood.
b. A soft green stick is rubbed between the hands against a hardwood board.
c. A straight stick of wood is quickly rubbed back and forth against a dead tree.
d. Two sticks (one being the bow, the other the drill) are struck to create a spark.

9-9. It occurs to you that you can also use the fire as a distress signal. How do you form the international distress signal with fire?

a. Fires in random order
b. Fires in a square
c. Fires in a cross
d. Fires in a line

9-10. You are very thirsty. You go to a nearby stream and collect some water in the small metal cup you have in your backpack. How long should you boil the water?

a. 15 minutes
b. A few seconds
c. 1 minute
d. It depends on the altitude.

9-11. You are very hungry, so you decide to eat what appear to be edible berries. When performing the universal edibility test, what should you do?

a. Do not eat for 2 hours before the test.
b. If the plant stings your lip, confirm the sting by holding it under your tongue for 15 minutes.
c. If nothing bad has happened 2 hours after digestion, eat half a cup of the plant and wait again.
d. Separate the plant into its basic components and eat each component, one at a time.

9-12. Next, you decide to build a shelter for the evening. In selecting a site, what do you *not* have to consider?

a. It must contain material to make the type of shelter you need.
b. It must be free of insects, reptiles, and poisonous plants.
c. It must be large enough and level enough for you to lie down comfortably.
d. It must be on a hill so you can signal rescuers and keep an eye on your surroundings.

9-13. In the shelter, you notice a spider. You heard from a fellow hiker that black widow spiders populate the area. How do you identify a black widow spider?

a. Its head and abdomen are black; its thorax is red.
b. It is attracted to light.
c. It runs away from light.
d. It is dark with a red or orange marking on the female's abdomen.

9-14. After getting some sleep, you notice that the night sky has cleared, so you decide to try to find your way back to base camp. You believe you can use the North Star for navigation. How do you locate the North Star?

a. Hold your right hand up as far as you can and look between your index and middle fingers.
b. Find Sirius and look 60 degrees above it and to the right.
c. Look for the Big Dipper and follow the line created by its cup end.
d. Follow the line of Orion's belt.

9-15. You come across a fast-moving stream. What is the best way to cross it?

a. Find a spot downstream from a sandbar, where the water will be calmer.
b. Build a bridge.
c. Find a rocky area, because the water will be shallow and you will have hand- and footholds.
d. Find a level stretch where it breaks into a few channels.

9-16. After walking for about an hour, you feel several spiders in your clothes. You don't feel any pain, but you know some spider bites are painless. Which of these spider bites is painless?

a. Black widow
b. Brown recluse
c. Wolf spider
d. Harvestman (daddy longlegs)

9-17. You decide to eat some insects. Which insects should you avoid?

a. Adults that sting or bite
b. Caterpillars and insects that have a pungent odor
c. Hairy or brightly colored ones
d. All the above

Group Task

Next, break into groups of five or six people. Once the group comes to an agreement for what to do in each situation, write your decision on the same sheet of paper you used for your individual answers.

Scoring Your Answers

Your instructor will provide you with the correct answers, which are based on expert judgments in these situations. Once you have received the answers, calculate (A) your individual score, (B) your group's score, (C) the average individual score in the group, and (D) the best individual score in the group. Write these down and consult with your group to ensure that they are accurate.

A. Your individual score ______________
B. Your group's score ______________
C. Average individual score in group ______________
D. Best individual score in group ______________

Discussion Questions

9-18. How did your group (B) perform relative to yourself (A)?

9-19. How did your group (B) perform relative to the average individual score in the group (C)?

9-20. How did your group (B) perform relative to the best individual score in the group (D)?

9-21. Compare your results with those of other groups. Did some groups do a better job of outperforming individuals than others?

9-22. What do these results tell you about the effectiveness of group decision making?

9-23. What can groups do to make group decision making more effective?

9-24. What circumstances might cause a group to perform worse than its best individual?

ETHICAL DILEMMA It's Obvious, They're Chinese.

The antithesis of social loafing was brought into sharp focus back in 2009 when Shanghai became the first Chinese region to enter the Programme for International Student Assessment (PISA). In its first entry year, Shanghai came top in mathematics, science, and reading by a considerable margin. PISA looks at the attainments of 15-year-olds, and by 2012, Shanghai had cemented their position as the top performing student groups.

The latest set of figures (2015) has seen Singapore replace Shanghai at the top of the ranks. This is due to the fact that Shanghai is no longer a separate entry; they are now part of the combined figures for the country based on four provinces. China is still ranked sixth with Macao (appearing as a separate entry). Three of the top five and seven of the top 10 countries are in the Far East.

A typical Chinese 15-year-old has eight 40-minute classes each day. Despite this heavy workload, the teacher-led sessions, according to observers, are performed with total pupil concentration even though classes can be up to 60 in strength. Age-old Chinese folktales recount the successes of those who show diligence and hard work. Concepts such as being gifted or talented have far less currency than simply working hard. For generations, Chinese students have worked hard to achieve good grades in their gaokao examinations. These are the key to university entrance.

The combination of hard work and high-stakes examinations mean that an average Chinese 15-year-old does 3 hours of homework every night. There is no time for social loafing; individual and cultural motivators drive the students forward.

Questions

9-25. Why does social loafing cause ethical dilemmas? What is it about social loafing that makes it difficult to cope with on a one-to-one basis if one of your colleagues does it?

9-26. Social loafing is exposed in performance appraisals and other methods of assessing productivity and output. How should it be handled when it is exposed?

9-27. Most Chinese 15-year-olds spurn television, social media, and console gaming. On the other hand, many of the students do not excel in creative thinking or problem-solving. To what extent might this be an issue compared to other societies that might focus on these aspects?

Sources: National Center for Education Statistics, Program for International Student Assessment, http://nces.ed.gov/surveys/pisa/index.asp, accessed January 23, 2014; "Shanghai Population 2015," WPR, http://worldpopulationreview.com/world-cities/shanghai-population/.

CASE INCIDENT 1 The Dangers of Groupthink

Sometimes, the desire to maintain group harmony overrides the importance of making sound decisions. When that occurs in a team, its members are said to engage in groupthink. Here is an example.

A civilian worker at a large air force base recalls a time when groupthink overcame her team's decision-making ability. She was a member of a process-improvement team that an air force general had formed to develop a better way to handle the base's mail, which included important letters from high-ranking military individuals. The team was composed mostly of civilians, and it took almost a month to come up with a plan. The problem: the plan was not a process improvement. "I was horrified," the civilian worker remarked. "What used to be 8 steps was now 19."

The team had devised a system that resulted in each piece of mail being read by several middle managers before reaching its intended recipient. The new plan slowed down the mail considerably, with an average delay of two weeks. Though the team members all knew that the new system was worse than its predecessor, no one wanted to disrupt the team's solidarity. The problems lasted almost an entire year. It wasn't until the general who formed the team complained about the mail that the system was changed.

This may seem like a trivial matter, but groupthink is found at the lowest to the highest levels of organizations, governments, and industries. For example, groupthink has been cited as contributing to the 2008 global financial crisis, the Challenger space shuttle disaster, the collapse of the Swiss airline Swissair, and the Enron scandal.

Questions

9-28. What are some of the factors that led to groupthink in the case described here?

9-29. What can teams do to help avoid groupthink from occurring?

9-30. The group in the case was composed of air force and civilian personnel. Do you think there may have been a perceived difference in status that could have contributed to the groupthink?

Sources: Based on C. Hawn, "Fear and Posing," *Forbes*, March 25, 2002, pp. 22–25; J. Sandberg, "Some Ideas Are So Bad That Only Team Efforts Can Account for Them," *Wall Street Journal*, September 29, 2004, p. B1; and H. L. Bouygues, "The Problem of Groupthink: How to Encourage More Independent Thinking," www.forbes.com, April 20, 2019.

CASE INCIDENT 2 Intragroup Trust and Survival

When 10 British Army soldiers on a 10-day training exercise descended into Low's Gully, a narrow chasm that cuts through Mt. Kinabalu in Borneo, each knew "the golden rule for such expeditions—never split up." Yet the fittest three struggled out of the jungle with concussions, malaria, and infected wounds 19 days later, two more terribly ill soldiers found a village the next day, and the remaining five emaciated and injured men were rescued from a cave by a helicopter on day 33. What happened?

On a surface level, the near-tragic fracturing of the group began with a logical division of labor, according to the training's initiators, Lieutenant Colonel Neill and Major Foster:

> Because the group would be one of mixed abilities, and the young British and NCOs [non-commissioned officers] were likely to be fitter and more experienced than the Hong Kong soldiers, the team would work in two halves on the harder phases of the descent. The British, taking advantage of Mayfield's expertise (in rock climbing), would set up ropes on the difficult sections, while he [Neill] and Foster would concentrate on bringing the Hong Kong soldiers down. Every now and then the recce (reconnaissance) party would report back, and the expedition would go on down in one unit until another reconnaissance party became necessary.

The men reported that from then on, perilous climbing conditions, debilitating sickness, and monsoon rains permanently divided the group. A review board found differently, blaming Neill's and Foster's leadership and their decision to take some less-experienced soldiers on the exercise.

No rulings were made about the near-catastrophic decision to divide the group, but closer inquiries show that this temporary work group of diverse members who were not previously acquainted started out with a high level of intragroup trust that dissolved over time. The resulting faultlines, based on members' similarities and differences and the establishment of ad hoc leaders, may have been inevitable.

Initially, all group members shared the common ground of soldier training, clear roles, and volunteer commitment to the mission. When the leaders ignored the soldiers' concerns about the severity of conditions, lack of preparation, and low level of communication, however, trust issues divided the group into subgroups. The initial reconnaissance party established common ground and trust that allowed them to complete the mission and reach safety, even though they divided yet again. Meanwhile, the main group that stayed with the leaders in the cave under conditions of active distrust fractured further.

We will never know whether it would have been better to keep the group together. However, we do know that this small group of soldiers trained to stay together for survival fractured into at least four subgroups because they didn't trust their leaders or their group, thus endangering all their lives.

Questions

9-31. How was the common ground established by the reconnaissance subgroups different from the common ground established by the cave subgroups?

9-32. Do you think the group should have fractured as it did? Why or why not?

9-33. When the exercise was designed, Neill created a buddy system based on similarity of soldiers' backgrounds (rank, unit, age, fitness, skills level). The first group out of the jungle was assigned buddies and one other: two lance corporals and one corporal from the same unit (regular army), ages 24–26 with good fitness levels, all top roping and abseiling (TR&A) instructors. The second group out was assigned buddies: a sergeant and a lance corporal from the same unit (elite regular army), ages 25 and 37, good fitness levels, both with Commando Brigade skills. The group left in the cave split into: a lieutenant colonel and a major (buddies), one from the regular army and one from the part time territorial army, ages 46 and 54, fair fitness level, one TR&A and one ski instructor. The second faction was the three from the Hong Kong unit—a lance corporal and two privates, ages 24–32, fair to good fitness levels, one with jungle training and two novices. Would you have set up the buddy system Neill did? Why or why not, and if not, what would you have changed?

Sources: Based on M. A. Korsgaard, H. H. Brower, and S. W. Lester, "It Isn't Always Mutual: A Critical Review of Dyadic Trust," *Journal of Management* 41, no. 1 (2014): 47–70; R. L. Priem and P. C. Nystrom, "Exploring the Dynamics of Workgroup Fracture: Common Ground, Trust-with-Trepidation, and Warranted Distrust," *Journal of Management* 40, no. 3 (2014): 764–95; and "The Call of Malaysia's 'Conquerable' Mount Kinabalu," *BBC*, June 5, 2015, http://www.bbc.com/news/world-asia-33020356.

ENDNOTES

[1] E. J. Boothby, M. S. Clark, and J. A. Bargh, "Shared Experiences Are Amplified," *Psychological Science* 25, no. 12 (2014): 2209–16.

[2] B. Bastien, J. Jetten, and L. J. Ferris, "Pain as Social Glue: Shared Pain Increases Cooperation," *Psychological Science* 25, no. 11 (2014): 2079–85.

[3] See H. Tajfel and J. C. Turner, "The Social Identity Theory of Inter Group Behavior," in S. Worchel & W. G. Austin (eds.), *Psychology of Intergroup Relations* (Chicago, IL: Nelson, 1986); and N. Karelaia and L. Guillen, "Me, a Woman and a Leader: Positive Social Identity and Identity Conflict," *Organizational Behavior and Human Decision Processes* 125, no. 2 (2014): 204–19; S. V. Bentley, K. H. Greenaway, S. Alexander Haslam, T. Cruwys, N. K. Steffens, C. Haslam, and B. Cull, "Social Identity Mapping Online," *Journal of Personality and Social Psychology* 118, no. 2 (2020): 213–41; H. Tajfel and J. C. Turner, "An Integrative Theory of Intergroup Conflict," in W. G. Austin and S. Worchel (eds.), *The Social Psychology of Intergroup Relations* (Monterey, CA: Brooks/Cole, 1979): 33–47.

[4] P. Belmi, R. C. Barragan, M. A. Neale, and G. L. Cohen, "Threats to Social Identity Can Trigger Social Deviance," *Personality and Social Psychological Bulletin* 41, no. 4 (2015): 467–84.

[5] H. Takahashi, M. Kato, M. Matsuura, D. Mobbs, T. Suhara, and Y. Okubo, "When Your Gain Is My Pain and Your Pain Is My Gain: Neural Correlates of Envy and Schadenfreude," *Science* 323, no. 5916 (2009): 937–39; and C. W. Leach, R. Spears, N. R. Branscombe, and B. Doosje, "Malicious Pleasure: Schadenfreude at the Suffering of Another Group," *Journal of Personality and Social Psychology* 84, no. 5 (2003): 932–43.

[6] Department of Justice and Equality, "Citizenship Updates and Announcements" (2017), http://www.inis.gov.ie/en/INIS/Pages/citizenship-updates (accessed February 13, 2018); P. McGarry, "Some 120,000 from Abroad Have Become Irish Citizens since 2011," *The Irish Times*, November 27, 2017, https://www.irishtimes.com/opinion/some-120-000-from-abroad-have-become-irish-citizens-since-2011-1.3307542 (Accessed February 13, 2018).

[7] Karelaia and Guillen, "Me, a Woman and a Leader."

[8] T. Cruwys, E. I. South, K. H. Greenaway, and S. A. Haslam, "Social Identity Reduces Depression by Fostering Positive Attributions," *Social Psychological and Personality Science* 6, no. 1 (2015): 65–74.

[9] T. Schmader, K. Block, and B. Lickel, "Social Identity Threat in Response to Stereotypic Film Portrayals: Effects on Self-Conscious Emotion and Implicit Ingroup Attitudes," *Journal of Social Issues* 71, no. 1 (2015): 54–72.

[10] A. S. Leonard, A. Mehra, & R. Katerberg, "The Social Identity and Social Networks of Ethnic Minority Groups in Organizations: A Crucial Test of Distinctiveness Theory," *Journal of Organizational Behavior* 29, no. 5 (2008): 573–89.

[11] S. Zhang, G. Chen, X.-P. Chen, D. Liu, and M. D. Johnson, "Relational versus Collective Identification within

Workgroups: Conceptualization, Measurement Development, and Nomological Network Building," *Journal of Management* 40, no. 6 (2014): 1700–31.
[12] C. G. Banks, S. Kepes, M. Joshi, and A. Seers, "Social Identity and Applicant Attraction: Exploring the Role of Multiple Levels of Self," *Journal of Organizational Behavior* 37 no. 3 (2016): 326–45.
[13] X. Qin, P. W. Hom, and M. Xu, "Am I a Peasant or a Worker? An Identity Strain Perspective on Turnover among Developing-World Migrants," *Human Relations* 72, no. 4 (2019): 801–33.
[14] M. B. Brewer, "Intergroup Discrimination: Ingroup Love or Outgroup Hate?" in C. Sibley and F. Barlow (eds.), *The Cambridge Handbook of the Psychology of Prejudice* (Cambridge, UK: Cambridge University Press, 2017): 90–110; L. Hamley, C. A. Houkamau, D. Osborne, F. Kate Barlow, and C. G. Sibley, "Ingroup Love or Outgroup Hate (or Both)? Mapping Distinct Bias Profiles in the Population," *Personality and Social Psychology Bulletin* 46, no. 2 (2020): 171–88.
[15] Islam, A., Prakashi, D. & Sahoo, S. (2022). "Gender-caste intersectionality in discrimination: Do patients care about doctor's social identity?" *Ideas For India (January 12, 2022).* Retrieved from https://www.ideasforindia.in (Accessed on April 21. 2022)
[16] G. J. Lewis and T. C. Bates, "Common Heritable Effects Underpin Concerns over Norm Maintenance and In-Group Favoritism: Evidence from Genetic Analyses of Right-Wing Authoritarianism and Traditionalism," *Journal of Personality* 82, no. 4 (2014): 297–309.
[17] A. L. Lando, L. Muthuri, and P. R. Odira, "The Importance of Interfaith Dialog in the Workplace for Achieving Organizational Goals: A Kenyan Case Study," *Language and Intercultural Communication* 15, no. 1 (2015): 62–75.
[18] J. Conrad Jackson, N. Castelo, and K. Gray, "Could a Rising Robot Workforce Make Humans Less Prejudiced?" *American Psychologist* (in press).
[19] T. C. Dennehy, A. Ben-Zeev, and N. Tanigawa, " 'Be Prepared': An Implemental Mindset for Alleviating Social-Identity Threat," *British Journal of Social Psychology* 53 (2014): 585–94.
[20] M. J. Garfield and A. R. Denis, "Toward an Integrated Model of Group Development: Disruption of Routines by Technology-Induced Change," *Journal of Management Information Systems* 29, no. 3 (2012): 43–86; M. J. Waller, J. M. Conte, C. B. Gibson, and M. A. Carpenter, "The Effect of Individual Perceptions of Deadlines on Team Performance," *Academy of Management Review* (October 2001): 586–600; A. Chang, P. Bordia, and J. Duck, "Punctuated Equilibrium and Linear Progression: Toward a New Understanding of Group Development," *Academy of Management Journal* (February 2003): 106–17; and C. J. Gersick. "Time and Transition in Work Teams: Toward a New Model of Group Development," *Academy of Management Journal* 31, no. 1 (1988): 1–41.
[21] B. B. Morgan, E. Salas, and A. S. Glickman, "An Analysis of Team Evolution and Maturation," *The Journal of General Psychology* 120, no. 3 (1993): 277–291; and B. Tuckman, "Some Stages of Development in Groups," *Psychological Bulletin* 63, no. 1 (1965): 384–99.
[22] M. M. Kazmer, "Disengaging from a Distributed Research Project: Refining a Model of Group Departures," *Journal of the American Society for Information Science and Technology* (April 2010): 758–71.
[23] Y. Liu, T. Vriend, and O. Janssen, "To Be (Creative), or Not to Be (Creative)? A SenseMaking Perspective of Creative Role Expectations," *Journal of Business and Psychology* (in press).
[24] J. A.-M. Coyle-Shapiro, S. Pereira Costa, W. Doden, and C. Chang, "Psychological Contracts: Past, Present, and Future," *Annual Review of Organizational Psychology and Organizational Behavior*, 6 (2019): 145–69; K. Giese and A. Thiel, "The Psychological Contract in Chinese-African Informal Labor Relations," *International Journal of Human Resource Management* 26, no. 14 (2015): 1807–26; L. Sels, M. Janssens, and I. Van den Brande, "Assessing the Nature of Psychological Contracts: A Validation of Six Dimensions," *Journal of Organizational Behavior* (June 2004): 461–88; C. Hui, C. Lee, and D. M. Rousseau, "Psychological Contract and Organizational Citizenship Behavior in China: Investigating Generalizability and Instrumentality," *Journal of Applied Psychology* (April 2004): 311–21; and D. M. Rousseau, "Psychological and Implied Contracts in Organizations," *Employee Responsibilities and Rights Journal* 2, no. 2 (1989): 121–39.
[25] K. M. Mai, A. J. Ellis, J. S. Christian, and C.H. Porter, "Examining the Effects of Turnover Intentions on Organizational Citizenship Behaviors and Deviance Behaviors: A Psychological Contract Approach," *Journal of Applied Psychology* 101, no. 8 (2016): 1067–81.
[26] M. D. Collins, "The Effect of Psychological Contract Fulfillment on Manager Turnover Intentions and Its Role as a Mediator in a Casual, Limited-Service Restaurant Environment," *International Journal of Hospitality Management* 29, no. 4 (2010): 736–42; and J. M. Jensen, R. A. Opland, and A. M. Ryan, "Psychological Contracts and Counterproductive Work Behaviors: Employee Responses to Transactional and Relational Breach," *Journal of Business and Psychology* 25, no. 4 (2010): 555–68.
[27] Venkatesh, S. "How Lavanya Nalli gave a modern twist to Nalli's nine-decade legacy". *Outlook Business WOW.* Retrieved from https://wow.outlookbusiness.com (Accessed on April 29, 2022).
[28] D. C. Thomas, S. R. Fitzsimmons, E. C. Ravlin, K. Y. Au, B. Z. Ekelund, and C. Barzantny, "Psychological Contracts across Cultures," *Organization Studies* 31 (2010): 1437–58.
[29] R. L. Kahn, D. M. Wolfe, R. P. Quinn, J. D. Snoek, and R.A. Rosenthal, *Organizational Stress* (Oxford, England: Wiley, 1964); and K. S. Wilson and H. M. Baumann, "Capturing a More Complete View of Employees' Lives outside of Work: The Introduction and Development of New Interrole Conflict Constructs," *Personnel Psychology* 68, no. 2 (2015): 235–82.
[30] Ibid.
[31] See, for example, F. T. Amstad, L L. Meier, U. Fasel, A. Elfering, and N. K. Semmer, "A Meta-Analysis of Work-Family Conflict and Various Outcomes with a Special Emphasis on Cross-Domain versus Matching-Domain Relations," *Journal of Occupational Health Psychology* 16, no. 2 (2011): 151–69.
[32] Wilson and Baumann, "Capturing a More Complete View of Employees' Lives outside of Work."
[33] D. Vora and T. Kostova. "A Model of Dual Organizational Identification in the Context of the Multinational Enterprise," *Journal of Organizational Behavior* 28 (2007): 327–50.
[34] C. Reade, "Dual Identification in Multinational Corporations: Local Managers and Their Psychological Attachment to the Subsidiary versus the Global Organization," *International Journal of Human Resource Management* 12, no. 3 (2001): 405–24.
[35] S. Drury, S. A. Hutchens, D. E. Shuttlesworth, and C. L. White, "Philip G. Zimbardo on His Career and the Stanford Prison Experiment's 40th Anniversary,"

History of Psychology 15, no. 2 (2012): 161–70; S. A. Haslam and S. D. Reicher, "Contesting the 'Nature' of Conformity: What Milgram and Zimbardo's Studies Really Show," *Plos Biology* 10, no. 11 (2012): e1001426; and C. Haney, W. Banks, and P. Zimbardo. "Interpersonal Dynamics in a Simulated Prison," *International Journal of Criminology and Penology* 1, no. 1 (1973): 69–97.

[36] S. A. Haslam and S. Reicher, "Stressing the Group: Social Identity and the Unfolding Dynamics of Responses to Stress," *Journal of Applied Psychology* 91, no. 5 (2006): 1037–52; S. Reicher and S. A. Haslam, "Rethinking the Psychology of Tyranny: The BBC Prison Study," *British Journal of Social Psychology* 45, no. 1 (2006): 1–40; and P. G. Zimbardo, "On Rethinking the Psychology of Tyranny: The BBC Prison Study," *British Journal of Social Psychology* 45, no. 1 (2006): 47–53.

[37] Y. Huang, K. M. Kendrick, and R. Yu, "Conformity to the Opinions of Other People Lasts for No More Than 3 Days," *Psychological Science* 25, no. 7 (2014): 1388–93.

[38] M. S. Hagger, P. Rentzelas, and N. K. D. Chatzisrantis, "Effects of Individualist and Collectivist Group Norms and Choice on Intrinsic Motivation," *Motivation and Emotion* 38, no. 2 (2014): 215–23; and M. G. Ehrhart and S. E. Naumann, "Organizational Citizenship Behavior in Work Groups: A Group Norms Approach," *Journal of Applied Psychology* (December 2004): 960–74.

[39] A. Lieberman, K. E. Duke, and O. Amir, "How Incentive Framing Can Harness the Power of Social Norms," *Organizational Behavior and Human Decision Processes* 151 (2019): 118–31; D. B. Shank, Y. Kashima, K. Peters, Y. Li, G. Robins, and M. Kirley, "Norm Talk and Human Cooperation: Can We Talk Ourselves into Cooperation?" *Journal of Personality and Social Psychology* 117, no. 1 (2019): 99–123.

[40] E. Delvaux, N. Vanbeselaere, and B. Mesquita, "Dynamic Interplay between Norms and Experiences of Anger and Gratitude in Groups," *Small Group Research* 46, no. 3 (2015): 300–23.

[41] N. Pontus Leander, M. Agostini, W. Stroebe, J. Kreienkamp, R. Spears, T. Kuppens, M. Van Zomeren, S. Otten, and A. W. Kruglanski, "Frustration-Affirmation? Thwarted Goals Motivate Compliance with Social Norms for Violence and Nonviolence," *Journal of Personality and Social Psychology* (in press).

[42] R. B. Cialdini and N. J. Goldstein, "Social Influence: Compliance and Conformity," *Annual Review of Psychology* 55 (2004): 591–621.

[43] P. Kundu and D. D. Cummins, "Morality and Conformity: The Asch Paradigm Applied to Moral Decisions," *Social Influence* 8, no. 4 (2013): 268–79.

[44] Ibid.

[45] R. A. Griggs, "The Disappearance of Independence in Textbook Coverage of Asch's Social Pressure Experiments," *Teaching of Psychology* 42, no. 2 (2015): 137–42.

[46] S. Sansfacon and C. E. Amiot, "The Impact of Group Norms and Behavioral Congruence on the Internalization of an Illegal Downloading Behavior," *Group Dynamics: Theory Research and Practice* 18, no. 2 (2014): 174–88; L. Rosh, L. R. Offermann, and R. Van Diest, "Too Close for Comfort? Distinguishing between Team Intimacy and Team Cohesion," *Human Resource Management Review* (June 2012): 116–27; and R. B. Cialdini, R. C. A. Kallgren, and R. R. Reno, "A Focus Theory of Normative Conduct: A Theoretical Refinement and Reevaluation of the Role of Norms in Human Behavior," *Advances in Experimental Social Psychology* 24 (1998): 201–34.

[47] J. S. Hassard, "Rethinking the Hawthorne Studies: The Western Electric Research in Its Social, Political, and Historical Context," *Human Relations* 65, no. 11 (2012): 1431–61; and E. Mayo, *The Human Problems of an Industrial Civilization* (New York: MacMillan, 1933).

[48] M. K. Chin, D. C. Hambrick, and L .K. Treviño, "Political Ideologies of CEOs: The Influence of Executives' Values on Corporate Social Responsibility," *Administrative Science Quarterly* 58, no. 2 (2013): 197–232; and A. B. Carroll, "Corporate Social Responsibility," *Business & Society* 38, no. 1 (1999): 268–95.

[49] J. A. Goncalo, J. A. Chatman, M. M. Duguid, and J. A. Kennedy, "Creativity from Constraint? How the Political Correctness Norm Influences Creativity in Mixed-Sex Work Groups," *Administrative Science Quarterly* 60, no. 1 (2015): 1–30.

[50] E. Gonzalez-Mule, D. S. DeGeest, B. W. McCormick, et al., "Can We Get Some Cooperation around Here? The Mediating Role of Group Norms on the Relationship between Team Personality and Individual Helping Behaviors," *Journal of Applied Psychology* 99, no. 5 (2014): 988–99.

[51] C. Marino, A. Vieno, M. Pastore, I. P. Albery, D. Frings, and M. M. Spada, "Modeling the Contribution of Personality, Social Identity and Social Norms to Problematic Facebook Use in Adolescents," *Addictive Behaviours* 63 (2016): 51–56.

[52] See R. J. Bennett and S. L. Robinson, "The Past, Present, and Future of Workplace Deviance," in J. Greenberg (ed.), *Organizational Behavior: The State of the Science,* 2nd ed. (Mahwah, NJ: Erlbaum, 2003): 237–71; and C. M. Berry, D. S. Ones, and P. R. Sackett, "Interpersonal Deviance, Organizational Deviance, and Their Common Correlates: A Review and Meta-Analysis," *Journal of Applied Psychology* 92, no. 2 (2007): 410–24.

[53] M. A. Baysinger, K. T. Scherer, and J. M. LeBreton, "Exploring the Disruptive Effects of Psychopathy and Aggression on Group Processes and Group Effectiveness," *Journal of Applied Psychology* 99, no. 1 (2014): 48–65.

[54] T. C. Reich and M. S. Hershcovis, "Observing Workplace Incivility," *Journal of Applied Psychology* 100, no. 1 (2015): 203–15; and Z. E. Zhou, Y. Yan, X. X. Che, and L. L. Meier, "Effect of Workplace Incivility on End-of-Work Negative Affect: Examining Individual and Organizational Moderators in a Daily Diary Study," *Journal of Occupational Health Psychology* 20, no. 1 (2015): 117–30.

[55] See C. Pearson, L. M. Andersson, and C. L. Porath, "Workplace Incivility," in S. Fox and P. E. Spector (eds.), *Counterproductive Work Behavior: Investigations of Actors and Targets* (Washington, DC: American Psychological Association, 2005): 177–200.

[56] S. Lim, L. M. Cortina, and V. J. Magley, "Personal and Workgroup Incivility: Impact on Work and Health Outcomes," *Journal of Applied Psychology* 93, no. 1 (2008): 95–107.

[57] D. L. Ferris, J. R. Spence, D. J. Brown, and D. Heller, "Interpersonal Injustice and Workplace Deviance: The Role of Esteem Threat," *Journal of Management* 38 no. 6 (2012): 1788–811.

[58] M. S. Christian and A. P. J. Ellis, "Examining the Effects of Sleep Deprivation on Workplace Deviance: A Self-Regulatory Perspective," *Academy of Management Journal* 54, no. 5 (2011): 913–34.

[59] S. L. Robinson and A. M. O'Leary-Kelly, "Monkey See, Monkey Do: The Influence of Work Groups on the Antisocial Behavior of Employees," *Academy of Management Journal* 41, no. 6 (1998): 658–72; and T. M. Glomb and H. Liao, "Interpersonal Aggression in Workgroups: Social Influence, Reciprocal, and Individual Effects," *Academy of Management Journal* 46 (2003): 486–96.

[60] P. Bamberger and M. Biron, "Group Norms and Excessive Absenteeism: The Role of Peer Referent Others," *Organizational Behavior and Human Decision Processes* 103, no. 2 (2007): 179–96; and A. Väänänen, N. Tordera, M. Kivimäki,

A. Kouvonen, J. Pentti, A. Linna, and J. Vahtera, "The Role of Work Group in Individual Sickness Absence Behavior," *Journal of Health & Human Behavior* 49, no. 4 (2008): 452–67.
[61] M. S. Cole, F. Walter, and H. Bruch, "Affective Mechanisms Linking Dysfunctional Behavior to Performance in Work Teams: A Moderated Mediation Study," *Journal of Applied Psychology* 93, no. 5 (2008): 945–58.
[62] U. E. Kim, H. C. Triandis, C. E. Kagitçibaşi, S. C. E. Choi, and G. E. Yoon, *Individualism and Collectivism: Theory, Method, and Applications* (Thousand Oaks, CA: Sage Publications, 1994).
[63] M. Yoshie and D. A. Sauter, "Cultural Norms Influence Nonverbal Emotion Communication: Japanese Vocalizations of Socially Disengaging Emotions," *Emotion* 20, no. 3 (2020): 513–517.
[64] Hagger, Rentzelas, and Chatzisrantis, "Effects of Individualist and Collectivist Group Norms and Choice on Intrinsic Motivation."
[65] J. Dippong and W. Kalkhoff, "Predicting Performance Expectations from Affective Impressions: Linking Affect Control Theory and Status Characteristics Theory," *Social Science Research* 50 (2015): 1–14; A. E. Randel, L. Chay-Hoon, and P. C. Earley, "It's Not Just about Differences: An Integration of Role Identity Theory and Status Characteristics Theory," in M. C. T. Hunt (ed.), *Research on Managing Groups and Teams* (Bingley, UK: Emerald Insight, 2005): 23–42; and B. Anderson, J. Berger, B. Cohen, and M. Zelditch, "Status Classes in Organizations," *Administrative Science Quarterly* 11 no. 2 (1966): 264–283.
[66] Randel, Chay-Hoon, and Earley, "It's Not Just about Differences."
[67] R. R. Callister and J. A. Wall Jr., "Conflict across Organizational Boundaries: Managed Care Organizations versus Health Care Providers," *Journal of Applied Psychology* 86, no. 4 (2001): 754–63; and P. Chattopadhyay, W. H. Glick, and G. P. Huber, "Organizational Actions in Response to Threats and Opportunities," *Academy of Management Journal* 44, no. 5 (2001): 937–55.
[68] Business World (November 3, 2021). "Rahul Dravid appointed head coach of Indian men's cricket team: BCCI". Retrieved from https://www.business-standard.com (Accessed on April 21. 2022).
[69] P. F. Hewlin, "Wearing the Cloak: Antecedents and Consequences of Creating Facades of Conformity," *Journal of Applied Psychology* 94, no. 3 (2009): 727–41.
[70] B. Groysberg, J. T. Polzer, and H. A. Elfenbein, "Too Many Cooks Spoil the Broth: How High-Status Individuals Decrease Group Effectiveness," *Organization Science* (May–June 2011): 722–37.
[71] C. Bendersky and N. P. Shah, "The Cost of Status Enhancement: Performance Effects of Individuals' Status Mobility in Task Groups," *Organization Science* 23, no. 2 (2012): 308–22.
[72] B. Groysberg, J. T. Polzer, and H. A. Elfenbein, "Too Many Cooks Spoil the Broth: How High-Status Individuals Decrease Group Effectiveness," *Organization Science* 22, no. 3 (2011): 722–37.
[73] S. Yu and G. J. Kilduff, "Knowing Where Others Stand: Accuracy and Performance Effects of Individuals' Perceived Status Hierarchies," *Journal of Personality and Social Psychology* (in press).
[74] A. M. Christie and J. Barling, "Beyond Status: Relating Status Inequality to Performance and Health in Teams," *Journal of Applied Psychology* 95, no. 5 (2010): 920–34; and L. H. Nishii and D. M. Mayer, "Do Inclusive Leaders Help to Reduce Turnover in Diverse Groups? The Moderating Role of Leader-Member Exchange in the Diversity to Turnover Relationship," *Journal of Applied Psychology* 94, no. 6 (2009): 1412–26.
[75] V. Venkataramani, S. G. Green, and D. J. Schleicher, "Well-Connected Leaders: The Impact of Leaders' Social Network Ties on LMX and Members' Work Attitudes," *Journal of Applied Psychology* 95, no. 6 (2010): 1071–84.
[76] H. van Dijk and M. L. van Engen, "A Status Perspective on the Consequences of Work Group Diversity," *Journal of Occupational and Organizational Psychology* (June 2013): 223–41.
[77] J. D. Wellman, C. L. Wilkins, E. E. Newell, and D. Kamiya Stewart, "Conflicting Motivations: Understanding How Low-Status Group Members Respond to Ingroup Discrimination Claimants," *Personality and Social Psychology Bulletin* 45, no. 8 (2019): 1170–83.
[78] Based on J. B. Pryor, G. D. Reeder, and A. E. Monroe, "The Infection of Bad Company: Stigma by Association," *Journal of Personality and Social Psychology* 102, no. 2 (2012): 224–41; E. Goffman, *Stigma: Notes on the Management of Spoiled Identity* (New York, NY: Touchstone Digital, 2009); M. R. Hebl and L. M. Mannix, "The Weight of Obesity in Evaluating Others: A Mere Proximity Effect," *Personality and Social Psychology Bulletin* 29 (2003): 28–38; and M. Hernandez, D. R. Avery, S. Tonidandel, M. R. Hebl, A. N. Smith, and P. F. McKay, "The Role of Proximal Social Contexts: Assessing Stigma-by-Association Effects on Leader Appraisals," *Journal of Applied Psychology* 101, no. 1 (2016): 68–85.
[79] M. Cikara and J. J. Van Bavel, "The Neuroscience of Intergroup Relations: An Integrative Review," *Perspectives on Psychological Science* 9, no. 3 (2014): 245–74; and H. Tajfel, "Social Psychology of Intergroup Relations," *Annual Review of Psychology* 33, no. 1 (1982): 1–39.
[80] M. Rubin, C. Badea, and J. Jetten, "Low Status Groups Show In-Group Favoritism to Compensate for Their Low Status and Compete for Higher Status," *Group Processes & Intergroup Relations* 17, no. 5 (2014): 563–76.
[81] C. L. Wilkins, J. D. Wellman, L. G. Babbitt, N. R. Toosi, and K. D. Schad, "You Can Win but I Can't Lose: Bias against High-Status Groups Increases Their Zero-Sum Beliefs about Discrimination," *Journal of Experimental Social Psychology* 57 (2014): 1–14.
[82] T. J. Bouchard, J. Barsaloux, and G. Drauden, "Brainstorming Procedure, Group Size, and Sex as Determinants of the Problem-Solving Effectiveness of Groups and Individuals," *Journal of Applied Psychology* 59, no. 2 (1974): 135–8.
[83] R. B. Gallupe, A. R. Dennis, W. H. Cooper, J. S. Valacich, L. M. Bastianutti, and J. Nunamaker, "Electronic Brainstorming and Group Size," *Academy of Management Journal* 35, no. 2 (2012): 350–69.
[84] J. S. Valacich, B. C. Wheeler, B. E. Mennecke, and R. Wachter, "The Effects of Numerical and Logical Group Size on Computer-Mediated Idea Generation," *Organizational Behavior and Human Decision Processes* 62, no. 3 (1995): 318–29.
[85] R. M. Bray, N. L. Kerr, and R. S. Atkin, "Effects of Group Size, Problem Difficulty, and Sex on Group Performance and Member Reactions," *Journal of Personality and Social Psychology* 36 no. 11 (1978): 1224–40.
[86] R. B. Lount, Jr. and S. L. Wilk, "Working Harder or Hardly Working? Posting Performance Eliminates Social Loafing and Promotes Social Laboring in Workgroups," *Management Science* 60, no. 5 (2014): 1098–106; S. M. Murphy, S. J. Wayne, R. C. Liden, and B. Erdogan, "Understanding Social Loafing: The Role of Justice Perceptions and Exchange Relationships," *Human Relations* (January 2003): 61–84; R. C. Liden, S. J. Wayne, R. A. Jaworski, and N. Bennett, "Social Loafing: A Field

Investigation," *Journal of Management* (April 2004): 285–304; and W. Stroebe and B. S. Frey, "Self-Interest and Collective Action: The Economics and Psychology of Public Goods," *British Journal of Social Psychology* 21, no. 1 (1982): 121–37.
[87] A. W. Delton, L. Cosmides, M. Guemo, T. E. Robertson, and J. Tooby, "The Psychosemantics of Free Riding: Dissecting the Architecture of a Moral Concept," *Journal of Personality and Social Psychology* 102, no. 6 (2012): 1252–70.
[88] S. J. Karau and K. D. Williams, "Social Loafing: A Meta-Analytic Review and Theoretical Integration," *Journal of Personality and Social Psychology* 65 no. 4 (1993): 681–706.
[89] C. Rubino, D. R. Avery, S. D. Volpone, et al., "Does Teaming Obscure Low Performance? Exploring the Temporal Effects of Team Performance Diversity," *Human Performance* 27, no. 5 (2014): 416–34.
[90] Karau and Williams, "Social Loafing."
[91] D. L. Smrt and S. J. Karau, "Protestant Work Ethic Moderates Social Loafing," *Group Dynamics-Theory Research and Practice* (September 2011): 267–74.
[92] M. C. Schippers, "Social Loafing Tendencies and Team Performance: The Compensating Effect of Agreeableness and Conscientiousness," *Academy of Management Learning & Education* 13, no. 1 (2014): 62–81.
[93] A. Gunnthorsdottir and A. Rapoport, "Embedding Social Dilemmas in Intergroup Competition Reduces Free-Riding," *Organizational Behavior and Human Decision Processes* 101 (2006): 184–99; and E. M. Stark, J. D. Shaw, and M. K. Duffy, "Preference for Group Work, Winning Orientation, and Social Loafing Behavior in Groups," *Group and Organization Management* 32, no. 6 (2007): 699–723.
[94] Lount and Wilk, "Working Harder or Hardly Working?"
[95] M. Casey-Campbell and M. L. Martens, "Sticking It All Together: A Critical Assessment of the Group Cohesion-Performance Literature," *International Journal of Management Reviews* 11 (2009): 223–46; E. Salas, R. Grossman, A. M. Hughes, and C. W. Coultas, "Measuring Team Cohesion: Observations from the Science," *Human Factors* 57, no. 3 (2015): 365–74.
[96] Gunnthorsdottir and Rapoport, "Embedding Social Dilemmas in Intergroup Competition Reduces Free-Riding"; and Stark, Shaw, and Duffy, "Preference for Group Work, Winning Orientation, and Social Loafing Behavior in Groups."
[97] L. L. Greer, "Group Cohesion: Then and Now," *Small Group Research* (December 2012): 655–61.
[98] D. S. Staples and L. Zhao, "The Effects of Cultural Diversity in Virtual Teams versus Face-to-Face Teams," *Group Decision and Negotiation* (July 2006): 389–406.
[99] N. Chi, Y. Huang, and S. Lin, "A Double-Edged Sword? Exploring the Curvilinear Relationship between Organizational Tenure Diversity and Team Innovation: The Moderating Role of Team-Oriented HR Practices," *Group and Organization Management* 34, no. 6 (2009): 698–726.
[100] K. J. Klein, A. P. Knight, J. C. Ziegert, B. C. Lim, and J. L. Saltz, "When Team Members' Values Differ: The Moderating Role of Team Leadership," *Organizational Behavior and Human Decision Processes* 114, no. 1 (2011): 25–36; and G. Park and R. P. DeShon, "A Multilevel Model of Minority Opinion Expression and Team Decision-Making Effectiveness," *Journal of Applied Psychology* 95, no. 5 (2010): 824–33.
[101] J. S. Chun and J. N. Choi, "Members' Needs, Intragroup Conflict, and Group Performance," *Journal of Applied Psychology* 99, no. 3 (2014): 437–50.
[102] M. Rigoglioso, "Diverse Backgrounds and Personalities Can Strengthen Groups," *Stanford Knowledgebase*, August 15, 2006, www.stanford.edu/group/knowledgebase/.
[103] K. W. Phillips and D. L. Loyd, "When Surface and Deep-Level Diversity Collide: The Effects on Dissenting Group Members," *Organizational Behavior and Human Decision Processes* 99 (2006): 143–60; and S. R. Sommers, "On Racial Diversity and Group Decision Making: Identifying Multiple Effects of Racial Composition on Jury Deliberations," *Journal of Personality and Social Psychology* (April 2006): 597–612.
[104] Chun and Choi, "Members' Needs, Intragroup Conflict, and Group Performance."
[105] Y. Zhang and L. Hou, "The Romance of Working Together: Benefits of Gender Diversity on Group Performance in China," *Human Relations* 65, no. 11 (2012): 1487–508.
[106] E. Mannix and M. A. Neale, "What Differences Make a Difference? The Promise and Reality of Diverse Teams in Organizations," *Psychological Science in the Public Interest* (October 2005): 31–55.
[107] E. P. Apfelbaum, K. W. Phillips, and J. A. Richeson, "Rethinking the Baseline in Diversity Research: Should We Be Explaining the Effects of Homogeneity?," *Perspectives on Psychological Science* 9, no. 3 (2014): 235–44.
[108] See M. B. Thatcher and P. C. Patel, "Group Faultlines: A Review, Integration, and Guide to Future Research," *Journal of Management* 38, no. 4 (2012): 969–1009.
[109] K. Bezrukova, S. M. B. Thatcher, K. A. Jehn, and C. S. Spell, "The Effects of Alignments: Examining Group Faultlines, Organizational Cultures, and Performance," *Journal of Applied Psychology* 97, no. 1 (2012): 77–92.
[110] R. Rico, M. Sanchez-Manzanares, M. Antino, and D. Lau, "Bridging Team Faultlines by Combining Task Role Assignment and Goal Structure Strategies," *Journal of Applied Psychology* 97, no. 2 (2012): 407–20.
[111] D. Cooper, P. C. Patel, and S. B. Thatcher, "It Depends: Environmental Context and the Effects of Faultlines on Top Management Team Performance," *Organization Science* 25, no. 2 (2014): 633–52.
[112] B. Oc, M. R. Bashshur, and C. Moore, "Head above the Parapet: How Minority Subordinates Influence Group Outcomes and the Consequences They Face for Doing So," *Journal of Applied Psychology* 104, no. 7 (2019): 929–45.
[113] P. Satterstrom, J. T. Polzer, L. B. Kwan, O. P. Hauser, W. Wiruchnipawan, and M. Burke, "Thin Slices of Workgroups," *Organizational Behavior and Human Decision Processes* 151 (2019): 104–17.
[114] B. L. Bonner, S. D. Sillito, and M. R. Baumann, "Collective Estimation: Accuracy, Expertise, and Extroversion as Sources of Intra-Group Influence," *Organizational Behavior and Human Decision Processes* 103 (2007): 121–33.
[115] J. E. Kammer, W. Gaissmaier, T. Reimer, and C. C. Schermuly, "The Adaptive Use of Recognition in Group Decision Making," *Cognitive Science* 38, no. 5 (2014): 911–42.
[116] G. Stasser and S. Abele, "Collective Choice, Collaboration, and Communication," *Annual Review of Psychology* 71 (2020): 589–612.
[117] J. R. Mesmer-Magnus and L. A. DeChurch, "Information Sharing and Team Performance: A Meta-Analysis,"

Journal of Applied Psychology 94, no. 2 (2009): 535–46.
[118] Chun and Choi, "Members' Needs, Intragroup Conflict, and Group Performance."
[119] I. L. Janis, "Groupthink," *Psychology Today* 5, no. 6 (1971): 43–6.
[120] E. Burnstein, E. L. Miller, A. Vinokur, S. Katz, and I. Crowley, "Risky Shift Is Eminently Rational," *Journal of Personality and Social Psychology* 20, no. 1 (1971): 462–71.
[121] G. Park and R. P. DeShon, "A Multilevel Model of Minority Opinion Expression and Team Decision-Making Effectiveness," *Journal of Applied Psychology* 95, no. 5 (2010): 824–33.
[122] R. Benabou, "Groupthink: Collective Delusions in Organizations and Markets," *Review of Economic Studies* (April 2013): 429–62.
[123] J. A. Goncalo, E. Polman, and C. Maslach, "Can Confidence Come Too Soon? Collective Efficacy, Conflict, and Group Performance over Time," *Organizational Behavior and Human Decision Processes* 113, no. 1 (2010): 13–24.
[124] See N. Richardson Ahlfinger and J. K. Esser, "Testing the Groupthink Model: Effects of Promotional Leadership and Conformity Predisposition," *Social Behavior & Personality* 29, no. 1 (2001): 31–41; and S. Schultz-Hardt, F. C. Brodbeck, A. Mojzisch, R. Kerschreiter, and D. Frey, "Group Decision Making in Hidden Profile Situations: Dissent as a Facilitator for Decision Quality," *Journal of Personality and Social Psychology* 91, no. 6 (2006): 1080–93.
[125] See I. Yaniv, "Group Diversity and Decision Quality: Amplification and Attenuation of the Framing Effect," *International Journal of Forecasting* (January–March 2011): 41–49.
[126] M. P. Brady and S. Y. Wu, "The Aggregation of Preferences in Groups: Identity, Responsibility, and Polarization," *Journal of Economic Psychology* 31, no. 6 (2010): 950–63.
[127] Z. Krizan and R. S. Baron, "Group Polarization and Choice-Dilemmas: How Important Is Self-Categorization?," *European Journal of Social Psychology* 37, no. 1 (2007): 191–201.
[128] Stasser and Abele, "Collective Choice, Collaboration, and Communication."
[129] See R. P. McGlynn, D. McGurk, V. S. Effland, N. L. Johll, and D. J. Harding, "Brainstorming and Task Performance in Groups Constrained by Evidence," *Organizational Behavior and Human Decision Processes* (January 2004): 75–87; and R. C. Litchfield, "Brainstorming Reconsidered: A Goal-Based View," *Academy of Management Review* 33, no. 3 (2008): 649–68.
[130] N. L. Kerr and R. S. Tindale, "Group Performance and Decision-Making," *Annual Review of Psychology* 55 (2004): 623–55.
[131] C. Faure, "Beyond Brainstorming: Effects of Different Group Procedures on Selection of Ideas and Satisfaction with the Process," *Journal of Creative Behavior* 38 (2004): 13–34.
[132] P. L. Perrewe, K. L. Zellars, G. R. Ferris, A. M. Rossi, C. J. Kacmar, and D. A. Ralston, "Neutralizing Job Stressors: Political Skill As an Antidote to the Dysfunctional Consequences of Role Conflict," *Academy of Management Journal* (February 2004): 141–52.

10 Understanding Work Teams

Source: Shoja Lack/Alamy Stock Photo

LEARNING OBJECTIVES

After studying this chapter, you should be able to:

10-1 Analyze the continued popularity of teams in organizations.

10-2 Contrast groups and teams.

10-3 Contrast the five types of team arrangements.

10-4 Identify the characteristics of effective teams.

10-5 Explain how organizations can create team players.

10-6 Decide when to use individuals instead of teams.

Employability Skills Matrix (ESM)

	Myth or Science?	Career OBjectives	An Ethical Choice	Point/ Counterpoint	Experiential Exercise	Ethical Dilemma	Case Incident 1	Case Incident 2
Critical Thinking	✓			✓	✓	✓	✓	✓
Communication			✓		✓			✓
Collaboration		✓	✓	✓	✓	✓	✓	✓
Knowledge Application and Analysis	✓			✓	✓	✓	✓	✓
Social Responsibility		✓	✓			✓		

A SOLUTION TO GROWING PAINS

In 2015, Aytekin Tank was the CEO of Jotform, a global company that specializes in online form-building tools. After a decade of building his start-up, the company was expanding rapidly and doing well, in part to Tank's commitment to hiring talent. Despite a commitment to hiring top talent and fostering a supportive and innovative work culture, this growth came at a cost. Tank could see his company losing momentum, and the young entrepreneur could not put his finger on why. When Jotform began to grow, the CEO explored ways to recapture the advantages of having a smaller team. "I looked back to the time when we had around five people. I tried to figure out what had changed: why we moved so fast when we were five people, why we felt like a family when we were that small."

The solution, Tank found, was to restructure his organization into cross-functional teams. This approach was pioneered in the twenty-first century by Jack Welch (shown here), CEO of General Electric (GE), who believed dividing employees by function led to slower and poorer decisions. Welch's cross-functional or boundaryless organization created forums where employees with different roles within the company could meet and coordinate decision making. Welch found that GE became more efficient when employees from marketing, finance, engineering, and many other sectors had a chance to work together. It has been over twenty years since Welch popularized cross-functional teams, and many organizations have found that adopting a cross-functional structure gives them a competitive edge over more traditional companies.

Tank found that, by dividing his company into cross-functional teams, he was able to re-create the close-knit, efficient structure of the smaller organization that Jotform used to be. In this new structure, team members came from several different parts of the organization, allowing for better communication across different functions. Teams typically had a web designer, a programmer, and a marketing analyst (or similar position), all working on solutions to organizational problems. Once these teams were formed, Tank also made sure that each team had their own meeting space and a budget for fun activities like weekly lunches. Besides building morale, the Jotform leader believed that cross-functional teams allowed team members to bond and ultimately begin to trust each other. His goal was to breed cooperation rather than competition. Tank also made sure to keep Jotform's teams small, allowing employees to feel greater ownership over their successes and failures. By having team members from several different functions, employees could see how their work affected other parts of Jotform for better—or worse. The last ingredient in Tank's cross-functional teams was autonomy—freedom to make decisions that have an impact on other parts of the organization, tackle problems the way they want, and work the way they want.

Tank's decision has given his company the same edge it did when it was smaller. After restructuring the company, Jotform experienced increased productivity. By mixing different functions of the company into teams, employees could make decisions more quickly. Teams had more diverse skill sets, so they were able to tackle any problems the company faced with greater creativity by using varied perspectives from different parts of the company.

Even though the move was successful, Tank admits that he was afraid of trying something new in the beginning. Still, he realizes that in order to continue to grow the company, he had to take a risk. "Change can be difficult for people and for companies," Tank has said when discussing the move to cross-functional teams. "However, if your current system is not effective and you don't take the initiative to improve via change, staying the course can be disastrous."

Sources: Based on J. Boss, "5 Reasons Why This CEO Leverages Cross Functional Teams for Better Business Performance," *Forbes*, February 13, 2017, https://www.forbes.com/sites/deniserestauri/2017/07/19/how-this-woman-made-the-jump-and-beat-impostor-syndrome/#377b26a46460, accessed April 9, 2017; R. Ashkenas, "Jack Welch's Approach to Breaking Down Silos Still Works," *Harvard Business Review*, September 9, 2015, www.hbr.com/2015/09/jack-welchs-approach-to-breaking-down-silos-still-works, accessed April 9, 2017; and A. Tank, "How to Scale Your Company with Small Teams," *Entrepreneur*, December 9, 2016, www.entrepreneur.com/article/285917, accessed April 9, 2017.

IPM India Wholesale Trading Pvt. Ltd. (IPM India) is a joint venture between Philip Morris Brands—Sarl, Switzerland—and two Indian companies—Godfrey Phillips India Ltd (GPI) and K.K. Modi Investment & Financial Services Private Ltd. IPM has several firsts to its credit including being EQUAL-SALARY certified in 2018. The Great Place to Work Institute and the Top Employer Institute recognized IPM for its efforts to create a world class organization in 2020. The 110 employees of IPM, engaged in wholesale trading of cigarettes and other tobacco products either manufactured in India or imported into India, extensively work in cross-functional teams for projects of strategic importance to the company. Members of the finance, marketing, operation and HR teams work together. For example, on the project to bring smokeless projects to the millions of smokers in the world, members of IPM work in cross-national-functional teams of the parent company Phillips Morrison. Lorna Hosne Ara, the HR head of IPM shares that, superior solutions are found when cross functional teams work on issues such as how to increase customer engagement. To improve the functionality of cross-functional teams IPM provides support in terms of training and guidance to all employees on working collaboratively and listening to others point of view.[1]

Are cross-functional teams the best, as this story suggests? There are many different ways to build a successful team. In this chapter, we will consider different types of teams and how a team's composition, context, and team processes lead to success or failure.

Why Have Teams Become So Popular?

10-1 Analyze the continued popularity of teams in organizations.

Why are teams popular? In short, because we believe they are effective. "A team of people happily committed to the project and to one another will outperform a brilliant individual every time," writes *Forbes* publisher Rich Karlgaard.[2] In some ways, he's right. Teams can sometimes achieve feats an individual could never accomplish.[3] Teams are more flexible and responsive to changing events than traditional departments or other forms of permanent groupings. They can quickly assemble, deploy, refocus, and disband. They are an effective means to democratize organizations and increase employee involvement. And research indicates that our involvement in teams positively shapes the way we think as individuals, introducing a collaborative mindset about even our personal decision making.[4]

The fact that organizations have embraced teamwork doesn't necessarily mean teams are always effective. Team members, as humans, can be swayed by fads and herd mentality that can lead them astray from the best decisions. What conditions affect their potential? How do members work together? Do we even like teams? Maybe not, according to the OB Poll. To answer these questions, let's first distinguish between groups and teams.

Differences between Groups and Teams

10-2 Contrast groups and teams.

work group A group that interacts primarily to share information, make decisions, and help each group member perform within his or her area of responsibility.

Groups and teams are not the same thing. In Chapter 9, we defined a *group* as two or more individuals, interacting and interdependent, who work together to achieve particular objectives. A **work group** is a group that interacts primarily to share information, make decisions, and help each group member perform within his or her area of responsibility.

OB POLL

Is Teamwork a Good Thing?

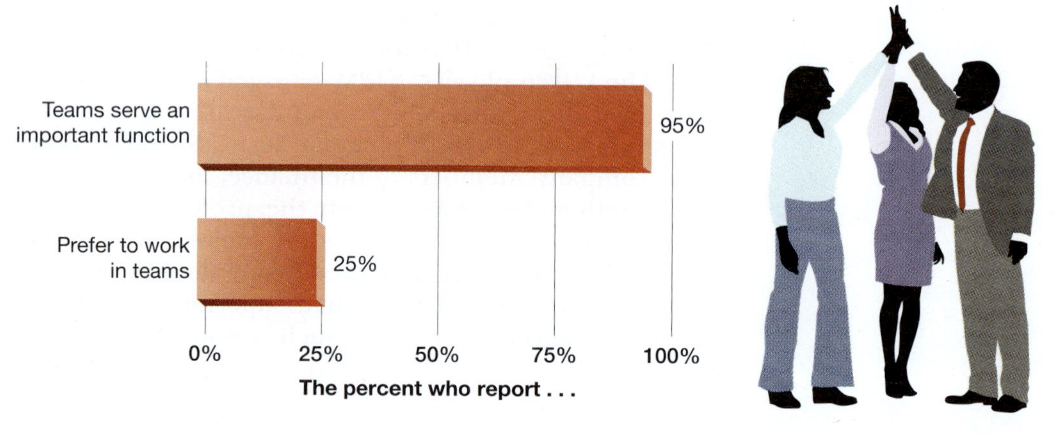

Source: Based on "University of Phoenix Survey Reveals Nearly Seven in Ten Workers Have Been Part of Dysfunctional Teams," downloaded on June 9, 2013, from www.prnewswire.com.

Work groups have no need or opportunity to engage in collective work with joint effort, so the group's performance is merely the summation of each member's individual contribution. There is no positive synergy that would create an overall level of performance greater than the sum of the inputs. A work group is a collection of individuals doing their work, albeit with interaction and/or dependency.

work team A group whose individual efforts result in performance that is greater than the sum of the individual inputs.

A **work team**, on the other hand, generates positive synergy through coordination.[5] The individual efforts result in a level of performance greater than the sum of the individual inputs. Teams are more likely to be constantly changing and adapting, rather than static entities—seeing teams as dynamic systems in this way has led many to focus more on *teaming* as a verb (i.e., on the processes or actions involved in engaging as a team) rather than on the team itself.[6]

In both work groups and work teams, there are often behavioral expectations of members, collective normalization efforts, active group dynamics, and some level of decision making (even if just informally about the scope of membership). Both may generate ideas, pool resources, or coordinate logistics such as work schedules; for the work group, however, this effort is limited to information gathering for decision makers outside the group.

Whereas we can think of a work team as a subset of a work group, the team is constructed to be purposeful (symbiotic) in its member interaction. The distinction between a work group and a work team should be kept even when the terms are mentioned interchangeably in different contexts. Exhibit 10-1 highlights the differences between them.

The definitions help clarify why organizations structure work processes by teams. Management is looking for positive synergy that will create increased performance. The extensive use of teams creates the *potential* for an organization to generate greater outputs with no increase in employee head count. Notice, however, that we said *potential.* There is nothing magical that ensures the achievement of positive synergy in the creation of teams. Merely calling a *group* a *team* doesn't automatically improve its performance. As we

Exhibit 10-1 Comparing Work Groups and Work Teams

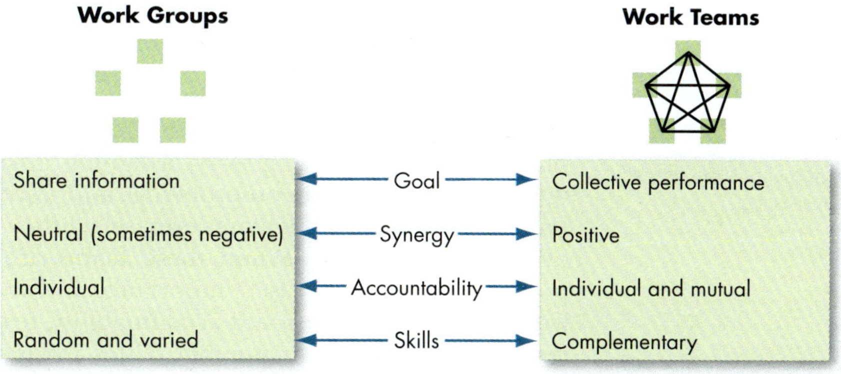

show later, effective teams have certain common characteristics. If management hopes to gain increases in organizational performance through the use of teams, their teams must possess these characteristics.

Types of Teams

10-3 Contrast the five types of team arrangements.

Teams can make products, provide services, negotiate deals, coordinate projects, offer advice, and make decisions.[7] In this section, we first describe four common types of teams in organizations: *problem-solving teams*, *self-managed work teams*, *cross-functional teams*, and *virtual teams* (see Exhibit 10-2). Then we will discuss *multiteam systems*, which utilize a "team of teams" and are becoming increasingly widespread as work increases in complexity.

Problem-Solving Teams

problem-solving teams Groups of five to twelve employees from the same department who meet for a few hours each week to discuss ways of improving quality, efficiency, and the work environment.

Quality-control teams have been in use for many years. Originally seen most often in manufacturing plants, these were permanent teams that generally met at a regular time, sometimes weekly or daily, to address quality standards and any problems with the products made. Also, the medical field in particular has recently implemented quality teams to improve their services in patient care. **Problem-solving teams** like these rarely have the authority to implement their suggestions unilaterally, but if their recommendations are paired with implementation processes, some significant improvements can be realized.

Exhibit 10-2 Four Types of Teams

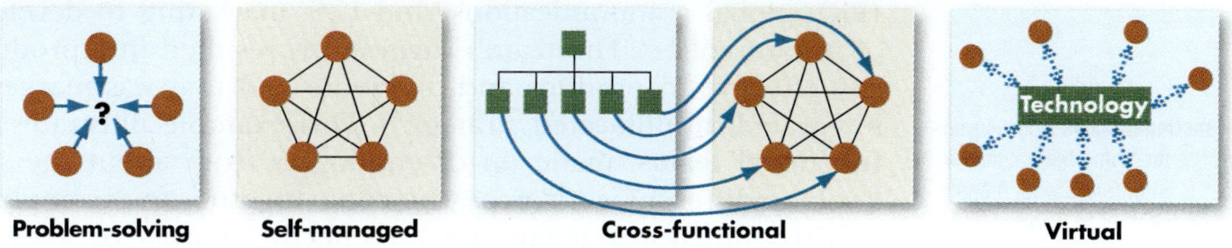

Self-Managed Work Teams

As we discussed, problem-solving teams only make recommendations. Some organizations have gone further and created teams that also implement solutions and take responsibility for outcomes.

self-managed work teams Groups of ten to fifteen people who autonomously implement solutions and take responsibility for the outcomes (responsibilities normally given to supervisors).

Self-managed work teams are groups of employees (typically 10 to 15 in number) who perform highly related or interdependent jobs; these teams take on some supervisory responsibilities.[8] The responsibilities usually include planning and scheduling work, assigning tasks to members, making operating decisions, taking action on problems, and working with suppliers and customers. Fully self-managed work teams even select their own members who evaluate each other's performance. When these teams are established, former supervisory positions take on decreased importance and are sometimes eliminated. However, with a lack of authority and accountability, teams may spend valuable time and resources aligning team member values and goals to "get on the same page."[9]

Research results on the effectiveness of self-managed work teams have not been uniformly positive. Some research indicates that self-managed teams may be more or less effective based on the degree to which team-promoting behaviors are rewarded. For example, one study of 45 self-managing teams found that when team members perceived that economic rewards such as pay depended on input from their teammates, performance improved for both individuals and the team as a whole.[10]

A second area of research focus has been the impact of conflict on self-managed work team effectiveness. Some research indicates that self-managed teams are not effective when there is conflict. When disputes arise, members often stop cooperating and power struggles ensue, which lead to lower group performance and learning, though this may depend on the structure of roles within the team.[11] However, other research indicates that when members feel confident that they can speak up without being embarrassed, rejected, or punished by other team members—in other words, when they feel psychologically safe—conflict can be beneficial and boost team performance.[12]

Research has also explored the effect of self-managed work teams on member behavior. Here again the findings are mixed. Although individuals on teams report higher levels of job satisfaction than other individuals, studies indicate they sometimes have higher absenteeism and turnover rates. One large-scale study of labor productivity in British establishments found that, although using teams improved individual (and overall) labor productivity, no evidence supported the claim that self-managed teams performed better than traditional teams with less decision-making authority.[13] On the whole, it appears that, for self-managing teams to be advantageous, a number of facilitating factors must be in place.

Cross-Functional Teams

Starbucks created a team of individuals from production, global public relations (PR), global communications, and U.S. marketing to develop the Via brand of instant coffee. The team's suggestions resulted in a product that would be cost-effective to produce and distribute and that was marketed with a tightly integrated, multifaceted strategy.[14] This example illustrates the use of **cross-functional teams**, made up of employees from about the same hierarchical level but different work areas who come together to accomplish a task.

cross-functional teams Employees from about the same hierarchical level but from different work areas who come together to accomplish a task.

Cross-functional teams are an effective means of allowing people from diverse areas within or even between organizations to exchange information, develop new ideas, solve problems, and coordinate complex projects. Due to the high need for coordination, however, cross-functional teams are not simple to manage. First, it makes sense for power shifts to occur when different expertise is needed because the members are at roughly the same level in the organization, which creates leadership ambiguity. A climate of trust thus needs to be developed before shifts can happen without undue conflict.[15] Second, the early stages of development are often long because members need to learn to work with higher levels of diversity and complexity. Third, it takes time to build trust and teamwork, especially among people with different experiences and perspectives.

Organizations have used horizontal, boundary-spanning teams for decades, and we would be hard-pressed to find a large organization or product launch that did not use them. Major automobile manufacturers—Toyota, Honda, Nissan, BMW, GM, Ford, and Chrysler—currently use this form of team to coordinate complex projects, as do other industries. For example, Cisco relies on specific cross-functional teams to identify and capitalize on new trends in several areas of the software market. Its teams are the equivalent of social-networking groups that collaborate in real time to identify new business opportunities in the field and then implement them from the bottom up.[16]

In sum, the strength of traditional cross-functional teams is the collaborative effort of individuals with diverse skills from a variety of disciplines. When the unique perspectives of these members are considered, these teams can be very effective.

Virtual Teams

virtual teams Teams that use technology to tie together physically dispersed members in order to achieve a common goal.

The teams described in the preceding section do their work face-to-face, whereas **virtual teams** use computer technology to unite physically dispersed members and achieve a common goal.[17] They collaborate online—using communication links such as wide-area networks, corporate social media, videoconferencing, and e-mail—whether members are nearby or continents apart. Nearly all teams do at least some of their work remotely.

Harley-Davidson Motor Company uses cross-functional teams at all levels of its organization in creating new products, such as its first electric motorcycle, shown here. From product conception to launch, cross-functional teams include Harley employees from product planning, engineering, design, marketing, manufacturing, and purchasing.

Source: Lucas Jackson/Reuters/Alamy Stock Photo

Virtual teams should be managed differently than face-to-face teams in an office, partially because virtual team members may not interact along traditional hierarchical patterns. For instance, virtual environments differ from face-to-face environments in the ways they convey social cues and foster a sense of distance between people.[18] Because of the complexity of interactions, research indicates that shared leadership of virtual teams may significantly enhance team performance, although the concept is still in development.[19] For virtual teams to be effective, management should ensure that (1) trust is established among members (one inflammatory remark in an e-mail can severely undermine team trust), (2) progress is monitored closely (so the team doesn't lose sight of its goals and no team member "disappears"), and (3) the efforts and products of the team are publicized throughout the organization (so the team does not become invisible).[20] Managers should also carefully select who will be a member of a virtual team because working on a virtual team may require different competencies.[21]

It would be a mistake to think virtual teams are an easy substitute for face-to-face teams. While the geographical reach and immediacy of online communication make virtual teams a natural development, managers must make certain this type of team is the optimal choice for the desired outcome and then maintain an oversight role throughout the collaboration.

Multiteam Systems

multiteam system A collection of two or more interdependent teams that share a superordinate goal; a team of teams.

The types of teams we've described so far are typically smaller, stand-alone teams, although their activities relate to the broader objectives of the organization. As tasks become more complex, teams often grow in size. Increases in team size are accompanied by higher coordination demands, creating a tipping point at which the addition of another member does more harm than good. To solve this problem, organizations use **multiteam systems**, collections of two or more interdependent teams that share a superordinate goal. In other words, multiteam systems are a "team of teams."[22]

To picture a multiteam system, imagine the coordination of response needed after a major car accident. There is the emergency medical services team, which responds first and transports the injured to the hospital. An emergency room team then takes over, providing medical care, followed by a recovery team. Although the emergency services team, emergency room team, and recovery team are technically independent, their activities are interdependent, and the success of one depends on the success of the others. Why? Because they all share the higher goal of saving lives.

Some factors that make smaller, more traditional teams effective do not necessarily apply to multiteam systems and can even hinder their performance. One study showed that multiteam systems performed better when they had "boundary spanners" whose jobs were to coordinate with members of the other subteams. This reduced the need for some team member communication, which was helpful because it reduced coordination demands.[23] Leadership of multiteam systems is also much different than for stand-alone teams. While leadership of all teams affects team performance, a multiteam leader must both facilitate coordination between teams and lead each team.[24] Research indicated teams that received more attention and engagement from the organization's leaders felt more empowered, which made them more effective as they sought to solve their own problems.[25] Multiteam systems may have higher performance when planning is decentralized, but they may also have more problems with coordination.[26]

An Ethical Choice

The Size of Your Meeting's Carbon Footprint

Despite being in different countries or even on different continents, many teams in geographically dispersed locations communicate without regularly meeting face-to-face, and their members may never meet each other in person. Although the merits of face-to-face versus electronic communication have been debated, there may be a strong ethical argument for virtual teams.

Keeping team members where they are, as opposed to having them travel every time they need to meet, may be in line with corporate social responsibility (CSR) initiatives. A very large proportion of airline, rail, and car transport is for business purposes and contributes greatly to global carbon dioxide emissions. When teams are able to meet virtually rather than face-to-face, they dramatically reduce their carbon footprint.

In a globally connected world, how might you minimize your organization's environmental impact from business travel? Several tips might get you started thinking about ways that virtual teams can be harnessed for greater sustainability:

1. **Encourage all team members to think about whether a face-to-face meeting is really necessary.** Try to utilize alternative communication methods whenever possible.
2. **Communicate as much as possible through virtual means.** This includes e-mail, telephone calls, and videoconferencing.
3. **When traveling to team meetings, choose the most environmentally responsible travel methods possible.** Also, check the environmental profile of hotels before booking rooms.
4. **If the environmental savings are not enough motivation to reduce travel, consider the financial savings.** According to one survey, businesses spend about 8 to 12 percent of their entire budget on travel. Communicating electronically can therefore result in two benefits: (1) it's cheaper and (2) it's good for the environment.

Sources: Based on P. Tilstone, "Cut Carbon ... and Bills," *Director,* May 2009, 54; L. C. Latimer, "6 Strategies for Sustainable Business Travel," *Greenbiz,* February 11, 2011, www.greenbiz.com; and F. Gebhart, "Travel Takes a Big Bite out of Corporate Expenses," *Travel Market Report,* May 30, 2013, downloaded June 9, 2013, from www.travelmarketreport.com.

In general, a multiteam system is the best choice either when a team has become too large to be effective or when teams with distinct functions need to be highly coordinated.

Creating Effective Teams

10-4 Identify the characteristics of effective teams.

Teams are often created deliberately but sometimes evolve organically. Take the rise of team "hives" over the past 5 years for an organic example. Freelancing is typically the solo work of people who are highly specialized in their fields and can provide expertise to organizations on a short-term basis. The difficulty is for the freelancers to market themselves effectively to organizations, and for organizations to find freelancers who fit their needs. To bridge this gap, freelancers form teams with other freelancers from complementary specialties to present a cohesive working unit—a hive—to clients. This team-based approach has proven very successful.[27]

Many people have tried to identify factors related to team effectiveness. To help, some studies have organized what was once a large list of characteristics into a relatively focused model.[28] Exhibit 10-3 summarizes what we currently know about what makes teams effective. As you'll see, it builds on many of the group concepts introduced in Chapter 9.

In considering the team effectiveness model, keep in mind two points. First, teams differ in form and structure. The model attempts to generalize across all

Exhibit 10-3 Team Effectiveness Model

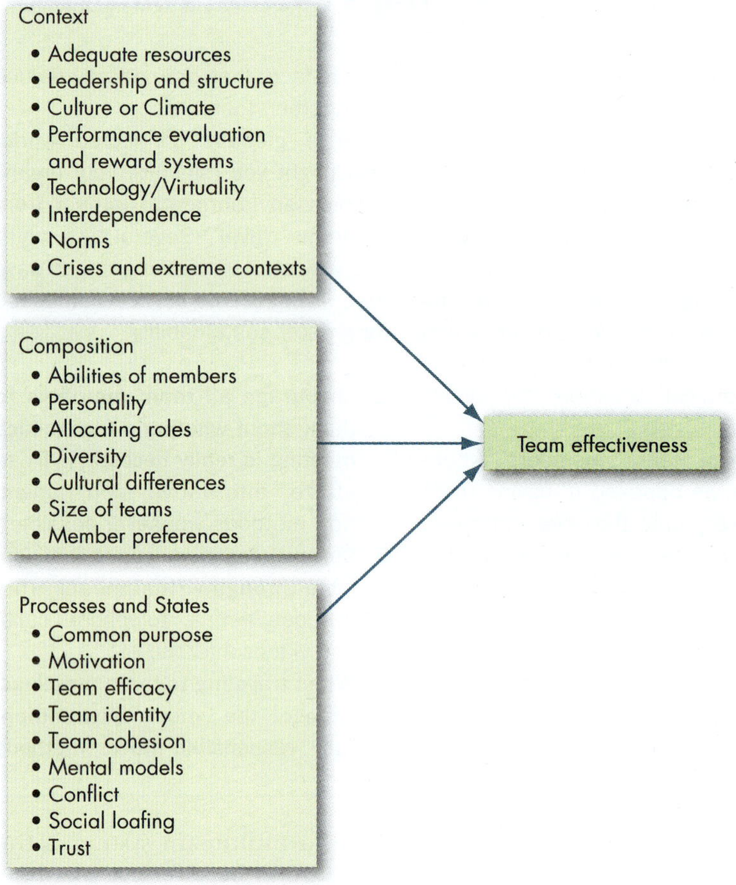

varieties of teams but avoids rigidly applying its predictions to all teams.[29] Use it as a guide. Second, the model assumes that teamwork is preferable to individual work. Creating "effective" teams when individuals can do the job better is like perfectly solving the wrong problem. Third, let's consider what *team effectiveness* means in this model. Typically, team effectiveness includes objective measures of the team's productivity, managers' ratings of the team's performance, and aggregate measures of member satisfaction.

We can organize the key components of effective teams into three general categories. First are the resources and other *contextual* influences that make teams effective. The second relates to the team's *composition*. Finally, *process* variables are events within the team that influence effectiveness. We will explore each of these components next.

Team Context: What Factors Determine Whether Teams Are Successful?

The five contextual factors most significantly related to team performance are adequate resources, effective leadership, culture or climate, a performance evaluation and reward system that reflects team contributions, and crises and extreme contexts.

Adequate Resources Teams are part of a larger organization system; every work team relies on resources outside the group to sustain it. A scarcity of resources directly reduces the ability of a team to perform its job effectively and achieve its goals. As one study concluded after looking at 13 factors related to group performance, "perhaps one of the most important characteristics of an effective work group is the support the group receives from the organization."[30] This support includes timely information, proper equipment, adequate staffing, encouragement, and administrative assistance. Racially diverse teams are less likely to be provided with the resources necessary for team performance.[31]

Leadership and Structure Teams function well if they properly allocate roles and ensure the workload is shared by all team members. Agreeing on the specifics of work and how they fit together to integrate individual skills requires leadership and structure, either from management or from team members themselves. In self-managed teams, members absorb many of the duties typically assumed by managers. A manager's job then becomes managing *outside* (rather than inside) the team. Leader personality, engagement, and leadership style all have an impact on team effectiveness.[32]

As we mentioned before, leadership is especially important in multiteam systems. Here, leaders need to delegate responsibility to teams and play the role of facilitator, making sure the teams work together rather than against one another.[33]

Culture or Climate Trust is the foundation of leadership; it allows a team to accept and commit to the leader's goals and decisions. Members of effective teams exhibit trust in their leaders.[34] They also trust each other. Interpersonal trust among team members facilitates cooperation, reduces the need to monitor each other's behavior, and bonds individuals through the belief that members won't take advantage of them. Members are more likely to take risks and expose vulnerabilities when they can trust others on their team. The overall level of trust in a team is important, but the way trust is dispersed among team members also matters. Trust levels that are asymmetric and imbalanced between team members can mitigate the performance advantages of a high overall level of trust—in such cases, coalitions form that often undermine the team as a whole.[35]

Trust is a perception that can be vulnerable to shifting conditions in a team environment. Also, trust is not unequivocally desirable. For instance, recent research in Singapore found that, in high-trust teams, individuals are less likely to claim and defend personal ownership of their ideas, but individuals who do still claim personal ownership are rated as lower contributors *by team members.*[36] This "punishment" by the team may reflect resentments that create negative relationships, increased conflicts, and reduced performance.

Performance Evaluation and Reward System Individual performance evaluations and incentives may interfere with the development of high-performance teams. Thus, in addition to evaluating and rewarding employees for their individual contributions, management should utilize hybrid performance systems that incorporate an individual member component to recognize individual contributions and a group reward to recognize positive team outcomes.[37] Group-based appraisals, profit sharing, small-group incentives, and other system modifications can reinforce team effort and commitment.

Crises and Extreme Contexts Crises and extreme contexts are a crucible in which the merits of teams can be put to the test. These contexts can unlock the potential of team members who do truly great things under stress. They can also lead to the unraveling of the team fabric, resulting in disaster. As an example, in the Mann Gulch fire of 1949, dozens of smokejumpers (i.e., elite firefighters who are airlifted to fight wildfires) led by foreman "Wag" Dodge were dispatched to an area south of the Mann Gulch valley in Montana after a lightning storm caused a wildfire.[38] Illustrating how quickly crises can escalate and unravel a team, Dodge saw the fire was moving toward them at 610 feet per minute with thirty-foot-high flames. The team turned around and headed up the 76 percent grade mountain toward the ridge. They were quickly losing ground, and Dodge yelled for everyone to drop their tools, lit a fire in front of them, and told them to lie down in the area he had burned. No one listened, and they all ran for the ridge. Twelve of the smokejumpers died. Dodge lived by lying down in the ashes of his escape fire.[39]

Disasters and extreme contexts alike have attracted a lot of research attention from OB researchers in the last several decades. From astronauts in long-duration space missions to health professional teams responding to crises during a worldwide pandemic, teams may find themselves in extreme, disastrous contexts and must act quickly together to perform their duties.[40] Research on multiteam systems in disaster environments demonstrate that people tend to default to gathering information rather than taking action—when they do take action, they do so without deliberately considering the context or options or even forming a plan.[41] Several factors play a role in influencing team success during crises. Leaders are extremely important in these contexts (just consider Dodge's role in the Mann Gulch fire). Leaders are most effective during disasters when they support team problem solving, are supportive of the team members, initiate structure and planning, delegate and coordinate, as well as help team members make sense of the situation.[42] Structure also plays an important role. *Team scaffolds* (i.e., fluid, underlying structures that establishes role types, shared responsibilities, and boundaries in teams) have been shown to help support coordination during crises because they establish accountability, a shared understanding, and a sense of identity or belonging.[43] Indeed, this fluidity and flexibility is important for teams in crisis, as higher-performing teams tend to be adaptable and exhibit few, short, and simple interaction patterns.[44] As for individual team members during times of crisis, positive affectivity (PA; see the discussion on personality and individual differences in Chapter 5) can help buffer the negative impact of the strain of the crisis situation.[45] Finally, informed decision-making is critical, as team members should know where to target decision making (e.g., toward the problem or the coordination of team members), how to share information effectively with team members, and when to reflect on team objectives, processes, and strategies before acting.[46]

Team Composition

Maria Contreras-Sweet, former head of the U.S. Small Business Administration, said, "When I'm building a team, I'm looking for people who are resourceful. I need people who are flexible, and I really need people who are discreet.... Discreetness also speaks to integrity."[47] These are good qualities, but they are not all that we should consider when staffing teams. The team composition category includes variables that relate to how teams should be staffed: the abilities and personalities of team members, allocation of roles, diversity, cultural differences, size of the team, and members' preferences for teamwork.

As you can expect, opinions vary widely about the type of members leaders want on their teams, and some evidence suggests that compositions may be more important at different stages of team development.

Abilities of Members It's true we occasionally read about an athletic team of mediocre players who, because of excellent coaching, determination, and precision teamwork, beat a far more talented group. But such cases make the news precisely because they are unusual. A team's performance depends in part on the knowledge, skills, and abilities of individual members.[48] Abilities set limits on what members can do and how effectively they will perform on a team.

Research reveals insights into team composition and performance. First, when solving a complex problem such as reengineering an assembly line, high-ability teams—composed of mostly intelligent members—do better than lower-ability teams. High-ability teams are also more adaptable to changing situations; they can apply existing knowledge more effectively to new problems.

Finally, the ability of the team's leader matters. Smart team leaders help less intelligent team members when they struggle with a task. A less intelligent leader can, conversely, neutralize the effect of a high-ability team.[49]

Personality of Members We demonstrated in Chapter 5 that personality significantly influences individual behavior. Some dimensions identified in the Big Five personality model are particularly relevant to team effectiveness.[50] Conscientiousness is especially important to teams. Conscientious people are good at backing up other team members and sensing when their support is truly needed. Conscientious teams also have other advantages—one study found that behavioral tendencies such as organization, achievement orientation, and endurance were all related to higher levels of team performance.[51]

Team composition can be based on individual personalities to good effect. Suppose an organization needs to create 20 teams of 4 people each and has 40 highly conscientious people and 40 who score low on conscientiousness. Would the organization be better off (1) forming 10 teams of highly

Members of a research team at the innovation lab of Swiss bank UBS are testing digital, virtual reality, and other new technologies to attract a young generation of investors and to help current clients visualize complex investment portfolios. Team members have the technical expertise and skills needed to function as a high-ability team.
Source: Arnd Wiegmann/Reuters

Myth or Science?

Team Members Who Are "Hot" Should Make the Play

Before we tell you whether this statement is true or false, we need to take a step back and ask: "Can individuals go on 'hot' streaks?" In teams, and especially in sports, we often hear about players who are on a streak and have the "hot hand." Basketball player LeBron James scores five baskets in a row, golfer Rory McIlroy makes three birdies in a row for the European Ryder Cup team, and tennis player Serena Williams hits four aces in a row during a doubles match with her sister Venus. Most people (around 90 percent) believe LeBron, Rory, and Serena score well because they are on a hot streak, performing above their average.

Although people believe in the hot hand, the scores tell the story. About half the relevant studies have shown that the hot hand is possible, while the remaining half show it is not. But perception can influence reality, so perhaps the more important question is whether belief in the hot hand affects teams' strategies. One study of volleyball players showed that coaches and players allocate more balls to players who are believed to have the hot hand. Is this a good strategy? If the hot player's performance is actually lower than her teammates', then giving her more balls to hit will hurt the team because the better players aren't getting enough chances to hit, while she gets more chances to perform.

Considering the research to date, the opening statement appears to be false.

Sources: Based on M. Raab, B. Gula, and G. Gigerenzer, "The Hot Hand Exists in Volleyball and Is Used for Allocation Decisions," *Journal of Experimental Psychology: Applied* 18, no. 1 (2012): 81–94; T Gilovich, R. Vallone, and A. Tversky, "The Hot Hand in Basketball: On the Misperception of Random Sequences," *Cognitive Psychology* 17 (1985): 295–314; and M. Bar-Eli, S. Avugos, and M. Raab, "Twenty Years of 'Hot Hand' Research: The Hot Hand Phenomenon: Review and Critique," *Psychology, Sport, and Exercise* 7 (2006): 525–53.

conscientious people and 10 teams of members low on conscientiousness, or (2) "seeding" each team with 2 people who scored high and 2 who scored low on conscientiousness? Perhaps surprisingly, evidence suggests option 1 is the best choice; performance across the teams will be higher if the organization forms 10 highly conscientious teams and 10 teams low in conscientiousness. The reason is that a team with varying conscientiousness levels will not work to the peak performance of its highly conscientious members. Instead, a group normalization dynamic (or simple resentment) will complicate interactions and force the highly conscientious members to lower their expectations, thus reducing the group's performance.[52]

What about the other traits? Teams with a high level of openness to experience tend to perform better, and research indicates that constructive task conflict *enhances* the effect. Open team members communicate better with one another and throw out more ideas, which makes teams composed of open people more creative and innovative.[53] Task conflict also enhances performance for teams with high levels of emotional stability.[54] It's not so much that the conflict itself improves performance for these teams, but that teams characterized by openness and emotional stability are able to handle conflict and leverage it to improve performance. The minimum level of team member agreeableness matters, too: Teams do worse when they have one or more highly disagreeable members, and a wide span in individual levels of agreeableness can lower productivity. Research is not clear on the outcomes of extraversion, but a recent study indicated that a high mean level of extraversion in a team can increase the level of helping behaviors, particularly in a climate of cooperation.[55] Thus the personality traits of individuals are as important to teams as the overall personality characteristics of the team.

Exhibit 10-4 Key Roles of Teams

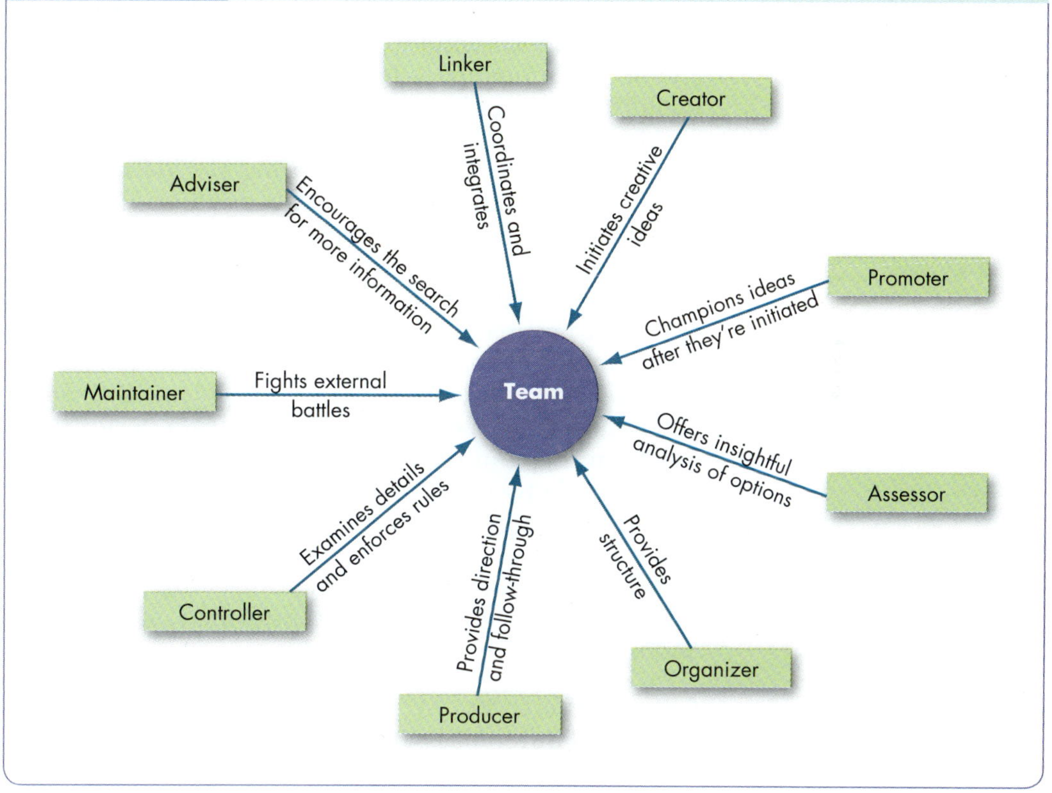

Allocation of Roles Teams have different needs, and members should be selected to ensure that all the various roles are filled. A study of 778 major league baseball teams over a 21-year period highlights the importance of assigning roles appropriately.[56] As you might expect, teams with more experienced and skilled members performed better. However, the experience and skill of those in core roles who handled more of the workflow of the team, and were central to all work processes (in this case, pitchers and catchers), were especially vital. In other words, put your most able, experienced, and conscientious workers in the most central roles in a team.

We can identify nine potential team roles (see Exhibit 10-4). Successful work teams have selected people to play all these roles based on their skills and preferences.[57] (On many teams, individuals will play multiple roles.) To increase the likelihood that team members will work well together, managers need to understand the individual strengths each person can bring to a team, select members with their strengths in mind, and allocate work assignments that fit with members' preferred styles.

organizational demography The degree to which members of a work unit share a common demographic attribute, such as age, sex, race, educational level, or length of service in an organization.

Diversity of Members In Chapter 9, we discussed the effect of diversity on groups. How does *team* diversity affect *team* performance? The degree to which members of a work unit (group, team, or department) share a common demographic attribute, such as age, sex, race, educational level, or length of service in the organization, is the subject of **organizational demography**. Organizational demography suggests that attributes such as age or the date of joining should help predict turnover. The logic goes like this: Turnover will be greater among those with dissimilar experiences because communication is more difficult and conflict is more likely. Increased conflict makes membership less attractive, so employees are more likely to quit. Similarly, the losers of a conflict are more apt to leave voluntarily or be forced out.[58] The conclusion is that diversity negatively affects team performance.

Many of us hold the optimistic view that diversity is a good thing—diverse teams should benefit from differing perspectives. Two meta-analytic reviews show, however, that demographic diversity is essentially unrelated to team performance, while a third review suggests that race and gender diversity are actually negatively related to team performance.[59] Other research findings are mixed. One qualifier is that gender and ethnic diversity have more negative effects in occupations dominated by white or male employees, but in more demographically balanced occupations or when attitudes toward diversity are more positive, diversity is less of a problem. Diversity in function, education, and expertise are positively related to team performance, but these effects are small and depend on the situation. Diversity may also have a negative effect when trust between members is already low.

Proper leadership can improve the performance of diverse teams.[60] For example, one study of 68 teams in China found that teams diverse in knowledge, skills, and ways of approaching problems were more creative but only when their leaders were transformational (see Chapter 12 for definition) and inspiring.[61]

Cultural Differences We have discussed research on team diversity regarding a number of differences. But what about cultural differences? Evidence indicates that cultural diversity interferes with team processes, at least in the short term,[62] but let's dig a little deeper: What about differences in cultural status? Though it's debatable, people with higher cultural status are usually in the majority or ruling race group of their nations. Researchers in the United Kingdom found that cultural status differences affected team performance whereby individuals in teams with more high cultural-status members than low cultural-status members realized improved performance . . . for *every* member.[63] This suggests not that diverse teams should be filled with individuals who have high cultural status in their countries but that we should be aware of how people identify with their cultural status even in diverse group settings.

In general, cultural diversity seems to be an asset for tasks that call for a variety of viewpoints. But culturally heterogeneous teams have more difficulty learning to work with each other and solving problems. The good news is that these difficulties seem to dissipate with time.

Size of Teams Most experts agree that keeping teams small is key to improving group effectiveness.[64] Amazon CEO Jeff Bezos uses the "two-pizza" rule, saying, "If it takes more than two pizzas to feed the team, the team is too big."[65] Psychologist George Miller claimed that "the magical number [is] seven, plus or minus two," for the ideal team size.[66] Author and *Forbes* publisher Rich Karlgaard writes, "Bigger teams almost never correlate with a greater chance of success" because the potential connections between people grow exponentially as team size increases, thus complicating communications.[67]

Generally speaking, the most effective teams have five to nine members. Experts suggest using the smallest number of people who can do the task. Unfortunately, managers often err by making teams too large. It may require

Career OBjectives

Is it wrong that I'd rather have guys on my team?

Please don't call me sexist; women are great colleagues and equally effective managers, but I'd rather have men on my team. It's more relaxing for me, and for the other guys I think, because we naturally understand each other and can talk freely. The teams with all men that I've been in have all been very productive.

—Jiten

Dear Jiten,

With all the talk currently focused on gender diversity in organizations, your viewpoint is refreshingly honest. And your preferences are not uncommon. Researchers who studied 8 years of employee surveys from a large U.S. organization found that individuals were happier on teams mainly of their own gender, whereas those on diverse teams reported less happiness, trust, and cooperation. Researcher Sara Fisher Ellison noted, "People are more comfortable around other people who are like them."

In some ways, the preference for our own gender in teams is an ugly truth. After all, if there hadn't been gender diversity initiatives and protections, a majority of professional positions may still be closed to women in masculine cultures like Japan, Austria, and Venezuela (see Hofstede's cultural values in Chapter 5). The value system in many countries has fortunately changed, with increased recognition of team diversity's potential for higher morale, trust, and satisfaction. Notice that these are *values* as opposed to the reported *reality* from the paragraph above. Ellison concluded that there is a "mismatch between the kind of workplace people think they would like and the actual workplace that would make them happier."

Don't think this is your ticket to male-only teams, though. Happiness aside, this study found that diverse teams realized significantly greater revenues, productivity, and performance. Other research in Spain indicated that gender-diverse teams realize novel solutions and radical innovation at a greater rate. Still other research suggested that gender-diverse teams perform better than male-dominated ones in sales and profits. The contextual climate is key, however. One meta-analysis found that gender equality and collectivism were important conditions for task performance in diverse teams, a Danish study indicated that diverse top management teams realized higher financial performance only when the structure supported cross-functional team work, and a study in South Korea indicated that cooperative group norms can lower the negative effects of gender diversity.

What all this means for you is that, while you may naturally prefer to work with men, it's not good for business. You would be better off putting your efforts into creating an egalitarian atmosphere and choosing your teammates based on what they can contribute to your team.

Sources: Based on C. Diaz-Garcia, A. Gonzalez-Moreno, and F. Jose Saez-Martinez, "Gender Diversity within R&D Teams: Its Impact on Radicalness of Innovation," *Innovation-Management Policy & Practice* 15, no. 2 (2013): 149–60; S. Hoogedoorn, H. Oosterbeek, and M. van Praag, "The Impact of Gender Diversity on the Performance of Business Teams: Evidence from a Field Experiment," *Management Science* 59, no. 7 (2013): 1514–28; N. Opstrup and A. R. Villadsen, "The Right Mix? Gender Diversity in Top Management Teams and Financial Performance," *Public Administration Review* (2015): 291–301; M. Schneid, R. Isidor, C. Li, et al., "The Influence of Cultural Context on the Relationship between Gender Diversity and Team Performance: A Meta-Analysis," *International Journal of Human Resource Management* 26, no. 6 (2015): 733–56; J. Y. Seong and D.-S. Hong, "Gender Diversity: How Can We Facilitate Its Positive Effects on Teams?" *Social Behavior and Personality* 41, no. 3 (2013): 497–508; and R. E. Silverman, "Do Men and Women Like Working Together?," *The Wall Street Journal*, December 16, 2014, D2.

The opinions provided here are of the managers and authors only and do not necessarily reflect those of their organizations. The authors or managers are not responsible for any errors or omissions, or for the results obtained from the use of this information. In no event will the authors or managers, or their related partnerships or corporations thereof, be liable to you or anyone else for any decision made or action taken in reliance on the opinions provided here.

only four or five members to develop an array of views and skills, and coordination problems can increase as team members are added. When teams have excess members, cohesiveness and mutual accountability decline, social loafing increases, and people communicate less. Members of large teams have trouble coordinating with one another, especially under time pressure. When a natural working unit is larger and you want a team effort, consider breaking the group into subteams.[68]

A Japanese nurse (left) served on a seven-member medical team formed by the International Committee of the Red Cross and deployed to the Philippines after a typhoon hit Mindanoa Island. The small team of health care workers had the capacity to respond quickly and effectively in providing patients with emergency medical care.
Source: KYDPL KYODO/AP Images

Member Preferences Not every employee is a team player. Given the option, many employees will select themselves *out* of team participation. When people who prefer to work alone are required to team up, there is a direct threat to the team's morale and to individual member satisfaction.[69] This suggests that, when selecting team members, managers should consider individual preferences along with abilities, personalities, and skills. High-performing teams are likely to be composed of people who prefer working as part of a group.

Team Processes

The final category related to team effectiveness includes process variables such as member commitment to a common purpose, establishment of specific team goals, team efficacy, team identity, team cohesion, mental models, a managed level of conflict, and minimized social loafing. These variables are especially important in larger teams and in teams that are highly interdependent.[70]

Why are processes important to team effectiveness? Teams should create outputs greater than the sum of their inputs. Exhibit 10-5 illustrates how group processes can have an impact on a group's actual effectiveness.[71] Teams are often used in research laboratories because they can draw on the diverse skills of various individuals to produce more meaningful research than researchers working independently—that is, they produce positive synergy, and their process gains exceed their process losses.

Exhibit 10-5 **Effects of Group Processes**

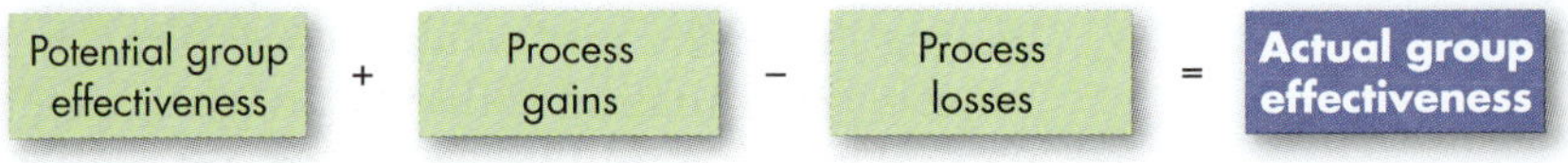

Common Plan and Purpose Effective teams begin by analyzing the team's mission, developing goals to achieve that mission, and creating strategies for achieving the goals. Teams that consistently perform better have a clear sense of what needs to be done and how.[72] This sounds obvious, but many teams ignore this fundamental process.

Members of successful teams put a tremendous amount of time and effort into discussing, shaping, and sharing a purpose that belongs to them collectively and individually. This common purpose, when accepted by the team, becomes what GPS is to a ship captain: It provides direction and guidance under any conditions. Like a ship following the wrong course, teams that don't have good planning skills are doomed, executing the wrong plan.[73] Teams should agree on whether their purpose is to learn about and master a task or simply to perform the task; evidence suggests that differing perspectives on learning versus performance lead to lower levels of team performance overall. Teams that emphasize learning are also more likely to agree on common goals, and identification with a team is also easier when members strongly identify with the team.[74]

reflexivity A team characteristic of reflecting on and adjusting the master plan when necessary.

Effective teams show **reflexivity**, meaning they reflect on and adjust their purpose when necessary. A team must have a good plan, but team members need to be willing and able to adapt when conditions call for it.[75] Reflexivity is especially important for teams that have had poor performance in the past.[76] Some evidence suggests that teams high in reflexivity are better able to adapt to conflicting plans and goals among team members.[77]

Motivation Successful teams translate their common purpose into specific, measurable, and difficult (yet realistic) performance goals that align with team objectives. Specific goals facilitate clear communication. They help teams maintain their focus on getting results.

Consistent with the research on individual goals, team goals should be challenging. Difficult but achievable goals raise team performance on those criteria for which they're set. For instance, goals for quantity tend to increase quantity, goals for accuracy increase accuracy, and so on.[78] Furthermore, motivational factors beyond goals matter. For instance, beyond goal setting, the actual experience of striving toward a goal involves wins, setbacks, and conservation of energy. Teams that are geared toward achievement tend to perform better over time.[79] Furthermore, teams that are strategic in how they allocate their resources and energy tend to perform better. For example, one study of five U.S. National Hockey League (NHL) seasons suggest that the teams' strategy in when they bench their most valuable players predicts their end-of-season record.[80]

team efficacy A team's collective belief that they can succeed at their tasks.

Team Efficacy Effective teams have confidence in themselves; they believe they can succeed. We call this **team efficacy**.[81] Teams that have been successful raise their beliefs about future success, which in turn motivates them to work harder. In addition, teams that have a shared knowledge of individual capabilities can strengthen the link between team members' self-efficacy and their individual creativity because members can solicit informed opinions from their teammates more effectively.[82]

What can management do to increase team efficacy? Two options are helping the team achieve small successes that build confidence and providing training to improve members' technical and interpersonal skills. The greater the abilities of team members, the more likely the team will develop confidence and the ability to deliver on that confidence.

Team Identity In Chapter 9, we discussed the important role of social identity in people's lives. When people connect emotionally with the groups they're in, they are more likely to invest in their relationship with those groups. It's the same with teams.[83] For example, research with soldiers in the Netherlands indicated that individuals who felt included and respected by team members became more willing to work hard for their teams, even though as soldiers they were already called upon to be dedicated to their units. Similarly, when team identity is strong, team members who are highly motivated by performance goals are more likely to direct their efforts toward team goals rather than individual goals. Therefore, by recognizing individuals' specific skills and abilities, as well as creating a climate of respect and inclusion, leaders and members can foster positive **team identity** and improved team outcomes.[84] Managers should pay special attention to fostering team identity in virtual teams. Team identity may be lower in virtual teams, which can lead to lower effort on the part of virtual team members.[85]

team identity A team member's affinity for and sense of belongingness to their team.

Organizational identity is important, too. Rarely do teams operate in a vacuum—more often teams interact with other teams, requiring interteam coordination. Individuals with a positive team identity but without a positive organizational identity can become fixed to their teams and unwilling to coordinate with other teams within the organization.[86]

Team Cohesion Have you ever been a member of a team that really gelled, one in which team members felt connected? The term **team cohesion** describes a situation in which members are emotionally attached to one another and motivated toward the team because of their attachment. Team cohesion is a useful tool to predict team outcomes. For example, a large study in China recently indicated that if team cohesion is high and tasks are complex, costly investments in promotions, rewards, training, and so forth, yield greater profitable team creativity. Teams with low cohesion and simple tasks, on the other hand, are not likely to respond to incentives with greater creativity.[87]

team cohesion A situation when team members are emotionally attached to one another and motivated toward the team because of their attachment.

Team cohesion is a strong predictor of team performance such that when cohesion is harmed, performance may be, too. Negative relationships are one driver of reduced cohesion. To mitigate this effect, teams can foster high levels of interdependence and high-quality interpersonal interactions. Team cohesion is higher in teams with female team leaders when teams are larger and more functionally diverse. Team cohesion is also higher in teams with shared leadership and when leaders are fair.[88]

Mental Models The members of an effective team share accurate **mental models**—organized mental representations of the key elements within a team's environment that team members share.[89] (Team mission and goals pertain to *what* a team needs to be effective; mental models pertain to *how* a team does its work.) If team members have the wrong mental models, which is particularly likely in teams under acute stress, their performance suffers.[90] One review of 65 independent studies found that teams with shared mental models engaged in more frequent interactions with one another, were more motivated, had more positive attitudes toward their work, and had higher levels of objectively rated performance.[91] If team members have different ideas about how to do things, however, the team will fight over methods rather than focus on what needs to be done.[92] Teams should also develop *transactive memory systems*, which represent a shared model of information relevant to the team. For example, these types of teams enable team members to know "who knows what and is

mental model Team members' knowledge and beliefs about how the work gets done by the team.

best at what" so that the most-skilled members are assigned tasks they are best suited for and the most knowledgeable are consulted for advice on issues they are experts in.[93] Transactive memory systems are important for performance, especially in collectivist and high-power distance cultures and in environments that are particularly volatile (e.g., times of crisis).[94]

Individuals who normally function in *action teams*—teams with specialists engaged in intense, interdependent, and unpredictable tasks—are likely to share mental models. Even though they are often under acute stress, their performance levels can be high because the stress has been normalized through the expected context. These action teams have learned that the best way to share mental models is to voice them. An anesthetic team in a hospital is one example of an action team with shared mental models. For example, research in Switzerland found that anesthetic teams communicated two distinct types of messages while in an operation: vocally monitoring each others' performance (not to criticize but to keep a vocal record of events), and "talking to the room" (announcements to everyone such as "Patient's blood pressure is dropping"). The study found that high- and low-performing teams communicated in these ways equally often; what mattered to performance was the sequencing of the communication to maintain a shared mental model. High-performing teams followed up monitoring dialogue with assistance and instructions, and talking-to-the-room dialogue with further team dialogue.[95] The message seems simple: To maintain shared mental models, share conversation about what is happening while the team is in operation!

Conflict Levels Conflict has a complex relationship with team performance, and it's not necessarily bad. *Relationship conflicts*—those based on interpersonal incompatibility, tension, and animosity toward others—are almost always dysfunctional. However, when teams are performing nonroutine activities, disagreements about task content—called *task conflicts*—stimulate discussion, promote critical assessment of problems and options, and can lead to better team decisions, though it may not lead to more innovative products. The positive (and negative) effects of conflict on performance may be smaller or larger depending on many factors, such as the task type, setting, and how performance is measured.[96] Task conflict is beneficial when members are open to experience and emotionally stable.[97] Task conflict may also be beneficial when some team members perceive high task conflict while other team members perceive low task conflict.[98] According to one study conducted in China, moderate levels of task conflict during the initial phases of team performance were positively related to team creativity, but both very low and very high levels of task conflict were negatively related to team performance.[99] In other words, both too much and too little disagreement about how a team should initially perform a creative task can inhibit performance.

The way conflicts are resolved can make the difference between effective and ineffective teams. A study of ongoing comments made by 37 autonomous work groups showed that effective teams resolved conflicts by explicitly discussing the issues, whereas ineffective teams had unresolved conflicts that were focused more on personalities and the way things were said.[100]

Which teams are more likely to have conflicts than others? It's not a simple answer. While we may presume that diversity increases conflicts, the answer is likely to be much more subtle than that. For example, recent research in Spain found that when individual team members varied greatly in their perceptions of organizational support, task conflict increased, communication decreased, and ultimately team performance suffered.[101] If the researchers had instead compared only the average level of organizational support given to the team rather than how members perceived the support, they would have missed the correct causal links. A study of Chinese teams found that teams high in social capital experienced higher task conflict and lower relationship conflict, but this was only true after the group had been established for several years.[102] Thus we need to be careful not to overgeneralize.

Social Loafing As we noted earlier, individuals can engage in social loafing and coast on the group's effort when their particular contributions (or lack thereof) can't be identified. Effective teams undermine this tendency by making members individually and jointly accountable for the team's purpose, goals, and approach.[103] Therefore, members should be clear on what they are individually and jointly responsible for on the team.

Team Trust During the COVID-19 pandemic, it was clear just how important trust is to the successful operation of teams. Lindsay Kaplan, co-founder and CEO of Chief, a private network for powerful women, recounts life as a virtual manager during this time after a household emergency with her baby: "I text the marketing team that I'll likely be late to our team meeting … trust in my team is what's getting me through. I believe in hiring slowly, and it's rewarding to see our carefully curated team operate self-sufficiently."[104] Trust in teams entails a mutual, positive state of positive expectations between team members. When you trust a team member, you believe in their reliability and dependability and are genuinely concerned for their welfare (and vice versa). Trust can be broken; but it can also be repaired.[105] Team trust has been shown to have a sizeable effect on team performance, especially in virtual teams.[106] Team trust evolves over time as members share with one another, put effort into the team, and monitor one another's performance.[107]

Turning Individuals into Team Players

10-5 Explain how organizations can create team players.

We've made a case for the value and growing popularity of teams. But many people are not inherently team players, and many organizations have historically nurtured individual accomplishments. Teams often fit well in countries that score high on collectivism, but what if an organization wants to introduce teams into a work population of individuals born and raised in an individualistic society?

Here are options for managers trying to turn individuals into team players.

Selecting: Hiring Team Players

Some people already possess the interpersonal skills to be effective team players. When hiring team members, be sure candidates can fulfill their team roles as well as technical requirements.[108]

Creating teams often means resisting the urge to hire the best talent no matter what. For example, the New York Knicks professional basketball team pays Carmelo Anthony well because he scores a lot of points for his team, but statistics show he takes more shots than other highly paid players in the league, which means fewer shots for his teammates.[109]

As a final consideration, personal traits appear to make some people better candidates for working in diverse teams. Teams made of members who like to work through difficult mental puzzles also seem more effective and able to capitalize on the multiple points of view that arise from diversity in age and education.[110]

Training: Creating Team Players

Training specialists conduct exercises that allow employees to experience the satisfaction that teamwork can provide. Workshops help employees improve their problem-solving, communication, negotiation, conflict management, and coaching skills. L'Oréal, for example, found that successful sales teams required much more than a staff of high-ability salespeople. "What we didn't account for was that many members of our top team in sales had been promoted because they had excellent technical and executional skills," said L'Oréal's senior vice president David Waldock. As a result of introducing purposeful team training, Waldock says, "We are no longer a team just on paper, working independently. We have a real group dynamic now, and it's a good one."[111] An effective team doesn't develop overnight—it takes time, but good team training has positive tangible effects on performance regardless of employee and training characteristics, as evidenced by a recent review of 112 studies of medical team training programs.[112]

Rewarding: Providing Incentives to Be a Good Team Player

A traditional organization's reward system must be reworked to encourage cooperative efforts rather than competitive ones.[113] Hallmark Cards Inc. added to its basic individual incentive system an annual bonus based on the achievement of team goals. Whole Foods directs most of its performance-based rewards toward team performance. As a result, teams select new members carefully so they will contribute to team effectiveness (and thus team bonuses).[114] It is usually best to set a cooperative tone as soon as possible in the life of a team. As we already noted, teams that switch from competitive to cooperative do not immediately share information, and they still tend to make rushed, poor-quality decisions.[115] Apparently, the low trust typical of the competitive group will not be readily replaced by high trust with a quick change in reward systems.

Promotions, pay raises, and other forms of recognition should be given to individuals who work effectively as team members by training new colleagues, sharing information, helping resolve team conflicts, and mastering needed new skills. This doesn't mean individual contributions should be ignored; rather, they should be balanced with selfless contributions to the team.

Finally, don't forget the intrinsic rewards, such as camaraderie, that employees can receive from teamwork. It's exciting to be part of a successful team. The opportunity for personal development of oneself and teammates can be a very satisfying and rewarding experience.

Beware! Teams Aren't Always the Answer

10-6 Decide when to use individuals instead of teams.

Teamwork takes more time and often more resources than individual work. Teams have increased communication demands, conflicts to manage, and meetings to run. So the benefits of using teams have to exceed the costs, and that's not always possible.[116]

How do you know whether the work of your group would be better done in teams? You can apply three tests.[117] First, can the work be done better by

New engineering employees of India's Tata Consultancy Services (TCS) work in teams to construct paper boats during a team-building exercise at the firm's training center. Creating team players is essential to the success of TCS because employees must collaborate and work cohesively in providing information technology (IT) consulting services and business solutions for global clients.
Source: Namas Bhojani/Bloomberg/Getty Images

more than one person? Good indicators are the complexity of the work and the need for different perspectives. Simple tasks that don't require diverse input are probably better left to individuals. Second, does the work create a common purpose or set of goals for the people in the group that is more than the aggregate of individual goals? Many service departments of new-vehicle dealers have introduced teams that link customer service people, mechanics, parts specialists, and sales representatives. Such teams can better manage collective responsibility for ensuring that customer needs are properly met.

The final test is to determine whether the members of the group are interdependent. Using teams makes sense when there is interdependence among tasks—the success of the whole depends on the success of each one, *and* the success of each one depends on the success of the others. Soccer, for instance, is an obvious *team* sport. Success requires a great deal of coordination among interdependent players. Conversely, swim teams (except possibly for relays) are not really teams. They are groups of individuals performing individually and whose total performance is merely the aggregate summation of their individual performances.

Summary

Few trends have influenced jobs as much as the massive movement of teams into the workplace. Working on teams requires employees to cooperate with others, share information, confront differences, and sublimate personal interests for the greater good of the team. Understanding the distinctions between problem-solving, self-managed, cross-functional, and virtual teams as well as multiteam systems helps determine the appropriate applications for team-based work. Concepts such as reflexivity, team efficacy, team identity, team cohesion, and mental models bring to light important issues relating to team context, composition, and processes. For teams to function optimally, careful attention must be given to hiring, creating, and rewarding team players. Still, effective organizations recognize that teams are not always the best method for getting the work done efficiently. Careful discernment and an understanding of organizational behavior are needed.

Implications for Managers

- Effective teams have adequate resources, effective leadership, a climate of trust, and a performance evaluation and reward system that reflects team contributions. These teams have individuals with technical expertise and the right traits and skills.
- Effective teams tend to be small. They have members who fill role demands and who prefer to be part of a group.
- Effective teams have members who believe in the team's capabilities, are committed to a common plan and purpose, and have an accurate shared mental model of what is to be accomplished.
- Select individuals who have the interpersonal skills to be effective team players, provide training to develop teamwork skills, and reward individuals for cooperative efforts.
- Do not assume that teams are always needed. When tasks will not benefit from interdependency, individuals may be the better choice.

To Get the Most Out of Teams, Empower Them

POINT

If you want high-performing teams with members who like each other and their jobs, here's a simple solution: Remove the leash tied to them by management and let them make their own decisions. In other words, empower them. This trend started a long time ago, when organizations realized that creating layers of bureaucracy thwarts innovation, slows progress to a trickle, and merely provides hoops for people to jump through in order to get anything done.

You can empower teams in two ways. One way is structurally, by transferring decision making from managers to team members and giving teams the official power to develop their own strategies. The other way is psychologically, by enhancing team members' beliefs that they have more authority, even though legitimate authority still rests with the organization's leaders. Structural empowerment leads to heightened feelings of psychological empowerment, giving teams (and organizations) the best of both worlds.

Research suggests that empowered teams benefit in a number of ways. Members are more motivated. They exhibit higher levels of commitment to the team and the organization. And they perform much better. Empowerment sends a signal to the team that it is trusted and doesn't have to be constantly micromanaged by upper leadership. And when teams get the freedom to make their own choices, they accept more responsibility for and take ownership of both the good and the bad.

Granted, responsibility also means that empowered teams must take the initiative to foster their ongoing learning and development, but teams entrusted with the authority to guide their own destiny do just that. So do yourself (and your company) a favor and make sure that teams, rather than needless layers of middle managers, are the ones making the decisions that count.

COUNTERPOINT

Empowerment can do some good in certain circumstances, but it's certainly not a cure-all.

Yes, organizations have become flatter over the past several decades, paving the way for decision-making authority to seep into lower levels of the organization. But consider that many teams are "empowered" simply because the management ranks have been so thinned that there is no one left to make the key calls. Empowerment is then just an excuse to ask teams to take on more responsibility without an accompanying increase in tangible benefits like pay.

In addition, the organization's leadership already has a good idea of what it would like its teams (and individual employees) to accomplish. If managers leave teams to their own devices, how likely is it that those teams will always choose what the manager wanted? Even if the manager offers suggestions about how the team might proceed, empowered teams can easily ignore that advice. Instead, they need direction on what goals to pursue and how to pursue them. That's what effective leadership is all about.

When decision-making authority is distributed among team members, each member's role is less clear, and members lack a leader to whom they can go for advice. And finally, when teams are self-managed, they become like silos, disconnected from the rest of the organization and its mission. Simply handing people authority is no guarantee they will use it effectively. So leave the power to make decisions in the hands of those who were assigned leadership roles. After all, they became leaders for a reason, and they can best guide the team to stay focused and perform at top levels to maximize organizational outcomes.

Sources: Based on S. I. Tannenbaum, J. Mathieu, E. Salas, and D. Cohen, "Teams Are Changing: Are Research and Practice Evolving Fast Enough?" *Industrial and Organizational Psychology* 5 (2012): 2–24; and R. Ashkenas, "How to Empower Your Team for Non-Negotiable Results," *Forbes*, April 24, 2013, downloaded June 10, 2013, from www.forbes.com.

CHAPTER REVIEW

QUESTIONS FOR REVIEW

10-1 How do you explain the growing popularity of teams in organizations?

10-2 What is the difference between a group and a team?

10-3 What are the five types of team arrangements?

10-4 What conditions or context factors determine whether teams are effective?

10-5 How can organizations create team players?

10-6 When is work performed by individuals preferred over work performed by teams?

APPLICATION AND EMPLOYABILITY

Teamwork is a pivotal part of the modern workplace. Unlike work groups, teams are meant to create a level of performance greater than the sum of individual efforts. In this chapter, you learned some of the reasons a team may be successful or unsuccessful in meeting this goal, based on the team's context, composition, and various processes the team goes through. A strong understanding of how to build a strong team and be a strong team member can help you perform better in any team environment, from virtual to cross-functional teams and beyond. In this chapter, you improved your collaboration skills and social responsibility by learning to understanding the value of working with members of both genders and how to communicate with team members in an eco-conscious way. You also applied your knowledge and utilized critical thinking skills by taking a second look at the hot hand phenomena as well as assessing the merits and drawbacks of empowerment. In the following chapter, you will further develop these skills, along with communication skills, as you decide whether or not to hire a "star" employee, figure out how to structure teams after a merger, try to build trust on virtual teams, and learn about what makes a team smart.

EXPERIENTIAL EXERCISE How to Resolve Social Loafing in Your Team?

Assume that you have been recently appointed as team leader in the research and development unit of an important pharmaceutical company. The team you are heading has been stuck for several months in the development of a new drug due to some delay in the clinical trial process. The deadline set by the managing director of the company is approaching. After a few weeks, you noticed social loafing in the team as some members systematically put less effort in the development of the new drug, blaming the delay in the trial process as solely responsible for this situation and never taking the initiative to resolve the impasse with creative solutions. The top performers of your team have privately complained to you about this situation, which is causing significant stress due to overload. They are even threatening to leave the company. You must decide how to manage this critical situation: should you report the cases of social loafing for possible disciplinary measures or seek to resolve the situation yourself?

10-7. What could be the reasons behind such attitudes from some team members? How could this issue be resolved?

10-8. What would you change, if at all, about the way the team functions to ensure more active participation of all team members? Why?

10-9. As a recently appointed head of the team, what will be the most appropriate solution in this case, trying to resolve this situation yourself or reporting the case to general direction for possible disciplinary measures? Examine the pros and cons of each alternative individually and then discuss your analysis within your team to find a common solution.

ETHICAL DILEMMA When Your Cycling Skills Matter!

Within the foodtech industry landscape, new ordering and delivering platforms, marketplaces, and channels have recently been introduced. Of particular interest are the case of Deliveroo and Uber Eats and the business model they follow. In the UK marketplace, food delivery is a big market that is growing rapidly. Most restaurants and takeaways have their in-house delivery service, but they will not always cater to all areas within a given city. Restaurants or takeaways that do not have an in-house delivery service may be at a severe disadvantage against the competition. Deliveroo and Uber Eats offer a solution by providing delivery services for all restaurants and takeaways that subscribe to their services, thanks to the delivery radius and wide coverage enabled by their cyclists. These cyclists are easy riders who can deliver food orders to most locations within a city. However, considering how new all of this is to the economy, how do teamwork and performance figure in the new model?

To begin with, the model is a rather self-managed set-up. Riders are classed as self-employed contractors who are not entitled to protections granted to employees and "workers." They are not entitled to collective bargaining rights. Nevertheless, they are part of a team and of the broader company's group. They are paid a flat rate per order they deliver without any time restriction, which means that they can work flexible hours (with the bonus of keeping their bodies physically fit!). Therefore, the ones who accomplish the most deliveries will get a good day's earnings. There are issues, of course: one is if the deliveries are great distances from each other, and another is the weather, which can slow down deliveries and thus restrict the earnings of the day for individual cyclists.

Supervision over self-management and self-sustained contractors can be challenging with regard to overall group performance, but the way the reward system works could act as a further positive reinforcement for better performance individually and, therefore, as an entity of a particular group setting. But perhaps the most interesting aspect here is the matter of trust in the working relationships between the cyclists and their supervisor—how these are built and sustained is the big question. Complicating this setup further is the fact that there are no physical supervisors delegating tasks to the riders; a algorithm calculates variables such as distance, time, etc., possibly diluting team spirit.

In contrast to the model above, other companies, such as Marks & Spencer and Moneypenny (the United Kingdom's leading telephone company), pride themselves on their team-driven incentives and team-bonding activities. Yet all these companies perform very well in their individual industries despite their different reward system models and activities. Thus, the question of whether it is better to praise individual work or group work, for which performance and under which circumstances, still offers food for thought.

Questions

10-10. Would you consider the Deliveroo and Uber Eats model a work-group or a work-team environment? Justify your answer based on the characteristics of groups and teams.

10-11. What type of group or team are cyclists working for a supervisor for Deliveroo? Justify your answer.

10-12. In the cases discussed above, where do you think you would perform better, and why? Justify your answer by taking into account efficiency factors, reward systems, the context, and your individual perceptions.

Sources: Anna Tims, "Gig Economy Ruling Has Deliveroo Riders without Rights and Buying Their Own Kit," *The Guardian*, November 21, 2017, https://www.theguardian.com/business/2017/nov/19/gig-economy-ruling-deliveroo-riders-equipment-basic-employment-rights; Tim Wallace, "Deliveroo Offers Workers Pay per Trip in Bid to Defuse Self Employment Row," *The Telegraph*, June 1, 2017, http://www.telegraph.co.uk/business/2017/05/31/deliveroo-offers-workers-pay-per-trip-bid-defuse-self-employment/; "M&S in £10m Team Building Dance Exercise," *The Telegraph*, December 20, 2017, http://www.telegraph.co.uk/news/1499954/MandS-in-10m-team-building-dance-exercise.html; The Business of Tech, "Deliveroo," May 8, 2016, https://thebusinessoftech.wordpress.com/2016/05/08/deliveroo/; RideSharingDriver, "Driving for UberEats: What It's Like Delivering Food for Uber," March 29, 2016, https://www.ridesharingdriver.com/driving-for-ubereats-what-its-like-delivering-food-for-uber/; MoneyPenny, "Moneypenny HQ Named Best Corporate Workplace at BCO Awards," April 11, 2017, https://www.moneypenny.com/uk/news/moneypenny-hq-named-best-corporate-workplace/.

CASE INCIDENT 1 Trusting Someone You Can't See

One of the greatest determinants of a successful team is trust. For a team to be successful, employees must trust that their team members are reliable and capable. They have to have faith that their teammates will work toward the goals of the team rather than their own goals. Trust can be built in teams by creating an environment where team members are not scared to admit that they have made a mistake and feel comfortable providing their input rather than agreeing with the team leader or assertive team members. Building trust among teammates is important, but what if you never see your teammates?

Trust is especially important but also more difficult to build in virtual teams. In a recent review of 52 independent studies, researchers found that the link between trust and team performance is stronger for virtual teams than face-to-face teams! According to the same review, managers can counteract some of the negative effects of low trust in virtual teams by carefully documenting team interactions. This practice shows that team members are held accountable for the work they do in virtual teams and makes sure that team members are recognized for their contributions.

Compensating for a lack of trust may only be a Band-Aid for a larger problem because trust is one of the most important factors in determining team effectiveness. Another review of 112 separate studies found that trust was one of the strongest predictors of team performance, regardless of the team members' past performance or trust in the team's manager. The same researchers found that trust may be especially important in teams with varied skill sets or interdependent roles. Trust is also just as important for short-term teams because team members do not have the same adjustment period to learn more about their teammates before having faith that they will contribute to team goals.

Questions

10-13. Recall a time when you felt like you could not trust members on your team. Why did you feel that way? How did that affect the team's performance?

10-14. Can you think of strategies that can help build trust among virtual team members?

10-15. Imagine you are a manager at a national corporation. You have been asked to select employees for a virtual problem-solving team. What types of employees would you include and why?

Sources: Based on W. Vanderbloemen, "Is Your Staff a High-Trust Team?," Entrepreneurs, March 21, 2017, https://www.forbes.com/sites/williamvanderbloemen/2017/03/21/is-your-staff-a-high-trust-team/#2997197230cd, accessed April 9, 2016; D. B. Nast, "Trust and Virtual Teams," The Huffington Post, March 28, 2017, http://www.huffingtonpost.com/entry/trust-and-virtual-teams_us_58da7e2be4b0e96354656eb5, accessed April 9, 2017; L. L. Gilson, M. T. Maynard, N. C. J. Young, M. Vartiainen, and M. Hakonen, "Virtual Teams Research: 10 Years, 10 Themes, and 10 Opportunities," Journal of Management 41, no. 4 (2015): 1313–37; and B. A. De Jong, K. T. Dirks, and N. Gillespie, "Trust and Team Performance: A Meta-Analysis of Main Effects, Moderators, and Covariates," Journal of Applied Psychology 101, no. 8 (2016): 1134–50.

CASE INCIDENT 2 Smart Teams and Dumb Teams

In this chapter, we've identified how some of the characteristics we use to describe individuals can also describe teams. For example, individuals can be high in the trait of openness, as can a team. Along the same lines, have you noticed that some teams seem to be smart, while others seem, um, dumb? This characteristic has nothing to do with the average IQ of the team members but instead reflects the functionality of the whole team. Teams that are synergistic excel in logical analysis, brainstorming, coordination, planning, and moral reasoning. And teams that are dumb? Think of long unproductive meetings, social loafing, and interpersonal conflicts.

You might be remembering a few teams you've witnessed that are in the dumb category, but we hope you can think of a few that excelled. Smart teams tend to be smart in everything—for any task, they will find a workable solution. But what makes them smart? Researchers in a Massachusetts Institute of Technology (MIT) study grouped 697 subjects into teams of 2 to 5 members to solve tasks, looking for the characteristics of smart teams (they weren't all smart). Here are the findings:

1. **Smart teams did not allow individual members to dominate.** Instead, there were more equal

contributions from members than in other teams.

2. **Smart teams had more members who were able to read minds.** Just kidding! But the members were able to read complicated emotions by looking into the eyes of others. There is a test for this ability called Reading the Mind in the Eyes.
3. **Smart teams had more women.** It's not that smart teams had more gender equality; these teams simply had more women. This result might be partly due to the fact that more women scored higher in the Reading the Mind in the Eyes test.

The researchers recently replicated the study using 68 teams and again found that some teams were smarter than others. This study added a new angle to the research: How would teams working in person differ from teams working online? Surprisingly, there was little difference: All smart teams had more equal member communication (and plenty of it) and were good at emotion reading. When the online collaborators could not see each other, they practiced theory of mind, remembering and reacting to the emotional cues they were able to detect through any mode of communication. Theory of mind is related to emotional intelligence (EI), which we discussed in Chapter 4.

When we have the opportunity to hand-pick team members, we can look for those who listen as much as they speak, express empathy, and remember what others tell them about themselves. For teams to which we are assigned, we can seek these attributes in others and help guide the team toward its best self. As for IQ? Here's the good news: Recent research indicates that our membership in a team actually makes us smarter decision makers as individuals!

Questions

10-16. From your experiences in teams, do you agree with the researchers' findings on the characteristics of smart teams? Why or why not?

10-17. On the highly functioning teams in which you've been a member, what other characteristics might have contributed to success?

10-18. The authors who suggested that membership in a team makes us smarter found that teams were more rational and quicker at finding solutions to difficult probability problems and reasoning tasks than were individuals. After participation in the study, team members were much better at decision making on their own, even up to 5 weeks later. Do you think this spillover effect would happen equally for people in smart teams and dumb teams? Why or why not?

Sources: Based on E. E. F. Bradford, I. Jentzsch, and J.-C. Gomez, "From Self to Cognition: Theory of Mind Mechanisms and Their Relation to Executive Functioning," Cognition 138 (2015): 21–34; B. Maciejovsky, M. Sutter, D. V. Budescu, et al., "Teams Make You Smarter: How Exposure to Teams Improves Individual Decisions in Probability and Reasoning Tasks," Management Science 59, no. 6 (2013): 1255–70; and A. Woolley, T. W. Malone, and C. Chabris, "Why Some Teams Are Smarter Than Others," The New York Times, January 18, 2015, 5.

ENDNOTES

[1] Kashyap, K. (2019). "How India Philip Morris offers a cross-functional training to its employees". *HRKatha (November 29, 2019).* Retrieved from https://www.hrkatha.com (Accessed on April 21, 2022).

[2] R. Karlgaard, "Think (Really!) Small," *Forbes,* April 13, 2015, 32.

[3] J. C. Gorman, "Team Coordination and Dynamics: Two Central Issues," *Current Directions in Psychological Science* 23, no. 5 (2014): 355–60.

[4] Ibid.

[5] D. Chan, "Team-Level Constructs," *Annual Review of Organizational Psychology and Organizational Behavior* 6 (2019): 325–48; J. E. Mathieu, P. T. Gallagher, M. A. Domingo, and E. A. Klock, "Embracing Complexity: Reviewing the Past Decade of Team Effectiveness Research," *Annual Review of Organizational Psychology and Organizational Behavior* 6 (2019): 17–46.

[6] A. C. Edmondson, *Teaming: How Organizations Learn, Innovate, and Compete in the Knowledge Economy* (San Francisco, CA: Wiley, 2012); A. C. Edmondson, "The Three Pillars of a Teaming Culture," *Harvard Business Review,* December 17, 2013, https://hbr.org/2013/12/the-three-pillars-of-a-teaming-culture; K. Einola and M. Alvesson, "The Making and Unmaking of Teams," *Human Relations* 72, no. 12 (2019): 1891–919; Mathieu et al., "Embracing Complexity."

[7] J. Mathieu, M. T. Maynard, T. Rapp, and L. Gilson, "Team Effectiveness 1997–2007: A Review of Recent Advancements and a Glimpse into the Future," *Journal of Management* 34, no. 3 (2008): 410–76.

[8] See, for example, A. Erez, J. A. LePine, and H. Elms, "Effects of Rotated Leadership and Peer Evaluation on the Functioning and Effectiveness of Self-Managed Teams: A Quasi-Experiment," *Personnel Psychology* (Winter 2002): 929–48.

[9] A. Nederveen Pieterse, J. R. Hollenbeck, D. van Knippenberg, M. Spitzmüller, N. Dimotakis, E. P. Karam, and D. J. Sleesman, "Hierarchical Leadership versus Self-Management in Teams: Goal Orientation Diversity as Moderator of Their Relative Effectiveness," *The Leadership Quarterly* (in press).

[10] G. L. Stewart, S. H. Courtright, and M. R. Barrick, "Peer-Based Control in Self-Managing Teams: Linking Rational and Normative Influence with Individual and Group Performance," *Journal of Applied Psychology* 97, no. 2 (2012): 435–47.

[11] C. W. Langfred, "The Downside of Self-Management: A Longitudinal Study of the Effects of Conflict on Trust, Autonomy, and Task Interdependence in Self-Managing Teams," *Academy of Management Journal* 50, no. 4 (2007): 885–900; and J. S. Bunderson and P. Boumgarden, "Structure and Learning in Self-Managed Teams: Why 'Bureaucratic' Teams Can Be Better Learners," *Organization Science* 21 no. 3 (2010): 609–24.
[12] B. H. Bradley, B. E. Postlethwaite, A. C. Klotz, M. R. Hamdani, and K. G. Brown, "Reaping the Benefits of Task Conflict in Teams: The Critical Role of Team Psychological Safety Climate," *Journal of Applied Psycholog* 97, no. 1 (2012): 151–58.
[13] J. Devaro, "The Effects of Self-Managed and Closely Managed Teams on Labor Productivity and Product Quality: An Empirical Analysis of a Cross-Section of Establishments," *Industrial Relations* 47, no. 4 (2008): 659–98.
[14] A. Shah, "Starbucks Strives for Instant Gratification with Via Launch," *PRWeek* (December 2009): 15.
[15] F. Aime, S. Humphrey, D. S. DeRue, and J. B. Paul, "The Riddle of Heterarchy: Power Transitions in Cross-Functional Teams," *Academy of Management Journal* 57, no. 2 (2014): 327–52.
[16] B. Freyer and T. A. Stewart, "Cisco Sees the Future," *Harvard Business Review* (November 2008): 73–79.
[17] See, for example, L. L. Martins, L. L. Gilson, and M. T. Maynard, "Virtual Teams: What Do We Know and Where Do We Go from Here?," *Journal of Management* (November 2004): 805–35; and B. Leonard, "Managing Virtual Teams," *HRMagazine*, June 2011, 39–42.
[18] J. Eisenberg and N. DiTomaso, "Structural Decisions about Configuration, Assignments, and Geographical Distribution in Teams: Influences on Team Communications and Trust," *Human Resource Management Review* (in press); M. G. Moore, "Theory of Transactional Distance" in D. Keegan (ed.), *Theoretical Principles of Distance Education* (New York: Routledge, 1993).
[19] J. E. Hoch and S. W. J. Kozlowski, "Leading Virtual Teams: Hierarchical Leadership, Structural Supports, and Shared Team Leadership," *Journal of Applied Psychology* 99, no. 3 (2014): 390–403.
[20] A. Malhotra, A. Majchrzak, and B. Rosen, "Leading Virtual Teams," *Academy of Management Perspectives* (February 2007): 60–70; J. M. Wilson, S. S. Straus, and B. McEvily, "All in Due Time: The Development of Trust in Computer-Mediated and Face-to-Face Teams," *Organizational Behavior and Human Decision Processes* 19 (2006): 16–33; and C. Breuer, J. Hüffmeier, and G. Hertel, "Does Trust Matter More in Virtual Teams? A Meta-Analysis of Trust and Team Effectiveness Considering Virtuality and Documentation as Moderators," *Journal of Applied Psychology* 101 no. 8 (2016): 1151–77.
[21] P. Balkundi and D. A. Harrison, "Ties, Leaders, and Time in Teams: Strong Inference about Network Structure's Effects on Team Viability and Performance," *Academy of Management Journal* 49, no. 1 (2006): 49–68; G. Chen, B. L. Kirkman, R. Kanfer, D. Allen, and B. Rosen, "A Multilevel Study of Leadership, Empowerment, and Performance in Teams," *Journal of Applied Psychology* 92, no. 2 (2007): 331–46; L. A. DeChurch and M. A. Marks, "Leadership in Multiteam Systems," *Journal of Applied Psychology* 91, no. 2 (2006): 311–29; A. Srivastava, K. M. Bartol, and E. A. Locke, "Empowering Leadership in Management Teams: Effects on Knowledge Sharing, Efficacy, and Performance," *Academy of Management Journal* 49, no. 6 (2006): 1239–51; and J. E. Mathieu, K. K. Gilson, and T. M. Ruddy, "Empowerment and Team Effectiveness: An Empirical Test of an Integrated Model," *Journal of Applied Psychology* 91, no. 1 (2006): 97–108.
[22] K. Lanaj, J. R. Hollenbeck, D. R. Ilgen, C. M. Barnes, and S. J. Harmon, "The Double-Edged Sword of Decentralized Planning in Multiteam Systems," *Academy of Management Journal* 56, no. 3 (2013): 735–57.
[23] R. B. Davison, J. R. Hollenbeck, C. M. Barnes, D. J. Sleesman, and D. R. Ilgen, "Coordinated Action in Multiteam Systems," *Journal of Applied Psychology* 97, no. 4 (2012): 808–24.
[24] D. R. Carter, K. L. Cullen-Lester, J. M. Jones, A. Gerbasi, D. Chrobot-Mason, and E. Young Nae, "Functional Leadership in Interteam Contexts: Understanding 'What' in the Context of Why? Where? When? and Who?," *The Leadership Quarterly* (in press).
[25] M. M. Luciano, J. E. Mathieu, and T. M. Ruddy, "Leading Multiple Teams: Average and Relative External Leadership Influences on Team Empowerment and Effectiveness," *Journal of Applied Psychology* 99, no. 2 (2014): 322–31.
[26] S. Krumm, J. Kanthak, K. Hartmann, and G. Hertel. "What Does It Take to Be a Virtual Team Player? The Knowledge, Skills, Abilities, and Other Characteristics Required in Virtual Teams," *Human Performance* 29, no. 2 (2016): 123–42.
[27] R. Greenwald, "Freelancing Alone—but Together," *The Wall Street Journal*, February 3, 2014, R5.
[28] V. Gonzalez-Roma and A. Hernandez, "Climate Uniformity: Its Influence on Team Communication Quality, Task Conflict, and Team Performance," *Journal of Applied Psychology* 99, no. 6 (2014): 1042–58; C. F. Peralta, P. N. Lopes, L. L. Gilson, P. R. Lourenco, and L. Pais, "Innovation Processes and Team Effectiveness: The Role of Goal Clarity and Commitment, and Team Affective Tone," *Journal of Occupational and Organizational Psychology* 88, no. 1 (2015): 80–107; L. Thompson, *Making the Team* (Upper Saddle River, NJ: Prentice Hall, 2000), 18–33; and J. R. Hackman, *Leading Teams: Setting the Stage for Great Performance* (Boston: Harvard Business School Press, 2002).
[29] See G. L. Stewart and M. R. Barrick, "Team Structure and Performance: Assessing the Mediating Role of Intrateam Process and the Moderating Role of Task Type," *Academy of Management Journal* (April 2000): 135–48.
[30] D. E. Hyatt and T. M. Ruddy, "An Examination of the Relationship between Work Group Characteristics and Performance: Once More Into the Breech," *Personnel Psychology* 50, no. 3 (1997): 553–85; and A. W. Richter, G. Hirst, G., D. van Knippenberg, and M. Baer, "Creative Self-Efficacy and Individual Creativity in Team Contexts: Cross-Level Interactions with Team Informational Resources," *Journal of Applied Psychology* 97, no. 6 (2012): 1282–90.
[31] J. Hu and Judge, "Leader-Team Complementarity: Exploring the Interactive Effects of Leader Personality Traits and Team Power Distance Values on Team Processes and Performance," *Journal of Applied Psychology* 102, no. 6 (2017): 935–55; N. Wirtz, T. Rigotti, K. Otto, and C. Loeb, "What about the Leader? Crossover of Emotional Exhaustion and Work Engagement from Followers to Leaders," *Journal of Occupational Health Psychology* 22, no. 1 (2016): 86–97; and Y. Dong, K. M. Bartol, Z. Zhang, and C. Li, "Enhancing Employee Creativity via Individual Skill Development and Team Knowledge Sharing: Influences of Dual-Focused Transformational Leadership," *Journal of Organizational Behavior* 38, no. 3 (2017): 439–58.
[32] R. J. Lount, O. J. Sheldon, F. Rink, and K. W. Phillips, "Biased Perceptions of Racially Diverse Teams and Their Consequences for Resource Support," *Organization Science* 26, no. 5 (2015): 1351–64.

[33] P. Balkundi and D. A. Harrison, "Ties, Leaders, and Time in Teams: Strong Inference about Network Structure's Effects on Team Viability and Performance," *Academy of Management Journal* 49, no. 1 (2006): 49–68; G. Chen, B. L. Kirkman, R. Kanfer, D. Allen, and B. Rosen, "A Multilevel Study of Leadership, Empowerment, and Performance in Teams," *Journal of Applied Psychology* 92, no. 2 (2007): 331–46; L. A. DeChurch and M. A. Marks, "Leadership in Multiteam Systems," *Journal of Applied Psychology* 91, no. 2 (2006): 311–29; A. Srivastava, K. M. Bartol, and E. A. Locke, "Empowering Leadership in Management Teams: Effects on Knowledge Sharing, Efficacy, and Performance," *Academy of Management Journal* 49, no. 6 (2006): 1239–51; and J. E. Mathieu, K. K. Gilson, and T. M. Ruddy, "Empowerment and Team Effectiveness: An Empirical Test of an Integrated Model," *Journal of Applied Psychology* 91, no. 1 (2006): 97–108.

[34] K. T. Dirks, "Trust in Leadership and Team Performance: Evidence from NCAA Basketball," *Journal of Applied Psychology* (December 2000): 1004–12; M. Williams, "In Whom We Trust: Group Membership as an Affective Context for Trust Development," *Academy of Management Review* (July 2001): 377–96; and J. Schaubroeck, S. S. K. Lam, and A. C. Peng, "Cognition-Based and Affect-Based Trust as Mediators of Leader Behavior Influences on Team Performance," *Journal of Applied Psychology* 96, no.4 (2011): 863–71.

[35] B. A. De Jong and K. T. Dirks, "Beyond Shared Perceptions of Trust and Monitoring in Teams: Implications of Asymmetry and Dissensus," *Journal of Applied Psychology* 97, no. 2 (2012): 391–406; and B. A. De Jong, K. T. Dirks, and N. Gillespie, "Trust and Team Performance: A Meta-Analysis of Main Effects, Moderators, and Covariates," *Journal of Applied Psychology* 101, no. 8 (2016): 1134–50.

[36] G. Brown, C. Crossley, and S. L. Robinson, "Psychological Ownership, Territorial Behavior, and Being Perceived as a Team Contributor: The Critical Role of Trust in the Work Environment," *Personnel Psychology* 67 (2014): 463–85.

[37] See F. Aime, C. J. Meyer, and S. E. Humphrey, "Legitimacy of Team Rewards: Analyzing Legitimacy as a Condition for the Effectiveness of Team Incentive Designs," *Journal of Business Research* 63, no. 1 (2010): 60–66; P. A. Bamberger and R. Levi, "Team-Based Reward Allocation Structures and the Helping Behaviors of Outcome-Interdependent Team Members," *Journal of Managerial Psychology* 24, no. 4 (2009): 300–27; and M. J. Pearsall, M. S. Christian, and A. P. J. Ellis, "Motivating Interdependent Teams: Individual Rewards, Shared Rewards, or Something in Between?," *Journal of Applied Psychology* 95, no. 1 (2010): 183–91.

[38] N. MacLean, *Young Men and Fire* (Chicago, IL: Chicago University Press, 1992); K. E. Weick, "The Collapse of Sensemaking in Organizations: The Mann Gulch Disaster," *Administrative Science Quarterly* 38 (1993): 628–52.

[39] Ibid.

[40] T. Driskell, E. Salas, and J. E. Driskell, "Teams in Extreme Environments: Alterations in Team Development and Teamwork," *Human Resource Management Review* 28 (2018): 434–49; S. J. Golden, C.-H. D. Chang, and S. W. J. Kozlowski, "Teams in Isolated, Confined, and Extreme (ICE) Environments: Review and Integration," *Journal of Organizational Behavior* 39 (2018): 701–15; L. B. Landon, K. J. Slack, and J. D. Barrett, "Teamwork and Collaboration in Long-Duration Space Missions: Going to Extremes," *American Psychologist* 73, no. 4 (2018): 563–75; N. Power, "Extreme Teams: Toward a Greater Understanding of Multiagency Teamwork during Major Emergencies and Disasters," *American Psychologist* 73, no. 4 (2018): 478–90; Red Cross, *Red Cross Disaster Teams Still Serving Communities during COVID-19*, March 26, 2020, https://www.redcross.org/about-us/news-and-events/news/2020/red-cross-disaster-teams-still-serving-communities-during-covid-19.html

[41] L. Alison, N. Power, C. van den Heuvel, M. Humann, M. Palasinksi, and J. Crego, "Decision Inertia: Deciding between Least Worst Outcomes in Emergency Response to Disasters," *Journal of Occupational and Organizational Psychology* 88 (2015): 295–321; S. Waring, J.-L. Moran, and R. Page, "Decision-Making in Multiagency Multiteam Systems Operating in Extreme Environments," *Journal of Occupational and Organizational Psychology* (in press).

[42] C. Shawn Burke, M. L. Shuffler, and C. W. Wiese, "Examining the Behavioral and Structural Characteristics of Team Leadership in Extreme Environments," *Journal of Organizational Behavior* 39 (2018): 716–30; K. J. Klein, J. C. Ziegert, A. P. Knight, and Y. Xiao, "Dynamic Delegation: Shared, Hierarchical, and Deindividualized Leadership in Extreme Action Teams," *Administrative Science Quarterly* 51 (2006): 590–621; F. Tschan, N. K. Semmer, D. Gautschi, P. Hunziker, M. Spychiger, and S. U. Marsch, "Leading to Recovery: Group Performance and Coordinative Activities in Medical Emergency Driven Groups," *Human Performance* 19, no. 3 (2006): 277–304.

[43] M. A. Valentine and A. C. Edmondson, "Team Scaffolds: How Mesolevel Structures Enable Role-Based Coordination in Temporary Groups," *Organization Science* 26, no. 2 (2015): 405–22.

[44] A. A. Stachowski, S. A. Kaplan, and M. J. Waller, "The Benefits of Flexible Team Interaction during Crises," *Journal of Applied Pscyhology* 94, no. 6 (2009): 1536–43.

[45] S. Kaplan, K. Laport, and M. J. Waller, "The Role of Positive Affectivity in Team Effectiveness during Crisis," *Journal of Organizational Behavior* 34 (2013): 473–91; G. R. Leon, R. Kanfer, R. G. Hoffman, and L. Dupre, "Interrelationships of Personality and Coping in a Challenging Extreme Situation," *Journal of Research in Personality* 25 (1991): 357–71; S. Razinskas and M. Hoegl, "A Multilevel Review of Stressor Research in Teams," *Journal of Organizational Behavior* 41 (2020): 185–209.

[46] L. Alison, N. Power, C. van den Heuvel, and S. Waring, "A Taxonomy of Endogenous and Exogenous Uncertainty in High-Risk, High-Impact Contexts," *Journal of Applied Psychology* 100, no. 4 (2015): 1309–18; J. B. Schmutz, Z. Lei, W. J. Eppich, and T. Manser, "Reflection in the Heat of the Moment: The Role of In-action Team Reflexivity in Health Care Emergency Teams," *Journal of Organizational Behavior* 39 (2018): 749–65; S. Uitdewilligen and M. J. Waller, "Information Sharing and Decision-Making in Multidisciplinary Crisis Management Teams," *Journal of Organizational Behavior* 39 (2018): 731–48.

[47] A. Bryant, "Taking Your Skills with You," *The New York Times*, May 31, 2015, 2; and J. E. Mathieu, S. I. Tannenbaum, J. S. Donsbach, and G. M. Alliger, "A Review and Integration of Team Composition Models: Moving Toward a Dynamic and Temporal Framework," *Journal of Management* 40, no. 1 (2017): 130–60.

[48] R. R. Hirschfeld, M. H. Jordan, H. S. Feild, W. F. Giles, and A. A. Armenakis, "Becoming Team Players: Team Members' Mastery of Teamwork Knowledge as a Predictor of Team Task Proficiency and Observed Teamwork Effectiveness," *Journal of Applied Psychology* 91, no. 2 (2006): 467–74; and K. R. Randall, C. J. Resick, and L. A. DeChurch, "Building Team Adaptive Capacity: The Roles of Sensegiving and Team Composition," *Journal of Applied Psychology* 96, no. 3 (2011): 525–40.

[49] H. Moon, J. R. Hollenbeck, and S. E. Humphrey, "Asymmetric Adaptability: Dynamic Team Structures as One-Way Streets," *Academy of Management Journal* 47, no. 5 (October 2004): 681–95; A. P. J. Ellis, J. R. Hollenbeck, and D. R. Ilgen, "Team Learning: Collectively Connecting the Dots," *Journal of Applied Psychology* 88, no. 5 (October 2003): 821–35; C. L. Jackson and J. A. LePine, "Peer Responses to a Team's Weakest Link: A Test and Extension of LePine and Van Dyne's Model," *Journal of Applied Psychology* 88, no. 3 (June 2003): 459–75; and J. A. LePine, "Team Adaptation and Postchange Performance: Effects of Team Composition in Terms of Members' Cognitive Ability and Personality," *Journal of Applied Psychology* 88, no. 1 (February 2003): 27–39.
[50] C. C. Cogliser, W. L. Gardner, M. B. Gavin, and J. C. Broberg, "Big Five Personality Factors and Leader Emergence in Virtual Teams: Relationships with Team Trustworthiness, Member Performance Contributions, and Team Performance," *Group & Organization Management* 37, no. 6 (2012): 752–84; and S. T. Bell, "Deep-Level Composition Variables as Predictors of Team Performance: A Meta-Analysis," *Journal of Applied Psychology* 92, no. 3 (2007): 595–615.
[51] T. A. O'Neill and N. J. Allen, "Personality and the Prediction of Team Performance," *European Journal of Personality* 25, no. 1 (2011): 31–42.
[52] S. E. Humphrey, J. R. Hollenbeck, C. J. Meyer, and D. R. Ilgen, "Personality Configurations in Self-Managed Teams: A Natural Experiment on the Effects of Maximizing and Minimizing Variance in Traits," *Journal of Applied Psychology* 41, no. 7 (2011): 1701–32.
[53] Ellis, Hollenbeck, and Ilgen, "Team Learning"; C. O. L. H. Porter, J. R. Hollenbeck, and D. R. Ilgen, "Backing Up Behaviors in Teams: The Role of Personality and Legitimacy of Need," *Journal of Applied Psychology* 88, no. 3 (June 2003): 391–403; and J. A. Colquitt, J. R. Hollenbeck, and D. R. Ilgen, "Computer-Assisted Communication and Team Decision-Making Performance: The Moderating Effect of Openness to Experience," *Journal of Applied Psychology* 87, no. 2 (April 2002): 402–10.
[54] B. H. Bradley, A. C. Klotz, B. E. Postlethwaite, and K. G. Brown, "Ready to Rumble: How Team Personality Composition and Task Conflict Interact to Improve Performance," *Journal of Applied Psychology* 98, no. 2 (2013): 385–92.
[55] E. Gonzalez-Mule, D. S. DeGeest, B. W. McCormick, J. Y. Seong, and K. G. Brown, "Can We Get Some Cooperation around Here? The Mediating Role of Group Norms on the Relationship between Team Personality and Individual Helping Behaviors," *Journal of Applied Psychology* 99, no. 5 (2014): 988–99.
[56] S. E. Humphrey, F. P. Morgeson, and M. J. Mannor, "Developing a Theory of the Strategic Core of Teams: A Role Composition Model of Team Performance," *Journal of Applied Psychology* 94, no. 1 (2009): 48–61.
[57] C. Margerison and D. McCann, *Team Management: Practical New Approaches* (London: Mercury Books, 2000).
[58] A. Joshi, "The Influence of Organizational Demography on the External Networking Behavior of Teams," *Academy of Management Review* (July 2006): 583–95.
[59] A. Joshi and H. Roh, "The Role of Context in Work Team Diversity Research: A Meta-Analytic Review," *Academy of Management Journal* 52, no. 3 (2009): 599–627; S. K. Horwitz and I. B. Horwitz, "The Effects of Team Diversity on Team Outcomes: A Meta-Analytic Review of Team Demography," *Journal of Management* 33, no. 6 (2007): 987–1015; A. C. Homan, C. Buengeler, R. A. Eckhoff, W. P. van Ginkel, and S. C. Voelpel, "The Interplay of Diversity Training and Diversity Beliefs on Team Creativity in Nationality Diverse Teams," *Journal of Applied Psychology* 100, no. 5 (2015): 1456–67; S. T. Bell, A. J. Villado, M. A. Lukasik, L. Belau, and A. L. Briggs, "Getting Specific about Demographic Diversity Variable and Team Performance Relationships: A Meta-Analysis," *Journal of Management* 37, no. 3 (2011): 709–43; and S. Y. Cheung, Y. Gong, M. Wang, L. Zhou, and J. Shi, "When and How Does Functional Diversity Influence Team Innovation? The Mediating Role of Knowledge Sharing and the Moderation Role of Affect-Based Trust in a Team," *Human Relations* 69, no. 7 (2016): 1507–31.
[60] S. J. Shin and J. Zhou, "When Is Educational Specialization Heterogeneity Related to Creativity in Research and Development Teams? Transformational Leadership as a Moderator," *Journal of Applied Psychology* 92, no. 6 (2007): 1709–21; and K. J. Klein, A. P. Knight, J. C. Ziegert, B. C. Lim, and J. L. Saltz, "When Team Members' Values Differ: The Moderating Role of Team Leadership," *Organizational Behavior and Human Decision Processes* 114, no. 1 (2011): 25–36.
[61] S. J. Shin, T. Kim, J. Lee, and L. Bian, "Cognitive Team Diversity and Individual Team Member Creativity: A Cross-Level Interaction," *Academy of Management Journal* 55, no. 1 (2012): 197–212.
[62] S. Mohammed and L. C. Angell, "Surface- and Deep-Level Diversity in Workgroups: Examining the Moderating Effects of Team Orientation and Team Process on Relationship Conflict," *Journal of Organizational Behavior* (December 2004): 1015–39.
[63] Y. F. Guillaume, D. van Knippenberg, and F. C. Brodebeck, "Nothing Succeeds Like Moderation: A Social Self-Regulation Perspective on Cultural Dissimilarity and Performance," *Academy of Management Journal* 57, no. 5 (2014): 1284–308.
[64] D. Coutu, "Why Teams Don't Work," *Harvard Business Review* (May 2009): 99–105. The evidence in this section is described in Thompson, *Making the Team*, pp. 65–67. See also L. A. Curral, R. H. Forrester, and J. F. Dawson, "It's What You Do and the Way That You Do It: Team Task, Team Size, and Innovation-Related Group Processes," *European Journal of Work & Organizational Psychology* 10, no. 2 (June 2001): 187–204; and R. C. Liden, S. J. Wayne, and R. A. Jaworski, "Social Loafing: A Field Investigation," *Journal of Management* 30, no. 2 (2004): 285–304.
[65] R. Karlgaard, "Think (Really!) Small," *Forbes*, April 13, 2015, 32.
[66] Ibid.
[67] Ibid.
[68] "Is Your Team Too Big? Too Small? What's the Right Number?," *Knowledge@Wharton*, June 14, 2006, http://knowledge.wharton.upenn.edu/article/is-your-team-too-big-too-small-whats-the-right-number-2/; see also A. M. Carton and J. N. Cummings, "A Theory of Subgroups in Work Teams," *Academy of Management Review* 37, no. 3 (2012): 441–70.
[69] Hyatt and Ruddy, "An Examination of the Relationship between Work Group Characteristics and Performance"; J. D. Shaw, M. K. Duffy, and E. M. Stark, "Interdependence and Preference for Group Work: Main and Congruence Effects on the Satisfaction and Performance of Group Members," *Journal of Management* 26, no. 2 (2000): 259–79; and S. A. Kiffin-Peterson and J. L. Cordery, "Trust, Individualism, and Job Characteristics of Employee Preference for Teamwork," *International Journal of Human Resource Management* (February 2003): 93–116.
[70] J. A. LePine, R. F. Piccolo, C. L. Jackson, J. E. Mathieu, and J. R. Saul, "A Meta-Analysis of Teamwork Processes: Tests of a

Multidimensional Model and Relationships with Team Effectiveness Criteria," *Personnel Psychology* 61 (2008): 273–307.

[71] J. F. Dovidio, "Bridging Intragroup Processes and Intergroup Relations: Needing the Twain to Meet," *British Journal of Social Psychology* 52, no. 1 (2013): 1–24; and J. Zhou, J. Dovidio, and E. Wang, "How Affectively-Based and Cognitively-Based Attitudes Drive Intergroup Behaviours: The Moderating Role of Affective-Cognitive Consistency," *Plos One* 8, no. 11 (2013): article e82150.

[72] LePine, Piccolo, Jackson, Mathieu, and Saul, "A Meta-Analysis of Teamwork Processes"; and J. E. Mathieu and T. L. Rapp, "Laying the Foundation for Successful Team Performance Trajectories: The Roles of Team Charters and Performance Strategies," *Journal of Applied Psychology* 94, no. 1 (2009): 90–103.

[73] J. E. Mathieu and W. Schulze, "The Influence of Team Knowledge and Formal Plans on Episodic Team Process–Performance Relationships," *Academy of Management Journal* 49, no. 3 (2006): 605–19.

[74] A. N. Pieterse, D. van Knippenberg, and W. P. van Ginkel, "Diversity in Goal Orientation, Team Reflexivity, and Team Performance," *Organizational Behavior and Human Decision Processes* 114, no. 2 (2011): 153–64; and M. J. Pearsall and V. Venkataramani, "Overcoming Asymmetric Goals in Teams: The Interactive Roles of Team Learning Orientation and Team Identification," *Journal of Applied Psychology* 100, no. 3 (2015): 735–48.

[75] A. Gurtner, F. Tschan, N. K. Semmer, and C. Nagele, "Getting Groups to Develop Good Strategies: Effects of Reflexivity Interventions on Team Process, Team Performance, and Shared Mental Models," *Organizational Behavior and Human Decision Processes* 102 (2007): 127–42; M. C. Schippers, D. N. Den Hartog, and P. L. Koopman, "Reflexivity in Teams: A Measure and Correlates," *Applied Psychology: An International Review* 56, no. 2 (2007): 189–211; and C. S. Burke, K. C. Stagl, E. Salas, L. Pierce, and D. Kendall, "Understanding Team Adaptation: A Conceptual Analysis and Model," *Journal of Applied Psychology* 91, no. 6 (2006): 1189–207.

[76] M. C. Schippers, A. C. Homan, and D. Van Knippenberg, "To Reflect or Not to Reflect: Prior Team Performance as a Boundary Condition of the Effects of Reflexivity on Learning and Final Team Performance," *Journal of Organizational Behavior* 34, no. 1 (2013): 6–23.

[77] A. N. Pieterse, D. van Knippenberg, and W. P. van Ginkel, "Diversity in Goal Orientation, Team Reflexivity, and Team Performance," *Organizational Behavior and Human Decision Processes* 114, no. 2 (2011): 153–64.

[78] See R. P. DeShon, S. W. J. Kozlowski, A. M. Schmidt, K. R. Milner, and D. Wiechmann, "A Multiple-Goal, Multilevel Model of Feedback Effects on the Regulation of Individual and Team Performance," *Journal of Applied Psychology* (December 2004): 1035–56.

[79] Acton et al., "Built for Unity"; N. L. Larson, M. J. W. McLarnnon, and T. A. O'Neill, "Challenging the 'Static' Quo: Trajectories of Engagement in Team Processes toward a Deadline," *Journal of Applied Psychology* (in press).

[80] J. W. Beck, A. M. Schmidt, and M. W. Natali, "Efficient Proximal Resource Allocation Strategies Predict Distal Team Performance: Evidence from the National Hockey League," *Journal of Applied Psychology* 104, no. 11 (2019): 1387–403.

[81] K. Tasa, S. Taggar, and G. H. Seijts, "The Development of Collective Efficacy in Teams: A Multilevel and Longitudinal Perspective," *Journal of Applied Psychology* 92, no. 1 (2007): 17–27; D. I. Jung and J. J. Sosik, "Group Potency and Collective Efficacy: Examining Their Predictive Validity, Level of Analysis, and Effects of Performance Feedback on Future Group Performance," *Group & Organization Management* (September 2003): 366–91; and R. R. Hirschfeld and J. B. Bernerth, "Mental Efficacy and Physical Efficacy at the Team Level: Inputs and Outcomes among Newly Formed Action Teams," *Journal of Applied Psychology* 93, no. 6 (2008): 1429–37.

[82] A. W. Richter, G. Hirst, D. van Knippenberg, and M. Baer, "Creative Self-Efficacy and Individual Creativity in Team Contexts: Cross-Level Interactions with Team Informational Resources," *Journal of Applied Psychology* 97, no. 6 (2012): 1282–90.

[83] T. L. Rapp and J. E. Mathieu, "Team and Individual Influences on Members' Identification and Performance per Membership in Multiple Team Membership Arrangements," *Journal of Applied Psychology* 104, no. 3 (2019): 303–20.

[84] N. Ellemers, E. Sleebos, D. Stam, and D. de Gilder, "Feeling Included and Valued: How Perceived Respect Affects Positive Team Identity and Willingness to Invest in the Team," *British Journal of Management* 24 (2013): 21–37; and B. Dietz, D. van Knippenberg, G. Hirst, and S. D. Restubog, "Outperforming Whom? A Multilevel Study of Performance-Prove Goal Orientation, Performance, and the Moderating Role of Shared Team Identification," *Journal of Applied Psychology* 100, no. 6 (2015): 1811–24.

[85] D. L. Shapiro, S. A. Furst, G. M. Spreitzer, and M. A. Von Glinow, "Transnational Teams in the Electronic Age: Are Team Identity and High Performance at Risk?," *Journal of Organizational Behavior* 23 (2002): 455–67.

[86] T. A. De Vries, F. Walter, G. S. Van Der Vegt, and P. J. M. D. Essens, "Antecedents of Individuals' Interteam Coordination: Broad Functional Experiences as a Mixed Blessing," *Academy of Management Journal* 57, no. 5 (2014): 1334–59.

[87] S. Chang, L. Jia, R. Takeuchi, and Y. Cai, "Do High-Commitment Work Systems Affect Creativity? A Multilevel Combinational Approach to Employee Creativity," *Journal of Applied Psychology* 99, no. 4 (2014): 665–80.

[88] C. Post, "When Is Female Leadership an Advantage? Coordination Requirements, Team Cohesion, and Team Interaction Norms," *Journal of Organizational Behavior* 36, no. 8 (2015): 1153–75; J. E. Mathieu, M. R. Kukenberger, L. D'Innocenzo, and G. Reilly, "Modeling Reciprocal Team Cohesion–Performance Relationships, as Impacted by Shared Leadership and Members' Competence," *Journal of Applied Psychology* 100, no. 3 (2015): 71–34; and A. C. Stoverink, E. E. Umphress, R. G. Gardner, and K. N. Milner, "Misery Loves Company: Team Dissonance and the Influence of Supervisor-Focused Interpersonal Justice Climate on Team Cohesiveness," *Journal of Applied Psychology* 99, no. 6 (2014): 1059–73.

[89] S. Mohammed, L. Ferzandi, and K. Hamilton, "Metaphor No More: A 15-Year Review of the Team Mental Model Construct," *Journal of Management* 36, no. 4 (2010): 876–910.

[90] A. P. J. Ellis, "System Breakdown: The Role of Mental Models and Transactive Memory on the Relationships between Acute Stress and Team Performance," *Academy of Management Journal* 49, no. 3 (2006): 576–89.

[91] L. A. DeChurch and J. R. Mesmer-Magnus, "The Cognitive Underpinnings of Effective Teamwork: A Meta-Analysis," *Journal of Applied Psychology* 95, no. 1 (2010): 32–53.

[92] S. W. J. Kozlowski and D. R. Ilgen, "Enhancing the Effectiveness of Work Groups and Teams," *Psychological Science in*

the Public Interest (December 2006): 77–124; and B. D. Edwards, E. A. Day, W. Arthur Jr., and S. T. Bell, "Relationships among Team Ability Composition, Team Mental Models, and Team Performance," *Journal of Applied Psychology* 91, no. 3 (2006): 727–36.

[93] D. G. Bachrach, K. Lewis, Y. Kim, P. C. Patel, M. C. Campion, and S. M. B. Thatcher, "Transactive Memory Systems in Context: A Meta-Analytic Examination of Contextual Factors in Transactive Memory Systems Development and Team Performance," *Journal of Applied Psychology* 104, no. 3 (2019): 464–93; K. Lewis and B. Herndon, "Transactive Memory Systems: Current Issues and Future Research Directions," *Organization Science* 22 (2011): 1254–65.

[94] Ibid.

[95] M. Kolbe, G. Grote, M. J. Waller, J. Wacker, B. Grande, and D. R. Spahn, "Monitoring and Talking to the Room: Autochthonous Coordination Patterns in Team Interaction and Performance," *Journal of Applied Psychology* 99, no. 6 (2014): 1254–67.

[96] R. Sinha, N. S. Janardhanan, L. L. Greer, D. E. Conlon, and J. R. Edwards, "Skewed Task Conflicts in Teams: What Happens When a Few Members See More Conflict Than the Rest?" *Journal of Applied Psychology* 101, no. 7 (2016): 1045–55.

[97] T.A. O'Neill, N. J. Allen, and S. E. Hastings, "Examining the 'Pros' and 'Cons' of Team Conflict: A Team-Level Meta-Analysis of Task, Relationship, and Process Conflict," *Human Performance* 26, no. 3 (2013): 236–60.

[98] Bradley, Klotz, Postlethwaite, and Brown, "Ready to Rumble."

[99] J. Farh, C. Lee, and C. I. C. Farh, "Task Conflict and Team Creativity: A Question of How Much and When," *Journal of Applied Psychology* 95, no. 6 (2010): 1173–80.

[100] K. J. Behfar, R. S. Peterson, E. A. Mannix, and W. M. K. Trochim, "The Critical Role of Conflict Resolution in Teams: A Close Look at the Links between Conflict Type, Conflict Management Strategies, and Team Outcomes," *Journal of Applied Psychology* 93, no. 1 (2008): 170–88.

[101] V. Gonzalez-Roma and A. Hernandez, "Climate Uniformity: Its Influence on Team Communication Quality, Task Conflict, and Team Performance," *Journal of Applied Psychology* 99, no. 6 (2014): 1042–58.

[102] M. Chang, "On the Relationship between Intragroup Conflict and Social Capital in Teams: A Longitudinal Investigation in Taiwan," *Journal of Organizational Behavior* 38, no. 1 (2017): 3–27.

[103] K. H. Price, D. A. Harrison, and J. H. Gavin, "Withholding Inputs in Team Contexts: Member Composition, Interaction Processes, Evaluation Structure, and Social Loafing," *Journal of Applied Psychology* 91, no. 6 (2006): 1375–84.

[104] E. Sherberg, "In Her Own Words: Lindsay Kaplan, Co-founder of Chief, a Private Network for Powerful Women, Sees Herself as a Stay-at-Home Mom. It's Hard Work." *Bizwomen* (April 21, 2020), https://www.bizjournals.com/bizwomen/news/latest-news/2020/04/in-her-own-words-lindsay-kaplan-co-founder-of.html?page=all.

[105] A. Cristina Costa, C. Ashley Fulmer, and N. R. Anderson, "Trust in Work Teams: An Integrative Review, Multilevel Model, and Future Research Directions," *Journal of Organizational Behavior* 39 (2018): 169–84.

[106] C. Breuer, J. Hüffmeier, and G. Hertel, "Does Trust Matter More in Virtual Teams? A Meta-Analysis of Trust and Team Effectiveness Considering Virtuality and Documentation as Moderators," *Journal of Applied Psychology* 101, no. 8 (2016): 1151–77; B. A. De Jong, K. T. Dirks, and N. Gillespie, "Trust and Team Performance: A Meta-Analysis of Main Effects, Moderators, and Covariates," *Journal of Applied Psychology* 101, no. 8 (2016): 1134–50; J. Feitosa, R. Grossman, W. S. Kramer, and E. Salas, "Measuring Team Trust: A Critical and Meta-Analytical Review," *Journal of Organizational Behavior* (in press).

[107] R. Grossman and J. Feitosa, "Team Trust over Time: Modeling Reciprocal and Contextual Influences in Action Teams," *Human Resource Management Review* 28 (2018): 395–410.

[108] G. Hertel, U. Konradt, and K. Voss, "Competencies for Virtual Teamwork: Development and Validation of a Web-Based Selection Tool for Members of Distributed Teams," *European Journal of Work and Organizational Psychology* 15, no. 4 (2006): 477–504.

[109] T. V. Riper, "The NBA's Most Overpaid Players," *Forbes*, April 5, 2013, http://www.forbes.com/sites/tomvanriper/2013/04/05/the-nbas-most-overpaid-players/.

[110] E. Kearney, D. Gebert, and S. C. Voelpel, "When and How Diversity Benefits Teams: The Importance of Team Members' Need for Cognition," *Academy of Management Journal* 52, no. 3 (2009): 581–98.

[111] H. M. Guttman, "The New High-Performance Player," *The Hollywood Reporter*, October 27, 2008, www.hollywoodreporter.com.

[112] A. M. Hughes, M. E. Gregory, D. L. Joseph, S. C. Sonesh, S. L. Marlow, C. N. Lacerenza, L. E. Benishek, H. B. King, and E. Salas, "Saving Lives: A Meta-Analysis of Team Training in Healthcare," *Journal of Applied Psychology* 101, no. 9 (2016): 1266–304.

[113] C. H. Chuang, S. Chen, and C. W. Chuang, "Human Resource Management Practices and Organizational Social Capital: The Role of Industrial Characteristics," *Journal of Business Research* (May 2013): 678–87; and L. Prusak and D. Cohen, "How to Invest in Social Capital," *Harvard Business Review* (June 2001): 86–93.

[114] T. Erickson and L. Gratton, "What It Means to Work Here," *BusinessWeek*, January 10, 2008, www.businessweek.com.

[115] M. D. Johnson, J. R. Hollenbeck, S. E. Humphrey, D. R. Ilgen, D. Jundt, and C. J. Meyer, "Cutthroat Cooperation: Asymmetrical Adaptation to Changes in Team Reward Structures," *Academy of Management Journal* 49, no. 1 (2006): 103–19.

[116] C. E. Naquin and R. O. Tynan, "The Team Halo Effect: Why Teams Are Not Blamed for Their Failures," *Journal of Applied Psychology* (April 2003): 332–40.

[117] E. R. Crawford and J. A. LePine, "A Configural Theory of Team Processes: Accounting for the Structure of Taskwork and Teamwork," *Academy of Management Review* (January 2013): 32–48.

11 Power and Politics

Source: Kim Hong-Ji/Reuters/Alamy Stock Photo

LEARNING OBJECTIVES

After studying this chapter, you should be able to:

11-1 Contrast leadership and power.

11-2 Explain the three bases of formal power and the two bases of personal power.

11-3 Explain the role of dependence in power relationships.

11-4 Identify power or influence tactics and their contingencies.

11-5 Identify the causes and consequences of abuse of power.

11-6 Describe how politics work in organizations.

11-7 Identify the causes, consequences, and ethics of political behavior.

Employability Skills Matrix (ESM)

	Myth or Science?	Career OBjectives	An Ethical Choice	Point/ Counterpoint	Experiential Exercise	Ethical Dilemma	Case Incident 1	Case Incident 2
Critical Thinking	✓	✓		✓	✓	✓	✓	✓
Communication			✓		✓			✓
Collaboration		✓			✓			
Knowledge Application and Analysis	✓		✓	✓	✓	✓	✓	✓
Social Responsibility		✓					✓	✓

A TALE OF PRESIDENTIAL CORRUPTION

Answer quickly: If someone were given the ability to exert his or her will over others for his or her self-interest, would this person do it?

On Wednesday, December 19, 2012, Park Guen-hye became the first female president of South Korea. Park was considered a trailblazer in South Korean politics and the heir to a long political legacy. The 60-year-old politician was the daughter of former South Korean president Park Chung-hee. Guen-hye had begun her political career at a young age when, at the age of 22, she took on first lady duties after her mother's assassination by a North Korean gunman. When she became president of South Korea, she made many promises, making many citizens hopeful that she would revive the country's slowing economic growth. These promises included pushing for regulations of some of South Korea's largest companies, such as Samsung and Hyundai. Park ran and won based on pledges to support and build small and medium-sized businesses while encouraging more exports.

Within four years, Park Guen-hye was impeached and tried on charges of corruption. Park had always been close to Choi Soon-sil, the daughter of another public figure. Soon-sil's father was the head of the Church of Eternal Life and a close family friend of former president Park Chung-hee. It seems Choi used her long-time friendship with the president to force Samsung and many other large companies to donate to her charities. The scandal goes much deeper than bribes, however. Choi had an unusual amount of power over the leader of South Korea. Besides using her relationship with the president to gain $70 million in donations to her nonprofit foundations, Choi also was given illegal access to confidential documents and edited presidential speeches.

Park Guen-hye won the election partly because she was seen as less corrupt than her predecessors. In the last 30 years of democracy in South Korea, two presidents have already been jailed. President Lee Myung-bak was also implicated in a bribery scandal before leaving office. Similar to Park, Lee's friend and brother Sang-deuk used his connection to the president to collect bribes from two Korean banks. Several of Lee's former aides were also charged with receiving bribes.

So what caused Park's transformation from South Korea's seemingly least corrupt politician to an impeached president charged with corruption? Some South Koreans believe that Choi's power as a religious leader and family friend is to blame. Did Choi have influence over the new president because she held the keys to her salvation? Or was Park corrupted by receiving tremendous power?

The tale of Park's downfall is not unique to South Korea. Political parties are considered the most corrupt public institutions, according to Transparency International's 2013 survey on global corruption. The organization found that a quarter of survey respondents had paid a bribe to politicians in the past year. Around the globe, from India to southern Europe to the United States, there are stories of political leaders using their power for their own self-interest. This phenomenon occurs at all levels. In Florida, former Opa-locka commissioner Luis Santiago used his position to gain $40,000 in bribes. In Maryland, state senator Nathaniel T. Oaks was caught pushing through legislation for a fake real estate project in exchange for $15,000 in bribes.

In all these stories, officials were elected to serve the interests of the public, yet they used their power to serve their own interests instead. Many of these citizens were elected because they claimed they could clean up a corrupt system. Then, when they gained power themselves, they used their influence to further their own goals. As we can see from Park Guen-hye's story, however, there are other ways of gaining power besides obtaining a leadership position in politics. Cho Soon-sil obtained power through religious institutions and personal connections. Many of the bribery scandals described above were possible because someone controlled resources such as wealth or economic power.

Sources: Based on M. Park, P. Hancocks and K. J. Kwon, "Park Guen-hye Claims South Korea Presidential Victory," *CNN*, December 19, 2012, http://www.cnn.com/2012/12/18/world/

asia/south-korea-presidential-election/; K. J. Kwon and M. Park, "South Korean President Apologizes for Bribery Scandals in His Inner Circle," *CNN*, July 24, 2012, http://www.cnn.com/2012/07/24/world/asia/south-korean-president-apology/index.html; Associated Press, "Impeached South Korean President Indicted, Faces Trial," *New York Post*, April 17, 2017, http://nypost.com/2017/04/17/impeached-south-korean-president-indicted/; BBC Profiles, "Profile: South Korean President Park Guen-hye," *BBC News*, March 10, 2017, http://www.bbc.com/news/world-asia-20787271; A. E. Marimow and O. Wiggins, "Code Word 'Lollipop': That Was Bribe Cue for Maryland State Senator, Investigators Charge," *The Washington Post*, April 7, 2017; J. Weaver, "Opa-locka Politician Pleads Guilty to Bribery, as FBI Continues Corruption Probe," *Miami Herald*, January 10, 2017, http://www.miamiherald.com/news/local/article125617409.html; R. Jennings, "Five Things to Know about South Korea's Presidential Scandal," *Forbes*, November 9, 2016, https://www.forbes.com/sites/ralphjennings/2016/11/09/5-sad-and-creepy-things-you-should-know-about-south-koreas-presidential-scandal/#59a510541556; and K. Rapoza, "Transparency International Spells It Out: Politicians Are the Most Corrupt," *Forbes*, July 9, 2013, https://www.forbes.com/sites/kenrapoza/2013/07/09/transparency-international-spells-it-out-politicians-are-the-most-corrupt/#7497bca21c33.

In this chapter, we will learn about power, including how a person obtains power and the tactics employees use to exert their will over others. We will also learn the role of political behavior in maintaining power within an organization. Power in organizations is a compelling force: People who have power deny it, people who want it try not to look like they're seeking it, and those who are good at getting it are secretive about how they do so.[1] We begin by exploring our natural association of power with leadership.

Power and Leadership

11-1 Contrast leadership and power.

power The capacity, discretion, and means to enforce one's will over others.

dependence The extent to which people depend or rely upon a powerful person.

In organizational behavior (OB), **power** refers to the capacity that *A* has to influence the behavior of *B* so that *B* acts in accordance with *A*'s wishes.[2] Someone can thus have power but not use it; it is a capacity or potential. Probably the most important aspect of power is that it is a function of **dependence**.[3] The greater *B*'s dependence on *A*, the greater *A*'s power in the relationship. Dependence, in turn, is based on alternatives that *B* perceives and the importance *B* places on the alternative(s) that *A* controls. A person can have power over you only if he or she controls something you desire. If you want a college degree and have to pass a certain course to get it, and your current instructor is the only faculty member in the college who teaches that course, she has power over you because your alternatives are highly limited and you place a high degree of importance on the outcome. Similarly, if you're attending college on funds provided by your parents, you probably recognize the power they hold over you. But once you're out of school, have a job, and are making a good income, your parents' power is reduced significantly.

Money is a powerful variable for dependence. Who among us has not heard of a rich relative who controls family members merely through the implicit or explicit threat of "writing them out of the will"? Another example is found on Wall Street, where portfolio manager Ping Jiang allegedly was able to coerce his subordinate, analyst Andrew Tong, into taking female hormones and wearing lipstick and makeup. Why such power? Jiang controlled Tong's access to day trading and thus his livelihood.[4]

A careful comparison of our description of power with our description of leadership in Chapter 13 reveals the concepts are closely intertwined. *Leaders* use *power* as a means of attaining group goals. How are the two terms, *leadership* and *power*, different? Power does not require goal compatibility, just dependence. Leadership, on the other hand, requires some congruence between the goals of the leader and those being led. A second difference relates to the direction of influence. Leadership research focuses on the downward influence on followers. It minimizes the importance of lateral and upward influence patterns. Power research takes all factors into consideration. For a third difference, leadership research often emphasizes style. It seeks answers to questions such as: "How supportive should a leader be?" and "How much decision making should be shared with followers?" In contrast, the research on power focuses on tactics for gaining compliance. Leadership concentrates on the individual leader's influence, while the study of power acknowledges that groups as well as individuals can use power to control other individuals or groups.

You may have noted that, for a power situation to exist, one person or group needs to have control over resources that the other person or group values. This is usually the case in established leadership situations. However, power relationships are possible in all areas of life, and power can be obtained in many ways. Let's explore the various sources of power next.

Bases of Power

11-2 Explain the three bases of formal power and the two bases of personal power.

Where does power come from? What gives an individual or a group influence over others? We answer these questions by dividing the bases or sources of power into two general groupings—formal and personal—and breaking down each into more specific categories.[5]

Formal Power

Formal power is based on an individual's position in an organization. It can come from the ability to coerce or reward, or from formal authority.

coercive power A power base that depends on fear of the negative results from failing to comply.

Coercive Power The **coercive power** base depends on the target's fear of negative results from failing to comply. On the physical level, coercive power rests on the application, or the threat of application, of bodily distress through the infliction of pain, the restriction of movement, or the withholding of basic physiological or safety needs.

At the organizational level, *A* has coercive power over *B* if *A* can dismiss, suspend, or demote *B*, assuming *B* values her job. If *A* can assign *B* work activities *B* finds unpleasant, or treat *B* in a manner *B* finds embarrassing, *A* possesses coercive power over *B*. Coercive power comes also from withholding key information. People in an organization who have data or knowledge that others need can make others dependent on them. When subordinates are being abused by supervisors, coercive power is the main force that keeps them from retaliating.[6]

reward power Compliance achieved based on the ability to distribute rewards that others view as valuable.

Reward Power The opposite of coercive power is **reward power**, which people comply with because it produces positive benefits; someone who can distribute rewards that others view as valuable has power over them. These rewards can be financial—such as controlling pay rates, raises, and bonuses—or nonfinancial, including recognition, promotions, interesting work assignments, friendly colleagues, and preferred work shifts or sales territories.[7]

legitimate power The power a person receives as a result of his or her position in the formal hierarchy of an organization.

Legitimate Power In formal groups and organizations, probably the most common access to one or more of the power bases is through **legitimate power**. It represents the formal authority to control and use organizational resources based on the person's structural position in the organization.

Legitimate power is broader than the power to coerce and reward. Specifically, it includes members' acceptance of the authority of a hierarchical position.[8] We associate power so closely with the concept of hierarchy that just drawing longer lines in an organization chart leads people to infer the leaders are especially powerful.[9] In general, when school principals, bank presidents, or army captains speak, teachers, tellers, and first lieutenants usually comply.

Personal Power

Many of the most competent and productive chip designers at Intel have power, but they aren't managers and they have no formal power. What they have is *personal power*, which comes from an individual's unique characteristics.[10] There are two bases of personal power: expertise and the respect and admiration of others. Personal power is not mutually exclusive from formal power, but it can be independent.

expert power Influence based on special skills or knowledge.

Expert Power **Expert power** is influence wielded as a result of expertise, special skills, or knowledge.[11] As jobs become more specialized, we become dependent on experts to achieve goals. It is generally acknowledged that physicians have expertise and hence expert power: Most of us follow our doctor's advice. Computer specialists, tax accountants, economists, industrial psychologists, and other specialists wield power as a result of their expertise.

Internet entrepreneur Mark Zuckerberg, cofounder and CEO of Facebook, has expert power. Shown here talking with employees, Zuckerberg earned the title "software guy" during college because of his expertise in computer programming. Today, Facebook depends on his expertise to achieve company goals.
Source: Tony Avelar/FR155217/AP Images

referent power Influence based on identification with a person who has desirable resources or personal traits.

Referent Power **Referent power** is based on identification with a person who has desirable resources or personal traits.[12] If I like, respect, and admire you, you can exercise power over me because I want to please you.

Referent power develops out of admiration of another and a desire to be like that person. It helps explain, for instance, why celebrities are paid millions of dollars to endorse products in commercials. Marketing research shows people such as LeBron James and Tom Brady have the power to influence your choice of athletic shoes and credit cards. With a little practice, you and I could probably deliver as smooth a sales pitch as these celebrities, but the buying public doesn't identify with us. Some people who are not in formal leadership positions have referent power and exert influence over others because of their charismatic dynamism, likability, and emotional appeal.[13]

Which Bases of Power Are Most Effective?

Of the three bases of formal power (coercive, reward, legitimate) and two bases of personal power (expert, referent), which are most important? Research suggests the personal sources of power are most effective. Both expert and referent power are positively related to employees' satisfaction with supervision, their organizational commitment, and their performance, whereas reward and legitimate power seem to be unrelated to these outcomes. One source of formal power—coercive power—can be damaging.

Referent power can be a powerful motivator. Consider Steve Stoute's company, Translation, which matches pop-star spokespersons with corporations that want to promote their brands. Stoute has paired Justin Timberlake with McDonald's, Beyoncé with Tommy Hilfiger, and Jay-Z with Reebok. Stoute's business seems to be all about referent power. His firm aims to use the credibility of artists and performers to reach youth culture.[14] The success of these well-known companies attests to Stoute's expectation that the buying public identifies with and emulates his spokespersons and therefore thinks highly of the represented brands.

Dependence: The Key to Power

11-3 Explain the role of dependence in power relationships.

The most important aspect of power is that it is a function of dependence. In this section, we show how understanding dependence helps us understand the degrees of power.

The General Dependence Postulate

Let's begin with a general postulate: *The greater* B*'s dependence on* A, *the more power* A *has over* B. When you possess anything others require that you alone control, you make them dependent on you and therefore you gain power over them.[15] As the old saying goes, "In the land of the blind, the one-eyed man is king!" But if something is plentiful, possessing it will not increase your power. Therefore, the more you can expand your own options, the less power you place in the hands of others. This explains why most organizations develop multiple suppliers rather than give their business to only one. It also explains why so many people aspire to financial independence. Independence reduces the power others can wield to limit our access to opportunities and resources.

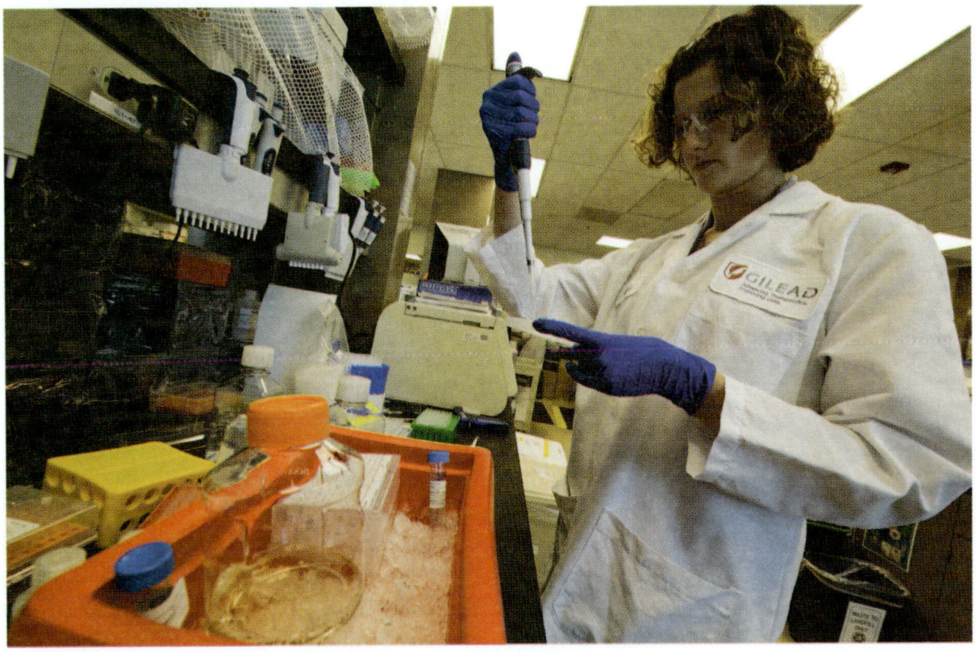

Scientist Maria Kovalenko is in a position of power at Gilead Sciences, a research-based biopharmaceutical firm. Scientists are in a powerful occupational group at Gilead because they discover and develop medicines that improve the lives of patients and contribute to Gilead's growth and success.
Source: David Paul Morris/Bloomberg/Getty Images

What Creates Dependence?

Dependence increases when the resource you control is important, scarce, and nonsubstitutable.[16]

Importance If nobody wants what you have, it's not going to create dependence. Note, however, that there are many degrees of importance, from needing the resource for survival to wanting a resource that is in fashion or adds to convenience.

Scarcity Ferruccio Lamborghini, who created the exotic supercars that still carry his name, understood the importance of scarcity and used it to his advantage during World War II. When Lamborghini was in Rhodes with the Italian army, his superiors were impressed with his mechanical skills because he demonstrated an almost uncanny ability to repair tanks and cars no one else could fix. After the war, he admitted his ability was largely due to his having been the first person on the island to receive the repair manuals, which he memorized and then destroyed to make himself indispensable.[17]

We see the scarcity–dependence relationship in the power situation of employment. Where the supply of labor is low relative to demand, workers can negotiate compensation and benefits packages far more attractive than those in occupations with an abundance of candidates. For example, today, college administrators have no problem finding English instructors because there is a high supply and low demand. In contrast, the market for network systems analysts is comparatively tight, with demand high and supply limited. The resulting bargaining power of computer-engineering faculty members allows them to negotiate higher salaries, lighter teaching loads, and other benefits.

Nonsubstitutability The fewer viable substitutes for a resource, the more power a person controlling that resource has. At universities that value faculty publishing, for example, the more recognition the faculty member receives through publication, the more control that person has because other universities want faculty members who are highly published and visible.

Social Network Analysis: A Tool for Assessing Resources

One tool to assess the exchange of resources and dependencies within an organization is *social network analysis*.[18] This method examines patterns of communication among organizational members to identify how information flows between them. Within a social network, or connections between people who share professional interests, each individual or group is called a node, and the links between nodes are called ties. When nodes communicate or exchange resources frequently, they are said to have very strong ties. Other nodes that are not engaged in direct communication with one another achieve resource flows through intermediary nodes. In other words, some nodes act as brokers between otherwise unconnected nodes. A graphical illustration of the associations among individuals in a social network is called a *sociogram* and functions like an informal version of an organization chart. The difference is that a formal organization chart shows how authority is supposed to flow, whereas a sociogram shows how resources *really* flow in an organization. An example of a sociogram is shown in Exhibit 11-1.

Networks can create substantial power dynamics, such as enforcing norms (see Chapter 9) or creating change within an organization. Thus, employees who have many connections to an organizational social network are less likely to engage in corruption.[19] Those in the position of brokers tend to have more power because they can leverage the unique resources they can acquire from different groups. In other words, many people depend on brokers,

Exhibit 11-1 An Organizational Sociogram

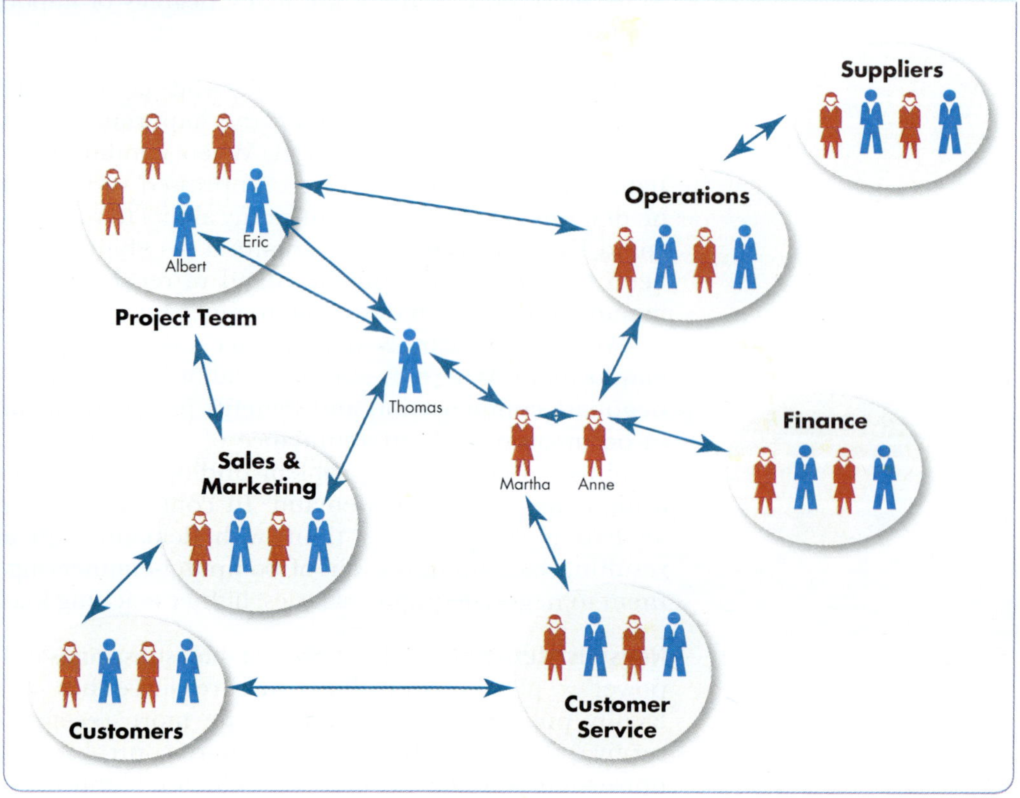

which gives the brokers more power. For example, organizational culture changes such as corporate social responsibility (CSR) awareness often begin in a single connected group of individuals, grow in strength, and then slowly move to other connected groups through brokers over time.[20] Data from the United Kingdom's National Health Service show that change agents—people entrusted with helping an organization to make a significant change—have more success if they are information brokers.[21] These functions are not without cost, however. One study found that people identified as central to advice networks were more likely to quit their jobs, possibly because they did a great deal of extra work without reward.[22]

A social network analysis in an organization can be implemented in many ways.[23] Some organizations keep track of the flow of e-mail communications or document sharing across departments. These big-data tools are an easy way to gather objective information about how individuals exchange information. Other organizations look at data from human resources (HR) information systems, analyzing how supervisors and subordinates interact with one another. These data sources can produce sociograms showing how resources and power flow. Leaders can then identify powerful brokers who exert the strongest influence on many groups, and address these key individuals.

Power Tactics

11-4 Identify power or influence tactics and their contingencies.

power tactics Ways in which individuals translate power bases into specific actions.

What **power tactics** do people use to translate power bases into specific action? What options do they have for influencing their bosses, coworkers, or employees? Research has identified nine distinct influence tactics:[24]

- *Legitimacy.* Relying on your authority position or saying that a request is in accordance with organizational policies or rules.
- *Rational persuasion.* Presenting logical arguments and factual evidence to demonstrate that a request is reasonable.
- *Inspirational appeals.* Developing emotional commitment by appealing to a target's values, needs, hopes, and aspirations.
- *Consultation.* Increasing support by involving the target in deciding how to accomplish your plan.
- *Exchange.* Rewarding the target with benefits or favors in exchange for acceding to a request.
- *Personal appeals.* Asking for compliance based on friendship or loyalty.
- *Ingratiation.* Using flattery, praise, or friendly behavior prior to making a request.
- *Pressure.* Using warnings, repeated demands, and threats.
- *Coalitions.* Enlisting the aid or support of others to persuade the target to agree.

Using Power Tactics

Some tactics are more effective than others. Rational persuasion, inspirational appeals, and consultation tend to be the most effective, especially when the audience is highly interested in the outcomes of a decision process. The pressure tactic tends to backfire and is typically the least effective of the nine.[25] You can increase your chance of success by using two or more tactics together or sequentially, as long

Exhibit 11-2 Preferred Power Tactics by Influence Direction

Upward Influence	Downward Influence	Lateral Influence
Rational persuasion	Rational persuasion Inspirational appeals Ingratiation Legitimacy	Rational persuasion Consultation Ingratiation Exchange Legitimacy Personal appeals Coalitions

as your choices are compatible.[26] Using ingratiation and legitimacy together can lessen negative reactions, but only when the audience does not really care about the outcome of a decision process or the policy is routine.[27]

Let's consider the most effective way of getting a raise. You can start with a rational approach—figure out how your pay compares to that of your organizational peers, land a competing job offer, gather data that testify to your performance, or use salary calculators like Salary.com to compare your pay with others in your occupation—then share your findings with your manager. The results can be impressive. Kitty Dunning, a vice president at Don Jagoda Associates, landed a 16 percent raise when she e-mailed her boss numbers showing she had increased sales.[28] Using rational persuasion to make a case to your supervisor about a possible raise, or even a alternative work arrangement (see Chapter 8), may be effective because it fosters a mutual sense of respect between you and your supervisor.[29]

While rational persuasion may work in this situation, the effectiveness of some influence tactics depends on the direction of influence,[30] and of course on the audience. As Exhibit 11-2 shows, rational persuasion is the only tactic effective at both upwardly and downwardly influencing, although it is stronger when it is used for downward influence attempts. Inspirational appeals work best as a downward-influencing tactic with subordinates. Ingratiation is most effective as lateral influence, although it can also be effective in downward influence.[31] Other factors relating to the effectiveness of influence include the sequencing of tactics, a person's skill in using the tactic, and the organizational culture.

In general, you're more likely to be effective if you begin with "softer" tactics that rely on personal power, such as personal and inspirational appeals, rational persuasion, and consultation. If these fail, you can move to "harder" tactics, such as exchange, coalitions, and pressure, which emphasize formal power and incur greater costs and risks.[32] A single soft tactic is more effective than a single hard tactic, and combining two soft tactics or a soft tactic and rational persuasion is more effective than any single tactic or combination of hard tactics.[33]

As we mentioned, the effectiveness of tactics depends on the audience.[34] People especially likely to comply with soft power tactics tend to be more reflective and intrinsically motivated; they have high self-esteem and a greater desire for control. Those likely to comply with hard power tactics are more action-oriented and extrinsically motivated, and more focused on getting along with others than on getting their own way.

Cultural Preferences for Power Tactics

Preference for power tactics varies across cultures.[35] Those from individualist countries tend to see power in personalized terms and as a legitimate means of advancing their personal ends, whereas those in collectivist countries see power in social terms and as a legitimate means of helping others.[36] A study comparing managers in the United States and China found U.S. managers preferred rational appeal, whereas Chinese managers preferred coalition tactics.[37] Reason-based tactics are consistent with the U.S. preference for direct confrontation and rational persuasion to influence others and resolve differences, while coalition tactics align with the Chinese preference for meeting difficult or controversial requests with indirect approaches.

Applying Power Tactics

political skill The ability to influence others in such a way as to enhance one's objectives.

People differ in their **political skill**, or their ability to influence others to attain their own objectives.[38] The politically skilled are more effective users of all influence tactics, and draw on their knowledge of others' demands, resources, and preferences to do so.[39] People who are politically skilled have higher self-efficacy, job satisfaction, work productivity, and career success. They are less likely to be victims of workplace aggression. Political skill is also more effective when the stakes are high, such as when the individual is accountable for important organizational outcomes. Finally, the politically skilled are able to exert their influence without others detecting it, a key element in effectiveness (it's damaging to be labeled political).[40] These individuals are able to use their political skills in environments with low levels of procedural and distributive justice. Politically skilled individuals tend to receive higher performance ratings when they ask strategically for feedback in a way that enhances their image in the organization.[41] However, when an organization has fairly applied rules, free of favoritism or biases, political skill is actually negatively related to job performance ratings.[42]

We know cultures within organizations differ markedly—some are warm, relaxed, and supportive; others are formal and conservative. Some encourage participation and consultation, some encourage reason, and still others rely on pressure. People who fit the culture of the organization tend to obtain more influence.[43] Specifically, extraverts tend to be more influential in team-oriented organizations, and highly conscientious people are more influential in organizations that value working alone on technical tasks. People who fit the culture are influential because they can perform especially well in the domains deemed most important for success. Thus, the organization itself influences which subset of power tactics is viewed as acceptable for use.

How Power Affects People

11-5 Identify the causes and consequences of abuse of power.

Until this point, we've discussed what power is and how it is acquired. But we've not yet answered one important question: "Does power corrupt?"

There is certainly evidence that there are corrupting aspects of power. Power leads people to place their own interests ahead of others' needs or goals. Why does this happen? Power not only leads people to focus on their self-interests because they can, it liberates them to focus inward and thus come to place greater weight on their own aims and interests. Power also appears to lead individuals to "objectify" others (to see them as tools to obtain their instrumental goals) and to see relationships as more peripheral.[44]

That's not all. Powerful people react—especially negatively—to any threats to their competence. People in positions of power hold on to power when they can, and individuals who face threats to their power are exceptionally willing to take actions to retain it whether their actions harm others or not. Those given power are more likely to make self-interested decisions when faced with a moral hazard, such as when hedge fund managers take more risks with other people's money because they're rewarded for gains but less often punished for losses. People in power are more willing to denigrate others. Power also leads to overconfident decision making.[45]

Frank Lloyd Wright, perhaps the greatest U.S. architect, is a good example of power's corrupting effects. Early in his career, Wright worked for and was mentored by a renowned architect, Louis Sullivan (sometimes known as the father of the skyscraper). Before Wright achieved greatness, he was generous in his praise for Sullivan. Later in his career, that praise faded, and Wright even took credit for one of Sullivan's noted designs. Wright was never a benevolent man, but as his power accumulated, so did his potential to behave in a "monstrous" way toward others.[46]

Power Variables

As we've discussed, power does appear to have some important disturbing effects on us. But that is hardly the whole story—power is more complicated than that. It doesn't affect everyone in the same way, and there are even positive effects of power. Let's consider each of these in turn.

First, the toxic effects of power depend on the wielder's personality. Research suggests that if we have an anxious personality, power does not corrupt us because we are less likely to think that using power benefits us.[47] Second, the corrosive effect of power can be contained by organizational systems. One study found, for example, that while power made people behave in a self-serving manner, when accountability for this behavior was initiated, the self-serving behavior stopped. Third, we have the means to blunt the negative effects of power. One study showed that simply expressing gratitude toward powerful others makes them less likely to act aggressively against us. Finally, remember the saying that those with little power abuse what little they have? There seems to be some truth to this in that the people most likely to abuse power are those who start low in status and gain power. Why? It appears having low status is threatening, and the fear this creates is used in negative ways if power is later given.[48]

As you can see, some factors can moderate the negative effects of power. But there can be general positive effects. Power energizes and increases motivation to achieve goals. It can also enhance our motivation to help others. One study found, for example, that a desire to help others translated into actual work behavior when people felt a sense of power.[49]

This study points to an important insight about power. It is not so much that power corrupts as it *reveals what we value*. Supporting this line of reasoning, another study found that power led to self-interested behavior only in those with a weak moral identity (the degree to which morals are core to someone's identity). In those with a strong moral identity, power enhanced their moral awareness and willingness to act.[50]

Sexual Harassment: Unequal Power in the Workplace

sexual harassment Any unwanted activity of a sexual nature that affects an individual's employment and creates a hostile work environment.

Sexual harassment is defined as any unwanted activity of a sexual nature that affects an individual's employment or creates a hostile work environment.[51] According to the U.S. Equal Employment Opportunity Commission (EEOC), sexual harassment happens when a person encounters "unwelcome sexual advances, requests for sexual favors, and other verbal or physical conduct of a sexual nature" on the job that disrupts work performance or that creates an "intimidating, hostile, or offensive" work environment.[52] Although the definition changes from country to country, most nations have at least some policies to protect workers. Whether the policies or laws are followed is another question, however. Equal employment opportunity legislation is established in Pakistan, Bangladesh, and Oman, for example, but studies suggest it might not be well implemented.[53]

Generally, sexual harassment is more prevalent in male-dominated societies. For example, a study in Pakistan found that up to 93 percent of female workers were sexually harassed.[54] In Singapore, up to 54 percent of workers (women and men) reported they were sexually harassed.[55] The percentages in the United States and some other countries are generally much lower but still troubling. Surveys indicate about one-quarter of U.S. women and 10 percent of men have been sexually harassed.[56] Data from the EEOC suggest that sexual harassment is decreasing: Sexual harassment claims now make up 10 percent of all discrimination claims, compared with 20 percent in the mid-1990s. Of this percentage, though, claims from men have increased from 11 percent of total claims in 1997 to 17.5 percent today.[57] Sexual harassment is disproportionately prevalent for women in certain types of jobs. In the restaurant industry, for instance, 80 percent of female wait staff reported having been sexually harassed by coworkers or customers, compared to 70 percent of male wait staff.[58]

Most studies confirm that power is central to understanding sexual harassment.[59] This seems true whether the harassment comes from a

A federal jury awarded this woman a $95 million judgment in a sexual harassment lawsuit against her employer for harassment from her supervisor that included unwanted physical contact. The jury found the supervisor guilty of assault and battery, and the company liable for negligent supervision and sexual harassment.
Source: Bill Greenblatt/UPI/Newscom

supervisor, coworker, or employee. And sexual harassment is more likely to occur when there are large power differentials. The supervisor–employee dyad best characterizes an unequal power relationship, where formal power gives the supervisor the capacity to reward and coerce. Because employees want favorable performance reviews, salary increases, and the like, supervisors control resources most employees consider important and scarce. When there aren't effective controls to detect and prevent sexual harassment, abusers are more likely to act. Also vitally important are effective controls to give voice to whistleblowers and protect them from retaliation.[60] The #MeToo and Time's Up movements were formed to establish a coalition giving voice to sexual harassment and abuse survivors to quell the tide of sexual harassment in organizations and communities.[61]

Sexual harassment can have a detrimental impact on individuals and the organization, but it can be avoided. The manager's commitment to the process and responsibility is critical:[62]

1. *Make sure an active policy defines what constitutes sexual harassment, informs employees they can be fired for inappropriate behavior, and establishes procedures for making complaints.*
2. *Reassure employees that they will not encounter retaliation if they file a complaint.*
3. *Investigate every complaint, and inform the legal and HR departments.*
4. *Make sure offenders are disciplined or terminated.*
5. *Set up in-house training to raise employee awareness of sexual harassment issues.*

The bottom line is that managers have a responsibility to protect their employees from a hostile work environment. They may easily be unaware that one of their employees is being sexually harassed, but being unaware does not protect them or their organization. If investigators believe a manager could have known about the harassment, both the manager and the company can be held liable.

Prevention of sexual harassment at the workplace is important to encourage women to feel safe and thus participate in the workplace. The National Commission for Women, an autonomous body constituted by the Indian government, is an apex body to help address concerns for women in the formal and informal sector. 624 complaints of sexual harassment against women in the workplace in 2021.[63]

Politics: Power in Action

11-6 Describe how politics work in organizations.

Whenever people get together in groups, power will be exerted. People in organizations want to carve out a niche to exert influence, earn rewards, and advance their careers. If they convert their power into action, we describe them as being engaged in *politics.* Those with good political skills have the ability to use their bases of power effectively.[64] Politics are not only inevitable; they might be essential, too (see OB Poll).

Definition of Organizational Politics

There is no shortage of definitions of *organizational politics.* Essentially, this type of politics focuses on the use of power to affect decision making in an organization, sometimes for self-serving and organizationally unsanctioned

political behavior Activities that are not required as part of a person's formal role in the organization but that influence, or attempt to influence, the distribution of advantages and disadvantages within the organization.

behaviors.[65] For our purposes, **political behavior** in organizations consists of activities that are not required as part of an individual's formal role but that influence, or attempt to influence, the distribution of advantages and disadvantages within the organization.[66]

This definition encompasses what most people mean when they talk about organizational politics. Political behavior is outside specified job requirements. It requires some attempt to use power bases. It includes efforts to influence the goals, criteria, or processes used for decision making. Our definition is broad enough to include varied political behaviors such as withholding key information from decision makers, joining a coalition, whistle-blowing, spreading rumors, leaking confidential information to the media, exchanging favors with others for mutual benefit, and lobbying on behalf of or against a particular individual or decision alternative. In this way, political behavior is often negative, but not always.

The Reality of Politics

Interviews with experienced managers show that most believe political behavior is a major part of organizational life.[67] Many managers report some use of political behavior is ethical, as long as it doesn't directly harm anyone else. They describe politics as necessary and believe someone who never uses political behavior will have a hard time getting things done. Most also indicate that they have never been trained to use political behavior effectively. But why, you may wonder, must politics exist? Isn't it possible for an organization to be politics-free? It's *possible*—but unlikely.

Organizations have individuals and groups with different values, goals, and interests.[68] This sets up the potential for conflict over the allocation of limited resources, such as budgets, work space, and salary and bonus pools. If resources were abundant, all constituencies within an organization could satisfy their goals. But because they are limited, not everyone's interests can be satisfied.

OB POLL

Importance of Organizational Politics

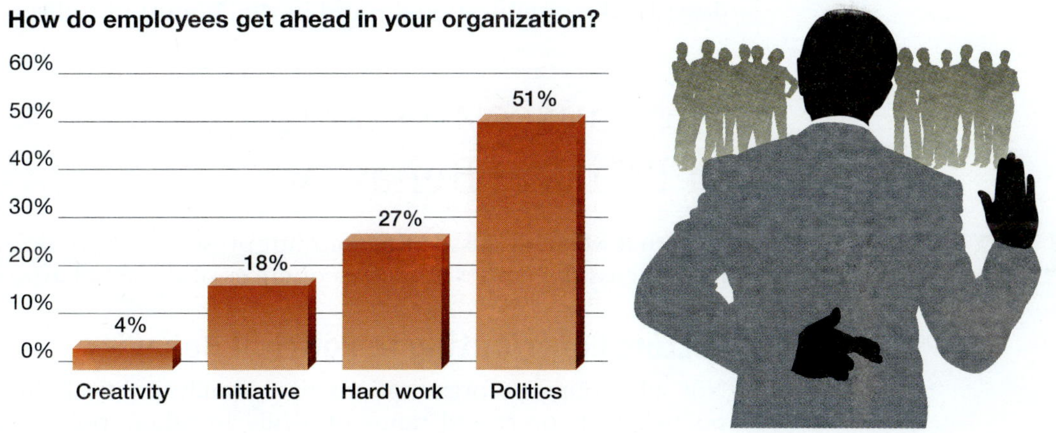

Source: Based on D. Crampton, "Is How Americans Feel about Their Jobs Changing?" (September 28, 2012), http://corevalues.com/employee-motivation/is-how-americans-feel-about-their-jobs-changing.

Furthermore, gains by one individual or group are often *perceived* as coming at the expense of others within the organization (whether they are or not). These forces create competition among members for the organization's limited resources.

For instance, Abhishek Mishra of MW High Tech Projects who worked in MW High Tech Projects reported unethical practices with respect to statutory dues. The CBI enquiry lead by the Central Vigilance Committee lead to the company withdrawing its Indian operations. The case is still being heard in the courts and in the meanwhile attempts have been made on Abhishek Mishra's life. Abhishek has also not been able to find work because of his reputation of being a whistleblower.[69]

Maybe the most important factor leading to politics within organizations is the realization that most of the "facts" used to allocate limited resources are open to interpretation. When allocating pay based on performance, for instance, what is *good* performance? What's an *adequate* improvement? What constitutes an *unsatisfactory* job? The manager of any major league baseball team knows a .400 hitter is a high performer and a .125 hitter is a poor performer. You don't need to be a baseball genius to know you should play your .400 hitter and send the .125 hitter back to the minors. But what if you have to choose between players who hit .280 and .290? Then less objective factors come into play: fielding expertise, attitude, potential, ability to perform in a clutch, loyalty to the team, and so on. More managerial decisions resemble the choice between a .280 and a .290 hitter than between a .125 hitter and a .400 hitter. It is in this large and ambiguous middle ground of organizational life—where the facts don't speak for themselves—that politics flourish.

Because most decisions have to be made in a climate of ambiguity—where facts are rarely objective and thus open to interpretation—people within organizations will use whatever influence they can to support their goals and interests. That, of course, creates the activities we call *politicking*. One person's "selfless effort to benefit the organization" is seen by another as a "blatant attempt to further his or her interest."[70]

Therefore, to answer the question of whether it is possible for an organization to be politics-free, we can say yes—if all members of that organization hold the same goals and interests, if organizational resources are not scarce, and if performance outcomes are completely clear and objective. But that doesn't describe the organizational world in which most of us live.

The Causes and Consequences of Political Behavior

11-7 Identify the causes, consequences, and ethics of political behavior.

Now that we've discussed the constant presence of politicking in organizations, let's discuss the causes and consequences of these behaviors.

Factors Contributing to Political Behavior

Not all groups or organizations are equally political. In some organizations, politicking is overt and rampant, while in others politics plays a small role in influencing outcomes. Why this variation? Research and observation have identified a number of factors that appear to encourage political behavior. Some are individual characteristics, derived from the qualities of the people employed

Exhibit 11-3 **Factors That Influence Political Behavior**

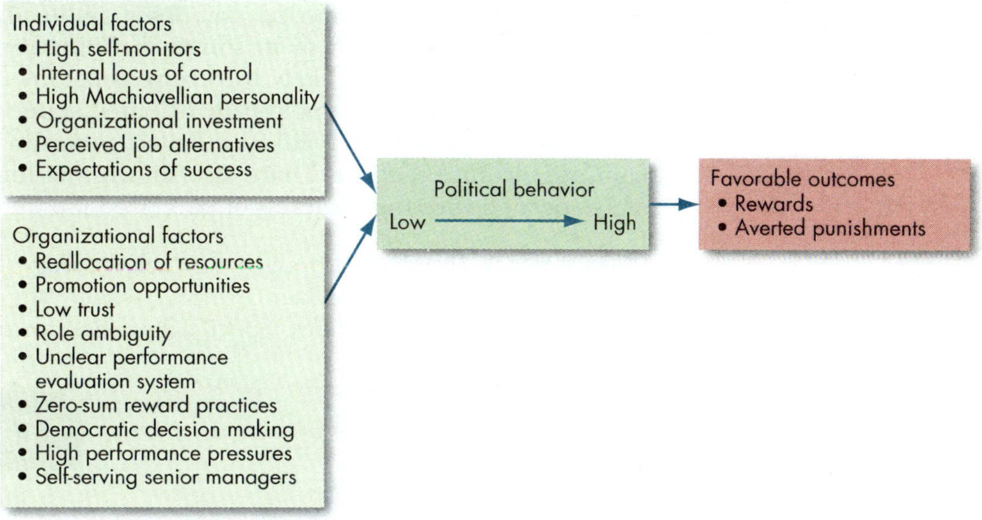

by the organization; others are a result of the organization's culture or internal environment. Exhibit 11-3 illustrates how both individual and organizational factors can increase political behavior and provide favorable outcomes (increased rewards and averted punishments) for individuals and groups in the organization.

Individual Factors At the individual level, researchers have identified certain personality traits, needs, and other factors likely to be related to political behavior. In terms of traits, we find that employees who are high self-monitors, possess an internal locus of control, and have a high need for power are more likely to engage in political behavior. The high self-monitor is more sensitive to social cues, exhibits higher levels of social conformity, and is more likely to be skilled in political behavior than the low self-monitor. Because they believe they can control their environment, individuals with an internal locus of control are more prone to take a proactive stance and attempt to manipulate situations in their favor. Not surprisingly, the Machiavellian personality trait—characterized by the will to manipulate and the desire for power—is consistent with using politics as a means to further personal interests.

An individual's investment in the organization and perceived alternatives influence the degree to which he or she will pursue illegitimate means of political action.[71] The more a person expects increased future benefits from the organization, and the more that person has to lose if forced out, the less likely he or she is to use illegitimate means. Conversely, the more alternate job opportunities an individual has—due to a favorable job market, possession of scarce skills or knowledge, prominent reputation, or influential contacts outside the organization—the more likely the person is to employ politics.

An individual with low expectations of success from political means is unlikely to use them. High expectations from such measures are most likely to be the province of both experienced and powerful individuals with polished political skills, and inexperienced and naïve employees who misjudge their chances.

Some individuals engage in more political behavior because they simply are better at it. Such individuals read interpersonal interactions well, fit their behavior to situational needs, and excel at networking.[72] These people are often indirectly rewarded for their political efforts. For example, a study of a construction firm in southern China found that politically skilled subordinates were more likely to receive recommendations for rewards from their supervisors and that politically oriented supervisors were especially likely to respond positively to politically skilled subordinates.[73] Other studies from countries around the world have also shown that higher levels of political skill are associated with higher levels of perceived job performance.[74]

Organizational Factors Although we acknowledge the role that individual differences can play, the evidence more strongly suggests that certain situations and cultures promote politics. Specifically, when an organization's resources are

Career OBjectives

Should I become political?

My office is so political! Everyone is just looking for ways to get ahead by plotting and scheming rather than doing the job. Should I just go along with it and develop my own political strategy?

— Julia

Dear Julia:

There's definitely a temptation to join in when other people are behaving politically. If you want to advance your career, you need to think about social relationships and how to work with other people in a smart and diplomatic way. But that doesn't mean you have to give in to pressure to engage in organizational politics.

Of course, in many workplaces, hard work and achievement aren't recognized, which heightens politicking and lowers performance. But politics aren't just potentially bad for the company. People who are seen as political can be gradually excluded from social networks and informal communication. Coworkers can sabotage a person with a reputation for dishonesty or manipulation so they don't have to deal with him or her. It's also likely that a political person will be the direct target of revenge from those who feel they've been wronged.

If you want to provide a positive alternative to political behavior in your workplace, there are a few steps you can take:

- *Document your work efforts, and find data to back up your accomplishments.* Political behavior thrives in an ambiguous environment where standards for success are subjective and open to manipulation. The best way to shortcut politics is to move the focus toward clear, objective markers of work performance.
- *Call out political behavior when you see it.* Political behavior is, by its very nature, secretive and underhanded. By bringing politics to light, you limit this capacity to manipulate people against one another.
- *Try to develop a network with only those individuals who are interested in performing well together.* This makes it hard for a very political person to get a lot done. On the other hand, trustworthy and cooperative people will be able to find many allies who are genuinely supportive. These support networks will result in performance levels that a lone political person simply cannot match.

Remember, in the long run a good reputation can be your greatest asset!

Sources: Based on A. Lavoie "How to Get Rid of Toxic Office Politics," *Fast Company*, April 10, 2014, http://www.fastcompany.com/3028856/work-smart/how-to-make-office-politicking-a-lame-duck; C. Conner, "Office Politics: Must You Play?," *Forbes*, April 14, 2013, http://www.forbes.com/sites/cherylsnappconner/2013/04/14/office-politics-must-you-play-a-handbook-for-survivalsuccess/; and J. A. Colquitt and J. B. Rodell, "Justice, Trust, and Trustworthiness: A Longitudinal Analysis Integrating Three Theoretical Perspectives," *Academy of Management Journal* 54 (2011): 1183–206.

The opinions provided here are of the managers and authors only and do not necessarily reflect those of their organizations. The authors or managers are not responsible for any errors or omissions, or for the results obtained from the use of this information. In no event will the authors or managers, or their related partnerships or corporations thereof, be liable to you or anyone else for any decision made or action taken in reliance on the opinions provided here.

declining, when the existing pattern of resources is changing, and when there is opportunity for promotions, politicking is more likely to surface.[75] When resources are reduced, people may engage in political actions to safeguard what they have. Also, *any* changes, especially those implying significant reallocation of resources within the organization, are likely to stimulate conflict and increase politicking.

Cultures characterized by low trust, role ambiguity, unclear performance evaluation systems, zero-sum (win–lose) reward allocation practices, democratic decision making, high pressure for performance, and self-serving senior managers will also create breeding grounds for politicking.[76] Because political activities are not required as part of the employee's formal role, the greater the role ambiguity, the more employees can engage in unnoticed political activity. Role ambiguity means that the prescribed employee behaviors are not clear; therefore, there are fewer limits to the scope and functions of the employee's political actions.

zero-sum approach An approach that treats the reward "pie" as fixed so that any gains by one individual are at the expense of another.

The more an organizational culture emphasizes the zero-sum or win–lose approach to reward allocations (which often begins as a result of financial vulnerability), the more employees will be motivated to engage in politicking.[77] The **zero-sum approach** treats the reward "pie" as fixed, so any gain one person or group achieves comes at the expense of another person or group. For example, if $15,000 is distributed among five employees for raises, any employee who gets more than $3,000 takes money away from one or more of the others. Such a practice encourages making others look bad and increasing the visibility of what you do.

There are also political forces at work in the relationships *between* organizations, where politics work differently depending on the organizational cultures.[78] One study showed that when two organizations with very political environments interacted with one another, the political interactions between them hurt performance in collaborative projects. On the other hand, when

Organizations foster politicking when they reduce resources. By announcing plans to downsize its global workforce of 100,000 employees in an effort to increase its competitiveness, French pharmaceutical firm Sanofi stimulated political activity among employees who organized protests against the job cuts.
Source: Robert Pratta/Reuters

Myth or Science?

Powerful Leaders Keep Their (Fr)Enemies Close

This statement appears to be true.

We all have heard the term *frenemies* to describe friends who are also rivals or people who act like friends but secretly dislike each other. Some observers have argued that frenemies are increasing at work due to the "abundance of very close, intertwined relationships that bridge people's professional and personal lives."

Keeping enemies close may be one reason Barack Obama appointed Hillary Clinton secretary of state after their bitter battle for the U.S. presidency, or in the business world, why one entrepreneur decided not to sue a former college classmate who, after working for her startup as a consultant, took that knowledge and started his own, competing company.

Is it really wise to keep your enemies close? And, if so, why?

New research suggests answers to these questions. Three experimental studies found individuals chose to work in the same room as their rival even when informed they would probably perform better apart, sit closer to rivals when working together, and express an explicit preference to be closer to the rival. The researchers further found the primary reason for the "being closer" effect was the desire to monitor the rival's behavior and performance.

The researchers also found the "keeping enemies closer" effect was strong under certain conditions—when the individual was socially dominant, when the individual felt more competition from the team member, and when rewards and the ability to serve as leader were dependent on performance.

These results suggest the concept of frenemies is very real and that we choose to keep our rivals close so we can keep an eye on the competition they bring.

Sources: Based on M. Thompson, "How to Work with Your Startup Frenemies," *VentureBeat*, December 22, 2012, http://venturebeat.com/2012/12/22/frenemies/; and N. L. Mead and J. K. Maner, "On Keeping Your Enemies Close: Powerful Leaders Seek Proximity to Ingroup Power Threats," *Journal of Personality and Social Psychology* 102 (2012): 576–91.

companies with less internal political behavior interacted with one another, even political disputes between them did not lead to lower performance in collaborative projects. This study shows companies should be wary of forming alliances with companies that have high levels of internal political behavior.

How Do People Respond to Organizational Politics?

Trish loves her job as a writer on a weekly U.S. television comedy series but hates the internal politics. "A couple of the writers here spend more time kissing up to the executive producer than doing any work. And our head writer clearly has his favorites. While they pay me a lot and I get to really use my creativity, I'm sick of having to be on alert for backstabbers and constantly having to self-promote my contributions. I'm tired of doing most of the work and getting little of the credit." We all know friends or relatives like Trish who regularly complain about the politics at their jobs. But how do people in general react to organizational politics? Let's look at the evidence.

For most people who have modest political skills or are unwilling to play the politics game, outcomes tend to be predominantly negative. See Exhibit 11-4 for a diagram of this situation. However, very strong evidence indicates perceptions of organizational politics are negatively related to job satisfaction.[80] Politics may lead to self-reported declines in employee performance, perhaps because employees perceive political environments to be unfair, which demotivates them.[81] Not surprisingly, when politicking becomes too much to handle, it can lead employees to quit.[82] When employees of two agencies in a study in Nigeria

Exhibit 11-4 Employee Responses to Organizational Politics

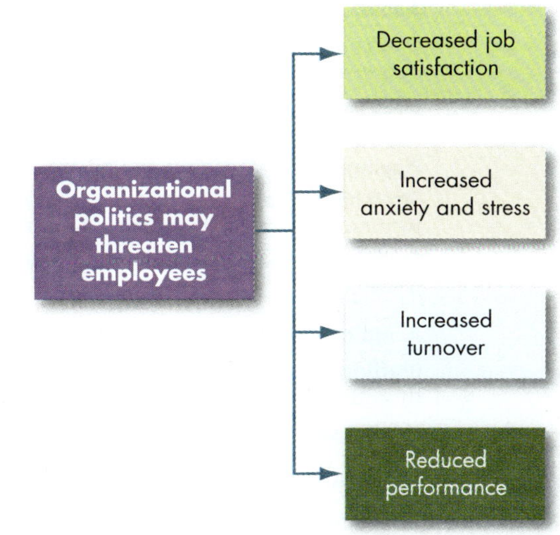

viewed their work environments as political, they reported higher levels of job distress and were less likely to help their coworkers. Thus, although developing countries such as Nigeria present perhaps more ambiguous and therefore more political environments in which to work, the negative consequences of politics appear to be the same as in the United States.[83]

There are some qualifiers. First, the politics–performance relationship appears to be moderated by an individual's understanding of the hows and whys of organizational politics. Researchers noted, "An individual who has a clear understanding of who is responsible for making decisions and why they were selected to be the decision makers would have a better understanding of how and why things happen the way they do than someone who does not understand the decision-making process in the organization."[84] When both politics and understanding are high, performance is likely to increase because these individuals see political activity as an opportunity. This is consistent with what you might expect for individuals with well-honed political skills. But when understanding is low, individuals are more likely to see politics as a threat, which can have a negative effect on job performance.[85]

Second, political behavior at work moderates the effects of ethical leadership.[86] One study found that male employees were more responsive to ethical leadership and showed the most citizenship behavior when levels of both politics and ethical leadership were high. Women, on the other hand, appeared most likely to engage in citizenship behavior when the environment was consistently ethical and *apolitical.*

defensive behaviors Reactive and protective behaviors to avoid action, blame, or change.

Third, when employees see politics as a threat, they often respond with **defensive behaviors**—reactive and protective behaviors to avoid action, blame, or change.[87] (Exhibit 11-5 provides some examples.) In the short run, employees may find that defensiveness protects their self-interest, but in the long run it wears them down. People who consistently rely on defensiveness find that eventually it is the only way they know how to behave. At that point, they lose the trust and support of their peers, bosses, employees, and clients.

Exhibit 11-5 Defensive Behaviors

Avoiding Action

Overconforming. Strictly interpreting your responsibility by saying things like "The rules clearly state..."or "This is the way we've always done it."

Buck passing. Transferring responsibility for the execution of a task or decision to someone else.

Playing dumb. Avoiding an unwanted task by falsely pleading ignorance or inability.

Stretching. Prolonging a task so that one person appears to be occupied—for example, turning a two-week task into a 4-month job.

Stalling. Appearing to be more or less supportive publicly while doing little or nothing privately.

Avoiding Blame

Bluffing. Rigorously documenting activity to project an image of competence and thoroughness, known as "covering your rear."

Playing safe. Evading situations that may reflect unfavorably. It includes taking on only projects with a high probability of success, having risky decisions approved by superiors, qualifying expressions of judgment, and taking neutral positions in conflicts.

Justifying. Developing explanations that lessen one's responsibility for a negative outcome and/or apologizing to demonstrate remorse, or both.

Scapegoating. Placing the blame for a negative outcome on external factors that are not entirely blameworthy.

Misrepresenting. Manipulation of information by distortion, embellishment, deception, selective presentation, or obfuscation.

Avoiding Change

Prevention. Trying to prevent a threatening change from occurring.

Self-protection. Acting in ways to protect one's self-interest during change by guarding information or other resources.

Impression Management

We know people have an ongoing interest in how others perceive and evaluate them. For example, North Americans spend billions of dollars on diets, health club memberships, cosmetics, and plastic surgery—all intended to make them more attractive to others. Being perceived positively by others has benefits in an organizational setting. It might, for instance, help us initially to get the jobs we want in an organization and, once hired, to get favorable evaluations, superior salary increases, and more rapid promotions. The process by which individuals attempt to control the impressions that others form of them is called **impression management (IM)**.[88]

impression management (IM) The process by which individuals attempt to control the impressions that others form of them.

Who might we predict will engage in IM? No surprise here. It's our old friend, the high self-monitor.[89] Low self-monitors tend to present images of themselves that are consistent with their personalities, regardless of the beneficial or detrimental effects for them. In contrast, high self-monitors are good at reading situations and molding their appearances and behavior to fit each situation. If you want to control the impressions others form of you, what IM techniques can you use? Exhibit 11-6 summarizes some of the most popular with examples.

Keep in mind that when people engage in IM, they are sending a false message that might be true under other circumstances.[90] Excuses, for instance, may be offered with sincerity. Referring to the example in Exhibit 11-6, you

Exhibit 11-6 Impression Management (IM) Techniques

Conformity

Agreeing with someone else's opinion to gain his or her approval is a *form of ingratiation.*

Example: A manager tells his boss, "You're absolutely right on your reorganization plan for the western regional office. I couldn' t agree with you more."

Favors

Doing something nice for someone to gain that person' s approval is a *form of ingratiation.*

Example: A salesperson says to a prospective client, "I've got two tickets to the theater tonight that I can't use. Take them. Consider it a thank-you for taking the time to talk with me."

Excuses

Explaining a predicament-creating event aimed at minimizing the apparent severity of the predicament is a *defensive IM technique.*

Example: A sales manager says to her boss, "We failed to get the ad in the paper on time, but no one responds to those ads anyway."

Apologies

Admitting responsibility for an undesirable event and simultaneously seeking to get a pardon for the action is a *defensive IM technique.*

Example: An employee says to his boss, "I'm sorry I made a mistake on the report. Please forgive me."

Self-Promotion

Highlighting your best qualities, downplaying your deficits, and calling attention to your achievements is a *self-focused IM technique.*

Example: A salesperson tells his boss, "Matt worked unsuccessfully for three years to try to get that account. I sewed it up in six weeks. I'm the best closer this company has."

Enhancement

Claiming that something you did is more valuable than most other members of the organizations would think is a *self-focused IM technique.*

Example: A journalist tells his editor, "My work on this celebrity divorce story was really a major boost to our sales" (even though the story only made it to page 3 in the entertainment section).

Flattery

Complimenting others about their virtues in an effort to make yourself appear perceptive and likeable is an *assertive IM technique.*

Example: A new sales trainee says to her peer, "You handled that client's complaint so tactfully! I could never have handled that as well as you did."

Exemplification

Doing more than you need to in an effort to show how dedicated and hard working you are is an *assertive IM technique.*

Example: An employee sends e-mails from his work computer when he works late so that his supervisor will know how long he's been working.

Source: Based on M. C. Bolino, K. M. Kacmar, W. H. Turnley, and J. B. Gilstrap, "A Multi-Level Review of Impression Management Motives and Behaviors," *Journal of Management* 34, no. 6 (2008): 1080–109.

can *actually* believe that ads contribute little to sales in your region. But misrepresentation can have a high cost. If you cry wolf once too often, no one is likely to believe you when the wolf really comes. So the impression manager must be cautious not to be perceived as insincere or manipulative.[91]

One study found that when managers attributed an employee's citizenship behaviors to impression management, they actually felt angry (probably because they felt manipulated) and gave subordinates lower performance ratings. When managers attributed the same behaviors to prosocial values and concern about the organization, they felt happy and gave higher performance ratings.[92] In sum, people don't like to feel others are manipulating them through impression management, so such tactics should be employed with caution. Not all impression management consists of talking yourself up, either. Recent research suggests modesty, in the form of generously providing credit to others and understating your own contributions to success, may create a more positive impression on others.[93]

Most of the studies to test the effectiveness of IM techniques have related IM to two criteria: interview success and performance evaluations. Let's consider each of these.

Interviews and IM The evidence indicates that most job applicants and interviewers alike use IM techniques in interviews and that it works, in part

An Ethical Choice

How Much Should You Manage Interviewer Impressions?

Almost everyone agrees that dressing professionally, highlighting previous accomplishments, and expressing interest in the job are reasonable impression management tactics to improve your presentation in an interview. Strategies like flattering the interviewer and using positive nonverbal cues like smiling and nodding are also often advised.

Is there an upside to such impression management? Research generally shows there is. The more effort applicants put into highlighting their skills, motivation, and admiration for the organization, the more likely they are to be hired. A recent study in Taiwan examined this relationship, finding that interviewers saw applicants who talked confidently about their qualifications as a better fit for the job, and applicants who said positive things about the organization as a better fit for the organization. Positive nonverbal cues improved interviewer moods, which also improved the applicant's ratings.

Despite evidence that making an effort to impress an interviewer can pay off, you can go too far. Evidence that a person misrepresented qualifications in the hiring process is usually grounds for immediate termination. Even so-called white lies are a problem if they create unfounded expectations. For example, if you noted that you managed budgets in the past when all you were doing was tracking expenditures, you lack skills your boss will expect you to have. When you fail to deliver, it will look very bad for you. However, if you describe your experience more accurately but note your desire to learn, the company will know you need additional training and that you'll need a bit of extra time.

So what does an ethical, effective interview strategy entail? The key is to find a positive but truthful way to manage impressions. Don't be afraid to let an employer know about your skills and accomplishments, and be sure to show your enthusiasm for the job. At the same time, keep your statements as accurate as possible, and be careful not to overstate your abilities. In the long run, you're much more likely to be happy and successful in a job where both you and the interviewer can assess fit honestly.

Sources: Based on C. Chen and M. Lin, "The Effect of Applicant Impression Management Tactics on Hiring Recommendations: Cognitive and Affective Processes," *Applied Psychology: An International Review* 63, no. 4, (2014): 698–724; J. Levashina, C. J. Hartwell, F. P. Morgeson, and M. A. Campion "The Structured Employment Interview: Narrative and Quantitative Review of the Research Literature," *Personnel Psychology* (Spring 2014): 241–93; and M. Nemko, "The Effective, Ethical, and Less Stressful Job Interview," *Psychology Today*, March 25, 2014, https://www.psychologytoday.com/blog/how-do-life/201503/the-effective-ethical-and-less-stressful-job-interview.

because they increase interviewer perceptions of the applicants' warmth and competence.[94] Interviewers are rarely able to detect when an individual is engaging in impression management, especially when applicants are using deception to engage in impression management.[95] To develop a sense of how effective different IM techniques are in interviews, one study grouped data from thousands of recruiting and selection interviews into appearance-oriented efforts (like looking professional), explicit tactics (like flattering the interviewer or talking up your own accomplishments), and verbal cues (like using positive terms and showing general enthusiasm).[96] Across all the dimensions, it was quite clear that IM was a powerful predictor of how well people did. However, there was a twist. When interviews were highly structured, meaning the interviewer's questions were written out in advance and focused on applicant qualifications, the effects of IM were substantially weaker. Manipulative behaviors like IM are more likely to have an effect in ambiguous and unstructured interviews. In addition, the effectiveness of impression management depends on the applicants' ability to correctly identify what traits or skills the interviewer is looking for.[97]

Performance Evaluations and IM In terms of performance evaluations, the picture is quite different. Ingratiation is positively related to performance ratings, meaning those who ingratiate themselves with their supervisors get higher performance evaluations. However, self-promotion appears to backfire: Those who self-promote actually may receive *lower* performance ratings.[98] There is an important qualifier to these general findings. It appears that individuals high in political skill are able to translate IM into higher performance appraisals, whereas those lower in political skill are more likely to be hurt by their IM attempts.[99] Another study of 760 boards of directors found that individuals who ingratiated themselves with current board members (e.g., expressed agreement with the director, pointed out shared attitudes and opinions, complimented the director) increased their chances of landing on a board.[100] Interns who attempted to use ingratiation with their supervisors in one study were usually disliked—unless they had high levels of political skill. For those who had this ability, ingratiation led to higher levels of liking from supervisors and higher performance ratings.[101]

What explains these consistent results across multiple studies and contexts? If you think about them, they make sense. Ingratiating always works because everyone—both interviewers and supervisors—likes to be treated nicely. However, self-promotion may work only in interviews and backfire on the job: The interviewer has little idea whether you're blowing smoke about your accomplishments, but the supervisor knows because it's his or her job to observe you.

Are our conclusions about responses to politics valid around the world? Should we expect employees in Israel, for instance, to respond the same way to workplace politics that employees in the United States do? Almost all our conclusions on employee reactions to organizational politics are based on studies conducted in North America. The few studies that have included other countries suggest some minor modifications.[102] One study of managers in U.S. culture and three Chinese cultures (People's Republic of China, Hong Kong, and Taiwan) found U.S. managers evaluated "gentle persuasion" tactics such as consultation and inspirational appeal as more effective than did their Chinese counterparts.[103] Other research suggests effective U.S. leaders achieve influence by focusing on the personal goals of group members and the tasks at hand (an analytical approach), whereas influential East Asian leaders focus on relationships among group members and meeting the demands of people around them (a holistic approach).[104] Another study of Chinese supervisors and subordinates found that subordinates were seen as more agreeable and conscientious when they engaged in self-effacing behaviors, but only if these behaviors made them appear modest rather than supplicating.[105]

The Ethics of Behaving Politically

Although there are no clear-cut ways to differentiate ethical from unethical politicking, there are some questions you should consider. For example, what is the utility of engaging in politicking? Sometimes we do it for little good reason. Senior leaders in organizations across India display their education from reputed institutions such as IIM Ahmedabad in their social media profiles such as, Linkedin. However, the fact is that they would have attended just a two-day management training at the said institution. Likewise, there are corporate leaders who would have claimed to have worked in a company which may not be true in many cases. Outright lies like this may be a rather rare and extreme example of impression management, but many of us have at least distorted information to make a favorable impression. One thing to keep in mind is whether it's worth the risk. Another issue to consider is whether the utility of engaging in the political behavior will balance out harm (or potential harm) to others. Complimenting a supervisor on her appearance in order to curry favor is probably much less harmful than grabbing credit for a project that others deserve.

Finally, does the political activity conform to standards of equity and justice? Sometimes it is difficult to weigh the costs and benefits of a political action, but its ethicality is clear. The department head who inflates the performance evaluation of a favored employee and deflates the evaluation of a disfavored employee—and then uses these evaluations to justify giving the former a big raise and the latter nothing—has treated the disfavored employee unfairly.

Unfortunately, powerful people can become very good at explaining self-serving behaviors in terms of the organization's best interests. They can persuasively argue that unfair actions are really fair and just. Those who are powerful, articulate, and persuasive are most vulnerable to ethical lapses because they are more likely to get away with them. When faced with an ethical dilemma regarding organizational politics, try to consider whether playing politics is worth the risk and whether others might be harmed in the process. If you have a strong power base, recognize the ability of power to corrupt. Remember it's a lot easier for the powerless to act ethically, if for no other reason than they typically have very little political discretion to exploit.

Mapping Your Political Career

As we have seen, politics is not just for politicians. You can use the concepts presented in this chapter in some very tangible ways in your organization. However, they also have another application: you.

One of the most useful ways to think about power and politics is in terms of your own career.[106] What are your ambitions? Who has the power to help you achieve them? What is your relationship to these people? The best way to answer these questions is with a political map, which can help you sketch out your relationships with the people on whom your career depends. Exhibit 11-7 contains such a political map.[107] Let's walk through it.

Exhibit 11-7 Drawing Your Political Map

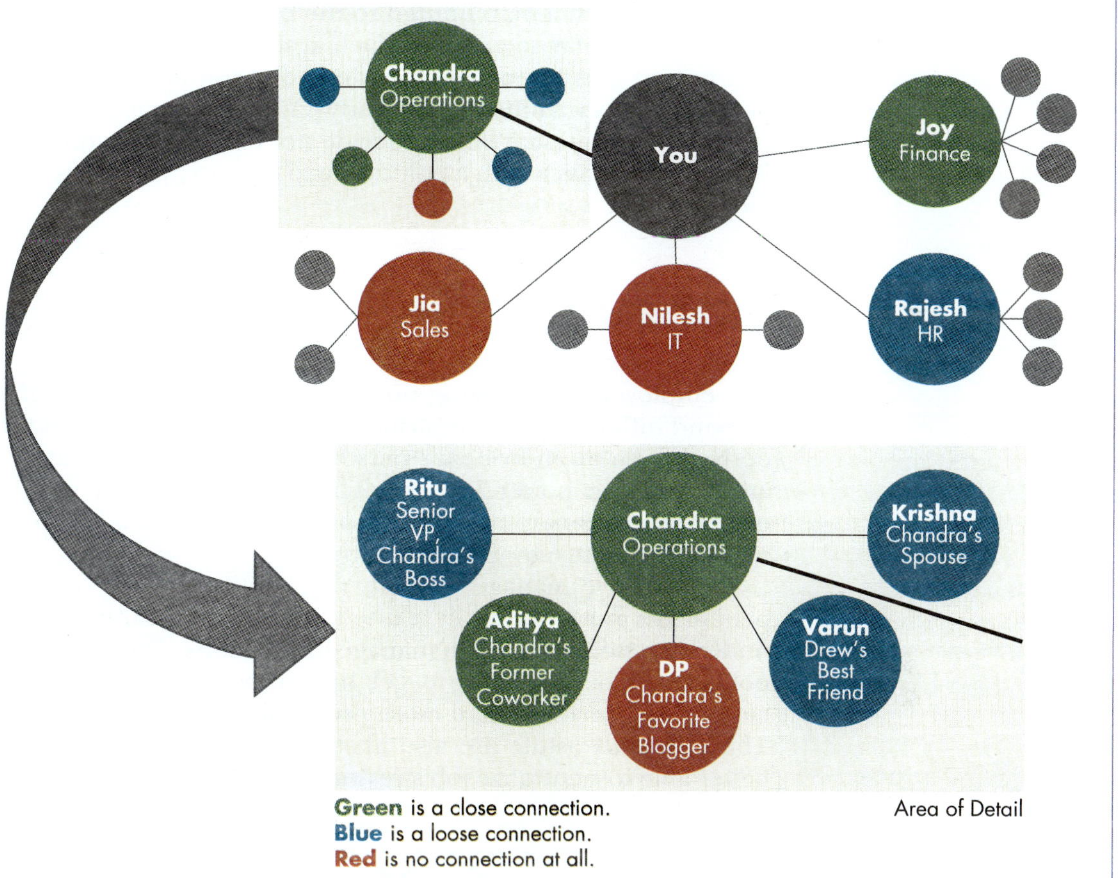

Source: Based on D. Clark, "A Campaign Strategy for Your Career," *Harvard Business Review* (November 2012): 131–4.

Assume your future promotion depends on five people, including Chandra, your immediate supervisor. As you can see in the exhibit, you have a close relationship with Chandra (you would be in real trouble otherwise). You also have a close relationship with Joy in finance. However, with the others, you have either a loose relationship (Rajesh) or none at all (Jia, Nilesh). One obvious implication of this map is the need to formulate a plan to gain more influence over, and a closer relationship with, these people. How might you do that?

The map also provides for a useful way to think about the power network. Assume the five individuals all have their own networks. In this case, though, assume these aren't so much power networks like yours as they are influence networks of the people who influence the individuals in power positions.

One of the best ways to influence people is indirectly. What if you played in a tennis league with Aditya, Chandra's former coworker who you know remains friends with Chandra? To influence Aditya, in many cases, may also be to influence Nilesh. In addition, why not post an entry on CJ's blog? You can complete a similar analysis for the other four decision makers and their networks.

Of course, this map doesn't show you everything you need to know—no map does. For example, rarely would all five people have the same amount of power. Maps are also harder to construct in the era of large social networks. Try to keep such a map limited to the people who *really* matter to your career.

All of this may seem a bit Machiavellian to you. Remember, however, only one person gets the promotion, and your competition may have a map of his or her own. As we noted in the early part of the chapter, power and politics are part of organizational life. To decide not to play is deciding not to be effective. Better to be explicit with a political map than to proceed as if power and politics didn't matter.

Summary

Few employees relish being powerless in their jobs and organizations. People respond differently to the various power bases. Expert and referent power are derived from an individual's personal qualities. In contrast, coercion, reward, and legitimate power are essentially organizationally granted. Competence especially appears to offer wide appeal, and its use as a power base results in high performance by group members.

An effective manager accepts the political nature of organizations. Some people are more politically astute than others, meaning they are aware of the underlying politics and can manage impressions. Those who are good at playing politics can be expected to get higher performance evaluations and hence larger salary increases and more promotions than the politically naïve or inept. The politically astute are also likely to exhibit higher job satisfaction and be better able to neutralize job stressors.

Implications for Managers

- To maximize your power, increase others' dependence on you. For instance, increase your power in relation to your boss by developing a needed knowledge or skill for which there is no ready substitute.
- You will not be alone in attempting to build your power bases. Others, particularly employees and peers, will be seeking to increase your dependence on them while you are trying to minimize it and increase their dependence on you.
- Try to avoid putting others in a position where they feel they have no power.
- By assessing behavior in a political framework, you can better predict the actions of others and use that information to formulate political strategies that will gain advantages for you and your work unit.
- Consider that employees who have poor political skills or are unwilling to play the politics game generally relate perceived organizational politics to lower job satisfaction and self-reported performance, increased anxiety, and higher turnover. Therefore, if you are adept at organizational politics, help others understand the importance of becoming politically savvy.

Everyone Wants Power

POINT

We don't admit to everything we want. For instance, one psychologist found people would seldom admit to wanting money, but they thought everyone else wanted it. They were half right—everyone wants money. And everyone wants power.

Harvard psychologist David McClelland was justifiably famous for his study of underlying motives. McClelland measured people's motivation for power based on how they described pictures (this method is called the Thematic Apperception Test [TAT]). Why didn't he simply ask people how much they wanted power? Because he believed that many more people really wanted power than would admit it or even consciously realize. And that's exactly what he found.

Why do we want power? Because it is good for us. It gives us more control over our own lives. It gives us more freedom to do as we wish. There are few things worse in life than feeling helpless and few better than feeling in charge of your destiny. Research shows people with power and status command more respect from others, have higher self-esteem (no surprise there), and enjoy better health than those of less stature.

Take Steve Cohen, founder of SAC Capital Advisors and one of the most powerful men on Wall Street. Worth $11.1 billion, Cohen buys Picassos, lives in a mansion, has white-gloved butlers, and travels the world first class. People will do almost anything to please him—or even to get near him. One writer notes, "Inside his offices, vast fortunes are won and lost. Careers are made and unmade. Type-A egos are inflated and crushed, sometimes in the space of hours." All this is bad for Steve Cohen how?

Usually, people who tell you power doesn't matter are those who have no hope of getting it. Wanting power, like being jealous, can be one of those secrets people just won't admit to.

COUNTERPOINT

Of course it's true that some people desire power—and often behave ruthlessly to get it. For most of us, however, power is not high in priority, and for some, it's actually undesirable.

Research shows that most individuals feel uncomfortable when placed in powerful positions. One study asked individuals, before they began work in a four-person team, to "rank, from 1 [highest] to 4 [lowest], in terms of status and influence within the group, what rank you would like to achieve." Only about one-third (34 percent) of participants chose the highest rank. In a second study, researchers focused on employees participating in Amazon's Mechanical Turk online service. They found that the main reason people wanted power was to earn respect. If they could get respect without gaining power, that was preferred. In a third study, researchers found that individuals desired power only when they had high ability—in other words, when their influence helped their groups.

These studies suggest that we often confuse the desire for power with other things—like the desire to be respected and to help our groups and organizations succeed. In these cases, power is something most of us seek for more benevolent ends—and only when we think it does good.

Another study confirmed that most people want respect from their peers, not power. Cameron Anderson, the author of this research, sums it up nicely: "You don't have to be rich to be happy, but instead be a valuable contributing member to your groups. What makes a person high in status in a group is being engaged, generous with others, and making self-sacrifices for the greater good."

Oh, and about Steve Cohen ... you realize he pleaded guilty and paid a $1.2 billion fine for failing to prevent insider trading and then had to shut down SAC, right?

Sources: Based on B. Burrough and B. McLean, "The Hunt for Steve Cohen," *Vanity Fair*, June 2013, http://www.vanityfair.com/news/business/2013/06/steve-cohen-insider-trading-case; C. Anderson, R. Willer, G. J. Kilduff, and C. E. Brown, "The Origins of Deference: When Do People Prefer Lower Status?," *Journal of Personality and Social Psychology* 102 (2012): 1077–88; C. Anderson, M. W Kraus, A. D. Galinsky, and D. Keltner, "The Local-Ladder Effect: Social Status and Subjective Well-Being," *Psychological Science 23*(7) (2012): 764–71; S. Kennelly, "Happiness Is about Respect, Not Riches," *Greater Good,* July 13, 2012, http://greatergood.berkeley.edu/article/item/happiness_is_about_respect_not_riches; and P. Lattman and B. Protess, "$1.2 Billion Fine for Hedge Fund SAC Capital in Insider Case," *The New York Times Dealbook*, November 4, 2013, http://dealbook.nytimes.com/2013/11/04/sac-capital-agrees-to-plead-guilty-to-insider-trading/?_r=0.

CHAPTER REVIEW

QUESTIONS FOR REVIEW

11-1 How is leadership different from power?

11-2 What are the similarities and differences among the five bases of power?

11-3 What is the role of dependence in power relationships?

11-4 What power or influence tactics and their contingencies are identified most often?

11-5 What are the causes and consequences of abuse of power?

11-6 How do politics work in organizations?

11-7 What are the causes, consequences, and ethics of political behavior?

APPLICATION AND EMPLOYABILITY

Power is an important part of organizational behavior. Who has power (and who doesn't) shapes which employees make decisions and advance in their careers. There are many tactics that people can use to gain power and to influence those in power. Individuals can also influence others through political behaviors. In this chapter, you used many different skills that are important to your employability while learning about power and politics. You learned critical thinking skills while reading about the debate over whether most people want power, studying research on keeping enemies closer, and learning how to avoid politics. You also applied your knowledge to using impression management techniques in job interviews. In the next section, you will further apply your knowledge and critical thinking skills to addressing office romances, promoting gender diversity on executive boards, and learning the drawbacks to ingratiating oneself to a boss.

EXPERIENTIAL EXERCISE The Dark Side of Power

Form groups of three or four and reflect on the following study from 1998 by psychologist Dacher Keltner and his team at UC Berkeley in California. Keltner wanted to examine the consequences of power on people's behavior. He invited participants to a lab study and divided them into groups of three each. In each team, one person was randomly assigned the role of the leader and the team then was asked to work on some boring tasks. During the execution of such tasks, the researchers brought out a plate with four chocolate cookies, and each team member took one. Thus, each team had a cookie remaining on the plate. Researchers observed that the person appointed as a leader claimed the last cookie without even asking others. They also displayed other impolite behaviors, such as eating with their mouths open or in a manner that many crumbs fell on their sweater. This experiment, also known as the Cookie Monster study, demonstrates that people with power tend to lose touch with other people and take on disrespectful behaviors. Consider the following questions as a team.

Questions

11-8. Discuss the possible reasons that leaders may be led to abuse their position and ignore others' needs. What lessons about power does this study teach?

11-9. Discuss whether any of you has ever behaved like the participants in the experiment under any circumstances. Each team member is also invited to share relevant stories. Did they ever realize that the people they know had started to behave differently when they had power? Did all people react to the influence of power in the same way? Which individuals are less prone to corruptive power?

11-10. As a team, propose three or four possible interventions that could help mitigate such adverse consequences of power in the workplace.

ETHICAL DILEMMA Sexual Harassment and Office Romances

In this chapter, we talked about sexual harassment and how uneven power dynamics can contribute to sexual harassment. Sexual harassment often occurs because one employee, such as a supervisor, can use his or her control of resources to reward or coerce another employee into sexual behaviors. For example, when a manager asks a female subordinate to go on a date with him, the female subordinate is more likely to say yes because he has control over resources in the organization. If she declines his request, he could retaliate and withhold privileges from her.

Many companies try to prevent sexual harassment by forbidding coworkers from dating. Some have slightly softer rules. They forbid employees from dating their direct supervisors or coworkers in the same department, presumably so that employees cannot use their power to perpetrate sexual harassment. These less stringent policies do not account for informal power that may exist in organizations. An employee can be in a junior position and still be able withhold access to resources, or this employee can have enough political skill to harm another employee's career.

On the other hand, it may be impractical to enforce a policy against office romances. Most people who go out to work spend one-third of their lives working, so it is likely that an employee with meet a mate at their workplace. In a survey conducted by Randstad in 2012, seventy percent of Indian employees reported that they had a romantic brush with a co-worker.[108] There is openness among Indian IT organizations towards dating coworkers and couples working in the same organization.

Is it worth discouraging office romances? The same survey revealed that almost one-third of office relationships resulted in marriage. And what should you do if Cupid's arrow strikes you in the breakroom? National workplace expert Lynn Taylor has this advice, "Policy or no policy, love happens. So in the absence of written rules...there's one common barometer: your common sense."

Questions

11-11. Do you think offices should include rules about office romances in their sexual harassment policies? Why or why not?

11-12. Is it ever okay for a supervisor to date a subordinate? What if someone becomes their romantic partner's supervisor after the relationship was already initiated?

11-13. Why might 36 percent of the survey respondents say that they hid their romantic relationships from coworkers? How does this relate to what we learned about office gossip in Chapter 9?

Sources: Based on J. Smith, "Eight Questions to Ask Yourself before You Start Dating a Coworker," *Business Insider*, May 29, 2016, http://www.businessinsider.com/questions-to-ask-before-you-start-dating-a-coworker-2016-5/#-1; J. Grasz, "Workers Name Their Top Office Romance Deal Breakers in New CareerBuilder Survey," *CareerBuilder*, February 11, 2015, http://www.careerbuilder.com/share/aboutus/pressreleasesdetail.aspx?sd=2%2F11%2F2015&id=pr868&ed=12%2F31%2F2015.

CASE INCIDENT 1 Power and Gender Diversity

Only 17.3% of the board seats are occupied by women in Indian listed companies.[109] In Malta, Greece, and Estonia, the figure is less than 10 percent. This disparity highlights the discrimination and the glass ceiling that many women continue to face, but more and more research is showing that it may also be bad for business.

In Chapter 9, we learned that diverse groups may be more creative and innovative, and decision making is more accurate when a group has a variety of perspectives. This principle appears to hold true when it comes to diverse executive boards. A review of 140 studies found that having women on an executive board boosted returns, especially in countries with stronger shareholder protections. The same review found that having female board members helped companies' marketplace performance in countries with higher gender equality. In addition, boards with greater gender diversity are better at monitoring company performance and engage in more strategic involvement. Other research suggests that diverse executive boards are not always beneficial; in most circumstances, having women with greater power on a board led to more strategic change in the organization, but this is only true when the company is not threatened by low performance.

Some countries are trying to improve their economies by creating quotas that promote more gender-diverse boards. France passed legislation in 2011 to promote gender-diverse boards and has a quota of 40 percent. As a result, 44 percent of board members in the country are women, the highest in the European Union.

Questions

11-14. Why do you think having women on a board changes a firm's performance?

11-15. Do you think using a quota system to promote gender diversity is a good idea? Why or why not?

11-16. Why do you think some countries have more gender-diverse boards than others?

Sources: Based on S. H. Jeong and D. A. Harrison, "Glass Breaking, Strategy Making, and Value Creating: Meta-Analytic Outcomes of Females as CEOs and TMT Members," *Academy of Management Journal*, 60, no.4 (2016); C. Post and C. J. Byron, "Women on Boards and Firm Financial Performance: A Meta-Analysis," *Academy of Management Journal* 58, no. 5 (2015): 1546–71; T. M. del Carmen, T. L. Miller, and T. M. Trzebiatowski, "The Double-Edged Nature of Board Gender Diversity: Diversity, Firm Performance, and the Power of Women Directors as Predictors of Strategic Change," *Organization Science* 25, no. 2 (2014): 609–32; and M. Liautaud, "Breaking Through: Stories and Best Practices from Companies That Help Women Succeed," *Huffington Post*, April 29, 2016, http://www.huffingtonpost.com/martine-liautaud/stories-and-best-practices-from-companies-that-help-women-succeed_b_9722518.html; and European Commission, "2019 Report on Equality between Women and Men in the EU," Luxembourg: Publications Office of the European Union, 2019.

CASE INCIDENT 2 Where Flattery Will Get You

One of the various impression management techniques that people use in the workplace is flattering or complimenting a person. Many people believe that flattery has a positive impact on career prospects. Vicky Oliver, author of *301 Smart Answers to Tough Interview Questions*, suggests using flattery to ask for a raise. Oliver advises employees to use other impression management techniques, such as self-promotion (e.g., highlighting your accomplishments) and enhancement (e.g., showing how your work is superior to your peers), but she also suggests complimenting or strategically "flattering" the boss before sitting down to talk about a salary raise.

Does flattery always work? The answer is yes and no. Flattery may influence someone in power but only if they see the flattery as sincere. Seeming sincere may be especially difficult, however, because people who have the most power are often the hardest to fool. After all, they have more experience with people flattering them. Recent research suggests that there may be a way to make flattery more effective: Try to convince yourself that you actually like the person you are flattering. In the study, employees who spent more time considering what they had in common with their boss were more likely to obtain their goal through flattery.

Even if an employee is successful using flattery, it has one major drawback. Another recent study found that executives who flatter their CEOs are more likely to resent their CEO later on. Though CEOs do not require their employees to compliment them, many employees feel demeaned when they go to great lengths to strategically flatter the boss. Employees who complimented their CEOs were also more likely to complain to third parties about their boss. Some even complained to journalists.

Questions

11-17. What are some other consequences of using flattery at work? Why do these consequences occur?

11-18. The study described in this case also found that executives resented directing flattery toward female and minority CEOs more than white males. Why do you think this finding is true?

11-19. Are there impression management techniques that are more effective than flattery?

Sources: Based on V. Oliver, "How to Suck Up to Your Boss and Get a Raise," *Fortune*, January 9, 2017, http://fortune.com/2017/01/09/pay-raise-career-advice-leadership-self-promotion-boss/; C. Romm, "How to Suck Up Without Being Obvious About It," *NY Magazine*, July 5, 2016, http://nymag.com/scienceofus/2016/07/how-to-suck-up-without-being-obvious-about-it.html; and J. McGregor, "Bosses Be Warned: Your Biggest Kiss-Up Could Be Your Biggest Backstabber," *Daily Herald*, April 19, 2017, http://www.dailyherald.com/business/20170416/bosses-be-warned-your-biggest-kiss-up-could-be-your-biggest-backstabber; M. G. McIntyre, "Disgruntlement Won't Advance Your Career," *Pittsburgh Post-Gazette*, September 2.

ENDNOTES

[1] D. A. Buchanan, "You Stab My Back, I'll Stab Yours: Management Experience and Perceptions of Organization Political Behavior," *British Journal of Management* 19, no. 1 (2008): 49–64.

[2] B. Oc, M. R. Bashshur, and C. Moore, "Speaking Truth to Power: The Effect of Candid Feedback on How Individuals with Power Allocate Resources," *Journal of Applied Psychology* 100, no. 2 (2015): 450–63; and R. E. Sturm and J. Antonakis, "Interpersonal Power: A Review, Critique, and Research Agenda," *Journal of Management* 41, no. 1 (2015): 136–63.

[3] C. Anderson and S. Brion, "Perspectives on Power in Organizations," *Annual Review of Organizational Psychology and Organizational Behavior* 1 (2014): 67–97.

[4] M. Gongloff, "Steve Cohen, Super-Rich and Secretive Trader, Faces Possible SEC Investigation," *Huffington Post,* November 28, 2012, http://www.huffingtonpost.com/2012/11/28/steven-cohen-sac-capital_n_2205544.html.

[5] E. Landells and S. L. Albrecht, "Organizational Political Climate: Shared Perceptions about the Building and Use of Power Bases," *Human Resource Management Review* 23, no. 4 (2013): 357–65; P. Rylander, "Coaches' Bases of Power: Developing Some Initial Knowledge of Athletes' Compliance with Coaches in Team Sports," *Journal of Applied Sport Psychology* 27, no. 1 (2015): 110–21; and G. Yukl, "Use Power Effectively," in E. A. Locke (ed.), *Handbook of Principles of Organizational Behavior* (Malden, MA: Blackwell, 2004): 242–47.

[6] H. Lian, D. J. Brown, D. L. Ferris, L. H. Liang, L. M. Keeping, and R. Morrison, "Abusive Supervision and Retaliation: A Self-Control Framework," *Academy of Management Journal* 57, no. 1 (2014): 116–39.

[7] E. A. Ward, "Social Power Bases of Managers: Emergence of a New Factor," *Journal of Social Psychology* (February 2001): 144–47; and J. French and B. Raven, "The Bases of Social Power," in D. Cartwright (ed.), *Studies in Social Power* (Ann Arbor: University of Michigan Press, 1959): 150–67.

[8] See, for instance, G. D. Granic and A. K. Wagner, "Where Power Resides in Committees," *The Leadership Quarterly* (in press).

[9] French and Raven, "The Bases of Social Power"; and S. R. Giessner and T. W. Schubert, "High in the Hierarchy: How Vertical Location and Judgments of Leaders' Power Are Interrelated," *Organizational Behavior and Human Decision Processes* 104, no. 1 (2007): 30–44; Ward, "Social Power Bases of Managers."

[10] M. Van Djike and M. Poppe, "Striving for Personal Power as a Basis for Social Power Dynamics," *European Journal of Social Psychology* 27, no. 1 (2006): 537–56.

[11] French and Raven, "The Bases of Social Power."

[12] Ibid.

[13] J. D. Kudisch, M. L. Poteet, G. H. Dobbins, M. C. Rush, and J. A. Russell, "Expert Power, Referent Power, and Charisma: Toward the Resolution of a Theoretical Debate," *Journal of Business and Psychology* 10, no. 1 (1995): 177–95.

[14] S. Perman, "Translation Advertising: Where Shop Meets Hip Hop," *Time,* August 30, 2010, http://content.time.com/time/magazine/article/0,9171,2011574,00.html.

[15] Sturm and Antonakis, "Interpersonal Power."

[16] M. C. J. Caniels and A. Roeleveld, "Power and Dependence Perspectives on Outsourcing Decisions," *European Management Journal* 27, no. 6 (2009): 402–17; R.-J. Bryan, D. Kim, and R. S. Sinkovics, "Drivers and Performance Outcomes of Supplier Innovation Generation in Customer-Supplier Relationships: The Role of Power-Dependence," *Decision Sciences* 43, no. 6 (2012): 1003–38; and R. M. Emerson, "Power-Dependence Relations," *American Sociological Review* 27, no. 1 (1962): 31–40.

[17] N. Foulkes, "Tractor Boy," *High Life* (October 2002): 90.

[18] R. S. Burt, M. Kilduff, and S. Tasselli, "Social Network Analysis: Foundations and Frontiers on Advantage," *Annual Review of Psychology* 64 (2013): 527–47; M. A. Carpenter, M. Li, and H. Jiang, "Social Network Research in Organizational Contexts: A Systematic Review of Methodological Issues and Choices," *Journal of Management* (July 1, 2012): 1328–61; and M. Kilduff and D. J. Brass, "Organizational Social Network Research: Core Ideas and Key Debates." *Academy of Management Annals* (January 1, 2010): 317–57.

[19] B. L. Aven, "The Paradox of Corrupt Networks: An Analysis of Organizational Crime at Enron," *Organization Science* 26, no. 4 (2015): 980–96.

[20] J. Gehman, L. K. Treviño, and R. Garud, "Values Work: A Process Study of the Emergence and Performance of Organizational Values Practices," *Academy of Management Journal* (February 1, 2013): 84–112.

[21] J. Battilana and T. Casciaro, "Change Agents, Networks, and Institutions: A Contingency Theory of Organizational Change," *Academy of Management Journal* (April 1, 2012): 381–98.

[22] S. M. Soltis, F. Agneessens, Z. Sasovova, and G. Labianca, "A Social Network Perspective on Turnover Intentions: The Role of Distributive Justice and Social Support," *Human Resource Management* (July 1, 2013): 561–84.

[23] R. Kaše, Z. King, and D. Minbaeva, "Using Social Network Research in HRM: Scratching the Surface of a Fundamental Basis of HRM," *Human Resource Management* (July 1, 2013): 473–83; and R. Cross and L. Prusak, "The People Who Make Organizations Go—or Stop," *Harvard Business Review* (June 2002): https://hbr.org/2002/06/the-people-who-make-organizations-go-or-stop.

[24] See, for example, D. M. Cable and T. A. Judge, "Managers' Upward Influence Tactic Strategies: The Roll of Manager Personality and Supervisor Leadership Style," *Journal of Organizational Behavior* 24, no. 2 (2003): 197–214; M. P. M. Chong, "Influence Behaviors and Organizational Commitment: A Comparative Study," *Leadership and Organization Development Journal* 35, no. 1 (2014): 54–78; and G. Blickle, "Influence Tactics Used by Subordinates: An Empirical Analysis of the Kipnis and Schmidt Subscales," *Psychological Reports* (February 2000): 143–54.

[25] G. R. Ferris, W. A. Hochwarter, C. Douglas, F. R. Blass, R. W. Kolodinksy, and D. C. Treadway, "Social Influence Processes in Organizations and Human Resource Systems," in G. R. Ferris and J. J. Martocchio (eds.), *Research in Personnel and Human Resources Management,* vol. 21 (Oxford, UK: JAI Press/Elsevier, 2003): 65–127; C. A. Higgins, T. A. Judge, and G. R. Ferris, "Influence Tactics and Work Outcomes: A Meta-Analysis," *Journal of Organizational Behavior* (March 2003): 89–106; and M. Uhl-Bien, R. E. Riggio, K. B. Lowe, and M. K. Carsten. "Followership Theory: A Review and Research Agenda," *The Leadership Quarterly* (February 2014): 83–104.

[26] Chong, "Influence Behaviors and Organizational Commitment."

[27] R. E. Petty and P. Briñol, "Persuasion: From Single to Multiple to Metacognitive

Processes," *Perspectives on Psychological Science* 3, no. 2 (2008): 137–47.
[28] J. Badal, "Getting a Raise from the Boss," *The Wall Street Journal*, July 8, 2006, B1, B5.
[29] N. Clarke, N. Alshenalfi, and T. Garavan, "Upward Influence Tactics and Their Effects on Job Performance Ratings and Flexible Work Arrangements: The Mediating Roles of Mutual Recognition Respect and Mutual Appraisal Respect," *Human Resource Management* 58 (2019): 397–416.
[30] Lee et al., "How Do I Get My Way?"
[31] Ibid.
[32] Ibid.
[33] O. Epitropaki and R. Martin, "Transformational-Transactional Leadership and Upward Influence: The Role of Relative Leader-Member Exchanges (RLMX) and Perceived Organizational Support (POS), *Leadership Quarterly* 24, no. 2 (2013): 299–315.
[34] A. W. Kruglanski, A. Pierro, and E. T. Higgins, "Regulatory Mode and Preferred Leadership Styles: How Fit Increases Job Satisfaction," *Basic and Applied Social Psychology* 29, no. 2 (2007): 137–49; and A. Pierro, L. Cicero, and B. H. Raven, "Motivated Compliance with Bases of Social Power," *Journal of Applied Social Psychology* 38, no. 7 (2008): 1921–44.
[35] P. P. Fu and G. Yukl, "Perceived Effectiveness of Influence Tactics in the United States and China," *Leadership Quarterly* (Summer 2000): 251–66; O. Branzei, "Cultural Explanations of Individual Preferences for Influence Tactics in Cross-Cultural Encounters," *International Journal of Cross Cultural Management* (August 2002): 203–18; G. Yukl, P. P. Fu, and R. McDonald, "Cross-Cultural Differences in Perceived Effectiveness of Influence Tactics for Initiating or Resisting Change," *Applied Psychology: An International Review* (January 2003): 66–82; P. P. Fu, T. K. Peng, J. C. Kennedy, and G. Yukl, "Examining the Preferences of Influence Tactics in Chinese Societies: A Comparison of Chinese Managers in Hong Kong, Taiwan, and Mainland China," *Organizational Dynamics* 33, no. 1 (2004): 32–46; and S. Aslani, J. Ramirez-Marin, J. Brett, J. Yao, Z. Semnani-Azad, Z.-X. Zhang, … and W. Adair, "Dignity, Face, and Honor Cultures: A Study of Negotiation Strategy and Outcomes in Three Cultures," *Journal of Organizational Behavior* 37, no. 8 (2016): 1178–201.
[36] C. J. Torelli and S. Shavitt, "Culture and Concepts of Power," *Journal of Personality and Social Psychology* 99, no. 4 (2010): 703–23.
[37] Fu and Yukl, "Perceived Effectiveness of Influence Tactics in the United States and China."; C. Man Zhang and H. R. Greve, "Dominant Coalitions Directing Acquisitions: Different Decision Makers, Different Decisions," *Academy of Management Journal* 62, no. 1 (2019): 44–65.
[38] G. R. Ferris, D. C. Treadway, P. L. Perrewé, R. L. Brouer, C. Douglas, and S. Lux, "Political Skill in Organizations," *Journal of Management* 33, no. 3 (2007): 290–320; G. R. Ferris, B. Parker Ellen III, C. P. McAllister, and L. P. Maher, "Reorganizing Organizational Politics Research: A Review of the Literature and Identification of Future Research Directions," *Annual Review of Organizational Psychology and Organizational Behavior* 6 (2019): 299–323; G. R. Ferris, D. C. Treadaway, R. W. Kolodinsky, W. A. Hochwater, C. J. Kacmar, C. Douglas, and D. D. Fink, "Development and Validation of the Political Skill Inventory," *Journal of Management* 31, no. 1 (2005): 126–52.
[39] S. Granger, L. Neville, and N. Turner, "Political Knowledge at Work: Conceptualization, Measurement, and Applications to Follower Proactivity," *Journal of Occupational and Organizational Psychology* (in press).
[40] T. P. Munyon, J. K. Summers, K. M. Thompson, and G. R. Ferris, "Political Skill and Work Outcomes: A Theoretical Extension, Meta-Analytic Investigation, and Agenda for the Future,". *Personnel Psychology* 68, no. 1 (2015): 143–84; G. R. Ferris, D. C. Treadway, P. L. Perrewé, R. L. Brouer, C. Douglas, and S. Lux, "Political Skill in Organizations," *Journal of Management* (June 2007): 290–320; K. J. Harris, K. M. Kacmar, S. Zivnuska, and J. D. Shaw, "The Impact of Political Skill on Impression Management Effectiveness," *Journal of Applied Psychology* 92, no. 1 (2007): 278–85; W. A. Hochwarter, G. R. Ferris, M. B. Gavin, P. L. Perrewé, A. T. Hall, and D. D. Frink, "Political Skill as Neutralizer of Felt Accountability–Job Tension Effects on Job Performance Ratings: A Longitudinal Investigation," *Organizational Behavior and Human Decision Processes* 102 (2007): 226–39; D. C. Treadway, G. R. Ferris, A. B. Duke, G. L. Adams, and J. B. Tatcher, "The Moderating Role of Subordinate Political Skill on Supervisors' Impressions of Subordinate Ingratiation and Ratings of Subordinate Interpersonal Facilitation," *Journal of Applied Psychology* 92, no. 3 (2007): 848–55; and Z. E. Zhou, L. Yang, and P. E. Spector, "Political Skill: A Proactive Inhibitor of Workplace Aggression Exposure and an Active Buffer of the Aggression-Strain Relationship," *Journal of Occupational Health Psychology* 20, no. 4 (2015): 405–19.
[41] J. J. Dahling and B. G. Whitaker, "When Can Feedback-Seeking Behavior Result in a Better Performance Rating? Investigating the Moderating Role of Political Skill," *Human Performance* 29, no. 2 (2016): 73–88.
[42] M. C. Andrews, K. M. Kacmar, and K. J. Harris, "Got Political Skill? The Impact of Justice on the Importance of Political Skills for Job Performance," *Journal of Applied Psychology* 94, no. 6 (2009): 1427–37.
[43] C. Anderson, S. E. Spataro, and F. J. Flynn, "Personality and Organizational Culture as Determinants of Influence," *Journal of Applied Psychology* 93, no. 3 (2008): 702–10.
[44] Y. Cho and N. J. Fast, "Power, Defensive Denigration, and the Assuaging Effect of Gratitude Expression," *Journal of Experimental Social Psychology* 48 (2012): 778–82.
[45] I. Vitanova, "Nurturing Overconfidence: The Relationship between Leader Power, Overconfidence and Firm Performance," *The Leadership Quarterly* (in press).
[46] A. Grant, "Yes, Power Corrupts, but Power Also Reveals," *Government Executive*, May 23, 2013, http://www.huffingtonpost.com/adam-grant/yes-power-corrupts-but-po_b_3085291.html.
[47] J. K. Maner, M. T. Gaillot, A. J. Menzel, and J. W. Kunstman, "Dispositional Anxiety Blocks the Psychological Effects of Power," *Personality and Social Psychology Bulletin* 38 (2012): 1383–95.
[48] N. J. Fast, N. Halevy, and A. D. Galinsky, "The Destructive Nature of Power without Status," *Journal of Experimental Social Psychology* 48 (2012): 391–94.
[49] T. Seppälä, J. Lipponen, A. Bardi, and A. Pirttilä-Backman, "Change-Oriented Organizational Citizenship Behaviour: An Interactive Product of Openness to Change Values, Work Unit Identification, and Sense of Power," *Journal of Occupational and Organizational Psychology* 85 (2012): 136–55.
[50] K. A. DeCelles, D. S. DeRue, J. D. Margolis, and T. L. Ceranic, "Does Power Corrupt or Enable? When and Why Power Facilitates Self-Interested Behavior," *Journal of Applied Psychology* 97 (2012): 681–89.
[51] J. C. Quick and M. Ann McFadyen, "Sexual Harassment: Have We Made Any Progress?" *Journal of Occupational Health Psychology* 22, no. 3 (2017): 286–98;

A. E. Tenbrunsel, M. R. Rees, and K. A. Diekmann, "Sexual Harassment in Academia: Ethical Climates and Bounded Ethicality," *Annual Review of Psychology* 70 (2019): 245–70.

[52] "Facts about Sexual Harassment," The U.S. Equal Employment Opportunity Commission, www.eeoc.gov/facts/fs-sex.html, accessed June 19, 2015.

[53] F. Ali and R. Kramar, "An Exploratory Study of Sexual Harassment in Pakistani Organizations," *Asia Pacific Journal of Management* 32, no. 1 (2014): 229–49.

[54] Ibid.

[55] Workplace Sexual Harassment Statistics, Association of Women for Action and Research, 2015, http://www.aware.org.sg/ati/wsh-site/14-statistics/.

[56] R. Ilies, N. Hauserman, S. Schwochau, and J. Stibal, "Reported Incidence Rates of Work-Related Sexual Harassment in the United States: Using Meta-Analysis to Explain Reported Rate Disparities," *Personnel Psychology* (Fall 2003): 607–31; and G. Langer, "One in Four U.S. Women Reports Workplace Harassment," *ABC News,* November 16, 2011, http://abcnews.go.com/blogs/politics/2011/11/one-in-four-u-s-women-reports-workplace-harassment/.

[57] "Sexual Harassment Charges," Equal Employment Opportunity Commission, from www.eeoc.gov/eeoc/statistics/, accessed August 20, 2015.

[58] B. Popken, "Report: 80% of Waitresses Report Being Sexually Harassed," *USA Today,* October 7, 2014, http://www.today.com/money/report-80-waitresses-report-being-sexually-harassed-2D80199724.

[59] L. M. Cortina and S. A. Wasti, "Profiles in Coping: Responses to Sexual Harassment across Persons, Organizations, and Cultures," *Journal of Applied Psychology* (February 2005): 182–92; K. Jiang, Y. Hong, P. F. McKay, D. R. Avery, D. C. Wilson, and S. D. Volpone, "Retaining Employees through Anti-Sexual Harassment Practices: Exploring the Mediating Role of Psychological Distress and Employee Engagement," *Human Resource Management* 54, no. 1 (2015): 1–21; and J. W. Kunstman, "Sexual Overperception: Power, Mating Motives, and Biases in Social Judgment," *Journal of Personality and Social Psychology* 100, no. 2 (2011): 282–94.

[60] See, for example, M. E. Bergman, R. Day Langhout, P. A. Palmieri, L. M. Cortina, and L. F. Fitzgerald, "The (Un) reasonableness of Reporting: Antecedents and Consequences of Reporting Sexual Harassment," *Journal of Applied Psychology* 87, no. 2 (2002): 230–42; D. Fernando and A. Prasad, "Sex-Based Harassment and Organizational Silencing: How Women Are Led to Reluctant Acquiescence in Academia," *Human Relations* 72, no. 10 (2019): 1565–94.

[61] A. E. Dastagir, "It's Been Two Years Since the #MeToo Movement Exploded. Now What?," *USA Today,* September 30, 2019, https://www.usatoday.com/story/news/nation/2019/09/30/me-too-movement-women-sexual-assault-harvey-weinstein-brett-kavanaugh/1966463001/; A. Langone, "#MeToo and Time's Up Founders Explain the Difference Between the 2 Movements—and How They're Alike," *Time,* March 22, 2018, https://time.com/5189945/whats-the-difference-between-the-metoo-and-times-up-movements/; #MeToo [website], accessed April 30, 2020, https://metoomvmt.org/; Time's Up [website], accessed April 30, 2020, https://timesupnow.org/.

[62] H. Kwan Cheung, C. B. Goldberg, E. B. King, and V. J. Magley, "Are They True to the Cause? Beliefs about Organizational and Unit Commitment to Sexual Harassment Awareness Training," *Group & Organization Management* 43, no. 4 (2018): 531–60; Quick and McFadyen, "Sexual Harassment"; M. V. Roehling and J. Huang, "Sexual Harassment Training Effectiveness: An Interdisciplinary Review and Call for Research," *Journal of Organizational Behavior* 39 (2018): 134–50.

[63] National Commission for Women. "Statistical Overview of Complaints". *©Government of India. Retrieved from* http://ncwapps.nic.in (Accessed on April 16, 2022)

[64] G. R. Ferris, D. C. Treadway, R. W. Kolokinsky, W. A. Hochwarter, C. J. Kacmar, and D. D. Frink, "Development and Validation of the Political Skill Inventory," *Journal of Management* (February 2005): 126–52.

[65] A. Pullen and C. Rhodes, "Corporeal Ethics and the Politics of Resistance in Organizations," *Organization* 21, no. 6 (2014): 782–96.

[66] G. R. Ferris and W. A. Hochwarter, "Organizational Politics," in S. Zedeck (ed.), *APA Handbook of Industrial and Organizational Psychology,* vol. 3 (Washington, DC: American Psychological Association, 2011): 435–59.

[67] D. A. Buchanan, "You Stab My Back, I'll Stab Yours: Management Experience and Perceptions of Organization Political Behavior," *British Journal of Management* 19, no. 1 (2008): 49–64.

[68] J. Pfeffer, *Power: Why Some People Have It—And Others Don't* (New York: Harper Collins, 2010).

[69] Layak, S. (2019). "The whistleblowers: In the absence of a comprehensive law, here's how employee whistleblowers fare". *The Economic Times (November 24, 2019).* Retrieved from https://economictimes.indiatimes.com (Accessed on April 16, 2022).

[70] S. M. Rioux and L. A. Penner, "The Causes of Organizational Citizenship Behavior: A Motivational Analysis," *Journal of Applied Psychology* (December 2001): 1306–14; M. A. Finkelstein and L. A. Penner, "Predicting Organizational Citizenship Behavior: Integrating the Functional and Role Identity Approaches," *Social Behavior & Personality* 32, no. 4 (2004): 383–98; and J. Schwarzwald, M. Koslowsky, and M. Allouf, "Group Membership, Status, and Social Power Preference," *Journal of Applied Social Psychology* 35, no. 3 (2005): 644–65.

[71] See, for example, J. Walter, F. W. Kellermans, and C. Lechner, "Decision Making within and between Organizations: Rationality, Politics, and Alliance Performance," *Journal of Management* 38, no. 5 (2012): 1582–610.

[72] G. R. Ferris, D. C. Treadway, P. L. Perrewe, R. L. Grouer, C. Douglas, and S. Lux, "Political Skill in Organizations," *Journal of Management* 33 (2007): 290–320.

[73] J. Shi, R. E. Johnson, Y. Liu, and M. Wang, "Linking Subordinate Political Skill to Supervisor Dependence and Reward Recommendations: A Moderated Mediation Model," *Journal of Applied Psychology* 98 (2013): 374–84.

[74] W. A. Gentry, D. C. Gimore, M. L. Shuffler, and J. B. Leslie, "Political Skill as an Indicator of Promotability among Multiple Rater Sources," *Journal of Organizational Behavior* 33 (2012): 89–104; I. Kapoutsis, A. Paplexandris, A. Nikolopoulous, W. A. Hochwarter, and G. R. Ferris, "Politics Perceptions as a Moderator of the Political Skill-Job Performance Relationship: A Two-Study, Cross-National, Constructive Replication," *Journal of Vocational Behavior* 78 (2011): 123–35.

[75] M. Abbas, U. Raja, W. Darr, and D. Bouckenooghe, "Combined Effects of Perceived Politics and Psychological Capital on Job Satisfaction, Turnover Intentions, and Performance," *Journal of Management* 40, no. 7 (2014): 1813–30; and C. C. Rosen, D. L. Ferris, D. J. Brown, and W.-W. Yen, "Relationships among Perceptions

of Organizational Politics (POPs), Work Motivation, and Salesperson Performance," *Journal of Management and Organization* 21, no. 2 (2015): 203–16.

[76] See, for example, M. D. Laird, P. Harvey, and J. Lancaster, "Accountability, Entitlement, Tenure, and Satisfaction in Generation Y," *Journal of Managerial Psychology* 30, no. 1 (2015): 87–100; J. M. L. Poon, "Situational Antecedents and Outcomes of Organizational Politics Perceptions," *Journal of Managerial Psychology* 18, no. 2 (2003): 138–55; and K. L. Zellars, W. A. Hochwarter, S. E. Lanivich, P. L. Perrewe, and G. R. Ferris, "Accountability for Others, Perceived Resources, and Well Being: Convergent Restricted Non-Linear Results in Two Samples," *Journal of Occupational and Organizational Psychology* 84, no. 1 (2011): 95–115.

[77] T. He, R. Derfler-Rozin, and M. Pitesa, "Financial Vulnerability and the Reproduction of Disadvantage in Economic Exchanges," *Journal of Applied Psychology* 105, no. 1 (2020): 80–96.

[78] J. Walter, F. W. Kellermanns, and C. Lechner, "Decision Making within and between Organizations: Rationality, Politics, and Alliance Performance," *Journal of Management* 38 (2012): 1582–610.

[79] W. A. Hochwarter, C. Kiewitz, S. L. Castro, P. L. Perrewe, and G. R. Ferris, "Positive Affectivity and Collective Efficacy as Moderators of the Relationship between Perceived Politics and Job Satisfaction," *Journal of Applied Social Psychology* (May 2003): 1009–35; C. C. Rosen, P. E. Levy, and R. J. Hall, "Placing Perceptions of Politics in the Context of Feedback Environment, Employee Attitudes, and Job Performance," *Journal of Applied Psychology* 91, no. 1 (2006): 211–30; and Abbas, Raja, Darr, and Bouckenooghe, "Combined Effects of Perceived Politics and Psychological Capital on Job Satisfaction, Turnover Intentions, and Performance."

[80] S. Aryee, Z. Chen, and P. S. Budhwar, "Exchange Fairness and Employee Performance: An Examination of the Relationship between Organizational Politics and Procedural Justice," *Organizational Behavior & Human Decision Processes* (May 2004): 1–14.

[81] C. Kiewitz, W. A. Hochwarter, G. R. Ferris, and S. L. Castro, "The Role of Psychological Climate in Neutralizing the Effects of Organizational Politics on Work Outcomes," *Journal of Applied Social Psychology* (June 2002): 1189–207; M. C. Andrews, L. A. Witt, and K. M. Kacmar, "The Interactive Effects of Organizational Politics and Exchange Ideology on Manager Ratings of Retention," *Journal of Vocational Behavior*, April 2003, 357–69; and C. Chang, C. C. Rosen, and P. E. Levy, "The Relationship between Perceptions of Organizational Politics and Employee Attitudes, Strain, and Behavior: A Meta-Analytic Examination," *Academy of Management Journal* 52, no. 4 (2009): 779–801.

[82] O. J. Labedo, "Perceptions of Organisational Politics: Examination of the Situational Antecedent and Consequences among Nigeria's Extension Personnel," *Applied Psychology: An International Review* 55, no. 2 (2006): 255–81.

[83] K. M. Kacmar, M. C. Andrews, K. J. Harris, and B. Tepper, "Ethical Leadership and Subordinate Outcomes: The Mediating Role of Organizational Politics and the Moderating Role of Political Skill," *Journal of Business Ethics* 115, no. 1 (2013): 33–44.

[84] Ibid.

[85] K. M. Kacmar, D. G. Bachrach, K. J. Harris, and S. Zivnuska, "Fostering Good Citizenship through Ethical Leadership: Exploring the Moderating Role of Gender and Organizational Politics," *Journal of Applied Psychology* 96 (2011): 633–42.

[86] C. Homburg and A. Fuerst, "See No Evil, Hear No Evil, Speak No Evil: A Study of Defensive Organizational Behavior towards Customer Complaints," *Journal of the Academy of Marketing Science* 35, no. 4 (2007): 523–36.

[87] See, for instance, M. C. Bolino and W. H. Turnley, "More Than One Way to Make an Impression: Exploring Profiles of Impression Management," *Journal of Management* 29, no. 2 (2003): 141–60; S. Zivnuska, K. M. Kacmar, L. A. Witt, D. S. Carlson, and V. K. Bratton, "Interactive Effects of Impression Management and Organizational Politics on Job Performance," *Journal of Organizational Behavior* (August 2004): 627–40; and M. C. Bolino, K. M. Kacmar, W. H. Turnley, and J. B. Gilstrap, "A Multi-Level Review of Impression Management Motives and Behaviors," *Journal of Management* 34, no. 6 (2008): 1080–109.

[88] D. J. Howard and R. A. Kerin, "Individual Differences in the Name Similarity Effect: The Role of Self-Monitoring," *Journal of Individual Differences* 35, no. 2 (2014): 111–18.

[89] D. H. M. Chng, M. S. Rodgers, E. Shih, and X.-B. Song, "Leaders' Impression Management during Organizational Decline: The Roles of Publicity, Image Concerns, and Incentive Compensation," *The Leadership Quarterly* 26, no. 2 (2015): 270–85; and L. Uziel, "Life Seems Different with You Around: Differential Shifts in Cognitive Appraisal in the Mere Presence of Others for Neuroticism and Impression Management," *Personality and Individual Differences* 73 (2015): 39–43.

[90] J. Ham and R. Vonk, "Impressions of Impression Management: Evidence of Spontaneous Suspicion of Ulterior Motivation," *Journal of Experimental Social Psychology* 47, no. 2 (2011): 466–71; and W. M. Bowler, J. R. B. Halbesleben, and J. R. B. Paul, "If You're Close with the Leader, You Must Be a Brownnose: The Role of Leader–Member Relationships in Follower, Leader, and Coworker Attributions of Organizational Citizenship Behavior Motives," *Human Resource Management Review* 20, no. 4 (2010): 309–16.

[91] J. R. B. Halbesleben, W. M. Bowler, M. C. Bolino, and W. H Turnley, "Organizational Concern, Prosocial Values, or Impression Management? How Supervisors Attribute Motives to Organizational Citizenship Behavior," *Journal of Applied Social Psychology* 40, no. 6 (2010): 1450–89.

[92] G. Blickle, C. Diekmann, P. B. Schneider, Y. Kalthöfer, and J. K. Summers, "When Modesty Wins: Impression Management through Modesty, Political Skill, and Career Success—A Two-Study Investigation," *European Journal of Work and Organizational Psychology* (December 1, 2012): 899–922.

[93] Amaral et al., "Why Does Impression Management Positively Influence Interview Ratings?"; K. Yang Trevor Yu, "Influencing How One Is Seen by Potential Talent: Organizational Impression Management among Recruiting Firms," *Journal of Applied Psychology* 104, no. 7 (2019): 888–906; L. A. McFarland, A. M. Ryan, and S. D. Kriska, "Impression Management Use and Effectiveness across Assessment Methods," *Journal of Management* 29, no. 5 (2003): 641–61; C. A. Higgins and T. A. Judge, "The Effect of Applicant Influence Tactics on Recruiter Perceptions of Fit and Hiring Recommendations: A Field Study," *Journal of Applied Psychology* 89, no. 4 (2004): 622–32; and W. C. Tsai, C.-C. Chen, and S. F. Chiu, "Exploring Boundaries of the Effects of Applicant Impression Management Tactics in Job Interviews," *Journal of Management* (February 2005): 108–25.

[94] N. Roulin, A. Bangerter, and J. Levashina, "Honest and Deceptive Impression Management in the

Employment Interview: Can It Be Detected and How Does It Impact Evaluations?," *Personnel Psychology* 68, no. 2 (2015): 395–444.

[95] M. R. Barrick, J. A. Shaffer, and S. W. DeGrassi. "What You See May Not Be What You Get: Relationships among Self-Presentation Tactics and Ratings of Interview and Job Performance," *Journal of Applied Psychology* 94, no. 6 (2009): 1394–411.

[96] B. Griffin, "The Ability to Identify Criteria: Its Relationship with Social Understanding, Preparation, and Impression Management in Affecting Predictor Performance in a High-Stakes Selection Context," *Human Performance* 27, no. 4 (2014): 147–64.

[97] E. Molleman, B. Emans, and N. Turusbekova, "How to Control Self-Promotion among Performance-Oriented Employees: The Roles of Task Clarity and Personalized Responsibility," *Personnel Review* 41 (2012): 88–105.

[98] K. J. Harris, K. M. Kacmar, S. Zivnuska, and J. D. Shaw, "The Impact of Political Skill on Impression Management Effectiveness," *Journal of Applied Psychology* 92, no. 1 (2007): 278–85; and D. C. Treadway, G. R. Ferris, A. B. Duke, G. L. Adams, and J. B. Thatcher, "The Moderating Role of Subordinate Political Skill on Supervisors' Impressions of Subordinate Ingratiation and Ratings of Subordinate Interpersonal Facilitation," *Journal of Applied Psychology* 92, no. 3 (2007): 848–55.

[99] J. D. Westphal and I. Stern, "Flattery Will Get You Everywhere (Especially if You Are a Male Caucasian): How Ingratiation, Boardroom Behavior, and Demographic Minority Status Affect Additional Board Appointments of U.S. Companies," *Academy of Management Journal* 50, no. 2 (2007): 267–88.

[100] Y. Liu, G. R. Ferris, J. Xu, B. A. Weitz, and P. L. Perrewé, "When Ingratiation Backfires: The Role of Political Skill in the Ingratiation-Internship Performance Relationship," *Academy of Management Learning and Education* 13 (2014): 569–86.

[101] See, for example, E. Vigoda, "Reactions to Organizational Politics: A Cross-Cultural Examination in Israel and Britain," *Human Relations* (November 2001): 1483–518; and Y. Zhu and D. Li, "Negative Spillover Impact of Perceptions of Organizational Politics on Work-Family Conflict in China," *Social Behavior and Personality* 43, no. 5 (2015): 705–14.

[102] J. L. T. Leong, M. H. Bond, and P. P. Fu, "Perceived Effectiveness of Influence Strategies in the United States and Three Chinese Societies," *International Journal of Cross Cultural Management* (May 2006): 101–20.

[103] Y. Miyamoto and B. Wilken, "Culturally Contingent Situated Cognition: Influencing Other People Fosters Analytic Perception in the United States but Not in Japan," *Psychological Science* 21, no. 11 (2010): 1616–22.

[104] Y. Wang and S. Highhouse, "Different Consequences of Supplication and Modesty: Self-Effacing Impression Management Behaviors and Supervisory Perceptions of Subordinate Personality," *Human Performance* 29, no. 5 (2016): 394–407.

[105] See, for instance, G. Blickle, K. Oerder, and J. K. Summers, "The Impact of Political Skill on Career Success of Employees' Representatives," *Journal of Vocational Behavior* 77 (2010): 383–90; G. Blickle, N. Schütte, and A. Wihler, "Political Will, Work Values, and Objective Career Success: A Novel Approach—The Trait-Reputation-Identity Model," *Journal of Vocational Behavior* 107 (2018): 42–56; Y. Liu, J. Liu, and L. Wu, "Are You Willing and Able? Roles of Motivation, Power, and Politics in Career Growth," *Journal of Management* 36, no. 6 (2010): 1432–60.

[106] D. Clark, "A Campaign Strategy for Your Career," *Harvard Business Review* (November 2012): 131–34.

[107] Dhar, S. (2013). "Love at work: Relationships in the workplace common in India". *The Economic Times (May 26, 2013).* Retrieved from https://economictimes.indiatimes.com (Accessed on April 16, 2022).

[108] Press Trust of India (2021). "At 17.3%, India Inc badly lags presence of women board members: Report". *Business Standard (September 28, 2021) ©PTI.* Retrieved from https://www.business-standard.com (Accessed on April 16, 2022).

12 Communication

Source: Image Source/Alamy Stock Photo

LEARNING OBJECTIVES

After studying this chapter, you should be able to:

12-1 Describe the functions and process of communication.

12-2 Contrast downward, upward, and lateral communication through small-group networks and the grapevine.

12-3 Contrast oral, written, and nonverbal communication.

12-4 Describe how channel richness underlies the choice of communication method.

12-5 Differentiate between automatic and controlled processing of persuasive messages.

12-6 Identify common barriers to effective communication.

12-7 Discuss how to overcome the potential problems of cross-cultural communication.

Employability Skills Matrix (ESM)

	Myth or Science?	Career OBjectives	An Ethical Choice	Point/ Counterpoint	Experiential Exercise	Ethical Dilemma	Case Incident 1	Case Incident 2
Critical Thinking			✓	✓	✓	✓	✓	✓
Communication	✓	✓	✓		✓		✓	✓
Collaboration		✓			✓		✓	✓
Knowledge Application and Analysis	✓	✓	✓	✓	✓	✓	✓	✓
Social Responsibility		✓	✓	✓		✓	✓	

WORKPLACE COMMUNICATION: TOO MUCH OF A GOOD THING?

It wasn't long ago that communicating with colleagues meant gathering around a table for a meeting or chatting next to the water cooler. But times have changed, and the pace of that change has accelerated due to COVID-19. On a typical day, the digital agency Manifesto has only about 20 of its 45 staff in the office. The rest are elsewhere but still working on the same projects, using collaboration tools such as Slack, Trello, Confluence, and Google Drive. Collaborative working is not new, but how it is being done is possible due to readily available, inexpensive, user-friendly tech tools. Even e-mail is becoming passé, with apps like Yammer and Google Hangouts increasing in popularity.

The range of methods of communication available today is almost overwhelming, but is communication itself getting more effective and efficient in modern organizations? Or is it too much of a good thing? Proponents of high-tech business communication tools cite improvements in productivity, idea generation, employee engagement, and speed of decision making, among many other benefits. But not everyone is convinced. Others claim it creates stress and decreases productivity because of communication overload and constant disruptions and even increases bullying and harassment. Furthermore, these tools may not have significantly reduced the barriers to effective communication as is commonly believed. In a report by the Economist Intelligence Unit, respondents to a survey said that communication barriers are leading to delays or failures in completion of projects (44 percent), low morale (31 percent), missed performance goals (25 percent), and even lost sales (18 percent).

And what about social media in the workplace? The pros and cons are similar. Properly used, the positives include potential gains in productivity, better employee engagement, a wider audience reach outside of the firm, reinforcement of organizational culture, and effective dissemination of the company's vision. When used by senior executives, social media can help communicate the financial and strategic direction of a company, attract potential employees, and retain current ones. Used badly, social media in the workplace is nothing more than a major distraction, an encouragement to cyberloaf, and a security risk for both the employee and the organization. Consider these two examples:

When a branch manager at an industrial supply company tweeted criticism of the company's choice of holiday gift for the Christmas Season, a barbecue scraper and sauce, he was fired before New Year's Day. When questioned, the company's CEO confirmed that the employee was terminated and said that the company's policy about acceptable standards of conduct is given to every employee and posted on the company website. News of the firing went viral and prompted a backlash on social media, with many customers saying they would no longer buy from the firm.

In another widely publicized case, despite having the highest possible security settings on her Facebook profile, Angela Gibbins was dismissed for gross misconduct from the British Council after publishing an offensive post about Prince George. An employment tribunal upheld the dismissal, finding that she had breached her employer's advice on social media use that employees should be cautious about what they post even if the message is intended to be private.

Sources: F. Regalado, "Asia's Social Media-Shy CEOs Fade behind US, EU Counterparts: Survey," *Nikkei Asia Review*, December 20, 2019; R. Rigby, "How Popular Tech Tools Are Transforming the Workplace," *Financial Times*, May 2, 2017; D. DePass, "Employee Mocks Company Holiday Gift on Twitter, Gets Fired," *The Seattle Times*, January 14, 2020; E. Jacobs, "Money, Trolls, Timewasting: The Impact of Social Media on Work," *Financial Times*, December 16, 2019; and The Economist Intelligence Unit, "Communication Barriers in the Modern Workplace," available at https://eiuperspectives.economist.com/sites/default/files/EIU_Lucidchart-Communication%20barriers%20in%20the%20modern%20workplace.pdf, accessed February 26, 2020.

In this chapter, we will explore communication in the modern workplace. We will learn more about the communication process and how this process can go awry. We will also learn about types of communication and how these types are shaped by recent technologies.

communication The transfer and the understanding of meaning.

Communication must include both the *transfer* and *the understanding* of meaning. Communicating is more than merely imparting meaning; that meaning must also be understood. It is only thus that we can convey information and ideas. In perfect communication, if it existed, a thought would be transmitted so the receiver understood the same mental picture the sender intended. Though it sounds elementary, perfect communication is never achieved in practice for reasons we shall see.

Functions of Communication

12-1 Describe the functions and process of communication.

Communication serves five major functions within a group or organization: management, feedback, emotional sharing, persuasion, and information exchange.[1]

Communication acts to *manage* member behavior in several ways.[2] Organizations have authority hierarchies and formal guidelines that employees are required to follow. When employees follow their job descriptions or comply with company policies, communication performs a management function. Informal communication controls behavior too. When work groups tease or harass a member who produces too much (and makes the rest of the members look bad), they are informally communicating, and managing, the member's behavior.

Communication creates *feedback* by clarifying to employees what they must do, how well they are doing it, and how they can improve their performance. We saw this operating in goal-setting theory in Chapter 7. Formation of goals, feedback on progress, and reward for desired behavior all require communication and stimulate motivation.

The work group is a primary source of social interaction for many employees. Communication is a fundamental mechanism by which members show satisfaction and frustration. Therefore, communication provides for the *emotional sharing* of feelings and fulfillment of social needs. For example, after a white police officer shot an unarmed black man in Ferguson, Missouri, in 2015, software engineer Carl Jones wanted to process his feelings through talking with his coworkers at his corporation. As a second example, Starbucks had baristas write "Race Together" on coffee cups to start conversations about race relations. In both cases, the initial communications were awkward—so awkward that Starbucks pulled the campaign—but Jones and others have forged solid relationships from their emotional sharing.[3]

Like emotional sharing, *persuasion* can be good or bad depending on if, say, a leader is trying to persuade a work group to believe in the organization's commitment to corporate social responsibility (CSR) or, conversely, to persuade the work group to break the law to meet an organizational goal. These may be extreme examples, but it's important to remember that persuasion can benefit or harm an organization.

The final function of communication is *information exchange* to facilitate decision making. Communication provides the information that individuals

Exhibit 12-1 The Communication Process

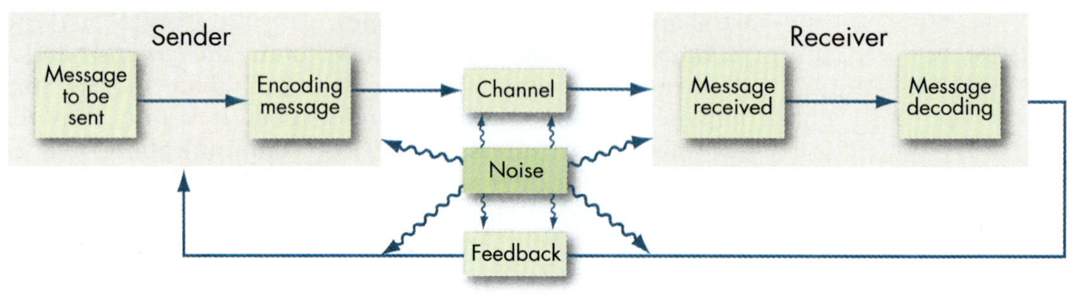

and groups need to make decisions by transmitting the data needed to identify and evaluate choices.

Almost every communication interaction that takes place in a group or organization performs one or more of these functions, and none of the five is more important than the others. To perform effectively, groups need to maintain some control over members, provide feedback to stimulate members to perform, allow emotional expression, monitor the persuasive efforts of individuals, and encourage information exchange.

Before communication can take place it needs a purpose, a message to be conveyed between a sender and a receiver. The sender encodes the message (converts it to a symbolic form) and passes it through a medium (channel) to the receiver, who decodes it. The result is a transfer of meaning from one person to another.[4]

communication process The steps between a source and a receiver that result in the transfer and understanding of meaning.

Exhibit 12-1 depicts this **communication process**. The key parts of this model are (1) the sender, (2) encoding, (3) the message, (4) the channel, (5) decoding, (6) the receiver, (7) noise, and (8) feedback.

formal channels Communication channels established by an organization to transmit messages related to the professional activities of members.

informal channels Communication channels that are created spontaneously and that emerge as responses to individual choices.

The *sender* initiates a message by encoding a thought. The *message* is the actual physical product of the sender's *encoding*. When we speak, the speech is the message. When we write, the writing is the message. When we gesture, the movements of our arms and the expressions on our faces are the message. The *channel* is the medium through which the message travels. The sender selects it, determining whether to use a formal or informal channel. **Formal channels** are established by the organization and transmit messages related to the professional activities of members. They traditionally follow the authority chain within the organization. Other forms of messages, such as personal or social, follow **informal channels**, which are spontaneous and subject to individual choice.[5] The *receiver* is the person(s) to whom the message is directed, who must first translate the symbols into understandable form. This step is the *decoding* of the message. *Noise* represents communication barriers that distort the clarity of the message, such as perceptual problems, information overload, semantic difficulties, or cultural differences. The final link in the communication process is a feedback loop. *Feedback* is the check on how successful we have been in transferring our messages as originally intended. It determines whether understanding has been achieved. This final link may or may not be achieved, depending upon whether the receiver engages in closed-loop communication (i.e., when the receiver acknowledges, verbally or nonverbally, that they heard and/or understood the message).[6]

Direction of Communication

12-2 Contrast downward, upward, and lateral communication through small-group networks and the grapevine.

Communication can flow vertically or laterally, through formal small-group networks or the informal grapevine. We subdivide the vertical dimension into downward and upward directions.[7] For instance, you may think of a CEO or founder establishing a vision for an entire organization (see Chapter 13)—however, in reality, communication transforms this vision as it travels downward, laterally, and upward throughout the organization, resulting in separate sub-visions.[8]

Downward Communication

Communication that flows from one level of a group or organization to a lower level is *downward communication.* Group leaders and managers use it to assign goals, provide job instructions, explain policies and procedures, point out problems that need attention, and offer feedback. More informally, group leaders and managers may also convey signals of their rank (e.g., prestige or dominance) through downward communication.[9]

In downward communication, managers must explain the reasons *why* a decision was made. Although this may seem like common sense, many managers feel they are too busy to explain things or that explanations will raise too many questions. Evidence clearly indicates, though, that explanations increase employee commitment and the support of decisions.[10] Managers might think that sending a message once is enough to get through to lower-level employees, but research suggests managerial communications must be repeated several times and through a variety of different media to be truly effective.[11]

Another problem in downward communication is its one-way nature; generally, managers inform employees but rarely solicit their advice or opinions. Research revealed that nearly two-thirds of employees said their boss rarely or never asks their advice. The study noted, "Organizations are always striving for higher employee engagement, but evidence indicates they unnecessarily create fundamental mistakes. People need to be respected and listened to." The way advice is solicited also matters. Employees will not provide input, even when conditions are favorable, if doing so seems against their best interests.[12]

In downward communication, the delivery mode and the context of the information exchange are of high importance. We will talk more about communication methods later, but consider the ultimate downward communication: the performance review. Alan Buckelew, CEO of Carnival Cruise Lines, says, "A review is probably the one time when you want to be physically present." Samsonite's CEO agrees: "A conference call cannot substitute for face-to-face interactions." Automated performance reviews have allowed managers to review their subordinates without discussions, which is efficient but misses critical opportunities for growth, motivation, and relationship building.[13] In general, employees subjected to less than direct, personalized communication are less likely to understand the intentions of the message correctly.

The best communicators explain the reasons behind their downward communications but also solicit communication from the employees they supervise. That leads us to the next direction: upward communication.

Burger King improved lateral communication among its executives by eliminating their closed-door offices and organizing their desks in an open-space setting. Shown here, from left, are executives Jonathan Fitzpatrick, Jose Tomas, and Daniel Schwartz communicating in their new work area at company headquarters in Miami.
Source: C.W. Griffin/Miami Herald/MCT/Newscom

Upward Communication

Upward communication flows to a higher level in the group or organization. It's used to provide feedback to higher-ups, inform them of progress toward goals, and relay current problems. Upward communication keeps managers aware of how employees feel about their jobs, coworkers, and the organization in general. Managers also rely on upward communication for ideas on how conditions can be improved. It is also important for subordinates to give honest, authentic feedback, because if managers are not given reasonable negative feedback about allocating resources, they are more likely to make self-interested decisions at the expense of their surbordinates.[14]

Given that most managers' job responsibilities have expanded, upward communication is increasingly difficult because managers can be overwhelmed and easily distracted. To engage in effective upward communication, try to communicate in short summaries rather than long explanations, support your summaries with actionable items, and prepare an agenda to make sure you use your boss's attention well.[15] And watch what you say, especially if you are communicating something to your manager that will be unwelcome. If you're turning down an assignment, for example, be sure to project a can-do attitude while asking advice about your workload dilemma or inexperience with the assignment.[16] Your delivery can be as important as the content of your communication.

Lateral Communication

When communication occurs between members of the same work group, members at the same level in separate work groups, or any other horizontally equivalent workers, we describe it as *lateral communication.*[17]

Lateral communication saves time and facilitates coordination. Some lateral relationships are formally sanctioned. On the other hand, some lateral communication can also be informal, such as when coworkers witness the emotional expression of another coworker.[18] For example, witnessing a crying coworker leaving the manager's office can present a powerful message to the rest of the office. Lateral communication occurring with management's knowledge and support can be beneficial. But dysfunctional conflict can result when formal vertical channels are ignored, such as when managers find actions have been taken or decisions made without their knowledge. Therefore, both lateral and vertical communication should be used in organizations.

Whether to have an open office or an office with private spaces in organizations is dependent on the nature of work carried out by an organization. In a university faculty need to have private spaces to be able to carry out their work, an ad agency may have a mix between open and closed spaces, a claims processing department of an insurance agency can work out of an open office. Open offices make it easy for people to communicate with each other.

Formal Small-Group Networks

Formal organizational networks can be complicated, including hundreds of people and a half-dozen or more hierarchical levels. We've condensed these networks into three common small groups of five people each (see Exhibit 12-2): chain, wheel, and all-channel.

The *chain* rigidly follows the formal chain of command; this network approximates the communication channels you might find in a rigid three-level organization. The *wheel* relies on a central figure to act as the conduit for all group communication; it simulates the communication network you might find on a team with a strong leader. The *all-channel* network permits group members to actively communicate with each other; it's most often characterized by self-managed teams, in which group members are free to contribute and no single person takes on a leadership role. Many organizations today like to consider themselves all-channel, meaning that anyone can communicate with anyone (but sometimes they shouldn't).

As Exhibit 12-3 demonstrates, the effectiveness of each network is determined by the dependent variable that concerns you. The structure of the wheel facilitates the emergence of a leader, the all-channel network is best if you desire high member satisfaction, and the chain is best if accuracy is most important. Exhibit 12-3 leads us to the conclusion that no single network will be best for all occasions.

Exhibit 12-2 Three Common Small-Group Networks

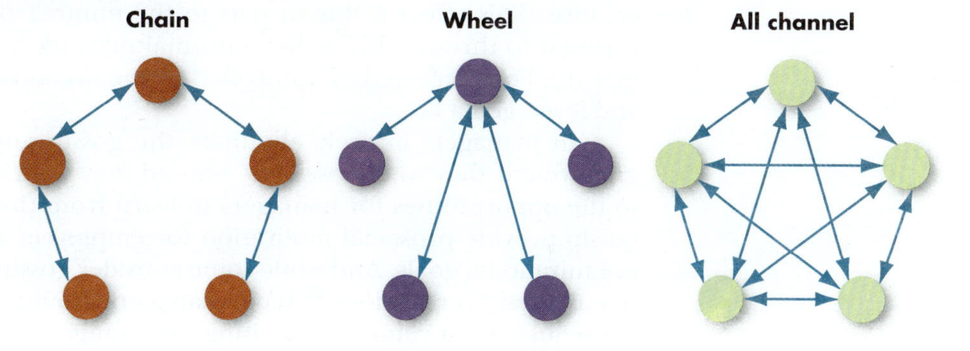

Exhibit 12-3 Small-Group Networks and Effective Criteria

Criteria	Networks		
	Chain	*Wheel*	*All-Channel*
Speed	Moderate	Fast	Fast
Accuracy	High	High	Moderate
Emergence of a leader	Moderate	High	None
Member satisfaction	Moderate	Low	High

The Grapevine

grapevine An organization's informal communication network.

The informal communication network in a group or organization is called the **grapevine.**[19] Typically, the grapevine and gossip are viewed negatively by most people. Indeed, research shows that untrustworthy gossip can cause people to unfairly judge and dislike others.[20] Overall, the grapevine is a double-edged sword, leading to positive performance because of the sense of social pressure it produces while also undermining employee well-being.[21] Furthermore, rumors and gossip transmitted through the grapevine may be an important source of information for employees and job applicants.[22] Grapevine or word-of-mouth information from peers about a company has important effects on whether job applicants join an organization,[23] even over and above informal ratings on websites like Glassdoor.

The grapevine is an important part of any group or organization communication network. It serves employees' needs: Small talk creates a sense of closeness and friendship among those who share information, although research suggests it often does so at the expense of those in the outgroup.[24] It also gives managers a feel for the morale of their organization, identifies issues employees consider important, and helps them tap into employee anxieties. Evidence indicates that managers can study the gossip driven largely by employee social networks to learn more about how positive and negative information is flowing through the organization.[25] Managers can also identify influencers (highly networked people trusted by their coworkers[26]) by noting which individuals are small talkers (those who regularly communicate about insignificant, unrelated issues). Small talkers tend to be influencers. One study found that social talkers are so influential that they were significantly more likely to retain their jobs during layoffs.[27] Other research has found that individuals who are connected through the office grapevine tend to be more creative. This effect is due in part to the number of unique ideas a person is exposed to through his or her informal network.[28] Thus, while the grapevine may not be sanctioned or controlled by the organization, it can be understood and leveraged a bit.

Can managers entirely eliminate the gossip and rumors common to the grapevine if they so choose? No. Should they want to? Maybe not; in addition to the opportunities for managers to learn from the grapevine, some forms of gossip provide prosocial motivation for employees to help each other achieve organizational goals. And while some consider gossiping to be deviant behavior, not all gossip is malicious.[29] What managers should do is minimize the negative consequences of rumors by limiting their range and impact. Exhibit 12-4 offers a few practical suggestions.

Exhibit 12-4 **Dealing with Gossip and Rumors**

1. **Share** the information you have, and the information you don't—where there is good formal communication with much information, there is no need for rumors. When you don't know information that others are seeking, discuss when you will know and follow up.
2. **Explain,** explain, explain. As a manager, discuss what decisions are made and why they were made, as well as the plan going forward.
3. **Respond** to rumors noncommittally, and then verify for yourself the truths you can. Make certain to gather all sides of the story.
4. **Invite** employees to discuss their concerns, ideas, suggestions, thoughts, and feelings about organizational matters. Help them frame their thoughts into more objective viewpoints.

Modes of Communication

12-3 Contrast oral, written, and nonverbal communication.

How do group members transfer meaning among themselves? They rely on oral, written, and nonverbal communication. This much is obvious, but as we will discuss, the choice between modes can greatly enhance or detract from the way the perceiver reacts to the message. Certain modes are highly preferred for specific types of communication. We will cover the latest thinking and practical application.

Oral Communication

A primary means of conveying messages is oral communication. Speeches, formal one-on-one and group discussions, and the informal rumor mill or grapevine are popular forms of oral communication.

The advantages of oral communication are speed, feedback, and exchange. We can convey a verbal message and receive a response in minimal time. As one professional put it, "Face-to-face communication on a consistent basis is still the best way to get information to and from employees."[30] If the receiver is unsure of the message, rapid feedback allows the sender to detect and correct it quickly. The feedback we receive includes information and emotional content; however, we should acknowledge that we are usually bad listeners. Researchers indicate that we are prone to "listener burnout," in which we tune the other person out and rush to offer advice. "Good listeners overcome their natural inclination to fix the other's problems and to keep the conversation brief," said Professor Graham Bodie. Active listening—in which we remove distractions, lean in, make eye contact, paraphrase, and encourage the talker to continue[31]—helps us learn more and build trust if we are genuine and not judgmental.[32] The exchange given through oral communication has social, cultural, and emotional components. Cultural social exchange, in which we purposefully share social exchanges that transcend cultural boundaries, can build trust, cooperation, and agreement between individuals and teams.[33]

One major disadvantage of oral communication surfaces whenever a message has to pass through a number of people: the more people, the greater the potential distortion. If you've ever played the game Telephone, you know the problem. Each person interprets the message in their own way. The message's content, when it reaches its destination, is often very different from the original, even when we think the message is simple and straightforward. Therefore, oral communication "chains" are generally more of a liability than an effective tool in organizations. Let's discuss some popular oral communication applications in more detail.

Meetings Meetings can be formal or informal, include two or more people, and take place in almost any venue. Although 11 million meetings take place in the United States daily, some people hate them. So we try to make them more effective: Amazon CEO Jeff Bezos begins meetings with 30 minutes of attendees silently reading his report to themselves, Twitter and Apple have meetings only on Mondays, BuzzFeed has 2 no-meeting days per week, and some organizations limit the duration of meetings.[34]

Framing even our casual business interactions as meetings helps us stay focused on progress. Every meeting is an opportunity to "get stuff done," as BetterWorks CEO Kris Duggan said, and to "sparkle." He noted, "You may be an expert in your field, but if you don't communicate well, or if you don't get people excited, or you're not passionate or enthusiastic, that's going to be a hindrance."[35] Other stumbling blocks to effective meetings are overuse of jargon[36] and qualifiers that undermine your words (for example, phrases like "to be perfectly honest" or "to tell the truth" imply that you aren't truthful the other 99 percent of the time!).[37]

Good interpersonal communication is key to making meetings effective. Some experts recommend using humor as an ice breaker; public relations firm Peppercomm even offers stand-up comedy workshops to help businesses teach people how to use humor. Using humor in meetings even predicts team performance two years later.[38] But what if you don't have a voice in meetings? We don't mean someone who is speaking or hearing disabled, as we discuss in Career OBjectives. *Voice* refers to the ability to contribute words of value to the meeting or other forum in the workplace.[39] By definition, voice challenges the status quo, supports others' viewpoints, adds constructively, or is defensive/destructive.[40] As you can see, voice refers to the input and reactions of a person within the meeting, and the lack of voice creates a barrier to input (when no one is speaking, few people want to be the first to break the silence). A person without voice may have nothing to say, but research indicates that women in particular don't speak up in meetings even when they are in leadership

John T. Chambers, former CEO of Cisco System, had the habit of organizing early breakfast meetings with different groups of employees. Such meetings gave employees a chance to ask John important questions about the strategy and overall functioning of the company and John occasion to express gratitude to employees for their daily effort.
Source: MTP/Alamy Stock Photo

positions, suggesting that certain group dynamics inhibit equal participation.[41] In addition, voice may also be affected by employees' self-evaluation, personal initiative, sense of responsibility, and engagement, as well as workplace climate and the emotions and behavior of their supervisor.[42] Without equitable participation, the benefits of meetings are questionable.

Videoconferencing and Conference Calling *Videoconferencing* permits employees and clients to conduct real-time meetings with people at different locations. Live audio and video images let us see, hear, and talk with each other without being physically in the same location. *Conference calling* is generally limited to telephone exchanges where some people may gather around one speaker phone, and others call in through a secure line. There may be some shared files or videos everyone can see on their computers. Both modes are used selectively, according to the application.

Peter Quirk, an information technology director with EMC Corporation, uses videoconferencing to hold monthly meetings of employees at various locations while saving travel expenses and time. He notes it's important to stimulate questions and involve all participants in this forum deliberately to avoid having someone who is on the call but disengaged (a common problem). Other leaders wish they had that problem; instead, they have to mediate between callers who talk over one another, and address those who make too much noise. Mahesh Prasad told his colleague, during a zoom meeting of his department, "Your daughter sings beautifully but I would rather hear your views than your daughter's singing in the background".

You might assume people prefer videoconferencing to conference calling because video offers a more "live" experience, but 65 percent of all remote meetings are done via audio only. For reasons not clearly understood (besides some people's reluctance to be on camera), the time people spend on audio-only calls may be growing almost 10 percent per year.[43] To address the pitfalls of videoconferencing and conference calls, experts offer the following suggestions:

1. **Set more explicit agendas and firmer rules than for face-to-face meetings.**
2. **Have callers begin by introducing themselves, their roles in the project, and what they are looking for in the meeting.** They should also state their names each time they speak.
3. **Leaders should talk 40 percent of the time and listen 60 percent of the time.**
4. **Distribute discussion questions before the meeting, and note the responses of each participant during the meeting.**
5. **Assign a moderator for the meeting (not the leader) and a secretary (again, not the leader).**
6. **Understand people's preferences for videoconferencing versus conference calling before the meeting and make sure everyone understands the technology.** "I cannot tell you how many times I've heard people say, 'I don't know what's wrong with my webcam, so I'm just going to be here in voice'" when they might just prefer conference calling, said Laura Stack, author of *Execution Is the Strategy*.[44]

Telephone The telephone has been around so long that we can overlook its efficiency as a mode of communication. Communication by telephone is fast, effective, and less ambiguous than e-mail. However, telephone messages can be

Career OBjectives

Isn't this disability too much to accommodate?

I thought it was a good, responsible move when my manager hired a guy who is hearing-impaired ... but now I'm not so sure. We do okay in communicating with him, mostly thanks to e-mail and texting. None of us knows sign language but sometimes we spell out words with our hands. The problem is that the guy makes a LOT of inappropriate noises—farts, burps, coughs, moans, you name it. Isn't this too much to put up with?

— *Vandana*

Dear Vandana:
In short: No. Workplace accommodation means more than simply tolerating a disabled worker's presence. Perhaps you might consider this from your deaf coworker's point of view (by the way, *deaf* is the preferred term, according to the National Association of the Deaf):

- *How are the communication conditions in which he has to work?* Are you being sure to include him in discussions by, say, assigning one of you to write down the important points for him and ask his opinions in meetings? Search for "10 Annoying Habits of Hearing People" online to get a glimpse of his perspective.
- *Do you know what he thinks about your "hand spelling"?* You may not know that American Sign Language (ASL) is not simply English. Your coworker probably doesn't appreciate your "pigeon" sign language and may be offended by your attempts, but he would likely appreciate an effort for the group to learn some ASL and/or use a translator. There are apps and online translators where you can type in a phrase and see someone sign your words on the screen, for instance. Similarly, new technology from MotionSavvy translates signs into written speech.
- *It seems you might be attributing emotions to your coworker when he makes noises, emotions he may not feel.* Do you think he is uncaring about his listening coworkers? It's much more likely that he simply doesn't realize he is making noises or thinks they are quieter than they are. Consider what it's like when you are in a loud room; you're probably less aware of your sounds than when you're in a quiet room where everyone can react.

If you can get past the barrier of thinking about how he should accommodate himself to your environment and instead show him how your group is willing to work to communicate with him, you may begin to develop an understanding of one another. Then, and only then, it would make sense to approach the noise problem respectfully and kindly, with a nonoffensive one-on-one. But before you do, search the Internet for tips on communicating with the deaf, and show him some respect.

Sources: Based on C. Swinbourne, "The 10 Annoying Habits of Hearing People," *The Huffington Post*, September 17, 2013, http://www.huffingtonpost.com/charlie-swinbourne/the-10-annoying-habits-of_b_3618327.html; National Association of the Deaf website, www.nad.org, accessed June 30, 2015; and R. Walker, "An Office Distraction," *The New York Times*, March 22, 2015, 8.

The opinions provided here are of the managers and authors only and do not necessarily reflect those of their organizations. The authors or managers are not responsible for any errors or omissions, or for the results obtained from the use of this information. In no event will the authors or managers, or their related partnerships or corporations thereof, be liable to you or anyone else for any decision made or action taken in reliance on the opinions provided here.

easily overlooked, and a lack of functions has made the phone difficult to use without electronic follow-up. Recently, however, a number of software options have come to the rescue to make phoning more versatile.

Written Communication

Written communication includes letters, e-mail, instant messaging, organizational periodicals, and any other method that conveys written words or symbols. Written business communication today is usually conducted via letters, PowerPoint, e-mail, instant messaging, text messaging, social media, apps, and blogs. We are all familiar with these methods, but let's consider the unique current business communication applications of them.

Letters With all the technology available, why would anyone write and send a letter? Of all the forms of written communication, letter writing is the oldest—and the most enduring. Letter writing can be used to great effect in business, adding a personal touch to a communication or, alternately, creating a lasting document to signal an official communication. Research indicates that when we write by hand, the content is much more memorable to us than when we type.[45]

PowerPoint PowerPoint and other slide formats like Prezi can be an excellent mode of communication because slide-generating software combines words with visual elements to engage the reader and help explain complex ideas. PowerPoint is often used in conjunction with oral presentations, but its appeal is so intuitive that it can serve as a primary mode of communication. It is not without its detractors, however, who argue that it is too impersonal, disengaging, and frequently hard to follow.

E-Mail The growth of e-mail since its inception nearly 50 years ago has been spectacular, and its use is so pervasive it's hard to imagine life without it. There are more than 3.1 billion active e-mail accounts worldwide, and corporate employees average 105 e-mails each day.[46] Exhibit 12-5 shows the time that managers and professionals spend daily on various tasks. Many managers report they spend too much time on e-mail. Do you?

The business benefits of e-mail messages are obvious: they can be written, edited, sent, and stored quickly and cheaply. E-mail is not without cost, however. In fact, according to e-mail software company Messagemind, corporations lose $650 billion each year from time spent processing unnecessary e-mails.[47] One study also indicated that people focus longer on tasks and are less stressed when they are cut off from checking e-mail, although other research suggests that e-mail is only stressful for employees when their workload is already heavy.[48]

Exhibit 12-5 Allocation of Time at Work for Managers and Professionals

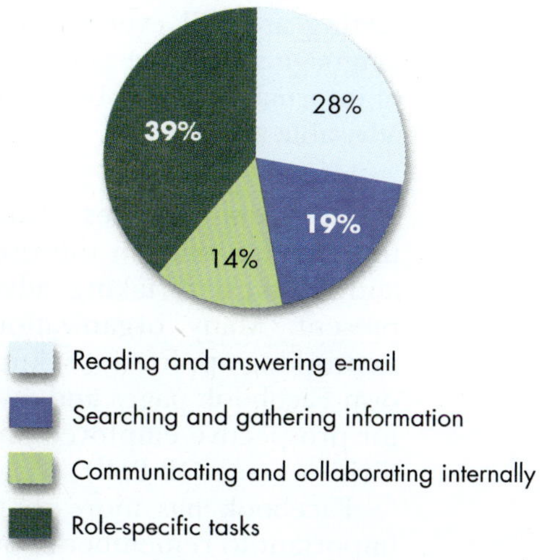

Source: Based on M. Chui et al., "The Social Economy: Unlocking Value and Productivity through Social Technologies," McKinsey & Company, July 2012, http://www.mckinsey.com/insights/high_tech_telecoms_internet/the_social_economy.

Despite the costs, e-mail is likely here to stay, and is "often the first impression that others get of you," according to executive coach and etiquette expert Jaqueline Whitmore.[49] Still, even seasoned e-mail aficionados struggle with striking the proper tone in their communications.

Whitmore offers the following advice:

1. **Don't skip the subject line, but make it short and topic-related.**
2. **Give a greeting/salutation.** "Dear" and "hello" are good starting points. In later exchanges, "hi" may be appropriate. Use the person's name. "Err on the side of being more formal" in your greeting and the body of the e-mail, Whitmore advises. Same for your closing; "Best regards" is more formal.
3. **Keep sentences, paragraphs, and thoughts short.** Use bullet points when possible.
4. **However, don't be curt.** "No one can see your facial expressions or hear your tone of voice, so the only way they're gauging your emotions is the tone that you use in that e-mail," she said.
5. **Don't use text language.** "Even if you've just graduated from college and you're now out in the workforce," Whitmore observed, "remember that a lot of your clients may be baby boomers. It's important for you to stay professional."
6. **Check your spelling.** Check it again.
7. **When people write back, reply within 24 hours.** "Even if you don't have an answer for someone, reply anyway," she said.[50]

Instant Messaging Like e-mail, instant messaging (IM) is usually done via computer. There are distinct pros and cons to IM, but there are mostly negatives for business interactions. If you are present when the IM comes in, you can respond in real time to engage in online typed dialogue, but the conversation will not be saved for later reference. If you miss the incoming IM, you may be alerted when you next log on that a person tried to reach you, which may be long after a response was needed.

Text Messaging Text messaging may be a little bit better than IM but has many of the same pitfalls in business usage. The guidelines for the business use of texting are still evolving, but experts continually caution that business text language should be as formal as any other business communication. The level of informality and abbreviations we use in personal text messages is usually not advisable at work.[51]

Social Media Websites Nowhere has online communication been more transformed than in the rise of social networks like Facebook and LinkedIn, and business is taking advantage of the opportunities these social media present. Many organizations have developed their own in-house social-networking applications, known as *enterprise social software,* and most have their own Facebook pages and Twitter feeds.[52] Social networking has become a tool for prospective employees, hiring managers, employees, and human resources divisions (see OB Poll).

Facebook has more than 1.44 billion active users per month,[53] and it's important to remember in business that users can send messages to other users either by posting on their walls (public), sending messages, or setting up chats (private). They can also communicate with multiple other users ("friends") by posting status updates, videos, and photos. Some of the modes of communication

OB POLL

Do You Use Social-Networking Sites to Research Job Candidates?

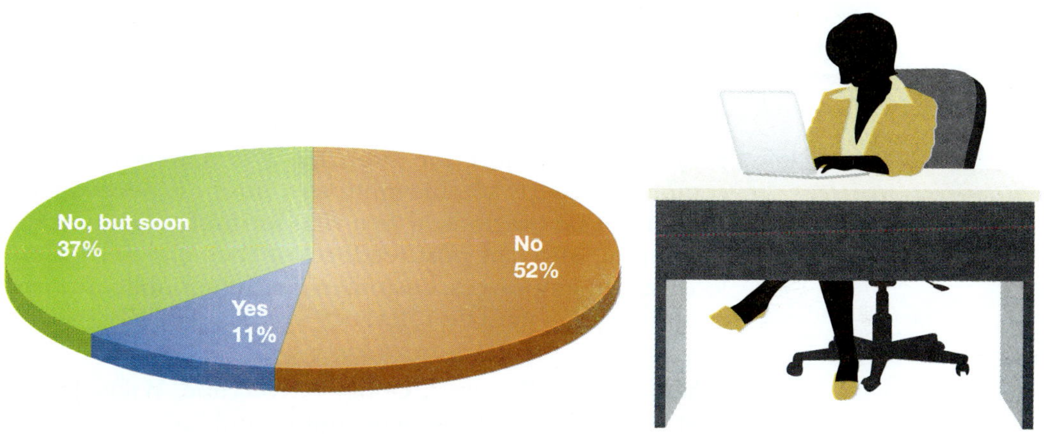

Note: CareerBuilder survey of over 2,000 hiring professionals.
Source: Based on CareerBuilder at http://www.careerbuilder.com/JobPoster/Resources/page.aspx?pagever=2012SocialMedia&template=none.

may be appropriate for business application (such as an organization's Facebook page), but many are not. Research has found that none of the world's 50 most profitable companies' CEOs are using Facebook.[54] This represents a dramatic shift from 2010, when these CEOs were using Facebook, LinkedIn, and Twitter quite equally. Leslie Gaines-Ross, who represents the study, observed, "I think that CEOs are identifying which platform really works for them."[55] Privacy remains a high concern for many Facebook users, and some regions of the world do not have access to it.[56]

Unlike many social media venues, LinkedIn was created as an online business network and now has 187 million active users per month.[57] User profiles on the site are like virtual résumés. Communication is sometimes limited to endorsements of others' skills and establishment of business connections, though direct private communication is available and users can form and belong to groups. LinkedIn is used increasingly by top CEOs and is the top popular network for them (22 percent of the top 50 companies' CEOs use LinkedIn).[58]

Twitter is a hybrid social-networking service for users to post microblog entries of 140 characters to their subscribers about any topic, including work. Twitter has 236 million active users monthly on average[59] and is growing as a business venue. While only 10 percent of the top companies' CEOs are on Twitter,[60] some have many followers, such as President Donald Trump, who has 29.7 million, and Richard Branson of Virgin Group, who has 5.99 million. As former Medtronic CEO Bill George noted, "Can you think of a more cost-effective way of getting to your customers and employees?"[61] Having many followers can be an advantage to a firm or a manager, but a huge liability when posts (tweets) are badly written or negative.

Apps LinkedIn and Twitter are two of the most widely used social media platforms for businesses, but they are not the only ones. Apps—easily accessed mobile-friendly platforms—are increasingly the forum of choice for the public. Some websites have apps, while other apps exist without corresponding websites. One of the biggest apps is WhatsApp, at 450 million active monthly users. Apps are most popular in regions where mobile phone usage is primary.[62] Asia has the world's largest number of social media users, and apps play a large role in that part of the world through Line (Japan), WeChat (China), and Kakao (South Korea).[63]

Blogs A *blog* (short for "web log") is a website about a single person or company. Experts see blogging as a business necessity for organizations, so it should not be overlooked as a vital form of communication to employees and customers, who can post feedback if they choose.[64] However, outdated blogs look bad to employees, customers, and the public, so new ones must be added continually to maintain relevancy.

Others Flickr, Pinterest, Google+, YouTube, Wikis, Jive, Socialtext, and Social Cast are just a few of the many public and industry-specific platforms, with new ones launching daily. Some are designed for only one type of posting: YouTube accepts only videos, for instance, and Flickr only videos and images. Other sites

Myth or Science?

Today, Writing Skills Are More Important Than Speaking Skills

Never before have the writing skills of managers and employees been more on display. Whether we are tapping on a keyboard or a screen, this communication with others is often unedited. (Thank goodness for spell-check.) With all the written communication methods we currently employ, it would be easy to think upper management values writing skills over speaking skills. However, evidence suggests that this is not the case.

As we discussed in Chapter 1, soft skills matter most to employers, regardless of industry. According to Nick Schultz of the American Enterprise Institute, "Considerable evidence suggests that many employers would be happy just to find applicants who have the sort of 'soft' skills that used to be almost taken for granted." Though soft skills refer to all interpersonal skills evident through speaking and writing, they are most on display in one-on-one discussions, interviews, meetings, and presentations. The ability to speak well, particularly in English, has become a job prerequisite for many multinational corporations.

The good news is that speaking ability—knowledge of when to speak, how to speak, how to sound, what to say—can be improved through training. According to leadership coach and author Kristi Hedges, most people can train on their own and do not need formal presentation classes. You can make significant improvements by researching speaking techniques, watching videos of practice sessions, and practicing new techniques in meetings. If learning to speak a foreign language fluently is a problem, full immersion courses and overseas assignments can be helpful if they are options, as are listening to and mimicking television and radio broadcasts in the language. Speaking well hinges on clarity and sincerity of expression.

While it is a mistake to believe writing skills have become more important than speaking skills, we can all make significant improvements in our verbal communications relatively quickly.

Sources: Based on R. J. Aldrick and J. Kasuku, "Escaping from American Intelligence: Culture, Ethnocentrism and the Anglosphere," *International Affairs*, September 2012, 1009–28; K. Hedges, "Confessions of a Former Public Speaking Trainer: Don't Waste Your Money," *Forbes*, April 19, 2012, www.forbes.com/sites/work-in-progress/2012/04/19/public-speaking-trainer-confesses-dont-waste-your-money-on-this/; and N. Schultz, "Hard Unemployment Truths about 'Soft' Skills," *The Wall Street Journal*, September 20, 2012, A15.

have a particular culture, such as Pinterest's informal posts sharing recipes or decorating tips. The business applications have not been fully realized yet, but soon there will probably be at least one social media site tailored to every type of business communication.

Nonverbal Communication Every time we deliver a verbal message, we also impart an unspoken message.[65] No discussion of communication would thus be complete without consideration of *nonverbal communication*—which includes body movements, the intonations or emphasis we give to words, facial expressions, and the physical distance between the sender and receiver.[66]

We could argue that every *body movement* has meaning, and no movement is accidental (though some are unconscious). We act out our state of being with nonverbal body language. For example, we smile to project trustworthiness, uncross our arms to appear approachable, and stand to signal authority.[67] We may also engage in nonverbal communication unconsciously and automatically—when events happen, we react and express our emotions—the bystanders perceiving our emotions then make appraisals based on the emotional expressions.[68]

Body language can convey status, level of engagement, and emotional state.[69] Body language adds to, and often complicates, verbal communication. In fact, studies indicate that people read much more about another's attitude and emotions from their nonverbal cues than their words! If nonverbal cues conflict with the speaker's verbal message, the cues are sometimes more likely to be believed by the listener.[70]

If you read the minutes of a meeting, you wouldn't grasp the impact of what was said the same way as if you had been there or could see the meeting on video. Why is this so? There is no record of nonverbal communication, and the emphasis given to words or phrases is missing. Both make the meaning clearer. Exhibit 12-6 illustrates how *intonations* can change the meaning of a message. *Facial expressions* also convey meaning. Facial expressions, along with intonations, can show arrogance, aggressiveness, fear, shyness, and other characteristics.

Physical distance also has meaning. What is considered proper spacing between people largely depends on cultural norms. For example, a businesslike distance in some European countries feels intimate in many parts of North

Exhibit 12-6 **Intonations: It's the Way You Say It!**

Change your tone and you change your meaning:

Placement of the Emphasis	What It Means
Why don't I take **you** to dinner tonight?	I was going to take someone else.
Why don't **I** take you to dinner tonight?	Instead of the guy you were going with.
Why **don't** I take you to dinner tonight?	I'm trying to find a reason why I **shouldn't** take you.
Why don't I take you to dinner tonight?	Do you have a problem with me?
Why don't I **take** you to dinner tonight?	Instead of going on your own.
Why don't I take you to **dinner** tonight?	Instead of lunch tomorrow.
Why don't I take you to dinner **tonight**?	Not tomorrow night.

Source: Reproduced in A. Huczynski and D. Buchanan, *Organizational Behavior*, 4th ed. (Essex, UK: Pearson Education, 2001), 194.

America. If someone stands closer to you than is considered appropriate, it may indicate aggressiveness or sexual interest; if the person stands farther away, it may signal disinterest or displeasure with what is being said.

Choice of Communication

12-4 Describe how channel richness underlies the choice of communication method.

Now that we've discussed various modes of business communication, why do people choose one channel of communication over another? A model of media richness helps explain channel selection among managers.[71]

Channel Richness

channel richness The amount of information that can be transmitted during a communication episode.

Channels differ in their capacity to convey information.[72] Some are *rich* in that they can (1) handle multiple cues simultaneously, (2) facilitate rapid feedback, and (3) be very personal. Others are *lean* in that they score low on these factors. As Exhibit 12-7 illustrates, face-to-face conversation scores highest in **channel richness** because it transmits the most information per communication episode—multiple information cues (words, postures, facial expressions, gestures, intonations), immediate feedback (both verbal and nonverbal), and the personal touch of being present. Impersonal written media such as formal reports and bulletins rate lowest in richness.

In sum, rich channels give us the chance to observe. The unconscious aspects of communication help us understand the full meaning of a message. When these aspects are missing, we must look for other clues to deduce the sender's emotions and attitudes.

Choosing Communication Methods

The choice of channel depends on whether the message is routine. Routine messages tend to be straightforward and have minimal ambiguity; channels low in richness can carry them efficiently. Nonroutine communications are likely

Exhibit 12-7 **Information Richness and Communication Channels**

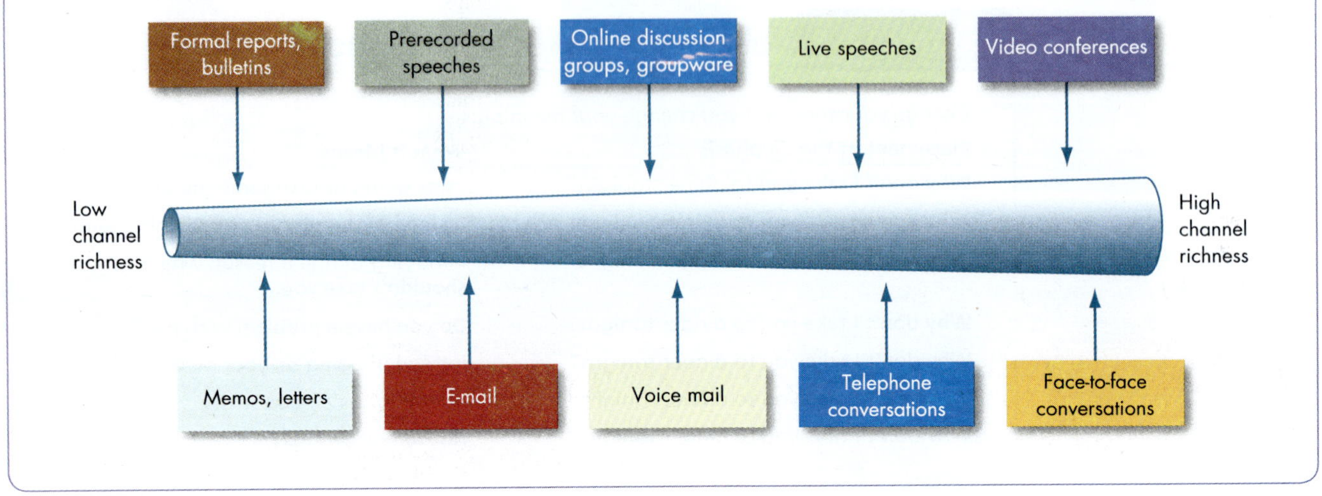

Source: Reproduced from R. L. Daft and R. A. Noe, *Organizational Behavior* (Fort Worth, TX: Harcourt, 2001), 311.

to be complicated and have the potential for misunderstanding. Managers can communicate them effectively only by selecting the appropriate channel for the message.[73]

Channel richness is a helpful framework for choosing your mode of communication. It is not always easy to know when to choose oral rather than written communication, for instance. Experts say oral communication or "face-to-face" communication with coworkers, clients, and upper management is the key to success. However, if you seek out the CEO just to say hello, you may be remembered as an annoyance rather than a star, and signing up for every meeting on the calendar to increase your face-to-face interactions is counterproductive to getting the work of the organization done. Your communication choice is worth a moment's thought: Is the message you need to communicate better suited to a discussion? A diagram? Let's explore some decision points.

Whenever you need to gauge the receiver's receptivity, *oral communication* is usually the better choice. The marketing plan for a new product, for instance, may need to be worked out with clients in person, so you can see their reactions to each idea you propose. Also consider the receiver's preferred mode of communication; some individuals focus on content better in written form and others prefer discussion. For example, if your manager requests a meeting with you, you may not want to ask for an e-mail exchange instead. The pace of your work environment matters, too. A fast-paced workplace may thrive on pop-by meetings, while a deadline-heavy team project may progress faster with scheduled Skype videoconferences.

Much of what we communicate face-to-face is in the delivery, so also consider your speaking skills when choosing your communication method. Research indicates the sound of your voice is twice as important as what you are saying. A good speaking voice—clear, moderated—can be a help to your career, while loud, questioning, irritating, immature, falsetto, breathy, or monotone voice tones can hinder you. If your voice is problematic, your work teams can help you raise your awareness so you can make changes, or you may benefit from the help of a voice coach.[74]

Written communication is generally the most reliable mode for complex and lengthy communications, and it can be the most efficient method for short messages when, for instance, a two-sentence text can take the place of a 10-minute phone call. But keep in mind that written communication can be limited in its emotional expression.

Choose written communication when you want the information to be tangible, verifiable, and "on the record." People are usually forced to think more thoroughly about what they want to convey in a written message than in a spoken one, so your written communications can be well thought out, logical, and clear. But be aware that, as with oral communication, your delivery is just as important as the content. We discussed the level of formality, but note that managers report grammar mistakes and lack of business formality are unprofessional—and unacceptable. "People get passionate about grammar," corporate writing instructor and author Jack Appleman noted, and one study found that 45 percent of employers were adding training programs to teach grammar and communication skills.[75] On the other hand, some experts argue that the use of social media jargon and abbreviations is good for business. Overall, for your professional success, know your audience when possible, and use good grammar.

Letters are used in business primarily for networking purposes and when signatures need to be authentic. A handwritten thank-you note is never a wrong choice for an applicant to send after an employment interview, for instance,

Several doctors during COVID-19 started consulting their regular patients (asthma, blood pressure, diabetics) over phone on a weekly basis to be able to keep in touch with patients and yet not expose them to the risks involved in visiting a clinic/hospital.
Source: WESTOCK PRODUCTIONS.shutterstock.com

and handwritten envelopes often are put right on the receiver's desk unopened by administrative staff. Although electronic written communication provides authentication by indicating the sender and date/time sent, a handwritten signature is still preferred and sometimes required for letters and contracts. *E-mails* are often less formal forms of written communication, and perhaps used the most frequently in business contexts. E-mails are used to informally communicate information that does not require a meeting but is too long or information-dense to be conveyed through a text or instant message. However, how the message is worded is important—nonverbal cues are often lost in these messages, and the sender could be perceived as rude, egocentric, or even culturally insensitive.[76]

In general, you should respond to *instant messages* only when they are professional and initiate them only when you know they will be welcome. Remember that your conversation will not be stored for later reference.

There are significant gains and challenges from *text messaging* in business settings. Texts are cheap to send and receive, and the willingness to be available for quick communications from clients and managers is conducive to good business. However, some users—and managers—view text messaging as intrusive and distracting. The rules of business etiquette are not yet established, resulting in offenses ranging from texts sent at unreasonable hours to serial texting in bursts of short messages that keep receivers' phones buzzing annoyingly. Such a continual presence can also make it hard for employees to concentrate and stay focused. Consider these recent research findings from a survey of professionals:

- *Eighty-four percent think it's inappropriate to write texts or e-mails during formal meetings.*
- *Seventy-five percent think it's inappropriate to read texts or e-mails during formal meetings.*
- *Sixty-six percent think it's inappropriate to write texts or e-mails during any meetings.*
- *At least 22 percent think it's inappropriate to use phones during any meetings.*[77]

As you can see, it is best to strictly limit personal text messages during office hours and be cautious in using texting for business purposes. You should discuss using texting for business with people before you text them for the first time, set up general availability ground rules, and take your cues about when to text from the other person. For longer messages, it is better to use e-mail; even though the receiver still might scroll through the message on a smartphone, the option of viewing—and saving—your message on a computer is preferable.

On the corporate level, the returns on using *social media* are mixed. Some of the most spectacular gains are in the sales arena, both business-to-public and business-to-business. For instance, one sales representative for virtual-meetings company PGi landed his fastest sale ever by instantly connecting with a potential client after TweetDeck alerted him that a CEO was tweeting his frustration about web conferencing.[78] Companies are also developing their own internal social-networking platforms to encourage employees to collaborate and to improve training, reporting a 300 percent annual increase in corporate network activity.

Some organizations have policies governing the use of social media, but many don't. It is difficult for management to control the content that employees post; even well-intentioned employees post comments that could be construed as harmful to their organization's reputation or that reveal confidential or sensitive information. Software that mines social media sites can check on a job applicant, and the growing field of digital forensics helps investigate potential problems with current employees; however, cybersleuthing can be time-consuming and expensive.[79] And acting on violations of an organization's social media policy is tricky. Thus, if you want to use social media for business purposes, make certain you are connected with all levels of management engaged in the effort. And if you would like to mention your business in your personal social media, communicate with your organization about what you would like to do, and what you think the potential return for the company may be. Use discretion about which personal social media platforms and *apps* are acceptable for business communication. And know your company's social media policies about corporate confidentiality and your company's view on your privacy.[80]

As an individual, you may choose to post a *blog* on your own blog page, or you may choose to comment on another person's blog. Both options are more public than you may think, and your words are easily reachable by your name via search engines like Google. If others in the company happen to read a critical or negative blog entry or post, there is nothing to keep them from sharing that information with management. You could be dismissed as a result.

It's important to be alert to *nonverbal* aspects of communication and look for these cues as well as the literal meaning of a sender's words. You should be particularly aware of contradictions between the messages. Someone who frequently glances at her wristwatch is giving the message that she would prefer to terminate the conversation no matter what she actually says, for instance. We misinform others when we express one message verbally, such as trust, but nonverbally communicate a contradictory message that reads, "I don't have confidence in you."

Information Security

Security is a huge concern for nearly all organizations with private or proprietary information about clients, customers, and employees. Organizations worry about the security of electronic information they seek to protect such as

An Ethical Choice

Using Employees in Organizational Social Media Strategy

Social media are good for business communication, but their use is an ethical minefield for employers and employees. In a study of 24 industries in 115 countries, 63 percent of managers believed social media will be important to their businesses in 3 years. Research suggests that social media use may be an indicator of an organization's profitability. Companies at the forefront include McDonald's, IBM, Salesforce, SAP, and Yammer. Social media can turn customers into fans through increased and personalized communication, and quick and appropriate responses to customers' communication can turn those fans—and employees—into spokespeople for the brand. The key is forming emotional bonds or capitalizing on current relationships to spread the good word about the company to potential clients.

Social media sites pose a host of business ethical concerns. Employees with a huge online presence who use social media for both personal and company promotion (known as co-branded employees) become a liability if they leak corporate information, present a bad image, or leave the company. There are also ethical concerns about employees' privacy and right to free speech: Let's say that an employee who monitors the company Twitter feed wins a customer over; she later tweets from her personal account, "Score for us: another happy customer." That may present no concern, but she would hurt the company if she lost the customer and tweeted, "Epic fail: We blew it again."

Other employer tasks with few tested ethical guidelines include ensuring employees make proper use of company time, compensating them for time they spend promoting the company through their personal social media connections, clarifying who should own personal devices used for company promotion, setting limits on company expectations of employees' promotion efforts, dealing with permissions/attributions, and clearing any legal hurdles.

Experts advise organizations to draft social media policies that reflect their company ethics rather than seek to "cover all the bases" of potential liabilities. While an organization could require job applicants to share their online passwords, for instance, this may violate trust and personal privacy rules. Policies that define ethical expectations for employee online behavior, discuss monitoring, define consequences for nonconformance, and explain the logic of the guidelines will be the most effective. Even still, the National Labor Relations Board (NLRB) finds many corporate policies aimed at the ethics of social media usage violate the National Labor Relations Act. A good social media policy can affirm the ethical expectations of the corporation and improve its organizational culture.

Sources: Based on S. F. Gale, "Policies Must Score a Mutual Like," *Workforce Management* (August 2012): 18; B. Giamanco and K. Gregoire, "Tweet Me, Friend Me, Make Me Buy," *Harvard Business Review* (July–August 2012): 88–93; D. Kiron, D. Palmer, A. N Phillips, and N. Kruschwitz, "What Managers Really Think about Social Business," *MIT Sloan Management Review* (Summer 2012): 51–60; X. Luo, J. Zhang, and W. Duan, "Social Media and Firm Equity Value," *Information Systems Research* (March 2013): 146–63; C. M. Sashi, "Customer Engagement, Buyer-Seller Relationships, and Social Media," *Management Decision* 50 (2012): 253–72; and A. Smith, "NLRB Finds Social Media Policies Unlawful," *HR Magazine* (August 2012): 18.

hospital patient data,[81] physical information they still keep in file cabinets, and information they entrust their employees with knowing. Most companies actively monitor employee Internet use and e-mail records, and some even use video surveillance and record phone conversations. Necessary though they may be, such practices can seem invasive to employees, who may lash out as a result.[82] An organization can relieve employee concerns by engaging them in the creation of information-security policies and giving them some control over how their personal information is used.[83]

Persuasive Communication

12-5 Differentiate between automatic and controlled processing of persuasive messages.

We've discussed a number of methods for communication up to this point. Now we turn our attention to one of the functions of communication—persuasion—and the features that might make messages more or less persuasive to an audience.

Automatic and Controlled Processing

To understand the process of persuasion, it is useful to consider two different ways we process information.[84] Think about the last time you bought a can of soda. Did you carefully research brands, or did you reach for the can that had the most appealing advertising? If we're honest, we'll admit glitzy ads and catchy slogans have an influence on our choices as consumers. We often rely on **automatic processing**, a relatively superficial consideration of evidence and information making use of heuristics like those we discussed in Chapter 6. Automatic processing takes little time and low effort, so it makes sense to use it for processing persuasive messages related to topics you don't care much about. The disadvantage is that it lets us be fooled easily by a variety of tricks, like a cute jingle or glamorous photo.

automatic processing A relatively superficial consideration of evidence and information making use of heuristics.

Now consider the last time you chose a place to live. You probably sourced experts who knew something about the area, gathered information about prices, and considered the costs and benefits of renting versus buying. You were engaging in more effortful **controlled processing**, a detailed consideration of evidence and information relying on facts, figures, and logic. Controlled processing requires effort and energy, but it's harder to fool someone who has taken the time and effort to engage in it. So what makes someone engage in either shallow or deep processing? Let's explore how we might determine what types of processing an audience will use.

controlled processing A detailed consideration of evidence and information relying on facts, figures, and logic.

Interest Level One of the best predictors of whether people will use an automatic or controlled process for reacting to a persuasive message is their level of interest in it.[85] Interest levels reflect the impact a decision will have on your life. When people are very interested in the outcome of a decision, they're more likely to process information carefully. That's probably why people look for so much more information when deciding about something important (like where to live) than something relatively unimportant (like what color t-shirt to wear).

One way you can enhance interest in what a sender is communicating is through storytelling. For example, even though structured job interviews are much more valid than unstructured ones, HR professionals tend to use unstructured interviews more often. A recent study has found that stories or testimonials about the successes of structured interviews can persuade HR professionals to adopt more structured approaches.[86]

Prior Knowledge People who are well informed about a subject area are more likely to use controlled processing strategies. They have already thought through various arguments for or against a specific course of action and therefore won't readily change their position unless very good, thoughtful reasons are provided. On the other hand, people who are poorly informed about a topic can change their minds more readily, even in the face of fairly superficial arguments presented without a great deal of evidence. A better-informed audience is likely to be much harder to persuade.

need for cognition A personality trait of individuals depicting the ongoing desire to think and learn.

Personality Do you read at least five reviews of a movie before deciding whether to see it? Perhaps you even research films by the same stars and director. If so, you are probably high in **need for cognition**, a personality trait of individuals who are most likely to be persuaded by evidence and facts.[87] Those who are lower in their need for cognition are more likely to use automatic processing strategies, relying on intuition and emotion to guide their evaluation of persuasive messages.

Message Characteristics Another factor that influences whether people use an automatic or controlled processing strategy is the characteristics of the message itself. Messages provided through relatively lean communication channels, with little opportunity for users to interact with the content of the message, encourage automatic processing. Conversely, messages provided through richer communication channels encourage more deliberative processing. These messages vary through nuanced pitch, volume, intonation, and speech rate, which can convey confidence (and thus lead the messages to be perceived as more persuasive).[88]

Choosing the Message The most important implication is to match your persuasive message to the type of processing your audience is likely to use.[89] When audience members are not interested in a persuasive message topic, when they are poorly informed, when they are low in need for cognition, and when information is transmitted through relatively lean channels, they'll be more likely to use automatic processing. In these cases, use messages that are more emotionally laden and associate positive images with your preferred outcome. On the other hand, when audience members are interested in a

Managers of Germany's construction firm Hochtief relied on controlled processing during a meeting when they presented rational arguments about a takeover bid by another firm. Fearing that a takeover would put their jobs at risk, Hochtief employees had a high level of interest in learning about managers' plans to prevent it.

Source: Bernd Thissen/dpa/picture-alliance/Newscom

topic, when they are high in need for cognition, or when the information is transmitted through rich channels, then it is a better idea to focus on rational arguments and evidence to make your case.

Barriers to Effective Communication

12-6 Identify common barriers to effective communication.

Several barriers can slow or distort effective communication, barriers that we need to recognize and reduce. In this section, we highlight the most important.

Filtering

filtering A sender's manipulation of information so that it will be seen more favorably by the receiver.

Filtering refers to a sender's purposely manipulating information so the receiver will see it more favorably. A manager who tells his boss what he feels the boss wants to hear is filtering information.

The more vertical levels in the organization's hierarchy, the more opportunities there are for filtering. But some filtering will occur wherever there are status differences. Factors such as fear of conveying bad news and the desire to please the boss often lead employees to tell their superiors what they think they want to hear, thus distorting upward communications.[90]

Selective Perception

Selective perception is important because the receivers in the communication process selectively see and hear based on their needs, motivations, experience, backgrounds, and other personal characteristics. Receivers also project their interests and expectations into communications as they decode them. For example, an employment interviewer who expects a female job applicant to put her family ahead of her career is likely to see that characteristic in all female applicants, regardless of whether any of the women actually feel that way. As we said in Chapter 6, we don't see reality; we interpret what we see and call it reality.

Information Overload

information overload A condition in which information inflow exceeds an individual's processing capacity.

Although people integrate information from multiple sources to effectively make sense of information,[91] individuals have a finite capacity for processing data. When the information we have to work with exceeds our processing capacity, the result is **information overload**. We've seen in this text that dealing with it has become a huge challenge for individuals and for organizations. It's a challenge you can manage—to some degree—by following the steps outlined earlier in this chapter.

What happens when individuals have more information than they can sort and use? They tend to select, ignore, pass over, or forget it. Or they may put off further processing until the overload situation ends. In any case, lost information and less effective communication results, making it all the more important to deal well with overload.

More generally, as an Intel study shows, it may make sense to connect to technology less frequently, to, in the words of one article, "avoid letting the drumbeat of digital missives constantly shake up and reorder to-do lists." One radical way is to limit the number of devices you access. For example, insurance agents who used to use a paper-pencil and phone, have started using electronic pads for their work. and so have a pharma company moved all its employees from desktops to use of laptops and mobile phones. These moves have been effective in improving productivity.

As information technology and immediate communication have become a more prevalent component of modern organizational life, more employees find they are never able to get offline. For example, some business travelers were disappointed when airlines began offering wireless Internet connections in flight because they could no longer use their travel time as a rare opportunity to relax without a constant barrage of organizational communications. The negative impacts of these communication devices can spill over into employees' personal lives as well. Both workers and their spouses relate the use of electronic communication technologies outside work to higher levels of work–life conflict, though some research suggests that the level of conflict may depend on the characteristics of the employee.[92] Employees must balance the need for constant communication with their personal need for breaks from work, or they risk burnout from being on call 24 hours a day.

Emotions

You may interpret the same message differently when you're angry or distraught than when you're happy. For example, individuals in positive moods are more confident about their opinions after reading a persuasive message, so well-designed arguments have a stronger impact on their opinions.[93] People in negative moods are more likely to scrutinize messages in greater detail, whereas those in positive moods tend to accept communications at face value.[94] Extreme emotions such as fury are most likely to hinder effective communication.[95] In such instances, we are most prone to disregarding our controlled thinking processes.

Language

Even when we're communicating in the same language, words mean different things to different people. Age and context are two of the biggest factors that influence such differences. For example, when business consultant Michael

Communication barriers exist between these call center employees in Gurgaon, India and their U.S. and Canadian customers even though they all communicate in English. Training in pronunciation, intonation, vocabulary, and grammar helps employees convey messages effectively to their customers.
Source: Dondi Tawatao/Getty Images

Schiller asked his 15-year-old daughter where she was going with friends, he said, "You need to recognize your ARAs [ARA stands for "accountability, responsibility, and authority"] and measure against them." Schiller said that in response, his daughter "looked at him like he was from outer space." Those new to corporate lingo may find acronyms such as ARA, words such as *deliverables* (verifiable outcomes of a project), and phrases such as *get the low-hanging fruit* (deal with the easiest parts first) bewildering, in the same way parents may be mystified by teen slang.[96] The persuasiveness of language also depends on the person's initial agreement with a message. For example, concrete language is more persuasive when the audience has dissimilar political views to the message, while abstract language is more persuasive when political views are similar.[97]

Our use of language is far from uniform. If we knew how each of us modifies the language, we could minimize communication difficulties, but we usually don't know. Senders tend to assume—incorrectly—that the words and terms they use mean the same to the receivers as they do to them.

Silence

It's easy to ignore silence or lack of communication because it is defined by the absence of information. This is often a mistake, however—silence itself can be the message to communicate noninterest or the inability to deal with a topic.[98] Employees are more likely to be silent if they are being mistreated by managers, are experiencing frequent negative emotions and rumination, or feel like they have less power in the organization.[99] Silence can also be a simple outcome of information overload or a delaying period for considering a response. For whatever reasons, research suggests using silence and withholding communication are common and problematic.[100] One survey found that more than 85 percent of managers reported remaining silent about at least one issue of significant concern.[101] The impact of silence can be organizationally detrimental. Employee silence can mean managers lack information about ongoing operational problems; management silence can leave employees bewildered. Silence regarding discrimination, harassment, corruption, and misconduct means top management cannot take action to eliminate problematic behavior.

Communication Apprehension

communication apprehension
Undue tension and anxiety about oral communication, written communication, or both.

An estimated 20 percent of college students suffer from debilitating **communication apprehension**, or social anxiety.[102] These people experience undue tension and anxiety in oral communication, written communication, or both.[103] They may find it extremely difficult to talk with others face-to-face or become extremely anxious when they have to use the phone, relying on memos or e-mails when a phone call would be faster and more appropriate.

Oral-communication apprehensives avoid situations, such as teaching, for which oral communication is a dominant requirement.[104] But almost all jobs require *some* oral communication. Of greater concern is evidence that some oral-communication apprehensives distort the communication demands of their jobs in order to minimize the need for communication. Be aware that some people severely limit their oral communication and rationalize their actions by telling themselves communicating isn't necessary for them to do their jobs effectively.

Lying

Outright misrepresentation of information, or lying, is a barrier to effective information (it literally involves distortion of information).[105] People differ in their definition of a lie. For example, is deliberately withholding information about a mistake a lie, or do you actively have to deny your role in the mistake to pass the threshold? While the definition of a lie befuddles ethicists and social scientists, there is no denying the prevalence of lying. People may tell one to two lies per day, with some individuals telling considerably more.[106] Compounded across a large organization, this is an enormous amount of deception happening every day. Evidence shows people are more comfortable lying over the phone than face-to-face, and they are more comfortable lying in e-mails than when they have to write with pen and paper.[107]

Can you detect liars? Research suggests most people are not very good at detecting deception in others.[108] The problem is there are no nonverbal or verbal cues unique to lying—averting your gaze, pausing, and shifting your posture can also be signals of nervousness, shyness, or doubt. Most people who lie take steps to guard against being detected, so they might look a person in the eye when lying because they know that direct eye contact is (incorrectly) assumed to be a sign of truthfulness. Finally, many lies are embedded in truths; liars usually give a somewhat true account with just enough details changed to avoid detection.

In sum, the frequency of lying and the difficulty in detecting liars makes this an especially strong barrier to effective communication.

Communicating in Times of Crisis

The final barrier to effective communication can be found in the underlying context: communication becomes more challenging during times of crisis.[109] As an example, the devastation caused when Tsunami hit the eastern shores of India on December 26, 2004 has been frequently viewed as an exemplary case in how crises can be fraught with ineffective and inefficient communication.[110] Government agencies at all levels were taken by surprise when confronted with the threat of Hurricane Katrina approaching the United States and had difficulty coordinating a response to the crisis as well as coping with the uncertainty and ambiguity of the situation.

Effective communication during times of crisis involves breaking down crisis response into several stages: (1) communicating in anticipation of or preparation for crises, (2) managing responses to the crises while they are occurring, and (3) communicating with stakeholders after the crisis and catalyzing shared learning.[111] Collective motivations underlying communication change throughout these stages: people become driven to take control and dominate during times of war, whereas crises during times of peace tend to drive people toward being self-critical and fearful of negative consequences.[112] These shifting motivations need to be accounted for in crisis communication—control, domination, anxiety, and fear are not directly aligned with reassurance and grace under pressure.

What can be done to improve communication during times of crisis? Effective messaging that focuses on sharing facts, sharing interpretations of the facts, and projections for consequences of actions at all stages can be beneficial.[113] Furthermore, although motivations tend to shift more toward power and responsibility, people should try to work together in times of crisis instead of independently. For example, research shows that when people try to solve a problem separately (e.g., developing a vaccine for a virus), they may be overcome by confusion and an inability to learn from one another's failures. By coordinating and collaborating, they may be able to overcome the confusion and learn from one another.[114] Finally, technology can help communicate information rapidly and accurately to all those who may be (imminently) affected by a disaster, such as apps that help provide information quickly to response teams.[115] Technology can also be used to sound the crisis alarm. For instance, a Twitter alert was issued in 2018 for a potential ballistic missile threat. This alert proved to be a false alarm, yet an analysis of the 1.2 million tweets that followed suggested that anxiety remained heightened throughout the week as a result.[116] Therefore, people should remain sensitive to the impact of their communications on others during crises.

Cultural Factors

12-7 Discuss how to overcome the potential problems of cross-cultural communication.

Effective communication is difficult under the best of conditions. Cross-cultural factors clearly create the potential for increased communication problems. A gesture that is well understood and acceptable in one culture can be meaningless or lewd in another. Unfortunately, only 18 percent of companies have documented strategies for communicating with employees across cultures, and only 31 percent require that corporate messages be customized for consumption in other cultures.

Cultural Barriers

Several problems are related to difficulties in cross-cultural communications. First are *barriers caused by semantics.* Words mean different things to different people, particularly people from different national cultures. Some words don't translate between cultures. For instance, the Finnish word *sisu* means something akin to "guts" or "dogged persistence" but is essentially untranslatable into English. Capitalists in Russia may have difficulty communicating with British or Canadian counterparts because English terms such as *efficiency, free market,* and *regulation* have no direct Russian equivalents. Similarly, differences can be observed for some communicative behaviors beyond language, such as how people culturally differ in the expression of gratitude, including the use of bodily contact in individualist cultures.[117]

Second are *barriers caused by word connotations.* Understanding a word's suggestive meaning is important. The word *quality* is associated in America with "it works"; in Korea, it suggests "it's brand new"; in Japan, "it's perfect—zero defects"; and in China, "it gives status."[118]

Third are *barriers caused by tone differences.* In some cultures, language is formal; in others, it's informal. In some cultures, the tone changes depending on the context: People speak differently at home, in social situations, and at work.[119] Using a personal, informal style when a more formal style is expected can be inappropriate.

Fourth are *differences in tolerance for conflict and methods for resolving conflicts.* People from individualist cultures tend to be more comfortable with direct conflict and will make the source of their disagreements overt. Collectivists are more likely to acknowledge conflict only implicitly and avoid emotionally charged disputes. They may attribute conflicts to the situation more than to the individuals and therefore may not require explicit apologies to repair relationships, whereas individualists prefer explicit statements accepting responsibility for conflicts and public apologies to restore relationships.

In addition, while all cultures identify certain behaviors as overly aggressive, there are certain types of behaviors that are more likely to be identified as negative depending on the culture. In Israel, Pakistan, and Japan, there is a greater distinction between verbal and physical aggression. In the United States and Israel, behaviors that infringe on personal resources are considered aggressive, while Pakistan differentiates between different degrees of threats. Different standards for aggression reflect the ways that a certain country may interpret or respond to a conflict.[120]

Cultural Context

high-context cultures Cultures that rely heavily on nonverbal and subtle situational cues in communication.

low-context cultures Cultures that rely heavily on words to convey meaning in communication.

Cultures tend to differ in the degree to which context influences the meaning individuals take from communication.[121] In **high-context cultures** such as China, Korea, Japan, and Vietnam, people rely heavily on nonverbal and subtle situational cues in communicating with others, and a person's official status, place in society, and reputation carry considerable weight. What is *not* said may be more significant than what *is* said. In contrast, people from Europe and North America reflect their **low-context cultures**. They rely essentially on spoken and written words to convey meaning; body language and formal titles are secondary (see Exhibit 12-8).

Contextual differences mean quite a lot in terms of communication. Communication in high-context cultures implies considerably more trust by both parties. What may appear to be casual and insignificant conversation in fact reflects the desire to build a relationship and create trust. Oral agreements imply strong commitments in high-context cultures. And who you are—your age, seniority, rank in the organization—is highly valued and heavily influences your credibility. Managers can therefore "make suggestions" rather than give orders. But in low-context cultures, enforceable contracts tend to be in writing, precisely worded, and highly legalistic. Similarly, low-context cultures value directness. Managers are expected to be explicit and precise in conveying intended meaning.

Exhibit 12-8 High- versus Low-Context Cultures

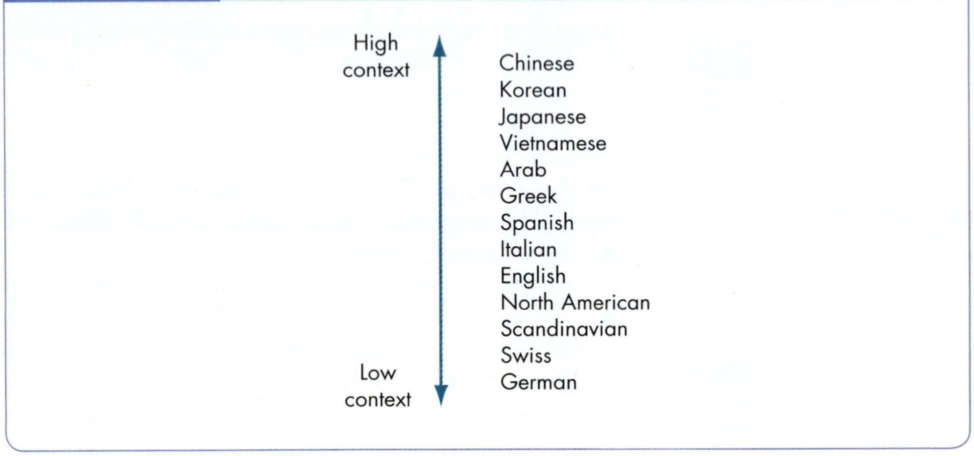

A Cultural Guide

There is much to be gained from business intercultural communications. It is safe to assume that every one of us has a different viewpoint that is culturally shaped. Because we do have differences, we have an opportunity to reach the most creative solutions possible with the help of others if we communicate effectively.

According to Fred Casmir, a leading expert in intercultural communication research, we often do not communicate well with people outside our culture because we tend to generalize from only their cultural origin. This can be insensitive and potentially disastrous, especially when we make assumptions based on observable characteristics. Many of us have a richly varied ethnic background and would be offended if someone addressed us according to what culture our physical features might favor, for instance. Also, attempts to be culturally sensitive to another person are often based on stereotypes propagated by media. These stereotypes usually do not have a correct or current relevance.

Casmir noted that, because there are far too many cultures for anyone to understand completely, and individuals interpret their own cultures differently, intercultural communication should be based on sensitivity and pursuit of common goals. He found the ideal condition is an ad hoc "third culture" that a group can form when its members seek to incorporate aspects of each member's cultural communication preferences. The norms that this subculture establishes through appreciating individual differences create a common ground for effective communication. Intercultural groups that communicate effectively can be highly productive and innovative.

When communicating with people from a different culture, what can you do to reduce misinterpretations? Casmir and other experts offer the following suggestions:

1. **Know yourself.** Recognizing your own cultural identity and biases is critical to understanding the unique viewpoints of other people.
2. **Foster a climate of mutual respect, fairness, and democracy.** Clearly establish an environment of equality and mutual concern. This will be your "third culture" context for effective intercultural communication that transcends each person's cultural norms.
3. **State facts, not your interpretation.** Interpreting or evaluating what someone has said or done draws more on your own culture and background than on the observed situation. If you state only facts, you will have the opportunity to benefit from the other person's interpretation. Delay judgment until you've had sufficient time to observe and interpret the situation from the differing perspectives of all concerned.
4. **Consider the other person's viewpoint.** Before sending a message, put yourself in the recipient's shoes. What are their values, experiences, and frames of reference? What do you know about their education, upbringing, and background that can give you added insight? Try to see the people in the group as they really are first, and take a collaborative problem-solving approach whenever potential conflicts arise.
5. **Proactively maintain the identity of the group.** Like any culture, the establishment of a common-ground "third culture" for effective intercultural communication takes time and nurturing. Remind members of the group of your common goals, mutual respect, and need to adapt to individual communication preferences.[122]

Summary

You've probably discovered the link between communication and employee satisfaction in this chapter: the less uncertainty, the greater the satisfaction. Distortions, ambiguities, and incongruities between verbal and nonverbal messages all increase uncertainty and reduce satisfaction. Careful attention to the methods and modes for each communication ensures that the message is interpreted properly by the receiver.

Implications for Managers

- Remember that your communication mode will partly determine your communication effectiveness.
- Obtain feedback to make certain your messages—however they are communicated—are understood.
- Remember that written communication creates more misunderstandings than oral communication; communicate with employees through in-person meetings when possible.
- Make sure you use communication strategies appropriate to your audience and the type of message you're sending.
- Keep in mind communication barriers such as gender and culture.

We Should Use Employees' Social Media Presence

POINT

Everyone uses social media. Well, almost everyone: A Pew Research Center study found that the highest percentage of adults who use social-networking sites was in Israel, at 53 percent, followed by 50 percent in the United States, 43 percent in Russia and Great Britain, and 42 percent in Spain.

Business is social, and using employees' social contacts to increase business has always been a facet of marketing. Organizations that don't follow their employees' social media presence are missing an opportunity to expand their business and strengthen their workforce. For example, the Honda employee who once told 30 friends that Honda is best can now tell 300 Facebook friends and 500 Twitter followers about the latest model. Employees' savvy about social media can have a substantial positive effect on the bottom line.

Monitoring employees' social media presence can also strengthen the workforce by identifying the best talent. Managers can look for potential online celebrities—frequent bloggers and Twitter users with many followers—to approach for co-branding partnerships. Scrutiny can also help employers spot problems. For example, consider the employee who is fired one day and turns violent. A manager who had been monitoring the employee's social media posts may be able to detect warning signs. A human resources department monitoring employees' social media activity may be able to identify a substance abuse problem and provide help for the employee through the company's intervention policies.

A job candidate's social media presence provides one more input to hiring and retention decisions that many organizations already take advantage of. In reality, there is no difference between the employee and the person—they are one and the same, on or off working hours.

Employers that monitor social media can also identify employees who use their platforms to send out bad press or who leak proprietary information. For this reason, managers may someday be *required* to monitor employees' social media postings and to act on infringements of company policies. Many do so already.

Managers should therefore develop enforceable social media policies and create a corporate infrastructure to research and monitor social media activity regularly. The potential increase in business and limit on liability is ample return for dedicating staff and work hours to building a successful social media program.

COUNTERPOINT

There is little to be gained and much to be lost when organizations follow candidates' and employees' presence on social media. Managers may be able to learn more about individuals through their online activity, and organizations may be able to catch some good press from employee postings, but the risk of liability for this intrusion on privacy is inescapable. Managers are ill-equipped to monitor, interpret, and act on employees' social media postings, and few have any experience with relating the medium to business use.

Managers may also easily misinterpret the information they find. Few companies have training programs for the proper use of social media; only 40 percent have social media policies of any kind. Those that do are skating on thin ice because monitoring policies can conflict with privacy regulations.

An employee's online image doesn't reveal much that is relevant to the job, certainly not enough to warrant the time and money that a business would spend on monitoring. Most users view social media as a private, recreational venue, and their membership on Facebook and other sites should be regarded with the same respect as would membership in a club. In this light, monitoring employees' social media accounts is an unethical violation of their right to privacy.

Equal employment opportunity laws require companies to hire without respect to race, age, religion, national origin, or disability. But managers who check into candidates' social media postings often find out more than the candidate wanted to share, and then there is no way to keep that information from affecting the hiring decision. Searching through social media can therefore expose a company to a costly discrimination claim.

Using employees' personal social media presence as a marketing tool through company-supportive postings is unethical from many standpoints. First, it is unethical to expect employees to expand the company's client base through their personal contacts. Second, it is unreasonable to expect them to endorse the company after working hours. And the practice of asking employees for their social media passwords is an obvious intrusion into their personal lives.

In sum, people have a right to a professional and a private image. Unless the employee is offering to "friend" the company in a social media partnership, there is no question that employers should stay out of their personal business.

Sources: Based on S. F. Gale, "Policies Must Score a Mutual Like," *Workforce Management* 91, no. 8 (2012): 18-9; R. Huggins and S. Ward, "Countries with the Highest Percentage of Adults Who Use Social Networking Sites," *USA Today*, February 8, 2012, 1A; A. L. Kavanaugh et al., "Social Media Use by Government: From the Routine to the Critical," *Government Information Quarterly* (October 2012): 480–91; and S. Johnson, "Those Facebook Posts Could Cost You a Job," *San Jose Mercury News*, January 16, 2012, www.mercurynews.com/business/ci_19754451.

CHAPTER REVIEW

QUESTIONS FOR REVIEW

12-1 What are the functions and process of communication?

12-2 What are the communication differences between downward, upward, and lateral communication sent through small-group networks and the grapevine?

12-3 What are the methods of oral communication, written communication, and nonverbal communication?

12-4 How does channel richness underlie the choice of communication method?

12-5 What is the difference between automatic and controlled processing of persuasive messages?

12-6 What are some common barriers to effective communication?

12-7 How do you overcome the potential problems of cross-cultural communication?

APPLICATION AND EMPLOYABILITY

The ability to communicate messages to others effectively is vital to succeeding in the workplace. Communication allows us to manage group members, provide and receive feedback, share our emotions, persuade others, and exchange information. A strong understanding of how to communicate effectively with others can help you be a better coworker by allowing you to set goals, coordinate with a team, and continuously improve through feedback. In this chapter, you learned better communication and analysis skills by assessing whether organizations still value oral communication, understanding how to communicate with someone who is deaf, and studying the pros and cons of employees using social media. In the next part of the chapter, you will learn about the difficulties of emotional sharing through e-mail, examine the use of personal devices in workplaces, learn about gender differences in communication style, and learn some techniques for managing gossip.

EXPERIENTIAL EXERCISE Choosing the Right Modes of Communication

Pair up with someone you never worked with before. In this exercise, you will pretend to be Sanjeev, the head of the accounting department in the company. During an intense week, you receive the following email from the human resources director.

Subject: A difficult situation with an employee

Dear Sanjeev,

I am writing to inform you about a difficult situation we are handling among the personnel. An employee from the marketing department is experiencing interpersonal tensions with the boss and two colleagues, due to which he is frequently absent from work. As he is a valued employee with good performance records in the past, we've realized that changing offices could be beneficial for him and the company.

We believe that your department would be a good environment for this employee to feel more engaged on the job. Two colleagues from HR will assist you and the employee in the transition process, which we hope to begin next month. All the people involved so far have demonstrated great collaboration with us, and we are sure you will do the same. Sorry for the short notice, but we are facing strict deadlines this month.

Do not hesitate to contact me if you have further questions. We will be monitoring the situation with monthly check-ins. I would like to thank you in advance for the welcome you will be giving the employee.

Thanks,
Rakesh Mishra
HR Director

You are both surprised by and disappointed by this email for several reasons, including the decision to communicate such an important information via email, the short notice period, and above all, the fact that you were not consulted in the decision. However, you also know that helping the organization to retain its talents is the right thing to do. Take 5 minutes and write draft replies to Michel individually telling him whether you will accept the employee. Then try to come to an agreement about the definitive reply to send the HR director and discuss the following questions.

Questions

12-8. Were you two in agreement about the reply to send the HR director?

12-9. What alternative modes of communication would you have used in similar circumstances? Why?

12-10. Discuss with your partner the possible impact on Sanjeev's reputation and career if he accepts or denies the HR director's request. What changes in HR practices could avoid this situation in the future?

ETHICAL DILEMMA BYOD

"What's your cell phone number? Good, I'll call you about the meeting." If you're like many people in the world who have used a smartphone for years, or one of the 1.3 billion people who bought one recently, chances are you've used it for work. In fact, your employer may have even invited—or asked—you to use your smartphone, tablet, or laptop in your job. Such is the bring-your-own-device (BYOD) trend, which started out of friendly convenience but now carries major ethical issues. For instance:

- *Did you know your employer can wipe your personal devices clean?* Remotely? With no warning? It happens, and not just at the 21 percent of organizations that erase devices when employees are terminated. Any time an organization has a privacy concern, it may wipe all devices clean to prevent a further breach of its cyberdefenses. Health care consultant Michael Irvin lost his personal e-mail accounts, apps, music, contacts, and photos suddenly one day, leaving his multiuse iPhone "like it came straight from the factory." Another individual lost pictures of a relative who had died.
- *Is your device part of your employment contract, either explicitly or by understanding?* If so, who pays for the device? Well, you did, and you continue to pay for the service. If the device breaks, who pays for the replacement device? Can you lose your job if you can't afford the device and service?
- *Can you use your device for all work-related communications?* The cloud has brought opportunities for people to send classified work information anywhere, anytime. Organizations are concerned about what social media, collaboration, and file-sharing applications are in use, which is fair, but some policies can limit how you use your own device.
- *Once you use your personal device for work, where are the boundaries between work and home life?* Research indicates that intensive smartphone users, for instance, need to disengage in their off-hours to prevent work–home stress and burnout. Yet not everyone can do this, even if they are allowed to; research indicates that a significant proportion of smartphone users felt pressured to access their devices around the clock, whether or not that pressure was warranted.

The clear dilemma for employees is whether to acknowledge you own a smart device, and whether to offer its use for your employer's convenience. Put that way, it seems obvious to say no: Why would you risk possibly losing everything to a corporate swipe? But the convenience of carrying one phone is real. Some people think it's better to carry two phones—one for work, another for personal use. Attorney Luke Cocalis tried it and concluded, "It frankly keeps me saner."

Questions

12-11. Do you use your smartphone or other personal devices for work? If so, do you think this adds to your stress level or helps you by providing convenience?

12-12. Cocalis likes the two-phone lifestyle and says that his boss has his personal phone number only for emergencies. But assistant talent manager Chloe Ifshin reports that it doesn't work so well in practice. "I have friends who are clients and clients who are friends," she says, so work contacts end up on her personal phone and friends call her work phone. How does this consideration affect your thinking about using your own device for both work and leisure?

12-13. Organizations are taking steps to protect themselves from what employees might be doing on their personal devices through allowing only approved computer programs and stricter policies, but no federal regulations protect employees from these restrictions. What ethical initiatives might organizations adopt to make this situation fair for everyone?

Sources: Based on S. E. Ante, "Perilous Mix: Cloud, Devices from Home," *The Wall Street Journal*, February 20, 2014, B4; D. Derks and A. B. Bakker, "Smartphone Use, Work-Home Interference, and Burnout: A Diary Study on the Role of Recovery," *Applied Psychology: An International Review* 63, no. 3 (2014): 411–40; L. Duxbury, C. Higgins, R. Smart, and M. Stevenson, "Mobile Technology and Boundary Permeability," *British Journal of Management* 25 (2014): 570–88; E. Holmes, "When One Phone Isn't Enough," *The Wall Street Journal*, April 2, 2014, D1, D2; C. Mims, "2014: The Year of Living Vulnerably," *The Wall Street Journal*, December 22, 2014, B1, B2; L. Weber, "Leaving a Job? Better Watch Your Cellphone," *The Wall Street Journal*, January 22, 2014; and E. Yost, "Can an Employer Remotely Wipe an Employee's Cellphone?" *HR Magazine* (July 2014): 19.

CASE INCIDENT 1 Do Men and Women Speak the Same Language?

We have talked a lot about how culture affects communication style. Did you know that within cultures, men and women may be socialized to have different communication styles? Just as there are cultural communication barriers, there may also be gender-based communication barriers.

When Boston Consulting Group tried to discover why their female employees were less satisfied with their male employees, the answer seemed to be different communication styles. Many women felt that, in order to fit into the predominantly male culture, they had to adopt a more masculine communication style. Carol Kinsey Goman, author of *The Nonverbal Advantage: Body Language at Work* and founder of Kinsey Consulting, has found many ways men's and women's communication style tends to vary. Goman believes that there are advantages and disadvantages to stereotypically male and female communication. Female communication styles typically involve reading body language and interpreted nonverbal cues, good listening skills, and displaying empathy. On the other hand, female communication styles may be too roundabout and submissive. Males are encouraged to be authoritative by taking up space, being quick and concise, and emphasizing power. Yet the stereotypical male communication style also has many weaknesses. Sometimes, by emphasizing conciseness, masculine communication may seem too blunt, insensitive, and overly confident.

Is one communication style more effective? Not according to Goman. The key is to use the full spectrum of communication and not adopt an extremely masculine or feminine style. The male communication style is better in situations that require decisiveness, while the female style is more effective in collaborative environments. By tailoring communication styles to the situation, employees can be more effective. And by finding a happy medium between the two styles, an employee, male or female, can appear assertive as well as compassionate to their intended audience.

Following this advice, Boston Consulting Group launched a training program to teach upper management how to use both communication styles. While going through the training program, many senior partners realized that they had been encouraging their younger female staff members to adopt a more male communication style without recognizing the advantages of female communication styles. One senior consultant recalled telling a female employee that she would seem more charismatic if she "took up more space." He also realized that, by being domineering in interactions, he was making it harder for women to speak up during their interactions.

Questions

12-14. What are some other situations where having a stereotypically male communication style may be advantageous? What about situations where having a stereotypically female communication style may be more advantageous?

12-15. How might male and female communication styles differ across cultures?

12-16. Do you feel like your communication style corresponds with your gender? Why or why not?

Sources: Based on C. K. Goman, "Is Your Communication Style Dictated By Your Gender?" *Forbes*, March 31, 2016, https://www.forbes.com/sites/carolkinseygoman/2016/03/31/is-your-communication-style-dictated-by-your-gender/2/#6832ffe555b9, accessed April 13, 2017; and A. Elejalde-Ruiz, "To Retain Women, Consulting Firms Target Gender Communication Differences," *The Chicago Tribune*, September 6, 2016, http://www.chicagotribune.com/business/ct-bcg-women-communication-0906-biz-20160906-story.html, accessed April 13, 2017.

CASE INCIDENT 2 Shoulders Back, It's Interview Time

First impressions in a job interview, which usually form within the first few minutes, can be a major factor in the recruiters' decision to hire. In a CareerBuilder survey conducted by The Harris Poll in the United States, it was found that as many as 49 percent of the 1,014 hiring managers who participated in the study make their hiring decisions within the first five minutes of the job interview. This is not to say that work experience and education are unimportant in hiring decisions, but first impressions in a job interview clearly play a prime role in the hiring process. Indeed, a study involving 273 managers and 3,286 employees by UK-based recruitment website Monster revealed that, after work experience, the second most important factor that employers consider when making a hiring decision is the first impression.

The first impressions that a job candidate leaves on the recruiter are not only based on what the candidate says in an interview but also includes nonverbal communication—body language. According to research by psychologist Albert Mehrabian at the University of California, nonverbal expressions make up 93 percent of the first impression. The biggest body language mistakes that can ruin the first impression and weaken job hiring chances range from failing to make eye contact, to having a bad posture, to making a weak handshake with the interviewer.

In an article in *The Irish Times*, Eimear Nolan, an assistant professor at Trinity College Dublin, recommends that candidates appearing for interviews wear a smile and sit in a high-power pose (an expansive posture, in contrast to a low-power pose, where the legs are crossed and the body leans inward). Ronald E. Riggio, a professor at Claremont McKenna College, adds that verbal and nonverbal communication should reinforce each other and go hand-in-hand to create the right impression—an interviewee has to be *consistent* in what they say and how they say it during the job interview. For example, Riggio says, a job candidate who verbally expresses their interest in the job they are interviewing for must also ensure that their body language conveys the same expression of interest: body leaning slightly forward, no yawning, maintaining eye contact, and being attentive.

Questions

12-17. How easy do you think it is for interviewers to detect that a candidate is engaging in impression management during a job interview?

12-18. When do interviewees go too far in using impression management? Would high self-monitors engage in more impression management techniques than low self-monitors?

12-19. What are some popular impression management techniques not mentioned in the case that one may use in a job interview?

Sources: Ronald E. Riggio, "Using Effective Nonverbal Communication in Job Interviews," *Psychology Today*, January 5, 2011, www.psychologytoday.com, accessed June 24, 2020; Eimear Nolan, "Importance of Making a Good First Impression at Interviews," *The Irish Times*, February 1, 2019, www.irishtimes.com, accessed June 24, 2020; "The Most Unusual Interview Mistakes and Biggest Body Language Mishaps, According to Annual CareerBuilder Survey," press release, CareerBuilder, February 22, 2018, press.careerbuilder.com, accessed June 25, 2020.

ENDNOTES

[1] J. Keyton, "Communication in Organizations," *Annual Review of Organizational Psychology and Organizational Behavior* 4 (2017): 501–26; M. Scott Poole, "Communication," in S. Zedeck (ed.), *APA Handbook of Industrial and Organizational Psychology* (Washington, DC: APA, 2011): 249–70.

[2] M. S. Poole, Chapter 7: "Communication," in S. Zedeck (ed.), *Handbook of Industrial and Organizational Psychology*, Vol. 3 (Washington, DC: APA Book, 2010).

[3] R. Swarns, "After Uneasy First Tries, Coworkers Find a Way to Talk about Race," *The New York Times*, March 23, 2015, A15.

[4] D. C. Barnlund, "A Transactional Model of Communication," in C. D. Mortenson (ed.), *Communication Theory* (New Brunswick, NJ: Transaction, 2008): 47–57; see K. Byron, "Carrying Too Heavy a Load? The Communication and Miscommunication of Emotion by E-Mail," *Academy of Management Review* 33, no. 2 (2008): 309–27.

[5] R. E. Kraut, R. S. Fish, R. W. Root, and B. L. Chalfonte, "Informal Communication in Organizations: Form, Function, and Technology," in S. Oskamp and S. Spacapan (eds.), *People's Reactions to Technology* (Beverly Hills, CA: Sage, 1990): 145–99; and A. Tenhiaelae and F. Salvador, "Looking inside Glitch Mitigation Capability: The Effect of Intraorganizational Communication Channels," *Decision Sciences* 45, no. 3 (2014): 437–66.

[6] E. Salas, D. E. Sims, and C. S. Burke, "Is There a 'Big Five' in Teamwork?" *Small Group Research* 36, no. 5 (2005): 555–99.
[7] S. Jhun, Z.-T. Bae, and S.-Y. Rhee, "Performance Change of Managers in Two Different Uses of Upward Feedback: A Longitudinal Study in Korea," *International Journal of Human Resource Management* 23, no. 20 (2012): 4246–64; J. W. Smither and A. G. Walker, "Are the Characteristics of Narrative Comments Related to Improvement in Multirater Feedback Ratings over Time?," *Journal of Applied Psychology* 89, no. 3 (June 2004): 575–81; and J. H. Bernardin and R. W. Beatty, "Can Subordinate Appraisals Enhance Managerial Productivity?," *Sloan Management Review* 28, no. 1 (1987): 63–73.
[8] A. Lewis and J. Clark, "Dreams within a Dream: Multiple Visions and Organizational Structure," *Journal of Organizational Behavior* 41 (2020): 50–76.
[9] Z. Witkower, J. L. Tracy, J. T. Cheng, and J. Henrich, "Two Signals of Social Rank: Prestige and Dominance Are Associated with Distinct Nonverbal Displays," *Journal of Personality and Social Psychology* 118, no. 1 (2020): 89–120.
[10] P. Dvorak, "How Understanding the 'Why' of Decisions Matters," *The Wall Street Journal,* March 19, 2007, B3.
[11] T. Neeley and P. Leonardi, "Effective Managers Say the Same Thing Twice (or More)," *Harvard Business Review* (May 2011): 38–39.
[12] H. A. Richardson and S. G. Taylor, "Understanding Input Events: A Model of Employees' Responses to Requests for Their Input," *Academy of Management Review* 37 (2012): 471–91.
[13] J. S. Lublin, "Managers Need to Make Time for Face Time," *The Wall Street Journal,* March 18, 2015, B6.
[14] B. Oc, M. R. Bashshur, and C. Moore, "Speaking Truth to Power: The Effect of Candid Feedback on How Individuals with Power Allocate Resources," *Journal of Applied Psychology* 100, no. 2 (2015): 450–63.
[15] E. Nichols, "Hyper-Speed Managers," *HR Magazine* (April 2007): 107–10.
[16] R. Walker, "Declining an Assignment, with Finesse," *The New York Times,* August 24, 2014, 8.
[17] D. Cray, G. R. Mallory, R. J. Butler, D. Hickson, and D. Wilson, "Sporadic, Fluid, and Constricted Processes: Three Types of Strategic Decision-Making in Organizations," *Journal of Management Studies* 25, no. 1 (1988): 13–39.
[18] S. B. Algoe, P. C. Dwyer, A. Younge, and C. Oveis, "A New Perspective on the Social Functions of Emotions: Gratitude and the Witnessing Effect," *Journal of Personality and Social Psychology* (in press).
[19] See, for example, N. B. Kurland and L. H. Pelled, "Passing the Word: Toward a Model of Gossip and Power in the Workplace," *Academy of Management Review* (April 2000): 428–38; and G. Michelson, A. van Iterson, and K. Waddington, "Gossip in Organizations: Contexts, Consequences, and Controversies," *Group and Organization Management* 35, no. 4 (2010): 371–90.
[20] J. Baum, M. Rabovsky, S. Benjamin Rose, and R. Abdel Rahman, "Clear Judgments Based on Unclear Evidence: Person Evaluation Is Strongly Influenced by Untrustworthy Gossip," *Emotion* 20, no. 2 (2020): 248–60.
[21] N. Tan, K. Chi Yam, P. Zhang, and D. J. Brown, "Are You Gossiping about Me? The Costs and Benefits of High Workplace Gossip Prevalence," *Journal of Business and Psychology* (in press).
[22] See, for instance, E. Martinescu, O. Janssen, and B. A. Nijstad, "Gossip as a Resource: How and Why Power Relationships Shape Gossip Behavior," *Organizational Behavior and Human Decision Processes* 153 (2019): 89–102.
[23] G. Van Hoye and F. Lievens, "Tapping the Grapevine: A Closer Look at Word-of-Mouth as a Recruitment Source," *Journal of Applied Psychology* 94, no. 2 (2009): 341–52.
[24] J. K. Bosson, A. B. Johnson, K. Niederhoffer, and W. B. Swann Jr., "Interpersonal Chemistry through Negativity: Bonding by Sharing Negative Attitudes about Others," *Personal Relationships* 13 (2006): 135–50.
[25] T. J. Grosser, V. Lopez-Kidwell, and G. Labianca, "A Social Network Analysis of Positive and Negative Gossip in Organizational Life," *Group and Organization Management* 35, no. 2 (2010): 177–212.
[26] R. Feintzeig, "The Boss's Next Demand: Make Lots of Friends," *The Wall Street Journal,* February 12, 2014, B1, B6.
[27] R. E. Silverman, "A Victory for Small Office Talkers," *The Wall Street Journal,* October 28, 2014, D2.
[28] G. Hirst, D. Van Knippenberg, J. Zhou, E. Quintane, and C. Zhu, "Heard It through the Grapevine: Indirect Networks and Employee Creativity," *Journal of Applied Psychology* 100, no. 2 (2015): 567–74.
[29] M. Feinberg, R. Willer, J. Stellar, and D. Keltner, "The Virtues of Gossip: Reputational Information Sharing as Prosocial Behavior," *Journal of Personality and Social Psychology* 102 (2012): 1015–30; D. L. Brady, D. J. Brown, and L. H. Liang, "Moving Beyond Assumptions of Deviance: The Reconceptualization and Measurement of Workplace Gossip," *Journal of Applied Psychology* 102, no. 1 (2017): 1–25.
[30] L. Dulye, "Get out of Your Office," *HR Magazine* (July 2006): 99–101; and T. Gordon, *P.E.T: Parent Effectiveness Training* (New York, NY: New American Library, 1975).
[31] E. Bernstein, "How Well Are You Listening?" *The Wall Street Journal,* January 13, 2015, D1.
[32] S. Shellenbarger, "Work & Family Mailbox," *The Wall Street Journal,* July 30, 2014, D2.
[33] E. C. Ravlin, A.-K. Ward, and D. C. Thomas, "Exchanging Social Information across Cultural Boundaries," *Journal of Management* 40, no. 5 (2014): 1437–65.
[34] A. Kessler, "Let's Call off the Meeting and Get Back to Work," *The Wall Street Journal,* January 2, 2015, A13.
[35] A. Bryant, "Getting Stuff Done: It's a Goal, and a Rating System," *The New York Times,* March 9, 2013, www.nytimes.com/2013/03/10/business/kris-duggan-of-badgeville-on-the-getting-stuff-done-index.html?pagewanted=all&_r=0.
[36] J. Queenan, "Fire Away!—Military Metaphors," *The Wall Street Journal,* March 28–29, 2015, C11.
[37] E. Bernstein, "What Verbal Tics May Be Saying about Us," *The Wall Street Journal,* January 21, 2014, D3.
[38] N. Lehmann-Willenbrock and J. A. Allen, "How Fun Are Your Meetings? Investigating the Relationship between Humor Patterns in Team Interactions and Team Performance," *Journal of Applied Psychology* 99, no. 6 (2014): 1278–87; M. Mihelich, "Bit by Bit: Stand-up Comedy as a Team-Building Exercise," *Workforce Management* (February 2013): 16; and "Comedy Experience," Peppercomm, http://peppercomm.com/services/comedy-experience, accessed July 1, 2015.
[39] A. Bryant, "Finding, and Owning, Their Voice," *The New York Times,* November 16, 2014, 6.
[40] T. D. Maynes and P. M. Podsakoff, "Speaking More Broadly: An Examination of the Nature, Antecedents, and Consequences of an Expanded Set of Employee Voice Behaviors," *Journal of Applied Psychology* 99, no. 1 (2014): 87–112.
[41] J. Lipman, "A Guide for Men," *The Wall Street Journal,* December 13–14, 2014, C1, C2.
[42] S. Aryee, F. O. Walumbwa, R. Mondejar, and C. L. Chu, "Core Self-Evaluations and Employee Voice Behavior: Test of

a Dual-Motivational Pathway," *Journal of Management* 43, no. 3 (2017): 946–66; W. Liu, Z. Song, X. Li, and Z. Liao, "Why and When Leaders' Affective States Influence Employee Upward Voice," *Academy of Management Journal* 60, no. 1 (2017): 236–63; and M. Chamberlin, D. W. Newton, and J. A. Lepine, "A Meta-Analysis of Voice and Its Promotive and Prohibitive Forms: Identification of Key Associations, Distinctions, and Future Research Directions," *Personnel Psychology* 70, no. 1 (2017): 11–71.

[43] Ibid.

[44] Ibid.

[45] P. A. Mueller and D. M. Oppenheimer, "The Pen Is Mightier Than the Keyboard: Advantages of Longhand over Laptop Note Taking," *Psychological Science* 25, no. 6 (2014): 1159–68.

[46] N. Bilton, "Disruptions: Life's Too Short for So Much E-Mail," *The New York Times,* July 8, 2012, http://bits.blogs.nytimes.com/2012/07/08/life%E2%80%99s-too-short-for-so-much-e-mail/.

[47] "Executive Summary," *Messagemind* (2012), www.messagemind.com.

[48] S. R. Barley, D. E. Meyerson, and S. Grodal, "E-Mail as a Source and Symbol of Stress," *Organization Science* 22, no. 4 (2011): 887–906; and G. J. Mark, S. Voida, and A. V. Cardello, "'A Pace Not Dictated by Electrons': An Empirical Study of Work without E-Mail," *Proceedings of the SIGCHI Conference on Human Factors in Computing Systems,* 2012, 555–64.

[49] C. L.-L. Tan, "Mind Your E-Mail Manners: No 'XOXO' or 'LOL' Allowed," *The Wall Street Journal,* April 21, 2015.

[50] Ibid.

[51] E. Bernstein, "The Miscommunicators," *The Wall Street Journal,* July 3, 2012, D1, D3.

[52] B. Roberts, "Social Media Gets Strategic," *HR Magazine* (October 2012): 30–38.

[53] "Number of Monthly Active Facebook Users Worldwide as of 1st Quarter 2015 (in Millions)," Statista/Facebook, http://www.statista.com/statistics/264810/number-of-monthly-active-facebook-users-worldwide/, accessed July 1, 2015.

[54] K. Wagner, "The World's Top CEOs Are Tweeting More, Facebooking Less," *Re/Code,* May 17, 2015, http://recode.net/2015/05/17/the-worlds-top-ceos-are-tweeting-more-facebooking-less/.

[55] Ibid.

[56] P. Mozur, J. Osawa, and N. Purnell, "Facebook and WhatsApp a Tough Sell in Asia," *The Wall Street Journal,* February 21, 2014, B4.

[57] C. Smith, "By the Numbers: 125+ Amazing LinkedIn Statistics," DMR, June 6, 2015, http://expandedramblings.com/index.php/by-the-numbers-a-few-important-linkedin-stats/.

[58] Wagner, "The World's Top CEOs Are Tweeting More, Facebooking Less."

[59] "Number of Monthly Active Twitter Users Worldwide from 1st Quarter 2010 to 1st Quarter 2015 (in Millions)," Statista/Twitter, http://www.statista.com/statistics/282087/number-of-monthly-active-twitter-users/, accessed July 1, 2015.

[60] Wagner, "The World's Top CEOs Are Tweeting More, Facebooking Less."

[61] L. Kwoh and M. Korn, "140 Characters of Risk: CEOs on Twitter," *The Wall Street Journal,* September 26, 2012, B1, B8.

[62] Mozur, Osawa, and Purnell, "Facebook and WhatsApp a Tough Sell in Asia."

[63] Ibid.

[64] O. Allen, "6 Stats You Should Know about Business Blogging in 2015," HubSpot Blogs, March 11, 2015, http://blog.hubspot.com/marketing/business-blogging-in-2015.

[65] L. Talley and S. Temple, "How Leaders Influence Followers through the Use of Nonverbal Communication," *Leadership & Organizational Development Journal* 36, no. 1 (2015): 69–80; J. A. Hall, T. G. Horgan, and N. A. Murphy, "Nonverbal Communication," *Annual Review of Psychology* 70 (2019): 271–94.

[66] N. Dargue, N. Sweller, and M. P. Jones, "When Our Hands Help Us Understand: A Meta-Analysis into the Effects of Gesture on Comprehension," *Psychological Bulletin* 145, no. 8 (765–84).

[67] C. K. Goman, "5 Body Language Tips to Increase Your Curb Appeal," *Forbes,* March 4, 2013, www.forbes.com/sites/carolkinseygoman/2013/03/14/5-body-language-tips-to-increase-your-curb-appeal/.

[68] C. F. Lima, A. Anikin, A. Catarina Monteiro, S. K. Scott, and S. Luís Castro, "Automaticity in the Recognition of Nonverbal Emotional Vocalizations," *Emotion* 19, no. 2 (2019): 219–33; K. R. Scherer, A. Dieckmann, M. Unfried, H. Ellgring, and M. Mortillaro, "Investigating Appraisal-Drive Facial Expression and Inference in Emotion Communication," *Emotion* (in press).

[69] A. Metallinou, A. Katsamanis, and S. Narayanan, "Tracking Continuous Emotional Trends of Participants During Affective Dyadic Interactions Using Body Language and Speech Information," *Image and Vision Computing,* February 2013, 137–52.

[70] J. Smith, "10 Nonverbal Cues That Convey Confidence at Work," *Forbes,* March 11, 2013, www.forbes.com/sites/jacquelynsmith/2013/03/11/10-nonverbal-cues-that-convey-confidence-at-work/.

[71] See L. K. Trevino, J. Webster, and E. W. Stein, "Making Connections: Complementary Influences on Communication Media Choices, Attitudes, and Use," *Organization Science* (March–April 2000): 163–82; N. Kock, "The Psychobiological Model: Towards a New Theory of Computer-Mediated Communication Based on Darwinian Evolution," *Organization Science* 15, no. 3 (May–June 2004): 327–48; and R. L. Daft and R. H. Lengel, "Organizational Information Requirements, Media Richness and Structural Design," *Management Science* 32, no. 5 (1986): 554–71.

[72] R. L. Daft and R. H. Lengel, "Information Richness: A New Approach to Managerial Behavior and Organizational Design," *Research in Organizational Behavior* 6 (1984): 191–233; R. L. Daft and R. H. Lengel, "Organizational Information Requirements, Media Richness and Structural Design," *Management Science* 32, no. 5 (1986): 554–71; K. Ishii, M. Madison Lyons, and S. A. Carr, "Revisiting Media Richness Theory for Today and Future," *Human Behavior and Emerging Technologies* 1, no. 2 (2019): 124–31.

[73] R. H. Lengel and R. L. Daft, "The Selection of Communication Media as an Executive Skill," *The Academy of Management Executive* 2, no. 3 (1988): 225–32; K. Patterson, J. Grenny, R. McMillan, and A. Switzler, *Crucial Conversations Tools for Talking When Stakes Are High,* 2nd edition (New York, NY: McGraw-Hill, 2012); S. G. Rogelberg, *The Surprising Science of Meetings: How You Can Lead Your Team to Peak Performance* (New York, NY: Oxford University Press, 2019).

[74] S. Shellenbarger, "Is This How You Really Talk?," *The Wall Street Journal,* April 24, 2013, D1, D3.

[75] S. Shellenbarger, "This Embarrasses You and I: Grammar Gaffes Invade the Office in an Age of Informal Email, Texting, and Twitter," *The Wall Street Journal,* June 20, 2012, https://www.wsj.com/articles/SB10001424052702303410404577466629192754 48, accessed April 12, 2017.

[76] G. W. Giumetti, A. L. Hatfield, J. L. Scisco, A. N. Schroeder, E. R. Muth, and R. M. Kowalski, "What a Rude E-mail! Examining the Differential Effects of Incivility versus Support on Mood, Energy, Engagement, and Performance in an Online Context," *Journal of Occupational*

Health Psychology 18, no. 3 (2013): 297–309; J. Kruger, N. Epley, J. Parker, and Z-W. Ng, "Egocentrism over E-mail: Can We Communicate as well as We Think?" *Journal of Personality and Social Psychology* 89, no. 6 (2005): 925–36; Y. Park and V. C. Haun, "The Long Arm of Email Incivility: Transmitted Stress to the Partner and Partner Work Withdrawal," *Journal of Organizational Behavior* 39 (2018): 1268–82; E. M. Richard and M. McFadden, "Saving Face: Reactions to Cultural Norm Violations in Business Request Emails," *Journal of Business and Psychology* 31 (2016): 307–21.

[77] K. Kruse, "Why Successful People Never Bring Smartphones into Meetings," *Forbes*, December 26, 2013, http://www.forbes.com/sites/kevinkruse/2013/12/26/why-successful-people-never-bring-smartphones-into-meetings/.

[78] B. Giamanco and K. Gregoire, "Tweet Me, Friend Me, Make Me Buy," *Harvard Business Review*, July–August 2012, 88–93.

[79] T. Lytle, "Cybersleuthing," *HR Magazine* (January 2012): 55–57.

[80] J. Segal, "Widening Web of Social Media," *HR Magazine* (June 2012): 117–18.

[81] V. Cheung-Blunden, K. Cropper, A. Panis, and K. Davis, "Functional Divergence of Two Threat-Induced Emotions: Fear-Based versus Anxiety-Based Cybersecurity Preferences," *Emotion* 19, no. 8 (2019): 1353–65.

[82] A. Brown Yost, T. S. Behrend, G. Howardson, J. Badger Darrow, and J. M. Jensen, "Reactance to Electronic Surveillance: A Test of Antecedents and Outcomes," *Journal of Business and Psychology* 34 (2019): 71–86.

[83] "At Many Companies, Hunt for Leakers Expands Arsenal of Monitoring Tactics," *The Wall Street Journal*, September 11, 2006, B1, B3; and B. J. Alge, G. A. Ballinger, S. Tangirala, and J. L. Oakley, "Information Privacy in Organizations: Empowering Creative and Extrarole Performance," *Journal of Applied Psychology* 91, no. 1 (2006): 221–32.

[84] R. E. Petty and P. Briñol, "Persuasion: From Single to Multiple to Metacognitive Processes," *Perspectives on Psychological Science* 3, no. 2 (2008): 137–47; and F. A. White, M. A. Charles, and J. K. Nelson, "The Role of Persuasive Arguments in Changing Affirmative Action Attitudes and Expressed Behavior in Higher Education," *Journal of Applied Psychology* 93, no. 6 (2008): 1271–86.

[85] K. L. Blankenship and D. T. Wegener, "Opening the Mind to Close It: Considering a Message in Light of Important Values Increases Message Processing and Later Resistance to Change," *Journal of Personality and Social Psychology* 94, no. 2 (2008): 196–213.

[86] D. C. Zhang, X. S. Zhu, K-J. Ritter, and A. Thiele, "Telling Stories to Communicate the Value of the Pre-employment Structured Job Interview," *International Journal of Selection and Assessment* 27 (2019): 299–314.

[87] See, for example, Y. H. M. See, R. E. Petty, and L. R. Fabrigar, "Affective and Cognitive Meta-Bases of Attitudes: Unique Effects of Information Interest and Persuasion," *Journal of Personality and Social Psychology* 94, no. 6 (2008): 938–55; M. S. Key, J. E. Edlund, B. J. Sagarin, and G. Y. Bizer, "Individual Differences in Susceptibility to Mindlessness," *Personality and Individual Differences* 46, no. 3 (2009): 261–64; and M. Reinhard and M. Messner, "The Effects of Source Likeability and Need for Cognition on Advertising Effectiveness under Explicit Persuasion," *Journal of Consumer Behavior* 8, no. 4 (2009): 179–91.

[88] J. J. Guyer, L. R. Fabrigar, and T. I. Vaughan-Johnston, "Speech Rate, Intonation, and Pitch: Investigating the Bias and Cue Effects of Vocal Confidence on Persuasion," *Personality and Social Psychology Bulletin* 45, no. 3 (2019): 389–405; A. B. Van Zant and J. Berger, "How the Voice Persuades," *Journal of Personality and Social Psychology* 118, no. 4 (2020): 661–82.

[89] V. S. Ferreira, "A Mechanistic Framework for Explaining Audience Design in Language Production," *Annual Review of Psychology* 70 (2019): 29–51.

[90] C. Heath, "Do People Prefer to Pass Along Good or Bad News? Valence and Relevance of News as Predictors of Transmission Propensity," *Organizational Behavior and Human Decision Processes* 68, no. 2 (1996): 79–94.

[91] M. T. Wallace, T. G. Woynaroski, and R. A. Stevenson, "Multisensory Integration as a Window into Orderly and Disrupted Cognition and Communication," *Annual Review of Psychology* 71 (2020): 193–219.

[92] D. Derks, D. van Duin, M. Tims, et al., "Smartphone Use and Work-Home Interference: The Moderating Role of Social Norms and Employee Work Engagement," *Journal of Occupational and Organizational Psychology* 88, no. 1 (2015): 155–77; and D. Derks, A. B. Bakker, P. Pascale, and P. van Wingerden, "Work-Related Smartphone Use, Work–Family Conflict and Family Role Performance: The Role of Segmentation Preference," *Human Relations* 96, no. 5 (2016): 1045–68.

[93] P. Briñol, R. E. Petty, and J. Barden, "Happiness versus Sadness as a Determinant of Thought Confidence in Persuasion: A Self-Validation Analysis," *Journal of Personality and Social Psychology* 93, no. 5 (2007): 711–27.

[94] R. C. Sinclair, S. E. Moore, M. M. Mark, A. S. Soldat, and C. A. Lavis, "Incidental Moods, Source Likeability, and Persuasion: Liking Motivates Message Elaboration in Happy People," *Cognition and Emotion* 24, no. 6 (2010): 940–61; and V. Griskevicius, M. N. Shiota, and S. L. Neufeld, "Influence of Different Positive Emotions on Persuasion Processing: A Functional Evolutionary Approach," *Emotion* 10, no. 2 (2010): 190–206.

[95] See, for instance, J. A. Frimer, M. J. Brandt, Z. Melton, and M. Motyl, "Extremists on the Left and Right Use Angry, Negative Language," *Personality and Social Psychology Bulletin* 45, no. 8 (2019): 1216–31.

[96] J. Sandberg, "The Jargon Jumble: Kids Have 'Skeds,' Colleagues, 'Needs,'" *The Wall Street Journal*, October 24, 2006, http://online.wsj.com/article/SB116165746415401680.html.

[97] M. Menegatti and M. Rubini, "Convincing Similar and Dissimilar Others: The Power of Language Abstraction in Political Communication," *Personality and Social Psychology Bulletin* 39, no. 5 (2013): 596–607.

[98] E. Nechanska, E. Hughes, and T. Dundon, "Towards an Integration of Employee Voice and Silence," *Human Resource Management Review* (in press).

[99] E. W. Morrison and F. J. Milliken, "Organizational Silence: A Barrier to Change and Development in a Pluralistic World," *Academy of Management Review* 25, no. 4 (2000): 706–25; and B. E. Ashforth and V. Anand, "The Normalization of Corruption in Organizations," *Research in Organizational Behavior* 25 (2003): 1–52.

[100] E. W. Morrison, K. E. See., and C. Pan, "An Approach–Inhibition Model of Employee Silence: The Joint Effects of Personal Sense of Power and Target Openness," *Personnel Psychology* 68, no. 3 (2015): 547–80; H. P. Madrid, M. G. Patterson, and P. I. Leiva, "Negative Core Affect and Employee Silence: How Differences in Activation, Cognitive Rumination, and Problem-Solving Demands Matter," *Journal of Applied Psychology* 100, no. 6 (2015): 1887–98; and C. Kiewitz, S. D. Restubog, M. K. Shoss, P. M. Garcia, and R. L. Tang, "Suffering in Silence: Investigating the Role of Fear in the Relationship between Abusive

Supervision and Defensive Silence," *Journal of Applied Psychology* 101, no. 5 (2016): 731–42.
[101] F. J. Milliken, E. W. Morrison, and P. F. Hewlin, "An Exploratory Study of Employee Silence: Issues That Employees Don't Communicate Upward and Why," *Journal of Management Studies* 40, no. 6 (2003): 1453–76.
[102] J. C. Pearson and P. E. Nelson, *An Introduction to Human Communication: Understanding and Sharing* (8th Ed., New York, NY: McGraw-Hill, 2000); L. A. Withers, and L. L. Vernon, "To Err Is Human: Embarrassment, Attachment, and Communication Apprehension," *Personality and Individual Differences* 40, no. 1 (2006): 99–110.
[103] See, for instance, S. K. Opt and D. A. Loffredo, "Rethinking Communication Apprehension: A Myers-Briggs Perspective," *Journal of Psychology* (September 2000): 556–70; and B. D. Blume, G. F. Dreher, and T. T. Baldwin, "Examining the Effects of Communication Apprehension within Assessment Centres," *Journal of Occupational and Organizational Psychology* 83, no. 3 (2010): 663–71.
[104] See, for example, T. L. Rodebaugh, "I Might Look OK, but I'm Still Doubtful, Anxious, and Avoidant: The Mixed Effects of Enhanced Video Feedback on Social Anxiety Symptoms," *Behaviour Research & Therapy* 42, no. 12 (December 2004): 1435–51.
[105] A. Vrij, M. Hartwig, and P. Anders Granhag, "Reading Lies: Nonverbal Communication and Deception," *Annual Review of Psychology* 70 (2019): 295–317.
[106] K. B. Serota, T. R. Levine, and F. J. Boster, "The Prevalence of Lying in America: Three Studies of Self-Reported Lies," *Human Communication Research* 36, no. 1 (2010): 2–25.
[107] B. M. DePaulo, D. A. Kashy, S. E. Kirkendol, M. M. Wyer, and J. A. Epstein, "Lying in Everyday Life," *Journal of Personality and Social Psychology* 70, no. 5 (1996): 979–95; and C. E. Naguin, T. R. Kurtzberg, and L. Y. Belkin, "The Finer Points of Lying Online: E-Mail versus Pen and Paper," *Journal of Applied Psychology* 95, no. 2 (2010): 387–94.
[108] A. Vrij, P. A. Granhag, and S. Porter, "Pitfalls and Opportunities in Nonverbal and Verbal Lie Detection," *Psychological Science in the Public Interest* 11, no. 3 (2010): 89–121.
[109] J. Bundy, M. D. Pfarrer, C. E. Short, and W. Timothy Coombs, "Crises and Crisis Management: Integration, Interpretation, and Research Development," *Journal of Management* 43, no. 6 (2017): 1661–92.
[110] T. W. Cole and K. L. Fellows, "Risk Communication Failure: A Case Study of New Orleans and Hurricane Katrina," *Southern Communication Journal* 73, no. 3 (2008): 211–28; A Gheytanchi, L. Joseph, E. Gierlach, S. Kimpara, J. Housley, Z. E. Franco, and L. E. Beutler, "The Dirty Dozen: Twelve Failures of the Hurricane Katrina Response and How Psychology Can Help," *American Psychologist* 62, no. 2 (2007): 118–30.
[111] Bundy et al., "Crises and Crisis Management"; D-Y. Liou and C-H. Lin, "Human Resource Planning on Terrorism and Crises in the Asia Pacific Region: Cross-National Challenge, Reconsideration, and Proposition from Western Experiences," *Human Resource Management* 47, no. 1 (2008): 49–72.
[112] D. G. Winter, "Power, Affiliation, and War: Three Tests of a Motivational Model," *Journal of Personality and Social Psychology* 65, no. 3 (1993): 532–45; D. G. Winter, "The Role of Motivation, Responsibility, and Integrative Complexity in Crisis Escalation: Comparative Studies of War and Peace Crises," *Journal of Personality and Social Psychology* 92, no. 5 (2007): 920–37.
[113] S. Uitdewilligen and M. J. Waller, "Information Sharing and Decision-Making in Multidisciplinary Crisis Management Teams," *Journal of Organizational Behavior* 39 (2018): 731–48.
[114] T. Knudsen and K. Srikanth, "Coordinated Exploration: Organizing Joint Search by Multiple Specialists to Overcome Mutual Confusion and Joint Myopia," *Administrative Science Quarterly* 59, no. 3 (2014): 409–41.
[115] See, for example, N. Kman, "How Disaster Apps Work—and Don't," *Fast Company*, August 11, 2016, https://www.fastcompany.com/3062786/how-disaster-apps-work-and-dont; L. G. Militello, C. E. Sushereba, M. Branlat, R. Bean, and V. Finomore, "Designing for Military Pararescue: Naturalistic Decision-Making Perspective, Methods, and Frameworks," *Journal of Occupational and Organizational Psychology* 88 (2015): 251–72.
[116] N. M. Jones and R. Cohen Silver, "This Is Not a Drill: Anxiety on Twitter Following the 2018 Hawaii False Missile Alert," *American Psychologist* (in press).
[117] Y. P. Chang and S. B. Algoe, "On Thanksgiving: Cultural Variation in Gratitude Demonstrations and Perceptions between the United States and Taiwan," *Emotion* (in press).
[118] Derek Sivers, "Same Word. Different Places? Different Meanings.", January 16, 2014, https://sivers.org/quality.
[119] See, for instance, M. Yoshie and D. A. Sauter, "Cultural Norms Influence Nonverbal Emotion Communication: Japanese Vocalizations of Socially Disengaging Emotions," *Emotion* 20, no. 3 (2020): 513–17.
[120] L. Severance, L. Bui-Wrzosinska, M. J. Gelfand, S. Lyons, A. Nowak, W. Borkowski, N. Soomro, N. Soomro, A. Rafaeli, D. E. Treister, C. Lin, and S. Tamaguchi, "The Psychological Structure of Aggression across Cultures," *Journal of Organizational Behavior* 34, no. 6 (2013): 835–65.
[121] See E. T. Hall, *Beyond Culture* (Garden City, NY: Anchor Press/Doubleday, 1976); W. L. Adair, "Integrative Sequences and Negotiation Outcome in Same- and Mixed-Culture Negotiations," *International Journal of Conflict Management* 14, no. 3–4 (2003): 1359–92; W. L. Adair and J. M. Brett, "The Negotiation Dance: Time, Culture, and Behavioral Sequences in Negotiation," *Organization Science* 16, no. 1 (2005): 33–51; E. Giebels and P. J. Taylor, "Interaction Patterns in Crisis Negotiations: Persuasive Arguments and Cultural Differences," *Journal of Applied Psychology* 94, no. 1 (2009): 5–19; and M. G. Kittler, D. Rygl, and A. Mackinnon, "Beyond Culture or Beyond Control? Reviewing the Use of Hall's High-/Low-Context Concept," *International Journal of Cross-Cultural Management* 11, no. 1 (2011): 63–82.
[122] M. C. Hopson, T. Hart, and G. C. Bell, "Meeting in the Middle: Fred L. Casmir's Contributions to the Field of Intercultural Communication," *International Journal of Intercultural Relations* (November 2012): 789–97.

13 Leadership

Source: M4OS Photos / Alamy Stock Photo

LEARNING OBJECTIVES

After studying this chapter, you should be able to:

13-1 Summarize the conclusions of trait theories of leadership.

13-2 Identify the central tenets and main limitations of behavioral theories.

13-3 Contrast contingency theories of leadership.

13-4 Describe the contemporary theories of leadership and their relationship to foundational theories.

13-5 Discuss the roles of leaders in creating ethical organizations.

13-6 Describe how leaders can have a positive impact on their organizations through building trust and mentoring.

13-7 Identify the challenges to our understanding of leadership.

Employability Skills Matrix (ESM)

	Myth or Science?	Career OBjectives	An Ethical Choice	Point/ Counterpoint	Experiential Exercise	Ethical Dilemma	Case Incident 1	Case Incident 2
Critical Thinking	✓		✓	✓	✓	✓	✓	✓
Communication		✓			✓	✓	✓	
Collaboration		✓			✓	✓	✓	
Knowledge Application and Analysis	✓	✓	✓	✓	✓	✓	✓	✓
Social Responsibility			✓		✓	✓		

FROM WACKY VISION TO TOTAL HOTEL INDUSTRY DISRUPTION

In 2008, Brian Chesky and Joe Gebbia, design school graduates in Silicon Valley, had a wacky idea. Gebbia's roommates suddenly moved out, and he needed people to fill the remaining rooms. The idea to host a home-sharing platform came to him and Chesky after Gebbia asked Chesky to take the remaining room. The result was Air Bed & Breakfast (Airbnb). From these humble (and sometimes rocky) beginnings, Airbnb bourgeoned to a $31 billion organization, nearly the same valuation as Marriott International, without owning a single room. To date, the company has housed over 150 million guests in over 65,000 cities in over 191 countries. It also has more than 3 million listings worldwide (including over 1,400 castles).

Part of the reason for the major success of Airbnb is its executive leadership and top management team. Chesky, as CEO (shown here meeting with an Airbnb host in South Africa), has guided the organization through remarkably turbulent times throughout its development, with no prior business experience. In 2017, Chesky has been listed as one of the World's Greatest Leaders by *Fortune*. The caring leadership style of Chesky offers a counterpoint to that exhibited by leadership in other sharing-economy brands, such as Uber, who have come under fire for an apparent aggressive and sexist culture and whose CEO, Travis Kalanick, was caught on video verbally berating an Uber driver.

Perhaps what drives the success of Chesky is the charisma, authenticity, and ethicality with which he meets leadership challenges. His mentor, Warren Buffett (CEO of Berkshire Hathaway), notes that Brian "feels it all the way through. I think he would be doing what he's doing if he didn't get paid a dime for it." A trait that Chesky believes is important for handling leadership challenges is humility. Chesky realizes that it is easy for leaders to become defensive when they are challenged, but sometimes leaders must take a step back and approach their challenges with humility and acceptance.

Leaders need guidance and help, too. Chesky recognizes that, as leaders, "we need to have mentors. I think I've always been pretty shameless about seeking out people much smarter and much more experienced than me from the very beginning ... and the more successful I got, the more leaders I started seeking out, whether it was investors, or Sheryl Sandberg at Facebook, or ... Warren Buffett." Perhaps the ethicality with which Chesky approaches Airbnb is reflected in the company's new vision statement: "Belong Anywhere." New leaders within the organization, such as Beth Axelrod, the new vice president of employee experience, are modeling this mission and enacting it "to create belonging everywhere" through recruitment, selection, employee engagement, and motivation at Airbnb.

Sources: Based on Airbnb, *About Us*, https://www.airbnb.com/about/about-us, accessed April 12, 2017; L. Gallagher, "Airbnb's IPO Runway," *Fortune*, March 17, 2017, http://fortune.com/2017/03/17/airbnbs-ipo-runway/; L. Gallagher, "Q&A with Brian Chesky: Disruption, Leadership, and Airbnb's Future," *Fortune*, March 27, 2017, http://fortune.com/2017/03/27/chesky-airbnb-leadership-uber/; L. Gallagher, *The Airbnb Story: How Three Ordinary Guys Disrupted an Industry, Made Billions ... and Created Plenty of Controversy* (New York, NY: Houghton Mifflin Harcourt, 2017); L. Gallagher, "Why Airbnb CEO Brian Chesky Is Among the World's Greatest Leaders," *Fortune*, March 24, 2017, http://fortune.com/2017/03/24/airbnb-brian-chesky-worlds-greatest-leaders/; and V. Zarya, "Exclusive: Meet the Woman Joining Airbnb's Executive Team," *Fortune*, January 13, 2017, http://fortune.com/2017/01/13/airbnb-executive-beth-axelrod/.

Leaders like Brian Chesky possess a special something that sets them apart. However, theirs is not the only type of effective leadership. In this chapter, we'll look at all types of leaders and what differentiates leaders from nonleaders. First, we'll present trait theories of leadership. Then, we'll discuss challenges to the meaning and importance of leadership. But before we begin, let's clarify what we mean by the term *leadership*.

leadership The ability to influence a group toward the achievement of a vision or set of goals.

We define **leadership** as the ability to influence a group toward the achievement of a vision or set of goals. But not all leaders are managers, nor are all managers leaders. Just because an organization provides its managers with certain formal rights does not mean that they will lead effectively. Leaders can emerge from within a group as well as by formal appointment. Nonsanctioned leadership—the ability to influence that arises outside the formal structure of the organization—is often as important, or more important, than formal influence.

Organizations need strong leadership *and* strong management for optimal effectiveness. We need leaders to challenge the status quo, create visions of the future, and inspire organizational members to achieve the visions. We need managers to formulate detailed plans, create efficient organizational structures, and oversee day-to-day operations.

Trait Theories

13-1 Summarize the conclusions of trait theories of leadership.

trait theories of leadership Theories that consider personal qualities and characteristics that differentiate leaders from nonleaders.

Throughout history, strong leaders have been described by their traits. Therefore, leadership research has long sought to identify the personality, social, physical, or intellectual attributes that differentiate leaders from nonleaders. **Trait theories of leadership** focus on personal qualities and characteristics.[1]

For personality, comprehensive reviews of the leadership literature organized around the Big Five framework have found extraversion to be the most predictive trait of effective leadership.[2] However, extraversion is perhaps more related to the way leaders emerge than it is related to their effectiveness. Sociable and dominant people are more likely to assert themselves in group situations, which can help extraverts be identified as leaders. However, effective leaders do not tend to be domineering. One study found that leaders who scored very high in assertiveness, a facet of extraversion, were less effective than those who were moderately high.[3] Extraverted leaders may be more effective when leading groups of passive employees rather than proactive employees.[4] Although extraversion can predict effective leadership, the relationship may be due to unique facets of the trait and the situation. As a caveat, however, being "too bold" or "too warm" can also hurt your chances of emerging as a leader.[5]

Unlike agreeableness and emotional stability, which do not seem to predict leadership, conscientiousness and openness to experience may predict leadership, especially leader effectiveness. For example, multi-source data (i.e., from employees, coworkers, and supervisors) from a Fortune 500 organization suggest that conscientiousness facets, such as achievement striving and dutifulness, are related to leader emergence.[6] Also, achievement striving and dependability were found to be related to effectiveness as a manager.[7] In sum, leaders who like being around people, who can assert themselves (extraverted), and who are disciplined and able to keep commitments they make (conscientious) have an apparent advantage when it comes to leadership.

What about the Dark Side personality traits of Machiavellianism, narcissism, and psychopathy (see Chapter 4)? Research indicates they're not all bad for leadership. A study in Europe and the United States found that normative (midrange) scores on the Dark Side personality traits were optimal, while low (and high) scores were associated with ineffective leadership. The study suggested that high emotional stability may accentuate the ineffective behaviors.[8] However, higher scores on Dark Side traits and emotional stability can contribute to leadership emergence. Thankfully, both this study and other international research indicate that building self-awareness and self-regulation skills may be helpful for leaders to control the effects of their Dark Side traits.[9]

Another trait that may indicate effective leadership is emotional intelligence (EI), discussed in Chapter 6. A core component of EI is empathy. Empathetic leaders can sense others' needs, listen to what followers say (and don't say), and read the reactions of others. A leader who displays and manages emotions effectively will find it easier to influence the feelings of followers by expressing genuine sympathy and enthusiasm for good performance, and by showing irritation when employees fail to perform.[10] Although the association between leaders' self-reported EI and transformational leadership (to be discussed later in this chapter) was moderate, it is much weaker when followers rate their leaders' leadership behaviors.[11] However, research has demonstrated that people high in EI are more likely to emerge as leaders, even after taking cognitive ability and personality into account.[12]

Based on the latest findings, we offer two conclusions. First, we can say that traits can predict leadership. Second, traits do a better job predicting the emergence of leaders than distinguishing between effective and ineffective leaders.[13] The fact that an individual exhibits the right traits and others consider that person a leader does not necessarily mean he or she will be an effective one.

Trait theories help us *predict* leadership, but they don't fully *explain* leadership. What do successful leaders do that makes them effective? Are different types of leader behaviors equally effective? Behavioral theories, discussed next, help us define the parameters of leadership.

Behavioral Theories

13-2 Identify the central tenets and main limitations of behavioral theories.

behavioral theories of leadership Theories proposing that specific behaviors differentiate leaders from nonleaders.

initiating structure The extent to which leaders define and structure their roles and those of their subordinates in pursuit of goal attainment.

consideration The extent to which a leader has job relationships that are characterized by mutual trust, respect for subordinates' ideas, and regard for their feelings.

Trait research provides a basis for *selecting* the right people for leadership. **Behavioral theories of leadership**, in contrast, imply we can *train* people to be leaders.[14]

The most comprehensive behavioral theories of leadership resulted from the Ohio State Studies,[15] which sought to identify independent dimensions of leader behavior. Beginning with more than a thousand dimensions, the studies narrowed the list to two that substantially accounted for most of the leadership behavior described by employees: *initiating structure* and *consideration.*

Initiating structure is the extent to which a leader defines and structures his or her role and those of the subordinates to facilitate goal attainment. It includes behavior that attempts to organize work, work relationships, and goals. A leader high in initiating structure is someone who assigns followers particular tasks, sets definite standards of performance, and emphasizes deadlines.

Consideration is the extent to which a leader has job relationships that are characterized by mutual trust, respect for employees' ideas, and regard for their feelings. A leader high in consideration helps employees with personal problems, is friendly and approachable, treats all employees as equals, and expresses appreciation and support (people-oriented). Most of us want to work for considerate leaders—when asked to indicate what most motivated them at work, 66 percent of U.S. employees surveyed mentioned appreciation.[16]

The results of behavioral theory studies have been fairly positive. For example, one review found the followers of leaders high in consideration (and, to a lesser degree, initiating structure) were more satisfied with their jobs, were more motivated, and had more respect for their leaders. Both consideration and initiating structure were found to be moderately related to leader and group performance along with ratings of leader effectiveness.[17] However, results of behavioral theory tests may vary across cultures. Research from the GLOBE program—a study of 18,000 leaders from 825 organizations in 62 countries that was discussed in Chapter 4—suggested there are international differences in the preference for initiating structure and consideration.[18] The study found that leaders high in consideration succeeded best in countries where cultural values did not favor unilateral decision making, such as Brazil. In contrast, the French

Career OBjectives

How can I get my boss to be a better leader?

My boss is the CEO, and she's a gossipy, in-your-business oversharer. She's always asking our top management team personal questions and sharing information with anyone. The other day, I caught her e-mailing my colleague about my salary and career prospects! What should I do about her poor leadership?

— Deepak

Dear Deepak,

Nobody likes an oversharer! Perhaps your boss isn't aware of the impact of her behavior and thinks she is just being friendly. Assuming this is the case, you might be able to make her think first before sharing. If you're comfortable addressing her, you may suggest a private meeting to discuss your concerns. You should bring a list of the types of information she solicits and shares—with an example or two—and, if she's open to discussion, problem-solve with her about her habit. She may see that her open-book approach is undermining her leadership effectiveness.

Another tactic might be starting with researching the best privacy practices, laws, and business guidelines. Be sure to source your organization's human resources handbook for any mentions of privacy expectations. Then, in your meeting, you could present your research findings.

With both direct approaches, you run the risk of offending your boss, which may very well happen if she becomes embarrassed. And she may defend her behavior and not see the problem if her oversharing is actually strategic gossip, which could have ramifications for what she then thinks and says about you!

These approaches still might be worth trying, but from what you've said about her, it's highly unlikely she will change her general behavior. Research indicates that her personal tendencies will prevail over time. It sounds like she is extraverted, for instance, and you're not going to change that. She may be clever and manipulative, purposefully leveraging her information for personal gain without a concern for others (high-Machiavellian or narcissistic). In that case self-awareness can help, but her behavior won't change unless she is willing to practice self-regulation.

Perhaps most important, it doesn't seem that you like your boss. This may be a real problem that you cannot surmount. How are you going to build a relationship of trust with her, trust that will be needed for you to continue to feel motivated and work hard? Unfortunately, if you cannot thrive in this environment, it may be best to move on.

Good luck for your best possible outcome!

Sources: Based on A. E. Colbert, M. R. Barrick, and B. H. Bradley, "Personality and Leadership Composition in Top Management Teams: Implications for Organizational Effectiveness," *Personnel Psychology* 67 (2014): 351–87; R. B. Kaiser, J. M. LeBreton, and J. Hogan, "The Dark Side of Personality and Extreme Leader Behavior," *Applied Psychology: An International Review* 64, no. 1 (2015): 55–92; and R. Walker, "A Boss Who Shares Too Much," *The New York Times*, December 28, 2014, 7.

The opinions provided here are of the managers and authors only and do not necessarily reflect those of their organizations. The authors or managers are not responsible for any errors or omissions, or for the results obtained from the use of this information. In no event will the authors or managers, or their related partnerships or corporations thereof, be liable to you or anyone else for any decision made or action taken in reliance on the opinions provided here.

have a more bureaucratic view of leaders and are less likely to expect them to be humane and considerate. A leader high in initiating structure (relatively task-oriented) will do best there and can make decisions in a relatively autocratic manner. In other cultures, both dimensions may be important—Chinese culture emphasizes being polite, considerate, and unselfish, but it has a high-performance orientation. Thus, consideration and initiating structure may both be important for a manager to be effective in China.

Summary of Trait Theories and Behavioral Theories

In general, research indicates there is validity for both the trait and behavioral theories. Parts of each theory can help explain facets of leadership emergence and effectiveness. However, identifying the exact relationships is not a simple task. The first difficulty is in correctly identifying whether a trait or a behavior predicts a certain outcome. The second is in exploring which combinations of traits and behaviors yield certain outcomes. The third challenge is to determine the causality of traits to behaviors so that predictions toward desirable leadership outcomes can be made.

As important as traits and behaviors are in identifying effective or ineffective leaders, they do not guarantee success. Some leaders may have the right traits or display the right behaviors and still fail. Context matters too, which has given rise to the contingency theories we discuss next.

Contingency Theories

13-3 Contrast contingency theories of leadership.

Some leaders seem to gain a lot of admirers when they take over struggling companies and lead them out of crises. However, predicting leadership success is more complex than finding a few "heroes" to help lift the organization out of the mire. Also, the leadership style that works in tough times doesn't necessarily translate to long-term success. According to Fred Fiedler, it appears that under condition *a,* leadership style *x* would be appropriate, whereas style *y* would be more suitable for condition *b,* and style *z* for condition *c.* But what *were* conditions *a, b,* and *c*? We next consider the Fiedler model, one approach to isolating situational variables.

The Fiedler Model

Fiedler contingency model The theory that effective groups depend on a proper match between a leader's style of interacting with subordinates and the degree to which the situation gives control and influence to the leader.

least preferred coworker (LPC) questionnaire An instrument that purports to measure whether a person is task- or relationship-oriented.

Fred Fiedler developed the first comprehensive contingency model for leadership.[19] The **Fiedler contingency model** proposes that group performance depends on the proper match between the leader's style and the degree to which the situation gives the leader control. According to this model, the individual's leadership style is assumed to be stable or permanent. The **least preferred coworker (LPC) questionnaire** identifies whether a person is *task-oriented* or *relationship-oriented* by asking respondents to think of all the coworkers they have ever had and describe the one they *least enjoyed* working with.[20] If you describe this person in favorable terms (a high LPC score), you are relationship-oriented. If you see your least-preferred coworker in unfavorable terms (a low LPC score), you are primarily interested in productivity and are task-oriented.

After finding a score, a fit must be found between the organizational situation and the leader's style for there to be leadership effectiveness. We can assess the situation in terms of three contingency or situational dimensions:

leader–member relations The degree of confidence, trust, and respect that subordinates have in their leader.

task structure The degree to which job assignments are regimented.

position power Influence derived from one's formal structural position in the organization; includes the power to hire, fire, discipline, promote, and give salary increases.

1. **Leader–member relations** is the degree of confidence, trust, and respect that members have in their leader.
2. **Task structure** is the degree to which the job assignments are regimented (that is, structured or unstructured).
3. **Position power** is the degree of influence a leader has over power variables such as hiring, firing, discipline, promotions, and salary increases.

According to the model, the higher the task structure, the more procedures are added, and the stronger the position power, the more control the leader has. A very favorable situation (in which the leader has a great deal of control) might include a payroll manager who has the respect and confidence of his or her employees (good leader–member relations);

Exhibit 13-1 **Findings from the Fiedler Model**

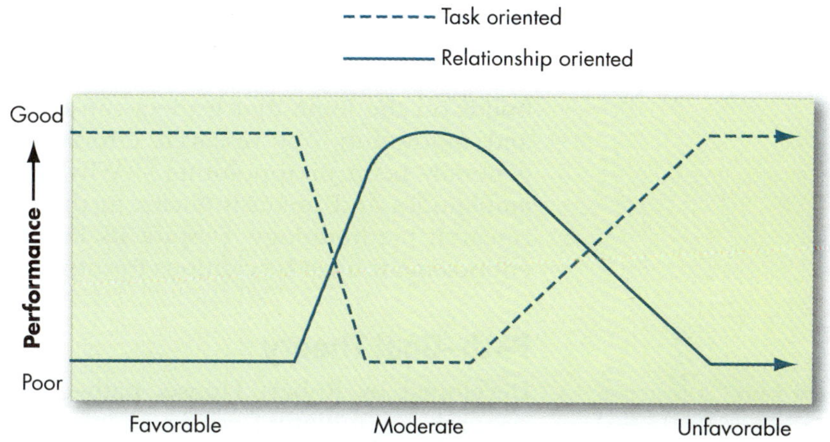

Category	I	II	III	IV	V	VI	VII	VIII
Leader–member relations	Good	Good	Good	Good	Poor	Poor	Poor	Poor
Task structure	High	High	Low	Low	High	High	Low	Low
Position power	Strong	Weak	Strong	Weak	Strong	Weak	Strong	Weak

activities that are clear and specific—such as wage computation, check writing, and report filing (high task structure); and considerable freedom to reward and punish employees (strong position power). The favorable situations are on the left side of the model in Exhibit 13-1. An unfavorable situation, to the right in the exhibit, might be that of the disliked chairperson of a volunteer United Way fundraising team (low leader–member relations, low task structure, low position power). In this job, the leader has very little control. When faced with a category I, II, III, VII, or VIII situation, task-oriented leaders perform better. Relationship-oriented leaders (represented by the solid line), however, perform better in moderately favorable situations—categories IV, V, and VI.

Studies testing the overall validity of the Fiedler model were initially supportive, but the model hasn't been studied much in recent years.[21] While it provides some insights that we should consider, its strict practical application is problematic.

Situational Leadership Theory

situational leadership theory (SLT) A contingency theory that focuses on followers' readiness to accomplish a specific task.

Situational leadership theory (SLT) focuses on the followers. It says that successful leadership depends on selecting the right leadership style contingent on the followers' *readiness,* the extent to which followers are willing and able to accomplish a specific task. A leader should choose one of four behaviors depending on follower readiness.[22]

If followers are *unable* and *unwilling* to do a task, the leader needs to give clear and specific directions; if they are *unable* but *willing,* the leader needs to display a high task orientation to compensate for followers' lack of ability, and high relationship orientation to get them to accept the leader's desires. If followers are *able* but *unwilling*, the leader needs to use a supportive and participative style; if they are both *able* and *willing*, the leader doesn't need to do much.

SLT has intuitive appeal. It acknowledges the importance of followers and builds on the logic that leaders can compensate for followers' limited ability and motivation. Yet research efforts to test and support the theory have generally been disappointing.[23] Why? Possible explanations include internal ambiguities and inconsistencies in the model itself, as well as problems with research methodology. Despite its intuitive appeal and wide popularity, any endorsement must be cautious for now.

Path–Goal Theory

path–goal theory A theory that states that it is the leader's job to assist followers by providing the necessary resources to achieve their goals, to ensure that the path to accomplishing these goals is understandable or clear, and to reduce any roadblocks that may be making goal achievement difficult.

Developed by Robert House, **path–goal theory** extracts elements from the research on initiating structure and consideration, and on the expectancy theory of motivation.[24] Path–goal theory suggests that it's the leader's job to provide followers with information, support, or other resources necessary to achieve goals. (The term *path–goal* implies effective leaders clarify followers' paths to their work goals and make the journey easier by reducing roadblocks.) The theory predicts the following:

- *Directive leadership yields greater employee satisfaction when tasks are ambiguous or stressful than when they are highly structured and well laid out.*
- *Supportive leadership results in high employee performance and satisfaction when employees are performing structured tasks.*
- *Directive leadership is likely to be perceived as redundant among employees with high ability or considerable experience.*

Like SLT, path–goal theory has intuitive appeal, especially from a goal attainment perspective. Also like SLT, the theory can be adopted only cautiously for application, but it is a useful framework in examining the vital role of leadership.[25]

Leader–Participation Model

leader–participation model A leadership theory that provides a set of rules to determine the form and amount of participative decision making in different situations.

The final contingency theory we cover argues that *the way* the leader makes decisions is as important as *what* he or she decides. The **leader–participation model** relates leadership behavior to subordinate participation in decision making.[26] Like path–goal theory, it says that leader behavior must adjust to reflect the task structure (such as routine, nonroutine, or in between), but it does not cover all leadership behaviors and is limited to recommending what types of decisions might be best made with subordinate participation. It lays the groundwork for the situations and leadership behaviors most likely to elicit acceptance from subordinates.

As one leadership scholar noted, "Leaders do not exist in a vacuum"; leadership is a symbiotic relationship between leaders and followers.[27] But the theories we've covered to this point assume that leaders use a homogeneous style with everyone in their work unit. Think about your experiences in groups. Did leaders often act very differently toward different people? Before we dig into differences between leaders, consider the OB Poll—and your own quest for leadership skills.

OB POLL

How Are You Developing Your Leadership Skills?

Note: Survey of 700 respondents.
Source: Based on J. Brox, "The Results Are In: How Do You Ensure You're Constantly Developing as a Leader?" May 14, 2013, http://www.refreshleadership.com/index.php/2013/05/results-ensure-youre-constantly-developing-leader/#more-4732.

Contemporary Theories of Leadership

13-4 Describe the contemporary theories of leadership and their relationship to foundational theories.

Leaders are important—to organizations, and to employees. The understanding of leadership is a constantly evolving science. Contemporary theories have been built on the foundation we've just established to discover unique ways leaders emerge, influence, and guide their employees and organizations. Let's explore some of the current leading concepts, and look for aspects of the theories we've discussed already throughout.

Leader–Member Exchange (LMX) Theory

leader–member exchange (LMX) theory A theory that suggests (1) leaders and followers have unique relationships that vary in quality and (2) these followers comprise ingroups and outgroups; subordinates with ingroup status will likely have higher performance ratings, less turnover, and greater job satisfaction.

Think of a leader you know. Does this leader have favorites who make up an ingroup? If you answered yes, you're acknowledging leader–member exchange theory.[28] **Leader–member exchange (LMX) theory** argues that, because of time pressures, leaders establish a special relationship with a small group of their followers. These individuals make up the ingroup—they are trusted, get a disproportionate amount of the leader's attention, and are more likely to receive special privileges. Other followers fall into the outgroup.

LMX theory proposes that early in the history of the interaction between a leader and a given follower, the leader implicitly categorizes the follower as an "in" or an "out"; that relationship becomes relatively stable over time. Leaders induce LMX by rewarding employees with whom they want a closer linkage and punishing those with whom they do not.[29] When leaders and followers interact with one another, research suggests that leaders and followers build social capital with one another—they contribute more to the relationship when they feel obligated to and will withhold contribution when they believe they have "done enough."[30] For the LMX relationship to remain intact, the leader and the follower must invest in the relationship.

Just how the leader chooses who falls into each category is unclear, but there is evidence that ingroup members have demographic, attitude, and

Exhibit 13-2 Leader–Member Exchange Theory

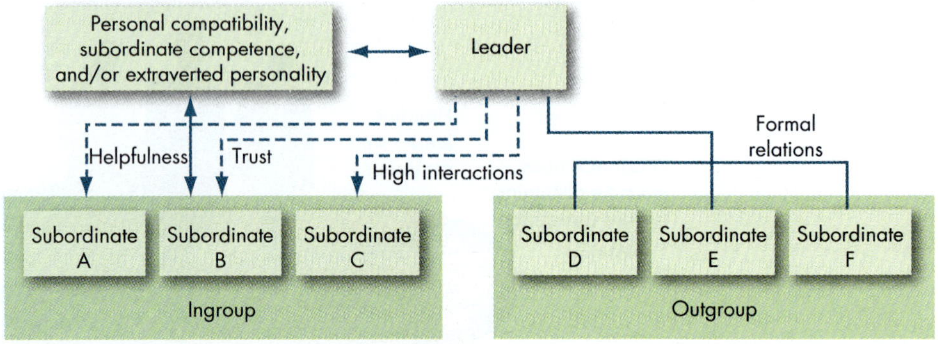

personality characteristics that are similar to those of their leader or a higher level of competence than outgroup members[31] (see Exhibit 13-2). Leaders and followers of the same gender tend to have closer (higher LMX) relationships than those of different genders.[32] Regardless of LMX quality perceptions, it is also true that LMX more or less varies in importance for leaders and followers (some employees value LMX less than others).[33]

Research to test LMX theory has been generally supportive, with substantive evidence that leaders do differentiate among followers. These disparities are far from random. Followers with ingroup status receive higher performance ratings, engage in more helping or citizenship behaviors at work, engage in less deviant or counterproductive behaviors at work, and report greater satisfaction with their superior.[34] LMX influences these work outcomes by improving employee trust, motivation, empowerment, and job satisfaction (although trust in the leader has the largest effect).[35] One study conducted in an entrepreneurial firm in southeast China found LMX is related to creative and innovative behavior.[36]

Recent research has also clarified how LMX changes over time, what happens when there is more than one leader supervising an employee, and whether the effects of LMX spreads outside the workplace. For one, it seems as if newer employees experience the development of LMX differently than employees who have been there longer—justice tends to matter more to the newer employees.[37] When employees have two leaders, the degree of LMX with both matters—and if an employee has high LMX with one leader and low LMX with the other, it matters more if the "primary" leader LMX is low.[38] Finally, recent research in India suggests that when employees who leave their organizations have good LMX with their old boss, they tend to have higher salaries, better responsibilities, and more goodwill toward their old company.[39]

When the treatment of the ingroup is starkly different from the treatment of the outgroup (e.g., when the leader plays favorites), research indicates that both the ingroup and the outgroup realize negative effects from LMX.[40] For example, a study in Turkey demonstrated that when leaders differentiated strongly among their followers in terms of their relationships (some followers had very positive leader–member exchange, others very poor), employees from both groups responded with more negative work attitudes and higher levels of withdrawal behavior.[41] One study in China and the United States indicated that differential leadership treatment hurts team trust and perceptions of procedural justice, especially when the team members work closely together.[42] Other research indicated that, although ingroup team members showed increased performance, the team as a whole became uncoordinated in the LMX environment and overall performance suffered.[43] Similar to substitutes for leadership theory (discussed later in the chapter), the quality of exchange between coworkers and colleagues can often substitute for or offset the negative impacts of low LMX in teams.[44] Close-knit teams may be able to help outgroup members to retain their confidence and self-efficacy by offering a supportive environment[45] at the cost of the relationship between employees and leaders.

Charismatic Leadership

Do you think leaders are born and not made, or made and not born? True, an individual may be literally born into a leadership position (think family heirs with surnames like Ford and Hilton), be endowed with a leadership position due to past accomplishments (like CEOs who worked their way up the organizational ranks), or be informally acknowledged as a leader (like a Twitter employee who knows everything because he was "there at the start"). But here, we are talking not about how leaders attain their roles; rather, we are focused on what makes great leaders extraordinary. Two contemporary leadership theories—charismatic leadership and transformational leadership—share a common theme in the great leader debate: They view leaders as individuals who inspire followers through words, ideas, and behaviors.

What Is Charismatic Leadership? Sociologist Max Weber defined *charisma* (from the Greek for "gift") as "a certain quality of an individual personality, by virtue of which he or she is set apart from ordinary people and treated as endowed with supernatural, superhuman, or at least specifically exceptional powers or qualities. These are not accessible to the ordinary person and are regarded as of divine origin or as exemplary, and on the basis of them the individual concerned is treated as a leader."[46]

charismatic leadership theory A leadership theory stating that followers make attributions of heroic or extraordinary leadership abilities when they observe certain behaviors in others.

The first researcher to consider charismatic leadership in terms of Organizational Behavior (OB) was Robert House. According to **charismatic leadership theory**, followers attribute heroic or extraordinary leadership abilities when they observe certain behaviors, and tend to give these leaders power.[47] A number of studies have attempted to identify the characteristics of charismatic leaders: They have a vision, have a sense of mission, are willing to take personal risks, are sensitive to their followers' needs, have confidence that their vision could be achieved, and engage in unconventional behaviors (i.e., they "go against the flow")[48] (see Exhibit 13-3).

Are Charismatic Leaders Born or Made? Are charismatic leaders born with their qualities? Or can people learn to be charismatic leaders? Yes, and yes.

Individuals *are* born with personality traits that make them more charismatic, on average. Personality is also related to charismatic leadership; charismatic leaders are likely to be emotionally stable and extraverted, although these traits are most likely to influence charismatic leader behaviors in stressful, fast-changing environments.[49] Consider the legendary qualities of

Exhibit 13-3 Key Characteristics of a Charismatic Leader

1. *Vision and articulation.* Has a vision—expressed as an idealized goal—that proposes a future better than the status quo; able to clarify the importance of the vision in terms that are understandable to others.
2. *Personal risk.* Willing to take on high personal risk, incur high costs, and engage in self-sacrifice to achieve the vision.
3. *Sensitivity to follower needs.* Perceptive of others' abilities and responsive to their needs and feelings.
4. *Unconventional behavior.* Engages in behaviors that are perceived as novel and counter to norms.

Source: Based on J. A. Conger and R. N. Kanungo, *Charismatic Leadership in Organizations* (Thousand Oaks, CA: Sage, 1998), 94.

leader such as Mahatma Gandhi, Subhash Chandra Bose, Indira Gandhi, Atal Bihari Vajpayee and APJ Abdul Kalam when they were in office: Whether you liked them or not, they are often compared because they all exhibited the qualities of charismatic leaders.

Research indicates that charismatic leadership is not only the province of world leaders—all of us can develop, within our own limitations, a more charismatic leadership style. One study of German managers suggests that training managers to be inspirational in their communications with followers was successful at increasing related charismatic behaviors.[50] To develop an aura of charisma, use your passion as a catalyst for generating enthusiasm. Speak in an animated voice, reinforce your message with eye contact and facial expressions, and gesture for emphasis. Bring out the potential in followers by tapping into their emotions, and create a bond that inspires them. Remember, enthusiasm is contagious!

vision A long-term strategy for attaining a goal or goals.

vision statement A formal articulation of an organization's vision or mission.

How Charismatic Leaders Influence Followers How do charismatic leaders influence followers? By articulating an appealing **vision**, a long-term strategy for attaining a goal by linking the present with a better future for the organization.[51] Desirable visions fit the organization's circumstances and reflect the uniqueness of the organization. Thus, followers are inspired not only by how passionately the leader communicates and their nonverbal cues (e.g., extended eye contact)[52]—there must be an underlying vision that appeals to followers as well.

A vision needs an accompanying **vision statement**, a formal articulation of an organization's vision or mission.[53] Charismatic leaders may use vision statements to imprint on followers an overarching goal and purpose. Through words and actions, the leader conveys a new set of values and sets an example for followers to imitate.

Research indicates that charismatic leadership works as followers "catch" the emotions that their leader is conveying, which leads them to identify affectively with the organization.[54] Another study examining archival data on U.S. presidential elections found that followers tend to attribute charismatic leadership qualities to the candidate when she or he has a history of charismatic leader behaviors; when the leadership history is unclear, followers compare the candidate with a mental prototype, or model, of a charismatic leader.[55] Notably, charismatic managers may seem to have an air of mystique and magnetism around them: These perceptions are aroused when they seem to be successful for mysterious reasons and when the effects of their charisma spread across followers.[56]

Some personalities are especially susceptible to charismatic leadership.[57] For instance, an individual who lacks self-esteem and questions his or her self-worth is more likely to absorb a leader's direction rather than establish an individual way of leading or thinking. For these people, the situation may matter much less than the charismatic qualities of the leader.

Does Effective Charismatic Leadership Depend on the Situation? Charismatic leadership has positive effects across many contexts. However, there are characteristics of followers, and of the situation, that enhance or somewhat limit its effects.

One factor that enhances charismatic leadership is stress. People are especially receptive to charismatic leadership when they sense a crisis or when they are under stress, perhaps because we think bold leadership is needed. Some of it, however, may be more primal. When people are psychologically aroused, even in laboratory studies, they are more likely to respond to charismatic leaders.[58] This may explain why, when charismatic leaders surface, it's likely to be in politics or religion, during wartime, or when a business is in its infancy or facing a threatening crisis. For example, in the 2022 elections in UP CM Yogi Adityanath offered a charismatic vision, "I want to make UP the most developed state in India. I want to generate employment to channelise youngsters who migrate to different states."[59] Sleep deprivation can have a big impact on both leaders and followers: Sleep deprivation can reduce charismatic leadership by reducing deep acting (see Chapter 6).[60]

You may wonder whether a situational factor limiting charisma is the person's level in the organization. Top executives create vision. You might assume that it is more difficult to utilize a person's charismatic leadership qualities in lower-level management jobs or to align his or her vision with specific top-management goals. While charismatic leadership may be more important in the upper echelons of organizations, it can be effective from a distance, or from close range.

The Dark Side of Charismatic Leadership Unfortunately, charismatic leaders who are larger than life don't necessarily act in the best interests of their organizations.[61] Research has shown that individuals who are narcissistic are also higher in some behaviors associated with charismatic leadership.[62] Many charismatic—but corrupt—leaders have allowed their personal goals to override the goals of their organizations. Leaders at Enron, Tyco, WorldCom, and HealthSouth recklessly used organizational resources for their personal benefit and unethically violated laws to inflate stock prices, and then cashed in millions of dollars in personal stock options. Some charismatic leaders—Hitler, for example—are all too successful at convincing their followers to pursue a disastrous vision. If charisma is power, then that power can be used for good and for ill.

It's not that charismatic leadership isn't effective; overall, it is. But a charismatic leader isn't always the answer. Success depends, to some extent, on the situation and on the leader's vision, and on the organizational checks and balances in place to monitor the outcomes.

Transactional and Transformational Leadership

transactional leaders Leaders who guide or motivate their followers in the direction of established goals by clarifying role and task requirements.

Charismatic leadership theory relies on leaders' ability to inspire followers to believe in them. In contrast, Fiedler's model, situational leadership theory, and path–goal theory describe **transactional leaders**, who guide their followers

Exhibit 13-4 Characteristics of Transactional and Transformational Leaders

Transactional Leader

Contingent Reward: Contracts exchange of rewards for effort, promises rewards for good performance, recognizes accomplishments.

Management by Exception (active): Watches and searches for deviations from rules and standards, takes corrective action.

Management by Exception (passive): Intervenes only if standards are not met.

Laissez-Faire: Abdicates responsibilities, avoids making decisions.

Transformational Leader

Idealized Influence: Provides vision and sense of mission, instills pride, gains respect and trust.

Inspirational Motivation: Communicates high expectations, uses symbols to focus efforts, expresses important purposes in simple ways.

Intellectual Stimulation: Promotes intelligence, rationality, and careful problem solving.

Individualized Consideration: Gives personal attention, treats each employee individually, coaches, advises.

Sources: Based on B. M. Bass, *Leadership and Performance Beyond Expectations* (New York, NY: Free Press, 1990); and T. A. Judge and R. F. Piccolo, "Transformational and Transactional Leadership: A Meta-Analytic Test of Their Relative Validity," *Journal of Applied Psychology* 89, no. 5 (2004): 755–68.

transformational leaders Leaders who inspire followers to transcend their own self-interests for the good of the organization.

toward established goals by clarifying role and task requirements. A stream of research has focused on differentiating transactional from **transformational leaders**,[63] who inspire followers to transcend their self-interests for the good of the organization. Transformational leaders and their teams and organizations perform well and can have an extraordinary effect on their followers, who respond with increased performance, organizational citizenship behavior (OCB), creativity, job satisfaction, mental health, and motivation.[64] Richard Branson of the Virgin Group is a good example of a transformational leader. He pays attention to the concerns and needs of individual followers, changes followers' awareness of issues by helping them look at old problems in innovative ways, and excites and inspires followers to put forth extra effort to achieve group goals. Research suggests that transformational leaders are most effective when their followers can see the positive impact of their work through direct interaction with customers or other beneficiaries.[65] Exhibit 13-4 briefly identifies and defines characteristics that differentiate transactional from transformational leaders.

Transactional and transformational leadership complement each other; they aren't opposing approaches to getting things done.[66] The best leaders are transactional *and* transformational. Transformational leadership *builds on* transactional leadership and produces levels of follower effort and performance beyond what transactional leadership alone can do. One review suggests that transformational and transactional leadership may be more or less important depending on the outcome. Although both tend to be important, it appears that transformational leadership is more important for group performance and satisfaction with the leader, whereas transactional leadership (primarily

Exhibit 13-5 Full Range of Leadership Model

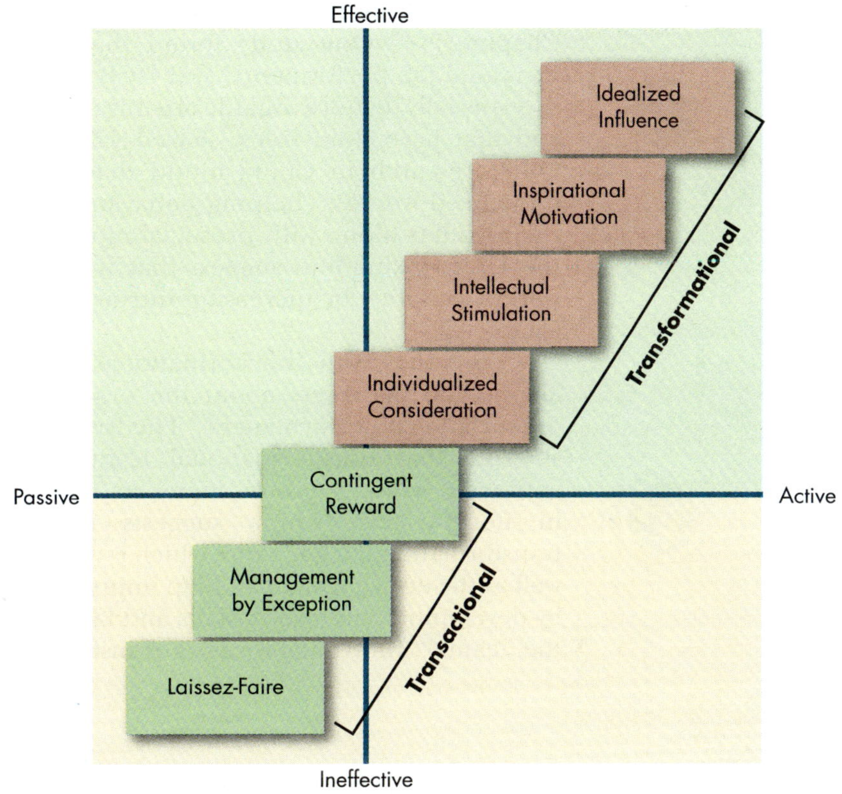

contingent reward) is more important for leader effectiveness and follower job satisfaction.[67]

full range of leadership model A model that depicts seven management styles on a continuum: laissez-faire, management by exception, contingent reward leadership, individualized consideration, intellectual stimulation, inspirational motivation, and idealized influence.

Full Range of Leadership Model Exhibit 13-5 shows the **full range of leadership model**. Laissez-faire, which literally means "let it be" (do nothing), is the most passive and therefore least effective of leader behaviors.[68] Management by exception (active or passive), in which leaders primarily "put out fires" when there are crisis exceptions to normal operating procedures, means they are often too late to be effective. Contingent reward leadership, which gives predetermined rewards for employee efforts, can be an effective style of leadership but will not get employees to go above and beyond the call of duty.

With the four remaining styles—all aspects of transformational leadership—leaders are best able to motivate followers to perform above expectations and transcend their self-interest for the sake of the organization. Individualized consideration, intellectual stimulation, inspirational motivation, and idealized influence (known as the "four I's") all result in excellent organizational outcomes.

How Transformational Leadership Works Overall, most research suggests that the reason transformational leadership works is that it inspires and motivates followers. For example, research in Germany and Switzerland found that transformational leadership improves employee job satisfaction, self-efficacy, and commitment to the leader by fulfilling follower autonomy, competence, and relatedness needs (see the discussion of self-determination theory in Chapter 7).[69] One study found that transformational leadership leads to increased job performance and OCB by empowering employees (see Chapter 3), especially in more organic organizations (i.e., organizations that are adaptive and that have fluid roles, shared values, and reciprocal communication).[70] Other research in China found that transformational leadership positively influenced workers' helping behaviors through improving employee trust in their leaders along with prosocial motivation.[71] Multiple studies in Israel and the United Kingdom suggest that transformational leadership can improve workplace safety by increasing intrinsic motivation and prevention focus (see Chapter 7).[72]

Companies with transformational leaders often show greater agreement among top managers about the organization's goals, which yields superior organizational performance.[73] The Israeli military has seen comparable results, showing that transformational leaders improve performance by building consensus among group members.[74] Research in high-tech organizations in northwestern China suggests that companies with a dual-focused transformational leadership, which is directed toward leading each employee as well as the entire team, can help improve employee outcomes such as creativity by developing employees' skills and facilitating knowledge sharing throughout the team.[75] Individual-focused transformational leadership is behavior that

Myth or Science?

Top Leaders Feel the Most Stress

Leaders of corporations fight pressures from their boards, customers, managers, and employees. Wouldn't it stand to reason they are the most stressed people in their organizations? Apparently not. According to studies from Harvard University, the University of California–San Diego, and Stanford University, leadership brings a blissful relief from the stress felt by individuals who are not in managerial roles. Not only did leaders report less anxiety than nonleaders, their cortisol (stress hormone) levels were also lower, indicating they were biologically less likely to register stress. Another study found that individuals in higher-status occupational groups registered less perceived stress and lower blood pressure readings than those in lower status occupations.

If you're thinking this is one more reason that it's better at the top, you may be right, if only partially. It is true that leaders appear to show fewer signs of stress by being leaders, regardless of higher income or longer job tenure. However, researchers found no "magic level" in an organization at which employees felt a reduction in stress levels.

One study indicated that stress reduction correlates with feelings of control. Leaders with more subordinates and greater power felt less stress than other individuals who knew they had less control over outcomes. Top leaders who control the resources of their corporations and have plenty of employees to carry out their directives therefore can fight stressors before they affect them.

Sources: Based on M. Korn, "Top-Level Leaders Have Less Stress Than Others," *The Wall Street Journal*, October 3, 2012, B6; G. D. Sherman, J. J. Lee, A. J. C. Cuddy, J. Renshon, C. Oveis, J. J. Gross, and J. S. Lerner, "Leadership Is Associated with Lower Levels of Stress," *Proceedings of the National Academy of Sciences of the United States of America* 109, no. 44 (2012): 17903–7; and E. Wiernik, B. Pannier, S. Czernichow, H. Nabi, O. Hanon, T. Simon, ... and C. Lemogne, "Occupational Status Moderates the Association between Current Perceived Stress and High Blood Pressure: Evidence from the IPC Cohort Study," *Hypertension* 61 (2013): 571–77.

Kiran Shaw Majumdar is an authentic leader. As the founder and CEO of Biocon (India's largest biopharma company), she is one of the most influential leaders. She is the driving force towards 'affordable innovation'—to provide universal access to all life-saving medicines. Globally Biocon has supplied more than two billion affordable doses of biosimilar insulins. Kiran has forged a culture where risk taking and learning from failures are not only tolerated but encouraged.[78]

Source: ZUMA Press, Inc. / Alamy Stock Photo

empowers individual followers to develop ideas, enhance their abilities, and increase self-efficacy. Team-focused transformational leadership emphasizes group goals, shared values and beliefs, and unified efforts. However, research in China suggested that, in team situations, the members' identification with the group could override the effects of transformational leadership.[76]

Evaluation of Transformational Leadership Transformational leadership has been supported at diverse job levels and occupations (school principals, teachers, marine commanders, ministers, presidents of MBA associations, military cadets, union shop stewards, sales representatives). In general, organizations perform better when they have transformational leaders.

The effect of transformational leadership on performance can vary by the situation. In general, transformational leadership has a greater impact on the bottom line in smaller, privately held firms than in more complex organizations.[77] A great deal of research suggests that the stress and demands surrounding the context affects whether or not transformational leadership improves health outcomes and work engagement (see Chapter 3). In particular, a study of Dutch elementary school teachers found that their principals' transformational behaviors were most effective at improving the teachers' engagement when the situations were cognitively demanding and when they had a high workload.[79] Transformational leaders helped reduce emotional exhaustion and improve perceptions of work-life balance in German information technology (IT) professionals when the time pressures were high.[80]

Transformational leadership may also be more effective when leaders can interact directly with the workforce to make decisions (when they have high task autonomy) than when they report to an external board of directors or deal with a complex bureaucratic structure. One study showed transformational leaders were more effective in improving group potency in teams higher in power distance and collectivism.[81]

The characteristics of the leader and the followers may also play roles in the effectiveness of transformational leadership. For example, transformational leadership can inspire employees to learn and thrive on the job, especially if they are high on openness to experience.[82] Another study suggests that IQ is important for transformational leadership perceptions—leaders who are "too intelligent" may be less transformational because their solutions may be too "sophisticated" to understand, they may use complex forms of communication that undermine their influence, and they may be seen as too "cerebral."[83] This doesn't mean that intelligence is not important for transformational leadership; it means that there is a "sweet spot" for intelligence in terms of leadership behaviors.

Another study on Dutch employees from a variety of occupations found that both the situation and individual can be important. For employees in positions with high job autonomy, transformational leadership was related to employee proactive behavior—but only when they were high in self-efficacy.[84]

Transformational versus Transactional Leadership When comparing transformational leadership with transactional leadership, research indicates transformational leadership is more strongly correlated than transactional leadership with a variety of workplace outcomes.[85] However, transformational leadership theory is not perfect. The full range of the leadership model shows a clear division between transactional and transformational leadership that may not fully exist in effective leadership, especially given that research suggests that transformational leadership is highly related to contingent reward leadership, to the point of being redundant.[86] Contrary to the full range of the leadership model, the four I's of transformational leadership are not always superior in effectiveness to transactional leadership; contingent reward leadership, in which leaders dole out rewards as certain goals are reached by employees, sometimes works as well as transformational leadership.[87] More research is needed, but the general supportable conclusion is that transformational leadership is desirable and effective, given the right application.

Transformational versus Charismatic Leadership In considering transformational and charismatic leadership, you surely noticed some commonalities. There are differences, too. Charismatic leadership places somewhat more emphasis on the way leaders communicate (are they passionate and dynamic?), while transformational leadership focuses more on what they are communicating (is it a compelling vision?). Still, the theories are more alike than different. At their heart, both focus on the leader's ability to inspire followers, and sometimes they do so in the same way. Because of this, some researchers believe the concepts are somewhat interchangeable.[88]

Responsible Leadership

13-5 Discuss the roles of leaders in creating ethical organizations.

Although the theories we've discussed so far have increased our understanding of effective leadership, they do not deal explicitly with the roles of ethics and trust, which are perhaps essential to complete the picture. These and the theories we discussed earlier are not mutually exclusive ideas (a transformational leader may also be a responsible one), but here, we consider contemporary concepts that explicitly address the role of leaders in creating ethical organizations.

Authentic Leadership

SAP's CEO Bill McDermott's motto is "Stay Hungry, Stay Humble," and he appears to practice what he preaches. Mark Zuckerberg, founder and CEO of Facebook, has resolved to halt the proliferation of fake news by adding fact checking and flagging to Facebook posts because it was the right thing to do. McDermott and Zuckerberg appear to be good exemplars of authentic leadership.[89]

authentic leaders Leaders who know who they are, know what they believe in and value, and act on those values and beliefs openly and candidly.

Authentic leadership focuses on the moral aspects of being a leader. **Authentic leaders** know who they are and what they believe in, and they act on those values and beliefs openly and candidly.[90] Their followers consider them ethical people and trust them as a result. Authentic leaders share information, encourage open communication, and stick to their ideals. Authentic leaders are also humble—research indicates that leaders who model humility help followers to understand the growth process for their own development.[91]

Authentic leadership, especially when shared among top management team members, creates a positive energizing effect that heightens teamwork, team productivity, and firm performance.[92] When leaders practice what they preach, or act on their values openly and candidly, followers tend to develop a strong affective commitment and trust in their leader and, to a lesser degree, to improve their performance and OCBs.[93] Not only is authenticity important for leaders, it is important for followers, too. In a study of Belgian service companies, the joint authenticity of both leaders and followers led to the satisfaction of basic needs (see the discussion of self-determination theory in Chapter 7), which in turn led to improvements in performance.[94] Much like the group- and individual-focused transformational leadership findings from the previous section, both group and individual perceptions of authenticity have an impact on follower outcomes.[95]

Brad Smith is an authentic leader. As the CEO of Intuit (one of the globe's biggest and most lucrative financial software companies), he is one of the most influential business leaders today, according to *Forbes* contributor and CEO of Fishbowl David K. Williams, and is known for his ethical entrepreneurial practices. Smith has forged a culture where risk taking and learning from failures are not only tolerated but encouraged.
Source: Christopher Victorio/The Photo Access/Alamy Stock Photo

Ethical Leadership

Leadership is not value-free. In assessing its effectiveness, we need to address the *means* that a leader uses to achieve goals as well as the content of those goals. The role of the leader in creating the ethical expectations for all members is crucial.[96] Ethical top leadership influences not only direct followers but spreads all the way down the command structure as well because top leaders set expectations and expect lower-level leaders to behave along ethical guidelines.[97]

Leaders rated as highly ethical tend to be evaluated very positively by their subordinates, who are also more satisfied and committed to their jobs, and experience less strain and turnover intentions.[98] Followers of such leaders are also more motivated, perform better, and engage in more OCBs and less counterproductive work behaviors (CWBs).[99] Ethical leaders can change norms: One reason why employees engage in more OCBs and less CWBs is because their perceptions on whether each is equitable (see the discussion of equity theory in Chapter 7) become altered so that OCBs are perceived as more equitable.[100] Ethical leaders also increase group awareness of moral issues, increase the extent to which the group is willing to speak up about ethical issues, and raise their empathic concern for others.[101] Research also found that ethical leadership reduced interpersonal conflicts.[102] Ethical leadership can matter for customer service outcomes, too—one study of bank tellers in Hong Kong found that when bank tellers display ethical leadership behaviors, and their coworkers see and recognize this, their coworkers adhere more to the customer service guidelines because their beliefs in what are appropriate and inappropriate change.[103] Ethical leadership has implications for financial outcomes as well. For example, one study of 111 U.S. retail stores found that ethical leadership can reduce "retail shrink," or the loss of merchandise primarily due to theft and shoplifting, because ethical leadership can reduce incivility among employees and customers.[104]

Ethical and charismatic leadership intersect at a number of junctures. To integrate ethical and charismatic leadership, scholars have advanced the idea of **socialized charismatic leadership**—conveying other-centered (not self-centered) values through leaders who model ethical conduct.[105] These leaders are able to bring employee values in line with their own values through their words and actions.[106]

socialized charismatic leadership A leadership concept stating that leaders convey values that are other-centered versus self-centered and who role-model ethical conduct.

Although every member of an organization is responsible for ethical behavior, many initiatives aimed at increasing organizational ethical behavior are focused on the leaders. Because top executives set the moral tone for an organization, they need to set high ethical standards, demonstrate them through their own behavior, and encourage and reward integrity in others while avoiding abuses of power.[107] Leadership training programs that incorporate cultural values should be especially mandated for leaders who take foreign assignments or manage multicultural work teams.[108] Despite the continued focus on the leader in ethical leadership, followers matter, too: One study on ethical leaders in Germany found that the effect of ethical leadership on follower OCBs was stronger for followers that were more mindful (see Chapter 6), suggesting that ethical leaders may be more effective if employees develop mindfulness through training or meditation techniques.[109]

For ethical leadership to be effective, it is not enough for the leader simply to possess high moral character. After all, there is no universal standard for ethical behavior, and ethical norms vary by culture, by industry, and even sometimes within an organization. Leaders must be willing to express their ethical beliefs and persuade others to follow their standards. To convey their beliefs, leaders should learn to express their moral convictions in statements that reflect values shared with their organization's members. Leaders can build on this foundation of trust to show their character, enhance a sense of unity, and create buy-in from followers. The leader's message should announce ambitious goals and express confidence that they can be reached.

Ethical leaders' statements are often positive messages, such as Winston Churchill's opening for his World War II victory speech: "This is your hour. This is not a victory of a party or of any class. It's a victory of the great British nation as a whole." An example of an ethical leader's negative message is this speech by Gandhi: "Even if all the United Nations opposes me, even if the whole of India forsakes me, I will say, 'You are wrong. India will wrench with nonviolence her liberty from unwilling hands.'" Positive and negative ethical leader statements can be equally effective when they deliver clear, moral, inclusive, goal-setting statements with persuasiveness. In fact, they can set trends in motion to make the seemingly far-fetched become real.[110]

Although ethical leadership has many positive outcomes, it can turn sour. For example, in a recent study, ethical leadership was found to lead to abusive supervision (discussed in the next section) on the following day. Sometimes behaving ethically can deplete our resources—we can even feel like, because we "behaved well" on the previous day, it gives us a license to behave poorly the next day.[111] However, followers do not necessarily react negatively to leader's

An Ethical Choice

Holding Leaders Ethically Accountable

Most people think that leaders should be held accountable for their actions. Leaders must balance many and conflicting stakeholder demands. The first demand is for strong financial performance; leaders are probably terminated more often for missing this goal than for all other factors combined. Leaders balance the extreme pressure for financial performance with the desire that most leaders should act ethically, even when there is no formal accountability. Given those competing aims, ethical leadership may be underrewarded and depend solely on the leader's innate decency.

Ethical leadership is a relatively new area of research attention. Demonstrating fairness and social responsibility even run counter to many old-school models of leadership. Consider, for example, legendary management guru Peter Drucker's advice from 1967: "It is the duty of the executive to remove ruthlessly anyone—and especially any manager—who consistently fails to perform with high distinction. To let such a man stay on corrupts the others." Modern ethical leadership guidelines say this cut-throat mindset fails to consider the moral implications of treating people as objects at an organization's disposal.

While few organizations still require "performance at all costs," financiers, shareholders, and boards have the reward power to teach leaders which outcomes to value. Ethical leadership resounds positively throughout all organizational levels, resulting in responsible and potentially highly profitable outcomes, but the ultimate ethical movement comes when shareholders—and leaders—show signs of balancing these accountabilities themselves.

Sources: Based on T. E. Ricks, "What Ever Happened to Accountability?," *Harvard Business Review,* October 2012, 93–100; J. M. Schaubroeck et al., "Embedding Ethical Leadership within and across Organizational Levels," *Academy of Management Journal* 55 (2012): 1053–78; and J. Stouten, M. van Dijke, and D. De Cremer, "Ethical Leadership," *Journal of Personnel Psychology* 11 (2012): 1–6.

unethical behavior: if the followers' values align with the leader's and they have a sense of mutual trust, they may be more likely to continue to support the leader.[112]

Abusive Supervision

It can happen to anyone—we're all capable of being abusive as managers.[113] Some research suggests that when it does occur, it can be costly. Current estimates suggest that it costs organizations in the United States about $23.8 billion per year.[114] The United States also has relatively low reported levels of abusive supervision in recent research—the highest ratings of abusive supervision are actually in the eastern hemisphere, including China, the Philippines, and Taiwan, with lower ratings in the United States, Canada, and India.[115] Although not a form of leadership in all cases, **abusive supervision** refers to the perception that a supervisor is hostile in his or her verbal and nonverbal behavior.[116]

abusive supervision Supervision that is hostile both verbally and nonverbally.

A recent review suggests that several factors are related to abusive supervision.[117] For one, nearly all forms of justice are negatively related to abusive supervision, suggesting that a sense of injustice is at the core of abusive supervision (especially for interpersonal justice). Although some personality traits such as agreeableness and conscientiousness appear to be negatively (but weakly) associated with perceptions of abusive supervision, negative affect is strongly linked with it. A family history of aggression has been shown to be related to engaging in abusive supervision across a variety of contexts in the Philippines.[118]

This same review also suggests that abusive supervision comes with dire consequences.[119] First and foremost, abusive supervision negatively affects health: It leads to increased depression, emotional exhaustion, and job tension perceptions. Second, it also leads to decreases in organizational commitment, job satisfaction, and perceived organizational support, along with increased work-family conflict. It can adversely affect employee performance and other employee behaviors. Victims of abusive supervision are more prone to engage in CWBs and other deviant behaviors (especially retaliatory ones directed toward their supervisors) and are less prone to engage in OCBs.

Abusive supervision often occurs in cycles. When employees are the victims of abusive supervision, they tend to lash out at the organization and the supervisor by engaging in CWB and deviant behaviors, and the supervisor then continues to be abusive to the employees in retaliation.[120] You may be wondering why the employee would lash out at the organization as well when it was the supervisor who was the one being abusive. Additional research suggests that employees often blame the organization when they are abused and see the supervisor as a representative of the organization as a whole.[121] When it comes to the experience of being a victim of abusive supervision, your personality and coping strategies matter. Conscientious employees tend to be able to cope with the abuse better, as are employees who cope by avoiding the issue.[122]

Servant Leadership

servant leadership A leadership style marked by going beyond the leader's own self-interest and instead focusing on opportunities to help followers grow and develop.

Scholars have recently considered ethical leadership from a new angle by examining **servant leadership**.[123] Servant leaders go beyond their self-interest and focus on opportunities to help followers grow and develop. Characteristic behaviors include listening, empathizing, persuading, accepting stewardship, and actively developing followers' potential. Because servant leadership focuses on serving the needs of others, research has focused on its outcomes for the well-being of followers. Perhaps not surprisingly, a study of 126 CEOs found that servant leadership is negatively correlated with the trait of narcissism.[124]

What are the effects of servant leadership? A study of 700 plus teachers working in government schools of Himachal Pradesh revealed that their job satisfaction was higher when they worked under school leaders displaying servant leadership.[125] In another study it was found that among young people working in a variety of organizations in India intention to stay was significantly higher among those who worked under managers who displayed servant leadership characteristics.[126] Another study of Chinese hairstylists found similar results, with servant leadership predicting customer satisfaction and stylists' service performance.[127] Second, there is a relationship between servant leadership and follower OCB that appears to be stronger when followers are encouraged to focus on being dutiful and responsible.[128] Third, servant leadership increases team potency (a belief that your team has above-average skills and abilities), which in turn leads to higher levels of team performance.[129] Fourth, a study with a nationally representative sample found higher levels of servant leadership were associated with a focus on growth and advancement, which in turn was associated with higher levels of creative performance.[130] Similar to authentic leadership, there appears to be an advantage for women who are servant leaders, because the leadership style stereotypically matches the gender role prototype. In other words, women who draw on servant leadership techniques tend to inspire their use in their followers, which leads to higher performance than when men exhibit the servant leadership style.[131]

Servant leadership may be more prevalent and effective in certain cultures.[132] When asked to draw images of leaders, for example, U.S. subjects tended to draw them in front of the group, giving orders to followers. Singaporeans tended to draw leaders at the back of the group, acting more to gather a group's opinions together and then unify them from the rear. This suggests that the East Asian prototype is more like a servant leader, which might mean servant leadership is more effective in these cultures.

13-6 Describe how leaders can have a positive impact on their organizations through building trust and mentoring.

Positive Leadership

In each of the theories we've discussed, you can see opportunities for the practice of good, bad, or mediocre leadership. Now let's think about the intentional development of positive leadership environments.

Trust

trust A psychological state of mutual positive expectations between people—both depend on each other and are genuinely concerned for each other's welfare.

Trust is a psychological state of mutual positive expectations between people—both depend on each other and are genuinely concerned for each other's welfare (see also the discussion in Chapters 9 and 10).[133] Although you aren't completely in control of the situation, you are willing to take a chance that the other person will come through for you. Trust is a primary attribute associated with leadership; breaking it can have serious adverse effects on a group's performance.[134]

Followers who trust a leader are confident that their rights and interests will not be abused.[135] Transformational leaders, for example, create support for their ideas in part by arguing that their direction will be in everyone's best interests. People are unlikely to look up to or follow someone they perceive as dishonest or likely to take advantage of them. Thus, as you might expect, transformational leaders generate higher levels of trust from their followers, which in turn are related to higher levels of team confidence and ultimately higher levels of team performance.[136]

In a simple contractual exchange of goods and services, your employer is legally bound to pay you for fulfilling your job description. But today's rapid reorganizations, diffusion of responsibility, and collaborative team-based work mean employment relationships are not stable long-term contracts with explicit terms. Rather, they are based more than ever before on trusting relationships. You must trust that if you show your supervisor a creative project you've been working on, he or she won't steal the credit behind your back. You must trust that the extra work you've been doing will be recognized in your performance appraisal. In contemporary organizations, where work is less closely documented and specified, voluntary employee contributions based on trust is absolutely necessary. Only a trusted leader will be able to encourage employees to reach beyond themselves to a transformational goal.

The Outcomes of Trust Trust between supervisors and employees has many specific advantages. Here are just a few from research:

- *Trust encourages taking risks.* Whenever leaders and employees decide to deviate from the usual way of doing things, or when employees decide to take their supervisor's word on a new direction, they are taking a risk. In both cases, a trusting relationship can facilitate that leap.[137]
- *Trust facilitates information sharing.* One big reason employees fail to express concerns at work is that they don't feel psychologically safe revealing their views. When managers demonstrate that they will give employees' ideas a fair hearing and actively make changes, employees are more willing to speak out.[138]
- *Trusting groups are more effective.* When a leader sets a trusting tone in a group, members are more willing to help each other and exert extra effort, which increases trust. Members of mistrusting groups tend to be suspicious of each other, constantly guard against exploitation, and restrict communication with others in the group. These actions tend to undermine and eventually destroy the group.[139]
- *Trust enhances productivity.* The bottom-line interest of companies appears to be positively influenced by trust. Employees who trust their supervisors tend to receive higher performance ratings, indicating higher productivity. People respond to mistrust by concealing information and secretly pursuing their own interests.[140]

Trust Development What key characteristics lead us to believe a leader is trustworthy? Evidence has identified three: integrity, benevolence, and ability (see Exhibit 13-6).[141]

Integrity refers to honesty and truthfulness. When 570 white-collar employees were given a list of 28 attributes related to leadership, they rated honesty the most important by far.[142] Integrity also means maintaining consistency between what you do and say.

Exhibit 13-6 The Nature of Trust

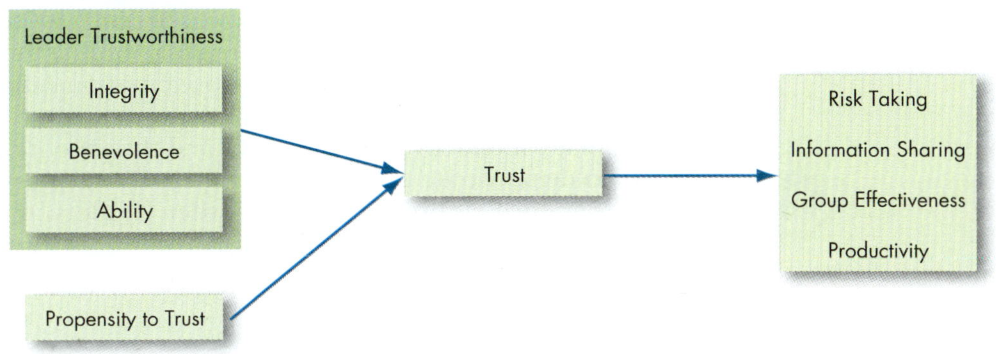

Benevolence means the trusted person has your interests at heart, even if your interests aren't necessarily in line with her or his interests. Caring and supportive behavior is part of the emotional bond between leaders and followers.

Ability encompasses an individual's technical and interpersonal knowledge and skills. You're unlikely to depend on someone whose abilities you don't believe in even if the person is highly principled and has the best intentions.

trust propensity How likely an employee is to trust a leader.

Trust Propensity Effective leadership is built on the trust of leaders and followers. **Trust propensity** refers to how likely a particular employee is to trust a leader. Some people are simply more likely to believe others can be trusted.[143] Those who carefully document every promise or conversation with their supervisors aren't very high in trust propensity, and they probably aren't going to take a leader's word for anything. Those who think most people are basically honest and forthright will be much more likely to seek evidence that their leaders have behaved in a trustworthy manner. Trust propensity is closely linked to the personality trait of agreeableness, and people with lower self-esteem are less likely to trust others.[144]

Trust and Culture Does trust look the same in every culture? Using the basic definition of trust, certainly it does. However, in the work context, trust in an employment relationship may be built on very different perceptions from culture to culture. For example, a recent study in Taiwan indicated that employees responded to paternalistic leadership when it is benevolent and ethical with increased trust performance.[145] This positive response to paternalism may be unique to the collectivistic context where the Confucian values of hierarchy and relationship predominate. In individualistic societies, we might expect that paternalistic leadership will rankle many employees who prefer not to see themselves as part of a hierarchical family work group. Employees in individualist cultures may build trust along dimensions of leadership support and consistency instead, for instance.

The Role of Time Time is the final component for building trust. We come to trust people by observing their behavior over a period of time.[146] To help, leaders need to demonstrate integrity, benevolence, and ability in situations where trust is important—say, where they could behave opportunistically or let employees down. Second, trust can be won in the ability domain by demonstrating competence and apologizing, not denying, when leaders' competence fails them.[147] Third, research with 100 companies around the world suggests that leaders can build trust by shifting their communication style from top-down commands to ongoing organizational dialogue.[148] Fourth, when leaders regularly create interpersonal conversations with their employees that are intimate, interactive, and inclusive and that intentionally follow an agenda, followers demonstrate trust with high levels of engagement.[149] Finally, followers can experience a breach of trust when leaders replace transformational leadership with laissez-faire leadership or when they are furious in response to an employee's unethical behavior—this breach of trust can cause followers to rate leaders as less effective as a result.[150]

Regaining Trust Managers who break the psychological contract with workers, demonstrating they aren't trustworthy leaders, will find employees are less satisfied and less committed, have a higher intent toward turnover, engage in less OCB, and have lower levels of task performance.[151]

Once it has been violated, trust can be regained, but only in certain situations and depending on the type of violation.[152] If the cause is lack of ability, it's usually best to apologize and recognize you should have done better. When lack of integrity is the problem, apologies don't do much good. Regardless of the violation, saying nothing or refusing to confirm or deny guilt is never an effective strategy for regaining trust. Trust can be restored when we observe a consistent pattern of trustworthy behavior by the transgressor. However, if the transgressor used deception, trust never fully returns, not even after apologies, promises, or a consistent pattern of trustworthy actions.[153]

Mentoring

mentor A senior employee who sponsors and supports a less-experienced employee, called a protégé.

Leaders often take responsibility for developing future leaders. A **mentor** is a senior employee who sponsors and supports a less-experienced employee, a protégé.[154] Successful mentors are good teachers. They present ideas clearly, listen well, and empathize with protégés' problems. Mentoring relationships serve career and psychosocial functions (see Exhibit 13-7).[155]

In formal mentoring relationships, protégé candidates are identified according to assessments of leadership potential and then matched with leaders in corresponding organizational functions. Informal mentoring relationships develop when leaders identify a less experienced, lower-level employee who appears to have potential for future development.[156] The protégé is often tested with a particularly challenging assignment. If performance is acceptable, the mentor develops the relationship. In both formal and informal mentoring, the goal is to show the protégé how the organization *really* works outside its formal structures and procedures.

Are all employees in an organization likely to participate in a mentoring relationship? Unfortunately, no.[157] However, research continues to indicate that employers should establish mentoring programs because they benefit both mentors and protégés.[158]

Although started with the best intentions, formal relationships are not as effective as informal ones,[159] perhaps due to poor planning, design, and communication. Mentors must see the relationship as beneficial to themselves and the protégé, and the protégé must have input into the

Exhibit 13-7 Career and Psychological Functions of the Mentoring Relationship

Career Functions	Psychosocial Functions
• Lobbying to get the protégé challenging and visible assignments	• Counseling the protégé to bolster his or her self-confidence
• Coaching the protégé to help develop his or her skills and achieve work objectives	• Sharing personal experiences with the protégé
• Providing exposure to influential individuals within the organization	• Providing friendship and acceptance
• Protecting the protégé from possible risks to his or her reputation	• Acting as a role model
• Sponsoring the protégé by nominating him or her for potential advances or promotions	
• Acting as a sounding board for ideas the protégé might be hesitant to share with a direct supervisor	

relationship.[160] Formal mentoring programs are also most likely to succeed if they appropriately match the work style, needs, and skills of protégé and mentor.[161]

Mentors may be effective not because of the functions they provide but because of the resources they can obtain; a mentor connected to a powerful network can build relationships that will help the protégé advance. Network ties, whether built through a mentor or not, are a significant predictor of career success.[162] If a mentor is not well connected or not a very strong performer, the best mentoring advice in the world will not be very beneficial.

You might assume that mentoring is valuable for objective outcomes like compensation and job performance, but research suggests the gains are primarily psychological. Thus, while mentoring can have an impact on career success, it is not as much of a contributing factor as ability and personality. It may *feel* nice to have a mentor, but it doesn't appear that having a good mentor, or any mentor, is critical to your career. The mentor is a boost to your confidence.

Leading in Times of Crisis

A popular English proverb states, "cometh the hour, cometh the [wo]man," suggesting that during times of crisis, leaders will emerge to bring order and understanding to the chaos.[163] Indeed, leaders can and do emerge during times of crisis, although there is variability in how effective they are at handling the situation. For example, during the COVID-19 outbreak of 2020, German Chancellor Angela Merkel has been praised for her impressive, decisive, firm, evidence-based, and effective leadership—and these are not merely attributions; under her leadership, Germany had one of the lowest fatality rates in the world when the virus broke out.[164] During times of peace and stability, women leaders tend to under-emerge due to the *glass cliff* phenomenon (see Chapter 2 for more discussion).[165] Because of this *think female–think crisis* effect, women are not seen as leaders during status-quo periods, often due to leader stereotypes of not displaying enough agency to prevent their emergence (despite little evidence indicating that they are either more or less effective than men). This phenomenon is just one of the many indicators that leadership in crisis is not as simple as the "cometh the hour" proverb would suggest—not to mention the time-pressure, complexity, and strain from the threat these stressful situations impose.[166]

Leaders in times of crisis, such as decorated combat heroes of World War II, are often thought of in mythical, heroic terms: eager, loyal, risk-taking, transformational, and so on.[167] Interestingly, one review of historical leadership incidents across several decades suggests that most of the successful leadership episodes involve *transactional* behaviors, such as strategizing (e.g., analyzing the situation, delegating, planning) and coordinating (e.g., orchestrating action, managing information flow).[168] Analyzing the situation appears to be particularly important, and research demonstrates that leaders managing crisis teams move quickly toward a shared mental model (see Chapter 10) of the crisis with followers over time.[169] Emotions also play a large role: for example, in one study, a leader responsible for a product recall that cost an organization a lot of money was rated more favorably when accepting responsibility and expressing sadness (as opposed to denial and anger).[170]

Of all the leadership styles during times of crisis, charismatic leadership has been studied the most frequently. During times of crisis, charismatic leadership can be *visionary* (e.g., starting with establishing a vision and then making a plea for action) or *crisis-responsive* (e.g., starting with a plea for action and, over time, justifying this action by communicating their effective results).[171] Both forms can be effective in different ways, although the crisis-responsive approach tends to be used less frequently once the crisis ends.[172] Followers are also highly attuned to the crisis, and this affects their leadership attributions. For example, analyses of presidential elections suggest that perceptions of crisis predict how voters rate a candidate's charisma as well as their intentions to vote for candidates who are charismatic.[173] The effects of charismatic and transformational leadership during times of crisis may even reverberate after the crisis is over. For example, a study of Army unit leaders suggests that transformational leaders observe less unit turnover after the crisis is over and that these soldiers feel more embedded in their unit due to their shared experiences.[174]

Challenges to Our Understanding of Leadership

13-7 Identify the challenges to our understanding of leadership.

"In the 1500s, people ascribed all events they didn't understand to God. Why did the crops fail? God. Why did someone die? God. Now our all-purpose explanation is leadership."[175] This may be an astute observation from management consulting, but, of course, much of an organization's success or failure is due to factors outside the influence of leadership. Sometimes it's a matter of being in the right or wrong place at a given time. In this section, we present challenges to the accepted beliefs about the value of leadership.

Leadership as an Attribution

attribution theory of leadership A leadership theory stating that leadership is merely an attribution that people make about other individuals.

As you may remember from Chapter 5, attribution theory examines how people try to make sense of cause-and-effect relationships. The **attribution theory of leadership** says that leadership is merely an attribution people make about other individuals.[176] We attribute the following to leaders: intelligence, outgoing personality, strong verbal skills, aggressiveness, understanding, and industriousness.[177] At the organizational level, we tend, rightly or wrongly, to see leaders as responsible for both extremely negative and extremely positive performance.[178]

Perceptions of leaders by their followers strongly affect leaders' ability to be effective. First, one study of 128 major U.S. corporations found that, whereas perceptions of CEO charisma did not lead to objectively better company performance, company performance did lead to perceptions of charisma.[179] Second, employee perceptions of leaders' behaviors are significant predictors of whether they blame the leader for failure, regardless of how the leader assesses him- or herself.[180] Third, a study of more than 3,000 employees from western Europe, the United States, and the Middle East found people who tended to "romanticize" leadership in general were more likely to believe their own leaders were transformational.[181]

We also make demographic assumptions about leaders. Respondents in a study assumed a leader described with no identifying racial information was white at a rate beyond the base rate of white employees in that company.[182] When identical leadership situations are described but the leaders' race is manipulated, white leaders are rated as more effective than leaders of other racial groups.[183] One large-scale summary found that many individuals hold stereotypes of men as having more leader characteristics than women, although, as you might expect, this tendency to equate leadership with masculinity has decreased over time.[184] Other data suggest women's perceived success as transformational leaders may be based on situations. Teams prefer male leaders when aggressively competing against other teams, but they prefer female leaders when the competition is within teams and calls for improving positive relationships within the group.[185]

Attribution theory suggests that what is important is projecting the *appearance* of being a leader rather than focusing on *actual accomplishments*. Leader-wannabes who can shape the perception that they're smart, personable, verbally adept, aggressive, hardworking, and consistent in their style can increase the probability that their bosses, colleagues, and employees will view them as effective leaders. It works both ways as well—coworkers and leaders alike can see a follower engaging in OCB toward the leader as being ingratiating or "sucking up."[186] Similarly, attributions that suggest the leader was only acting fairly for non-benevolent motives (e.g., desiring to exercise control or maintain their image) do not influence trust in the leader like a more benevolent motive would.[187]

Neutralizers of and Substitutes for Leadership

neutralizers Attributes that make it impossible for leader behavior to make any difference to follower outcomes.

substitutes Attributes, such as experience and training, that can replace the need for a leader's support or ability to create structure.

One theory of leadership suggests that, in many situations, leaders' actions are irrelevant.[188] **Neutralizers** such as indifference to rewards make it impossible for leader behavior to make any difference to follower outcomes (see Exhibit 13-8). On the other hand, experience and training are among the **substitutes** that can replace the need for a leader's support or ability to create structure. Organizations such as videogame producer Valve Corporation, Gore-Tex maker W. L. Gore, and collaboration-software firm GitHub have experimented with eliminating leaders and management. Governance in the "bossless" work environment is achieved through accountability to coworkers, who determine team composition and sometimes even pay.[189] Organizational characteristics such as explicit

Exhibit 13-8 Neutralizers of and Substitutes for Leadership

Defining Characteristics	Relationship-Oriented Leadership	Task-Oriented Leadership
Individual		
Experience/training	No effect on	Substitutes for
Professionalism	Substitutes for	Substitutes for
Indifference to rewards	Neutralizes	Neutralizes
Job		
Highly structured task	No effect on	Substitutes for
Provides its own feedback	No effect on	Substitutes for
Intrinsically satisfying	Substitutes for	No effect on
Organization		
Explicit formalized goals	No effect on	Substitutes for
Rigid rules and procedures	No effect on	Substitutes for
Cohesive work groups	Substitutes for	Substitutes for

Source: Based on K. B. Lowe and W. L. Gardner, "Ten Years of the Leadership Quarterly: Contributions and Challenges for the Future," *Leadership Quarterly* 11, no. 4 (2000): 459–514.

formalized goals, rigid rules and procedures, and cohesive work groups can replace formal leadership. At the same time, leadership can also substitute for the effects of policies, practices, and procedures. For example, ethical leadership can substitute for actual justice enactment, such that perceiving the leader as ethical matters more to followers than them actually enacting and enforcing justice.[190]

Sometimes the difference between substitutes and neutralizers is fuzzy. If I'm working on a task that's intrinsically enjoyable, theory predicts leadership will be less important because the task provides motivation. But does that mean intrinsically enjoyable tasks neutralize leadership effects, substitute for them, or both? Another problem is that, while substitutes for leadership (such as employee characteristics, the nature of the task, etc.) matter to performance, that doesn't necessarily mean leadership doesn't matter.[191] It's simplistic to think employees are guided to goal accomplishments solely by the actions of their leaders. We've introduced several variables—such as attitudes, personality, ability, and group norms—that affect employee performance and satisfaction. Leadership is simply another independent variable in our overall OB model.

Selecting Leaders

The process organizations go through to fill management positions is an exercise in the identification of effective leaders. You might begin by reviewing the knowledge, skills, and abilities needed to do the job effectively. Personality tests can identify traits associated with leadership—extraversion, conscientiousness, and openness to experience. High self-monitors (see Chapter 4) are better at reading situations and adjusting their behavior accordingly. Candidates with high emotional intelligence should have an advantage, especially in situations requiring transformational leadership.[192] Broad experience is a poor predictor of leader effectiveness, but situation-specific experience is relevant.

Because nothing lasts forever, the most important event an organization needs to plan for is a change in leadership. JCPenney hired a CEO with no department store experience who promptly changed its overall strategy, a

Situation-specific experience played a key role in selecting Satya Nadella (center) as Microsoft's new CEO. To strengthen its position in the growing cloud domain, Microsoft chose Nadella, who formerly led Microsoft's Cloud and Enterprise Group and was instrumental in transforming Microsoft's technology culture from client services to cloud infrastructure and services.
Source: PRNewsFoto/Microsoft Corp/AP Images

maneuver so disastrous that JCPenney's stock fell 69 percent in the roughly one year he lasted (after which JCPenney rehired the old CEO it had forced out, and he stayed until the company returned to a better standing). After that debacle, JCPenney seemed to learn its lesson by hiring Marvin Ellison, an executive from Home Depot who also had 15 years of experience at Target. The company's press release repeatedly described Ellison as "a highly-accomplished retail executive [with] an extensive knowledge of store operations."[193]

In general, organizations seem to spend no time on leadership succession and are surprised when their picks turn out poorly. HP is on its fourth CEO in under 10 years, including one who lasted a matter of months, causing observers to wonder whether its boards of directors had done their homework in leadership succession. Their choice of Meg Whitman, the current CEO, was based on her role as CEO of eBay, during which she was praised as a top-performing leader. She was also heavily invested in politics, having run for governor of California. Not long ago she was named the "Most Underachieving CEO" for her leadership of HP, although shares of HP have increased drastically over her tenure as she sought to undo the work of her predecessors.[194]

Training Leaders

Organizations spend billions of dollars on leadership training and development.[195] These efforts take many forms, from $50,000 executive leadership programs offered by universities such as Harvard to sailing trips with the Outward Bound program. Goldman Sachs is well known for developing leaders; at one point, *BusinessWeek* called it the "Leadership Factory."[196] Business schools are placing renewed emphasis on leadership development too.

How can managers get the most from their leadership-training budgets? First, leadership training is likely to be more successful with high self-monitors. Such individuals have the flexibility to change their behavior. Second, organizations can teach implementation skills. Third, skills such as trust building and mentoring can be taught. Leaders can be taught situational-analysis skills. They can learn how to evaluate situations, modify them to match their style more closely, and assess which leader behaviors might be most effective in given situations. BHP Billiton, Best Buy, Nokia, and Adobe have hired coaches to help top executives improve their interpersonal skills and act less autocratically.[197] The effectiveness of leadership training seems to hinge much more on outside characteristics than other types of training that are more closed or technical, such as computer software skills training.[198] Fourth, behavioral training through modeling exercises can increase an individual's ability to exhibit charismatic leadership qualities. Research also indicates that leaders should engage in regularly reviewing their leadership after key organizational events as part of their development. These after-event reviews are especially effective for leaders who are high in conscientiousness and openness to experience, and who are emotionally stable (low in neuroticism).[199] Finally, leaders can be trained in transformational leadership skills that have bottom-line results.

Summary

Leadership plays a central part in understanding group behavior because it's the leader who usually directs us toward our goals. Knowing what makes a good leader should thus be valuable toward improving group performance. The Big Five personality framework shows strong and consistent relationships between personality and leadership. The major contribution of the behavioral approach was narrowing leadership into task-oriented (initiating structure) and people-oriented (consideration) styles. By considering the situation in which the leader operates, contingency theories promised to improve on the behavioral approach. Contemporary theories have made major contributions to our understanding of leadership effectiveness, and studies of ethics and positive leadership offer exciting promise.

Implications for Managers

- For maximum leadership effectiveness, ensure that your preferences on the initiating structure and consideration dimensions are a match for your work dynamics and culture.
- Hire candidates who exhibit transformational leadership qualities and who have demonstrated success in working through others to meet a long-term vision. Personality tests can reveal candidates higher in extraversion, conscientiousness, and openness, which may indicate leadership readiness.
- Hire candidates whom you believe are ethical and trustworthy for management roles and train current managers in your organization's ethical standards to increase leadership effectiveness and reduce abusive supervision.
- Seek to develop trusting relationships with followers because, as organizations have become less stable and predictable, strong bonds of trust are replacing bureaucratic rules in defining expectations and relationships.
- Consider investing in leadership training such as formal courses, workshops, and mentoring.

CEOs Start Early

POINT

If you really get down to specifics, you can see that CEOs start in leadership roles early in life. They have similar backgrounds, childhood challenges, and coping strategies. In fact, it's easy to see a CEO-in-the-making at your neighborhood lemonade stand.

What's the profile of burgeoning CEOs? It starts with their parents, who are almost all successful through industriousness. For example, Linda Zecher, the former CEO of publisher Houghton Mifflin Harcourt, grew up in a household in which her father ran several businesses. Brent Frei, CEO of software company Smartsheet.com, grew up on an 800-acre farm that his father owned and ran. Aspera CEO Michelle Munson's mother was a professor and her father was the fifth-generation leader of her farm.

Second, future CEOs are raised with responsibilities. Susan Story, CEO of utility company American Water, learned as a child that "no matter how bad things get, it's about working hard and taking personal responsibility, because nobody owes you anything." Frei "had an opportunity to do big things early on. When I was 6 years old, my dad . . . put me in the pickup, put it in first gear, and I drove it home with my 5-year-old sister in the passenger seat." Many CEOs grow up working on family farms or taking care of their siblings.

Third, burgeoning CEOs are successful leaders when they're young. Ruth Rathblott, CEO of Harlem Educational Activities Fund, was president of her seventh-grade class, then president of the middle school; Brad Jefferson, CEO of video slide show service Animoto, was the high school quarterback, captain of the football team, and senior class president; and Hannah Paramore, founder of digital agency Paramore, "was always the one in charge. I was always captain of this and captain of that."

Clearly, CEOs start early.

COUNTERPOINT

CEOs who start early have good stories to tell when they become successful, but that doesn't necessarily mean they represent the majority. Let's look at a few other aspects of the tender years of CEOs.

First, we know that much of our personality is attributable to genetics, but it's incorrect to infer that we can (a) map the genetic trail for a personality trait from ancestors to CEO or (b) tell where a young person's traits will lead. Likewise, we can't say that if the parents are successful through industriousness, their children will be. Story's parents worked in a cotton mill and a wastewater plant, and they "didn't have a lot of money." Frei's family farm "was a little bit below the threshold for break-even." Mitch Rothschild, CEO of website Vitals, observed, "Parents influence you either because you want to be like them or because you want to not be like them."

Second, what child is raised without responsibilities? None, even if all they have to do is go to school. There are plenty of CEOs who had a lot of responsibilities growing up, and others who did not. Munson's parents "emphasized two things. One was education, and the other was participating in 4-H." Zecher "had a paper route. [She] was a girl scout, and [she] was involved in a lot of clubs and sports in high school."

Third, it would be a mistake to conclude that CEOs start as young leaders. The ones who don't simply don't talk about it. Ron Kaplan, CEO of manufacturer Trex, was a marksmanship competitor. Zecher didn't have a plan or a leadership role until after college.

The stories of CEOs who start early make for good press reports, but CEOs do not by definition start early. What we can say, though, is that genetics and experiences both shape young people, and that the relationship between those factors and CEO success is complex.

Sources: Based on A. Bryant, "A Good Excuse Doesn't Fix a Problem," *The New York Times*, December 28, 2014, 2; A. Bryant, "Always Respect the Opportunity," *The New York Times*, October 19, 2014, 2; A. Bryant, "Don't Let Your Strengths Run Amok," *The New York Times*, May 18, 2014, 2; A. Bryant, "Knowing Your Company's Heartbeat," *The New York Times*, May 30, 2014, B2; A. Bryant, "The Danger of 'One Size Fits All,'" *The New York Times*, March 29, 2015, 2; A. Bryant, "The Job Description Is Just the Start," *The New York Times*, September 14, 2014, 2; A. Bryant, "Making Judgments, Instead of Decisions," *The New York Times*, May 4, 2014, 2; A. Bryant, "Pushing Beyond Comfort Zones," *The New York Times*, January 25, 2015, 2; A. Bryant, "Tell Me What's Behind Your Title," *The New York Times*, April 11, 2014, B2; and C. Crossland, J. Zyung, N. J. Hiller, and D. C. Hambrick, "CEO Career Variety: Effects on Firm-Level Strategic and Social Novelty," *Academy of Management Journal* 57, no. 3 (2014): 652–74.

CHAPTER REVIEW

QUESTIONS FOR REVIEW

13-1 What are the conclusions of trait theories of leadership?

13-2 What are the central tenets and main limitations of behavioral theories of leadership?

13-3 What are the contingency theories of leadership?

13-4 How do the contemporary theories of leadership relate to earlier foundational theories?

13-5 In what ways can leaders create ethical organizations?

13-6 How can leaders have a positive impact on their organizations through building trust and mentoring?

13-7 What are the challenges to our understanding of leadership?

APPLICATION AND EMPLOYABILITY

Understanding how leaders emerge, what makes leaders effective, and how to lead and influence people to pursue a vision and achieve organizational goals are invaluable skills. These skills will help you become more employable and perhaps improve your chances of being promoted in your job. Not only is this information important for knowing how to lead, it is also important for knowing how to interact and communicate effectively with your manager or supervisor. From this chapter, we know leadership is a multifaceted concept: Our personality traits can affect whether we become a leader (and if we will tend to be good at it). This may be important when you are in a position where you have a say in appointing a leader to your team or department. You should now have a better idea about what leaders do and how situations constrain them. You also know how important newer conceptualizations of leadership have focused on the specific relationships that managers have with their subordinates and how charisma, authenticity, ethicality, and transformational leadership styles tend to be the most effective. Clearly, you can see that being a leader and being a manager are two separate things—by inspiring and challenging your subordinates, you build trust and develop them so that they not only grow as employees but also help the organization achieve its goals. In this chapter, you improved your critical thinking and your knowledge application and analysis skills by debunking the myth that leaders experience the most stress, learning how to confront an oversharing boss, navigating the tension between ethical leadership and older schools of leadership, and debating whether CEOs start leadership roles earlier in life. In the following section, you will develop these skills, along with your communication and collaboration skills, by identifying examples of leaders from multiple different contexts, considering the ethical obligations of CEOs to their employees when CEOs consider leaving, analyzing the effectiveness of shared leadership, and considering the use of leadership algorithms for leadership development.

EXPERIENTIAL EXERCISE What's in a Leader?

Break the class into (or allow the class to volunteer to join) one of the following five groups:

GROUP A: Government leaders (president, senator, governor, representative, assemblyperson)

GROUP B: Business leaders (CEO, president, leader in business)

GROUP C: University leaders (university president, provost, dean, professor)

GROUP D: Sports leaders (coach, informal team leader, team captain)

GROUP E: Social/thought leaders (activists, whistle-blowers, authors)

Questions

13-8. Each group selects one leader from popular culture or history to serve as an example that is appropriate for the group. The group discusses that person, identifying the defining characteristics or traits of the leader, not simply by brainstorming but by drawing on examples that most of the group members agree are defining characteristics of the person.

13-9. Reconvene the class. The instructor will draw on the board one column for each of the five groups and list the selected person and his or her characteristics in each column. For each person selected by the groups, decide whether the person's traits or attributions would lead to good or bad leader effectiveness for the group's type of leader. Why or why not? What would the results of the *opposite* or *alternative* strategies in those contexts be, and why? What similarities do you see between the lists? From the results of this exercise, does it appear that what it takes to be a good leader is different depending on the context? For each context, does it appear that what makes for leader emergence within the context is different from what makes leaders effective?

ETHICAL DILEMMA Innocent, but What about Trust?

Innocent Drinks is a London-based company operating in the beverages industry worldwide. The business idea was conceived in 1998 by three Cambridge University graduates, and the company made its début in 1999. The three friends led the business idea by having a clear vision, and they took personal risks to achieve it. Their goal was to produce 100-percent natural smoothies that "do good." The uniqueness of the company's products and the unique leadership style combining visionary and charismatic elements became the brand's selling point. With an inspirational and ethical leadership stance, a business approach that emphasized social responsibility and ethical sources, an employee-led innovation culture, and its stated purpose of "doing good," Innocent established a reputation and became successful in the market. Since 2014, Innocent has thrived in 15 European countries.

Notwithstanding this success, Innocent recorded losses in 2008 due to the economic downturn, and in 2009 they announced plans to sell 10 percent of the company to Coca-Cola. Following this announcement, Innocent experienced a fall in their Ethiscore from 12.5 to 6.5. Since 2013, Coca-Cola Company has come to hold over 90 percent of Innocent Drinks, leaving very little scope for the former leadership of the company to lead the future of Innocent Drinks. Despite the positive strategic implications for global expansion and product development (including the launch of its coconut water products and Innocent Bubble in 2015), debates have raged over the trustworthiness and the authenticity of the current leadership, leading to a simple question about the brand: can we still trust its innocence?

Questions

13-10. In what way are Innocent's charismatic, transformational, and transactional elements of leadership now at stake?

13-11. What is ethical leadership, and how could ethical leadership be evidenced in the case of Innocent Drinks?

13-12. Why has the authenticity of ethical leadership of Innocent Drinks come under scrutiny?

Sources: Innocent Drinks Official Site, "Innocent and Coca-Cola Agree Deal for Further Investment," October, 8, 2015, http://www.innocentdrinks.co.uk/us/press/release/130222-innocent-and-coca-cola-agree-deal-for-further-investment; Personnel Today, "Innocent's Business Approach Inspires Leaders to Adopt New Ways of Working," May 20, 2010, http://www.personneltoday.com/hr/innocents-business-approach-inspires-leaders-to-adopt-new-ways-of-working/; L. Lucas, "Coca-Cola Swallows Most of Innocent," *Financial Times*, February, 22, 2013, http://www.ft.com/cms/s/0/0b01403a-7d0e-11e2-adb6-00144feabdc0.html#axzz3nz109fiw; Ethical Consumer Magazine, "Innocent Smoothies' Ethiscore Cut by Half," April, 7, 2009, http://www.ethicalconsumer.org/latestnews/tabid/62/entryid/290/innocent-smoothies-ethiscore-cut-by-half.aspx; L. Cummings, "Just an Innocent Business?", July 9, 2003, http://news.bbc.co.uk/1/hi/business/3014477.stm; W. A. Shahlman and D. Heath, "Innocent Drinks," *Harvard Business Review*, November 24, 2004.

CASE INCIDENT 1 Sharing Is Performing

While most people believe that there can be only one leader at a time, in the recent past we have seen examples of captaincy in the Indian Cricket Team between Anil Kumble, MS Dhoni and Virat Kohli on two different occasions. In the political field the chief minister MK Stalin has empowered the eminently qualified Palanivel Thiagarajan, Finance Minister of the State, to strategize in making Tamil Nadu an economically thriving state.[200] In the corporate world, the founder and current chairman emeritus of the Godrej Group, Adi Godrej, has successfully created the structures for shared leadership among members of the family and professionals in the Godrej Group.[201]

As Declan Fitzsimons suggests in a *Harvard Business Review* article, the twenty-first century moves too quickly and is too dynamic to be handled by one person. By sharing leadership among multiple individuals, the organization can respond more adaptively to challenges, share disparate but complementary perspectives, and ease the burden experienced by the traditional charismatic leader figurehead. However, sharing leadership leads to its own issues and obstacles, which are apparent in the multiple relationships between team members, subordinates, and other employees. Not only do individual identities become involved, but so do collective identities shared as a group. It is also important to recognize that shared leadership is not about delegation but about putting in effort to coordinate and collaborate, along with balancing individual and collective goals.

Recent reviews of the research on shared leadership suggest that, overall, shared leadership is effective at improving team performance, attitudes, and behaviors, especially when the leadership is transformational or charismatic and when the team tasks are complex.

Questions

13-13. What kind of obstacles can you foresee in taking a shared leadership approach? How might they (or can they) be solved?

13-14. How would you implement a shared leadership initiative in a company where you were the CEO? What elements of job design and redesign might you draw on to increase the effectiveness of the shared leadership initiative?

13-15. Can you think of any instances in which nonshared, traditional approaches to leadership would be preferable to a shared leadership approach? What are they, and how are they preferable? What sort of situational or individual factors lead to the traditional approach being more effective in these instances?

Sources: Based on J. Bell, P. Cubías, and B. Johnson, "Five Insights from Directors Sharing Power," *Nonprofit Quarterly,* March 28, 2017, https://nonprofitquarterly.org/2017/03/28/five-insights-directors-sharing-power/; D. Fitzsimons, "How Shared Leadership Changes Our Relationships at Work," *Harvard Business Review,* May 12, 2016, https://hbr.org/2016/05/how-shared-leadership-changes-our-relationships-at-work; N. Morrison, "Two Heads Are Better Than One: A Model of Shared Leadership," *Forbes,* December 21, 2013, https://www.forbes.com/sites/nickmorrison/2013/12/21/two-heads-are-better-than-one-a-model-of-shared-leadership/#d3bfeec540ac; D. Wang, D. A. Waldman, and Z. Zhang, "A Meta-Analysis of Shared Leadership and Team Effectiveness," *Journal of Applied Psychology* 99, no. 2 (2014): 181–98; and T. Watanabe and R. Xia, "UC Berkeley's new Chancellor Is Hailed as a 'Brilliant Choice,'" *Los Angeles Times,* March 13, 2017, http://www.latimes.com/local/lanow/la-me-ln-uc-berkeley-new-chancellor-20170313-story.html.

CASE INCIDENT 2 Andrea Illy: Leading a Family Company Responsibly

Founded in 1933 in Trieste, Italy, by Francesco Illy, the Illycaffè coffee dynasty is led today by the third generation of the family, with Chairperson Andrea Illy at its head. The firm operates in over 140 countries and has a turnover of about €500 million. More than 100,000 retailers serve Illy coffee, and the aim is to double that figure by 2027—but not at any cost. Mr. Illy is a firm believer in responsible business.

The 56-year-old has emerged as one of the most outspoken Italian business leaders. He has long espoused a sort of pick-and-mix version of capitalism, resolutely refusing to focus only on sales and profits. However, he rejects the notion his style of capitalism is charity, arguing instead that what he does is just good business.

This view has been shaped by the coffee sector itself, where issues such as sustainability have become a major concern. For decades, the company has paid its growers 30 percent higher than the average market value in order to maintain its supply of top Arabica beans. "This is not just good for society and workers but it is good for business," Illy says. "It is about shared values. It builds a long-term relationship with growers, which is good for customers, because of the quality of the coffee, and for our business too."

"This is about social responsibility," he insists, "but the real one and not the fake one. This is about being a stakeholder model and not a shareholder one. The business leader is always asking people to do things for him, but instead he should be asking: 'What can I do for you?'"

The Illy family is a supporter of arts and culture, including Trieste's annual sailing regatta, the Barcolana, where hundreds of boats race across the bay. Illy says this creates a virtuous circle: the more attractive Trieste becomes, the more talented people Illy can attract to work for the company, and the more visitors come to the city, raising its brand profile.

A portrait of his father Ernesto, one of his leadership heroes, hangs opposite his desk. "I put the painting there to ask him to control what I do," Illy says. But what has Illy learned from his family? "Society is made by the private sector, mostly," he says. "And if you want to improve society, then we need to be able to pursue long-term goals which are beyond profitability, and then you have to be free and accountable only to yourself."

Questions

13-16. Based on the concepts in this chapter, what is Andrea Illy's approach to leadership?

13-17. What evidence is there to suggest that his approach can be successful?

13-18. Identify some other business leaders who have similar leadership ideas. Have they been successful?

13-19. What arguments can you offer against responsible leadership?

Sources: Illy Shop website, www.illy.com, accessed August 11, 2020; and R. Sanderson, "Andrea Illy: Adapting a Family Business to a Multinational World," *Financial Times*, July 21, 2019.

ENDNOTES

[1] For a review, see D. S. Derue, J. D. Nahrgang, N. Wellman, and S. E. Humphrey, "Trait and Behavioral Theories of Leadership: An Integration and Meta-Analytic Test of Their Relative Validity," *Personnel Psychology* 64 (2011): 7–52.

[2] Derue, Nahrgang, Wellman, and Humphrey, "Trait and Behavioral Theories of Leadership"; and T. A. Judge, J. E. Bono, R. Ilies, and M. W. Gerhardt, "Personality and Leadership: A Qualitative and Quantitative Review," *Journal of Applied Psychology* (August 2002): 765–80.

[3] D. R. Ames and F. J. Flynn, "What Breaks a Leader: The Curvilinear Relation between Assertiveness and Leadership," *Journal of Personality and Social Psychology* 92, no. 2 (2007): 307–24.

[4] A. M. Grant, F. Gino, and D. A. Hofmann, "Reversing the Extraverted Leadership Advantage: The Role of Employee Proactivity," *Academy of Management Journal* 54, no. 3 (2011): 528–50.

[5] J. Hu, Z. Zhang, K. Jiang, and W. Chen, "Getting Ahead, Getting Along, and Getting Prosocial: Examining Extraversion Facets, Peer Reactions, and Leadership Emergence," *Journal of Applied Psychology* 104, no. 11 (2019): 1369–86.

[6] S. V. Marinova, H. Moon, and D. Kamdar, "Getting Ahead or Getting Along? The Two-Facet Conceptualization of Conscientiousness and Leadership Emergence," *Organization Science* 24, no. 4 (2012): 1257–76.

[7] Y. Wang, C.-H. Wu, and W. H. Mobley, "The Two Facets of Conscientiousness: Interaction of Achievement Orientation and Dependability in Predicting Managerial Execution Effectiveness," *Human Performance* 26 (2013): 275–96.

[8] R. B. Kaiser, J. M. LeBreton, and J. Hogan, "The Dark Side of Personality and Extreme Leader Behavior," *Applied Psychology: An International Review* 64, no. 1 (2015): 55–92.

[9] B. H. Gaddis and J. L. Foster, "Meta-Analysis of Dark Side Personality Characteristics and Critical Work Behaviors among Leaders across the Globe: Findings and Implications for Leadership Development and Executive Coaching," *Applied Psychology: An International Review* 64, no. 1 (2015): 25–54.

[10] R. H. Humphrey, J. M. Pollack, and T. H. Hawver, "Leading with Emotional Labor," *Journal of Managerial Psychology* 23 (2008): 151–68; and S. Melwani, J. S. Mueller, and J. R. Overbeck, "Looking Down: The Influence of Contempt and Compassion on Emergent Leadership Categorizations," *Journal of Applied*

Psychology 97, no. 6 (2012): 1171–85; M. A. Clark, M. M. Robertson, and S. Young, "'I Feel Your Pain': A Critical Review of Organizational Research on Empathy," *Journal of Organizational Behavior* 40 (2019): 166–92.

[11] P. D. Harms and M. Credé, "Emotional Intelligence and Transformational and Transactional Leadership: A Meta-Analysis," *Journal of Leadership & Organizational Studies* 17, no. 1 (2010): 5–17.

[12] S. Côté, P. N. Lopez, P. Salovey, and C. T. H. Miners, "Emotional Intelligence and Leadership Emergence in Small Groups," *Leadership Quarterly* 21 (2010): 496–508.

[13] N. Ensari, R. E. Riggio, J. Christian, and G. Carslaw, "Who Emerges as a Leader? Meta-Analyses of Individual Differences as Predictors of Leadership Emergence," *Personality and Individual Differences* 51, no. 4 (2011): 532–36.

[14] C. N. Lacerenza, D. L. Reyes, S. L. Marlow, D. L. Joseph, and E. Salas, "Leadership Training Design, Delivery, and Implementation: A Meta-Analysis," *Journal of Applied Psychology* 102, no. 12 (2017): 1686–718.

[15] T. A. Judge, R. F. Piccolo, and R. Ilies, "The Forgotten Ones? The Validity of Consideration and Initiating Structure in Leadership Research," *Journal of Applied Psychology* 89, no. 1 (2004): 36–51.

[16] D. Akst, "The Rewards of Recognizing a Job Well Done," *The Wall Street Journal,* January 31, 2007, D9.

[17] Judge, Piccolo, and Ilies, "The Forgotten Ones?"

[18] M. Javidan, P. W. Dorfman, M. S. de Luque, and R. J. House, "In the Eye of the Beholder: Cross Cultural Lessons in Leadership from Project GLOBE," *Academy of Management Perspectives* 20, no. 1 (2006): 67–90.

[19] F. E. Fiedler, "A Contingency Model of Leadership Effectiveness," *Advances in Experimental Social Psychology* 1 (1964): 149–90; for more current discussion on the model, see R. G. Lord, D. V. Day, S. J. Zaccaro, B. J. Avolio, and A. H. Eagly, "Leadership in Applied Psychology: Three Waves of Theory and Research," *Journal of Applied Psychology* 102, no. 3 (2017): 434–51.

[20] Ibid.

[21] L. H. Peters, D. D. Hartke, and J. T. Pohlmann, "Fiedler's Contingency Theory of Leadership: An Application of the Meta-Analysis Procedures of Schmidt and Hunter," *Psychological Bulletin* 97, no. 2 (1985): 274–85; and C. A. Schriesheim, B. J. Tepper, and L. A. Tetrault, "Least Preferred Co-Worker Score, Situational Control, and Leadership Effectiveness: A Meta-Analysis of Contingency Model Performance Predictions," *Journal of Applied Psychology* 79, no. 4 (1994): 561–73.

[22] R. P. Vecchio, "Situational Leadership Theory: An Examination of a Prescriptive Theory," *Journal of Applied Psychology* 72, no. 3 (1987): 444–51; and V. H. Vroom and A. G. Jago, "The Role of the Situation in Leadership," *American Psychologist* 62, no. 1 (2007): 17–24.

[23] See, for instance, G. Thompson and R. P. Vecchio, "Situational Leadership Theory: A Test of Three Versions," *Leadership Quarterly* 20, no. 5 (2009): 837–48; and R. P. Vecchio, C. R. Bullis, and D. M. Brazil, "The Utility of Situational Leadership Theory—a Replication in a Military Setting," *Small Group Research* 37, no. 5 (2006): 407–24.

[24] R. J. House, "A Path-Goal Theory of Leader Effectiveness," *Administrative Science Quarterly* 16 (1971): 321–38; and R. J. House and G. Dessler, "The Path-Goal Theory of Leadership: Some *Post Hoc* and A Priori Tests," in J. G. Hunt and L. L. Larson (eds.), *Contingency Approaches to Leadership* (Carbondale, IL: Southern Illinois University Press, 1974): 29–55.

[25] S. H. Malik, H. Sikandar, H. Hassan, and S. Aziz, "Path Goal Theory: A Study of Job Satisfaction in the Telecom Sector," in C. Dan (ed.), *Management and Service Science* 8 (2001): 127–34; and R. R. Vecchio, J. E. Justin, and C. L. Pearce, "The Utility of Transactional and Transformational Leadership for Predicting Performance and Satisfaction within a Path-Goal Theory Framework," *Journal of Occupational and Organizational Psychology* 81 (2008): 71–82.

[26] For a review, see Vroom and Jago, "The Role of the Situation in Leadership."

[27] W. Bennis, "The Challenges of Leadership in the Modern World," *American Psychologist* 62, no. 1 (2007): 2–5.

[28] F. Dansereau, G. B. Graen, and W. Haga, "A Vertical Dyad Linkage Approach to Leadership in Formal Organizations," *Organizational Behavior and Human Performance* 13 (1975): 46–78; and R. Martin, Y. Guillaume, G. Thomas, A. Lee, and O. Epitropaki, "Leader-Member Exchange (LMX) and Performance: A Meta-Analytic Review," *Personnel Psychology* 69 (2016): 67–121.

[29] S. J. Wayne, L. M. Shore, W. H. Bommer, and L. E. Tetrick, "The Role of Fair Treatment and Rewards in Perceptions of Organizational Support and Leader–Member Exchange," *Journal of Applied Psychology* 87, no. 3 (2002): 590–98.

[30] Z. Liao, W. Liu, X. Li, and Z. Song, "Give and Take: An Episodic Perspective on Leader-Member Exchange," *Journal of Applied Psychology* 104, no. 1 (2019): 34–51.

[31] M. Uhl-Bien, "Relationship Development as a Key Ingredient for Leadership Development," in S. E. Murphy and R. E. Riggio (eds.), *Future of Leadership Development* (Mahwah, NJ: Lawrence Erlbaum, 2003): 129–47.

[32] R. Vecchio and D. M. Brazil, "Leadership and Sex-Similarity: A Comparison in a Military Setting," *Personnel Psychology* 60 (2007): 303–35.

[33] A. Lee, G. Thomas, R. Martin, Y. Guillaume, and A. F. Marstand, "Beyond Relationship Quality: The Role of Leader-Member Exchange Importance in Leader-Follower Dyads," *Journal of Occupational and Organizational Psychology* 92 (2019): 736–63.

[34] Z. Chen, W. Lam, and J. A. Zhong, "Leader–Member Exchange and Member Performance: A New Look at Individual-Level Negative Feedback-Seeking Behavior and Team-Level Empowerment Culture," *Journal of Applied Psychology* 92, no. 1 (2007): 202–12; R. Ilies, J. D. Nahrgang, and F. P. Morgeson, "Leader–Member Exchange and Citizenship Behaviors: A Meta-Analysis," *Journal of Applied Psychology* 92, no. 1 (2007): 269–77; and Martin, Guillaume, Thomas, Lee, and Epitropaki, "Leader-Member Exchange (LMX) and Performance." For a critique of the LMX literature, see R. K. Gottfredson, S. L. Wright, and E. D. Heaphy, "A Critique of the Leader-Member Exchange Construct: Back to Square One," *The Leadership Quarterly* (in press).

[35] Martin, Guillaume, Thomas, Lee, and Epitropaki, "Leader-Member Exchange (LMX) and Performance."

[36] X.-H. Wang, Y. Fang, I. Qureshi, and O. Janssen, "Understanding Employee Innovative Behavior: Integrating the Social Network and Leader-Member Exchange Perspectives," *Journal of Organizational Behavior* 36, no. 3 (2015): 403–20.

[37] S. Park, M. C. Sturman, C. Vanderpool, and E. Chan, "Only Time Will Tell: The Changing Relationships between LMX, Job Performance, and Justice," *Journal of Applied Psychology* 100, no. 3 (2015): 660–80.

[38] P. R. Vidyarthi, B. Erdogan, S. Anand, R. C. Liden, and A. Chaudhry, "One Member,

Two Leaders: Extending Leader-Member Exchange Theory to a Dual Leadership Context," *Journal of Applied Psychology* 99, no. 3 (2014): 468–83.

[39] S. Raghuram, R. S. Gajendran, X. Liu, and D. Somaya, "Boundaryless LMX: Examining LMX's Impact on External Career Outcomes and Alumni Goodwill," *Personnel Psychology* 70, no. 2 (2017): 399-428.

[40] A. Lee, A. Gerbasi, G. Schwarz, and A. Newman, "Leader-Member Exchange Social Comparisons and Follower Outcomes: The Roles of Felt Obligation and Psychological Entitlement," *Journal of Occupational and Organizational Psychology* 92 (2019): 593–617.

[41] B. Erdogan and T. N. Bauer, "Differentiated Leader-Member Exchanges: The Buffering Role of Justice Climate," *Journal of Applied Psychology* 95, no. 6 (2010): 1104–20.

[42] D. Liu, M. Hernandez, and L. Wang, "The Role of Leadership and Trust in Creating Structural Patterns of Team Procedural Justice: A Social Network Investigation," *Personnel Psychology* 67 (2014): 801–45.

[43] A. N. Li and H. Liao, "How Do Leader-Member Exchange Quality and Differentiation Affect Performance in Teams? An Integrated Multilevel Dual Process Model," *Journal of Applied Psychology* 99, no. 5 (2014): 847–66.

[44] L. C. Wang and J. R. Hollenbeck, "LMX in Team-Based Contexts: TMX, Authority Differentiation, and Skill Differentiation as Boundary Conditions for Leader Reciprocation," *Personnel Psychology* 72 (2019): 271–90.

[45] J. Hu and R. C. Liden, "Relative Leader-Member Exchange within Team Contexts: How and When Social Comparison Impacts Individual Effectiveness," *Personnel Psychology* 66 (2013): 127–72.

[46] M. Weber, *The Theory of Social and Economic Organization*, A. M. Henderson and T. Parsons (trans.), (Eastford, CT: Martino Fine Books, 2012).

[47] R. J. House, "A 1976 Theory of Charismatic Leadership," in J. G. Hunt and L. L. Larson (eds.), *The Cutting Edge* (Carbondale, IL: Southern Illinois University Press, 1977): 189–207; see also J. Antonakis, N. Bastardoz, P. Jacquart, and B. Shamir, "Charisma: An Ill-Defined and Ill-Measured Gift," *Annual Review of Organizational Psychology and Organizational Behavior* 3 (2016): 293–319; L. L. Watts, L. M. Steele, and M. D. Mumford, "Making Sense of Pragmatic and Charismatic Leadership Stories," *The Leadership Quarterly* 30 (2019): 243–59.

[48] Antonakis, Bastardoz, Jacquart, and Shamir, "Charisma"; and J. A. Conger and R. N. Kanungo, *Charismatic Leadership in Organizations* (Thousand Oaks, CA: Sage, 1998).

[49] A. H. B. De Hoogh and D. N. Den Hartog, "Neuroticism and Locus of Control as Moderators of the Relationships of Charismatic and Autocratic Leadership with Burnout," *Journal of Applied Psychology* 94, no. 4 (2009): 1058–68; A. H. B. De Hoogh, D. N. Den Hartog, and P. L. Koopman, "Linking the Big-Five Factors of Personality to Charismatic and Transactional Leadership; Perceived Dynamic Work Environment as a Moderator," *Journal of Organizational Behavior* 26 (2005): 839–65; and S. Oreg and Y. Berson, "Personality and Charismatic Leadership in Context: The Moderating Role of Situational Stress," *Personnel Psychology* 68 (2015): 49–77.

[50] M. Frese, S. Beimel, and S. Schoenborn, "Action Training for Charismatic Leadership: Two Evaluations of Studies of a Commercial Training Module on Inspirational Communication of a Vision," *Personnel Psychology* 56 (2003): 671–97.

[51] Antonakis, Bastardoz, Jacquart, and Shamir, "Charisma"; and Conger and Kanungo, *Charismatic Leadership in Organizations.*

[52] T. Maran, M. Furtner, S. Liegl, S. Kraus, and P. Sachse, "In the Eye of a Leader: Eye-directed Gazing Shapes Perceptions of Leaders' Charisma," *The Leadership Quarterly* (in press).

[53] Y. Berson, D. A. Waldman, and C. L. Pearce, "Enhancing Our Understanding of Vision in Organizations: Toward an Integration of Leader and Follower Processes," *Organizational Psychology Review* 6, no. 2 (2016): 171–91. For reviews on the role of vision in leadership, see S. J. Zaccaro, "Visionary and Inspirational Models of Executive Leadership: Empirical Review and Evaluation," in S. J. Zaccaro (ed.), *The Nature of Executive Leadership: A Conceptual and Empirical Analysis of Success* (Washington, DC: American Psychological Association, 2001): 259–78; and M. Hauser and R. J. House, "Lead Through Vision and Values," in E. A. Locke (ed.), *Handbook of Principles of Organizational Behavior* (Malden, MA: Blackwell, 2004): 257–73.

[54] A. Erez, V. F. Misangyi, D. E. Johnson, M. A. LePine, and K. C. Halverson, "Stirring the Hearts of Followers: Charismatic Leadership as the Transferal of Affect," *Journal of Applied Psychology* 93, no. 3 (2008): 602–15; and A. Xenikou, "The Cognitive and Affective Components of Organisational Identification: The Role of Perceived Support Values and Charismatic Leadership," *Applied Psychology: An International Review* 63, no. 4 (2014): 567–88.

[55] P. Jacquart and J. Antonakis, "When Does Charisma Matter for Top-Level Leaders? Effect of Attributional Ambiguity," *Academy of Management Journal* 58, no. 4 (2015): 1051–74.

[56] M. J. Young, M. W. Morris, and V. M. Scherwin, "Managerial Mystique: Magical Thinking in Judgments of Managers' Vision, Charisma, and Magnetism," *Journal of Management* 39, no. 4 (2013): 1044–61.

[57] F. Cohen, S. Solomon, M. Maxfield, T. Pyszczynski, and J. Greenberg, "Fatal Attraction: The Effects of Mortality Salience on Evaluations of Charismatic, Task-Oriented, and Relationship-Oriented Leaders," *Psychological Science* 15, no. 12 (2004): 846–51; and M. G. Ehrhart and K. J. Klein, "Predicting Followers' Preferences for Charismatic Leadership: The Influence of Follower Values and Personality," *Leadership Quarterly* 12, no. 2 (2001): 153–79; K. Breevaart and R. E. de Vries, "Followers' HEXACO Personality Traits and Preferences for Charismatic, Relationship-Oriented, and Task-Oriented Leadership," *Journal of Business and Psychology* (in press).

[58] J. C. Pastor, M. Mayo, and B. Shamir, "Adding Fuel to Fire: The Impact of Followers' Arousal on Ratings of Charisma," *Journal of Applied Psychology* 92, no. 6 (2007): 1584–96.

[59] Dhawan, B. (2018). "Want to make UP most developed state in India: CM Yogi". *Inshorts (February 28, 2018).* Retrieved from https://inshorts.com (Accessed on April 12, 2022).

[60] C. M. Barnes, C. L. Guarana, S. Nauman, and D. T. Kong, "Too Tired to Inspire or Be Inspired: Sleep Deprivation and Charismatic Leadership," *Journal of Applied Psychology* 101, no. 8 (2016): 1191–9.

[61] See, for instance, R. Khurana, *Searching for a Corporate Savior: The Irrational Quest for Charismatic CEOs* (Princeton, NJ: Princeton University Press, 2002); and J. A. Raelin, "The Myth of Charismatic Leaders," *Training & Development* (March 2003): 47–54.

[62] B. M. Galvin, D. A. Waldman, and P. Balthazard, "Visionary Communication Qualities as Mediators of the Relationship between Narcissism and Attributions of Leader Charisma," *Personnel Psychology* 63, no. 3 (2010): 509–37.
[63] See, for instance, B. M. Bass, *Leadership and Performance Beyond Expectations* (New York, NY: Free Press, 1990); B. M. Bass, "Two Decades of Research and Development in Transformational Leadership," *European Journal of Work and Organizational Psychology* 8 (1999): 9–32; and B. M. Bass and R. E. Riggio, *Transformational Leadership*, 2nd ed. (Mahwah, NJ: Lawrence Erlbaum, 2006).
[64] T. A. Judge and R. F. Piccolo, "Transformational and Transactional Leadership: A Meta-Analytic Test of Their Relative Validity," *Journal of Applied Psychology* 89, no. 5 (2004): 755–68; D. Montano, A. Reeske, F. Franke, and J. Hüffmeier, "Leadership, Followers' Mental Health and Job Performance in Organizations: A Comprehensive Meta-Analysis from an Occupational Health Perspective," *Journal of Organizational Behavior* 38 (2017): 32–50; and G. Wang, I.-S. Oh, S. H. Courtright, and A. E. Colbert, "Transformational Leadership and Performance across Criteria and Levels: A Meta-Analytic Review of 25 Years of Research," *Group & Organization Management* 36, no. 2 (2011): 223–70. For a critique, see N. Siangchokyoo, R. L. Klinger, and E. D. Campion, "Follower Transformation as the Linchpin of Transformational Leadership Theory: A Systematic Review and Future Research Agenda," *The Leadership Quarterly* (in press).
[65] A. M. Grant, "Leading with Meaning: Beneficiary Contact, Prosocial Impact, and the Performance Effects of Transformational Leadership," *Academy of Management Journal* 55 (2012): 458–76.
[66] M. A. Robinson and K. Boies, "Different Ways to Get the Job Done: Comparing the Effects of Intellectual Stimulation and Contingent Reward Leadership on Task-Related Outcomes," *Journal of Applied Social Psychology* 46 (2016): 336–53.
[67] Derue, Nahrgang, Wellman, and Humphrey, "Trait and Behavioral Theories of Leadership."
[68] Ibid.
[69] S. Kovjanic, S. C. Schuh, K. Jonas, N. Van Quauqebeke, and R. van Dick, "How Do Transformational Leaders Foster Positive Employee Outcomes? A Self-Determination-Based Analysis of Employees' Needs as Mediating Links," *Journal of Organizational Behavior* 33, no. 8 (2012): 1031–52.
[70] S. B. Dust, C. J. Resick, and M. B. Mawritz, "Transformational Leadership, Psychological Empowerment, and the Moderating Role of Mechanistic-Organic Contexts," *Journal of Organizational Behavior* 35, no. 3 (2014): 413–33.
[71] Y. Zhu and S. Akhtar, "How Transformational Leadership Influences Follower Helping Behavior: The Role of Trust and Prosocial Motivation," *Journal of Organizational Behavior* 35, no. 3 (2014): 373–92.
[72] S. M. Conchie, "Transformational Leadership, Intrinsic Motivation, and Trust: A Moderated-Mediated Model of Workplace Safety," *Journal of Occupational Health Psychology* 18, no. 2 (2013): 198–210; and R. Kark, T. Katz-Navon, and M. Delegach, "The Dual Effects of Leading for Safety: The Mediating Role of Employee Regulatory Focus," *Journal of Applied Psychology* 100, no. 5 (2015): 1332–48.
[73] A. E. Colbert, A. E. Kristof-Brown, B. H. Bradley, and M. R. Barrick, "CEO Transformational Leadership: The Role of Goal Importance Congruence in Top Management Teams," *Academy of Management Journal* 51, no. 1 (2008): 81–96.
[74] D. Zohar and O. Tenne-Gazit, "Transformational Leadership and Group Interaction as Climate Antecedents: A Social Network Analysis," *Journal of Applied Psychology* 93, no. 4 (2008): 744–57.
[75] Y. Dong, K. M. Bartol, Z.-X. Zhang, and C. Li, "Enhancing Employee Creativity via Individual Skill Development and Team Knowledge Sharing: Influences of Dual-Focused Transformational Leadership," *Journal of Organizational Behavior* 38, no. 3 (2017): 439–58.
[76] N. Li, D. S. Chiaburu, B. L. Kirkman, and Z. Xie, "Spotlight on the Followers: An Examination of Moderators of Relationships between Transformational Leadership and Subordinates' Citizenship and Taking Charge," *Personnel Psychology* 66 (2013): 225–60; and X. Wang and J. M. Howell, "Exploring the Dual-Level Effects of Transformational Leadership on Followers," *Journal of Applied Psychology* 95, no. 6 (2010): 1134–44.
[77] Y. Ling, Z. Simsek, M. H. Lubatkin, and J. F. Veiga, "The Impact of Transformational CEOs on the Performance of Small- to Medium-Sized Firms: Does Organizational Context Matter?," *Journal of Applied Psychology* 93, no. 4 (2008): 923–34.
[78] Gautam, V. (2022). "Women's Day Special: Meet 10 Indian Women Leaders Who Are Heading Global Companies". *India Times (March 8, 2022).* Retrieved from https://www.indiatimes.com (Accessed on April 12, 2022).
[79] K. Breevaart and A. B. Bakker, "Daily Job Demands and Employee Work Engagement: The Role of Daily Transformational Leadership Behavior," *Journal of Occupational Health Psychology* (in press).
[80] C. J. Syrek, E. Apostel, and C. H. Antoni, "Stress in Highly Demanding IT Jobs: Transformational Leadership Moderates the Impact of Time Pressure on Exhaustion and Work-Life Balance," *Journal of Occupational Health Psychology* 18, no. 3 (2013): 252–61.
[81] J. Schaubroeck, S. S. K. Lam, and S. E. Cha, "Embracing Transformational Leadership: Team Values and the Impact of Leader Behavior on Team Performance," *Journal of Applied Psychology* 92, no. 4 (2007): 1020–30.
[82] K. Hildenbrand, C. A. Sacramento, and C. Binnewies, "Transformational Leadership and Burnout: The Role of Thriving and Followers' Openness to Experience," *Journal of Occupational Health Psychology* (in press).
[83] J. Antonakis, R. J. House, and D. K. Simonton, "Can Super Smart Leaders Suffer from Too Much of a Good Thing? The Curvilinear Effect of Intelligence on Perceived Leadership Behavior," *Journal of Applied Psychology* 102, no. 7 (2017): 1003–21.
[84] D. N. Den Hartog and F. D. Belschak, "When Does Transformational Leadership Enhance Employee Proactive Behavior? The Role of Autonomy and Role Breadth Self-Efficacy," *Journal of Applied Psychology* 97, no. 1 (2012): 194–202.
[85] Judge and Piccolo, "Transformational and Transactional Leadership"; Montano, Reeske, Franke, and Hüffmeier, "Leadership, Followers' Mental Health and Job Performance in Organizations"; and Wang, Oh, Courtright, and Colbert, "Transformational Leadership and Performance across Criteria and Levels."
[86] Judge and Piccolo, "Transformational and Transactional Leadership."
[87] Derue, Nahrgang, Wellman, and Humphrey, "Trait and Behavioral Theories of Leadership."

[88] Lord, Day, Zaccaro, Avolio, and Eagly, "Leadership in Applied Psychology."
[89] R. Safian, "Facebook, Airbnb, Uber, and the Struggle to Do the Right Thing," *Fast Company*, April 11, 2017, https://www.fastcompany.com/40397294/facebook-airbnb-uber-and-the-struggle-to-do-the-right-thing; and C. Tan, "CEO Pinching Penney in a Slowing Economy," *The Wall Street Journal*, January 31, 2008, 1–2.
[90] F. Luthans and B. J. Avolio, "Authentic Leadership Development," in K. S. Cameron, J. E. Dutton, and R. Quinn (eds.), *Positive Organizational Scholarship: Foundations of a New Discipline* (San Francisco, CA: Barrett-Koehler, 2003): 241–61; and F. O. Walumbwa, B. J. Avolio, W. L. Gardner, T. S. Wernsing, and S. J. Peterson, "Authentic Leadership: Development and Validation of a Theory-Based Measure?," *Journal of Management* 34 (2008): 89–126. For a critique, see M. Alvesson and K. Einola, "Warning for Excessive Positivity: Authentic Leadership and Other Traps in Leadership Studies," *The Leadership Quarterly* 30 (2019): 383–95.
[91] B. P. Owens and D. R. Hekman, "Modeling How to Grow: An Inductive Examination of Humble Leader Behaviors, Contingencies, and Outcomes," *Academy of Management Journal* 55 (2012): 787–818.
[92] S. T. Hannah, F. O. Walumbwa, and L. W. Fry, "Leadership in Action Teams: Team Leader and Members' Authenticity, Authenticity Strength, and Team Outcomes," *Personnel Psychology* 64 (2011): 771–802; and K. M. Hmieleski, M. S. Cole, and R. A. Baron, "Shared Authentic Leadership and New Venture Performance," *Journal of Management*, 2012, 1476–99.
[93] T. Simons, H. Leroy, V. Collewaert, and S. Masschelein, "How Leader Alignment of Words and Deeds Affects Followers: A Meta-Analysis of Behavioral Integrity Research," *Journal of Business Ethics* 132 (2015): 831–44.
[94] H. Leroy, F. Anseel, W. L. Gardner, and L. Sels, "Authentic Leadership, Authentic Followership, Basic Need Satisfaction, and Work Role Performance," *Journal of Management* 41, no. 6 (2015): 1677–97.
[95] C. Gill and A. Caza, "An Investigation of Authentic Leadership's Individual and Group Influences on Follower Responses," *Journal of Management* (in press).
[96] J. Stouten, M. van Dijke, and D. De Cremer, "Ethical Leadership: An Overview and Future Perspectives," *Journal of Personnel Psychology* 11 (2012): 1–6.
[97] J. M. Schaubroeck, S. T. Hannah, B. J. Avolio, S. W. J. Kozlowski, R. G. Lord, L. K. Treviño … and A. C. Peng, "Embedding Ethical Leadership within and across Organization Levels," *Academy of Management Journal* 55, no. 5 (2012): 1053–78.
[98] T. W. H. Ng and D. C. Feldman, "Ethical Leadership: Meta-Analytic Evidence of Criterion-Related and Incremental Validity," *Journal of Applied Psychology* 100, no. 3 (2015): 948–65; T. W. H. Ng, Mo Wang, D. Y. Hsu, and C. Su, "Changes in Perceptions of Ethical Leadership: Effects on Associative and Dissociative Outcomes," *Journal of Applied Psychology* (in press).
[99] Ibid.
[100] C. J. Resick, M. B. Hargis, P. Shao, and S. B. Dust, "Ethical Leadership, Moral Equity Judgments, and Discretionary Workplace Behavior," *Human Relations* 66, no. 7 (2013): 951–72.
[101] L. Huang and T. A. Paterson, "Group Ethical Voice: Influence of Ethical Leadership and Impact on Ethical Performance," *Journal of Management* 43, no. 4 (2017): 1157–84; and K. Kalshoven, D. N. Den Hartog, and A. H. B. De Hoogh, "Ethical Leadership and Follower Helping and Courtesy: Moral Awareness and Empathic Concern as Moderators," *Applied Psychology: An International Review* 62, no. 2 (2013): 211–35.
[102] D. M. Mayer, K. Aquino, R. L. Greenbaum, and M. Kuenzi, "Who Displays Ethical Leadership, and Why Does It Matter? An Examination of Antecedents and Consequences of Ethical Leadership," *Academy of Management Journal* 55 (2012): 151–71.
[103] M. Schaubroeck, S. S. K. Lam, and A. C. Peng, "Can Peers' Ethical and Transformational Leadership Improve Coworkers' Service Quality? A Latent Growth Analysis," *Organizational Behavior and Human Decision Processes* 133 (2016): 45–68.
[104] J. M. Jensen, M. S. Cole, and R. S. Rubin, "Predicting Retail Shrink from Performance Pressure, Ethical Leader Behaivor, and Store-level Incivility," *Journal of Organizational Behavior* 40 (2019): 723–39.
[105] M. E. Brown and L. K. Treviño, "Socialized Charismatic Leadership, Values Congruence, and Deviance in Work Groups," *Journal of Applied Psychology* 91, no. 4 (2006): 954–62.
[106] M. E. Brown and L. K. Treviño, "Leader-Follower Values Congruence: Are Socialized Charismatic Leaders Better Able to Achieve It?," *Journal of Applied Psychology* 94, no. 2 (2009): 478–90.
[107] B. Ogunfowora, "It's All a Matter of Consensus: Leader Role Modeling Strength as a Moderator of the Links between Ethical Leadership and Employee Outcomes," *Human Relations* 67, no. 12 (2014): 1467–90.
[108] S. A. Eisenbeiss and S. R. Giessner, "The Emergence and Maintenance of Ethical Leadership in Organizations," *Journal of Personnel Psychology* 11 (2012): 7–19.
[109] S. A. Eisenbeiss and D. van Knippenberg, "On Ethical Leadership Impact: The Role of Follower Mindfulness and Moral Emotions," *Journal of Organizational Behavior* 36, no. 2 (2015): 182–95.
[110] J. Antonakis, M. Fenley, and S. Liechti, "Learning Charisma," *Harvard Business Review* (June 2012): 127–30.
[111] S.-H. Lin, J. Ma, and R. E. Johnson, "When Ethical Leader Behavior Breaks Bad: How Ethical Leader Behavior Can Turn Abusive via Ego Depletion and Moral Licensing," *Journal of Applied Psychology* 101, no. 6 (2016): 815–30.
[112] R. Fehr, A. Fulmer, and F. T. Keng-Highberger, "How Do Employees React to Leaders' Unethical Behavior? The Role of Moral Disengagement," *Personnel Psychology* 73 (2020): 73–93.
[113] M. Mawritz, R. L. Greenbaum, M. Butts, and K. Graham, "We're All Capable of Being an Abusive Boss," *Harvard Business Review*, October 14, 2016, https://hbr.org/2016/10/were-all-capable-of-being-an-abusive-boss.
[114] B. J. Tepper, M. K. Duffy, C. A. Henle, and L. S. Lambert, "Procedural Injustice, Victim Precipitation, and Abusive Supervision," *Personnel Psychology* 59, no. 1 (2006): 101–23.
[115] J. D. Mackey, R. E. Frieder, J. R. Brees, and M. J. Martinko, "Abusive Supervision: A Meta-Analysis and Empirical Review," *Journal of Management* 43, no. 6 (2017): 1940–65.
[116] B. J. Tepper, "Consequences of Abusive Supervision," *Academy of Management Journal* 43 (2000): 178–90.
[117] Mackey, Frieder, Brees, and Martinko, "Abusive Supervision."
[118] P. Raymund, J. M. Garcia, S. L. D. Restuborg, C. Kiewitz, K. L. Scott, and R. L. Tang, "Roots Run Deep: Investigating Psychological Mechanisms between History of Family Aggression and Abusive Supervision," *Journal of Applied Psychology* 99, no. 5 (2014): 883–97.

[119] Mackey, Frieder, Brees, and Martinko, "Abusive Supervision."
[120] L. S. Simon, C. Hurst, K. Kelley, and T. A. Judge, "Understanding Cycles of Abuse: A Multimotive Approach," *Journal of Applied Psychology* 100, no. 6 (2015): 1798–810.
[121] M. K. Shoss, R. Eisenberger, S. L. D. Restubog, and T. J. Zagenczyk, "Blaming the Organization for Abusive Supervision: The Roles of Perceived Organizational Support and Supervisor's Organizational Embodiment," *Journal of Applied Psychology* 98, no. 1 (2013): 158–68.
[122] A. K. Nandkeolyar, J. A. Shaffer, A. Li, S. Ekkirala, and J. Bagger, "Surviving an Abusive Supervisor: The Joint Roles of Conscientiousness and Coping Strategies," *Journal of Applied Psychology* 99, no. 1 (2014): 138–50.
[123] D. van Dierendonck, "Servant Leadership: A Review and Synthesis," *Journal of Management* 37, no. 4 (2011): 1228–61; N. Eva, M. Robin, S. Sendjaya, D. van Dierendonck, and R. C. Liden, "Servant Leadership: A Systematic Review and Call for Future Research," *The Leadership Quarterly* 30 (2019): 111–32.
[124] S. J. Peterson, F. M. Galvin, and D. Lange, "CEO Servant Leadership: Exploring Executive Characteristics and Firm Performance," *Personnel Psychology* 65 (2012): 565–96.
[125] Singh, Sonika & Ryhal, Piar. (2020). How Does Servant Leadership Behaviour Affect Job Satisfaction? A Study on Indian Academia. *FIIB Business Review.* 10. 231971452096869. 10.1177/231971452096869.
[126] Kashyap, V. "Impact of Servant Leadership Style on Employee's Intentions to Stay in Indian Organizations". *Indian Institute of Ahmedabad.* Retrieved from http://vslir.iima.ac.in (Accessed on April 12, 2022).
[127] Z. Chen, J. Zhu, and M. Zhou, "How Does a Servant Leader Fuel the Service Fire? A Multilevel Model of Servant Leadership, Individual Self Identity, Group Competition Climate, and Customer Service Performance," *Journal of Applied Psychology* 100, no. 2 (2015): 511–21.
[128] D. De Cremer, D. M. Mayer, M. van Dijke, B. C. Schouten, and M. Bardes, "When Does Self-Sacrificial Leadership Motivate Prosocial Behavior? It Depends on Followers' Prevention Focus," *Journal of Applied Psychology* 94, no. 4 (2009): 887–99.
[129] J. Hu and R. C. Liden, "Antecedents of Team Potency and Team Effectiveness: An Examination of Goal and Process Clarity and Servant Leadership," *Journal of Applied Psychology* 96, no. 4 (July 2011): 851–62.
[130] M. J. Neubert, K. M. Kacmar, D. S. Carlson, L. B. Chonko, and J. A. Roberts, "Regulatory Focus as a Mediator of the Influence of Initiating Structure and Servant Leadership on Employee Behavior," *Journal of Applied Psychology* 93, no. 6 (2008): 1220–33.
[131] G. James Lemoine and T. C. Blum, "Servant Leadership, Leader Gender, and Team Gender Role: Testing a Female Advantage in a Cascading Model of Performance," *Personnel Psychology* (in press).
[132] T. Menon, J. Sim, J. Ho-Ying Fu, C. Chiu, and Y. Hong, "Blazing the Trail versus Trailing the Group: Culture and Perceptions of the Leader's Position," *Organizational Behavior and Human Decision Processes* 113, no. 1 (2010): 51–61.
[133] D. M. Rousseau, S. B. Sitkin, R. S. Burt, and C. Camerer, "Not So Different after All: A Cross-Discipline View of Trust," *Academy of Management Review* 23, no. 3 (1998): 393–404; and J. A. Simpson, "Psychological Foundations of Trust," *Current Directions in Psychological Science* 16, no. 5 (2007): 264–68; A. Cristina Costa, C. Ashley Fulmer, and N. R. Anderson, "Trust in Work Teams: An Integrative Review, Multilevel Model, and Future Research Directions," *Journal of Organizational Behavior* 39 (2018): 169–84.
[134] See, for instance, K. T. Dirks and D. L. Ferrin, "Trust in Leadership: Meta-Analytic Findings and Implications for Research and Practice," *Journal of Applied Psychology* 87, no. 4 (2002): 611–28; Martin, Guillaume, Thomas, Lee, and Epitropaki, "Leader-Member Exchange (LMX) and Performance."
[135] R. C. Mayer, J. H. Davis, and F. D. Schoorman, "An Integrative Model of Organizational Trust: Past, Present, and Future," *Academy of Management Review* 32, no. 2 (2007): 344–54.
[136] J. Schaubroeck, S. S. K. Lam, and A. C. Peng, "Cognition-Based and Affect-Based Trust as Mediators of Leader Behavior Influences on Team Performance," *Journal of Applied Psychology* 96, no. 4 (2011): 863–71.
[137] J. A. Colquitt, B. A. Scott, and J. A. LePine, "Trust, Trustworthiness, and Trust Propensity: A Meta-Analytic Test of Their Unique Relationships with Risk Taking and Job Performance," *Journal of Applied Psychology* 92, no. 4 (2007): 909–27; and S. R. Giessner and D. van Knippenberg, "'License to Fail': Goal Definition, Leader Group Prototypicality, and Perceptions of Leadership Effectiveness after Leader Failure," *Organizational Behavior and Human Decision Processes* 105, no. 1 (2008): 14–35.
[138] S. M. Conchie, P. J. Taylor, and I. J. Donald, "Promoting Safety Voice with Safety-Specific Transformational Leadership: The Mediating Role of Two Dimensions of Trust," *Journal of Occupational Health Psychology* 17, no. 1 (2012): 105–15; and J. R. Detert and E. R. Burris, "Leadership Behavior and Employee Voice: Is the Door Really Open?," *Academy of Management Journal* 50, no. 4 (2007): 869–84; S. Loretta Kim, "Enticing High Performers to Stay and Share Their Knowledge: The Importance of Trust in Leader," *Human Resource Management* 58 (2019): 341–51.
[139] B. A. De Jong, K. T. Dirks, and N. Gillespie, "Trust and Team Performance: A Meta-Analysis of Main Effects, Moderators, and Covariates," *Journal of Applied Psychology* 101, no. 8 (2016): 1134–50.
[140] Colquitt, Scott, and LePine, "Trust, Trustworthiness, and Trust Propensity."
[141] Colquitt, Scott, and LePine, "Trust, Trustworthiness, and Trust Propensity"; and Mayer, Davis, and Schoorman, "An Integrative Model of Organizational Trust."
[142] Cited in D. Jones, "Do You Trust Your CEO?," *USA Today,* February 12, 2003, 7B.
[143] Mayer, Davis, and Schoorman, "An Integrative Model of Organizational Trust."
[144] J. A. Simpson, "Foundations of Interpersonal Trust," in A. W. Kruglanski and E. T. Higgins (eds.), *Social Psychology: Handbook of Basic Principles,* 2nd ed. (New York: Guilford, 2007): 587–607.
[145] X.-P. Chen, M. B. Eberly, T.-J. Chiang, J.-L. Farh, and B.-Shiuan Cheng, "Affective Trust in Chinese Leaders: Linking Paternalistic Leadership to Employee Performance," *Journal of Management* 40, no. 3 (2014): 796–819.
[146] J. A. Simpson, "Foundations of Interpersonal Trust."
[147] P. H. Kim, C. D. Cooper, K. T. Dirks, and D. L. Ferrin, "Repairing Trust with Individuals vs. Groups," *Organizational Behavior and Human Decision Processes* 120, no. 1 (2013): 1–14.
[148] B. Groysberg and M. Slind, "Leadership Is a Conversation," *Harvard Business Review* (June 2012): 76–84.
[149] Ibid.
[150] K. Breevaart and H. Zacher, "Main and Interactive Effects of Weekly

Transformational and Laissez-Faire Leadership on Followers' Trust in the Leader and Leader Effectiveness," *Journal of Occupational and Organizational Psychology* 92 (2019): 384–409; B. Shao, "Moral Anger as a Dilemma? An Investigation on How Leader Moral Anger Influences Follower Trust," *The Leadership Quarterly* 30 (2019): 365–82.

[151] H. Zhao, S. J. Wayne, B. C. Glibkowski, and J. Bravo, "The Impact of Psychological Contract Breach on Work-Related Outcomes: A Meta-Analysis," *Personnel Psychology* 60 (2007): 647–80.

[152] D. L. Ferrin, P. H. Kim, C. D. Cooper, and K. T. Dirks, "Silence Speaks Volumes: The Effectiveness of Reticence in Comparison to Apology and Denial for Responding to Integrity- and Competence-Based Trust Violations," *Journal of Applied Psychology* 92, no. 4 (2007): 893–908; and Kim, Cooper, Dirks, and Ferrin, "Reparing Trust with Individuals vs. Groups."

[153] M. E. Schweitzer, J. C. Hershey, and E. T. Bradlow, "Promises and Lies: Restoring Violated Trust," *Organizational Behavior and Human Decision Processes* 101, no. 1 (2006): 1–19.

[154] K. E. Kram, "Phases of the Mentor Relationship," *Academy of Management Journal* 26 (1983): 608–25; and K. E. Kram, *Mentoring at Work: Developmental Relationships in Organizational Life* (Glenview, IL: Foresman, 1985).

[155] T. A. Scandura, "Mentorship and Career Mobility: An Empirical Investigation," *Journal of Organizational Behavior* 13 (1992): 169–74.

[156] C. R. Wanberg, E. T. Welsh, and S. A. Hezlett, "Mentoring Research: A Review and Dynamic Process Model," in G. R. Ferris and J. J. Martocchio (eds.), *Research in Personnel and Human Resources Management*, vol. 22 (Greenwich, CT: Elsevier Science, 2003): 39–124; and T. D. Allen, "Protégé Selection by Mentors: Contributing Individual and Organizational Factors," *Journal of Vocational Behavior* 65, no. 3 (2004): 469–83.

[157] See, for example, R. Ghosh, "Antecedents of Mentoring Support: A Meta-Analysis of Individual, Relational, and Structural or Organizational Factors," *Journal of Vocational Behavior* 84, no. 3 (2014): 367–84; and K. E. O'Brien, A. Biga, S. R. Kessler, and T. D. Allen, "A Meta-Analytic Investigation of Gender Differences in Mentoring," *Journal of Management* 36, no. 2 (2010): 537–54.

[158] See, for instance, T. D. Allen, L. T. Eby, M. L. Poteet, E. Lentz, and L. Lima, "Career Benefits Associated with Mentoring for Protégés: A Meta-Analysis," *Journal of Applied Psychology* 89, no. 1 (2004): 127–36; L. T. D. Eby, T. D. Allen, S. C. Evans, T. Ng, and D. L. DuBois, "Does Mentoring Matter? A Multidisciplinary Meta-Analysis Comparing Mentored and Non-Mentored Individuals," *Journal of Vocational Behavior* 72, no. 2 (2008): 254–67; L. T. D. Eby, T. D. Allen, B. J. Hoffman, L. E. Baranik, J. B. Sauer, S. Baldwin, ... and S. C. Evans, "An Interdisciplinary Meta-Analysis of the Potential Antecedents, Correlates, and Consequences of Protégé Perceptions of Mentoring," *Psychological Bulletin* 139, no. 2 (2013): 441–76; R. Ghosh and T. G. Reio Jr., "Career Benefits Associated with Mentoring for Mentors: A Meta-Analysis," *Journal of Vocational Behavior* 83, no. 1 (2013): 106–16; and C. M. Underhill, "The Effectiveness of Mentoring Programs in Corporate Settings: A Meta-Analytical Review of the Literature," *Journal of Vocational Behavior* 68, no. 2 (2006): 292–307.

[159] Underhill, "The Effectiveness of Mentoring Programs in Corporate Settings."

[160] T. D. Allen, E. T. Eby, and E. Lentz, "The Relationship between Formal Mentoring Program Characteristics and Perceived Program Effectiveness," *Personnel Psychology* 59 (2006): 125–53; T. D. Allen, L. T. Eby, and E. Lentz, "Mentorship Behaviors and Mentorship Quality Associated with Formal Mentoring Programs: Closing the Gap between Research and Practice," *Journal of Applied Psychology* 91, no. 3 (2006): 567–78; and M. R. Parise and M. L. Forret, "Formal Mentoring Programs: The Relationship of Program Design and Support to Mentors' Perceptions of Benefits and Costs," *Journal of Vocational Behavior* 72, no. 2 (2008): 225–40.

[161] L. T. Eby and A. Lockwood, "Protégés' and Mentors' Reactions to Participating in Formal Mentoring Programs: A Qualitative Investigation," *Journal of Vocational Behavior* 67, no. 3 (2005): 441–58; G. T. Chao, "Formal Mentoring: Lessons Learned from Past Practice," *Professional Psychology: Research and Practice* 40, no. 3 (2009): 314–20; and C. R. Wanberg, J. D. Kammeyer-Mueller, and M. Marchese, "Mentor and Protégé Predictors and Outcomes of Mentoring in a Formal Mentoring Program," *Journal of Vocational Behavior* 69 (2006): 410–23.

[162] M. K. Feeney and B. Bozeman, "Mentoring and Network Ties," *Human Relations* 61, no. 12 (2008): 1651–76; N. Bozionelos, "Intra-Organizational Network Resources: How They Relate to Career Success and Organizational Commitment," *Personnel Review* 37, no. 3 (2008): 249–63; and S. A. Hezlett and S. K. Gibson, "Linking Mentoring and Social Capital: Implications for Career and Organization Development," *Advances in Developing Human Resources* 9, no. 3 (2007): 384–412.

[163] D. Robson, "COVID-19: What Makes a Good Leader during a Crisis?" *BBC: Worklife*, blog, March 27, 2020, https://www.bbc.com/worklife/article/20200326-covid-19-what-makes-a-good-leader-during-a-crisis.

[164] Z. Marks, "In a Global Emergency, Women Are Showing How to Lead," *The Washington Post*, April 21, 2020, https://www.washingtonpost.com/opinions/2020/04/21/global-emergency-women-are-showing-how-lead/; S. Miller, "The Secret to Germany's COVID-19 Success: Angela Merkel Is a Scientist," *The Atlantic*, April 20, 2020, https://www.theatlantic.com/international/archive/2020/04/angela-merkel-germany-coronavirus-pandemic/610225/; N. Yancey-Bragg, "Female World Leaders Are Handling Coronavirus Crisis 'in a Really Impressive Manner,' Experts Say," *USA Today*, April 17, 2020, https://www.usatoday.com/story/news/world/2020/04/17/coronavirus-women-world-leaders-praised-handling-crisis/5144421002/.

[165] S. Alexander Haslam and M. K. Ryan, "The Road to the Glass Cliff: Differences in the Perceived Suitability of Men and Women for Leadership Positions in Succeeding and Failing Organizations," *The Leadership Quarterly* 19 (2008): 530–46; C. Kulich, V. Iacoviello, F. Lorenzi-Cioldi, "Solving the Crisis: When Agency Is the Preferred Leadership for Implementing Change," *The Leadership Quarterly* 29 (2018): 295–308; M. K. Ryan, S. Alexander Haslam, T. Morgenroth, F. Rink, J. Stoker, and K. Peters, "Getting on Top of the Glass Cliff: Reviewing a Decade of Evidence, Explanations, and Impact," *The Leadership Quarterly* 27 (2016): 446–55.

[166] S. T. Hannah, M. Uhl-Bien, B. J. Avolio, and F. L. Cavaretta, "A Framework for Examining Leadership in Extreme Contexts," *The Leadership Quarterly* 20

(2009): 897–919; E. Hayes James and L. Perry Wooten, *Leading Under Pressure: From Surviving to Thriving Before, During, and After a Crisis* (New York, NY: Routledge, 2010).
[167] B. Wansink, C. R. Payne, K. van Ittersum, "Profiling the Heroic Leader: Empirical Lessons from Combat-Decorated Veterans of World War II," *The Leadership Quarterly* 19 (2008): 547–55.
[168] L. A. DeChurch, C. Shawn Burke, M. L. Shuffler, R. Lyons, D. Doty, and E. Salas, "A Historiometric Analysis of Leadership in Mission Critical Multiteam Environments," *The Leadership Quarterly* 22 (2011): 152–69; see also M. D. Mumford, T. L. Friedrich, J. J. Caughron, and C. L. Byrne, "Leader Cognition in Real-World Settings: How Do Leaders Think about Crises?," *The Leadership Quarterly* 18 (2007): 515–43; J. I. Stoker, H. Garretsen, and D. Soudis, "Tightening the Leash after a Threat: A Multilevel Event Study on Leadership Behavior Following the Financial Crisis," *The Leadership Quarterly* 30 (2019): 199–214.
[169] D. J. Carrington, I. A. Combe, and M. D. Mumford, "Cognitive Shifts within Leader and Follower Teams: Where Consensus Develops in Mental Models during an Organizational Crisis," *The Leadership Quarterly* 30 (2019): 335–50; I. A. Combe and D. J. Carrington, "Leaders' Sensemaking under Crises: Emerging Cognitive Consensus over Time within Management Teams," *The Leadership Quarterly* 26 (2015): 307–22.
[170] J. M. Madera and D. B. Smith, "The Effects of Leader Negative Emotions on Evaluations of Leadership in a Crisis Situation: The Role of Anger and Sadness," *The Leadership Quarterly* 20 (2009): 103–14.
[171] M. C. Bligh, J. C. Kohles, and J. R. Meindl, "Charisma under Crisis: Presidential Leadership, Rhetoric, and Media Responses before and after the September 11th Terrorist Attacks," *The Leadership Quarterly* 15, no. 2 (2004): 211–39; K. M. Davis and W. L. Gardner, "Charisma under Crisis Revisited: Presidential Leadership, Perceived Leader Effectiveness, and Contextual Influences," *The Leadership Quarterly* 23 (2012): 918–33; J. G. Hunt, K. B. Boal, and G. E. Dodge, "The Effects of Visionary and Crisis-Responsive Charisma on Followers: An Experimental Examination of Two Kinds of Charismatic Leadership," *The Leadership Quarterly* 10, no. 3 (1999): 423–48.
[172] Ibid.
[173] E. A. Williams, R. Pillai, B. Deptula, and K. B. Lowe, "The Effects of Crisis, Cynicism about Change, and Value Congruence on Perceptions of Authentic Leadership and Attributed Charisma in the 2008 Presidential Election," *The Leadership Quarterly* 23 (2012): 324–41; E. A. Williams, R. Pillai, K. B. Lowe, D. Jung, and D. Herst, "Crisis, Charisma, Values, and Voting Behavior in the 2004 Presidential Election," *The Leadership Quarterly* 20 (2009): 70–86.
[174] M. B. Eberly, D. J. Bluhm, C. Guarana, B. J. Avolio, and S. T. Hannah, "Staying after the Storm: How Transformational Leadership Relates to Follower Turnover Intentions in Extreme Contexts," *Journal of Vocational Behavior* 102 (2017): 72–85.
[175] Comment by Jim Collins, cited in J. Useem, "Conquering Vertical Limits," *Fortune*, February 19, 2001, 94.
[176] See, for instance, S. G. Green and T. R. Mitchell, "Attributional Processes of Leaders in Leader-Member Interactions," *Organizational Behavior & Human Performance* 23, no. 3 (1979): 429–58; and B. Schyns, J. Felfe, and H. Blank, "Is Charisma Hyper-Romanticism? Empirical Evidence from New Data and a Meta-Analysis," *Applied Psychology: An International Review* 56, no. 4 (2007): 505–27.
[177] J. H. Gray and I. L. Densten, "How Leaders Woo Followers in the Romance of Leadership," *Applied Psychology: An International Review* 56, no. 4 (2007): 558–81; M. J. Martinko, P. Harvey, D. Sikora, and S. C. Douglas, "Perceptions of Abusive Supervision: The Role of Subordinates' Attribution Styles," *Leadership Quarterly* 22, no. 4 (2011): 751–64; J. R. Meindl and S. B. Ehrlich, "The Romance of Leadership and the Evaluation of Organizational Performance," *Academy of Management Journal* 30, no. 1 (1987): 91–109; and J. R. Meindl, S. B. Ehrlich, and J. M. Dukerich, "The Romance of Leadership," *Administrative Science Quarterly* 30 (1985): 78–102.
[178] M. C. Bligh, J. C. Kohles, C. L. Pearce, J. E. Justin, and J. F. Stovall, "When the Romance Is Over: Follower Perspectives of Aversive Leadership," *Applied Psychology: An International Review* 56, no. 4 (2007): 528–57.
[179] B. R. Agle, N. J. Nagarajan, J. A. Sonnenfeld, and D. Srinivasan, "Does CEO Charisma Matter?," *Academy of Management Journal* 49, no. 1 (2006): 161–74.
[180] Bligh, Kohles, Pearce, Justin, and Stovall, "When the Romance Is Over."
[181] Schyns, Felfe, and Blank, "Is Charisma Hyper-Romanticism?"
[182] A. S. Rosette, G. J. Leonardelli, and K. W. Phillips, "The White Standard: Racial Bias in Leader Categorization," *Journal of Applied Psychology* 93, no. 4 (2008): 758–77.
[183] Ibid.
[184] A. M. Koenig, A. H. Eagly, A. A. Mitchell, and T. Ristikari, "Are Leader Stereotypes Masculine? A Meta-Analysis of Three Research Paradigms," *Psychological Bulletin* 137, no. 4 (2011): 616–42.
[185] M. Van Vugt and B. R. Spisak, "Sex Differences in the Emergence of Leadership during Competitions within and between Groups," *Psychological Science* 19, no. 9 (2008): 854–58.
[186] W. Matthew Bowler, J. B. Paul, and J. R. Halbesleben, "LMX and Attributions of Organizational Citizenship Behavior Motives: When Is Citizenship Perceived as Brownnosing?" *Journal of Business and Psychology* 34 (2019): 139–52.
[187] F. K. Matta, T. B. Sabey, B. A. Scott, S.-H. J. Lin, and J. Koopman, "Not All Fairness Is Created Equal: A Study of Employee Attributions of Supervisor Justice Motives," *Journal of Applied Psychology* 105, no. 3 (2020): 274–93.
[188] S. Kerr and J. M. Jermier, "Substitutes for Leadership: Their Meaning and Measurement," *Organizational Behavior & Human Performance* 22, no. 3 (1978): 375–403.
[189] R. E. Silverman, "Who's the Boss? There Isn't One," *The Wall Street Journal*, June 20, 2012, B1, B8.
[190] J. Koopman, B. A. Scott, F. K. Matta, D. E. Conlon, and T. Dennerlein, "Ethical Leadership as a Substitute for Justice Enactment: An Information Processing Perspective," *Journal of Applied Psychology* 104, no. 9 (2019): 1103–16.
[191] S. D. Dionne, F. J. Yammarino, L. E. Atwater, and L. R. James, "Neutralizing Substitutes for Leadership Theory: Leadership Effects and Common-Source Bias," *Journal of Applied Psychology* 87 (2002): 454–64; and J. R. Villa, J. P. Howell, P. W. Dorfman, and D. L. Daniel, "Problems with Detecting Moderators in Leadership Research Using Moderated Multiple Regression," *Leadership Quarterly* 14 (2002): 3–23.
[192] B. M. Bass, "Cognitive, Social, and Emotional Intelligence of Transformational Leaders," in R. E. Riggio, S. E. Murphy, and F. J. Pirozzolo (eds.), *Multiple Intelligences*

and Leadership (Mahwah, NJ: Lawrence Erlbaum, 2002): 113–14.

[193] "JCPenney Names Marvin Ellison President and CEO-Designee," JCPenney Press Release, August 1, 2015, http://ir.jcpenney.com/phoenix.zhtml?c=70528&p=irol-newsArticle&ID=1976923.

[194] "Most Underachieving: CEOs," *Bloomberg*, 2013, http://www.bloomberg.com/visual-data/best-and-worst//most-underachieving-ceos; and B. Darrow, "Meg Whitman and HP Five Years Later: Mission Accomplished?," *Fortune*, September 27, 2016, http://fortune.com/2016/09/27/whitman-hp-five-year/.

[195] See, for instance, P. Dvorak, "M.B.A. Programs Hone 'Soft Skills,'" *The Wall Street Journal*, February 12, 2007, B3.

[196] J. Weber, "The Leadership Factory," *BusinessWeek* (June 12, 2006): 60–64.

[197] D. Brady, "The Rising Star of CEO Consulting," *Bloomberg Businessweek*, November 24, 2010, www.businessweek.com.

[198] B. D. Blume, J. K. Ford, T. T. Baldwin, and J. L. Huang, "Transfer of Training: A Meta-Analytic Review," *Journal of Management* 36, no. 4 (2010): 1065–105.

[199] D. S. DeRue, J. D. Nahrgang, J. R. Hollenbeck, and K. Workman, "A Quasi-Experimental Study of After-Event Reviews and Leadership Development," *Journal of Applied Psychology* 97 (2012): 997–1015.

[200] The Times of India (September 13, 2021). "Captains for courses: *Shared leadership is actually much more widespread than we tend to think.* Retrieved from https://timesofindia.indiatimes.com (Accessed on April 12, 2022).

[201] Vijayaraghavan, K. (2021). "Adi Godrej has created good working climate for shared leadership". *The Economic Times (August 16, 2021).* Retrieved from https://economictimes.indiatimes.com (Accessed on April 12, 2022).

14 Foundations of Organization Structure

Source: Stephen Barnes/Travel/Alamy Stock Photo

LEARNING OBJECTIVES

After studying this chapter, you should be able to:

14-1 Identify seven elements of an organization's structure.

14-2 Identify the characteristics of the functional structure, the bureaucracy, and the matrix structure.

14-3 Identify the characteristics of the virtual structure, the team structure, and the circular structure.

14-4 Describe the effects of downsizing on organizational structures and employees.

14-5 Contrast the reasons for using mechanistic versus organic structural models.

14-6 Analyze the behavioral implications of different organizational designs.

Employability Skills Matrix (ESM)

	Myth or Science?	Career OBjectives	An Ethical Choice	Point/ Counterpoint	Experiential Exercise	Ethical Dilemma	Case Incident 1	Case Incident 2
Critical Thinking	✓	✓	✓	✓	✓	✓	✓	✓
Communication					✓			
Collaboration	✓		✓	✓	✓		✓	
Knowledge Application and Analysis	✓	✓	✓	✓	✓	✓	✓	✓
Social Responsibility			✓			✓	✓	✓

SAMSUNG: TRANSFORMING A HIERARCHY

Samsung Group is an international leader in electronics—in 2017, nearly one quarter of the global smartphone market was owned by the South Korean conglomerate. While they have had an even higher market share before, this is a significant climb from just 3 percent in 2009. Since then, other big names in the mobile phone market have fallen away, leaving only Apple as a strong competitor.

However, this climb to the top has not been without turbulence. In 2016, Samsung announced a global recall of the Note 7 after several owners discovered their phones on fire. The replacement phones did not solve the problem, and production was halted. As if things couldn't get worse, the heir to the Samsung Group, Jay Y. Lee, was jailed for corruption in early 2017. There was a public outcry, and the firm's reputation was at stake.

Faced with a leadership vacuum, investors demanded a review of the corporate structure. Strategic, operational, financial, legal, tax, and accounting considerations had to be scrutinized to determine the optimal structure for the conglomerate. Clearly there were issues of quality (as in the Note 7 debacle) and transparency (as in the Lee bribery and embezzlement scandal). In spite of all this, Samsung's share price has held; in fact, it has risen. While the decision was taken not to change the fundamental corporate structure, the structures have undergone change internally.

Much attention was given to the Future Strategy Office, the centralized headquarters of Samsung. The Office was referred to as the Control Tower and played an important role in lobbying the government on policy issues. The centralized headquarters also enabled Lee to maneuver as he did, and as a response to his conviction, and for scrutiny of decision making, the Future Strategy Office was dismantled.

This decision promises to provide more autonomy to the subsidiaries. On the face of it, these structural changes appear to address concerns over abuse of power. However, with 59 subsidiaries and 500,000 employees in the Group, questions have been raised as to how organized the Group will be without its central authority in place. The fact is that all group-wide projects and tasks were halted as a result of the decision to disband the Office. Collaboration across the entities is predicted to become more difficult without a central coordinating body.

Will other structural adjustments be on the horizon? With the cut-throat level of hyper-competition in the electronics sector, the ability to innovate is at a premium. Can Samsung attract the innovative talent needed into its still very hierarchical structures?

Sources: Song Su-hyun, "Samsung Prepares Organizational Change Focused on R&D Convergence," *The Korea Herald*, November 17, 2017, http://www.koreaherald.com/view.php?ud=20171117000626; Manny Reyes, "Samsung Sets Up Dedicated AI Center as Part of Restructuring," Android Headlines, November 23, 2017, https://www.androidheadlines.com/2017/11/samsung-sets-up-dedicated-ai-center-as-part-of-restructuring.html; "Samsung Smartphone Market Share Worldwide 2009-2017," Statistic, https://www.statista.com/statistics/276477/global-market-share-held-by-samsung-smartphones/; F. Richter, "The Size and Scope of Samsung's Business. Manufacturing Business Technology," 2016, retrieved from https://search-proquest-com.ezproxy.lancs.ac.uk/docview/1828409455?accountid=11979; Samsung, "Galaxy Note7 Safety Recall and Exchange Program," July 19, 2017, http://www.samsung.com/us/note7recall/; "Samsung Confirms Battery Faults as Cause of Note 7 Fires," BBC News, January 23, 2017, http://www.bbc.com/news/business-38714461; "Samsung Heir Lee Jae-Yong Jailed for Corruption," BBC News, August 25, 2017, http://www.bbc.com/news/business-41033568; "Samsung Electronics Completes Review of Optimal Corporate Structure," Samsung Global Newsroom, April 27, 2017, https://news.samsung.com/global/samsung-electronics-completes-review-of-optimal-corporate-structure; "Samsung Damps Investor Hopes of Structural Changes," *Financial Times*, March 24, 2017, https://www.ft.com/content/08393d8c-1060-11e7-b030-768954394623; Hansoo Choi, "Conviction, and How Business in South Korea Is Changing," HBR, September 29, 2017, https://hbr.org/2017/09/samsung-lee-jae-yongs-conviction-and-how-business-in-south-korea-is-changing.

Even for a start-up with only a few employees, choosing an organizational structure requires far more than simply deciding who is the boss and how many employees are needed. The organization's structure determines what relationships form, the formality of those relationships, and many work outcomes. The structure may also change as organizations grow and shrink, as management trends dictate, and as research uncovers better ways of maximizing productivity.

Structural decisions are arguably the most fundamental ones that a leader must make toward sustaining organizational growth.[1] In this chapter, we'll explore how structure affects employee behavior and the organization as a whole.

What Is Organizational Structure?

14-1 Identify seven elements of an organization's structure.

organizational structure The way in which job tasks are formally divided, grouped, and coordinated.

An **organizational structure** defines how job tasks are formally divided, grouped, and coordinated.[2] Seven key elements should be considered when designing an organization's structure: work specialization, departmentalization, chain of command, span of control, centralization and decentralization, formalization, and boundary spanning.[3] Exhibit 14-1 presents each element as the answer to an important structural question, and the following sections describe each one.

Work Specialization

Early in the twentieth century, Henry Ford became rich by building automobiles using an assembly line. Every worker was assigned a specific, repetitive task such as putting on the right front wheel or installing the right front door. By dividing jobs into small standardized tasks that could be performed over and over, Ford was able to produce a car every 10 seconds, using employees with relatively limited skills.[4]

work specialization The degree to which tasks in an organization are subdivided into separate jobs.

Work specialization, or *division of labor*, describes the degree to which activities in the organization are divided into separate jobs.[5] The essence of work specialization is to divide a job into several steps, each completed by a separate

Exhibit 14-1 Key Design Questions and Answers for Designing the Proper Organizational Structure

The Key Question	The Answer Is Provided by
1. To what degree are activities subdivided into separate jobs?	Work specialization
2. On what basis will jobs be grouped together?	Departmentalization
3. To whom do individuals and groups report?	Chain of command
4. How many individuals can a manager efficiently and effectively direct?	Span of control
5. Where does decision-making authority lie?	Centralization and decentralization
6. To what degree will there be rules and regulations to direct employees and managers?	Formalization
7. Do individuals from different areas need to regularly interact?	Boundary spanning

Exhibit 14-2 Economies and Diseconomies of Work Specialization

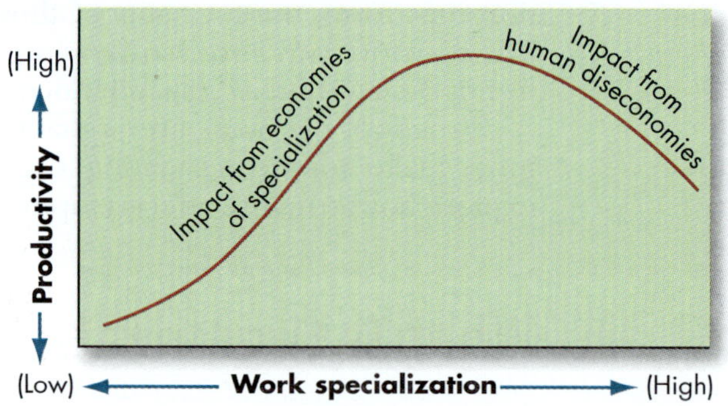

individual. Individuals specialize in doing part of an activity rather than the entirety. Specialization is a means of making the most efficient use of employees' skills and even successfully improving them through repetition. Less time is spent changing tasks, putting away tools and equipment from a prior step, and getting ready for another.

By the 1960s, it increasingly seemed that the good news of specialization could be carried too far. Human diseconomies began to surface in the form of boredom, fatigue, stress, low productivity, inferior quality, increased absenteeism, and high turnover, which more than offset the economic advantages (see Exhibit 14-2).[6] Productivity could be increased now by enlarging, rather than narrowing, the scope of job activities. Giving employees a variety of activities to do, allowing them to do a whole and complete job, and putting them into teams with interchangeable skills often achieved significantly higher output, with increased employee satisfaction.[7]

Ford demonstrated that work can be performed more efficiently if work is specialized, and the practice still has applications in many industries. For example, could you build a car by yourself? Not likely! Equally important, it's easier and less costly to find and train workers to do specific tasks, especially in highly sophisticated and complex operations. Work specialization increases efficiency and productivity by encouraging the creation of customized inventions and machinery.

Most managers today recognize the economies that specialization provides in certain jobs and the problems when it's carried too far. High work specialization helps fast-food restaurants make and sell hamburgers and fries efficiently, and aids medical specialists in most health maintenance organizations. Wherever job roles can be broken down into specific tasks or projects, specialization is possible. Specialization may still confer advantages outside manufacturing, particularly where job sharing and part-time work are prevalent.[8] Amazon's Mechanical Turk program, TopCoder, and others like it have facilitated a new trend in microspecialization, e-lancing, or crowd sourcing in which extremely small pieces of programming, data processing, or evaluation tasks are delegated to a global network of individuals by a program manager who then assembles the results.[9] This opens the way for employers to use online platforms to assign multiple workers to tasks in a broader functional role like marketing.[10] Automation and the use of computers and information systems within organizations are creating a new form of work specialization in which computers take on specialized work.[11]

Thus, whereas specialization of yesteryear focused on breaking manufacturing tasks into specific duties within the same plant, today's specialization judiciously breaks complex tasks into specific elements by technology, expertise, and region. The core principle, however, is the same.

Departmentalization

Once jobs have been divided through work specialization, they must be grouped so common tasks can be coordinated and complexity can be reduced. The basis by which jobs are grouped is called **departmentalization.**[12]

departmentalization The basis by which jobs in an organization are grouped together.

One of the most popular ways to group activities is by the *functions* performed. A manufacturing manager might organize a plant into engineering, accounting, manufacturing, human resources (HR), and supply chain departments. A hospital might have departments for research, surgery, intensive care, accounting, and so forth. A professional football franchise might have departments for player personnel, ticket sales, and travel and accommodations. The major advantage of this type of functional departmentalization is efficiencies gained from putting specialists that focus on similar areas together.

Jobs can also be departmentalized by the type of *product* or *service* the organization produces. Procter & Gamble places each major product—such as Tide, Pampers, Charmin, and Pringles—under an executive who has complete global responsibility for it. The major advantage here is increased accountability for performance because all activities related to a specific product or service are under the direction of a single manager.[13] But for this type of departmentalization to be effective, it is also important for the department or team to have a broader understanding of the organization outside of their own product specialization (e.g., knowing what the other teams and departments work on over time).[14]

When a firm is departmentalized based on *geography*, or territory, each function (for example, sales) may have western, southern, midwestern, and eastern regions. This form is valuable when an organization's customers are scattered over a large geographic area and have similar needs within their locations. For this reason, Toyota changed its management structure into geographic regions "so that they may develop and deliver ever better products," said CEO Akio Toyoda.[15] When organizations departmentalize by region, these departments and co-located teams form their own identities and practices.[16] These regional teams affect the coordination and performance across locations, as well as how information is acquired and shared throughout the organization.[17] Organizations with geographical departmentalization should pay special attention to inter-region communication and knowledge sharing, which can be made easier through virtual communications and knowledge management systems.

Process departmentalization works for processing customers as well as products. If you've ever been to a state motor vehicle office to get a driver's license, you probably went through several departments before receiving your license. In one typical state, applicants go through three steps, each handled by a separate department: (1) validation by the motor vehicles division, (2) processing by the licensing department, and (3) payment collection by the treasury department. A final category of departmentalization uses the particular type of *customer* the organization seeks to reach.

Organizations do not always stay with the basis of departmentalization they first adopt. Microsoft, for instance, used customer departmentalization for years, organizing around its customer bases: consumers, large corporations, software developers, and small businesses. However, in a June 2013 letter from CEO Steve Ballmer to all employees, he announced a restructuring to functional departmentalization, citing a need to foster continuing innovation. The new departments grouped jobs by traditional functions, including engineering, marketing, business development, strategy and research, finance, HR, and legal.[18]

Ballmer expected the change in Microsoft's organizational structure to "reshape how we interact with our customers, developers, and key innovation partners, delivering a more coherent message and family of product offerings."[19] As we see throughout this text, whenever changes are deliberately made in organizations to align practices with organizational goals, particularly the goals of strong leaders, a good execution of the changes creates a much higher probability for improvement. In Microsoft's case, the results are not yet determined—Ballmer, who is a strong leader, announced his retirement 2 months later (he officially left Microsoft in 2014), and further changes ensued. Microsoft continued to struggle with the reorganization, announcing additional changes in its leadership personnel and team structure less than a year later. These changes included, for example, product specialization and functional specialization; for instance, the PowerPoint, Excel, and Access teams have been reorganized into content creation and data visualization teams.[20]

Chain of Command

While the chain of command was once a basic cornerstone in the design of organizations, it has far less importance today. But managers should still consider its implications, particularly in industries that deal with potential

A global firm that operates on a local scale in more than 200 countries, The Coca-Cola Company is organized into five geographic segments: North America, Latin America, Europe, the Middle East and Africa, and Asia Pacific. The structure enables it to tailor its strategy to markets in different stages of economic development and with differing consumer tastes and buying behavior.

Source: Kim Kyung-Hoon/Reuters

life-or-death situations when people need to rely quickly and suddenly on decision makers. The **chain of command** is an unbroken line of authority that extends from the top of the organization to the lowest echelon and clarifies who reports to whom.

chain of command The unbroken line of authority that extends from the top of the organization to the lowest echelon and clarifies who reports to whom.

authority The rights inherent in a managerial position to give orders and to expect the orders to be obeyed.

unity of command The idea that a subordinate should have only one superior to whom they are directly responsible to.

We can't discuss the chain of command without also discussing *authority* and *unity of command.* **Authority** refers to the rights inherent in a managerial position to give orders and expect them to be obeyed.[21] To facilitate coordination, each managerial position is given a place in the chain of command, and each manager is given a degree of authority to meet their responsibilities. In chains of command in which most of the authority is vested in one person, LMX (see Chapter 13) becomes more important, as the leader's "buy-in" becomes more important to getting things done.[22] The principle of **unity of command** helps preserve the concept of an unbroken line of authority. It says that a person should have one and only one superior to whom he or she is directly responsible. If the unity of command is broken, an employee might have to cope with conflicting demands or priorities from several superiors, as is often the case in an organization chart's dotted-line reporting relationships depicting an employee's accountability to multiple managers.[23] Although unity of command is more common than having multiple supervisors, if you do find yourself in the situation where you report to multiple people, be aware of your own workload, conflicting messages, who has the "final say" in disputes, and loyalty expectations.[24] Furthermore, you should try to be proactive about your workload, foster communication between your supervisors, and set up boundaries and norms for effective communication and workflow.

Times change, however, and so do the basic tenets of organizational design. A low-level employee today can access information in seconds that was available only to top managers a generation ago, and many employees are empowered to make decisions previously reserved for management.[25] Add the popularity of self-managed and cross-functional teams (see Chapter 10) as well as structural designs that include multiple bosses, and you can see why authority and unity of command may appear to hold less relevance. Yet many organizations still find that they are the most productive when they enforce a chain of command. Indeed, one survey of more than 1,000 managers found that 59 percent agreed with the statement, "There is an imaginary line in my company's organizational chart. Strategy is created by people above this line, while strategy is executed by people below the line." However, this same survey found that lower-level employees' buy-in (agreement and active support) to the organization's overall, big-picture strategy was inhibited by their reliance on the hierarchy for decision making.[26] Maybe instead of viewing the chain of command as a line, it should be seen more as a pyramid? Indeed, one study found that people who see the chain of command in this way are more likely to acknowledge the collective contributions of lower-level employees as well as experience enhanced group performance and social relationships.[27]

Span of Control

span of control The number of subordinates that a manager can direct efficiently and effectively.

How many employees can a manager direct efficiently and effectively? The **span of control** describes the number of levels (also referred to as layers) and managers in an organization.[28] All things being equal, the wider or larger the span, the fewer the levels, and the more employees at each level, the more efficient the organization.[29]

Exhibit 14-3 Contrasting Spans of Control

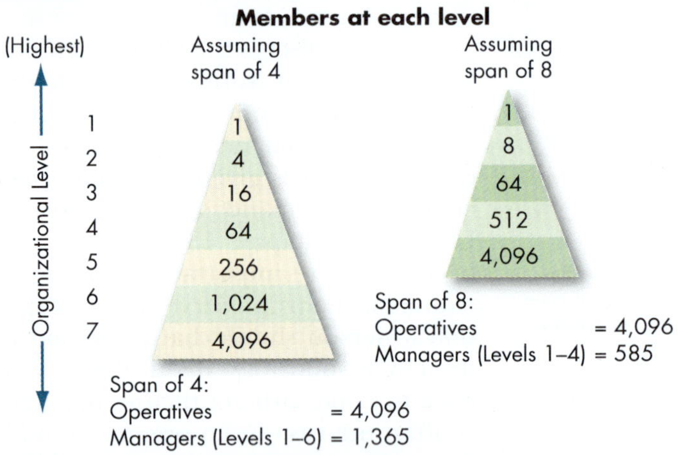

Assume two organizations each have about 4,100 operative-level employees. One has a uniform span of 4 and the other a span of 8. As Exhibit 14-3 illustrates, the wider span of 8 will have two fewer levels and approximately 800 fewer managers. If the average manager makes ₹600,000 a year, the wider span will save ₹4.8 crore a year in management salaries! Obviously, wider spans are more efficient in terms of cost. However, when supervisors no longer have time to provide subordinates with the necessary leadership and support, effectiveness declines and employee performance suffers.[30]

Narrow or small spans have their advocates. By keeping the span of control to five or six employees, a manager can maintain close control.[31] But narrow spans have three major drawbacks.[32] First, they're expensive because they add levels of management. Second, they make vertical communication in the organization more complex. The added levels of hierarchy slow down decision making and can isolate upper management. Third, narrow spans encourage overly tight supervision and discourage employee autonomy.

The trend in recent years has been toward wider spans of control.[33] They're consistent with firms' efforts to reduce costs, cut overhead, speed decision making, increase flexibility, get closer to customers, and empower employees. To ensure that performance doesn't suffer because of these wider spans, however, organizations might invest heavily in employee training because managers recognize they can handle a wider span best when employees know their jobs well or can turn to coworkers with questions.

Centralization and Decentralization

centralization The degree to which decision making is concentrated at a single point in an organization.

Centralization refers to the degree to which decision making is concentrated at a single point in the organization.[34] In *centralized* organizations, top managers make all the decisions, and lower-level managers merely carry out their directives. In organizations at the other extreme, *decentralized* decision making is pushed down to the managers closest to the action or to workgroups.[35] The concept of centralization includes only formal authority—that is, the rights inherent to a position.

An organization characterized by centralization is different structurally from one that's decentralized. A decentralized organization can act more quickly to solve problems, more people provide input into decisions, and employees are less likely to feel alienated from those who make decisions that affect their work lives.[36] The effects of centralization and decentralization can be predicted: Centralized organizations are better for avoiding commission errors (bad choices), while decentralized organizations are better for avoiding omission errors (lost opportunities).[37]

Management efforts to make organizations more flexible and responsive have produced a trend toward decentralized decision making by lower-level managers, who are closer to the action and typically have more detailed knowledge about problems than top managers. When Procter & Gamble empowered small groups of employees to make decisions about new-product development independent of the usual hierarchy, it was able to rapidly increase the proportion of new products ready for market.[38] Concerning creativity, research investigating a large number of Finnish organizations demonstrated that companies with decentralized research and development (R&D) offices in multiple locations were better at producing innovation than companies that centralized all R&D in a single office.[39] Decentralization can have unintended consequences. A study of Italian physicians revealed that decentralization may lead to role overload, role conflict, and role ambiguity. The physicians were confident in their abilities but less interested in roles that are excessively demanding and ill-defined.[40]

Decentralization is often necessary for companies with offshore sites because localized decision making is needed to respond to each region's profit opportunities, client base, and specific laws, while centralized oversight is needed to hold regional managers accountable. Failure to successfully balance these priorities can harm not only the organization but also its relationships with foreign governments.[41]

With more than 7,000 neighborhood and airport locations throughout North America and Europe, Enterprise Rent-A-Car empowers employees at the local level to make decisions that affect their work. Decentralization gives Enterprise a competitive advantage by enabling employees to provide personalized service that results in high customer satisfaction.

Source: Islandstock/Alamy Stock Photo

Formalization

formalization The degree to which jobs within an organization are standardized.

Formalization refers to the degree to which jobs within the organization are standardized.[42] If a job is highly formalized, the employee has a minimal amount of discretion over what to do and when and how to do it, resulting in consistent and uniform output. There are explicit job descriptions, lots of organizational rules, and clearly defined procedures covering work processes. Formalization eliminates the possibility of employees engaging in alternative behaviors, and it removes the need for them to consider alternatives. Conversely, where formalization is low, job behaviors are relatively unprogrammed and employees have a great deal of freedom to exercise discretion in their work.

The degree of formalization can vary widely between and within organizations. Research from 94 high-technology Chinese firms indicated that formalization is a detriment to team flexibility in decentralized organization structures, suggesting that formalization does not work as well where duties are inherently interactive or where there is a need to be flexible and innovative.[43] For example, publishing representatives who call on college professors to inform them of their company's new publications have a great deal of freedom in their jobs. They have a general standardized sales pitch, which they tailor as needed, and rules and procedures governing their behavior may be little more than suggestions on what to emphasize about forthcoming titles and the requirement to submit a weekly sales report. At the other extreme, clerical and editorial employees in the same publishing houses may need to be at their desks by 8:00 A.M. and follow a set of precise procedures dictated by management.

Boundary Spanning

We've described ways that organizations create well-defined task structures and chains of authority. These systems facilitate control and coordination for specific tasks, but if there is too much division within an organization, attempts to coordinate across groups can be disastrous. One way to overcome this sense of compartmentalization and retain the benefits of structure is to encourage or create boundary-spanning roles.

boundary spanning Individuals forming relationships outside their formally assigned groups.

Within a single organization, **boundary spanning** occurs when individuals form relationships with people outside their formally assigned groups.[44] An HR executive who frequently engages with the IT group is engaged in boundary spanning, as is a member of an R&D team who implements ideas from a production team. These activities help prevent formal structures from becoming too rigid and, not surprisingly, enhance organization and team creativity, decision making, knowledge sharing, and performance.[45]

Boundary-spanning activities occur not only within but also between organizations. Positive results are especially strong in organizations that encourage extensive internal communication; in other words, external boundary spanning is most effective when it is followed up with internal boundary spanning.[46] In addition, research on 225 manufacturer–distributor dyads in China suggests that ties between salespersons and buyers across organizations are linked with greater relationship quality between two organizations than are ties between executives across organizations, but when there are strong relationships between executives and employees, there may be cooperation and better conflict resolution.[47]

Organizations can use formal mechanisms to facilitate boundary-spanning activities. One method is to assign formal liaison roles or develop committees of individuals from different areas of the organization.[48] Development activities

BMW encourages all employees, including this production worker at its plant in Jakarta, Indonesia, to build relationships throughout the global company. Boundary spanning at BMW links R&D, design, production, and marketing individuals to speed problem solving and innovation and to adapt to market fluctuations.
Source: Dadang Tri/Bloomberg/Getty Images

can also facilitate boundary spanning. Employees with experience in multiple functions, such as accounting and marketing, are more likely to engage in boundary spanning.[49] Many organizations may try to set the stage for these sorts of positive relationships by creating job rotation programs so new hires get a better sense of different areas of the organization. Another method to encourage boundary spanning is to bring attention to overall organizational goals, such as efficiency and innovation, and shared identity concepts.[50]

You probably have personal experience with at least some of the results of decisions that leaders have made in your school or workplace that were related to the elements of organizational structure. The organizational framework, which can be depicted by drawing an organizational chart, can help you clarify these leaders' decisions. We'll discuss them next.

Common Organizational Frameworks and Structures

14-2 Identify the characteristics of the functional structure, the bureaucracy, and the matrix structure.

Organizational designs are known by many names and are constantly evolving in response to changes in the way work is done. We will start with three of the more common organizational frameworks: the *simple structure*, the *bureaucracy*, and the *matrix structure.*

The Simple Structure

simple structure An organizational structure characterized by a low degree of departmentalization, wide spans of control, authority centralized in a single person, and little formalization.

What do a small retail store, an electronics firm run by a hard-driving entrepreneur, and an airline's war room during a pilot's strike have in common? They probably all use the simple structure.[51] The **simple structure** has a low degree of departmentalization, wide spans of control, authority centralized in a single person, and little formalization. It is a flat organization; it usually has

Exhibit 14-4 A Simple Structure (Rakesh Mehra's Men's Store)

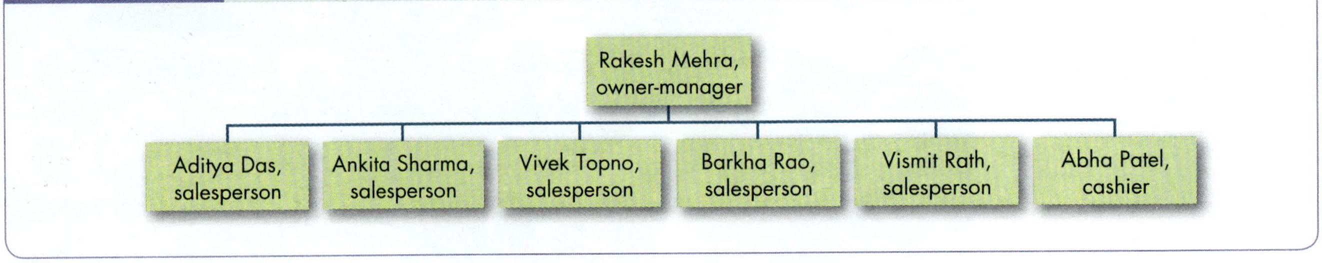

only two or three vertical levels, a loose body of employees, and one individual with decision-making authority. Most companies start as a simple structure, and many innovative technology-based firms with short life spans, like cell phone app development firms, remain compact by design.[52]

Exhibit 14-4 is an organization chart for a retail men's store owned and managed by Rakesh Mehra. Rakesh employs five full-time salespeople, a cashier, and extra workers for weekends and holidays, but he "runs the show." Although this type of organization is typical for a small business, in times of crisis large companies often simplify their structures (though not to this degree) as a means of focusing their resources.

The strength of the simple structure lies, of course, in its simplicity. It's fast, flexible, and inexpensive to operate, and accountability is clear. One major weakness is that it becomes increasingly inadequate as an organization grows because its low formalization and high centralization tend to create information overload at the top. Decision making typically becomes slower as the single executive tries to continue doing it all. This proves the undoing of many small businesses. If the structure isn't changed and made more elaborate, the firm often loses momentum and can eventually fail.[53] The simple structure's other weakness is that it's risky—everything depends on one person. An illness for the owner-manager can literally halt the organization's information and decision-making capabilities.[54]

The Bureaucracy

Standardization! That's the key concept that underlies all bureaucracies. Consider the bank where you keep your checking account; the store where you buy clothes; or the government entities that collect your taxes, enforce health regulations, or provide local fire protection. They all rely on standardized work processes for coordination and control.

bureaucracy An organizational structure with highly routine operating tasks achieved through specialization, very formalized rules and regulations, tasks that are grouped into functional departments, centralized authority, narrow spans of control, and decision making that follows the chain of command.

The **bureaucracy** is characterized by highly routine operating tasks achieved through specialization, strictly formalized rules and regulations, tasks grouped into units, centralized authority, narrow spans of control, and decision making that follows the chain of command.[55] Bureaucracy incorporates all the strongest degrees of departmentalization described earlier.

Bureaucracy is a dirty word in many people's minds. However, this type of organization does have advantages, primarily the ability to perform standardized activities very efficiently. Putting like specialties together in units results in economies of scale, minimum duplication of people and equipment, and a common language employees all share. Bureaucracies can get by with less talented—and hence less costly—middle- and lower-level managers because

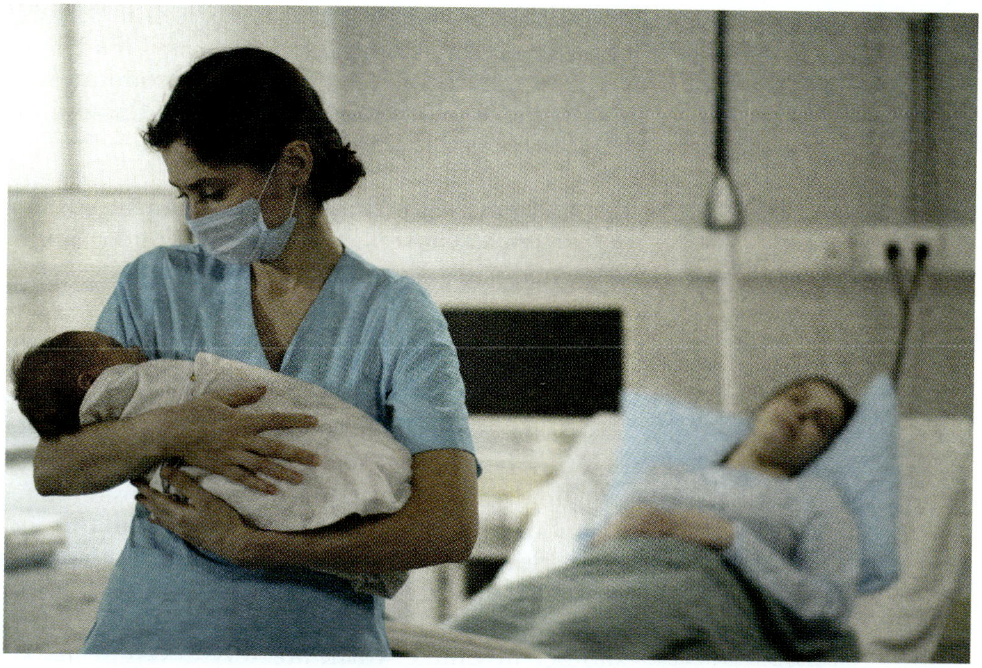

Hospitals benefit from standardized work processes and procedures common to a bureaucratic structure because they help employees perform their jobs efficiently. At leading hospitals in India, nurses follow formal rules and regulations in caring for mothers and newborns.
Source: TommyStockProject.shutterstock.com

rules and regulations substitute for managerial discretion. There is little need for innovative and experienced decision makers below the level of senior executives, and innovative employees often do not mesh well with bureaucracy.[56]

Listen to this conversation among four executives in one company: "You know, nothing happens in this place until we *produce* something," said the production executive. "Wrong," commented the R&D manager, "Nothing happens until we *design* something!" "What are you talking about?" asked the marketing executive, "Nothing happens until we *sell* something!" The exasperated accounting manager responded, "It doesn't matter what you produce, design, or sell. No one knows what happens until we *tally up the results*!" This conversation highlights how bureaucratic specialization can create conflicts in which the unit perspectives override the overall goals of the organization.

The other major weakness of a bureaucracy is something we've all witnessed: obsessive concern with following the rules. When cases don't fit the rules precisely, there is no room for modification. The bureaucracy is efficient only if employees confront familiar problems with programmed decision rules.[57] The standardization and rule adherence that benefit it also result in drawbacks: bureaucratic structures may result in diminished autonomy and motivation for employees within these systems, making it difficult to develop and maintain motivation.[58] There are two types of bureaucracies we should explore: functional and divisional structures.

functional structure An organizational structure that groups employees by their similar specialties, roles, or tasks.

The Functional Structure The **functional structure** groups employees by their similar specialties, roles, or tasks.[59] An organization organized into production, marketing, HR, and accounting departments is an example. Many large organizations utilize this structure, although this is evolving to allow for quick changes in response to business opportunities. One advantage of the functional structure is that specialists may be able to become experts more easily than if they worked in diversified units. Employees can also be motivated by a clear career path to the top of the organization chart specific to their specialties.

The functional structure works well if the organization is focused on one product or service. Unfortunately, it creates rigid, formal communications because the hierarchy dictates the communication protocol. Coordination among many units is a problem, and infighting in units and between units can lead to reduced motivation.

divisional structure An organizational structure that groups employees into units by product, service, customer, or geographical market area.

The Divisional Structure The **divisional structure** groups employees into units by product, service, customer, or geographical market area.[60] It is highly departmentalized. Sometimes this structure is known by the type of division structure it uses: *product/service organizational structure* (for example, units for cat food, dog food, and bird food that report to an animal food producer), *customer organizational structure* (for example, units for outpatient care, inpatient care, and pharmacy that report to hospital administration), or *geographic organizational structure* (for example, units for Europe, Asia, and South America that report to corporate headquarters).

The divisional structure has the opposite benefits and disadvantages of the functional structure. It facilitates coordination in units to achieve their goals while addressing the specific concerns of each unit. It provides clear responsibility for all activities related to a product but with duplication of functions and costs. Sometimes this is helpful, say, when the organization has a unit in Spain and another in China, which are very different markets, and a marketing strategy is needed for a new product. Marketing experts in both places can incorporate the appropriate cultural perspectives into their region's marketing campaign. However, the organization's marketing function employees in two places may represent an increased cost because they are doing basically the same task in two different countries. It appears as if organizations can shift from a divisional to a functional structure, and vice versa; however, those who shift from a functional to a divisional structure tend to perform the best.[61]

The Matrix Structure

matrix structure An organizational structure that creates dual lines of authority and combines functional and product departmentalization.

The **matrix structure** combines the functional and product structures, and we find it in advertising agencies, aerospace firms, R&D laboratories, construction companies, hospitals, government agencies, universities, management consulting

Exhibit 14-5 Matrix Structure for a College of Business Administration

Academic Departments \ Programs	Undergraduate	Master's	Ph.D.	Research	Executive Development	Community Service
Accounting						
Finance						
Decision and Information Systems						
Management						
Marketing						

firms, and entertainment companies.[62] Companies that use matrixlike structures include ABB, Boeing, BMW, IBM, and P&G.

The most obvious structural characteristic of the matrix is that it breaks the unity-of-command concept. Employees in the matrix have two bosses: their functional department managers and their product managers. Exhibit 14-5 shows the matrix for a college of business administration. The academic departments of accounting, decision and information systems, marketing, and so forth, are functional units. Overlaid on them are specific programs (that is, products). Thus, members in a matrix structure have a dual chain of command: to their functional department and to their product groups. A professor of accounting teaching an undergraduate course may report to the director of undergraduate programs as well as to the chairperson of the accounting department.

The strength of the matrix is its ability to facilitate coordination when the organization has many complex and interdependent activities.[63] Direct and frequent contacts between different specialties in the matrix can let information permeate the organization and reach the people who need it more quickly. The matrix reduces so-called bureaupathologies—its dual lines of authority limit people's tendency to protect their territories at the expense of the organization's goals.[64] A matrix also achieves economies of scale and facilitates the allocation of specialists by both providing the best resources and ensuring that they are efficiently used.[65]

The major disadvantages of the matrix lie in the confusion it creates, its tendency to foster power struggles, and the stress it places on individuals.[66] For individuals who desire security and absence from ambiguity, this work climate can be stressful. Reporting to more than one boss introduces role conflict, and unclear expectations introduce role ambiguity. Without the unity-of-command concept, ambiguity about who reports to whom is significantly increased and often leads to conflict and power struggles between functional and product managers.

Alternate Design Options

14-3 Identify the characteristics of the virtual structure, the team structure, and the circular structure.

In the ever-increasing trend toward flatter structures, many organizations have been developing new options with fewer layers of hierarchy and more emphasis on opening the boundaries of the organization.[67] In this section, we describe three such designs: the *virtual structure*, the *team structure*, and the *circular structure*.

The Virtual Structure

virtual structure A small, core organization that outsources major business functions.

Why own when you can rent? That question captures the essence of the **virtual structure** (also sometimes called the *network*, or *modular*, structure), typically a small, core organization that outsources its major business functions.[68] The virtual structure is highly centralized, with little or no departmentalization.

The prototype of the virtual structure is today's filmmaking organization. In Bollywood, movies were made by huge, vertically integrated corporations. Studios such as Ranjit Studios and Bombay Talkies owned large movie lots and employed thousands of full-time specialists—set designers, camera people, film editors, directors, and actors. Today, most movies are made by a collection of

Exhibit 14-6 A Virtual Structure

individuals and small companies who come together and make films project by project. This structural form allows each project to be staffed with the talent best suited to its demands rather than just with the people employed by the studio. It minimizes bureaucratic overhead because there is no lasting organization to maintain. It lessens long-term risks and their costs because there is no long term—a team is assembled for a finite period and then disbanded.

Exhibit 14-6 shows a virtual structure in which management outsources all the primary functions of the business. The core of the organization is a small group of executives whose job is to oversee directly any activities done in-house and to coordinate relationships with organizations that manufacture, distribute, and perform other crucial functions. The dotted lines represent the relationships typically maintained under contracts. Managers in virtual structures spend most of their time coordinating and controlling external relations.

Network organizations often take many forms.[69] Some of the more traditional forms include the *franchise form*, in which there are managers, systems, and other experts in the central node (i.e., executive group), and customer sales and services are carried out by franchise units. This popular form of network organization is very common in service business models, such as 7-Eleven, McDonald's, Jimmy John's, and Dunkin' Donuts, Barbeque Nation, Social and Pizza Hut. In this form, however, franchisees do not tend to collaborate or coordinate with one another, are difficult to influence by the executive group, and may actually be in direct competition for resources from the executive group. For instance, one study of franchises found that there is variability in how mission statements are formed at each franchise along with how well they consider ethical standards. These differences subsequently impact how much discrimination is experienced at each franchise.[70] Another example is the *starburst form*, in which a parent firm splits off one of its functions into a spinoff firm.[71] For example, in 2012, Netflix split off its DVD function into a separate entity, now DVD.com.[72]

The major advantage of the virtual structure is its flexibility, which allows individuals with an innovative idea and little money to successfully compete against larger, more established organizations. The structure also saves a great deal of money by eliminating permanent offices and hierarchical roles for outsourced functions.[73] The drawbacks have become increasingly clear as popularity has grown.[74] Virtual organizations are in a state of perpetual flux and reorganization, which means roles, goals, and responsibilities are unclear, setting the stage for increased political behavior.

The Team Structure

team structure An organizational structure that replaces departments with empowered teams, and that eliminates horizontal boundaries and external barriers between customers and suppliers.

The **team structure** seeks to eliminate the chain of command and replace departments with empowered teams.[75] This structure removes vertical and horizontal boundaries in addition to breaking down external barriers between the company and its customers and suppliers.

By removing vertical boundaries, management flattens the hierarchy and minimizes status and rank. Cross-hierarchical teams (which include top executives, middle managers, supervisors, and operative employees),

Career OBjectives

What structure should I choose?

I'm running a small but growing business and need help figuring out how to keep positions flexible as we expand. What advice can you give me about designing job structures that will help combine my success today with growth for tomorrow?

—*Anika*

Dear Anika:

A surprising number of small businesses fail right at the point where they begin to grow, and for many reasons, including financing deficits and competitors that copy their clever ideas. However, a frequent problem is that the structure that the company began with is simply not right for a larger firm.

There are ways to meet the challenge. Start by looking at individual jobs and their responsibilities. Make a list for each job. When job roles and responsibilities aren't defined, you can pick up a great deal of flexibility, assigning employees to tasks exactly when needed. Unfortunately, this flexibility also means it's hard to determine which skills are available or to identify gaps between planned strategy and available human resources.

Second, you may want to define roles based on broad sets of competencies that span multiple levels of organizational functioning. In this *strategic competency model*, job roles and incentives are defined based on a clear structure. Here are the steps:

- *Look at the top level and think about the future.* In the competency model, you should use the mission statement and overall organizational strategies to evaluate your organization's future needs.
- *Once you've identified the organization's future needs, figure out a smart way to assign responsibilities to individuals.* You'll obviously need some specialization, but at the same time, consider general skills that will be useful for both growth and long-term sustainability.
- *As your business grows, identify applicants with the potential to meet future needs, and develop employee incentives to encourage broad skills profiles.* You'll want to structure your plan so employees increase in competency as they move up the organization chart.

The most important thing to remember is that you aren't creating a job structure just for today—make sure it's ready to grow and change with your business. Grow well!

Sources: Based on G. W. Stevens, "A Critical Review of the Science and Practice of Competency Modeling," *Human Resource Development Review* 12 (March 2013): 86–107; P. Capelli and J. R. Keller, "Talent Management: Conceptual Approaches and Practical Challenges," *Annual Review of Organizational Psychology and Organizational Behavior* 1 (March 2014): 305–31; and C. Fernández-Aráoz, "21st Century Talent Spotting," *Harvard Business Review*, June 2014, https://hbr.org/2014/06/21st-century-talent-spotting.

The opinions provided here are of the managers and authors only and do not necessarily reflect those of their organizations. The authors or managers are not responsible for any errors or omissions, or for the results obtained from the use of this information. In no event will the authors or managers, or their related partnerships or corporations thereof, be liable to you or anyone else for any decision made or action taken in reliance on the opinions provided here.

participative decision-making practices, and the use of 360-degree performance appraisals (in which peers and others evaluate performance) can be used. For example, at the Danish firm Oticon A/S, the world's largest hearing aid manufacturer, all traces of hierarchy have disappeared.[76] Everyone works at uniform mobile workstations, and project teams, not functions or departments, coordinate work.

As previously discussed, functional departments create horizontal boundaries between functions, product lines, and units. The way to reduce them is to replace functional departments with cross-functional teams and organize activities around processes. Xerox, for instance, develops new products through multidisciplinary teams that work on a single process instead of on narrow functional tasks.[77]

When fully operational, the team structure may break down geographic barriers. Today, most large U.S. companies see themselves as team-oriented global corporations; many, like Coca-Cola and McDonald's, do as much business

An Ethical Choice

Flexible Structures, Deskless Workplaces

Once upon a time, students fresh from business schools couldn't wait for that first cubicle to call home, midlevel managers aspired to an office of their own, and executives coveted the corner office. These days, the walls are coming down. As organizational structures change, so do their physical environments. Many organizations have been trying to make the physical environment reflect the organizational structures they adopt.

At online retailer Zappos, not even the CEO wants an office, and all 1,500 employees are welcome throughout the open spaces. Firms like Google have workplace designs of public rooms with lounge areas and large, multiperson tables. According to Edward Danyo, manager of workplace strategy at pharmaceuticals firm GlaxoSmithKline, shared environments create efficient work gains, including what he estimates is a 45 percent increase in the speed of decision making. But there are ethical concerns about the dismantling of the physical and mental organizational structure:

- *Where will confidential discussions take place?* In some contemporary workplace designs, ad hoc conference rooms address the need for separate gatherings. This may not be optimal if the walls are made of glass, if employees will feel stigmatized when called into a meeting room, or if they become reluctant to approach human resources staff with issues because of privacy concerns.
- *How can differences in personality traits be overcome?* Employees high in extraversion will be more comfortable building collaborative relationships without assigned workspaces, while introverted individuals may be uncomfortable without an established office structure where they can get to know others over time.
- *How can personal privacy be maintained?* Zappos gives employees personal lockers, asks employees to angle laptop screens away from neighbors, and tries to make open spaces more private by encouraging ear buds to create a sound barrier between working employees.
- *How can you assure your clients about confidentiality?* Even walled, soundproof rooms for virtual or live meetings may not provide the desired level of security for clients who need to know their business will stay on a need-to-know basis.
- *How will expectations and accountabilities be enforced?* In an environment without offices and sometimes without job titles, there is an even greater need for clearly assigned goals, roles, and expectations. Otherwise, open collaborative structures may foster diffusion of responsibility and confusion.

Sources: Based on S. Henn, "'Serendipitous Interaction' Key to Tech Firm's Workplace Design," NPR, March 13, 2013, www.npr.org/blogs/alltechconsidered/2013/03/13/174195695/serendipitous-interaction-key-to-tech-firms-workplace-design; H. El Nasser, "What Office? Laptops Are Workspace," *USA Today*, June 6, 2012, 1B–2B; R. W. Huppke, "Thinking Outside the Cubicle," *Chicago Tribune*, October 29, 2012, 2-1, 2-3; "Inside the New Deskless Office," *Forbes*, July 16, 2012, 34; and E. Maltby, "My Space Is Our Space," *The Wall Street Journal*, May 21, 2012, R9.

overseas as in the United States, and some struggle to incorporate geographic regions into their structure. In other cases, the team approach is need-based. Such is the case with Chinese companies, which made 93 acquisitions in the oil and gas industry in five years—incorporating each acquisition as a new team unit—to meet forecasted demand that their resources in China could not meet.[78] The team structure provides a solution because it considers geography as more of a tactical, logistical issue than a structural one. In short, the goal may be to break down cultural barriers and open opportunities.

Some organizations create teams incorporating their employees and their customers or suppliers. For example, to ensure that important product parts are made reliably and to exacting specifications by its suppliers, Honeywell International partners some of its engineers with managers at those suppliers.

The Circular Structure

circular structure An organizational structure in which executives are at the center, spreading their vision outward in rings grouped by function (managers, then specialists, then workers).

Picture the concentric rings of an archery target. In the center are the executives, and radiating outward in rings grouped by function are the managers, then the specialists, then the workers. This is the **circular structure**.[79] Does it seem like organizational anarchy? There is still a hierarchy, but top management is at the very heart of the organization, with its vision spreading outward.

The circular structure has intuitive appeal for creative entrepreneurs, and some small innovative firms have claimed it. As in many of the current hybrid approaches, however, employees are apt to be unclear about whom they report to and who is running the show. We are still likely to see the popularity of the circular structure spread. The concept may have intuitive appeal for spreading a vision of corporate social responsibility (CSR), for instance.

The Leaner Organization: Downsizing

14-4 Describe the effects of downsizing on organizational structures and employees.

downsizing A systematic effort to make an organization leaner by closing locations, reducing staff, or selling off business units that do not add value.

The goal of some organizational structures we've described is to improve agility by creating a lean, focused, and flexible organization. *Downsizing* is a systematic effort to make an organization leaner by closing locations, reducing staff, de-layering (i.e., narrowing span of control by reducing the number of levels in a hierarchy), or selling off business units that don't add value.[80] Downsizing doesn't necessarily mean physically shrinking the size of your office, although that's been happening, too (see OB Poll).

The radical shrinking of Motorola Mobility in 2012 and 2013 is a case of downsizing to survive after its 2011 $12.5 billion acquisition by Google. In response to declining demand for its smartphones, Motorola cut its workforce by 20 percent in August 2012. When the company posted a $350 million fourth-quarter loss in 2012, with a 40 percent revenue decline, it cut the workforce again, by 10 percent. Google called this rightsizing.[81] Motorola Mobility was then sold to China's Lenovo in 2014 for $2.91 billion.

Other firms downsize to direct all their efforts toward their core competencies. American Express claims to have been doing this in a series of layoffs over more than a decade: 7,700 jobs in 2001, 6,500 jobs in 2002, 7,000 jobs (10 percent of its workforce) in 2008, and 4,000 jobs in 2009. The 2013 cut of 5,400 jobs (8.5 percent of the remaining workforce) represented "its biggest retrenchment in a decade," with an additional sizable layoff of around 4,000 jobs in 2015. Each layoff has been accompanied by a restructuring, to

OB POLL

The Incredible Shrinking Office

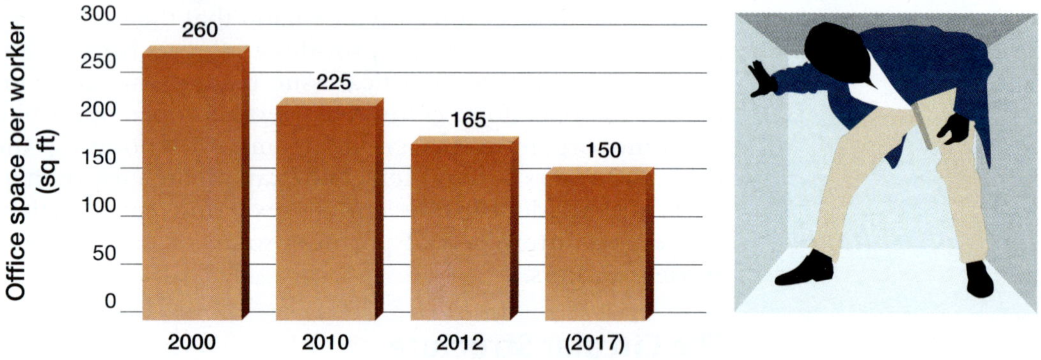

Source: Based on February 28, 2012, press release "Office Space per Worker Will Drop to 100 Square Feet or Below," http://www.corenetglobal.org/files/home/info_center/global_press_releases/pdf/pr120227_officespace.pdf.

reflect changing customer preferences, away from personal customer service and toward online customer service. According to CEO Ken Chennault, "Our business and industry continue to become transformed by technology. Because of these changes, we have the need and the opportunity to evolve our organization and cost structure."[82] However, other firms do not have a choice and implement downsizing measures because of outside forces. For example, organizations may engage in downsizing, along with work restructuring, wage, and employment freezes during times of natural disaster, pandemics (such as those that occurred during the COVID-19 pandemic), and economic recessions.[83]

Many companies have also laid off large numbers of employees to remain afloat during the pandemic. IBM, Accenture, Cognizant Technologies are among some of the organizations that have laid off employees in the last 20 months.[84]

Some companies focus on lean management techniques to reduce bureaucracy and speed decision making.[85] Starbucks adopted lean initiatives in 2009, which encompassed all levels of management and focused on faster barista techniques and manufacturing processes.[86] Customers generally applauded the shortened wait times and improved product consistency.

Despite the advantages of being a lean organization, the impact of downsizing on organizational performance is not without controversy. Reducing the size of the workforce perhaps has positive outcomes in the long run, although the majority of the evidence suggests that downsizing has a negative impact on stock returns the year of downsizing (although this may be contingent on the organization's goals for downsizing along with other contextual factors).[87] An example of these contingencies can be found in the case of Russia's Gorky Automobile Factory (GAZ), which realized a profit for the first time in many years after President Bo Andersson fired 50,000 workers, half the workforce.[88] Eventually, however, the rampant downsizing policy caught up with Andersson when he was CEO of Russia's largest car maker, AvtoVAZ. From 2014 to 2016, downsizing at its plant in Togliatti led to tens of thousands of workers losing their jobs. At the time, Sergei Chemezov, an ally of President Vladmir Putin, told Andersson that he was "playing with fire."[89] Eventually, Andersson was removed as CEO for his tactics in 2016—what tended to be standard practice in the West (downsizing) was frowned upon in Russia, where the auto industry is revered with nationalistic pride and jobs tend to be preserved rather than cut.[90]

Part of the problem is the effect of downsizing on employee attitudes.[91] From a broad perspective, many have argued that the prominence of downsizing has led employees across the world to be insecure about their jobs and uncertain about their careers.[92] Employees who remain often feel worried about future layoffs, may be less committed to the organization, and may experience a greater amount of stress and strain.[93] Downsizing can also lead to psychological withdrawal and more voluntary turnover, so vital human capital is lost.[94] The result is a company that is more anemic than lean. Paradoxically, some research suggests that the victims may even fare better than the survivors, experiencing higher control perceptions and less stress.[95]

Companies can reduce the negative impact of downsizing by preparing in advance, thus alleviating some employee stress and strengthening support for the new direction. Here are some effective strategies for downsizing:

- *Invest.* Companies that downsize to focus on core competencies are more effective when they invest in high-involvement work practices afterward.
- *Communicate.* When employers make efforts to discuss downsizing with employees early, employees are less worried about the outcomes and feel the company is taking their perspective into account.
- *Participate.* Employees worry less if they can participate in the process in some way. Voluntary early-retirement programs or severance packages can help achieve leanness without layoffs.
- *Assist.* Severance, extended health care benefits, and job search assistance demonstrate that a company cares about its employees and honors their contributions.

In short, companies that make themselves lean can be more agile, efficient, and productive—but only if they make cuts carefully and help employees through the process.

14-5 Contrast the reasons for using mechanistic versus organic structural models.

mechanistic model A structure characterized by extensive departmentalization, high formalization, a limited information network, and centralization.

organic model A structure that is flat, uses cross-hierarchical and cross-functional teams, has low formalization, possesses a comprehensive information network, and relies on participative decision making.

Why Do Structures Differ?

We've described many organization design options. Exhibit 14-7 recaps our discussions by presenting two extreme models of organizational design.[96] One model is the **mechanistic model**. It's generally synonymous with the bureaucracy in that it has highly standardized processes for work, high formalization, and more managerial hierarchy. The other extreme is the **organic model**. It's flat, has fewer formal procedures for making decisions, has multiple decision makers, and favors flexible practices.[97]

With these two models in mind, let's ask a few questions. Why are some organizations structured along more mechanistic lines whereas others follow organic characteristics? What forces influence the choice of design? In this section, we present major causes or determinants of an organization's structure.[98]

Exhibit 14-7 Mechanistic versus Organic Models

The Mechanistic Model

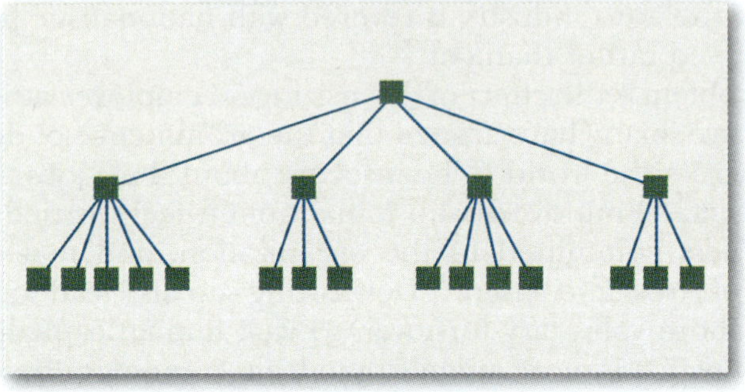

- High specialization
- Rigid departmentalization
- Clear chain of command
- Narrow spans of control
- Centralization
- High formalization

The Organic Model

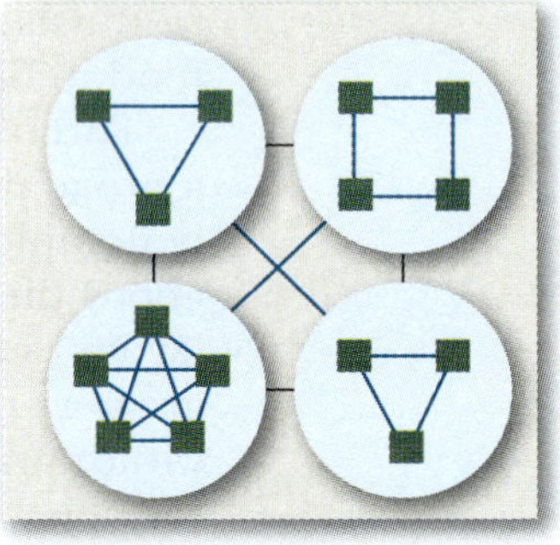

- Cross-functional teams
- Cross-hierarchical teams
- Free flow of information
- Wide spans of control
- Decentralization
- Low formalization

Organizational Strategies

Because structure is a means to achieve objectives, and objectives derive from the organization's overall strategy, it's only logical that structure should follow strategy. If management significantly changes the organization's strategy or its values, the structure must change to accommodate. For example, recent research indicates that aspects of organizational culture may influence the success of corporate social responsibility (CSR) initiatives.[99] If the culture is supported by the structure, the initiatives are more likely to have clear paths toward application. Most current strategy frameworks focus on three strategy dimensions—innovation, cost minimization, and imitation—and the structural design that works best with each.[100]

innovation strategy A strategy that emphasizes the introduction of major new products and services.

To what degree does an organization introduce major new products or services? An **innovation strategy** strives to achieve meaningful and unique innovations.[101] Obviously, not all firms pursue innovation. Apple and 3M do, but conservative retailer Marks & Spencer doesn't. Innovative firms use competitive pay and benefits to attract top candidates and motivate employees to take risks. Some degree of the mechanistic structure can actually benefit innovation. Well-developed communication channels, policies for enhancing long-term commitment, and clear channels of authority all may make it easier for rapid changes to occur smoothly.

cost-minimization strategy A strategy that emphasizes tight cost controls, avoidance of unnecessary innovation or marketing expenses, and price cutting.

An organization pursuing a **cost-minimization strategy** controls costs tightly, refrains from incurring unnecessary expenses, and cuts prices in selling a basic product.[102] This describes the strategy pursued by Walmart and the makers of generic or store-label grocery products. Cost-minimizing organizations usually pursue fewer policies meant to develop commitment among their workforce.

imitation strategy A strategy that seeks to move into new products or new markets only after their viability has already been proven.

Organizations following an **imitation strategy** try to minimize risk and maximize opportunity for profit, moving new products or entering new markets only after innovators have proven their viability.[103] Mass-market fashion manufacturers that copy designer styles follow this strategy, as do firms such as Hewlett-Packard and Caterpillar. They follow smaller and more innovative competitors with superior products but only after competitors

Chumbak, started as an India-inspired souvenirs brand in 2010 first started with putting out its products in modern brand outlets. In a span of 12 years, Chumbak has opened 70 stores and a formidable digital presence. In 2022 Chumbak plans to double its revenues by spending on marketing and opening more stores in cities across India.[104,105]

Source: Rahul Ramachandram.shutterstock.com

have demonstrated that a market exists. Italy's Moleskine SpA, a small maker of fashionable notebooks, is another example of imitation strategy but in a distinct way: Looking to open more retail shops around the world, it imitates the expansion strategies of larger, successful fashion companies Salvatore Ferragamo SpA and Brunello Cucinelli.[106]

Exhibit 14-8 describes the structural option that best matches each strategy. Innovators need the flexibility of the organic structure (although, as we noted, they may use some elements of the mechanistic structure as well), whereas cost minimizers seek the efficiency and stability of the mechanistic structure. Imitators combine the two structures. They use a mechanistic structure to maintain tight controls and low costs in their current activities but create organic subunits in which to pursue new undertakings.

Organization Size

An organization's size significantly affects its structure.[107] Organizations that employ 2,000 or more people tend to have more specialization, more departmentalization, more vertical levels, and more rules and regulations

Exhibit 14-8 **The Strategy–Structure Relationship**

Strategy	Structural Option
Innovation	**Organic:** A loose structure; low specialization, low formalization, decentralized
Cost minimization	**Mechanistic:** Tight control; extensive work specialization, high formalization, high centralization
Imitation	**Mechanistic and organic:** Mix of loose with tight properties; tight controls over current activities and looser controls for new undertakings

than do small organizations. However, size becomes less important as an organization expands. Why? At around 2,000 employees, an organization is already mechanistic; 500 more employees won't have much impact. But adding 500 employees to an organization of only 300 is likely to significantly shift it toward a more mechanistic structure.

Technology

technology The way in which an organization transfers its inputs into outputs.

Technology describes the way an organization transfers inputs into outputs. Every organization has at least one technology for converting financial, human, and physical resources into products or services. For example, the Chinese consumer electronics company Haier (the owners of GE Appliances) uses an assembly-line process for mass-produced products, which is complemented by more flexible and innovative structures to respond to customers and design new products.[108] Regardless, organizational structures adapt to their technology—and vice versa.[109] Organizational structure and culture can become inscribed in the data structure, software, and hardware that an organization uses.[110]

Environment

environment Forces outside an organization that potentially affect the organization's structure.

An organization's **environment** includes outside institutions or forces that can affect its structure, such as suppliers, customers, competitors, and public pressure groups.[111] Dynamic environments create significantly more uncertainty for managers than do static ones. To minimize uncertainty in key market arenas, managers may broaden their structure to sense and respond to threats. Most companies, for example Pepsi and Southwest Airlines, have added social media departments to counter negative information posted on blogs.

Any organization's environment has three dimensions: capacity, volatility, and complexity.[112] *Capacity* refers to the degree to which the environment can support growth. Rich and growing environments generate excess resources, which can buffer the organization in times of relative scarcity.

Volatility describes the degree of instability in the environment. A dynamic environment with a high degree of unpredictable change makes it difficult for management to make accurate predictions. Because information technology changes at such a rapid pace, more organizations' environments are becoming volatile.

Complexity is the degree of heterogeneity and concentration among environmental elements. Simple environments—like the tobacco industry where the methods of production, competitive and regulatory pressures, and the like, haven't changed in quite some time—are homogeneous and concentrated. Environments characterized by heterogeneity and dispersion—like the broadband industry—are complex and diverse, with numerous competitors.

Exhibit 14-9 summarizes our definition of the environment along its three dimensions. The arrows indicate movement toward higher uncertainty. Thus, organizations that operate in environments characterized as scarce, dynamic, and complex face the greatest degree of uncertainty because they have high unpredictability, little room for error, and a diverse set of elements in the environment to monitor constantly.

Given this three-dimensional definition of *environment,* we can offer some general conclusions about environmental uncertainty and structural arrangements. The more scarce, dynamic, and complex the environment, the more organic a structure should be. The more abundant, stable, and simple the environment, the more the mechanistic structure will be preferred.

Exhibit 14-9 Three-Dimensional Model of the Environment

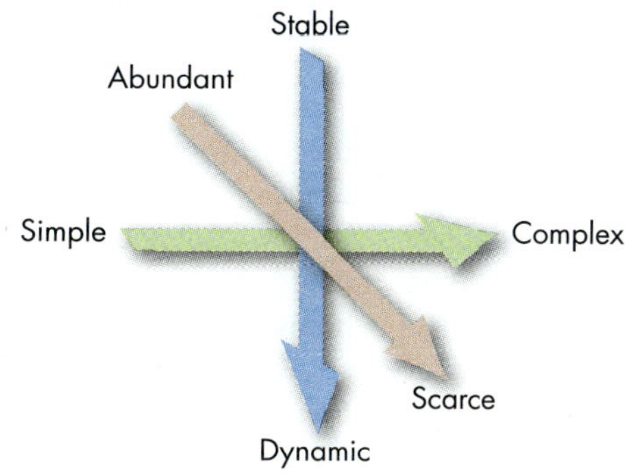

Institutions

institutions Cultural factors, especially those factors that might not lead to adaptive consequences, that lead many organizations to have similar structures.

Another factor that shapes organizational structure is **institutions**. These are cultural factors that act as guidelines for appropriate behavior.[113] Institutional theory describes some of the forces that lead many organizations to have similar structures and, unlike the theories we've described so far, focuses on pressures that aren't necessarily adaptive. In fact, many institutional theorists try to highlight the ways in which corporate behaviors sometimes *seem* to be performance-oriented but are guided by unquestioned social norms and conformity.

The most obvious institutional factors come from regulatory pressures; certain industries under government contracts, for instance, must have clear reporting relationships and strict information controls. Sometimes simple inertia determines an organizational form—companies can be structured in a particular way just because that's the way things have always been done. Organizations in countries with high power distance might have a structural form with strict authority relationships because it's seen as more legitimate in that culture. Some have attributed problems in adaptability in Japanese organizations to the institutional pressure to maintain authority relationships.

Sometimes organizations start to have a particular structure because of fads or trends. Organizations can try to copy other successful companies just to look good to investors and not because they need that structure to perform better. Many companies have recently tried to copy the organic form of a company like Google only to find that such structures are a very poor fit with their operating environment. Institutional pressures are often difficult to see specifically because we take them for granted, but that doesn't mean they aren't powerful.

Organizational Designs and Employee Behavior

14-6 Analyze the behavioral implications of different organizational designs.

We opened this chapter by implying that an organization's structure can have significant effects on its members. What might those effects be?

A review of the evidence leads to a pretty clear conclusion: You can't generalize! Not everyone prefers the freedom and flexibility of organic structures. Several factors stand out in different structures as well. In highly formalized, heavily structured mechanistic organizations, the level of fairness in formal policies and procedures (organizational justice) is a very important

Myth or Science?

Employees Can Work Just as Well from Home

This statement is true—but not unequivocally. Employees who work from home even part of the time report they are happier, and as we saw in Chapter 3, happier employees are likely to be more productive than dissatisfied counterparts. From an organization's perspective, companies are realizing gains of 5 to 7 extra work hours a week for each employee working from home. There are also cost savings, from reduced overhead for office space and utilities to elimination of unproductive social time. Employers of a home-based workforce can establish work teams and organizational reporting relationships with little attention to office politics, making it possible to assign roles and responsibilities more objectively. These may be some of the reasons organizations have increasingly endorsed the concept of telecommuting, to the point where 3.1 million U.S. payrolled employees work from home.

Although we can all think of jobs that may never be conducive to working from home (such as many in the service industry), not all positions that *could* be based from home *should* be. Research indicates that the success of a work-from-home position depends on the job's structure even more than on its tasks. The amount of interdependence needed between employees within a team or in a reporting relationship sometimes requires *epistemic interdependence*, which is each employee's ability to predict what other employees will do. Organization consultants pay attention to how employee roles relate in the *architecture* of the organization chart, realizing that intentional relationship building is key. Thus, while an employee may complete the tasks of a job well by working alone from home, the benefits of teamwork can be lost. We don't yet fully understand the impact of working at a physical distance without sharing time or space with others, but it is perhaps the reason that Yahoo!, Best Buy, and other corporations have brought their employees back into the office.

The success of a work-from-home program depends on the individual, job, and culture of the organization. Work from home can be satisfying for employees and efficient for organizations, but we are learning it has limits.

Sources: Based on M. Mercer, "Shirk Work? Working at Home Can Mean Longer Hours," *TriCities.com*, March 4, 2013, www.tricities.com/news/opinion_columns/article_d04355b8-83cb-11e2-bc31-0019bb30f31a.html; P. Puranam, M. Raveendran, and T. Knudsen, "Organization Design: The Epistemic Interdependence Perspective," *Academy of Management Review* 37, no. 3 (2012): 419–40; N. Shah, "More Americans Working Remotely," *The Wall Street Journal*, March 6, 2013, A3; and R. E. Silverman and Q. Fottrell, "The Home Office in the Spotlight," *The Wall Street Journal*, February 27, 2013, B6.

predictor of satisfaction. In more personal, individually adaptive organic organizations, employees value interpersonal justice more.[114] Some people are most productive and satisfied when work tasks are standardized and ambiguity is minimized—that is, in mechanistic structures. So any discussion of the effect of organizational design on employee behavior should address individual differences. To do so, let's consider employee preferences for work specialization, span of control, and centralization.[115]

The evidence generally indicates that *work specialization* contributes to higher employee productivity—but at the price of job satisfaction. However, work specialization is not an unending source of higher productivity. Problems start to surface, and productivity begins to suffer, when the human diseconomies of doing repetitive and narrow tasks overtake the economies of specialization. As the workforce has become more highly educated and desirous of jobs that are intrinsically rewarding, we seem to reach the point at which productivity begins to decline as a function of specialization more quickly than in the past. While decreased productivity often prompts companies to add oversight and inspection roles, the better answer may be to reorganize work functions and accountability.[116]

A segment of the workforce still prefers the routine and repetitiveness of highly specialized jobs. Some individuals want work that makes minimal intellectual demands and provides the security of routine; for them, high work specialization is a source of job satisfaction. The question is whether they represent 2 percent of the workforce or 52 percent. Given that some self-selection operates in the choice of careers, we might conclude that negative behavioral outcomes from high specialization are most likely to surface in professional jobs occupied by individuals with high needs for personal growth and diversity.

It is probably safe to say that no evidence supports a relationship between *span of control* and employee satisfaction or performance. Although it is intuitively attractive that large spans might lead to higher employee performance because they provide more distant supervision and more opportunity for personal initiative, there is a lack of research to support this notion. Some people like to be left alone; others prefer the security of a boss who is available at all times. Consistent with several of the contingency theories of leadership discussed in Chapter 13, we would expect factors such as employees' experiences and abilities, and the degree of structure in their tasks, to explain when wide or narrow spans of control are likely to contribute to performance and job satisfaction. However, some evidence indicates that large spans of control are related to more unsafe behaviors and accidents in the workplace.[117]

We also find evidence linking *centralization* and job satisfaction.[118] This is partly because, in general, less centralized organizations have a greater amount of autonomy. But, again, while one employee may value freedom, another may find autonomous environments frustratingly ambiguous.

We can draw one obvious insight: People don't select employers randomly. They are attracted to, are selected by, and stay with organizations that suit their personal characteristics.[119] Job candidates who prefer predictability are likely to seek out and take employment in mechanistic structures, and those who want autonomy are more likely to end up in organic structures. Thus, the effect of structure on employee behavior is undoubtedly reduced when the selection process facilitates proper matching of individual characteristics with organizational characteristics. Companies should strive to establish, promote, and maintain the unique identity of their structures, because skilled employees may quit because of dramatic changes.[120]

Research on preferences for job formalization across cultures from subsidiaries of a high-technology company in Taiwan, France, Germany, Italy, Holland, and Britain found that the level of job satisfaction of employees from high-power-distance cultures was dependent on the congruence between the degree of formalization and cultural norms.[121] So consider cultural differences along with individual differences when predicting how structure will affect employee performance and satisfaction.

The changing landscape of organizational structure designs has implications for the individual progressing on a career path. Research with managers in Japan, the United Kingdom, and the United States indicated that employees who weathered downsizing and resulting hybrid organizational structures considered their future career prospects diminished. While this may or may not have been correct, their thinking shows that organizational structure does affect the employee and thus must be designed carefully.[122]

Summary

The theme of this chapter is that an organization's internal structure contributes to explaining and predicting behavior. That is, in addition to individual and group factors, the structural relationships in which people work have a bearing on employee attitudes and behavior. What's the basis for this argument? To the degree that an organization's structure reduces ambiguity for employees and answers questions such as "What am I supposed to do?," "How am I supposed to do it?," "To whom do I report?," and "To whom do I go if I have a problem?," it shapes their attitudes and facilitates and motivates them to higher levels of performance. Exhibit 14-10 summarizes what we've discussed.

Implications for Managers

- Specialization can make operations more efficient, but remember that excessive specialization can create dissatisfaction and reduced motivation.
- Avoid designing rigid hierarchies that overly limit employees' empowerment and autonomy.
- Balance the advantages of remote work against the potential pitfalls before adding flexible workplace options into the organization's structure.
- Downsize your organization to realize major cost savings, and focus the company around core competencies—but only if necessary, because downsizing can have a significant negative impact on employee affect.
- Consider the scarcity, dynamism, and complexity of the environment, and balance organic and mechanistic elements when designing an organizational structure.

Exhibit 14-10 Organizational Structure: Its Determinants and Outcomes

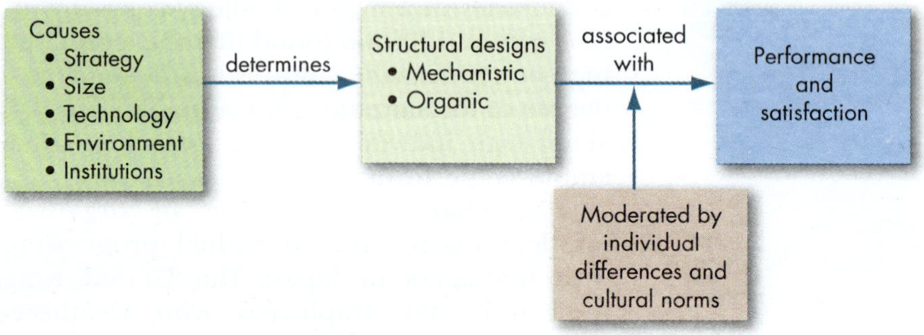

Open-Air Offices Inspire Creativity and Enhance Productivity

POINT

Eric Prum, cofounder of W&P Design in Brooklyn, New York, and the rest of his 12 coworkers share a single room on the fourth floor of an open-air, converted warehouse. Although it can occasionally be noisy, the layout has led to some very productive brainstorming sessions. In fact, their latest project, ¡Buenos Nachos!, was a direct result of the open-air office plan. The cofounders were discussing the idea for a hipster nacho cookbook in the office while the coworkers eavesdropped. What turned into a spontaneous idea quickly became a productive brainstorming session. From this open-air plan emerged a cookbook with over 75 recipes from famous chefs and celebrities, including Bill Hader, Andrew Zimmern, and Rachael Ray.

Aside from cost minimization, the logic of the open-air office is that it is meant to tear down the physical barriers between people in the workplace. The functional communication among employees is maximized when these barriers are removed. Starting with the organization's functional goals in mind, an open-air workplace can be tailored so that it accomplishes these goals by setting aside certain areas or spaces so that they are well suited to accomplish specific functions (e.g., a meeting area, a reading area, etc.). For example, the New York branding firm Collins altered aspects of the environment to work around any limitations of an open-air office, including arranging the tables so that no person faces another employee. Overall, Collins found, in their own internal research, that the open-air office improves a sense of shared vision and mission, community, and creativity perceptions. Additional research also suggests that these open-air plans can reduce the amount of time spent in meetings.

COUNTERPOINT

"Our new, modern Tribeca office was beautifully airy, and yet remarkably oppressive. Nothing was private. On the first day, I took my seat at the table assigned to our creative department, next to a nice woman who I suspect was an air horn in a former life. All day, there was constant shuffling, yelling, and laughing, along with loud music piped through a PA system." The picture Lindsey Kaufman, a Brooklyn advertising professional, described highlights the strain and dissatisfaction employees in open-air office environments can experience, even when there are cubicles granting at least some privacy. The creator of the cubicle, Robert Probst, envisioned something very different in 1964: a freespace where employees could customize their workplace to accommodate their level of privacy, space needs, and flexibility, and to give them a sense of autonomy in an open office. This "action office" became mass-produced and limited in size, quality, and customizability, leading to what we would now call the modern-day cubicle.

Studies on the open-air office and the confinement cubicles of modern offices paint a dismal picture of their effectiveness. One study reviewing hundreds of office environments found that, despite their cohesion benefits, open-air offices reduced workers' attention spans, productivity, creative thinking, and satisfaction. One of the biggest factors responsible is the level of noise, which leads to decreased motivation and potential posture issues. The satisfaction levels related to noise, sound privacy, ease of interaction, among others, across 42,764 observations from over 300 office buildings were analyzed by researchers using the Post-Occupancy Evaluation (POE) database from the University of California at Berkeley. They found a clear disparity between satisfaction in open offices versus private offices, and drastically more satisfaction with the latter. And they found that ease of interaction (a goal of open-office plans) was no greater in open offices than in private offices.

Sources: Based on D. Burkus, "Why Your Open Office Workspace Doesn't Work," *Forbes*, June 21, 2016, https://www.forbes.com/sites/davidburkus/2016/06/21/why-your-open-office-workspace-doesnt-work/#336a42f6435f; G. W. Evans and D. Johnson, "Stress and Open-Office Noise," *Journal of Applied Psychology* 85, no. 5 (2000): 779–83; L. Kaufman, "Google Got It Wrong. The Open-Office Trend Is Destroying the Workplace," *The Washington Post*, December 30, 2014, https://www.washingtonpost.com/posteverything/wp/2014/12/30/google-got-it-wrong-the-open-office-trend-is-destroying-the-workplace/?utm_term=.d716ef9fe41a; S. Khetarpal, "The Popular 'Open Office' Design Has Many Disadvantages, but Some Employers Are Going Beyond It to Create an Empowering Environment at the Workplace," *Business Today*, March 12, 2017, 100–6; M. Konnikova, "The Open-Office Trap," *The New Yorker*, January 7, 2014, http://www.newyorker.com/business/currency/the-open-office-trap; P. Rosenberg and K. Campbell, "An Open Office Experiment That Actually Worked," *Harvard Business Review* (October 3, 2014); R. Saunderson, "Learning in an Open Office Environment," *Training*, January 1, 2016, 134–5; D. Ward, "Beyond the Open Office," *HR Magazine*, April 1, 2015, 30–5; and M. D. Zalesny and R. V. Farace, "Traditional versus Open Offices: A Comparison of Sociotechnical, Social Relations, and Symbolic Meaning Perspectives," *Academy of Management Journal* 30, no. 2 (1987): 240–59.

CHAPTER REVIEW

QUESTIONS FOR REVIEW

14-1 What seven key elements define an organization's structure?

14-2 What are the characteristics of the functional, bureaucracy, and matrix structures?

14-3 What are the characteristics of the virtual structure, the team structure, and the circular structure?

14-4 How might downsizing affect organizational structures and employees?

14-5 How are mechanistic and organic structural models similar and different?

14-6 What are the behavioral implications of different organizational designs?

APPLICATION AND EMPLOYABILITY

Knowing the ins and outs of the structure of your organization can help you improve your employability in the future by improving how you make strategic and ethical decisions along with how you collaborate and communicate with others in the workplace. Different forms of organizational structure have different consequences for employee, manager, and customer behaviors; recognizing these effects can help you behave more adaptively. Perhaps some day you will be starting your own organization from the ground up, or you may collaborate to restructure or redesign the work in an organization. Understanding these different forms of structure will help you improve your skills for use in those situations. In this chapter, you improved your critical thinking as well as your knowledge application and analysis skills by determining whether employees can work just as well from home, considering what type of structure to choose for a small and growing business, considering the ethics of flexibility and structural changes in the workplace, and debating the effectiveness of open-air offices.

In the next section, you will develop these skills, along with your social responsibility knowledge, by participating in the Experiential Exercise: The Sandwich Shop, examining the ethicality behind employment fluidity in the current job market, considering creative deviance and its anti-hierarchical benefits to organizations, and questioning the effectiveness of the bureaucratic structure for a major airline carrier.

EXPERIENTIAL EXERCISE The Sandwich Shop

Form groups of at least four individuals. Use the following information as background for the exercise.

The managers of a new chain of sandwich shops need to determine what types of sandwiches consumers want and find recipes and ingredients. Ingredient sources, prices, and other logistical requirements (like refrigeration) need to be determined, purchasing decisions are ongoing, and supplier relationships need to be managed. Financing must also be arranged at this early phase. With this groundwork, the company will move to the next stage of marketing, including pricing and the development of advertising materials. Finally, selecting and training workers will occur. Each group creates the following.

A Simple Structure

Determine what a simple structure would look like for this organization. Recall that a simple structure is one in which there is little hierarchy, wide spans of control, and centralized decision making. To whom would the various tasks described in the background above be assigned? What sort of delegation might take place? Who would coordinate the multiple operations? About how many people would be acting in an administrative role, and what sort of spans of control would they have? What challenges will the organization face as it grows?

A Bureaucracy

Determine what a bureaucratic structure would look like for this organization. Bureaucracies are marked by more hierarchy, small spans of control, and specialized decision making. Establish task assignments, delegation, coordination, and the number of individuals required. Also consider possibilities for future growth with a bureaucratic system.

A Virtual Structure

Determine what a virtual structure would look like for this organization if many of the aspects of the business are outsourced. Consider which tasks can be performed adequately by individuals who do not work within the restaurant chain and which tasks should be kept in house.

Debriefing

After all groups have developed different structural options, convene for class discussion for groups to describe how they created responsibilities for different individuals. Then the class should talk about which system of organization seems most beneficial for this business.

ETHICAL DILEMMA Postmillennium Tensions in the Flexible Organization

The message from the business press has been consistent: Don't count on long-term employment. For years, job seekers have been told they should expect to be responsible for their own careers and prepare for the possibility that they will be changing jobs frequently. A simple look at employment trends also confirms that highly routine and well-defined jobs have been decreasing in number.

The shift has often been described in positive terms. Managers work to create organizations that have laudable characteristics like adaptability, flexibility, and creativity. Author Micha Kaufman notes that doing well in contemporary business environments means "having the flexibility to let go of the ideas of the past, the courage to constantly reevaluate plans for the future, and the presence of mind to adapt to life, as it is, in the moment." There is a lot of appeal in creating your own future at work.

At the same time, many workers land in precarious positions. Researchers find that individuals who feel insecure or uncertain about future employment experience higher levels of psychological strain and worry. Insecure workers also get sick more frequently. Contrary to the positive image of the freelance worker with boundless energy and creativity, evidence shows that for many individuals, a lack of job security can result in exhaustion and an apprehensive approach to work problems.

Corporate leaders ask themselves what their role in creating job security should be. Some note that companies built around stability and security are less likely to compete successfully and may go out of business. Many organizations try to maintain flexibility *and* a certain level of security. For example, Scripps Health has maintained a pool of internal transfer opportunities and training assignments for individuals whose job functions are no longer needed. As a result, even within the highly volatile health care industry, it has been able to avoid layoffs. However, systems that provide job security do not come cheaply nor are they feasible for all companies.

Questions

14-7. Do you think that stability is good or bad for employees? Explain your answer.

14-8. Do employers have an ethical responsibility to provide security for employees or just a warning about a lack of security?

14-9. If long-term employment security isn't feasible, what alternatives might employers provide to help employees make smoother transitions?

Sources: Based on M. Kaufman, "The Wisdom of Job Insecurity," *Forbes*, October 3, 2014, http://www.forbes.com/sites/michakaufman/2014/10/03/the-wisdom-of-job-insecurity-dont-be-lulled-by-falling-unemployment/; C. Van Gorder, "A No-Layoffs Policy Can Work, Even in an Unpredictable Economy," *Harvard Business Review*, January 26, 2015, https://hbr.org/2015/01/a-no-layoffs-policy-can-work-even-in-an-unpredictable-economy; J. Zumbrun, "Is Your Job 'Routine'? If So, It's Probably Disappearing," *Wall Street Journal*, April 8, 2015, http://blogs.wsj.com/economics/2015/04/08/is-your-job-routine-if-so-its-probably-disappearing/; and U. Kinnunen, A. Mäkikangas, S. Mauno, N. De Cuyper, and H. De Witte, "Development of Perceived Job Insecurity across Two Years: Associations with Antecedents and Employee Outcomes," *Journal of Occupational Health Psychology* 19 (2014): 243–58.

CASE INCIDENT 1 Kuuki: Reading the Atmosphere

Most Japanese businesses have very complex vertically structured organizations. Indeed, each of the key departments of the organization has its own vertical structure and operates rather like individual businesses. There is very little inter-relationship between departments, each of which has very clearly defined roles.

When the business interacts with customers, it is the sales and marketing departments that handle negotiations. Even when the customer needs technical information and support, sales and marketing are often involved as an intermediary between the company's engineers and the customer. It is common for sales specialists to take on the role of negotiators on behalf of the manufacturing department or research and development. Inter-departmental communications are infrequent.

One of the problems with this situation is that salespeople rarely have technical expertise. The majority of salespeople would not have studied science and technology and are more likely to be qualified in the arts; they are chosen for the sales role due to their social skills. The common perception is that engineers and technical specialists are not as sociable and are therefore not good sellers.

Japanese companies have relied on other ways to make up for this. In their offices, larger Japanese companies tend to have open-plan spaces. This allows the departmental head to learn what other people do and to ensure that they share information. In smaller Japanese businesses, it is common for the business owner to also be situated in an open-plan environment.

The key to success is "reading the air," or reading the *kuuki*. Being alert to what is being said and what is being done means that Japanese managers have instant access to up-to-date information—they know what individual employees know. Individuals in a department are comfortable with this situation; informal information sharing is seen as an effective and vital process.

Questions

14-10. Complex vertical organizational structures are very hierarchical in nature. They are very rigid, with each department having clearly defined roles. Is such an organization capable of being agile and responsive, or is it a disadvantage?

14-11. What are the problems with such strictly defined roles?

14-12. Is reading the air just eavesdropping and spying on others? Would most employees be comfortable with this situation?

Sources: John Spacey, "Why You Need to Read the Air in Japan," *Japan Talk*, http://www.japan-talk.com/jt/new/kuuki-yomenai (accessed January 24, 2014).

CASE INCIDENT 2 Turbulence on United Airlines

The beginning of 2017 was not good for United Airlines. Several incidents involving United Airlines personnel enforcing a variety of rules, regulations, and protocols in employees' interactions with customers caused international outcry. The first incident involved two teenagers who were wearing leggings for their flight from Minneapolis to Denver. They were stopped by the gate agent and not allowed to board for violating the United Airlines travel perk program. These travel perk passes hinge on a requirement for users of the passes to dress themselves so that the airline is presented in a favorable light. United defended its decision via Twitter: "Leggings are not inappropriate attire except in the case of someone traveling as a pass rider." Comedian Seth Rogan tweeted, "We here at @United are just trying to police the attire of the daughters of our employees! That's all! Cool, right?"

A second, more severe incident occurred when David Dao, a doctor who needed to see his patients the following morning, was aboard a Louisville-bound flight from Chicago in April. Four United employees needed to get to Louisville at the last minute, and it was announced that four people needed to give up their seats or else the flight would be cancelled. Attendants called the police after no one complied. The police approached Dao and forcibly removed him from the plane. Dao suffered a broken nose and concussion after his head smashed into an armrest. United policy allowed for the involuntary removal of passengers from flights, although this time United was not as defensive. Dao later filed a lawsuit against United for its actions.

A third incident, in Houston, involved a soon-to-be-married couple, Michael and Amber, headed to Costa Rica for their wedding. When they entered the plane, they noticed a man sleeping in the row where their seats were assigned. Instead of disturbing him, they found some seats three rows up and sat there instead. They were soon asked by an attendant to return to their seats and they complied. A U.S. marshall approached them soon after and ejected them from the plane. According to United statements, the couple "repeatedly" tried to sit in upgraded seats and would not follow the instructions of the attendants and crew members, and, as such, they were within their power to eject the passengers.

These incidents suggest that, starting with the structure as created by the CEO, United employees do not have much latitude or flexibility when dealing with day-to-day policy breaches. Taking cost-minimization and efficiency-boosting strategies to the extreme may also have had an effect given that the focus drifted from the customer and toward rule following. Many attribute this inflexibility to the strict, rule-following bureaucracy created by United managers. In this bureaucracy, their 85,000 employees may be reluctant to deviate from the rules—intracompany historical precedent suggests that many employees face termination if they break the rules.

Questions

14-13. How do you think United Airlines should have handled the recent string of incidents? Do you think that United Airlines was within its power to have removed these people from the flights? Why or why not?

14-14. What are the pros and cons of having a bureaucratic organizational structure for an airline? Do you think the pros and cons are justified for United Airlines and that they should keep the structure they have? Why or why not?

14-15. What do you think United Airlines should do in the future? Do you have any suggestions for enhancements or improvements to the United Airlines organizational structure? Would you consider restructuring? Why or why not?

Sources: Based on S. Carey, "Behind United Airlines' Fateful Decision to Call Police; Airline's Rules-Based Culture in Spotlight after Man Was Dragged off Flight by Law Enforcement," *The Wall Street Journal*, April 17, 2017; J. Disis and J. Ostrower, "United Airlines in Twitter Trouble over Leggings Rule," *CNN Money*, March 27, 2017, money.cnn.com/2017/03/26/news/united-airlines-twitter-dress-code/; A. Hartung, "Why United Airlines Abuses Customers: The Risks of Operational Excellence," *Forbes*, April 10, 2017, https://www.forbes.com/sites/adamhartung/2017/04/10/why-united-airlines-abuses-customers-the-risks-of-operational-excellence/#78a1af3fbb10; M. Hiltzik, "At United Airlines and Wells Fargo, Toxic Corporate Culture Starts with the CEO," *Los Angeles Times*, April 17, 2017, http://www.latimes.com/business/hiltzik/la-fi-hiltzik-toxic-united-wells-20170411-story.html; and E. C. McLaughlin, "Man Dragged off United Flight Has Concussion, Will File Suit, Lawyer Says." *CNN*, April 14, 2017, http://www.cnn.com/2017/04/13/travel/united-passenger-pulled-off-flight-lawsuit-family-attorney-speak/.

ENDNOTES

[1] F. A. Csaszar, "An Efficient Frontier in Organization Design: Organizational Structure as a Determinant of Exploration and Exploitation," *Organization Science* 24, no. 4 (2013): 1083–101; G. P. Huber, "Organizations: Theory, Design, Future," in S. Zedeck (ed.), *APA Handbook of Industrial and Organizational Psychology: Vol. 1, Pt. II: Perspectives on Designing Organizations and Human Resource Systems* (Washington, DC: APA, 2011): 117–60; and B. McEvily, G. Soda, and M. Tortoriello, "More Formally: Rediscovering the Missing Link between Formal Organization and Informal Social Structure," *The Academy of Management Annals* 8, no. 1 (2014): 299–345.

[2] Huber, "Organizations."

[3] See, for instance, R. L. Daft, *Organization Theory and Design*, 12th ed. (Boston, MA: Cengage, 2015).

[4] T. Hindle, *Guide to Management Ideas and Gurus* (London, UK: Profile Books/The Economist Newspaper, 2008).

[5] See, for instance, E. Penrose, *The Theory of the Growth of the Firm*, 4th ed. (Oxford, UK: Oxford, 2009); and D. G. Ross, "An Agency Theory of the Division of Managerial Labor," *Organization Science* 25, no. 2 (2013): 494–508.

[6] For a review, see J. A. Häusser, S. Schulz-Hardt, T. Schultze, A. Tomaschek, and A. Mojzisch, "Experimental Evidence for the Effects of Task Repetitiveness on Mental Strain and Objective Work Performance," *Journal of Organizational Behavior* 35, no. 5 (2014): 705–21.

[7] J. R. Hackman and G. R. Oldham, "Motivation through the Design of Work: Test of a Theory," *Organizational Behavior and Human Performance* 16 (1976): 250–79.

[8] J. G. Miller, "The Real Women's Issue: Time," *The Wall Street Journal*, March 9–10, 2013, C3.

[9] P. Hitlin, "Research in the Crowdsourcing Age, a Case Study," *Pew Research Center: Internet, Science & Technology*, July 11, 2016, http://www.pewinternet.org/2016/07/11/research-in-the-crowdsourcing-age-a-case-study/; and T. W. Malone, R. J. Laubacher, and T. Johns, "The Age of

Hyperspecialization," *Harvard Business Review* (July–August 2011): 56–65.
[10] J. Schramm, "A Cloud of Workers," *HR Magazine* (March 2013): 80.
[11] F. Levy and R. J. Murnane, *The New Division of Labor: How Computers Are Creating the Next Job Market* (New York, NY: Sage, 2004).
[12] See, for instance, J. L. Price, "The Impact of Departmentalization on Interoccupational Cooperation," *Human Organization* 27, no. 4 (1968): 362–8.
[13] N. Kumar, "Kill a Brand, Keep a Customer," *Harvard Business Review*, December 2003, https://hbr.org/2003/12/kill-a-brand-keep-a-customer.
[14] See, for instance, S. Postrel, "Islands of Shared Knowledge: Specialization and Mutual Understanding in Problem-Solving Teams," *Organization Science* 13, no. 3 (2002): 303–20.
[15] C. Woodyard, "Toyota Brass Shakeup Aims to Give Regions More Control," *USA Today*, March 6, 2013, www.usatoday.com/story/money/cars/2013/03/06/toyota-shakeup/1966489/.
[16] J. T. Polzer, C. Brad Crisp, S. L. Jarvenpaa, and J. W. Kim, "Extending the Faultline Model to Geographically Dispersed Teams: How Collocated Subgroups Can Impair Group Functioning," *Academy of Management Journal* 49, no. 4 (2006): 679–92; E. Romanelli and O. M. Khessina, "Regional Industry Identity: Cluster Configurations and Economic Development," *Organization Science* 16, no. 4 (2005): 344–58.
[17] W. Fong Boh, Y. Ren, S. Kiesler, and R. Bussjaeger, "Expertise and Collaboration in the Geographically Dispersed Organization," *Organization Science* 18, no. 4 (2007): 595–612; K. Laursen, F. Masciarelli, and A Prencipe, "Regions Matter: How Localized Social Capital Affects Innovation and External Knowledge Acquisition," *Organization Science* 23, no. 1 (2012): 177–93; S. Tallman and A. Phene, "Leveraging Knowledge across Geographic Boundaries," *Organization Science* 18, no. 2 (2007): 252–60.
[18] S. Ballmer, "One Microsoft: Company Realigns to Enable Innovation at Greater Speed, Efficiency," Microsoft, July 11, 2013, http://blogs.microsoft.com/firehose/2013/07/11/one-microsoft-company-realigns-to-enable-innovation-at-greater-speed-efficiency/.
[19] Ibid.
[20] M. Weinberger, "Why This Microsoft Exec Totally Shook up the Team That Makes One of Its Most Important Products," *Business Insider*, June 14, 2016, http://www.businessinsider.com/microsoft-office-team-reorganization-2016-6; and A. Wilhelm, "Microsoft Shakes Up Its Leadership and Internal Structure as Its Fiscal Year Comes to a Close," *TechCrunch*, June 17, 2015, http://techcrunch.com/2015/06/17/microsoft-shakes-up-its-leadership-and-internal-structure-as-its-fiscal-year-comes-to-a-close/#.mcn4eo:OnA3.
[21] J. R. Hollenbeck, B. Beersma, and M. E. Schouten, "Beyond Team Types and Taxonomies: A Dimensional Scaling Conceptualization for Team Description," *Academy of Management Review* 37 (2012): 82–106.
[22] L. C. Wang and J. R. Hollenbeck, "LMX in Team-Based Contexts: TMX, Authority Differentiation, and Skill Differentiation as Boundary Conditions for Leader Reciprocation," *Personnel Psychology* 72 (2019): 271–90.
[23] See, for instance, S. Finkelstein and R. A. D'Aveni, "CEO Duality as a Double-Edged Sword: How Boards of Directors Balance Entrenchment Avoidance and Unity of Command," *Academy of Management Journal* 37, no. 5 (1994): 1079–1108; and J. Pfeffer, "Management as Symbolic Action: The Creation and Maintenance of Organizational Paradigms," in L. L. Cummings and B. M. Staw (eds.), *Research in Organizational Behavior*, Vol. 3 (Greenwich, CT: JAI, 1981): 1–52.
[24] "The Multiple Boss Dilemma: Is It Possible to Please More Than One?" *Knowledge@Wharton*, blogpost, September 2, 2016, https://knowledge.wharton.upenn.edu/article/multiple-boss-dilemma-possible-please-one/; A. Gallo, "Managing Multiple Bosses," *Harvard Business Review*, August 18, 2011, https://hbr.org/2011/08/managing-multiple-bosses.html.
[25] P. Hinds and S. Kiesler, "Communication across Boundaries: Work, Structure, and Use of Communication Technologies in a Large Organization," *Organization Science* 6, no. 4 (1995): 373–93.
[26] See, for instance, "How Hierarchy Can Hurt Strategy Execution," *Harvard Business Review* (July–August 2010): 74–75.
[27] S. Yu, L. L. Greer, N. Halevy, and L. van Bunderen, "On Ladders and Pyramids: Hierarchy's Shape Determines Relationships and Performance in Groups," *Personality and Social Psychology Bulletin*, 45, no. 12 (2019): 1717–33.
[28] For a review, see D. D. Van Fleet and A. G. Bedeian, "A History of the Span of Management," *Academy of Management Review* 2, no. 3 (1977): 356–72.
[29] E. Appelbaum and R. Batt, *The New American Workplace* (Ithaca, NY: ILR, 1994); and C. Heckscher and A. Dornellor (eds.), *The Post-Bureaucratic Organization* (Thousand Oaks, CA: Sage, 1994).
[30] B. Brady, "It's Time to Stop Trying to Do It All," *Fortune*, May 26, 2016, http://fortune.com/2016/05/26/fortune-500-principal-financial-time-management/.
[31] See, for instance, J. H. Gittell, "Supervisory Span, Relational Coordination, and Flight Departure Performance: A Reassessment of Postbureaucracy Theory," *Organization Science* 12, no. 4: (2001): 468–83.
[32] Society for Human Resource Management (SHRM), "Span of Control: What Factors Should Determine How Many Direct Reports a Manager Has?," *SHRM: HR Q&S*, April 25, 2013, https://www.shrm.org/resourcesandtools/tools-and-samples/hr-qa/pages/whatfactorsshoulddetermine howmanydirectreportsamanagerhas.aspx.
[33] J. Morgan, *The Future of Work: Attract New Talent, Build Better Leaders, and Create a Competitive Organization* (Hoboken, NJ: Wiley, 2014); and J. Morgan, "The 5 Types of Organizational Structures: Part 3, Flat Organizations," *Forbes*, July 13, 2015, https://www.forbes.com/sites/jacobmorgan/2015/07/13/the-5-types-of-organizational-structures-part-3-flat-organizations/#5b9001926caa.
[34] Huber, "Organizations."
[35] Ibid.
[36] Huber, "Organizations"; and Society for Human Resource Management (SHRM), "Understanding Organizational Structures," *SHRM: Toolkits*, November 30, 2015, https://www.shrm.org/resourcesandtools/tools-and-samples/toolkits/pages/understanding organizationalstructures.aspx.
[37] F. A. Csaszar, "Organizational Structure as a Determinant of Performance: Evidence from Mutual Funds," *Strategic Management Journal* 33, no. 6 (2012): 611–32.
[38] B. Brown and S. D. Anthony, "How P&G Tripled Its Innovation Success Rate," *Harvard Business Review* (June 2011): 64–72.
[39] A. Leiponen and C. E. Helfat, "Location, Decentralization, and Knowledge Sources for Innovation," *Organization Science* 22, no. 3 (2011): 641–58.
[40] D. Mascia, S. Dello Russo, and F. Morandi, "Exploring Professionals' Motivation to Lead: A Cross-Level Study in the Healthcare Sector," *The International*

Journal of Human Resource Management 26, no. 12 (2015): 1622–44.
[41] K. Parks, "HSBC Unit Charged in Argentine Tax Case," *The Wall Street Journal*, March 19, 2013, C2.
[42] Huber, "Organizations"; and McEvily, Soda, and Tortoriello, "More Formally."
[43] P. Hempel, Z.-X. Zhang, and Y. Han, "Team Empowerment and the Organizational Context: Decentralization and the Contrasting Effects of Formalization," *Journal of Management* 38, no. 2 (2012): 475–501.
[44] M. L. Tushman and T. J. Scanlan, "Characteristics and External Orientations of Boundary Spanning Individuals," *Academy of Management Journal* 24 (1981): 83–98.
[45] J. E. Perry-Smith and C. E. Shalley, "A Social Composition View of Team Creativity: The Role of Member Nationality-Heterogeneous Ties outside of the Team," *Organization Science* 25 (2014): 1434–52; J. Han, J. Han, and D. J. Brass, "Human Capital Diversity in the Creation of Social Capital for Team Creativity," *Journal of Organizational Behavior* 35 (2014): 54–71; M. Tortoriello, R. Reagans, and B. McEvily, "Bridging the Knowledge Gap: The Influence of Strong Ties, Network Cohesion, and Network Range on the Transfer of Knowledge between Organizational Units," *Organization Science* 23, no. 4 (2012): 1024–39; and X. Zou and P. Ingram, "Bonds and Boundaries: Network Structure, Organizational Boundaries, and Job Performance," *Organizational Behavior and Human Decision Processes* 120, no. 1 (2013): 98–109.
[46] N. J. Foss, K. Laursen, and T. Pedersen, "Linking Customer Interaction and Innovation: The Mediating Role of New Organizational Practices," *Organization Science* 22 (2011): 980–99; N. J. Foss, J. Lyngsie, and S. A. Zahra, "The Role of External Knowledge Sources and Organizational Design in the Process of Opportunity Exploitation," *Strategic Management Journal* 34 (2013): 1453–71; and A. Salter, P. Crisuolo, and A. L. J. Ter Wal, "Coping with Open Innovation: Responding to the Challenges of External Engagement in R&D," *California Management Review* 56 (Winter 2014): 77–94.
[47] Y. Huang, Y. Luo, Y. Liu, and Q. Yang, "An Investigation of Interpersonal Ties in Interorganizational Exchanges in Emerging Markets," *Journal of Management* 42, no. 6 (2016): 1557–87.
[48] H. Aldrich and D. Herker, "Boundary Spanning Roles and Organization Structure," *Academy of Management Review* 2, no. 2 (1977): 217–30.
[49] T. A de Vries, F. Walter, G. S. Van der Vegt, and P. J. M. D. Essens, "Antecedents of Individuals' Interteam Coordination: Broad Functional Experiences as a Mixed Blessing," *Academy of Management Journal* 57 (2014): 1334–59.
[50] R. Cross, C. Ernst, D. Assimakopoulos, and D. Ranta, "Investing in Boundary-Spanning Collaboration to Drive Efficiency and Innovation," *Organizational Dynamics* 44, no. 3 (2015): 204–16.
[51] Huber, "Organizations"; and H. Mintzberg, *Structure in Fives: Designing Effective Organizations* (Englewood Cliffs, NJ: Prentice Hall, 1983).
[52] A. Murray, "Built Not to Last," *The Wall Street Journal*, March 18, 2013, A11.
[53] B. Sugarman, "Stages in the Lives of Organizations," *Administration and Policy in Mental Health* 1, no. 2 (1989): 59–66.
[54] See, for instance, M. Myatt, "Businesses Don't Fail—Leaders Do," *Forbes*, January 12, 2012, https://www.forbes.com/sites/mikemyatt/2012/01/12/businesses-dont-fail-leaders-do/#7ad1d7596c97.
[55] Huber, "Organizations"; and Mintzberg, *Structure in Fives.*
[56] J.-F. Harvey, P. Cohendet, L. Simon, and L.-E. Dubois, "Another Cog in the Machine: Designing Communities of Practice in Professional Bureaucracies," *European Management Journal* 31, no. 1 (2013): 27–40.
[57] D. Graeber, *The Utopia of Rules: On Technology, Stupidity, and the Secret Joys of Bureaucracy* (New York, NY: Melville House, 2015).
[58] V. Gauri, J. C. Jamison, N. Mazar, and O. Ozier, "Motivating Bureaucrats through Social Recognition: External Validity—A Tale of Two States," *Organizational Behavior and Human Decision Processes* (in press); C. Wolf, "Not Lost in Translation: Managerial Career Narratives and the Construction of Protean Identities," *Human Relations* 72, no. 3 (2019): 505–33.
[59] J. H. Gittell and A. Douglass, "Relational Bureaucracy: Structuring Reciprocal Relationships into Roles," *Academy of Management Review* 37, no. 4 (2012): 709–33.
[60] For a quick overview, see J. Davoren, "Functional Structure Organization Strength and Weakness," *Small Business Chronicle*, http://smallbusiness.chron.com/functional-structure-organization-strength-weakness-60111.html, accessed June 25, 2015; and Huber, "Organization."
[61] H. Moon, J. R. Hollenbeck, S. E. Humphrey, D. R. Ilgen, B. West, A. P. J. Ellis, and C. O. L. H. Porter, "Asymmetric Adaptability: Dynamic Team Structures as One-Way Streets," *Academy of Management Journal* 47, no. 5 (2004): 681–95.
[62] J. R. Galbraith, *Designing Matrix Organizations That Actually Work: How IBM, Procter & Gamble, and Others Design for Success* (San Francisco: Jossey Bass, 2009); Huber, "Organization"; and E. Krell, "Managing the Matrix," *HRMagazine* (April 2011): 69–71.
[63] R. C. Ford, "Cross-Functional Structures: A Review and Integration of Matrix Organization and Project Management," *Journal of Management* 18, no. 2 (1992): 267–94.
[64] See, for instance, M. Bidwell, "Politics and Firm Boundaries: How Organizational Structure, Group Interests, and Resources Affect Outsourcing," *Organization Science* (November–December 2012): 1622–42.
[65] Ford, "Cross-Functional Structures."
[66] See, for instance, T. Sy and L. S. D'Annunzio, "Challenges and Strategies of Matrix Organizations: Top-Level and Mid-Level Managers' Perspectives," *Human Resource Planning* 28, no. 1 (2005): 39–48; and T. Sy and S. Côté, "Emotional Intelligence: A Key Ability to Succeed in the Matrix Organization," *Journal of Management Development* 23, no. 5 (2004): 437–55.
[67] N. Anand and R. L. Daft, "What Is the Right Organization Design?," *Organizational Dynamics* 36, no. 4 (2007): 329–44.
[68] Huber, "Organizations."
[69] Ibid.
[70] D. Kanze, M. A. Conley, and E. Tory Higgins, "The Motivation of Mission Statements: How Regulatory Mode Influences Workplace Discrimination," *Organizational Behavior and Human Decision Processes* (in press).
[71] Huber, "Organizations"; and J. B. Quinn and P. Anderson, "Leveraging Intellect," *Academy of Management Executive* 10 (1996): 7–27.
[72] E. Steel, "Netflix Refines Its DVD Business, Even as Streaming Unit Booms," *The New York Times*, July 26, 2015, https://www.nytimes.com/2015/07/27/business/while-its-streaming-service-booms-netflix-streamlines-old-business.html?_r=0.
[73] J. Schramm, "At Work in a Virtual World," *HR Magazine* (June 2010): 152.
[74] See, for instance, C. B. Gibson and J. L. Gibbs, "Unpacking the Concept of Virtuality: The Effects of Geographic Dispersion, Electronic Dependence,

Dynamic Structure, and National Diversity on Team Innovation," *Administrative Science Quarterly* 51, no. 3 (2006): 451–95; H. M. Latapie and V. N. Tran, "Subculture Formation, Evolution, and Conflict between Regional Teams in Virtual Organizations," *The Business Review* (Summer 2007): 189–93; and S. Davenport and U. Daellenbach, "'Belonging' to a Virtual Research Center: Exploring the Influence of Social Capital Formation Processes on Member Identification in a Virtual Organization," *British Journal of Management* 22, no. 1 (2011): 54–76.

[75] See, for instance, M. A. West and L. Markiewicz, *Building Team-Based Working: A Practical Guide to Organizational Transformation* (Malden, MA: Blackwell, 2004).

[76] D. Herath, "Mess Is Good for Business: Some Companies Would Do Better if They Embraced Disorganization," *Newsweek*, February 28, 2017, http://www.newsweek.com/organization-skills-business-efficiency-561985; S. Stevenson, "Who's the Boss? No one." *Slate*, June 2, 2014, http://www.slate.com/articles/business/psychology_of_management/2014/06/the_bossless_office_how_well_do_workplaces_without_managers_function.html; and Schumpeter, "The Holes in Holacracy," *The Economist*, July 5, 2014, http://www.economist.com/news/business/21606267-latest-big-idea-management-deserves-some-scepticism-holes-holacracy.

[77] A. Grasso, Y. Hoppenot, and C. Privault, "Experience Design: The Path from Research to Business," *Xerox Research Centre Europe* (Press Release), 2013, http://www.xrce.xerox.com/About-XRCE/History/20-Years-of-Innovation-in-Europe/Articles/Experience-Design-the-path-from-research-to-business.

[78] J. Scheck, L. Moloney, and A. Flynn, "Eni, CNPC Link Up in Mozambique," *The Wall Street Journal*, March 15, 2013, B3.

[79] A. G. L. Romme, "Domination, Self-Determination and Circular Organizing," *Organization Studies* 20, no. 5 (1999): 801–31.

[80] D. K. Datta, J. P. Guthrie, D. Basuil, and A. Pandey, "Causes and Effects of Employee Downsizing: A Review and Synthesis," *Journal of Management* 36, no. 1 (2010): 281–348.

[81] S. Ghosh, "Google's Motorola Mobility Layoffs: Sweeping Changes Axe 4,000 Jobs," *Reuters*, August 13, 2012, http://www.huffingtonpost.com/2012/08/13/google-motorola-mobility-layoffs-cuts-employees_n_1771692.html.

[82] L. Gensler, "American Express to Slash 4,000 Jobs on Heels of Strong Quarter," *Forbes*, January 21, 2015, http://www.forbes.com/sites/laurengensler/2015/01/21/american-express-earnings-rise-11-on-increased-cardholder-spending/.

[83] T. Borden, "The Coronavirus Outbreak Has Triggered Unprecedented Mass Layoffs and Furloughs. Here Are the Major Companies That Have Announced They Are Downsizing Their Workforces," *Business Insider*, April 29, 2020, https://www.businessinsider.com/coronavirus-layoffs-furloughs-hospitality-service-travel-unemployment-2020; S. Wood, G. Michaelides, and C. Ogbonnaya, "Recessionary Actions and Absence: A Workplace-Level Study," *Human Resource Management* (in press).

[84] Baruah, A. (2020). "IT companies resort to layoffs as pressure mounts due to COVID" *The Mint (July 7, 2020)*. Retrieved from https://www.livemint.com (Accessed on April 15, 2022).

[85] B. Fotsch and J. Case, "Transforming Your Service Business with Lean Management," *Forbes*, March 7, 2017, https://www.forbes.com/sites/fotschcase/2017/03/07/transforming-your-service-business-with-lean-management/#66b5134254e8; and L. McCann, J. S. Hassard, E. Granter, and P. J. Hyde, "Casting the Lean Spell: The Promotion, Dilution and Erosion of Lean Management in the NHS," *Human Relations* 68, no. 10 (2015): 1557–77.

[86] J. Jargon, "Latest Starbucks Buzzword: 'Lean' Japanese Techniques," *The Wall Street Journal*, August 4, 2009, https://www.wsj.com/articles/SB124933474023402611.

[87] Datta, Guthrie, Basuil, and Pandey, "Causes and Effects of Employee Downsizing."

[88] L. I. Alpert, "Can Imported CEO Fix Russian Cars?," *The Wall Street Journal*, March 20, 2013, http://www.wsj.com/articles/SB10001424127887323639604578370121394214736.

[89] R. Handfield, "Bo Andersson's Supply Strategy Collides with Vladmir Putin's Russia: The Performance Triangle Collapses," *Supply Chain View From the Field*, NC State Poole College of Management, Supply Chain Resource Cooperative, April 11, 2016, https://scm.ncsu.edu/blog/2016/04/11/bo-anderssons-supply-strategy-collides-with-vladimir-putins-russia-the-performance-triangle-collapses/.

[90] G. Stolyarov and C. Lowe, "In Russia's Detroit, Layoffs Are Blamed on Foreign Interlopers," *Reuters: Business News*, April 27, 2016, http://www.reuters.com/article/us-russia-avtovaz-idUSKCN0XO0EE.

[91] D. Van Dierendonck and G. Jacobs, "Survivors and Victims: A Meta-Analytical Review of Fairness and Organizational Commitment after Downsizing," *British Journal of Management* 23 (2012): 96–109.

[92] W. M. Foster, J. S. Hassard, J. Morris, and J. Wolfram Cox, "The Changing Nature of Managerial Work: The Effects of Corporate Restructuring on Management Jobs and Careers," *Human Relations* 72, no. 3 (2019): 473–504.

[93] J. R. B. Halbesleben, A. R. Wheeler, and S. C. Paustian-Underdahl, "The Impact of Furloughs on Emotional Exhaustion, Self-Rated Performance, and Recovery Experiences," *Journal of Applied Psychology* 98, no. 3 (2013): 492–503; R. Kalimo, T. W. Taris, and W. B. Schaufeli, "The Effects of Past and Anticipated Future Downsizing on Survivor Well-Being: An Equity Perspective," *Journal of Occupational Health Psychology* 8, no. 2 (2003): 91–109; and Van Dierendonck and Jacobs, "Survivors and Victims."

[94] G. M. Spreitzer and A. K. Mishra, "To Stay or Go: Voluntary Survivor Turnover Following an Organizational Downsizing," *Journal of Organizational Behavior* 23, no. 6 (2002): 707–29; C. O. Trevor and A. J. Nyberg, "Keeping Your Headcount When All About You Are Losing Theirs: Downsizing, Voluntary Turnover Rates, and the Moderating Role of HR Practices," *Academy of Management Journal* 51, no. 2 (2008): 259–76.

[95] K. Devine, T. Reay, L. Stainton, and R. Collins-Nakai, "Downsizing Outcomes: Better a Victim Than a Survivor?," *Human Resources Management* 42, no. 2 (2003): 109–24.

[96] T. Burns and G. M. Stalker, *The Management of Innovation* (London, UK: Tavistock, 1961).

[97] K. Walker, N. Ni, and B. Dyck, "Recipes for Successful Sustainability: Empirical Organizational Configurations for Strong Corporate Environmental Performance," *Business Strategy and the Environment* 24, no. 1 (2015): 40–57.

[98] See, for instance, A. Drach-Zahavy and A. Freund, "Team Effectiveness under Stress: A Structural Contingency Approach," *Journal of Organizational Behavior* 28, no. 4 (2007): 423–50.

[99] K. Walker, N. Ni, and B. Dyck, "Recipes for Successful Sustainability: Empirical Organizational Configurations for Strong Corporate Environmental Performance," *Business Strategy and the Environment* 24, no. 1 (2015): 40–57.

[100] See, for instance, S. M. Toh, F. P. Morgeson, and M. A. Campion, "Human Resource Configurations: Investigating Fit with the Organizational Context," *Journal of Applied Psychology* 93, no. 4 (2008): 864–82.
[101] G. P. Pisano, "You Need an Innovation Strategy," *Harvard Business Review*, June 2015, https://hbr.org/2015/06/you-need-an-innovation-strategy.
[102] See, for instance, R. Robinson, "Costs and Cost-Minimisation Analysis," *British Medical Journal* 307 (1993): 726–8.
[103] See, for instance, J. C. Naranjo-Valencia, D. Jiménez-Jiménez, and R. Sanz-Valle, "Innovation or Imitation? The Role of Organizational Culture," *Management Decision* 49, no. 1 (2011): 55–72.
[104] Sharma, K. (2021). "Chumbak plans to double its turnover by the end of FY22 by doubling down on marketing". *Advertising and Media Insider India (March 17, 2021).* Retrieved from https://www.businessinsider.in (Accessed on April 15, 2022).
[105] Kashyaap, S. (2015). "From a souvenir store to a lifestyle brand, in five years Chumbak has seen 300 per cent growth YOY". *Your Story (July 29, 2015).* Retrieved from https://yourstory.com (Accessed on April 15, 2022).
[106] M. Mesco, "Moleskine Tests Appetite for IPOs," *The Wall Street Journal*, March 19, 2013, B8.
[107] M. Josefy, S. Kuban, R. D. Ireland, and M. A. Hitt, "All Things Great and Small: Organizational Size, Boundaries of the Firm, and a Changing Environment," *The Academy of Management Annals* 9, no. 1 (2015): 715–802.
[108] J. Backaler, "Haier: A Chinese Company That Innovates," *Forbes*, June 17, 2010, http://www.forbes.com/sites/china/2010/06/17/haier-a-chinese-company-that-innovates/.
[109] T. A. Kochan, C. A. Riordan, A. M. Kowalski, M. Khan, and D. Yang, "The Changing Nature of Employee and Labor-Management Relationships," *Annual Review of Organizational Psychology and Organizational Behavior* 6 (2019): 195–219.
[110] A. Mutch, "Technology, Organization, and Structure—A Morphogenetic Approach," *Organization Science* 21, no. 2 (2010): 507–20.
[111] Huber, "Organizations."
[112] See, for instance, J. A. Cogin and I. O. Williamson, "Standardize or Customize: The Interactive Effects of HRM and Environment Uncertainty on MNC Subsidiary Performance," *Human Resource Management* 53, no. 5 (2014): 701–21; and G. Kim and M.-G. Huh, "Exploration and Organizational Longevity: The Moderating Role of Strategy and Environment," *Asia Pacific Journal of Management* 32, no. 2 (2015): 389–414.
[113] R. Greenwood, C. R. Hinings, and D. Whetten, "Rethinking Institutions and Organizations," *Journal of Management Studies,* 51 (2014): 1206–20; D. Chandler and H. Hwang, "Learning from Learning Theory: A Model of Organizational Adoption Strategies at the Microfoundations of Institutional Theory," *Journal of Management* 41 (2015): 1446–76.
[114] C. S. Spell and T. J. Arnold, "A Multi-Level Analysis of Organizational Justice and Climate, Structure, and Employee Mental Health," *Journal of Management* 33, no. 5 (2007): 724–51; and M. L. Ambrose and M. Schminke, "Organization Structure as a Moderator of the Relationship between Procedural Justice, Interactional Justice, Perceived Organizational Support, and Supervisory Trust," *Journal of Applied Psychology* 88, no. 2 (2003): 295–305.
[115] See, for instance, Spell and Arnold, "A Multi-Level Analysis of Organizational Justice Climate, Structure, and Employee Mental Health"; J. D. Shaw and N. Gupta, "Job Complexity, Performance, and Well-Being: When Does Supplies-Values Fit Matter?," *Personnel Psychology* 57, no. 4 (2004): 847–79; and C. Anderson and C. E. Brown, "The Functions and Dysfunctions of Hierarchy," *Research in Organizational Behavior* 30 (2010): 55–89.
[116] See, for instance, T. Martin, "Pharmacies Feel More Heat," *The Wall Street Journal*, March 16–17, 2013, A3.
[117] R. Hechanova-Alampay and T. A. Beehr, "Empowerment, Span of Control, and Safety Performance in Work Teams after Workforce Reduction," *Journal of Occupational Health Psychology* 6, no. 4 (2001): 275–82.
[118] S. Bhargava and A. Kelkar, "Prediction of Job Involvement, Job Satisfaction, and Empowerment from Organizational Structure and Corporate Culture," *Psychological Studies* 45, nos. 1–2 (2000): 43–50; A. P. Kakabadse and R. Worrall, "Job Satisfaction and Organizational Structure: A Comparative Study of Nine Social Service Departments," *The British Journal of Social Work* 8, no. 1 (1978): 51–70; E. G. Lambert, E. A. Paoline III, and N. L. Hogan, "The Impact of Centralization and Formalization on Correctional Staff Job Satisfaction and Organizational Commitment: An Exploratory Study," *Criminal Justice Studies* 19, no. 1 (23–44); and G. S. Rai, "Job Satisfaction among Long-Term Care Staff: Bureaucracy Isn't Always Bad," *Administration in Social Work* 37, no. 1 (2013): 90–9.
[119] See, for instance, R. E. Ployhart, J. A. Weekley, and K. Baughman, "The Structure and Function of Human Capital Emergence: A Multilevel Examination of the Attraction-Selection-Attrition Model," *Academy of Management Journal* 49, no. 4 (2006): 661–77; and B. Schneider, "The People Make the Place," *Personnel Psychology* 40, no. 3 (1987): 437–53.
[120] J. B. Stewart, "A Place to Play for Google Staff," *The New York Times*, March 16, 2013, B1.
[121] Y. Lee and J. Antonakis, "When Preference Is Not Satisfied but the Individual Is. How Power Distance Moderates Person–Job Fit," *Journal of Management* 40, no. 3 (2014): 641–75.
[122] J. Hassard, J. Morris, and L. McCann, "'My Brilliant Career?' New Organizational Forms and Changing Managerial Careers in Japan, the UK, and USA," *Journal of Management Studies* 49, no. 3 (2012): 571–99.

15 Organizational Culture

Source: Chris Batson/Alamy Stock Photo

LEARNING OBJECTIVES

After studying this chapter, you should be able to:

15-1 Describe the common characteristics of organizational culture.

15-2 Show how culture is transmitted to employees.

15-3 Identify the factors that create and sustain an organization's culture.

15-4 Compare the functional and dysfunctional effects of organizational culture on people and the organization.

15-5 Describe the similarities and differences in creating an ethical culture, a positive culture, and a spiritual culture.

15-6 Show how national culture can affect the way organizational culture is transported to another country.

Employability Skills Matrix (ESM)

	Myth or Science?	Career OBjectives	An Ethical Choice	Point/ Counter-point	Experi-ential Exercise	Ethical Dilemma	Case Incident 1	Case Incident 2
Critical Thinking	✓			✓	✓	✓	✓	✓
Communication	✓	✓	✓		✓	✓	✓	
Collaboration	✓	✓			✓		✓	
Knowledge Application and Analysis	✓			✓	✓	✓	✓	✓
Social Responsibility			✓			✓		✓

"UNIFORM" CULTURE

For a long time, a job in law, banking, or accounting required a uniform just as much as a job in the police or fire service. There is a very strong visual link between the professional culture of an organization and the traditional corporate suit. A typical example is PricewaterhouseCoopers (PwC). The PwC network, formed in 1998 from the merger of Price Waterhouse and Coopers & Lybrand, focuses on delivering assurance, tax, and advisory services. The professional nature of an organization like PwC is often reinforced by a traditional suit, smart shirt, and tie for men, and appropriate alternatives for women. In sharp contrast, high-profile and successful companies like Google are going casual—no. 9 on "Ten Things We Know to Be True," Google's manifesto, is "You can be serious without a suit." In the new hiring landscape, does an established firm like PwC need to change?

In 2015, Nicola Thorp was employed as a temporary worker at a PwC office in the United Kingdom. Arriving for work on her first day, she was told that she was not following the dress code with regard to footwear. She was given the option to go shopping and replace her flat shoes with ones that have a two- to four-inch heel. Thorp refused, and she was sent home without pay. After speaking to her friends, she decided to start a petition calling for a change in the law to make it illegal for a company to insist that a female worker should wear high heels. Having received enough signatures, a Parliamentary report considered the petition and concluded that this incident, along with many others identified in other companies, was an example of gender discrimination in the workplace. PwC argued that the requirement to wear high heels was specified by the agency, and in response to the Parliamentary report, it stressed that they had a flexible approach to work attire and were committed to values of equality, respect, and inclusion.

PwC is a truly global organization, employing over 236,000 staff in 158 countries, and in June 2016, PwC Australia announced a radical change to their dress code. The old code had very specific guidelines for everything from the suit to business socks; the new policy accepted the employee's judgment of what is appropriate. Move on to 2017, and the once-conservative employer looks very different and is ranked no. 1 on LinkedIn's Top Companies list in Australia. The dress code was just one of many changes; there are a whole range of new initiatives, including treadmill meetings, table tennis tables in the office, and flexible work spaces. Sue Horlin, a partner at PwC Australia, said that these initiatives were not a direct result of the UK incident but more of a strategy to help them recruit the best staff in a competitive environment. Taking a lead from many of the tech companies, PwC believes that giving talented people the space to work as they want to will attract and retain the best.

LinkedIn's poll suggests that this philosophy is working; evidently, staff and clients in Australia are ready to accept a more casual corporate culture. However, what about the other 157 countries where PwC operates? How do you manage a change in different national cultures? It has yet to be seen whether the high-heels incident will lead the United Kingdom and other countries to follow Australia and move toward a more relaxed dress code and working environment.

Sources: Nadia Khomami, "Receptionist 'Sent Home from PwC for Not Wearing High Heels,'" *The Guardian*, https://www.theguardian.com/uk-news/2016/may/11/receptionist-sent-home-pwc-not-wearing-high-heels-pwc-nicola-thorp; "PwC Response to High Heels and Workplace Dress Codes Report," January 25, 2017, https://www.pwc.co.uk/press-room/press-releases/pwc-response-to-high-heels-and-workplace-dress-codes-report.html; Dana McCauley, "PwC Named Australia's Top Company to Work for by LinkedIn," News Limited, http://www.news.com.au/finance/work/careers/pwc-named-australias-top-company-to-work-for-by-linkedin/news-story/e1a36acf32b2081c7079385ef853e1dd; Chris Pash, *Business Insider*, June 1, 2016, https://www.businessinsider.com.au/pwc-has-ditched-its-old-dress-code-for-staff-in-australia-2016-6/; PwC, "Culture," https://www.pwc.co.uk/careers/experienced-jobs/aboutpwc/culture.html; Google, "Ten Things We Know to Be True," https://www.google.com/about/philosophy.html; PwC, "About Us," https://www.pwc.com/gx/en/about.html.

Organizations have values, beliefs, assumptions, and norms that govern how members behave. We call these expectations the *organizational culture.* Every organization has a culture that, depending on its strength, can have a considerable influence on the attitudes and behaviors of organization members, even if that effect is hard to measure precisely. In this chapter, we'll discuss what organizational culture is, how it affects employee attitudes and behavior, where it comes from, and whether it can be changed.

What Is Organizational Culture?

15-1 Describe the common characteristics of organizational culture.

An executive once was asked what he thought *organizational culture* meant. He replied, "in a great place to work, the culture becomes the CEO". In this section, we propose one definition and review several related ideas.[1]

A Definition of Organizational Culture

organizational culture A system of shared meaning held by an organization's members that distinguishes the organization from others.

Organizational culture refers to a system of shared meaning held by members that distinguishes the organization from other organizations.[2] This system of shared meaning includes values, beliefs, and assumptions that characterize the organization. Six primary characteristics seem to capture the essence of an organization's culture:[3]

1. **Adaptability.** The degree to which employees are encouraged to be innovative and flexible as well as to take risks and experiment.
2. **Detail orientation.** The degree to which employees are expected to exhibit precision, analysis, and attention to detail.
3. **Results/outcome orientation.** The degree to which management focuses on results or outcomes rather than on the techniques and processes used to achieve them.
4. **People/customer orientation.** The degree to which management decisions consider the effect of outcomes on people within and outside the organization.
5. **Collaboration/team orientation.** The degree to which work activities are organized around teams rather than individuals.
6. **Integrity.** The degree to which people exhibit integrity and high ethical standards in their work.

Each of these characteristics exists on a continuum from low to high. Appraising an organization on the strength of each provides a basis for the shared understanding that members have about the organization, how things are done in it, and the way they are supposed to behave. Exhibit 15-1 contrasts two companies that are very different along these six dimensions.

Another common culture framework groups organizations into one of four types, each with its own assumptions, beliefs, values, material symbols, and even criteria for effectiveness:[4]

1. **"The Clan."** A culture based on human affiliation. Employees value attachment, collaboration, trust, and support.
2. **"The Adhocracy."** A culture based on change. Employees value growth, variety, attention to detail, stimulation, and autonomy.
3. **"The Market."** A culture based on achievement. Employees value communication, competence, and competition.
4. **"The Hierarchy."** A culture based on stability. Employees value communication, formalization, and routine.

The differences between these cultures are reflected in their internal versus external focus and their flexibility and stability.[5] For instance, clans are internally focused and flexible, adhocracies are externally focused and flexible, markets are externally focused and stable, and hierarchies are internally

Exhibit 15-1 Contrasting Organizational Cultures

Organization A

This organization is a manufacturing firm. Managers are expected to fully document all decisions, and "good managers" are those who can provide detailed data to support their recommendations. Creative decisions that incur significant change or risk are not encouraged. Because managers of failed projects are openly criticized and penalized, managers try not to implement ideas that deviate much from the status quo. One lower-level manager quoted an often-used phrase in the company: "If it ain't broke, don't fix it."

There are extensive rules and regulations in this firm that employees are required to follow. Managers supervise employees closely to ensure there are no deviations. Management is concerned with high productivity, regardless of the impact on employee morale or turnover.

Work activities are designed around individuals. There are distinct departments and lines of authority, and employees are expected to minimize formal contact with other employees outside their functional area or line of command. Performance evaluations and rewards emphasize individual effort, although seniority tends to be the primary factor in the determination of pay raises and promotions.

Organization B

This organization is also a manufacturing firm. Here, however, management encourages and rewards risk taking and change. Decisions based on intuition are valued as much as those that are well rationalized. Management prides itself on its history of experimenting with new technologies and its success in regularly introducing innovative products. Managers or employees who have a good idea are encouraged to "run with it." And failures are treated as "learning experiences." The company prides itself on being market driven and rapidly responsive to the changing needs of its customers.

There are few rules and regulations for employees to follow, and supervision is loose because management believes that its employees are hardworking and trustworthy. Management is concerned with high productivity but believes that this comes through treating its people right. The company is proud of its reputation as being a good place to work.

Job activities are designed around work teams, and team members are encouraged to interact with people across functions and authority levels. Employees talk positively about the competition between teams. Individuals and teams have goals, and bonuses are based on achievement of these outcomes. Employees are given considerable autonomy in choosing the means by which the goals are attained.

focused and stable. Reviews of hundreds of studies have helped summarize the findings on the cultures from the competing values framework.[6] As shown in Exhibit 15-2, the various cultures differ regarding how they influence organizational outcomes. Although we note that many of these outcomes are also heavily influenced by leadership and organizational structure (see their respective chapters for more information), culture adds more to the picture than leadership or structure. A strategic approach to culture would suggest that cultures would ideally match the organization's objectives. Most cultures have a positive effect on employee attitudes, performance, innovation, product/service quality, and operational efficiency, but it is clear that a clan or market culture is perhaps best aligned with customer-oriented outcomes and that a hierarchical culture is best for profitability and revenue growth.

Although the competing values approach is one of the most frequently studied ways of examining organizational culture, other frameworks have been introduced. For example, the *Organizational Culture Inventory* groups cultures into 3 categories: (1) *constructive cultures* that value affiliation, encouragement, and achievement; (2) *passive-defensive cultures* that avoid accountability, seek validation and approval from others, and are conventional; and (3)

Exhibit 15-2 The Effect of Culture on Organizational Outcomes

Culture	Employee Attitudes & Performance	Innovation	High Quality Products/ Services & Operational Efficiency	Customer Satisfaction & Market Share	Profitability & Revenue Growth
Clan	+*	+*	0	+*	-
Adhocracy	+*	+	+*	-	0
Market	0	+	+*	+*	0
Hierarchy	+*	-	+*	0	+*

Note: + corresponds with a positive effect on the outcome, - corresponds with a negative effect on the outcome, 0 corresponds with a zero, or null, effect on the outcome, * suggests the culture is strongly related to the outcome.

Source: Based on findings from C. A. Hartnell, A. Y. Ou, A. J. Kinicki, D. Choi, and E. P. Karam, "A Meta-Analytic Test of Organizational Culture's Association with Elements of an Organization's System and Its Relative Predictive Validity on Organizational Outcomes," *Journal of Applied Psychology* 104, no. 6 (2019): 832–50.

aggressive-defensive cultures that are competitive, perfectionist, and power-oriented.[7] Another widely used framework is the *Organizational Culture Profile* (OCP).[8] The OCP draws upon a novel survey method in which employees sort a set of values based on how closely they represent their organization. The OCP suggests an organizational culture can be described by eight dimensions: (1) *innovation*, (2) *attention to detail*, (3) *decisiveness*, (4) *team-orientation*, (5) *outcome-orientation*, (6) *aggressiveness*, (7) *supportiveness*, and (8) *rewards-emphasis.*

Culture Is a Descriptive Term

If you've ever been in an organization (certainly you've been in many!), you probably noticed a pervasive culture among the members. *Organizational culture* describes how employees perceive the characteristics of an organization, not whether they like those characteristics. In other words, it's a descriptive term. Research on organizational culture has sought to measure how employees see their organization: Does it encourage teamwork? Does it reward innovation? Does it stifle initiative? In contrast, job satisfaction seeks to measure how employees feel about the organization's expectations, reward practices, and the like. Although the two terms have overlapping characteristics, keep in mind that *organizational culture* is descriptive in that it describes an organization, much like how personality traits describe employees. On the other hand, *job satisfaction* is evaluative because it can be positive or negative (as is the case with job dissatisfaction).

Do Organizations Have Uniform Cultures?

Organizational culture represents a perception that the organization's members share. Statements about organizational culture are valid only if individuals with different backgrounds or at different levels in the organization describe the culture in similar terms.[9] For example, the purchasing department can have a subculture

Myth or Science?

An Organization's Culture Is Forever

This statement is not true. Although organizational culture is difficult to change and a notable change can take a long time, it can be done. Sometimes it is essential for survival. For years, Wisconsin's Wellspring system provided nursing homes in which inpatients had little input about their care, and the organizational culture allowed lax standards to prevail. Then the network of 11 nursing homes launched a culture change initiative. Management focused on caregiver collaboration, education, accountability, and empowerment. The results were excellent. Wellspring realized fewer state standards infractions and higher employee retention rates at the facilities, and the results for the patients were even greater: fewer bedridden residents, less use of restraints and psychoactive medication, less incontinence, and fewer tube feedings than in other nursing homes.

The Wellspring program illustrates the significant effect that positive organizational culture change can achieve. CEO Bob Flexon of Dynegy Inc., a Houston-based electric utility giant that emerged from bankruptcy, saved his company by changing the organizational culture. First, he ditched the cushy CEO office suite, $15,000 marble desk, and Oriental rugs for a small cubicle on a warehouse-style floor shared with all 235 headquarters employees. Next, he visited company facilities, trained "culture champions," reinstated annual performance reviews, and increased employee collaboration. He created a plaque as a reminder to "Be Here Now" instead of multitasking and banned smartphones from meetings. Flexon said, "The idea was to instill a winning spirit," and he counts on his visibility as CEO to broadcast the culture change down to the lowest levels of the widespread organization.

Positive results at Dynegy have included a reduction in turnover from 8 percent in 2011 to 5.8 percent in the turnaround of 2012. Flexon said, "People are cautiously beginning to believe that we can win again." The company continues to report massive earnings losses, but Flexon is optimistic about Dynegy's rebound. He says, "Our ongoing focus on culture is what will make the difference." Through substantial growth following its bankruptcy, Dynegy makes around $5.5 billion annually as of 2017.

Sources: Based on J. Bellot, "Nursing Home Culture Change: What Does It Mean to Nurses?," *Research in Gerontological Nursing* (October 2012): 264–73; T. Linquist, "Interview with Bob Flexon, CEO of Dynegy in Houston," *Leadership Lyceum: A CEO's Virtual Mentor* [podcast], https://www.linkedin.com/pulse/part-1-2-interview-bob-flexon-ceo-dynegy-houston-thomas-linquist; J. S. Lublin, "This CEO Used to Have an Office," *The Wall Street Journal*, March 13, 2013, B1, B8; and J. Molineux, "Enabling Organizational Cultural Change Using Systemic Strategic Human Resource Management—A Longitudinal Case Study," *International Journal of Human Resource Management* (April 1, 2013): 1588–612.

dominant culture A culture that expresses the core values that are shared by a majority of the organization's members.

core values The primary or dominant values that are accepted throughout the organization.

subcultures Minicultures within an organization, typically defined by department designations and geographical separation.

that includes the core values of the dominant culture, such as aggressiveness, plus additional values unique to members of that department, such as risk taking.

The **dominant culture** expresses the **core values** that a majority of members share and that give the organization its distinct personality.[10] **Subcultures** tend to develop in large organizations in response to common problems or experiences that a group of members face in the same department or location.[11] Most large organizations have a dominant culture and numerous subcultures.[12] Sometimes the subcultures can be so strong, however, that they subtly reject the "official" culture and do not conform.[13]

If organizations were composed only of subcultures, the dominant organizational culture would be significantly less powerful. It is the "shared meaning" aspect of culture that makes it a potent device for guiding and shaping behavior. That's what allows us to say, for example, that the Zappos culture values customer care and dedication over speed and efficiency, which explains the behavior of Zappos executives and employees.[14]

Strong versus Weak Cultures

It's possible to differentiate between strong and weak cultures.[15] If most employees have the same opinions about the organization's mission and values, the culture is strong; if opinions vary widely, the culture is weak.

strong culture A culture in which the core values are intensely held and widely shared.

In a **strong culture,** the organization's core values are both intensely held and widely shared.[16] The more members who accept the core values and the greater their commitment, the stronger the culture and the greater its influence on member behavior. Nordstrom employees know exactly what is expected of them, for example, and these expectations go a long way toward shaping their behavior.

A strong culture should more directly affect organizational outcomes because it demonstrates high agreement about what the organization represents. Such unanimity of purpose builds cohesiveness, loyalty, meaning, and organizational commitment. For example, with high cultural consensus and intensity surrounding the adaptability dimension of culture, organizations in one study experienced gains in net income, revenue, and operating cash flow.[17] A study of nearly 90,000 employees from 137 organizations found that culture strength or consistency was related to numerous financial outcomes when there was a strong sense of mission and high employee involvement.[18]

How Employees Learn Culture

15-2 Show how culture is transmitted to employees.

Culture is transmitted to employees in several forms, the most potent being stories, rituals, material symbols, and language.

Stories

When Henry Ford II was chair of Ford Motor Company, you would have been hard-pressed to find a manager who hadn't heard how he reminded his executives, when they got too arrogant, "It's my name that's on the building." The message was clear: Henry Ford II ran the company.

Today, a number of senior Nike executives spend much of their time serving as corporate storytellers.[19] When they tell how cofounder (and Oregon track coach) Bill Bowerman went to his workshop and poured rubber into a waffle iron to create a better running shoe, they're talking about Nike's spirit of innovation. When new hires hear tales of Oregon running star Steve Prefontaine's battles to make running a professional sport and attain better performance equipment, they learn of Nike's commitment to helping athletes.

Stories such as these circulate through many organizations, anchoring the present in the past and legitimizing current practices.[20] They typically include narratives about the organization's founders, rule breaking, rags-to-riches successes, workforce reductions, relocations of employees, reactions to past mistakes, and organizational coping.[21] Employees also create their own narratives about how they came either to fit or not to fit with the organization during the process of socialization, including first days on the job, early interactions with others, and first impressions of organizational life.[22]

rituals Repetitive sequences of activities that express and reinforce the key values of the organization, which goals are most important, which people are important, and which are expendable.

Rituals

Rituals are repetitive sequences of activities that express and reinforce the key values of the organization—what goals are most important, and/or which people are important versus which are expendable.[23] Some companies have nontraditional rituals to help support the values of their cultures. Kimpton Hotels & Restaurants, one of *Fortune*'s 100 Best Companies to Work For, maintains its customer-oriented culture with traditions like a Housekeeping Olympics that includes blindfolded bedmaking and vacuum races.[24] At marketing firm United Entertainment Group, employees work unusual hours a few times a year, arriving in the late afternoon and working until early morning. CEO Jarrod Moses does this to support a culture of creativity. He says, "You mess with somebody's internal clock, and some interesting ideas come out."[25]

Symbols

material symbols Physical objects, or artifacts, that symbolize values, beliefs, or assumptions inherent in the organization's culture.

The layout of corporate headquarters, the types of automobiles top executives are given, and the presence or absence of corporate aircraft are a few examples of **material symbols**, sometimes also known as artifacts.[26] Others include the size of offices, the elegance of furnishings, perks, and attire.[27] These convey to employees who is important; the degree of egalitarianism top management desires; and the kinds of behavior that are appropriate, such as risk taking, and conservative, authoritarian, participative, individualistic, or social behavior. Material symbols also offer a sense of connection and stir emotions in employees who make sense of the symbols.[28]

One example of the intentional use of material symbols is Texas electric company Dynegy. Dynegy's headquarters doesn't look like a typical operation. There are few individual offices, even for senior executives. The space is essentially made up of cubicles, common areas, and meeting rooms. This informality conveys to employees that Dynegy values openness, equality, creativity, and flexibility. While some organizations provide their top executives with chauffeur-driven limousines and a corporate jet, other CEOs drive the company car themselves and travel in airlines' economy section. At some firms, like Chicago shirtmaker Threadless, an "anything goes" atmosphere helps emphasize a creative culture. At Threadless, meetings are held in an Airstream camper parked inside the company's converted FedEx warehouse, while employees in shorts and flip-flops work in bullpens featuring disco balls and garish decorations chosen by each team.[29]

Some cultures are known for the perks in their environments, such as Google's bocce courts, Factset Research's onsite pie/cheese/cupcake trucks, software designer Autodesk's bring-your-dog-to-work days, SAS's free health care clinic, Microsoft's organic spa, and adventure-gear specialist REI's free equipment rentals. Other companies communicate the values of their cultures through the gift of time to think creatively, either with leaders or offsite. For instance, Biotech leader Genentech and many other top companies provide paid sabbaticals. Genentech offers every employee 7 weeks' paid leave for every 5 years of service to support a culture of equitability and innovative thinking.[30]

Language

Many organizations and subunits within them use language to help members identify with the culture, attest to their acceptance of it, and help preserve it.[31] Unique terms describe equipment, officers, key individuals, suppliers, customers, or products that relate to the business. New employees may be overwhelmed at first by acronyms and jargon that, once assimilated, act as a common denominator to unite members of a given culture or subculture.

An Ethical Choice

A Culture of Compassion

In the world of banking, success and ethical culture don't necessarily go hand in hand. Leaders who desire ethical cultures in their organizations must choose to build ethics into the company's definition of success in ways that translate into ethical actions for managers and employees. Contrast two financial success stories, Goldman Sachs and JP Morgan Chase & Company. Both megabanks are among the Fortune 100 (the largest U.S. companies ranked by revenue). They are also two of *Fortune*'s World's Most Admired Companies, a list that ranks the largest companies in revenue by nine criteria including social responsibility. Yet their organizational cultures appear to be vastly different. Goldman Sachs seems to struggle to achieve an ethical culture for its employees and clients, while JP Morgan Chase seems to emanate a culture of compassion. Consider some headlines:

- *Mefit "Mike" Mecevic was a loyal janitor for Goldman Sachs when Superstorm Sandy hit New York in 2012.* Mecevic and his coworkers rode out the storm in the company's Manhattan skyscraper and worked nonstop for days to keep floodwaters back. Then a Goldman Sachs manager threw him out without explanation. Mecevic said to him, "'I live in Staten Island, there's a state of emergency, there are no cars, no trains, no lights. The water is up to our necks.' I was begging for my life. But he said, 'Leave the building.'" Mecevic left but was later fired anyway. "I worked day and night," Mecevic said. "They destroyed my life for nothing. Nothing."
- Jamie Dimon, CEO of JP Morgan Chase & Company, proclaims, "People are our most important asset. The long-term growth and success of JP Morgan Chase depends on our ability to attract and retain our employees. Maintaining a diverse and inclusive workplace where everyone can thrive is not only the smart thing to do—it's the right thing to do." The culture of JP Morgan Chase is driven by performance and merit, partnership and inclusion, and directness. It has programs that support the success of women and minorities.

Organizational culture is where leaders' ethical choices demonstrate their expectations for others' decisions throughout the company. These examples suggest that the two cultures may make very different ethical choices.

Sources: Based on JP Morgan Chase & Co., "People and Culture," https://www.jpmorganchase.com/corporate/About-JPMC/ab-people-culture.htm, accessed April 18, 2017; B. Ross, A. Ng, and C. Siemaszko, "Ex-Goldman Sachs Janitor Sues for Being Forced into Post-Hurricane Sandy Destruction," *New York Daily News*, June 7, 2013, www.nydailynews.com/new-york/janitor-sues-tossed-aftermath-hurricane-sandy-article-1.1366334; and M. Schifrin and H. Touryalai, "The Bank That Works," *Forbes*, February 13, 2012, 66–74.

Despite providing a unique, descriptive window into the culture of organizations, values and beliefs can be conveyed *through* stories, rituals, material symbols, and language. For example, in one study of Fortune 500 mission statements, organizations that communicated that they believe people can grow and improve tended to have more positive culture ratings on Glassdoor than companies that believe people do not change. In subsequent studies of employees at Fortune 1000 companies, this perception of culture impacted employee trust and commitment.[32]

Creating and Sustaining Culture

15-3 Identify the factors that create and sustain an organization's culture.

An organization's culture doesn't pop out of thin air and, once established, it rarely fades away. What influences the creation of a culture? What reinforces and sustains it once in place?

How a Culture Begins

An organization's customs, traditions, and general way of doing things are largely due to what it has done before and how successful it was in doing it. This leads us to the ultimate source of an organization's culture: the founders.[33] Founders have a vision of what the organization should be, and the firm's initial small size makes it easy to enact that vision with all members.

Culture creation occurs in three ways.[34] First, founders hire and keep only employees who think and feel the same way they do. Second, they socialize employees to their way of thinking and feeling. And finally, the founders' own behavior encourages employees to identify with them and internalize their beliefs, values, and assumptions. When the organization succeeds, the founders' personalities become embedded in the culture. For example, the fierce, competitive style and disciplined, authoritarian nature of Hyundai, the giant Korean conglomerate, exhibits the same characteristics often used to describe founder Chung Ju-Yung.[35] Other founders with sustaining impact on their organization's culture include Jamsetji Tata at the Tata Group, Dhirubhai Ambani of the Reliance Group, Sajjan Jindal of the JSW Group, Bill Gates at Microsoft, Ingvar Kamprad at IKEA, Herb Kelleher at Southwest Airlines, Fred Smith at FedEx, and Richard Branson at the Virgin Group.

Exhibit 15-3 summarizes how an organization's culture is established and sustained. The original culture derives from the founders' philosophy and strongly influences hiring criteria as the firm grows. The success of socialization depends on the deliberateness of matching new employees' values to those of the organization in the selection process and on top management's commitment to socialization programs. Top managers' actions signal what is valued, including what is acceptable behavior and what is not, thus directly influencing the socialization process and the culture. The culture then becomes linked and entrenched within the organizational structures and systems, and is perpetuated by leadership. In the most comprehensive study of organizational culture to date (an impressive study of more than 500,000 employees from over 26,000 organizations), culture was found strongly related to the current leadership, practices, and structures that comprise the organization.[36]

Keeping a Culture Alive

Once a culture is in place, practices within the organization maintain it by giving employees a set of similar experiences.[37] The selection process, performance evaluation criteria, training and development activities, and promotion

Exhibit 15-3 How Organizational Cultures Form

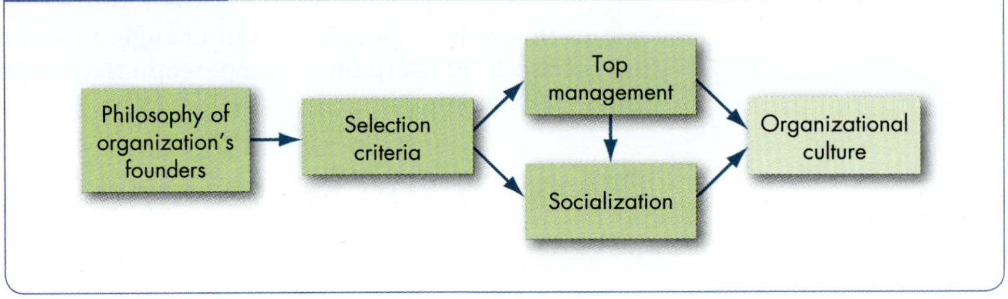

procedures (all discussed in Chapter 17) ensure those hired fit in with the culture, reward those employees who support it, and penalize (or even expel) those who challenge it.[38] Three forces play a particularly important part in sustaining a culture: selection or hiring practices, actions of top management, and socialization or onboarding methods (e.g., teaching and including new employees). Let's look at each.

Selection The explicit goal of the selection process is to identify and hire individuals with the knowledge, skills, and abilities to perform successfully. The final decision, because it is significantly influenced by the decision maker's judgment of how well candidates will fit into the organization, identifies people whose values are consistent with at least a good portion of the organization's.[39] The selection process also provides information to applicants. Those who perceive a conflict between their values and those of the organization can remove themselves from the applicant pool, or even fake their way into the organization by pretending that they share the organization's values.[40] Selection thus becomes a two-way street, with both employers and applicants as active participants in determining the value fit between the applicant and the organization.

Decathlon India, a mutli-sportsware store which works with the mission of providing access to sports for all, is largely flat and encourages intrapreneurship among its employees.[41] All its staff are enthusiastic about sports and excel in at least one sport. Sportsmanship, helping the other win, and team collaboration are some of the values that are the core to Decathlon. Selection of teammates starts with playing a sport and the selection committee observing the potential employees play. Interviews are held to ensure that the person being selected holds values of Decathlon. The selection process emphasizes on culture fit.[42]

Top Management The actions of top management have a major impact on the organization's culture.[43] Through words and behavior, senior executives establish norms that filter through the organization about, for instance, whether risk taking is desirable, how much freedom managers give employees, the uniforms employees should wear, and what behavior is desired and rewarded.

The culture of Kalyan Jewellers has been shaped by its owner—TS Kalyanaraman. Transparency, trust, and customer satisfaction are primary values of the organization. Until 1993, the family owned textile shops in Kerala. Customers visiting the stores for wedding shopping expressed their wish to buy gold jewelry under one roof along with the clothes. Taking a small loan, Kalyanraman started Kalyan Jewellers, pioneering the concept of large showrooms with readymade jewelry on display that had detailed rate-cards and educated the customers. He started a campaign, "My Gold My Right." Customers were satisfied with the design, prices, and helpfulness of the shop staff. The company believes in taking care of its employees. During the COVID-19 pandemic, a ' Goldsmith Relief Fund' was started to support 50,000 artisans and daily wage earners who worked in the gems and jewelry industry. The culture of trust and transparency is sustained by the actions of its founding members.[44 &45] In addition, no salary deductions were made for the non-operational stores during the pandemic.[46]

socialization A process that enables new employees to acquire the social knowledge and necessary skills in order to adapt to the organization's culture.

Socialization No matter how good a job the organization does in recruiting and selection, new employees need help adapting to the prevailing culture. This help comes in the form of **socialization** practices.[47] Socialization can help alleviate the problem many employees report when their new jobs are different from what they expected (see OB Poll). For example, the consulting firm Booz Allen Hamilton begins its process of bringing new employees onboard even before their first day of work. New recruits go to an internal Web portal to learn about the company and understand the culture. After they start work, a social networking application links them with more established members of the firm and helps ensure that the culture is reinforced over time.[48] Clear Channel Communications, Facebook, Google, and other companies are adopting fresh onboarding (new hire acclimation) procedures, including assigning "peer coaches," holding socializing events, personalizing orientation programs, and giving out immediate work assignments. "When we can stress the personal identity of people, and let them bring more of themselves at work, they are more satisfied with their job and have better results," researcher Francesca Gino of Harvard said.[49]

We can think of socialization as a process with three stages: prearrival, encounter, and metamorphosis.[50] This process, shown in Exhibit 15-4, has an impact on the new employee's work productivity, commitment to the organization's objectives, and decision to stay with the organization.

prearrival stage The period of learning in the socialization process that occurs before a new employee joins the organization.

The **prearrival stage** recognizes that each individual arrives with a set of values, attitudes, and expectations about both the work and the organization. One major purpose of a business school, for example, is to socialize students to the attitudes and behaviors that companies desire in future employees. Newcomers to high-profile organizations with strong market positions have their own assumptions about what it's like to work there.[51] Most new recruits will expect Nike to be dynamic and exciting, and a stock brokerage firm to be high in pressure and rewards. How accurately people judge an organization's culture before they join the organization, how positive, adaptive, and proactive their personalities are, and their anticipated "psychological contract" with the organization become critical predictors of how well they adjust.[52]

encounter stage The stage in the socialization process in which a new employee sees what the organization is really like and confronts the possibility that expectations and reality may diverge.

The selection process can help inform prospective employees about the organization as a whole. Upon entry into the organization, the new member enters the **encounter stage** and confronts the possibility that expectations—about the job, coworkers, boss, and organization in general—may differ from reality.[53] If expectations were accurate, this stage merely cements earlier perceptions. However, this is not often the case. At the extreme, a new member may become disillusioned enough to resign. Proper recruitment, selection, and socialization (e.g., giving a realistic preview of the job) should significantly reduce this outcome, along with encouraging friendship ties in the organization—newcomers are more committed when friendly coworkers help them "learn the ropes."[54]

metamorphosis stage The stage in the socialization process in which a new employee changes and adjusts to the job, work group, and organization.

Finally, to work out any problems discovered during the encounter stage, the new member changes or goes through the **metamorphosis stage**.[55] The options presented in Exhibit 15-5 are alternatives designed to bring about metamorphosis. Most research suggests two major "bundles" of socialization practices.[56] The more management relies on formal, collective, fixed, and serial socialization programs while emphasizing divestiture, the more likely newcomers' differences will be stripped away and replaced by standardized predictable behaviors. These *institutional* practices are common in police departments, fire departments, and

OB POLL

Job Is Not as Good as Advertised

Source: Based on S. Bates, "Majority of New Hires Say Job Is Not What They Expected," *Society for Human Resource Management*, May 28, 2012, http://www.shrm.org/hrdisciplines/employeerelations/articles/pages/newhiresfeelmisled.aspx.

other organizations that value rule following and order. Programs that are informal, individual, variable, and random while emphasizing investiture are more likely to give newcomers a sense of their roles and methods of working. Creative fields such as research and development, advertising, and filmmaking rely on these *individual* practices.[57] Most research suggests that high levels of institutional practices encourage person–organization fit, high levels of commitment, and improved role clarity, whereas individual practices produce more role innovation, improve motivation, and lead to social integration.[58]

The three-part entry socialization process is complete when new members have internalized and accepted the norms of the organization and their work groups, are confident in their competence, and feel trusted and valued by their peers. They understand the system—not only their own tasks but the rules, procedures, and informally accepted practices as well. Finally, they know what is expected of them and what criteria will be used to measure and evaluate their work. As Exhibit 15-4 showed earlier, successful metamorphosis should have a positive impact on new employees' productivity and their commitment to the organization, and reduce their propensity to leave the organization (turnover).

Researchers examine how employee attitudes change during socialization by measuring at several points over the first few months. Several studies have now documented patterns of "honeymoons" and "hangovers" for new workers, showing that the period of initial adjustment is often marked by decreases in job satisfaction as idealized hopes come into contact with the reality of organizational life.[59] Newcomers may find that the level of social support they receive from supervisors and coworkers is gradually withdrawn over the first few weeks on the job, as everyone returns to "business as usual."[60] Role conflict and role overload may rise for newcomers over time, and workers with the largest increases in these role problems experience the

Exhibit 15-4 A Socialization Model

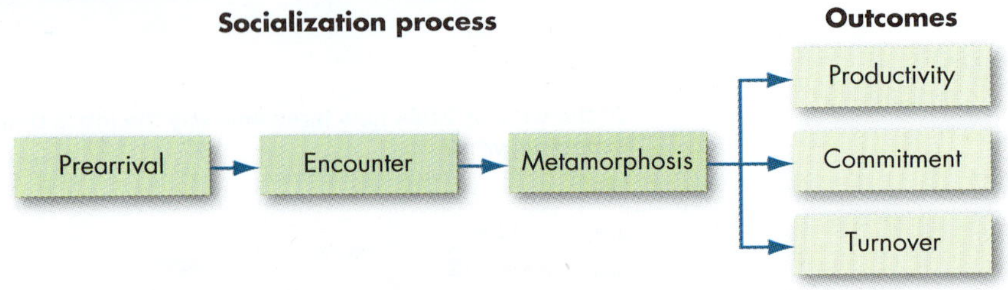

Exhibit 15-5 Entry Socialization Options

Formal vs. Informal The more a new employee is segregated from the ongoing work setting and differentiated in some way to make explicit his or her newcomer's role, the more socialization is formal. Specific orientation and training programs are examples. Informal socialization puts the new employee directly into the job, with little or no special attention.

Individual vs. Collective New members can be socialized individually. This describes how it's done in many professional offices. They can also be grouped together and processed through an identical set of experiences, as in military boot camp.

Fixed vs. Variable This refers to the time schedule in which newcomers make the transition from outsider to insider. A fixed schedule establishes standardized stages of transition. This characterizes rotational training programs. It also includes probationary periods, such as the 8- to 10-year "associate" status used by accounting and law firms before deciding on whether or not a candidate is made a partner. Variable schedules give no advance notice of their transition timetable. Variable schedules describe the typical promotion system, in which one is not advanced to the next stage until one is "ready."

Serial vs. Random Serial socialization is characterized by the use of role models who train and encourage the newcomer. Apprenticeship and mentoring programs are examples. In random socialization, role models are deliberately withheld. New employees are left on their own to figure things out.

Investiture vs. Divestiture Investiture socialization assumes that the newcomer's qualities and qualifications are the necessary ingredients for job success, so these qualities and qualifications are confirmed and supported. Divestiture socialization tries to strip away certain characteristics of the recruit. Fraternity and sorority "pledges" go through divestiture socialization to shape them into the proper role.

largest decreases in commitment and satisfaction.[61] The initial adjustment period for newcomers may present increasing demands and difficulties, at least in the short term.

15-4 Compare the functional and dysfunctional effects of organizational culture on people and the organization.

What Do Cultures Do?

Let's discuss the role that culture performs and whether it can ever be a liability for an organization.

The Functions of Culture

Culture defines "the rules of the game." First, it has a boundary-defining role: It creates distinctions between organizations. Second, it conveys a sense of identity for organization members. Third, culture facilitates commitment to something larger than individual self-interest. Fourth, it enhances the stability of the social system. Culture is the social glue that helps hold the organization together by providing standards for what employees should say and do. Finally, it is a sense-making and control mechanism that guides and shapes employees' attitudes and behavior. This last function is of particular interest to us.[62]

A strong culture ensures that employees will act in a relatively uniform and predictable way. Today's trend toward decentralized organizations (see Chapter 15) makes culture more important than ever, but ironically it also makes establishing a strong culture more difficult. When formal authority and control systems are reduced through decentralization, culture's *shared meaning* can point everyone in the same direction. Decentralization also highlights the role climate plays in linking organizational culture to organizational and employee outcomes. However, employees organized in teams may show greater allegiance to their team and its values than to the organization. Strong leadership that fosters a strong culture by communicating frequently about common goals and priorities may be especially important for organizations. Research on hundreds of CEOs and top management team (TMT) members suggests that more positive organizational outcomes are achieved when the culture and leadership styles are *complementary in content* and not *redundant*.[63] When leadership behaviors and an organization's cultural values are redundant, the leaders have less of an effect on organizational outcomes. However, when leaders provide something that is lacking in the organization's culture, they can substitute or fill in for the element that is missing. For example, a transformational leader in a bureaucratic, hierarchical culture would be more effective than a transactional leader in the same type of culture.

Individual–organization "fit"—that is, whether the applicant's or employee's attitudes and behavior are compatible with the culture—strongly influences who gets a job offer, a favorable performance review, or a promotion.[64] It's no coincidence that Disney theme park employees appear almost universally attractive, clean, and wholesome and smile brightly. The company selects employees who will maintain that image.

Culture Creates Climate

organizational climate The shared perceptions organizational members have about their organization and work environment; particularly, the policies, practices, and procedures that are in place.

If you've worked with someone whose positive attitude inspired you to do your best, or if you have worked with a lackluster team that drained your motivation, you've experienced the effects of climate. **Organizational climate** refers to the shared perceptions that organizational members have about their organization's policies, procedures, and practices.[65] Although it may appear difficult on the surface to distinguish organizational culture from climate, culture and climate are "two crucial building blocks for organizational description."[66] One meta-analysis found that, across dozens of different samples, psychological climate was strongly related to individuals' level of job satisfaction, involvement, commitment, and motivation.[67] A positive workplace climate has been linked to higher customer satisfaction and organizational financial performance as well.[68]

Employees of French video-game publisher Ubisoft Entertainment are shown working on "Just Dance 3" at the firm's creative studio near Paris. Ubisoft's 26 creative studios around the world share a climate of creative collaboration that reflects the diversity of team members.
Source: Charles Platiau/Reuters

Recent theory also suggests that there is a difference between *espoused* (i.e., adopted on-the-surface) and *enacted* (i.e., actually put into practice) cultural values, beliefs, and assumptions and that this difference has implications for how climate emerges.[69] Today, researchers agree that organizational climate represents the more readily observable "behavioral evidence" for an organization's culture.[70] It directly links what the organization values and believes with explicit practices, policies, and procedures. In other words, it puts the "what we believe and value" (like what you would find in a mission statement) and links it to what employees perceive is *actually* supported, rewarded, and practiced. In making sense of their environments, employees draw a distinction between what they "hear" or "see" being supported by organizational leaders in meetings, memos, rulebooks, and so on, and what they "actually" see being enacted. Climate, then, is a function of what employees perceive is being rewarded. Research in Australia suggests that when there is alignment between espoused and enacted organizational values, employees have higher organizational commitment.[71]

An example might help illustrate this culture-climate distinction.[72] Let us say the captain of a cargo ship was running behind in departing from port. The captain tried to increase speed and take a more direct course to make up for the delay. On its way to the destination, the ship ran aground, suffering damage, and thousands of dollars in expensive cargo was ruined. If we were to interview the captain, the captain might say, "I feel a tremendous sense of pressure to make sure the cargo gets to where it needs to be on time. Our company values timeliness above everything else, and top management constantly reiterates this to us. Besides, we are rewarded for getting to the port on time. Policy permits us to increase speed and alter routes to get to port on time, and every other captain I work with at this company makes similar decisions when we're running behind!" These statements reflect the policies, practices, and procedures that represent a climate of timeliness. But when asked about safety, the captain shrugs and says "it's just not important to them"—this says a lot. An organization with a strong safety culture (valuing safety and believing safety matters) and a strong safety climate (prohibiting speed and direction changes, incorporating technology to detect and prevent collisions, using proper safety equipment, and requiring safety training for captains) may have avoided this incident altogether.

Dozens of dimensions of climate have been studied, including innovation, creativity, communication, warmth and support, involvement, safety, justice, diversity, and customer service.[73] For example, someone who encounters a safety climate will have higher levels of job satisfaction and organizational commitment, have better health, and be more prone to engage in safety behaviors.[74] Climate influences the habits that people adopt. If there is a climate of safety, everyone wears safety gear and follows safety procedures even if individually they wouldn't normally think very often about being safe. Indeed, many studies have shown that a safety climate decreases the number of documented injuries on the job.[75] Climates can also interact with one another to produce various outcomes. For example, a climate of worker empowerment can lead to higher levels of performance in organizations that also have a climate of personal accountability.[76] Exhibit 15-6 depicts the impact of organizational culture. Employees form an overall subjective perception of the organization based on leader and member behaviors, the organizational structure, the organization's values and beliefs, as well as artifacts, stories, and symbols. This overall perception represents, in effect, the organization's culture, which varies in its strength (or degree to which others perceive the culture in the same way). The culture is then revealed through organizational climates, which manifest the culture's underlying values and beliefs. The climates then affect employee performance and satisfaction, along with other outcomes relevant to organization.

The Ethical Dimension of Culture

ethical culture The shared concept of right and wrong behavior in the workplace that reflects the true values of the organization and shapes the ethical decision making of its members.

Organizational cultures are not neutral in their ethical orientation, even when they are not openly pursuing ethical goals. **Ethical culture** develops over time as the shared concept of right and wrong behavior in the workplace. The ethical culture reflects the true values of the organization and shapes the ethical decision making of its members.[77] Research indicates that ethical cultures espouse clear ethical standards, with ethical behavior modeled by leadership and with employees who are capable of and committed to behaving ethically. Employees and managers are open to discuss ethical issues and are reinforced for their ethical behavior.[78]

Researchers have developed *ethical climate theory (ECT)* to measure the shared perceptions of ethical policies, practices, and procedures.[79] Ethical climates are heavily influenced by the values and beliefs leaders hold about ethical behavior as well as the collective sense of identity people forge around their shared ethics.[80]

An organization's ethical climate is a powerful influence on the way its individual members feel they should behave, so much so that researchers have been able to predict organizational outcomes.[81] Ethical climates that emphasize self-interest are negatively associated with employee job satisfaction and organizational commitment, even though those climates appeal to helping oneself versus others. These climates are also positively associated with turnover intentions, workplace bullying, and deviant behavior.[82] Ethical climates that emphasize caring for one another and establishing rules may bring greater job satisfaction as well as reduce employee turnover intentions, workplace bullying,

Exhibit 15-6 How Organizational Cultures Have an Impact on Employee Performance and Satisfaction

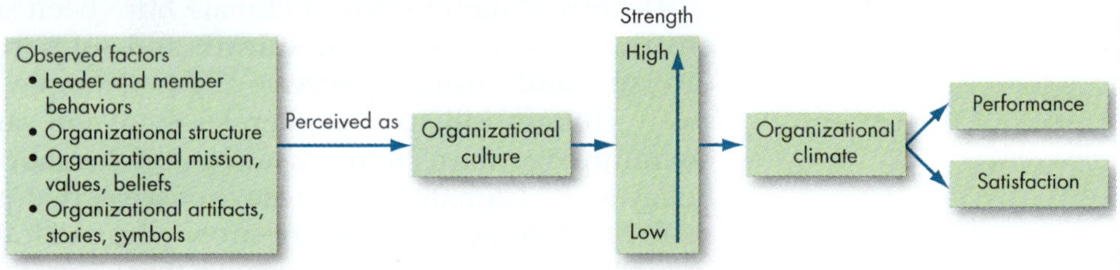

and dysfunctional behavior. Recent research also suggests that ethical climates have a strong influence on sales growth over time when there is also a customer service climate to support it.[83]

Industries with exacting standards, such as engineering, accounting, and law, tend to have a climate with an insistence on laws and codes. Industries that thrive on competitiveness, such as financial trading, often have a climate focused on self-interest. Industries with missions of benevolence are likely to have a caring climate, even if they are for-profit, as in an environmental protection firm. We cannot conclude, however, that climates emphasizing self-interest are bad or that those based on caring for one another are good. An emphasis on self-interest may foster the individual-level successes their companies need to thrive, for example, and they may help underperformers to recognize that their self-interest is better served elsewhere. Managers who prioritize mutual care may be thwarted in making the best decisions when only choices that serve the greatest number of employees are acceptable.[84] The ECI, first introduced in 2010, is one way researchers are seeking to understand the context of ethical drivers in organizations. By measuring the collective levels of moral sensitivity, judgment, motivation, and character of our organizations, we may be able to determine the strength of the influence that our ethical climates have on us.[85]

Although ECT was first introduced more than 25 years ago, researchers have been recently studying ethics in organizations more closely to determine not only how ethical climates behave but also how they might be fostered or even changed.[86] Eventually, we may be able to provide leaders with clear blueprints for designing effective ethical climates.

Culture and Sustainability

sustainability Maintaining organizational practices over a long period of time because the tools or structures that support them are not damaged by the processes.

Sustainability refers to maintaining practices over very long periods of time[87] because the tools or structures that support the practices are not damaged by the processes. One survey found that a substantial majority of executives saw sustainability as an important part of future success.[88] Concepts of sustainable management have their origins in the environmental movement, so processes that are in harmony with the natural environment are encouraged. *Social sustainability* practices address the ways that social systems are affected by an organization's actions over time and how changing social systems may affect the organization.

For example, farmers in Australia have been working collectively to increase water use efficiency, minimize soil erosion, and implement tilling and harvesting methods that ensure long-term viability for their farm businesses.[89] In a very different context, 3M has an innovative pollution-prevention program rooted in cultural principles of conserving resources, creating products that have minimal effects on the environment, and collaborating with regulatory agencies to improve environmental effects.[90]

Sustainable management doesn't need to be purely altruistic. Systematic reviews of the research literature show a generally positive relationship between sustainability and financial performance.[91] However, there is often a strong moral and ethical component that shapes organizational culture and which must be a genuine value for the relationship to exist.

To create a truly sustainable business, an organization must develop a long-term culture and put its values into practice.[92] In other words, there needs to be a sustainable system for creating sustainability! In one workplace study, a company seeking to reduce energy consumption found that soliciting group feedback reduced energy use significantly more than simply issuing reading materials about the importance of conservation.[93] In other words, talking about energy conservation and building the value into the organizational culture resulted in positive employee behavioral changes. Like other cultural practices we've discussed, sustainability needs time and nurturing to grow.

Culture and Innovation

The most innovative companies are often characterized by their open, unconventional, collaborative, vision-driven, accelerating cultures.[94] Start-up firms often have innovative cultures because they are usually small, agile, and focused on solving problems to survive and grow. Consider digital music leader Echo Nest, recently bought by Spotify. As a start-up, the organization was unconventional, flexible, and open; it hosted music app "hack" days for users and fostered a music culture.[95] All these are hallmarks of Spotify's culture, too, making the fit rather seamless.[96] Because of the similar organizational cultures, Echo Nest and Spotify may be able to continue their start-up level of innovation. Research on companies such as these has found that innovation-friendly practices (support for new ideas, openness to change, and providing resources to be creative—which make up an innovation climate) leads to boosts in creativity at work, the creation and implementation of novel ideas, and increased performance.[97]

At the other end of the start-up spectrum, consider 30-year-old Intuit, one of the World's 100 Most Innovative Companies according to *Forbes*. Intuit employees attend workshops to teach them how to think creatively and unconventionally. Sessions have led to managers talking through puppets and holding bake sales to sell prototype apps with their cupcakes. The culture stresses open accountability. "I saw one senior guy whose idea they'd been working on for nine months get disproved in a day because someone had a better way. He got up in front of everyone and said, 'This is my bad. I should have checked my hypothesis earlier,'" said Eric Ries, author of *The Lean Startup*. As a consultant for entrepreneurs, Ries considers the older software company equally innovative to start-ups because of its culture.[98]

Alexion Pharmaceuticals is also one of *Forbes'* Most Innovative and, like Intuit, it has been in operation long past the usual innovation life-cycle stage. Unlike Intuit, though, this maker of life-saving medicines is not known for unconventional management practices. The key to its continuing innovation

Visitors to "The Crystal" in London, which is the largest exhibition about the future of the world's cities and one of the most sustainable buildings in the world. The Crystal was created by Siemens, an international conglomerate who prides itself on being the most energy-efficient firm in its industry and who took the top spot in the 2017 Global 100 list of most sustainable organizations in the world.
Source: Julio Etchart/Alamy Stock Photo

is a culture of caring, which drives it to develop medicines that save victims of rare diseases, even when the patients affected are few, the cost of development is prohibitively high, and the probability of success is low.[99]

Israeli research suggests that CEOs who value self-direction can lead to the formation of a creative culture, which in turn, is related to employee innovative behavior *and* employees recognizing creative solutions more readily.[100]

Culture as an Asset

As we have discussed, organizational culture can foster a positive environment, with organizational climates that put values in action. Culture can also contribute significantly to an organization's bottom line in many ways.

It is because of its mission to serve the best tea to the customer that a small regional brand, Wagh Bakri, is now the 3rd largest tea packaging company in India. The Desais, who are the owners of the company believe in serving quality tea and not profit. In fact, they have consistently kept their profits in single digits and reduced prices of tea if they have started earning profit. Employees working at Wagh Bakri are encouraged to understand the customer needs and preferences, and maintain integrity at all costs.[101] When Mr. A. N. Radhakrishnan took charge as the managing director of Chennai Meenakshi SuperSpeciality Hospitals (a 46 year old 100 bed hospital), he had taken over a loss making hospital. Radhakrishan analysed that because of their inability to provide the best medical care, patients were not choosing them. He increased more than double the spend on human resources, from training doctors and paramedical staff to hiring a large number of specialist doctors. Efforts were also made to ethically sell the services of the hospitals. In a span of four years, the hospital was turned around and continues to be profitable and a preferred place of work by doctors in Chennai.[102] Tihar Central Jail in Delhi was infamous and not a preferred

Founded in 1969, Samsung Electronics of South Korea is past the usual innovation life cycle stage yet continues to foster a climate of creativity and idea generation. Samsung emulates a start-up culture through its Creative Labs, where employees like engineer Ki Yuhoon, shown here, take up to a year off from their regular jobs to work on innovative projects.
Source: Lee Jin-man/AP Images

posting for senior police officers. At that time, Kiran Bedi accepted the post as the Inspector General of Police. In her two-year tenure during 1993 -1995, she successfully uplifted the prison conditions from a place of incarceration to reformation. Attention was paid to the physical and mental well-being of the prisoners. Inmates were used to help other inmates to follow discipline. Criminal elements operating within the prison were identified and punished. The staff of the prison was trained to work alongside each other and inmates to improve the conditions of the prison. Suggestions were sought from all stakeholders including the inmate.[103]

Culture as a Liability

Culture can enhance organizational commitment and increase the consistency of employee behavior, which clearly benefits an organization. Culture is valuable to employees too because it spells out what's important. But we shouldn't ignore the potentially dysfunctional aspects of culture, especially a strong one, on an organization's effectiveness. Hewlett-Packard, once known as a premier computer manufacturer, rapidly lost market share and profits as dysfunction in its TMT trickled down, leaving employees disengaged, uncreative, unappreciated, or in a polarized environment.[104] Let's unpack some of the major factors that signal a negative organizational culture, beginning with institutionalization.

institutionalization A condition that occurs when an organization takes on a life of its own, apart from any of its members.

Institutionalization When an organization undergoes **institutionalization**—that is, it becomes valued for itself and not for the goods or services it produces—it takes on a life of its own, apart from its founders or members.[105] Institutionalized organizations often don't go out of business even if the original goals are no longer relevant. Acceptable modes of behavior may become largely self-evident to members; although this isn't entirely negative, it does mean behaviors and habits go unquestioned, which can stifle innovation and make maintaining the organization's culture an end in itself.

Barriers to Change Culture is a liability when shared values don't agree with those that further the organization's effectiveness. This is most likely when an organization's environment is undergoing rapid change, and its entrenched culture may no longer be appropriate.[106] Consistency of behavior, an asset in a stable environment, may then burden the organization and make it difficult to respond to changes.

Barriers to Diversity Hiring new employees who differ from the majority in race, age, gender, disability, or other characteristics creates a paradox:[107] Management wants to demonstrate support for the differences that these employees bring to the workplace, but newcomers who wish to fit in are usually pressured to accept the organization's core culture. Second, because diverse behaviors and unique strengths are likely to diminish as people assimilate, strong cultures can become liabilities when they effectively eliminate the advantages of diversity. Third, a strong culture that condones prejudice, supports bias, becomes insensitive, or overemphasizes differences can undermine formal corporate diversity policies or the positive effects of demographic diversity.[108] It seems that these barriers to diversity can start at the community level: One study of nearly 150 retail bank locations in the United States found that the demographic composition of the community serves as an important signal in setting the diversity norms that are adopted and made part of an organization's culture and climate.[109] Barriers to diversity can, in part, be addressed through cultures and climates of inclusion—by showing the organization values and enacts an inclusive environment, diversity may flourish within the organization and employees may be more committed to the organization.[110] On the other hand, people from various backgrounds may perceive the culture and climates differently, undermining the effect positive cultures and climates may have on organizational outcomes.[111]

Toxicity and Dysfunctions In general, we've discussed cultures that cohere around a positive set of values and beliefs. This consensus can create powerful forward momentum. However, coherence around negative and dysfunctional values in a corporation can produce downward forces that are equally powerful yet toxic. For example, research on 862 bank employees in about 150 branches of a large bank in the United States suggests that branch managers model conflict management styles, which then shape conflict cultures within each branch.[112] Collaborative cultures (i.e., encouraging proactive, constructive, and collaborative conflict resolution) tended to increase the cohesion and satisfaction of the branch and decrease levels of burnout. Dominating cultures (i.e., encouraging active confrontation and aggressive competition among employees when there is conflict) tend to reduce branch cohesion and customer service performance. Avoidance cultures (i.e., those that passively avoid conflict) tend to be less creative.

Barriers to Acquisitions and Mergers Historically, when management looked at acquisition or merger decisions, the key decision factors were potential financial advantage and product synergy. In recent years, cultural compatibility has become the primary concern.[113] All things being equal, whether the acquisition works seems to have much to do with how well the two organizations' cultures match up. When they don't mesh well, the organizational cultures of both become a liability to the whole new organization. A study conducted by Bain and Company found that 70 percent of mergers failed to increase shareholder values, and Hay Group found that more than 90 percent of mergers in Europe failed to reach financial goals.[114] Considering this dismal rate of success, Lawrence Chia from Deloitte Consulting observed, "One of the biggest failings is people. The people at Company A have a different way of doing things from Company B . . . you can't find commonality in goals."

Culture clash was commonly argued to be one of the causes of AOL Time Warner's problems. The $183 billion merger between America Online (AOL) and Time Warner in 2001 was the largest in U.S. corporate history. It was also a disaster. Only 2 years later, the new company saw its stock fall an astounding 90 percent, and it reported what was then the largest financial loss in U.S. history—it has since been acquired by Verizon and is being merged, yet again, with Yahoo under the umbrella company "Oath."[115]

Recent research on acquisitions in the Taiwanese electronics industry suggests that the success of mergers and acquisitions hinge on *how* the acquisition was acquired, the organizational structure (e.g., centralization and divisional integration), *and* the organizational culture.[116]

Influencing an Organizational Culture

15-5 Describe the similarities and differences in creating an ethical culture, a positive culture, and a spiritual culture.

As we discussed, the culture of an organization is set by its founders and is often difficult to change afterward. It's true that the ideal scenario is a strong founder or founders who carefully plan the organization's culture beforehand. That's seldom the case, though; organizational culture usually grows organically over time. When we think of the development of culture as ongoing and conducted through each employee, we can see ways to increase the ethical, positive, and/or spiritual aspects of the environment, which we discuss next.

Developing an Ethical Culture

Despite differences across industries and cultures, ethical organizational cultures share some common values and processes.[117] Therefore, managers can create a more ethical culture and more ethical climates by adhering to the following principles:[118]

- *Be a visible role model.* Employees will look to the actions of top management as a benchmark for appropriate behavior, but everyone can be a role model to positively influence the ethical atmosphere. Send a positive message.
- *Communicate ethical expectations.* Whenever you serve in a leadership capacity, minimize ethical ambiguities by sharing a code of ethics that states the organization's primary values and the judgment rules employees must follow.
- *Provide ethical training.* Set up seminars, workshops, and training programs to reinforce the organization's standards of conduct, clarify what practices are permissible, and address potential ethical dilemmas.

- *Visibly reward ethical acts and punish unethical ones.* Evaluate subordinates on how their decisions compare with the organization's code of ethics. Review the means as well as the ends. Visibly reward those who act ethically and conspicuously punish those who don't.
- *Provide protective mechanisms.* Seek formal mechanisms so everyone can discuss ethical dilemmas and report unethical behavior without fear of reprimand. These might include identifying ethical counselors, ombudspeople, or ethical officers for liaison roles.

A widespread positive ethical climate must start at the top of the organization.[119] When top management emphasizes strong ethical values, supervisors are more likely to practice ethical leadership. Clear expectations transfer down to line employees, who show lower levels of deviant behavior and higher levels of cooperation and assistance. Several other studies have come to the same general conclusion: The values of top management are a good predictor of ethical behavior among employees. For example, one study involving auditors found perceived pressure from organizational leaders to behave unethically was associated with increased intentions to engage in unethical practices.[120] Clearly the wrong type of organizational culture can negatively influence employee ethical behavior. Conversely, ethical leadership has been shown to improve group ethical voice, or the extent to which employees feel comfortable speaking up about issues that seem unethical to them, through improvements in ethical culture.[121] Finally, employees whose ethical values are similar to those of their department are more likely to be promoted, so we can think of ethical culture as flowing from the bottom up as well.[122]

For instance, Arpan, an NGO which works on Child Sexual Abuse prevention founded in 2006, has impacted over 900,000 children and adults, directly and indirectly across the country. The founder, Pooja, says the secret to their large impact is "their incredible team". Pooja believes, "that it is this 'people' element that has been critical to helping the organization unlock its potential to create a 'World Free of Child Sexual Abuse.'"[123]

Developing a Positive Culture

At first, creating a positive culture may sound hopelessly naïve or like a Dilbert-style conspiracy. The one thing that makes us believe this trend is here to stay, however, are signs that management practice and Organizational Behavior (OB) research are converging. A **positive organizational culture** values building on employee strengths, rewards more than it punishes, and encourages individual vitality and growth.[124] Let's consider each of these areas.

positive organizational culture A culture that values building on employee strengths, rewards more than it punishes, and encourages individual vitality and growth.

Building on Employee Strengths Although a positive organizational culture does not ignore problems, it does emphasize showing workers how they can capitalize on their strengths. As management guru Peter Drucker said, "Most Americans do not know what their strengths are. When you ask them, they look at you with a blank stare, or they respond in terms of subject knowledge, which is the wrong answer."[125] Wouldn't it be better to be in an organizational culture that helped you discover your strengths and how to make the most of them?

As CEO and founder of Looks Salon –one of the fastest growing salons in Delhi-NCR –Mr. Sanjay Dutta, decided to take care of his employees during the COVID-19 pandemic. While the salon business was really affected by the raging pandemic with difficulty in paying salaries to all his staff, Mr. Dutta sold one of his salons located in a prime location to support his employees. He decided to continue to focus on the training and education of his employees so that when

Brunello Cucinelli, an Italian luxury cashmere brand, believes in the dignity of work and importance of leisure time. The firm prefers to have a lower profit than its competitors in order to offer employees high salaries and decent working conditions. Moreover, Brunello, the founder, invites all employees to leave the office at 5 P.M. in order to participate in their numerous non-working activities, and he encourages the managers of the company to do the same.
Source: Dpa picture alliance/Alamy Stock Photo

the times improved, the employees would be better trained, and thus, be able to charge higher prices for their services.[126]

Rewarding More Than Punishing Although most organizations are sufficiently focused on extrinsic rewards such as pay and promotions, they often forget about the power of smaller (and cheaper) rewards such as praise. Part of creating a positive organizational culture is "catching employees doing something right." Many managers withhold praise because they're afraid employees will coast or because they think praise is not valued. Employees generally don't ask for praise, and managers usually don't realize the costs of failing to give it.

In organizations that have downsized, there is often a decrease in morale. In such organizations, keeping the engagement of those who have survived, requires special strategies. In a study of managers who worked in IT organizations where extensive downsizing was carried out it was found that communication was an effective tool to manage employee engagement. Open, frequent, transparent communication, access to information and senior managers was helpful in employee engagement. Acknowledging that fear is rampant among employees during and after downsizing and explicitly creating mechanisms for people to feel safe helps in employee growth and productivity.[127]

Encouraging Vitality and Growth No organization will get the best from employees who see themselves as mere cogs in the machine. A positive culture recognizes the difference between a job and a career. It supports not only what the employee contributes to organizational effectiveness but how the organization can make the employee more effective—personally and professionally. Top companies recognize the value of helping people grow. Radixweb a software solution provider based out of Ahmedabad over the last 20 years has gone from strength to strength to help their clients achieve their vision. Divyesh Patel, the founder and chief technical leader of the company, encourages his team to work hard and balance family needs. Women employees are supported during their pregnancy and are supported fully to come back to their work and positions.[128&129]

It may take more creativity to encourage employee growth in some industries. From the Masterfoods headquarters in Brussels, Philippe Lescornez led a team of sales promoters, including Didier Brynaert, who worked in Luxembourg, nearly 150 miles away. Lescornez decided Brynaert's role could be improved if he were an expert on the unique features of the Luxembourg market. So Lescornez asked Brynaert for information he could share with the home office. "I started to communicate much more what he did internally to other people [within the company], because there's quite some distance between the Brussels office and the section he's working in. So I started to communicate, communicate, communicate. The more I communicated, the more he started to provide material," he said. As a result, "Now he's recognized as the specialist for Luxembourg—the guy who is able to build a strong relationship with the Luxembourg clients," says Lescornez. What's good for Brynaert was, of course, also good for Lescornez, who got credit for helping Brynaert grow and develop.[130]

Limits of Positive Culture Is a positive culture a cure-all? Though many companies have embraced aspects of a positive organizational culture, it is a new enough idea for us to be uncertain about how and when it works best.

Not all national cultures value being positive as much as the U.S. culture does and, even within U.S. culture, there surely are limits to how far organizations should go. The limits may need to be dictated by the industry and society. For example, Admiral, a British insurance company, has established a Ministry of Fun in its call centers to organize poem writing, foosball, conkers (a British game involving chestnuts), and fancy-dress days, which may clash with an industry value of more serious cultures. When does the pursuit of a positive culture start to seem coercive? As one critic notes, "Promoting a social orthodoxy of positiveness focuses on a particular constellation of desirable states and traits but, in so doing, can stigmatize those who fail to fit the template."[131] There may be benefits to establishing a positive culture, but an organization also needs to be objective and not pursue it past the point of effectiveness.

A Spiritual Culture

What do Aravind Eye Care, Hewlett-Packard, Provident Fund Officers, Tata Steel, Sarvanna Bhawan have in common? They're among a growing number of organizations that have embraced workplace spirituality.

What Is Spirituality? Workplace spirituality is *not* about organized religious practices. It's not about God or theology. **Workplace spirituality** recognizes that people have an inner life that nourishes and is nourished by meaningful work in the context of community.[132] Organizations that support a spiritual culture recognize that people seek to find meaning and purpose in their work and desire to connect with other human beings as part of a community. Many of the topics we have discussed—ranging from job design to corporate social responsibility (CSR)—are well matched to the concept of organizational spirituality. When a company emphasizes its commitment to paying Third World suppliers a fair (above-market) price for their products to facilitate community development—as did Starbucks—or encourages employees to share prayers or inspirational messages through e-mail—as did Interstate Batteries—it may encourage a more spiritual culture and climate.[133]

Why Spirituality Now? As noted in our discussion of emotions in Chapter 4, the myth of rationality assumed that the well-run organization eliminated people's feelings. Concern about an employee's inner life had no role in the perfectly rational model. But just as we realize that the study of emotions improves our understanding of OB, an awareness of spirituality can help us better understand employee behavior.

workplace spirituality The recognition that people have an inner life that nourishes and is nourished by meaningful work that takes place in the context of community.

Of course, employees have always had an inner life. So why has the search for meaning and purposefulness in work surfaced now? We summarize the reasons in Exhibit 15-7.

Characteristics of a Spiritual Organization The concept of workplace spirituality draws on our previous discussions of values, ethics, motivation, and leadership. Although research remains preliminary, several cultural values tend to be evident in spiritual organizations:[134]

- *Benevolence.* Spiritual organizations value kindness toward others and the happiness of employees and other organizational stakeholders.
- *Strong sense of purpose.* Spiritual organizations build their cultures around a meaningful purpose. Although profits may be important, they're not the primary value.
- *Trust and respect.* Spiritual organizations are characterized by mutual trust, honesty, and openness. Employees are treated with esteem and value, consistent with the dignity of each individual.
- *Open-mindedness.* Spiritual organizations value flexible thinking and creativity among employees.

Achieving Spirituality in the Organization Many organizations have grown interested in spirituality but have had trouble putting principles into practice. Several types of practices can facilitate a spiritual climate,[135] including those that support work-life balance. Leaders can demonstrate values, attitudes, and behaviors that trigger intrinsic motivation and a sense of fulfilling a calling through work. Encouraging employees to consider how their work provides a sense of purpose can help achieve a spiritual workplace; often this is done through group counseling and organizational development, the latter of which we take up in Chapter 18.

Exhibit 15-7 Reasons for the Growing Interest in Spirituality

- Spirituality can counterbalance the pressures and stress of a turbulent pace of life. Contemporary lifestyles—single-parent families, geographic mobility, the temporary nature of jobs, new technologies that create distance between people—underscore the lack of community many people feel and increase the need for involvement and connection.
- Formalized religion hasn't worked for many people, and they continue to look for anchors to replace lack of faith and to fill a growing feeling of emptiness.
- Job demands have made the workplace dominant in many people's lives, yet they continue to question the meaning of work.
- People want to integrate personal life values with their professional lives.
- An increasing number of people are finding that the pursuit of more material acquisitions leaves them unfulfilled.

Criticisms of Spirituality Critics of the spirituality movement in organizations[136] have focused on three issues. First is the question of scientific foundation. What really is workplace spirituality? Is spirituality just a new management buzzword? Second, are spiritual organizations legitimate? Specifically, do organizations have the right to claim spiritual values? Third is the question of economics: Are spirituality and profits compatible?

First, there is comparatively little research on workplace spirituality. Spirituality has been defined so broadly in some sources that practices from job rotation to corporate retreats at meditation centers have been identified as spiritual. Questions need to be answered before the concept gains full credibility.

Second, an emphasis on spirituality can clearly make some employees uneasy. Critics have argued that secular institutions, especially business firms, should not impose spiritual values on employees.[137] This criticism is undoubtedly valid

Career OBjectives

How do I learn to lead?

I'll be starting a new job in a few weeks. It's my first time working as a leader for a team, and I know I have a lot to learn. Is there any way I can be sure I'll achieve success as a leader?

—Ganesh

Dear Ganesh:

Learning about a new job is always complicated. Learning how to be a leader is doubly complicated. It's expected that you have the capacity to provide direction and purpose for employees and that you will respect the existing culture of the group as well as the capacities of individual members. Here are a few key insights toward making your transition into leadership successful:

- *Ask questions.* New leaders are often anxious about asking questions of employees who report directly to them for fear of being seen as incompetent or weak. However, inquiring about how things have been done in the past and asking about individual goals signals that you are concerned about the team members. Familiarizing yourself with the group's culture and practices can also help you develop techniques to harness the team's strengths and overcome challenges.
- *Build relationships with other leaders.* Remember—you were put into this role for a reason, and the company wants to see you succeed, so make the most of the resources of others. Take detailed notes regarding specific activities and strategies that were successful, and schedule a check-in to discuss how these strategies have worked over time. If you can show you are truly engaged in the learning process, you'll find others are more willing to provide you with assistance and advice.
- *Start small.* Much has been written about the importance of gaining small wins early to build your reputation. The old saying "You never get a second chance to make a first impression" definitely holds true in the workplace. Try to develop new initiatives with clear outcomes that will allow you to demonstrate your leadership traits.

The best leadership transitions include learning what the situation calls for and setting your team up for success from the start.

Be proactive!

Sources: Based on T. B. Harris, N. Li, W. R. Boswell, X. Zhang, and Z. Xie, "Getting What's New from Newcomers: Empowering Leadership, Creativity, and Adjustment in the Socialization Context," *Personnel Psychology* 67 (2014): 567–604; Y. H. Ji, N. A. Cohen, A. Daly, K. Finnigan, and K. Klein, "The Dynamics of Voice Behavior and Leaders' Network Ties in Times of Leadership Successions," *Academy of Management Proceedings* (2014): 16324; and B. Eckfeldt, "5 Things New CEOS Should Focus On," *Business Insider*, June 1, 2015, http://www.businessinsider.com/5-things-new-ceos-should-focus-on-2015-6.

The opinions provided here are of the managers and authors only and do not necessarily reflect those of their organizations. The authors or managers are not responsible for any errors or omissions, or for the results obtained from the use of this information. In no event will the authors or managers, or their related partnerships or corporations thereof, be liable to you or anyone else for any decision made or action taken in reliance on the opinions provided here.

when spirituality is defined as bringing religion and God into the workplace. However, it seems less stinging when the goal is limited to helping employees find meaning and purpose in their work lives. If the concerns listed in Exhibit 15-7 truly characterize a large segment of the workforce, then perhaps organizations can help.

Third, whether spirituality and profits are compatible objectives is a relevant concern for managers and investors in business. The evidence, although limited, indicates they are. In one study, organizations that provided their employees with opportunities for spiritual development outperformed those that didn't.[138] Other studies reported that spirituality in organizations was positively related to creativity, employee satisfaction, job involvement, and organizational commitment.[139]

15-6 Show how national culture can affect the way organizational culture is transported to another country.

The Global Context

We considered global cultural values (collectivism–individualism, power distance, and so on) in Chapter 5. Here our focus is a bit narrower: How is organizational culture affected by the global context? Organizational culture is so powerful that it often transcends national boundaries. But that doesn't mean organizations should, or could, ignore local culture.

Organizational cultures often reflect national culture.[140] The culture at AirAsia, a Malaysian-based airline, emphasizes openness and friendships. The carrier has lots of parties, participative management, and no private offices, reflecting Malaysia's relatively collectivistic culture. The culture of many U.S. airlines does not reflect the same degree of informality. If a U.S. airline were to merge with AirAsia, it would need to take these cultural differences into account. Organizational culture differences are not always due to international culture differences, however. One of the chief challenges of the merger of HP and Compaq was the sales driven quick decision making culture of Compaq with the engineering driven consensus seeking decision making culture of HP. [141]

One of the primary things employees can do is to be culturally sensitive. Some ways in which employees can be culturally sensitive include being aware of one's actions and how they may be perceived by others and to consider others' backgrounds, perspectives, and emotions before speaking or acting.

The management of ethical behavior is one area where national culture can rub against corporate culture.[142] U.S. managers and employees often endorse the supremacy of anonymous market forces as a moral obligation for business organizations. This worldview sees bribery, nepotism, and favoring personal contacts as highly unethical. They also value profit maximization, so any action that deviates from profit maximization may suggest inappropriate or corrupt behavior. In contrast, managers in developing economies are more likely to see ethical decisions as embedded in the social environment. That means doing special favors for family and friends is not only appropriate but possibly even an ethical responsibility. Managers in many nations view capitalism skeptically and believe the interests of workers should be put on a par with the interests of shareholders, which may limit profit maximization.

Creating a multinational organizational culture can initiate strife between employees of traditionally competing countries. When Swedish, Norwegian, Finnish, and Danish banks combined to form Nordea Bank AB, the stereotypes some employees held based on the countries' historical relationships created tensions. Finland had originally been a colony of Sweden, and Norway had been a part of Denmark and then of Sweden. The fact that none of the employees had yet been born when their countries were colonies didn't matter; complex alliances within Nordea formed along nationalistic lines. To bridge these gaps, Nordea employed storytelling to help employees identify with positive aspects of their shared geographical *region.* The organization reinforced the shared identity through press releases, corporate correspondence, equal country representation in top management, and championing of shared values. Although the organization continues to struggle with a multinational culture, the successes it has enjoyed can be attributed to careful attention to national differences.[143]

As national organizations seek to employ workers in overseas operations, management must decide whether to standardize many facets of organizational culture. For example, should organizations offer wellness plans and work-life balance initiatives from the home country to the satellite offices, or should they tailor the plans for the norms of each society? Either can be problematic. For instance, when U.S. company Rothenberg International introduced its alcohol abuse remediation plan to Russian employees as part of its employee assistance program (EAP), it didn't foresee that Russians resist the concept of "assistance" and prefer "support" instead. Rothenberg could adjust, but sometimes local laws intercede (as a help or a hindrance) when employers roll out homeland plans. Brazil has a government anti-HIV plan that employers can use, for instance, and the United Kingdom's National Health Service pays for smoking cessation programs, while in Germany private insurance must pay for wellness plans.[144] At this point, there is no clear consensus on the best course of action, but the first step is for companies to be sensitive to differing standards.

Summary

Organizational cultures have an immense impact on behavior in organizations. Although the "essence" of an organization is often hard to describe, we can peer into the world of organizational life by examining an organization's shared values and beliefs, material symbols, rituals, stories, and language. Several culture frameworks have demonstrated that values and beliefs can have a substantial effect on organizational outcomes and that different cultural values affect different strategic outcomes. Cultures can also cut across organizations because employees differ in how strongly they agree on their organization's culture—these differences can lead to the creation of subcultures, which have implications for why people do things differently in different branches, departments, or teams.

The influence of founders on organizations' cultures is strong and undeniable. Founders set the tone and establish the foundation for what is valued, which leads them to hire people who share these values (and exclude those who do not). Over time, support from top management and socialization processes perpetuate the organizational culture, making it very difficult to change.

Cultures serve several functions for organizations. They define boundaries, convey a sense of identity, facilitate commitment to something larger than the self, and enhance the stability of the organizational system (acting as the "glue that holds the organization together"). The way the culture establishes tangible, concrete roots in organizations is through the establishment of climates, or policies, practices, and procedures that reinforce cultural values and beliefs. These climates then influence organizational outcomes such as performance and attitudes. Notably, a plethora of types of cultures and climates have been studied in OB to date. Of these, safety, ethical, sustainable, and innovation cultures and climates are particularly important and relevant for organizations. Furthermore, cultures and climates can be construed as both assets and liabilities, depending upon the values and practices considered. To enhance their value as assets, managers and employees alike can seek to foster positive, ethical, and spiritual cultures and climates that may help make their organization a re-affirming and positive place to work. As a caveat, you should always be aware of how national and organizational cultures may sometimes clash, especially when it comes to ethical issues.

Implications for Managers

- Realize that organizational culture is a complex, descriptive, and information-rich aspect of organizations that has a major influence on important outcomes. It is relatively fixed in the short term. To effect change, involve top management and strategize a long-term plan.
- Hire individuals whose values align with those of the organization (unless the objective is to introduce a diversity of perspectives); these employees will tend to remain committed and satisfied. Not surprisingly, "misfits" have considerably higher turnover rates.
- Understand that employees' performance and socialization depend to a considerable degree on their knowing what is valued and what is practiced in the organization. Train your employees well and keep them informed of changes to their job roles.
- You can shape the culture of your work environment, sometimes as much as it shapes you. All managers can do their part to create the desired culture by focusing on establishing policies, practices, and procedures that reinforce the desired or emphasized values.
- Be aware that your company's organizational culture may not be "transported" easily to other countries. Understand the cultural relevance of your organization's norms before introducing new plans or initiatives overseas.

Organizational Culture Can Be "Measured"

POINT

Greg Besner, the CEO of CultureIQ, has spent 15 years as an entrepreneur and leader following hundreds of companies to be able to accurately measure organizational culture. CultureIQ focuses on measuring and managing organizational culture using a software package, and they have found, over time, what they believe are 10 indicators that help a company assess their organizational cultures (especially the mission and values aspect). Besner suggests that companies should assess all of the following:

1. Communication, including employee voice and downward communication from leaders
2. Innovation, including employee creativity and organizational receptiveness to new ideas
3. Agility, including employee perceptions of whether the organization adapts to changes
4. Wellness, including the mental and physical well-being of employees
5. Environment, including the comfort and usability of the office space
6. Collaboration, including how well employees work with one another
7. Support, including the assistance that employees get from their supervisors, coworkers, and organization as a whole
8. Performance orientation, including role clarity, rewards, and employee recognition
9. Responsibility, including employee accountability and autonomy
10. Mission and values, including awareness and implementation

Beyond Besner's approach, a variety of other researchers and practitioners have claimed to assess organizational culture accurately. Primarily, they have used surveys and interviews to assess organizational culture and have amassed evidence that the surveys and interviews measure what they should and measure them consistently. One example of these measures asks employees to respond to questions related to the dimensions of organizational culture discussed at the beginning of the chapter (the same "objective factors" listed in Exhibit 15-6) and to compare how their stance on these values aligns with those of the organization.

COUNTERPOINT

Can something so complex, so deep, and so difficult to define clearly be measured by asking someone about his or her organization's culture in an interview or a survey? Probably not, according to some researchers. As Professor John Traphagan notes, "The problem with the term 'culture' is that it tends to essentialize groups: It simplistically represents a group of people as a unified whole that share simple common values, ideas, practices, and beliefs." Not only does it reduce complex systems to unified wholes, organizational culture is also deterministic, meaning that it is a given, complete entity that changes slowly and tends to have a strong, straightforward effect on behavior. But the reality is that these assumptions are probably not grounded.

The survey measures and interviews that are employed to assess organizational culture often fail to "meet the mark" because either they assess other phenomena that we inappropriately call "culture" (e.g., communication, performance, attitudes, etc.) or they do not fully capture the deep complexities of organizational culture. For example, should organizational culture assessments focus on myths? Stories? Values? Behavior? Artifacts? Beliefs? Underlying assumptions? Although it is easy to see how values, behavior, and beliefs can be assessed with surveys, it is perhaps very difficult to make sense of the organization's stories, artifacts, and underlying assumptions. Furthermore, how can we distinguish reliably between the effect of subcultures or the national culture and the overall culture as a whole?

A final issue can be found in *what* we should measure. As can be seen throughout this chapter, many different forms of organizational culture and dimensions have been forwarded by organizational behavior researchers over many decades. Which ones are correct? The answer to this question plays into the question of how we should measure organizational culture. It seems clear that, although organizational cultures appear to be real and to influence people, it is incredibly difficult to "measure" them.

Sources: Based on N. M. Ashkanasy, L. E. Broadfoot, and S. Falkus, "Questionnaire Measures of Organizational Culture," in N. M. Ashkanasy, C. P. M. Wilderom, and M. F. Peterson (eds.), *Handbook of Organizational Culture and Climate* (Thousand Oaks, CA: Sage, 2000): 131–46; G. Besner, "The 10 Company Culture Metrics You Should Be Tracking Right Now," *Entrepreneur*, June 3, 2015, https://www.entrepreneur.com/article/246899; C. Ostroff, A. J. Kinicki, and R. S. Muhammad, "Organizational Culture and Climate," in I. B. Weiner (ed.), *Handbook of Psychology*, 2nd ed. (Hoboken, NJ: Wiley, 2012): 643–76; B. Schneider, M. G. Ehrhart, and W. H. Macey, "Organizational Climate and Culture," *Annual Review of Psychology* 64 (2013): 361–88; and J. Traphagan, "Why 'Company Culture' Is a Misleading Term," *Harvard Business Review*, April 21, 2015, https://hbr.org/2015/04/why-company-culture-is-a-misleading-term.

CHAPTER REVIEW

QUESTIONS FOR REVIEW

15-1 What is organizational culture, and what are its common characteristics?

15-2 How is culture transmitted to employees?

15-3 What factors create and sustain an organization's culture?

15-4 What are the functional and dysfunctional effects of organizational culture?

15-5 What are the similarities and differences in creating an ethical culture, a positive culture, and a spiritual culture?

15-6 How does national culture affect what happens when an organizational culture is transported to another country?

APPLICATION AND EMPLOYABILITY

In this chapter, you were introduced to organizational culture and climate as well as their differentiating characteristics. You should also know now that they matter—a poor organizational culture, in many ways, can be a make-or-break factor for an organization. Organizational cultures are often taken very seriously by organizations. By learning about organizational cultures and how they work, you are improving your employability by enabling you to adapt to distinct types of cultures, to craft positive organizational cultures if you are to be in a leadership position, and to demonstrate your fit with the values of a company at which you are interviewing. You are also aware of the negative aspects of organizational culture, which will help you avoid or circumvent potentially troublesome situations when you are either on the job or applying to an organization that might have a negative organizational culture. In this chapter, you improved your communication skills by considering the forces of organizational culture change, learning how to be a better leader, differentiating between compassionate cultures in the banking industry, and debating whether it is possible to "measure" organizational culture. In the next section, you will improve your critical thinking and knowledge application and analysis skills by designing an organizational culture of your own, examining how cultures can encourage dishonesty or corruption, discussing how aspects of office and organizational design contribute to organizational culture, and questioning the pros and cons of an active culture.

EXPERIENTIAL EXERCISE Creating a Green Culture

Form groups of three or four students. Each group will be the founder of a new organization based in a different country. Drawing from the content developed in this chapter, your goal is to create a company with a strong organizational culture that emphasizes sustainability, attention to internal as well as external stakeholders, and promotion of ethical behaviors. Consider the term "sustainability" in its broader meaning, which encompasses not only attention toward the environment and a more conscious use of natural resources but also takes into account employees' well-being, workload, and work–life balance. Each group needs to provide the following information about their new organization and culture and be ready to justify their decision in class:

- *Name of the organization*
- *Products or services provided*
- *Primary country chosen for the headquarters*
- *Founding members*
- *Mission or vision statement*
- *Three primary values guiding the organization*
- *Five core beliefs that guide the conduct of business in the organization*

- *Three examples of organizational policies that enable the organization's vision to be accomplished or which reinforce its values*
- *One or more artifacts or symbols that represent the organization's mission or values*

Questions

15-7. Was it easy for your team to consider sustainability in its broader meaning to focus on both environmental protection and employees' well-being? Why or why not?

15-8. Paradoxically, contemporary organizations seem to commit greater attention and resources toward the protection of the environment than the care of people working for them. As a team, discuss three possible reasons behind this paradox and possible remedies to foster greater attention toward employees' well-being at work.

15-9. What specific organizational interventions could be implemented to help employees achieve greater work–life balance in their lives?

ETHICAL DILEMMA Culture of Deceit

We have noted throughout the text that honesty is generally the best policy in managing OB. But that doesn't mean honest dealing is always the rule in business.

Studies have found, in fact, that whole industries may encourage dishonesty. In one experiment, subjects were first asked either to think about their professional identities or to complete a generic survey. They were then asked to report on a series of coin flips; they were told in advance that the more times the coin showed heads, the more money they would make. The bankers who took the generic survey were about as honest in reporting coin flips as people who worked in other fields. The bankers told to think about their professional identities, however, exaggerated how often the coin turned up heads. People in other professions didn't do so—the tie between professional identity and dishonesty was unique to those who worked in banking. These results are certainly not limited to the banking industry. Many other ways of priming people to think about financial transactions seem to generate more dishonesty. And studies have also found that many individuals feel pressured to engage in dishonest behavior to meet the bottom line. Money provides powerful motives for dishonesty.

Money motivations are strong in professional sports. For example, the number of top leaders in FIFA (Fédération Internationale de Football Association, the international governing body of association football [soccer], futsal, and beach soccer) who were indicted in 2015 suggests that behaving dishonestly has been accepted within FIFA and covering up for the dishonesty of others has been encouraged. Domenico Scala, FIFA's audit and compliance committee chair, noted, "To support the change we need a culture that censures inappropriate behavior and enforces rules vigorously, fairly, and [is] responsive." There is consensus that to overcome corruption, those in positions of authority must demonstrate commitment to an ethical culture. As Scala noted, "It is the leaders' tone that ensures it is embedded at all levels of the organization. This must be honest and communicated with sincerity in both words and actions." There may well be a tendency to become dishonest when there's money to be made, so leaders may need to be especially vigilant and communicate clear expectations for ethical behavior.

Fortunately, evidence shows that asking people to focus on relationships and the way they spend their time can make them behave more honestly and helpfully. This suggests that a focus on the social consequences of our actions can indeed help to overcome corruption.

Questions

15-10. What are the negative effects of a culture that encourages dishonesty and corruption on an organization's reputation and its employees?

15-11. Why might some organizations push employees to behave in a dishonest or corrupt manner? Are there personal benefits to corruption that organizational culture can counteract?

15-12. What actions can you take as a new employee if you are pressured to violate your own ethical standards at work? How might midlevel employees' responses to this question differ from those of more senior managers?

Sources: Based on F. Gino, "Banking Culture Encourages Dishonesty," *Scientific American*, December 30, 2014, http://www.scientificamerican.com/article/banking-culture-encourages-dishonesty/; A. Cohn, E. Fehr, and M. A. Maréchal, "Business Culture and Dishonesty in the Banking Industry," *Nature*, 2014, doi:10.1038/nature13977; L. Geggel, "FIFA Scandal: The Complicated Science of Corruption," *Scientific American*, May 31, 2015, http://www.scientificamerican.com/article/fifa-scandal-the-complicated-science-of-corruption/; and K. Radnedge, "Culture Change Required if FIFA Is to Eliminate Wrongdoing," *World Soccer*, May 29, 2015, http://www.worldsoccer.com/columnists/keir-radnedge/culture-change-required-if-fifa-is-to-eliminate-wrongdoing-362278.

CASE INCIDENT 1 Culture of Fear

A Sports Direct store is a fixture in nearly every town in the United Kingdom. Founded by Mike Ashley in 1982, the retailing group has grown to become Britain's largest sporting goods retailer, with approximately 465 stores and 29,000 employees. However, a number of reports, most recently by *The Guardian* newspaper in 2015, revealed a number of questionable work practices. It seems that the company's success may have been underpinned by a culture of fear.

Undercover *Guardian* reporters at the company's Derbyshire warehouse found individual employees being told to work faster via a public-address system and security searches at the end of a shift (taking place after employees had clocked out). Most disturbing was the warning system, referred to as the "six strikes." You could receive a "strike" for a number of reasons, including errors in your work, having long toilet breaks, or a period of reported sickness. Receiving six strikes over a six-month period would result in your contract being terminated.

In 2016, a Parliamentary committee was set up to investigate the claims from *The Guardian* and other sources. They concluded that the success of Sports Direct had been achieved through a culture that allowed some employees to be treated without dignity or respect. Although the committee did concede that there were probably other organizations guilty of employee mistreatment, they identified Sports Direct as a particularly bad example of this type of exploitation.

Reviewing evidence regarding the "six strikes" policy, the committee heard from a union representative who described people coming to work ill as they feared that they would receive a strike for calling in sick. This increase in presenteeism—going to work when you are too ill to do so—thus poses health and safety risks. Between January 1, 2013, and April 19, 2016, a total of 110 ambulances or paramedics were dispatched to the warehouse. Of these, 50 cases were classed as life-threatening, including a woman giving birth in the toilet. Although strikes were often given in a very arbitrary manner, the committee concluded that workers were unlikely to argue as they were employed as agency workers and protest could mean that they would probably not be given as many hours work in the future.

The strict control systems in force suggest a strong culture; however, it is difficult to say whether this case highlights a subculture specific to the warehouse or a dominant culture demonstrating core values across the organization. It is clear that there was a negative workplace climate at the warehouse that was affecting the health and wellbeing of the employees. After the committee, Ashley agreed to look into a number of issues, including the "six strikes'" policy and allegations of bullying and physical intimidation. As the founder of the company, a cultural change has to be driven by him.

A year on and some things have clearly changed. The company has a staff wellbeing service and a staff listening group as well as an employee representative who attends board meetings.

Questions

15-13. How would you describe the culture at the Sports Direct warehouse? How might this culture be a liability to the organization?

15-14. What does the case study tell you about the six characteristics of organizational culture at Sports Direct?

15-15. With so many stores and employees, how do you change the organizational culture at Sports Direct? What action do you think should be taken and by whom?

Sources: Simon Goodley and Jonathan Ashby, "Revealed: How Sports Direct Effectively Pays below Minimum Wage," *The Guardian*, December 9, 2015, https://www.theguardian.com/business/2015/dec/09/how-sports-direct-effectively-pays-below-minimum-wage-pay; Jeff Farrell, "Sports Direct 'Identifies Staff by Fingerprint' after Asking Them to Press Happy or Sad Face Emoji," *Independent*, 2 September 2017, http://www.independent.co.uk/news/uk/home-news/sports-direct-sad-happy-face-emoji-unite-steve-turner-nottingham-protest-mike-ashley-work-conditions-a7925401.html; House of Commons, Employment Practices at Sports Direct, Business, Innovation and Skills Committee (July 21 2016), https://publications.parliament.uk/pa/cm201617/cmselect/cmbis/219/21902.htm?utm_source=219&utm_medium=fullbullet&utm_campaign=modulereports7; Sports Direct International plc, Reports and Presentations, http://www.sportsdirectplc.com/investor-relations/reports-and-presentations/rp-2017.aspx.

CASE INCIDENT 2 Active Cultures

Employees at many successful companies start the day by checking the economic forecast. Patagonia's Ventura, California, employees start the day by checking the surf forecast. The outdoor clothing company encourages its workforce to take time from the workday to get outside and get active. For Patagonia, linking employees with the natural environment is a major part of the culture.

New hires are introduced to this mindset very quickly. Soon after starting at Patagonia, marketing executive Joy Howard was immediately encouraged to go fly fishing, surfing, and rock climbing all around the world. She notes that all this vacationing is not just playing around—it's an important part of her job. "I needed to be familiar with the products we market," she said. Other practices support this outdoors-oriented, healthy culture. The company has an on-site organic café featuring locally grown produce. Employees at all levels are encouraged through an employee discount program to try out activewear in the field. And highly flexible hours ensure that employees feel free to take the occasional afternoon off to catch the waves or get out of town for a weekend hiking trip.

Are there bottom-line benefits to this organizational culture? Some corporate leaders think so. As Neil Blumenthal, one of the founders of Warby Parker eyewear, observes, "[T]hey've shown that you can build a profitable business while thinking about the environment and thinking about your team and community." As Patagonia CEO Rose Marcario says, "People recognize Patagonia as a company that's ... looking at business through a more holistic lens other than profit." However, she is quick to add, "Profit is important; if it wasn't you wouldn't be talking to me."

Patagonia's culture obviously makes for an ideal workplace for some people—but not for others who don't share its values. People who are just not outdoor types would likely feel excluded. While the unique mission and values of Patagonia may not be for everyone, for its specific niche in the product and employment market, the culture fits like a glove.

Questions

15-16. What do you think are the key dimensions of culture that make Patagonia successful? How does the organization help to foster this culture?

15-17. Does Patagonia use strategies to build its culture that you think could work for other companies? Is the company a useful model for others that aren't so tied to a lifestyle? Why or why not?

15-18. What are the drawbacks of Patagonia's culture? Might it sometimes be a liability and, if so, in what situations?

Sources: Based on J. Murphy, "At Patagonia, Trying New Outdoor Adventures Is a Job Requirement," *Wall Street Journal*, March 10, 2015, http://www.wsj.com/articles/at-patagonia-trying-new-outdoor-adventures-is-a-job-requirement-1425918931; B. Schulte, "A Company That Profits as It Pampers Workers," *Washington Post*, October 25, 2014, http://www.washingtonpost.com/business/a-company-that-profits-as-it-pampers-workers/2014/10/22/d3321b34-4818-11e4-b72e-d60a9229cc10_story.html; and D. Baer, "Patagonia CEO: 'There's No Way I Should Make One Decision Based on Quarterly Results,'" *Business Insider*, November 19, 2014, http://www.businessinsider.com/patagonia-ceo-interview-2014-11.

ENDNOTES

[1] Rao, M. (2018). 'In a great place to work, the culture becomes the CEO' – 45 quotes from Indian startup journeys. *Yourstory (November 19, 2018)*. Retrieved from https://yourstory.com (Accessed on April 22, 2022)

[2] See, for example, B. Schneider, M. G. Ehrhart, and W. H. Macey, "Organizational Climate and Culture," *Annual Review of Psychology* 64 (2013): 361–88.

[3] J. A. Chatman, D. F. Caldwell, C. A. O'Reilly, and B. Doerr, "Parsing Organizational Culture: How the Norm for Adaptability Influences the Relationship between Culture Consensus and Financial Performance in High Technology Firms," *Journal of Organizational Behavior* 35, no. 6 (2014): 785–808.

[4] C. A. Hartnell, A. Y. Ou, and A. Kinicki, "Organizational Culture and Organizational Effectiveness: A Meta-Analytic Investigation of the Competing Values Framework," *Journal of Applied Psychology* 96 (2011): 677–94; and R. E. Quinn and J. Rohrbaugh, "A Special Model of Effectiveness Criteria: Toward a Competing Values Approach to Organizational Analysis," *Management Science* 29 (1983): 363–77.

[5] Schneider, Ehrhart, and Macey, "Organizational Climate and Culture."

[6] Hartnell et al., "Organizational Culture and Organizational Effectiveness"; C. A. Hartnell, A. Y. Ou, A. J. Kinicki, D. Choi, and E. P. Karam, "A Meta-Analytic Test of Organizational Culture's Association with Elements of an Organization's System and Its Relative Predictive Validity on Organizational Outcomes," *Journal of Applied Psychology* 104, no. 6 (2019): 832–50.

[7] R. A. Cooke and J. C. Lafferty, *Organizational Culture Inventory* (Plymouth, MA: Human Synergistics, 1987); R. A. Cooke and J. L. Szumal, "Measuring Normative Beliefs and Shared Behavioral Expectations in Organizations: The Reliability and Validity of the Organizational Culture Inventory," *Psychology Reports* 72 (1993): 1299–330; R. A. Cooke and J. L. Szumal, "Using the Organizational Culture Inventory to Understand the Operating Cultures of Organizations," in N. M. Ashkanasy, C. P. M. Wilderom, and M. F. Peterson (eds.), *Handbook of Organizational Culture & Climate* (Thousand Oaks, CA: Sage, 2000): 147–62.

[8] N. M. Ashkanasy, L. E. Broadfoot, and S. Falkus, "Questionnaire Measures of Organizational Culture," in N. M. Ashkanasy, C. P. M. Wilderom, and M. F. Peterson (eds.), *Handbook of Organizational Culture & Climate* (Thousand Oaks, CA: Sage, 2000): 131–46; C. A. O'Reilly III, J. A. Chatman, and D. F. Caldwell, "People and Organizational Culture: A Profile Comparison Approach to Assessing Person-Organization Fit," *Academy of Management Journal* 34 (1991): 487–516.

[9] See, for example, C. Ostroff, A. J. Kinicki, and R. S. Muhammad, "Organizational Culture and Climate," in I. B. Weiner (ed.), *Handbook of Psychology*, 2nd ed. (Hoboken, NJ: Wiley, 2012): 643–76.

[10] D. A. Hoffman and L. M. Jones, "Leadership, Collective Personality, and Performance," *Journal of Applied Psychology* 90, no. 3 (2005): 509–22.

[11] J. Martin, *Organizational Culture: Mapping the Terrain* (Thousand Oaks, CA: Sage, 2002).

[12] P. Lok, R. Westwood, and J. Crawford, "Perceptions of Organisational Subculture and Their Significance for Organisational Commitment," *Applied Psychology: An International Review* 54, no. 4 (2005): 490–514; and B. E. Ashforth, K. M. Rogers, and K. G. Corley, "Identity in Organizations: Exploring Cross-Level Dynamics," *Organization Science* 22 (2011): 1144–56.

[13] J. M. Jermier, J. W. Slocum Jr., L. W. Fry, and J. Gaines, "Organizational Subcultures in a Soft Bureaucracy: Resistance behind the Myth and Façade of an Official Culture," *Organization Science* 2, no. 2 (1991): 170–94.

[14] T. Hsieh, "Zappos's CEO on Going to Extremes for Customers," *Harvard Business Review* (July/August 2010): 41–45.

[15] For discussions of how culture can be evaluated as a shared perception, see D. Chan, "Multilevel and Aggregation Issues in Climate and Culture Research," in B. Schneider and K. M. Barbera (eds.), *The Oxford Handbook of Organizational Climate and Culture* (New York: Oxford University Press, 2014): 484–95; and J. B. Sorensen, "The Strength of Corporate Culture and the Reliability of Firm Performance," *Administrative Science Quarterly* (March 2002): 70–91.

[16] B. Schneider, A. N. Salvaggio, and M. Subirats, "Climate Strength: A New Direction for Climate Research," *Journal of Applied Psychology* 87 (2002): 220–29; L. M. Kotrba, M. A. Gillespie, A. M. Schmidt, R. E. Smerek, S. A. Ritchie, and D. R. Denison, "Do Consistent Corporate Cultures Have Better Business Performance: Exploring the Interaction Effects," *Human Relations* 65 (2012): 241–62; and M. W. Dickson, C. J. Resick, and P. J. Hanges, "When Organizational Climate Is Unambiguous, It Is Also Strong," *Journal of Applied Psychology* 91 (2006): 351–64.

[17] Chatman, Caldwell, O'Reilly, and Doerr, "Parsing Organizational Culture."

[18] L. M. Kotrba, M. A. Gillespie, A. M. Schmidt, R. E. Smerek, S. A. Ritchie, and D. R. Denison, "Do Consistent Corporate Cultures Have Better Business Performance? Exploring the Interaction Effects," *Human Relations* 65, no. 2 (2012): 241–62.

[19] E. Ransdell, "The Nike Story? Just Tell It!," *Fast Company* (January–February 2000): 44–46; and A. Muccino, "Exclusive Interview with Chuck Eichten," *Liquid Brand Summit Blog*, February 4, 2011, http://blog.liquidbrandsummit.com/.

[20] R. Garud, H. A. Schildt, and T. K. Lant, "Entrepreneurial Storytelling, Future Expectations, and the Paradox of Legitimacy," *Organization Science* 25, no. 5 (2014): 1479–92; and G. A. Rosile, D. M. Carlon, S. Downs, and R. Saylors, "Storytelling Diamond: An Antenarrative Integration of the Six Facets of Storytelling in Organization Research Design," *Organizational Research Methods* 16, no. 4 (2013): 557–80.

[21] S. L. Dailey and L. Browning, "Retelling Stories in Organizations: Understanding the Functions of Narrative Repetition," *Academy of Management Review* 39 (2014): 22–43.

[22] A. J. Shipp and K. J. Jansen, "Reinterpreting Time in Fit Theory: Crafting and Recrafting Narratives of Fit in Medias Res," *Academy of Management Review* 36, no. 1 (2011): 76–101.

[23] See G. Islam and M. J. Zyphur, "Rituals in Organizations: A Review and Expansion of Current Theory," *Group and Organization Management* 34, no. 1 (2009): 114–39; and M. J. Rossano, "The Essential Role of Ritual in the Transmission and Reinforcement of Social Norms," *Psychological Bulletin* 138, no. 3 (2012): 529–49.

[24] Great Place to Work, "Kimpton Hotels & Restaurants," http://reviews.greatplacetowork.com/kimpton-hotels-restaurants, accessed April 18, 2017; and S. Halzack, "At Kimpton Hotels, Employees Bond through Housekeeping Olympics," *The Washington Post*, January 6, 2013, https://www.washingtonpost.com/business/capitalbusiness/at-kimpton-hotels-employees-bond-through-housekeeping-olympics/2013/01/04/3a212b2c-535c-11e2-bf3e-76c0a789346f_story.html?utm_term=.c3e004bef157.

[25] A. Bryant, "Take the Bus, and Watch the Ideas Flow," *The New York Times*, September 16, 2012, 2.

[26] C. Jones, *How Matter Matters: Objects, Artifacts, and Materiality in Organization Studies* (Oxford, UK: Oxford University Press, 2013); and E. H. Schein, *Organizational Culture and Leadership*, 4th ed. (San Francisco, CA: Jossey-Bass, 2010).

[27] M. G. Pratt and A. Rafaeli "Artifacts and Organizations: Understanding Our Objective Reality," in A. Rafaeli and M. G. Pratt (eds.), *Artifacts and Organizations: Beyond Mere Symbolism* (Mahwah, NJ: Lawrence Erlbaum, 2006): 279–88.

[28] A. Rafaeli and I. Vilnai-Yavetz, "Emotion as a Connection of Physical Artifacts and Organizations," *Organization Science* 15, no. 6 (2004): 671–86.

[29] B. Gruley, "Relaxed Fit," *Bloomberg Businessweek*, September 17–23, 2012, 98–99.

[30] Great Place to Work, "Genentech," http://reviews.greatplacetowork.com/genentech, accessed April 18, 2017.

[31] Z. Kalou and E. Sadler-Smith, "Using Ethnography of Communication in Organizational Research," *Organizational Research Methods* 18, no. 4 (2015): 629–55; and H. M. Trice and J. M. Beyer, *The Cultures of Work Organizations* (Englewood Cliffs, NJ: Prentice Hall, 1993).

[32] E. A. Canning, M. C. Murphy, K. T. U. Emerson, J. A. Chatman, C. S. Dweck, and L. J. Kray, "Cultures of Genius at Work: Organizational Mindsets Predict Cultural Norms, Trust, and Commitment," *Personality and Social Psychology Bulletin* 46, no. 4 (2020): 626–42.

[33] For a review, see Schneider, Ehrhart, & Macey, "Organizational Climate and Culture."

[34] E. H. Schein, *Organizational Culture and Leadership*, Vol. 2 (New York: John Wiley & Sons, 2010).

[35] R. M. Steers, *Made in Korea: Chung Ju Yung and the Rise of Hyundai* (New York, NY: Routledge, 1999).

[36] J. Basque and A. Langley, "Invoking Alphonse: The Founder Figure as a Historical Resource for Organizational Identity Work," *Organizational Studies* 39, no. 12

(2018): 1685–708; S. Oreg and Y. Berson, "The Impact of Top Leaders' Personalities: The Process through Which Organizations Become Reflections of Their Leaders," *Current Directions in Psychological Science* 27, no. 4 (2018): 241–48; Ostroff et al., "Organizational Culture and Climate"; D. Katz and R. L. Kahn, *The Social Psychology of Organizations*, 2nd ed. (New York, NY: Wiley, 1978); Hartnell et al., "A Meta-Analytic Test of Organizational Culture's Association with Elements of an Organization's System and Its Relative Predictive Validity on Organizational Outcomes."

[37] See, for example, D. E. Bowen and C. Ostroff, "The 'Strength' of the HRM System, Organizational Climate Formation, and Firm Performance," *Academy of Management Review* 29 (2004): 203–21.

[38] D. D. Warrick, J. F. Milliman, and J. M. Ferguson, "Building High Performance Cultures," *Organizational Dynamics* 45 (2016): 64–70.

[39] W. Arthur Jr., S. T. Bell, A. J. Villado, and D. Doverspike, "The Use of Person-Organization Fit in Employment Decision Making: An Assessment of Its Criterion-Related Validity," *Journal of Applied Psychology* 91, no. 4 (2006): 786–801; W. Li, Y. Wang, P. Taylor, K. Shi, and D. He, "The Influence of Organizational Culture on Work-Related Personality Requirement Ratings: A Multilevel Analysis," *International Journal of Selection and Assessment* 16, no. 4 (2008): 366–84; and A. M. Saks and B. E. Ashforth, "Is Job Search Related to Employment Quality? It All Depends on the Fit," *Journal of Applied Psychology* 87, no. 4 (2002): 646–54.

[40] See, for instance, B. R. Dineen, S. R. Ash, and R. A. Noe, "A Web of Applicant Attraction: Person-Organization Fit in the Context of Web-Based Recruitment," *Journal of Applied Psychology* 87, no. 4 (2002): 723–34.

[41] @workplace. "Best practice retail connection and collaboration: Decathlon". *From Meta.* Retrieved from https://www.workplace.com (Accessed on April; 21, 2022)

[42] Referring to the reply of Krishna Jha, Sales Manager at Decathlon Sports India, at Quora.com (March 4, 2019) for the query "What is the hiring process in Decathlon? Which types of jobs are there?" Retrieved from https://www.quora.com (Accessed on April 29, 2022)

[43] D. C. Hambrick, "Upper Echelons Theory: An Update," *Academy of Management Review* 32 (2007): 334–43; M. A. Carpenter, M. A. Geletkanycz, and W. G. Sanders, "Upper Echelons Research Revisited: Antecedents, Elements, and Consequences of Top Management Team Composition," *Journal of Management* 30, no. 6 (2004): 749–78; and H. Wang, A. S. Tsui, and K. R. Xin, "CEO Leadership Behaviors, Organizational Performance, and Employees' Attitudes," *The Leadership Quarterly* 22, no. 1 (2011): 92–105.

[44] Meghani, V. (2017). "How Kalyan Jewellers rose to international prominence". *Forbes India (March 28, 2017).* Retrieved from https://www.forbesindia.com (Accessed on April 23, 2022)

[45] Business Line (2020). "Kalyan Jewellers to support daily-wage workers". *The Hindu Business Line (Apr 09, 2020).* Retrieved from https://www.thehindubusinessline.com (Accessed on April 23, 2022)

[46] Moneycontrol News (2020). "Coronavirus pandemic | No salary cuts at non-operational showrooms, Kalyan Jewellers assures employees". *Money Control (March 26, 2020).* Retrieved from https://www.moneycontrol.com (Accessed on April 23, 2022)

[47] T. D. Allen, L. T. Eby, G. T. Chao, and T. N. Bauer, "Taking Stock of Two Relational Aspects of Organizational Life: Tracing the History and Shaping the Future of Socialization and Mentoring Research," *Journal of Applied Psychology* 102, no. 3 (2017): 324–37; and T. N. Bauer, T. Bodner, B. Erdogan, D. M. Truxillo, and J. S. Tucker, "Newcomer Adjustment during Organizational Socialization: A Meta-Analytic Review of Antecedents, Outcomes, and Methods," *Journal of Applied Psychology* 92, no. 3 (2007): 707–21.

[48] G. Kranz, "Training That Starts before the Job Begins," *Workforce Management*, July 2009, www.workforce.com.

[49] R. E. Silverman, "Companies Try to Make the First Day for New Hires More Fun," *The Wall Street Journal*, May 28, 2013, http://online.wsj.com/article/SB1000142412788732333610457850163147593 4850.html.

[50] D. M. Cable, F. Gino, and B. R. Staats, "Breaking Them in or Eliciting Their Best? Reframing Socialization around Newcomers' Authentic Self-Expression," *Administrative Science Quarterly* 58 (2013): 1–36; and M. Tuttle, "A Review and Critique of Van Maanen and Schein's 'Toward a Theory of Organizational Socialization' and Implications for Human Resource Development," *Human Resource Development Review* 1 (2002): 66–90.

[51] C. J. Collins, "The Interactive Effects of Recruitment Practices and Product Awareness on Job Seekers' Employer Knowledge and Application Behaviors," *Journal of Applied Psychology* 92, no. 1 (2007): 180–90.

[52] N. Delobbe, H. D. Cooper-Thomas, and R. De Hoe, "A New Look at the Psychological Contract during Organizational Socialization: The Role of Newcomers' Obligations at Entry," *Journal of Organizational Behavior* 37, no. 6 (2016): 845–67; J. D. Kammeyer-Mueller and C. R. Wanberg, "Unwrapping the Organizational Entry Process: Disentangling Multiple Antecedents and Their Pathways to Adjustment," *Journal of Applied Psychology* 88 (2003): 779–94; E. W. Morrison, "Longitudinal Study of the Effects of Information Seeking on Newcomer Socialization," *Journal of Applied Psychology* 78 (2003): 173–83; and M. Wang, Y. Zhan, E. McCune, and D. Truxillo, "Understanding Newcomers' Adaptability and Work-Related Outcomes: Testing the Mediating Roles of Perceived P-E Fit Variables," *Personnel Psychology* 64, no. 1 (2011): 163–89.

[53] See, for instance, C. Woodrow and D. E. Guest, "Pathways through Organizational Socialization: A Longitudinal Qualitative Study Based on the Psychological Contract," *Journal of Occupational and Organizational Psychology* 93 (2020): 110–33.

[54] Bauer, Bodner, Erdogan, Truxillo, and Tucker, "Newcomer Adjustment during Organizational Socialization"; E. W. Morrison, "Newcomers' Relationships: The Role of Social Network Ties during Socialization," *Academy of Management Journal* 45 (2002): 1149–60; and A. M. Saks, K. L. Uggerslev, and N. E. Fassina, "Socialization Tactics and Newcomer Adjustment: A Meta-Analytic Review and Test of a Model," *Journal of Vocational Behavior* 70 (2007): 413–46.

[55] B. Schneider, H. W. Goldstein, and D. B. Smith, "The ASA Framework: An Update," *Personnel Psychology* 48 (1995): 747–73.

[56] Saks, Uggerslev, and Fassina, "Socialization Tactics and Newcomer Adjustment"; and J. Van Maanen and E. Schein, "Toward a Theory of Organizational Socialization," in B. M. Staw (ed.), *Research in Organizational Behavior*, Vol. 1 (Greenwich, CT: JAI, 1979).

[57] O. C. Richard, D. R. Avery, A. Luksyte, O. Dorian Boncoeur, and C. Spitzmueller, "Improving Organizational Newcomers' Creative Job Performance through Creative Process Engagement: The Moderating Role of a Synergy Diversity Climate," *Personnel Psychology* 72 (2019): 421–44.

[58] Bauer, Bodner, Erdogan, Truxillo, and Tucker, "Newcomer Adjustment during Organizational Socialization"; J. X. Y. Chong, G. Beenen, M. Gagné, and P. D. Dunlop, "Satisfying Newcomers' Needs: The Role of Socialization Tactics and Supervisor Autonomy Support," *Journal of Business and Psychology* (in press); M. Ikram Nasr, A. El Akremi, and J. A.-M. Coyle-Shapiro, "Synergy or Substitution? The Interactive Effects of Insiders' Fairness and Support and Organizational Socialization Tactics on Newcomer Role Clarity and Social Integration," *Journal of Organizational Behavior* 40 (2019):

758–78; and Saks, Uggerslev, and Fassina, "Socialization Tactics and Newcomer Adjustment."

[59] W. R. Boswell, A. J. Shipp, S. C., Payne, and S. S. Culbertson, "Changes in Newcomer Job Satisfaction over Time: Examining the Pattern of Honeymoons and Hangovers," *Journal of Applied Psychology* 94, no. 4 (2009): 844–58; W. R. Boswell, J. W. Boudreau, and J. Tichy, "The Relationship between Employee Job Change and Job Satisfaction: The Honeymoon-Hangover Effect," *Journal of Applied Psychology* 90 (2005): 882–92; and Y. Zhou, M. Zou, M. Williams, and V. Tabvuma, "Is the Grass Greener on the Other Side? A Longitudinal Study of the Impact of Employer Change and Occupational Change on Job Satisfaction," *Journal of Vocational Behavior* 99 (2017): 66–78.

[60] J. D. Kammeyer-Mueller, C. R. Wanberg, A. L. Rubenstein, and Z. Song, "Support, Undermining, and Newcomer Socialization: Fitting in during the First 90 Days," *Academy of Management Journal* 56 (2013): 1104–24; and M. Jokisaari and J. Nurmi, "Change in Newcomers' Supervisor Support and Socialization Outcomes after Organizational Entry," *Academy of Management Journal* 52 (2009): 527–44.

[61] C. Vandenberghe, A. Panaccio, K. Bentein, K. Mignonac, and P. Roussel, "Assessing Longitudinal Change of and Dynamic Relationships among Role Stressors, Job Attitudes, Turnover Intention, and Well-Being in Neophyte Newcomers," *Journal of Organizational Behavior* 32, no. 4 (2011): 652–71.

[62] See S. Maitlis and M. Christianson, "Sensemaking in Organizations: Taking Stock and Moving Forward," *The Academy of Management Annals* 8 (2014): 57–125; and K. Weber and M. T. Dacin, "The Cultural Construction of Organizational Life," *Organization Science* 22 (2011): 287–98.

[63] C. A. Hartnell, A. J. Kinicki, L. S. Lambert, M. Fugate, and P. D. Corner, "Do Similarities or Differences between CEO Leadership and Organizational Culture Have a More Positive Effect on Firm Performance? A Test of Competing Predictions," *Journal of Applied Psychology* 101, no. 6 (2016): 846–61.

[64] A. L. Kristof-Brown, R. D. Zimmerman, and E. C. Johnson, "Consequences of Individuals' Fit at Work: A Meta-Analysis of Person-Job, Person-Organization, Person-Group, and Person-Supervisor Fit," *Personnel Psychology* 58 (2005): 281–342.

[65] Schneider, Ehrhart, and Macey, "Organizational Climate and Culture."

[66] E. H. Schein, "Sense and Nonsense about Culture and Climate," in N. M. Ashkanasy, C. P. M. Wilderom, and M. F. Peterson (eds.), *Handbook of Organizational Culture & Climate* (Thousand Oaks, CA: Sage, 2000): xxxiii–xxx; Schneider et al., "Organizational Climate and Culture."

[67] J. Z. Carr, A. M. Schmidt, J. K. Ford, and R. P. DeShon, "Climate Perceptions Matter: A Meta-Analytic Path Analysis Relating Molar Climate, Cognitive and Affective States, and Individual Level Work Outcomes," *Journal of Applied Psychology* 88, no. 4 (2003): 605–19.

[68] M. Schulte, C. Ostroff, S. Shmulyian, and A. Kinicki, "Organizational Climate Configurations: Relationships to Collective Attitudes, Customer Satisfaction, and Financial Performance," *Journal of Applied Psychology* 94, no. 3 (2009): 618–34.

[69] D. Zohar and D. A. Hofmann, "Organizational Culture and Climate," in S. W. J. Kozlowski (ed.), *The Oxford Handbook of Organizational Psychology*, Vol. 1 (Oxford, UK: Oxford University Press, 2012): 317–34.

[70] Ostroff et al., "Organizational Culture and Climate"; Schneider, Ehrhart, and Macey, "Organizational Climate and Culture"; D. Zohar and D. A. Hofmann, "Organizational Culture and Climate," in S. W. J. Kozlowski (ed.), *The Oxford Handbook of Organizational Psychology*, Vol. 1 (Oxford, UK: Oxford University Press, 2012): 1–41.

[71] A. Howell, A. Kirk-Brown, and B. K. Cooper, "Does Congruence between Espoused and Enacted Organizational Values Predict Affective Commitment in Australian Organizations?," *The International Journal of Human Resource Management* 23, no. 4 (2012): 731–47.

[72] See, for instance, K. Fitzgerald, "Safety Culture, Climate and Performance Improvement," *HazardEx*, October 22, 2018, http://www.hazardexonthenet.net/article/162743/Safety-Culture–Climate-and-Performance-Improvement.aspx#; Maritime Knowledge, "Safety Management: Safety Culture vs Safety Climate—What's the Difference?", *Safety4SEA*, blogpost, March 1, 2019, https://safety4sea.com/cm-safety-management-safety-culture-vs-safety-climate-whats-the-difference/.

[73] M. Kuenzi and M. Schminke, "Assembling Fragments into a Lens: A Review, Critique, and Proposed Research Agenda for the Organizational Work Climate Literature," *Journal of Management* 35, no. 3 (2009): 634–717; and Schneider, Ehrhart, and Macey, "Organizational Climate and Culture."

[74] S. Clarke, "The Relationship between Safety Climate and Safety Performance: A Meta-Analytic Review," *Journal of Occupational Health Psychology* 11, no. 4 (2006): 315–27; and S. Clarke, "An Integrative Model of Safety Climate: Linking Psychological Climate and Work Attitudes to Individual Safety Outcomes Using Meta-Analysis," *Journal of Occupational and Organizational Psychology* 83 (2010): 553–78.

[75] J. M. Beus, S. C. Payne, M. E. Bergman, and W. Arthur, "Safety Climate and Injuries: An Examination of Theoretical and Empirical Relationships," *Journal of Applied Psychology* 95, no. 4 (2010): 713–27.

[76] J. C. Wallace, P. D. Johnson, K. Mathe, and J. Paul, "Structural and Psychological Empowerment Climates, Performance, and the Moderating Role of Shared Felt Accountability: A Managerial Perspective," *Journal of Applied Psychology* 96, no. 3 (2011): 840–50.

[77] M. Kaptein, "Developing and Testing a Measure for the Ethical Culture of Organizations: The Corporate Ethical Virtues Model," *Journal of Business Ethics* 29 (2008): 923–47; and L. K. Trevino and G. R. Weaver, *Managing Ethics in Business Organizations: Social Scientific Perspectives* (Stanford, CA: Stanford University Press, 2003).

[78] Kaptein, "Developing and Testing a Measure for the Ethical Culture of Organizations."

[79] A. Arnaud and M. Schminke, "The Ethical Climate and Context of Organizations," *Organization Science* 23, no. 6 (2012): 1767–80; A. Simha and J. B. Cullen, "Ethical Climates and Their Effects on Organizational Outcomes: Implications from the Past and Prophecies for the Future," *Academy of Management Perspectives* 26, no. 4 (2012): 20–34; and B. Victor and J. B. Cullen, "The Organizational Bases of Ethical Work Climates," *Administrative Science Quarterly* 33, no. 1 (1988): 101–25.

[80] M. Kuenzi, D. M. Mayer, and R. L. Greenbaum, "Creating an Ethical Organizational Environment: The Relationship between Ethical Leadership, Ethical Organizational Climate, and Unethical Behavior," *Personnel Psychology* 73 (2020): 43–71.

[81] Kuenzi et al., "Creating an ethical organizational environment"; Simha and Cullen, "Ethical Climates and Their Effects on Organizational Outcomes."

[82] Kuenzi et al., "Creating an Ethical Organizational Environment."

[83] A. T. Myer, C. N. Thoroughgood, and S. Mohammed, "Complementary or Competing Climates? Examining the Interactive Effect of Service and Ethical Climates on Company-Level Financial Performance," *Journal of Applied Psychology* 101, no. 8 (2016): 1178–90.

[84] Simha and Cullen, "Ethical Climates and Their Effects on Organizational Outcomes."

[85] A. Arnaud, "Conceptualizing and Measuring Ethical Work Climate Development and Validation of the Ethical Climate Index," *Business & Society*, June 2010, 345–458.
[86] Arnaud and Schminke, "The Ethical Climate and Context of Organizations."
[87] J. Howard-Greenville, S. Bertels, and B. Lahneman, "Sustainability: How It Shapes Organizational Culture and Climate," in B. Schneider and K. M. Barbera (eds.), *The Oxford Handbook of Organizational Climate and Culture* (New York: Oxford University Press, 2014): 257–75.
[88] P. Lacy, T. Cooper, R. Hayward, and L. Neuberger, "A New Era of Sustainability: UN Global Compact–Accenture CEO Study 2010," June 2010, www.uncsd2012.org/content/documents/Accenture_A_New_Era_of_Sustainability_CEO_study.pdf.
[89] B. Fitzgerald, "Sustainable Farming Will Be Next 'Revolution in Agriculture,'" *Australian Broadcasting Company*, May 29, 2015, http://www.abc.net.au/news/2015-05-29/state-of-tomorrow-sustainable-farming/6504842.
[90] A. A. Marcus and A. R. Fremeth, "Green Management Matters Regardless," *Academy of Management Perspectives* 23 (2009): 17–26.
[91] H. R. Dixon-Fowler, D. J. Slater, J. L. Johnson, A. E. Ellstrand, and A. M. Romi, "Beyond 'Does It Pay to Be Green?' A Meta-Analysis of Moderators of the CEP-CFP Relationship," *Journal of Business Ethics* 112 (2013): 353–66.
[92] P. Bansal, "From Issues to Actions: The Importance of Individual Concerns and Organizational Values in Responding to Natural Environmental Issues," *Organization Science 14* (2003): 510–27; P. Bansal, "Evolving Sustainably: A Longitudinal Study of Corporate Sustainable Development," *Strategic Management Journal* 26 (2005): 197–218; and J. Howard-Grenville and A. J. Hoffman, "The Importance of Cultural Framing to the Success of Social Initiatives in Business," *Academy of Management Executive* 17 (2003): 70–84.
[93] A. R. Carrico and M. Riemer, "Motivating Energy Conservation in the Workplace: An Evaluation of the Use of Group-Level Feedback and Peer Education," *Journal of Environmental Psychology* 31 (2011): 1–13.
[94] J. P. Kotter, "Change Management: Accelerate!" *Harvard Business Review* (November 2012): 44–58.
[95] R. Walker, "Behind the Music," *Fortune*, October 29, 2012, 57–58.
[96] J. P. Titlow, "How Spotify's Music-Obsessed Culture Keeps Employees Hooked," *Fast Company*, August 20, 2014, http://www.fastcompany.com/3034617/how-spotifys-music-obsessed-culture-makes-the-company-rock.
[97] A. Newman, H. Round, S. Wang, and M. Mount, "Innovation Climate: A Systematic Review of the Literature and Agenda for Future Research," *Journal of Occupational and Organizational Psychology* 93 (2020): 73–109.
[98] E. Ries, *The Lean Startup* (New York: Crown Business, 2011).
[99] M. Herper, "Niche Pharma," *Forbes*, September 24, 2012, 80–89.
[100] Y. Berson, S. Oreg, and T. Dvir, "CEO Values, Organizational Culture and Firm Outcomes," *Journal of Organizational Behavior* 29 (2008): 615–33; and J. Zhou, X. M. Wang, L. J. Song, and J. Wu, "Is It New? Personal and Contextual Influences on Perceptions of Novelty and Creativity," *Journal of Applied Psychology* 102, no. 2 (2017): 180–202.
[101] Gangal, N. (2021). "Wagh Bakri: The good blend". Forbes India (February 16, 2021). Retrieved from https://www.forbesindia.com (Accessed on April 21, 2022)
[102] Dhuri, Maithili. (2018). Turnaround Strategies of Indian Companies-Case study of a Chennai Meenakshi Multispecialty Hospital Ltd. Review of literature on Turnaround strategy. Available at https://www.researchgate.net (Accessed on April 21, 2022)
[103] Bhatia, C. (2018). "The Tihar transformer: Kiran Bedi". DNA India (March 22, 2022). Retrieved from https://www.dnaindia.com (Accessed on April 21, 2022)
[104] J. Bandler and D. Burke, "How HP Lost Its Way," *Fortune*, May 21, 2012, 147–64.
[105] G. F. Lanzara and G. Patriotta, "The Institutionalization of Knowledge in an Automotive Factory: Templates, Inscriptions, and the Problems of Durability," *Organization Studies* 28, no. 5 (2007): 635–60; and J. W. Meyer and B. Rowan, "Institutionalized Organizations: Formal Structure as Myth and Ceremony," *American Journal of Sociology* 83, no. 2 (1977): 340–63.
[106] See, for instance, P. Bate, R. Khan, and A. Pye, "Towards a Culturally Sensitive Approach to Organizational Structuring: Where Organizational Design Meets Organizational Development," *Organization Science* 11, no. 2 (2000): 197–211; and G. F. Latta, "Modeling the Cultural Dynamics of Resistance and Facilitation: Interaction Effects in the OC3 Model of Organizational Change," *Journal of Organizational Change Management* 28, no. 6 (2015): 1013–37.
[107] See D. L. Stone, E. F. Stone-Romero, and K. M. Lukaszewski, "The Impact of Cultural Values on the Acceptance and Effectiveness of Human Resource Management Policies and Practices," *Human Resource Management Review* 17, no. 2 (2007): 152–65; D. R. Avery, "Support for Diversity in Organizations: A Theoretical Exploration of Its Origins and Offshoots," *Organizational Psychology Review* 1 (2011): 239–56; and A. Groggins and A. M. Ryan, "Embracing Uniqueness: The Underpinnings of a Positive Climate for Diversity," *Journal of Occupational and Organizational Psychology* 86 (2013): 264–82.
[108] J. A. Chatman, J. T. Polzer, S. G. Barsade, and M. A. Neale, "Being Different yet Feeling Similar: The Influence of Demographic Composition and Organizational Culture on Work Processes and Outcomes," *Administrative Science Quarterly* 43 (1998): 749–80.
[109] S. D. Pugh, J. Dietz, A. P. Brief, and J. W. Wiley, "Looking Inside and Out: The Impact of Employee and Community Demographic Composition on Organizational Diversity Climate," *Journal of Applied Psychology* 93, no. 6 (2008): 1422–28.
[110] Y. Li, S. Perera, C. T. Kulik, and I. Metz, "Inclusion Climate: A Multilevel Investigation of Its Antecedents and Consequences," *Human Resource Management* 58 (2019): 353–69.
[111] M. Reinwald, H. Huettermann, and H. Bruch, "Beyond the Mean: Understanding Firm-Level Consequences of Variability in Diversity Climate Perceptions," *Journal of Organizational Behavior* 40 (2019): 472–91.
[112] M. J. Gelfand, L. M. Leslie, K. Keller, and C. de Dreu, "Conflict Cultures in Organizations: How Leaders Shape Conflict Cultures and Their Organizational-Level Consequences," *Journal of Applied Psychology* 97, no. 6 (2012): 1131–47.
[113] See, for instance, F. Bauer and K. Matzler, "Antecedents of M&A Success: The Role of Strategic Complementarity, Cultural Fit, and Degree and Speed of Integration," *Strategic Management Journal* 35 (2014): 269–91; I. H. Gleibs, A. Mummendey, and P. Noack, "Predictors of Change in Postmerger Identification during a Merger Process: A Longitudinal Study," *Journal of Personality and Social Psychology* 95, no. 5 (2008): 1095–112; C. Pike, *Mergers and Acquisitions: Managing Culture and Human Resources* (Stanford, CA: Stanford University Press, 2005); and R. A. Weber and C. F. Camerer, "Cultural Conflict and Merger Failure: An Experimental Approach," *Management Science* (April 2003): 400–12.
[114] K. Voigt, "Mergers Fail More Often Than Marriages," *CNN*, May 22, 2009, http://edition.cnn.com/2009/BUSINESS/05/21/merger.marriage/.
[115] Y. Chen, "Will It Blend? Oath Will Combine Disparate AOL-Yahoo Ad Tech Assets," *Digiday*, April 13, 2017, https://digiday.com/media/will-blend-oath-will-

combine-disparate-aol-yahoo-ad-tech-assets/; R. G. McGrath, "15 Years Later, Lessons from the Failed AOL–Time Warner Merger," *Fortune*, January 10, 2015, http://fortune.com/2015/01/10/15-years-later-lessons-from-the-failed-aol-time-warner-merger/.

[116] L.-H. Lin, "Organizational Structure and Acculturation in Acquisitions: Perspectives of Congruence Theory and Task Interdependence," *Journal of Management* 40, no. 7 (2014): 1831–56.

[117] A. Ardichvilli, J. A. Mitchell, and D. Jondle, "Characteristics of Ethical Business Cultures," *Journal of Business Ethics* 85, no. 4 (2009): 445–51; D. M. Mayer, "A Review of the Literature on Ethical Climate and Culture," in B. Schneider and K. M. Barbera (eds.), *The Oxford Handbook of Organizational Climate and Culture* (New York: Oxford University Press, 2014): 415–40.

[118] J. P. Mulki, J. F. Jaramillo, and W. B. Locander, "Critical Role of Leadership on Ethical Climate and Salesperson Behaviors," *Journal of Business Ethics* 86, no. 2 (2009): 125–41; M. Schminke, M. L. Ambrose, and D. O. Neubaum, "The Effect of Leader Moral Development on Ethical Climate and Employee Attitudes," *Organizational Behavior and Human Decision Processes* 97, no. 2 (2005): 135–51; and M. E. Brown, L. K. Treviño, and D. A. Harrison, "Ethical Leadership: A Social Learning Perspective for Construct Development and Testing," *Organizational Behavior and Human Decision Processes* 97, no. 2 (2005): 117–34.

[119] D. M. Mayer, M. Kuenzi, R. L. Greenbaum, M. Bardes, and S. Salvador, "How Low Does Ethical Leadership Flow? Test of a Trickle-Down Model," *Organizational Behavior and Human Decision Processes* 108, no. 1 (2009): 1–13; L. J. Christensen, A. Mackey, and D. Whetten, "Taking Responsibility for Corporate Social Responsibility: The Role of Leaders in Creating, Implementing, Sustaining, or Avoiding Socially Responsible Firm Behaviors," *Academy of Management Perspectives* 28 (2014): 164–78; and J. M. Schaubroeck, S. T. Hannah, B. J. Avolio, S. W. J. Kozlowski, R. G. Lord, L. K. Treviño, ... and A. C. Peng, "Embedding Ethical Leadership within and across Organization Levels," *Academy of Management Journal* 55, no. 5 (2012): 1053–78.

[120] B. Sweeney, D. Arnold, and B. Pierce, "The Impact of Perceived Ethical Culture of the Firm and Demographic Variables on Auditors' Ethical Evaluation and Intention to Act Decisions," *Journal of Business Ethics* 93, no. 4 (2010): 531–51.

[121] L. Huang and T. A. Paterson, "Group Ethical Voice: Influence of Ethical Leadership and Impact on Ethical Performance," *Journal of Management* 43, no. 4 (2017): 1157–84.

[122] M. L. Gruys, S. M. Stewart, J. Goodstein, M. N. Bing, and A. C. Wicks, "Values Enactment in Organizations: A Multi-Level Examination," *Journal of Management* 34, no. 4 (2008): 806–43.

[123] Dasra (2019). "People First: Scaling Impact through Talent Management". Pp.10. Dasra: Mumbai. Available at https://www.dasra.org (Accessed on April 12, 2022)

[124] D. L. Nelson and C. L. Cooper (eds.), *Positive Organizational Behavior* (London: Sage, 2007); K. S. Cameron, J. E. Dutton, and R. E. Quinn (eds.), *Positive Organizational Scholarship: Foundations of a New Discipline* (San Francisco: Berrett-Koehler, 2003); and F. Luthans and C. M. Youssef, "Emerging Positive Organizational Behavior," *Journal of Management* 33, no. 3 (2007): 321–49.

[125] M. Buckingham and D. O. Clifton, *Now, Discover Your Strengths* (Washington, D. C.: Gallup, 2001).

[126] Personal communication

[127] Binita Tiwari, Usha Lenka, Employee engagement: A study of survivors in Indian IT/ITES sector, IIMB Management Review, Volume 32, Issue 3, 2020, Pages 249-266, ISSN 0970-3896, https://doi.org/10.1016/j.iimb.2019.10.003. Available at https://www.sciencedirect.com (Accessed on April 12, 2022)

[128] Startup Talky (December 29, 2021). "Top 6 Best Work Culture Companies In India Offering Better Work-Life Balance". Retrieved from https://startuptalky.com (Accessed on March 12, 2022)

[129] Radix."Leadership". Retrieved from https://radixweb.com (Accessed on March 12, 2022)

[130] R. Wagner and J. K. Harter, "Performance Reviews without the Anxiety," *Gallup Leadership Journal*, July 12, 2007, 1–4; and Wagner and Harter, *12: The Elements of Great Managing.*

[131] S. Fineman, "On Being Positive: Concerns and Counterpoints," *Academy of Management Review* 31, no. 2 (2006): 270–91.

[132] E. Poole, "Organisational Spirituality: A Literature Review," *Journal of Business Ethics* 84, no. 4 (2009): 577–88.

[133] L. W. Fry and J. W. Slocum, "Managing the Triple Bottom Line through Spiritual Leadership," *Organizational Dynamics* 37, no. 1 (2008): 86–96.

[134] See, for example, C. L. Jurkiewicz and R. A. Giacalone, "A Values Framework for Measuring the Impact of Workplace Spirituality on Organizational Performance," *Journal of Business Ethics* 49, no. 2 (2004): 129–42.

[135] See, for example, B. S. Pawar, "Workplace Spirituality Facilitation: A Comprehensive Model," *Journal of Business Ethics* 90, no. 3 (2009): 375–86; and L. Lambert, *Spirituality Inc.: Religion in the American Workplace* (New York: New York University Press, 2009).

[136] See, for instance, S. Chan-Serafin, A. P. Brief, and J. M. George, "How Does Religion Matter and Why? Religion and the Organizational Sciences," *Organization Science* 24, no. 5 (2013): 1585–600.

[137] M. Lips-Miersma, K. L. Dean, and C. J. Fornaciari, "Theorizing the Dark Side of the Workplace Spirituality Movement," *Journal of Management Inquiry* 18, no. 4 (2009): 288–300.

[138] J.-C. Garcia-Zamor, "Workplace Spirituality and Organizational Performance," *Public Administration Review* 63, no. 3 (2003): 355–63; and L. W. Fry, S. T. Hannah, M. Noel, and F. O. Walumbwa, "Impact of Spiritual Leadership on Unit Performance," *Leadership Quarterly* 22, no. 2 (2011): 259–70.

[139] A. Rego and M. Pina e Cunha, "Workplace Spirituality and Organizational Commitment: An Empirical Study," *Journal of Organizational Change Management* 21, no. 1 (2008): 53–75; R. W. Kolodinsky, R. A. Giacalone, and C. L. Jurkiewicz, "Workplace Values and Outcomes: Exploring Personal, Organizational, and Interactive Workplace Spirituality," *Journal of Business Ethics* 81, no. 2 (2008): 465–80; M. Gupta, V. Kumar, and M. Singh, "Creating Satisfied Employees through Workplace Spirituality: A Study of the Private Insurance Sector in Punjab India," *Journal of Business Ethics* 122 (2014): 79–88.

[140] For a review, see Schneider, Ehrhart, and Macey, "Organizational Climate and Culture."

[141] Oberoi, S. (2020). "6 Examples of Merger Failures Owing to Cultural Incompatibility". *Toolbox|hr (August 20, 2020).* Retrieved from https://www.toolbox.com (Accessed on April 21, 2022)

[142] D. J. McCarthy and S. M. Puffer, "Interpreting the Ethicality of Corporate Governance Decision in Russia: Utilizing Integrative Social Contracts Theory to Evaluate the Relevance of Agency Theory Norms," *Academy of Management Review* 33, no. 1 (2008): 11–31.

[143] P. Monin, N. Noorderhavin, E. Vaara, and D. Kroon, "Giving Sense to and Making Sense of Justice in Postmerger Integration," *Academy of Management Journal* (February 2013): 256–84; A. Simha and J. B. Cullen, "Ethical Climates and Their Effects on Organizational Outcomes: Implications from the Past and Prophecies for the Future," *Academy of Management Perspectives* (November 2011): 20–34; and E. Vaara and J. Tienari, "On the Narrative Construction of Multinational Corporations: An Antenarrative Analysis of Legitimation and Resistance in a Cross-Border Merger," *Organization Science* (March–April 2011): 370–90.

[144] R. Vesely, "Seven Seas Change," *Workforce Management* (September 2012): 20–21.

16 Organizational Change and Stress Management

Source: ferli/123RF

LEARNING OBJECTIVES

After studying this chapter, you should be able to:

16-1 Contrast the forces for change and planned change.

16-2 Describe ways to overcome resistance to change.

16-3 Compare the four main approaches to managing organizational change.

16-4 Demonstrate three ways of facilitating change.

16-5 Identify the potential environmental, organizational, and personal sources of stress at work and the role of individual and cultural differences.

16-6 Identify the physiological, psychological, and behavioral symptoms of stress at work.

16-7 Describe individual and organizational approaches to managing stress at work.

Employability Skills Matrix (ESM)

	Myth or Science?	Career OBjectives	An Ethical Choice	Point/ Counter-point	Experi-ential Exercise	Ethical Dilemma	Case Incident 1	Case Incident 2
Critical Thinking			✓	✓	✓	✓	✓	✓
Communication		✓			✓			✓
Collaboration		✓	✓		✓			✓
Knowledge Application and Analysis	✓			✓	✓	✓	✓	✓
Social Responsibility		✓	✓	✓		✓	✓	✓

STRESS AND WELL-BEING

Straight out of college, Naoya Nishigaki joined a large Japanese telecommunications company. He would work until he could catch the last train, and if he missed it, he would sleep at his desk. In some cases, he would work through the night until the following evening—a 37-hour stretch. After a few years of this, he died of an overdose of medication. His death was ruled a case of *karoshi*, a term used in Japan to describe the phenomena of working oneself to death.

There are many other examples in Japan of overwork leading to suicide, heart attacks, and strokes. In the recession that followed the collapse of the economic bubble in the late 1980s, many companies downsized, forcing the remaining staff to work harder. According to a 2017 BBC World report, the Japanese government is intervening, but it is difficult to change national and organizational cultures where many employees are clocking over 80 hours a month of overtime as a matter of course. Critics say that not enough is being done to address these issues, and that short-term profits are taking priority.

Meanwhile, in the other hemisphere, stress levels have been on the rise in New Zealand. According to a 2017 report by *The New Zealand Herald*, employees stress levels have risen by more than 20 percent within the last two years, and in companies with more than 50 staff, the figures rose to more than 30 percent. They say that the change is due to the increase in demand for goods as a result of a newly signed free-trade agreement with China. Demand for production is up, and this, coupled with external factors such as the disruption caused by the earthquakes in Wellington and Christchurch, has played a role in the higher levels of stressed employees.

In these examples, we can see how changes in market conditions, an organization's structure, or even factors such as natural catastrophes can contribute to stress for people in organizations. However, greater recognition of these issues and further research and investment by companies in stress management is making a difference. Ingrid Ozols, Managing Director of MentalHealth@Work, cites the case of Andrew, an employee in Australia, who spoke to his boss about his feelings of anxiety since the last round of organizational restructuring. He was experiencing difficulty in concentrating, which resulted in his taking time off every week. Eventually, he was treated with medication and cognitive behavioral therapy, and after a couple of months, Andrew's level of anxiety was under control and he was fully back at work. He was later promoted to a senior executive position and has never missed a day of work since that anxiety attack. Now thriving, he was able to move on with his career despite all stress-related issues.

Recent approaches to change management support a shift from traditional to more resilience-building initiatives by firms to address issues of employee stress. Here we see a move from top-down change management to more increased engagement of staff. Financial incentives as a form of motivation take a back seat to specific initiatives that build resilience. Performance management becomes more integrated in the change process and involves HR managers and staff-development initiatives. At a strategic level, a firm will move away from compliance to policies and toward a longer-term view of embedding well-being into everyday behavior in the organization.

According to the Black Dog Institute, organizational change such as restructuring or downsizing can result in increased job strain. Employees who are not at risk of job loss can also experience mental illness, sickness absence, and disability. The Institute suggests that better planning of changes can lead to more job satisfaction and improved moods. This, of course, goes much deeper than simply providing fitness classes or placing fruit bowls by the coffee machine; it has to involve leadership as well as business processes and strategy.

Sources: Edwin Lane, "The Young Japanese Working Themselves to Death," BBC World Service, June 2, 2017, http://www.bbc.com/news/business-39981997; Tamsyn Parker, "Employee Stress Levels Up More Than 20pc in Two Years," *NZ Herald*, August 1, 2017, http://www.nzherald.co.nz/business/news/article.cfm?c_id=3&objectid=11897146; Caitlin Fitzsimmons, "Yoga and Free Fruit Won't Solve the Scourge of Workplace Stress," *The Sydney Morning Herald*, June 14, 2017, https://www.smh.com.au/national/yoga-and-free-fruit-wont-solve-the-scourge-of-workplace-stress-20170613-gwq6ap.html; Robertsoncooper, "Embedding Well-Being and Resilience to Support Change Management," http://www.robertsoncooper.com/files/download/Wellbeing_to_support_change_download.pdf; Jocelyn Lowinger, "Your Workplace and Its Impact on Your Mental Health," ABC Health & Wellbeing, http://www.abc.net.au/health/features/stories/2014/07/07/4040588.htm; Black Dog Institute, "Workplace Wellbeing," https://www.blackdoginstitute.org.au/docs/default-source/factsheets/workplacewellbeing; K. Roy, "The Personal Costs of Organizational Change: A Qualitative Study," *Public Performance & Management Review* 39, no. 1 (2016): 223–47; Roy Smollan and Edwina Pio, "Organisational Change, Identity and Coping with Stress," *New Zealand Journal of Employment Relations* 43, no. 1 (2018): 56–82.

Many changes bring about a great deal of stress. As Andrew's experiences highlight, it is extremely important to know how to deal with change: Think strategically about choosing a career, seek out learning and development opportunities that can hone your career skills, work hard, and be resilient and adaptive in handling the many stressors that are sent your way. In this chapter, we describe environmental forces that require firms and people to change, the reasons people and organizations often resist change, and the way this resistance can be overcome. We review processes for managing organizational change. Then we move to the topic of stress and its sources and consequences. In closing, we discuss what individuals and organizations can do to better manage stress levels and realize positive outcomes for organizational behavior (OB), which, after all, is the purpose of this text.

Change

16-1 Contrast the forces for change and planned change.

No company today is in a particularly stable environment. Even those with a dominant market share must change, sometimes radically. For example, the market for smartphones has been especially volatile.[1] During the fourth quarter of 2016, 77 million iPhones were sold, compared with 76.8 million Samsung sales.[2] Contrast this with the fourth quarter of 2015, in which considerably fewer (71.5 million) iPhones were sold, versus considerably more (83.4 million) Samsung phones.[3] At the same time, the Chinese mobile phone company Oppo, and its parent company, BBK Electronics, have been moving rapidly into the market: Collectively they hold only 6 percent less market share than either Samsung or Apple.[4] A look just a few years further back shows formerly dominant players like Nokia, Xiaomi, or Research in Motion (makers of the Blackberry) shrinking dramatically in size. In this and many markets, competitors are constantly entering and exiting the field, gaining and losing ground quickly.

Forces for Change

"Change or die!" is the rallying cry among today's managers worldwide.[5] Exhibit 16-1 summarizes six specific forces that stimulate change.

Throughout the text, we've discussed the *changing nature of the workforce.* Almost every organization must adjust to a multicultural environment, demographic changes, immigration, and outsourcing. *Technology* is continually changing jobs and organizations.[6] It is not difficult to imagine the idea of an office becoming an antiquated concept in the near future.

Economic shocks also have a significant impact on organizations. During the great recession of 2007 to 2009, millions of jobs were lost worldwide; home values dropped dramatically; and many large, well-known corporations like Merrill Lynch, Countrywide Financial, and Ameriquest disappeared or were acquired.[7] Recovery has occurred in many countries, and with it has come new job prospects and investments. Other countries, like Greece, struggle to regain their economic footing, limiting the economic viability of many Greek organizations.[8]

Competition is changing. Competitors are as likely to be across the ocean as across town. Successful organizations are fast on their feet, capable of developing new products rapidly and getting them to market quickly. In other words, they are flexible and require an equally flexible and responsive workforce.[9]

Social trends don't remain static either. Organizations must therefore adjust product and marketing strategies continually to be sensitive to changing social

Exhibit 16-1 Forces for Change

Force	Examples
Nature of the workforce	More cultural diversity
	Aging population
	Increased immigration and outsourcing
Technology	Faster, cheaper, and more mobile computers and handheld devices
	Emergence and growth of social-networking sites
	Deciphering of the human genetic code
Economic shocks	Rise and fall of global housing market
	Financial sector collapse
	Global recession
Competition	Global competitors
	Mergers and consolidations
	Increased government regulation of commerce
Social trends	Increased environmental awareness
	Liberalization of attitudes toward gay, lesbian, and transgender employees
	More multitasking and connectivity
World politics	Rising health care costs
	Negative social attitudes toward business and executives
	Opening of new markets worldwide

trends, as Instagram did when it debuted "Instagram Stories," media (e.g., pictures, videos, text) that disappears some time after sending, essentially re-creating "Snapchat Stories."[10] Consumers, employees, and organizational leaders are also becoming increasingly sensitive to environmental concerns. Green practices seem like they are now expected rather than optional.[11]

Not even globalization's strongest proponents could have imagined the change in *world politics* in recent years. We've seen a major set of financial crises that have rocked global markets, a worldwide pandemic,[12] a dramatic rise in the power and influence of China, populism and nationalist movements gaining headway in Europe and the United States, and intense shakeups in governments across the Arab world. Throughout the industrialized world, businesses—particularly in the banking and financial sectors—have come under new scrutiny.

Planned Change

A group of housekeeping employees who work for a small hotel confronted the owner: "It's very hard for most of us to maintain 7-to-4 work hours," said their spokeswoman. "Each of us has significant family and personal responsibilities. Rigid hours don't work for us. We're going to begin looking for someplace else to work if you don't set up flexible work hours." The owner listened thoughtfully to the group's ultimatum and agreed to make changes. The next day, a flextime plan for these employees was introduced.

A major automobile manufacturer spent several billion dollars to install state-of-the-art robotics. One area that received the new equipment was quality control, where sophisticated computers significantly improved the company's ability to find and correct defects. Because the new equipment dramatically changed the jobs in the quality-control area, and because management anticipated considerable employee resistance to it, executives developed a program to help people become familiar with the change and deal with any anxieties they might be feeling.

change When things become different from the way they were.

planned change Change activities that are intentional and goal-oriented.

Both of these scenarios are examples of **change**, or making things different. However, only the second scenario describes **planned change**.[13] Many changes are like the one that occurred at the hotel: They just happen. Some organizations treat all change as an accidental occurrence. In this chapter, we address change as an intentional, goal-oriented activity.

What are the goals of planned change? First, it seeks to improve the ability of the organization to adapt to changes in its environment. Second, it seeks to change employee behavior.

change agents Persons who act as catalysts and assume the responsibility for managing change activities.

Who in organizations is responsible for managing change activities? The answer is **change agents**.[14] They see a future for the organization others have not identified, and they are able to motivate, invent, and implement this vision.[15] Change agents can be managers or nonmanagers, current or new employees, or outside consultants.

Some change agents look to transform old industries to meet new capabilities and demands. For instance, Sandy Jen, Cameron Ring, Monica Lo, and Seth Sternberg are working together to apply social marketplace concepts to online business—a concept exemplified by rideshare company Uber and crowdfunding firm Kickstarter. The group has created an innovative service for senior care called Honor.[16] In contrast to older methods of matching seniors and their families with services through nursing facilities, Honor uses an online marketplace. Caregivers list qualifications and desired job attributes, and seniors specify the type of services they need. Then Honor facilitates meeting the needs. This new model could alter the entire field of care, based on the vision of a core group of dedicated leaders.

Finding true change agents in long-established organizations can pose unique challenges. General Motors (GM) expects its human resources (HR) managers to be change agents and its top HR executive to set the tone. Experts attributed some of the failed changes at GM to Kathleen Barclay's stint as global HR vice president. GM next hired Mary Barra, a manufacturing executive they thought could bring about better changes. Barra seemed like a change agent, but even then-CEO Dan Akerson said, "It was the worst application of talent I've ever seen." Barra was later named as GM's new CEO, displacing Akerson.[17] For the top HR spot, GM next selected Cynthia Brinkley, who supposedly had the right combination of skills to be a change agent. Yet she had no HR background[18] and was replaced shortly afterward by John Quattrone. Quattrone has over 25 years of experience in HR (and over 40 years of tenure with GM).[19] Time will tell.

Many change agents fail because organizational members resist change. In the next section, we discuss resistance to change and what managers can do about it.

Resistance to Change

16-2 Describe ways to overcome resistance to change.

Our egos are fragile, and we often see change as threatening. Even when employees are shown data that suggest they need to change, they latch onto whatever data they can find that suggest they are okay and don't need to change.[20] Employees who feel negatively toward a change cope by not thinking about it, increasing their use of sick time, or quitting. All these reactions can sap the organization of vital energy when it is most needed.[21] Resistance to change doesn't come only from lower levels of the organization. In many cases, higher-level managers resist changes proposed by subordinates, especially if these leaders are focused on immediate performance. Conversely, when leaders are more focused on mastery and exploration, they are more willing to hear and adopt subordinates' suggestions for change.[22] Furthermore, during an acquisition, employee and middle manager resistance to change can be reduced through a slow, rather than fast, transition.[23]

Resistance to change can be positive if it leads to open discussion and debate.[24] These responses are usually preferable to apathy or silence and can indicate that members of the organization are engaged in the process, providing change agents an opportunity to explain the change effort. Change agents can also monitor the resistance to modify the change to fit the preferences of members of the organization.

Resistance doesn't necessarily surface in standardized ways. It can be overt, implicit, immediate, or deferred.[25] It's easiest for management to deal with overt and immediate resistance such as complaints, a work slowdown, or a strike threat. The greater challenge is managing resistance that is implicit or deferred because these responses—loss of loyalty or motivation, increased errors or absenteeism—are more subtle and more difficult to recognize for what they are. Deferred actions also cloud the link between the change and the reaction to it, sometimes surfacing weeks, months, or even years later. Or a single change of little inherent impact may be the straw that breaks the camel's back because resistance to earlier changes has been deferred and stockpiled.

Exhibit 16-2 summarizes major forces for resistance to change, categorized by their sources. Individual sources reside in human characteristics such as perceptions, personalities, and needs. Organizational sources reside in the structural makeup of organizations themselves.

It's worth noting that not all change is good. Rapid, transformational change is risky, so change agents need to think through the full implications carefully. Speed can lead to bad decisions, and sometimes those initiating change fail to realize the full magnitude of the effects or their true costs.

Overcoming Resistance to Change

Eight tactics can help change agents deal with resistance to change.[26] Let's review them briefly.

Communication Communication is more important than ever in times of change. One study of German companies revealed changes are most effective when a company communicates a rationale that balances the interests of various stakeholders (shareholders, employees, community, customers) rather than those of shareholders only.[27] Other research on a changing organization in the Philippines found that formal information sessions decreased employees' anxiety about the change, while providing high-quality information about the change increased their commitment to it.[28]

Participation It's difficult to resist a change decision in which we've participated. Assuming participants have the expertise to make a meaningful contribution, their involvement can reduce resistance, obtain commitment, and increase the quality of the change decision.[29] However, these advantages sometimes come with potential negatives: the potential for a poor solution and a great consumption of time.

Building Support and Commitment When managers or employees have low emotional commitment to change, they resist it and favor the status quo.[30]

Exhibit 16-2 Sources of Resistance to Change

Individual Sources

Habit—To cope with life's complexities, we rely on habits or programmed responses. But when confronted with change, this tendency to respond in our accustomed ways becomes a source of resistance.

Security—People with a high need for security are likely to resist change because it threatens their feelings of safety.

Economic factors—Changes in job tasks or established work routines can arouse economic fears if people are concerned that they won't be able to perform the new tasks or routines to their previous standards, especially when pay is closely tied to productivity.

Fear of the unknown—Change substitutes ambiguity and uncertainty for the unknown.

Selective information processing—Individuals are guilty of selectively processing information in order to keep their perceptions intact. They hear what they want to hear, and they ignore information that challenges the world they've created.

Organizational Sources

Structural inertia—Organizations have built-in mechanisms—such as their selection processes and formalized regulations—to produce stability. When an organization is confronted with change, this structural inertia acts as a counterbalance to sustain stability.

Limited focus of change—Organizations consist of a number of interdependent subsystems. One can't be changed without affecting the others. So limited changes in subsystems tend to be nullified by the larger system.

Group inertia—Even if individuals want to change their behavior, group norms may act as a constraint.

Threat to expertise—Changes in organizational patterns may threaten the expertise of specialized groups.

Threat to established power relationships—Any redistribution of decision-making authority can threaten long-established power relationships within the organization.

Employees are also more accepting of changes when they are committed to the organization as a whole.[31] Motivating employees and emphasizing their commitment to the organization overall can help them commit emotionally to the change rather than embrace the status quo.[32] When employees' fear and anxiety are high, counseling and therapy, new-skills training, or a short paid leave of absence may facilitate adjustment to change.

Develop Positive Relationships People are more willing to accept changes if they trust the managers implementing them and see them as legitimate.[33] One study surveyed 235 employees from a large housing corporation in the Netherlands that was experiencing a merger. Those who had a more positive relationship with their supervisor, and who felt that the work environment supported development, were much more positive about the change process.[34] Underscoring the importance of social context, other work shows that even individuals who are generally resistant to change will be more willing to accept new and different ideas (and can even experience less stress) when they feel supported by their coworkers and believe the environment is safe for taking risks.[35] Another set of studies found that individuals who usually resisted change felt more positive about it if they trusted the change agent.[36] This research suggests that if managers are able to facilitate positive relationships, they may be able to overcome resistance to change even among those who ordinarily don't like changes.

Implementing Changes Fairly One way organizations can minimize negative impact is to make sure change is implemented fairly. As we saw in Chapter 7, procedural fairness is especially important when employees perceive an outcome as negative, so it's crucial that employees see the reason for the change, are kept informed about its progress, and perceive its implementation as consistent and fair.[37] However, research on 26 large-scale planned change projects in the Netherlands reveals that change recipients are not always self-interested: They focus on the impact that change has on their coworkers, the organization, and other parties.[38] Some resistance might be inevitable, particularly when the change affects the employees' freedoms, although fairness perceptions still help alleviate this resistance.[39]

Manipulation and Cooptation *Manipulation* refers to covert influence attempts.[40] Twisting facts to make them more attractive, withholding information, and creating false rumors to get employees to accept change are all examples of manipulation. If management threatens to close a manufacturing plant whose employees are resisting an across-the-board pay cut, and if the threat is actually unfounded, management is using manipulation. *Cooptation*, on the other hand, combines manipulation and participation.[41] It seeks to buy off the leaders of a resistance group by giving them a key role, seeking their advice not to find a better solution but to get their endorsement. Both manipulation and cooptation are relatively inexpensive ways to gain the support of adversaries, but they can backfire if the targets become aware that they are being tricked or used. Once that's discovered, the change agent's credibility may drop to zero.

Selecting People Who Accept Change Research suggests the ability to accept and adapt easily to *change* is related to personality—some people are simply more receptive to change.[42] Individuals who are emotionally stable, have high core self-evaluations, are willing to take risks, and are flexible in their behavior are prime candidates.[43] This seems to be universal. One study of managers in the United States, Europe, and Asia found those with a positive self-concept and high risk tolerance coped better with organizational change.[44] Individuals higher in general mental ability are also better able to learn and to adapt to changes in the workplace.[45] In sum, an impressive body of evidence shows organizations can facilitate change by selecting people predisposed to accept it.

Besides selecting individuals who are willing to accept changes, it is also possible to select teams that are more adaptable. In general, teams that are strongly motivated by learning about and mastering tasks, are high in cognitive ability, and have collectivistic values are better able to adapt to changing environments.[46] It may thus be necessary to consider not just individual motivation but also group motivation when trying to implement changes. A meta-analytic review of hundreds of teams suggests that teams whose members are high in cognitive ability and motivated to master their tasks tend to be the most adaptable.[47]

Coercion Last on the list of tactics is *coercion,* the application of direct threats or force on the resisters.[48] If management is determined to close a manufacturing plant whose employees don't acquiesce to a pay cut, the company is using coercion. Other examples include threatening employees with transfers, blocked promotions, negative performance evaluations, and poor letters of recommendation. Coercion is most effective when some force or pressure is enacted on at least some resisters—for instance, if an employee is publicly refused a promotion request, the threat of blocked promotions will become a real possibility in the minds of other employees. The advantages and drawbacks of coercion are approximately the same as for manipulation and cooptation.

The Politics of Change

No discussion of resistance would be complete without a brief mention of the politics of change.[49] Because change invariably threatens the status quo, it inherently implies political activity.

Politics suggests the impetus for change is more likely to come from outside change agents, employees new to the organization (who have less invested in the status quo), or managers slightly removed from the main power structure. Managers who have spent a long time with an organization and who have achieved a senior position in the hierarchy are often major impediments to change. For them, change can be a very real threat to their status and position. Yet they may be expected to implement changes to demonstrate they're not merely caretakers. By acting as change agents, they can convey to stockholders, suppliers, employees, and customers that they are addressing problems and adapting to a dynamic environment. Of course, as you might guess, when forced to introduce change, these longtime power holders tend to implement incremental changes. Radical change is often considered too threatening. This explains why boards of directors that recognize the imperative for rapid and radical change frequently turn to outside candidates for new leadership.[50]

Approaches to Managing Organizational Change

16-3 Compare the four main approaches to managing organizational change.

We now turn to several approaches to managing change: Lewin's classic three-step model of the change process, Kotter's eight-step plan, action research, and organizational development.

Lewin's Three-Step Model of the Change Process

Kurt Lewin argued that successful change in organizations should follow three steps: *unfreezing* the status quo, *movement* to a desired end state, and *refreezing* the new change to make it permanent[51] (see Exhibit 16-3).

driving forces Forces that direct behavior away from the status quo.

restraining forces Forces that hinder movement from the existing equilibrium.

By definition, status quo is an equilibrium state. To move from equilibrium—to overcome the pressures of both individual resistance and group conformity—unfreezing must happen in one of three ways (see Exhibit 16-4). For one, the **driving forces**, which direct behavior away from the status quo, can be increased. For another, the **restraining forces**, which hinder movement away from equilibrium, can be decreased. A third alternative is to combine the first two approaches. Companies that have been successful in the past are likely to encounter restraining forces because people question the need for change.[52]

Exhibit 16-3 Lewin's Three-Step Change Model

Exhibit 16-4 **Unfreezing the Status Quo**

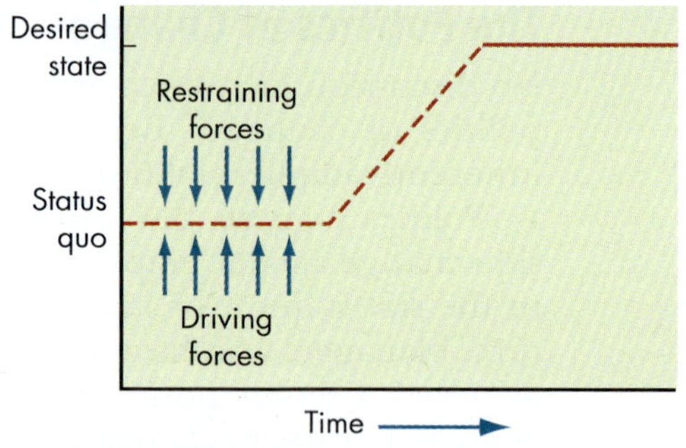

Once the movement stage begins, it's important to keep the momentum going. Organizations that build up to change do less well than those that get to and through the movement stage quickly. When change has been implemented, the new situation must be refrozen so it can be sustained over time. Without this last step, change will likely be short-lived and employees will attempt to revert to the previous equilibrium state. The objective of refreezing, then, is to stabilize the new situation by balancing the driving and restraining forces.

Kotter's Eight-Step Plan

John Kotter of Harvard Business School built on Lewin's three-step model to create a more detailed approach for implementing change.[53] Kotter began by listing common mistakes managers make when trying to initiate change. They may fail to create a sense of urgency about the need for change, a coalition for managing the change process, and a vision for change, and they may fail to communicate effectively about it and/or to anchor the changes into the organization's culture. They also may fail to remove obstacles that could impede the vision's achievement and/or provide short-term and achievable goals. Finally, they may declare victory too soon.

Kotter established eight sequential steps to overcome these problems. They are listed in Exhibit 16-5.

Exhibit 16-5 **Kotter's Eight-Step Plan for Implementing Change**

1. Establish a sense of urgency by creating a compelling reason for why change is needed.
2. Form a coalition with enough power to lead the change.
3. Create a new vision to direct the change and strategies for achieving the vision.
4. Communicate the vision throughout the organization.
5. Empower others to act on the vision by removing barriers to change and encouraging risk taking and creative problem solving.
6. Plan for, create, and reward short-term "wins" that move the organization toward the new vision.
7. Consolidate improvements, reassess changes, and make necessary adjustments in the new programs.
8. Reinforce the changes by demonstrating the relationship between new behaviors and organizational success.

Source: Based on J. Kotter, *Leading Change* (Boston, MA: Harvard Business School, 1996).

Notice how Kotter's first four steps essentially extrapolate Lewin's unfreezing stage. Steps 5, 6, and 7 represent movement, and the final step works on refreezing. So Kotter's contribution lies in providing managers and change agents with a more detailed guide for successfully implementing change.

Action Research

action research A change process based on systematic collection of data and then selection of a change action based on what the analyzed data indicate.

Action research is a change process based on the systematic collection of data and selection of a change action based on what the analyzed data indicate.[54] Its value is in providing a scientific methodology for managing planned change. Action research consists of five steps (note how they closely parallel the scientific method): diagnosis, analysis, feedback, action, and evaluation.

The change agent, often an outside consultant in action research, begins by gathering information about problems, concerns, and needed changes from members of the organization. This *diagnosis* is analogous to the physician's search to find specifically what ails a patient. In action research, the change agent asks questions, reviews records, and interviews employees by actively listening to their concerns.

Diagnosis is followed by *analysis*. What problems do people focus on? What patterns do these problems seem to take? The change agent synthesizes this information into primary concerns, problem areas, and possible actions.

Action research requires the people who will participate in a change program to help identify the problem and determine the solution. So the third step—*feedback*—requires sharing with employees what has been found from the first and second steps. The employees, with the help of the change agent, develop action plans for bringing about needed change.

Now the *action* part of action research is set in motion. The employees and the change agent carry out the specific actions they have identified to correct the problem.

The final step, consistent with the scientific underpinnings of action research, is *evaluation* of the action plan's effectiveness, using the initial data gathered as a benchmark.

Action research provides at least two specific benefits. First, it's problem-focused. The change agent objectively looks for problems, and the type of problem determines the type of change action. This is a process that makes intuitive sense. Unfortunately, in reality, change activities can become solution-centered and therefore erroneously predetermined. The change agent has a favorite solution—for example, implementing flextime, teams, or a process reengineering program—and then seeks out problems that the solution fits.

A second benefit of action research is the lowering of resistance. Because action research engages employees so thoroughly in the process, it reduces resistance to change. Once employees have actively participated in the feedback stage, the change process typically takes on a momentum of its own.

Organizational Development

organizational development (OD) A collection of planned change interventions, built on humanistic-democratic values, that seeks to improve organizational effectiveness and employee well-being.

Organizational development (OD) is a collection of change methods that try to improve organizational effectiveness and employee well-being.[55] OD methods value human and organizational growth, collaborative and participative processes, and a spirit of inquiry.[56] Contemporary OD borrows heavily from postmodern philosophy in placing heavy emphasis on the subjective ways people see and make sense of their work environment. The change agent may take the lead in OD, but there is a strong emphasis on collaboration.

What are some OD techniques or interventions for bringing about change? Here are six.

sensitivity training Training that seeks to change behavior through unstructured group interaction.

Sensitivity Training A variety of names—for example, **sensitivity training**, laboratory training, encounter groups, and training groups (T-groups)—all refer to an early method of changing behavior through unstructured group interaction.[57] Current organizational interventions such as diversity training, executive coaching, and team-building exercises are descendants of this early OD intervention technique.

In classic sensitivity training, members were brought together in a free and open environment in which participants discussed themselves and their interactive processes; they were loosely directed by a professional behavioral scientist who created the opportunity to express ideas, beliefs, and attitudes without taking any leadership role. The group was process-oriented, which means that individuals learned through observing and participating rather than being told. With all forms of OD, caution must be taken so the unstructured groups are not intimidating, chaotic, and damaging to work relationships.

survey feedback The use of questionnaires to identify discrepancies among member perceptions; discussion follows, and remedies are suggested.

Survey Feedback One tool for assessing the attitudes of organizational members, identifying discrepancies among member perceptions, and solving differences is the **survey feedback** approach.[58]

Everyone in an organization can participate in survey feedback, but of key importance is the organizational "family"—the manager of any given unit and the employees who report directly to him or her. All usually complete a questionnaire about their perceptions and attitudes on a range of topics, including decision-making practices; communication effectiveness; coordination among units; and satisfaction with the organization, job, peers, and immediate supervisor.

Data from questionnaires are tabulated along with data pertaining to an individual's specific organizational "family" and the entire organization, and then distributed to employees. These data become the springboard for identifying problems and clarifying issues that may be creating difficulties for people. Particular attention is given to encouraging discussion and ensuring it focuses on issues and ideas, not on attacking individuals. For instance, are people listening? Are new ideas being generated? Can decision making, interpersonal relations, or job assignments be improved? Answers should lead the group to commit to various remedies for the problems.

The survey feedback approach can be helpful to keep decision makers informed about the attitudes of employees toward the organization. However, individuals are influenced by many factors when they respond to surveys, which may make some findings unreliable. Managers who use the survey feedback approach should therefore monitor their organization's current events and employee response rates.

process consultation (PC) A meeting in which a consultant assists a client in understanding process events with which they must deal and identifying processes that need improvement.

Process Consultation Managers often sense that their unit's performance can be improved but are unable to identify what to improve and how. The purpose of **process consultation (PC)** is for an outside consultant to assist a client, usually a manager, through crafting "a relationship through a continuous effort of 'jointly deciphering what is going on' … to make coauthored choices about how to go on."[59] These events might include workflow, informal relationships among unit members, and formal communication channels.

PC is similar to sensitivity training in assuming we can improve organizational effectiveness by dealing with interpersonal problems and in emphasizing involvement. But PC is more task-directed, and consultants do not solve the organization's problems but rather guide or coach the client to solve his or her own problems after *jointly* diagnosing what needs improvement. The client develops the skill to analyze processes within his or her unit and can therefore use the skill long after the consultant is gone. Because the client actively participates in both the diagnosis and the development of alternatives, he or she arrives at a greater understanding of the process and the remedy, and becomes less resistant to the action plan chosen.

team building High interaction among team members to increase trust and openness.

Team Building We've noted throughout this text that organizations increasingly rely on teams to accomplish work tasks. **Team building** uses high-interaction group activities to increase trust and openness among team members, improve coordination efforts, and increase team performance.[60] Here, we emphasize the intragroup level, meaning within organizational families (command groups) as well as committees, project teams, self-managed teams, and task groups.

Team building typically includes goal setting, development of interpersonal relations among team members, role analysis to clarify each member's role and responsibilities, and team process analysis. It may emphasize or exclude certain activities, depending on the purpose of the development effort and the specific problems the team is confronting. Basically, however, team building uses high interaction among members to increase trust and openness. In these times when organizations increasingly rely on teams, team building is an important topic.

intergroup development Organizational development (OD) efforts to change the attitudes, stereotypes, and perceptions that groups have of each other.

Intergroup Development A major area of concern in OD is dysfunctional conflict among groups. **Intergroup development** seeks to change groups' attitudes, stereotypes, and perceptions about each other.[61] Here, training sessions closely resemble diversity training, except rather than focusing on demographic

The Indian Cricket team often plays and spends time together as part of their effort to bond and build teams. In 2019, the Indian team lead by Virat Kohli, just ahead of their world cup opening match against South Africa, played paintball.[62]
Source: James Boardman / Alamy Stock Photo

differences, they focus on differences among occupations, departments, or divisions within an organization.

In one organization, for example, the engineers saw the accounting department as composed of shy and conservative types, and the HR department as having a bunch of "ultra-liberals more concerned that some protected group of employees might get their feelings hurt than with the company making a profit." Such stereotypes can have an obvious negative impact on coordination efforts among departments.

Among several approaches for improving intergroup relations, a popular one emphasizes problem solving.[63] Each group meets independently to list its perceptions of itself and another group and how it believes the other group perceives it. The groups then share their lists, discuss similarities and differences, and look for causes of disparities. Are the groups' goals at odds? Are the perceptions distorted? On what basis were stereotypes formulated? Have some differences been caused by a misunderstanding of intentions? Have words and concepts been defined differently by each group? Answers to questions like these clarify the exact nature of the conflict.

Once they have identified the causes of discrepancies, the groups move to the integration phase—developing solutions to improve relations between them. Subgroups of members from each of the conflicting groups can conduct further diagnoses and formulate alternative solutions.

appreciative inquiry (AI) An approach that seeks to identify the unique qualities and special strengths of an organization, which can then be built on to improve performance.

Appreciative Inquiry Most OD approaches are problem-centered. They identify a problem or set of problems, then look for a solution. **Appreciative inquiry (AI)** instead accentuates the positive. Rather than looking for problems to fix, it seeks to identify the unique qualities and special strengths of an organization, which members can build on to improve performance.[64] That is, AI focuses on an organization's successes rather than its problems.

The AI process consists of four steps—discovery, dreaming, design, and destiny—often played out in a large-group meeting over 2 to 3 days and overseen by a trained change agent. *Discovery* sets out to identify what people think are the organization's strengths. Employees recount times they felt the organization worked best or when they specifically felt most satisfied with their jobs. In *dreaming*, employees use information from the discovery phase to speculate on possible futures, such as what the organization will be like in 5 years. In *design*, participants find a common vision of how the organization will look in the future and agree on its unique qualities. For the fourth step, participants seek to define the organization's *destiny* or how to fulfill their dream, and they typically write action plans and develop implementation strategies.

AI has proven to be an effective change strategy in organizations such as GTE, Roadway Express, American Express, and the U.S. Navy.[65] American Express used AI to revitalize its culture during a lean economy. In workshops, employees described how they already felt proud of working at American Express and were encouraged to create a change vision by describing how the company could be better in the future. The efforts led to some concrete improvements. Senior managers were able to use employees' information to better their methods of making financial forecasts, improve information technology (IT) investments, and create new performance-management tools for managers. The end result was a renewed culture focused on winning attitudes and behaviors.[66]

Facilitating Change

16-4 Demonstrate three ways of creating a culture for change.

We've considered how organizations can *adapt* to change. But recently, some OB scholars have focused on a more proactive approach—how organizations can *embrace* change by transforming their cultures. In this section, we review three approaches: managing paradox, stimulating innovation, and creating a learning organization. We also address the issue of organizational change and stress.

Managing Paradox

In a *paradox* situation, we are required to balance tensions across various courses of action. There is a constant process of finding a balancing point, a dynamic equilibrium, among shifting priorities over time.[67] Think of riding a bicycle: You must maintain forward momentum or you'll fall over. From this perspective, there is no such thing as a separate discipline of "change management" because all management is dealing with constant change and adaptation.

The idea of paradox sounds abstract, but more specific concepts have begun to emerge from a growing body of research.[68] Several key paradoxes have been identified. *Learning* is a paradox because it requires building on the past while rejecting it at the same time. *Organizing* is a paradox because it calls for setting direction and leading while requiring empowerment and flexibility. *Performing* is a paradox between creating organization-wide goals to concentrate effort and recognizing the diverse goals of stakeholders inside and outside the organization. And finally, *belonging* is a paradox between establishing a sense of collective identity and acknowledging our desire to be recognized and accepted as unique individuals.

paradox theory The theory that the key paradox in management is that there is no final optimal status for an organization.

Managers can learn a few lessons from **paradox theory**,[69] which states that the key paradox in management is that there is no final optimal status for an organization.[70] The first lesson is that, as the environment and members of the organization change, different elements take on more or less importance. For example, sometimes a company needs to acknowledge past success and learn how it worked, while at other times looking backward only hinders progress. There is some evidence that managers who think holistically and recognize the importance of balancing paradoxical factors are more effective, especially in generating adaptive and creative behavior in those they are managing.[71] However, leaders who adopt paradoxical approaches may fall into the trap of escalation of commitment (see Chapter 5) given that they may be more optimistic that the current state of affairs will swing toward a more desirable one.[72]

Stimulating Innovation

How can an organization become more innovative? An excellent model is W. L. Gore & Associates, the $2.9-billion-per-year company best known as the maker of Gore-Tex fabric.[73] Gore has developed a reputation as one of the most innovative companies by developing a stream of diverse products—including guitar strings, vacuum cleaner filters, industrial sealants, and fuel cell components.

What's the secret of Gore's success? What can other organizations do to duplicate its track record for innovation? Gore pioneered a flat, unique, lattice-type organizational structure (now termed an open allocation structure)[74] run by employees (associates) working in self-organized project groups.[75] Gore also allocates 10 percent of each emlpoyee's day to creative tasks and idea generation.[76] Although there is no guaranteed formula, certain characteristics surface repeatedly

Delhivery, the largest and fastest growing, fully integrated logistics company in India, has successfully fulfilled over 1 billion orders across India since its inception 11 years ago. Its founders Kapil Bharati, Mohit Tandon, Sahil Barua, Suraj Saharan, and Bhavesh Manglani believe that their team of over 66000 people spread across the country understand the values of the company and work together to deliver reliable, resilient, and agile supply chains at lowest cost.[77]

Source: Rahbar Stock.shutterstock.com

when researchers study innovative organizations. They are structural, cultural, and human resources characteristics. Change agents should consider introducing these characteristics into their organizations to create cultures and climate for innovation and creativity. Let's start by clarifying what we mean by innovation.

innovation A new idea applied to initiating or improving a product, process, or service.

Definition of *Innovation* We said change refers to making things different. **Innovation**, a specialized kind of change, is applied to initiating or improving a product, process, or service, in other words, a better solution.[78] So all innovations imply change, but not all changes introduce new ideas or lead to significant improvements. Innovations can range from incremental improvements, such as tablets, to radical breakthroughs, such as Nissan's electric Leaf car.

Sources of Innovation *Structural variables* are one potential source of innovation.[79] A comprehensive review of the structure–innovation relationship leads to the following conclusions:

1. **Organic structures positively influence innovation.** Because they're lower in vertical differentiation, formalization, and centralization, organic organizations facilitate the flexibility, adaptation, and cross-fertilization that make the adoption of innovations easier.[80]
2. **Innovation-contingent rewards positively influence innovation.** When creativity is rewarded, firms tend to become more innovative—especially when employees are given feedback on their performance in addition to autonomy in doing their jobs.[81]
3. **Innovation is nurtured when there are slack resources.** Having an abundance of resources, including an equal distribution of wealth, allows an organization to afford to purchase or develop innovations, bear the cost of instituting them, and absorb failures.[82]
4. **Interunit communication is high in innovative organizations.** These organizations are heavy users of committees, task forces, cross-functional teams, and other mechanisms that facilitate interaction across departmental lines.[83]

Context and Innovation Innovative organizations tend to have similar *cultures*. They encourage experimentation and reward both successes and failures. They celebrate mistakes.[84] Unfortunately, in too many organizations, people are rewarded for the absence of failures rather than for the presence of successes. Such cultures extinguish risk taking and innovation.[85] Innovative organizations have a shared sense of purpose[86] and also tend to be cohesive, mutually supportive, and encouraging of innovation.[87]

Within the *human resources* category, innovative organizations actively promote the training and development of their members so they keep current, offer high job security so employees don't fear getting fired for making mistakes, and encourage individuals to become champions of change.[88] A study of organizations in the manufacturing sector in the United Kingdom looked at the relationship between teamwork and organizational innovation and the moderating role of HRM systems. It was found that widespread use of teamwork increases innovation and that HRM systems can act to facilitate or constrain teams in organizations.[89]

idea champions Individuals who take an innovation and actively and enthusiastically promote the idea, build support, overcome resistance, and ensure that the idea is implemented.

Idea Champions and Innovation Once a new idea has been developed, **idea champions** actively and enthusiastically promote it, build support, overcome resistance, and ensure it is implemented.[90] Champions often have similar personality characteristics:[91] extremely high self-confidence, persistence, energy, and a tendency to take risks. They usually display traits associated with transformational leadership—they inspire and energize others with their vision of an innovation's potential and their strong personal conviction about their mission. Situations can also influence the extent to which idea champions are forces for change. For example, passion for change among entrepreneurs is greatest when work roles and the social environment encourage them to put their creative identities forward. On the flip side, work roles that push creative individuals to do routine management and administration tasks diminish both the passion for and implementation of change.[92] Idea champions are good at gaining the commitment of others, and their jobs should provide considerable decision-making discretion. This autonomy helps them introduce and implement innovations[93] when the context is supportive.

Do successful idea champions do things differently in varied cultures? Yes, they do.[94] Generally, people in collectivist cultures prefer appeals for cross-functional support for innovation efforts; people in high power-distance cultures prefer champions to work closely with those in authority to approve innovative activities before work is begun; and the higher the uncertainty avoidance of a society, the more champions should work within the organization's rules and procedures to develop the innovation. These findings suggest that effective managers alter their organization's innovation strategies to reflect cultural values. For instance, although idea champions in Russia might succeed by ignoring budgetary limitations and working around confining procedures, idea champions in Austria, Denmark, Germany, or other cultures high in uncertainty avoidance will be more effective by closely following budgets and procedures.

Harsha Engineers International Limited (Harsha) since 1986 has established itself as the largest manufacturer of precision bearing cages in organized sector in India and holds a market share of approximately 5% to 6% in the organized segment of the global brass, steel, polyamide bearing cages in terms of revenue. Its customers include the who's who of bearing manufacturers in the world. The promoters, Harish Rangwala and Rajendra Shah, who built the company from scratch with strong focus on research and development and use of latest technology to meet customer requirements. Both the promoters continue to be the idea champions in the company.[95]

Creating a Learning Organization

Another way an organization can proactively manage change is to make continuous growth part of its culture—to become a learning organization.[96]

learning organization An organization that has developed the continuous capacity to adapt and change.

What Is a Learning Organization? Just as individuals learn, so too do organizations. A **learning organization** has developed the continuous capacity to adapt and change. The Dimensions of the Learning Organization Questionnaire (DLOQ) has been adopted and adapted internationally to assess the degree of commitment to learning organization principles.[97]

Exhibit 16-6 summarizes the five basic characteristics of a learning organization—one in which people put aside their old ways of thinking, learn to be open with each other, understand how their organization really works, form a plan or vision everyone can agree on, and work together to achieve that vision.[98]

Proponents of the learning organization envision it as a remedy for three fundamental problems of traditional organizations: fragmentation, competition, and reactiveness.[99] First, *fragmentation* based on specialization creates "walls" and "chimneys" that separate different functions into independent and often warring fiefdoms. Second, an overemphasis on *competition* often undermines collaboration. Managers compete over who is right, who knows more, or who is more persuasive. Divisions compete when they ought to cooperate and share knowledge. Team leaders compete to show who the best manager is. And third, *reactiveness* misdirects management's attention to solving problems rather than creating. The problem solver tries to make something go away, while a creator tries to bring something new into being. An emphasis on reactiveness to problems pushes out innovation and continuous improvement and, in its place, encourages people to concentrate on quick fixes as problems emerge.

Managing Learning What can managers do to make their firms learning organizations? Here are some suggestions:

- ***Establish a strategy.*** Management needs to make explicit its commitment to change, innovation, and continuous improvement.

Exhibit 16-6 Characteristics of a Learning Organization

1. There exists a shared vision that everyone agrees on.
2. People discard their old ways of thinking and the standard routines they use for solving problems or doing their jobs.
3. Members think of all organizational processes, activities, functions, and interactions with the environment as part of a system of interrelationships.
4. People openly communicate with each other (across vertical and horizontal boundaries) without fear of criticism or punishment.
5. People sublimate their personal self-interest and fragmented departmental interests to work together to achieve the organization's shared vision.

Source: Based on P. M. Senge, *The Fifth Discipline: The Art and Practice of the Learning Organization*, 2nd ed. (New York: Random House, 2006).

- ***Redesign the organization's structure.*** The formal structure can be a serious impediment to learning. Flattening the structure, eliminating or combining departments, and increasing the use of cross-functional teams reinforce interdependence and reduce boundaries.
- ***Reshape the organization's culture.*** Managers must demonstrate by their actions that taking risks and admitting failures are desirable. This means rewarding people who take chances and make mistakes. They also need to encourage functional conflict.

Organizational Change and Stress

Think about the times you have felt stressed during your work life. Look past the everyday stress factors that can spill over to the workplace, like a traffic jam that makes you late for work or a broken coffee machine that keeps you from your morning java. What were your more memorable and lasting stressful times at work? For many people, these were caused by organizational change.

Researchers are increasingly studying the effects of organizational change on employees. We are interested in determining the specific causes and mitigating factors of stress to learn how to manage organizational change effectively.[100] The overall findings are that organizational changes that incorporate OB knowledge of how people react to stressors may yield more effective results than organizational changes that are managed only objectively through goal-setting plans.[101]

Not surprisingly, we also find that the role of leadership is critical. One study indicated that transformational leaders can help shape employee affect so employees stay committed to the change and do not perceive it as stressful.[102] Other research indicated that a positive orientation toward change *before* new initiatives are planned decreases employees' stress when they go through organizational changes and increases their positive attitudes.[103] Managers can be continually working to increase employees' self-efficacy, change-related attitudes, and perceived control over the situation to create this positive change orientation. For instance, they can use role clarification and continual rewards to increase self-efficacy, and they can enhance employees' perceived control and positive attitudes toward change by including them from the planning stages to the application of new processes. Another study added the need for increasing the amount of communication to employees during change, assessing and enhancing employees' psychological resilience through offering social support, and training employees in emotional self-regulation techniques.[104] Through these methods, managers can help employees keep their stress levels low and their commitment high.

Often, organizational changes are stressful because some employees perceive aspects of the changes as threatening. These employees are more likely to quit, partially in reaction to their stress. To reduce the perception of threat, employees need to perceive the organizational changes as fair. Research indicates that those who have a positive change orientation before changes are planned are less likely to perceive changes as unfair or threatening.

16-5 Identify the potential environmental, organizational, and personal sources of stress at work and the role of individual and cultural differences.

Stress at Work

Friends say that they're stressed from greater workloads and longer hours because of downsizing at their organizations. Parents worry about the lack of job stability and reminisce about a time when a job with a large corporation implied

Exhibit 16-7 Work Is One of the Top Sources of Stress

What area of your life causes you the most stress?

Area	Causes Most Stress
Nation's future	63%
Money	62%
Work	61%
Political Climate	57%
Crime (e.g., violence)	51%

Source: "Stress in America: The State of Our Nation," *American Psychological Association*, November 1, 2017, https://www.apa.org/news/press/releases/stress/2017/state-nation.pdf.

lifetime security. Employees complain about the stress of trying to balance work and family responsibilities. Harris, Rothenberg International, a leading provider of employee assistance programs (EAPs), finds that employees are having mental breakdowns and needing professional help at higher rates than ever.[105] Indeed, as Exhibit 16-7 shows, work is a major source of stress in most people's lives. (Recent surveys also show that access to healthcare and the threat of sexual harassment are also major sources of stress.[106]) What are the causes and consequences of stress, and how can individuals and organizations reduce it?

What Is Stress?

stress A psychological process in which an individual is confronted with an opportunity, demand, or resource related to what the individual desires and for which the outcome is perceived to be both uncertain and important (e.g., stressors).

Do you feel stressed? If so, join the crowd (see OB Poll). **Stress** is a dynamic condition in which an individual is confronted with an opportunity, demand, or resource related to what the individual desires and for which the outcome is perceived to be both uncertain and important.[107] This is a complicated definition. Let's look at its components more closely.

Although stress is typically discussed in a negative context, it also has a positive purpose.[108] In response to stress, your nervous system, hypothalamus, pituitary, and adrenal glands supply you with stress hormones to cope. Your heartbeat and breathing accelerate to increase oxygen, while your muscles tense for action.[109] This is a time when stress offers potential gain. Consider, for example, the superior performance that an athlete or stage performer gives in a clutch situation. Such individuals often use stress positively to rise to the occasion and perform at their maximum. Similarly, many professionals see the pressures of heavy workloads and deadlines as positive challenges that enhance the quality of their work and the satisfaction they get from their job. However, when the situation is negative, stress is harmful and may hinder your progress by elevating your blood pressure uncomfortably and creating an erratic heart rhythm as you struggle to speak and think logically.[110]

challenge stressors Stressors associated with workload, pressure to complete tasks, and time urgency.

hindrance stressors Stressors that keep you from reaching your goals, for example, red tape, office politics, and confusion over job responsibilities.

Stressors Researchers have argued that **challenge stressors**—or stressors associated with workload, pressure to complete tasks, and time urgency—operate quite differently from **hindrance stressors**—or stressors that keep you from reaching your goals (for example, red tape, office politics, confusion over job responsibilities).[111] Evidence suggests that both challenge and hindrance stressors lead to strain, although hindrance stressors lead to increased levels of strain.[112] Challenge stressors (when they are stable over time) lead to more motivation, engagement, and performance than hindrance stressors.[113] Hindrance stressors, on the

OB POLL

Many Employees Feel Extreme Stress

Source: Based on J. Hudson, "High Stress Has Employees Seeking Both Wellness and Employee Assistance Help," ComPsych Corporation press release, November 12, 2014, http://www.compsych.com/press-room/press-releases-2014/818-nov-12-2014.

other hand, appear to have more of a negative effect on safety compliance and participation, employee engagement, job satisfaction, organizational commitment, performance, and withdrawal than do challenge stressors.[114]

Researchers have sought to clarify the conditions under which each type of stress exists. It appears that time pressure and learning demands both act as challenge stressors that can help employees learn and thrive in organizations.[115] Unnecessary tasks block the potentially positive nature of the normally challenging stressors, such as time pressure.[116] Hindrances (e.g., a lack of resources to complete your job) serve to block goal attainment and should be distinguished from threats, which can result in personal harm (e.g., corrections officers fearing harm from inmates).[117]

demands Responsibilities, pressures, obligations, and even uncertainties that individuals face in the workplace.

resources Factors within an individual's control that can be used to resolve demands.

Demands and Resources More typically, stress is associated with demands and resources. **Demands** are responsibilities, pressures, obligations, and uncertainties that individuals face in the workplace. **Resources** are factors within an individual's control that he or she can use to resolve the demands. Let's discuss what this demands–resources model means.[118]

When you take a test at school or undergo your annual performance review at work, you feel stress because you confront opportunities and performance pressures. A good performance review may lead to a promotion, greater responsibilities, and a higher salary. A poor review may prevent you from getting a promotion. An extremely poor review might even result in your being fired. To the extent you can apply resources to the demands on you—such as preparing for the review, putting the review in perspective (it's not the end of the world), or obtaining social support—you will feel less stress.[119] In fact, this last resource—social support—may be more important on an ongoing basis than anything else. According to recent research on Dutch elementary school teachers, when school principals exhibit transformational leadership behaviors (see Chapter 12), their teachers' engagement is sustained in the presence of challenge stressors and buffered from negative effects when hindrance demands are present.[120] Overall, under the demands–resources perspective, having resources to cope with stress is just as important in offsetting stress as demands are in increasing it.[121]

Allostasis The discussion so far may give you the impression that individuals are seeking a steady state in which demands match resources perfectly. While early research tended to emphasize such a *homeostatic*, or balanced, equilibrium perspective, it has now become clear that no single ideal state exists. Instead, it's more accurate to talk about *allostatic* models in which demands shift, resources shift, and systems of addressing imbalances shift.[122] By **allostasis**, we work to find stability by changing our behaviors and attitudes. It all depends on the allostatic load, or the cumulative effect of stressors on us given the resources we draw upon.[123] For example, if you're feeling especially confident in your abilities and have lots of support from others, you may increase your willingness to experience strain and be better able to mobilize coping resources. This would be a situation where the allostatic load was not too great; in other cases where the allostatic load is too great and too prolonged, we may experience psychological or physiological stress symptoms.

allostasis Working to change behavior and attitudes to find stability.

Stress preferences change in cycles. You've experienced this when you sometimes just feel like relaxing and recovering, while at other times you welcome more stimulation and challenge. Much like organizations are in a constant state of change and flux, we respond to stress processes by continually adapting to both internal and external sources, and our stability is constantly redefined.

Potential Sources of Stress at Work

What causes stress? Let's examine the model in Exhibit 16-8.

Environmental Factors Just as environmental uncertainty influences the design of an organization's structure, it also influences stress levels among employees in that organization. Indeed, uncertainty is the biggest reason people have

Exhibit 16-8 A Model of Stress

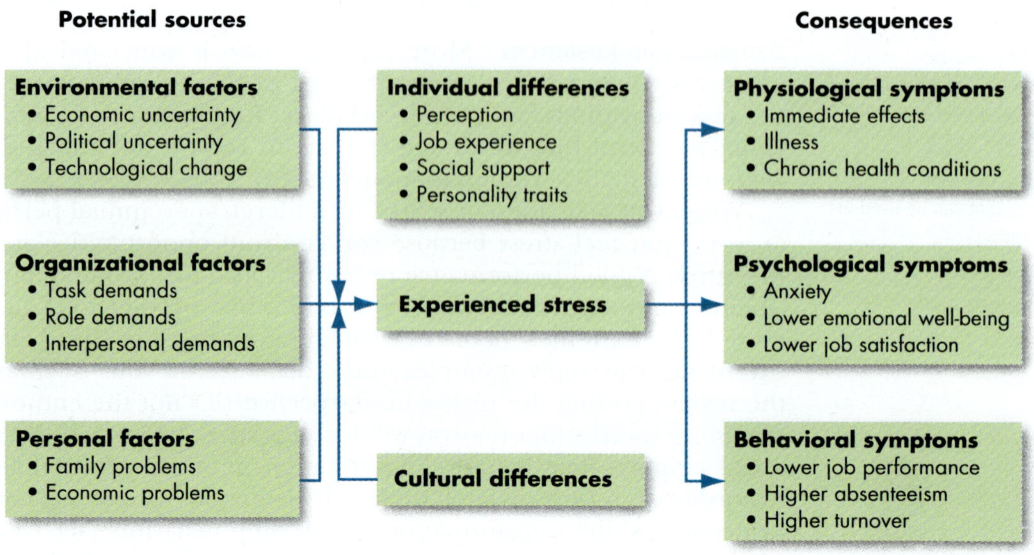

trouble coping with organizational changes.[124] There are three main types of environmental uncertainty: economic, political, and technological.

Changes in the business cycle create *economic uncertainties.* When the economy is contracting, for example, people become increasingly anxious about their job security. *Political uncertainties* don't tend to create stress among U.S citizens and Canadians as much as they do for employees in countries such as Haiti or Venezuela. The obvious reason is that the United States and Canada have more stable political systems, in which change is typically implemented in an orderly manner. Yet political threats and changes in all countries can induce stress. Because innovations can make an employee's skills and experience obsolete in a very short time, keeping up with new computer programs, robotics, automation, and similar forms of *technological change* is an additional challenge for many people at work that causes them stress.

Organizational Factors There is no shortage of factors within an organization that can cause stress. Pressures to avoid errors or complete tasks in a limited time, work overload, a demanding and insensitive boss, and unpleasant coworkers are a few examples. We've categorized these factors around task, role, and interpersonal demands.

Task demands relate to a person's job. They include the design of the job (including its degree of autonomy, task variety, and automation), working conditions, and the physical work layout. One factor consistently related to stress in the workplace is the amount of work that needs to be done, followed closely by the presence of looming deadlines.[125] Working in an overcrowded room or a visible location where noise and interruptions are constant can also increase anxiety and stress.[126]

Role demands relate to pressures placed on a person as a function of the particular role he or she plays in the organization.[127] Role conflicts create expectations that may be hard to reconcile or satisfy. Role overload occurs when the employee is expected to take on too much. Role ambiguity means role expectations are not clearly understood and the employee is not sure what to do. Unfortunately, individuals who face high situational constraints by their roles (such as fixed work hours or demanding job responsibilities) are less able to engage in the proactive coping behaviors, like taking a break, that reduce stress levels.[128] When faced with problems at work, they not only have higher levels of distress at the time, but they are also less likely to take steps to eliminate stressors in the future.

Interpersonal demands are pressures created by other employees. Some pressures are expected, but a rapidly growing body of research has shown that negative coworker and supervisor behaviors, including fights, bullying, incivility, abusive supervision, and racial/sexual harassment, are very strongly related to stress at work.[129] Interpersonal mistreatment can have effects at a physiological level, with one study finding that unfair treatment in a controlled setting triggered the release of cortisol, a hormone involved in the stress-reaction process.[130] Individuals who believe they are experiencing a social climate of discrimination from multiple sources over time have higher levels of psychological strain, even after accounting for differing baseline levels of well-being.[131] Social exclusion, perhaps as a form of interpersonal mistreatment, can also be a significant source of psychological strain. One study found that experiences of ostracism may have even more negative effects than experiences of interpersonal conflict.[132]

Personal Factors The typical individual may work between 40 and 50 hours a week. But the experiences and problems people encounter in the other

Career OBjectives

How can I bring my team's overall stress level down?

My coworkers and I are under a lot of pressure because we have a huge deadline coming up. We're working a lot of extra hours, and tensions are starting to ramp up to arguments. Is there any way I can get my team to chill out?

— Hakim

Dear Hakim:

It sounds like you're facing some of the core issues that produce stress at work: high demands, critical outcomes, and time pressure. There's no question tempers can start to flare under these conditions. While it may not even be desirable to get your team to relax, or chill out as you say, lowering your team's aggregate stress level will increase your group's effectiveness. Fortunately, there are some well-established ways to help lower stress in groups. Some of the most effective are directly related to getting people to recommit to the team:

- *To help minimize infighting, get the group to focus on a common goal.* Shared objectives are one of the most effective ways to reduce conflict in times of stress, and they remind everyone that cooperation is key.
- *Review what the team has done and what steps toward the goal remain.* When the team can see how much work they have accomplished, they will naturally feel better.
- *When the team feels most tense, take a collective temporary break.* It can be difficult to step away from a project with heavy time demands, but working at a point of maximum tension and conflict is often counterproductive. A chance to stop and gain perspective helps everyone recharge and focus.

Remember that minimizing team stress shouldn't happen through lowering standards and accepting lower-quality work but through reducing counterproductive organizational behavior. A positive work environment with high member engagement will do a lot to move the group forward. A combination of focus, progress, and perspective will ultimately be the best approach to limiting your stress.

Sources: Based on P. M. Poortvliet, F. Anseel, and F. Theuwis, "Mastery-Approach and Mastery-Avoidance Goals and Their Relation with Exhaustion and Engagement at Work: The Roles of Emotional and Instrumental Support," *Work & Stress* 29 (April 2015): 150–70; J. P. Trougakos, D. J. Beal, B. H. Cheng, I. Hideg, and D. Zweig, "Too Drained to Help: A Resource Depletion Perspective on Daily Interpersonal Citizenship Behaviors," *Journal of Applied Psychology* 100 (2015): 227–36; and J. P. Trougakos, I. Hideg, B. H. Cheng, and D. J. Beal, "Lunch Breaks Unpacked: The Role of Autonomy as a Moderator of Recovery during Lunch," *Academy of Management Journal* 57 (2014): 405–21.

The opinions provided here are of the managers and authors only and do not necessarily reflect those of their organizations. The authors or managers are not responsible for any errors or omissions, or for the results obtained from the use of this information. In no event will the authors or managers, or their related partnerships or corporations thereof, be liable to you or anyone else for any decision made or action taken in reliance on the opinions provided here.

120-plus hours can spill over to the job. The final category of sources of stress at work includes factors of an employee's personal life: family issues and personal economic problems.

National surveys consistently show that people hold family and personal relationships dear.[133] *Family issues*, even good ones, can cause stress that has a significant impact on individuals.[134] Family issues are often closely related to work–life conflict. The relationship becomes a vicious cycle: Work–life conflict affects stress levels, which in turn affect work–life conflict.[135]

Regardless of income level, financial issues can be a major source of stress. People who make $100,000 per year seem to have as much trouble handling their finances as those who earn $20,000, although recent research indicates that those who make under $50,000 per year do experience more stress.[136] The *personal economic problems* of overextended financial resources create stress and siphon attention away from work.

Stressors Are Additive When we review stressors individually, it's easy to overlook that stress is an additive phenomenon—it builds up.[137] For example, when you experience incivility from customers or coworkers, this can lead you to have a poor night's sleep and experience additional strain beyond the incivility you just experienced.[138] Each new and persistent stressor adds to an individual's stress level. So a single stressor may be relatively unimportant in and of itself, but if added to an already high level of stress, it can be too much. To appraise the total amount of stress an individual is under, we have to add all of the sources and severity levels of that person's stress. Because this cannot be easily quantified or observed, managers should remain aware of the potential stress loads from organizational factors in particular. Many employees are willing to express their perceived stress load at work to a caring manager.

Individual Differences

Some people thrive on stressful situations, while others are overwhelmed by them. What differentiates people in terms of their ability to handle stress? What individual variables moderate the relationship between *potential* stressors and *experienced* stress? At least four are relevant—perception, job experience, social support, and personality traits.

Perception In Chapter 6, we demonstrated that employees react in response to their perception of reality rather than to reality itself. *Perception* moderates the relationship between a potential stress condition and an employee's reaction to it. Layoffs may cause one person to fear losing his job, while another sees an opportunity to get a large severance allowance and start her own business. Those who perceive a stressful event as a small blip in an otherwise long timeline (and who take to heart phrases such as "this, too, shall pass" and "time heals all wounds") tend to cope better than those who focus on immediate circumstances.[139] So stress potential doesn't lie in objective conditions; rather, it lies in an employee's interpretation of those conditions.

During the pandemic the importance of physical and mental health of the patients became very important at Wipro. The company launched an employee wellness app to support employees' physical and emotional wellbeing. Other programs that were also started included employee assistance programmes, availability of counselors, and indoor fitness challenges.[140]

Source: Sundry Photography.shutterstock.com

Job Experience *Experience* on the job tends to be negatively related to work stress. Why? Two explanations have been offered.[141] First is selective withdrawal. Voluntary turnover is more probable among people who experience more stress. Therefore, people who remain with an organization longer are those with more stress-resistant traits or those more resistant to the stress characteristics of the organization. Second, people eventually develop coping mechanisms to deal with stress. Because this takes time, senior members of the organization are more likely to be fully adapted and should experience less stress.

Social Support *Social support*—collegial relationships with coworkers or supervisors—can buffer the impact of stress.[142] This is among the best-documented relationships in the stress literature. Social support acts as a palliative, mitigating the negative effects of even high-strain jobs.[143]

Personality Traits Stress symptoms expressed on the job may originate in the person's personality.[144] Perhaps the most widely studied *personality trait* in research on stress is neuroticism, which we discussed in Chapter 5. As you might expect, neurotic individuals are more prone to experience psychological strain.[145] Evidence suggests that neurotic individuals are more likely to find stressors in their work environments, so they believe their environments are more threatening. They also tend to select less adaptive coping mechanisms, relying on avoidance as a way of dealing with problems rather than attempting to resolve them.[146]

Workaholism is another personal characteristic related to stress levels.[147] Workaholics are people obsessed with their work; they put in an enormous number of hours, think about work even when not working, and create additional work responsibilities to satisfy an inner compulsion to work more. In some ways, they might seem like ideal employees. That's probably why, when most people are asked in interviews what their greatest weakness is, they reflexively say, "I just work too hard." However, there is a difference between working hard and working compulsively. Workaholics are not necessarily more productive than other employees, despite their extreme efforts. The strain of putting in such a high level of work effort eventually begins to wear on the person, leading to higher levels of work–life conflict and psychological burnout.[148]

Cultural Differences

Research suggests that the job conditions that cause stress show some differences across cultures. One study revealed that, whereas U.S. employees were stressed by a lack of control, Chinese employees were stressed by job evaluations and lack of training.[149] It doesn't appear that personality effects on stress are different across cultures, however. One study of employees in Hungary, Italy, the United Kingdom, Israel, and the United States found Type A personality traits (see Chapter 5) predicted stress equally well across countries.[150] A study of over 5,000 managers from 20 countries found individuals from individualistic countries such as the United States, Canada, and the United Kingdom experienced higher levels of stress due to work interfering with family than did individuals from collectivist countries in Asia and Latin America.[151] The authors proposed that this may occur because, in collectivist cultures, working extra hours is seen as a sacrifice to help the family, whereas in individualistic cultures, work is seen as a means of personal achievement that takes away from the family.

Consequences of Stress at Work

16-6 Identify the physiological, psychological, and behavioral symptoms of stress at work.

Strain shows itself in a number of ways, such as high blood pressure, ulcers, irritability, difficulty making routine decisions, changes in appetite, accident proneness, and the like. Refer back to Exhibit 8-8. These symptoms fit under three general categories: physiological, psychological, and behavioral symptoms.

Physiological Symptoms Most early concern with stress was directed at physiological symptoms because most researchers were specialists in the health and medical sciences. Their work led to the conclusion that stress could create changes in metabolism, increase heart and breathing rates and blood pressure, bring on headaches, and induce heart attacks.[152]

Evidence now clearly suggests stress may have other harmful physiological effects, including backaches, headaches, eye strain, sleep disturbances, dizziness, fatigue, loss of appetite, and gastrointestinal problems.[153] A study of hourly care workers showed that negative interactions with their supervisors led to heightened blood pressure and poor recovery from work (in other words, an inability to "re-charge" after work).[154] Still another study conducted with Canadian day-shift workers found that higher levels of psychological demands and overcommitment were related to significantly increased variation in cortisol levels.[155] Many other studies have shown similar results linking work stress to a variety of indicators of poor health.

The effects of stress and strain on sleep (see also Myth or Science?) have piqued the interests of researchers in particular, with the majority of studies suggesting that strain has a moderate impact on job attitudes (especially when it comes to sleep quality over quantity).[156] A variety of different types of work-related stressors have been shown to impair sleep quality; such stressors include unfinished work tasks. Social stressors and conflict between part-time work demands and school demands can have a great impact on sleep for college students.[157] Additional research suggests that, beyond the obvious solution of getting more, good-quality sleep, physical activity and recovery experiences with social support groups can help.[158]

Psychological Symptoms Job dissatisfaction is an obvious symptom of stress. But stress shows itself in other psychological states—for instance, tension, anxiety, irritability, boredom, and procrastination. One study that tracked physiological responses of employees over time found that stress due to high workloads was related to lower emotional well-being.[159]

Jobs that make multiple and conflicting demands or that lack clarity about the employee's duties, authority, and responsibilities increase both strain and dissatisfaction.[160] Similarly, the less control people have over the pace of their work, the greater their strain and dissatisfaction, a finding that has been replicated across 63 countries.[161] Jobs that provide a low level of variety, significance, autonomy, feedback, and identity appear to create strain and reduce satisfaction and involvement in the job.[162] Not everyone reacts to autonomy in the same way, however. For those with an external locus of control, increased job control increases the tendency to experience strain and exhaustion.[163]

Behavioral Symptoms Research on behavior and stress has been conducted across several countries and over time, and the relationships appear relatively consistent. Behavior-related stress symptoms include reductions in productivity; increases in absences, safety incidents, and turnover; changes in eating

Myth or Science?

When You're Working Hard, Sleep Is Optional

This statement is false. Individuals who do not get enough sleep are unable to perform well on the job. One study found that sleeplessness costs U.S. employers $63.2 billion per year, almost $2,300 per employee, partially due to decreased productivity and increased safety issues. Sleep deprivation has been cited as a contributing factor in heart disease, obesity, stroke, and cancer. It can also lead to disastrous accidents. For example, U.S. military researchers report that sleep deprivation is one of the top causes of friendly fire (when soldiers mistakenly fire on their own troops), and 20 percent of auto accidents are due to drowsy drivers. More than 160 people on Air India Flight 812 from Dubai to Mangalore were killed when pilot Zlatko Glusica awoke from a nap and, suffering from sleep inertia, overshot the runway in one of India's deadliest air crashes.

Sleeplessness affects the performance of millions of workers. According to research, one-third of U.S. employees in most industries, and more than one-quarter of workers in the finance and insurance industry, are sleep deprived, getting fewer than 6 hours of sleep per night (7 to 9 are recommended). More than 50 percent of U.S. adults age 19 to 29, 43 percent age 30 to 45, and 38 percent age 46 to 64 report that they rarely or never get a good night's sleep on weekdays.

Research has shown that lack of sleep impairs our ability to learn skills and find solutions, which may be part of the reason law enforcement organizations, Super Bowl–winning football teams, and half the Fortune 500 companies employ so-called fatigue management specialists as performance consultants.

Along with sleeplessness, insomnia has been a growing problem. Recent research in Norway indicated that up to 34 percent of motor vehicle deaths during the 14-year study period might have been prevented if the people involved in the crashes hadn't displayed insomnia symptoms. Managers and employees increasingly take prescription sleep aids, attend sleep labs, and consume caffeine in efforts to either sleep better or reduce the effects of sleeplessness on their performance. These methods often backfire. Studies indicate that prescription sleep aids increase sleep time by only 11 minutes and cause short-term memory loss. The effects of sleep labs may not be helpful after the sessions are over. And the diminishing returns of caffeine, perhaps the most popular method of fighting sleep deprivation (74 percent of U.S. adults consume caffeine every day), require the ingestion of increasing amounts to achieve alertness, which can make users jittery before the effect wears off and leave them exhausted.

When you're working hard, it's easy to consider using sleep hours to get the job done and to think that the stress and adrenaline from working will keep you alert. It's also easy to consider artificial methods in attempts to counteract the negative impact of sleep deprivation. However, research indicates that when it comes to maximizing performance and reducing accidents, we are not good at assessing our impaired capabilities when we are sleep deprived. In the end, there is no substitute for a solid night's sleep.

Sources: Based on M. J. Breus, "Insomnia Could Kill You—By Accident," *The Huffington Post*, May 9, 2015, http://www.huffingtonpost.com/dr-michael-j-breus/insomnia-could-kill-you-by-accident_b_7235264.html; D. K. Randall, "Decoding the Science of Sleep," *The Wall Street Journal*, August 4–5, 2012, C1–C2; M. Sallinen, J. Onninen, K. Tirkkonen, M.-L. Haavisto, M. Harma, T. Kubo, et al., "Effects of Cumulative Sleep Restriction on Self-Perceptions While Multitasking," *Journal of Sleep Research* (June 2012): 273–81; and P. Walker, "Pilot Was Snoring before Air India Crash," *The Guardian*, November 17, 2010, www.guardian.co.uk/world/2010/nov/17/sleepy-pilot-blamed-air-india-crash.

habits; increased smoking or consumption of alcohol; rapid speech; fidgeting; and sleep disorders.[164]

A significant amount of research has investigated the stress–performance relationship. One proposed pattern of this relationship is the inverted U shown in Exhibit 16-9.[165] The logic underlying the figure is that low to moderate levels of stress stimulate the body and increase its ability to react. Individuals may perform tasks better, more intensely, or more rapidly. But too much stress places unattainable demands on a person, which result in lower performance. In spite

Exhibit 16-9 **The Proposed Inverted-U Relationship between Stress and Job Performance**

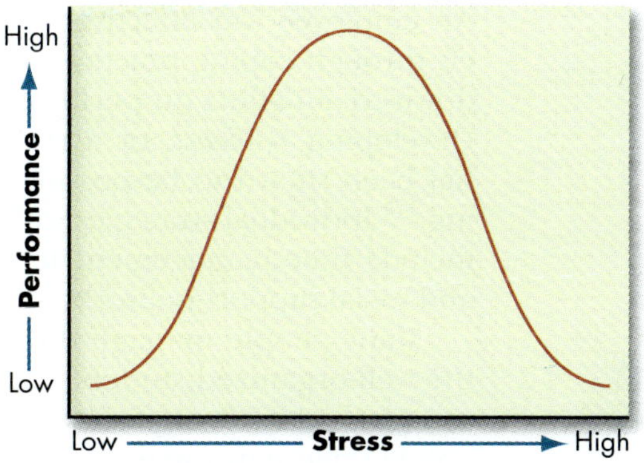

of its popularity and intuitive appeal, the inverted-U model hasn't earned a lot of empirical support.[166] Maybe the model misses links between stressors and felt stress and job performance, meaning that sometimes there are reasons we could be stressed but we feel fine because of positive moderating factors. We may be able to avoid letting stress affect our job performance.[167] For example, one study indicated that individuals with high emotional intelligence (EI; discussed in Chapter 4) may be able to mitigate the effects of job stress on performance.[168] Therefore, this model may be a good, neutral starting point from which to study differences.

As we mentioned earlier, researchers have begun to differentiate challenge and hindrance stressors, showing that these two forms of stress have opposite effects on job behaviors, especially job performance. A meta-analysis of responses from more than 35,000 individuals showed role ambiguity, role conflict, role overload, job insecurity, environmental uncertainty, and situational constraints were all consistently and negatively related to job performance.[169] There is also evidence that challenge stress improves job performance in a supportive work environment, whereas hindrance stress reduces job performance in all work environments.[170]

Managing Stress

16-7 Describe individual and organizational approaches to managing stress at work.

What should we do about stress? Should we do anything? Because low to moderate levels of stress can be functional and lead to higher performance, management may not be concerned when employees experience them; however, employees are likely to perceive even low levels of stress as undesirable. It's not unlikely, therefore, that employees and management have different notions of what constitutes an acceptable level of stress on the job. What management may consider to be "a positive stimulus that keeps the adrenaline running" is very likely to be seen as "excessive pressure" by the employee. Regardless, stress can lead to poor outcomes that even managers should be aware of; for example, research on over 4,000 caregivers across 35 different hospitals suggested that during a typical 12-hour shift without breaks, hand-washing and safety compliance reduced by 8.7 percent.[171] Keep this example in mind as we discuss individual and organizational approaches toward managing stress.[172]

Individual Approaches

An employee can effectively take personal responsibility for reducing stress levels through coping practices and recovery experiences, and doing so can have a downstream effect on performance, OCB, CWB, attitudes, and health at work.[173] Developing *resilience*, or a resistance to the adverse effects of stress and strain, has been shown to be possible over time through practice, coaching, and training.[174] Individual strategies within a resilience program that have proven effective include time management techniques, physical exercise, relaxation techniques, and social support networks.[175]

Many people manage their time poorly. The well-organized employee, like the well-organized student, may very well accomplish twice as much as the person who is poorly organized. A few of the best-known *time management techniques* are: (1) maintaining to-do lists; (2) scheduling activities based on priorities, not what you can accomplish; (3) doing the hard tasks first; and (4) scheduling distraction-free time to accomplish tasks. These time management skills can help minimize procrastination by focusing efforts on immediate goals and boosting motivation even in the face of tasks that are less enjoyable.[176] Furthermore, psychological techniques such as self-distancing from future stressors can help you adaptively cope with time pressure.[177]

Physicians have recommended noncompetitive *physical exercise*, such as aerobics, walking, jogging, swimming, and riding a bicycle, as a way to deal with excessive stress levels. These activities decrease the detrimental physiological responses to stress and allow us to recover from stress more quickly.[178]

Individuals can teach themselves to reduce tension through *relaxation techniques* such as meditation, mindfulness, and deep breathing.[179] The objective is to reach a state of deep physical relaxation in which you focus all your energy on the release of muscle tension.[180] Interestingly, the body's natural response of crying may help induce a state of self-soothing through deep breathing and heart rate regulation.[181] Deep relaxation for 20 minutes a day, twice a day, releases strain; provides a pronounced sense of peacefulness; and produces significant changes in heart rate, blood pressure, and other physiological factors.[182]

A growing body of research shows that simply taking breaks from work at routine intervals (e.g., lunch breaks, walks in the park) can facilitate psychological recovery, can reduce stress significantly, and may improve job performance, and these effects are even greater if relaxation techniques are employed.[183] Even very short *microbreaks* have been demonstrated to have an effect on employee stress relief and energy.[184] Furthermore, use of relaxation techniques during the day (and a lack of frustrating events) can help you relax when you get home—otherwise, you may have trouble doing so.[185] You might be tempted to think that complete detachment from work, or stiff boundaries between your work and leisure life, is good; however, research suggests that those who are *recovering ponderers*, or who do not completely detach and ponder over problems they need to resolve at work (but still engage in relaxation activities), tend to be *both* engaged *and* experience a substantial decrease in stress.[186]

As we have noted, friends, family, or work colleagues can provide an outlet when stress levels become excessive.[187] Expanding your *social support network* enables you to find someone to hear your problems and offer a more objective perspective on a stressful situation. Sometimes, however, these networks produce the opposite effect: If you do not try to expand your network and instead ruminate with similarly stressed friends, you can get caught in a vicious cycle.[188] That's why it is so important to be proactive and try to address your stress head on. But apart from rumination, support from family, friends, or spouses who help you recover from stressful work experiences can be mutually beneficial.[189]

Organizational Approaches

Several organizational factors that cause stress—particularly task and role demands—can be controlled by management. Strategies to consider include improved employee selection and job placement, training, goal setting,

An Ethical Choice

Manager and Employee Stress during Organizational Change

When organizations are in a state of change, employees feel the stress. In fact, a recent study indicated that job pressures, often due to downsizing and other organizational changes, are the second-leading cause of stress. Dealing with that stress was previously the domain of workers alone, who could turn to constructive (counselors, health professionals, support networks) or destructive (alcohol, gossip, counterproductive work behaviors) options as coping mechanisms. Employees who couldn't cope with stress suffered job burnout and headed to the unemployment line.

Beneficent employers provided employee assistance programs (EAPs) through subcontracted counselors or in-house HR departments to counsel employees dealing with stress. Managers simply steered individuals toward these resources when workplace problems indicated a need for intervention. This help often arrived too late to mitigate the negative outcomes of stress such as lost productivity and burnout—and sometimes it arrived too late to save the employee's job. Research suggests that continually occurring job stressors, such as when organizations are in the midst of change, reduce employee engagement because workers are deprived of recovery periods. Employee stress thus needs to be addressed proactively at the manager level if it is to be effective, before negative work outcomes appear.

Are managers ethically obligated to alleviate employee stress? On the one hand, managers are responsible for maximizing productivity and realize that organizations increase profitability when fewer employees produce and perform more. On the other hand, overwork will increase employee stress, particularly when the organization is in a state of change due to downsizing or growth. Managers who keep head count low and workloads high may realize short-term gains from lower workforce costs but long-term losses from negative stress outcomes, such as increased turnover and lowered productivity. Experts recommend that managers consider hiring the workers they need to keep employee workloads reasonable, adding reward programs to keep top employees engaged, and cutting nonworkforce costs to maintain profitability. Less conspicuous methods, such as teaching employees stress reduction techniques and creating a greenery room for a nature retreat from the office environment, can also be helpful. Managers must make the ethical choice between spending more money now on labor costs and stress reduction methods versus spending it later on the more hidden but salient costs of employee stress.

As research increasingly indicates, when employees react to stress, they and their organizations suffer the consequences. Therefore, managers must consider their opportunity to help alleviate the stress before it's too late.

Sources: Based on E. Frauenheim, "Stressed & Pressed," *Workforce Management* (January 2012): 18–22; J. B. Oldroyd and S. S. Morris, "Catching Falling Stars: A Human Resource Response to Social Capital's Detrimental Effect of Information Overload on Star Employees," *Academy of Management Review* 37 (2012): 396–418; and S. Sonnentag, E. J. Mojza, E. Demerouti, and A. B. Bakker, "Reciprocal Relations between Recovery and Work Engagement: The Moderating Role of Job Stressors," *Journal of Applied Psychology* 97 (2012): 42–53.

redesign of jobs, increased organizational communication, employee involvement, employee sabbaticals, and corporate wellness programs.

Selection and Placement, and Training Certain jobs are more stressful than others but, as we've seen, individuals differ in their response to stressful situations. We know individuals with little experience or an external locus of control tend to be more prone to stress. *Selection and placement* decisions should consider these factors. Obviously, management shouldn't hire only experienced individuals with an internal locus, but such individuals may adapt better to high-stress jobs and perform those jobs more effectively. Unfortunately, temporary employees who have the possibility of being hired are often at risk for experiencing heightened levels of stress associated with uncertainty and role ambiguity, which can in turn affect their chances of being hired.[190] Employees in these situations would do well to manage their impressions and develop a tolerance for ambiguity. Similarly, *training* can increase an individual's resilience and thus lessen job strain in these situations.[191]

Goal Setting We discussed *goal setting* in Chapter 7. Individuals perform better when they have specific and challenging goals and receive feedback on their progress toward these goals. Goals can reduce stress as well as provide motivation.[192] Employees who are highly committed to their goals and who see purpose in their jobs experience less stress because they are more likely to perceive stressors as challenges rather than hindrances. The type of goal also matters: When given a developmental, learning goal after negative feedback, employees tend to experience less tension and better performance than when they are given a performance target goal.[193] The employees' personality also matters: Goal setting and goal-focused leadership tend to be more successful in reducing stress for the conscientious but not for those who are low on emotional stability.[194]

Redesigning Jobs *Redesigning jobs* to give employees more responsibility, more meaningful work, more autonomy, and increased feedback can reduce stress because these factors give employees greater control over work activities and lessen dependence on others.[195] But as we noted in our discussion of work design, not all employees want enriched jobs. The right redesign for employees with a low need for growth might include less responsibility and increased specialization. If individuals prefer structure and routine, reducing skill variety should reduce uncertainties and stress levels. Organizations should be careful when deciding to structure work and organizations so that employees are on call 24 hours a day: Research suggests that workplace telepressure can impede the effectiveness of employee recovery experiences and increase stress.[196]

Employee Involvement Role stress is detrimental to a large extent because employees feel uncertain about goals, expectations, how they'll be evaluated, and the like. By giving employees a voice in the decisions that directly affect their job performance, management can increase employee control and reduce role stress. Thus, managers should consider increasing *employee involvement* in decision making because evidence clearly shows that increases in employee involvement and empowerment practices reduce psychological strain.[197]

Organizational Communication Increasing formal *organizational communication* with employees reduces uncertainty by lessening role ambiguity and role conflict.[198] Given the importance that perceptions play in moderating the stress–response relationship, management can also use effective communications as

Kingfisher B&Q employees undertake compulsory motivational exercises before the store opens. These last for around 20 minutes and have been brought in across the whole of the superstore network.
Source: 67photo/Alamy Stock Photo

a means to shape employee perceptions. Remember that what employees categorize as demands, threats, or opportunities at work is an interpretation and that interpretation can be affected by the symbols and actions communicated by management.

wellness programs Organizationally supported programs that focus on the employee's total physical and mental condition.

Employee Sabbaticals Some employees need an occasional escape from the frenetic pace of their work. Companies including Infosys, BCG, TCS, Accenture, PricewaterhouseCoopers (PwC), Goldman Sachs, The Cheesecake Factory Inc., VMware, and Adobe Systems have begun to provide extended voluntary leaves.[199] These *sabbaticals*—ranging in length from a few weeks to several months—allow employees to travel, relax, or pursue personal projects that consume time beyond normal vacations. One study of university faculty members suggests that sabbaticals increase job resources and well-being, especially when they have greater autonomy in how they spend their sabbatical.[200]

Wellness Programs Our final suggestion is organizationally supported **wellness programs**. These typically provide workshops to help people quit smoking, control alcohol use, lose weight, eat better, and develop a regular exercise program; they focus on the employee's total physical and mental condition.[201] Some programs help employees improve their psychological health as well. At the Phillips Innovation Centre in Bangalore, yoga sessions are held daily for employees to join voluntarily. Many employees feel that the practice of yoga makes them proactive and positive.[202] A meta-analysis of 36 programs designed to reduce stress (including wellness programs) showed that interventions to help employees reframe stressful situations and use active coping strategies appreciably reduced stress levels.[203] Wellness programs that help employees focus on developing the "good" kind of stress and becoming challenged through their work have also been introduced.[204] Most wellness programs assume that employees need to take personal responsibility for their physical and mental health and that the organization is merely a means to that end.

Most firms that have introduced wellness programs have found significant benefits. In a poll conducted by cult.fit, respondents said employee health and wellness programs improved employee engagement and employee productivity.[205] A study by ASSOCHAM shows that Indian companies can save up to $20 billion in a year if they adopt corporate wellness programs. The calculation is made by computing the 1 percent reduction in absenteeism.[205] However, the benefits workers experience appear to be contingent on how much they put into the program, the extent to which they participate, and their attitudes upon entering the program.[206] Other research sponsored by the U.S. Department of Labor and Department of Health and Human Services indicated that organizational wellness programs create healthier employees with fewer health risk factors.[207]

Summary

The need for change has been implied throughout this text. For instance, think about attitudes, motivation, work teams, communication, leadership, organizational structures, HR practices, and organizational cultures. Change was an integral part in our discussion of each. If environments were perfectly static, if employees' skills and abilities were always up to date and incapable of deteriorating, and if tomorrow were always exactly the same as today, organizational change would have little or no relevance to managers. But the real world is turbulent, requiring organizations and their members to undergo dynamic change if they are to perform at competitive levels. Coping with all these changes can be a source of stress, but with effective management, challenge can enhance engagement and fulfillment, leading to the high performance that is one major goal of the study of organizational behavior (OB), as you've discovered in this text.

Implications for Managers

- Consider that, as a manager, you are a change agent in your organization. The decisions you make and your role-modeling behaviors will help shape the organization's change culture.
- Your management policies and practices will determine the degree to which the organization learns and adapts to changing environmental factors.
- Some stress is good. Increasing challenges brought by autonomy and responsibility at work will lead to some stress, but they will also increase feelings of accomplishment and fulfillment. Hindrance stressors like bureaucracy and interpersonal conflicts, on the other hand, are entirely negative and should be eliminated.
- You can help alleviate harmful workplace stress for your employees by accurately matching workloads to employees, providing employees with stress-coping resources, and responding to employees' concerns.
- You can identify extreme stress in your employees when performance declines, turnover increases, health-related absenteeism increases, and engagement declines. By the time these symptoms are visible, however, it may be too late to be helpful, so stay alert for early indicators and be proactive.

Companies Should Encourage Stress Reduction

POINT

Companies make substantial investments in their employees, so the health and well-being of the workforce is a central concern. One of the most direct ways to provide assistance to employees is to engage in one of the stress-reduction interventions.

One major financial benefit of stress reduction programs is a reduction in health-related costs. Workplace stress leads to dozens of negative and expensive health-related consequences. Stress weakens the immune system, leading to increased illness and sick days. If employees feel extreme stress related to work, they may be more likely to come to work when they are contagious, leading to sickness for many others. Over the longer run, stress levels can also contribute to conditions like heart disease, which ultimately result in very expensive medical treatments. These medical treatments increase employer health insurance expenses.

Reductions in employee stress can facilitate job performance. Employees who are overburdened have difficulty concentrating, can lose energy and motivation at work, and find it difficult to think of new and creative ideas. Stress can also create conflicts with coworkers and lead to rude or hostile treatment of clients or customers. Ultimately, employees who are experiencing high levels of stress may leave, so all the costs of turnover are incurred.

Stress reduction programs also have an ethical component. The workplace generates a great deal of stress for many employees, so employers have a certain responsibility to offset its negative consequences. Stress reduction programs are a direct way to help employees feel better. When employers show concern for employees by helping reduce stress, employees feel more committed.

COUNTERPOINT

While employers may have a direct financial interest in certain elements of stress reduction, it's worth asking whether investing in stress reduction programs is actually a good idea.

The first problem is operational. Some stress reduction interventions are expensive, requiring professional facilitators or exercise equipment. These can take a long time to show financial returns, and the up-front costs of researching, designing, and implementing them are substantial. A growing number of corporations report that the expected returns on investment in wellness programs have failed to materialize. And the time employees spend in stress reduction interventions is time they spend not working.

Another problem is that stress reduction programs are invasive. Should your boss or other individuals in the workplace tell you how you're supposed to feel? Many stress reduction programs step even further into employees' personal lives by encouraging open discussions about sources of stress. Do you really want your manager and coworkers to know why you're experiencing stress? The more that sensitive topics related to stress are discussed, the harder it is to keep work relationships professional.

A final concern is that it is too hard to draw the line between stress from work and general life stress. A company's stress reduction program may try to target problems of work overload or social conflict, but these issues often affect other areas of life. How should a stress reduction program operate when the reasons for employee stress come, say, from a sick relative or conflicts with family members?

Organizations often mean well, but it may be more important to let employees keep their private lives private.

Sources: Based on L. Vanderkam, "The Dark Side of Corporate Wellness Programs," *Fast Company*, June 8, 2015, http://www.fastcompany.com/3047115/the-dark-side-of-corporate-wellness-programs; D. R. Stover and J. Wood, "Most Company Wellness Programs Are a Bust," *Gallup Business Journal*, February 4, 2015, http://www.gallup.com/businessjournal/181481/company-wellness-programs-bust.aspx; and A. Frakt and A. E. Carroll, "Do Wellness Programs Work? Usually Not," *New York Times*, September 11, 2014, http://www.nytimes.com/2014/09/12/upshot/do-workplace-wellness-programs-work-usually-not.html.

CHAPTER REVIEW

QUESTIONS FOR REVIEW

16-1 What are the differences between the forces for change and planned change?

16-2 How can resistance to change be overcome?

16-3 What are the four main approaches to managing organizational change?

16-4 How can managers create a culture for change?

16-5 What are the potential environmental, organizational, and personal sources of stress at work and the role of individual and cultural differences?

16-6 What are the physiological, psychological, and behavioral symptoms of stress at work?

16-7 What are the individual and organizational approaches to managing stress?

APPLICATION AND EMPLOYABILITY

In this chapter, you were introduced to the many ways in which change affects organizations, including the development of employee stress and strain. You learned about several techniques to manage your stress levels. Understanding organizational change can help you become more employable because change is a constant in organizations. Learning to adapt and manage change can help you progress and succeed at work. One day, you may be behind a major organizational change effort. If you find yourself in that position, you can draw on your knowledge of organizational change management efforts to make sure that the change is implemented smoothly. Knowing how to manage your stress levels can help you become more employable because you will be able to be productive in spite of the stress. Also, challenging stressors and goals can help motivate you and lead to great accomplishments. If you find yourself managing people someday, you have learned a variety of options for helping your employees manage their stress levels. In this chapter, you have improved your social responsibility skills by becoming aware of the dangers of a lack of sleep, considered how to handle team stress and conflict, learned how to manage stress during organizational change, and debated whether or not companies should be involved in stress reduction efforts. In the next section, you will continue to build these skills, along with your critical thinking and knowledge application and analysis skills, by reflecting on major events at work and how they influence your understanding of business, considering the negative effects of presenteeism, learning how organizations can improve employee stress levels, and becoming aware of the adverse effects of employee loneliness and what to do about it.

EXPERIENTIAL EXERCISE Making Employees Less Resistant to Change

As mentioned in this chapter, employees are often resistant to change as they are afraid of losing the status quo and the privileges accumulated over the course of their career. Now, let us suppose that your team, which has several years of experience in change management, has been hired by a leading business school that is facing an imminent merger with one of its competitors, located 500 miles away from the historical campus site.

The management of the school told you that the merger is essential to survive and compete in the market of higher education due to increasing competition and greater mobility of students who encounter fewer and fewer barriers to studying abroad. After some informal meetings with professors and other staff, you realized that professors have mixed feelings about the merger. Some are worried about the possibility that the school management will ask them to move or teach in the other campus. Many others are excited about the merger as they have already developed research relationships with colleagues in the other university. In general, your team feels that it won't be a problem to convince the others to support the change, and you have picked out two or three influential professors who can help you convince all the others.

The staff worries you more, as it is generally more negative about the change and, in several instances, they consciously acted to sabotage the merger. Many are afraid of losing their job, especially those holding positions of responsibility, as these positions are already filled in the other institution, and most think that the merger will cause extra work since new procedures need to be developed or old ones updated. Many people are skeptical about the reasons for the change and complain about the lack of information received so far. For example, many do not understand why a change is needed right now given that the number of students has been increasing year after year. Some have told you they have no faith in the management and believe the merger is just a way to scale and reduce costs. A general concern is that all managerial positions will be assigned to new people or those coming from the other institution.

Your team is worried about the success of the merger, but you believe that, with the right actions and choices, the staff's resistance can be won. On the basis of what you have read in this chapter and your experience of change in life, think of a possible plan to communicate to the management of the business school how they can make employees more willing to embrace the changes to come. Make a list of interventions, dividing them on the basis of priority and necessary people involved.

Questions

16-8. Was it easy for your team to reach a consensus about the recommendations to propose to the management of the business school? Which were the elements on which you disagreed, if any? How did you handle such disagreement?

16-9. How do you think organizations can train their employees to be less resistant to change? Why do you think faculty members are more willing to change than administrative staff?

16-10. Staff complained about the lack of information from the management before and during the merger process. How can managers of organizations involved in such delicate operations balance the need to inform employees and the need to maintain confidentiality?

ETHICAL DILEMMA The Fear of Redundancy and Ceasing Operations

Better.com, Cognizant, SpiceJet, Eli Lilly, BookMyShow, Bajaj Electricals are among the thousands of organizations that laid off employees in the last two years. According to the records of Registrar of Companies, more than 10,000 companies have closed down and their workers laid off in 2021 itself. All these companies have faced financial troubles and strains on their existence. As the companies have struggled, so have the people who worked for them. This is because some of these companies have ceased operations and trading while others have announced massive redundancies in anticipation of economic struggles and uncertainty, political instability or industry decline, or even unexpected increase in operating costs, all of which have led to employee layoffs.

In the case of Spice Jet and Better.com thousands of employees were made redundant within a short period of time. Some of these were introduced as planned and incremental changes, but most of these changes were abrupt, drastic, and rather forced, acting as a shock to the workforce staff. Situations like this constitute a stressful situation for both the management and the employees, as they can challenge trust relations and jeopardize individual and group performance as well as disrupt and confuse the group dynamics in many ways. Redundancy can also impede motivation for the staff remaining in their posts and generate stress for both those being made redundant as well as those who have to pick up after the former—not an easily accepted situation for those leaving or those remaining. In the new responsibilities and the workload, the remaining staff are also left worrying about their own future. In both cases, the stress created needs to be managed in the best possible manner. Support, mentoring, and consultations are vital for enhancing the skills and knowledge required in the new state of affairs as well as enhancing employee morale. Additionally, change needs to be planned and prepared for to the extent possible, rather than carrying it out abruptly and at the expense of employees.

Questions

16-11. Which were the main forces for change in the organizations presented above? How could these changes have been managed? How could the companies have resisted change?

16-12. How could Appreciative Inquiry be applied in the case of a redundancy period to motivate and improve performance of the remaining staff?

16-13. What type of stressors could be created in a redundancy scenario, and where are these generated? Discuss how a company that is undergoing redundancy procedures can manage the stress generated for all affected parties.

Sources: Alan Tovey, "Steel Industry Suffers New Blow with More Job Cuts in Sheffield," *The Telegraph,* March 16, 2016, http://www.telegraph.co.uk/business/2016/03/14/steel-industry-suffers-new-blow-with-more-job-cuts-in-sheffield/; James Field "Birmingham Cuts Jobs ahead of REF 2021," Research Fortnight, March 9, 2016, http://www.researchresearch.com/news/article/?articleId=1358723; Phillip Inman, "HSBC Starts Laying Off 840 IT Staff in UK," *The Guardian,* May 16, 2016, https://www.theguardian.com/business/2016/may/16/hsbc-job-losses-840-it-staff-uk; Dan Milmo, "Easyjet Cuts Luton East Midlands Flights," *The Guardian,* September 3, 2009, https://www.theguardian.com/business/2009/sep/03/easyjet-cuts-luton-east-midlands-flights; ITV News, "Thousands of BHS Staff to Be Told of Redundancies," July 26, 2017, http://www.itv.com/news/2016-07-25/thousands-of-bhs-staff-to-be-told-of-redundancies/; BBC News, "Monarch Flights Cancelled as Airline Ceases Trading," October 2, 2017, http://www.bbc.co.uk/news/business-41464934; Ravender Sembhy, "EasyJet Confirms Acquisition of Air Berlin Assets," *The Independent,* December 18, 2017, http://www.independent.co.uk/news/business/news/easyjet-air-berlin-deal-buy-tegel-airport-opeations-flying-crew-landing-slots-bankrupt-airline-a8116046.html, Frances Perraudin, "Manchester University Professors Sign Letter of No Confidence Over Cuts," *The Guardian,* June 5, 2017, https://www.theguardian.com/education/2017/jun/05/manchester-university-job-cuts-professors-sign-letter-no-confidence.

CASE INCIDENT 1 Sprucing Up Walmart

For more than half a century, Walmart has prided itself on providing value to customers by being a low-price leader. But the consumer mindset is changing. Now "value" also means convenience, ease of finding what you want, and the ability to get exactly what you want when you want it. Nationwide dollar-store chains often have lower prices than Walmart, so that point of competitive advantage is fading. And thanks to Amazon.com and other online retailers, consumers can shop from home whenever they like, compare prices, and know immediately what is available.

Contrast this with the experience many Walmart shoppers previously had when they entered a store—low inventory, disorganized aisles, unhelpful staff, and an overall depressing atmosphere. The company's online presence was about the same. The site was difficult to navigate, and attempts to search for products were frustrating at best and more often fruitless.

Named Walmart's CEO in 2014, Doug McMillon set out to change this situation. "What people think about the company is important," he noted. And at the moment, people weren't thinking about value and low prices when they thought about Walmart. McMillon enacted a number of changes. First, the company had earned a reputation of treating its store employees poorly—low wages, few benefits—while profits were in the billions of dollars, so Walmart announced it would increase its minimum wage.

Second, the company asked for and paid more attention to employee feedback. Recurring issues included the dress code, store music, and even store temperatures. So clothing rules were relaxed, more variety in music was introduced, and thermostats were adjusted. The company hopes improving employee morale will translate into a better experience for customers, thereby changing some of the negative images.

Walmart's Web presence was another target for big changes. Amazon is the store's biggest competitor, and McMillon wanted to offer customers more items, pickup options, and ways to meet their needs and demands—for example, an online grocery ordering service. This means a new way of thinking about marketing and inventory across the board.

McMillon was able to see how consumers have changed not only what they want but also the way they want it—whether from the hands of happy employees or with the simple click of a mouse. The question remains: Will his actions be enough to change the way consumers see Walmart?

Questions

16-14. What key factors do you think prompted Walmart to change? Do these factors exemplify the change pressures discussed in the chapter? Why or why not?

16-15. What results from Walmart's changes do you predict?

16-16. Describe how McMillon acted as a change agent in this situation.

Sources: Based on S. Halzack, "Why Walmart Is Ditching Its Celine Dion Soundtrack and Getting a DJ," *Washington Post*, June 3, 2015, http://www.washingtonpost.com/news/business/wp/2015/06/03/why-Walmart-is-ditching-its-celine-dion-soundtrack-and-getting-a-deejay/; B. Ritholtz, "Walmart Learns to Live without Everyday Poverty Wages," *Bloomberg View*, June 11, 2015, http://www.bloombergview.com/articles/2015-06-11/Walmart-lives-without-everyday-poverty-wages; and B. O'Keefe, "The Man Who's Reinventing Walmart," *Fortune*, June 4, 2015, http://fortune.com/2015/06/04/walmart-ceo-doug-mcmillon/.

CASE INCIDENT 2 Sweat the Stress

According to a 2016 report by the Health and Safety Executive, a public body in the United Kingdom, stress, depression, and anxiety cost UK industries £12.5 million in lost sick days. This accounted for 49 percent of all days lost due to ill health, and the trend is rising. The Institute of Directors, another British organization, reports that 98 percent of business leaders believe that good mental health is important to the performance of their organization. With 54 percent of its members saying that have been approached by staff suffering from mental ill health, it is clear that organizations need to develop new ways to address this increasing problem.

Like many large employers, the University of Leeds takes the health and well-being of its staff very seriously, providing a range of support services aimed at improving their psychological health. However, a new Wellness Programme aims to provide a different type of support. The pilot scheme, based in the Faculty of Engineering, offers employees a 12-week program that provides one-on-one support with exercises, stress management, sleep management, and healthy lifestyle management. Those on the program have access to on-site gym facilities and bespoke training programs followed by a further six-month premium gym membership.

The more commonly known impacts of stress are on our psychological health, leading to a number of problems such as tension or anxiety. However, it can also lead to physiological problems, ranging from loss of appetite to heart attacks. The benefits of exercise to those suffering from mental health issues are well documented. The Mayo Clinic has touted the stress-busting benefits of exercise, and a review by the Society of Occupational Medicine found that workplace physical activity programs can have a positive impact on anxiety, symptoms of depression, and stress.

The targeted Wellness Programme at the University of Leeds aims to tackle the issues of stress at the earliest stage, before the negative effects are felt by the individual or the business. Heather Swinsco, the human resources professional who proposed the program, sees the issue of mental health as something which needs to be taken seriously. In a recent survey, the mental health charity Mind found that 30 percent of staff would not feel comfortable talking to a line manager about being stressed, while 14 percent said they had resigned as a result of stress, with a worrying further 42 percent saying they had considered it. The inability to talk about stress may result in still higher levels of sickness as the issues are not being addressed, and staying at work may have a negative impact on other employees, who now have to deal with their stressed co-worker. Swinsco felt that identifying individuals at this earlier stage and making direct referrals to the Wellness Programme would limit these negative effects.

Referral to the program was based on certain criteria, such as the length of time that the individual was expected to experience mental ill-health and whether they were willing and able to engage with the activities. Members of the pilot program will be monitored during the initial 12 weeks and after to assess the impact of the exercise on their mental wellbeing. Initial reports are encouraging, and overall positive outcomes may lead to the program being taken up by other areas of the University.

Questions

16-16. To what extent is this Wellness Programme tackling the causes of stress? How should employees be selected for this type of program? What issues might this cause?

16-18. Do you see any challenges in a full implementation of this sort of Wellness Programme for the organization? Explain your answer.

16-19. This type of program aims to reduce stress across the organization. What issues may impact successful uptake by staff?

Source: Health and Safety Executive, "Work-related Stress, Depression or Anxiety Statistics in Great Britain 2017," November 2017, http://www.hse.gov.uk/statistics/causdis/stress/stress.pdf; A. H. Y. Chu, D. Koh, F. M. Moy, and F. Müller-Riemenschneider, "Do Workplace Physical Activity Interventions Improve Mental Health Outcomes?", *Occupational Medicine* 64, no. 4, June 1, 2014: pp. 235–45, retrieved from https://academic.oup.com/occmed/article/64/4/235/1465341; Mayo Clinic Staff, "Exercise and Stress: Get moving to Manage Stress," Mayo Foundation for Medical Education and Research, March 8, 2018, https://www.mayoclinic.org/healthy-lifestyle/stress-management/in-depth/exercise-and-stress/art-20044469; Mind, "Taking Care of Your Staff," https://www.mind.org.uk/workplace/mental-health-at-work/taking-care-of-your-staff/; Director magazine, "Mental health: IoD calls for 'a little more conversation,'" March 2, 2017, https://www.director.co.uk/news-mental-health-iod-calls-little-conversation-2386/.

ENDNOTES

[1] A. Chowdhry, "Apple Surpassed Samsung as Global Phone Market Leader, Says Report," *Forbes*, March 3, 2015, http://www.forbes.com/sites/amitchowdhry/2015/03/04/apple-passes-samsung/.

[2] L. Goadsduff and A. A. Forni, "Gartner Says Worldwide Sales of Smartphones Grew 7 Percent in the Fourth Quarter of 2016," *Gartner: Newsroom* [Press Release], February 15, 2017, http://www.gartner.com/newsroom/id/3609817.

[3] Ibid.

[4] Ibid.

[5] A. Deutschman, "Change or Die," *Fast Company*, May 1, 2005, https://www.fastcompany.com/52717/change-or-die; A. Deutschman, *Change or Die: The Three Keys to Change at Work and in Life* (New York, NY: Harper Collins, 2007); and M. L. Stallard, "Will Your Company Navigate Change or Die?" *Fox Business*, March 24, 2015, http://www.foxbusiness.com/features/2015/03/24/will-your-company-navigate-change-or-die.html.

[6] W. F. Cascio and R. Montealegre, "How Technology Is Changing Work and Organizations," *Annual Review of Organizational Psychology and Organizational Behavior* 3 (2016): 349–75; D. L. Stone, D. L. Deadrick, K. M. Lukaszewski, and R. Johnson, "The Influence of Technology on the Future of Human Resource Management," *Human Resource Management Review* 25 (2015): 216–31.

[7] N. Fligstein and A. Goldstein, "The Roots of the Great Recession," in D. B. Grusky, B. Western, and C. Wimer (eds.), *The Great Recession* (New York, NY: Russell Sage Foundation, 2011): 21–56; B. Okay-Somerville and D. Scholarios, "A Multilevel Examination of Skills-Oriented Human Resource Management and Perceived Skill Utilization during Recession: Implications for the Well-Being of all Workers," *Human Resource Management* 58 (2019): 139–54; R. Rich, "The Great Recession," *Federal Reserve History*, November 22, 2013, https://www.federalreservehistory.org/essays/great_recession_of_200709; H. Smith, "A Year After the Crisis Was Declared Over, Greece Is Still Spiralling Down," *The Guardian*, August 13, 2016, https://www.theguardian.com/business/; and S. Wood, G. Michaelides, and C. Ogbonnaya, "Recessionary Actions and Absence: A Workplace-Level Study," *Human Resource Management* (in press).

[8] H. Smith, "A Year after the Crisis Was Declared Over, Greece Is Still Spiralling Down," *The Guardian*, August 13, 2016, https://www.theguardian.com/business/2016/aug/13/greek-economy-still-spiralling-down-year-after-crisis-declared-over.

[9] D. Clark, "How to Increase Your Corporate Agility," *Forbes*, November 24, 2014, https://www.forbes.com/sites/dorieclark/2014/11/24/how-to-increase-your-corporate-agility/#56f09028772d; and A. Setili, *The Agility Advantage: How to Identify and Act on Opportunities in a Fast-Changing World* (San Francisco, CA: Wiley, 2014).

[10] P. Mohan, "Clone Wars: Why Instagram Will Legally Get Away with Copying Snapchat Stories," *Fast Company*, August 5, 2016, https://www.fastcompany.com/3062593/clone-wars-why-instagram-will-legally-get-away-with-copying-snapchat-stories.

[11] P. Bansal and H.-C. Song, "Similar but Not the Same: Differentiating Corporate Sustainability from Corporate Responsibility," *Academy of Management Annals* 11, no. 1 (2017): 106–49.

[12] B. Casselman, P. Cohen, S. Cowley, C. Dougherty, N. Kulish, D. McCabe, and K. Weise, "Coronavirus Cost to Businesses and Workers: 'It Has All Gone to Hell,'" *The New York Times*, March 15, 2020, https://www.nytimes.com/2020/03/15/business/economy/coronavirus-economy-impact.html.

[13] D. L. Bradford and W. W. Burke (eds.), *Reinventing Organization Development: New Approaches to Change in Organizations* (San Francisco, CA: Pfeiffer, 2005).

[14] See, for instance, J. Birkinshaw, G. Hamel, and M. J. Mol, "Management Innovation," *Academy of Management Review* 33, no. 4 (2008): 825–45; and J. Welch and S. Welch, "What Change Agents Are Made Of," *BusinessWeek*, October 20, 2008, 96.

[15] See, for instance, S. Konlechner, M. Latzke, W. H. Güttel, E. Höfferer,

"Prospective Sensemaking, Frames and Planned Change Interventions: A Comparison of Change Trajectories in Two Hospital Units," *Human Relations* 72, no. 4 (2019): 706–32.

[16] M. Helft, "How the Tech Elite Plans to Reinvent Senior Care," *Forbes*, April 2, 2015, http://www.forbes.com/sites/miguelhelft/2015/04/02/how-the-tech-elite-plans-to-reinvent-senior-care.

[17] General Motors website, http://www.gm.com/company/corporate-officers/mary-barra, accessed July 22, 2015.

[18] R. J. Grossman, "Accelerating Change at GM," *HR Magazine* (June 2012): 58–64.

[19] General Motors website, http://www.gm.com/company/aboutGM/GM_Corporate_Officers/John_Quattrone.html, accessed July 22, 2015.

[20] See, for instance, P. G. Audia and S. Brion, "Reluctant to Change: Self-Enhancing Responses to Diverging Performance Measures," *Organizational Behavior and Human Decision Processes* 102 (2007): 255–69.

[21] M. Fugate, A. J. Kinicki, and G. E. Prussia, "Employee Coping with Organizational Change: An Examination of Alternative Theoretical Perspectives and Models," *Personnel Psychology* 61, no. 1 (2008): 1–36.

[22] R. B. L. Sijbom, O. Janssen, and N. W. Van Yperen, "How to Get Radical Creative Ideas into a Leader's Mind? Leader's Achievement Goals and Subordinates' Voice of Creative Ideas," *European Journal of Work and Organizational Psychology* 24 (2015): 279–96.

[23] D. R. King, F. Bauer, Q. D. Weng, S. Schriber, and S. Tarba, "What, When, and Who: Manager Involvement in Predicting Employee Resistance to Acquisition Integration," *Human Resource Management* 59 (2020): 63–81.

[24] J. D. Ford, L. W. Ford, and A. D'Amelio, "Resistance to Change: The Rest of the Story," *Academy of Management Review* 33, no. 2 (2008): 362–77.

[25] Q. N. Huy, K. G. Corley, and M. S. Kraatz, "From Support to Mutiny: Shifting Legitimacy Judgments and Emotional Reactions Impacting the Implementation of Radical Change," *Academy of Management Journal* 57, no. 6 (2014): 165–80.

[26] R. K. Smollan, "The Multi-Dimensional Nature of Resistance to Change," *Journal of Management & Organization* 17, no. 6 (2011): 828–49.

[27] P. C. Fiss and E. J. Zajac, "The Symbolic Management of Strategic Change: Sensegiving via Framing and Decoupling," *Academy of Management Journal* 49, no. 6 (2006): 1173–93.

[28] A. E. Rafferty and S. L. D. Restubog, "The Impact of Change Process and Context on Change Reactions and Turnover during a Merger," *Journal of Management* 36, no. 5 (2010): 1309–38.

[29] S. Fuchs and R. Prouska, "Creating Positive Employee Change Evaluation: The Role of Different Levels of Organizational Support and Change Participation," *Journal of Change Management* 14, no. 3 (2014): 361–83.

[30] Q. N. Huy, "Emotional Balancing of Organizational Continuity and Radical Change: The Contribution of Middle Managers," *Administrative Science Quarterly* (March 2002): 31–69; D. M. Herold, D. B. Fedor, and S. D. Caldwell, "Beyond Change Management: A Multilevel Investigation of Contextual and Personal Influences on Employees' Commitment to Change," *Journal of Applied Psychology* 92, no. 4 (2007): 942–51; and G. B. Cunningham, "The Relationships among Commitment to Change, Coping with Change, and Turnover Intentions," *European Journal of Work and Organizational Psychology* 15, no. 1 (2006): 29–45.

[31] R. Peccei, A. Giangreco, and A. Sebastiano, "The Role of Organizational Commitment in the Analysis of Resistance to Change: Co-predictor and Moderator Effects," *Personnel Review* 40, no. 2 (2011): 185–204.

[32] K. Alfes, A. D. Shantz, C. Bailey, E. Conway, K. Monks, and N. Fu, "Perceived Human Resource System Strength and Employee Reactions toward Change: Revisiting Human Resource's Remit as Change Agent," *Human Resource Management* 58 (2019): 239–52; Turgut et al., "Dispositional Resistance to Change and Emotional Exhaustion."

[33] Huy, Corley, and Kraatz, "From Support to Mutiny"; and J. P. Kotter, "Leading Change: Why Transformational Efforts Fail," *Harvard Business Review* 85 (January 2007): 96–103.

[34] K. van Dam, S. Oreg, and B. Schyns, "Daily Work Contexts and Resistance to Organisational Change: The Role of Leader-Member Exchange, Development Climate, and Change Process Characteristics," *Applied Psychology: An International Review* 57, no. 2 (2008): 313–34.

[35] A. H. Y. Hon, M. Bloom, and J. M. Crant, "Overcoming Resistance to Change and Enhancing Creative Performance," *Journal of Management* 40 (2014): 919–41; and S. Turgut, A. Michel, L. M. Rothenhöfer, and K. Sonntag, "Dispositional Resistance to Change and Emotional Exhaustion: Moderating Effects at the Work-Unit Level," *European Journal of Work and Organizational Psychology* 25, no. 5 (2016): 735–50.

[36] S. Oreg and N. Sverdlik, "Ambivalence toward Imposed Change: The Conflict between Dispositional Resistance to Change and the Orientation toward the Change Agent," *Journal of Applied Psychology* 96, no. 2 (2011): 337–49.

[37] M. De Ruiter, R. Schalk, J. Schaveling, and D. van Gelder, "Psychological Contract Breach in the Anticipatory Stage of Change: Employee Responses and the Moderating Role of Supervisory Informational Justice," *The Journal of Applied Behavioral Science* 53, no. 1 (2017): 66–88; B. Fedor, S. Caldwell, and D. M. Herold, "The Effects of Organizational Changes on Employee Commitment: A Multilevel Investigation," *Personnel Psychology* 59 (2006): 1–29; and R. D. Foster, "Resistance, Justice, and Commitment to Change," *Human Resource Development Quarterly* 21, no. 1 (2010): 3–39.

[38] G. Jacobs and A. Keegan, "Ethical Considerations and Change Recipients' Reactions: 'It's Not All about Me,'" *Journal of Business Ethics* (in press).

[39] D. A. Nesterkin, "Organizational Change and Psychological Reactance," *Journal of Organizational Change Management* 26, no. 3 (2013): 573–94.

[40] See, for instance, D. E. Krause, "Consequences of Manipulation in Organizations: Two Studies on Its Effects on Emotions and Relationships," *Psychological Reports* 111, no. 1 (2012): 199–218.

[41] J. Battilana and T. Casciaro, "Overcoming Resistance to Organizational Change: Strong Ties and Affective Cooptation," *Management Science* 59, no. 4 (2013): 819–36.

[42] S. Oreg, "Personality, Context, and Resistance to Organizational Change," *European Journal of Work and Organizational Psychology* 15, no. 1 (2006): 73–101.

[43] S.-H. Chung, Y.-F. Su, and S.-W. Su, "The Impact of Cognitive Flexibility on Resistance to Organizational Change," *Social Behavior and Personality* 40, no. 5 (2012): 735–46; I. B. Saksvik and H. Hetland, "Exploring Dispositional Resistance to Change," *Journal of Leadership & Organizational Studies* 16, no. 2 (2009): 175–83; H. Toch and J. D. Grant, *Reforming Human Services Change Through Participation* (Beverly Hills, CA: Sage, 1982); and C. R. Wanberg and J. T. Banas, "Predictors and Outcomes of Openness to Changes in a Reorganizing Workplace," *Journal of Applied Psychology* 85, no. 1 (2000): 132–42.

[44] T. A. Judge, C. J. Thoresen, V. Pucik, and T. M. Welbourne, "Managerial Coping with

Organizational Change: A Dispositional Perspective," *Journal of Applied Psychology* 84, no. 1 (1999): 107–22.

[45] J. W. B. Lang and P. D. Bliese, "General Mental Ability and Two Types of Adaptation to Unforeseen Change: Applying Discontinuous Growth Models to the Task-Change Paradigm," *Journal of Applied Psychology* 94, no. 2 (2009): 411–28.

[46] C. O. L. H. Porter, J. W. Webb, and C. I. Gogus, "When Goal Orientations Collide: Effects of Learning and Performance Orientation on Team Adaptability in Response to Workload Imbalance," *Journal of Applied Psychology* 95, no. 5 (2010): 935–43; and K. R. Randall, C. J. Resick, and L. A. DeChurch, "Building Team Adaptive Capacity: The Roles of Sensegiving and Team Composition," *Journal of Applied Psychology* 96, no. 3 (2011): 525–40.

[47] J. S. Christian, M. S. Christian, M. J. Pearsall, and E. C. Long, "Team Adaptation in Context: An Integrated Conceptual Model and Meta-Analytic Review," *Organizational Behavior and Human Decision Processes* 140 (2017): 62–89.

[48] D. G. Erwin and A. N. Garman, "Resistance to Organizational Change: Linking Research and Practice," *Leadership & Organization Development Journal* 31, no. 1 (2010): 39–56.

[49] V. E. Schein, "Organizational Realities: The Politics of Change," *Training & Development Journal* 39, no. 2 (1985): 37–41.

[50] See, for instance, A. Karaevli, "Performance Consequences for New CEO 'Outsiderness': Moderating Effects of Pre- and Post-Succession Contexts," *Strategic Management Journal* 28, no. 7 (2007): 681–706.

[51] K. Lewin, "Frontiers in Group Dynamics: Concept, Method and Reality in Social Science: Equilibrium and Social Change," *Human Relations* 1, no. 1 (1947): 5–41. Compare with S. Cummings, T. Bridgman, and K. G. Brown, "Unfreezing Change as Three Steps: Rethinking Kurt Lewin's Legacy for Change Management," *Human Relations* 69, no. 1 (2016): 33–60.

[52] P. G. Audia, E. A. Locke, and K. G. Smith, "The Paradox of Success: An Archival and a Laboratory Study of Strategic Persistence Following Radical Environmental Change," *Academy of Management Journal* 43, no. 5 (2000): 837–53; and P. G. Audia and S. Brion, "Reluctant to Change: Self-Enhancing Responses to Diverging Performance Measures," *Organizational Behavior and Human Decision Processes* 102, no. 2 (2007): 255–69.

[53] J. Kotter, *Leading Change* (Boston, MA: Harvard Business School, 1996); J. Kotter, *Our Iceberg Is Melting* (New York, NY: St. Martin's, 2005); J. Kotter, *A Sense of Urgency* (Boston, MA: Harvard Business School, 2008); and J. Pollack and R. Pollack, "Using Kotter's Eight Stage Process to Manage an Organisational Change Program: Presentation and Practice," *Systemic Practice and Action Research* 28, no. 1 (2015): 41–66.

[54] For reviews, see I. Bleijenbergh, J. van Mierlo, and T. Bondarouk, "Closing the Gap between Scholarly Knowledge and Practice: Guidelines for HRM Action Research," *Human Resource Management Review* (in press); C. Cassell and P. Johnson, "Action Research: Explaining the Diversity," *Human Relations* 59, no. 6 (2006): 783–814.

[55] Bradford and Burke (eds.), *Reinventing Organization Development*; M.-Y. Cheung-Judge and L. Holbeche, *Organization Development: A Practitioner's Guide for OD and HR* (London, UK: Kogan, 2011); and B. Burnes and B. Cooke, "The Past, Present and Future of Organization Development: Taking the Long View," *Human Relations* 65, no. 11 (2012): 1395–429.

[56] See, for instance, Burnes and Cooke, "The Past, Present and Future of Organization Development."

[57] S. Highhouse, "A History of the T-Group and Its Early Application in Management Development," *Group Dynamics: Theory, Research, & Practice* 6, no. 4 (2002): 277–90.

[58] See, for instance, R. J. Solomon, "An Examination of the Relationship between a Survey Feedback O.D. Technique and the Work Environment," *Personnel Psychology* 29 (1976): 583–94.

[59] F. Lambrechts, S. Grieten, R. Bouwen, and F. Corthouts, "Process Consultation Revisited: Taking a Relational Practice Perspective," *Journal of Applied Behavioral Science* 45, no. 1 (2009): 39–58; E. H. Schein, *Process Consultation—Volume 1: Its Role in Organization Development*, 2nd ed. (Reading, MA: Addison Wesley, 1988); and E. H. Schein, *Process Consultation Revisited: Building the Helping Relationship* (Reading, MA: Addison Wesley, 1999).

[60] W. W. G. Dyer, W. G. Dyer, and J. H. Dyer, *Team Building: Proven Strategies for Improving Team Performance* (Hoboken, NJ: Jossey-Bass, 2007); and M. L. Shuffler, D. DiazGranados, and E. Salas, "There's a Science for That: Team Development Interventions in Organizations," *Current Directions in Psychological Science* 20, no. 6 (2011): 365–72.

[61] See, for instance, W. A. Randolph and B. Z. Posner, "The Effects of an Intergroup Development OD Intervention as Conditioned by the Life Cycle State of Organizations: A Laboratory Experiment," *Group & Organization Studies* 7, no. 3 (1982): 335–52.

[62] Times Now News (May 31, 2019). "Virat Kohli-led Indian cricket team play paintball ahead of their World Cup 2019 opener vs South Africa". Retrieved from https://www.timesnownews.com (Accessed on April 19, 2022)

[63] U. Wagner, L. Tropp, G. Finchilescu, and C. Tredoux (eds.), *Improving Intergroup Relations* (New York: Wiley-Blackwell, 2008).

[64] R. Fry, F. Barrett, J. Seiling, and D. Whitney (eds.), *Appreciative Inquiry and Organizational Transformation: Reports from the Field* (Westport, CT: Quorum, 2002); R. J. Ridley-Duff and G. Duncan, "What Is Critical Appreciation? Insights from Studying the Critical Turn in an Appreciative Inquiry," *Human Relations* 68, no. 10 (2015): 1579–99; and D. van der Haar and D. M. Hosking, "Evaluating Appreciative Inquiry: A Relational Constructivist Perspective," *Human Relations* 57, no. 8 (2004): 1017–36.

[65] Case Western Reserve University, *Appreciative Inquiry Commons*, https://appreciativeinquiry.case.edu/, accessed April 20, 2017.

[66] G. Giglio, S. Michalcova, and C. Yates, "Instilling a Culture of Winning at American Express," *Organization Development Journal* 25, no. 4 (2007): P33–P37.

[67] See, for instance, G. T. Fairhurst, W. K. Smith, S. G. Banghart, M. W. Lewis, L. L. Putnam, S. Raisch, and J. Schad, "Diverging and Converging: Integrative Insights on a Paradox Meta-Perspective," *The Academy of Management Annals* 10, no. 1 (2016): 173–82.

[68] W. K. Smith and M. W. Lewis, "Toward a Theory of Paradox: A Dynamic Equilibrium Model of Organizing," *Academy of Management Review* 36 (2011): 381–403.

[69] J. Schad, M. W. Lewis, S. Raisch, and W. K. Smith, "Paradox Research in Management Science: Looking Back to Move Forward," *The Academy of Management Annals* 10, no. 1 (2016): 5–64; and D. A. Waldman, L. L. Putnam, E. Miron-Spektor, and D. Siegel, "The Role of Paradox Theory in Decision Making and Management Research, *Organizational Behavior and Human Decision Processes* 155 (2019): 1–9.

[70] J. Jay, "Navigating Paradox as a Mechanism of Change and Innovation in Hybrid Organizations," *Academy of Management Journal* 56 (2013): 137–59.

[71] M. Pina e Cunha, E. Gomes, K. Mellahi, A. S. Miner, and A. Rego, "Strategic Agility through Improvisational Capabilities: Implications for a Paradox-Sensitive HRM,"

Human Resource Management Review (in press); D. A. Waldman and D. E. Bowen, "Learning to Be a Paradox-Savvy Leader," *Academy of Management Perspectives* 30, no. 3 (2016): 316–27; Y. Zhang and Y-L. Han, "Paradoxical Leader Behavior in Long-Term Corporate Development: Antecedents and Consequences," *Organizational Behavior and Human Decision Processes* 155 (2019): 42–54; and Y. Zhang, D. A. Waldman, Y. Han, and X. Li, "Paradoxical Leader Behaviors in People Management: Antecedents and Consequences," *Academy of Management Journal* 58 (2015): 538–66.

[72] D. J. Sleesman, "Pushing through the Tension while Stuck in the Mud: Paradox Mindset and Escalation of Commitment," *Organizational Behavior and Human Decision Processes* 155 (2019): 83–96.

[73] A. Harrington, "Who's Afraid of a New Product?," *Fortune*, November 10, 2003, 189–92; D. K. Williams, "Do These 4 Things to Foster New Creativity," *Forbes*, October 17, 2016, https://www.forbes.com/sites/davidkwilliams/2016/10/17/do-these-4-things-to-foster-new-creativity/#47dcf67d902f; and C. C. Manz, F. Shipper, and G. L. Stewart, "Everyone a Team Leader: Shared Influence at W. L. Gore and Associates," *Organizational Dynamics* 38, no. 3 (2009): 239–44.

[74] "A Team-Based, Flat Lattice Organization," Gore website, http://www.gore.com/en_xx/aboutus/culture/index.html, accessed July 23, 2015.

[75] S. Caulkin, "Gore-Text Gets Made without Managers," *The Observer*, November 1, 2008, http://www.theguardian.com/business/2008/nov/02/gore-tex-textiles-terri-kelly.

[76] Williams, "Do These 4 Things to Foster New Creativity."

[77] N. Anderson, K. Potočnik, and J. Zhou, "Innovation and Creativity in Organizations: A State-of-the-Science Review, Prospective Commentary, and Guiding Framework," *Journal of Management* 40, no. 5 (2014): 1297–333; G. P. Pisano, "You Need an Innovation Strategy," *Harvard Business Review* (June 2015): 44–54; and J. Zhou and I. J. Hoever, "Research on Workplace Creativity: A Review and Redirection," *Annual Review of Organizational Psychology and Organizational Behavior* 1 (2014): 333–59.

[78] Delhivery. "About Us". Retrieved from https://www.delhivery.com (Accessed on April 18, 2022)

[79] Anderson, Potočnik, and Zhou, "Innovation and Creativity in Organizations"; and H. W. Volberda, F. A. J. Van den Bosch, and C. V. Heij, "Management Innovation: Management as Fertile Ground for Innovation," *European Management Review* (2013): 1–15.

[80] Anderson, Potočnik, and Zhou, "Innovation and Creativity in Organizations."

[81] K. Byron and S. Khazanchi, "Rewards and Creative Performance: A Meta-Analytic Test of Theoretically Derived Hypotheses," *Psychological Bulletin* 138, no. 4 (2012): 809–30; A. Lee, A. Legood, D. Hughes, A. Wei Tian, A. Newman, and C. Knight, "Leadership, Creativity, and Innovation: A Meta-Analytic Review," *European Journal of Work and Organizational Psychology* 29, no. 1 (2020): 1–35.

[82] See, for instance, V. Mueller, N. Rosenbusch, and A. Bausch, "Success Patterns of Exploratory and Exploitative Innovation: A Meta-Analysis of the Influence of Institutional Factors," *Journal of Management* 39, no. 6 (2013): 1606–36.

[83] U. R. Hülsheger, N. Anderson, and J. F. Salgado, "Team-Level Predictors of Innovation at Work: A Comprehensive Meta-Analysis Spanning Three Decades of Research," *Journal of Applied Psychology* 94, no. 5 (2009): 1128–45; and P. Schepers and P. T. van den Berg, "Social Factors of Work-Environment Creativity," *Journal of Business and Psychology* 21, no. 3 (2007): 407–28.

[84] M. Frese and N. Keith, "Action Errors, Error Management, and Learning in Organizations," *Annual Review of Psychology* 66 (2015): 661–87.

[85] R. S. Friedman and J. Förster, "The Effects of Promotion and Prevention Cues on Creativity," *Journal of Personality and Social Psychology* 81, no. 6 (2001): 1001–13.

[86] Hülsheger, Anderson, and Salgado, "Team-Level Predictors of Innovation at Work."

[87] Ibid.

[88] Anderson, Potočnik, and Zhou, "Innovation and Creativity in Organizations."

[89] D. Fay, H. Shipton, M.A. West, and M. Patterson, "Teamwork and Organizational Innovation: The Moderating Role of the HRM Context," *Creativity and Innovation Management* 24, no. 2 (2015): 261–77.

[90] See, for instance, M. E. Mullins, S. W. J. Kozlowski, N. Schmitt, and A. W. Howell, "The Role of the Idea Champion in Innovation: The Case of the Internet in the Mid-1990s," *Computers in Human Behavior* 24, no. 2 (2008): 451–67.

[91] J. M. Howell and C. A. Higgins, "Champions of Technological Innovation," *Administrative Science Quarterly* 35 (1990): 317–41.

[92] C. Y. Murnieks, E. Mosakowski, and M. S. Cardon, "Pathways of Passion Identity Centrality, Passion, and Behavior among Entrepreneurs," *Journal of Management* 40 (2014): 1583–606.

[93] S. C. Parker, "Intrapreneurship or Entrepreneurship?," *Journal of Business Venturing* 26, no. 1 (2011): 19–34.

[94] M. Černe, M. Jaklič, and M. Škerlavaj, "Decoupling Management and Technological Innovations: Resolving the Individualism-Collectivism Controversy," *Journal of International Management* 19, no. 2 (2013): 103–17; and S. Shane, S. Venkataraman, and I. MacMillan, "Cultural Differences in Innovation Championing Strategies," *Journal of Management* 21, no. 5 (1995): 931–52.

[95] Harsha Engineers. "Abiut Us". Retrieved from http://harshaengineers.com (Accessed on April 19, 2022)

[96] P. M. Senge, *The Fifth Discipline: The Art & Practice of the Learning Organization*, 2nd ed. (New York, NY: Random House, 2006); V. I. Sessa and M. London, *Continuous Learning in Organizations: Individual, Group, and Organizational Perspectives* (Mahwah, NJ: Lawrence Erlbaum, 2006); and J. H. Song and T. J. Chermack, "A Theoretical Approach to the Organizational Knowledge Formation Process: Integrating Concepts of Individual Learning and Learning Organization Culture," *Human Resource Development Review* 7, no. 4 (2008): 424–42.

[97] J. Kim, T. Egan, and H. Tolson, "Examining the Dimensions of the Learning Organization Questionnaire: A Review and Critique of Research Utilizing the DLOQ," *Human Resource Development Review* 14, no. 1 (2015): 91–112.

[98] Senge, *The Fifth Discipline.*

[99] R. Chiva and J. Habib, "A Framework for Organizational Learning: Zero, Adaptive, and Generative Learning," *Journal of Management & Organization* 21, no. 3 (2015): 350–68; and Kim, Egan, and Tolson, "Examining the Dimensions of the Learning Organization Questionnaire."

[100] A. Michel and M. G. González-Morales, "Reactions to Organizational Change: An Integrated Model of Health Predictors, Intervening Variables, and Outcomes," in S. Oreg, A. Michel, and R. T. By (eds.), *The Psychology of Organizational Change: Viewing Change from the Employee's Perspective* (New York, NY: Cambridge University Press, 2013).

[101] D. Meinert, "Wings of Change," *HR Magazine* (November 2012): 30–36; Michel and González-Morales, "Reactions to Organizational Change."

[102] M.-G. Seo, M. S. Taylor, N. S. Hill, X. Zhang, P. E. Tesluk, and N. M. Lorinkova, "The Role of Affect and Leadership during Organizational Change," *Personnel Psychology* 65 (2012): 121–65.

[103] M. Fugate, G. E. Prussia, and A. J. Kinicki, "Managing Employee Withdrawal

during Organizational Change: The Role of Threat Appraisal," *Journal of Management* (May 2012): 890–914.

[104] J. Shin, M. S. Taylor, and M.-G. Seo, "Resources for Change: The Relationships of Organizational Inducements and Psychological Resilience to Employees' Attitudes and Behaviors toward Organizational Change," *Academy of Management Journal* 55 (2012): 727–48.

[105] B. Mirza, "Workplace Stress Hits Three-Year High," *HR Magazine* (April 2012): 15.

[106] "Stress in America 2019," *American Psychological Association*, November 2019, https://www.apa.org/news/press/releases/stress/2019/stress-america-2019.pdf.

[107] C. L. Cooper, P. J. Dewe, and M. P. O'Driscoll, *Organizational Stress: A Review and Critique of Theory, Research, and Applications* (Thousand Oaks, CA: Sage, 2002).

[108] M. B. Hargrove, W. S. Becker, and D. F. Hargrove, "The HRD Eustress Model: Generating Positive Stress with Challenging Work," *Human Resource Development Review* 14, no. 3 (2015): 279–98.

[109] S. Shellenbarger, "When Stress Is Good for You," *The Wall Street Journal*, January 24, 2012, D1, D5.

[110] Ibid.

[111] J. A. LePine, M. A. LePine, and C. L. Jackson, "Challenge and Hindrance Stress: Relationships with Exhaustion, Motivation to Learn, and Learning Performance," *Journal of Applied Psychology* 89, no. 5 (2004): 883–91; K. E. O'Brien and T. A. Beehr, "So Far, So Good: Up to Now, the Challenge-Hindrance Framework Describes a Practical and Accurate Distinction," *Journal of Organizational Behavior* 40 (2019): 962–72; P. E. Spector, "Introduction: The Challenge-Hindrance Stressor Model," *Journal of Organizational Behavior* 40 (2019): 947–48.

[112] N. P. Podsakoff, J. A. LePine, and M. A. LePine, "Differential Challenge-Hindrance Stressor Relationships with Job Attitudes, Turnover Intentions, Turnover, and Withdrawal Behavior: A Meta-Analysis," *Journal of Applied Psychology* 92, no. 2 (2007): 438–54; C. C. Rosen, N. Dimotakis, M. S. Cole, S. G. Taylor, L. S. Simon, T. A. Smith, and C. S. Reina, "When Challenges Hinder: An Investigation of When and How Challenge Stressors Impact Employee Outcomes," *Journal of Applied Psychology* (in press).

[113] E. R. Crawford, J. A. LePine, and B. L. Rich, "Linking Job Demands and Resources to Employee Engagement and Burnout: A Theoretical Extension and Meta-Analytic Test," *Journal of Applied Psychology* 95, no. 5 (2010): 834–48; J. A. LePine, N. P. Podsakoff, and M. A. LePine, "A Meta-Analytic Test of the Challenge Stressor-Hindrance Stressor Framework: An Explanation for Inconsistent Relationships among Stressors and Performance," *Academy of Management Journal* 48, no. 5 (2005): 764–75; C. C. Rosen, N. Dimotakis, M. S. Cole, S. G. Taylor, L. S. Simon, T. A. Smith, and C. S. Reina, "When Challenges Hinder: An Investigation of When and How Challenge Stressors Impact Employee Outcomes," *Journal of Applied Psychology* (in press).

[114] S. Clarke, "The Effect of Challenge and Hindrance Stressors on Safety Behavior and Safety Outcomes: A Meta-Analysis," *Journal of Occupational Health Psychology* 17, no. 4 (2012): 387–97; LePine, Podsakoff, and LePine, "A Meta-Analytic Test of the Challenge Stressor-Hindrance Stressor Framework"; and Podsakoff, LePine, and LePine, "Differential Challenge-Hindrance Stressor Relationships with Job Attitudes, Turnover Intentions, Turnover, and Withdrawal Behavior."

[115] R. Prem, S. Ohly, B. Kubicek, and C. Korunka, "Thriving on Challenge Stressors? Exploring Time Pressure and Learning Demands as Antecedents of Thriving at Work," *Journal of Organizational Behavior* 38, no. 1 (2017): 108–23.

[116] M. Kronenwett and T. Rigotti, "When Do You Face a Challenge? How Unnecessary Tasks Block the Challenging Potential of Time Pressure and Emotional Demands," *Journal of Occupational Health Psychology* 24, no. 5 (2019): 512–26.

[117] M. R. Tuckey, B. J. Searle, C. M. Boyd, A. H. Winefield, and H. R. Winefield, "Hindrances Are Not Threats: Advancing the Multidimensionality of Work Stress," *Journal of Occupational Health Psychology* 20, no. 2 (2015): 131–47.

[118] See, for instance, A. B. Bakker and E. Demerouti, "Job Demands–Resources Theory: Taking Stock and Looking Forward," *Journal of Occupational Health Psychology* 22, no. 3 (2017): 273–85; A. B. Bakker, E. Demerouti, and A. I. Sanz-Vergel, "Burnout and Work Engagement: The JD–R Approach," *Annual Review of Organizational Psychology and Organizational Behavior* 1 (2014): 389–411.

[119] See, for instance, M. Mathieu, K. J. Eschleman, and D. Cheng, "Meta-Analytic and Multiwave Comparison of Emotional Support and Instrumental Support in the Workplace," *Journal of Occupational Health Psychology* 24, no. 3 (2019): 387–409.

[120] K. Breevaart and A. B. Bakker, "Daily Job Demands and Employee Work Engagement: The Role of Daily Transformational Leadership Behavior," *Journal of Occupational Health Psychology* (in press).

[121] G. M. Alarcon, "A Meta-Analysis of Burnout with Job Demands, Resources, and Attitudes," *Journal of Vocational Behavior* 79, no. 2 (2011): 549–62; Bakker and Demerouti, "Job Demands-Resources Theory"; and Crawford, LePine, and Rich, "Linking Job Demands and Resources to Employee Engagement and Burnout."

[122] D. C. Ganster and C. C. Rosen, "Work Stress and Employee Health: A Multidisciplinary Review," *Journal of Management* 39 (2013): 1085–122.

[123] P. Sterling, "Allostasis: A Model of Predictive Regulation," *Physiology & Behavior* 106, no. 1 (2012): 5–15.

[124] A. E. Rafferty and M. A. Griffin, "Perceptions of Organizational Change: A Stress and Coping Perspective," *Journal of Applied Psychology* 71, no. 5 (2007): 1154–62.

[125] R. Ilies, N. Dimotakis, and I. E. De Pater, "Psychological and Physiological Reactions to High Workloads: Implications for Well-Being," *Personnel Psychology* 63, no. 2 (2010): 407–36; A. B. Bakker, E. Demerouti, and A. I. Sanz-Vergel, "Burnout and Work Engagement: The JD–R Approach," *Annual Review of Organizational Psychology and Organizational Behavior* 1 (2014): 389–411.

[126] T. L. Smith-Jackson and K. W. Klein, "Open-Plan Offices: Task Performance and Mental Workload," *Journal of Environmental Psychology* 29, no. 2 (2009): 279–89.

[127] M. A. Griffin and S. Clarke, "Stress and Well-Being at Work," in S. Zedeck (ed.), *APA Handbook of Industrial and Organizational Psychology: Maintaining, Expanding, and Contracting the Organization*, Vol. 3 (Washington, DC: American Psychological Association, 2011): 359–397.

[128] C. Fritz and S. Sonnentag, "Antecedents of Day-Level Proactive Behavior: A Look at Job Stressors and Positive Affect during the Workday," *Journal of Management* 35, no. 1 (2009): 94–111.

[129] N. A. Bowling and T. A. Beehr, "Workplace Harassment from the Victim's Perspective: A Theoretical Model and Meta-Analysis," *Journal of Applied Psychology* 91, no. 5 (2006): 998–1012; M. B. Nielsen and S. Einarsen, "Outcomes of Exposure to Workplace Bullying: A Meta-Analytic Review," *Work & Stress* 26, no. 4 (2012): 309–32; and C. R. Willness, P. Steel, and K. Lee, "A Meta-Analysis of the Antecedents and Consequences of Workplace Sexual Harassment," *Personnel Psychology* 60, no. 1 (2007): 127–62.

[130] L. Yang, J. Bauer, R. E. Johnson, M. W. Groer, and K. Salomon, "Physiological

Mechanisms That Underlie the Effects of Interactional Unfairness on Deviant Behavior: The Role of Cortisol Activity," *Journal of Applied Psychology* 99 (2014): 310–21.

131 M. T. Schmitt, N. R. Branscombe, T. Postmes, and A. Garcia, "The Consequences of Perceived Discrimination for Psychological Well-Being: A Meta-Analytic Review," *Psychological Bulletin* 140 (2014): 921–48.

132 J. O'Reilly, S. L. Robinson, J. L. Berdahl, and S. Banki, "Is Negative Attention Better Than No Attention? The Comparative Effects of Ostracism and Harassment at Work," *Organization Science* (2014): 774–93.

133 "Stress in America: Paying with Our Health," *American Psychological Association*, February 4, 2015, http://www.apa.org/news/press/releases/stress/2014/stress-report.pdf.

134 F. T. Amstad, L. L. Meier, U. Fasel, A. Elfering, and N. K. Semmer, "A Meta-Analysis of Work-Family Conflict and Various Outcomes with a Special Emphasis on Cross-Domain Versus Matching-Domain Relations," *Journal of Occupational Health Psychology* 16, no. 2 (2011): 151–69.

135 C. Nohe, L. L. Meier, K. Sonntag, and A. Michel, "The Chicken or the Egg? A Meta-Analysis of Panel Studies of the Relationship between Work-Family Conflict and Strain," *Journal of Applied Psychology* 100, no. 2 (2015): 522–36.

136 "Stress in America."

137 M. T. Ford, R. A. Matthews, J. D. Wooldridge, V. Mishra, U. M. Kakar, and S. R. Strahan, "How Do Occupational Stressor-Strain Effects Vary with Time? A Review and Meta-Analysis of the Relevance of Time Lags in Longitudinal Studies," *Work & Stress* 28, no. 1 (2014): 9–30; and Q. Hu, W. B. Schaufeli, and T. W. Taris, "The Job Demands–Resources Model: An Analysis of Additive and Joint Effects of Demands and Resources," *Journal of Vocational Behavior* 79, no. 1 (2011): 181–90.

138 C. A. Demsky, C. Fritz, L. B. Hammer, and A. E. Black, "Workplace Incivility and Employee Sleep: The Role of Rumination and Recovery Experiences," *Journal of Occupational Health Psychology* 24, no. 2 (2019): 228–40; Y. Park and S. Kim, "Customer Mistreatment Harms Nightly Sleep and Next-Morning Recovery: Job Control and Recovery Self-Efficacy as Cross-Level Moderators," *Journal of Occupational Health Psychology* 24, no. 2 (2019): 256–69.

139 E. Bruehlman-Senecal and O. Ayduk, "This Too Shall Pass: Temporal Distance and the Regulation of Emotional Distress," *Journal of Personality and Social Psychology* 108, no. 2 (2015): 354–75.

140 Business Today. "India's Coolest Workplaces". Retrieved from https://www.businesstoday.in (Accessed on April 18, 2022)

141 Crawford, LePine, and Rich, "Linking Job Demands and Resources to Employee Engagement and Burnout."

142 See J. B. Halbesleben, "Sources of Social Support and Burnout: A Meta-Analytic Test of the Conservation of Resources Model," *Journal of Applied Psychology* 91, no. 5 (2006): 1134–45; N. Bolger and D. Amarel, "Effects of Social Support Visibility on Adjustment to Stress: Experimental Evidence," *Journal of Applied Psychology* 92, no. 3 (2007): 458–75; and C. Fernet, M. Gagné, and S. Austin, "When Does Quality of Relationships with Coworkers Predict Burnout over Time? The Moderating Role of Work Motivation," *Journal of Organizational Behavior* 31 (2010): 1163–80.

143 Mathieu et al., "Meta-Analytic and Multiwave Comparison of Emotional Support and Instrumental Support in the Workplace."

144 See, for instance, B. W. Swider and R. D. Zimmerman, "Born to Burnout: A Meta-Analytic Path Model of Personality, Job Burnout, and Work Outcomes," *Journal of Vocational Behavior* 76, no. 3 (2010): 487–506; and Q. Wang, N. A. Bowling, and K. J. Eschleman, "A Meta-Analytic Examination of Work and General Locus of Control," *Journal of Applied Psychology* 95, no. 4 (2010): 761–8.

145 See, for example, C. M. Middeldorp, D. C. Cath, A. L. Beem, G. Willemsen, and D. I. Boomsma, "Life Events, Anxious Depression, and Personality: A Prospective and Genetic Study," *Psychological Medicine* 38, no. 11 (2008): 1557–65; Swider and Zimmerman, "Born to Burnout"; and A. A. Uliaszek, R. E. Zinbarg, S. Mineka, M. G. Craske, J. M. Sutton, J. W. Griffith … and C. Hammen, "The Role of Neuroticism and Extraversion in the Stress-Anxiety and Stress-Depression Relationships," *Anxiety, Stress, and Coping* 23, no. 4 (2010): 363–81.

146 J. D. Kammeyer-Mueller, T. A. Judge, and B. A. Scott, "The Role of Core Self-Evaluations in the Coping Process," *Journal of Applied Psychology* 94, no. 1 (2009): 177–95.

147 For a review, see M. A. Clark, J. S. Michel, L. Zhdanova, S. Y Pui, and B. B. Baltes, "All Work and No Play? A Meta-Analytic Examination of the Correlates and Outcomes of Workaholism," *Journal of Management* 42, no. 7 (2016): 1836–73.

148 R. J. Burke, A. M. Richardson, and M. Mortinussen, "Workaholism among Norwegian Managers: Work and Well-Being Outcomes," *Journal of Organizational Change Management* 7 (2004): 459–70; Clark, Michel, Zhdanova, Pui, and Baltes, "All Work and No Play?"; and W. B. Schaufeli, T. W. Taris, and W. van Rhenen, "Workaholism, Burnout, and Work Engagement: Three of a Kind or Three Different Kinds of Employee Well-Being," *Applied Psychology: An International Review* 57, no. 2 (2008): 173–203.

149 C. Liu, P. E. Spector, and L. Shi, "Cross-National Job Stress: A Quantitative and Qualitative Study," *Journal of Organizational Behavior* 28, no. 2 (2007): 209–39.

150 J. Chen, C. Silverthorne, and J. Hung, "Organization Communication, Job Stress, Organizational Commitment, and Job Performance of Accounting Professionals in Taiwan and America," *Leadership & Organization Development Journal* 27, no. 4 (2006): 242–49.

151 P. E. Spector, T. D. Allen, S. A. Y. Poelmans, L. M. Lapierre, C. L. Cooper, M. O'Driscoll, et al., "Cross National Differences in Relationships of Work Demands, Job Satisfaction, and Turnover Intention with Work-Family Conflict," *Personnel Psychology* 60, no. 4 (2007): 805–35.

152 P. J. Gianaros and T. D. Wager, "Brain-Body Pathways Linking Psychological Stress and Physical Health," *Current Directions in Psychological Science* 24, no. 4 (2015): 313–21.

153 A. E. Nixon, J. J. Mazzola, J. Bauer, J. R. Krueger, and P. E. Spector, "Can Work Make You Sick? A Meta-Analysis of the Relationships between Job Stressors and Physical Symptoms," *Work & Stress* 25, no. 1 (2011): 1–22.

154 J. H. K. Wong and E. K. Kelloway, "What Happens at Work Stays at Work? Workplace Supervisory Social Interactions and Blood Pressure Outcomes," *Journal of Occupational Health Psychology* 21, no. 2 (2016): 133–41.

155 A. Marchand, R.-P. Juster, P. Durand, and S. J. Lupien, "Work Stress Models and Diurnal Cortisol Variations: The SALVEO Study," *Journal of Occupational Health Psychology* 21, no. 2 (2016): 182–93.

156 B. Litwiller, L. A. Snyder, W. D. Tay, and L. M. Steele, "The Relationship between Sleep and Work: A Meta-Analysis," *Journal of Applied Psychology* 102, no. 4 (2017): 682–99.

157 D. Pereira and A. Elfering, "Social Stressors at Work and Sleep during Weekends: The Mediating Role of Psychological Detachment," *Journal of Occupational Health Psychology* 19, no. 1 (2014): 85–95; Y. Park and J. M. Sprung, "Weekly Work-School Conflict, Sleep Quality, and Fatigue: Recovery Self-Efficacy as a Cross-Level Moderator," *Journal of Organizational Behavior* 36,

no. 1 (2015): 112–27; and C. J. Syrek, O. Weigelt, C. Peifer, and C. H. Antoni, "Zeigarnik's Sleepless Nights: How Unfinished Tasks at the End of the Week Impair Employee Sleep on the Weekend through Rumination," *Journal of Occupational Health Psychology* 22, no. 2 (2017): 225–38.

[158] L. Flueckiger, R. Lieb, A. H. Meyer, C. Witthauer, and J. Mata, "The Importance of Physical Activity and Sleep for Affect on Stressful Days: Two Intensive Longitudinal Studies," *Emotion* 16, no. 4 (2016): 488–97; and J. Pow, D. B. King, E. Stephenson, and A. DeLongis, "Does Social Support Buffer the Effects of Occupational Stress on Sleep Quality Among Paramedics? A Daily Diary Study," *Journal of Occupational Health Psychology* 22, no. 1 (2017): 71–85.

[159] R. Ilies, N. Dimotakis, and I. E. De Pater, "Psychological and Physiological Reactions to High Workloads: Implications for Well-Being," *Personnel Psychology* 63, no. 2 (2010): 407–36.

[160] D. Örtqvist and J. Wincent, "Prominent Consequences of Role Stress: A Meta-Analytic Review," *International Journal of Stress Management* 13, no. 4 (2006): 399–422.

[161] R. Fischer and D. Boer, "What Is More Important for National Well-Being: Money or Autonomy? A Meta-Analysis of Well-Being, Burnout, and Anxiety Across 63 Societies," *Journal of Personality and Social Psychology* 101, no. 1 (2011): 164–84; and P. E. Spector, "Perceived Control by Employees: A Meta-Analysis of Studies Concerning Autonomy and Participation at Work," *Human Relations* 39, no. 11 (1986): 1005–16.

[162] J. J. Hakanen, A. B. Bakker, and M. Jokisaari, "A 35-Year Follow-Up Study on Burnout among Finnish Employees," *Journal of Occupational Health Psychology* 16, no. 3 (2011): 345–60; Crawford, LePine, and Rich, "Linking Job Demands and Resources to Employee Engagement and Burnout"; and G. A. Chung-Yan, "The Nonlinear Effects of Job Complexity and Autonomy on Job Satisfaction, Turnover, and Psychological Well-Being," *Journal of Occupational Health Psychology* 15, no. 3 (2010): 237–51.

[163] L. L. Meier, N. K. Semmer, A. Elfering, and N. Jacobshagen, "The Double Meaning of Control: Three-Way Interactions between Internal Resources, Job Control, and Stressors at Work," *Journal of Occupational Health Psychology* 13, no. 3 (2008): 244–58.

[164] E. M. de Croon, J. K. Sluiter, R. W. B. Blonk, J. P. J. Broersen, and M. H. W. Frings-Dresen, "Stressful Work, Psychological Job Strain, and Turnover: A 2-Year Prospective Cohort Study of Truck Drivers," *Journal of Applied Psychology* (June 2004): 442–54; R. Cropanzano, D. E. Rupp, and Z. S. Byrne, "The Relationship of Emotional Exhaustion to Work Attitudes, Job Performance, and Organizational Citizenship Behaviors," *Journal of Applied Psychology* (February 2003): 160–69; Griffin and Clarke, "Stress and Well-Being at Work"; and S. Diestel and K. Schmidt, "Costs of Simultaneous Coping with Emotional Dissonance and Self-Control Demands at Work: Results from Two German Samples," *Journal of Applied Psychology* 96, no. 3 (2011): 643–53.

[165] R. M. Yerkes and J. D. Dodson, "The Relation of Strength of Stimulus to Rapidity of Habit-Formation," *Journal of Comparative Neurology and Psychology* 18 (1908): 459–82.

[166] H. S. Field, "Has the Inverted-U Theory of Stress and Job Performance Had a Fair Test?," *Human Performance* 16, no. 4 (2003): 349–64.

[167] See, for example, L. W. Hunter and S. M. B. Thatcher, "Feeling the Heat: Effects of Stress, Commitment, and Job Experience on Job Performance," *Academy of Management Journal* 50, no. 4 (2007): 953–68; and J. C. Vischer, "The Effects of the Physical Environment on Job Performance: Towards a Theoretical Model of Workplace Stress," *Stress and Health* 23, no. 3 (2007): 175–84.

[168] Y.-C. Wu, "Job Stress and Job Performance among Employees on the Taiwanese Finance Sector: The Role of Emotional Intelligence," *Social Behavior and Personality* 39, no. 1 (2011): 21–31. This study was replicated with similar results in U. Yozgat, S. Yurtkoru, and E. Bilginoglu, "Job Stress and Job Performance among Employees in Public Sector in Istanbul: Examining the Moderating Role of Emotional Intelligence," in E. Eren (ed.), *Procedia Social and Behavioral Sciences*, Vol. 75 (2013): 518–24.

[169] S. Gilboa, A. Shirom, Y. Fried, and C. L. Cooper, "A Meta-Analysis of Work Demand Stressors and Job Performance: Examining Main and Moderating Effects," *Personnel Psychology* 61, no. 2 (2008): 227–71.

[170] J. C. Wallace, B. D. Edwards, T. Arnold, M. L. Frazier, and D. M. Finch, "Work Stressors, Role-Based Performance, and the Moderating Influence of Organizational Support," *Journal of Applied Psychology* 94, no. 1 (2009): 254–62.

[171] H. Dai, K. L. Milkman, D. A. Hofmann, and B. R. Staats, "The Impact of Time at Work and Time off from Work on Rule Compliance," *Journal of Applied Psychology* 100, no. 3 (2015): 846–62.

[172] K. M. Richardson and H. R. Rothstein, "Effects of Occupational Stress Management Intervention Programs: A Meta-Analysis," *Journal of Occupational Health Psychology* 13, no. 1 (2008): 69–93.

[173] Y. Zhang, T. W. H. Ng, and S. S. K. Lam, "Promotion- and Prevention-Focused Coping: A Meta-Analytic Examination of Regulatory Strategies in the Work Stress Process," *Journal of Applied Psychology* 104, no. 10 (2019): 1296–323.

[174] A. J. Vanhove, M. N. Herian, A. L. U. Perez, P. D. Harms, and P. B. Lester, "Can Resilience Be Developed at Work? A Meta-Analytic Review of Resilience-Building Programme Effectiveness," *Journal of Occupational and Organizational Psychology* 89 (2016): 278–307.

[175] A. Häfner, A. Stock, L. Pinneker, and S. Ströhle, "Stress Prevention through a Time Management Training Intervention: An Experimental Study," *Educational Psychology* 34, no. 3 (2014): 403–16; S. Sonnentag, L. Venz, and A. Casper, "Advances in Recovery Research: What Have We Learned? What Should be Done Next?," *Journal of Occupational Health Psychology* 22, no. 3 (2017): 365–80; and M. Virgili, "Mindfulness-Based Interventions Reduce Psychological Distress in Working Adults: A Meta-Analysis of Intervention Studies," *Mindfulness* 6, no. 2 (2015): 326–37.

[176] R. W. Renn, D. G. Allen, and T. M. Huning, "Empirical Examination of Individual-Level Personality-Based Theory of Self-Management Failure," *Journal of Organizational Behavior* 32, no. 1 (2011): 25–43; and P. Gröpel and P. Steel, "A Mega-Trial Investigation of Goal Setting, Interest Enhancement, and Energy on Procrastination," *Personality and Individual Differences* 45, no. 5 (2008): 406–11.

[177] J. H. Riskind and E. Calvete, "Anxiety and the Dynamic Self as Defined by the Prospection and Mental Simulation of Looming Future Threats," *Journal of Personality* 88 (2020): 31–44; R. E. White, M. M. Kuehn, A. L. Duckworth, E. Kross, and Ö. Ayduk, "Focusing on the Future Self from Afar: Self-Distancing from Future Stressors Facilitates Adaptive Coping," *Emotion* 19, no. 5 (2019): 903–16.

[178] E. E. Bernstein, J. E. Curtiss, G. W. Y. Wu, P. J. Barreira, and R. J. McNally, "Exercise and Emotion Dynamics: An Experience Sampling Study," *Emotion* 19, 4 (2019): 637–44; Sonnentag, Venz, and Casper, "Advances in Recovery Research"; M. L. M. van Hooff, R. M. Benthem de Grave, and S. A. E. Geurts, "No Pain, no Gain? Recovery and Strenuousness of

Physical Activity," *Journal of Occupational Health Psychology* 24, no. 5 (2019): 499–511.
[179] Eby et al., "Mindfulness-Based Training Interventions for Employees"; U. R. Hülsheger, J. W. B. Lang, F. Depenbrock, C. Fehrmann, F. R. H. Zijlstra, and H. J. E. M. Alberts, "The Power of Presence: The Role of Mindfulness at Work for Daily Levels and Change Trajectories of Psychological Detachment and Sleep Quality," *Journal of Applied Psychology* 99, no. 6 (2014): 1113–28; V. Perciavalle, M. Blandini, P. Fecarotta, A. Buscemi, D. Di Corrado, L. Bertolo ... and M. Coco, "The Role of Deep Breathing on Stress," *Neurological Sciences* 38, no. 3 (2017): 451–8; and R. Q. Wolever, K. J. Bobinet, K. McCabe, E. R. Mackenzie, E. Fekete, C. A. Kusnick, and M. Baime, "Effective and Viable Mind-Body Stress Reduction in the Workplace: A Randomized Controlled Trial," *Journal of Occupational Health Psychology* 17, no. 2 (2012): 246–58.
[180] Richardson and Rothstein, "Effects of Occupational Stress Management Intervention Programs."
[181] L. S. Sharman, G. A. Dingle, A. J. J. M. Vingerhoets, and E. J. Vanman, "Using Crying to Cope: Physiological Responses to Stress Following Tears of Sadness," *Emotion* (in press).
[182] S. Reddy, "Doctor's Orders: 20 Minutes of Meditation Twice a Day," *The Wall Street Journal*, April 15, 2013, https://www.wsj.com/articles/SB10001424127887324345804578424863782143682.
[183] V. C. Hahn, C. Binnewies, S. Sonnentag, and E. J. Mojza, "Learning How to Recover from Job Stress: Effects of a Recovery Training Program on Recovery, Recovery-Related Self-Efficacy, and Well-Being," *Journal of Occupational Health Psychology* 16, no. 2 (2011): 202–16; J. Krajewski, R. Wieland, and M. Sauerland, "Regulating Strain States by Using the Recovery Potential of Lunch Breaks," *Journal of Occupational Health Psychology* 15, no. 2 (2010): 131–9; and M. Sianoja, C. J. Syrek, J. de Bloom, K. Korpela, and U. Kinnunen, "Enhancing Daily Well-Being at Work through Lunchtime Park Walks and Relaxation Exercises: Recovery Experiences as Mediators," *Journal of Occupational Health Psychology* 23, no. 3 (2018): 428–42.
[184] S. Kim, Y. Park, and Q. Niu, "Micro-Break Activities at Work to Recover from Daily Work Demands," *Journal of Organizational Behavior* 38 (2017): 28–44; and H. Zacher, H. A. Brailsford, and S. L. Parker, "Micro-Breaks Matter: A Diary Study on the Effects of Energy Management Strategies on Occupational Well-Being," *Journal of Vocational Behavior* 85 (2014): 287–97.
[185] S. L. Parker, S. Sonnentag, N. L. Jimmieson, and C. J. Newton, "Relaxation during the Evening and Next-Morning Energy: The Role of Hassles, Uplifts, and Heart Rate Variability during Work," *Journal of Occupational Health Psychology* 25, no. 2 (2020): 83–98.
[186] A. A. Bennett, A. S. Gabriel, C. Calderwood, J. J. Dahling, and J. P. Trougakos, "Better Together? Examining Profiles of Employee Recovery Experiences," *Journal of Applied Psychology* 101, no. 12 (2016): 1635–54.
[187] I. Brissette, M. F. Scheier, and C. S. Carver, "The Role of Optimism in Social Network Development, Coping, and Psychological Adjustment during a Life Transition," *Journal of Personality and Social Psychology* 82, no. 1 (2002): 102–11.
[188] Y. Kalish, G. Luria, S. Toker, and M. Westman, "Till Stress Do Us Part: On the Interplay between Perceived Stress and Communication Network Dynamics," *Journal of Applied Psychology* 100, no. 6 (2015): 1737–51.
[189] L. K. Kammrath, B. F. Armstrong III, S. P. Lane, M. K. Francis, M. Clifton, K. M. McNab, and O. M. Baumgarten, "What Predicts Who We Approach for Social Support? Tests of the Attachment Figure and Strong Ties Hypotheses," *Journal of Personality and Social Psychology* 118, no. 3 (2020): 481–500; Y. Park and C. Fritz, "Spousal Recovery Support, Recovery Experiences, and Life Satisfaction Crossover among Dual-Earner Couples," *Journal of Applied Psychology* 100, no. 2 (2015): 557–66.
[190] T. N. Bauer and D. M. Truxillo, "Temp-to-Permanent Employees: A Longitudinal Study of Stress and Selection Success," *Journal of Occupational Health Psychology* 5, no. 3 (2000): 337–46.
[191] Vanhove et al., "Can Resilience Be Developed at Work?"
[192] P. Miquelon and R. J. Vallerand, "Goal Motives, Well-Being, and Physical Health: Happiness and Self-Realization as Psychological Resources under Challenge," *Motivation and Emotion* 30, no. 4 (2006): 259–72.
[193] A. M. Cianci, H. J. Klein, and G. H. Seijts, "The Effect of Negative Feedback on Tension and Subsequent Performance: The Main and Interactive Effects of Goal Content and Conscientiousness," *Journal of Applied Psychology* 95, no. 4 (2010): 618–30.
[194] Cianci, Klein, and Seijts, "The Effect of Negative Feedback on Tension and Subsequent Performance"; and S. J. Perry, L. A. Witt, L. M. Penney, and L. Atwater, "The Downside of Goal-Focused Leadership: The Role of Personality in Subordinate Exhaustion," *Journal of Applied Psychology* 95, no. 6 (2010): 1145–53.
[195] P. W. Lichtenthaler and A. Fischbach, "A Meta-Analysis of Promotion- and Prevention-Focused Job Crafting," *European Journal of Work and Organizational Psychology* 28, no. 1 (2019): 30–50.
[196] L. K. Barber and A. M. Santuzzi, "Please Respond ASAP: Workplace Telepressure and Employee Recovery," *Journal of Occupational Health Psychology* 20, no. 2 (2015): 172–89.
[197] M. M. Butts, R. J. Vandenberg, D. M. DeJoy, B. S. Schaffer, and M. G. Wilson, "Individual Reactions to High Involvement Work Processes: Investigating the Role of Empowerment and Perceived Organizational Support," *Journal of Occupational Health Psychology* 14, no. 2 (2009): 122–36; K. S. Mackie, C. K. Holahan, and N. H. Gottlieb, "Employee Involvement Management Practices, Work Stress, and Depression in Employees of a Human Services Residential Care Facility," *Human Relations* 54, no. 8 (2001): 1065–92; and S. Wood, M. Van Veldhoven, M. Croon, and L. M. de Menezes, "Enriched Job Design, High Involvement Management and Organizational Performance: The Mediating Roles of Job Satisfaction and Well-Being," *Human Relations* 65, no. 4 (2012): 419–45.
[198] Griffin and Clarke, "Stress and Well-Being at Work."
[199] L. Shen, "These 19 Great Employers Offer Paid Sabbaticals," *Fortune*, March 7, 2016, http://fortune.com/2016/03/07/best-companies-to-work-for-sabbaticals/.
[200] O. B. Davidson, D. Eden, M. Westman, Y. Cohen-Charash, L. B. Hammer, A. N. Kluger, ... and P. E. Spector, "Sabbatical Leave: Who Gains and How Much?," *Journal of Applied Psychology* 95, no. 5 (2010): 953–64.
[201] H. De La Torre and R. Goetzel, "How to Design a Corporate Wellness Plan That Actually Works," *Harvard Business Review*, March 31, 2016, https://hbr.org/2016/03/how-to-design-a-corporate-wellness-plan-that-actually-works; M. R. Frone, *Alcohol and Illicit Drug Use in the Workforce and Workplace* (Washington, DC: American Psychological Association, 2013); and A. Kohll, "8 Things you Need to Know about Employee Wellness Programs," *Forbes*, April 21, 2016, https://www.forbes.com/sites/alankohll/2016/04/21/8-things-you-need-to-know-about-employee-wellness-programs/#38054a8840a3;

C. J. Ott-Holland, W. J. Shepherd, and A. Marie Ryan, "Examining Wellness Programs over Time: Predicting Participation and Workplace Outcomes," *Journal of Occupational Health Psychology* 24, no.1 (2019): 163–79.
[202] The New Indian Express (June 19, 2019). "Bengaluru firms turn to yoga for enhancing employee health, productivity". Retrieved from https://www.newindianexpress.com (Accessed on April 20, 2022)
[203] Richardson and Rothstein, "Effects of Occupational Stress Management Intervention Programs."
[204] M. B. Hargrove, D. L. Nelson, and C. L. Cooper, "Generating Eustress by Challenging Employees: Helping People Savor Their Work," *Organizational Dynamics* 42, no. 1 (2013): 61–9.
[205] People Matters. "Better late than never: Creating effective employee health and wellness plan". Retrieved from https://www.peoplematters.in (Accessed on April 20, 2022)
[206] ASSOCHAM. "News". Retrieved from https://www.assocham.org (Accessed on April 20, 2022)
[207] Ott-Holland et al., "Examining Wellness Programs over Time."
[208] S. Mattke, L. Hangsheng, J. P. Caloyeras, C. Y. Huan, K. R. Van Busum, D. Khodyakov, and V. Shier, *Workplace Wellness Programs Study* (Santa Monica, CA: RAND, 2013).

17 Conflict and Negotiation

Source: To come

LEARNING OBJECTIVES

After studying this chapter, you should be able to:

17-1 Describe the three types of conflict and the three loci of conflict.

17-2 Outline the conflict process.

17-3 Contrast distributive and integrative bargaining.

17-4 Apply the five steps of the negotiation process.

17-5 Show how individual differences influence negotiations.

17-6 Assess the roles and functions of third-party negotiations.

Employability Skills Matrix (ESM)

	Myth or Science?	Career OBjectives	An Ethical Choice	Point/ Counter-point	Experi-ential Exercise	Ethical Dilemma	Case Incident 1	Case Incident 2
Critical Thinking				✓	✓	✓	✓	✓
Communication	✓	✓			✓		✓	
Collaboration	✓	✓	✓		✓	✓	✓	
Knowledge Application and Analysis		✓		✓	✓	✓	✓	✓
Social Responsibility			✓			✓		✓

BARGAINING CHIPS

What gives someone the ability to negotiate? Power? Money? Relationships? Can someone with seemingly no power, little access to the outside world, and almost no economic resources still have the power to bargain? Yes.

Raghu seemed to have nothing to negotiate with. The Tihar Jail inmate was serving a sentence for armed robbery at a state prison in Delhi, in April 2017. His sentence would last for over two decades. But with such a long sentence, Raghu knew he could not live in the inhumane conditions offered by the prison. While officials claimed that conditions in the prisons were meant to maintain security because of gang activity, many residents of the prison felt they were being subjected to cruel treatment. Many inmates were kept in lockdown for days at a time, despite laws that require at least a few hours of recreational activity a week. At the same time, limits on visitors meant that many inmates could rarely see family and friends.

In addition, the physical conditions also needed to be improved in the facility. Inmates complained of unhygienic conditions too. On top of this, the prison did not have air ventilation, which could be dangerous for inmates when temperatures soared high in the summer.

One inmate commented, "It's a violation of our rights. What's more disappointing is there is no action taken by the authorities," The inmates tried to negotiate by using the only bargaining chip they had: their stomachs. The inmates began refusing to eat, knowing that health problems from starvation would draw press and state officials' attention. The tactic proved successful. By the end of the month, Raghu and the rest of the protesting inmates were transferred to a prison with better conditions.

Lakshmi, Raghu's wife, was very relieved. "[We] have been trying to get my husband transferred from Tihar Central Jail for over a year. If we had known a hunger strike would get him transferred, then he should have gotten on it a year ago," she told a reporter.

A hunger strike may seem extreme, but it is a relatively common strategy when prisoners want to negotiate better conditions. They occur frequently in Indian prisons. A couple of years prior to when Raghu and many other inmates were striking in Tihar, hundreds of inmates took part in a hunger strike in Goalpara District Jail in Assam. Inmates at the Goalpara District Jail were especially vulnerable because they were undocumented immigrants without the same legal rights as the prisoners in Tihar. They complained about wage inequality. Similarly, the inmates of Beur Central jail seemed to have nothing to negotiate with. During the COVID-19 pandemic, all physical meetings with family members had been stopped. For the past eighteen months the inmates had not seen their family members and had to suffice with e-mulaqat (e-meeting) for 15 minutes a week. Some inmates complained even that was not allowed to them. Around 2000 inmates had written letters to the jail authorities. To draw attention of the jail authorities, the inmates began refusing to eat. The tactic proved successful. The inmates were allowed to meet their family members from October 2021.

Around the globe, the same tactic was being used by Palestinian inmates in Israeli prisons. Unlike the strikes in Indian prisons, the Palestinian hunger strike was especially political in nature. Led by a prominent Palestinian figure, Marwan Barghouti, the strike was meant to draw attention to persecution of Palestinian citizens in Israel. Besides leading the hunger strike, Barghouti was also punished for smuggling essays on Palestinian resistance to *The New York Times*.

Hunger strikes highlight many of the concepts we will cover in this chapter. First, they highlight a response to conflict. In the cases above, the conflicts between inmates and prison officials were dysfunctional. As you will learn from this text, however, some conflict is beneficial, and even necessary, because it enhances creativity and drives change in organizations. Second, the negotiation process tended to alleviate the conflict. By using their health as a bargaining tool, inmates in Tihar were able to gain better conditions. Would the same tactic always be successful in every context? Not necessarily. We will also explain many factors, from emotions to personality, that influence the success of negotiation techniques across situations.

Sources: Based on I. Fisher, "Over 1,000 Palestinian Prisoners in Israel Stage Hunger Strike," *New York Times*, April 17, 2017, https://www.nytimes.com/2017/04/17/world/middleeast/marwan-barghouti-hunger-strike-israel.html; PTI (2013). "40 Tihar Jail inmates go on hunger strike, claims activist". The Business Standard (January 20, 2013). Retrieved from https://www.business-standard.com; J. Amy, and Karmakar, R. (2018). "'Foreigners' in Assam detention camp on hunger strike". The Hindu *(March 21, 2018)*. Retrieved from https://www.thehindu.com (Accessed on April 15, 2022), Kumar A. (2021). "After hunger strike, prisoners in Bihar allowed to meet kin, get outside food". Hindustan Times (October 28, 2021). Retrieve from https://www.hindustantimes.com (Accessed on April 29, 2022)

A Definition of Conflict

17-1 Describe the three types of conflict and the three loci of conflict.

conflict A process that begins when one party perceives that another party has negatively affected or is about to negatively affect something that the first party cares about.

There has been no shortage of definitions for the word *conflict*,[1] but common to most is the idea that conflict is a perception. If no one is aware of a conflict, then it is generally agreed no conflict exists. Also needed to begin the conflict process are opposition or incompatibility, and interaction.

We define **conflict** broadly as a process that begins when one party perceives that another party has affected or is about to negatively affect something the first party cares about. Conflict describes the point in ongoing activity when interaction becomes disagreement. People experience a wide range of conflicts in organizations over an incompatibility of goals, differences in interpretations of facts, disagreements over behavioral expectations, and the like. Our definition covers the full range of conflict levels, from overt and violent acts to subtle forms of disagreement.

There is no consensus over the role of conflict in groups and organizations. In the past, researchers tended to argue about whether conflict was uniformly good or bad. Such simplistic views eventually gave way to approaches recognizing that not all conflicts are the same and that different types of conflict have different effects.[2]

functional conflict Conflict that supports the goals of the group and improves its performance.

dysfunctional conflict Conflict that hinders group performance.

Contemporary perspectives differentiate types of conflict based on their effects. **Functional conflict** supports the goals of the group, improves its performance, and is thus a constructive form of conflict.[3] For example, a debate among members of a work team about the most efficient way to improve production can be functional if unique points of view are discussed and compared openly. Conflict that hinders group performance is destructive or **dysfunctional conflict**.[4] A highly personal struggle for control in a team that distracts from the task at hand is dysfunctional. Exhibit 17-1 provides an overview depicting the effect of levels of conflict. To understand different types of conflict, we will discuss next the *types* of conflict and the *loci* of conflict.

Types of Conflict

task conflict Conflict over content and goals of the work.

relationship conflict Conflict based on interpersonal relationships.

process conflict Conflict over how work gets done.

One means of understanding conflict is to identify the *type* of disagreement, or what the conflict is about. Is it a disagreement about goals? Is it about people who just do not get along well with one another? Or is it about the best way to get things done? Although each conflict is unique, researchers have classified conflicts into three categories: task, relationship, or process. **Task conflict** relates to the content and goals of the work. **Relationship conflict** focuses on interpersonal relationships. **Process conflict** is about how the work gets done.[5]

Studies demonstrate that relationship conflicts, at least in work settings, are almost always dysfunctional[6] (although they may improve creativity under

Exhibit 17-1 **Conflict and Unit Performance**

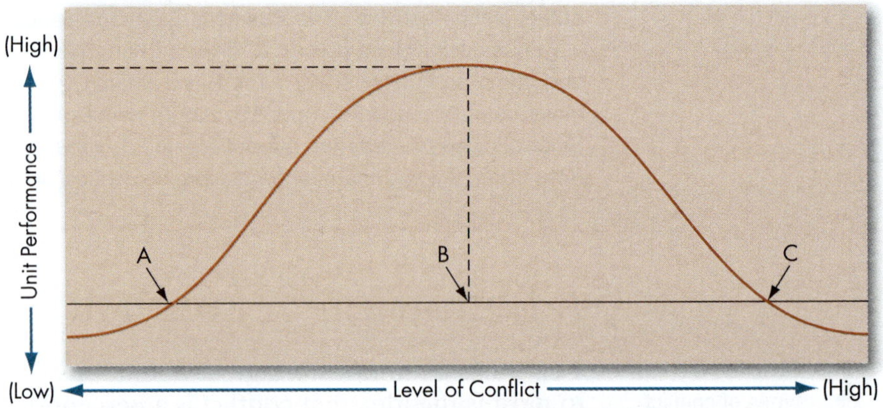

Situation	Level of Conflict	Type of Conflict	Unit's Internal Characteristics	Unit Performance Outcome
A	Low or none	Dysfunctional	Apathetic Stagnant Nonresponsive to change Lack of new ideas	Low
B	Optimal	Functional	Viable Self-critical Innovative	High
C	High	Dysfunctional	Disruptive Chaotic Uncooperative	Low

some circumstances).[7] Why? It appears that the friction and interpersonal hostilities inherent in relationship conflicts increase personality clashes and decrease mutual understanding, which hinders the completion of organizational tasks. Of the three types, relationship conflicts also appear to be the most psychologically exhausting for individuals.[8] This type of conflict can also be very problematic for employees who are new to the organization because newcomers rely on coworkers to learn information about the job.[9] Because they tend to revolve around personalities, you can see how relationship conflicts can become destructive. After all, we can't expect to change our coworkers' personalities, and we would generally take offense at criticisms directed at who we *are* as opposed to how we behave.

While scholars agree that relationship conflict is dysfunctional, there is considerably less agreement about whether task and process conflicts are functional. Early research suggested that task conflict within groups correlated to higher group performance, but a review of 116 studies found that generalized task conflict was essentially unrelated to group performance. However, there were factors of the conflict that could create a relationship between conflict and performance.[10] One such factor was whether the conflict included top management or occurred lower in the organization. Task conflict among top management teams was positively associated with performance, whereas conflict lower in the organization was negatively associated with group performance, perhaps because people in top positions may not feel as threatened in their organizational roles by conflict. This review also found that it mattered whether other types of conflict were occurring at the same time. If task and relationship conflict occurred together, task conflict was more likely negative, whereas if task conflict occurred by itself, it more likely was positive. Also, some scholars have argued that the strength of conflict is important—if task conflict is very low, people aren't really engaged or addressing the important issues. If task conflict is too high, however, infighting quickly degenerates into relationship conflict. Moderate levels of task conflict may thus be optimal. Supporting this argument, one study in China found that moderate levels of task conflict in the early development stage increased creativity in groups, but high levels decreased team performance.[11]

The personalities of the teams appear to matter. One study demonstrated that teams of individuals who are, on average, high in openness and emotional stability are better able to turn task conflict into increased group performance.[12] The reason may be that open and emotionally stable teams can put task conflict in perspective and focus on how the variance in ideas can help solve the problem rather than letting it degenerate into relationship conflicts.

What about process conflict? Researchers found that process conflicts are about delegation and roles. Conflicts over delegation often revolve around the perception of some members as shirking, and conflicts over roles can leave some group members feeling marginalized. Thus, process conflicts often become highly personalized and quickly devolve into relationship conflicts. It's also true, of course, that arguing about how to do something takes time away from actually doing it. We've all been part of groups in which the arguments and debates about roles and responsibilities seem to go nowhere.

Loci of Conflict

dyadic conflict Conflict that occurs between two people.

intragroup conflict Conflict that occurs within a group or team.

intergroup conflict Conflict between different groups or teams.

Another way to understand conflict is to consider its *locus*, or the framework within which the conflict occurs. Here, too, there are three basic types. **Dyadic conflict** is conflict between two people. **Intragroup conflict** occurs *within* a group or team. **Intergroup conflict** is conflict *between* groups or teams.[13]

Nearly all the literature on task, relationship, and process conflict considers intragroup conflict (within the group). That makes sense given that groups and teams often exist only to perform a particular task. However, it doesn't necessarily tell us all we need to know about the context and outcomes of conflict. For example, research has found that for intragroup task conflict to influence performance within the team positively, it is important that the team has a supportive climate in which mistakes aren't penalized and every team member "[has] the other's back."[14] Similarly, the personal needs of group members may determine when task conflict has a positive impact on performance. In a study of Korean work groups, task conflict was beneficial for performance when members were high on the need for achievement.[15]

But is this concept applicable to the effects of intergroup conflict? Think about, say, the teams in the Indian premier League (IPL). For a team to adapt and improve, perhaps a certain amount of intragroup conflict (but not too much) is good for team performance, especially when the team members support one another. But would we care whether members from one IPL team conflicted with members from another team? Probably not. In fact, if groups are competing with one another so that only one team can "win," interteam conflict seems almost inevitable. Still, it must be managed. Intense intergroup conflict can be quite stressful to group members and might well affect the way they interact. One study found, for example, that high levels of conflict between teams caused individuals to focus on complying with norms within their teams.[16]

It may surprise you that a group member's network position is important during intergroup conflicts. One study that focused on intergroup conflict found an interplay between an individual's position within a group and the way that individual managed conflict between groups. Group members who were relatively peripheral in their own group were better at resolving conflicts between their group and another one. But this happened only when those peripheral members were still accountable to their group.[17] Thus, being at the core of your work group does not necessarily make you the best person to manage conflict with other groups.

Another intriguing question about loci is whether conflicts interact with or buffer one another. Assume, for example, that Jia and Marcus are on the same team. What happens if they don't get along interpersonally (dyadic conflict) *and* their team also has high task conflict? Progress might be halted. What happens to their team if two other team members, Shawna and Justin, do get along well? The team might still be dysfunctional, or the positive relationship might prevail.

Thus, understanding functional and dysfunctional conflict requires not only that we identify the type of conflict; we also need to know where it occurs. It's possible that while the concepts of task, relationship, and process conflict are useful in understanding intragroup or even dyadic conflict, they are less useful in explaining the effects of intergroup conflict. But how do we make conflict as productive as possible? A better understanding of the conflict process, discussed next, will provide insight about potential controllable variables.

The Conflict Process

17-2 Outline the conflict process.

The conflict process has five stages: potential opposition or incompatibility, cognition and personalization, intentions, behavior, and outcomes (see Exhibit 17-2).[18]

Stage I: Potential Opposition or Incompatibility

The first stage of conflict is the appearance of conditions—causes or sources—that create opportunities for it to arise. These conditions may *not* lead directly to conflict, but one of them is necessary if it is to surface. We group the conditions into three general categories: communication, structure, and personal variables.

Communication Shailey had worked in a supply chain management firm for three years. She enjoyed her work largely because her manager, Satish, was a great boss. Then Satish was promoted and Kishore took his place. Six months later, Shailey says her job is frustrating. "Satish and I were on the same wavelength. It's not that way with Kishore. He tells me something, and I do it. Then he tells me I did it wrong. I think he means one thing but says something else. It's been like this since the day he arrived. I don't think a day goes by when he isn't yelling at me for something. You know, there are some people you just find it easy to communicate with. Well, Kishore isn't one of those!"

Exhibit 17-2 The Conflict Process

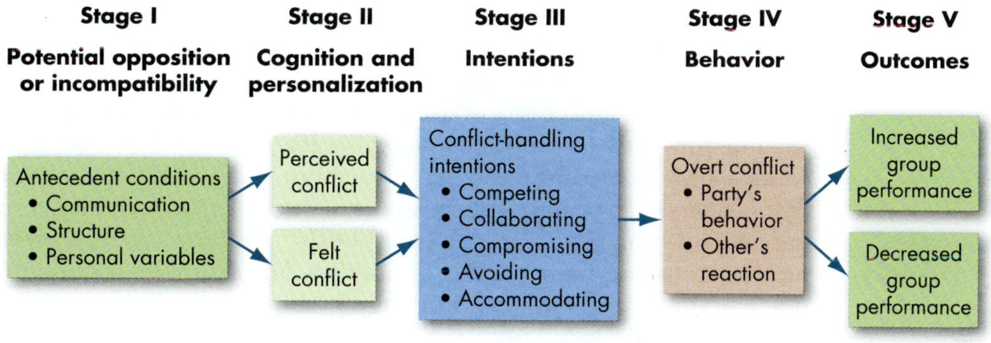

Shailey comments illustrate that communication can be a source of conflict.[19] Her experience represents the opposing forces that arise from semantic difficulties, misunderstandings, and "noise" in the communication channel (see Chapter 11). These factors, along with jargon and insufficient information, can be barriers to communication and may be potential antecedent conditions to conflict. The potential for conflict has also been found to increase with too little or *too much* communication. Communication is functional up to a point, after which it is possible to overcommunicate, increasing the potential for conflict.

Structure Gargi is a salesperson and Madhu is the company credit manager at Royal Oak, a large discount furniture retailer. The women have known each other for years and have much in common: They live two blocks apart, and their oldest daughters attend the same middle school and are best friends. If Gargi and Madhu had different jobs, they might be friends, but at work they constantly disagree. Gargi's job is to sell furniture, and she does it well. Most of her sales are made on credit. Because Madhu's job is to minimize credit losses, she regularly has to turn down the credit applications of Gargi's customers. It's nothing personal between the women; the requirements of their jobs just bring them into conflict.

The conflicts between Gargi and Madhu are structural in nature. The term *structure* in this context includes variables such as the size of the group, degree of specialization in tasks assigned to group members, role clarity, member–goal compatibility, leadership styles, reward systems, and degree of dependence between groups or group members. The larger the group and the more specialized its activities, the greater the likelihood of intragroup conflict. Tenure and conflict are inversely related, meaning that the longer a person stays with an organization, the less likely intragroup conflict becomes. Therefore, the potential for intragroup conflict is greatest when group members are younger and when turnover is high. However, intergroup conflict can self-perpetuate, actually imbuing *meaning* and *identity* to the groups experiencing conflict.[20]

Personal Variables Have you ever met someone you immediately disliked? Perhaps you disagreed with most of his opinions. Even insignificant characteristics—his voice, facial expressions, or word choice—may have annoyed you. Sometimes our impressions are negative. When you have to work with people you don't like, the potential for conflict arises.

Our last category of potential sources of conflict is personal variables, which include personality, emotions, and values. People high in the personality traits of disagreeableness, neuroticism, or self-monitoring (see Chapter 5) are prone to tangle with other people more often—and to react poorly when conflicts occur.[21] Emotions can cause conflict even when they are not directed at others. An employee who shows up to work irate from her hectic morning commute may carry that anger into her workday, which can result in a tension-filled meeting.[22] Incompatibilities in emotions can also lead to conflict—for example, if your supervisor is more optimistic than you about your work, you are more likely (than if you had similar optimistic–pessimistic outlooks) to experience more conflict, become less engaged, and perform poorly.[23] Differences in preferences and values can generate higher levels of conflict. For example, a study in Korea found that when group members didn't agree about their desired achievement levels, there was more task conflict; when group members didn't agree about their desired interpersonal closeness, there was more relationship conflict; and when group members didn't have similar desires for power, there was more conflict over status.[24]

Stage II: Cognition and Personalization

If the conditions cited in Stage I negatively affect something one party cares about, then the potential for opposition or incompatibility becomes actualized in the second stage.

perceived conflict Awareness by one or more parties of the existence of conditions that create opportunities for conflict to arise.

felt conflict Emotional involvement in a conflict that creates anxiety, tenseness, frustration, or hostility.

As we noted in our definition of conflict, one or more of the parties must be aware that antecedent conditions exist. However, just because a disagreement is a **perceived conflict** does not mean it is personalized. It is at the **felt conflict** level, when individuals become emotionally involved, that they experience anxiety, tension, frustration, or hostility.

Stage II is important because it's where conflict issues tend to be defined, where the parties decide what the conflict is about.[25] The definition of conflict is important because it delineates the set of possible settlements. Most evidence suggests that people tend to default to cooperative strategies in interpersonal interactions unless there is a clear signal that they are faced with a competitive person. However, if our salary disagreement is a zero-sum situation (the increase in pay you want means there will be that much less in the raise pool for me), I am going to be far less willing to compromise than if I can frame the conflict as a potential win–win situation (the dollars in the salary pool might be increased so both of us could get the added pay we want).

Second, emotions play a major role in shaping perceptions.[26] Negative emotions lead us to oversimplify issues, lose trust, and put negative interpretations on the other party's behavior.[27] When you perceive conflict, sometimes you may turn to a confidant within your group to vent or talk about what you are feeling. Paradoxically, if this person is responsive and reaffirming, your confidant may validate your perspective, which might undermine the resolution of conflict as a result.[28] In contrast, positive feelings increase our tendency to see potential relationships among elements of a problem, take a broader view of the situation, and develop innovative solutions.[29] Negative emotions are natural and perhaps inevitable—before conflict escalates, taking time to reflect and reappraise how you are feeling may help you approach the conflict more constructively (but don't ruminate!).[30] Ultimately, a state of mindfulness (see Chapter 17) might be a good emotional state to aspire toward, given it facilitates constructive conflict management.[31]

Stage III: Intentions

intentions Decisions to act in a particular way.

Intentions intervene between people's perceptions and emotions, and their overt behavior. They are decisions to act in a particular way.[32]

Intentions are a distinct stage because we have to infer the other's intent to know how to respond to behavior. Many conflicts escalate simply because one party attributes the wrong intentions to the other. There is slippage between intentions and behavior, so behavior does not always reflect a person's intentions accurately.

We can also think of conflict-handling intentions as falling along two dimensions. These two dimensions—*assertiveness* (the degree to which one party attempts to satisfy his or her own concerns) and *cooperativeness* (the degree to which one party attempts to satisfy the other party's concerns)—can help us identify five conflict-handling intentions: *competing* (assertive and uncooperative), *collaborating* (assertive and cooperative), *avoiding* (unassertive and uncooperative), *accommodating* (unassertive and cooperative), and *compromising* (midrange on both assertiveness and cooperativeness).[33]

competing A desire to satisfy one's interests, regardless of the impact on the other party to the conflict.

Competing When one person seeks to satisfy his or her own interests regardless of the impact on the other parties in the conflict, that person is **competing**.[34] We are more apt to compete when resources are scarce. We have competition-prone personalities when we are close to satisfying our own interests (e.g., the "finish line is near"), or when the culture or climate supports competition.[35]

collaborating A situation in which the parties in a conflict each desires to satisfy fully the concerns of all parties.

Collaborating When parties in conflict each desire to fully satisfy the concerns of all parties, there is cooperation and a search for a mutually beneficial outcome. In **collaborating**, parties intend to solve a problem by clarifying differences rather than by accommodating various points of view.[36] If you attempt to find a win–win solution that allows both parties' goals to be completely achieved, that's collaborating. Collaboration is more likely if the party is seen as competent, rational, and open to collaborating.[37]

avoiding The desire to withdraw from or suppress a conflict.

Avoiding A person may recognize that a conflict exists and want to withdraw from or suppress it. Examples of **avoiding** include trying to ignore a conflict and keeping away from others with whom you disagree.

accommodating The willingness of one party in a conflict to place the negotiation partner's interests above their own.

Accommodating A party who seeks to appease a negotiation partner may be willing to place the negotiation partner's interests above their own, sacrificing to maintain the relationship. We refer to this intention as **accommodating**. Supporting someone else's opinion despite your reservations about it, for example, is accommodating.

compromising A situation in which each party to a conflict is willing to give up something to resolve the conflict.

Compromising In **compromising**, there is no winner or loser. Rather, there is a willingness to rationalize the object of the conflict and accept a solution with incomplete satisfaction of both parties' concerns. The distinguishing characteristic of compromising therefore is that each party intends to give up something.

Stage IV: Behavior

When most people think of conflict, they tend to focus on Stage IV because this is where conflicts become visible. The behavior stage includes statements, actions, and reactions made by conflicting parties, usually as overt attempts

Exhibit 17-3 **Conflict-Intensity Continuum**

Annihilatory conflict
- Overt efforts to destroy the other party
- Aggressive physical attacks
- Threats and ultimatums
- Assertive verbal attacks
- Overt questioning or challenging of others
- Minor disagreements or misunderstandings

No conflict

Sources: Based on S. P. Robbins, *Managing Organizational Conflict: A Nontraditional Approach* (Upper Saddle River, NJ: Prentice Hall, 1974): 93–97; and F. Glasi, "The Process of Conflict Escalation and the Roles of Third Parties," in G. B. J. Bomers and R. Peterson (eds.), *Conflict Management and Industrial Relations* (Boston: Kluwer-Nijhoff, 1982): 119–40.

to implement their own intentions. As a result of miscalculations or unskilled enactments, overt behaviors sometimes deviate from original intentions.[38]

Stage IV is a dynamic process of interaction. For example, you make a demand on me, I respond by arguing, you threaten me, I threaten you back, and so on. Exhibit 17-3 provides a way of visualizing conflict behavior. All conflicts exist somewhere along this continuum. At the lower end are conflicts characterized by subtle, indirect, and highly controlled forms of tension, such as a student challenging a point the instructor has made. Conflict intensities escalate as they move upward along the continuum until they become highly destructive. Strikes, riots, and wars clearly fall in this upper range. Conflicts that reach the upper range of the continuum are almost always dysfunctional. Functional conflicts are typically confined to the lower range of the continuum.

Intentions that are brought into a conflict are eventually translated into behaviors. *Competing* brings out active attempts to contend with team members, and more individual effort to achieve ends without working together. *Collaborating* creates investigation of multiple solutions with other members of the team and trying to find a solution that satisfies all parties as much as possible. *Avoidance* is seen in behavior like refusals to discuss issues and reductions in effort toward group goals. People who *accommodate* put their relationships ahead of the issues in the conflict, deferring to others' opinions and sometimes acting as a subgroup with them. When people *compromise,* they both expect to (and do) sacrifice parts of their interests, hoping that if everyone does the same, an agreement will emerge.

A review that examined the effects of the four sets of behaviors across multiple studies found that openness and collaborating were both associated with superior group performance, whereas avoiding and competing strategies were associated with significantly worse group performance.[39] These effects were nearly as large as the effects of relationship conflict. Collaboration may be especially effective for tasks that require innovation, but it can lead to mistrust and conflict when groups are splintered into smaller groups of two or three based on task.[40] Individuals who have been assigned power tend to have a more difficult time using collaborative strategies.[41] This further demonstrates that it is not just the existence of conflict or even the type of conflict that creates

Exhibit 17-4 Conflict Management Techniques

Conflict-Resolution Techniques	
Problem solving	Meeting face to face for the purpose of identifying the problem and resolving it through open discussion.
Superordinate goals	Creating a shared goal that cannot be attained without the cooperation of each of the conflicting parties.
Expansion of resources	Expanding the supply of a scarce resource (for example, money, promotion, opportunities, office space).
Avoidance	Withdrawing from or suppressing the conflict.
Smoothing	Playing down differences while emphasizing common interests between the conflicting parties.
Compromise	Having each party to the conflict give up something of value.
Authoritative command	Letting management use its formal authority to resolve the conflict and then communicating its desires to the parties involved.
Altering the human variable	Using behavioral change techniques such as human relations training to alter attitudes and behaviors that cause conflict.
Altering the structural variables	Changing the formal organization structure and the interaction patterns of conflicting parties through job redesign, transfers, creation of coordinating positions, and the like.
Conflict-Stimulation Techniques	
Communication	Using ambiguous or threatening messages to increase conflict levels.
Bringing in outsiders	Adding employees to a group whose backgrounds, values, attitudes, or managerial styles differ from those of present members.
Restructuring the organization	Realigning work groups, altering rules and regulations, increasing interdependence, and making similar structural changes to disrupt the status quo.
Appointing a devil's advocate	Designating a critic to purposely argue against the majority positions held by the group.

Source: Based on S. P. Robbins, *Managing Organizational Conflict: A Nontraditional Approach* (Upper Saddle River, NJ: Prentice Hall, 1974): 59–89.

problems but rather the ways people respond to conflict and manage the process once conflicts arise.

If a conflict is dysfunctional, what can the parties do to deescalate it? Or, conversely, what options exist if conflict is too low to be functional and needs to be increased? This brings us to techniques of **conflict management**. Exhibit 17-4 lists the major resolution and stimulation techniques that allow managers to control conflict levels. We have already described several as conflict-handling intentions. Under ideal conditions, a person's intentions should translate into comparable behaviors.

conflict management The use of resolution and stimulation techniques to achieve the desired level of conflict.

Stage V: Outcomes

The action–reaction interplay between conflicting parties creates consequences. As our model demonstrates (see Exhibit 17-1), these outcomes may be functional if the conflict improves the group's performance, or dysfunctional if it hinders performance.

Functional Outcomes How might conflict act as a force to increase group performance? It is hard to visualize a situation in which open or violent aggression could be functional. But it's possible to see how low or moderate levels of conflict could improve group effectiveness. Note that all our examples focus on task and process conflicts and exclude the relationship variety.

Conflict is constructive when it improves the quality of decisions, stimulates creativity and innovation, encourages interest and curiosity among group

Lean production, pioneered by Toyota, creates a sense of creative tension within the workforce. They have to be creative in order to solve complex problems and address challenges, driving the success, productivity, and profitability of the business.

Source: jeremy sutton-hibbert/Alamy Stock Photo

members, provides the medium for problems to be aired and tensions released, and fosters self-evaluation and change. Mild conflicts also may generate energizing emotions so members of groups become more active, energized, and engaged in their work.[42]

Dysfunctional Outcomes The destructive consequences of conflict on the performance of a group or an organization are generally well known: Uncontrolled opposition breeds discontent, which acts to dissolve common ties and eventually leads to the destruction of the group. And, of course, a substantial body of literature documents how dysfunctional conflicts can reduce group effectiveness.[43] Among the undesirable consequences are poor communication, reductions in group cohesiveness, and subordination of group goals to the primacy of infighting among members. All forms of conflict—even the functional varieties—appear to reduce group member satisfaction and trust.[44] When active discussions turn into open conflicts between members, information sharing between members decreases significantly.[45] At the extreme, conflict can bring group functioning to a halt and threaten the group's survival.

Managing Functional Conflict If managers recognize that conflict can be beneficial in some situations, what can they do to manage conflict effectively in their organizations? In addition to knowing the principles of conflict motivation we just discussed, there are some practical guidelines for managers.

In anticipating and managing conflict, organizations can target three specific domains: *strategy* (e.g., designing conflict management activities with an understanding of their effect on the organization system, garnering managerial support for and application of conflict management strategies), *function* (e.g., encouraging the systemic adoption of conflict management practices, understanding employees' needs, job design to reduce conflict), and *worker* (e.g., improving employee perceptions of conflict, fostering ties and cohesion between people, adaptively addressing conflict as it emerges).[46] For example, if the conflict is expected to be perpetual and ongoing, a strategic conflict management strategy might not target resolving the conflict completely but instead focus on how people can adaptively address the conflict over time.[47]

Under ideal conditions, a person's intentions should translate into comparable behaviors. However, conditions are not always ideal, and the findings from research on conflict management have been inconsistent.[48] First, strategies appropriate for resolving one form of conflict may backfire and cause more conflict in another area.[49] For example, adopting a shared identity and improving relationship quality may unintentionally result in blurred distinctions between people's roles, stimulating task conflict. Second, strategies appropriate for managing one form of conflict may spill over into another domain.[50] For example, clearly outlining differences in what people do in the presence of task conflict can spill over to stimulate relational conflict. This is where strategic conflict management (as mentioned earlier) may come into play.

One of the keys to minimizing counterproductive conflicts is recognizing when there really is a disagreement. Many apparent conflicts are due to people using different verbiage to discuss the same general course of action. For example, someone in marketing might focus on "distribution problems," while someone from operations will talk about "supply chain management" to describe essentially the same issue. Successful conflict management recognizes these different approaches and attempts to resolve them by encouraging open, frank discussion focused on interests rather than issues.

Another approach is to have opposing groups pick parts of the solution that are most important to them and then focus on how each side can get its top needs satisfied. Neither side may get exactly what it wants, but each side will achieve the most important parts of its agenda.[51]

Third, groups that resolve conflicts successfully discuss differences of opinion openly and are prepared to manage conflict when it arises.[52] The most disruptive conflicts are those that are never addressed directly. An open discussion makes it much easier to develop a shared perception of the problems at hand; it also allows groups to work toward a mutually acceptable solution.

Fourth, managers need to emphasize shared interests in resolving conflicts so groups that disagree with one another don't become too entrenched in their points of view and start to take the conflicts personally. Groups with cooperative conflict styles and a strong underlying identification with the overall group goals are more effective than groups with a competitive style.[53]

Differences across countries in conflict resolution strategies may be based on collectivist tendencies and motives.[54] Collectivist cultures see people as deeply embedded in social situations, whereas individualist cultures see them as autonomous. As a result, collectivists are more likely to seek to preserve relationships and promote the good of the group as a whole. They avoid the direct expression of conflict, preferring indirect methods for resolving differences of opinion. Collectivists may also be more interested in demonstrations of concern and working through third parties to resolve disputes, whereas individualists are more likely to confront differences of opinion directly and openly.

Some research supports this theory. Compared to collectivist Japanese negotiators, their more individualist U.S. counterparts are more likely to see offers as unfair and to reject them. Another study revealed that, whereas U.S. managers were more likely to use competing tactics in the face of conflicts, compromising and avoiding were the most preferred methods of conflict management in China.[55] Interview data suggest, however, that top management teams in Chinese high-technology firms prefer collaboration even more than compromising and avoiding.[56]

Cross-cultural negotiations can also create issues of trust.[57] One study of Indian and U.S. negotiators found that respondents reported having less trust in their cross-culture negotiation counterparts. The lower level of trust was associated with less discovery of common interests between parties, which occurred because cross-culture negotiators were less willing to disclose and solicit information. Another study found that both U.S. and Chinese negotiators tended to have an ingroup bias, which led them to favor negotiating partners from their own cultures. For Chinese negotiators, this was particularly true when accountability requirements were high.

Having considered conflict—its nature, causes, and consequences—we now turn to negotiation, which often resolves conflict.

Negotiation

17-3 Contrast distributive and integrative bargaining.

Negotiation permeates the interactions of almost everyone in groups and organizations. There's the obvious: Labor bargains with management. There's the not-so-obvious: Managers negotiate with employees, peers, and bosses; salespeople negotiate with customers; purchasing agents negotiate with suppliers. And there's the subtle: An employee agrees to cover for a colleague for a few minutes in exchange for a future benefit. In today's loosely structured organizations, in which members work with colleagues over whom they have no direct authority and with whom they may not even share a common boss, negotiation skills are critical.

negotiation A process in which two or more parties exchange goods or services and attempt to agree on the exchange rate for them.

We can define **negotiation** as a process that occurs when two or more parties decide how to allocate scarce resources.[58] Although we commonly think of the outcomes of negotiation in one-shot transactional terms, like negotiating over the price of a car, every negotiation in organizations also affects the relationship between negotiators and the way negotiators feel about themselves.[59] Depending on how much the parties are going to interact with one another, sometimes maintaining the social relationship and behaving ethically will be just as important as achieving an immediate outcome of bargaining. Note that we use the terms *negotiation* and *bargaining* interchangeably.

Bargaining Strategies

There are two general approaches to negotiation—*distributive bargaining* and *integrative bargaining*.[60] As Exhibit 17-5 shows, they differ in their goal and motivation, focus, interests, information sharing, and duration of relationship. Let's define each and illustrate the differences.

Distributive Bargaining You see a used car advertised for sale online that looks great. You go see the car. It's perfect, and you want it. The owner tells you the

distributive bargaining Negotiation that seeks to divide up a fixed amount of resources; a win-lose situation.

fixed pie The belief that there is only a set amount of goods or services to be divvied up between or among the parties.

asking price. You don't want to pay that much. The two of you negotiate. The negotiating strategy you're engaging in is called **distributive bargaining**. Its identifying feature is that it operates under zero-sum conditions—that is, any gain I make is at your expense, and vice versa. Every dollar you can get the seller to cut from the car's price is a dollar you save, and every dollar the seller can get from you comes at your expense. The essence of distributive bargaining is negotiating over who gets what share of a fixed pie. By **fixed pie**, we mean a set amount of goods or services to be divvied up. When the pie is fixed, or the parties believe it is, they tend to engage in distributive bargaining.

The essence of distributive bargaining is depicted in Exhibit 17-6. Parties *A* and *B* represent two negotiators. Each has a *target point* that defines what he or she would like to achieve. Each also has a *resistance point*, which marks the lowest acceptable outcome—the point beyond which the party would break off negotiations rather than accept a less favorable settlement. The area between these two points makes up each party's *aspiration range*. As long as there is some overlap between *A*'s and *B*'s aspiration ranges, there exists a settlement range in which each one's aspirations can be met.

When you are engaged in distributive bargaining, one of the best things you can do is make the first offer, and make it an aggressive one. Making the first offer shows power; individuals in power are much more likely to make initial offers, speak first at meetings, and thereby gain the advantage. Another reason

Exhibit 17-5 Distributive versus Integrative Bargaining

Bargaining Characteristic	Distributive Bargaining	Integrative Bargaining
Goal	Get as much of the pie as possible	Expand the pie so that both parties are satisfied
Motivation	Win–lose	Win–win
Focus	Positions ("I can't go beyond this point on this issue.")	Interests ("Can you explain why this issue is so important to you?")
Interests	Opposed	Congruent
Information sharing	Low (Sharing information will only allow other party to take advantage.)	High (Sharing information will allow each party to find ways to satisfy interests of each party.)
Duration of relationship	Short term	Long term

Exhibit 17-6 Staking Out the Bargaining Zone

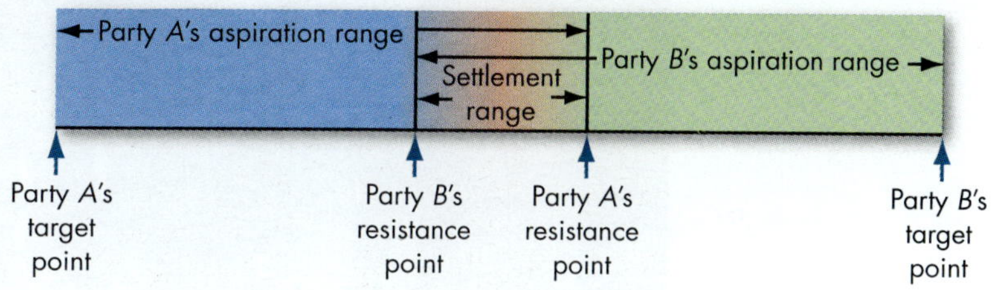

this is a good strategy is the anchoring bias, mentioned in Chapter 6. People tend to fixate on initial information. Once that anchoring point has been set, they fail to adequately adjust it based on subsequent information. A savvy negotiator sets an anchor with the initial offer, and scores of negotiation studies show that such anchors greatly favor the person who sets them.[61] However, framing matters: if you frame the first proposal as a *request* (i.e., I request your B for my A) instead of an *offer* (i.e., I offer my A for your B), it can be detrimental to your negotiation success by highlighting a "loss" rather than a "gain" for the negotiation partner.[62]

Say that you have a job offer, and your prospective employer asks you what sort of starting salary you want. You've just been given a gift—you have a chance to set the anchor, meaning you should ask for the highest salary you think the employer could reasonably offer. Asking for a million dollars is only going to make most of us look ridiculous, which is why we suggest being on the high end of what you think is *reasonable.* Too often, we err on the side of caution, afraid of scaring off the employer and thus settling for far too little. It *is* possible to scare off an employer, and it's true employers don't like candidates to be assertive in salary negotiations, but liking isn't the same as doing what it takes to hire or retain someone.[63] What happens much more often is that we ask for less than we could have obtained.

Not showing up for a meeting is a tactic that is used by many negotiators to put the other party on a backfoot. RPG Chairman Sanjeev Goenka recalls that the Spencer Group after having asked for a meeting at midnight never showed up for the meeting.[64]

Integrative Bargaining Jake was a Chicago luxury boutique owned by Jim Wetzel and Lance Lawson. In the early days of the business, Wetzel and Lawson moved millions of dollars of merchandise from many up-and-coming designers. They developed such a good rapport that many designers would send allotments to Jake without requiring advance payment. When the economy soured in 2008, Jake had trouble selling inventory, and designers were not being paid for what they had shipped to the store. Despite the fact that many designers were willing

Officials of General Motors and United Auto Workers participate in the ceremonial handshake that opens new contract negotiations. They are committed to integrative bargaining and work toward negotiating win–win settlements that boost GM's competitiveness. From left are GM CEO Mary Barra, UAW president Dennis Williams, GM VP Cathy Clegg, and UAW VP Cindy Estrada.
Source: Paul Sancya/AP Images

to work with the store on a delayed payment plan, Wetzel and Lawson stopped returning their calls. Lamented one designer, Doo-Ri Chung, "You kind of feel this familiarity with people who supported you for so long. When they have cash-flow issues, you want to make sure you are there for them as well."[65] Chung's attitude shows the promise of **integrative bargaining**. In contrast to distributive bargaining, integrative bargaining assumes that one or more of the possible settlements can create a win–win solution. Of course, as the Jake example shows, both parties must be engaged for integrative bargaining to work.

integrative bargaining Negotiation that seeks one or more settlements that can create a win-win solution.

Exhibit 17-7 illustrates how the two bargaining strategies can be utilized within the same negotiation episode. Early on in the episode, integrative strategies can be used, while later in the episode, distributive strategies can be used. Continuing with the previous example, if Wetzel and Lawson agreed to work with Chung to resolve their inventory dilemma, Chung could first clarify her needs to Wetzel and Lawson then articulate her interests in maintaining their relationship, all while trying to not come to a compromise right away. Once all of the needs and interests are established for both parties, she could then switch to a distributive strategy where she sets goals aligned with her needs and interests and attempts to maximize the extent to which these goals are met.

In terms of intraorganizational behavior, integrative bargaining is preferable to distributive bargaining because the former builds long-term relationships. Integrative bargaining bonds negotiators and allows them to leave the bargaining table feeling they have achieved a victory. Distributive bargaining, however, leaves one party a loser. It tends to build animosity and deepen divisions when people have to work together on an ongoing basis. Research shows that, over repeated bargaining episodes, a losing party who feels positively about the negotiation outcome is much more likely to bargain cooperatively in subsequent negotiations.

Why, then, don't we see more integrative bargaining in organizations? The answer lies in the conditions necessary for it to succeed. Evidence from a study of nearly 200,000 people found that the financially vulnerable are more likely to construe the negotiation in zero-sum terms, curtailing their ability to come to integrative solutions. Furthermore, negotiating parties who are open with information and candid about concerns are sensitive to other's needs and trust, and maintain flexibility tend to foster integrative bargaining.[66] Because these conditions seldom exist in organizations, negotiations often take a win-at-any-cost dynamic. Employees' personal characteristics and perceived accountability also play a role in whether negotiators come to an integrative solution. The use and effectiveness of negotiation strategies may depend on the regulatory focus of the parties involved (i.e., promotion or prevention focus; see Chapter 7) and accountability

Exhibit 17-7 Integration of Two Bargaining Strategies within a Negotiation Episode

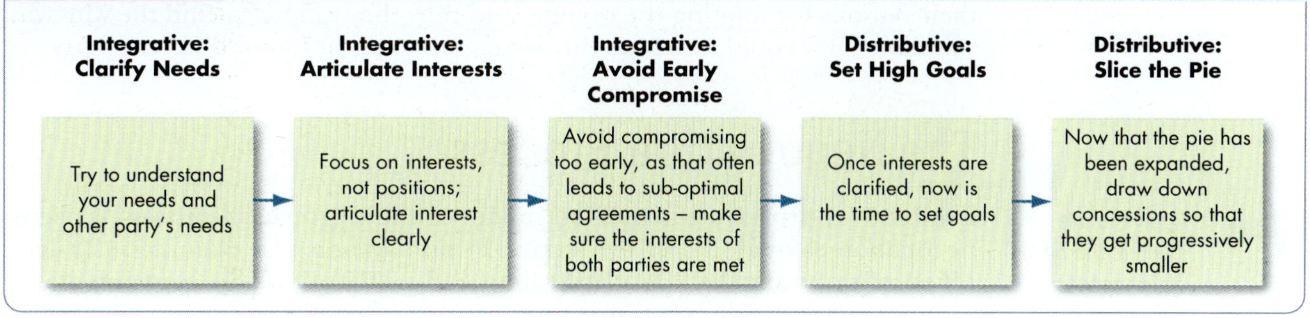

Myth or Science?

Teams Negotiate Better Than Individuals in Collectivistic Cultures

According to a recent study, this statement appears to be false.

In general, the literature has suggested that teams negotiate more effectively than individuals negotiating alone. Some evidence indicates that team negotiations create more ambitious goals, and that teams communicate more with each other than individual negotiators do.

Common sense suggests that if this is indeed the case, it is especially true in collectivistic cultures, where individuals are more likely to think of collective goals and be more comfortable working in teams. A study of the negotiation of teams in the United States and in Taiwan, however, suggests that this common sense is wrong. The researchers conducted two studies comparing two-person teams with individual negotiators. They defined negotiating effectiveness as the degree to which the negotiation produced an optimal outcome for both sides. U.S. teams did better than solo individuals in both studies. In Taiwan, solo individuals did better than teams.

Why did this happen? The researchers determined that, in Taiwan, norms respecting harmony already exist, and negotiating in teams only amplifies that tendency. This poses a problem because teams "satisfice" (settle for a satisfactory but less than optimal solution) to avoid conflict when norms for cooperation are exceptionally high. When Taiwanese individuals negotiate solo, at least they can clearly represent their own interests. In contrast, because the United States is individualistic, solo negotiators may focus on their own interests, which makes reaching integrative solutions more difficult. When Americans negotiate in teams, they become less inclined to focus on individual interests and therefore can reach solutions.

Overall, these findings suggest that negotiating individually works best in collectivistic cultures, and negotiating in teams works best in individualistic cultures.

Sources: Based on M. J. Gelfand, et al., "Toward a Culture-by-Context Perspective on Negotiation: Negotiating Teams in the United States and Taiwan," *Journal of Applied Psychology* 98 (2013): 504–13; and A. Graf, S. T. Koeszegi, and E.-M. Pesendorfer, "Electronic Negotiations in Intercultural Interfirm Relationships," *Journal of Managerial Psychology* 25 (2010): 495–512.

to a third party, such as a supervisor. Individuals are also more likely to use integrative bargaining when the other party expresses emotional ambivalence.[67]

Compromise may be your worst enemy in negotiating a win–win agreement. Compromising reduces the pressure to bargain integratively. After all, if you or your opponent caves in easily, no one needs to be creative to reach a settlement. People then settle for less than they could have obtained if they had been forced to consider the other party's interests, trade off issues, and be creative.[68] Consider a classic example in which two siblings are arguing over who gets an orange. Unknown to them, one sibling wants the orange to drink the juice, whereas the other wants the orange peel to bake a cake. If one capitulates and gives the other the orange, they will not be forced to explore their reasons for wanting the orange, and thus they will never find the win–win solution: They could *each* have the orange because they want different parts.

The Negotiation Process

17-4 Apply the five steps of the negotiation process.

Exhibit 17-8 provides a simplified model of the negotiation process. It views negotiation as made up of five steps: (1) preparation and planning, (2) definition of ground rules, (3) clarification and justification, (4) bargaining and problem solving, and (5) closure and implementation.[69]

Exhibit 17-8 **The Negotiation**

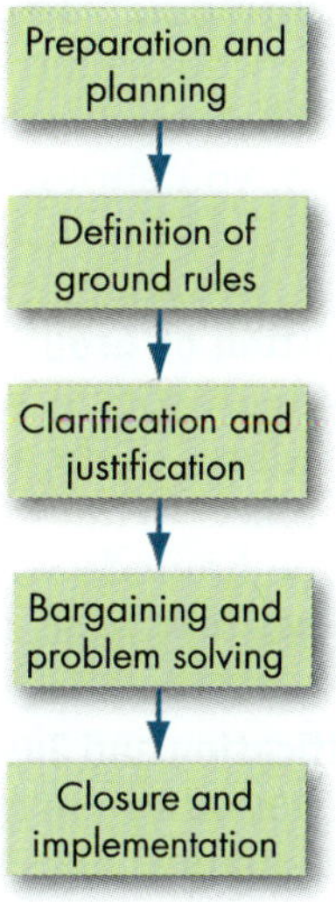

Preparation and Planning Before you start negotiating, do your homework. What's the nature of the conflict? What's the history leading up to this negotiation? Who's involved and what are their perceptions of the conflict? What do you want from the negotiation? What are *your* goals? If you're a supply manager at Dell Computer, for instance, and your goal is to get a significant cost reduction from your keyboard supplier, make sure this goal stays paramount in discussions and doesn't get overshadowed by other issues. It helps to put your goals in writing and develop a range of outcomes—from "most hopeful" to "minimally acceptable"—to keep your attention focused.

You should also assess what you think are the other party's goals. What is he or she likely to ask? How entrenched is his or her position likely to be? What intangible or hidden interests may be important to him or her? On what might he or she be willing to settle? When you can anticipate your opponent's position, you are better equipped to counter arguments with facts and figures that support your position.

Relationships change as a result of negotiation, so take that into consideration. If you could "win" a negotiation but push the other side into resentment or animosity, it might be wiser to pursue a more compromising style. If preserving the relationship will make you seem easily exploited, you may consider a more aggressive style. As an example of how the tone of a relationship in negotiations matters, people who feel good about the *process* of a job offer negotiation are more satisfied with their jobs and are less likely to leave the job a year later regardless of their actual *outcomes* from these negotiations.[70]

BATNA The best alternative to a negotiated agreement; the least a party in a negotiation should accept.

Once you've gathered your information, develop a strategy. You should determine your and the other side's best alternative to a negotiated agreement (**BATNA**). Your BATNA determines the lowest value acceptable to you for a negotiated agreement. Any offer you receive that is higher than your BATNA is better than an impasse.

In nearly all cases, the party with superior alternatives will do better in a negotiation, so experts advise negotiators to solidify their BATNA prior to any interaction. There is an interesting exception to this general rule—negotiators with absolutely no alternative to a negotiated agreement sometimes "go for broke" because they don't even consider what would happen if the negotiation falls through.[71] Think carefully about what the other side is willing to give up. People who underestimate their negotiating partner's willingness to give on key issues before the negotiation even starts end up with lower outcomes.[72] Conversely, you shouldn't expect success in your negotiation effort unless you're able to make the other side an offer it finds more attractive than its BATNA.

Definition of Ground Rules Once you've done your planning and developed a strategy, you're ready to define with the other party the ground rules and procedures of the negotiation itself. Who will do the negotiating? Where will it take place? What time constraints, if any, will apply? To what issues will negotiation be limited? Will you follow a specific procedure if an impasse is reached? During this phase, the parties will exchange their initial proposals or demands.

Clarification and Justification When you have exchanged initial positions, you and the other party will explain, amplify, clarify, bolster, and justify your original demands. This step needn't be confrontational. Rather, it's an opportunity for educating each other on the issues, why they are important, and how you arrived at your initial demands. Provide the other party with any documentation that supports your position.

Bargaining and Problem Solving The essence of the negotiation process is the actual give-and-take in trying to hash out an agreement. This is where both parties need to make concessions.

Closure and Implementation The final step in the negotiation process is formalizing your agreement and developing procedures necessary for implementing and monitoring it.[73] For major negotiations—from labor–management negotiations to bargaining over lease terms—this requires hammering out the specifics in a formal contract. For other cases, closure of the negotiation process is nothing more formal than a handshake.

Individual Differences in Negotiation Effectiveness

17-5 Show how individual differences influence negotiations.

Are some people better negotiators than others? The answer is complex. Four factors influence how effectively individuals negotiate: personality, mood/emotions, culture, and gender.

Personality Traits in Negotiations Can you predict a negotiation partner's negotiating tactics if you know something about his or her personality? Because personality and negotiation outcomes are related but only weakly, the answer is, at best, sort of.[74] Most research has focused on the Big Five trait of agreeableness, for obvious reasons—agreeable individuals are cooperative, compliant, kind, and conflict-averse. We might think such characteristics make agreeable individuals easy prey in negotiations, especially distributive ones. The evidence suggests, however, that overall agreeableness is weakly related to negotiation outcomes. Why is this so?

It appears that the degree to which agreeableness, and personality more generally, affects negotiation outcomes depends on the situation. The importance of being extraverted in negotiations, for example, very much depends on how the other party reacts to someone who is assertive and enthusiastic. One complicating factor for agreeableness is that it has two facets: The tendency to be cooperative and compliant is one, but so is the tendency to be warm and empathetic.[75] It may be that while the former is a hindrance to negotiating favorable outcomes, the latter helps. Empathy, after all, is the ability to take the perspective of another person and gain insight into and an understanding of him or her. We know perspective taking benefits integrative negotiations, so perhaps the null effect for agreeableness is due to the two tendencies pulling against one another. If this is the case, then the best negotiator is a competitive but empathetic one, and the worst is a gentle but empathetic one. Recent research also suggests that personality traits such as agreeableness and extraversion do have an effect, but the effect depends on personality similarity between parties, not overall levels. For example, if both parties are disagreeable, they will negotiate with each other more effectively than if one party was disagreeable and the other were agreeable.[76]

The type of negotiations may matter as well. In one study, agreeable individuals reacted more positively and felt less stress (measured by their cortisol levels) in integrative negotiations than in distributive ones. Low levels of stress, in turn, made for more effective negotiation outcomes.[77] Similarly, in hard-edged distributive negotiations, where giving away information leads to a disadvantage, extraverted negotiators do less well because they tend to share more information than they should.[78]

Self-efficacy is one individual-difference variable that seems to relate consistently to negotiation outcomes.[79] This is a fairly intuitive finding—it isn't too surprising to hear that those who believe they will be more successful in negotiation situations tend to perform more effectively. Maybe individuals who are more confident stake out stronger claims, are less likely to back down from their positions, and exhibit confidence that intimidates others. Although the exact mechanism is not yet clear, it does seem that negotiators may benefit from trying to get a boost in confidence before going to the bargaining table.

Research suggests intelligence predicts negotiation effectiveness, but, as with personality, the effects aren't especially strong.[80] In a sense, these weak links mean you're not severely disadvantaged, even if you're an agreeable extravert, when it's time to negotiate. We all can learn to be better negotiators.[81]

Moods and Emotions in Negotiations Do moods and emotions influence negotiation? They do, but the way they work depends on the emotion as well as the context. A negotiator who shows anger can induce concessions, for instance, because the other negotiator believes no further concessions from the angry party are possible. One factor that governs this outcome, however, is power—you should show anger in negotiations only if you have at least as much power as your counterpart. If you have less, showing anger actually seems to provoke hardball reactions from the other side.[82] Evoking emotions, such as sympathy, or expressing other emotions like sadness may also be used to persuade others.[83]

Another factor is how genuine your anger is—"faked" anger, or anger produced from surface acting (see Chapter 4), is not effective, but showing anger

Career OBjectives

How can I get a better job?

I feel like my career is at a standstill, and I want to talk to my boss about getting a more developmental assignment. How can I negotiate effectively for a better job position?

— Sugandha

Dear Sugandha:

You're certainly starting out on the right foot. A lot of people focus on salary as a way to achieve success and negotiate for the best short-run offer. There's obviously an advantage to this strategy in the short run, but sustained career growth has better payoffs in the long run. Developing skills can help put you on track for multiple salary increases. A strong skill set from developmental assignments will also give you a better position for future negotiations because you will have more career options.

Long-term career negotiations based on developmental assignments are also often easier to bring up with a supervisor. That's because salary negotiations are often a zero-sum situation, but career development negotiations can bring positive outcomes to both sides. When negotiating for a developmental assignment, make sure you emphasize a few points with your supervisor:

- *When it comes to salary negotiations, either you get the money, or the company keeps the money.* Given that, your interests and the interests of your managers are directly opposed. On the other hand, negotiating for developmental assignments usually means finding ways to improve not just your skills but also your contribution to the company's bottom line. You can, in complete honesty, frame the discussion around these mutual benefits.
- *Let your supervisor know that you are interested in getting better at your job and that you are motivated to improve through a developmental assignment.* Asking your supervisor for opportunities to grow is a clear sign that you are an employee worth investing in.
- *Be open to creative solutions.* It's possible that there are some idiosyncratic solutions (also called I-deals) for enhancing both your interests and those of your supervisor. One of the best things about an integrative bargaining situation like this is that you and your negotiation partner can find novel solutions that neither would have imagined separately.

Think strategically about your career, and you'll likely find you can negotiate not just for a better paycheck tomorrow but for a paycheck that keeps increasing in the years to come.

Sources: Based on Y. Rofcanin, T. Kiefer, and K. Strauss, "How I-Deals Build Resources to Facilitate Reciprocation: Mediating Role of Positive Affective States," *Academy of Management Proceedings* (August 2014), doi:10.5465/AMBPP.2014.16096abstract; C. Liao, S. J. Wayne, and D. M. Rousseau, "Idiosyncratic Deals in Contemporary Organizations: A Qualitative and Meta-Analytical Review," *Journal of Organizational Behavior* (October 16, 2014), doi:10.1002/job.1959; and V. Brenninkmeijer and M. Hekkert-Koning, "To Craft or Not to Craft," *Career Development International* 20 (2015): 147–62.

The opinions provided here are of the managers and authors only and do not necessarily reflect those of their organizations. The authors or managers are not responsible for any errors or omissions, or for the results obtained from the use of this information. In no event will the authors or managers, or their related partnerships or corporations thereof, be liable to you or anyone else for any decision made or action taken in reliance on the opinions provided here.

that is genuine (deep acting) is.[84] It also appears that having a history of showing anger induces more concessions because the other party perceives the negotiator as tough.[85] Finally, culture seems to matter. For instance, one study found that when East Asian participants showed anger, it induced more concessions than when the negotiator expressing anger was from the United States or Europe, perhaps because of the stereotype of East Asians as refusing to show anger.[86]

Another relevant emotion is disappointment. Generally, a negotiator who perceives disappointment from his or her counterpart concedes more. In one study, Dutch students were given 100 chips to bargain over. Negotiators who expressed disappointment were offered 14 more chips than those who didn't. In a second study, showing disappointment yielded an average concession of 12 chips. Unlike a show of anger, the relative power of the negotiators made no difference in either study.[87]

An Ethical Choice

Using Empathy to Negotiate More Ethically

You may have noticed that much of our advice for negotiating effectively depends on understanding the perspective and goals of the person with whom you are negotiating. Preparing checklists of your negotiation partner's interests, likely tactics, and BATNA have all been shown to improve negotiation outcomes. Can these steps make you a more ethical negotiator as well? Studies suggest that they might.

Researchers asked respondents to indicate how much they tended to think about other people's feelings and emotions and to describe the types of tactics they engaged in during a negotiation exercise. More empathetic individuals consistently engaged in fewer unethical negotiation behaviors like making false promises and manipulating information and emotions.

When considering how to improve your ethical negotiation behavior, follow these guidelines:

1. **Try to understand your negotiation partner's perspective.** This isn't accomplished just by understanding cognitively what the other person wants but by empathizing with the emotional reaction he or she will likely have to the possible outcomes.
2. **Be aware of your own emotions because many moral reactions are fundamentally emotional.** One study found that engaging in unethical negotiation strategies increased feelings of guilt so, by extension, feeling guilty in a negotiation may mean you are engaging in behavior you'll regret later.
3. **Beware of empathizing so much that you work against your own interests.** Just because you try to understand the motives and emotional reactions of the other side does not mean you have to assume the other person is going to be honest and fair in return. So be on guard.

Sources: Based on T. R. Cohen, "Moral Emotions and Unethical Bargaining: The Differential Effects of Empathy and Perspective Taking in Deterring Deceitful Negotiation," *Journal of Business Ethics* 94, no. 4 (2010): 569–79; and R. Volkema, D. Fleck, and A. Hofmeister, "Predicting Competitive-Unethical Negotiating Behavior and Its Consequences," *Negotiation Journal* 26, no. 3 (2010): 263–86.

People generally negotiate more effectively within cultures than between them. Politeness and positivity characterize the typical conflict-avoidant negotiations in Japan, such as with labor union leader Hidekazu Kitagawa (right), shown here presenting wage and benefits demands to Ikuo Mori, president of Fuji Heavy Industries, which makes Subaru vehicles.
Source: */Kyodo/Newscom

Anxiety also appears to have an impact on negotiation. For example, one study found that individuals who experienced more anxiety about a negotiation used more deceptions in dealing with others.[88] Another study found that anxious negotiators expect lower outcomes, respond to offers more quickly, and exit the bargaining process more quickly, leading them to obtain worse outcomes.[89]

As you can see, emotions—especially negative ones—matter to negotiation. Even emotional unpredictability affects outcomes; researchers have found that negotiators who express positive and negative emotions in an unpredictable way extract more concessions because this behavior makes the other party feel less in control.[90] As one negotiator put it, "Out of the blue, you may have to react to something you have been working on in one way, and then something entirely new is introduced, and you have to veer off and refocus."[91]

Culture in Negotiations Do people from different cultures negotiate differently? The simple answer is the obvious one: Yes, they do. However, there are many nuances in the way this works. It isn't as simple as "these negotiators are the best"; indeed, success in negotiations depends on the context.

So what can we say about culture and negotiations? First, it appears that people generally negotiate more effectively within cultures than between them. For example, a Colombian is apt to do better negotiating with a Colombian than with a Sri Lankan. Second, it appears that in cross-cultural negotiations, it is especially important that the negotiators be high in openness. This suggests a good strategy is to choose cross-cultural negotiators who are high on openness to experience, and to avoid factors such as time pressure that tend to inhibit learning about the other party.[92] Third, people are more likely to use certain negotiation strategies depending on what culture they belong to. For example, people from China and Qatar are more likely to use a competitive negotiation strategy than do people from the United States.[93]

Because emotions are culturally sensitive, negotiators need to be especially aware of the emotional dynamics in cross-cultural negotiation. One study, for example, explicitly compared how U.S. and Chinese negotiators reacted to an angry counterpart. Chinese negotiators increased their use of distributive negotiating tactics, whereas U.S. negotiators decreased their use of these tactics. That is, Chinese negotiators began to drive a harder bargain once they saw that their negotiation partner was becoming angry, whereas U.S. negotiators capitulated somewhat in the face of angry demands. Why the difference? It may be that individuals from East Asian cultures feel that using anger to get their way in a negotiation is not a legitimate tactic, so they refuse to cooperate when their negotiation partners become upset.[94]

Gender Differences in Negotiations There are many areas of organizational behavior (OB) in which men and women are not that different. Negotiation is not one of them. It seems fairly clear that men and women negotiate differently, men and women are treated differently by negotiation partners, and these differences affect outcomes (see OB Poll).

A popular stereotype is that women are more cooperative and pleasant in negotiations than men. Though this is controversial, there is some merit to it. Men tend to place a higher value on status, power, and recognition, whereas women tend to place a higher value on compassion and altruism. Women do tend to value relationship outcomes more than men, and men tend to value economic outcomes more than women.[95]

OB POLL

Men Ask More

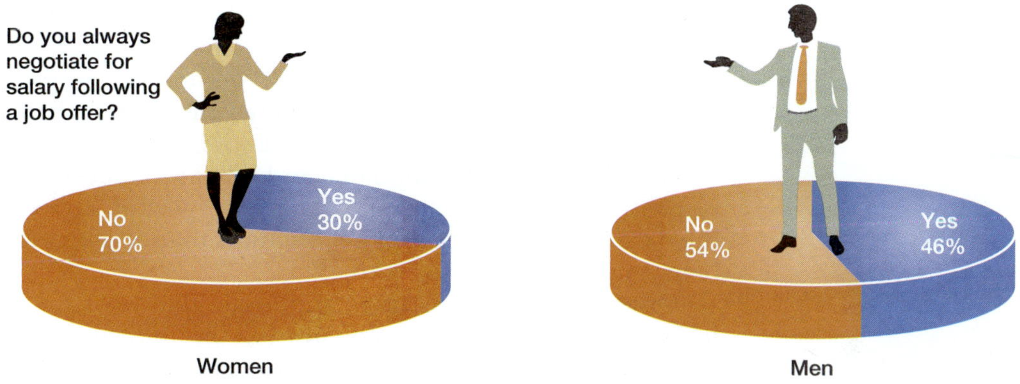

Source: Based on A. Gouveia, "Why Americans Are Too Scared to Negotiate Salary," *San Francisco Chronicle*, April 3, 2013, downloaded May 30, 2013, from http://www.sfgate.com/jobs/.

These differences affect both negotiation behavior and negotiation outcomes. Compared to men, women tend to behave in a less assertive, less self-interested, and more accommodating manner. As one review concluded, women "are more reluctant to initiate negotiations, and when they do initiate negotiations, they ask for less, are more willing to accept [the] offer, and make more generous offers to their negotiation partners than men do."[96] A study of MBA students at Carnegie-Mellon University found that the male students took the step of negotiating their first offer 57 percent of the time, compared to 4 percent for the female students. The net result? A $4,000 difference in starting salaries.[97]

One comprehensive literature review suggests that the tendency for men to receive better negotiation outcomes in some situations does not cover *all* situations.[98] Indeed, evidence suggested women and men bargained more equally in certain situations, women sometimes outperformed men, and men and women obtained more nearly equal outcomes when negotiating on behalf of someone else. In other words, everyone was better at advocating for others than they were at advocating for themselves. Another review of 123 studies found that gender differences are smaller when negotiators have experience with negotiating. Women also perform better in situations with low role incongruity.[99]

Factors that increased the predictability of negotiations also tended to reduce gender differences. When the range of negotiation settlements was well defined, men and women were more equal in outcomes. When more experienced negotiators were at the table, men and women were also more nearly equivalent. The study authors proposed that when situations are more ambiguous, with less well-defined terms and less experienced negotiators, stereotypes may have stronger effects, leading to larger gender differences in outcomes.

So what can be done to change this troublesome state of affairs? First, organizational culture plays a role. If an organization, even unwittingly, reinforces gender-stereotypic behaviors (men negotiating competitively, women negotiating cooperatively), it will negatively affect negotiations when anyone goes against stereotype. Men and women need to know that it is acceptable for each to show a full range of negotiating behaviors. Thus, a female negotiator who behaves competitively and a male negotiator who behaves cooperatively need to know that they are not violating expectations. Making sure negotiations are designed to focus on well-defined and work-related terms also has promise for reducing gender differences by minimizing the ambiguous space for stereotypes to operate. This focus on structure and work relevance also obviously helps focus negotiations on factors that improve the organization's performance.

Research is less clear on whether women can improve their outcomes by showing some gender-stereotypic behaviors. Researchers Laura Kray and colleagues suggested that female negotiators who were instructed to behave with "feminine charm" (be animated in body movements, make frequent eye contact with their partners, smile, laugh, be playful, and frequently compliment their partners) did better in negotiations than women not so instructed. These behaviors didn't work for men.[100]

Other researchers disagree and argue that what can best benefit women is to break down gender stereotypes for the individuals who hold them.[101] It's possible this is a short-term/long-term situation: In the short term, women can gain an advantage in negotiation by being both assertive and charming, but in the long term, their interests are best served by eliminating these sorts of sex role stereotypes.

Evidence suggests women's own attitudes and behaviors hurt them in negotiations. Managerial women demonstrate less confidence than men in anticipation of negotiating and are less satisfied with their performance afterward, even when their performance and the outcomes they achieve are similar to those for men.[102] Women are also less likely to see an ambiguous situation as an opportunity for negotiation. Women may unduly penalize themselves by failing to engage in negotiations that would be in their best interests. Some research suggests that women are less aggressive in negotiations because they are worried about backlash from others.

Negotiating in a Social Context

17-6 Assess the roles and functions of third-party negotiations.

We have been mostly discussing negotiations that occur among parties that meet only once and in isolation from other individuals. In organizations, however, many negotiations are open-ended and public. When you are trying to figure out who in a work group should do a tedious task, negotiating with your boss to get a chance to travel internationally, or asking for more money for a project, there's a social component to the negotiation. You are probably negotiating with someone you already know and will work with again, and the negotiation and its outcome are likely to be topics people will talk about. To understand negotiations in practice, then, we must consider the social factors of reputation and relationships.

Reputation

Your reputation is the way other people think and talk about you. When it comes to negotiation, having a reputation for being trustworthy matters. In short, trust in a negotiation process opens the door to many forms of integrative negotiation strategies that benefit both parties.[103] The most effective way to build trust is to behave in an honest way across repeated interactions. Then others will feel more comfortable making open-ended offers with many different outcomes. This helps to achieve win–win outcomes because both parties can work to achieve what is most important to themselves while still benefitting the other party.

Sometimes we either trust or distrust people based on word of mouth about a person's characteristics. What type of characteristics help a person develop a trustworthy reputation? A combination of competence and integrity.[104] Negotiators higher in self-confidence and cognitive ability are seen as more competent by negotiation partners.[105] They are also considered better able to describe accurately a situation and their own resources, and they are more credible when they make suggestions for creative solutions to impasses. Individuals who have a reputation for integrity can also be more effective in negotiations.[106] They are seen as more likely to keep their promises and present information accurately, so others are more willing to accept their promises as part of a bargain. This opens many options for the negotiator that wouldn't be available to someone who is not seen as trustworthy. Finally, individuals who have more solid reputations are better liked and have more friends and allies—in other words, they have more social resources, which may give them more implicit power in negotiations.

Relationships

There is more to repeated negotiations than just reputation. The social, interpersonal component of relationships with repeated negotiations means that individuals go beyond valuing what is simply good for themselves and instead start to think about what is best for the other party and the relationship as a whole.[107] Repeated negotiations built on a foundation of trust also broaden the range of options because a favor or concession today can be offered in return for some repayment further down the road.[108] Repeated negotiations also facilitate integrative problem solving. This occurs partly because people begin to see their negotiation partners in a more personal way over time and come to share emotional bonds.[109] Repeated negotiations also make integrative approaches more workable because a sense of trust and reliability has been built up.[110]

In sum, it's clear that an effective negotiator needs to think about more than just the outcomes of a single interaction. Negotiators who consistently act in a way that demonstrates competence, honesty, and integrity usually have better outcomes in the long run.

Third-Party Negotiations

Until this point, we've discussed bargaining in terms of direct negotiations. Occasionally, however, individuals or group representatives reach a stalemate and are unable to resolve their differences through direct negotiations. In such cases, they may turn to a third party to help them find a solution. There are three basic third-party roles: mediator, arbitrator, and conciliator.

mediator A neutral third party who facilitates a negotiated solution by using reasoning, persuasion, and suggestions for alternatives.

A **mediator** is a neutral third party who facilitates a negotiated solution by using reasoning and persuasion, suggesting alternatives, and the like. Mediators are widely used in labor–management negotiations and in civil court disputes. Their overall effectiveness is fairly impressive. For example, the Equal Employment Opportunity Commission (EEOC) reported a settlement rate through mediation at 72.1 percent.[111] But the situation is the key to whether mediation will succeed; the conflicting parties must be motivated to bargain and resolve their conflict. In addition, conflict intensity can't be too high; mediation is most effective under moderate levels of conflict. Finally, perceptions of the mediator are important; to be effective, the mediator must be perceived as neutral and noncoercive.

arbitrator A third party to a negotiation who has the authority to dictate an agreement.

An **arbitrator** is a third party with the authority to dictate an agreement. Arbitration can be voluntary (requested by the parties) or compulsory (forced on the parties by law or contract). The big plus of arbitration over mediation is that it always results in a settlement. Whether there is a downside depends on how heavy-handed the arbitrator appears. If one party is left feeling overwhelmingly defeated, that party is certain to be dissatisfied and the conflict may resurface at a later time.

conciliator A trusted third party who provides an informal communication link between the negotiator and the negotiation partner.

A **conciliator** is a trusted third party who provides an informal communication link between the negotiator and the negotiation partner. Agreeable individuals with a concern for others tend to adopt the role of conciliator, and they tend to be respected and admired by their peers as a result.[112] This role was made famous by Robert Duval in the first *Godfather* film. As Don Corleone's adopted son and a lawyer by training, Duval acted as an intermediary between the Corleones and the other Mafioso families. Comparing conciliation to mediation in terms of effectiveness has proven difficult because the two overlap a great deal. In practice, conciliators typically act as more than mere communication conduits. They also engage in fact finding, interpret messages, and persuade disputants to develop agreements.

Summary

While many people assume conflict lowers group and organizational performance, this assumption is frequently incorrect. Conflict can be either constructive or destructive to the functioning of a group or unit. Levels of conflict can be either too high or too low to be constructive. Either extreme hinders performance. An optimal level is one that prevents stagnation, stimulates creativity, allows tensions to be released, and initiates the seeds of change without being disruptive or preventing the coordination of activities.

Implications for Managers

- Choose an authoritarian management style in emergencies, when unpopular actions need to be implemented (such as cost cutting, enforcement of unpopular rules, discipline), and when the issue is vital to the organization's welfare. Be certain to communicate your logic when possible to make certain others remain engaged and productive.
- Seek integrative solutions when your objective is to learn, when you want to merge insights from people with different perspectives, when you need to gain commitment by incorporating concerns into a consensus, and when you need to work through feelings that have interfered with a relationship.
- You can build trust by accommodating others when you find you're wrong, when you need to demonstrate reasonableness, when other positions need to be heard, when issues are more important to others than to

yourself, when you want to satisfy others and maintain cooperation, when you can build social credits for later issues, to minimize loss when you are outmatched and losing, and when others should learn from their own mistakes.

- Consider compromising when goals are important but not worth potential disruption, when opponents with equal power are committed to mutually exclusive goals, and when you need temporary settlements to complex issues.
- Distributive bargaining can resolve disputes, but it often reduces the satisfaction of one or more negotiators because it is confrontational and focused on the short term. Integrative bargaining, in contrast, tends to provide outcomes that satisfy all parties and build lasting relationships.

Nonunion Positions and the Gig Economy Are Bad for Workers

POINT

What do Uber, Etsy, and Amazon Turk all have in common? All of these platforms are fuel for short-term freelance work, and a reflection of what economists have dubbed the gig economy. Fifty years ago, employers expected workers to stay with a company for 30 years. In exchange for their loyalty, employees were given more opportunities and a pension. Unlike the labor market of today, companies promoted from within. As this practice fell by the wayside, employers hired employees for shorter and shorter periods. Now, many new jobs are not long-term or even short-term positions: They're gigs. Employees work as independent contractors, using third-party platforms to connect to clients. Because these employees do not have a traditional employment contract, they have complete flexibility: They can work as much or as little as they want.

Unfortunately, many of these platforms have a dirty secret. Unlike regular employment, people who are employed primarily through gigs do not have the benefits of a traditional job. Because they're considered self-employed, they do not get paid for overtime, do not receive benefits, and have no collective bargaining power. There's also evidence that they're replacing rather than supplementing more stable employment. For example, Uber and Lyft drivers tripled in Silicon Valley from 2012 to 2014, while payrolled cab and limo jobs decreased by 31 percent in the same time period.

Without the ability to collectively bargain, the labor market is akin to the Wild West. That's why many freelancers on these platforms are trying to unionize. In New York and Seattle, labor unions are trying to allow gig employees that work as rideshare drivers, house cleaners, and delivery persons the ability to create collective bargaining units. Doing so will allow employees to demand health benefits and overtime. It will also ensure that these employees make a living hourly wage, which is rare for gig employees based on recent research. Many employees, despite working 60 hours a week, still do not make as much as a traditional employee.

Yes, it's great for employers to sell younger generations on the flexibility of these positions. But in exchange for flexibility, they are also losing the power to negotiate for fair working conditions. Let's stop pretending that freelance work platforms like Uber are good for the economy, and leave the gig economy trend at the curb.

COUNTERPOINT

While the gig economy has its drawbacks, these platforms exist for a reason. Employers and employees alike are fed up with traditional employment. Yes, some people who work through freelance apps use it as a primary source of income. But there are just as many, if not more, who just want a flexible second job to get a little extra cash. If these positions were like the services they are replacing (e.g., cab companies), then gig employees would have to agree to specific policies regarding sick days and work a set schedule.

I'm also skeptical of this idea that freelancers are replacing traditional employment. Yes, some city-level data shows that gig-based jobs increased while payroll jobs decreased. But there are also more data from 2010 to 2014 that suggest that contractor and payroll jobs have increased in most sectors that support freelance platforms. For example, while use of freelance platforms like Airbnb increased over four years, payroll jobs in hospitality also increased. The same is true for the transportation industry over the same time period. If anything, the reason these freelance platforms have been so successful is because these industries are growing. It's not that they're replacing traditional services—they're meeting the demand that traditional services cannot fulfill.

The benefits of having a collective bargaining agreement may also be exaggerated. Whenever a group tries to create a collective bargaining agreement, it causes conflict. A 2016 poll indicates that most employees (80 percent) believe leaders will not protect the interests of the group as a whole. Instead, leaders usually use their power in numbers to protect their own self-interests in negotiations.

Collective bargaining doesn't just hurt businesses—it also hurts the public. For example, the International Civil Aviation Organization has been trying to put cameras in commercial airline cockpits. These cameras would allow authorities and employers to monitor pilots on the job. These videos can help piece together why plane crashes occur. Yet pilots have been using collective bargaining techniques to fight the initiative on grounds that it violates airline pilots' privacy. They also insist that it could be used to "lead investigators away from accurate conclusions" regarding employees' performance.

Yes, traditional employment allows employees to bargain for rights as a group. But this also leads to concessions and conflict that do not benefit employees or their employers.

Sources: Based on A. Nunes, "Unions Are Hurting Public Safety," *Forbes*, April 10, 2017, https://www.forbes.com/sites/ashleynunes/2017/04/10/unions-are-hurting-public-safety/2/#396682da516e; Rasmussen Polling, "Most Say Union Leaders Out of Touch with Members," *Rasmussen Reports*, August 10, 2016, http://www.rasmussenreports.com/public_content/politics/general_politics/august_2016/most_say_union_leaders_out_of_touch_with_members; D. DeMay, "Driver Union, for Lyft, Uber, Forces Seattle to Ask Tough Questions about 'Gig' Economy," *Seattle Post-Intelligencer*, December 19, 2016, http://www.seattlepi.com/local/transportation/article/Driver-union-for-Lyft-Uber-forces-Seattle-to-10797019.php; M. Murro, "The Gig Economy: Complement or Cannibal?," *Brookings*, November 17, 2016, https://www.brookings.edu/blog/the-avenue/2016/11/17/the-gig-economy-complement-or-cannibal/; Reuters, "Unions and the Gig Economy Are Gearing Up for Battle in This State," *Fortune*, November 28, 2016, http://fortune.com/2016/11/28/unions-gig-economy-new-york/; and K. Kokalitcheva, "Uber Lost Hundreds of Millions in the Most Recent Quarter," *Fortune*, December 19, 2016, http://fortune.com/2016/12/19/uber-financials-2016/.

CHAPTER REVIEW

QUESTIONS FOR REVIEW

17-1 What are the three types of conflict and the three loci of conflict?

17-2 What are the steps in the conflict process?

17-3 What are the differences between distributive and integrative bargaining?

17-4 What are the five steps in the negotiation process?

17-5 How do individual differences influence negotiations?

17-6 What are the roles and functions of third-party negotiations?

APPLICATION AND EMPLOYABILITY

Conflict is an inevitable part of every workplace. As you learned in this chapter, conflict is also beneficial in certain contexts. You also learned about negotiation, and how and when certain negotiation and conflict resolution strategies may be used. While exploring these topics, you used many skills that can help you be more employable. You learned collaboration while exploring why collectivist teams are not better negotiators, learned how to use concepts from the chapter to move forward in your career, and assessed how to be a more empathetic negotiator. You also applied your knowledge of bargaining to America's growing gig economy. In the next section, you will develop these skills further while also using your critical thinking skills to evaluate the pros and cons of unions, resolve a conflict between coworkers, assess how to deal with an overly assertive employee, and take part in a negotiation role play.

EXPERIENTIAL EXERCISE A Negotiation Role Play

You will consider two scenarios for this case: One is more distributive, the other more integrative. Form pairs, with one of you taking the role of the engineering director, and the other taking the role of the marketing director. Read only your own side's specific information for the two negotiation processes. The overall situation is the same for both scenarios, but the priorities and outlook for the parties change depending on whether you are negotiating the "contested resources" scenario or the "combined future" scenario.

The Case

Cytrix develops integrated bicycle and running performance systems. Runners and bikers wear the Cytrix watch, which uses GPS signals to identify their location and the distance they've covered. This information can then be uploaded to the Cytrix Challenge website, where users record their performance over time. Social media tools also allow them to compare their performance relative to that of friends. The majority of users are either amateur student athletes or committed adult hobbyists like marathon runners.

The organization needs to determine how to allocate a fixed pool of resources for future development between the marketing and engineering groups. Rather than making an executive decision about resource allocation, the top management team has asked the respective teams to allocate $30 million for planned future development and decide who will run different parts of the project.

Specific Information for the Marketing Group

Only the marketing manager should read this section.

The marketing group has been tracking the major areas of sales and has come to the conclusion that Cytrix has saturated the market. New sources of customers, especially general consumers who are interested in health but are not committed athletes, will need to be considered for future growth. Research into sales of competitive products and areas where competitors are failing to meet consumer demands is needed. The marketing group's primary goal is to allocate sufficient resources to finance the research. The group also wants to retain control over which new products will be developed. Marketing would prefer to see engineering act in a consulting role, determining how best to manufacture the devices that fit the needs identified above.

Specific Information for the Engineering Group

Only the engineering manager should read this section.

The engineering group has recently been tracking the development of new hardware that will improve the accuracy of distance and speed estimates in remote areas. Several other companies are already experimenting with similar designs. To realize this improvement fully, engineering believes it will be necessary to develop the technology further so it is both lightweight and inexpensive to produce. The engineering group's primary goal is to allocate sufficient resources to develop these new technologies. The engineers would prefer to see marketing act in a consulting role, determining how best to advertise and deliver the new devices.

Contested Resources Scenario

The marketing and engineering departments are locked in a struggle for power. Your side (either marketing or engineering) should try to direct the largest possible proportion of both money and authority toward your proposed program. You still need to think of a solution in which the other side ultimately agrees to assist you in implementing the program. If you can't reach an agreement for shared resources, the CEO will appoint new directors for both groups.

Combined Future Scenario

The marketing and engineering departments are eager to find a positive solution. Both sides should try to see that the company's future needs are met. You know that to achieve success everyone needs to work together, so you'd like to find a way to divide the money and resources that benefits both marketing and engineering. Plans can incorporate multiple techniques for sharing and collaborating with resources.

The Negotiation

At the start of the negotiation, the instructor randomly assigns half the groups to the contested resources scenario and the other half to the combined future scenario. Begin the process by outlining the goals and resources for your side of the negotiation. Then negotiate over the terms described in your scenario, attempting to advocate for a solution that matches your perspective.

Debriefing

Afterward, you will get together with the other students to discuss the processes used. Especially consider the differences in outcomes between the contested resources and combined future scenarios. Either scenario could arise in a real work environment, so think about how different negotiation situations give rise to different strategies, tactics, and outcomes.

ETHICAL DILEMMA The Case of the Overly Assertive Employee

In this chapter, we learned about several conflict-handling intentions. Each of these intentions involved two dimension—assertiveness (the degree to which one party attempts to satisfy his or her own concerns) and cooperativeness (the degree to which one party attempts to satisfy the other party's concerns). Consider these dimensions, and then put yourself in the shoes of the manager described below.

Tom is a manager at a small copy supply firm. Their marketing team consists mainly of two employees: Janna and Kim. Kim is incredibly assertive, while Janna is incredibly cooperative. Though you are their manager, they sometimes have the discretion to negotiate with each other over who is responsible for which task in a project. You notice that Janna seems always to do the most tedious, unpleasant tasks. When you've asked Janna in the past if she is happy with what she contributes to projects, she meekly replies, "I don't mind. I don't want to make any waves."

You sense that Janna is unhappy but also scared of a confrontation with Kim. Kim is getting more recognition and compliments from the CEO because she does high-profile work. You know this puts Janna at a disadvantage in her career. On the other hand, Kim is overly assertive. You know that if you ask her to be more cooperative, it could cause more conflict in the office.

As we learned about relationship conflict, it's almost never beneficial. Yes, it may be unfair to Janna, but you don't want to disrupt the team by bringing conflict into the office. You also know that conflict tends to spread in the office—if Kim and Janna are at odds with each other, it may distract people on other teams.

Questions

17-7. If Tom does nothing, is that ethical? Does he have a responsibility to Janna to make sure her concerns are addressed?

17-8. In this chapter, you learned about mediators, arbitrators, and conciliators. Is it possible for Tom to act in one of these roles? Why or why not?

17-9. If Tom does nothing in this situation, how do you think the situation between Janna and Kim will play out? Do you think there will be problems with conflict?

CASE INCIDENT 1 Disorderly Conduct

The sound of Mohit and Pankaj's arguing is familiar to everyone in the office by now. In an effort to make the best use of space and ensure a free flow of discussion and ideas, the founder of Markay Design had decided to convert the one-floor office of the company to an open plan with no walls between workers. The goal of such a layout is to eliminate boundaries and enhance creativity. But for Mohit and Pankaj, the new arrangement creates a growing sense of tension.

The argument boils down to the question of workspace order and organization. Pankaj prefers to keep his desk completely clean and clear, and he keeps a stack of cleaning wipes in a drawer to eliminate any dust or dirt. Mohit, on the other hand, likes to keep all his work visible on his desk, so sketches, plans, magazines, and photos are scattered everywhere, alongside boxes of crackers and coffee cups. Pankaj finds it hard to concentrate when he sees Mohit's piles of materials everywhere, while Mohit feels he can be more creative and free flowing when he's not forced to clean and organize constantly. Many of Mohit and Pankaj's coworkers wish they'd just let the issue drop. The men enjoyed a good working relationship in the past, with Pankaj's attention to detail and thorough planning serving to rein in some of Mohit's wild inspirations. But of late, their collaborations have been derailed in disputes.

Everyone knows it's not productive to engage in conflicts over every small irritant in the workplace. However, completely avoiding conflict can be equally negative. An emerging body of research has examined so-called conflict cultures in organizations. The findings suggest having a culture that actively avoids and suppresses conflicts is associated with lower levels of creativity. Cultures that push conflict underground but do not succeed in reducing the underlying tensions can become passive-aggressive, marked by underhanded behavior against other coworkers.

Ultimately, finding a way through the clutter dispute is probably going to be an ongoing process to find a balance between perspectives. Both Mohit and Pankaj worry that if they can't find a solution, their usually positive work relationship will be too contentious to bear. And that would be a real mess.

Questions

17-10. Describe some of the factors that led this situation to become an open conflict.

17-11. Do you think this is an issue worth generating conflict over? What are the potential costs and benefits of Mohit and Pankaj having an open discussion of the issues?

17-12. How can Mohit and Pankaj develop an active problem-solving discussion to resolve this conflict? What could effectively be changed, and what is probably going to remain a problem?

Sources: Based on S. Shellenbarger, "Clashing over Office Clutter," *Wall Street Journal,* March 19, 2014, http://www.wsj.com/articles/SB10001424052702304747404579447331212245004; S. Shellenbarger, "To Fight or Not to Fight? When to Pick Workplace Battles," *Wall Street Journal,* December 17, 2014, http://www.wsj.com/articles/picking-your-workplace-battles-1418772621; and M. J. Gelfand, J. R. Harrington, and L. M. Leslie, "Conflict Cultures: A New Frontier for Conflict Management Research and Practice," in N. M. Ashkanasy, O. B. Ayoko, and K. A. Jehn (eds.), *Handbook of Conflict Management Research* (Northampton, MA: Edward Elgar, 2014): 109–35.

CASE INCIDENT 2 Start-up Stress

Nikolay Storonsky, a British-Russian entrepreneur, prides himself on straight answers. Despite conventional wisdom, the co-founder and CEO of Revolut says that he has little time for work–life balance. According to him, the concept has no place while building a start-up, when the focus should be on competing with established and better-funded firms, attracting customers, and working with limited resources—on winning the "game."

After a funding round raised nearly €500 million, Revolut became one of the world's most valuable financial technology firms in 2020, with a valuation of €5 billion. It's an extraordinary achievement as it was founded just five years prior, has yet to make a profit, and lost €36 million in 2018. Fast growth has also brought problems. Revolut is grappling with the difficulties of finding and retaining the right staff as it transforms itself from a tiny, scrappy business into one with 2,000 employees, forecast to grow to 5,000 by the end of 2020.

The company has earned a reputation for a tough working environment where employees work long hours at the office, sometimes during weekends as well. Those in the tech start-up sector expect to work for long hours, but working at Revolut is known for being particularly demanding. Storonsky says that he is in the office from 8 am to 10 pm on a typical day. He dismisses the suggestion that his staff are overworked, but he acknowledges that he is demanding. "As you make the world better you will need to break walls," he says. "And to break walls you really need to try hard, and unfortunately trying hard means in many cases you need to spend time on it." He claims he has never come across a burnt-out employee and pledges to pay for a two-week holiday for any of his staff who feels overwhelmed by the demands of their job.

Nevertheless, one former executive claims to have left because Storonsky seemed to micromanage his senior management team and had little interest in his staff's work–life balance. "You can sacrifice your life," the executive said. "But you can't do it forever."

Questions

17-13. What might be the potential sources of stress at Revolut?

17-14. Do you think Nikolay Storonsky's attitudes toward work–life balance are valid for start-ups? Why?

17-15. What could be the long-term consequences if Revolut's employees are expected to work long hours in a highly competitive environment?

17-16. What would you recommend to the company to manage stress?

Sources: K. Shubber, "Revolut's Nikolay Storonsky on Long Hours and High Staff Turnover," *Financial Times*, February 18, 2018; and I. Withers, "British Fintech Revolut Hits $5.5 billion Valuation after Funding Round," *Reuters*, February 25, 2020.

ENDNOTES

[1] See, for instance, D. Tjosvold, A. S. H. Wong, and N. Y. F. Chen, "Constructively Managing Conflicts in Organizations," *Annual Review of Organizational Psychology and Organizational Behavior* 1 (March 2014): 545–68; and M. A. Korsgaard, S. S. Jeong, D. M. Mahony, and A. H. Pitariu, "A Multilevel View of Intragroup Conflict," *Journal of Management* 34, no. 6 (2008): 1222–52.

[2] C. K. W. De Dreu, "Conflict at Work: Basic Principles and Applied Issues," in S. Zedeck (ed.), *APA Handbook of Industrial and Organizational Psychology* (Washington, DC: APA Press, 2012): 461–93.

[3] B. Brehmer, "Social Judgment Theory and the Analysis of Interpersonal Conflict," *Psychological Bulletin* 83, no. 1 (1976): 985–1003.

[4] Ibid.

[5] K. A. Jehn, "A Qualitative Analysis of Conflict Types and Dimensions in Organizational Groups," *Administrative Science Quarterly* 42, no. 1 (1997): 530–57.

[6] F. R. C. de Wit, L. L. Greer, and K. A. Jehn, "The Paradox of Intragroup Conflict: A Meta-Analysis," *Journal of Applied Psychology* 97, no. 2 (2012): 360–90; and N. Gamero, V. González-Romá, and J. M. Peiró, "The Influence of Intra-Team Conflict on Work Teams' Affective Climate: A Longitudinal Study," *Journal of Occupational and Organizational Psychology* 81, no. 1 (2008): 47–69.

[7] E. J. Jung and S. Lee, "The Combined Effects of Relationship Conflict and the Relational Self on Creativity," *Organizational Behavior and Human Decision Processes* 130, no. 1 (2016): 44–57.

[8] N. Halevy, E. Y. Chou, and A. D. Galinsky, "Exhausting or Exhilarating? Conflict as Threat to Interests, Relationships and Identities," *Journal of Experimental Social Psychology* 48 (2012): 530–37.

[9] S. S. Nifadkar and T. N. Bauer, "Breach of Belongingness: Newcomer Relationship Conflict, Information, and Task-Related Outcomes during Organizational Socialization," *Journal of Applied Psychology* 101, no. 1 (2016): 1–13.

[10] F. R. C. de Wit, L. L. Greer, and K. A. Jehn, "The Paradox of Intragroup Conflict: A Meta-Analysis," *Journal of Applied Psychology* 97 (2012): 360–90.

[11] J. Farh, C. Lee, and C. I. C. Farh, "Task Conflict and Team Creativity: A Question of How Much and When," *Journal of Applied Psychology* 95, no. 6 (2010): 1173–80.

[12] B. H. Bradley, A. C. Klotz, B. F. Postlethwaite, and K. G. Brown, "Ready to Rumble: How Team Personality Composition and Task Conflict Interact to Improve Performance," *Journal of Applied Psychology* 98 (2013): 385–92.

[13] K. A. Jehn and C. Bendersky, "Intragroup Conflict in Organizations: A Contingency Perspective on the Conflict-Outcome Relationship," *Research in Organizational Behavior* 25, no. 1 (2003): 187–242.

[14] B. H. Bradley, B. F. Postlethwaite, A. C. Klotz, M. R. Hamdani, and K. G. Brown, "Reaping the Benefits of Task Conflict in Teams: The Critical Role of Team Psychological Safety Climate," *Journal of Applied Psychology* 97 (2012): 151–58.

[15] J. S. Chun, S. Jinseok, and J. N. Choi, "Members' Needs, Intragroup Conflict, and

Group Performance," *Journal of Applied Psychology* 99, no. 3 (2014): 437–50.
[16] S. Benard, "Cohesion from Conflict: Does Intergroup Conflict Motivate Intragroup Norm Enforcement and Support for Centralized Leadership?," *Social Psychology Quarterly* 75 (2012): 107–30.
[17] G. A. Van Kleef, W. Steinel, and A. C. Homan, "On Being Peripheral and Paying Attention: Prototypicality and Information Processing in Intergroup Conflict," *Journal of Applied Psychology* 98 (2013): 63–79.
[18] K. W. Thomas, "Conflict and Negotiation Processes in Organizations," in M. D. Dunnette and L. M. Hough (eds.), *Handbook of Industrial and Organizational Psychology* (Palo Alto, CA: Consulting Psychologist's Press, 1992): 651–717.
[19] R. S. Peterson and K. J. Behfar, "The Dynamic Relationship between Performance Feedback, Trust, and Conflict in Groups: A Longitudinal Study," *Organizational Behavior & Human Decision Processes* (September–November 2003): 102–12.
[20] See, for instance, D. R. Rovenpor, T. C. O'Brien, A. Roblain, L. De Guissmé, P. Chekroun, and B. Leidner, "Intergroup Conflict Self-Perpetuates via Meaning: Exposure to Intergroup Conflict Increases Meaning and Fuels a Desire for Further Conflict," *Journal of Personality and Social Psychology* 116, no. 1 (2019): 119–40.
[21] J. Deventer, J. Wagner, O. Lüdtke, and U. Trautwein, "Are Personality Traits and Relationship Characteristics Reciprocally Related? Longitudinal Analyses of Codevelopment in the Transition out of High School and Beyond," *Journal of Personality and Social Psychology* 116, no. 2 (2019): 331–47; T. M. Glomb and H. Liao, "Interpersonal Aggression in Work Groups: Social Influence, Reciprocal, and Individual Effects," *Academy of Management Journal* 46, no. 4 (2003): 486–96; and V. Venkataramani and R. S. Dalal, "Who Helps and Harms Whom? Relational Aspects of Interpersonal Helping and Harming in Organizations," *Journal of Applied Psychology* 92, no. 4 (2007): 952–66.
[22] R. Friedman, C. Anderson, J. Brett, M. Olekalns, N. Goates, and C. C. Lisco, "The Positive and Negative Effects of Anger on Dispute Resolution: Evidence from Electronically Mediated Disputes," *Journal of Applied Psychology* (April 2004): 369–76; J. A. Yip and M. E. Schweitzer, "Losing Your Temper and Your Perspective: Anger Reduces Perspective-taking," *Organizational Behavior and Human Decision Processes* 150 (2019): 28–45.
[23] X. Parent-Rocheleau, K. Bentein, G. Simard, and M. Tremblay, "Leader-Follower (Dis)similarity in Optimism: Its Effect on Followers' Role Conflict, Vigor and Performance," *Journal of Business and Psychology* (in press).
[24] J. S. Chun and J. N. Choi, "Members' Needs, Intragroup Conflict, and Group Performance," *Journal of Applied Psychology* 99 (2014): 437–50.
[25] See, for instance, J. R. Curhan, "What Do People Value When They Negotiate? Mapping the Domain of Subjective Value in Negotiation," *Journal of Personality and Social Psychology* (September 2006): 117–26; and N. Halevy, E. Chou, and J. K. Murnighan, "Mind Games: The Mental Representation of Conflict," *Journal of Personality and Social Psychology* 102 (2012): 132–48.
[26] A. M. Isen, A. A. Labroo, and P. Durlach, "An Influence of Product and Brand Name on Positive Affect: Implicit and Explicit Measures," *Motivation & Emotion* (March 2004): 43–63.
[27] Ibid.
[28] E. P. Lemay Jr., J. E. Ryan, R. Fehr, and M. J. Gelfand, "Validation of Negativity: Drawbacks of Interpersonal Responsiveness during Conflicts with Outsiders," *Journal of Personality and Social Psychology* (in press).
[29] M. Lu, X. Yang, H. H. Fung, and T. Hamamura, "Is Positive Emotion an Amplifier or a Buffer? It Depends: Dialectical Thinking Moderates the Impact of Positive Emotion on Intergroup Conflicts," *Emotion* 20, no. 4 (2020): 700–12; C. Montes, D. Rodriguez, and G. Serrano, "Affective Choice of Conflict Management Styles," *International Journal of Conflict Management* 23 (2012): 6–18.
[30] K. Brans, P. Koval, P. Verduyn, Y. Lin Lim, and P. Kuppens, "The Regulation of Negative and Positive Affect in Daily Life," *Emotion* 13, no. 5 (2013): 926–39; S. Nolen-Hoeksema, B. E. Wisco, and S. Lyubomirsky, "Rethinking Rumination," *Perspectives of Psychological Science* 3, no. 5 (2008): 400–24.
[31] A. A. Kay and D. P. Skarlicki, "Cultivating a Conflict-Positive Workplace: How Mindfulness Facilitates Constructive Conflict Management," *Organizational Behavior and Human Decision Processes* (in press).
[32] M. A. Rahim, *Managing Conflict in Organizations*, 4th ed. (New Brunswick, NJ: Transaction Publishers, 2011).
[33] Rahim, *Managing Conflict in Organizations*; K. W. Thomas and R. H. Kilmann, *The Thomas-Kilmann Conflict Mode Instrument* (Mountain View, CA: CPP, 1974).
[34] R. Gabrielle Swab and P. D. Johnson, "Steel Sharpens Steel: A Review of Multilevel Competition and Competitiveness in Organizations," *Journal of Organizational Behavior* 40 (2019): 147–65.
[35] Gabrielle Swab and Johnson, "Steel Sharpens Steel"; S-C. Huang, S. C. Lin, and Y. Zhang, "When Individual Goal Pursuit Turns Competitive: How We Sabotage and Coast," *Journal of Personality and Social Psychology* 117, no. 3 (2019): 605–20.
[36] G. Stasser and S. Abele, "Collective Choice, Collaboration, and Communication," *Annual Review of Psychology* 71 (2020): 589–612.
[37] M-H. Tsai, N. Velda Melia, and V. B. Hinsz, "The Effects of Perceived Decision-Making Styles on Evaluations of Openness and Competence That Elicit Collaboration," *Personality and Social Psychology Bulletin* 46, no. 1 (2020): 124–39.
[38] Rahim, *Managing Conflict in Organizations*; K. W. Thomas and R. H. Kilmann, *The Thomas-Kilmann Conflict Mode Instrument* (Mountain View, CA: CPP, 1974).
[39] L. A. DeChurch, J. R. Mesmer-Magnus, and D. Doty, "Moving beyond Relationship and Task Conflict: Toward a Process-State Perspective," *Journal of Applied Psychology* 98 (2013): 559–78.
[40] J. P. Davis, "The Group Dynamics of Interorganizational Relationships: Collaborating with Multiple Partners in Innovation Ecosystems," *Administrative Science Quarterly* 61, no. 4 (2016): 621–61.
[41] J. D. Hildreth and C. Anderson, "Failure at the Top: How Power Undermines Collaborative Performance," *Journal of Personality and Social Psychology* 110, no. 2 (2016): 261–86.
[42] G. Todorova, J. B. Bear, and L. R. Weingart, "Can Conflict Be Energizing? A Study of Task Conflict, Positive Emotions, and Job Satisfaction," *Journal of Applied Psychology* 99 (2014): 451–67.
[43] P. J. Hinds and D. E. Bailey, "Out of Sight, Out of Sync: Understanding Conflict in Distributed Teams," *Organization Science* (November–December 2003): 615–32.
[44] K. A. Jehn, L. Greer, S. Levine, and G. Szulanski, "The Effects of Conflict Types, Dimensions, and Emergent States on Group Outcomes," *Group Decision and Negotiation* 17, no. 6 (2005): 777–96.
[45] M. E. Zellmer-Bruhn, M. M. Maloney, A. D. Bhappu, and R. B. Salvador, "When and How Do Differences Matter? An Exploration of Perceived Similarity in Teams," *Organizational Behavior and Human Decision Processes* 107, no. 1 (2008): 41–59.
[46] A. Avgar, "Integrating Conflict: A Proposed Framework for the Interdisciplinary Study of Workplace Conflict and Its Management," *Industrial and Labor Relations Review* 73, no. 2 (2020): 281–311.
[47] B. Mayer, *Staying with Conflict: A Strategic Approach to Ongoing Disputes* (San Francisco, CA: Wiley, 2009).
[48] A. M. Carton and B. A. Tewfik, "A New Look at Conflict Management in Work Groups," *Organization Science* 27, no. 5 (2016): 1125–41.

[49] Ibid.

[50] Ibid.

[51] J. Fried, "I Know You Are, but What Am I?," *Inc.* (July/August 2010): 39–40.

[52] K. J. Behfar, R. S. Peterson, E. A. Mannix, and W. M. K. Trochim, "The Critical Role of Conflict Resolution in Teams: A Close Look at the Links between Conflict Type, Conflict Management Strategies, and Team Outcomes," *Journal of Applied Psychology* 93, no. 1 (2008): 170–88; and A. G. Tekleab, N. R. Quigley, and P. E. Tesluk, "A Longitudinal Study of Team Conflict, Conflict Management, Cohesion, and Team Effectiveness," *Group and Organization Management* 34, no. 2 (2009): 170–205.

[53] A. Somech, H. S. Desivilya, and H. Lidogoster, "Team Conflict Management and Team Effectiveness: The Effects of Task Interdependence and Team Identification," *Journal of Organizational Behavior* 30, no. 3 (2009): 359–78.

[54] H. Ren and B. Gray, "Repairing Relationship Conflict: How Violation Types and Culture Influence the Effectiveness of Restoration Rituals," *Academy of Management Review* 34, no. 1 (2009): 105–26.

[55] M. J. Gelfand, M. Higgins, L. H. Nishii, J. L. Raver, A. Dominguez, F. Murakami, S. Yamaguchi, and M. Toyama, "Culture and Egocentric Perceptions of Fairness in Conflict and Negotiation," *Journal of Applied Psychology* (October 2002): 833–45; and Z. Ma, "Chinese Conflict Management Styles and Negotiation Behaviours: An Empirical Test," *International Journal of Cross Cultural Management* (April 2007): 101–19.

[56] P. P. Fu, X. H. Yan, Y. Li, E. Wang, and S. Peng, "Examining Conflict-Handling Approaches by Chinese Top Management Teams in IT Firms," *International Journal of Conflict Management* 19, no. 3 (2008): 188–209.

[57] W. Liu, R. Friedman, and Y. Hong, "Culture and Accountability in Negotiation: Recognizing the Importance of In-Group Relations," *Organizational Behavior and Human Decision Processes* 117 (2012): 221–34; and B. C. Gunia, J. M. Brett, A. K. Nandkeolyar, and D. Kamdar, "Paying a Price: Culture, Trust, and Negotiation Consequences," *Journal of Applied Psychology* 96, no. 4 (2010): 774–89.

[58] M. H. Bazerman, J. R. Curhan, D. A. Moore, and K. L. Valley, "Negotiation," *Annual Review of Psychology* 51 (2000): 279–314.

[59] See, for example, D. R. Ames, "Assertiveness Expectancies: How Hard People Push Depends on the Consequences They Predict," *Journal of Personality and Social Psychology* 95, no. 6 (2008): 1541–57; and J. R. Curhan, H. A. Elfenbein, and H. Xu, "What Do People Value When They Negotiate? Mapping the Domain of Subjective Value in Negotiation," *Journal of Personality and Social Psychology* 91, no. 3 (2006): 493–512.

[60] R. Lewicki, D. Saunders, and B. Barry, *Negotiation,* 6th ed. (New York: McGraw-Hill/Irwin, 2009).

[61] J. C. Magee, A. D. Galinsky, and D. H. Gruenfeld, "Power, Propensity to Negotiate, and Moving First in Competitive Interactions," *Personality and Social Psychology Bulletin* (February 2007): 200–12.

[62] J. M. Majer, R. Trötschel, A. D. Galinsky, and D. D. Loschelder, "Open to Offers, but Resisting Requests: How the Framing of Anchors Affects Motivation and Negotiated Outcomes," *Journal of Personality and Social Psychology* (in press).

[63] H. R. Bowles, L. Babcock, and L. Lei, "Social Incentives for Gender Differences in the Propensity to Initiative Negotiations: Sometimes It Does Hurt to Ask," *Organizational Behavior and Human Decision Processes* 103 (2007): 84–103.

[64] Ganguly, D. (2011). "The art of smart negotiation: From Ratan Tata, Kumar Birla to RPG, Anchor and Wartsila". *The Economic Times (July 22, 2011).* Retrieved from https://economictimes.indiatimes.com (Accessed on April 20, 2022).

[65] E. Wilson, "The Trouble with Jake," *The New York Times,* July 15, 2009, www.nytimes.com.

[66] T. He, R. Derfler-Rozin, and M. Pitesa, "Financial Vulnerability and the Reproduction of Disadvantage in Economic Exchanges," *Journal of Applied Psychology* 105, no. 1 (2020): 80–96.

[67] A. C. Peng, J. Dunn, and D. E. Conlon, "When Vigilance Prevails: The Effect of Regulatory Focus and Accountability on Integrative Negotiation Outcomes," *Organizational Behavior and Human Decision Processes* 126, no. 1 (2016): 77–87; N. B. Rothman and G. B. Northcraft, "Unlocking Integrative Potential: Expressed Emotional Ambivalence and Negotiation Outcomes," *Organizational Behavior and Human Decision Processes* 126, no. 1 (2015): 65–76; and C. K. W. De Dreu, L. R. Weingart, and S. Kwon, "Influence of Social Motives on Integrative Negotiation: A Meta-Analytic Review and Test of Two Theories," *Journal of Personality & Social Psychology* (May 2000): 889–905.

[68] This model is based on R. J. Lewicki, D. Saunders, and B. Barry, *Negotiation,* 7th ed. (New York: McGraw Hill, 2014).

[69] J. R. Curhan, H. A. Elfenbein, and G. J. Kilduff, "Getting off on the Right Foot: Subjective Value versus Economic Value in Predicting Longitudinal Job Outcomes from Job Offer Negotiations," *Journal of Applied Psychology* 94, no. 2 (2009): 524–34.

[70] L. L. Thompson, J. Wang, and B. C. Gunia. "Negotiation," *Annual Review of Psychology* 61, (2010): 491–515.

[71] Michael Schaerer, Roderick I. Swaab, and Adam D. Galinsky, "Anchors Weigh More Than Power: Why Absolute Powerlessness Liberates Negotiators to Achieve Better Outcomes," *Psychological Science* (December 2014), doi:10.1177/0956797614558718.

[72] R. P. Larrick and G. Wu, "Claiming a Large Slice of a Small Pie: Asymmetric Disconfirmation in Negotiation," *Journal of Personality and Social Psychology* 93, no. 2 (2007): 212–33.

[73] A. A. Mislin, R. L. Campagna, and W. P. Bottom, "After the Deal: Talk, Trust Building and the Implementation of Negotiated Agreements," *Organizational Behavior and Human Decision Processes* 115 (2011): 55–68.

[74] H. A. Elfenbein, "Individual Difference in Negotiation: A Nearly Abandoned Pursuit Revived," *Current Directions in Psychological Science* 24 (2015): 131–36.

[75] T. A. Judge, B. A. Livingston, and C. Hurst, "Do Nice Guys—and Gals—Really Finish Last? The Joint Effects of Sex and Agreeableness on Income," *Journal of Personality and Social Psychology* 102 (2012): 390–407.

[76] K. S. Wilson, D. S. DeRue, F. K. Matta, M. Howe, and D. E. Conlon, "Personality Similarity in Negotiations: Testing the Dyadic Effects of Similarity in Interpersonal Traits and the Use of Emotional Displays on Negotiation Outcomes," *Journal of Applied Psychology* 101, no. 10 (2016): 1405–21.

[77] N. Dimotakis, D. E. Conlon, and R. Ilies, "The Mind and Heart (Literally) of the Negotiator: Personality and Contextual Determinants of Experiential Reactions and Economic Outcomes in Negotiation," *Journal of Applied Psychology* 97 (2012): 183–93.

[78] E. T. Amanatullah, M. W. Morris, and J. R. Curhan, "Negotiators Who Give Too Much: Unmitigated Communion, Relational Anxieties, and Economic Costs in Distributive and Integrative Bargaining," *Journal of Personality and Social Psychology* 95, no. 3 (2008): 723–38; and D. S. DeRue, D. E. Conlon, H. Moon, and H. W. Willaby, "When Is Straightforwardness a Liability in Negotiations? The Role of Integrative Potential and Structural Power," *Journal of Applied Psychology* 94, no. 4 (2009): 1032–47.

[79] S. Sharma, W. Bottom, and H. A. Elfenbein, "On the Role of Personality, Cognitive Ability, and Emotional Intelligence in Predicting Negotiation Outcomes: A Meta-Analysis," *Organizational Psychology Review* 3 (2013): 293–336.

[80] H. A. Elfenbein, J. R. Curhan, N. Eisenkraft, A. Shirako, and L. Baccaro, "Are Some Negotiators Better Than Others? Individual

Differences in Bargaining Outcomes," *Journal of Research in Personality* (December 2008): 1463–75.

[81] A. Zerres, J. Hüffmeier, P. A. Freund, K. Backhaus, and G. Hertel, "Does It Take Two to Tango? Longitudinal Effects of Unilateral and Bilateral Integrative Negotiation Training," *Journal of Applied Psychology* 98 (2013): 478–91.

[82] G. Lelieveld, E. Van Dijk, I. Van Beest, and G. A. Van Kleef, "Why Anger and Disappointment Affect Other's Bargaining Behavior Differently: The Moderating Role of Power and the Mediating Role of Reciprocal Complementary Emotions," *Personality and Social Psychology Bulletin* 38 (2012): 1209–21.

[83] A. Shirako, G. J. Kilduff, and L. J. Kray, "Is There a Place for Sympathy in Negotiation? Finding Strength in Weakness," *Organizational Behavior and Human Decision Processes* 131, no. 1 (2015): 95–109; and M. Sinaceur, S. Kopelman, D. Vasiljevic, and C. Haag, "Weep and Get More: When and Why Sadness Expression Is Effective in Negotiations," *Journal of Applied Psychology* 100, no. 6 (2016): 1847–71.

[84] S. Côté, I. Hideg, and G. A. van Kleef, "The Consequences of Faking Anger in Negotiations," *Journal of Experimental Social Psychology* 49 (2013): 453–63.

[85] G. A. Van Kleef and C. K. W. De Dreu, "Longer-Term Consequences of Anger Expression in Negotiation: Retaliation or Spillover?," *Journal of Experimental Social Psychology* 46, no. 5 (2010): 753–60.

[86] H. Adam and A. Shirako, "Not All Anger Is Created Equal: The Impact of the Expresser's Culture on the Social Effects of Anger in Negotiations," *Journal of Applied Psychology* 98, no. 5 (2013): 785–98.

[87] Lelieveld, Van Dijk, Van Beest, and Van Kleef, "Why Anger and Disappointment Affect Other's Bargaining Behavior Differently."

[88] M. Olekalns and P. L Smith, "Mutually Dependent: Power, Trust, Affect, and the Use of Deception in Negotiation," *Journal of Business Ethics* 85, no. 3 (2009): 347–65.

[89] A. W. Brooks and M. E. Schweitzer, "Can Nervous Nellie Negotiate? How Anxiety Causes Negotiators to Make Low First Offers, Exit Early, and Earn Less Profit," *Organizational Behavior and Human Decision Processes* 115, no. 1 (2011): 43–54.

[90] M. Sinaceur, H. Adam, G. A. Van Kleef, and A. D. Galinsky, "The Advantages of Being Unpredictable: How Emotional Inconsistency Extracts Concessions in Negotiation," *Journal of Experimental Social Psychology* 49 (2013): 498–508.

[91] K. Leary, J. Pillemer, and M. Wheeler, "Negotiating with Emotion," *Harvard Business Review* (January–February 2013): 96–103.

[92] L. A. Liu, R. Friedman, B. Barry, M. J. Gelfand, and Z. Zhang, "The Dynamics of Consensus Building in Intracultural and Intercultural Negotiations," *Administrative Science Quarterly* 57 (2012): 269–304.

[93] S. Aslani, J. Ramirez-Marin, J. Brett, J. Yao, Z. Semnani-Azad, Z. Zhang, ... and W. Adair, "Dignity, Face, and Honor Cultures: A Study of Negotiation Strategy and Outcomes in Three Cultures," *Journal of Organizational Behavior* 37, no. 8 (2016): 1178–201.

[94] M. Liu, "The Intrapersonal and Interpersonal Effects of Anger on Negotiation Strategies: A Cross-Cultural Investigation," *Human Communication Research* 35, no. 1 (2009): 148–69; and H. Adam, A. Shirako, and W. W. Maddux, "Cultural Variance in the Interpersonal Effects of Anger in Negotiations," *Psychological Science* 21, no. 6 (2010): 882–89.

[95] P. D. Trapnell and D. L. Paulhus, "Agentic and Communal Values: Their Scope and Measurement," *Journal of Personality Assessment* 94 (2012): 39–52.

[96] C. T. Kulik and M. Olekalns, "Negotiating the Gender Divide: Lessons from the Negotiation and Organizational Behavior Literatures," *Journal of Management* 38 (2012): 1387–415.

[97] C. Suddath, "The Art of Haggling," *Bloomberg Businessweek* (November 26, 2012): 98.

[98] J. Mazei, J. Hüffmeier, P. A. Freund, A. F. Stuhlmacher, L. Bilke, and G. Hertel, "A Meta-Analysis on Gender Differences in Negotiation Outcomes and Their Moderators," *Psychological Bulletin* 141, no. 1 (2015): 85–104.

[99] Ibid.

[100] L. J. Kray, C. C. Locke, and A B. Van Zant, "Feminine Charm: An Experimental Analysis of Its Costs and Benefits in Negotiations," *Personality and Social Psychology Bulletin* 38 (2012): 1343–57.

[101] S. de Lemus, R. Spears, M. Bukowski, M. Moya, and J. Lupiáñez, "Reversing Implicit Gender Stereotype Activation as a Function of Exposure to Traditional Gender Roles," *Social Psychology* 44 (2013): 109–16.

[102] D. A. Small, M. Gelfand, L. Babcock, and H. Gettman, "Who Goes to the Bargaining Table? The Influence of Gender and Framing on the Initiation of Negotiation," *Journal of Personality and Social Psychology* 93, no. 4 (2007): 600–13.

[103] D. T. Kong, K. T. Dirks, and D. L. Ferrin, "Interpersonal Trust within Negotiations: Meta-Analytic Evidence, Critical Contingencies, and Directions for Future Research," *Academy of Management Journal* 57 (2014): 1235–55.

[104] G. R. Ferris, J. N. Harris, Z. A. Russell, B. P. Ellen, A. D. Martinez, and F. R. Blass, "The Role of Reputation in the Organizational Sciences: A Multilevel Review, Construct Assessment, and Research Directions," *Research in Personnel and Human Resources Management* 32 (2014): 241–303.

[105] R. Zinko, G. R. Ferris, S. E. Humphrey, C. J. Meyer, and F. Aime, "Personal Reputation in Organizations: Two-Study Constructive Replication and Extension of Antecedents and Consequences," *Journal of Occupational and Organizational Psychology* 85 (2012): 156–80.

[106] A. Hinshaw, P. Reilly, and A. Kupfer Schneider, "Attorneys and Negotiation Ethics: A Material Misunderstanding?," *Negotiation Journal* 29 (2013): 265–87; and N. A. Welsh, "The Reputational Advantages of Demonstrating Trustworthiness: Using the Reputation Index with Law Students," *Negotiation Journal* 28 (2012): 117–45.

[107] J. R. Curhan, H. A. Elfenbein, and X. Heng, "What Do People Value When They Negotiate? Mapping the Domain of Subjective Value in Negotiation," *Journal of Personality and Social Psychology* 91 (2006): 493–512.

[108] W. E. Baker and N. Bulkley, "Paying It Forward vs. Rewarding Reputation: Mechanisms of Generalized Reciprocity," *Organization Science* 25 (June 17, 2014): 1493–510.

[109] G. A. Van Kleef, C. K. W. De Dreu, and A. S. R. Manstead, "An Interpersonal Approach to Emotion in Social Decision Making: The Emotions as Social Information Model," *Advances in Experimental Social Psychology* 42 (2010): 45–96.

[110] F. Lumineau and J. E. Henderson, "The Influence of Relational Experience and Contractual Governance on the Negotiation Strategy in Buyer–Supplier Disputes," *Journal of Operations Management* 30 (2012): 382–95.

[111] U.S. Equal Employment Opportunity Commission, http://www.eeoc.gov/eeoc/mediation/qanda.cfm, accessed June 9, 2015.

[112] N. Halevy, E. Halali, and T. R. Cohen, "Brokering Orientations and Social Capital: Influencing Others' Relationships Shapes Status and Trust," *Journal of Personality and Social Psychology* (in press).

Appendix Research in Organizational Behavior

A number of years ago, a friend of mine was excited because he had read about the findings from a research study that finally, once and for all, resolved the question of what it takes to make it to the top in a large corporation. I doubted there was any simple answer to this question but, not wanting to dampen his enthusiasm, I asked him to tell me about what he had read. The answer, according to my friend, was *participation in college athletics*. To say I was skeptical of his claim is a gross understatement, so I asked him to tell me more.

The study encompassed 1,700 successful senior executives at the 500 largest U.S. corporations. The researchers found that half of these executives had played varsity-level college sports.[1] My friend, who happens to be good with statistics, informed me that since fewer than 2 percent of all college students participate in intercollegiate athletics, the probability of this finding occurring by mere chance is less than 1 in 10 million! He concluded his analysis by telling me that, based on this research, I should encourage my management students to get into shape and to make one of the varsity teams.

My friend was somewhat perturbed when I suggested that his conclusions were likely to be flawed. These executives were all males who attended college in the 1940s and 1950s. Would his advice be meaningful to females in the twenty-first century? These executives also weren't your typical college students. For the most part, they had attended elite private colleges such as Princeton and Amherst, where a large proportion of the student body participates in intercollegiate sports. And these "jocks" hadn't necessarily played football or basketball; many had participated in golf, tennis, baseball, cross-country running, crew, rugby, and similar so-called minor sports. Moreover, maybe the researchers had confused the direction of causality. That is, maybe individuals with the motivation and ability to make it to the top of a large corporation are drawn to competitive activities like college athletics.

My friend was guilty of misusing research data. Of course, he is not alone. We are all continually bombarded with reports of experiments that link certain substances to cancer in mice and surveys that show changing attitudes toward sex among college students, for example. Many of these studies are carefully designed, with great caution taken to note the implications and limitations of the findings. But some studies are poorly designed, making their conclusions at best suspect, and at worst meaningless.

Rather than attempting to make you a researcher, the purpose of this appendix is to increase your awareness as a consumer of behavioral research. A knowledge of research methods will allow you to appreciate more fully the care in data collection that underlies the information and conclusions presented in this text. Moreover, an understanding of research methods will make you a more skilled evaluator of the OB studies you will encounter in business and professional journals. So, an appreciation of behavioral research is important because (1) it's the foundation on which the theories in this text are built, and (2) it will benefit you in future years when you read reports of research and attempt to assess their value.

Purposes of Research

Research is concerned with the systematic gathering of information. Its purpose is to help us in our search for the truth. Although we will never find ultimate truth—in our case, that would be to know precisely how any person or group would behave in any organizational context—ongoing research adds to our body of OB knowledge by supporting some theories, contradicting others, and suggesting new theories to replace those that fail to gain support.

Research Terminology

Researchers have their own vocabulary for communicating among themselves and with outsiders. The following briefly defines some of the more popular terms you're likely to encounter in behavioral science studies.[2]

Variable

A *variable* is any general characteristic that can be measured and that changes in amplitude, intensity, or both. Some examples of OB variables found in this textbook are job satisfaction, employee productivity, work stress, ability, personality, and group norms.

Hypothesis

A tentative explanation of the relationship between two or more variables is called a *hypothesis*. My friend's statement that participation in college athletics leads to a top executive position in a large corporation is an example of a hypothesis. Until confirmed by empirical research, a hypothesis remains only a tentative explanation.

Dependent Variable

A *dependent variable* is a response that is affected by an independent variable. In terms of the hypothesis, it is the variable that the researcher is interested in explaining. Referring back to our opening example, the dependent variable in my friend's hypothesis was executive succession. In organizational behavior research, the most popular dependent variables are productivity, absenteeism, turnover, job satisfaction, and organizational commitment.[3]

Independent Variable

An *independent variable* is the presumed cause of some change in the dependent variable. Participating in varsity athletics was the independent variable in my friend's hypothesis. Popular independent variables studied by OB researchers include intelligence, personality, job satisfaction, experience, motivation, reinforcement patterns, leadership style, reward allocations, selection methods, and organization design.

You may have noticed that we said that job satisfaction is frequently used by OB researchers as both a dependent and an independent variable. This is not an error. It merely reflects that the label given to a variable depends on its place in the hypothesis. In the statement "Increases in job satisfaction lead to reduced turnover," job satisfaction is an independent variable. However, in the statement "Increases in money lead to higher job satisfaction," job satisfaction becomes a dependent variable.

Moderating Variable

A *moderating variable* abates the effect of the independent variable on the dependent variable. It might also be thought of as the contingency variable: If X (independent variable), then Y (dependent variable) will occur, but only under conditions Z (moderating variable). To translate this into a real-life example, we might say that if we increase the amount of direct supervision in the work area (X), then there will be a change in worker productivity (Y), but this effect will be moderated by the complexity of the tasks being performed (Z).

Causality

A hypothesis, by definition, implies a relationship. That is, it implies a presumed cause and effect. This direction of cause and effect is called *causality*. Changes in the independent variable are assumed to cause changes in the dependent variable. In behavioral research, however, it's possible to make an incorrect assumption of causality when relationships are found. For example, early behavioral scientists found a relationship between employee satisfaction and productivity. They concluded that a happy worker was a productive worker. Follow-up research has supported the relationship, but disconfirmed that high productivity leads to satisfaction rather than the other way around.

Correlation Coefficient

It's one thing to know that there is a relationship between two or more variables. It's another to know the *strength* of that relationship. The term *correlation coefficient* is used to indicate that strength, and it is expressed as a number between −1.00 (a perfect negative relationship) and +1.00 (a perfect positive correlation).

When two variables vary directly with one another, the correlation will be expressed as a positive number. When they vary inversely—that is, one increases as the other decreases—the correlation will be expressed as a negative number. If the two variables vary independently of each other, we say that the correlation between them is zero.

For example, a researcher might survey a group of employees to determine the satisfaction of each with his or her job. Then, using company absenteeism reports, the researcher could correlate the job satisfaction scores against individual attendance records to determine whether employees who are more satisfied with their jobs have better attendance records than their counterparts who indicated lower job satisfaction. Let's suppose the researcher found a correlation coefficient of +0.50 between satisfaction and attendance. Would that be a strong association? There is, unfortunately, no precise numerical cutoff separating strong and weak relationships. A standard statistical test would need to be applied to determine whether the relationship was a significant one.

A final point needs to be made before we move on: A correlation coefficient measures only the strength of association between two variables. A high value does *not* imply causality. The length of women's skirts and stock market prices, for instance, have long been noted to be highly correlated, but one should be careful not to infer that a causal relationship between the two exists. In this instance, the high correlation is more happenstance than predictive.

Theory

The final term we introduce in this section is *theory*. Theory describes a set of systematically interrelated concepts or hypotheses that purports to explain and predict phenomena. In OB, theories are also frequently referred to as *models*. We use the two terms interchangeably.

There are no shortages of theories in OB. For instance, we have theories to describe what motivates people, the most effective leadership styles, the best way to resolve conflicts, and how people acquire power. In some cases, we have half a dozen or more separate theories that purport to explain and predict a given phenomenon. In such cases, is one right and the others wrong? No! They tend to reflect science at work—researchers testing previous theories; modifying them; and, when appropriate, proposing new models that may prove to have higher explanatory and predictive powers. Multiple theories attempting to explain common phenomena merely attest to the fact that OB is an active discipline, still growing and evolving.

Evaluating Research

As a potential consumer of behavioral research, you should follow the dictum of *caveat emptor*—let the buyer beware! In evaluating any research study, you need to ask three questions.[4]

Is it valid? Is the study actually measuring what it claims to be measuring? A number of psychological tests have been discarded by employers in recent years because they have not been found to be valid measures of the applicants' ability to do a given job successfully. But the validity issue is relevant to all research studies. So, if you find a study that links cohesive work teams with higher productivity, you want to know how each of these variables was measured and whether it is actually measuring what it is supposed to be measuring.

Is it reliable? Reliability refers to consistency of measurement. If you were to have your height measured every day with a wooden yardstick, you'd get highly reliable results. On the other hand, if you were measured each day by an elastic tape measure, there would probably be considerable disparity between your height measurements from one day to the next. Your height, of course, doesn't change from day to day. The variability is due to the unreliability of the measuring device. So, if a company asked a group of its employees to complete a reliable job satisfaction questionnaire and then repeat the questionnaire six months later, we'd expect the results to be very similar—provided nothing changed in the interim that might significantly affect employee satisfaction.

Is it generalizable? Are the results of the research study generalizable to groups of individuals other than those who participated in the original study? Be aware, for example, of the limitations that might exist in research that uses college students as subjects. Are the findings in such studies generalizable to full-time employees in real jobs? Similarly, how generalizable to the overall work population are the results from a study that assesses job stress among 10 nuclear power plant engineers in the hamlet of Mahone Bay, Nova Scotia?

Research Design

Doing research is an exercise in trade-offs. Richness of information typically comes with reduced generalizability. The more a researcher seeks to control for confounding variables, the less realistic his or her results are likely to be. High precision, generalizability, and control almost always translate into higher costs. When researchers make choices about whom they'll study, where their research will be done, the methods they'll use to collect data, and so on, they must make some concessions. Good research designs are not perfect, but they do carefully reflect the questions being addressed. Keep these facts in mind as we review the strengths and weaknesses of five popular research designs: case studies, field surveys, laboratory experiments, field experiments, and aggregate quantitative reviews.

Case Study

You pick up a copy of Soichiro Honda's autobiography. In it he describes his impoverished childhood; his decisions to open a small garage, assemble motorcycles, and eventually build automobiles; and how this led to the creation of one of the largest and most successful corporations in the world. Or you're in a business class and the instructor distributes a 50-page handout covering two companies: Walmart and Kmart. The handout details the two firms' histories; describes their corporate strategies, management philosophies, and merchandising plans; and includes copies of their recent balance sheets and income statements. The instructor asks the class members to read the handout, analyze the data, and determine why Walmart has been so much more successful than Kmart in recent years.

Soichiro Honda's autobiography and the Walmart and Kmart handouts are case studies. Drawn from real-life situations, case studies present an in-depth analysis of one setting. They are thorough descriptions, rich in details about an individual, a group, or an organization. The primary source of information in case studies is obtained through observation, occasionally backed up by interviews and a review of records and documents.

Case studies have their drawbacks. They're open to the perceptual bias and subjective interpretations of the observer. The reader of a case is captive to what the observer/case writer chooses to include and exclude. Cases also trade off generalizability for depth of information and richness of detail. Because it's always dangerous to generalize from a sample of one, case studies make it difficult to prove or reject a hypothesis. On the other hand, you can't ignore the in-depth analysis that cases often provide. They are an excellent device for initial exploratory research and for evaluating real-life problems in organizations.

Field Survey

A lengthy questionnaire was created to assess the use of ethics policies, formal ethics structures, formalized activities such as ethics training, and executive involvement in ethics programs among billion-dollar corporations. The public affairs or corporate communications office of all Fortune 500 industrial firms and 500 service corporations were contacted to get the name and address of the "officer most responsible for dealing with ethics and conduct issues" in each firm. The questionnaire, with a cover letter explaining the nature of the study, was mailed to these 1,000 officers. Of the total, 254 returned a completed questionnaire, for a response rate just above 25 percent. The results of the survey found, among other things, that 77 percent had formal codes of ethics and 54 percent had a single officer specifically assigned to deal with ethics and conduct issues.[5]

The preceding study illustrates a typical field survey. A sample of respondents (in this case, 1,000 corporate officers in the largest U.S. publicly held corporations) was selected to represent a larger group that was under examination (billion-dollar U.S. business firms). The respondents were then surveyed using a questionnaire or interviewed to collect data on particular characteristics (the content and structure of ethics programs and practices) of interest to the researchers. The standardization of response items allows for data to be easily quantified, analyzed, and summarized, and for the researchers to make inferences from the representative sample about the larger population.

The field survey provides economies for doing research. It's less costly to sample a population than to obtain data from every member of that population. (There are, for instance, more than 5,000 U.S. business firms with sales in excess of a billion dollars, and since some of these are privately held and don't release financial data to the public, they are excluded from the *Fortune* list.) Moreover, as the ethics study illustrates, field surveys provide an efficient way to find out how people feel about issues or how they say they behave. These data can then be easily quantified.

But the field survey has a number of potential weaknesses. First, mailed questionnaires rarely obtain 100 percent returns. Low response rates call into question whether conclusions based on respondents' answers are generalizable to nonrespondents. Second, the format is better at tapping respondents' attitudes and perceptions than behaviors. Third, responses can suffer from social desirability, that is, people saying what they think the researcher wants to hear. Fourth, because field surveys are designed to focus on specific issues, they're a relatively poor means of acquiring depth of information. Finally, the quality of the generalizations is largely a factor of the population chosen. Responses from executives at Fortune 500 firms, for instance, tell us nothing about small- or medium-sized firms or nonprofit organizations. In summary, even a well-designed field survey trades off depth of information for breadth, generalizability, and economic efficiencies.

Laboratory Experiment

The following study is a classic example of the laboratory experiment. A researcher, Stanley Milgram, wondered how far individuals would go in following commands. If subjects were placed in the role of a teacher in a learning experiment and told by an experimenter to administer a shock to a learner each time that learner made a mistake, would the subjects follow the commands of the experimenter? Would their willingness to comply decrease as the intensity of the shock was increased?

To test these hypotheses, Milgram hired a set of subjects. Each was led to believe that the experiment was to investigate the effect of punishment on memory. Their job was to act as teachers and administer punishment whenever the learner made a mistake on the learning test.

Punishment was administered by an electric shock. The subject sat in front of a shock generator with 30 levels of shock—beginning at zero and progressing in 15-volt increments to a high of 450 volts. The demarcations of these positions ranged from "Slight Shock" at 15 volts to "Danger: Severe Shock" at 450 volts. To increase the realism of the experiment, the subjects received a sample shock of 45 volts and saw the learner—a pleasant, mild-mannered man about 50 years old—strapped into an "electric chair" in an adjacent room. Of course, the learner was an actor, and the electric shocks were phony, but the subjects didn't know this.

Taking his seat in front of the shock generator, the subject was directed to begin at the lowest shock level and to increase the shock intensity to the next level each time the learner made a mistake or failed to respond.

When the test began, the shock intensity rose rapidly because the learner made many errors. The subject got verbal feedback from the learner: At 75 volts, the learner began to grunt and moan; at 150 volts, he demanded to be released from the experiment; at 180 volts, he cried out that he could no longer stand the pain; and at 300 volts, he insisted that he be let out, yelled about his heart condition, screamed, and then failed to respond to further questions.

Most subjects protested and, fearful they might kill the learner if the increased shocks were to bring on a heart attack, insisted they could not go on with their job. Hesitations or protests by the subject were met by the experimenter's statement, "You have no choice; you must go on! Your job is to punish the learner's mistakes." Of course, the subjects did have a choice. All they had to do was stand up and walk out.

The majority of the subjects dissented. But dissension isn't synonymous with disobedience. Sixty-two percent of the subjects increased the shock level to the maximum of 450 volts. The average level of shock administered by the remaining 38 percent was nearly 370 volts.[6]

In a laboratory experiment such as that conducted by Milgram, an artificial environment is created by the researcher. Then the researcher manipulates an independent variable under controlled conditions. Finally, because all other things are held equal, the researcher is able to conclude that any change in the dependent variable is due to the manipulation or change imposed on the independent variable. Note that, because of the controlled conditions, the researcher is able to imply causation between the independent and dependent variables.

The laboratory experiment trades off realism and generalizability for precision and control. It provides a high degree of control over variables and precise measurement of those variables. But findings from laboratory studies are often difficult to generalize to the real world of work. This is because the artificial laboratory rarely duplicates the intricacies and nuances of real organizations. In addition, many laboratory experiments deal with phenomena that cannot be reproduced or applied to real-life situations.

Field Experiment

The following is an example of a field experiment. The management of a large company is interested in determining the impact that a 4-day workweek would have on employee absenteeism. To be more specific, management wants to know if employees working four 10-hour days have lower absence rates than similar employees working the traditional 5-day week of 8 hours each day. Because the company is large, it has a number of manufacturing plants that employ essentially similar workforces. Two of these are chosen for the experiment, both located in the greater Cleveland area. Obviously, it would not be appropriate to compare two similar-sized plants if one is in rural Mississippi and the other is in urban Copenhagen because factors such as national culture, transportation, and weather might be more likely to explain any differences found than changes in the number of days worked per week.

In one plant, the experiment was put into place—workers began the 4-day week. At the other plant, which became the control group, no changes were made in the employees' 5-day week. Absence data were gathered from the company's records at both locations for a period of 18 months. This extended time period lessened the possibility that any results would be distorted by the mere novelty of changes being implemented in the experimental plant. After 18 months, management found that absenteeism had dropped by 40 percent at the experimental plant, and by only 6 percent in the control plant. Because of the design of this study, management believed that the larger drop in absences at the experimental plant was due to the introduction of the compressed workweek.

The field experiment is similar to the laboratory experiment except it is conducted in a real organization. The natural setting is more realistic than the laboratory setting, and this enhances validity but hinders control. In addition, unless control groups are maintained, there can be a loss of control if extraneous forces intervene—for example, an employee strike, a major layoff, or a corporate restructuring. Maybe the greatest concern with field studies has to do with organizational selection bias. Not all organizations are going to allow outside researchers to come in and study their employees and operations. This is especially true of organizations that have serious problems. Therefore, because most published studies in OB are done by outside researchers, the selection bias might work toward the publication of studies conducted almost exclusively at successful and well-managed organizations.

Our general conclusion is that, of the four research designs we've discussed to this point, the field experiment typically provides the most valid and generalizable findings and, except for its high cost, trades off the least to get the most.[7]

Aggregate Quantitative Reviews

What's the overall effect of organizational behavior modification (OB Mod) on task performance? There have been a number of field experiments that have sought to throw light on this question. Unfortunately, the wide range of effects from these various studies makes it hard to generalize.

To try to reconcile these diverse findings, two researchers reviewed all the empirical studies they could find on the impact of OB Mod on task performance over a 20-year period.[8] After discarding reports that had inadequate information, had non-quantitative data, or didn't meet all conditions associated with principles of behavioral modification, the researchers narrowed their set to 19 studies that included data on 2,818 individuals. Using an aggregating technique called *meta-analysis,* the researchers were able to synthesize the studies quantitatively and to conclude that the average person's task performance will rise from the 50th percentile to the 67th percentile after an OB Mod intervention.

The OB Mod–task performance review done by these researchers illustrates the use of meta-analysis, a quantitative form of literature review that enables researchers to look at validity findings from a comprehensive set of individual studies and then to apply a formula to them to determine if they consistently produced similar results.[9] If results prove to be consistent, it allows researchers to conclude more confidently that validity is generalizable. Meta-analysis is a means for overcoming the potentially imprecise interpretations of qualitative reviews and to synthesize variations in quantitative studies. In addition, the technique enables researchers to identify potential moderating variables between an independent and a dependent variable.

In the past 25 years, there has been a surge in the popularity of this research method. Why? It appears to offer a more objective means for doing traditional literature reviews. Although the use of meta-analysis requires researchers to make a number of judgment calls, which can introduce a considerable amount of subjectivity into the process, there is no denying that meta-analysis reviews have now become widespread in the OB literature.

Ethics in Research

Researchers are not always tactful or candid with subjects when they do their studies. For instance, questions in field surveys may be perceived as embarrassing by respondents or as an invasion of privacy. Also, researchers in laboratory studies have been known to deceive participants about the true purpose of their experiment "because they felt deception was necessary to get honest responses."[10]

The "learning experiments" conducted by Stanley Milgram, which were conducted more than 30 years ago, have been widely criticized by psychologists on ethical grounds. He lied to subjects, telling them his study was investigating learning, when, in fact, he was concerned with obedience. The shock machine he used was a fake. Even the "learner" was an accomplice of Milgram's who had been trained to act as if he were hurt and in pain. Yet ethical lapses continue. For instance, in 2001, a professor of organizational behavior at Columbia University sent out a common letter on university letterhead to 240 New York City restaurants in which he detailed how he had eaten at this restaurant with his wife in celebration of their wedding anniversary, how he had gotten food poisoning, and that he had spent the night in his bathroom throwing up.[11] The letter closed with: "Although it is not my intention to file any reports with the Better Business Bureau or the Department of Health, I want you to understand what I went through in anticipation that you will respond accordingly. I await your response." The fictitious letter was part of the professor's study to determine how restaurants responded to complaints. But it created culinary chaos among many of the restaurant owners, managers, and chefs as they reviewed menus and produce deliveries for possibly spoiled food, and questioned kitchen workers about possible lapses. A follow-up letter of apology from the university for "an egregious error in judgment by a junior faculty member" did little to offset the distress it created for those affected.

Professional associations like the American Psychological Association, the American Sociological Association, and the Academy of Management have published formal guidelines for the conduct of research. Yet the ethical debate continues. On one side are those who argue that strict ethical controls can damage the scientific validity of an experiment and cripple future research. Deception, for example, is often necessary to avoid contaminating results. Moreover, proponents of minimizing ethical controls note that few subjects have been appreciably harmed by deceptive experiments. Even in Milgram's highly manipulative experiment, only 1.3 percent of the subjects reported negative feelings about their experience. The other side of this debate focuses on the rights of participants. Those favoring strict ethical controls argue that no procedure should ever be emotionally or physically distressing to subjects, and that, as professionals, researchers are obliged to be completely honest with their subjects and to protect the subjects' privacy at all costs.

Summary

The subject of organizational behavior is composed of a large number of theories that are research based. Research studies, when cumulatively integrated, become theories, and theories are proposed and followed by research studies designed to validate them. The concepts that make up OB, therefore, are only as valid as the research that supports them.

The topics and issues in this book are for the most part research-derived. They represent the result of systematic information gathering rather than merely hunch, intuition, or opinion. This doesn't mean, of course, that we have all the answers to OB issues. Many require far more corroborating evidence. The generalizability of others is limited by the research methods used. But new information is being created and published at an accelerated rate. To keep up with the latest findings, we strongly encourage you to review regularly the latest research in organizational behavior. More academic work can be found in journals such as the *Academy of Management Journal, Academy of Management Review, Administrative Science Quarterly, Human Relations, Journal of Applied Psychology, Journal of Management, Journal of Organizational Behavior,* and *Leadership Quarterly.* For more practical interpretations of OB research findings, you may want to read the *California Management Review, Harvard Business Review, Organizational Dynamics,* and the *Sloan Management Review.*

Endnotes

1. J. A. Byrne, "Executive Sweat," *Forbes,* May 20, 1985, 198–200.
2. See D. P. Schwab, *Research Methods for Organizational Behavior* (Mahwah, NJ: Lawrence Erlbaum Associates, 1999); and S. G. Rogelberg (ed.), *Blackwell Handbook of Research Methods in Industrial and Organizational Psychology* (Malden, MA: Blackwell, 2002).
3. B. M. Staw and G. R. Oldham, "Reconsidering Our Dependent Variables: A Critique and Empirical Study," *Academy of Management Journal* 21, no. 4 (1978): 539–59; and B. M. Staw, "Organizational Behavior: A Review and Reformulation of the Field's Outcome Variables," in M. R. Rosenzweig and L. W. Porter (eds.), *Annual Review of Psychology,* vol. 35 (Palo Alto, CA: Annual Reviews, 1984), 627–666.
4. R. S. Blackburn, "Experimental Design in Organizational Settings," in J. W. Lorsch (ed.), *Handbook of Organizational Behavior* (Upper Saddle River, NJ: Prentice Hall, 1987), 127–128; and F. L. Schmidt, C. Viswesvaran, and D. S. Ones, "Reliability Is Not Validity and Validity Is Not Reliability," *Personnel Psychology* 53, no. 4 (2000): 901–912.
5. G. R. Weaver, L. K. Treviño, and P. L. Cochran, "Corporate Ethics Practices in the Mid-1990's: An Empirical Study of the Fortune 1000," *Journal of Business Ethics* 18, no. 3 (1999): 283–294.
6. S. Milgram, *Obedience to Authority* (New York: Harper & Row, 1974). For a critique of this research, see T. Blass, "Understanding Behavior in the Milgram Obedience Experiment: The Role of Personality, Situations, and Their Interactions," *Journal of Personality and Social Psychology* 60, no. 3 (1991): 398–413.
7. See, for example, W. N. Kaghan, A. L. Strauss, S. R. Barley, M. Y. Brannen, and R. J. Thomas, "The Practice and Uses of Field Research in the 21st Century Organization," *Journal of Management Inquiry* 8, no. 1 (1999): 67–81.
8. A. D. Stajkovic and F. Luthans, "A Meta-Analysis of the Effects of Organizational Behavior Modification on Task Performance, 1975–1995," *Academy of Management Journal* 40, no. 5 (1997): 1122–1149.
9. See, for example, K. Zakzanis, "The Reliability of Meta Analytic Review," *Psychological Reports* 83, no.1 (1998): 215–222; C. Ostroff and D. A. Harrison, "Meta-Analysis, Level of Analysis, and Best Estimates of Population Correlations: Cautions for Interpreting Meta-Analytic Results in Organizational Behavior," *Journal of Applied Psychology* 84, no. 2 (1999): 260–270; R. Rosenthal and M. R. DiMatteo, "Meta-Analysis: Recent Developments in Quantitative Methods for Literature Reviews," *Annual Review of Psychology* 52 (2001): 59–82; and F. L. Schmidt and J. E. Hunter, "Meta-Analysis," in N. Anderson, D. S. Ones, H. K. Sinangil, and C. Viswesvaran (eds.), *Handbook of Industrial, Work & Organizational Psychology,* vol. 1 (Thousand Oaks, CA: Sage, 2001), 51–70.
10. For more on ethical issues in research, see T. L. Beauchamp, R. R. Faden, R. J. Wallace, Jr., and L. Walters (eds.), *Ethical Issues in Social Science Research* (Baltimore, MD: Johns Hopkins University Press, 1982); and J. G. Adair, "Ethics of Psychological Research: New Policies, Continuing Issues, New Concerns," *Canadian Psychology* 42, no. 1 (2001): 25–37.
11. J. Kifner, "Scholar Sets Off Gastronomic False Alarm," *New York Times* (September 8, 2001), A1.

Comprehensive Cases

CASE 1 Managing Motivation in a Difficult Economy

Learning Goals

In this case, you'll have an opportunity to assess a motivational program designed to reenergize a troubled company's workforce. Acting on behalf of the company's executive board, you'll evaluate the board's current strategy based on survey data. You'll also advise board members about improving the effectiveness of this program based on what you've learned about goal setting and motivation in organizations.

Major Topic Areas

- Changing nature of work
- Diversity and age
- Goal setting
- Organizational downsizing
- Organizational justice

The Scenario

Morgan-Moe's drugstores are in trouble. As a major regional player in the retail industry, the company has hundreds of stores in the upper Midwest. Unfortunately, a sharp decline in the region's manufacturing economy has put management in a serious financial bind. Revenues have been consistently dwindling. Customers spend less, and the stores have had to switch their focus to very low-margin commodities, such as milk and generic drugs, rather than the high-margin impulse-buy items that used to be the company's bread and butter. The firm has closed quite a few locations, reversing its expansion plans for the first time since it incorporated.

Because this is uncharted territory for the company, Jim Claussen, vice president for human relations, had been struggling with how to address the issue with employees. As the company's fortunes worsened, he could see that employees were becoming more and more disaffected. Their job insecurity was taking a toll on their job attitudes. The company's downsizing was big news, and the employees didn't like what they were hearing.

Media reports of Morgan-Moe's store closings have focused on the lack of advance notice or communication from the company's corporate offices, as well as the lack of severance payments for departing employees. In the absence of official information, rumors and gossip have spread like wildfire among the remaining employees. A few angry blogs developed by laid-off employees, like IHateMorganMoe.blogspot.com, have made the morale and public relations picture even worse.

Morgan-Moe is changing in other ways as well. The average age of its workforce is increasing rapidly. A couple of factors have contributed to this shift. First, fewer qualified young people are living in the area because many families have moved away to find jobs. Second, stores have been actively encouraged to hire older workers, such as retirees looking for supplemental income. Managers are very receptive to these older workers because they are more mature, miss fewer days of work, and do not have child care responsibilities. They are also often more qualified than younger workers because they have more experience, sometimes in the managerial or executive ranks.

These older workers have been a great asset to the company in troubled times, but they are especially likely to leave if things get bad. If these older workers start to leave the company, taking their hard-earned experience with them, it seems likely that Morgan-Moe will sink deeper toward bankruptcy.

The System

Claussen wasn't sure how to respond to employees' sense of hopelessness and fear until a friend gave him a book entitled *Man's Search for Meaning*. The book was written by a psychologist named Victor Frankl, who survived the concentration camps at Auschwitz. Frankl found that those who had a clear sense of purpose, a reason to live, were more likely to persevere in the face of nearly unspeakable suffering. Something about this book, and its advocacy of finding meaning and direction as a way to triumph over adversity, really stuck with Claussen. He thought he might be able to apply its lessons to his workforce. He proposed the idea of a new direction for management to the company's executive committee, and they reluctantly agreed to try his suggestions.

Over the last 6 months, stores throughout the company have used a performance management system that, as Claussen says, "gets people to buy into the idea of performing so that they can see some real results in their stores. It's all about seeing that your work serves a broader purpose. I read about how some companies have been sharing store performance information with employees to get them to understand what their jobs really mean and participate in making changes, and I thought that was something we'd be able to do."

The human resources (HR) team came up with five options for the management system. Corporate allowed individual managers to choose the option they thought would work best with their employees so that managers wouldn't feel too much like a rapid change was being forced on them. Program I is opting out of the new idea, continuing to stay the course and providing employees with little to no information or opportunities for participation. Program II tracks employee absence and sick leave data and shares that information with individual employees, giving them feedback about things they can control. Management takes no further action. Program III tracks sales and inventory replacement rates across shifts. As in Program II, information is shared with employees, but without providing employee feedback about absence and sick leave data. Program IV, the most comprehensive, tracks the same information as Programs II and III. Managers communicate it in weekly brainstorming sessions, during which employees try to determine what they can do better in the future and make suggestions for improving store performance. Program V keeps the idea of brainstorming but doesn't provide employees with information about their behavior or company profits.

Since implementing the system, Claussen has spoken with several managers about what motivated them to choose the program they did. Artie Washington, who chose Program IV, said, "I want to have my employees' input on how to keep the store running smoothly. Everybody worries about their job security in this economy. Letting them know what's going on and giving them ways to change things keeps them involved."

Betty Alvarez couldn't disagree more. She selected Program I. "I would rather have my employees doing their jobs than going to meetings to talk about doing their jobs. That's what management is for." Michael Ostremski, another proponent of Program I, added, "It's okay for the employees to feel a little uncertain—if they think we're in the clear, they'll slack off. If they think we're in trouble, they'll give up."

Cal Martins also questions the need to provide information to the whole team, but he chose Program II. "A person should know where he or she stands in the job, but they don't have to know about everyone else. It creates unnecessary tension."

This is somewhat similar to Cindy Ang's reason for picking Program V. "When we have our brainstorming meetings, I learn what they [the employees] think is most pressing, not what some spreadsheet says. It gives me a better feel for what's going on in my store. Numbers count, of course, but they don't tell you everything. I was also a little worried that employees would be upset if they saw that we aren't performing well."

Results to Date

Claussen is convinced that the most elaborate procedure (Program IV) is the most effective, but not everyone in the executive committee is won over by his advocacy. Although they have supported the test implementation of the system because it appears to have relatively low costs, others on the committee want to see results. CEO Jean Masterson has asked for a complete breakdown of the performance of the various stores over the past 4 years. She's especially interested in seeing how sales figures and turnover rates have been affected by the new program.

The company has been collecting data in spreadsheets on sales and turnover rates, and it prepared the following report, which also estimates the dollar cost of staff time taken up in each method. These costs are based on the number of hours employees spend working on the program multiplied by their wage rate. Estimates of turnover, profit, and staff time are collected per store. Profit and turnover data include means and standard deviations across locations; profit is net of the monthly time cost. Turnover information refers to the percentage of employees who either quit or are terminated in a month.

To see if any patterns emerged in managers' selection of programs, the company calculated relationships between program selection and various attributes of the stores. Program I was selected most frequently by the oldest stores and those in the most economically distressed areas. Programs II and III were selected most frequently by stores in urban areas and in areas where the workforce was younger on average. Programs IV and V were selected most frequently in stores in rural areas, and especially where the workforce is older on average.

Program	Methods	Number of Stores	Average Turnover	Weekly Profit per Month	Monthly Staff Time Cost
Program I	Traditional management	83	Mean = 30% SD = 10%	Mean = $5,700 SD = $3,000	None
Program II	Share absence and sick leave	27	Mean = 23% SD = 14%	Mean = $7,000 SD = $5,800	$1,960
Program III	Share sales and inventory	35	Mean = 37% SD = 20%	Mean = $11,000 SD = $2,700	$2,440
Program IV	Share information and brainstorm	67	Mean = 17% SD = 20%	Mean = $13,000 SD = $3,400	$3,420
Program V	Brainstorm without sharing information	87	Mean = 21% SD = 12%	Mean = $14,000 SD = $2,400	$2,750

Your Assignment

Your task is to prepare a report for the company's executive committee on the effectiveness of these programs. Make certain it is in the form of a professional business document. Your audience won't necessarily know about the organizational principles you're describing, so make sure you provide detailed explanations that someone in a real business can understand.

When you write, make sure you touch on the following points:

CC-1. Consider the five management systems as variables in an experiment. Identify the independent and dependent variables, and explain how they are related to one another.

CC-2. Based on the discussion of independent and dependent variables in the text, is there anything else you'd like to measure as an outcome?

CC-3. Look over the data and decide which method of management appears most effective in generating revenues and reducing turnover, and why. Which methods appear least effective, and why?

CC-4. Are there any concerns you have about these data?

CC-5. Does a comparison of the number of stores using each method influence your conclusions at all?

CC-6. Does the fact that managers are selecting the specific program to use (including Program I, which continues the status quo) affect the inferences you can draw about program success?

CC-7. What are the advantages of randomly assigning different conditions to the stores instead of using this self-selection process?

CC-8. How does the changing nature of the workforce and the economy, described in your text and in the case, affect your conclusions about how to manage retail employees? Does the participation of a more experienced workforce help or hurt these programs? Why might these programs work differently in an economy that isn't doing so poorly?

CC-9. Claussen essentially designed the program on his own, with very little research into goal setting and motivation. Based on your text, how well has he done? Which parts of the program appear to fit well with research evidence on goal setting? What parts would you change to get more substantial improvements in employee motivation?

CC-10. Describe the feelings that employees might have when these systems are implemented that could help or hinder the program's success. What advice would you give managers about how to implement the programs so they match the principles of organizational justice described in your text?

CASE 2 Repairing Jobs That Fail to Satisfy

Learning Goals

Companies often divide work as a way to improve efficiency, but specialization can lead to negative consequences. DrainFlow is a company that has effectively used specialization to reduce costs relative to its competitors' costs for years, but rising customer complaints suggest the firm's strong position may be slipping. After reading the case, you will suggest some ways it can create more interesting work for employees. You'll also tackle the problem of finding people qualified and ready to perform the multiple responsibilities required in these jobs.

Major Topic Areas

- Job design
- Job satisfaction
- Personality
- Emotional labor

The Scenario

DrainFlow is a large residential and commercial plumbing maintenance firm that operates around the United States. It has been a major player in residential plumbing for decades, and its familiar rhyming motto, "When Your Drain Won't Go, Call DrainFlow," has been plastered on billboards since the 1960s.

Lee Reynaldo has been a regional manager at DrainFlow for about 2 years. She used to work for a newer competing chain, Lightning Plumber, which has been drawing more and more customers from DrainFlow. Although her job at DrainFlow pays more, Reynaldo isn't happy with the way things are going. She's noticed the work environment just isn't as vital or energetic as the environment she saw at Lightning.

Reynaldo thinks the problem is that employees aren't motivated to provide the type of customer service Lightning Plumber employees offer. She recently sent surveys to customers to collect information about performance, and the data confirmed her fears. Although 60 percent of respondents said they were satisfied with their experience and would use DrainFlow again, 40 percent felt their experience was not good, and 30 percent said they would use a competitor the next time they had a plumbing problem.

Reynaldo is wondering whether DrainFlow's job design might be contributing to its problems in retaining customers. DrainFlow has about 2,000 employees in four basic job categories: plumbers, plumber's assistants, order processors, and billing representatives. This structure is designed to keep costs as low as possible. Plumbers make very high wages, whereas plumber's assistants make about one-quarter of what a licensed plumber makes. Using plumber's assistants is therefore a very cost-effective strategy that has enabled DrainFlow to undercut the competition easily when it comes to price. Order processors make even less than assistants but about the same as billing processors. All work is very specialized, but employees are often dependent on another job category to perform at their most efficient level.

Like most plumbing companies, DrainFlow gets business mostly from the Yellow Pages and the Internet. Customers either call in to describe a plumbing problem or submit an online request for plumbing services, receiving a return call with information within 24 hours. In either case, DrainFlow's order processors listen to the customer's description of the problem to determine whether a plumber or a plumber's assistant should make the service call. The job is then assigned accordingly, and a service provider goes to the location. When the job has been completed, a billing representative relays the fee to the service representative via cell phone, who presents a bill to the customer for payment. Billing representatives can take customers' credit card payments by phone, or they can e-mail an invoice for online payment.

The Problem

Although specialization does cut costs significantly, Reynaldo is worried about customer dissatisfaction. According to her survey, about 25 percent of customer contacts ended in no service call because customers were confused by the diagnostic questions the order processors asked and because the order processors did not have sufficient knowledge or skill to explain the situation. That means fully one in four people who call DrainFlow to hire a plumber are worse than dissatisfied: They aren't customers at all! The remaining 75 percent of calls that did end in a customer service encounter resulted in other problems.

The most frequent complaints Reynaldo found in the customer surveys were about response time and cost, especially when the wrong person was sent to a job. A plumber's assistant cannot complete a more technically complicated job. The appointment has to be rescheduled, and the customer's time and the staff's time have been wasted. The resulting delay often caused customers in these situations to decline further contact with DrainFlow—many of them decided to go with Lightning Plumber.

"When I arrive at a job I can't take care of," says plumber's assistant Jim Larson, "the customer gets ticked off. They thought they were getting a licensed plumber, since they were calling for a plumber. Telling them they have to have someone else come out doesn't go over well."

On the other hand, when a plumber responds to a job easily handled by a plumber's assistant, the customer is still charged at the plumber's higher pay rate. Licensed plumber Luis Berger also does not like being in the position of giving customers bad news. "If I get called out to do something like snake a drain, the customer isn't expecting a hefty bill. I'm caught between a rock and a hard place—I don't set the rates or make the appointments, but I'm the one who gets it from the customer." Plumbers also resent being sent to do such simple work.

Susie McCarty is one of DrainFlow's order processors. She's frustrated too when the wrong person is sent to a job but feels she and the other order processors are doing the best they can. "We have a survey we're supposed to follow with the calls to find out what the problem is and who needs to take the job," she explains. "The customers don't know that we have a standard form, so they think we can answer all their questions. Most of us don't know any more about plumbing than the caller. If they don't use the terms on the survey, we don't understand what they're talking about. A plumber would, but we're not plumbers; we just take the calls."

Customer service issues also involve the billing representatives. They are the ones who have to keep contacting customers about payment. "It's not my fault the wrong guy was sent," says Elizabeth Monty. "If two guys went out, that's two trips. If a plumber did the work, you pay plumber rates. Some of these customers don't get that I didn't take their first call, and so I get yelled at." The billing representatives also complain that they see only the tail end of the process, so they don't know what the original call entailed. The job is fairly impersonal, and much of the work is recording customer complaints. Remember—40 percent of customers aren't satisfied, and it's the billing representatives who take the brunt of their negative reactions on the phone.

As you can probably tell, all employees have to engage in emotional labor, as described in this text, and many lack the skills or personality traits to complete the customer interaction component of their jobs. They aren't trained to provide customer service, and they see their work mostly in technical, or mechanical, terms. Quite a few are actually anxious about speaking directly with customers. The office staff (order processors and billing representatives) realize customer service is part of their job, but they also find dealing with negative feedback from customers and coworkers taxing.

A couple of years ago a management consulting company was hired to survey DrainFlow worker attitudes. The results showed they were less satisfied than workers in other comparable jobs. The following table provides a breakdown of respondent satisfaction levels across a number of categories:

	DrainFlow Plumbers	DrainFlow Plumber's Assistants	DrainFlow Office Workers	Average Plumber	Average Office Worker
I am satisfied with the work that I am asked to do.	3.7	2.5	2.5	4.3	3.5
I am satisfied with my working conditions.	3.8	2.4	3.7	4.1	4.2
I am satisfied with my interactions with coworkers.	3.5	3.2	2.7	3.8	3.9
I am satisfied with my interactions with my supervisor.	2.5	2.3	2.2	3.5	3.4

The information about average plumbers and average office workers is taken from the management consulting company's records of other companies. They aren't exactly surprising, given some of the complaints DrainFlow employees have made. Top managers at DrainFlow are worried about these results, but they haven't been able to formulate a solution. The traditional DrainFlow culture has been focused on cost containment, and the "soft stuff" like employee satisfaction hasn't been a major issue.

The Proposed Solution

The company is in trouble, and as revenues shrink and the cost savings that were supposed to be achieved by dividing work fail to materialize, a change seems to be in order.

Reynaldo is proposing using cash rewards to improve performance among employees. She thinks if employees were paid based on work outcomes, they'd work harder to satisfy customers. Because it's not easy to measure how satisfied people are with the initial call-in, Reynaldo would like to give the order processors a small reward for every 20 calls successfully completed. For the hands-on work, she'd like to have each billing representative collect information about customer satisfaction for each completed call. If no complaints are made and the job is handled promptly, a moderate cash reward would be given to the plumber or plumber's assistant. If the customer indicates real satisfaction with the service, a larger cash reward would be provided.

Reynaldo also wants to find people who are a better fit with the company's new goals. Current hiring procedure relies on unstructured interviews with each location's general manager, and little consistency is found in the way these managers choose employees. Most lack training in customer service and organizational behavior. Reynaldo thinks it would be better if hiring methods were standardized across all branches in her region to help managers identify recruits who can actually succeed in the job.

Your Assignment

Your task is to prepare a report for Reynaldo on the potential effectiveness of her cash reward and structured-interview programs. Make certain it is in the form of a professional business document that you'd actually give to an experienced manager at this level of a fairly large corporation. Reynaldo is very smart when it comes to managing finances and running a plumbing business, but she won't necessarily know about the organizational behavior principles you're describing. Because any new proposals must be passed through top managers, you should also address their concerns about cost containment. You'll need to make a strong, evidence-based financial case that changing the management style will benefit the company.

When you write, make sure you touch on the following points:

CC-11. Although it's clear employees are not especially satisfied with their work, do you think this is a reason for concern? Does research suggest satisfied workers are actually better at their jobs? Are any other behavioral outcomes associated with job satisfaction?

CC-12. Using job characteristics theory, explain why the present system of job design may be contributing to employee dissatisfaction. Describe some ways you could help employees feel more satisfied with their work by redesigning their jobs.

CC-13. Reynaldo has a somewhat vague idea about how to implement the cash rewards system. Describe some of the specific ways you would make the reward system work better, based on the case.

CC-14. Explain the advantages and disadvantages of using financial incentives in a program of this nature. What, if any, potential problems might arise if people are given money for achieving customer satisfaction goals? What other types of incentives might be considered?

CC-15. Create a specific plan to assess whether the reward system is working. What are the dependent variables that should change if the system works? How will you go about measuring success?

CC-16. What types of hiring recommendations would you make to find people better suited for these jobs? Which Big Five personality traits would be useful for the customer service responsibilities and emotional labor?

CASE 3 Building a Coalition

Learning Goals

Many of the most important organizational behavior challenges require coordinating plans and goals among groups. This case describes a multiorganizational effort, but the same principles of accommodation and compromise also apply when trying to work with multiple divisions within a single organization. You'll create a blueprint for managing a complex development team's progress in order to steer team members away from negative conflicts and toward productive discussion. You'll also be asked to help create a new message for executives so they can lead effectively.

Major Topic Areas

- Group dynamics
- Maximizing team performance
- Organizational culture
- Integrative bargaining

The Scenario

The Woodson Foundation, a large nonprofit social service agency, is teaming up with the public school system in Washington, D.C., to improve student outcomes. There's ample room for improvement. The schools have problems with truancy, low student performance, and crime. New staff members quickly burn out as their initial enthusiasm for helping students is blunted by the harsh realities they encounter in the classroom. Turnover among new teachers is very high, and many of the best and brightest are the most likely to leave for schools that aren't as troubled.

The plan is to create an experimental afterschool program that will combine the Woodson Foundation's skills of raising private money and coordinating community leaders with the educational expertise of school staff. Ideally, the system will be financially self-sufficient, which is important because less money is available for schools than in the past. After several months of negotiation, the leaders of the Woodson Foundation and the school system have agreed that the best course is to develop a new agency that will draw on resources from both organizations. The Woodson Foundation will provide logistical support and program development and measurement staff; the school system will provide classrooms and teaching staff.

The first stage in bringing this new plan to fruition is the formation of an executive development team. This team will span multiple functional areas and establish the operating plan for improving school performance. Its cross-organizational nature means representatives from both the Woodson Foundation and the school district must participate. The National Coalition for Parental Involvement in Education (NCPIE) is also going to be a major partner in the program, acting as a representative for parents on behalf of the PTA.

Conflict and Agreement in the Development Team

While it would be perfect if all the groups could work together easily to improve student outcomes, there is little doubt some substantive conflicts will arise. Each group has its own interests, and, in some cases, these are directly opposed to one another.

School district representatives want to ensure that the new jobs will be unionized and will operate in a way that is consistent with current school board policies. They are very concerned that if Woodson assumes too dominant a role, the school board won't be able to control the operations of the new system. The complexity of the school system has led to the development of a highly complex bureaucratic structure over time, and administrators want to make sure their policies and procedures will still hold for teachers in these programs even outside the regular school day. They also worry that jobs going into the new system will take funding from other school district jobs.

Woodson, founded by entrepreneur Theodore Woodson around 1910, still bears the hallmarks of its founder's way of doing business. Woodson emphasized efficiency and experimentation in everything he did. Many of the foundation's charities have won awards for minimizing costs while still providing excellent services. Their focus on using hard data to measure performance for all their initiatives is not consistent with the school district culture.

Finally, the NCPIE is driven by a mission to increase parental control. The organization believes that when communities are able to drive their own educational methods, students and parents are better able to achieve success together. The organization is strongly committed to celebrating diversity along racial, gender, ethnic, and disability status categories. Its members are most interested in the process by which changes are made, ensuring that everyone has the ability to weigh in.

Some demographic diversity issues complicate the team's situation. Most of the students served by the Washington, D.C., school district are African American, along with large populations of Caucasians and Hispanics. The NCPIE makeup generally matches the demographic diversity of the areas served by the public schools. The Woodson Foundation, based in northern Virginia, is predominantly staffed by Caucasian professionals. There is some concern that this new group that will be so involved in this major change in educational administration does not understand the demographic concerns of the community. The leadership of the new program will have to be able to present an effective message for generating enthusiasm for the program across diverse stakeholder groups.

Although the groups differ in important ways, it's also worth considering what they have in common. All are interested in meeting the needs of students. All would like to increase student learning. The school system does benefit from anything that increases student test scores. The Woodson Foundation and NCPIE are united in their desire to see more parents engaged in the system.

Candidates for the Development Team

The development team will consist of three individuals—an HR representative from the Woodson Foundation, one from the school system, and one from the NCPIE—who have prepared the following list of potential candidates for consideration.

Victoria Adams is the superintendent of schools for Washington, D.C. She spearheaded the initial communication with the Woodson Foundation and has been building support among teachers and principals. She thinks the schools and the foundation need to have larger roles than the parents and communities. "Of course, we want their involvement and support, but as professionals, we should have more say when it comes to making decisions and implementing programs. We don't want to shut anyone out, but we have to be realistic about what the parents can do."

Duane Hardy has been a principal in the Washington area for more than 15 years. He also thinks the schools should have the most power. "We're the ones who work with these kids every day. I've watched class sizes get bigger, and scores and graduation rates go down. Yes, we need to fix this, but these outside groups can't understand the limitations we're dealing with. We have the community, the politicians, the taxpayers—everyone watching what we're doing, everyone thinking they know what's best. The parents, at least, have more of a stake in this."

"The most important thing is the kids," says second-year teacher Ari Kaufman, who is well liked by his students but doesn't get along well with other faculty members. He's seen as a "squeaky wheel." "The schools need change so badly. And how did they get this way? From too little outside involvement."

Community organizer Mason Dupree doesn't like the level of bureaucracy either. He worries that the school's answer to its problems is to throw more money at them. "I know these kids. I grew up in these neighborhoods. My parents knew every single teacher I had. The schools wanted our involvement then. Now all they want is our money. And I wouldn't mind giving it to them if I thought it would be used responsibly, not spent on raises for people who haven't shown they can get the job done."

Meredith Watson, with the Woodson Foundation, agrees the schools have become less focused on the families. A former teacher, she left the field of education after being in the classroom for 6 years. "There is so much waste in the system," she complains. "Jobs are unnecessarily duplicated, change processes are needlessly convoluted. Unless you're an insider already, you can't get anything done. These parents want to be involved. They know their kids best."

Unlike her NCPIE colleagues, Candace Sharpe thinks the schools are doing the best they can. She is a county social worker, relatively new to the D.C. area. "Parents say they want to be involved but then don't follow through. *We* need to step it up, *we* need to lead the way. Lasting change doesn't come from the outside, it comes from the home."

Victor Martinez has been at the Woodson Foundation for 10 years, starting as an intern straight out of college. "It's sometimes hard to see a situation when you're in the thick of it," he explains. "Nobody likes to be told they're doing something wrong, but sometimes it has to be said. We all know there are flaws in the system. We can't keep the status quo. It just isn't cutting it."

Strategies for the Program Team

Once the basic membership and principles for the development team have been established, the program team would also like to develop a handbook for those who will be running the new program. Ideally, this set of principles can help train new leaders to create an inspirational message that will facilitate success. The actual content of the program and the nature of the message will be hammered out by the development team, but it is still possible to generate some overriding principles for the program team in advance of these decisions.

Your Assignment

The Woodson Foundation, the NCPIE, and the schools have asked you to provide some information about how to form teams effectively. They would like your response to explain what should be done at each step of the way, from the selection of appropriate team members to setting group priorities and goals, setting deadlines, and describing effective methods for resolving conflicts that arise. After this, they'd like you to prepare a brief set of principles for leaders of the newly established program. That means you will have two audiences: the development team, which will receive one report on how it can effectively design the program, and the program team, which will receive one report on how it can effectively lead the new program.

The following points should help you form a comprehensive message for the development team:

CC-17. The development team will be more effective if members have some idea about how groups and teams typically operate. Review the dominant perspectives on team formation and performance from the chapters in the text for the committee so it can know what to expect.

CC-18. Given the profiles of candidates for the development team, provide suggestions for who would likely be a good group member and who might be less effective in this situation. Be sure you are using the research on groups and teams in the text to defend your choices.

CC-19. Using principles from the chapters on groups and teams, describe how you will advise the team to manage conflict effectively.

CC-20. Describe how integrative negotiation strategies might achieve joint goals for the development team.

The following points should help you form a message for the program team:

CC-21. Leaders of the new combined organization should have a good idea of the culture of the school district, the NCPIE, and the Woodson Foundation because they will need to manage relationships with all three groups on an ongoing basis. How would you describe the culture of these various stakeholder organizations? Use concepts from the chapter on organizational culture to describe how they differ and how they are similar.

CC-22. Consider how leaders of the new program can generate a transformational message and encourage employee and parent trust. Using material from the chapter on leadership, describe how you would advise leaders to accomplish these ends.

CC-23. Given the potential for demographic faultlines in negotiating these changes, what would you advise as a strategy for managing diversity issues for program leaders?

CASE 4 Boundaryless Organizations

Learning Goals

The multinational organization is an increasingly common and important part of the economy. This case takes you into the world of a cutting-edge music software business seeking success across three very different national and organizational cultures. Its managers need to make important decisions about how to structure work processes so employees can be satisfied and productive doing very different tasks.

Major Topic Areas

- Organizational structure and boundaryless organizations
- Organizational culture
- Human resources
- Organizational socialization

The Scenario

Newskool Grooves is a transnational company developing music software. The software is used to compose music, play music in clubs, and produce albums. Founder and CEO Gerd Finger is, understandably, the company's biggest fan. "I started this company from nothing, from just me, my ideas, and my computer. I love music—love playing music, love writing programs for making music, love listening to music—and the money is nice, too." Finger says he never wanted to work for someone else, to give away his ideas and let someone else profit from them. He wanted to keep control over them, and their image. "Newskool Grooves is always ahead of the pack. In this business, if you can't keep up, you're out. And we are the company everyone else must keep up with. Everyone knows when they get something from us, they're getting only the best and the newest."

The company headquarters are in Berlin, the nerve center for the organization, where new products are developed and the organizational strategy is established. Newskool outsources a great deal of its coding work to programmers in Kiev, Ukraine. Its marketing efforts are increasingly based in its Los Angeles offices. This division of labor is at least partially based on technical expertise and cost issues. The German team excels at design and production tasks. Because most of Newskool's customers are English speakers, the Los Angeles office has been the best group to write ads and market products. The Kiev offices are filled with outstanding programmers who don't require the very high rates of compensation you'd find in German or U.S. offices. The combination of high-tech software, rapid reorganization, and outsourcing makes Newskool the very definition of a boundaryless organization.

Finger also makes the final decision on hiring every employee for the company and places a heavy emphasis on independent work styles. "Why would I want to put my company in the hands of people I can't count on?," he asks with a laugh. "They have to believe in what we're doing here, really understand our direction and be able to go with it. I'm not the babysitter, I'm not the school master handing out homework. School time is over. This is the real world."

The Work Culture

Employees want to work at this company because it's cutting edge. Newskool's software is used by a number of electronic dance music (EDM) DJs, who have been the firm's core market, seeing it as a relatively expensive but very high-quality and innovative brand. Whenever the rest of the market for music software goes in one direction, it seems like Newskool heads in a completely different direction in an effort to keep itself separate from the pack. This strategy has tended to pay off. While competitors develop similar products and therefore need to lower their prices continually to compete with one another, Newskool has kept revenues high by creating completely new types of products that don't face this type of price competition.

Unfortunately, computer piracy has eroded Newskool's ability to make money with just software-based music tools, and it has had to move into the production of hardware, such as drum machines and amplifiers that incorporate its computer technology. Making this massive market change might be challenging for some companies, but for an organization that reinvents itself every 2 or 3 years like Newskool does, the bigger fight is a constant war against stagnation and rigidity.

The organization has a very decentralized culture. With only 115 employees, the original management philosophy of allowing all employees to participate in decision making and innovation is still the lifeblood of the company's culture. One developer notes, "At Newskool, they want you to be part of the process. If you are a person who wants to do what you're told at work, you're in trouble. Most times, they can't tell you what they want you to do next—they don't even know what comes next! That's why they hire employees who are creative, people who can try to make the next thing happen. It's challenging, but a lot of us think it's very much an exciting environment."

The Boundaryless Environment

Because so much of the work can be performed on computers, Finger decided early to allow employees to work outside the office. The senior management in Berlin and Los Angeles are both quite happy with this arrangement. Because some marketing work does require face-to-face contact, the Los Angeles office has weekly in-person meetings. Employees who like Newskool are happiest when they can work through the night and sleep most of the day, firing up their computers to get work done at the drop of a hat. Project discussions often happen via social networking on the company's intranet.

The Kiev offices have been less eager to work with the boundaryless model. Managers say their computer programmers find working with so little structure rather uncomfortable. They are more used to the idea of a strong leadership structure and well-defined work processes.

"When I started," says one manager, "Gerd said getting in touch with him would be no problem, getting in touch with L.A. would be no problem. We're small, we're family, he said. Well, it is a problem. When I call L.A., they say to wait until their meeting day. I can't always wait until they decide to get together. I call Gerd—he says, 'Figure it out.' Then when I do, he says it isn't right and we have to start again. If he just told me in the first place, we would have done it."

Some recent events have also shaken up the company's usual way of doing business. Developers in the corporate offices had a major communications breakdown about their hardware DJ controller, which required many hours of discussion to resolve. It seems that people who seldom met face-to-face had all made progress—but had moved in opposite directions. To test and design the company's hardware products, employees apparently need to do more than send each other code; sometimes they need to collaborate face to face. Some spirited disagreements have been voiced within the organization about how to move forward in this new environment.

The offices are experiencing additional difficulties. Since the shift to newer products, Sandra Pelham in the Los Angeles office has been more critical of the company. "With the software, we were more limited in the kinds of advertising media we could access. So now, with the hardware—real instruments—we finally thought, 'All right, this is something we can work with!' We had a whole slate of musicians and DJs and producers to contact for endorsements, but Gerd said, 'No way.' He didn't want customers who only cared that a celebrity liked us. He scrapped the whole campaign. He says we're all about creativity and doing our own thing—until we don't want to do things his way."

Although the organization is not without problems, there is little question Newskool has been a standout success in the computer music software industry. While many are shuttering their operations, Newskool is using its market power to push forward the next generation of electronic music-making tools. As Gerd Finger puts it, "Once the rest of the industry has gotten together and figured out how they're all going to cope with change, they'll look around and see that we're already three miles ahead of them down the road to the future."

Your Assignment

Finger has asked for your advice on how to keep his organization successful. He wants to have some sort of benchmark for how other boundaryless organizations in the tech sector stay competitive despite the challenge of so many workers heading in so many different directions. You will need to prepare a report for the company's executive committee. Your report should read like a proposal to a corporate executive who has a great deal of knowledge about the technical aspects of his company but might not have much knowledge of organizational behavior.

When you write, make sure you touch on the following points:

CC-24. Identify some of the problems likely to occur in a boundaryless organization like Newskool Grooves. What are the advantages of boundaryless organizations?

CC-25. Consider some of the cultural issues that will affect a company operating in such different parts of the world and whose employees may not be representative of the national cultures of each country. Are the conflicts you observe a function of the different types of work people have to perform?

CC-26. Based on what you know about motivation and personality, what types of people are likely to be satisfied in each area of the company? Use concepts from job characteristics theory and the emerging social relationships perspective on work to describe what might need to change to increase employee satisfaction in all areas.

CC-27. What types of human resources practices need to be implemented in this sort of organization? What principles of selection and hiring are likely to be effective? Which Big Five traits and abilities might Newskool supervisors want to use for selection?

CC-28. What kind of performance measures might you want to see for each office?

CC-29. How can the company establish a socialization program that will maximize employee creativity and independence? Do employees in all its locations need equal levels of creativity?

CASE 5 The Stress of Caring

Learning Goals

One of the most consistent changes in the structure of work over the past few decades has been a shift from a manufacturing economy to a service economy. More workers are now engaged in jobs that include providing care and assistance, especially in education and medicine. This work is satisfying for some people, but it can also be highly stressful. In the following scenario, consider how a company in the nursing care industry is responding to the challenges of the new environment.

Major Topic Areas

- Stress
- Organizational change
- Emotions
- Leadership

The Scenario

Parkway Nursing Care is an organization facing a massive change. The company was founded in 1972 with just two nursing homes in Phoenix, Arizona. The company was very successful, and throughout the 1980s it continued to turn a consistent profit while slowly acquiring or building 30 more units. This low-profile approach changed forever in 1993 when venture capitalist Robert Quine decided to make a major investment in expanding Parkway in return for a portion of its profits over the coming years. The number of nursing homes exploded, and Parkway was operating 180 homes by the year 2000.

The company now has 220 facilities in the southwestern United States, with an average of 115 beds per facility and a total of nearly 30,000 employees. In addition to health care facilities, it also provides skilled in-home nursing care. Parkway is seen as one of the best care facilities in the region, and it has won numerous awards for its achievements in the field.

As members of the baby boom generation become senior citizens, the need for skilled care will only increase. Parkway wants to make sure it is in a good position to meet this growing need. This means the company must continue expanding rapidly.

The pressure for growth is one significant challenge, but it's not the only one. The nursing home industry has come under increasing government scrutiny following investigations that turned up widespread patient abuse and billing fraud. Parkway has always had outstanding patient care, and no substantiated claim of abuse or neglect in any of its homes has ever been made, but the need for increased documentation will still affect the company. As the federal government tries to trim Medicare expenses, Parkway may face a reduction in funding.

The Problem

As growth continues, Parkway has remained committed to maintaining the dignity and health of all residents in its facilities. The board of directors wants to see renewed commitment to the firm's mission and core values, not a diffusion of its culture. Its members are worried there might be problems to address. Interviews with employees suggest there's plenty to worry about.

Shift leader Maxine Vernon has been with Parkway for 15 years. "Now that the government keeps a closer eye on our staffing levels, I've seen management do what it can to keep positions filled, and I don't always agree with who is hired. Some of the basic job skills can be taught, sure, but how to *care* for our patients—a lot of these new kids just don't pick up on that."

"The problem isn't with staff—it's with Parkway's focus on filling the beds," says nurse's aide Bobby Reed. "When I started here, Parkway's reputation was still about the service. Now it's about numbers. No one is intentionally negligent—there just are too many patients to see."

A recent college graduate with a B.A. in psychology, Dalton Manetti is more stressed than he expected he would be. "These aren't the sweet grannies you see in the movies. Our patients are demanding. They complain about everything, even about being called patients, probably because most of them think they shouldn't be here in the first place. A lot of times, their gripes amount to nothing, but we have to log them in anyway."

Carmen Frank has been with Parkway almost a year and is already considering finding a new job. "I knew there were going to be physical parts to this job, and I thought I'd be able to handle that. It's not like I was looking for a desk job, you know? I go home after every shift with aches all over—my back, my arms, and my legs. I've never had to take so much time off from a job because I hurt. And then when I come back, I feel like the rest of the staff thinks I'm weak."

Year	Number of Patients	Injuries per Staff Member	Incidents per Patient	Certified Absences per Staff Member	Other Absences per Staff Member	Turnover Rate
2000	21,200	3.32	4.98	4.55	3.14	0.31
2001	22,300	3.97	5.37	5.09	3.31	0.29
2002	22,600	4.87	5.92	4.71	3.47	0.28
2003	23,100	4.10	6.36	5.11	3.61	0.35
2004	23,300	4.21	6.87	5.66	4.03	0.31
2005	23,450	5.03	7.36	5.33	3.45	0.28
2006	23,600	5.84	7.88	5.28	4.24	0.36
2007	24,500	5.62	8.35	5.86	4.06	0.33
2008	24,100	7.12	8.84	5.63	3.89	0.35
2009	25,300	6.95	9.34	6.11	4.28	0.35

"I started working here right out of high school because it was the best-paid of the jobs I could get," says Niecey Wilson. "I had no idea what I was getting myself into. Now I really like my job. Next year I'm going to start taking some night classes so I can move into another position. But some of the staff just think of this as any other job. They don't see the patients as people, more like inventory. If they want to work with inventory, they should get a job in retail."

Last month, the company's human resources department pulled the above information from its records at the request of the board of directors. The numbers provide some quantitative support for the concerns voiced by staff.

Injuries to staff occur mostly because of back strain from lifting patients. Patient incidents reflect injuries due to slips, falls, medication errors, or other accidents. Certified absences are days off from work due to medically verified illnesses or injuries. Other absences are days missed that are not due to injuries or illnesses; these are excused absences (unexcused absences are grounds for immediate firing).

Using Organizational Development to Combat Stress and Improve Performance

The company wants to use organizational development methods such as appreciative inquiry (AI) to create change and reenergize its sense of mission. As the chapter on organizational change explains, AI procedures systematically collect employee input and then use this information to create a change message everyone can support. The human resources department conducted focus groups, asking employees to describe some of their concerns and suggestions for the future. The focus groups highlighted a number of suggestions, although they don't all suggest movement in the same direction.

Many suggestions concerned schedule flexibility. One representative comment was this: "Most of the stress on this job comes because we can't take time off when we need it. The LPNs [licensed practical nurses, who do much of the care] and orderlies can't take time off when they need to, but a lot of them are single parents or primary caregivers for their own children. When they have to leave for child care responsibilities, the work suffers and there's no contingency plan to help smooth things over. Then everyone who is left has to work extra hard. The person who takes time off feels guilty, and there can be fights over taking time off. If we had some way of covering these emergency absences, we'd all be a lot happier, and I think the care would be a lot better."

Other suggestions proposed better methods for communicating information across shifts. Most of the documentation for shift work is done in large spiral notebooks. When a new shift begins, staff members say they don't have much time to check on what happened in the previous shift. Some younger caregivers would like to have a method that lets them document patient outcomes electronically because they type faster than they can write. The older caregivers are more committed to the paper-based process, in part because they think switching systems would require a lot of work. (Government regulations on health care reporting require that any documentation be made in a form that cannot be altered after the fact, to prevent covering up abuse, so specialized software systems must be used for electronic documentation.)

Finally, the nursing care staff believes its perspectives on patient care are seldom given an appropriate hearing. "We're the ones who are with the patients most of the time, but when it comes to doing this the right way, our point of view gets lost. We really could save a lot of money by eliminating some of these unnecessary routines and programs, but it's something management always just says it will consider."

Staff members seem to want some way to provide suggestions for improvement, but it isn't clear what method they would prefer.

Your Assignment

Parkway has taken some initial steps in this new direction, but clearly it has a lot of work left to do. You've been brought in as a change management consultant to help the company change its culture and respond to the stress that employees experience. Remember to create your report as if for the leadership of a major corporation.

When you write your recommendations, make sure you touch on the following points:

CC-30. What do the data on employee injuries, incidents, absences, and turnover suggest to you? Is there reason for concern about the company's direction?

CC-31. The company is going to be making some significant changes based on the AI process, and most change efforts are associated with resistance. What are the most common forms of resistance, and which would you expect to see at Parkway?

CC-32. Given the board of directors' desire to reenergize the workforce, what advice would you provide for creating a leadership strategy? What leader behaviors should nursing home directors and nurse supervisors demonstrate?

CC-33. What are the major sources of job stress at Parkway? What does the research on employee stress suggest you should do to help minimize the experience of psychological strain for employees? Create a plan for how to reduce stress among employees.

CC-34. Based on the information collected in the focus groups, design a survey to hand out to employees. What sort of data should the survey gather? What types of data analysis methods would you like to employ for these data?

Glossary

ability An individual's capacity to perform the various tasks in a job.

accommodating The willingness of one party in a conflict to place the negotiation partner's interests above their own.

action research A change process based on the systematic collection of data and the selection of a change action based on what the analyzed data indicate.

affect A term used to describe a broad range of feelings that people experience.

affect intensity Individual differences in the strength with which individuals experience their emotions.

affective component The emotional or feeling segment of an attitude.

affective events theory (AET) A model that suggests that workplace events cause emotional reactions on the part of employees, which then influence workplace attitudes and behaviors.

agreeableness A personality dimension that describes someone who is good natured, cooperative, and trusting.

allostasis Working to change behavior and attitudes to find stability.

anchoring bias A tendency to fixate on initial information, from which one then fails to adequately adjust for subsequent information.

anthropology The study of societies to learn about human beings and their activities.

appreciative inquiry An approach that seeks to identify the unique qualities and special strengths of an organization, which can then be built on to improve performance.

arbitrator A third party to a negotiation who has the authority to dictate an agreement.

attitudes Evaluative statements or judgments concerning objects, people, or events.

attribution theory An attempt to explain the ways we judge people differently, depending on the meaning we attribute to a behavior, such as determining whether an individual's behavior is internally or externally caused.

attribution theory of leadership A leadership theory that states that leadership is merely an attribution that people make about other individuals.

authentic leaders Leaders who are self-aware and are anchored by their mission, consider others' opinions and all relevant information before acting, and display their true selves when interacting with employees.

authority The rights inherent in a managerial position to give orders and to expect the orders to be obeyed.

automatic processing A relatively superficial consideration of evidence and information that takes little time or effort and makes use of heuristics.

autonomy The degree to which a job provides substantial freedom and discretion to the individual in scheduling the work and in determining the procedures to be used in carrying it out.

availability bias The tendency for people to base their judgments on information that is readily available to them.

avoiding The desire to withdraw from or suppress a conflict.

BATNA The **b**est **a**lternative **t**o a **n**egotiated **a**greement; the least the individual should accept.

behavioral component An intention to behave in a certain way toward someone or something.

behavioral ethics Analyzing how people behave when confronted with ethical dilemmas.

behavioral theories of leadership Theories proposing that specific behaviors differentiate leaders from nonleaders.

behaviorism A theory that behavior follows stimuli in a relatively unthinking manner.

big five model A personality model that proposes five basic dimensions encompass most of the differences in human personality.

biographical characteristics Personal characteristics—such as age, gender, race, and length of tenure—that are objective and easily obtained from personnel records. These characteristics are representative of surface-level diversity.

bonus A pay plan that rewards employees for recent performance rather than historical performance.

boundary spanning When individuals form relationships outside their formally assigned groups.

bounded rationality A simplified process of making decisions by perceiving and interpreting the essential features of problems without capturing their complexity.

brainstorming An idea-generation process that specifically encourages any and all alternatives while withholding any criticism of those alternatives.

bureaucracy An organization structure with highly routine operating tasks achieved through specialization, very formalized rules and regulations, departmentalization, centralized authority, narrow spans of control, and decision making that follows the chain of command.

centralization The degree to which decision making is concentrated at a single point in an organization.

chain of command The unbroken line of authority that extends from the top of the organization to the lowest echelon and clarifies who reports to whom.

challenge stressors Stressors associated with workload, pressure to complete tasks, and time urgency.

change When things become different from the way they were.

change agents People who act as catalysts and assume the responsibility for managing change activities.

channel richness The amount of information that can be transmitted during a communication episode.

charismatic leadership theory A leadership theory that states that followers make attributions of heroic or extraordinary leadership abilities when they observe certain behaviors.

circular structure An organization structure in which executives are at the center, spreading their vision outward in rings grouped by function (managers, then specialists, then workers).

coercive power A power base that is dependent on fear of the negative results from failing to comply.

cognitive component The opinion or belief segment of an attitude.

cognitive dissonance Any incompatibility between two or more attitudes or between behavior and attitudes.

cognitive evaluation theory A sub-theory of self-determination theory in which extrinsic rewards for behavior tend to decrease the overall level of motivation, if the rewards are seen as controlling or reduce their sense of competence.

cohesiveness The shared bond driving group members to work together and to stay in the group.

collaborating A situation in which the parties in a conflict each desires to satisfy fully the concerns of all parties.

collectivism A national culture attribute that describes a tight social framework in which people expect others in groups of which they are a part to look after them and protect them. Collectivistic countries/cultures are those in which people see themselves as interdependent and seek community and group goals. Collectivistic values are found in Asia, Africa, and South America, for example.

communication The transfer and the understanding of meaning.

communication apprehension Undue tension and anxiety about oral communication, written communication, or both.

communication process The steps between a source and a receiver that result in the transfer and understanding of meaning.

competing A desire to satisfy one's interests, regardless of the impact on the other party to the conflict.

compromising A situation in which each party to a conflict is willing to give up something.

conciliator A trusted third party who provides an informal communication link between the negotiator and the negotiation partner.

confirmation bias The tendency to seek out information that reaffirms past choices and current views, and to discount information that challenges them.

conflict A process that begins when one party perceives that another party has negatively affected, or is about to negatively affect, something that the first party cares about.

conflict management The use of resolution and stimulation techniques to achieve the desired level of conflict.

conformity The adjustment of one's behavior to align with the norms of the group.

conscientiousness A personality dimension that describes someone who is responsible, dependable, persistent, and organized.

consideration The extent to which a leader is likely to have job relationships characterized by mutual trust, respect for subordinates' ideas, and regard for their feelings.

contingency variables Situational factors or variables that moderate the relationship between two or more variables.

contrast effect Evaluation of a person's characteristics that is affected by comparisons with other people recently encountered who rank higher or lower on the same characteristics.

controlled processing A detailed consideration of evidence and information relying on facts, figures, and logic.

core self-evaluation (CSE) Believing in one's inner worth and basic competence.

core values The primary or dominant values that are accepted throughout the organization.

corporate social responsibility (CSR) An organization's self-regulated actions to benefit society or the environment beyond what is required by law.

cost-minimization strategy A strategy that emphasizes tight cost controls, avoidance of unnecessary innovation or marketing expenses, and price cutting.

counterproductive work behavior (CWB) Actions that actively damage the organization, including stealing, behaving aggressively toward co-workers, or being late or absent.

creativity The ability to produce novel and useful ideas.

cross-functional teams Employees from about the same hierarchical level, but from different work areas, who come together to accomplish a task.

dark triad A constellation of negative personality traits consisting of Machiavellianism, narcissism, and psychopathy.

decisions Choices made from among two or more alternatives.

deep acting Trying to modify one's true inner feelings based on display rules.

deep-level diversity Differences in values, personality, and work preferences that become progressively more important for determining similarity as people get to know one another better.

defensive behaviors Reactive and protective behaviors to avoid action, blame, or change.

demands Responsibilities, pressures, obligations, and even uncertainties that individuals face in the workplace.

deonance A perspective in which ethical decisions are made because you "ought to" in order to be consistent with moral norms, principles, standards, rules, or laws.

departmentalization The basis by which jobs in an organization are grouped together.

dependence The extent to which people depend or rely upon a powerful person.

deviant workplace behavior Voluntary behavior that violates significant organizational norms and, in so doing, threatens the well-being of the organization or its members. Also called antisocial behavior or workplace incivility.

discrimination Noting a difference between things; often we refer to unfair discrimination, which means making judgments about individuals based on stereotypes regarding their demographic group.

displayed emotions Emotions that are organizationally required and considered appropriate in a given job.

distributive bargaining Negotiation that seeks to divide up a fixed amount of resources; a win–lose situation.

distributive justice Perceived fairness of the amount and allocation of rewards among individuals.

diversity The extent to which members of a group are similar to, or different from, one another.

diversity management The process and programs by which managers make everyone more aware of and sensitive to the needs and differences of others.

dominant culture A culture that expresses the core values that are shared by most of the organization's members.

downsizing A systematic effort to make an organization leaner by closing locations, reducing staff, or selling off business units that do not add value.

driving forces Forces that direct behavior away from the status quo.

dyadic conflict Conflict that occurs between two people.

dysfunctional conflict Conflict that hinders group performance.

effectiveness The degree to which an organization meets the needs of its clientele or customers.

efficiency The degree to which an organization can achieve its ends at a low cost.

emotion regulation The process of identifying and modifying felt emotions.

emotional contagion The process by which people's emotions are caused by the emotions of others.

emotional dissonance Inconsistencies between the emotions people feel and the emotions they project.

emotional intelligence (EI) The ability to detect and to manage emotional cues and information.

emotional labor An employee's organizationally desired emotions during interpersonal transactions at work.

emotional stability A personality dimension that characterizes someone as calm, self-confident, and secure (positive) versus nervous, anxious, and insecure (negative).

emotions Intense, discrete, and short-lived feeling experiences that are often caused by a specific event.

employee engagement The degree of enthusiasm an employee feels for the job.

employee involvement and participation (EIP) A participative process that uses the input of employees to increase employee commitment to organizational success.

employee recognition program A plan to encourage specific employee behaviors by formally appreciating specific employee contributions.

employee stock ownership plan (ESOP) A company-established benefits plan in which employees acquire stock, often at below-market prices, as part of their benefits.

encounter stage The stage in the socialization process in which a new employee sees what the organization is really like and confronts the possibility that expectations and reality may diverge.

environment Forces outside an organization that potentially affect the organization's structure.

equity theory A theory stating that individuals compare their job inputs and outcomes with those of others and then respond to eliminate any inequities.

escalation of commitment An increased commitment to a previous decision, despite negative information.

ethical culture The shared concept of right and wrong behavior in the workplace that reflects the true values of the organization and shapes the ethical decision making of its members.

ethical dilemmas and ethical choices Situations in which individuals are required to define right and wrong conduct.

evidence-based management (EBM) The basing of managerial decisions on the best available scientific evidence.

exit Dissatisfaction expressed through behavior directed toward leaving the organization.

expectancy The probability perceived by the individual that exerting a given amount of effort will lead to performance.

expectancy theory A theory that the strength of a tendency to act in a certain way depends on the strength of an expectation that the act will be followed by a given outcome and on the attractiveness of that outcome to the individual.

expert power Power based in influence through possessing expertise, special skills, or knowledge.

extraversion A personality dimension describing someone who is sociable, gregarious, and assertive.

faultlines The perceived divisions that split groups into two or more subgroups based on individual differences such as sex, race, age, work experience, language, and education.

feedback The degree to which carrying out the work activities required by a job results in the individual obtaining direct and clear information about the effectiveness of their performance.

felt conflict Emotional involvement in a conflict that creates anxiety, tension, frustration, or hostility.

felt emotions An individual's actual emotions.

femininity A national culture attribute that indicates little differentiation between male and female roles; a high rating indicates that women are treated as the equals of men in all aspects of the society.

Fiedler contingency model The theory that effective groups depend on a proper match between a leader's style of interacting with subordinates and the degree to which the situation gives control and influence to the leader.

filtering The manipulation of information so that it will be seen more favorably by the receiver.

fixed pie The belief that there is only a set amount of goods or services to be divvied up between the parties.

flexible benefits A benefits plan that allows each employee to put together a benefits package individually tailored to their own needs and situation.

flextime Flexible work hours.

formal channels Communication channels established by an organization to transmit messages related to the professional activities of members.

formal group A designated workgroup defined by an organization's structure.

formalization The degree to which a job is standardized.

full range of leadership model A model that depicts seven leadership styles on a continuum: laissez-faire, management by exception, contingent reward leadership, individualized consideration, intellectual stimulation, inspirational motivation, and idealized influence.

functional conflict Conflict that supports the goals of the group and improves its performance.

fundamental attribution error The tendency to underestimate the influence of external factors and overestimate the influence of internal factors when making judgments about the behavior of others.

general mental ability (GMA) An overall factor of intelligence, as suggested by the positive correlations among specific intellectual ability dimensions.

globalization The process in which worldwide integration and interdependence is promoted across national borders.

goal-setting theory A theory that specific and difficult goals, with feedback, lead to higher performance.

grapevine An organization's informal communication network.

group Two or more individuals, interacting and interdependent, who have come together to achieve certain objectives.

group cohesion The extent to which members of a group support and validate one another while at work.

group functioning The quantity and quality of a group's work output.

groupshift A change between a group's decision and an individual decision that a member within the group would make; the shift can be toward either conservatism or greater risk, but it generally is toward a more extreme version of the group's original position.

groupthink A phenomenon in which the norm for consensus overrides the realistic appraisal of alternative courses of action.

halo effect The tendency to draw a general impression about an individual based on a single characteristic.

hierarchy of needs Abraham Maslow's hierarchy of five needs—physiological, safety, social, esteem, and self-actualization—in which, as each need is well-satisfied, the next need becomes dominant.

high-context cultures Cultures that rely heavily on nonverbal and subtle situational cues in communication.

hindrance stressors Stressors that keep you from reaching your goals (for example, red tape, office politics, confusion over job responsibilities).

hindsight bias The tendency to believe falsely, after an outcome of an event is known, that one would have accurately predicted that outcome.

horns effect The tendency to draw a negative general impression about an individual based on a single characteristic.

hygiene factors Factors—such as company policy and administration, supervision, and salary—that, when adequate in a job, placate workers and limit job dissatisfaction.

idea champions Individuals who take an innovation and actively and enthusiastically promote the idea, build support, overcome resistance, and ensure that the idea is implemented.

idea evaluation The process of creative behavior involving the evaluation of potential solutions to problems to identify the best one.

idea generation The process of creative behavior that involves developing possible solutions to a problem from relevant information and knowledge.

illusory correlation The tendency of people to associate two events when in reality there is no connection.

imitation strategy A strategy that seeks to move into new products or new markets only after their viability has already been proven.

impression management (IM) The process by which individuals attempt to control the impression others form of them.

individualism A national culture attribute that describes the degree to which people prefer to act as individuals rather than as members of groups.

influence tactics Ways in which individuals translate power bases into specific actions.

informal channels Communication channels that are created spontaneously and that emerge as responses to individual choices.

informal group A group that is not defined by an organization's structure; such a group appears in response to other needs, such as social clubs or interest groups.

information gathering The stage of creative behavior when possible solutions to a problem incubate in an individual's mind.

information overload A condition in which information inflow exceeds an individual's processing capacity.

informational justice The degree to which employees are provided truthful explanations for decisions.

ingroup The members of a group we belong to. We tend to play favorites with our ingroup.

initiating structure The extent to which leaders define and structure their roles and those of their subordinates in pursuit of goal attainment.

innovation A new idea applied to initiating or improving a product, process, or service.

innovation strategy A strategy that emphasizes the introduction of major new products and services.

inputs Variables like personality, group structure, and organizational culture that lead to processes.

institutionalization A condition that occurs when an organization takes on a life of its own, apart from any of its members, and acquires immortality.

institutions Cultural factors, especially those factors that might not lead to adaptive consequences, that lead many organizations to have similar structures.

instrumentality The degree to which the individual believes performing at a certain level will lead to the attainment of a desired outcome.

instrumental values Preferable modes of behavior or means of achieving one's terminal values.

integrative bargaining Negotiation that seeks one or more settlements that can create a win–win solution.

intellectual abilities The capacity to do mental activities—thinking, reasoning, and problem solving.

intentions Decisions to act in a particular way.

interacting groups Typical groups in which members interact with each other, relying on both verbal and nonverbal communication.

interactional justice Sensitivity to the quality of interpersonal treatment.

intergroup conflict Conflict between different groups or teams.

intergroup development Organizational development efforts to change the attitudes, stereotypes, and perceptions that groups have of each other.

interpersonal justice The degree to which employees are treated with dignity and respect.

interrole conflict A situation in which the expectations of an individual's different, separate groups are in opposition.

intragroup conflict Conflict that occurs within a group or team.

intuition An instinctive feeling not necessarily supported by research.

intuitive decision making An unconscious process created out of distilled experience.

job characteristics model (JCM) A model that proposes that any job can be described in terms of five core job dimensions: skill variety, task identity, task significance, autonomy, and feedback.

job design The way the elements in a job are organized.

job engagement The investment of an employee's physical, cognitive, and emotional energies into job performance.

job enrichment Adding high-level responsibilities to a job to increase intrinsic motivation.

job involvement The degree to which a person identifies with a job, actively participates in it, and considers performance important to their self-worth.

job rotation The periodic shifting of an employee from one task to another.

job satisfaction A positive feeling about one's job resulting from an evaluation of its characteristics.

job sharing An arrangement that allows two or more individuals to split a traditional full-time job.

leader–member exchange (LMX) theory A theory that suggests (1) leaders and followers have unique relationships that vary in quality and (2) these followers comprise ingroups and outgroups; subordinates with ingroup status will likely have higher performance ratings, less turnover, and greater job satisfaction.

leader–member relations The degree of confidence, trust, and respect subordinates have in their leader.

leader-participation model A leadership theory that provides a set of rules to determine the form and amount of participative decision making in different situations.

leadership The ability to influence a group toward the achievement of a vision or set of goals.

learning organization An organization that has developed the continuous capacity to adapt and change.

least preferred coworker (LPC) questionnaire An instrument that measures whether a person is task or relationship oriented.

legitimate power Power based on a person's position in the formal hierarchy of an organization.

long-term orientation A national culture attribute that emphasizes the future, thrift, and persistence.

low-context cultures Cultures that rely heavily on words to convey meaning in communication.

loyalty Dissatisfaction expressed by passively waiting for conditions to improve.

Machiavellianism The degree to which an individual is pragmatic, maintains emotional distance, and believes that ends can justify means.

management by objectives (MBO) A program that encompasses specific goals, participatively set, for an explicit time period and including feedback on goal progress.

masculinity A national culture attribute that describes the extent to which the culture favors traditional masculine work roles of achievement, power, and control. Societal values are characterized by assertiveness and materialism.

material symbols Physical objects, or artifacts, that symbolize values, beliefs, or assumptions inherent in the organization's culture.

matrix structure An organization structure that creates dual lines of authority and combines functional and product departmentalization.

mechanistic model A structure characterized by extensive departmentalization, high formalization, a limited information network, and centralization.

mediator A neutral third party who facilitates a negotiated solution by using reasoning, persuasion, and suggestions for alternatives.

mental models Team members' knowledge and beliefs about how the work gets done by the team.

mentor A senior employee who sponsors and supports a less-experienced employee, called a protégé.

merit-based pay plan A pay plan based on performance appraisal ratings.

metamorphosis stage The stage in the socialization process in which a new employee changes and adjusts to the job, workgroup, and organization.

model An abstraction of reality, a simplified representation of some real-world phenomenon.

moods Feelings that tend to be longer lived and less intense than emotions and that lack a contextual stimulus.

moral emotions Emotions that have moral implications because of our instant judgment of the situation that evokes them.

motivating potential score (MPS) A predictive index that suggests the motivating potential in a job.

motivation The processes that account for an individual's intensity, direction, and persistence of effort toward attaining a goal.

multiteam system A collection of two or more interdependent teams that share a superordinate goal; a team of teams.

Myers-Briggs Type Indicator (MBTI) A personality test that taps four characteristics and classifies people into one of sixteen personality types.

narcissism The tendency to be arrogant, have a grandiose sense of self-importance, require excessive admiration, and have a sense of entitlement.

need for achievement (nAch) The need to excel or achieve to a set of standards.

need for affiliation (nAff) The need to establish friendly and close interpersonal relationships.

need for autonomy The need to feel in control and autonomous at work.

need for cognition A personality trait of individuals depicting the ongoing desire to think and learn.

need for competence The need to feel like we are good at what we do and proud of it.

need for power (nPow) The need to make others behave in a way in which they would not have behaved otherwise.

negative affect A mood dimension that consists of emotions such as nervousness, stress, and anxiety at the high end and relaxation and calmness at the low end.

neglect Dissatisfaction expressed through allowing conditions to worsen.

negotiation A process in which two or more parties exchange goods or services and attempt to agree on the exchange rate for them.

neutralizers Attributes that make it impossible for leader behavior to make any difference to follower outcomes.

nominal group technique A group decision-making method in which individual members meet face to face to pool their judgments in a systematic but independent fashion.

norms Acceptable standards of behavior within a group that are shared by the group's members.

openness to experience A personality dimension that characterizes someone in terms of imagination, artistic sensitivity, and curiosity.

organic model A structure that is flat, uses cross-hierarchical and cross-functional teams, has low formalization, possesses a comprehensive information network, and relies on participative decision making.

organizational behavior A field of study that investigates the impact individuals, groups, and structure have on behavior within organizations, for the purpose of applying such knowledge toward improving an organization's effectiveness.

organizational citizenship behavior (OCB) Discretionary behavior that contributes to the psychological and social environment of the workplace.

organizational climate The shared perceptions organizational members have about their organization and work environment; particularly, the policies, practices, and procedures that are in place.

organizational commitment The degree to which an employee identifies with a particular organization and its goals and wishes to maintain membership in the organization.

organizational culture A system of shared meaning held by members that distinguishes the organization from other organizations. This system is characterized by values, beliefs, and underlying assumptions that serve several purposes.

organizational demography The degree to which members of a work unit share a common demographic attribute, such as age, sex, race, educational level, or length of service in an organization.

organizational development (OD) A collection of planned change interventions, built on humanistic–democratic values, that seeks to improve organizational effectiveness and employee well-being.

organizational identification The extent to which employees define themselves by the same characteristics that define one's organization, forming the basis for which attitudes are engendered.

organizational justice An overall perception of what is fair in the workplace, composed of distributive, procedural, informational, and interpersonal justice.

organizational structure The way in which job tasks are formally divided, grouped, and coordinated.

organizational survival The degree to which an organization is able to exist and grow over the long term.

outcomes Key factors that are affected by some other variables.

outgroup The inverse of an ingroup; an outgoup can mean anyone outside the group, but more usually it is an identified other group.

overconfidence bias A tendency to be overconfident about our own abilities or the abilities of others.

paradox theory The theory that the key paradox in management is that there is no final optimal status for an organization.

participative management A process in which subordinates share a significant degree of decision-making power with their immediate superiors.

path–goal theory A theory that states that it is the leader's job to assist followers by providing the necessary resources to achieve their goals, to ensure that the path to accomplishing these goals is understandable or clear, and to reduce any roadblocks that may be making goal achievement difficult.

perceived conflict Awareness by one or more parties of the existence of conditions that create opportunities for conflict to arise.

perceived organizational support (POS) The degree to which employees believe an organization values their contribution and cares about their well-being.

perception A process by which individuals organize and interpret their sensory impressions in order to give meaning to their environment.

personality The sum total of ways in which an individual reacts to and interacts with others.

personality traits Enduring characteristics that describe an individual's behavior.

personality–job fit theory A theory that identifies six personality types and proposes that the fit between personality type and occupational environment determines satisfaction and turnover.

person–organization fit A theory that people are attracted to and selected by organizations that match their values and leave when there is no compatibility.

physical abilities The capacity to do tasks that demand stamina, dexterity, strength, and similar characteristics.

piece-rate pay plan A pay plan in which workers are paid a fixed sum for each unit of production completed.

planned change Change activities that are proactive, intentional, and goal oriented.

political behavior Activities that are not required as part of a person's formal role in the organization but that influence, or attempt to influence, the distribution of advantages and disadvantages within the organization.

political skill The ability to influence others in such a way as to enhance one's objectives.

position power Influence derived from one's formal structural position in the organization; includes power to hire, fire, discipline, promote, and give salary increases.

positive affect A mood dimension that consists of specific positive emotions such as excitement, enthusiasm, and elation at the high end and boredom, sluggishness, and tiredness at the low end.

positive organizational culture A culture that values building on employee strengths, rewards more than it punishes, and encourages individual vitality and growth.

positive organizational scholarship An area of OB research that concerns how organizations develop human strengths, foster vitality and resilience, and unlock potential.

positivity offset The tendency of most individuals to experience a mildly positive mood at zero input (when nothing in particular is going on).

power The capacity, discretion, and means to enforce one's will over others.

power distance A national culture attribute that describes the extent to which a society accepts that power in institutions and organizations is distributed unequally.

prearrival stage The period of learning in the socialization process that occurs before a new employee joins the organization.

prevention focus A self-regulation strategy that involves striving for goals by fulfilling duties and obligations.

proactive personality People who identify opportunities, show initiative, take action, and persevere until meaningful change occurs.

problem A discrepancy between the current state and some desired state.

problem formulation The stage of creative behavior that involves identifying a problem or opportunity requiring a solution that is as yet unknown.

problem-solving teams Groups of five to twelve employees from the same department who meet for a few hours each week to discuss ways of improving quality, efficiency, and the work environment.

procedural justice The perceived fairness of the process used to determine the distribution of rewards.

process conflict Conflict over how work gets done.

process consultation (PC) A meeting in which a consultant assists a client in understanding process events with which they must deal and identifying processes that need improvement.

processes Actions that individuals, groups, and organizations engage in as a result of inputs and that lead to certain outcomes.

productivity The combination of the effectiveness and efficiency of an organization.

profit-sharing plan An organization-wide program that distributes compensation based on some established formula designed around a company's profitability.

promotion focus A self-regulation strategy that involves striving for goals through advancement and accomplishment.

psychological contract An unwritten agreement between employees and employers that establishes mutual expectations.

psychological empowerment Employees' belief in the degree to which they affect their work environment, their competence, the meaningfulness of their job, and their perceived autonomy in their work.

psychology The science that seeks to measure, explain, and sometimes change the behavior of humans and other animals.

psychopathy The tendency for a lack of concern for others and a lack of guilt or remorse when actions cause harm.

punctuated equilibrium model A set of phases that temporary groups go through that involve transitions between inertia and activity.

randomness error The tendency of individuals to believe that they can predict the outcome of random events.

rational A style of decision making characterized by making consistent, value-maximizing choices within specified constraints.

rational decision-making model A decision-making model that describes how individuals should behave in order to maximize some outcome.

reference groups Important groups to which individuals belong or hope to belong, and which adopt norms with which individuals are likely to conform.

referent power Power based on identification with a person who has desirable resources or personal traits.

reflexivity A team characteristic of reflecting on and adjusting their purpose or plan when necessary.

reinforcement theory A theory that behavior is a function of its consequences.

relational job design Constructing jobs so employees see the positive difference they can make in the lives of others directly through their work.

relationship conflict Conflict based on interpersonal relationships.

representative participation A system in which workers participate in organizational decision making through a small group of representative employees.

resources Things within an individual's control that can be used to resolve demands.

restraining forces Forces that hinder movement from the existing equilibrium.

reward power Power based on the ability to distribute rewards that others view as valuable.

risk aversion The tendency to prefer a sure gain of a moderate amount over a riskier outcome, even if the riskier outcome might have a higher expected payoff.

rituals Repetitive sequences of activities that express and reinforce the key values of the organization, which goals are most important, which people are important, and which are expendable.

role A function assumed by someone occupying a given position in a group.

role conflict A situation in which an individual is confronted by divergent role expectations.

role expectations How others believe a person should act in a given situation.

role perception An individual's view of how they are supposed to act in a given situation.

selective perception The tendency to selectively interpret what one sees based on one's interests, background, experience, and attitudes.

self-concordance The degree to which people's reasons for pursuing goals are consistent with their interests and core values.

self-determination theory A meta-theory of motivation at work that is concerned with autonomy, intrinsic motivation, extrinsic motivation, and the satisfaction of psychological work needs.

self-efficacy theory An individual's belief that they are capable of performing a task.

self-managed work teams Groups of ten to fifteen people who autonomously implement solutions and take responsibility for the outcomes (responsibilities normally given to supervisors).

self-monitoring A personality trait that measures an individual's ability to adjust their behavior to external, situational factors.

self-serving bias The tendency for individuals to attribute their own successes to internal factors and put the blame for failures on external factors.

sensitivity training Training that seeks to change behavior through unstructured group interaction.

servant leadership A leadership style marked by going beyond the leader's own self-interest and instead focusing on opportunities to help followers grow and develop.

sexual harassment Any unwanted activity of a sexual nature that affects an individual's employment and creates a hostile work environment.

short-term orientation A national culture attribute that emphasizes the present and accepts change.

simple structure An organization structure characterized by a low degree of departmentalization, wide spans of control, authority centralized in a single person, and little formalization.

situation strength theory A theory indicating that the way personality translates into behavior depends on the strength of the situation.

situational leadership theory (SLT) A contingency theory that focuses on followers' readiness, or the extent to which they are willing and able to accomplish a specific task.

skill variety The degree to which a job requires a variety of activities using different skills or talents.

social identity theory A perspective that considers when and why individuals consider themselves members of groups.

social loafing The tendency for individuals to expend less effort when working collectively than when working individually.

social psychology An area of psychology that blends concepts from psychology and sociology to focus on the influence of people on one another.

socialization A process that enables new employees to acquire the social knowledge and necessary skills in order to adapt to the organization's culture.

social-learning theory The view that we can learn through both observation and direct experience.

sociology The study of people in relation to their social environment or culture.

span of control The number of subordinates a manager can efficiently and effectively direct.

status A socially defined position or rank given to groups or group members by others.

status characteristics theory A theory that states that differences in status characteristics create status hierarchies within groups.

stereotype threat The degree to which we are concerned with being judged by or treated negatively based on a certain stereotype.

stereotyping Judging someone based on one's perception of the group to which that person belongs.

strain A psychological and physical unpleasant response due to an appraisal of the stressor.

stress A psychological process in which an individual is confronted with an opportunity, demand, or resource related to what the individual desires and for which the outcome is perceived to be both uncertain and important (e.g., stressors).

strong culture A culture in which the core values are intensely held and widely shared.

subcultures Minicultures within an organization, typically defined by department designations or geographical separation.

substitutes Attributes, such as experience and training, that can replace the need for a leader's support or ability to create structure.

surface acting Hiding one's inner feelings and forgoing emotional expressions in response to display rules.

surface-level diversity Differences in easily perceived characteristics such as gender, race, ethnicity, age, or disability, that do not necessarily reflect the ways people think or feel but that may activate certain stereotypes.

survey feedback technique The use of questionnaires to listen to members and identify discrepancies among member perceptions; discussion follows and remedies are suggested.

sustainability Organization practices that can be sustained over a long period of time because the tools or structures that support them are not damaged by the processes.

systematic study Looking at relationships, attempting to attribute causes and effects, and drawing conclusions based on scientific evidence.

task conflict Conflict over content and goals of the work.

task identity The degree to which a job requires completion of a whole and identifiable piece of work.

task performance The combination of effectiveness and efficiency at doing core job tasks.

task significance The degree to which a job has a substantial impact on the lives or work of other people.

task structure The degree to which job assignments follow a specific procedure.

team building High interaction among team members to increase trust and openness.

team cohesion A situation when team members are emotionally attached and bonded to one another and committed toward the team.

team efficacy A team's collective belief among team members that they can succeed at their tasks.

team identity A team member's affinity for and sense of belongingness to their team.

team structure An organization structure that replaces departments with empowered teams, and that eliminates horizontal boundaries and external barriers between customers and suppliers.

technology The way in which an organization transfers its inputs into outputs.

telecommuting Working from home at least two days a week through virtual devices that are linked to the employer's office.

terminal values Desirable end-states of existence; the goals a person would like to achieve during their lifetime.

threat of technological unemployment A situation in which professional decision makers resist certain decision-making improvements (e.g., AI and structured approaches alike), because they reduce the extent the decision makers are relied on for expert judgment, lessening the value they provide the organization.

trait activation theory (TAT) A theory that predicts that some situations, events, or interventions "activate" a trait more than others.

trait theories of leadership Theories that consider personal qualities and characteristics that differentiate leaders from nonleaders.

transactional leaders Leaders who guide or motivate their followers in the direction of established goals by clarifying role and task requirements, allocating rewards and punishment where needed, and (passively or actively) intervening when the situation calls for it.

transformational leaders Leaders who inspire followers to transcend their own self-interests for the good of the organization.

trust A psychological state of mutual positive expectations between people—both depend on each other and are genuinely concerned for each other's welfare.

trust propensity How likely an employee is to trust a leader.

two-factor theory A theory that relates intrinsic factors to job satisfaction and associates extrinsic factors with dissatisfaction. Also called motivation–hygiene theory.

uncertainty avoidance A national culture attribute that describes the extent to which a society feels threatened by uncertain and ambiguous situations and tries to avoid them.

(un)ethical leadership The idea that leaders serve as ethical role models to followers, and thus demonstrate appropriate (or inappropriate) behavior by using their power in (un)ethical ways and/or by treating others fairly (or unfairly).

unity of command The idea that a subordinate should have only one superior to whom they are directly responsible to.

utilitarianism An ethical perspective in which decisions are made to provide the greatest good for all.

valence The degree to which organizational rewards satisfy an individual's personal goals or needs and the attractiveness of those potential rewards for the individual.

value system A hierarchy based on a ranking of an individual's values in terms of their intensity.

values Basic convictions that a specific mode of conduct or end-state of existence is personally or socially preferable to an opposite or converse mode of conduct or end-state of existence.

variable-pay program A pay plan that bases a portion of an employee's pay on some individual and/or organizational measure of performance.

virtual structure A small, core organization that outsources major business functions.

virtual teams Teams that use technology to tie together physically dispersed members in order to achieve a common goal.

vision A long-term strategy for attaining a goal or goals.

vision statement A formal articulation of an organization's vision or mission.

voice Dissatisfaction expressed through active and constructive attempts to improve conditions.

wellness programs Organizationally supported programs that focus on the employee's total physical and mental condition.

whistleblowers Individuals who report unethical practices by their employer to outsiders.

withdrawal behavior The set of actions employees take to separate themselves from the organization.

work specialization The degree to which tasks in an organization are subdivided into separate jobs.

work team A group whose individual efforts result in performance that is greater than the sum of the individual inputs.

workforce diversity The concept that organizations are becoming more heterogeneous in terms of gender, age, race, ethnicity, sexual orientation, and other characteristics.

workgroup A group that interacts primarily to share information and make decisions to help all members perform within their respective areas of responsibility.

workplace spirituality The recognition that people have an inner life that nourishes and is nourished by meaningful work that takes place in the context of community.

zero-sum approach An approach to reward allocation that treats the reward "pie" as fixed, so any gain one person or group achieves comes at the expense of another person or group.

Name Index

C

D

E

F

G

H

L

M

N

O

Q

R

S

T

W

X

Y

Z

Organization Index

Subject Index

P

T